THE BUILDINGS OF ENGLAND

FOUNDING EDITOR: NIKOLAUS PEVSNER

WORCESTERSHIRE

ALAN BROOKS AND NIKOLAUS PEVSNER

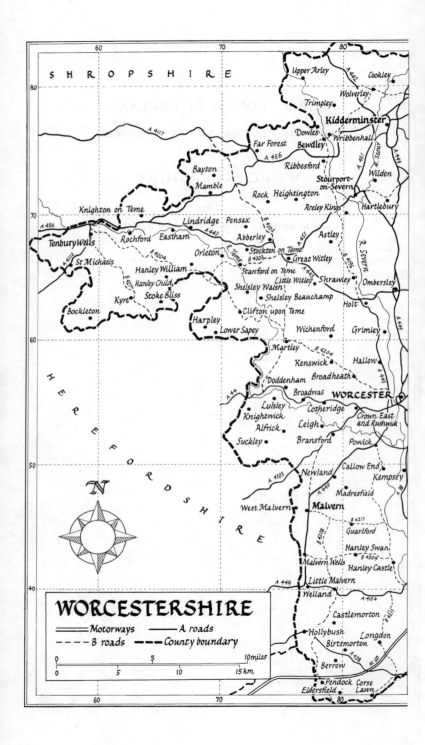

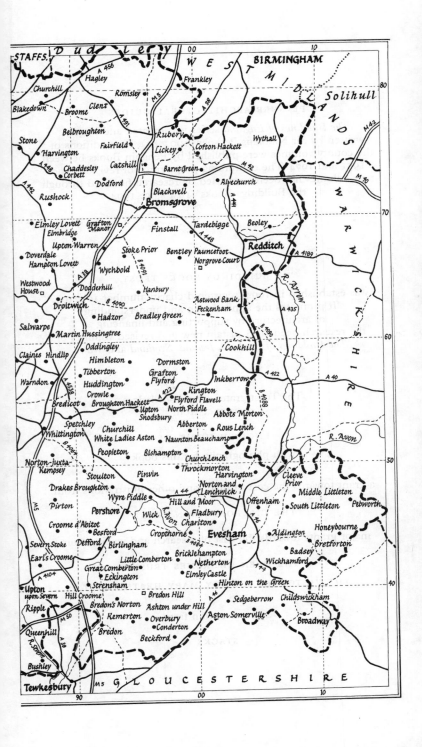

PEVSNER ARCHITECTURAL GUIDES

The Buildings of England series was created and largely
written by Sir Nikolaus Pevsner (1902–83). First editions of
the county volumes were published by Penguin Books between
1951 and 1974. The continuing programme of revisions and
new volumes has been supported by research financed through
the Buildings Books Trust since 1994

THE BUILDINGS BOOKS TRUST

was established in 1994, registered charity number 1042101.
It promotes the appreciation and understanding
of architecture by supporting and financing
the research needed to sustain new and revised volumes of
The Buildings of England, Ireland, Scotland and *Wales*

The Trust gratefully acknowledges
assistance from

ENGLISH HERITAGE

with photography for this book

a grant towards the cost of maps and other illustrations from

THE C.J. ROBERTSON TRUST

major grants towards the cost of research and writing from

THE OPEN CHURCHES TRUST
THE VICTORIAN SOCIETY MARY HEATH TRUST

and a donation from

STACKS

Worcestershire

BY

ALAN BROOKS

AND

NIKOLAUS PEVSNER

THE BUILDINGS OF ENGLAND

YALE UNIVERSITY PRESS

NEW HAVEN AND LONDON

YALE UNIVERSITY PRESS
NEW HAVEN AND LONDON
302 Temple Street, New Haven CT 06511
47 Bedford Square, London WC1B 3DP
www.pevsner.co.uk
www.lookingatbuildings.org
www.yalebooks.co.uk
www.yalebooks.com
for
THE BUILDINGS BOOKS TRUST

Published by Yale University Press 2007
2 4 6 8 10 9 7 5 3 1

ISBN 978 0 300 11298 6

Printed in China
through World Print
Set in Monotype Plantin

CONTENTS

LIST OF TEXT FIGURES AND MAPS

Every effort has been made to contact or trace all copyright holders. The publishers will be glad to make good any errors or omissions brought to our attention in future editions.

MAPS

PHOTOGRAPHIC ACKNOWLEDGEMENTS

We are grateful to English Heritage and its photographer James O. Davies for taking most of the photographs in this volume (© English Heritage Photo Library) and also to the sources of the remaining photographs as shown below. We are grateful for permission to reproduce them as appropriate.

Andor Gomme: 72
Judy Mainwearing/Photoworks: 69, 97

MAP REFERENCES

The numbers printed in italic type in the margin against the place names in the gazetteer of the book indicate the position of the place in question on the index map (pp. ii–iii), which is divided into sections by the 10-kilometre reference lines of the National Grid. The reference given here omits the two initial letters (formerly numbers) which in a full grid reference refer to the 100-kilometre squares into which the county is divided. The first two numbers indicate the *western* boundary, and the last two the *southern* boundary, of the 10-kilometre square in which the place in question is situated. For example, Abberley (reference 7060) will be found in the 10-kilometre square bounded by grid lines 70 (on the *west*) and 80, and 60 (on the *south*) and 70; Wythall (reference 0070) in the square bounded by the grid lines 00 (on the *west*) and 10, and 70 (on the *south*) and 80.

The map contains all those places, whether towns, villages, or isolated buildings, which are the subject of separate entries in the text.

FOREWORD AND ACKNOWLEDGEMENTS

This book is a revision and expansion of Nikolaus Pevsner's architectural guide to Worcestershire, published in 1968, the thirty-fifth volume in his series *The Buildings of England*. The preparatory work for this first edition was undertaken by Jennifer Sherwood, with financial support from the Leverhulme Trust. Pevsner's 'companion, driver, helper, and dogsbody' on his journeys through the county was Neil Stratford, who was also able to incorporate, mostly as footnotes, much of his detailed study of Worcestershire's Norman sculpture. For this new edition these footnotes have, with permission, been updated and included within the main text, as has Mr Stratford's introduction to Norman Sculpture. The late F.W.B. ('Freddie') Charles also contributed to the introduction and provided many entries on timber-framed houses for the gazetteer, to a standard which Pevsner himself acknowledged had not been reached in earlier books in the series. These also, with permission, have been updated and incorporated into the main gazetteer text. The inclusion of these two noteworthy contributions, together of course with those of others who assisted Pevsner in his work, have added much to the present book.

Before acknowledging the help received for this volume, it is necessary to say something about the difference in boundaries. The boundaries of Worcestershire have been tinkered with more than those of most counties, but for this revised edition they coincide happily with those of the current local authority of that name (as reconstituted in 1998, after the dissolution of the short-lived county of Hereford and Worcester). They differ from Pevsner's in that the NE extremity of the historic county, since 1974 included in the Metropolitan Boroughs of Dudley and Sandwell in the County of the West Midlands, has been excluded. The area in question, including Cradley, Halesowen, Oldswinford, Pedmore and Stourbridge, as well as certain other built-up districts which Pevsner treated with them under the heading of Birmingham Outer Western Suburbs (most of which belonged historically to Staffordshire), will be included in a future *Buildings of England* volume devoted to Birmingham and the Black Country.

The list of people to thank in respect of this volume is long and omissions may be inevitable – my apologies to anyone who has been inadvertently excluded. I should firstly like to thank those who have provided specialist sections for the introduction. Peter Oliver, of the Herefordshire and Worcestershire Earth

Heritage Trust, contributed the section on geology and building stones; Malcolm Atkin, the County Archaeologist, provided those on Worcestershire archaeology. The section on the domestic timber-framed tradition is the work of Stephen Price and Nicholas Molyneux. Stephen Price in addition fed me with further information on Worcestershire timber-framed buildings, so that this introduction and the gazetteer could be co-ordinated. I am also most grateful to Brian and Moira Gittos for extensive notes on medieval church monuments, and to Geoffrey Fisher for commenting on C17–C18 monuments by London sculptors, with many new attributions for anonymous works, marked (GF) in the gazetteer. Ian Dungavell provided information on the work of Aston Webb; Michael Kerney numerous stained-glass references extracted from C19 journals; and Dennis Hadley a detailed list of work by James Powell & Sons. Mike Wall provided a long list concerning buildings throughout the county, Michael Speak a list of references from Herefordshire sources, and George McHardy notes on selected churches.

Now for those who have helped on specific buildings. Both Richard K. Morris and Ute Engel kindly read through my draft on Worcester Cathedral, and offered many useful suggestions. Chris Guy, the Cathedral archaeologist was also most helpful. Dr Morris also read through the entry on Pershore Abbey, David Cox that on Evesham Abbey, and Heather Gilderdale Scott that on Great Malvern Priory. For Stanbrook Abbey, Michael Hill kindly gave me a copy of his conservation plan prepared for the Benedictine community there, and Sister Margaret Truran, the community's archivist, gave me the benefit of a conducted tour as well as her extensive knowledge of the site. Andor and Susan Gomme, and Alison Maguire, allowed me to benefit greatly from their study of Norgrove Court; Andor Gomme also provided other leads and an invaluable last-minute update on Westwood House. Michael Hodgetts read through and made comments on my entry for Harvington Hall. Jennie McGregor-Smith provided me with much detailed information on Bromsgrove and the surrounding district. Others who have helped with information on specific places include Pat Hughes (Worcester and South Littleton), Nat Alcock (Mere Hall, Hanbury), Nigel Gilbert (Kidderminster), Andrew Harris (Hanbury), Charles Hudson (Wick), Norman Rosser (Malvern College), Scott Pettitt (Kidderminster), Eric Pritchard (Upper Arley), and Melvyn Thompson (on Kidderminster Mills). Help on specific architects was received from Kerry Bristol (James Stuart), Andy Foster (Birmingham architects), Charles Keighley (Randall Wells), and Alan Teulon (S.S. Teulon). David Park kindly facilitated access to the files on wall paintings at the Courtauld Institute of Art. I should also like to acknowledge contributions, amongst others, from Oliver Bradbury, Geoff Brandwood, Robert Coatsworth, Sir Howard Colvin, Peter Cormack, Alan Crawford, Patrick Farman, Catherine Gordon, Peter Howell, Susan Jenkins, Annette Leech, and Chris Pickford. Peter Hughes arranged for me to have access to the archives at Madresfield Court, and district councils throughout the county were most helpful in retrieving information from their, now mostly computerized, records. At Worcester I should particularly like to thank the conservation officers, Will Scott and John Kirwan. James Dinn, the Worcester City archaeological officer, read through and updated parts of my Worcester text. Graham Reddie, former Chief Architect and Planning Officer of Redditch Development Corporation, was also especially helpful.

Much of my own research was carried out at the Worcester-shire County Record Office and I should like to thank the staff there for their expert and always good-natured help. I should also like to thank staff at the Worcestershire Library and History Centre and at several other public libraries, notably Evesham, Malvern, Kidderminster, Bromsgrove, and Redditch. Also those at Birmingham Central Library, at the National Monuments Records Centre, Swindon, and at the RIBA Drawings Collection at the Victoria and Albert Museum, London. Special thanks should be extended to Karen Evans, who searched out informa-tion for me at the Public Record Office and various other London libraries and archives.

Many practising architects provided information about their buildings, as did numerous owners of houses and other build-ings. I am particularly grateful to those who invited me into their homes. Churchwardens and incumbents have also been unfail-ingly helpful. Worcestershire churches seem to be locked more frequently than those in most neighbouring counties, but nowhere did I meet with any major difficulties in obtaining access.

Despite this plethora of help, it should be pointed out that the responsibility for any mistakes in the text is mine. I should be delighted to be informed of any errors, either directly or through the publishers, so that they can be corrected in any future edition.

This volume was carefully edited by Simon Bradley who sug-gested numerous improvements, tempered by his great architec-tural knowledge. Funds towards travel and other expenses were provided, through Gavin Watson, by the Buildings Books Trust. The team at Yale University Press was ably led by Sally Salvesen. Emily Winter was the managing editor and Emily Wraith the picture researcher. Reg and Marjorie Piggott drew the county map; other maps and plans are by Alan Fagan. Nearly all the splendid photographs were taken by James O. Davies of English Heritage.

Finally I should like to thank my wife Jean for her support and her tolerance of my obsession with the architecture of the South-west Midlands.

Alan Brooks
November 2006

INTRODUCTION

Worcestershire is one of the smaller English counties and surprisingly varied. A summary of its popular images readily reveals
this: orchards, with a liberal scattering of black-and-white timber-
framed cottages; Worcester city, with its cathedral dramatically
sited above the River Severn; the magical Malvern Hills, forming
an emphatically memorable boundary with Herefordshire;
Bredon Hill, the largest Cotswold outlier, a prominent and
equally loved landscape feature; and Broadway, where Worcestershire makes one deep salient right into Gloucestershire, up
onto the Cotswold scarp itself. There is even more variety than
this. The north-western uplands, stretching from the Abberley
Hills, a northern continuation of the Malverns, far W towards
Herefordshire and Shropshire, are one of the most delightful
areas in the county. To the N and NE the Clent and Lickey hills,
ideal walking country, form a vital bulwark against the Black
Country and especially Birmingham, the expanding influence of
which hangs like a threat over this part of the county. For Worcestershire is predominately a West Midlands county, like its rather
larger neighbours to the N and E: Shropshire, Staffordshire, Warwickshire. Only towards its western and southern boundaries,
with Herefordshire and Gloucestershire, does Birmingham feel
really distant. The NW tip of the county in fact lies only some
fifteen miles from the Welsh border. The River Severn, bisecting
the county N to S, with its access to the sea at Bristol, provided
also a major connection with the West Country. Its tributaries,
the Stour (from Staffordshire), the Teme (from Shropshire) and
the Avon (from Warwickshire), emphasize the West Midlands
connections, as well as all being significant landscape elements
in their own right.

In shape Worcestershire resembles a parallelogram with irregular edges (once even more irregular; *see* below). Its form, closer
to a geographical entity than most counties, can be compared to
a shallow basin, surrounded by an upland rim. Only in the central
area around Worcester, and in the Vale of Evesham to the SE, does
the landscape appear particularly flat. Elsewhere few parts are
without some low-lying undulations, and the surrounding hills,
including the (Redditch) Ridgeway forming the E boundary with
Warwickshire, enhance the upland perception from almost anywhere within the county.

This landscape of course reflects the underlying geology, more
fully dealt with below. The youngest rocks, the oolitic Jurassic
limestones of Bredon Hill and the extreme SE, provide by far the

best building stones. The rest of the SE quarter, on the Lower Lias, provides only a shaly stone, usually used only for higher-grade buildings (in the absence of any better quality local stone). The soft red marls of the centre and eastern edge gives way in the N of the county to Triassic sandstones, then to some of the Carboniferous and Devonian periods. The oldest rocks, notably those of the Malvern Hills, were particularly hard to work, and were only used systematically from the Victorian period. This general inadequacy of the county's building stones accounts for the predominance of timber-framed buildings until the C18. The prevalent redness of the buildings where sandstone was used provides a further leitmotif, reinforced by the fact that the bricks that eventually superseded timber framing are also almost invariably quite deep red in colour.

Worcestershire was created as an administrative (and defensive) unit in 918, taking into account the huge estates held by the Bishop of Worcester and the great abbeys of Evesham and Pershore. Few counties have been subject to so many subsequent boundary changes, albeit mostly minor. Bewdley was only specifically assigned to the county (rather than Shropshire) in 1544. There were further adjustments in 1844 and in the 1890s, but the most sweeping changes occurred in the C20. Yardley, Northfield and King's Norton were absorbed by Birmingham in 1911. Dudley, formerly a detached island of Worcestershire and its second largest town, became an independent county borough in 1929. Further changes, mostly in 1931, transferred other detached islands to Warwickshire and tidied up the boundary with Gloucestershire. The most radical change, in 1974, amalgamated the county with Herefordshire, and removed the remaining Worcestershire parts of the Black Country (notably Stourbridge and Halesowen) to the Borough of Dudley within the new, confusingly named, West Midlands Metropolitan County. The annulment of Hereford and Worcester County Council in 1998 returned Worcestershire to something like its traditional form (the area covered by this book, i.e. without the Black Country areas to the NE), but its singularly tattered original outline, with nine detached enclaves, now belongs to the past.

Traces of human activity in Worcestershire have been discovered from the Palaeolithic period onwards, but visible prehistoric remains are remarkably scarce, apart from a number of Iron Age hill-forts on the hills around its boundaries. Roman remains are even scarcer, though it is clear that Droitwich was then already an important centre for salt production. Soon after, Worcester had become predominant as a major religious centre; its huge diocese included most of Gloucestershire until the Reformation, and Warwickshire until the early C20. Medieval remains in the city, apart from the cathedral, are, however, few; it will probably be remembered as being predominately of Georgian red brick. Of other towns, those in the N, Bromsgrove, Kidderminster, even Droitwich, have suffered from the proximity of Birmingham; Redditch was specifically expanded as a new town to cater for

Birmingham overspill. Bewdley is the most attractive town in this ₅ area, though Stourport remains notable as a creation of the canal age. The towns of the s (Pershore, Evesham, Upton upon Severn) and of the far NW (Tenbury Wells) all possess notable individual character. Great Malvern, with its remarkable hillside setting, is a case apart, an exceptionally well-preserved Victorian spa town, with a major late medieval abbey church. Of VILLAGES the variety is enormous; which ought to be called the finest in Worcestershire will always remain a matter of personal choice. Broadway, pure Cotswold in character, would probably be in ₄ everyone's top three, though some might think that it has too little that is out of place, or at least too little that is left alone. Other villages that rank high are Ombersley and Chaddesley Corbett, both also with main streets, Overbury and Cropthorne, with a more complex structure, and the curious Wolverley, particularly distinctive with its church on a steep hill and little square down below dominated by the Sebright School of 1829. Also ₁₀₂ worth noting, for different reasons, are Bredon, Clent, Clifton upon Teme, Elmley Castle, Feckenham, Fladbury, Hanbury, Hartlebury, Rous Lench and Upper Arley, though this is inevitably a somewhat subjective list. The tendency seems to be for villages to become less nucleated as one travels w towards Herefordshire.

GEOLOGY AND BUILDING STONES

by Peter Oliver

Worcestershire geology covers some 700 million years. Throughout this vast period the story is one of moving sections of the Earth's crust, a process known as plate tectonics. The resulting upheaval of mountains with volcanoes and cataclysmic earthquakes, the erosion of the land, the creation of new oceans and closing of others, all gave rise to a great variety of rock formations, which has been a major influence on the shaping of the landscape. These rocks have also been the source of building stones, providing the investigator and visitor with a pleasant journey through geological time in the villages and towns of the county.

The first glimpse of the rocks in their natural setting is always as a result of a view of the landscape, which is stunning. No-one can fail to be impressed by the natural beauty of Worcestershire when seen from its hilltops. The HILLS rise on three sides, neatly enveloping the vale of the River Severn and its tributaries, and leaving only the s as an opening to the Bristol Channel. In the w the Malvern Hills form the border with Herefordshire. Stretch- ₂ ing for 7½ m. from North Hill at 1303 ft (398 metres) to Chase Hill, they dominate the skyline with some of the oldest rocks in England: Precambrian igneous rocks of granite and diorite. This geological structure, known as the Malvern Axis, continues northwards as the sedimentary Silurian limestones and shales of the Suckley and Abberley hills, where Woodbury Hill rises to 902 ft (276 metres). The rocks of these hills are now dipping vertically, producing wonderful ridge-and-vale topography. These give way in the northernmost part of the county to the younger rocks of the Wyre Forest coalfield, with its hard Carboniferous sandstones together with clays and thin coals. The high ground continues eastwards into the Clent Hills and Lickey Hills (997 and 955 ft, 304 and 291 metres, respectively) with their Carboniferous and Triassic sandstones and mudstones and Permian breccias. In the Lickey Hills these sit juxtaposed against hard resistant Ordovician quartzites. Towards the boundary with Warwickshire, s of Redditch, the Arden Sandstone escarpment, a harder component of the Triassic mudstones that underlie much of central Worcestershire, forms the line of higher ground. This eventually gives way eastwards to the glacial deposits, which form a feature known as the Ridgeway, which rises to 489 ft (149 metres). Finally, rising into Gloucestershire to the s e can be seen the impressive Cotswold Escarpment of Jurassic limestones. Only a small part of the Cotswolds falls within the county, but the isolated outlier of Bredon Hill at 962 ft (293 metres), with similar geology, imposing and slab like, stands sentinel above the valley of the Avon.

These hills with their distinctive topographies look down upon the WORCESTER PLAIN, shaped by the rivers Severn, Teme, Stour and Avon and the meltwaters of the vast Pleistocene ice sheets that poured from the n and w some 15,000 years ago. Most of the lower ground to the n of the county is underlain by distinctive red sandstones of Permian and Triassic age, some of which are resistant enough to form prominent ridges. To the s and e these sandstones change to the much softer mudstones of the Triassic and Jurassic, giving rise to the broad sweeping vale of the lower Severn. Great spreads of fluvial sands, gravels and alluvium make up the terraces of the Severn, Avon, Teme and Stour, and rise step-like up the valley sides, each rise taking us further back into periods of torrential meltwaters as the climate warmed. The Ice Age legacy is also present across much of the lower ground of the county in the form of glacial till (boulder clay) and outwash sand and gravel.

The county's native BUILDING STONES can now be described, largely in order of decreasing age. The PRECAMBRIAN rocks of the Malvern Hills are divided into the MALVERNS COMPLEX and the overlying Warren House Formation. The former, predominantly igneous, are mainly diorites, tonalites and granites but with some ultrabasic material, a variety of metamorphic rocks and dykes and veins of microdiorite and pegmatite. This area is one of the largest exposures of Precambrian rocks in England, which are believed to be the root of a volcanic island arc above a zone where one plate of the Earth's crust plunged beneath another. The rocks were intruded about 677 million years ago, a date fixed by studying the decay of uranium isotopes. These hard rocks were quarried until the 1970s, predominantly for

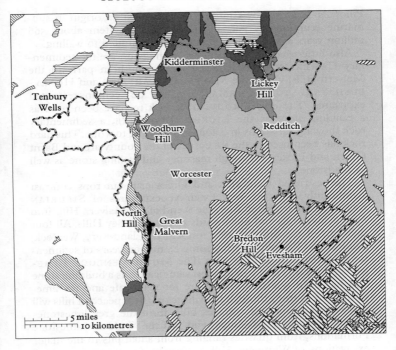

▨ INFERIOR OOLITE GROUP

▨ LOWER LIAS GROUP

▨ MERCIA MUDSTONE GROUP

▨ SHERWOOD SANDSTONE GROUP

▨ PERMIAN

▨ CARBONIFEROUS

☐ OLD RED SANDSTONE MADE UP OF THE RAGLAN MUDSTONE (MAINLY SILURIAN), THE BISHOP'S FROME LIMESTONE, THE ST MAUGHANS AND THE BROWNSTONES FORMATIONS (ALL DEVONIAN)

▨ SILURIAN (LIMESTONES AND SHALES)

▨ LICKEY QUARTZITE

■ PRECAMBRIAN

Geological map of Worcestershire

roadstone. Many of the large scars can still be seen and are a paradise for the researching geologist. Many houses, churches and walls in Great Malvern, Malvern Wells and West Malvern also provide excellent examples of the rock, with pink granite blocks contrasting with the grey diorites. The irregular shapes of the stones, caused by variable jointing within the rock, gives a very distinctive pattern to the walls in that area. The WARREN HOUSE FORMATION, seen on Broad Down and Hangman's Hill, is volcanic; lavas of basalt and rhyolite as well as pyroclastic ashes.

Pillow lavas at nearby Clutter's Cave suggest an origin in submarine eruptions as part of an island arc system about 566 million years ago. Use as building stone is limited to walling.

Also little-used, except locally as aggregates, are the sedimentary CAMBRIAN strata exposed in the southern parts of the Malvern Hills, where the MALVERN QUARTZITE and HOLLY-BUSH SANDSTONE FORMATIONS can be seen in restricted exposures. The only ORDOVICIAN rock to have been used as a building stone is the LICKEY QUARTZITE, a sedimentary rock showing variations in colour from purple to white. This hard rock has been used in the NE corner of the county around Barnt Green and Lickey, for rough masonry and walling stone as well as roadstone.

The restricted Cambrian and Ordovician outcrops contrast significantly with the very extensive exposures of SILURIAN rocks. The latter stretch from the N end of the Malvern Hills into the Suckley Hills and northwards to the Abberley Hills. All four divisions of the Silurian are represented: Llandovery, Wenlock, Ludlow and Pridoli, covering some 25 million years of sedimentation in tropical shallow seas. The MUCH WENLOCK LIMESTONE FORMATION is of greatest significance as a building stone and has been quarried even more for aggregate and for limeburning. A journey through the villages of these peaceful hills will throw up examples of cottages built from the grey limestones of the Aymestry, Woolhope and Much Wenlock Limestone Formations, from quarries ranging from small pits to the major excavations of Whitmans Hill, Woodbury (disused since 2000) and Shavers End. Investigation of the garden walls will reveal a wealth of fossil trilobites, corals, crinoids, brachiopods, gastropods and bryozoans.

The upper Silurian marks a change from marine to terrestrial conditions with the fluvial deposits of the RAGLAN MUDSTONE FORMATION. With its brownish red colour it is in great contrast to the grey and beige of the underlying limestones and shales just described. These rocks, often also referred to as the OLD RED SANDSTONE, pass upwards without a break into the rocks of the DEVONIAN period. The Raglan Mudstone Formation and the overlying St Maughan's Formation surround the valley of the River Teme upstream from Knightwick to Tenbury Wells. The ST MAUGHAN'S FORMATION, which consists of red-brown sandstones, mudstones and conglomerates, also gives rise to the Bromyard Plateau to the W of the River Teme. Many of the sandstones have been used for building. They can be seen in their many colours in the church at Shelsley Beauchamp, where the walls of the nave make their poor quality very obvious, whilst the more resistant Triassic orange-red sandstones make up the impressive tower. As the site is at the foot of the Silurian Abberley Hills, the boundary walls are built of grey limestones and siltstones.

In the same locality the junction between the Raglan Mudstone and St Maughan's formations is marked by the BISHOP'S FROME LIMESTONE. The last is only a few metres thick at best, and was used for lime-burning and as a roadstone. It also played a major part in forming the tufa deposits (probably in the last 10,000 years) that run along the escarpment on the W side of the Teme valley. Groundwater percolating through the St Maughan's Formation limestones here dissolved out calcium carbonate and then re-precipitated it when forced to the surface by the underlying impermeable Raglan Mudstone Formation. Impressive cliffs of tufa are to be seen at Southstone Rock and in the woodlands of the escarpment in locations with spine-chilling names such as Witchery Hole, Hell Hole and Devil's Dingle. This tufa with its free carving and lightness can be seen to great effect in Shelsley Walsh and Eastham churches, as well as in local houses and walls. It was also used in vaulting the transepts of Worcester Cathedral.

The upper CARBONIFEROUS period can be seen in the Wyre Forest coalfield, where the Coal Measures Group and the overlying Warwickshire Group outcrop. Of the Warwickshire Group, the sandstones of the HALESOWEN FORMATION have been used to great effect. Much evidence of their extraction can still be seen in the old quarries alongside the Severn, especially just N of the county boundary into Shropshire where the best-known variety, the Highley Sandstone, a massive greenish-grey rock, is exposed. Similar rock in the Mamble area reaches 100 ft (30 metres) thick. Sometimes called the THICK SANDSTONE, it has been used in buildings in Mamble, Bayton and Abberley, where the rock frequently displays goethite (iron oxide) deposits on the joint surfaces and staining. The fast-weathering sandstone quarried alongside the river was used in considerable quantities in the construction of Worcester Cathedral, where it is being replaced by a much harder sandstone of similar colour, also of Carboniferous age, from the Forest of Dean. Highley Sandstone has also been used in other churches along the River Severn such as the tower of St Anne, Bewdley, and also for bridges across the river and over the Severn Valley Railway. The Guildhall entrance in Bewdley is another good example of the use of the stone and its weathering characteristics. Other varieties within the Warwickshire Group include the red sandstones of the SALOP FORMATION, which was supplied from Hextons quarry just N of Arley. Blocks of cut rock can still be seen here, abandoned by the remains of a wharf on the bank of the Severn. Such rock was transported down river and probably used in the Cathedral.

The PERMIAN rocks of the county are present in the CLENT FORMATION, a reddish breccia with fragments mainly of volcanic origin set in a mudstone matrix. Formed as alluvial fans at the base of rising mountains, the rock can be seen capping the Abberley Hills (where it is known as the Haffield Breccia), at Osebury Rock (a riverside cliff on the Teme) and in the Clent Hills. Nowhere is it used as a building stone.

Younger Permian strata pass conformably upwards into the TRIASSIC deposits. Both these groups of sedimentary rocks have a major impact on the topography and buildings of the central and NE parts of the county. They stretch from the Abberley and

Malvern hills in the W to the edge of the South Staffordshire coal-field and the Birmingham Plateau in the N, and to the Lickey and Clent hills in the NE; they pass eastwards into Warwickshire where they continue to be significant; they abut the lower Jurassic rocks and Cotswold Hills to the E and SE; and they spread down the Severn Valley towards Gloucester. The Permian rocks are present as the BRIDGNORTH SANDSTONE FORMATION, extensive dune-bedded sandstone representing part of one of the biggest deserts the Earth has ever seen. They outcrop between Bewdley and Kidderminster and run northwards into Staffordshire. The rock is quite soft and does not make a good building stone, but it has been used in walls and doorsteps, good examples of which can be seen in Bewdley. Overlying the Permian rocks is the Sher-wood Sandstone Group of the Triassic, a sequence of fluvial deposits of red-brown sandstones and conglomerates making up the Kidderminster Formation, the Wildmoor Formation and the Bromsgrove Formation. The KIDDERMINSTER FORMATION conglomerates are resistant enough to form a significant ridge running through Kidderminster and high ground NE of Broms-grove, rising towards the Clent Hills. The large liver-coloured quartzite pebbles of these conglomerates, reworked by the rivers flowing southwards at the end of the Ice Age, can often be seen in some of the old pavement setts across central Worcestershire. Rocks from the WILDMOOR FORMATION have been used in buildings, but the rock of choice from these red Sherwood Sand-stones comes from the BROMSGROVE SANDSTONE FORMA-TION. It was extensively used for churches, of which notable examples are the parish churches at Bromsgrove and Tardebigge. Some of the best Bromsgrove Sandstone came from quarries in the Ombersley area, where some rock horizons gave hard pink, cream and grey-white stone. The best examples are dotted about amongst the black-and-white buildings of Ombersley, but the material was also put to great use in many parts of the county. It is yet another stone used in Worcester Cathedral.

The Triassic period is further represented by the Mercia Mudstone Group. These mudstones, siltstones, evaporites and sandstones represent the deposition of water- and wind-borne materials laid down in shallow subaqueous environments, com-parable to those which produced the salt deposits of Droitwich. One constituent of the Group is the ARDEN SANDSTONE FORMATION, which consists of mudstones, siltstones, and fine-grained sandstones changing in colour from grey-green to pale grey. It varies in thickness from less than 3 ft (1 metre) N of Worcester to 36 ft (11 metres) just over the boundary in Warwickshire. None of the quarries for this rock in Worcester-shire were very large, but the long winding outcrop of the sand-stone between Redditch and Worcester produced some notable examples of its use, including the church, cottages and walls of Inkberrow. Hanbury Hall a little further W uses the stone to good effect, but its sometimes poor quality is also apparent.

The Mercia Mudstone Group is succeeded by the PEN-ARTH GROUP, which represents a change from a continental environment to a shallow marine sea. Its predominantly grey fossiliferous mudstones, sandstones and limestones distinguish it from the earlier Triassic rocks. A prominent N–S escarpment can be seen E of the Severn in the S part of the county, from which some churches such as the one at Himbleton may have sourced their building stone.

JURASSIC strata are confined to the E and SE parts of the county. They are represented by the Lias Group and the Inferior Oolite Group. These mark the beginning of a significant accumulation of marine deposits most of which occur to the E and SE in Gloucestershire. The Lias Group is subdivided into five formations of which the lowest division is the BLUE LIAS FORMATION, which has at its base the Wilmcote limestone. The latter was much quarried although probably mainly for lime-burning. The full succession of the Jurassic in Worcestershire, including part of the overlying INFERIOR OOLITE FORMATION, can be seen on the geological outlier that is Bredon Hill. In the settlements here and in the nearby village of Broadway the full glory of the honey-coloured oolitic limestones can be seen. There were many quarries in the area, and the large one on Fish Hill, just inside the county, is still operating. The lower beds of the quarry are freestones, so called because they can easily be cut and shaped for building purposes. The higher beds of less massive limestones are typical of the rocks that have been used for drystone walling. Many of the old quarries also supplied the thinner beds of limestone for roofing purposes. All of these types of use can be seen at the foot of the Cotswold escarpment and even some way W of the source of the rock itself.

Any account of building materials would not be complete without reference to BRICK. It is ever-present in the county and has its own geological story. Worcestershire has considerable clay deposits for brickmaking and there were many small brick pits supplying the demands of the C19 and C20. Mudstones from the Raglan Mudstone and St Maughan's Formations were used, as were many clays within the terrace deposits along the many rivers. Clays of the Wyre Forest coalfield were also used for brickmaking, and of course the clays of the Carboniferous Etruria Formation in the South Staffordshire coalfield of the Black Country produced the hard blue bricks that are still so obvious in some buildings across the county, such as the fine cottage terrace in Wilden. Disused clay pits are common in the Vale of Evesham where clays from the Lower Lias Clay Formation were worked, and where one operation continued at Honeybourne until recent times. In the last sixty years Mercia Mudstone deposits were worked at locations such as Norton near Worcester, at Redditch, and at Belmont in Great Malvern. It is this surface outcrop of clay that provides the dominant red brick to be seen throughout the county. Today there is only one working brickworks, at Hartlebury (Baggeridge Brick), where significant quantities of the same material are excavated each year.

A modern assessment of the building stones of town centres is not complete without a look at the IMPORTED STONES that have been used either structurally or as a facing in the many commercial and public buildings. Some are ubiquitous: Norwegian Larvikite, pink Aberdeenshire granite, Millstone Grit paving slabs from the Pennines, white granite from Cornwall, dolerite setts from Clee Hill and Rowley Regis, oolitic Portland stone, Bath stone, and roofing slate from North Wales. Used in banks, shops and departmental stores, in town halls and shopping malls, in colleges, police stations and hospitals, they all add to the variety and interest that is geodiversity.

WORCESTERSHIRE ARCHAEOLOGY FROM PREHISTORY TO THE MIDDLE AGES

by Malcolm Atkin

Our understanding of the early history of Worcestershire has been transformed since the first edition of this book in 1968. At that time only a few hundred archaeological sites were known. Now, the County Historic Environment Record contains over 17,000 sites, from Palaeolithic axe finds to Second World War pillboxes. There is now also much more emphasis on placing sites – whether buried remains or standing buildings – within the context of their historic landscapes.

Worcestershire in Prehistory

The paucity of upstanding major field monuments before the Iron Age belies the increasing evidence for dense occupation of Worcestershire from at least the Bronze Age. The small scatter of PALAEOLITHIC stone tools, mainly recovered from sand and gravel quarries, is now being related to the geological context, shedding new light on a Worcestershire that looked very different from the present county. At the time of the earliest likely human activity, 700,000–500,000 years ago, the area was drained by the pre-Anglian 'Bytham' river system, rising in the Vale of Evesham area and flowing eastwards into East Anglia. The first settlers appear to have used this routeway into the Midlands rather than coming from the S. There was then a hiatus during the Anglian glaciation, when Britain was abandoned by human occupation. Over thirty-eight hand axes of the Lower and Middle Palaeolithic are then known from Worcestershire, dating back up to 300,000 years but mainly from just before the last (Devensian) glaciation of 10,000–11,000 years ago, when the country was again abandoned. Fifteen of these axes came from just one find spot, in a quarry at Kemerton, suggesting that the known finds represent only a small percentage of the total.

The Holocene period brought rapid climatic improvement, with the emergence of forests and a new population of nomadic MESOLITHIC (10,000–3,500 B.C.) hunter-gatherers, using characteristic flint blades. The landscape was now more recognizably that of the present Worcestershire, drained by the Severn and Avon. At Lightmarsh Farm W of Kidderminster (*see* Wribbenhall) over 1,400 fragments of Mesolithic flint tools were found, in association with post-holes, a hearth, gullies and a pit. A radiocarbon date was obtained of 8,800 years (±80) before the present, making this of one of the earliest known occupation sites in the region. Pollen evidence from other sites also suggests that the people of this era were already starting to clear forest and grow crops before the conventional emergence of Neolithic farmers.

NEOLITHIC sites (3,500–2,000 B.C.) are comparatively widespread, mainly identified from cropmarks on the gravel terraces. The introduction of farming enabled the development of larger social groups within a more settled landscape. These SETTLEMENT SITES may be evidenced only by ephemeral post-holes, as of a rectangular structure found at Huntsman's Quarry, Kemerton. As in the rest of the country, most known monuments are elements of a ritual landscape. Such RITUAL SITES include a possible ceremonial cursus site near Fladbury: a pattern of rectilinear enclosures, possibly the focal point for a celestial clock. The period also provides the first surviving upstanding archaeological monument in the county: Whittington Tump, beside the M5 on the E outskirts of Worcester. This is interpreted as a natural hill artificially raised as a ceremonial monument (and not, as legend might have it, a large cairn to commemorate the Battle of Worcester in 1651, or even spoil from railway building). The discovery of polished stone axes from Cornwall, the Lake District and North Wales, and even from Brittany and North Italy/Switzerland, indicates the potential of trade in the period and the development of a more sophisticated economy than might otherwise be imagined. The Neolithic also saw the first appearance of pottery – a soft fabric fired at a low temperature in a bonfire. An important Late Neolithic/Early Bronze Age site found at Clifton (Severn Stoke) included pits containing Grooved-Ware pottery and stone axes, and a mound of fire-cracked stones (a burnt mound). These were the product of heating water in a trough using hot stones, either for cooking or to create a sweat lodge or sauna.

By the end of the BRONZE AGE (2,000–600 B.C.), with a growing population, it appears that farming extended over most of the area currently farmed, with farmsteads frequently moving location within tribal areas. Samples from peat deposits in the Avon valley, as at the Carrant Brook near Bredon Hill and at Birlingham, show a landscape largely cleared of woodland by the Early Bronze Age. The scarcity of cereal grains from excavations within this area suggests that the land may have been used mainly for cattle. One consequence of the reduction in tree cover was an increased build-up of alluvium on low-lying land, from the flooding of the rivers Avon and Severn.

This was a period of great change, in both social organization and in religious belief. There may have been a change from the enclosed small FARMSTEADS of the Middle Bronze Age, as represented by a site excavated at George Lane, Wyre Piddle, in a low-lying boggy area that suggests that all available better land had already been exploited, to more dispersed open settlements set within extensive field systems. The period also saw the emergence of the most striking collection of prehistoric archaeological monuments, the HILL-FORTS. Midsummer Hill and British Camp (both partly within Herefordshire) appear to be of Late Bronze Age origin. There are up to *c.* 20 possible surviving Bronze Age BARROWS in the county, with excavated examples at Holt and Wyre Piddle. A penannular palisaded enclosure 89 ft (27 metres) in diameter and with an E-facing entrance at the Perdiswell Park and Ride site, on the outskirts of Worcester, is dated to the Early to Middle Bronze Age and is interpreted as a ceremonial focus, perhaps with some surrounding funerary use. There is also evidence for burial in cremation fields, as at Wyre Piddle.

The difficulty of identifying OPEN SETTLEMENTS from aerial photography may suggest that they are more common than hitherto considered. That at Huntsman's Quarry, Kemerton, had round-houses, water holes, droveways and field boundaries, dating from the Late Bronze Age, with evidence for bronze casting and textile production. There is also increasing evidence, as from the Kemerton and Wyre Piddle areas, that many present field BOUNDARIES originated as sinuous Bronze Age land boundaries to control stock, which for the first time carved up the county into formal territorial units. To that extent, we are still living in a prehistoric landscape! A surviving Bronze Age boundary is the Shire Ditch on the Malvern Hills, which has recently been demonstrated to underlie the Late Bronze Age/Iron Age hill-forts of Midsummer Hill and British Camp, although reworked as a medieval deerpark boundary. Running off the Shire Ditch at right angles are the boundary ditches of a prehistoric field system, indicating that the early hill-fort did not lie in isolation from the farms below. At Childswickham, in south Worcestershire towards the Cotswolds, a substantial Bronze Age boundary seems to have been respected by Roman ditches on the same alignment.

IRON AGE (600 B.C.–43 A.D.) settlements included the HILL-FORTS which are so prominent in the landscape. Up to fifteen are known, from Wychbury in the N to Midsummer Hill in the S. Many are inter-visible, forming a network of power and control. There is also the promontory fort beside the Severn at Kempsey. From possible origins in the Late Bronze Age (*see* above), the group underwent much change, and may have served a variety of functions, from cattle enclosures, semi-permanent occupation sites, and meeting places to tribal strongholds. Detailed survey at British Camp has suggested the presence of large numbers of huts dug into the rock, although this is not in itself evidence for permanent occupation. Grain-storage pits have also been found within the Bredon and Conderton hill-forts. A hut circle was also excavated within Hanbury hill-fort, just outside the S boundary of the present churchyard.

There is, however, increasing evidence for widespread Iron Age occupation in the LOWLANDS, forming a continuum into the

Roman period. Excavations at Beckford in 1972–9, just S of Bredon Hill and beside the Carrant Brook, revealed a Middle Iron Age settlement (c. 400–c. 100 B.C.) extending over more than 10 acres (4 ha.), with a compact plan of conjoined enclosures defined by ditches. Some enclosures had been remodelled several times and one house had been rebuilt six times. In all, excavation revealed c. 50 houses, over a thousand grain-storage pits, and smaller internal compounds. Another excavation, on Albert Road, Evesham, revealed part of an extensive Middle Iron Age settlement, with a substantial enclosure ditch and a network of other boundary ditches, a complex of pits, and a cobbled yard area. Beyond the settlement enclosures would have been small fields, linked by a network of trackways.

This was still a mobile population, with little evidence for continuity of occupation on a single site over long periods. Instead, there may have been progressive movement of settlements, but constrained within local territories. In particular there appears to be a major shift at the end of the Middle Iron Age, when a number of lowland farms and hill-forts were abandoned.

The Iron Age also sees the first evidence for large-scale INDUSTRY in the county: the exploitation of the natural brine wells in Droitwich, which established the importance of the settlement until the later C19. There is well-preserved evidence of salt production in the form of boiling hearths and brine pits in the area of the present Vines Park. A network of saltways exported the product over a radius of c. 40 miles, identified by distribution of the characteristic storage vessels (briquetage). In the Middle Iron Age Worcestershire also became the centre of a regionally significant pottery industry based in the vicinity of the Malvern Hills, a tradition which continued into the post-medieval period.

Roman Worcestershire

The Late Iron Age was a time of mounting inter-tribal conflict, with the number of hill-forts declining and those that survived becoming more heavily defended. The Roman invaders took advantage of this to impose their own discipline. (A group of skeletons of men and boys found at the entrance to Bredon Hill Camp may have been massacred in inter-tribal fighting before the invasion, or by the Roman army itself.) Even so, Iron Age tribal organization in the region may have co-existed with Roman occupation for a considerable time, as is suggested by the continuation of 'native' pottery types beyond the end of the C1 A.D. and characteristic types of Iron Age round-house into the C3. Romanisation occurred to differing degrees and at different times according to how useful or important it was for the local population to undergo change.

Although ten possible ROMAN FORTS have been recorded in the county, Worcestershire was behind the 'front line' of campaigning in the W, and these are generally small bases to protect the road network. A succession of two forts is also known at Dodderhill, overlooking the continuing saltworks in Droitwich.

A further clue to the status of Droitwich is the presence at Bays Meadow of a classical VILLA-TYPE BUILDING with mosaic pavements. This may have been an imperial administrative centre for the saltworks or a military *mansio*. Evidence of similar buildings is rare in Worcestershire away from the edge of the Cotswolds. One outlier of the Cotswolds group of villas was partially excavated at Childswickham. For the majority, timber ROUND-HOUSES continued in use, together with buildings now represented only by metalled floor surfaces, which may have had clay or cob walling. These houses were set within rectangular enclosures, defined by bank and ditch.

Smaller-scale salt-working industries may also have existed across the Vale of Evesham, based around springs of a lower brine concentration. At one such Roman salt-processing site, at Lower Moor in the Vale, a spring fed into a carefully maintained pond with a complex series of sluices and channels. The presence of this important industry probably explains the unusually dense concentration of settlement sites in the vicinity.

Worcester also developed as a small industrial town during the Roman period, although there is no evidence of municipal buildings or the regular planning of larger towns. Iron-working was a major element in the economy, with scatters of iron slag found throughout the town, used as road metalling or dumped in peripheral areas. The ore was brought from the Forest of Dean in Gloucestershire. There may have been an early fort to guard the river crossing, and there is certainly evidence for a late Roman defence enclosing a horseshoe-shaped enclosure against the river, bounded approximately by Copenhagen Street, Friar Street and Severn Street. The Cathedral was later sited in the centre of this defensive circuit. There was an extensive suburb to the N and a burial ground to the S.

Early medieval archaeology

The collapse of the Roman administrative and military system exposed how thin was the veneer of Romanisation. Worcestershire probably remained linguistically and culturally largely British throughout the c6–c7, although archaeological evidence is sparse. Occupation continued in Worcester during the c5, although more as a cluster of farmsteads rather than anything urban in the accepted sense. Documentary evidence suggests that St Helen's church may have had a British origin as the centre of a large estate, whilst 'dark earth' deposits excavated on Deansway suggest that the area was intensively grazed from the c5 to the c10. Salt-working also continued in Droitwich in the sub-Roman and Anglo-Saxon periods.

In the rural areas, there is growing evidence for ANGLO-SAXON SETTLEMENT SITES and cemeteries in south Worcestershire, extending from the Cotswold edge to the banks of the Severn. Sites with both sunken-floored and aisled buildings are known from Kemerton, Fladbury, Ipsley (Redditch) and Ripple. Pagan cemeteries from as early as the c5 have been recorded in the same eastern areas, at Broadway, Offenham, Fladbury, and Beckford. Anglo-Saxon material is not, however, found in the W of the county until much later. By the C8 the evidence from surviving Anglo-Saxon charters points to a well-organized system of landholding, frequently referring to landmarks still visible in the landscape (such as Whittington Tump).

A major change came in the late Saxon period with the creation of a more settled society, heavily influenced by the CHURCH. This followed the creation of the see at Worcester in 679–80. Establishment of the two great minsters in the Vale of Evesham – at Pershore and Evesham – followed in the early C8. Sadly, little of the Saxon churches has survived later rebuilding (*see* pp. 17–18). Such remains are a reminder that a church may well have an older history than the date of the earliest surviving upstanding structure.

The development of first timber and then stone churches fossilized the previously mobile settlement pattern, and stimulated the creation of markets and TOWNS. Excavation at Worcester has revealed late C9 defences to the *burh* on Deansway. Only Worcester, Droitwich, Pershore and Evesham could be said to be truly urban before the Norman Conquest, but the majority of the twelve small medieval towns in Worcestershire also owe their origins to the influence of the Saxon Church (Alvechurch, Bewdley, Broadway, Bromsgrove, Clifton upon Teme, Droitwich, Evesham, Kidderminster, Pershore, Redditch, Tenbury Wells and Upton upon Severn).

The NORMAN CONQUEST brought a new military system to the county. There were over thirty CASTLES in Worcestershire, although they are less well-preserved, less well-known, and less investigated than the marcher castles of Herefordshire. They include the sheriff's castle at Worcester, built *c.* 1069 S of the Cathedral. It ceased to be of military importance from 1216, although it survived to be used as part of the C17 Civil War defences until final demolition in the C19. The sheriff's brother, Robert D'Abitôt, probably built Elmley Castle at the foot of Bredon Hill, later the seat of the Beauchamp family, which survives as an earthwork with fragmentary walls. The Beauchamps also built Bengeworth Castle, on the S side of Evesham, whose abbot destroyed it in the C12 to prevent attacks on the adjacent priory and lands by the 'lawless bands' that occupied it. Earthworks survive at Hanley Castle, built after 1206, with the surrounding great ditch dug in 1324. Other notable survivals are one late medieval tower from Caldwall Castle, Kidderminster, and a motte and bailey castle at Castlemorton Tump. A small castle or hunting lodge was also built on top of the Iron Age fort at British Camp. The castles of the county are discussed further on p. 33.

Much of the history of the medieval towns can still be read in the STREETSCAPES. At Worcester the pattern of streets and lanes encompassed by the circuit of medieval defences is still clear, with small suburbs beyond. In smaller towns, in particular at Evesham and Pershore, the bounds of the medieval town are still evident, dominated by the monastic precinct and centred on the

Norman market. Medieval tenement plots can still be identified from a detailed map, and on the ground from their narrow building frontages and from peeks down long alleyways beside the buildings. The Central Marches Historic Towns Survey in the mid 1990s highlighted the archaeological potential of such small towns, with their fragile medieval remains in shallow deposits close to the modern surface, and also some deeply stratified deposits, akin in character to the archaeology of Worcester. It is likely that fragments of many more medieval buildings survive, still unrecognized, behind later façades. Phases of church building and major alterations can also demonstrate the rise and fall of population and the prosperity of a settlement.

The VILLAGE, as we know it, evolved during the C7–C11 in association with the growth of regular field systems, although the majority of planned villages in Worcestershire probably date from the C11–C12, stimulated by the development of the parish system and construction of stone churches. There are strong contrasts in the medieval settlement pattern. The area to the NW around the Teme valley is one of predominantly dispersed settlement. This area was densely settled by Domesday (1086), but much woodland still remained. The NE of the county, still well wooded in 1086, has a mix of small nucleated and dispersed settlement. The Vale of Evesham and the S of the county is predominantly an area of nucleated villages with open fields.

Over two hundred DESERTED or SHRUNKEN MEDIEVAL SETTLEMENTS are known from the county, represented by earthwork lumps and bumps of the remains of houses, barns and lanes in pasture or grassland. Good examples are at Grafton Flyford, Ullington (Pebworth) and Woollashill (Eckington). The characteristic remains of medieval arable cultivation in the form of ridge-and-furrow and headlands survive throughout Worcestershire, but particularly in the SE of the county where fine examples can be seen around Honeybourne and Naunton Beauchamp.

Worcestershire has one of the largest concentration of medieval MOATED SITES in the country. Good examples can be seen at Inkberrow (and at Nobury in the same parish) and beside the church at Throckmorton. Moats were status symbols rather than being defensive, and many may have served a dual purpose as fishponds. There is a significant distribution of moated sites to the E and NE of the county.

From the C14–C15 there was a shrinking of settlement in both town and country, largely due to the effects of the famines and plagues of the C14. This occurred across the whole county and was not simply a retreat from marginal land. In both Pershore and Evesham there is evidence of tenement plots becoming gardens in the late C14 (and not recovering until the C19). By the end of the medieval period Redditch and Clifton upon Teme had entirely ceased to be urban in character. Worcester recovered more quickly, probably aided by increased migration from the countryside and smaller centres.

Medieval Worcestershire contained extensive areas of FOREST, including Wyre Forest, Feckenham Forest and Malvern Chase.

They were used for the hunting by the Church and nobility; the unusual earthworks of a royal hunting lodge survive at Feckenham. It is a mistake to think of these as composed simply of ancient trees. The presence of ridge-and-furrow within many areas of present woodland suggests that parts were farmed as arable land, perhaps until the late medieval decrease in population led to a reduced demand. Woodland was itself considered a crop, and was regularly coppiced and felled, as can be seen on the surviving areas of ancient coppicing. Woodland fuelled the pottery industry of the Hanley Castle area, the saltworks of Droitwich and the iron industry of north Worcestershire. Worcester Woods Country Park has good examples of both medieval ridge-and-furrow and coppicing.

The two great rivers, the Avon and Severn, were also part of the medieval farm management system. Evidence of extensive WATER MANAGEMENT FEATURES can be seen beside the Severn at Grimley, together with a series of medieval fishponds. These can also seen beside the medieval Bishop's Palace at Hartlebury and at Chaddesley Corbett.

Medieval Worcestershire had a strong INDUSTRIAL presence, which continued and expanded through the post-medieval period. There was pottery- and tile-making in the Malvern area and in many kilns in and around Worcester. Quay Lane at Hanley Castle led to a quay for the shipment of local pottery. Although no kilns survive, underwater archaeology here has revealed stratified deposits of broken pottery that failed to survive the journey from the kilns. The salt-working industry at Droitwich remained very conservative and the brine pit survived with only one major improvement from the C13 to the C18. In the N of the county, coal-working was established from the late C13, centred on villages such as Mamble, Bayton and Pensax. These early mines were typically bell-pits, and remains can still be seen in the fields around Mamble in the form of a raised spoil heap with a circular hollow in the middle. The coal was used for household fuel and brickmaking. The high sulphur content also made it useful for preserving hops. Iron-working became a feature of N and NE Worcestershire during the C17 and C18, with local specialisms such as metalworking at Churchill Forge, needle-making in the Redditch area and the manufacture of scythes and other tools at Belbroughton.

MEDIEVAL ECCLESIASTICAL ARCHITECTURE

Anglo-Saxon architecture and sculpture

Worcestershire has an almost total absence of Anglo-Saxon ARCHITECTURAL REMAINS. No surviving church fabric can be assigned with certainty to the period, though it has been claimed that the W wall at Sedgeberrow is of this date. Some fabric at, for example, Cropthorne and Leigh could also be Saxon; the surviving indent for a large rood of Romsey type at Salwarpe suggests such fabric may also survive there. Herringbone masonry, as in the chancel at Elmley Castle, could well be CII, but, like several other features, not necessarily pre-Conquest. One explanation for this Anglo-Saxon paucity may be that most of the county's churches were of timber, but this only partly satisfies.

Of Saxon SCULPTURE only two pieces might merit inclusion in a national survey: the Cropthorne cross-head and the Lechmere Stone kept at Severn End, Hanley Castle. The former is assigned to *c.* 825–50, the latter may be C9–C10; the former is of high quality, wonderfully preserved, the latter barbaric (despite apparent Byzantine influence), but all the more impressive for that. The two sum up the Anglo-Saxon alternatives: one a renaissance rather than continuation of the highly accomplished style of the Ruthwell and Bewcastle crosses of the late C7, with scrolls inhabited by birds and beasts and such classical motifs as the Greek key; the other along the Celtic lines of ferocious stylization. Byzantine influence is better seen in a mysterious stone at Rous Lench, with two peacocks drinking from a vase; this could be Anglo-Danish. Three (loose) fragments of window heads here are perhaps also pre-Conquest. Apart from these, Worcestershire has only a few parts of crosses with interlace (Stoke Prior, Tenbury Wells), some preserved pieces at Wyre Piddle, and possibly a few turned capitals from Oswald's late C10 Worcester Cathedral (St Mary), reused there in the slype. The N wall of this room, and other parts of the cloister outer walls, may incorporate Saxon fabric. Worcester Cathedral in the Saxon period consisted of two churches (the earlier dedicated to St Peter), still standing close together in the early CII; no further details are known. Excavation has also revealed foundations of an apsed chancel at Pershore Abbey, of *c.* 972, or more probably of the early CII.

Several other churches retain pre-Conquest DEDICATIONS. St Kenelm, the boy king of Mercia, was reputedly murdered at Romsley in 821, and the churches there, and at Clifton upon Teme and Upton Snodsbury, are dedicated to him. Abberton, Broadway, and Leigh are dedicated to St Eadburga (or Edburga) of Pershore; Honeybourne and Norton to St Ecgwin (Egwin) of Evesham. Other rare early dedications are St Cassian (Chaddesley Corbett), St Godwald (Finstall), and St Milburgh (Offenham).

Monastic foundations

Worcester Cathedral Priory and Pershore Abbey were Benedictine. The see of Worcester was founded *c.* 680, to serve the Saxon sub-kingdom of the Hwicce; Pershore was probably founded *c.* 689. Both became Benedictine under the auspices of Bishop Oswald, *c.* 961–72. The original foundation of the third great Benedictine house in Worcestershire, Evesham Abbey, was also very early, *c.* 701. Great Malvern Priory also claimed a pre-Conquest origin, but was probably founded *c.* 1085. Little Malvern Priory (C12 Benedictine) was dependent on Worcester.

Astley had a Benedictine priory attached to the Abbey of St Taurin (near Rouen), suppressed with other alien foundations in 1414.* The only other Benedictine establishment was Westwood Priory (for nuns), founded under the rule of Fontevrault in the mid C12; no trace remains. Bordesley Abbey (near Redditch), founded c. 1138, was an important Cistercian foundation; there were also small Cistercian priories, for nuns, at Whistones, or Whiteladies, founded c. 1240 just N of Worcester, and at Cookhill, probably late C12, re-founded 1260. Worcester also had houses of the Greyfriars (or Franciscans), established c. 1225–30, and of the Blackfriars (Dominicans), a late establishment of 1347.

The REMAINS of these foundations vary greatly. Worcester p. 703 Cathedral Priory has most: apart of course from the cathedral 38 church, there are monastic cloisters, chapter house, refectory, 9 ruins of the guesthouse, infirmary and reredorter, the great p. 699 gateway, and more. Of Pershore, only the E part of the church survives: chancel, tower and S transept. What remains at Evesham p. 288 is surprising; almost nothing of the church (though the plan has been recovered by excavation), but the chapter-house entrance, parts of two gateways, the almonry, and a complete detached 40 Late Perp *clocher* or bell-tower, close to two strangely placed parish churches. Great Malvern Priory church is intact, with out- p. 449 standing Norman and Perp work; otherwise there is only the restored gatehouse. Little Malvern has half the church and p. 432 notable remains of the prior's lodging. At Astley there is the 32 whole Norman church, indistinguishable now from any other parish church, except perhaps for its quality. Bordesley Abbey is a special case. Redditch Borough Council has undertaken ongoing excavation here which has so far exposed the founda- p. 551 tions of the chancel, crossing, S transept, and some of the nave; the site is completely undisturbed, so more revelations can be expected. There are also minor remains of the Cistercian nun-neries: parts of the E and W walls of the chapel at Whistones, built into the Royal Grammar School, even less of the church walls at Cookhill. Nothing survives of the two friaries at Worcester.

Norman architecture

EARLY NORMAN work is mostly confined to the major monas- tic sites. The crypt of Worcester Cathedral is a complete survival 8 of the 1080s. With its fifty or so short columns with their block or single-scallop or single-trumpet-scallop capitals and plain groin vaults, it represents to perfection the mood of those deter- mined and ruthless years. Of about the same date must be the slype, S of the S transept. The crypt allows us to reconstruct the p. 679 plan of the Cathedral's Norman E end. It must have had an apse with ambulatory and probably three radiating chapels; the SE chapel of the crypt, of irregular pentagonal form, has been exca- vated. There were also chapels E of the transepts. Above these

*An alien Augustinian priory at Beckford was suppressed even earlier. Droitwich had an Augustinian priory, from 1331.

chapels were galleries, as at Pershore Abbey. At that church the
11 S transept reveals most about the Early Norman building,
perhaps begun shortly before *c.* 1100. Earlier suggestions that it
had a four-tier elevation are no longer generally accepted. More
probably it had a three-tier elevation, without clerestory, beneath
a stone barrel vault. Such vaults may well have extended throughout the church, but it is clear from what little survives of the nave
that this had a different elevation from the E end, with high round
piers as at Tewkesbury and Gloucester; Pershore's were 25 ft (8
metres) high (as against 30 ft 6 in. (9.5 metres) in the Glouces-
10 tershire examples). The piers at Great Malvern Priory are round
too, though not so high. The naves of both Pershore and Great
Malvern are probably of *c.* 1120. The (re-tooled) foliage trails of
the capitals of the arch to the S transept chapel at Worcester
suggest approximately the same date. At this time, the cathedral
masons built in alternate courses of green and white stone. This
is the case also at the memorable chapter house, contemporary
9 or slightly earlier. This, round with a high central column, must
always have been vaulted, and is the earliest centrally planned
English chapter house; its successors were polygonal. Evesham
Abbey also has one reminder of those early Norman decades, its
Cemetery Gate, apparently the work of Abbot Reginald
(1130–49), but in its details looking decidedly pre-1130.

As regards later Norman PARISH CHURCHES, Worcestershire
is one of the richest of all counties; an unusually high proportion
of its Romanesque work survives. Nearly half the pre-Georgian
churches, i.e. about a hundred, have notable Norman fabric.
After the dearth of the Early Norman period, two main phases
can be easily distinguished, *c.* 1120–60, and *c.* 1160–90 and after;
closer attention to sculptural detail allows an attempt at a more
specific chronology (*see* below). The earlier phase has simple capitals, mostly block or single-scallop, and plainer doorways with
heavy roll mouldings; ornament is relatively flat. The later has as
its hallmark trumpet-scallop capitals or finely decorated multi-
scallop capitals, and often already crockets or even early stiff-
leaf.* Similarly the arches may already go pointed. But the
developmental logic of unmoulded-round, single-step-moulded-
round, and so on to pointed, is not at all consistently kept, and
earlier and later forms mix. Generally Norman sculpture of the
later phase is more lavish, often with figured capitals (Holt,
15 Rock), and an extravagant use of developed forms of chevron.
Work in the Transitional period (*see* below), notably at Bredon,
continued these trends.

One characteristic Worcestershire feature seems to have originated in the earlier phase. This is a group of churches, particularly in the NW of the county (Eastham, Knighton on Teme,
Martley, but also Grimley and Stoulton) with the doorway set in
a slightly projecting bay, a feature which evidently became
popular; cf. Abberley, Astley, Beckford, Bockleton, Hampton

*Dodderhill, consecrated 1220, still has trumpet scallops.

Lovett, Holt, Pirton, Rochford, and Rock. In addition four of these doorways (Bockleton, Eastham, Knighton, Stoulton) are topped by blank arcading, simple or interlaced, of a more or less elaborate form (*see also* Norman Sculpture, below, and compare the interlaced arcading of the Worcester chapter house). Such projecting entrance bays are rare elsewhere in England. There are some instances in northern Spain (though without arcading above), besides Moorish examples.

It is remarkable how large some of Worcestershire's Norman parish churches were. This prompts a consideration of their PLAN *p. 22–3* TYPES. The largest (as of course was the case with major monastic churches) were cruciform, preferably with a crossing tower. Ripple is a fairly complete example; Powick had E chapels to the transepts, like the monastic churches; unexpected parts of a cruciform church remain at Dodderhill. Three-cell churches could also have a central tower (without transepts), as at Beckford, Bredon, and Pirton, or instead a W tower, which seems generally to have been a later preference (Abberley, Cropthorne, Fladbury, Harvington, Tenbury). Two-cell churches, nave and chancel, were the commonest form. Remote little-altered examples are Eastham and Rochford. The ruined or disused churches at Netherton and Lower Sapey are of this type, but so are larger examples such as Holt, Rock, Martley and Stoulton. Aisles are rare before the C13; exceptions include Chaddesley Corbett, Cropthorne, Leigh, Overbury, and St Alban, Worcester. Of the simplest Norman form, the single-cell church, there are only some seven or eight, usually subordinate chapels; a disused example, easily missed, is at Belne near Belbroughton (p. 132).

A few other details should be noted. Bredon has an exceptional late C12 rib-vaulted porch. Astley has curious buttresses, in section semicircular above, but below of two semicircles with a keel moulding between. A remarkable amount of Norman sculpture survives (*see* below), not necessarily of high quality, much of it iconographically baffling. Its lavish display continued into Transitional work, even after *c.* 1200.

The *locus classicus* for the TRANSITIONAL period in Worcestershire is at Worcester Cathedral, after the fall of a tower in 1175. Probably this was a W tower, thus causing wholesale rebuilding of the two W bays of the nave. These bays, most likely executed *c.* 1180–5, have pointed arches and are decidedly idiosyncratic in 16 certain details. Three features in particular should be noted: the use of groups of three shafts; large foliage paterae in the *p. 24* spandrels (cf. the Lady Chapel at Glastonbury); and the use of continuous edge-roll mouldings alternating with normal orders on shafts with capitals. The S aisle here incidentally retains its original rib vault, the earliest in the Cathedral. There is similar work in the infirmary passage. Sophisticated patterns of undercut chevron, including diagonally set examples, also belong to this phase, as do trumpet-scallop capitals. Their first appearance may be as early as *c.* 1175 (on the Pershore font). Not earlier than 1185 purely French crocket capitals are introduced. There is also much Transitional work in the Cathedral's N and S transepts,

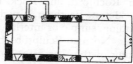

Shelsley Walsh

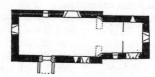

Lower Sapey

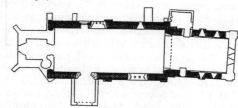

Shrawley

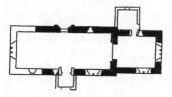

Rochford

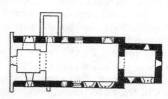

Earl's Croome

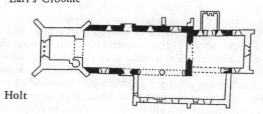

Holt

Norman churches.
Two-cell plans (above); cruciform and three-cell plans (right)

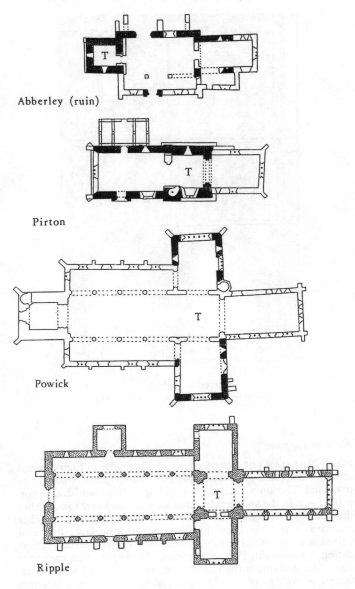

Abberley (ruin)

Pirton

Powick

Ripple

which goes closely with the new work at the w end, though on the whole seems marginally later, *c.* 1180–90. Frontal and diagonal chevron again appear, with, higher up, keeled shafts for intended vaulting, and stiff-leaf capitals; so here we have probably reached *c.* 1200. Of parish churches, Ripple best illustrates the development from Norman, through Transitional, to the Early English Gothic style.

Worcester Cathedral.
Interior elevation of two western bays of nave

Norman sculpture*

Much NORMAN SCULPTURE remains, but little of high quality;
survivals are often piecemeal, and chronology must remain controversial. The only fixed date available is the Cathedral crypt,
8 *c.* 1084–92. In the smaller churches little seems likely to be earlier
than *c.* 1120, an early C12 lacuna that can be paralleled in other
counties. A notable exception may be the fine large figure of
Christ at Leigh, which could be of *c.* 1100 or even earlier, but its
dating is uncertain; Pevsner for example proposed an early C13
date. The bulbous turned capitals in the Cathedral slype mentioned above (p. 18) could conceivably be C11 Saxo-Norman
overlap; the slype otherwise has block capitals. Among the block
capitals of the crypt (one with billet on the abacus) a few have
an elegant concave shape, unparalleled elsewhere, and curiously
prophetic of the trumpet scallops of nearly a hundred years later.
Block capitals also occur in the gateway at Evesham, *c.* 1130 or

---

*Largely based on the chapter by Neil Stratford in the first edition, 1968.

earlier. Here the shafts are grouped in threes, the earliest known
case of a motif typical of the Transitional style of the late C12 in
the West of England. The loss of Evesham Abbey causes the greatest gap in our knowledge of Norman sculpture in the county. At
Pershore we are more fortunate. Various decoration in transepts   11
and crossing includes simple volute, block, and scallop capitals
and one pair with interlace and six busts. The finest capitals,
probably c. 1120–40, are those of the E arch of the S transept in
the Cathedral, block capitals with acanthus foliage of Winchester type, also a dragon and angel; their connections are the Canterbury crypt and Romsey. Surviving stones suggest large areas
of diapered wall, as in other buildings of the first half of the C12.

The decoration of the second quarter of the C12 in smaller
churches is usually confined to fairly plain doorways and arches
with a heavy roll (Childswickham, Grimley, Stoulton), also sometimes simple saltire cross or star patterns. In the NW of the county
one team of masons worked at Stockton on Teme, Eastham,
Knighton on Teme, and Martley. Bockleton of the 1160s still
belongs to this group. Several of these churches have their doorways set in a wall projection (see above); Stockton and Eastham
also have small re-set carved panels with the Agnus Dei etc., the
original function of which is unknown. The richer decoration at
Ribbesford, including a tympanum carved with a hunting scene,
is probably Herefordshire School work, of c. 1140–50. Entirely
on its own in the county is the Christ in Majesty of c. 1140–50   12
at Rous Lench, the only ambitious figure of this date to survive,
and one with international connotations. It is close to the Prior's
Door at Ely Cathedral (c. 1135–40) and may be the work of a
sculptor from Northamptonshire. The tympanum at Rochford
has a Tree of Life, a motif frequent in the West of England. Other
interesting tympana are at Netherton, with a fine winged dragon,
and Little Comberton, with cross and four bulgy whorls. A
fragment at Chaddesley Corbett (by the same hand as the crude
tympanum at Pedmore, Stourbridge), and a Christ in Majesty
tympanum at Romsley (with the only example of beakhead in
Worcestershire) are also mid C12. The latter again shows influence from the Herefordshire School, but suffers from the carver's
naïve incomprehension of the iconographical models. Its broad
border of loose interlace seems still in the Anglo-Saxon tradition.

Sculpture of c. 1160–80 is on the whole much more lavish, particularly in its use of chevron (or zigzag). In the first half of the
C12 this is applied simply to the outer face of an order, or to both
outer and inner faces resulting in a lozenge shape (point-to-point
chevron), as at Bayton and Chaddesley Corbett. The chevron
may also be decorated with bobbins, pellets, or diamonds. The
earliest Worcestershire example of outward-pointing or frontal
chevron is at Rochford, c. 1150, but this motif only becomes
popular in the third quarter (Astley, Beckford, Castlemorton,   14
Earl's Croome, Pirton, Queenhill, Rock, Shelsley Walsh). At Holt
an order is decorated with more than one range of chevron
applied in steps. Already shortly before 1150 chevron begins to
be used elsewhere than on arches, e.g. window heads at Rous

32 Lench, then later at Holt and on jambs at Astley, Beckford and Rock. In the s of the county the chevron is usually furrowed, with alternately concave and convex ribs. At Holt (c. 1160–75) it is treated for the first time with slight undercutting. From then onwards undercut chevron develops an astonishing range of patterns (Worcester Cathedral, Bredon, Eckington, Elmbridge, Netherton, Shrawley). At this final stage of its evolution chevron is even found set diagonally (Worcester Cathedral, Bredon, Bricklehampton).

For other sculptural decoration we must return to c. 1150. The county at this date appears divided into two distinct areas, N and s, at about the latitude of Worcester. In the N (Astley, Bockleton, Holt, Rock N doorway) there are close connections with Here-
15 fordshire and Shropshire. The amazing chancel arch at Rock and
13 the Chaddesley Corbett font (see below), both c. 1160–70, must in fact be the work of Herefordshire carvers. They mark the high point of Romanesque sculpture in Worcestershire. The s is less clearly defined. Beckford alone (c. 1160–75), formerly in Glouces-tershire, survives with its sculpture nearly intact. This includes one tympanum with the Harrowing of Hell, another with a
14 strange Adoration of the Cross. The ornamental repertoire has much in common with Bricklehampton, Eldersfield, Pendock, Pirton etc., but adds some Italianate features. Earl's Croome (c. 1155–60) until the C19 had a richly arcaded W front. Its chancel arch and N doorway have capitals with foliage of a type unique in Worcestershire. One late C12 rarity, directly influenced by France, is the small Chartresque head of a queen at Defford.

Sculpture of the Transitional phase is heavily influenced by the
p. 24 motifs used in the two W bays of the Cathedral, see above; notable examples are at Bredon, Bricklehampton, Dodderhill, Ripple, and Shrawley. Further N three churches have trumpet-scallop and stiff-leaf capitals side by side but no undercut chevron (Dodderhill, Droitwich St Andrew, Stoke Prior). Undercut chevron continues in the Worcester area until after 1200, a date when the motif was otherwise still used only in the West of England. However, reactionary and progressive forms mix in such unexpected ways that dating must be hazardous. In the chancel at Pershore, as late as c. 1220, the extreme form of
23 trumpet scallop known as cornucopia capitals is still used with entirely post-Norman work. Similarly capitals at Bretforton with heads and a lively dragon inspired by the Wells Cathedral transept are probably as late as c. 1215–20.

In the context of Norman sculpture NORMAN FONTS should be considered here. Signally many are preserved, almost invari-ably the oldest fitting in a church. Most are plain, nearly all are round, some two dozen are decorated. Several have just a band or two of rope-moulding, plait or zigzag, or blank arches (Pinvin, Stoke Bliss); Broome adds grotesque heads. The notable Per-shore font has Christ and the Apostles set in the blank arcading; the earlier font at Overbury (perhaps altered in the C17–C18) also has two standing figures (cf. Coleshill, Warwickshire). Other fonts have just rosettes or a medallion with the Agnus Dei (Rock,

Bayton, Inkberrow, Bricklehampton). The finest and most ornate of all is at Chaddesley Corbett, in style an outlier of Hereford- 13 shire. The motifs here are four dragons. At least as impressive are the mighty dragons on the base of the Elmley Castle font, but they must be early C13. Big monster-heads are the motif at Holt, where the date is also mid-C12 or soon after.

Finally the two most interesting and finest pieces of C12 sculpture to survive, the LECTERNS at Crowle and Norton, the latter 7 from Evesham Abbey where a lectorium for the refectory is known to have been provided by an abbot who ruled in 1161–89. Strongly influenced by Italian ambones, both with central figures flanked by leaf scrolls, they are nevertheless absolutely native in style and foliage. Their date is probably c. 1190–1200; close parallels are to be found among the capitals at Wells. Both are of Wenlock Marble, resembling Purbeck (a similar lectern without figures has been excavated at Wenlock Priory). Heavy restoration somewhat lessens their value in a period from which large-scale figure sculpture has rarely survived.

The Early English and Decorated styles

The contrast between the lavish decoration of the Late Norman style and the refined austerity of the few examples of EARLY ENGLISH in the county is remarkable. Worcester Cathedral is of 20 course the major monument. Bishop William de Blois began its new E end in 1224 and this was perhaps completed c. 1260. It is large, of eight bays, with a pair of E transepts, and had a triforium, clerestory and quadripartite vaults with longitudinal ridge rib. There is plenty of Purbeck marble and plenty of sculpture, notably in the arcading at ground-floor level, best-preserved in 19 the SE transept. The whole is more conventional than Lincoln, but possesses for that very reason a reposeful though cool perfection. The feature nearest to Lincoln is the syncopation of the 21 triforium, where the rhythm of the arcading towards the choir differs from the blank background arcading. The rebuilding of the E end of Pershore Abbey, begun some twenty years earlier 23 than that of Worcester, was interrupted by a fire in 1223 and presumably completed at a consecration in 1239. The progress of the building is not easy to unravel. Work started at the E and ended near the E end. The plan is odd, with an ambulatory but p. 523 two square-ended chapels flanking the former Lady Chapel, all three facing due E. In addition there are a N and a S chapel as vestigial E transepts. The chancel itself has rich stiff-leaf capitals, and the wall passage taking the place of a triforium is architecturally pulled together with the clerestory much higher up, resulting in a two-tier elevation on the pattern of St Davids and 23 Llanthony. The E chapels and what remains of the Lady Chapel, i.e. the earliest parts, are alone distinguished by a display of Purbeck shafting.

In PARISH CHURCHES the demand must have been all but saturated when the Early English style set in. There is little to note here. Parts of St Andrew at Droitwich, notably the crossing, are 26

early C13. The noble chancels at Overbury and Kempsey are of
c. 1250. The former is rib-vaulted, the latter, on a grander scale,
is reminiscent of the work at Worcester Cathedral (the bishops
had a palace here). Bredon received a fine s aisle, known as the
Mitton Chapel, probably also c. 1250. The tower at Stoke Prior
is a good E.E. example, also parts at Ripple, both completions
of schemes begun earlier. There is other early to mid-C13 work
at Himbleton, Powick, Mamble and Knighton on Teme. Both the
latter two have bell-turrets supported by massive timber structures of four huge corner posts with diagonal bracing, secured in
place by lap dovetail joints. Dendrochronology (dates obtained
from tree rings) carried out at both indicates the early part of the
C13, comparable to the timber towers at Yarpole and Pembridge
in Herefordshire.

EARLY C13 SCULPTURE can be seen at its best in Worcester
Cathedral. There is the beautiful, though damaged, large seated
17 Christ in Majesty, of c. 1220–30, on the E wall of the refectory,
as well as outstanding monuments of about the same date. First
place must be given to the marvellous Purbeck marble monument to King John; he died in 1216 but his monument, the ear-
18 liest surviving royal tomb in England, may not have been carved
before c. 1230. The Purbeck monument to William of Blois †1236
is almost as fine, and there are in the cathedral other C13 monuments to bishops and ladies. In parish churches most C13 and
earlier monuments take the form of coffin-lids with crosses: good
examples are at Bredon, Overbury, Ribbesford and Stockton on
Teme.*

The DECORATED STYLE is hardly more frequent in Worcestershire than the Early English. In parish churches there is very
little; for really rewarding work one must go again to Pershore
and Worcester. Bredon's spacious chancel must be very early C14,
and the rebuilding of its central tower begun at about the same
time. There is also good Dec work at Martley. Of other parochial
jobs three are datable: Dodderhill chancel with a dedication in
1322 (though C19 restoration has obscured the issue); Sedgeberrow, a small church consecrated in 1331, much more satisfacto-
rily restored; and Broadwas, with a neat s chantry chapel of
1340–4. This last provides the best example of flowing (curvilinear) tracery. Generally speaking Worcestershire parish churches
provide limited enlightenment with regard to the progression
from Geometrical tracery (of late C13 derivation), through intersecting (c. 1300) and reticulated, to flowing tracery. The finest
chancel, the quite delightful and fully Dec example at Chaddes-
33 ley Corbett, has the most inventive tracery, making free use of
most forms. Hampton Lovett has probably the best of several
other C14 towers, Fladbury has a rib-vaulted porch. Also mid-
C14 probably is Worcestershire's one complete timber-framed
church, Besford, see p. 32. At Evesham Abbey the entry arch to
the chapter-house vestibule survives, with an order of seated and

---

*It is worth a note that Bishop Carpenter, who died in 1476, still chose (or had
chosen for him) a plain foliated cross as his memorial; this is at Alvechurch.

an order of standing figurines, perhaps *c.* 1290. Such figurines occur in the chapter-house entrance at Westminster Abbey and the s portal of the Lincoln Angel Choir. But Pershore again has far more substantial work: the revaulting of the chancel and the rebuilding of the crossing tower, after fire in 1287–8. If the vault at Pershore with its liernes opening and closing along the ridge in a scissor-like pattern is really as early as *c.* 1290–1300, it is, with the lower chapel of St Stephen's in the Palace of Westminster (1292–7), the earliest lierne vault in England. In any case it was certainly finished soon after *c.* 1300. The vault (with fine naturalistic bosses) achieves full harmony with the parts below, those that had been consecrated in 1239. The crossing tower is a very beautiful piece, with some similarities with Salisbury. It has plenty of ballflower (rare in Worcestershire), and so probably dates from *c.* 1320–30.

At WORCESTER CATHEDRAL rebuilding of the nave began at the NE end *c.* 1310–20. It was carried on speedily and consistently so that by the late 1370s the vaults were complete. Imperceptibly in the years of the third quarter Dec changed into Perp. The rebuilding of the cloister probably started in the 1380s, and work finished only in the C15. But one can see particularly in the earliest, E, range, how the reticulation motif of the Dec style, prominent in the embrasures of the windows and elsewhere, stands side by side with the Perp detail above the entry to the chapter house. The nave can be called Dec without hesitation. The general elevational theme is continued from the chancel, an interesting case of deliberate conformity. The result is a very satisfying harmony between builds separated by a century. The piers are complex, the windows have Dec tracery. The details, however, differ between N and S, making it clear that the N side was almost completed before work started on the S side; for in the latter the rich Dec band of knobbly foliage in the capitals is replaced by single thin, emphatically Perp capitals, and in the upper part this Perp thinning can also be observed (though the window tracery is still flowing, not yet Perp at all). The vault of the nave is remarkably simple, with ridge ribs, and only a single tierceron (clearly a last-minute compromise). Lierne ribs as well as tiercerons appear in the S transept and in the crossing-tower vaults, though externally the tower, finished in 1374, has Perp-looking detail on its lower, and rather more Dec details on its higher stage. The cloister vaults also had liernes from the start, and all four ranges bosses of interest. The best figural ones, in the cloister S range, may not have been provided until *c.* 1405. Purely Dec was the Guesten Hall, perhaps of *c.* 1338–9, which survives only as a ruin, though its elegant timber roof has been reconstructed at the Avoncroft Museum, Stoke Prior (*see* below). Dec also, probably again of the 1330s, is the refectory with its large, even windows and pretty vaulted canopy over the former reading pulpit. The seated Christ of *c.* 1220–30 on its E wall is surrounded by a bold C14 'reredos'.

Before moving on to the Perp style it may be useful to round up CHURCH FURNISHINGS and funerary monuments from

where we left them in the early C13 to where we have reached
now. There is not a great deal to record. A few beautiful pieces
of STAINED GLASS of the C14 survive: at Kempsey in the first
place (some pieces probably late C13, and also at Bredon, St Peter
49 Droitwich, Mamble, Sedgeberrow, Warndon, and Fladbury. Of
WALL PAINTINGS there is a beautiful early C14 female saint at
35 Kyre, more substantial remains of a cycle of *c.* 1300 at Pinvin,
and intriguing mixed C13–C14 survivals at Martley. An excellent
small piece of SCULPTURE of Moses, *c.* 1300, is at All Saints,
Evesham, and some fine heraldic TILES of the early C14 at
Bredon.

For MONUMENTS there is more to be said. Purbeck marble
ladies at Worcester Cathedral have been mentioned before. The
27 earliest and best of them is of *c.* 1250, a recumbent lady with a
curious (later?) limestone border of pierced stiff-leaf.★ The earliest knight, also mid-C13, a rather rigid flat figure, his legs not
yet crossed, is at Great Malvern Priory. Early cross-legged ones
28 are at Pershore, *c.* 1280–1300, and in Worcester Cathedral retrochoir; then there are, as everywhere, plenty with crossed legs
(Tenbury Wells, Chaddesley Corbett, Mamble, Clifton upon
Teme, Upper Arley, Alvechurch, the last an exceptionally fine
example of *c.* 1350.) The best late C14 monument in Worcestershire, though somewhat restored, is the Beauchamp tomb in the
Cathedral with its two recumbent effigies. The tomb-chest in the
Cathedral said to be of Bishop Godfrey de Giffard †1302, and
that the lady nearby of *c.* 1300, are noteworthy for their delicately
carved allegorical reliefs, though it is not clear how much here
has been reassembled. For reasons of its quite exceptional com-
29 position, an early or mid-C14 effigial slab at Bredon deserves
attention. It has a crucifix with lopped-off branches and at its top
busts of the husband and wife.

The Perpendicular style

The PERPENDICULAR STYLE also has not a great deal to show
quantitatively in the county, but some of what there is, is of the
1 highest order. That is true of the crossing tower of the Cathedral
(*see* above), of the N porch (said to be of 1386), and of the very
grand, if quite irregular, windows in the transepts. The most
complete impression of Perp, however, is to be had at Great
41 Malvern Priory. Here, from *c.* 1420 onwards, the E end was
10 rebuilt and transept and nave remodelled. Few monastic establishments in England did so much at so late a date. Inspiration
from Gloucester, especially with regard to the central tower, is
evident. At Evesham, Abbot Lichfield built in the most sumptu-
39 ous manner a fan-vaulted chapel in All Saints, a similar chapel
in St Lawrence (perhaps both when he was still prior, *c.* 1510),
40 and later the free-standing bell tower or *clocherium* with its two
main walls panelled all over, but its two other walls almost com-

───────────────

★The next best female effigy, of *c.* 1300, is at the time of writing hidden away in a
closed-off part of the crypt.

pletely bare. The panelling has its parallels in the gatehouse and (rebuilt) N porch at Great Malvern.

Of other buildings in this context Romsley has a specially attractive thin W tower and other detailing typical of the Perp style in the SW Midlands. Bromsgrove's splendid W tower and spire is equally typical, though the closest Worcestershire parallels (King's Norton and Yardley) are now within Birmingham. Martley also has a good tower, of very red sandstone. Other substantially Perp churches are Claines, Inkberrow and Hampton (in Evesham). Hampton and Honeybourne have porches with transverse stone ribs or arches, a type more usual in such counties as Nottinghamshire and Derbyshire. Little Malvern Priory also received a new E end (now partly ruined) in 1480–2, at the instigation of Bishop Alcock; the upper parts of its crossing tower may be slightly earlier. The largest and most ambitious Perp parish church is at Kidderminster. Its clerestoried nave and mighty SW tower are of c. 1500, mostly drastically renewed outside (almost as drastically as the whole exterior of the Cathedral). At its E end, exceptionally for a parish church,* there is a three-bay-long chantry chapel of c. 1530. The arcade piers of the Kidderminster nave are octagonal, with concave sides, a Cotswold motif. This occurs also in the S aisle at Rock; from a former inscription, this aisle and the lofty, square W tower are known to date from 1510. Other Perp arcades worth comment are octagonal, with one hollow in the diagonals (Bredon, Evesham All Saints, Pebworth – called 'new' in 1528), or quatrefoil, with each foil being three sides of an octagon (e.g. St John in Bedwardine, Worcester, where the sturdy W tower is said to be of 1461). Huddington has a stately Late Perp chancel, albeit on a small scale, and a good timber porch (*see* below).

There are many late medieval FUNERARY MONUMENTS of interest and quality. The best are either of brass (Strensham, c. 1390 and †1405; Kidderminster †1415; Fladbury †1445, still on its original Purbeck tomb-chest) or of alabaster (Bromsgrove, two, †1450 and †1490; Martley, a single knight †1460; Stanford on Teme, a couple †1493, already with kneeling children). The costume of both types helps to confirm their dates. Other good C15 monuments are at Kidderminster and Birtsmorton. But the finest monuments by far are both sculpture and architecture: the monument to Lady Joyce Beauchamp †1473 at Kidderminster and, in a class of its own, Prince Arthur's Chantry in Worcester Cathedral. This was begun in 1504 and has high walls with windows and panelling, a large number of statuettes, many of them unmutilated by the iconoclasts, a flat lierne vault inside, and a very rich reredos, but no effigy on the tomb-chest. The tomb-chest for King John (*see* above), renewed in 1529, is incidentally very similar in style.

This is the one major piece of Late Perp enrichment in the Cathedral. One has to go to Great Malvern Priory to see first-class CHURCH FURNISHINGS of the C15 and early C16. For

43

42

p. 432

p. 396

51

p. 399

p. 317

44

45

47

46

* But cf. Long Melford, Suffolk.

STAINED GLASS and tiles Malvern is among the most important
churches in England. The glass, considering its date, between
c. 1430 and c. 1500, is more complete than anywhere else in the
country, and its quality is high, though C15 glass nowhere
achieves, or aims at, the jewel-like colour of the C13 and the inten-
sity of emotion of the early C14. It is all rather cooler and more
matter-of-fact, and scenes from the lives of Christ or Saints suffer
from being hard to make out. But the totality of enclosure in pic-
tures remains. Little Malvern Priory also has good glass of
c. 1480–2. Otherwise what has remained is mostly bits and pieces,
though more than can be listed here; the best collections are
48   perhaps at Oddingley and Birtsmorton. The TILES at Great
p. 453 Malvern are entirely without English parallel. Some 1,300 have
been counted, to about a hundred patterns. They include, against
the outer sides of the stone choir screen walls, by far the best collection of wall tiles in England, rectangular and larger than those
used for flooring. The patterns throughout are attractive and
varied, shields, letters, ornamental motifs, even apparently the
name of a tiler, one *Whillar*. Malvern became a major centre for
the production of tiles in the C15 and very many parish churches
also have them; others were made at Droitwich.

Great Malvern has STALLS too, with MISERICORDS. In the
36   latter respect Worcestershire is lucky. The set of 1379 in the
Cathedral and that at Ripple, probably C15, are among the best
37   we have. Both include Labours of the Months, notably complete
at Ripple. For PAINTING there is one remarkable survival, but
not in a church: it is the room in the Commandery at Worcester,
presumably for the dying, which has religious paintings of
c. 1490, including a large representation of the Trinity on the
ceiling. Strensham has figures from a former rood screen re-set
on the front of a W gallery, but rustic work and over-restored.
SCREENS on the whole are minor. Worcester Cathedral has one
of stone, re-set and not outstanding, and those of wood in the
county are mostly of one-light divisions. Shelsley Walsh and Little
Malvern have also kept the rood beam or part of it, and Besford
the complete rood-loft parapet. Pershore Abbey has retained one
handsome stone REREDOS.

Timberwork in medieval churches

Finally a summary of the important part played by TIMBER in
Worcestershire churches. The county's one completely timber-
framed church, at Besford, has Dec detail and is probably of the
mid C14; its W front has bold curved wall-braces. Other completely timber-framed churches are known to have existed at
Whittington and Newland, the latter partly reconstructed as the
C19 mortuary of the Beauchamp Almshouses. For comparative
churches now one would have to look to Shropshire (Melverley,
Halston). Ribbesford has a tall late C15 arcade entirely of timber,
huge and impressive; Oddingley one timber arch (to the S
transept). Like Shropshire, Worcestershire also has timber-
framed towers as well as bell-turrets over the W end of the nave.

The supporting structures of the turrets at Mamble and Knighton on Teme, as we have seen (p. 28), have been dendro-dated to the early C13. Dating elsewhere is extremely hazardous, unless such confirmation can be obtained. The Pirton tower is perhaps the next oldest; it has two aisles, like Essex towers such as Margaretting, and the diagonal bracing of the main posts resembles huge cruck blades. That at Cotheridge is perhaps also C14. Others are probably C15–C16: towers at Dormston, Kington, and Warndon (1498 on tree-ring evidence); bell-turrets at White Ladies Aston and Himbleton. Several other churches rely on beams to carry the bell-turret, though the finely decorated beam in this position at Peopleton seems to be a re-set rood beam. Yet others have a whole timber-framed cross wall inside the w end of the nave, as if it were the internal wall of a house. This is so at Bransford, Knighton on Teme, and Mamble. At Martley there is instead a timber-framed tympanum between nave and chancel, more probably C17. The technique is that of timber-framed houses (on which *see* below). Internally the roof construction is often the most rewarding element of many churches. The most ornate example in a parish church is the chancel at Shelsley Walsh, with foils above the collar-beams, though some of this may be of 1859. Other good roofs include those at Stockton on Teme, Stoulton and Rock. The former chapel at Woodmanton Farm, Clifton upon Teme (where licence to crenellate was granted in 1332) has a wagon roof with curved ashlar pieces and a wholly timber substructure. Generally churches show a slight preference for such single-framed or rafter-type roofs over the double-framed or purlin-type that are characteristic of other timber-framed buildings. Of timber also are many porches. The earliest may be at Warndon, an archaic-looking structure of two slabs of oak forming an arch exactly following the grain. Crowle and Dormston have C14 detail, Huddington and Romsley are prob-ably Late Perp (the latter partly rebuilt in brick).

MAJOR MEDIEVAL SECULAR ARCHITECTURE

CASTLES are almost non-existent in Worcestershire; the county, well back from the front line against the Welsh, and dominated by its major religious houses, seems to have had little need of them. The largest was probably the Bishop of Worcester's quad-rangular Hartlebury Castle, begun *c.* 1255, but of its military past only part of the moat, the base of one tower, and much late C14 fabric, all hidden by C17–C18 work, remain. Of the royal motte and bailey castle raised at Worcester after the Norman Conquest there are only a few minor later remnants to be seen, tangled up with those of the Priory outbuildings; of Elmley Castle, first con-structed in the late C11, later a stronghold of the Beauchamps, only some impressive earthworks. Earthworks also give the sole indication of Hanley Castle, originally built as a hunting lodge for King John in 1207–12, of Castlemorton, and of one or two other baronial strongholds. That leaves two individual towers.

Holt Castle was built *c.* 1385 for John Beauchamp, but it is
p. 381 unclear whether the surviving tower belonged to a larger building or whether it stood alone. The hall and solar added behind
in the C15–C16 do little to clarify the issue. The octagonal tower
of Caldwall Castle, Kidderminster, probably formed part of a C14
upper-floor hall house, perhaps built for the Cokesay family
c. 1347.

STONE HOUSES of before the C16 are very rare, and most of
these are restricted to areas of easily quarried stone. The exception is the Bishop's Palace at Worcester, which appears entirely
early C18 from the street, but contains a great hall (remodelled
in the late C15) and below that and elsewhere extensive rib-
vaulted undercrofts of the late C13. The other notable medieval
stone house is also monastic, belonging to Pershore Abbey, the
fine C14 Abbot's Grange at Broadway; its hall (retaining three
p. 181 doorways to kitchen, buttery, and pantry) and solar are largely
intact despite extensive additions. Also at Broadway is the smaller
C14 Prior's Manse, said to have housed the Abbot's steward; a
good doorway survives, plus the basic layout of hall, solar and
service wing. Again early C14 is Bretforton Grange, which
belonged to Evesham Abbey; a little detail of its hall survives, but
more notably the tunnel-vaulted undercroft below, with three
rounded transverse arches. The core of the Old Rectory at
Bredon is a C15 stone house with central hall and big gabled
wings; the original roofs with wind-braces and arch-braced
collars survive.

Some of the grandest medieval secular buildings are BARNS,
particularly three built for monastic owners. All three are probably C14, two of stone, one timber-framed, and with notable
roofs. Bredon, 134 ft (41 metres) long, built for the Bishops of
Worcester *c.* 1340–50, is of oolitic limestone, with the only fully
aisled timber interior in the county; a rare survival is its upper
30 solar for the reeve above one of the large porches. Middle Lit-
p. 495 tleton, probably built very early in the C14, for Evesham Abbey,
is of coursed Lias, 136 ft (42 metres) long, with a splendid interior mostly of base-cruck construction (i.e. crucks reaching only
to collar-beam level), but with an aisled bay at each end. The
31 largest, over 140 ft (43 metres) long, at Leigh, built for Pershore
Abbey, is probably of *c.* 1325. This is entirely timber-framed, and
of full cruck construction, the largest such building in England
(and probably anywhere). Other good timber-framed barns
include Holiday's Farm, Berrow, of cruck construction (now a
house); the very long C15 one at Bretforton Grange; and several
later examples, e.g. Pirton Court, probably C17. Notable DOVE-
COTES could also be of stone or timber framing; the Lias available on Evesham Abbey's estates allowed it to build some
memorable circular examples (Wickhamford, North Littleton;
also Kinwarton, in Warwickshire).

MAJOR TIMBER-FRAMED HOUSES are of course far more
common in Worcestershire than stone-built ones. Similar construction techniques were employed for buildings of all sizes and
this is dealt with in far greater detail below. Cruck construction

in major buildings is usually an earlier form (though in smaller buildings it can continue into the C15 or even C16). In the building of wall units, rectangular panels were the normal framing method, but their proportions change, tending to become more vertical in later times. Heavy square framing is thus normally earlier than framing with emphasis on closely spaced studs. Close studding, more extravagant of course in its use of timbering, came into fashion from c. 1400. In Worcestershire the large curved or elbowed wall-braces, obtained by cleaving (not the straight sawn ones), precede close studding and were often combined with it through the C15, but curved forms become rare in the C16. Close studding, however, persists into the C17. From the mid C16 straight wall-braces and such ornamental motifs as herringbone strutting are introduced. Concave-sided lozenges, fleurs-de-lys, and other shapes, obtained by letting in between the studs a panel of solid board carved in relief, came later still, all not usually until the Elizabethan and early Jacobean periods.

The earliest surviving example of BASE-CRUCK CONSTRUCTION in a major domestic building is probably the fine great hall at Eastington Hall, Longdon, perhaps of before c. 1300. Other parts of the house, including the hall's spere-truss, are equally outstanding work of c. 1500, all somewhat masked by competent work of 1914–15. The Hyde, Stoke Bliss, also has, at least internally, a remarkably intact base-cruck hall plus cross-wing, perhaps of c. 1300 or soon after; there are also remnants of a base-cruck hall at Rectory Farm, Grafton Flyford.

Internally the ROOF CONSTRUCTION is often the most rewarding element of many houses. Double-framed or purlin-type roofs are the most lavish. This is the type of the roof of the Guesten p. 699 Hall of Worcester Cathedral, now re-set at its original pitch at the New Guesten Hall at Avoncroft Museum, Stoke Prior. The remaining window tracery at the Guesten Hall in Worcester suggests that the roof must date from the 1330s. It is in any case the first such roof known in the region, with arch-braced trusses without tie-beams, and three tiers of purlins on each roof slope with elaborate cusped wind-braces between each tier. Of the same type but smaller is the well-preserved early C14 roof of the hall at Little Malvern Court, the refectory of the prior's lodging of the Priory. This has a spere-truss and roof with cusped windbraces and trefoils in the top triangle of the trusses. Cusped windbraces are also in the roofs of The Hyde, Stoke Bliss. The Old Hall (formerly rectory) at Martley also has significant survivals p. 491 of an early C14 house, including spere-truss and hall roof.

Fine examples of CLOSE STUDDING are the very complete Round House or Booth Hall at Evesham, late C15, and The 54 Greyfriars at Worcester. The latter, a secular building despite its 56 name, was probably built c. 1480–1500, for a brewer. C17 alterations, including a twelve-light oriel window, have modified the original layout but not detracted from the beautiful curving street façade, 69 ft (21 metres) long, with cross-gables at either end, the l. one above a basically original archway leading into a small courtyard.

The Commandery at Worcester (together perhaps with The
p. 734 Greyfriars) is the most interesting timber-framed ensemble. This,
a hospital run by Augustinian canons, is also mostly late C15,
including a painted chamber (*see* above) and fine Great Hall
52 (of the 1470s) with timber-framed polygonal bay window and
originally a hammerbeam roof (later converted to tie-beam
construction). Cofton Hall, Cofton Hackett, retains a similar
53 hammerbeam roof, a remarkable mid- to late C15 survival incorporated into a house of *c*. 1800. Such hammerbeam roofs were
alien to the Worcestershire timber-framed tradition, as they
required masonry walls to resist their enormous thrusts. A plainer
late C15, arch-braced roof is at Tickenhill Manor, Bewdley.
Mention must also be made of Huddington Court, perhaps the
55 most picturesque timber-framed manor house in the county,
partly late C15 (including probably its richly decorated brick
chimneystack of Hampton Court type), and standing within a
moat. This house, however, is difficult to interpret and must be
a fragment of a larger building, probably altered *c*. 1584. Its great
parlour retains a moulded early C14 stone fireplace with spectacular frieze. Consideration of other notable large timber-
framed manor houses would lead us into the Elizabethan and
Jacobean periods (*see* below).

THE DOMESTIC TIMBER-FRAMED TRADITION
by Stephen Price and Nicholas Molyneux

Crucks and box frames

The classic definition of the two types of FRAMING found in most
of the county's timber buildings was offered by F.W.B. ('Freddie')
Charles (1912–2002), a pioneer in their study and understanding, in the first edition of this book:

'The two structural types most general in Worcestershire are
the "cruck" and the far more numerous "post-and-truss" buildings. The cruck frame consists of two huge limbs of oak, curved
in shape, or elbowed, which extend from the base of the outer
side walls to the ridge of the roof. A pair of cruck blades is
obtained by splitting the main branch and trunk of the oak tree
so that each blade exactly matches the other. The blades of the
internal frames of a building are always perfectly symmetrical,
even though the outer ones, seen in the gable walls, sometimes
have unmatched blades. The method of erecting a cruck building is by *rearing*. That is, the components of each frame, previously wrought and numbered in the carpenter's yard, are laid out
on the building plot, jointed, and pegged to make a rigid frame,
which is then raised through ninety degrees with the feet of the
blades resting on the sill beam. As it is reared a tenon projecting
from the bottom of the blade engages a mortice already cut in
the upper surface of this beam. Indeed no timber simply rests on
or against another one. The longitudinal members – wall-plates,

purlins and wind-braces – are used to locate and secure each frame as it is reared. Post-and-truss construction as found throughout Worcestershire and in all the West Midlands is very closely allied to cruck building. Of the many variations of this form, the most common consists of posts on either side of the building held across the top by a tie-beam. On to this beam are jointed the principal rafters held about halfway up by a collar. These members together form the roof-truss. Various secondary members such as knee-braces and struts strengthen the complete frame. The longitudinal members are, in principle and function, the same as in cruck construction, so also is the wall frame, though the arrangement of studs, rails, and braces is subject to almost unlimited variation of pattern. Apart from formal dissimilarities, the post-and-truss building differs from the cruck in being erected timber by timber, but each frame must still be put together on the ground, and the joints exactly cut and fitted, before being taken apart and re-assembled vertically. The pegging of joints is then the final operation.'

This analysis has withstood forty years of study of the subject. Whilst oak was the staple of the timber framer's trade, often moved by water down the arterial River Severn, poplar was occasionally used for crucks, whilst elm was used in both crucks and box frames.* As yet only a small number of buildings have been precisely dated by dendrochronology.

Of DOMESTIC BASE CRUCKS (really a different tradition from crucks, although they use large curved timbers) five have been discovered. Nos. 5–9 Stourport Road, Wribbenhall, is tree-ring-dated to 1302–24. It has a crown-post roof in the solar cross-wing. The Hyde, Stoke Bliss, is now cased in stone, but the timber structure is practically intact. The two-bay hall had a stupendous central arched base-cruck truss. Everything about the building – the huge timbers and their heavy cusping and moulding – points to an early date. Another impressive house, Rectory Farm at Grafton Flyford, retains the central base-cruck truss supporting a crown-post, all heavily smoke-blackened. The example at Eastington Hall, Longdon, appears flimsy, although achieving a wide span. The date of all of them is probably shortly after *c.* 1300.

By the late C14 the typical roof has side PURLINS with tie-beam trusses. The purlins are trenched into the back of the principal rafters. Cusping of struts and wind-braces is the normal decoration in the C14 and early C15, but it is generally less vigorous than in Herefordshire and Shropshire. The clasped purlin was used from the later C15 up to the later C16 in conjunction with arch-braced tie-beams. Often the principal rafters are diminished above the purlin, making it possible to insert the purlins

---

* The ship's timbers myth is universally recounted and rarely if ever demonstrable. It perhaps derives from the C17 reservation of timber for the Navy, and so is perhaps an affirmation of the quality of the timber rather than origin. A ship was so much more carpentered than a house that it can never have made economic sense to use a ship to make a house.

after the roof was erected (unlike later examples which would
have been complex to assemble).

Medieval WALL FRAMING developed from large rectangular
panels with curved tension braces to vertical studding, the
intervals decreasing as the C15 progressed. In the second half of
the C16 as main framing members got straighter a distinctive
range of decorative framing techniques emerged. Herringbone
bracing, often over close-studded ground floors, and square
framing with decorative quadrant bracing to the gables occur in
both town and country. At Bromsgrove the former Hop Pole Inn
(1572) displays the earliest known use in the county of quadrant
and wavy braces, together with the fleur-de-lys. Renaissance
influence was translated into wood by the builders of the Pheasant Inn (c. 1590) in New Street, Worcester, where Ionic pilasters
decorate the storey posts of the jettied façade. But within the bays
the carpenters maintained the tradition of close studding,
relieved in the end panels by herringbone framing. King
Charles's House in the Cornmarket, Worcester, 1577, has Ionic
pilasters, herringbone framing, and (lost) elaborate bargeboards
and finials.

Another common pattern from the end of the C16 was
the combination of square framing to the first floor over close
studding to the ground floor. These were combined with slightly
projecting windows, often flanked by smaller frieze lights, a
commonplace of the first half of the C17. In the C17 heavy, carved
console brackets supported the jetties. The main windows
had mullions and transoms, planted on the face of the wall and
bracketed beneath the sill. Bargeboards, rare at every period in
the countryside but more prevalent in towns, were also richly
carved.

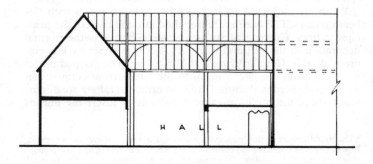

Stoke Prior, Avoncroft Museum.
House from Bromsgrove, section

Urban houses

Significant LATE MEDIEVAL BUILDINGS survive in Worcester (Friar Street particularly). The mid-C15 former Golden Lion occupies a narrow plot in a prime position in the High Street opposite the Guildhall. Behind the rendered C19 façade lies a medieval hall house which was jettied to the street, rising to four storeys. The front contained a shop with chambers above, while behind lay a two-bay open hall. A side passage, with a gallery over it, gave access to the service range at the back. The narrow frontage produced a 'squeezed' plan, the result of the central location where property values were high.

More relaxed planning was possible in secondary streets. Greyfriars in Friar Street, built as a merchant's house in the late 56 C15, proclaims its status with a continuous jettied frontage and a wide courtyard entrance. There is no structural evidence for an open hall, although there is a hint of a large hall in the documents. Significantly the upper chambers were ceiled from the outset. There is evidence for vaulted undercrofts in Worcester, reached by bulkheads from the street, with remnants of a C14 vault lying under No. 92 High Street.

In Bewdley economic decline in the C18 led to the survival of medieval houses hidden behind brick fronts, found in increasing numbers since the 1970s. Nos. 12–14 Wyre Hill has a generous frontage comprising a three-bay house parallel to the street with a central open hall. Nearer the centre, where building plots were at a premium, the plan was more compact; witness Nos. 59–60 High Street, a pair of open hall houses with the chamber or solar internally jettied into the open hall.

Inserted chimneys, floors, stairs and new frontages have altered these buildings, but their original form can be appreciated from the town house of *c.* 1475 from Bromsgrove, re-erected at the Avoncroft Museum of Buildings. It has a half-floored hall and two-bay solar wing, jettied towards the street. The timber-framed smoke-hood in the hall is mid-C16. The ground floor of the solar cross-wing may have been used for trading, although it lacks the distinctive shop window such as that at No. 32 Friar Street, Worcester, of *c.* 1500. This retains evidence for a two-light window from which falling shutters opened outwards to form a table for the display of shop wares.

No. 31 High Street, Droitwich (formerly known as Stephen's), *c.* 1400, has what Freddie Charles regarded as the finest medieval solar range in Worcestershire, comprising a three-bay block connected at first-floor level by an ante-chamber to a two-bay great chamber. The open-arched central truss of the great chamber is formed by impressive moulded knee-braces which connect the main posts, principals and collar. Two tiers of cusped wind-braces and a brattished wall-plate complete the visual feast.

A building type which might have been expected in an urban context is the Wealden house, with its recessed bay for the open hall. However, whilst these occur in Warwickshire to the E and Herefordshire to the W none have been found in Worcestershire.

Timber buildings were erected in large numbers in the towns during the LATE C16 AND EARLY C17. Bewdley and Worcester have the most, but there are also good examples in Bromsgrove, Tenbury, Upton upon Severn and Droitwich. In Worcester, Tudor House in Friar Street is a single continuously jettied range of the late C16 containing three two-storey houses. Each comprises a front parlour with a rear kitchen and a stair to one side of the chimney. Immediately behind were small framed structures which inventories identify as weaving shops. In the C16 the cumbersome broad looms were at ground-floor level, sometimes with substantial posts dug into the ground. From the last quarter of the C16 there is a significant change in the height of new houses in Worcester, so that even the lesser streets were soon boasting three- or four-storey houses. Nash House in New Street, 1605, is the best, three-and-a-half storeys; a reach-for-the-sky statement of the possibilities of timber framing, the front in close studding with continuous rows of windows. The Bailiff's House at Bewdley, 1610, is of the same type, though a storey lower, and in addition to the close studding has quadrant bracing at attic level. Both houses had timber-framed stair-turrets against the back wall.

The urban timber-framed tradition (at least externally) was virtually extinct by the late C17 when brick had become the walling material of choice. Brick buildings in Worcester are documented from the early C17, and had become the norm by 1660.

Rural houses and their plan forms

More than half of the surviving medieval rural houses have at their heart a CRUCK frame. The simplest are of two bays, such as Priest's Cottage, Huddington, but the more usual pattern was the four- or five-bay house with a two-bay open hall at the centre, as at the Fleece Inn, Bretforton or Cresswells, Ombersley. The main area for display was the arch-braced collar of the central truss and the associated wind-bracing of the purlins, which are very occasionally cusped for decorative effect, as at Butts Bank Farm, Broadwas (now a barn). These houses almost always had timber-framed walls, which, when they survive, are large rectangular panels with curved tension braces.

These houses are simple ranges without the elaboration of cross-wings, but usually with a cross-passage between the hall and the lower end. Cross-wings on other cruck-framed houses seem in most cases to be later additions. A few have early cross-wings, such as Pump House Farmhouse, Berrow (*see* Birtsmorton). But more often larger C16 and C17 additions aggrandize the cruck hall range, for example at Meneatt Farmhouse, Shelsley Kings, with its C16 cross-wing at the upper end.

At the modest end of the spectrum of BOX-FRAMED hall houses, Freddie Charles found the perfect miniature at Shell Cottage, Himbleton. The thatched C15 house has a two-bay hall with the solar and service bays built as outshuts. A meaner, and later, house at Orchard Cottage, Wick (near Pershore), has low side walls and a flimsy smoke-blackened roof.

Of slightly larger houses, the classic medieval H-plan with a hall flanked by cross-wings for the upper (solar) end is absent from the middling houses of the county. For example, Seechem Manor, Alvechurch, achieved an H-plan in the late C16, apparently by the replacement of in-line upper and lower ends by cross-wings. From time to time the only surviving section of the medieval house is the cross-wing, as at Shell Manor, Himbleton. Here a fully developed H-plan house was present by the late C16, but the jettied solar cross-wing is C15.

Higher up the social scale the plan forms are more developed. The intriguing Old Hall at Martley, the old rectory, is apparently an H-plan of C14 date. Internal inspection reveals that the solar cross-wing was separated from the hall by a 6-ft (2-metre) gap. The spectacularly picturesque Huddington Court (1493), still fortified by a water-filled moat, seems to have exhibited a similar plan form. There is a grand heated first-floor chamber, with the finest and probably earliest brick chimneyshafts in the county, and an attached kitchen block, but there is no trace of an attached hall, although there is plenty of space for such on the platform. p. 491

55

W.G. Hoskins dubbed the period c. 1570–1640 the 'Great Rebuilding', and sought explanations for it in increased prosperity and a desire for greater privacy and comfort amongst the lesser gentry, yeomen and husbandmen. The evidence for Worcestershire, where many open-hall farmhouses were changed by the insertion of upper floors or were completely rebuilt, clearly supports Hoskins' theory, but this rebuilding should be seen in the context of successive waves of alteration and renewal.

The NEW FARMHOUSES of the late C16 and early C17 added a distinct character to the Worcestershire landscape. These are of two or two-and-a-half storeys and exhibit decorative framing, often confined to the front elevation, as at Tanhouse Farm, Stoke Prior, of 1631, leaving the sides and rear relatively plain. First floors and attics, especially of parlour cross-wings, can be jettied, while a storeyed porch demarcates the entry. Brick chimneyshafts clustered in star plan, or as lozenges and squares set anglewise, tower above their roofs. The main body of the stack could also be decorated. Aston Hall Farm, White Ladies Aston, has four lozenges in rectangular panels (paralleled in an urban context at Priory House, Droitwich).

The most widespread ALTERATION was the insertion of a first floor into a former open hall, creating more space. The new floors, supported on spine beams, were inserted into existing frames by the use of the chased mortice. Sometimes one end of the new ceiling beam was supported by an internal chimneystack. The new ceilings were often richly decorated by moulded and stopped main beams and subsidiary joists. At Thorn Farm, Inkberrow, the Elizabethan ceiling inserted into the former open hall is much higher than normal. It is divided by main beams into quarters and the compartments have joists laid at right angles to each other, producing a chequerboard pattern.

Building a new chimney offered the opportunity to improve other facilities. Back-to-back HEARTHS provided warmth in rooms at each level either side of the stack. A recessed hearth with a fixed hood gave greater control over cooking than had been possible on an open hearth in the middle of a hall. It also offered the chance to build bread ovens into the sides or corners of the chimney as well as bacon-smoking chambers within the stack. Such curing chambers have been found at Brook Priory Farm, Inkford, Wythall and Seechem Manor, Alvechurch, and more must await discovery. A favoured position for the inserted stack was within the space formerly occupied by the through- or cross-passage, leaving a small lobby or baffle entry allowing access to the rooms either side. Frequently the matching space on the far side of the stack was used to house the staircase. Lateral stacks built against the back wall of the hall or the side of a parlour may be indicative of a more conservative plan form which retained the tradition of the hall, passage and solar. When the old roof was too low to house a new upper floor comfortably, additional space was provided by heightening the side walls on top of the wall-plate. A good example in a post-and-truss building can be seen at Whitney's Farm, Ombersley.

Deasland Farm, Heightington, a C15 cruck hall house replanned in 1611, is a microcosm of these developments. The date is carved on a porch with turned balusters added forward of the original ogee-headed doorway to the former cross-passage. The inserted chimneystack was accommodated within the old entry, which was reduced to the classic lobby. The new floor required additional headroom, provided by the raising of the roof, identifiable by the two rows of small square panels built on the old wall-plate. Within this new wall a gabled dormer with a large mullion-and-transom window threw light into the new chamber floor.

Tree-ring dating offers the opportunity for greater precision in the dating of these conversions. The floor inserted into the C14 base-cruck hall of The Hyde, Stoke Bliss (*see also* p. 35), produced a felling date of 1567/8, which was also the date of the stable block. This indicates that owners were not only improving their houses but upgrading their farm buildings too.

Adding a new or replacement wing was another option. At the Moat House, Longdon, a three-bay parlour cross-wing replaced the earlier solar around 1600. The new wing is characteristic of the period, with herringbone framing, jettied ends and moulded bressumers. The cross-wing at Seechem Manor, Alvechurch (close studding to the ground floor and square panels above) has been tree-ring dated to 1595.

Of PLAN FORM there are three types – a free-standing two- or three-bay range, the L- or T-plan house, and the H-plan. Blagrave's map of Feckenham in 1591 shows the three types in one parish. Much work remains to be done to link social status with this classification and to apply it more broadly to the rest of the county.

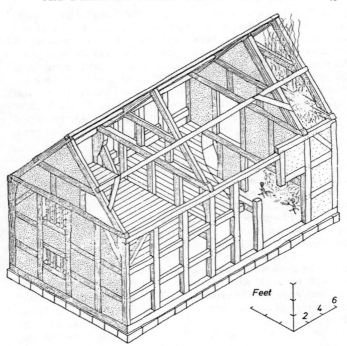

Wythall, Maypole Cottage.
Axonometric view

The SINGLE-RANGE PLAN is exemplified at Tanhouse Farm, Stoke Prior (1631), and Fosters Green Farm, Bentley Pauncefoot. Maypole Cottage at Wythall is one of the simplest, only one-and-a-half storeys with a two-and-a-half-bay plan, of one heated room and an inner room. The smoke bay at the gable end marks an intermediate stage towards the development of the chimneystack. Lower Blackstone Farm, Wribbenhall (1589), is altogether more impressive. Three bays long and two-and-a-half storeys high, its storeyed porch led to a lobby entry between parlour and hall, with a service room beyond.

When a wing was added to the first house type the plan could assume the L- or T-shape. This type is well suited to the baffle or lobby entry formed by the stack positioned against the junction of the ranges, providing heat to rooms either side. Keys Farm at Lower Bentley, Bentley Pauncefoot, is the archetypal T-plan house with a lobby between the parlour wing and the hall. Its modest parlour fireplace bears the date 1604, which must be very close to the house's construction. In contrast, the hall fireplace is 8 ft (2.5 metres) wide and was clearly used for cooking, turning hall into kitchen. In its first phase Barnt Green House p. 45

(*c.* 1620–30) had an L-plan, but here the front range displays precocious symmetry. Its axial stack and entrance were placed centrally in a narrow bay between the heated front rooms, which are demarcated by decorative gables rising from the wall-plate. An unheated rear wing completed the L-plan. Later examples of the symmetrical façade with storeyed porch and axial stack are Baston Hall Farm, Suckley, Fairfield House, Fairfield (1669) and Puddleford Farm, Eastham. Lower Tundridge Farm, Suckley (*c.* 1650), shows how the three-bay symmetrical façade developed as the front of an L-plan: the precursor of the Georgian brick farmhouses with one or more rear wings.

57   H-PLAN HOUSES such as Cattespool, Tardebigge (1639), were built with a cross-passage between the hall and service room, and show how long the tradition of the through-passage persisted into the C17 in a rural context. At Cattespool the hall is heated by a substantial stone chimney placed laterally against the back wall. Elsewhere, the axial stack has already arrived and is set close to the junction of one wing and the central range. At the Manor House, Bishampton, *c.* 1629, the stack is timber-framed and once tapered as a framed hood to the apex of the roof. The cross-wings may not be contemporary, as at Upper Beanhall Farm, which only assumed its H-plan when a second wing was added to the existing C16 T-plan in the C17. Gradually the central hall contracted to a central lobby; at Park Hall Farm, Hanbury, the bar of the H-plan is nothing more than an entry with an axial stack behind, all squeezed into a narrow bay between the two cross-wings which make up the four-room plan.

As in the towns, STAIR-TURRETS are a feature of the early C17. A stair-turret forms one of the rear wings of the Old House, Alvechurch (*c.* 1630), and at Manor Farm, Abbots Morton, one was added when the roof was raised in the C17.

In the NE of the county, where sandstone was readily available, a hybrid form of building using stone walls and internal framing developed in the 1670s. A two-and-a-half-storey stone house in St John Street, Bromsgrove, has exposed gable trusses and bears the date 1674 on its tie-beam, while in the countryside around Bromsgrove the pattern is represented by a substantial group of rebuilt farmhouses. Longmead (formerly Sandhills Farm) at Barnt Green is especially important, securely dated by a date-stone to 1678, displaying a symmetrical façade.

The DETACHED KITCHEN persisted into the C16 and C17. A handful of now one-and-a-half-storey single-bay detached buildings lying close to the service end of farmhouses across the county are likely to have started their lives as such. Illustrative evidence from the early C19 reinforces this impression. The detached single-storey outbuilding at Lower Grinsty Farm, Feckenham, is a former kitchen, while nearby at Meadow Farm (formerly Bordesley Lodge Farm), Redditch, the smoke-blackened bay of a two-bay range set at right angles to and almost touching the main house is a prime candidate.

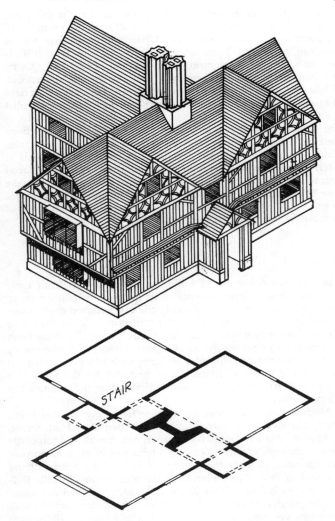

Barnt Green, Barnt Green House, *c.* 1620–30.
Isometric drawing and plan

The classic small black-and-white thatched COTTAGES of the 2
county beloved by the producers of calendars and postcards have
been the subject of a pioneering study by Richard Harris. They
are one- or two-cell buildings, one-and-a-half storeys high, their
framing usually comprising three square panels. They have
eyebrow thatch to the dormers, a half-hip to one end of the roof,
and an end chimney of brick or stone at the other. The two-cell

plan has one large heated room, usually entered in the gable end to one side of the stack or in the side wall near the corner, and an inner room housing the stairs. Upstairs the chamber may or may not be divided. These cottages are very small. One at Wadborough (Drakes Broughton) measured only 18 by 14 ft (5.5 by 4.3 metres), but still incorporated the two downstairs rooms. While earlier examples are properly framed, later examples have thin studs and rails, which are part-morticed and part-nailed halved joints. Downward straight braces are also characteristic of the later examples. A late framed example at Ripple has been dated *c*. 1800 from a 1795 penny lodged in the roof structure. Pairs of cottages were also popular. Two closely set cottages at Atch Lench are of two-room plan but have centrally placed entrances. The gap between them has since been infilled to make one large house. Semi-detached pairs of timber-framed cottages are more difficult to detect because of later amalgamations, but at least one example has been recorded.

Finishes

The external colouring of buildings was practised from early days, but there is little evidence of its nature. The blackening to which most timbers were subject in the C19 removed most traces of earlier colour: in the early C19 Bromsgrove was described as 'magpie' in appearance. Only rarely has detailed analysis been undertaken to discover the paint history. However, documentary evidence for the painting of a building with black-and-white in the C17 and visual evidence of the early C18 for the same at a house in Norton-juxta-Kempsey, indicates that the practice has a long history.

Medieval interiors seem generally to have been coloured red, which can survive extensively, as at the Golden Lion, High Street, Worcester. WALL PAINTINGS are often ephemeral, and can easily be lost through careless cleaning. Occasionally we find decorative schemes, such as the green and red on the beams of the remnant of Prior More's house at Battenhall (now Middle Battenhall Farmhouse), Outer Worcester, which matched the hangings he purchased in the late C15. The county's best secular wall paintings, covering many rooms in Dowles Manor, *c*. 1620, were lost after a fire in 1986. Vineyard scenes including the fox and grapes from Aesop are found at No. 3 Beale's Corner, Wribbenhall, while the early C18 floral and bird paintings at Yew Tree House, Northampton, Ombersley, are distinctly Chinese.

Decorative PLASTERWORK is now rare, although some of the subtler decoration can easily be missed. Ceilings sometimes have a simple scratch moulding around their edges, as at the Pheasant Inn in New Street, Worcester. More elaborate C17 plasterwork is to be found at the Tudor House, in Friar Street, at Cummin's Farm, Hindlip, and Harborough Hall, Blakedown. Plaster was also used for flooring. It is often found in attics where grain was stored, or sometimes in cheese rooms. The latter can be identified by the racks for close-set shelving for cheeses, as at Astwood Court Farm, Wychbold.

By the early C17 oak panelling was ubiquitous in the better houses in combination with arcaded overmantels, for example at Bittell Farm, Alvechurch, and The Greyfriars, Friar Street, Worcester. Pat Hughes's work on Worcester probate inventories shows that panelling was taking over from wall hangings as the C16 progressed.

FROM THE MID C16 TO THE MID C17

Major Elizabethan and Jacobean domestic architecture

Timber-framed MANOR HOUSES of some size continued to be built, as we have seen, throughout the C16 and for much of the C17. By the mid C16 almost all are of close-studded framing. Notable examples include Badge Court, Elmbridge; Birtsmorton Court, looking the picture of a medieval moated manor house but probably mostly remodelled for Giles Nanfan 1572–80; Salwarpe Court, probably rebuilt for Sir John Talbot *c.* 1580; and Besford Court, perhaps *c.* 1600. Prior's Court, Callow End, is a rare survival of a C16 house (with irregular framing) built round a small courtyard. The earliest dated example with the elaborate ornamentation that characterizes the last stage of timber-framed architecture is the former Hop Pole Inn at Bromsgrove, of 1572, quite early for its concave-sided lozenges and fleurs-de-lys motifs.* The most complete and finest timber-framed Jacobean manor house is probably Mere Hall, Hanbury, its main struc-   58 ture, with hall and cross-wings, dendrodated to *c.* 1611; its most intriguing feature is the continuous run of mullioned windows at attic level, clearly meant to reproduce the appearance of the fashionable long gallery. This feature was copied in smaller houses, especially at Middle Beanhall Farm, Bradley Green, dated 1635. Dowles Manor, near Bewdley, probably *c.* 1622, would also have merited inclusion here, had it not been shamefully demolished (together with its well-preserved decorative wall paintings) in the 1980s. The porch of the Tudor-looking Fairfield House carries the surprisingly late date of 1669.

Despite this continuance of high-quality timber-framed architecture, BRICK seems quite at home in Worcestershire by the later C16. The best-detailed, and probably first example, was Grafton   p. 48 Manor (near Bromsgrove), built in 1567–9. Much survived rebuilding of 1861, notably the porch and adjoining cross-wing with crowstepped gables. The Doric porch and pedimented   59 parlour window are among the best things of that moment in England, a date when there was great interest in classical motifs

---

*It must be noted, however, that in a wall painting of *c.* 1500 at Molesworth in Huntingdonshire a timber-framed house appears in the background with concave-sided lozenges.

Grafton Manor.
Drawing

(cf. Funerary monuments, below), which grew less when the Elizabethan style had developed into something more of its own, and when influence from the Netherlands had got a firmer hold. Also brick, with crowstepped gables, are what survives (before its
110 Victorian rebuilding) of Madresfield Court, 1584–93, namely its gatehouse range; and The Nash, Kempsey, probably mid-C16, altered *c.* 1600. Both have charming plaster ceilings with vine and rose decoration in chains of ogee reticulation units, and fine ornate chimneypieces, especially The Nash. Harvington Hall,
67 near Chaddesley Corbett, is an informal, moated, very picturesque Elizabethan brick house, probably mostly of *c.* 1580–1600, built round a C14–C15 timber-framed core. Best-known for its priest holes, the largest such collection in England, it is also notable for its wall paintings of *c.* 1600, the most outstanding by far in the county; some of them are extremely elegantly drawn, with nothing of the usual clumsy English naïvety. Worcestershire has only one major surviving JACOBEAN country house, West-
68 wood House, near Droitwich, begun *c.* 1612 as a hunting lodge for Sir John Pakington (who then lived at Hampton Lovett). Almost as soon as this was completed, perhaps before, Sir John
p. 655 decided to add four diagonal wings radially to this core, thus forming a unique and exciting ground plan. This work was probably completed before he died in 1625. The ornate central porch, a remarkably early attempt at copying the Arch of Constantine in Rome, and the delightful gatehouse, are probably also of *c.* 1620–5. The earliest surviving BRICK FARMHOUSE in the county incidentally is probably Warndon Court, of the early C17.

   Good STONE HOUSES are not quite confined to the extreme SE corner of the county. The late C16 Cleeve Prior Manor is

Woollas Hall.
Drawing of north front

mostly of Lias; Hillhampton House, Great Witley, early C17 E-
plan, is of sandstone, though with much Georgian remodelling.
But the most notable Jacobean houses are indeed of oolitic limestone, that is they are situated on the Cotswolds or nearby. They
are especially the Lygon Arms at Broadway, built as a manor
house probably *c.* 1620, and Woollas Hall, Eckington, at the foot
of Bredon Hill, built 1611. Both have asymmetrical gabled
façades, that of the Lygon Arms more convincingly composed.
The Great Chamber here has a striking stone chimneypiece and
some plasterwork; Woollas Hall retains its hall screen with Ionic
pilasters. The timber-framed Hill Court, Grafton Flyford, has
good plaster ceilings of *c.* 1630, probably by itinerant craftsmen
and executed from moulds identical to those used at Aston Hall,
Birmingham. Harborough Hall, Blakedown, of 1635, also has
good plaster ceilings. Apart from these, Elizabethan and Jacobean
PLASTERWORK is very modest (Mill Hall, Porter's Mill, Claines;
Pirton Court; and two houses in Friar Street, Worcester: Nos.
38–42, and No. 32 with a pretty strawberry trail). Many more
CHIMNEYPIECES of this age survive. The houses above again
have the best examples, especially the gorgeous timber one of
c. 1600 in the Great Chamber at Westwood House. Two at
Norgrove Court, *c.* 1600, are clearly derived from Vredeman de
Vries's *Caryatidum*, published 1565. One from Tickenhill Manor,
Bewdley, with the Prince of Wales' feathers, is displayed at 63
Hanbury Hall. Others to note are at the timber-framed Dormston Manor, and at St Peter's Manor, Droitwich, where the porch
carries the date 1618.

Funerary monuments

The comparative scarcity of Elizabethan and Jacobean houses
of consequence is in great contrast to the wealth of CHURCH

MONUMENTS. They illustrate all phases, all types, and all moods, starting with an alabaster monument to Sir John Talbot of Grafton Manor †1550, at Bromsgrove, where no Renaissance features are yet introduced. Yet in a tablet to Thomas Watson †1561 at Bengeworth (Evesham) we already find the characteristic elegant Renaissance details which were later as a rule either coarsened or anyway overlaid with Netherlandish strapwork, caryatids, and the like. The Bengeworth tablet has no figures at all, not even an effigy. Of the same year of death, 1561, was a Blount monument at Mamble, where the effigy (which alone survives) was replaced by a skeleton, a rare case in the Elizabethan age. A Blount monument of the same year of death, at Astley, shows the way from the Early Elizabethan classicism to the more rigid, more Mannerist stylization which is one trend of the mature Elizabethan style. The monument to Robert Blount †1573 at Astley, with Early Renaissance wreaths, has the rare distinction of a signature, *John Gildon* (or Guldo) of Hereford, who also signs a contemporary monument at Bosbury, Herefs. The mature Elizabethan style in its full panoply is represented, for example, by the monument to Bishop Freake †1591 at Worcester Cathedral; this is also prominently signed, though we do not know who *Anthony Tolly* was. The tomb-chest and back arch here are standard elements; cf. the richly detailed Acton monument of 1581 at Tenbury Wells. In many of the more lavish Worcestershire monuments they are combined with flanking columns and a top cornice with shields, obelisks, or the like. Good examples are two Sheldons †1570 and †1613 at Beoley; the earlier of these is more intricately carved, but the later appears decidedly more affluent, with greater use of colour. One of the finest is the double tomb of two generations of Sandys at Wickhamford with the date of death 1626. The type goes on till 1632 or later, see the Russell monument at Strensham. Both the Wickhamford monument and that at Strensham have been attributed to *Samuel Baldwin* of Gloucester (†1645), who may well have trained in London. So also have many others, probably too many, as his only documented work is a Berkeley monument of 1615 at Bristol Cathedral; but the distinct family likeness of them all is notable.

The Wickhamford and Strensham monuments are mostly of alabaster, and as a rule alabaster produced the best results. That is clearly shown by comparing them with the similar but clumsy wooden monuments to Walsh family members at Stockton on Teme †1593 and at Shelsley Walsh †1596, or with the later Washbourne monument at Wichenford of 1631; also with the stone Barneby monument of 1594 at Bockleton (probably by the Dutchman *Gerard Holleman*). Fine alabaster examples, all attributed to *Baldwin*, include the tomb-chest with Knotsford effigies at Great Malvern, *c.* 1615; the perfect Berkeley monument of 1614 at Spetchley; the sumptuous Reed monument †1611 at Bredon; the beautiful Savage monument at Elmley Castle, *c.* 1631; and the contemporary Savage monument at Inkberrow. The

underside of the canopy of the last is decorated with cusped quatrefoils, presumably Gothic Survival rather than Revival. The
same is true of the canopy underside at Wickhamford (†1626).
Comparison might be made with the low wooden rail round the
alabaster Harewell effigy at Besford (†1576), which has the
curious motif of horizontal reticulation units. Besford also has a
memorable Late Elizabethan monument, probably of the 1590s,
to another member of the Harewell family: a painted oak triptych with a kneeling figure and surrounding religious and alle-   62
gorical scenes and inscriptions. A similar monument at Burford,
Shropshire, is signed by *Melchior Salabossh* (though it seems more
suspect to attribute to him the wooden monuments at Stockton
and Shelsley Walsh, mentioned above). Of the type often used for
professional men, with a reclining figure nonchalantly propped
on one elbow, the only notable Worcestershire example is George
Wylde †1616 at Droitwich St Peter, wearing his red sergeant-at-
law robes, in a specially decorative, strapwork-enriched arched
recess. Kneeling effigies seen in profile were of course one of the
standard types of Elizabethan and Jacobean funerary art, and
there are many in the county. Three particularly worth noting are
the Hanford monument at Eckington (†1616), the Bigg monument at Norton (†1613), both these probably again by *Baldwin*,
and the Moore monument in Worcester Cathedral (also †1613);
here three men kneel in the front and three women behind them,
and the recess has a fan vault with pendants, another case of
chosen Gothicism, for whatever reason. In Worcestershire as
against other counties these monuments with kneelers were specially favoured about 1610–20: Salwarpe †1613, Leigh †1615,
Badsey †1617, All Saints Worcester †1621, Hanbury †1627, then
later examples at Leigh †1639 (with a little more individuality)
and at Cropthorne †1646.

Apart from these kneelers, the latest dates of death so far mentioned are 1631 and 1632, at Elmley Castle, Inkberrow, Wichenford and Strensham. Of †1633 is a modest Dowdeswell tablet at
Bushley, without figures and already post-Jacobean and classical
in its main elements. Another, †1639, at Ribbesford is also already
classical. So it seems that the Inigo Jones revolution, or, if you
like, the Carolean style, had reached Worcestershire by this date.
One needs to be cautious, however, when assuming too much
from the dates of death on monuments. The best such tablet,
Humfrey Pakington †1631, at Chaddesley Corbett, can be shown,   65
by careful reading of its inscription, to have been executed not
earlier than *c.* 1646. On the other hand the road to the Baroque
was opened with greater pomp and circumstance than nearly
anywhere in England with the monument to Thomas, first Baron
Coventry at Croome D'Abitot. He died in 1639, and if this was   66
indeed made shortly after his death, it is the ancestor of the most
frequent and characteristic type of monumental memorial of
about 1700, with reclining effigy flanked by standing or seated
figures. *Nicholas Stone* was probably responsible for this remarkably progressive piece.

Churches and church furnishings

Most of the major monastic foundations in Worcestershire were situated in the towns, so it was there that the DISSOLUTION of the 1530s had the greatest impact. Worcester Cathedral Priory found uses for most of its buildings (with the notable exception of its infirmary). At Evesham there were already two parish churches standing within the abbey precincts, so there was little hope of preserving the abbey itself; at least the detached bell-
40 tower survived (to great scenic effect). Pershore kept only the crossing tower and E end for parochial use, though Great Malvern, then much smaller, managed to retain the whole church. The greatest loss was at Redditch, where the whole Bordesley Abbey complex disappeared, apart from the gatehouse chapel, which the inhabitants maintained as their church. Little Malvern is the only significant case where the monastic buildings (the refectory or prior's hall) were adapted for secular use. Here again the church was reduced to the tower and E end.

There was, as was usual in England, little new CHURCH BUILDING in the period from *c.* 1550 to the mid to late C17. A conservative adherence to the Gothic style is the keynote of the few projects that survive: the Sheldon Chapel at Beoley of the late C16, with the elementarized Perp of its E window; the Berkeley Chapel of 1614 and much else at Spetchley; and the chancel at Ashton under Hill of 1624, with its Perp intention and incorrect, quite entertaining execution. Most notable is the still Perp work of 1674 at Hanley Castle, where Sir Nicholas Lechmere rebuilt the whole E end: central tower, chancel and N chapel. The material here is brick, but brick as we have seen had already been a viable option in the county for a hundred years or more. Of the shamefully neglected brick Blount Chapel of *c.* 1560 at Mamble hardly anything remains. The brick Berkeley Chapel at Cotheridge of *c.* 1620 is very modest indeed.

The most lavish CHURCH FURNISHINGS are PULPITS, quite understandable in Elizabethan and Jacobean England. Many average ones survive, with the usual squat blank arches, and with panels with arabesques, flowers, dragons, or just lozenges. Naunton Beauchamp's pulpit with loose cornucopia and leaf panels is probably of *c.* 1600 (hardly later than its benches with crude linenfold). Broadway St Michael, Honeybourne, Kidderminster Unitarian Church (dated 1621), and Ipsley (Redditch) have the most sumptuous examples, none of them incidentally at their original locations. That at Stoke Bliss is dated 1631, though the style is still purely Jacobean, and the same style continued as standard for many more years. A quite exceptional pulpit is at Worcester Cathedral, of 1641–2 by *Stephen Baldwin* (Samuel's son). This is of stone, and of the wine-glass form favoured in the C15; its delightful back panel, with its depiction of the New Jerusalem, also survives, though now detached from it. Wickhamford has perhaps the best ensemble of C17 (and C18) furnishings, including a remarkable C17 oak FONT, but much here has been brought in from elsewhere. The COMMUNION RAIL at

Castlemorton still has the Jacobean motif of flat openwork balusters, yet the dates inscribed on it are 1683 and 1684.

Civil War archaeology*

Worcestershire is famously the place where the Civil Wars of 1642–51 began and ended. Powick Bridge was the site of the first skirmish on 23 September 1642, and played a critical role in the Battle of Worcester on 3 September 1651. Worcester and Evesham were the main garrisons, but there were a number of smaller Royalist outposts, characteristically at medieval moated manor houses. That at Strensham (the home of Sir William Russell) survives, with artillery platforms built on the corners of the earthwork. Evidence of possible siege works from 1646 also survives in the parkland around Hartlebury Castle, and the classic Civil War battle landscape at Ripple (1643), where the opposing forces typically lined up in sight of each other in a single location, is intact. By contrast, the Battle of Worcester in 1651 was fought along an eight-mile front, with the final phase of bitter street fighting within Worcester itself. The Royalist Scots relied on the newly restored medieval defences (as best seen on City Walls Road), and on new works (the star-shaped Fort Royal, built 1643–6 and enlarged 1651; now an urban park). On the E side of the city, evidence of Parliamentary siege works can be seen in the form of an artillery position on Tamar Close.

SECULAR ARCHITECTURE, LATE C17 TO EARLY C19

Later C17 domestic architecture

The outstanding building of the COMMONWEALTH PERIOD in Worcestershire, is Norgrove Court near Redditch, probably p. 500 remodelled in 1649–51 for William Cookes, High Sheriff for the county in 1651. The abiding impression (despite odd irregularities and the surviving Jacobean detail within) is of a regular rectangular brick house with huge hipped roof, the earliest example of Inigo Jones' influence, or more probably of its sibling style, 'Artisan Mannerism', in the county. The Red House near Eldersfield, also of brick and said to date from 1647, is an intriguing but even more distant descendant of London mannerism.

Apart from these two cases, the CAROLEAN STYLE, or at least elements of the purer classicism of the Carolean age, came much later to domestic architecture than it did to church monuments. Both timber-framed and gabled stone houses went on for a remarkably long time. Of the latter a monumental example is Tudor House at Broadway of 1659–60, which, as against the Lygon Arms for example, is symmetrical, or nearly so. It still has

*By Malcolm Atkin.

mullioned windows, but has replaced the traditional individual hoodmoulds of the windows by dripcourses running through (cf. also Farnham House, Broadway). In dated small houses one can watch these changes as follows. The wing of a house in High Street, Broadway, dated 1687, still has mullioned windows and gables. Cross Cottages, Conderton, a former farmhouse of 1675, and Longmead, Barnt Green, 1678, still have mullioned windows but in a symmetrical arrangement, and this is so in cottages at Broadway even as amazingly late as 1718 and 1722. On the other hand, in Childswickham House, dated 1698, the windows, of course also symmetrically arranged, have mullioned-and-transomed crosses, and that can be regarded as the late C17 standard. They usually come with a hipped roof and represent the final turn from the informal to the formal.

The gables so far referred to have been straight-sided or stepped. SHAPED GABLES also appear, though surprisingly late. The earliest in Worcestershire, those at Westwood House, are probably of c. 1620. The next seem to be late C17 at the earliest: Bell End Farm, Belbroughton; The Grove, Stoke Bliss; and Stockton House, Stockton on Teme. The only dated example probably belongs to the remodelling of The Great House at Bickley, Knighton on Teme, 1709; the similar Stoke Court nearby, at Greete, Shropshire, is dated 1702. The first Dutch gables, i.e. shaped gables with a pediment on top, appear in the brick wings at Severn End, Hanley Castle. The date here is 1673, some fifty or sixty years after the introduction of this motif to London, and the name of the builder is known, one *John Avenant*. It is also worth noting that the main part of Severn End was being remodelled for Sir Nicholas Lechmere in the fanciest timber-framed style only some five years previously.

Altogether Worcestershire was conservative. We have to go to the remodelling of Hartlebury Castle for Bishop Fleetwood, begun c. 1675 by *Thomas Wood* of Oxford, especially its porch with semicircular pediment, to get a further inkling of the Jones-Pratt-May-Wren style (though it should be borne in mind that Hanbury Hall, *see* below, may well have been begun c. 1680–90). Dresden House, Evesham, dated 1692 with its symmetrical classical fenestration, its hipped roof, and its restraint in all decoration (except for the gloriously over-sized iron brackets flanking the doorway) fully belongs to this style. So does Berkeley's Hospital at Worcester, endowed 1692, though probably mostly not built until the first decade of the C18.

The outstanding INTERIORS of the late C17 in this new style are at Westwood House, perhaps reinstatement after Civil War damage. The staircase, probably of c. 1660–70, rises straight up to the upper floor in two parts with an intermediate landing. The splendid plaster ceiling of the Great Chamber is characteristic of progressive work of c. 1670: separate thickly moulded panels with foliage and wreaths. Good plaster ceilings of about the same date, on a far more modest scale, are in the parlour at Cummin's Farmhouse, Hindlip, and on the first floor at Greenstreet Farm, Hallow.

Secular architecture in the C18 and early C19

C18 HOUSES in Worcestershire are a large chapter. With the porch of Hartlebury Castle, Dresden House, Evesham, and the Berkeley Hospital the Wren style had established itself. Hanbury Hall is the finest example of it in the county, or more accurately of the type of house introduced by Sir Roger Pratt, a symmetrical restrained double-pile with hipped roof. It is dated 1701, but this may record its completion. The architect is unknown; the drawings that survive do not imply anyone of national significance. The most probable local influence was Robert Hooke's Ragley Hall in Warwickshire (1679–83), though Hanbury's stone centrepiece also shows precise knowledge of Thoresby Hall, Notts., of 1685–7 by William Talman. The remarkable wall paintings inside are slightly later, *c.* 1710, early work by *Sir James Thornhill*. On the whole, especially around the splendid staircase, they are better than those of Verrio and Laguerre, Thornhill's foreign competitors, the favourites of Court and nobility. There is also original plasterwork (and an outstanding overmantel of *c.* 1760). Wichenford Court is an excellent example of the smaller country house, in the Hanbury style, as it became popular throughout the country in the late C17 to early C18; here the date is probably *c.* 1710.

The rather more BAROQUE, i.e. less restrained, style of the Smiths of Warwick and others working in the same vein in the West Midlands is first encountered at the ruined shell of Hewell Grange, Tardebigge, 1711–12, probably by the brothers *William* and/or *Francis Smith*. The anonymous, quite ambitious Tutnall Hall nearby is in much the same style. The Bishop's Palace at Worcester, thoroughly remodelled in 1719–23 in a style that Colvin called 'bumbling Baroque', may also be by *William Smith*. Of far higher quality is Ombersley Court of 1723–6, a work of the abler *Francis Smith*; despite early C19 refacing, the interior remains astonishingly intact. Overbury Court, of 1739–43, perhaps by the younger *William Smith* (the son of Francis), has a grand entrance hall and excellent staircase. *William and David Hiorn* succeeded to the Smiths' business and were responsible for the remodelling of Kyre Park, 1753–6, and perhaps Wolverley House, *c.* 1749–52, and Broome House, *c.* 1760–70. Far more exuberant is what *Thomas White* did (or is said to have done) at Worcester, the spectacular and a little overdone Guildhall of 1721–4 (*see* below) and Britannia House of *c.* 1730, now part of the Alice Ottley School. The seated Britannia in the raised centre of the latter's parapet and the carved trophy at the Guildhall were certainly carved by White, but his status as an architect rests solely on a passage in Nash's *History of Worcestershire* (1782), parts of which are certainly inaccurate. The impressively Baroque w front of Kemerton Court, *c.* 1720–30, has also been attributed to White. The otherwise modest Manor House, South Littleton, begun *c.* 1712, might also be allowed into this paragraph because of the Vanbrughian effect of its open-arched chimneystacks.

Other SMALLER EARLY C18 COUNTRY HOUSES worth
mention include Doverdale Manor, Drayton House near Chaddesley Corbett, Knightwick Manor, Lickhill Manor near Stourport, and Wolverton Hall near Peopleton. Apsidal hoods over
doorways, especially with carved decoration, are a favourite
feature of Queen Anne or Early Georgian houses. The White
House at Suckley has an especially pretty one. Typical also of the
Early Georgian is the segment-headed window. Two neighbouring urban houses in Waterside, Upton upon Severn, have them:
one of *c.* 1740 in conjunction with a Gibbs surround to the
81 doorway (cf. the former church at Upton, of 1756–7); the other,
said to be of *c.* 1712, with a Venetian window, which is a mid-C18
motif in Worcestershire too, as we shall see presently.

NEO-PALLADIANISM, including an Inigo Jones revival, had
started in London already in 1715–20. It reached Worcestershire
p. 245 late. The paramount examples are Croome Court (Croome
D'Abitot) of 1751–2 by *Lancelot Brown* (apparently with some
88 assistance from *Sanderson Miller*) and Hagley Hall by *Miller*,
1754–60, assisted by a London architect, *John Sanderson*, and
others. Both are chaste and correct, and both have the corner
erections with pyramid roofs which Inigo Jones had introduced
at Wilton in Wiltshire, and William Kent had taken up at
Holkham Hall, Norfolk. It is curious that these two most purely
architectural houses should be by a garden designer and by the
Gothick specialist in the county. In Croome Court not a great
deal of the original interiors is preserved (the best the Long
93 Gallery by *Robert Adam*, 1761–6), but Hagley has a series of
extremely fine ones, some well restored after a fire in 1925; the
89 Entrance Hall and Saloon are especially memorable. A competent local exponent of the Neo-Palladian style was *Anthony Keck*
(1726–97), based in Gloucestershire. Bevere House, Claines, of
c. 1765 is the best survivor of his work in Worcestershire; Middle
Hill, Broadway, *c.* 1779, may also be his, and perhaps Ripple Hall,
of *c.* 1780–90, where the detail is decidedly Adamish. He carried
out some internal remodelling at Hanbury Hall, but his major
house in the county, Ham Court near Upton upon Severn, was
demolished in 1929.

Of the Neo-Palladian motifs of Croome and Hagley, the one
which became most popular in Worcestershire was the Venetian
window. It was used not, as in the Palladian mansions, as a rare,
significant accent, but all over façades, just to make them more
ornate. An unusually interesting case in a town is No. 61 Broad
Street at Worcester, one bay wide, four storeys high, with nothing
but Venetian windows and, incidentally, on the top a little lead-
domed belvedere with pointed windows. Other examples are at
96 Pershore, one commanding the w end of Broad Street; another,
much finer, in Bridge Street, Perrott House, built *c.* 1770, perhaps
by *T.F. Pritchard* of Shrewsbury. (This contains some excellent
plasterwork, good enough to be sometimes attributed to Robert
Adam who was busy at Croome Court at the same time.) An
amusing and historically telling variation on the theme is the
Gothick Venetian window, in which the raised middle part is

given an ogee arch. Often this motif is accompanied by ogee gables or a parapet treated as ogee gables. The best examples are the former Golden Lion Inn at Bromsgrove; one façade at Broome House, mentioned above (the other main front is classical, but probably contemporary); Tudor House at Chaddesley Corbett (probably by *James Rose*), The Pool House at Astley, especially delightful; and the refronting of the E side of the early C18 Old Trinity House at Worcester. This may be the earliest, *c.* 1750; the others seem to be of *c.* 1760–70. None unfortunately is dated.

Both Croome and Hagley have more PARK FURNISHINGS than any other house in the county, though the Picturesque in layouts and sentimental buildings had been introduced a little earlier at the poet William Shenstone's The Leasowes, Halesowen (formerly in Worcestershire); not much survives, though, of either his house or his garden furnishings. At Hagley the most important pieces are the Castle by *Sanderson Miller*, 1747–8, and the Temple of Theseus by *James 'Athenian' Stuart*, designed 1758–9, completed 1761–2, a remarkably early example of the baseless Athenian Doric order. Stuart and Nicholas Revett had been in Athens in 1751–5, but their *Antiquities of Athens* did not begin to appear until 1762 (and did not include the Hagley model, the so-called Theseion). Sanderson Miller's first effort at a medieval revival was the tower at Edge Hill in Warwickshire, on his own estate at Radway, built in 1745–7. Hagley also has a (now roofless) rotunda. Croome Court has a larger rotunda, called the Panorama Tower, by *James Wyatt*, 1801, based on an earlier design by *Robert Adam*, who provided other garden temples (he worked for Croome from 1760). Also his are the Temple Greenhouse, probably one other temple pavilion, and Dunstall Castle (*see* Earl's Croome) of 1766–7, looking very like a ruined castle by Miller. Other Croome garden features, including a grotto, are by *Lancelot 'Capability' Brown*, who laid out the grounds from 1751, his first complete landscape. The work at Croome Park (now again in splendid condition thanks to the National Trust, unlike the grounds at Hagley) belongs to the years of the sixth Earl of Coventry, who also built Broadway Tower, a prominent 'Saxon Hexagon Tower' with three higher round turrets, by *James Wyatt*,

Croome D'Abitot, Temple Greenhouse.
Elevation

1794–9. The Fish Inn on Broadway Hill was a summer house belonging to different owners, the Farncombe estate; this is of 1771, and classical in an entirely playful, if not barbaric way. Another tower, Leicester Tower, in the grounds of Abbey Manor, Evesham (*see* below), is much later, 1842. Castle Bourne, near Belbroughton, is also mid C19 but with a late C18 core, a ruined castle with two towers; another late C18 folly tower is at Clent Grove nearby.

Georgian HOUSES with less to distinguish them are to be found in all towns and in the countryside. C18 five-bay red brick houses throughout the county can hardly be counted and are not all included in the gazetteer; this is especially true of many isolated farmhouses, often as important a feature of the landscape as their timber-framed predecessors. In villages the outstanding Georgian buildings are often the PARSONAGES. Notable ones worth mentioning include Ripple, 1726, Eastham, 1735, Shelsley Beauchamp, 1784–5 (by *James Rose*), Lindridge, 1788 (by *Richard Morton*), Cropthorne, 1789 (by *Thomas Johnson*), and a stuccoed example, Tardebigge, 1815 (by *Thomas Cundy Sen.*). Worcester still has a few streets where Georgian houses easily dominate. This includes part of the main N–S spine, notably Foregate Street and The Tything. Bridge Street of 1788–92, part of *John Gwynne*'s approaches to his Worcester Bridge, is also worth noting. The best Georgian ensembles elsewhere are at Bewdley, Stourport-on-Severn, and Pershore. Bewdley has its bridge, waterside street, and the short Load Street running straight to the church. Stourport was created at the place where the Staffordshire and Worcestershire Canal reached the Severn (*see* Industrial Developments, below). At Pershore, Bridge Street provides an imposing, entirely Georgian brick entry to the town from the S. Several very good Georgian houses of stone at Broadway, mixed in almost imperceptibly with earlier and later examples, should also not be forgotten.

Of LATER C18 COUNTRY HOUSES, the most refined example is Craycombe House, Fladbury, by *George Byfield*, 1790–1, with a modest ashlar-faced exterior but an exceptionally elegant interior. Of his Perdiswell Hall of 1787–8, N of Worcester, only the gatepiers and stables survive. Beoley Hall, 1791, by *John Sanders*, Soane's first pupil, is also architecturally progressive and ambitious, but only the exterior is unaltered. Shakenhurst Hall near Bayton, much remodelled in 1798–9, is also worth mention, and perhaps the undated Bredon Manor. The outstanding early C19 house is the beautiful ashlar-faced Spetchley Park, built 1811–c. 1818 by *John Tasker*, a little-known London architect who worked mainly for Roman Catholic clients. It is now the only significant Worcestershire example of such domestic Grecian purity (since the sad demolition of Strensham Court, of 1824). Plans for the grandiose external remodelling of Ombersley Court by *John Nash*, 1808, were superseded by sober ashlar refacing by *John Webb* of Lichfield, 1812–14. Nash did, however, complete major additions at Witley Court, Great Witley, from c. 1806, notably two massive porticoes. Hadzor Hall, of 1779, is memorable for its portico of 1827 by *Matthew Habershon*, and even more for its interior and Schinkel-inspired garden layout by *Alexander Roos* from *c.* 1835. Other good early C19 houses are Hindlip Hall, *c.* 1820, now rather swamped by the West Mercia police headquarters, and the neat and modest Sodington Hall, Mamble, rebuilt *c.* 1807. Of GOTHIC REVIVAL HOUSES there are only two to note: the small, very pretty Bretforton Hall of *c.* 1800, emphatically of the Gothick variety, and Abbey Manor outside Evesham, 1816–17, still also entirely pre-archaeological in its use of Gothic motifs. Two houses fully in the castle style have not survived. Of the earlier, Lea Castle, near Cookley, probably by the 'architectural antiquary' *John Carter*, *c.* 1812–16, only lodges and boundary walls survive. Of the much later Arley Castle, Upper Arley, by *R. & J. Varden*, of 1843–4 and so really belonging to the Victorian section, all that remains is the fragment of one corner.

Several early C19 developments in WORCESTER also belong to this period. The best is Britannia Square, begun *c.* 1815, a variety 99 of stuccoed houses around a spacious green (in which the main house is placed). Lansdowne Crescent, begun *c.* 1835, and the smaller Lark Hill, *c.* 1819–24, are also stuccoed. At St George's Square, *c.* 1830–40, the stucco is given up and the brick once again exposed, pointing clearly towards the Victorian Age. Several early C19 stuccoed villas at Great Malvern, especially those along Worcester Road, also deserve mention here; so indeed does their focus, the stuccoed Library and Assembly Rooms by *John Deykes*, 1818–21.

Georgian PUBLIC BUILDINGS generally have so far been neglected. Only the Worcester Guildhall of 1721–4 has been mentioned. This is indeed as splendid an early C18 town hall as any 74 in England. *Thomas White* of Worcester, as has been said, was the most likely architect, but this is by no means certain. Its first-floor assembly room was handsomely remodelled in 1791 by *George Byfield* (whose other Worcester public building, the House of Industry, 1793–4, has disappeared). Georgian public buildings are in fact more scarce than one might expect. The former Worcester Royal Infirmary, brick and pedimented, by *Anthony* p. 724 *Keck*, 1766–70, survives more or less intact amongst later additions (and is soon to be absorbed into the University of Worcester). From the very end of the Georgian period is the fine Grecian ashlar-faced Shire Hall at Worcester by *Charles Day*, 1834–8, but this can equally well be included in a subsequent section of the Introduction. Outside Worcester there are only the small classical Guildhall at Bewdley, of 1808, probably by *John Simpson* of Shrewsbury, and the even more modest town halls at Droitwich, 1825–6, and Upton upon Severn, 1832; all three are in fact undetached terrace houses. Evesham's Town Hall is detached, and mostly of pre-Victorian dates, but not especially distinguished. No pre-C19 schools deserve particular mention, except perhaps Sir Thomas Cookes's Bromsgrove School of *c.* 1695 and Deacle's Charity School at Bengeworth (Evesham), of 1736 and now hideously disfigured. Part of the Sebright School at Wolverley

dates from 1787, but its main building, 1829–30, again fits better
into a later section. Bridges, also no doubt public buildings, are
discussed in the chapter on Industry and Transport.

CHURCHES FROM THE LATE C17 TO THE EARLY C19

C18 churches

The C17, as we have seen, was a lean period for church building
in Worcestershire. In contrast the C18, at least from the 1730s, is
especially rich, with several notable urban CHURCHES, especially
four in Worcester, and two or three rural ones of particular
quality. The outstanding Early Georgian example is that planned
by Lord Foley for his country estate at Great Witley and built in
1733–5; it replaced a large medieval parish church, as well as
serving as the chapel of his adjoining house. It is not known who
designed it; *James Gibbs* is the most likely candidate. It has a
78 quiet, restrained exterior, but the interior is gloriously Baroque,
79 thanks to *Antonio Bellucci*'s ceiling paintings, *Joshua Price*'s
80 stained glass, and the gold-on-white papier mâché decoration.
Paintings and glass were bought when the Duke of Chandos's
princely house at Canons (Middlesex) was sold off in 1747, and
the moulded decoration added at this date is certainly by *Gibbs*.
The result is the most Italian-looking church interior in Georgian England.

Great Witley has a w tower and round-arched windows. That
is the same with the four parish churches which Worcester built
(or rebuilt) between 1730 and 1770. They are externally all of the
same type, though St Nicholas, built by *Humphrey Hollins*
76 (perhaps to *Thomas White*'s design), 1730–5, and St Swithin by
Thomas & Edward Woodward of Chipping Campden, 1734–6, are
aisleless. All Saints, probably by *Richard Squire*, 1739–42, and St
Martin by *Anthony Keck*, 1768–72, both have aisles, the former
77 with Doric columns, continuous entablature, and an almost
semicircular plaster vault, the latter with slender unfluted Ionic
columns, each with its individual piece of entablature, and a flat
ceiling. The towers of All Saints and St Swithin are Perp in origin,
and in 1751 the Perp tower of St Andrew (all that now remains)
received a new spire by *Nathaniel Wilkinson*, with a Corinthian
capital instead of a finial. St Nicholas has an ambitious w front
towards the main street of Worcester; St Swithin, All Saints, and
St Martin all display fully developed E façades.

In the smaller towns two more Georgian churches soon
appeared, simple rectangles in plan, again with round-arched
windows and w towers. Bewdley, 1745–8, by *Thomas Woodward*,
82 also with Roman Doric columns and plaster tunnel vault inside,
has an earlier tower (1695–6). Of Upton upon Severn, by *John*
p. 642 *Willoughby*, 1756–7 (supervised by *Squire*), only a small fragment,
with doorway with Gibbs surround, and the stately C14 tower
remain. The tower, with its octagonal top stage and pepperpot

cap by *Keck*, 1769–70, is a fine and unexpected landmark. 81
Croome D'Abitot, of 1759–63, serving as an eyecatcher from the
house and almost certainly by *Lancelot Brown*, is of architectural
interest far beyond county concerns, not only because of *Robert
Adam*'s delightful Gothick interior. The archaeological exactitude 90
of its exterior, presaging the early C19, is also remarkable. The
tiny Rushock, by *Roger Eykyn* of Wolverhampton, 1756–8, and
Stanford on Teme, another eyecatcher, by *James Rose*, 1768–9,
are more typically Georgian Gothick, with the usual Y and intersecting varieties of tracery. *Rose* also supplied the splendidly dominating steeple at Chaddesley Corbett, 1778–9. Wolverley, 1770–2
by an unknown architect, is an even greater contrast to Croome;
frankly Georgian, unashamedly utilitarian, with its dark red
brick, round-arched windows, square w tower, and plain arcades:
a convinced, determined building. *Francis Hiorne* in 1776–7, and
now in great contrast to Wolverley, gave Tardebigge a superb,
decidedly Baroque steeple. The rebuilding of Longdon, 1786–7,
by a local architect, *William Marshall* of Bourton-on-the-Water
(Glos.), has some charming, rather naïve touches. Even more
charming is (or was) the small-scale Broome, as rebuilt in 1780.
Hanbury, mostly remodelled by *Thomas Johnson*, 1792–5, has
pointed windows and windows with Y-tracery. After that there is
little of note until the 1820s.

For CHURCH FURNISHINGS, few urban C18 churches can be
so complete and so pretty as St Swithin at Worcester. Croome 76
D'Abitot's interior is also remarkably well preserved, and *Robert
Adam*'s Gothick pulpit and classical mahogany font are individ-
ually as fine as any in England. The wonderful furnishings of
Great Witley have already been discussed. Little else survived the
reforming zeal of the Victorians. Exceptions include the mid-C18
wrought-iron altar table with marble top at Birtsmorton and the
wrought-iron sword rest in All Saints, Worcester (St Swithin has
another).

Church monuments

In FUNERARY MONUMENTS, as we have seen, the change
towards the classical ideal began *c*. 1630–40, not in the 1680s and
1690s. What happens in the second half of the C17 is that certain
monuments stay classical and shed what had still been impure in
the 1630s, while others go Baroque. The former trend is best
illustrated by three memorials to bishops of Worcester, all entirely
architectural, without figures, and with hardly any ornamental
details: bishops Blandford †1675, Fleetwood †1683, and Thomas
†1689 (though not made until *c*. 1710, and interestingly local
work, unlike probably the other two). The road to the Baroque
had already been opened with a flourish by *Nicholas Stone*'s spectacular monument to the first Baron Coventry at Croome 66
D'Abitot (*see* above). *Grinling Gibbons*'s Coventry monument of
1690, also at Croome, belongs to the same type, a reclining effigy
flanked by large symbolic figures. The figure carving, however, is
dull, as it is so often in Gibbons's work in stone. A Berkeley

monument at Spetchley, †1694, Sir Thomas Winford †1702 at Astley, and Bishop Stillingfleet †1699 in Worcester Cathedral are also attributed to him; there is in addition a documented tablet of 1689, at Clifton upon Teme, with good garlands, but not specially interesting otherwise. Other notable monuments with reclining effigies are at Elmley Castle (the first Earl of Coventry, made c. 1700 for Croome) by *William Stanton*, where again a large angel stands to either side; at Strensham by *Edward Stanton*, where the wife of Sir Francis Russell †1705 sits by his head; and at Bengeworth (Evesham): John Deacle †1709. And so on, right into the Georgian years, with reclining effigies at Hanbury – Thomas Vernon †1721 by *Edward Stanton* and *Christopher Horsnaile*, flanked by Justice and Learning – and at Hampton Lovett: Sir John Pakington †1727, by the elder *Joseph Rose*. Less effective, but meant to be fully in the Baroque mode, is the monument at Rous Lench to Francis Chaplin †1715 (sister of the architect Thomas Archer). Such major standing monuments, and of course some already of the first half of the C17, are of a size and especially height beyond anything medieval (except for Prince Arthur's Chantry at the Cathedral). As they were usually placed in the parish churches belonging to the estates, they tend to choke the buildings that host them.

Other more modest types of late C17 monument need only passing reference. One major tablet at Croome to the Hon. Henry Coventry †1686, attributed to *William Kidwell* or *Willam Stanton*, has large white caryatids l. and r. An intriguing monument to Elizabeth Talbot †1689 at Salwarpe has no effigies but two charity girls against the tomb-chest. A smaller tablet to Olave Talbot †1681 above this has twisted columns, like many others elsewhere. The best example is probably the Cookes monument, c. 1694, at Tardebigge, attributed to *James Hardy*. Other favourite late C17 forms for tablets had a gristly cartouche surround (cf. Peopleton †1682), or were provided with columns and pediments, sometimes broken and curly, and often with garlands of the Gibbons type; there is a batch at Beoley.

C18 MONUMENTS are plentiful. *J.M. Rysbrack*'s enormous and spectacular standing monument to the first Lord Foley, c. 1735 or soon after, at Great Witley, must be number one; it benefits greatly from its rare tailor-made setting, with the right unobstructed view. But *Roubiliac*'s Bishop Hough of 1744–7 in Worcester Cathedral is as fine in quality and more sophisticated in composition. He reclines no longer, but is seen rising, or being drawn up, to the higher spheres. Everything here is Rococo in the sense not so much of ornament as of subtly calculated asymmetry, resulting in a general zigzag movement through the whole monument. The other *Roubiliacs* in Worcestershire are far less sensational. That at Hagley, †1747, was designed by *Sir Charles Frederick*. That at Hanbury, c. 1740, based on Guelfi's Craggs monument in Westminster Abbey, has recently been reattributed to *Sir Henry Cheere*'s workshop; by the same perhaps are two Baylies monuments of c. 1754–60 at All Saints, Evesham. The earliest asymmetrical cartouche incidentally is on the fine monument, with reclining effigy, to Rear-Admiral William Caldwall †1718 (attributed to *Edward Stanton*) at Birtsmorton. *Prince Hoare*'s Bishop Maddox †1759, close to Bishop Hough's monument in the Cathedral, was no doubt made in opposition to Roubiliac; its large female figure is decently draped and phlegmatic.

Of sculptors of the late C18 and early years of the C19, *Joseph Wilton* is represented by the exquisite Adamish monument to Sir Thomas Street in Worcester Cathedral, of 1774, and *Joseph Nollekens* by two monuments with the busts in which he excelled: one to Bishop Johnson †1774 in the Cathedral, designed by *Adam*, the other †1797 in the Sandys Mausoleum at Ombersley. *Thomas Scheemakers* has an extremely fine monument, perhaps 84 his best, at Powick (Mary Russell †1786), and a more modest one at St Peter, Droitwich, †1779. By *John Bacon* is a beautiful piece, with Benevolence and Sensibility by a wreathed urn, at Astley (†1793). His earlier work in St Swithin, Worcester, *c.* 1770, is less memorable. The elder Bacon was also chief designer for Mrs *Coade*'s factory of moulded sculpture in artificial stone, and the two reliefs of Agriculture and Navigation, dated 1788, on the gatepiers of the former Perdiswell Hall, N of Worcester, have all the characteristics of his elegant, somewhat florid style of drapery. *John Bacon Jun.* has two similar tablets †1801 and †1806 at Astley, a good monument at Croome D'Abitot (†1809), and two ambitious ones in the Cathedral. That to Richard Solly †1803 85 is every bit as delicate as work by his father. The other is of the type of the memorials in St Paul's Cathedral to those killed in the Napoleonic wars; Sir Henry Ellis in fact fell at Waterloo. The two *Flaxmans*, at Wolverley (†1801) and Broome (†1804) are not particularly outstanding. *Sir Richard Westmacott*'s more intimate approach is demonstrated in his fine figure of a resting pilgrim on a tablet in Great Malvern Priory (*c.* 1830). Flaxman and Westmacott (together with his son *Richard Westmacott Jun.*) introduced purer Grecian forms to church monuments; many such were produced by the local firm *Stephens & Co.*, see below.

Sir Francis Chantrey more or less brings this section to an end. His white seated or kneeling female figures in profile, in relief, or in the round, pure and classical and at the same time sentimental, can be seen in the Cathedral (Charlotte Digby, 1823–5), 87 at Tardebigge (1835), and at Hanbury (1837). *Peter Hollins*'s monuments at Great Malvern (†1836 and †1841) are in exactly the same mood; Hollins worked at Birmingham. The most important Worcester monumental carvers were the Stephens family: *William Humphries Stephens* (born 1737), his son *Joseph Stephens the Elder* (1773–1834), and grandson *Joseph Stephens the Younger* (born 1808). They could do very good work, especially William: Elizabeth Eaton †1790, at Kempsey; Mary Hall †1794, at Worcester Cathedral. *Thomas White* (*c.* 1675–1748), whom we have met as a putative architect, was also a Worcester man, but probably trained in London; his tablets, though, are of limited interest. *Richard Squire* (1700–86), the probable designer of All Saints, Worcester, was also primarily a statuary, providing many good architectural tablets.

Nonconformist chapels

A postscript is necessary on the NONCONFORMIST denominations, whose earliest outstanding building, with a modest but dig-
101 nified ashlar-faced front with giant pilasters, is the Unitarian
Chapel at Evesham, of 1737. Equally impressive is the former
Presbyterian Church at Bewdley, of *c.* 1778, now Roman
Catholic: oblong, of brick, with two apsed ends. The same theme
was taken up in the large transeptal addition of 1815 to the
Countess of Huntingdon's Chapel at Worcester, the main part of
which is of 1804. Its interior, now a concert hall, is also largely
of 1815. The Baptist Chapel at Upton upon Severn was built in
1734, and there are Friends' Meeting Houses, modest as usual,
100 at Worcester, 1701, and Bewdley, 1706. A few unassuming late
C18–early C19 chapels, Baptist, Congregational or Wesleyan
(Methodist), also survive. No other early Nonconformist chapels,
however, need be recorded specifically here.

INDUSTRY AND TRANSPORT

Nationally significant INDUSTRIAL REMAINS are mostly confined to the larger towns in the northern part of the county,
Bromsgrove, Kidderminster and Redditch, and to Worcester
itself. Droitwich is (or was) a special case; the production of SALT
here was the mainstay of the town's economy from at least the
Iron Age or Roman periods. A reconstruction of the mid-C13
form of its principal brine well, Upwich Pit, has been erected in
Vines Park, but nearly all subsequent traces have disappeared
(peak production was reached in 1872). So sadly have most of
the buildings associated with the Droitwich brine spa, created
largely by John Corbett (cf. Chateau Impney, Dodderhill) when
he relocated salt production to his Stoke Works at Stoke Prior
(convenient for both canal and railway). Very little survives there
either. Nor does much remain of the major industry, at least from
the C17–C18, of the Bromsgrove area, the production of NAILS.
This was dependent on numerous, small-scale workshops: an
excellent C19 example (from Sidemoor) is preserved at the Avoncroft Museum, Stoke Prior. Such methods could not compete
with industrialized production elsewhere in the West Midlands,
particularly in the Black Country.
   Kidderminster is of course famous for the manufacture of
CARPETS, an industry apparently introduced to the town *c.* 1735.
It was slow to introduce power looms and reached its heyday only
in the later C19. By the late C20 little of the industry remained;
in addition the town suffered from the short-sightedness of its
municipal guardians – at the time of writing for example it
still awaits the establishment of a proper carpet museum. Some
good mill buildings do survive, however. The most impressive is
118 Thomas Lea's Slingfield Mills, of 1864 by *Lockwood & Mawson*
of Bradford. This multi-coloured brick leviathan, still remarkably

with its chimney more or less intact, was successfully converted
to retail use in 2004, a breakthrough for the town's industrial heritage. Other carpet mills remain s of the town centre around New
Road and Green Street, mostly the work of local architects.
Amongst these can be included *J.G. Bland* of Birmingham,
responsible for both Stour Vale Mills, built by Lord Ward, 1855–6,
to provide manufacturers with rentable space for power-loom
weaving, and Morton's Works, 1869–70, the most completely preserved complex, with buildings for yarn and pattern storage, dye
houses, weaving sheds, and finishing rooms. Some buildings also
remain of Brintons Ltd, the largest concern by the early C20. A
few others are now protected by listing, but a large number have
been allowed to disappear.

Redditch depended largely on the manufacture of needles, pins
and fish-hooks. A surprising amount remains, despite (perhaps
because of) the advent of the New Town in 1964. The origins of
NEEDLE-MAKING in the area, including Studley (in Warwickshire), are obscure. It was certainly the principal occupation of
the district by *c.* 1700; by *c.* 1850–60 Redditch was the national
centre for the industry. Forge Mill, converted to needle-scouring
c. 1730 and enlarged *c.* 1828, is preserved as a museum; other
early needle mills survive at Feckenham and Astwood Bank
(Double Century Works, partly of *c.* 1810–20). The Worcester
and Birmingham Canal which reached Tardebigge, three miles
away, in 1807, must have provided further stimulation to the
trade. British Mills, Prospect Hill, of *c.* 1840, are a good surviving steam-powered needle-mill complex, and there are also a few
later C19 examples, as well as buildings of related early C20 industries: spring production by Herbert Terry & Sons, s of the town,
and Royal Enfield motorcycles, to the N.

Most of the industries mentioned above depended on the production of iron and/or the availability of coal, imported mostly
by water (*see* below). There are some remains of the earlier IRON
INDUSTRY, though in landscape terms rather than buildings, at
Astley, where traces can be seen of the mid-C17 furnace and forge
traditionally associated with Andrew Yarranton. The ironworks at
Wilden, near Stourport, probably of similar antiquity, flourished
here or at other sites such as Cookley. Blakedown retains
the string of mill ponds that powered its iron foundries, and
Churchill Forge nearby is a remarkably intact example of a spade
and shovel works of *c.* 1800. Some industry developed along the
riverside at Stourport itself (including a large power station of
1925–6, now demolished). Remains of walls of the gas works
survive and rather more of Holbrook's Vinegar Brewery, established 1798, rebuilt 1882.

VINEGAR BREWING was one of the multifarious industries of
Worcester. It has left significant remains, notably the enormous
warehouse (or filling room) of Hill, Evans & Co., built *c.* 1865–70.
Its scale and materials, multi-coloured brick, are comparable to
the huge railway Engine Works that opened nearby in 1864 (*see*

below). Generally it is noteworthy how the industrial area that developed in the Blockhouse district, E of Worcester city centre, with the coming of the Worcester and Birmingham Canal in 1815, moved further E with the arrival of the railway at Shrub Hill in 1850. Lea & Perrins's Worcestershire Sauce factory, by *William Henman*, 1896–7, stands close to the latter. Others of the city's OLDER INDUSTRIES kept to the former location, for example Fownes's glove-making business, whose factory (by *Yeates & Jones*, 1882–4) is now a hotel. Yet older establishments retained their riverside sites. The most notable case is the famous Royal Worcester Porcelain Works, in Severn Street, which only ceased manufacturing porcelain in 2006. Its varied collection of mostly C19 buildings (several incidentally by architects from the Staffordshire Potteries) should be preserved.

Worcester also has the best remains of PUBLIC UTILITY INDUSTRIES. Its City Electricity Works of 1893–4, by Powick Bridge, the first permanent hydro-electric power station built by an English municipality, supplemented the waters of the River Teme with steam power as required. The buildings have been well converted to housing. Also of note are the city's water works at Barbourne, 1857–8 and later, now an environmental centre. Such utility buildings elsewhere have disappeared, including in 2006 the final remnants of Malvern's gas works, which supplied gas to the town's uniquely rich collection of C19 lamp-posts.

Most signs of industry in the county's smaller towns have also been erased. There are minimal remains, for example at Evesham, of the BREWERIES which once existed in nearly every town. At Wribbenhall (Bewdley) something remains *in situ* of the rope-works, mostly 1866–70. More is preserved at the Bewdley Museum, in Load Street, which also contains the town's C17–C18 brass foundry *in situ*.

RURAL INDUSTRY has not fared any better. A few early corn mills retain their gearing machinery (e.g at Wickhamford), and some of the larger mill buildings still look impressive, as at Wyre Piddle, *c.* 1800, and at Alvechurch, 1875 (by *E.A. Day*). The most impressive rural survivals are the brick hop kilns that dot the countryside, particularly towards the Herefordshire boundary (e.g. at Eardiston near Lindridge). Most are C19 and some form part of very large complexes, especially when combined with malthouses, as at Stockton on Teme and Suckley.

Transport

The RIVER SEVERN was the most powerful influence on industrial development in Worcestershire until at least the C19. It was England's busiest waterway, navigable from the sea as far inland as Welshpool in Wales. Bewdley and Worcester were the county's most important river ports. The Severn's tributaries were also navigable to some degree. The Avon improvement scheme by *William Sandys* of Fladbury, 1635–9, enabled boats to navigate from Tewkesbury (in Gloucestershire), through Pershore and Evesham, to Stratford-upon-Avon (Warwickshire). In the 1660s the Stour was improved to Stourbridge, and in the 1680s the Sal-warpe to Droitwich to facilitate the transport of salt. The Teme, however, was only navigable to Powick Bridge on the outskirts of Worcester. Navigation on the Severn began to deteriorate in the late c18 (mainly because of the enclosing and better drainage of water meadows). The major improvement scheme did not materialize until 1835–43, when work was undertaken between Stourport and Worcester. *Sir William Corbett* was the chief engineer, *Edward Leader Williams* the supervising engineer; the most telling reminders of the scale of their work are the locks at Lincomb (Hartlebury) and Holt, and the Diglis Severn Locks at Worcester.

Stourport, which replaced Bewdley as the major port in the N of the county, was a creation of the CANAL AGE. Canal build-ing in Worcestershire was driven by the need to link up with the Severn, particularly to provide outlets for the developing indus-tries of Birmingham and the Black Country. Stourport was built as a transhipment port at the Severn end of the Staffordshire and Worcestershire Canal, constructed 1766–71, with *James Brindley* as principal engineer. It ran 46 miles from the Trent and Mersey Canal near Wolverhampton, thus providing a significant link across the whole Midland region. Work on STOURPORT began c. 1768, and it remains the most important and best-preserved town built in England as a consequence of canal age. Its system of basins, locks and service buildings remains largely intact (and early c19 basins infilled c. 1960 are being reopened in 2006). Kid-derminster was also a significant beneficiary of this canal.

Contemporary with the Staffordshire and Worcestershire was Brindley's much more modest Droitwich Canal, which left the Severn at Hawford, and in 1853 was extended E to link up with the county's second major canal. This was the 30-mile-long Worcester and Birmingham Canal, the most expensive such undertaking in the Midlands. It was a relative latecomer, begun by Act in 1791, and reaching the Severn at Diglis, Worcester, only in 1815. Its Worcester outlet has little of the charm of Stourport but could be made much more attractive. Its most impressive canalscape is in Tardebigge parish, where thirty locks of 1812–13 take the canal up onto the Birmingham plateau. The only canal attempted W of the Severn, the Leominster Canal, begun from that Herefordshire town in 1791, was abandoned after the col-lapse of a tunnel near Mamble in 1794.

The earliest of the county's steam passenger RAILWAYS, the Birmingham & Gloucester, opened in 1840. Its major engineer-ing feat, the Lickey Incline, had to solve the same problem as the Worcester and Birmingham Canal's flight of locks, taking the system from the Severn valley up onto the Birmingham plateau; the engineer was Capt. *W. S. Moorsom*. Next, in time and impor-tance, was *Brunel*'s Oxford, Worcester & Wolverhampton Railway, which reached Worcester (Shrub Hill) in 1850 and Kiddermin-ster in 1852. Shrub Hill became a significant railway centre. Its Italianate station, rebuilt 1863–5, with a remarkable tiled waiting room, survives little altered, and the multicoloured brick exterior

116 of the enormous Worcester Engine Works of 1864 (by *Thomas Dickson*) is also largely intact. The Hereford & Worcester Railway of 1860 joined Malvern to Worcester Shrub Hill; its elegant bridge across the Severn was sadly altered in 1904, but Great
120 Malvern station, by *E. W. Elmslie*, 1860–2, with exotic platform ironwork, mostly survives, together with his enormous station hotel (now Malvern Girls' College). These three lines (later taken over by the Midland or Great Western railways) form the county's surviving rail network; Evesham station, rebuilt 1896, is a good example of a later GWR station.

Branch or cross-country lines have mostly disappeared, apart from the special case of the Severn Valley Railway, of 1861–2. Its section from Hartlebury through Stourport to Bewdley has gone, but the rest is still worked as a steam tourist railway, with a fine
119 iron bridge over the Severn at Upper Arley (engineer *John Fowler*), well-preserved stations at Arley and Bewdley, and even a Neo-Victorian pastiche station at Kidderminster. The Midland's loop line from Barnt Green to Ashchurch (Glos.), of 1859–68, is now curtailed at Redditch. Of their branch from Ashchurch to Great Malvern only the station of 1864 at Ripple remains (now converted to a house). Another unexpected survival is Hunnington station (Romsley), of 1883, on the branch from Northfield (Birmingham) to Halesowen. Almost all trace of the Tenbury & Bewdley Railway of 1863–4 (engineer *William Clarke*) has disappeared, apart from the dramatic ruin of its bridge across the Severn at Dowles, and the former station at Newnham Bridge (Knighton on Teme). Even less remains of the Worcester to Bromyard railway, completed 1877.

The most significant architectural legacy of ROAD TRAVEL in the county is its numerous BRIDGES. The Severn provided the major challenge, but the earliest surviving bridges are across the Teme, at Tenbury Wells and Powick, both basically late medieval; and across the Avon, of which Pershore's is partly medieval, and that at Eckington looks medieval but is a thoroughly old-fashioned rebuilding of 1729–30. Worcester's bridge across the Severn, by *John Gwynne*, 1771–80, suffered a diluted reconstruction in 1931–2, so the best stone bridge in the county is now
5 *Thomas Telford*'s Bewdley Bridge of 1797–9, with its three, elegantly Georgian, segmental arches. Telford's later Severn bridges are of iron: Mythe Bridge, near Bushley, 1824–6, and Holt Fleet Bridge, 1826–7, both with ironwork cast by *William Hazledine* of Shrewsbury. The replacement Powick Bridge, 1836–7, of the Telford type (*see* p. 777), is by *C. H. Capper* of Birmingham. Stourport's iron bridge, 1868–70, is by *Edward Wilson*, best known for his Liverpool Street Station in London. Evesham's Workman Bridge, of stone, by *James Samuel*, 1854–6, also merits a mention here.

Worcestershire's fine bridge-building tradition continued into the C20. Stanford Bridge, 1905 by *L. G. Mouchel*, is an early example of Hennebique's ferro-concrete system. *Joseph H. Garrett*, the first County Surveyor, was succeeded in 1911 by *Charles F. Gittings*, who designed the Abbey Bridge at Evesham, built 1925–8, a notable ferro-concrete period piece. Later bridges of note by the County Surveyor (also titled Bridgemaster from 1933) are Upton upon Severn, a steel cantilever design by *Bertram C. Hammond*, 1938–40, and Doddenham (Knightsford Bridge), an elegant concrete construction by *William R. Thomson*, 1956–8.

In contrast to bridge building, little remains of the age of TURNPIKE ROADS. The best example of a TOLL (or PIKE) HOUSE is that displayed at the Avoncroft Museum, Stoke Prior, of 1822, from Little Malvern. Very few remain *in situ*. The largest, octagonal in form, of 1814, is between the Ombersley and Droitwich roads in Outer Worcester. Others are on the Martley road near Great Witley, and at Pershore, a late Tudorish example of 1857. The major contribution of the late C20, with little to excite the architectural enthusiast, has been the buildings of MOTORWAYS. The M50, an early example of 1958–62, has a good bridge-cum-viaduct across the Severn at Queenhill, by *Sir Alexander Gibb & Partners*. The M5 was constructed in 1960–5 (*T.D. Wilson*, chief project engineer); the M42 in 1983–6.

CI9 AND EARLY C20 CHURCHES

Anglican churches

With the advent of the C19 it once again makes sense to consider ecclesiastical before secular buildings. Here the stylistic development is most easily recognized and most fully documented. Classical Georgian churches were first replaced by the rather pinched Gothic kind usually called the COMMISSIONERS' TYPE, characterized by aisles with galleries, short chancels, rather thin W towers, and high and thin windows separated by thin buttresses. The only Worcestershire church built under the first parliamentary grant of the Church Building Commission was in fact a far more lavish affair: St George, Kidderminster, of 1821–4 by *Francis Goodwin*. Its Perp style is amazingly accurate and substantial, with much use of cast-iron tracery and a landmark W tower; the interior was unfortunately burnt out in 1922. More typical of this period are Stone, 1831–2 by *William Knight* (clerk of works at St George, Kidderminster), Malvern Wells, 1835–6 by *R. W. Jearrad* of Cheltenham, and Elmley Lovett, 1837–40 by *John Mills* of Worcester.

Thomas Rickman is usually considered responsible for the acquisition of a greater degree of archaeological scholarship and its application to early C19 church design. Worcestershire has two particularly fine examples, Ombersley of 1825–9, with a remarkably unaltered pre-Ritualist interior, and Hartlebury, mostly of 1832–3. Equally notable for its seriousness and Perp exactitude is the church at Pensax, 1832–3, by *Thomas Jones* of Chester, most of whose comparable buildings are in North Wales.

The Commission's second parliamentary grant funded two surviving churches:* St John the Baptist, Kidderminster, Neo-Norman, by *George Alexander*, 1842–3, and the uninspiring Cat-shill, 1837–8, of standard type, by *Harvey Eginton* of Worcester (1809–49). Eginton's work is usually far better, and particularly progressive for its date. His best church in the county is St Michael, Broadway, 1839–40, with plaster rib vaults and full-length chancel. Many of his church restorations (e.g. at St Mary, Kidderminster) are of comparable quality. His Worcester contemporary, *Abraham Edward Perkins* (1807/8–73), a Rickman pupil, was far less forward-looking. His little-altered church at Whittington, 1842–4, is a notable period piece, but lacks the vigour of Eginton's work, and this is also true of his later career. Doddenham (now redundant), 1854–5, is perhaps his most attractive church. His major work was the restoration of Worces-ter Cathedral, particularly its exterior, from 1845. A late example of the Commissioners' type is Bushley, 1842–3, by *Edward Blore*; *G. G. Scott*'s solid replacement chancel, of 1856–7, forms a telling contrast.

Where the Church of England for some reason did not want to go Gothic, it had patent reasons not to be Italian, and so for a short time chose the NORMAN style. The great fashion for Neo-Norman was in the 1840s, but St Clement, Worcester, is as early as 1821–3. Its architect, *Thomas Lee Jun.*, must have been one of the first in the whole of England to make that choice (and the facing of the W front in Roman cement betrays the early date). St John the Baptist, Kidderminster, by *George Alexander*, 1842–3, is also Neo-Norman, as has already been said, but the best
105 example, vigorous as well as scholarly, is *Eginton*'s Trimpley, of 1844.

The change from Commissioners' Gothic to a fully under-stood, ARCHAEOLOGICALLY CORRECT GOTHIC is usually con-nected with the name of *A. W.N. Pugin*; Worcestershire has no church by him (only the very modest school at Spetchley of 1840–1). Pugin came to regard Perp, until then the most usual phase to be imitated, as debased, and pleaded, together with his Church of England contemporaries, the Cambridge Camden Society or Ecclesiologists, for 'Second Pointed' or 'Middle Pointed', i.e. the style of the late C13 and the early C14, with Geo-metrical or freer but not yet flowing tracery. A favourite architect of the Cambridge Camden Society was *R.C. Carpenter*, whose fine church at Kemerton, 1846–9, is an outstanding example of the sort they advocated. Among those whom Pugin convinced at once was *George Gilbert Scott* (later Sir Gilbert Scott), who from about 1841 designed churches in a competent Second Pointed. In Worcestershire his principal work is the internal restoration and furnishings of Worcester Cathedral, from 1863, the best sur-viving example of his cathedral work. His only surviving Worces-tershire church is Hanley Swan, 1871–3, characteristic but rather routine. More impressive was Stourport parish church, designed

---

* St George, Claines, Worcester, 1829–30, since replaced, was a third.

1875–6, and built posthumously by his son *John Oldrid Scott*. This was all but demolished in 1979–80.

In contrast to those who wanted to build convincingly medieval churches are those who refused to give up their own personality and believed in the possibility of a Gothic at once ancient and modern; there are signs that Pugin, before his early death in 1852, was moving in the same direction. *William Butterfield* was the leader in that trend. His Alvechurch, of 1857–61, is an outstanding example, with its vibrantly coloured brick inte- 112 rior. Sedgeberrow, 1867–8, also typical of his style and idiosyncracies, on a somewhat smaller scale, is technically a restoration, but shows how competent Butterfield could be with such work. Chaddesley Corbett, 1863–4, is another good example. *Henry Woodyer*'s style is often close to Butterfield. His outstanding work in the county is St Michael's College near Tenbury Wells, of 1854–6, with its crazily steep dormers. Its church (also a parish 113 church) is somewhat quieter, but has impressive roofs and a gratifyingly unaltered interior. His St Stephen, Redditch, of 1854–5, is rather less interesting. As a restorer Woodyer was as vigorous but less subtle than Butterfield. Good examples are Bockleton, 1861–2, Tenbury Wells, 1864–5, Bricklehampton, 1875–7, and Wick, 1892–3.

Of other leading HIGH VICTORIAN ARCHITECTS, the best represented in Worcestershire is *G.E. Street*. To his large restrained parish church of Hagley, 1856–8, he added a fine tower with broach spire in 1864–5. His West Malvern, 1870–1, is also impressive, but only his superb St Peter, Cowleigh (Malvern), of 1863–6, shows the hard and bold style of his early and most personal years. His rebuilt E end at Hanbury, 1860–1, is also powerful work. Like Butterfield, Street was a bold but competent church restorer: *see* Hanley Castle, 1858, and Shrawley, 1862. Birlingham church, 1871–2, is a late work by *Benjamin Ferrey*, unexpectedly muscular; his Fairfield, 1853–4, is more typical. *P.C. Hardwick* was responsible for Newland church, 1861–4, built in connection with his Beauchamp Almshouses there; it is richly furnished, with the most complete scheme of Victorian wall painting (by *Clayton & Bell*) in the county. *Arthur Blomfield* in his younger days was as bold as Butterfield or Street, but settled later in his career for a much safer style. Upton upon Severn of 1877–9 is a large and competent example, with a splendid steeple; his Wribbenhall, 1878–9, also looks promising, from outside. A late work by Blomfield is the large Perp-style chapel at Malvern College, of 1897–9, rather fussy outside but impressive within.

LOCAL ARCHITECTS played a much more significant role in church architecture in the C19 than they have been able to since. Eginton and Perkins have already been introduced. The two most prolific High Victorian architects in the county were *Frederick Preedy* (1820–98), and *William Jeffrey Hopkins* (1821–1901). *Preedy*, also notable (uniquely among C19 architects) for his stained-glass work, was a native of the county, born at Offenham, later living at Fladbury, though he moved his office to London in 1859. He probably trained with Harvey Eginton (where

Butterfield may also have been a pupil). His only brick church
124 in the county, Wythall, 1861–2 (now in commercial use), is vigorously Butterfieldian. His many stone churches also attempt to
be muscular, but often become formulaic. The best are probably
Hollybush, 1869, Madresfield, 1866–7, Offenham, 1860–1, and
St Stephen, 1861–2, and St Mary Magdalene, 1876–7, both at
Worcester (the latter with a notable steeple of 1888–9); Headless
Cross (Redditch) has a particularly well-preserved interior of
1867–8. His many church restorations often seem unnecessarily
ruthless. New churches by *Hopkins*, who trained with H.J. Under-
wood at Oxford, seem more successful. His masterpiece is no
doubt Hallow, of 1867–9, its spire only completed, to his designs,
in 1900. Suckley, 1876–9, is also very fine. Other typical churches
are Drakes Broughton, 1854–5, Bradley Green, 1864–5, and
Churchill near Blakedown, 1867–8. Tibberton, 1867–8, and
Abberton, 1881–2, have good patterned brick interiors. As a
restorer, Hopkins was more subtle than Preedy, but had an
alarming habit of moving piscinae, sedilia etc. to unexpected
locations. *Henry Day* of Worcester (†1869) designed churches at
Lickey, 1855–6, and Feckenham, 1866–7. His practice was
continued by his nephew *Ernest Augustus Day* (1846–1915), who
built St Barnabas, Worcester, 1884–5. The best church by *Lewis
Sheppard* (1845–1915), who succeeded Hopkins as Diocesan Surveyor, is Wychbold, 1887–8. *Henry Rowe Jun.* (*see* p. 671) designed
a good small church at North Piddle, 1875–6. For church architects based in other towns, *see* the introduction to each. The
two most important C19 architects based in Hereford both
contributed one typical new Worcestershire church: Lindridge,
1860–1, is by *Thomas Nicholson*; Harpley, 1876–7, by *F.R.
Kempson.**

This survey of the work of local architects has in places taken
us into the LAST QUARTER OF THE C19, a period characterized
by greater refinement, but also greater licence. It is the time on
the one hand of William Morris and of G.F. Bodley and J.L.
Pearson (neither of whom designed new churches in Worcestershire), and on the other of the Arts and Crafts and of, say, *J.D.
Sedding* (who designed a modest chancel at Hinton on the Green,
built 1894–5). It is quite difficult to unravel these two strands in
the most important late C19–early C20 churches in the county.
At St Paul, Worcester, 1885–6 by *A.E. Street* (son of G.E. Street),
it is even difficult to distinguish High from Late Victorian; the
muscularity of its patterned brick belongs to the former phase,
but the internal proportions are (or were, before subdivision)
highly reminiscent of Pearson's churches. Amongst the most
refined ecclesiastical works are *Temple Moore*'s remodelling of St
Stephen, Redditch, 1893–4; *Bucknall & Comper*'s superb chapel
at the former Convent of the Holy Name, Malvern Link, 1891–3,
with now sadly depleted *Comper* furnishings; and the striking

---

* *T.D. Barry & Sons* of Liverpool rather unexpectedly provided two large urban
churches, both in a bristly Dec style: Bengeworth (Evesham), 1871–2, and Christ
Church, Malvern, 1874–5.

tower of Wythall church, 1908, by *W.H. Bidlake* of Birmingham. 124
Bidlake was also involved with the private chapel at Madresfield
Court, a wonderful Arts and Crafts extravaganza undertaken by
Henry Payne and other Birmingham craftsmen, from 1902.
Church architecture at its best at the moment before abandon-
ing historicism is (Sir) *Aston Webb*'s large St George at Worcester,
of 1893–5, Gothic, but not imitated from any one building or
phase of style. Webb, who had family connections with Worcester, did quite a lot of work in the county, including adding the
fine outer aisle at Claines, 1886–7.

Worcester, St George.
Interior view

The most notable new EDWARDIAN CHURCHES are the
Ascension, Malvern, the most Bodleyesque in the county, an
early work of *Walter Tapper*, 1902–3, unassuming outside, noble
within; St Martin, Worcester, by *G.H. Fellowes Prynne*, 1903–15,
123 in his usual Free Dec style; and emphatically Dodford, 1907–8,
by *Arthur E. Bartlett*, a pupil of Sir Reginald Blomfield. This, a
delightful composition round a small courtyard, has excellent
Arts and Crafts detail, and excellent Arts and Crafts furnishings
mostly by the *Bromsgrove Guild* (*see* below). Barnt Green, by *A.S.*
p. 121 *Dixon*, 1909–13, represents another trend of Arts and Crafts
church architecture, particularly in its Birmingham manifesta-
tion, a brick reversion to the round arches of the Early Christian
or Byzantine style. The most interesting Worcester-based church
architect of the period is *Charles Arthur Ford Whitcombe*, about
whom very little is known, other than that he trained in the
United States. His only new church in the county is Broadheath,
1903–4, but he contributed numerous church furnishings in an
inventive Perp style. Before he disappears from the record,
c. 1912–13, he was briefly in partnership with the like-minded
William Gerald St John Cogswell, who designed the interesting
nave at Astwood Bank, 1911. Also of note is All Saints, The
Wyche, Malvern, 1902–3 by Elgar's friend (and Enigma Variation) *Arthur Troyte Griffith*.

Roman Catholic churches

In the early C19, following the Catholic Emancipation Act of
1829, the Roman Catholics could begin to build on a larger scale.
The development of their CHURCHES mirrors the Anglican
pattern, except that the first, St George, Worcester, by *Henry
Rowe*, 1828–9, is mildly Grecian, or Roman Baroque in its 1880s
remodelling (by *S.J. Nicholl*). The modest Harvington, 1825, is
very basic Gothic, and *Thomas Rickman*'s Our Lady of Mount
Carmel, Redditch, 1833–4, is like a Catholic version of a routine
Commissioners' church. Broadway, as remodelled for the Passionists in 1850, is even Neo-Norman. But by then the influence
of Pugin had already taken hold with two notable churches. St
Benet, Kemerton, by *M.E. Hadfield* of Sheffield, 1842–3, is a
little-altered invocation of the Puginian rural ideal. Our Lady,
Hanley Swan, 1844–6 by *Charles F. Hansom*, is not at all starved,
as Catholic churches so often had to be at this date, and has a
remarkably lavish interior. Hansom also provided the modest
church at Upton upon Severn, of 1850. By his talented pupil,
Benjamin Bucknall, is the splendidly bold Geometrical-style
church at Little Malvern, 1861–2. Other High Victorian Catholic
churches are by *Gilbert R. Blount*: Bromsgrove, 1858–60, little
altered, and Kidderminster, 1857–8, rather plainer; and by
Pugin's son, *E.W. Pugin*, the church at Stanbrook Abbey, Callow
End, 1869–71, with its pencil-like Sienese-Ruskinian tower. Stanbrook, scheduled to be vacated in 2007, is the best example of a
Roman Catholic abbey in Worcestershire. Established here in
1838, with surviving buildings by *Charles Day*, it is mostly by

Pugin & Pugin, from 1878. The same practice also provided typical Edwardian Roman Catholic churches at Great Malvern, 1904–5, now part of Malvern College, and Evesham, 1912.

Nonconformist chapels and cemeteries

The Nonconformists kept for a long time to their Georgian round-arched type in order not to appear churchy. RURAL CHAPELS exist throughout the county, but are increasingly at risk, whether from demolition, neglect or unsympathetic conversion. The Countess of Huntingdon's Chapel at Leigh Sinton (*see* Leigh), of 1831, is a sensitive example of domestic adaptation. The notable Baptist chapel at Atch Lench (Church Lench), sold for conversion to a house in 2005, has already lost its pews. Cookhill Baptist, 1841, survives in use at the time of writing. URBAN CHAPELS are also becoming increasingly rare. Far too many have been demolished, others converted, tactfully in the case of Astwood Bank Baptist, 1822; a minority, including Bromsgrove Congregational, 1832, remain in use. Other early C19 urban chapels were remodelled: Pershore Baptist, for example, of 1839–40 by *S. W. Daukes*, largely survives behind its later C19 frontages, while the Kingswood Meeting House, Wythall, is now mostly of 1874, and at the Wesley Methodist Church, Stourport, the sober late C18–early C19 exterior hides a lavish interior of 1894–6.

In the mid C19 some large Nonconformist congregations turned to an ITALIANATE STYLE, of which the best example is the former Congregational Church, Worcester, by the Nonconformist specialists *Poulton & Woodman* of Reading, 1858–9, with a remarkably intact interior beneath its current nightclub glitz (and a fine former Sunday School by *Aston Webb*, 1888). Or they chose GOTHIC, as at the Baptist church, Worcester, by *Pritchett & Son* of Darlington, 1863–4. Kidderminster retains two good later C19 Gothic examples, the Unitarian church, a remodelling of 1883, and the Baxter Congregational Church by *F. W. Tarring*, 1884–5, with a landmark spire. Great Malvern has the best collection of late C19 chapels, in particular the (Wesleyan) Methodist by *John Tarring*, 1865–6, Holly Mount Congregational by *James Tait* of Leicester, 1875–6, and Baptist by *Ingall & Son*, 1893–4. An early C20 Nonconformist speciality was a Free Gothic, especially Free Perp style. The only (rather mild) Worcestershire examples are the Methodist Church at Evesham, by *Frederic Foster* of Coventry, 1906–7, and the openwork stone spire of that at Headless Cross (Redditch) by *Ewen Harper*, 1896–7 (currently at risk).

CEMETERY CHAPELS, another Victorian building type at risk, deserve a brief paragraph. Kidderminster retains an early C19 classical example, probably of 1843, supplemented by a more typical Gothic chapel of 1876–8. The most usual Victorian form was a pair of chapels (one Anglican, one for Nonconformists) linked by an archway with tower and spire. Malvern has a very good example by *W.H. Knight* of Cheltenham, 1860–1. Others of note are at Upton upon Severn, 1865–6, and at Evesham and Pershore, both of 1874–5.

Furnishings and monuments

On VICTORIAN CHURCH FURNISHINGS little need be said. An indication of the architects who provided the best work has been given above. Both *Preedy* and *Hopkins* supplied excellent fittings to the churches they were involved with. Such High Victorian reredoses with figures in relief and mosaic, round stone pulpits, chunky fonts and metal screens are easily recognized (though increasingly subject to zealous reordering). The brothers *James Forsyth* (1827–1910) and *William Forsyth* (1834–1915) executed much of the best work. They trained in Edinburgh before moving s to work for G.G. Scott; James moved to London, but William remained in Worcester. Other notable Worcester carvers, *R.L. Boulton* and *H.H. Martyn*, relocated to Cheltenham, but carried out much work in the county. Worcester Cathedral has probably the best collection of C19 furnishings of any English cathedral, certainly the most complete of the many supervised by (*Sir*) *George Gilbert Scott*, who designed all the fittings here from 1863. An important Worcestershire contribution to church furnishing was the founding by *Walter Gilbert* of the Bromsgrove Guild of Applied Arts in 1898; the quality of their work sometimes depended on the architects involved, but the general standard was remarkably high until they closed in 1966.

The chief Victorian contribution to churches was STAINED GLASS. Almost nothing survives from the C18 or early C19, but huge quantities were produced in the mid- to late C19, much of it of high quality. Artists early in the field, from the 1840s, such as *Thomas Willement* (Kemerton, Evesham St Lawrence), *William Wailes* (Whittington), and *William Warrington* (Bushley), produced mostly brightly coloured windows in an attempt to imitate early medieval glass. The only Worcester-based glass stainer, *George Rogers* (1805–77), belongs with this group; his work, like theirs, shows little stylistic development (Bushley, Chaddesley Corbett). This was manifestly not the case with three major firms established in the late 1850s: *Clayton & Bell* (Hanbury, Hanley Castle, Pershore Abbey), *Lavers, Barraud & Westlake* (Earl's Croome, Feckenham, Powick, Worcester Cathedral), and *Heaton, Butler & Bayne* (Malvern Wells, Madresfield). Their work, distinguished *c*. 1860 by an astonishingly varied palette of intense colour, was severely toned down by *c*. 1870. Other prolific London firms included *O'Connor* (with a notably bright palette: Evesham St Lawrence), *Ward & Hughes* (often particularly sentimental: Charlton), and *James Powell & Sons* (who for much of the C19 employed mostly freelance designers such as *Henry Holiday*: Eldersfield, Evesham All Saints). The studio founded by *John Hardman* in Birmingham in 1845 (at the instigation of A.W.N. Pugin) followed a similar path, and was particularly prolific in Worcestershire; *John Hardman Powell*, the firm's chief designer from 1852 to 1895, had a particularly distinctive style (Doverdale, Kemerton, Salwarpe, Worcester Cathedral). Windows by *Frederick Preedy*, who at first worked with George Rogers, also show distinct stylistic development and are often more exciting than his architecture (Badsey, Church Lench, Fladbury, Offenham etc.). Such development was certainly not the case with Continental stained glass, as is shown by several windows by *J.B. Capronnier* of Brussels (Bromsgrove, Redditch St Stephen, Webheath) or *Mayer & Co.* of Munich (Pershore Abbey). The superiority of average English Victorian work received a tremendous boost from the founding of *William Morris*'s stained glass company in 1861, with *Edward Burne-Jones* as principal designer. A fine early example of 1865 is at Rochford; another, at Ribbesford, of 1877. Thanks to the ironmaster Alfred Baldwin, Worcestershire has a very rare example of a whole church filled with *Morris & Co.* glass, at Wilden, though all done from earlier designs after Morris's and Burne-Jones's deaths. Later Victorian glass generally became more 'refined' and translucent. Two firms particularly successful in this mode were that founded by *Charles Eamer Kempe* (Malvern College Chapel, Suckley, Welland), and *Burlison & Grylls*, set up at the instigation of G.F. Bodley (Claines, Crowle, North Piddle). An alternative was offered by stained glass in the Arts and Crafts mode, brightly coloured, intricately designed, and varied in texture. *Christopher Whall* was the leader in this field (Upton upon Severn, 1905). His pupil *Henry Albert Payne* (Malvern All Saints, Norton) established a whole school in this mode in Birmingham, whose works are a delight in many Worcestershire churches (Wythall; *see also* below).

From the late 1840s CHURCH MONUMENTS were largely superseded by stained-glass windows as memorials to the dead, especially in parish churches (hence the often disconcerting variety of Victorian stained glass in many of them). Memorial brasses however, many by *John Hardman & Co.*, underwent something of a revival (cf. Our Lady, Hanley Swan). Large monuments, especially with recumbent effigies, continued to be deemed suitable for major churches, and Worcester Cathedral has two of particular note, both by *James Forsyth* (Earl of Dudley, 1888), one at least designed by *G.G. Scott* (Lord Lyttelton, 1878). *Sir Thomas Brock* (born at Worcester) provided the large seated monument in the Cathedral to Bishop Philpott †1892.

SECULAR VICTORIAN AND EDWARDIAN ARCHITECTURE

Domestic architecture

Worcestershire provides a bumper crop of Victorian COUNTRY HOUSES. The first that calls for attention is Norton Park, Bredon's Norton, dated 1830 but probably not completed until 1839; it is in any case an amazingly early example of Tudor

Gothic as against Gothic Revival, already Victorian in its layout (with attached servants' quarters) as well as stylistic detail. This is equally true of the first on a large scale, Pull Court, Bushley, *p. 210* 1834–9, by *Edward Blore*, his first house in ELIZABETHAN OR JACOBEAN style, symmetrical, competent, highly monumental. *p. 211* The plan, with additional service facilities round a separate courtyard (somewhat altered for use as a school) could be a prototype for many later Victorian mansions; its Jacobethan style remained a favourite for much of the C19. Astley Hall of *c.* 1838 is another early example, also convincingly designed as one would expect from such an excellent local architect as *Harvey Eginton*. Such houses form an interesting contrast to the puzzling Ribbesford House, genuine C16 but apparently almost entirely reconstructed *c.* 1830. By *David Brandon*, a later specialist in inoffensive Jacobethan country houses, were the demolished Blackmore Park, Hanley Swan, 1861–3 (rebuilt 1881–2), and Rhydd Court, near Guarlford, mostly 1863–4, but so altered as to have lost whatever merit it originally had. Bockleton Court by *Henry Curzon*, 1866–7, is also basically Jacobean, though not without more muscular Gothic touches reminiscent of Curzon's friend *p. 159* William Burges. Bockleton's ground plan can be taken as the ideal for a High Victorian country house, with its large service range as big as the remainder of the house (though with lowergrade detail). The family end has been remarkably little altered despite years of educational use. A possible Worcestershire design by *William Burges* himself is the Italian-looking brick tower of 1881 in the grounds of Rous Lench Court, built for the Rev. Chafy Chafy. His house, picturesque black-and-white Tudor, was so thoroughly remodelled *c.* 1860 in half-timbered style as to seem largely Victorian, quite an early example of this later widespread fashion.

The ITALIANATE STYLE offered an alternative for country houses until the mid C19 and beyond. *Samuel Whitfield Daukes* provided the best examples in the county, all built for nouveaux riches, who had made their money in commerce or industry. The earliest is Abberley Hall, 1844–5, built for a Birmingham banker of Swiss extraction. It is copybook Italianate (like Prince Albert's contemporary Osborne), though it has sadly lost the typical open 107 top stage of its asymmetrical tower. The interior, again in educational use and remarkably well preserved, is exceptionally elegant, much of it the result of redecoration *c.* 1881 by *James Lamb* of Manchester. Also of this period (built for a cotton manufacturer from Oldham) is Abberley's most memorable feature, 106 the astonishing clock tower by *J.P. St Aubyn*, 1883–5, rather like an organic Big Ben, a landmark for much of West Worcestershire.* The second *Daukes* house, Bricklehampton Hall, 1848, built for a Pershore solicitor, is smaller and quieter but retains its Italianate tower intact. His grandest house, the grandest in the county, is Witley Court, Great Witley, thoroughly remodelled in

---

*Crown East Court, *c.* 1856, is an earlier example of Lancashire money funding a Worcestershire country house.

1854–60 for the first Earl of Dudley, whose fortune derived from Black Country coal mining and industry. It is now a spectacular Italianate ruin (cared for by English Heritage), incorporating truly gigantic porticoes by *John Nash* (c. 1806), but generally extremely restrained in its ornament, no doubt to keep in harmony with the attached church of 1733–5. Daukes, however, refaced this and all the rest in Bath stone ashlar. Only the curved wing towards the orangery takes as its pattern something more Baroquely Italian. The sumptuous terraces were laid out by *W.A. Nesfield*, who had established himself in collaboration with Charles Barry as the provider of Italian as against Anglo-Picturesque settings. The main feature of the grounds is Nesfield's spectacular 26-ft (8-metre) high fountain, carved by *James and William Forsyth*. The Italianate style was picked up, in more reticent form, for smaller houses. Some, for example Lower Hill at Wick, 1850, may also be by *Daukes*. Wheatfield, Callow End, a large merchant's villa in size, is an early example, probably mostly of 1836 by *Thomas Prosser* of Worcester. A late, aristocratic example is St James's House (now a school), which dominates West Malvern. Its present subdued form is the result of remodelling, by an unknown architect, for Lady Howard de Walden in 1890–1, at a cost of £100,000.

The most unexpected example of a country house funded by industry is Chateau Impney, Dodderhill, 1869–75, built for John Corbett of the Stoke Prior Salt Works, who also developed Droitwich as a brine spa. The surprise is that this really is a French château, designed by *Auguste Tronquois* of Paris (though the contribution of the executive architect *Richard Phené Spiers*, of London but with Beaux Arts training, should not be over-looked). One might think it all 'thoroughly debased', yet its exuberance is catching. Why Corbett wanted such a Francophile house is not entirely clear, though his wife was brought up in France. It certainly upstaged the safe, aristocratic, Neo-Tudor additions carried out by *P.C. Hardwick* for his political rival Sir John Pakington at Westwood House nearby. Other examples of local business funding country houses were provided by genuine Worcestershire sauce, that of Messrs Lea & Perrins. Charles Wheeley Lea built the gargantuan Gothic Bohun Court (now Parkfield), Hallow, c. 1870, the only country house by *W.J. Hopkins*; but only lodges, grounds and some notable garden pavilions survive. C.W. Dyson Perrins built Davenham, really a country house though situated at Great Malvern; originally of 1859 (by *Elmslie*), but hugely expanded in C15 Loire style by *William Henman* of Birmingham, c. 1900–5. Worcester also has a country house in an urban setting, Battenhall Mount (now St Mary's Convent School), originally Italianate of c. 1867, enormously expanded in the 1890s by the Worcester architect *J.H. Williams*, with fine interiors by *R.A. Briggs*; these bankrupted the owner, the Hon. Percy Allsopp (of the brewing family).

A house not to be missed, if only for its distant view, is Beaucastle, outside Bewdley, a multicoloured Ruskinian fantasy by *William Doubleday*, 1877, for a former Lord Mayor of

Birmingham. Yet the High Victorian country house that lingers
110 most in the memory is Madresfield Court, rebuilt and sweep-
p. 442 ingly enlarged within its moated site for the fifth Earl Beauchamp
by *P.C. Hardwick*, from 1863. He was not the most disciplined of
architects, and the result has tremendous, but often disjointed,
variety. The rebuilding was completed by others, and includes
some outstanding Edwardian interiors (*see* below).

111   The only outstanding LATE C19 COUNTRY HOUSE is Hewell
Grange, Tardebigge, by *Bodley & Garner*, 1884–91, for Lord
Windsor, later Earl of Plymouth, in lavish Jacobean style; *Thomas
Garner*, the operative partner, was the author of a standard work
on English domestic Tudor architecture (1911). The design is disciplined, knowledgeable, and yet not simply imitative; the contrast between this substantial mansion and Blore's so much
thinner Pull Court of fifty years before could not be greater.
p. 626 Hints in the external carving prepare one for the interior, where
the dominating influence is Italian Quattrocento, particularly in
the prodigious great hall that runs the whole length of the house.
It should all be better known, though this is difficult as it has
served as a prison since 1946. Other late C19 country houses pale
in comparison. Two worth mentioning are Wood Norton Hall
(Norton and Lenchwick) by *G.H. Hunt*, 1896–7, again Jacobethan but with French overtones, as it was built for the exiled
Duc d'Orléans, and Weatheroak Hall, Wythall, 1884–5 by *John
Cotton*, in florid Queen Anne style.

The QUEEN ANNE STYLE and other late C19 reflections of
what Philip Webb, Norman Shaw and others contributed to the
establishment of a more freely historicist, more elegant and delicate style of house, is found in Worcestershire in estate buildings
rather than in the country houses themselves. By *Shaw* himself
is the picturesque North Lodge of 1871–2 at Madresfield, as well
as his striking brick dovecote there. At Overbury, his additions
to the house have mostly been removed, but his Tudorish school,
1875–7, 'Old English' Post Office and Stores, 1879, and later, i.e.
more Baroque, village hall, 1895–6, all survive.

We need to backtrack here to consider URBAN HOUSING.
Great Malvern is the place to start. It started its career as a spa,
as we have seen, *c.* 1810, with mostly stuccoed development. After
1842 when the phenomenally successful German type of hydropathic treatment was introduced, and especially after the arrival
of the railway in 1859–60, an astonishing variety of villas was
erected: Tudor, Italianate, or Gothic; bargeboards are followed
by shaped gables, and they occasionally by embattled turrets.
Some of the largest were built as lodging houses. The former
Priessnitz House, 1845, is still classical; others of the early 1850s,
p. 473 in Tudor Gothic style, are surprisingly by *S.S. Teulon* (whose
'rogue' churches are entirely absent in the county). The majority
of Malvern's villas, however, are by local architects. *E.W. Elmslie*,
the architect of the railway station and its accompanying hotel
(*see* above), moved to the town *c.* 1854. His partners and succes-
121 sors, *Haddon Bros*, were especially busy. How large a Malvern
villa could be is shown by their swaggering Priory Park Mansion

of 1874–80, now well maintained as the Council House. The even bigger Davenham has already been mentioned.

Comparable areas of urban housing are difficult to find elsewhere in the county. In Worcester the best example is Battenhall, off the London Road (close to Battenhall Mount, mentioned above). Many large houses were provided here c. 1885–95, mostly by the local architect *John Henry Williams* (1851–1943), but these have been sadly depleted. Other towns (e.g. Bromsgrove) have suffered even more. Kidderminster has also lost most of its housing for the upper middle classes, though a notable group for carpet designers survives in Park Lane, and much terraced housing for artisans remains further N.

Victorian RURAL HOUSING tends to have a longer shelf life. The best examples are in those villages 'improved' by an enlightened landowner. Ombersley and Rous Lench are particularly good examples; Overbury has also been mentioned and will be again.

PARSONAGES, as in the Georgian period, are often the best C19 rural or urban building in their parishes. Some, for example *William Butterfield*'s excellent Alvechurch, 1855–6, and *Temple Moore*'s fine Redditch of 1892–3 (now Holmwood), were almost as large as a small country house. Good examples by local architects include Clifton upon Teme by *John Collins*, 1840, Tudor Gothic; Tenbury Wells by *Harvey Eginton*, 1843–4, still a stuccoed villa; and several by *A.E. Perkins*, who was perhaps better at parsonages than churches (Suckley 1850, Pensax 1855–6). Of many examples by *W.J. Hopkins*, the most notable are Worcester St Nicholas, 1861, its brick Gothic muscularity pointedly upsetting the stucco of Lansdowne Crescent, and Tibberton, 1884, where Hopkins tries hard to metamorphose his usual Gothic style into something more Queen Anne. Also of note are the former vicarages or rectories at Bushley, Jacobethan, by *Richard Armstrong*, 1850–2; Hanbury by *David Brandon*, 1861–2, and Defford by *H.R. Snelgrove*, 1866–7, both Gothic; Hinton on the Green by *J.A. Chatwin*, 1874–5, of patterned brick; and Wick, Free Tudor, by *Aston Webb*, 1888–9.

The final paragraph of this section must deal with the ARTS AND CRAFTS MOVEMENT. *C.F.A. Voysey*, inspired by the Webb–Shaw style but some twenty years younger than them, built his first medium-size country house in Worcestershire in 1890: Bannut Tree House (originally Walnut Tree Farm) at Castlemorton, still with the black-and-white gables he was soon to abandon, but already in all essentials in his sensible, pretty style. Oakhill (No. 54 Hillgrove Crescent, Kidderminster) is a typical small example, of 1899. Voysey also appears at his best, c. 1901, with his Lodge Cottages at Madresfield. Madresfield Court has already been referred to for the outstanding Arts and Crafts decoration of its chapel, begun in 1902 by *Henry Payne* and other craftsmen of the Birmingham Group. The adjoining Library has contemporary work, equally outstanding but much more sober, by *C.R. Ashbee* and his Guild of Handicraft from Chipping Campden. The identity of the designer of yet another

122

fine room, the Staircase Hall of *c.* 1908–13, is unclear, but *A. Randall Wells* was certainly involved at some stage. His most notable country house is in Worcestershire, Besford Court of 1912–14, one of the most imaginative and dramatic examples of the monumental, very freely historicist style one usually connects with Lutyens exclusively (*see* especially its main staircase). Two other large Edwardian houses of note are Eastham Grange by *Walter Tapper*, 1910–11, in Hampstead Garden Suburb style, and Hallow Park by *H.C. Corlette*, 1914, in quieter Neo-Georgian. For other notable Arts and Crafts work one must go to Overbury, Broadway, or Barnt Green. At Overbury *Ernest Newton* was employed extensively in the first decade of the C20 by the Martin family (in succession to Norman Shaw); his delightfully under-stated domestic style sets the tone for this beautiful village. Broadway became a centre for large and small Arts and Crafts houses after *Guy Dawber* described its charms in *The Builder* of 1888. Dawber at first had the lion's share of the work, though equally busy in the early C20 were the London-based Scot, *Andrew N. Prentice*, and *C.E. Bateman* from Birmingham. Bateman also built much at Barnt Green, an upmarket Birmingham commuter suburb that flourished at almost the same time. Many other Arts and Crafts houses here were provided by his fellow Birmingham architects; one of the most complete is Dale Cross Grange by *Crouch & Butler*, 1899–1900.

Public and commercial buildings

Charles Day's Grecian ashlar-faced Shire Hall at Worcester, of 1834–8, forms, as has already been said, a link between Georgian and Victorian PUBLIC BUILDINGS. Unfortunately it had few out-standing successors, either county or municipal, apart from the Shire Hall's neighbour, the Victoria Institute of 1894–6 by *John W. Simpson & E.J. Milner Allen*. This inventive mixed Tudor and Baroque building accommodates museum, art gallery and library; part of the same commission was the building of a large and equally lively School of Art and Science. Only Kidderminster has a municipal group that attempts similar grandeur, though the result can hardly be called subtle. The Municipal Buildings by *J.T. Meredith*, 1875–6, was rather hopefully called Free Italian by *The Builder*; the style of the nearby Corn Exchange and Public Rooms by *Bidlake & Lovatt*, 1853–4, is even more curious, though thoroughly enjoyable. Evesham's Town Hall is mostly a remodelling of 1884–7 by *G.H. Hunt*, who designed the small but dignified free Library and Public Hall nearby in 1908–9. Great Malvern's Public Library of 1905–6, by *Henry A. Crouch*, is even better.

A completely new type of public building was the UNION WORKHOUSE, built following the Poor Law Amendment Act of 1834. Of these buildings, deeply resented for the harshness of their regimes, few Worcestershire examples remain. Most were still minimally classical, such as the surviving central section of Bromsgrove, by *Bateman & Drury*, 1837–8. That at Tenbury

Wells, by the workhouse specialist *George Wilkinson* of Witney, 1836–7, is in a rather friendlier Tudor style, no doubt because of its unusually central location, right by the bridge over the Teme. The workhouse infirmary often developed into the town's general hospital, as at Bromsgrove, Evesham and Kidderminster, but the last town also built a new Infirmary, by *J.G. Bland*, 1870–1, in good High Victorian Gothic. The only other Victorian and Edwardian HOSPITALS to note are the Smallwood Hospital at Redditch, 1894–5 and the Community Hospital, Malvern, 1910–11, both by *William Henman*. The predecessor of the latter, Malvern Rural Hospital of 1868, also survives. The mentally ill were provided for by lunatic asylums at Powick (Italianate, by *Hamilton & Medland*, 1848–52) and Barnsley Hall near Bromsgrove (brick and terracotta by *G.T. Hine*, 1903–7); only fragments survive of both.

ALMSHOUSES in the C19 continued to be erected by private benefaction. The outstanding example is the Beauchamp Almshouses at Newland, picturesque Victorian Tudor by *P.C. Hardwick*, 1861–4, a bequest of the Beauchamps of Madresfield. Redditch again has an unexpectedly good example, the Smallwood Almshouses of 1896–7 by the local man, *C.G. Huins*. A cognate building is the former Royal Albert Orphanage at Henwick, Worcester, by *William Watkins* and *S. Dutton Walker*, 1868–9, impressive brick Gothic with stepped gables, but no doubt thoroughly intimidating for its young inmates.

Much more can be said about EDUCATIONAL BUILDINGS. The most impressive were provided by SCHOOLS FOR THE MIDDLE CLASSES. The earliest, the Sebright School at Wolverley, 1829–30, has an impressive Gothic centre which still dominates the village. The grandest by far is Malvern College, which received its very large Gothic or Early Tudor main buildings in 1863–6; the architect of this competent and impressive job was *Charles F. Hansom*. Later Victorian buildings, including boarding houses by *Hopkins*, *Haddon Bros*, and *Nevinson & Newton*, enhance the scenic potential of the site. Bromsgrove School's buildings are mostly later, but three in Worcester can be included here. The King's School, connected with the cathedral, built its huge raw School House in 1886–7, to designs by *Ewan Christian*, who also restored the monastic refectory as the school hall. The Royal Grammar School has a rather uptight Elizabethan Gothic building by *Perkins*, 1867–8, and many later ones by *A.H. Parker & Son*, including the fine Perrins Hall, of 1913–15. Alice Ottley School for Girls acquired the notable Britannia House of *c.* 1730 nearby, adding a suitably enhanced version of it by *Lewis Sheppard*, 1891–2. Kidderminster supplemented its Tudor Gothic grammar school of 1848 with a more Elizabethan High School for girls by *Pritchard & Pritchard*, 1912–13. Meanwhile good Wrenaissance-style grammar schools appeared at Evesham, Prince Henry's by *Buckland & Farmer*, 1909–10, and Bromsgrove, by *G.H. Gadd*, 1909–12.

ELEMENTARY SCHOOLS for most of the C19 were funded by the Church, aided by the National Society for Promoting the

102

p. 463

75

Education of the Poor in the Principles of the Established Church. The British and Foreign School Society provided the Nonconformist (or rather non-sectarian) response, though very few Worcestershire British Schools survive (cf. Pershore, dated 1847). Church schools, often designed by the same architects who worked on the churches themselves, can be of very good quality. *G.E. Street*, for example, designed schools at Hanbury and Shrawley, *Butterfield* at Alvechurch, *R.C. Carpenter* at Kemerton, and so on. Worthwhile church schools by local architects include Martley by *Eginton*; Church Lench and Fladbury, both by *Preedy*; Hallow and Crowle, both by *Hopkins*; Abberley and Feckenham, both by *Henry Day*; Great Malvern by *Elmslie*; Tenbury Wells by *James Cranston*; Eldersfield by *G.R. Clarke*; Broadway by *George Hunt*; and Salwarpe by *John Cotton*, 1882, the first to break away from Gothic forms. Many more could be added to this list.

The Education Act of 1870 allowed such voluntary schools to be supplemented by BOARD SCHOOLS, administered by locally elected school boards. Kidderminster and Bromsgrove had active school boards, but many other places shunned them as too radical. *Ernest A. Day* supplied the lion's share of rural Board Schools (Bradley Green, 1874, Inkberrow, 1876). County and city councils became responsible for elementary education in 1902. The best example of an early COUNCIL SCHOOL is Worcester's Stanley Road School, by *Alfred Parker*, 1914–15. Early schools for the County Council were designed by *Alfred B. Rowe* or by his son *A.V. Rowe* (cf. Evesham, Redditch etc.).

VICTORIAN AND EDWARDIAN COMMERCIAL BUILDINGS include some very fine examples of BANKS. First and foremost is *E.W. Elmslie*'s Lloyds Bank at Worcester, built for the Worcester City and County Bank in 1861–2. It is in Italian Renaissance style, handled with great finesse, the provincial bank at its most confidence-inspiring. The same bank also built a good Italianate

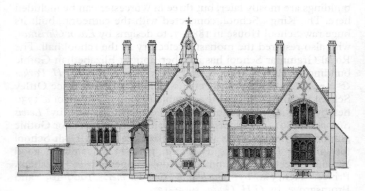

Tenbury Wells, National School.
Elevation

branch at Kidderminster in 1868–9 (by *H. & E.A. Day*). Also at Kidderminster, in the same style, is the Stourbridge & Kidderminster Bank (now HSBC) of 1856–7, by *Thomas Smith* of Stourbridge. A good later C19 example is Lloyds at Great Malvern by *J.A. Chatwin*, 1892. Edwardian banks tried to suggest equal security by turning to something more Baroque. This is the style of the former National Provincial Bank at Worcester, by *Charles Heathcote & Sons*, 1906–7.

The other noteworthy commercial buildings are also Edwardian Baroque and also in Worcester, most of them forming an outstanding range (including the two banks mentioned above) along the eastern side of The Cross and The Foregate. This ends impressively with the brick and terracotta Hop Market and Commercial Hotel, begun by *Alfred B. Rowe* in 1899, but not completed until 1909. The best such building however is a little further N, in The Tything: Messrs Kay & Co.'s Mail Order Stores of 1907, by *J.W. Simpson & Maxwell Ayrton*, thoroughly original for its date, combining boldness with functional soundness. Much more mainstream, but an unexpected survival, is the Palace Theatre at Redditch by *Bertie Crewe*, 1913, with a compact, little-altered, Neoclassical interior.

WORCESTERSHIRE SINCE 1914

Between the wars

One of the most popular interwar styles for CHURCHES was the Early Christian or Byzantine basilica, introduced to Worcestershire by *A.S. Dixon* at Barnt Green, in 1909–13. The Roman *p. 121* Catholic church at Droitwich, by *F. Barry Peacock*, 1919–21, would be a standard example, had its interior not been trans- 125 formed by an overwhelming display of mosaic work carried out by *Maurice Josey*, 1922–32, to the designs of *G.J. Pippet*; naïve this may be, but its overall impact is most satisfying. Also Early Christian is Holy Innocents at Kidderminster, by *W.E. Ellery Anderson*, 1937–8, sadly incomplete but with a very calm interior. Ellery Anderson, based in Cheltenham, began as an improver in Sir Ninian Comper's office; his church furnishings usually show this influence, *see* his fine reredos at Cropthorne, 1931–2. The final stage of the Arts and Crafts tradition is exemplified by Blackwell 126 church, 1939–40 by *Herbert Luck North* of Llanfairfechan in North Wales; its exterior, with a rather Scandinavian feel, conceals an impressive, finely crafted white interior. A third option for interwar churches was a continuation of the refined Gothic introduced by Bodley and others in the late C19. One of its greatest exponents was *Sir Giles Gilbert Scott*, the architect of Liverpool Cathedral. There are two notable examples of his work in Kidderminster: the Dec-style Whittall Chapel added to the chancel of the parish church (St Mary) in 1921–2; and the rebuilding, to a new design, of the burnt-out interior of St

George, 1923–5. Quite different, but equally impressive, is *Scott's* Memorial Chapel at Bromsgrove School, 1928–31, with an interior reminiscent of a medieval tithe barn.

Most good interwar STAINED GLASS followed either the refined Gothic or the Arts and Crafts mode. To the former type belong the windows of *Ninian Comper* and *Geoffrey Webb* (Himbleton, *c.* 1910, Evesham St Lawrence, 1938–44). It should also be remembered that C19 firms such as *Kempe & Co.* continued in business until the 1930s, others (*Burlison & Grylls, James Powell & Sons, Hardman*) for even longer. The most prolific Arts and Crafts artist was *Archibald John Davies* (1877–1953), a pupil of Henry Payne at Birmingham, who worked in close collaboration with the Bromsgrove Guild (Worcester St Stephen, *c.* 1920, Wychbold, 1927, Hallow 1936). His windows, if not of the highest class, are none the less attractive when not over-sentimental. Also based in Bromsgrove were *A.E. Lemmon* and his son *P.E. Lemmon*. Other successful local providers of good Arts and Crafts stained glass include *Alfred L. Pike* of Tardebigge (Redditch St George, 1920), and *Florence, Robert & Walter Camm*, also Payne pupils, who worked under the name of their father, *T.W. Camm* of Smethwick (Eckington, 1924–36, Strensham, 1926).

Most parishes erected WAR MEMORIALS in 1919 or soon after. The usual form, a tall shaft and cross, at its best, is exemplified by those at Malvern Wells, by *C.F.A Voysey*, with a pelican on top, and at Broadway, by *F.L. Griggs*. Many other parishes provided stained glass (as at Redditch St George) or memorial lychgates: an outstanding example is Overbury, by *Sir Herbert Baker*. Statues were another option: at Kidderminster, and Pershore Abbey, both by *Alfred Drury*, and Great Malvern by *R.R. Goulden*.

As regards PUBLIC BUILDINGS the most frequently encountered are SCHOOLS. Most public schools continued to add to their stock of buildings. The finest is the Memorial Library at Malvern College, 1923–4 by *Maurice Webb* (*Sir Aston Webb & Son*); its free treatment of Gothic and Tudor motifs, with many felicitous details, was not often matched at that moment. Webb also provided new buildings at Sebright School, Wolverley, 1930–1, in stripped Neo-Georgian style. Neo-Georgian was the preferred style for schools generally (Trinity High School, Redditch, by *H.W. Simister*, 1930–2). Almost all those erected for Worcestershire County Council by the County Architect, *Alfred Vernon Rowe* (†1940), are in this style. Rowe's largest Neo-Georgian effort was the County Buildings, Worcester, of 1929–30, built to provide extra accommodation for Shire Hall next door.* Some Worcester City schools verge more towards a jazzy Art Deco (Secondary School for Girls, Barbourne Road, by *William Ransom*, City Engineer, 1928–9; Christopher Whitehead School, Malvern Road, by *A.G. Parker*, 1937–8). For its only

---

*Rowe also designed several attractive Neo-Georgian POLICE STATIONS, e.g. at Evesham, 1937. But in his private practice, which he continued throughout his career, he favoured rather a Voysey-derived Arts and Crafts fashion.

major public buildings of the period, the City Police Headquarters and Fire Station in Deansway, 1939–41, the City Council stuck with Neo-Georgian, albeit in a rather more stylish version (by *Percy Thomas* of Cardiff) than most examples mentioned above. BANKS (not quite public buildings) might also be Neo-Georgian, or otherwise blend into the townscape (as at Broadway), or remain resolutely Neoclassical, as at Great Malvern (HSBC, 1920–1 by *J.A. Gotch*; NatWest, 1930–1 by *F.C.R. Palmer*).

The absence of any real hint of the MODERN MOVEMENT will have been noticed; the nearest Worcestershire usually came to it in the interwar period was its popularized, streamlined version, the DECO STYLE. The most striking, and least altered, commercial example is the brick offices (now Isaac Maddox House) built in 1937–8 by *Dyneley, Luker & Moore* for Messrs Heenan & Froude, in Shrub Hill Road, Worcester (an excellent foil to the former Engine Works opposite, which they had previously colonised). The Deco style of course is most often associated with CINEMAS, of which the county has several good examples. By far the best is the former Northwick, on the N suburban fringe of Worcester, by *C. Edmund Wilford*, 1938, with a stunning fantasy interior by *John Alexander*. Also worth mentioning, and little altered, is the Regal at Bengeworth (Evesham) by *Hurley Robinson*, 1932, which offers Neo-Egyptian touches. Even the tiny Regal Cinema at Tenbury Wells, by *Ernest S. Roberts*, 1937, provides the necessary internal exoticism with its painted Mediterranean scenes (by *George Legge*), an unusual survival.

Interwar HOUSING requires unfortunately little comment. The building of council houses mushroomed after the First World War, but whatever design flair was shown to begin with soon evaporated. Worcester City Council, under its surveyor *William Ransom*, was the most active, but as with most councils its designs soon became too standardized, with only occasional variations of style and layout, e.g. on and off Tolladine Road. Nor does much middle-class housing stand out, apart from its determination to be as little like council housing as possible, with endless safe variations of watered-down Tudorbethan or half-timbered styles. These same styles, plus the Neo-Georgian, met the needs of the very few examples of more expensive housing that were built during this period. The best large house built in imitation of C16–C17 timber framing is probably Wyke Manor at Wick, by *Cecil G. Hare* (of *Bodley & Hare*), 1923–4, picturesque and surprisingly evocative. Southcrest, S of Redditch, by *F.W.B. Yorke*, 1921, might have provided a good Neo-Georgian example, had it not been all but ruined by conversion to a hotel in the 1970s. A quite exceptional early Modern house at Bredon, overlooking the Avon valley, is Conigree, formerly Heatherdale, designed for himself by *Geoffrey Boumphrey* (of *The Listener* magazine) in 1935–7, but with every sign of having been thoroughly influenced by his consultant architect, *F.R.S. Yorke*, the famous Modernist and son of F.W.B. Yorke.

p. 88

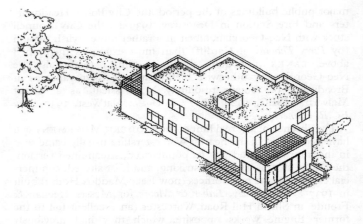

Bredon, Conigree (formerly Heatherdale).
Axonometric view

Over 550 sites related to 1939–42 ANTI-INVASION DEFENCES
have been recorded in Worcestershire.* The county was intended
as a place of retreat for national government and the royal family.†
Defences face both E and W, in case England was invaded via
Ireland and Wales. The basis of defence was a series of STOP
LINES, intended to slow any advance and provide opportunities
to counter-attack. Canals and rivers formed ready-made anti-
tank obstacles, with crossing points heavily defended, e.g. around
Pershore and Eckington bridges across the Avon. An example of
a pillbox facing W can be seen on the E bank of the Teme at Stanford Bridge, built into the bridge abutments. At Holt, on the
Severn, a well-preserved six-pound gun emplacement survives on
the E bank. Behind these stop lines, scattered throughout the
county, are the remains of other defences. A 'double-decker'
pillbox (incorporating an anti-aircraft defence as well as ground
fire) survives within the former Summerfields explosive factory,
Kidderminster (visible from Summerway Lane, near Wilden
Top), and a pillbox on Perdiswell golf course from the ring of
defences around Worcester. A number of underground hides,
intended for the carefully organized resistance forces, also survive
across the county. There were AIRFIELDS at Defford, Honeybourne and Throckmorton; the hospital buildings attached to
Defford airfield are being restored by the National Trust as
part of Croome Park. At Worcester, the campus of the University
and the DEFRA offices on Whittington Road retain buildings
from Ministry of Defence offices relocated from London. Most

* Paragraph by Malcolm Atkin.
† The work of the volunteer Defence of Britain Project under Mick Wilks and Colin
Jones (now Defence of Worcestershire Project) has transformed our understanding
of the military organization of the county during the Second World War.

unusually, perhaps, an underground aircraft engine factory was built under the hills at Drakelow (Wolverley). This was converted for use as a regional seat of government during the Cold War.

Architecture after 1945

When large-scale building began again, after the Second World War, MODERNISM could no longer be avoided. The priorities in Worcestershire were the building of houses and the provision of SCHOOLS. The newly appointed County Architect, *Leslie Clarson Lomas*, was of course deeply involved with the latter (though one suspects he might have preferred the Neo-Georgian; *see* his Kidderminster Police Station of 1954–5). The acceptably Modern school designs that emerged from his department (Witton, Droitwich, 1954–6) seem to have been the responsibility of his Deputy, *D. W. Sharpe*. More to the point, the County Council adopted the policy of commissioning schools from independent architects, including three inventive young practices from London. *Frederick Gibberd* provided the tidy, concrete-framed Sion Hill School at Kidderminster, and Ridgeway Middle School, Astwood Bank, both in 1957–8. By *Yorke, Rosenberg & Mardall* is the pleasantly functional Bewdley High School at Wribbenhall, 1953–5, though their bolder North Bromsgrove High School, 1961–71, has been tamed by later additions. The third, and most frequently employed, practice was *Richard Sheppard, Robson & Partners*. An early work is Evesham High School, 1951–2 (extended 1974); a stronger but equally friendly design is South Bromsgrove High School, of 1968, enlarged 1981 (currently under threat of replacement). The latter, as well as their work of 1953–71 at Pershore College, Wick, with its sharp diagonals and Corbusian truncated cylinder, make much use of attractive engineering brick. More severe and more controversial, because of its assertive 1960s self-confidence so close to the Cathedral, is their expansive Worcester College of Technology, 1960–73, faced in brown Hornton stone. The City of Worcester Training College, now the core of the University of Worcester, by *Holland W. Hobbiss & Partners*, 1961–4, undetermined whether to be Modern or traditional, forms an interesting contrast.

Hereford and Worcester County Council (County Architect, *Alan Meikle*) took over the mantle of school building from 1974, when the former Worcestershire and Herefordshire County Councils were amalgamated.* From then until 1998 (when the combined county was disbanded), a number of decent schools were produced, many of them of brick and with jagged forms. Some of the primary schools are particularly successful, often of two-tone brick, with the whole complex sheltering beneath a wide-spreading pitched roof. Swan Lane First School, Evesham, 1989–91, is perhaps the best example. The continuing popularity

---

* At the same date, Halesowen and Stourbridge became part of Dudley Metropolitan Borough, in the new West Midlands county.

of the form is shown by Matchborough First School, Redditch, 2002–3, by *Worcestershire Property Services*.

Brutalist raw concrete makes an unexpected appearance in Worcestershire schools thanks to *Michael Godwin* (1923–2001), of *Godwin & Cowper* of Stourport. His additions at the Alice Ottley School, Worcester (Sports Hall, 1971, Science Block, 1978) are quite strong stuff. So, at a more delicate primary level, is the practice's St Peter's First School at Droitwich, 1982, with its inward sloping shingle-clad walls. At Malvern Girls' College, *Godwin*'s concrete Parashell sports hall, the Edinburgh Dome, 1977–8, contrasts agreeably with Hatfield, a middle-school house of 1963–4 by *T.H.B. Burrough* of Bristol, similar to, but apparently not influenced by the 'Beehives' at St John's College, Oxford. Bromsgrove School has a notable and varied collection of late C20–early C21 buildings by *Associated Architects* of Birmingham: Library 1994 (*Richard Slawson*), Art and Design Centre, 1999–2000 (*J.T. Christophers*), and a sixth-form house of 2001–2 (*Adam Wardle*).

Now for other PUBLIC BUILDINGS. The most notable is the
130 County Hall built for the short-lived Hereford and Worcester County Council, on a semi-rural site at the E edge of Worcester, in 1974–8 (though Worcestershire had the design ready as early as 1972). The architects were *Robert Matthew, Johnson-Marshall & Partners*, who provided a relaxed elegant design, clad in reddish-brown brick, and capable of further expansion (which proved unnecessary when the Hereford and Worcester Council was abolished in 1998). Of district councils, the only ones to build entirely new premises after 1974 were Redditch, a Town Hall of 1981–2 by *Cassidy & Ashton* of Preston, heaped-up red brick, rather overbearing, and Wychavon, a rambling Neo-vernacular Civic Centre at Pershore of 1990–1, by their own chief architect. Wyre Forest District moved into the acceptable Civic Centre erected for Stourport UDC in 1963–6 by *Andrews & Hazzard*, low-key modern, in orange brick.

Amongst the most successful buildings of the late C20 have been PUBLIC LIBRARIES. *Hereford and Worcester County Architects Department* designed several very good brick ones, notably that at Kidderminster, 1996–7. A good earlier small example is Pershore, by *Darbourne & Darke*, 1974–5. Best of all is the contemporary library at Redditch by the *John Madin Design Group* of Birmingham, a strongly modelled brick design with a cleverly controlled interior, arguably the best C20 building in the town. Other types of building, including HOSPITALS, have been less successful, including the massive but far too mechanical-looking Worcestershire Royal Hospital, a PFI scheme of 1999–2001 by the American practice, *RTKL Associates*; it has, however, an impressive concourse, worthy of a mainline railway terminus.

Late C20 CHURCHES sadly need only a single paragraph. Only three call for attention. Rubery (really a Birmingham suburb) has
127 a fine Modernist example, with tall SW campanile, by *Richard Twentyman*, 1957–9. The same architect later designed the crematorium at Redditch, 1971–3, a model example for that class of

building. By *Maurice W. Jones*, the Diocesan Architect, is the inter-estingly planned Holy Trinity, Ronkswood, Worcester, built 1964–5, though this has suffered severely from having the strik-ing chequerboard patterning of its circular exterior removed. The rebuilding of Stourport, by *Adrian Thompson*, 1979–80 (extended 1988–9), is also of interest, particularly for the way it incorpo-rates walling retained from G.G. Scott's late C19 church (though one might well have scruples about this in principle). As for STAINED GLASS, only the colourfully semi-abstract windows of *Thomas Denny* remain in the memory; the best are at Martley, 1999, and two at Great Malvern Priory, 2003–4. Generally the late C20 tendency has been to remove fine earlier furnishings in the name of reordering, with little design input as to how to replace them or compensate for their loss. An alternative is to provide an attached CHURCH HALL. North Worcestershire has two satisfying recent examples: Blackwell, a circular parish room of 2003 by *J. T. Christophers* of *Associated Architects*; Alvechurch, a striking ark-shaped hall by *Graeme Beamish* (*Michael Reardon & Associates*), 2004, brick banded with stone, in tribute to the adjoining church by Butterfield. Also worth mentioning here, as it is attached to the nondescript Christ Church of 1940 at Tolla-dine, Outer Worcester (p. 768), is the Tolly (Community) Centre, a gritty example of early C21 'materiality', by *Meadowcroft Griffin Architects*, 2005–6.

Late C20 COMMERCIAL BUILDINGS that could be mentioned here range from shopping centres to OFFICE COMPLEXES. Of the latter, the best designed must be the extensive Britannic Assurance at Wythall by the *T.P. Bennett Partnership*, 1994–6, a 131 huge but crisply executed batwing plan, executed in High Tech style. Such glossy reworkings of the Modernist ethic are as pro-gressive as Worcestershire has so far become at the turn of the C21; free-form buildings have yet to appear and may well never do so. As regards Postmodernism, this has been largely confined to an urge to revert to the safe forms of the Neo-vernacular, as exemplified by the Wychavon Council Offices, Pershore, men-tioned above.

Of SHOPPING CENTRES only those in town centres seem occasionally to have had any serious design input or control. As regards the Lychgate Centre (by *Shingler Risdon Associates*) that obliterated much of Worcester's medieval street pattern in 1965–7, Pevsner's comment (of 1968) can be allowed to stand: it remains 'as acceptable as architecture as it is unacceptable as town planning'. The lesson was fortunately learnt by the time of the city's Crowngate Centre, 1989–92 by *Frederick Gibberd, Coombes & Partners*, which weaves in and out of the existing urban fabric, but not soon enough for the massive Kingfisher Centre at Redditch, by *Redditch Development Corporation*, 1970–5 and later, a huge fungous growth that has eradicated a signifi-cant part of that town's modest earlier centre.

Redditch must play a significant part in the last section of this introduction, which is devoted to late C20 HOUSING. Immediate post-war demand in the county was met by the same mix as before: a second mushrooming of council housing, usually of paler brick, in a more spacious setting (cf. the Warndon Estate, Worcester, begun *c.* 1955), and varied, usually uninspiring private housing (almost always sadly with little or no apparent architectural input). Council TOWER BLOCKS made a brief appearance, two groups at Kidderminster, 1963–7, one group of three in Worcester, *c.* 1967, until the collapse of the Ronan Point tower in East London in 1968 virtually put paid to this option. Particularly interesting council housing can be found at Pershore, where *Darbourne & Darke*, in 1973–7, carried out much redevel-

128 opment and infill of the S part of the town centre. The result is a model of its kind, varied, low-key, immaculately stitched into the existing fabric.

Redditch meanwhile had been designated a NEW TOWN in 1964. As with other 'second generation' New Towns, the brief,

p. 547 for the master planner *Hugh Wilson,* was to retain the existing town centre (or part of it) and its suburbs, and link these with new areas by a free-flowing traffic system. Architecturally it must be considered a mixed success, though in general the landscaping at least is excellent. The most interesting housing belongs to the later phase, *c.* 1970–80, when new areas were developed on a mostly virgin site E of the River Arrow (away from the existing town). There were three of these, Matchborough, Winyates, and Church Hill, with varied, often inventive and attractive housing clustering around so-called 'bead-centres'; these also tried to get to grips with the integration of pedestrian and motorized access. Oakenshaw, begun *c.* 1979 at the S end of western part of the town, has housing set in particularly generous landscaping. Imaginative landscaping might hopefully prove to be Redditch New Town's legacy to the county's problem of mass housing in the C21 (providing of course that it is not used as an excuse for later infill development). The Warndon Villages scheme on the E outskirts of Worcester, built 1988–2002 following guidelines laid down by *Worcester City Council,* is a well-planned example, though once again let down by the absence of innovative architectural input. It is also difficult to think of examples of larger-scale late C20 housing that could grace the end of this introduction to

132 Worcestershire. One at least is a hopeful pointer, Cobtun, on the N outskirts of Worcester, by *John T. Christophers* (of *Associated Architects*), 2000–1, a remarkable, ecologically designed house, utilizing *inter alia* traditional cob walling.

The final paragraph can deal with the PROFIT AND LOSS of architecturally notable buildings since the publication of the first edition of the Buildings of England volume for Worcestershire in 1968. In many respects the county has done rather well. The major post-war country house losses happened before the 1960s (Arley Castle, Upper Arley; The Park House, Elmley Castle; Perdiswell Hall, Worcester), though others that should have been preserved for the nation have been subdivided into apartments (as at Westwood House). The remarkable late C19 Hewell Grange, Tardebigge, currently a prison, remains in good enough condition to be considered for intact preservation. Churches mostly continue in use, though sometimes with unsatisfactory reorderings (St John the Baptist, Kidderminster). C19 monastic complexes (Stanbrook Abbey, Callow End; the former Convent of the Holy Name, Malvern Link) present the greatest challenge. Nonconformist chapels also continue at risk, urban ones from redevelopment, rural ones from unsympathetic domestic conversion. With regard to rural buildings generally the relisting of buildings of special architectural or historic interest in the 1980s has led to much greater awareness of their value. This does not, however, seem to be the case for many towns, particularly those in the Birmingham orbit, in the N of the county. Redditch, despite (or because of) its designation as a New Town, has probably fared better than others, notably Bromsgrove, Droitwich, and Kidderminster. Good C19 buildings (usually severely under-listed) are usually those most at risk. There is also as yet little appreciation of the quality of the better buildings of the C20; some of the excellent schools built under the County Council's post-war building programme, for example, remain under threat of the easy option of demolition and replacement, rather than being considered for inventive refurbishment.

FURTHER READING

There are two major pre-C19 COUNTY HISTORIES. Thomas Habington (1560–1647) of Hindlip, confined to Worcestershire after involvement in the Gunpowder Plot of 1605, spent the last forty years of his life delving into the history of the county. His *Survey of Worcestershire*, in two volumes, 1717 and 1723, was republished in 1895–9 in the *Worcestershire Historical Society Publications*. The Rev. Treadway Russell Nash (1725–1811) published his *Collections for the History of Worcestershire* in 1781–2. To these should be added the invaluable collection of drawings made by Peter Prattinton (1776–1840), consisting of thirty-five volumes, now in the library of the Society of Antiquaries in London.

There is remarkably little subsequent published material on Worcestershire generally. The main source is the *Victoria County History of Worcestershire* (VCH), published in four volumes from 1901 to 1924 (though prepared before the First World War). Its early date means that it has severely limited coverage after the early C18, worth comparing for example with *VCH Gloucestershire* Vol. VIII, of 1968, which covers four parishes formerly in that county (Ashton under Hill, Beckford, Hinton on the Green, Kemerton). There are no Worcestershire volumes published by the Royal Commission on Historical Monuments (RCHM). The archaeological periodical of the county is the *Transactions of the Worcestershire Archaeological Society* (W.A.S.), published from 1923. Its predecessor, originally the Worcester Diocesan Architectural Society, published papers from 1854 to 1922, some included in the *Reports and Papers of the Associated Architectural Societies*; these also contain useful accounts of contemporary church restorations and other buildings. The *Transactions and*

Proceedings of the Birmingham Archaeological Society also contain Worcestershire material. A short C20 summary is *A History of Worcestershire* by David Lloyd, 1993. This can be supplemented by *Cambridge County Geographies: Worcestershire* by L.J. Willis, 1911. Otherwise one would be advised to consult county directories, notably the always useful *Kelly's Directory*. Of general guides to the county the most readable by far is *Worcestershire: A Shell Guide* by James Lees-Milne, 1964.

WORCESTER CITY fares rather better for historical material, starting with *The History and Antiquities of the City and Suburbs of Worcester* by Valentine Green, 1796. Also useful is *Medieval Worcester: An Archaeological Framework*, edited by M.O.H. Carver (W.A.S., *Transactions*, 7, 1980) and *Old Worcester: People and Places* by H.W. Gwilliam, 1993. A neat summary is provided by *Worcester: A Pictorial History* by Tim Bridges and Charles Mundy, 1996; also *The Book of Worcester* by David Whitehead, 1976, and *The Buildings of Worcester* by Richard K. Morriss, 1994, with photographs by Ken Hoverd. Most contain further bibliographies. Booklets on *Friar Street* by Pat Hughes and Nicholas Molyneux, 1984, and *Blackfriars Street*, ed. Pat Hughes, 1986, are packed with information.

Of histories of OTHER TOWNS the best and most detailed are *A History of Malvern* by Brian S. Smith, 1964, and *A History of Kidderminster* by Nigel Gilbert, 2004. *Kidderminster since 1800* by K. Tomkinson and G. Hall, 1985, also contains much useful information. Good earlier histories include *History of Evesham* by George May, 1834, and *A History of Bewdley (with Concise Accounts of Some Neighbouring Parishes)* by J.R. Burton, 1883. Shorter pictorial histories (and compilations of photographs) have also proved helpful: *Droitwich* by Lyn Blewitt and Bob Field, 1994, and *Evesham* by A.H. Fryer and J. Jeremiah, 1994, amongst others; also *The Book of Pershore* by Philip Barrett, 1980. *Success in the Heart of England: A History of Redditch New Town* by Gordon Anstis, 1985, its tone revealed by its title, contains much useful information. Many VILLAGES also have their own histories. Very good compact examples are *Witley*, 1985, and *Hartlebury*, 1987, both edited by R.O. Walker. *Through Changing Scenes of Life: A Millennium History of Ombersley and Doverdale*, by Eugene Roelofsz, 1999, is particularly lavishly produced.

WORCESTER CATHEDRAL has of course the most extensive literature of any Worcestershire building. *The History and Antiquities of the Cathedral Church of Worcester* by John Britton, 1835, has fine engravings. Robert Willis's architectural account, published in the *Archaeological Journal* 20, 1863, remains invaluable. Also essential is *Medieval Art and Architecture at Worcester Cathedral*, 1978, i.e. the British Archaeological Association's Conference Transactions for 1975. The most recent monograph is *Die Kathedrale von Worcester* by Ute Engel, 2000; English translation forthcoming. The chapter on Worcester in *English Cathedrals: The Forgotten Centuries* by Gerald Cobb, 1980, is most enlightening. An excellent short account is provided by *A Short Architectural History of Worcester Cathedral* by Philip Barker, 1994. The volume on Worcester Cathedral by Edward F. Strange, 1904, in the *Bell's Cathedral Series*, is also still of use, as is its companion volume *Great Malvern Priory Church* by the Rev. A.C. Deane, 1914. An accessible detailed description of the Malvern stained glass is provided by *The Ancient Windows of Great Malvern Priory Church* by L.A. Hamand, 1947. The best published account of Pershore Abbey is *The Abbey Church, Pershore: An Architectural History* by Malcolm Thurlby, in the W.A.S. *Transactions* 15, 1996. On Bordesley Abbey there is *The History of Bordesley Abbey* by J.M. Woodward, 1866, which needs to be read in conjunction with the detailed B.A.R. (later C.B.A.) excavation reports: of 1976, 1983, and 1993.

For PARISH CHURCHES generally a readable account is provided by *Churches of Worcestershire* by Tim Bridges, 2000 (revised 2005). Norman churches are excellently covered by *Church and Parish in Norman Worcestershire* by C.J. Bond, chapter 10 in *Minsters and Parish Churches: The Local Church in Transition 950–1200*, ed. John Blair, 1988. *The Herefordshire School of Romanesque Sculpture* by Malcolm Thurlby, 1999, also deals with certain Worcestershire churches. For later medieval churches, articles in the W.A.S. *Transactions* are often the best source. Church guidebooks can often be helpful but vary greatly in quality. Model examples are *Evesham Abbey and the Parish Churches* by D.C. Cox, 1980, and those by J.A. Roper, e.g. *Himbleton*, 1978. For Georgian churches, *The Georgian Churches of Worcester* by David Whitehead (W.A.S. *Transactions* 13, 1992), must be supplemented by national studies. This applies also to C19 and later churches, for which local studies are severely limited; one needs to scour the contemporary journals (*The Ecclesiologist*, *The Builder*, *Building News* etc.) for detailed accounts. The annual volumes of the *Worcester Diocesan Calendar*, from 1862 until *c.* 1914, gave exceptionally valuable accounts of new churches, fittings, and related building such as schools and parsonages. A useful addition is the archive of plans held by the Incorporated Church Building Society, now on-line at www.churchplansonline.org. *Architectural Sketches* by J. Severn Walker, 1862, contains most useful drawings of churches (and some houses). Several Roman Catholic churches have excellent guidebooks by Michael Hodgetts.

On NONCONFORMIST CHAPELS there is only the RCHME volume *Nonconformist Chapels and Meeting Houses in Central England* by Christopher Stell, 1980. Some national church architects have relevant monographs, such as *William Butterfield* by Paul Thompson, 1971. LOCAL ARCHITECTS are poorly served, with the notable exception of *John Cotton: the Life of a Midlands Architect 1844–1934* by Jennie McGregor-Smith, 2002. There is also a brief account of *Frederick Preedy* by Gordon Barnes, 1984, which should be supplemented by *The Stained Glass of Frederick Preedy: A Catalogue of Designs* by Michael Kerney, 2001. Roy Albutt has produced two excellently illustrated studies: *Stained Glass Windows of Bromsgrove and Redditch*, 2002, and *Stained Glass Windows of A.J. Davies*, 2005. *The Bromsgrove Guild*, ed. Quintin Watt, 1999, contains much useful information but is inclined to

over-attribute. The best national study of C19 stained glass is
Victorian Stained Glass by Martin Harrison, 1980 (new edition
forthcoming).

On CHURCH MONUMENTS one can consult *Medieval Military
Effigies up to 1500 Remaining in Worcestershire* by Mark Downing
(W.A.S. *Transactions* 18, 2002) and *The Effigy Tombs of the Gentry
of Worcestershire 1500–1700* by Ralph Richardson (W.A.S. *Transactions* 19, 2004). The standard work on post-Reformation sculpture is *Sculpture in Britain: 1530–1830* by Margaret Whinney, 1988.
This can be supplemented by 'A Biographical Dictionary of
London Tomb Sculptors *c.* 1560–*c.* 1660' by Adam White, in the
Walpole Society 61, 1999. On Samuel Baldwin, there is the article
'Samuel Baldwin: Carver of Gloucester' by John Broome in
Church Monuments 10, 1995. Further details of the sculptors can
be found in Rupert Gunnis's invaluable *Dictionary of British
Sculptors 1660–1851*, revised 1968 (new edition by Ingrid Roscoe
forthcoming).

Detailed descriptions of churches and all other SURVIVING
BUILDINGS can be found in the revised *Lists of Buildings of
Special Architectural or Historic Interest*, published by the Department of the Environment (now Department of Culture, Media
and Sport) from the mid 1980s. The most comprehensive, the
two volumes for Worcester, 2001, are the latest. Others, such as
the old Pershore RDC and Malvern UDC areas, are hopelessly
out of date. Details of all listed buildings are also available on
English Heritage's *Images of England* website, *www.imagesofengland.org.uk*. Of other building types in Worcestershire, there is
rather limited literature for COUNTRY HOUSES. The best option,
as for most counties, is to search out articles in *Country Life.
Burke's and Savills Guide to Country Houses* Vol. 2, by Peter Reid,
1980, provides useful references, as well as many useful illustrations. *Illustrations of Old Worcestershire Houses* by W. Niven, 1873,
provides a valuable glimpse of the state of many houses before
the C20. Also most useful are *A Survey of Historic Parks and
Gardens in Worcestershire* by Richard Lockett, 1997, and *Historic
Gardens of Worcestershire* by Timothy Mowl, 2006. Two national
surveys of Victorian country houses contain Worcestershire
examples: *The Victorian Country House* by Mark Girouard, 1971,
and *The Gentleman's Country House and its Plan 1835–1914* by Jill
Franklin, 1981. The National Trust publishes an excellent guidebook on *Hanbury Hall*, English Heritage one on *Witley Court and
Gardens*. *The Coventrys of Croome* by Catherine Gordon, 2000, is
particularly strong on architectural information. A fine monograph on an architect particularly relevant to the Worcestershire
country house is *Smith of Warwick* by Andor Gomme, 2000.
Information about other architects can be found in *A Biographical Dictionary of British Architects 1600–1840* by Sir Howard
Colvin, 1995 (new edn 2007), and the *RIBA Directory of British
Architects 1834–1914* (2 vols), 2001. The latter unfortunately does
not contain lists of works, but can be supplemented by *Edwardian Architecture: A Biographical Dictionary* by A. Stuart Gray,

1985. A full general bibliography, including books on individual architects and artists, can be found at the reference section of the Pevsner Architectural Guides' website, *www.lookingatbuildings. org.uk*.

The pioneering study of the TIMBER-FRAMED TRADITION is *The Ancient Half-Timbered Houses of England* by Matthew Habershon, 1836 (the first use of the term half-timbered). Modern study of the county timber buildings was established by F.W.B. Charles with his *Medieval Cruck-Building and its Derivatives*, 1967; also helpful is his *Conservation of Timber Buildings*, 1984 (with Mary Charles). The compact *Discovering Timber-framed Buildings* by Richard Harris, 1978, uses several Worcestershire examples. *The VAG Spring Conference Handbook* to Worcestershire, 1995, is also extremely useful, as are the Hereford and Worcester Architecture Record Group files at the Worcestershire Record Office.

There are few specific books on Worcestershire GEOLOGY. One of the earliest is *The Rocks of Worcestershire* by George E. Roberts, 1860. *Geology of the Country Around Worcester* by the British Geological Survey, 1997, is particularly useful; other volumes cover the Droitwich and Redditch districts (1962 and 1991).

The county also desperately needs an up-to-date general account of its PREHISTORIC ARCHAEOLOGY. In 2006 the most modern summaries are contained in the West Midlands Regional Research Framework for Archaeology papers, which pending publication are available on-line at the Birmingham University Institute of Archaeology and Antiquity website at *www.arch-ant. bham.ac.uk/research*. *The Malvern Hills: An Ancient Landscape* by Mark Bowden, 2005, is an excellent summary for its area. Roman Worcestershire is now well served by the comprehensive C.B.A. publication *Roman Droitwich*, edited by Derek Hurst, 2006. A key text on the archaeology of Worcester is *Deansway Excavations 1988–9*, by Hal Dalwood and Rachel Edwards (CBA Research Report 139, 2004). For the Civil War period there is *Worcestershire Under Arms* by Malcolm Atkin, also 2004.

Finally INDUSTRY AND TRANSPORT. The history of the county's canals is put in context by *Canals of the West Midlands* by Charles Hadfield, 1966. Also useful are *Staffordshire and Worcestershire Canal (Towpath Guide No. 1)* by J. Ian Langford, 1974, and the comprehensive *Worcestershire and Birmingham Canal* by the Rev. Alan White, 2005. For railways, general histories of the Great Western and Midland railways provide the background information. Two books by Rex Christiansen fill in the local picture: *A Regional History of Railways of Great Britain*, Vol. 13, *Thames and Severn*, 1981, and *Forgotten Railways* Vol. 11, *Severn Valley and Welsh Border*, 1988. In addition, almost every line has its own individual history. As regards industry, the range of publications worth consulting is too varied to be listed here. An exception can be made for *Woven in Kidderminster* by Melvyn Thompson, 2002, as it contains much information on the buildings and layout of carpet mills.

GAZETTEER

ABBERLEY

Fine hill country, a northern extension of the Malverns. The extraordinary Clock Tower at Abberley Hall (*see* below) is a landmark against the sky for miles around. 106

ST MARY. Stately and quite large, of buff sandstone in late C13 style, on a knoll NW of the village. By *John J. Cole* of London, 1850–2, rebuilt by him, slightly more elaborately, in 1876–7, after a fire in 1873; some outer walls and the SW tower with broach spire survived. The aisles have repetitive Geometrical tracery; the larger E and W windows show more variety. Beneath the eaves, carved stone lettering, plus dogtooth on the S chapel and porch. Five-bay arcades with round piers of Devonshire marble; good stiff-leaf capitals (also Noah's Ark, Phoenix, and Pelican) carved by *Earp & Sons*. The chancel is given due prominence by marble shafting on the chancel arch and along the walls, detached in front of the side windows. Cusped arch to the N organ chamber; two-bay arcade to the S chapel, richly filled with tall two-light cusped openings with cinquefoils above. – Hexagonal FONT. 1852. – Most other FITTINGS of 1876. – Carved oak PULPIT and brass eagle LECTERN. 1889. – STAINED GLASS. All by *Lavers, Barraud & Westlake*: E and S chapel E 1876 (the latter a copy of *Wilmshurst*'s destroyed window of 1852); S aisle S *c.* 1890; N aisle N 1903. – LYCHGATE of 1888.

ST MICHAEL, the medieval church in the village centre, was restored in 1908. Only the chancel (with its narrow S chapel) is roofed; the lower courses of the nave, S aisle, and W tower also survive, but rise higher only above the S doorway and at the nave NE corner. The doorway is Norman, set in the usual Worcestershire wall projection; two orders, with plain tympanum with segmental intrados, the rest badly eroded. The E respond of the S arcade indicates a C13 aisle. The present W entry into the chancel (formerly the nave N doorway) is also Norman, with one order of shafts and arch with chevron. One Norman N window in the chancel, which was clearly lengthened in the C13 (see the twin NE lancets) and later heightened. Other openings *c.* 1800. Within, the outline of a Norman S window, blocked C15–C16 clerestory openings above, and a low C13 arch to the S chapel. Good arch-braced roof with cusped wind-braces, probably late C14, altered in the C15–C16. – p. 23

STAINED GLASS. In the E window traceries, early C19 Bromley heraldry by *Sir John Betton* of Shrewsbury. – Chancel S: heraldic oval, dated 1588. – MONUMENT. Elizabeth †1645 and Ann †1679, mother and wife of George Walsh, a double monument attributed to *William Stanton* (GF); three Ionic columns and joint segmental pediment. – BELL of *c.* 1500, said to have been brought from the North of England. – In the nave, a fine C13 COFFIN LID, with three incised crosses with encircled heads.

Immediately SE, the OLD RECTORY, apparently early C19; mostly roughcast, with two low storeys, shallow hipped roof (and bay windows, E side). In origin it is probably a C15–C16 hall house with S cross-wing, the W side of which still reveals timber framing. The hall roof survives above the upper floor. The slightly lower N extension, mostly of stone, may once have been a C14 detached kitchen.

The old church faces a small square. To its SW, THE JAYLANDS, mid-C18 brick, the mid windows stressed beneath a one-bay pediment: decorated first-floor lintel, quoins and pediment below. Altered by *E.A. Day*, 1880, see the N side with its half-timbered porch and Queen Anne windows. Opposite, THE OLD BAKEHOUSE, probably of 1686 (date on a fireplace lintel); of brick already laid in Flemish bond, with some blue brick diapering. Shaped gable-ends, the S one with a large chimney. Somewhat spoilt by a large half-timbered late C19 wing, NE. Next door, the mid-C19 MANOR ARMS, with an attractive display of applied heraldic shields.

Further SE, on the road to Astley, TOWN FARM is early C17: square-panelled framing, with gabled cross-wings, the E rebuilt in brick, the W jettied and projecting forward. C19 bargeboards and finials, also the porch and brick chimneys.

TUMP HOUSE (formerly Firleigh), ¼ m. W on the way to St Mary. Late C18, with rendered front of three wide bays. The centre projects beneath a pediment, with Venetian window below, and a big C20 balustraded bow window on the ground floor.

SCHOOL, ½ m. W on the B road, near the C19–C20 nucleus at Abberley Common, by *Henry Day*, 1859. Of sandstone with banded tile roof; early Dec, with plate-traceried end windows. Large additions 2003–4.

ABBERLEY HALL, 1 m. SW. A school since 1916. By *S. W. Daukes*, 1844–5, for J.L. Moilliet, a Birmingham banker of Swiss extraction.* Restored by *Daukes* in 1846, after a fire, and sold in 1867 to Joseph Jones, a colliery owner and cotton manufacturer from Oldham; altered and enlarged for his cousin J.J. Jones in 1880–8 by *J.P. St Aubyn*. The ashlar-faced house is Italianate in the manner of Charles Barry (cf. Prince Albert's Osborne, 1844–8), with the typical asymmetrical tower, now without its open top stage. The tower stands between the house and the

---

*The previous house, Abberley Lodge, was put up for auction by the Bromley family in 1837, but Moilliet only purchased it in 1844.

rendered service wing, at a lower level, and is largely hidden
by a matching billiard-room wing added at right angles in the
1880s. The main block, five plus three narrower E bays (formerly with a conservatory below), has round-arched ground-
floor windows with shell tympana; top balustrade. Deep porte
cochère of the 1880s, with fluted Doric columns. The garden
front, S, of nine bays with Ionic veranda along the ground floor
of the central five, was disfigured in the early 1970s by adding
a headmaster's house at the SE corner.

Elegant Neoclassical INTERIORS, very well preserved: basically of 1844–6, especially the ceilings and mahogany doors,
but greatly enriched by *James Lamb* of Manchester from
c. 1881. *Daukes* is most recognizable in the Grecian detail of
the entrance hall, with its screens of Siena scagliola Ionic   107
columns either end, and in the stone cantilever staircase (with
brass balustrade) to its W, beneath the tower. *Lamb* contributed
painted friezes, Lincrusta papering, most of the splendid chimneypieces, the fine bookcases in the library, and much other
surviving furniture.

Balustrading of the Italianate terraced GARDENS survives to
the S and especially E, where much remains of the rockery
created from artificial Pulhamite stone.

The former STABLES, NW, are also no doubt by *Daukes*;
brick, with an Italianate tower above the entrance arch, a
miniature version of that formerly on the house. Enlarged to
a quadrangular plan for Joseph Jones after 1867 (including a
well-preserved THEATRE, a rare country-house survival). The
quadrangle was adapted for school use in 1928, its W side filled
with a brick CHAPEL by *R.C. Foster* (of *Tooley & Foster*); long
nave and chancel with round-arched windows, tunnel-vaulted
interior. Painted reredos by *Reginald Hallward*; his also the four
sub-Arts and Crafts chancel windows, of 1932. The largest of
the later school buildings is the polygonal brick ASHTON
HALL by *Peter Cripwell*, 1978. Between this and the stables, a
small-scale CLOISTER of 1990 by *S.T. Walker & Partners*.

From Merritt's Hill, a little N, rises the amazing CLOCK TOWER   106
of 1883–5 by *J.P. St Aubyn*, 161 ft (50 metres) high and visible
for miles around; built by John Joseph Jones in memory of his
cousin Joseph. The lower half is of rock-faced Alveley sandstone, with redder trim; oriels at high level, with the rounded
stair-vice on the E face. Corbelled-out upper part of smoother
buff Ham Hill stone with projecting polygonal buttresses
ending in tall pinnacles. Recessed between them, the octagonal top stage, its gables reaching up into a short lucarned spire.
The whole is somewhat reminiscent of Big Ben at Westminster, but rather more organic.

The MAIN LODGE must be by *St Aubyn*: snecked yellow sandstone with red trim. Gatepiers topped with pairs of cast-metal
naked boys; fine iron gates and railings. The ELBATCH
LODGE, S, is very similar.

NORTH LODGE, ½ m. further NW, by *John Douglas* of Chester,
1881, is far more picturesque. Brick with mullioned windows,

half-timbering above; big octagonal corner tower with steep pyramidal roof. Two pairs of brick ESTATE COTTAGES opposite, with their typical first-floor lattice patterning, must also be by *Douglas*, who designed the former HOME FARM S of the lodge. This is of 1889, low and quadrangular, with more timberwork and latticing; farmhouse at the NE corner. The lane continues SE to the boldly timbered WEST LODGE of 1881, no doubt again by *Douglas*; small square stair-tower.

THE ELMS, 1¼ m. WSW; now a hotel. Roughcast with ashlar dressings and brick quoins. The big square core is claimed to be of 1710 and by *Thomas White*. In 1927–8 *B. Carpenter* of London added large projecting wings to the entrance front, E, for Sir Richard Brooke, Bt, then remodelled the core after it was gutted by fire. This has two-and-a-half storeys and 2+1+2 bays, the projecting centre broader with a brick-filled pediment (with stone carving by *Sprague & Evans*); Venetian window below, tripartite C20 doorway with pediment. Other windows have eared architraves; top balustrade. The wings (dining room, N, drawing room, S) are slightly lower and simpler, with round-arched upper windows and a tripartite end arrangement. Large, stark service wing, NW. Inside, most of the original block is filled by a huge staircase hall of *c.* 1928, beneath a glazed dome. Elsewhere, several good doorcases and chimneypieces (especially in the dining room) from Brooke's family home, Norton Priory, Cheshire (by *James Wyatt*, *c.* 1775–80; demolished 1928).

ABBERTON

ST EDBURGA. A medieval possession of Pershore Abbey. Rebuilt by *W.J. Hopkins*, 1881–2, for William Laslett of Abberton Hall. Of snecked sandstone, with W tower, nave and chancel in one, and open timber S porch. The strongly buttressed tower carried a broach spire, replaced by a feeble parapet in 1962, as it lay on the flight path of Pershore airfield (cf. Throckmorton). Elaborate Dec-style W and E windows, typical of Hopkins; mostly lancets elsewhere, trefoiled in the chancel. Dec nave NE window, reused from the medieval church. The interior is faced in buff-yellow brick, with a boldly patterned course of red brick bands enclosing green-glazed crosses. Nave and chancel are separated by a timber trefoiled arch with traceried spandrels, on foliage capitals carved by *Martyn & Emms*. Hopkins's surviving timber FITTINGS are also nicely carved. – FONT. Round Late Norman bowl, with two bands of zigzag: a narrow roll near the bottom, nested chevron beneath the rim (cf. Wyre Piddle). – REREDOS, now under the tower. Early Victorian, with the Royal Arms flanked by the Decalogue. – STAINED GLASS. Early C19 dove in the nave NE window tracery. – MONUMENTS. On the tower floor, early C18 ledgers to the Sheldon family, mostly with heraldry. – Two tablets with draped urns: Samuel Lesingham †1827, by

Lewis of Cheltenham; Lucy Sheldon †1839, by *Preece* of Worcester.

ABBERTON HALL, to the S, was mostly rebuilt in the mid C19; long, unexciting garden front, S, of yellow brick. Of the earlier house one or two internal timber-framed walls survive, plus two lateral stone chimney-breasts with brick star-stacks. The finer, at the W end, with three shafts, is dated 1619.

ABBOTS MORTON   0050

The large rectangular moat N of the church, now dry, is the site of a C13 rest house of Evesham Abbey; the pool closer to the church, NE, must have been its fishpond.

ST PETER. W tower, nave, N transept, and chancel. Mostly Dec, though the fabric of the nave is probably C12. Late C14 W tower with a two-light W window with flowing tracery, battlements, and arch to the nave with continuous hollow mouldings. The N transept has Dec N and E windows, the chancel a Dec E window; the date 1637 in the E gable probably refers to repairs, perhaps including the straight-headed SE window, of three lights with uncommonly pretty tracery, though this looks rather early C16. C15 timber-framed S porch, mostly rendered. Charming interior, well restored in 1913–14 by *Harold Brakspear*; he replaced the wooden nave SE window with a Perp stone one and renewed the N transept arch. Simple roofs, of roughly shaped timbers, with a lath and plaster tympanum instead of a chancel arch. NE vestry probably *c.* 1840. – COMMUNION RAILS. C17, with sturdy, close-set balusters. – Good timber SCREEN with attached PULPIT, by *Brakspear*. – BENCHES. Two, in the porch, with moulded top rails; C15–C16. – STAINED GLASS. In the N transept N window, C14–C15 fragments, with C18 Walker heraldry above. – The E window has two oblong Flemish medallions (Goliath and the Fiery Furnace), both dated 1590.

The VILLAGE consists predominately of black-and-white houses   2
and cottages, of an astonishing variety, with the church on a hill to the W. The more important houses are at this end of the village street, giving place gradually to more modest houses and cottages, some built end-on to the road. Several show how their timber frames were altered in the C17–C18, bringing their elevations up to date or raising the roofs.

The S side begins with the pretty CORNER THATCH, and the T-plan MANOR COTTAGE, much larger but also C17. The OLD RECTORY has a probably C15 core, with narrow studding and lobby entry, extended at each end in the C17. Then, behind a low brick wall, HIGH HOUSE FARM, C17, later extended W, all with exposed brick infill rather than the usual rendering.

The OLD MANOR, opposite, is more complicated. C16–C17, with narrow studding on the ground floor, square panelling above, then an early C18 hipped roof. Lobby entry, the stack behind with two brick star-stacks. Decorative bracing on the E cross-wing; gabled central stair-turret at the rear.

Further on, s side, the two most interesting smaller houses are LILAC and HIGH HOUSE COTTAGES, at right angles to each other and both probably C15. The former has some curved bracing; the latter, of cruck construction, was originally a two-bay open hall. MANOR FARM, N, is again larger, its C17 square panelling later heightened with skimpier timbering and a hipped roof. The C17 GABLE HOUSE, end-on to the road, is thatched, with tension bracing and decorative work in the gable. Finally cottages take over, two of them, CHESTNUT COTTAGE and CYMBELINE, late C17, again end-on to the road, their long narrow plots set very close together.

ABBOTS MORTON MANOR, at Goom's Hill ⅓ m. SW. Early C19, stuccoed, with shallow hipped roof. Pilastered E front, its projecting centre with recessed balcony.

0040
ALDINGTON
near Badsey

Fine ashlar-faced MANOR HOUSE of c. 1830, of 2+1+2 bays, the recessed centre filled on the ground floor by a Tuscan porch, its parapet with a ball finial; wings with plain giant angle pilasters. Shallow hipped slate roof. The lower, stuccoed, three-bay Manor Court adjoining, N, was presumably the earlier manor house, downgraded to a service wing for its successor. – At the rear, a nine-bay C17 BARN, coursed rubble, with three half-hipped wagon porches to the N, visible from Mill Lane.

Attractive group of houses by the manor house. CORNER COTTAGES, NW, is gabled Tudor Gothic of c. 1840, with an attached former FORGE. To the S, a nice mixed group: early C19 white-painted brick with bargeboards; a late C17 timber-framed and thatched cottage; the early C18 brick OLD HOUSE, with stone quoins; and an L-shaped one with C17 N wing with mullioned windows, dated 1686.

7050
ALFRICK

ST MARY MAGDALENE. A chapelry of Suckley until 1912. Long Norman nave with lower chancel added in the C13 or C14; square timber W bell-turret, with steep pyramidal roof (all re-shingled in 1988–9). Restored by *Aston Webb*, 1885; he rebuilt the timber S porch and the chancel S wall, and added a N transeptal chapel and vestry. Opposing Norman windows at the W end of the nave; also a Norman W window, slightly longer. Other windows of all medieval centuries: nicely pro-filed cusped lancets of c. 1300; another early Dec window, chancel SE; E window with three-light reticulation, becoming straight-sided in the Perp way; and a pretty straight-headed Perp window W of the porch, repeated by Webb to its E. Also his a cusped nave N window, copying those of c. 1300. The fine composition, on the N side, of his chapel and vestry should be noted, with its unequal gables, continuous string courses, and piquant corner chimney; inside both have broad segmentally arched openings. Rendered interior, with exposed C15 nave roof of wagon type.

PEWS by *Webb*, who also added the upper, Perp-style, part of the SCREEN; its C15–C16 dado has cusped panels with leaf spandrels. – PULPIT. Plain, late C17; renewed top rail. – Oak VESTRY SCREEN and ALTAR RAILS by *M. W. Jones*, 1951. – STAINED GLASS. Entirely reglazed in 1953 by *G. King & Son* of Norwich, who installed an excellent collection of C16–C18 Netherlandish panels, round and oblong. – MONUMENTS. William Estopp †1735 and his two wives; pretty rustic cartouche with cherubs, nicely regilded in 1953.

The N chapel FITTINGS were all brought from Lulsley church (q.v.) in 1974. – Small FONT, a strange shape with its conical bowl the mirror image of the flared stem, divided by tight roll moulding; base also roll moulded. Presumably late C12, though Pevsner questioned whether it might not be C17. – SCULPTURE (w wall). Small relief of a man, arms akimbo; perhaps early C12. – COMMUNION RAIL. C17, with heavy balusters and elongated knobs on top. – ALTAR TABLE of similar date.

The UPPER HOUSE, a little W of the church, is late C18, of three bays with hipped roof, like an upright dolls' house. Earlier timber-framed rear wing.

At CLAY GREEN, to the N, a WAR MEMORIAL CROSS of *c.* 1920, above average quality. To its NW, the former BOARD SCHOOL by *E.A. Day*, 1876, with stepped triplets of lancets and patterned brickwork. Further N in Folly Road, beyond the C17 CLAY GREEN FARM, the OLD VICARAGE, a large U-plan house of 1913–14 by *A.C. Martin* of London; rendered, with hipped roof with hipped dormers.

ALFRICK COURT, at the NW end of the village, is early C19 stuccoed, with a veranda on six Ionic columns.

At ALFRICK POUND, ½ m. SSE, a nice late C18–early C19 mill group on the Leigh Brook: three- to four-storey stone MILL, with brick-trimmed, segment-headed windows; lower three-bay house, painted white. All converted to housing.

ALVECHURCH   0070

King Offa of Mercia gave Alvechurch, in 780, to the bishops of Worcester, who had a palace here from at least the C12–C13. Only the moats remain, but its presence no doubt led to the founding of a market in 1196, an annual fair in 1239, and borough status by 1299. By this date a new town had been established, to the NE of the church on its hill. The market lapsed by the mid C16, and the borough was dissolved in 1868. Limited early C19 development was due to the Worcester and Birmingham Canal, which had wharves to the W and NW, plus a larger one at Hopwood 1½ m. N (*see* below). Later C19 (following the arrival of the railway in 1859) and C20 development resulted from the proximity of Birmingham.

ST LAURENCE. Almost entirely by *William Butterfield*, designed 1857–8, built 1860–1. His E.E.-to-Dec exterior is relatively conventional, built within the footprint of the medieval church apart from the lean-to s aisle, but the identity of the architect is revealed by the bold contrast of red sandstone with buff-white bands, together with diapering in the E gable, and perhaps by the way the height of the nave roof challenges that of the medieval tower. This is probably C15, *see* the Perp W window, but the upper part was remodelled by *Samuel & Thomas Richards* in 1676, especially the parapet with its flat balusters; restored in 1890–1 by *Butterfield*, who intended a lofty pyramidal cap. The N aisle and chapel are also medieval: E window with reticulated tracery (curtailed by Butterfield's NE vestry), and one Perp and two Dec N windows. Above the s aisle windows, large re-set medieval heads, and, within the timber s porch, a re-set Norman s doorway with one order of shafts. These have odd block capitals, with bundles of three lines at the corners, the inner ones converging into a small volute; rollmoulded arch, hoodmould with billet and saltire crosses.

Butterfield's interior is stunning, one of the best of his major surviving brick colour schemes (cf. Baldersby, North Yorkshire, and Penarth, Glamorgan). The nave walls are patterned with crisp white diaper against glowing red brick, but subservient to the white stone bands dominating the forceful clerestory. Arcades of alternating buff and pink sandstone, the three-bay N repeating the forms of its predecessor (the W respond capital is indeed C12): round piers with scallop capitals and stepped pointed arches. The s arcade, three bays plus a narrower W arch, has round piers with moulded capitals and chamfered arches. Chancel details typically Butterfieldian, especially the banded chapel arcades, with round piers and, in the spandrels, large octofoiled roundels infilled with brick patterns. Otherwise the chancel patterning is more restrained yet more compelling than the nave's; sanctuary divided off by a high cusped timber arch on tall wall-shafts. Typical roofs, that of the nave significantly higher than the surviving medieval roof-line. Here Butterfield tellingly links the grey stonework of the tower with the rest of his interior by two startling red brick bands. Broad, continuously double-chamfered tower arch. Other surviving medieval detail is C13. The vestry doorway (probably the former priest's doorway) has a continuous roll with broad fillet and hoodmould with dogtooth. Dogtooth and fillets also in the broad cusped sedilia (infilled with rich C19 polychromy).

Butterfield's FURNISHINGS mostly remain. Worth noting are the rich alabaster and tile REREDOS, the ALTAR RAILS and STALLS, the low carved and painted timber SCREEN (incorporating medieval work), timber Dec-traceried PULPIT, brass LECTERN, and strongly patterned octagonal FONT. In the chancel, above the bishop's chair, a flat wooden MITRE, probably also C19. – Butterfieldian PEWS by *George H. Chantrell* of

London, 1933–4. – Oak TOWER SCREEN, a war memorial of
1920 by *A. S. Dixon*. – Much of the STAINED GLASS conforms
to Butterfield's principles. By *Preedy*, 1860–1, are the N chapel
N window and the S aisle SW and W; his central S aisle window
is of 1870. – By *Alexander Gibbs*, 1861, the S aisle SE and large
E window, of 1873. – Later glass includes two by *Hardman*,
1876–7: N aisle NE and S chapel S (partly 1985); good chancel
side windows by *Powell & Sons*, 1890–1, the N to designs by
Henry Holiday, the S by *J. W. Brown*; two by *William Pearce Ltd*,
that in the tower, of 1897, portraying Queen Victoria and the
Bishop of Worcester; the S chapel E by *Jones & Willis*, 1934;
and, by far the best, the Arts and Crafts N aisle W window by
Alfred L. Pike, 1918.

MONUMENTS. In the N chapel, a large Dec niche with
cusped ogee arch contains the sandstone effigy of a cross-
legged knight, said to be Sir John Blanchfront. His head,
with the visor of the bascinet raised, lies on a pillow held by
two angels. The short kilted coat-armour can be dated to
c. 1345–50. It includes two breast chains and other rare details
comparable to the Giffard effigy at Leckhampton (Glos.) – In
the chancel a smaller niche with ogee-trefoiled arch, partly C19.
– Also a renewed C15 coffin lid, still with floriated cross, though
the flowers within it betray the real date. Shaft flanked by a
chalice and a shield with the arms of John Carpenter, Bishop
of Worcester 1443–76 (buried at Westbury-on-Trym, Bristol).
– N aisle. Good brass to Sir Philip Chatwyn †1525, a 28½ in.
(72 cm.) figure in armour, with shields at the corners of the
stone slab. – Edward Moore †1746. Large tablet of grey
marbles, with fluted Corinthian pilasters flanking the round-
arched centre. Above, an oval portrait medallion; at the foot,
heraldry in a fine Rococo cartouche.

Attached to the N aisle by a short glazed link is a remarkable, ark-shaped CHURCH HALL by *Michael Reardon & Associates*, 2004; job architect *Graeme Beamish*. The walls, brick
banded with stone, pay due tribute to Butterfield, but the
prow-like NW end is entirely glazed, producing a startling effect
within; glazed projections also midway along either flank.
Bridge-like mezzanine floor, SE (nearest the church).

In the CHURCHYARD, S, a C15 CROSS; a chunky TOMB to
Archdeacon John Sandford †1873, the client for the church
and rectory; and, also by *Butterfield*, a tall MEMORIAL CROSS
of 1861 to the two sons of Baroness Windsor of Hewell Grange
(*see* Tardebigge); Gothic, heavily detailed.

The former RECTORY, further S, now a nursing home, is by *Butterfield*, 1855–6. Big, of brick and half-timbering. The side
towards the church has a projecting gabled service wing, with
the entrance at the NW corner of the main range. Altered E
front, but the S, garden façade survives, a memorable attempt
at the Picturesque, with its broken forms, and contrast between
the brick and stone ground floor and the thinly half-timbered
upper storey. Its three gables denote, from W to E, library,
drawing room, and dining room.

PERAMBULATION

The VILLAGE preserves the layout of the C13 new town: a tri-angular marketplace pointing toward the church, entered by roads from the four cardinal directions. The vestigial central SQUARE has modest C18 to mid-C19 houses on its N and S sides with, across the main road to the W, a good display of C15–C16 timber framing partly infilling the apex of the former market-place at the foot of BEAR HILL. Here, set back, N side, the brick VILLAGE HALL by *Bloomer & Gough*, 1929. Nos. 1–3 opposite, L-plan, stuccoed, of *c.* 1830–40, housed the GRAMMAR SCHOOL; the narrow, well-windowed second storey, approached by an outer stair, served as its dormitory. Then a small green from which the ascent to the church begins.

Back on the N side, several nice houses climb the hill. VINE COTTAGE (Nos. 16–18) has segment-headed windows with moulded frames with imposts and key blocks, typical of the Birmingham area *c.* 1820–30. Nos. 20–22 are a small gabled brick pair by *John Cotton, c.* 1882. Nos. 24–28 is timber-framed with W cross-wing, all clad in brick or roughcast. Then the excellent OLD HOUSE, probably *c.* 1630, with exposed framing. It consists of a gabled hall range with gabled wings, the latter close-studded with overhangs (the W wing underbuilt in brick). The upper part of the recessed centre has wavy dec-orative bracing, the lower floor lean-to infill probably by *Bateman & Drury*, 1843–4, when the house was the Bear Inn.

In RED LION STREET, N from The Square, Nos. 1–3 also rep-resent a framed house with central range and cross-wings, probably C15. The S wing seems to be primary, the tension-braced N wing a few years later; both were jettied but are now underbuilt. No. 5 is also timber-framed, with narrow-studded rear wing, but the front entirely refaced in brick in the late C18. More narrow studding opposite, on the first floor of Nos. 6–8, a former C15 hall house now without its N service bay; floored in the C16–C17 with remains of a late C17 decorative ceiling in the room above the hall.

The rest of Red Lion Street is C19 brick, its best building the BAPTIST CHAPEL by *James Cranston*, 1860, red brick with blue banding, small but grittily Gothic. All the grouped lancet windows have saw-toothed arches and iron-latticed frames. Sharply canted NE stair to the E end gallery; broad canted W apse. Attached Sunday School by *Bloomer & Gough*, 1927–8. Then the RED LION itself, rebuilt by *S. T. Walker*, 1939–40, minimally Tudor brick.

SWAN STREET, S of The Square, is also named after its pub, rebuilt in the mid C19. In School Lane, off its SW end, is *Butterfield*'s brick SCHOOL of 1856–8, poorly altered in the late C19 (partly used, from 1971, as St Mary's R.C. church). The detached SCHOOL HOUSE, E, *c.* 1859, has typical half-hips and chimney set-offs.

Finally RADFORD ROAD, leading E from The Square. It begins with CROWN HOUSE, again a hall range with cross-wings,

probably C16, but over-restored. Round the bend, the FLOUR
MILL of 1875 by *E.A. Day*, quite substantial with three storeys
and attached gabled house, only slighter lower. Then, on a
steep bank across the River Arrow, the MOATED SITE of the
bishops' palace, two adjacent platforms some 175 ft (54 metres)
wide, the inner (SE) square and still entirely surrounded by
water; the late C19 Moat House stands at the NW corner of the
longer outer enclosure. Leland described the palace, *c.* 1540,
as a timber structure recently restored by Bishop Latimer; it
was demolished in the C18. An extensive medieval deerpark
extended to S and E.

FAIRFIELD, some distance further NE, is a tall house faced in
purple brick, by *Gerald McMichael*, 1906. Two sharp but differing gables between which the big tiled roof sweeps low over
the round-arched doorway.

SCARFIELD FARMHOUSE, ½ m. WSW. Early C17, timber-
framed. T-plan, with mixed square panelling and narrow studding. Wide cross-wing with N gable (to the road) and rear
parlour; good brick chimney with two star-shafts. Hall in the
stem, W. Close-studded NE addition.

The OLD RECTORY, ⅝ m. NNE, by the River Arrow. Large, early
C18 brick, to a broad H-plan, 1+7+1 bays with gabled wings;
altered in the C19, e.g. the N porch. It completely hides a late
C15 timber-framed structure, the main range with two-bay hall,
E, two-bay service range, W. The E cross-wing is also C15 (with
much framing exposed inside); later W wing.

HOPWOOD, 1½ m. N, became the interim terminus of the
WORCESTER AND BIRMINGHAM CANAL in 1802; begun in
1791, this reached Tardebigge (q.v.) in 1807, Worcester in 1815.
Of the wharf little remains apart from the plain brick
HOPWOOD HOUSE INN, of 1867. The best canalscape is ½ m.
further NNE, where the canal passes through a deep cutting
before entering the 1½ m.-long WAST HILLS TUNNEL (completed 1797). The impressive sandstone and brick BRIDGE
No. 69 provides a good viewpoint. Lower Bittell (and Cofton)
reservoirs, opened in 1813, maintained the flow of the Arrow;
Upper Bittell reservoir, of 1832, served the canal. Further S a
brick AQUEDUCT carries the canal over the narrow Aqueduct
Lane.

LITTLE STANNALLS, 1 m. NNW (just E of the canal). Large brick
house of Barnt Green (q.v.) type, mostly by *C.E. Bateman*,
c. 1920, with core by *Crouch & Butler*, *c.* 1900 (see the half-
timbering and gable at the N end of the garden front).

BITTELL FARM, L-plan, brick, N of Lower Bittell reservoir, is
mostly mid-C17. The SW front, with three wide bays of
segment-headed windows, rebuilt in the late C18, faces a walled
forecourt with fine rusticated gatepiers with ball finials. These,
like the rear NE parlour wing, may be late C17 additions. Good
panelling within.

Of other farms the best is BROADCROFT FARM, Lea End, 2 m.
NE. Early C19 brick, distinguished by portly single-storey bow
windows flanking the doorway.

WAST HILLS HOUSE, 2½ m. NNE, now a Birmingham University conference centre. By *Arthur E. McKewan*, 1905, for W.A. Cadbury; altered 1910. Roughcast, with gables (with diamond patterning) and green slate roofs, rather like over-scaled Voysey. Long garden front, S, with bay windows and timber balconies. Nice internal detail. – Matching W and NE lodges, the latter opposite contemporary cottages.

HOPWOOD PARK SERVICES, 1⅛ m. NE, at the junction of the M42 (opened 1986) and Alvechurch by-pass (opened 1994). By *J. Ward Associates Ltd*, 1998. Sleek flat-roofed exterior with wavy-form entrance canopy; open-plan interior.

At the mostly C20 ROWNEY GREEN, 1¼ m. ESE, a prominent early C19 stuccoed farmhouse, and small brick WESLEYAN CHAPEL of 1869, enlarged in the 1950s. This has an E window by *A.E. Lemmon*, 1951.

SEECHEM MANOR, ¾ m. further NE, formerly Rowney Green House, is timber-framed, to a T-plan, the two-bay hall range dendrodated to 1474, the NW parlour cross-wing to 1595. The former, now without its SE service wing, had a floor and central brick chimney inserted in the late C16, and its walls refaced in brick in the C18; the smoke-blackened late C15 roof survives, with cambered tie-beams and raking struts. The C16–C17 cross-wing has square framing above narrow studding, a conventional queenpost roof structure, and brick chimney-breast filling the SE return. Further altered *c.* 1840 when the cross-wing received bargeboards, hoodmoulded windows, and a big stuccoed Tudor NW porch. Inside, much early woodwork remains, including C17 panelling and a fine arched overmantel in the great chamber above the parlour, and an early C18 open-well stair behind the entrance hall.

LONGFIELD MANOR, N of the drive to Seechem, was rebuilt after a fire in 1893. Good late C17 stone gatepiers and brick farm buildings, probably of 1799.

WEATHEROAK HILL, 2 m. ENE. *See* Wythall.

8070

ARELEY KINGS
Stourport-on-Severn

ST BARTHOLOMEW. A chapelry of Martley, mostly red sandstone, on an elevated site. Rebuilt by *Preedy*, 1885–6, except for the tower and short chancel. The lower half of the S tower, of grey sandstone, is C14; see the mouldings of the entrance arch. The upper half, of red, is probably early C15. Norman chancel (with one S window), remodelled 1796: the E wall was then partly rebuilt in brick, with a Y-traceried window; various added buttresses. By *Preedy*, in brittle Geometrical Dec style, are the nave and N aisle, and the large N vestry; an oddity of this is its Neo-Norman E doorway, a copy of the destroyed nave N doorway. Tall four-bay N arcade with alternating round and octagonal piers, higher chancel arch, and arch-braced roofs.

FONT. Norman base with a probably C17 inscription 'Tempore La[y]amanni santi'. Layamon, author of the historical poem *Brut*, was a priest at Earnley-by-Severn, probably Areley Kings, *c.* 1200. Neo-Norman bowl of 1886, carved by *Robert Clarke* of Hereford. – Also his the eagle LECTERN and vestry SCREEN (1898). – Good HATCHMENT (N aisle). – STAINED GLASS. Chancel S window of 1899, also commemorating Layamon. – Colourful N aisle W by *John Petts* of Abergavenny, 1991, completed by *Jim Budd*. – MONUMENTS. Minor tablets, e.g. one of 1783 by *Perry* of Bewdley. – In the churchyard, WSW, a short stretch of stone wall, with a mixed Greek, Latin and English inscription to Sir Harry Coningsby †1701.

RECTORY, to the SE. Brick, early C17; remodelled probably *c.* 1728 (*see* below). The three Jacobean gables of the flat five-bay S front now look a little stunted because of the Georgian attic. To the churchyard, W, a neat four-bay early C18 façade. The blank opening l. of its doorway marks the fine open-well staircase, with three turned balusters to the tread. Contemporary panelling. Early C19 the N bay window and E service wing linking up to a formerly detached bakehouse, with shaped gables. The SUMMERHOUSE (or 'out-stout') at the end of the garden carries the Vernon arms and formerly the date 1728; still gabled, but the brickwork now in Flemish bond, with burnt headers. External stair towards the churchyard; semi-domed alcove below, facing the Severn. Restored 1904.

CHURCH HOUSE, S, was built in 1536, according to tree-ring dating. Of square-panelled framing, three bays, the first-floor jettied and open to the queen-strut roof. It became a school in the mid-C18, a stable in the C19. Restored by *Peter Taylor*, 2005. WAR MEMORIAL nearby, a wayside cross by *H.C. Corlette*, 1921.

On the N side of ARELEY LANE, a little E, are two or three large houses. ARELEY HALL, timber-framed and quite large, is said to be of 1605, built for Simon Mucklowe; remodelled and roughcast for Daniel Zachary, *c.* 1828. Three irregular gables at the rear, the outer two of C16–C17 origin, the NE one housing the staircase. On the entrance front, S, the overhang is still visible, and the doorway retains its original door, masked by a wide projecting bay on Doric columns, with later C19 timbered gable. Two similar gables link to a lower C16–C17 E range, probably originally detached; this, now Mucklowe House, became the C19 service wing. Almost opposite the former lodge, further E, is LOWER HOUSE, early C18 brick, square with hipped roof; former BARN nearby dated 1759.

ARELEY HOUSE, further SE, now a nursing home, is ashlar-faced, probably *c.* 1820. Five bays, the central three projecting beneath a pediment, with a porch of paired unfluted Ionic columns. Good entrance hall with a screen of two Corinthian columns; behind it, an oval room expressed outside by a full-height bow. – Former STABLES, SW, of brick, with three big round arches, the central one recessed.

At the N end of ARELEY COMMON, ⅜ m. S, a brick tower WIND-MILL of 1779, converted to a house with pyramidal cap *c.* 1902. The huge WALSHES ESTATE, centred on Hermitage Way, now covers most of the Common; low-cost 'Radburn' housing, of brick, planned for Stourport UDC by *Stephenson, Young & Partners* of Liverpool, built from 1953.

Redstone Lane leads E, past a caravan site, to the REDSTONE ROCK HERMITAGE, a system of chambers cut into the sandstone cliff by the Severn. A medieval ferry crossing here was served by the Brethren of the Redstone, founded in the C12. The apartments and cells are partly on two levels with internal stairs and various other cavities. In 1538 Bishop Latimer said they 'could lodge 500 men, as ready for thieves and traitors as true men'.

ASHTON UNDER HILL

Large village below the E slopes of Bredon Hill; transferred from Gloucestershire in 1931.

ST BARBARA. A chapelry of Beckford. Of the Norman nave only the simple S doorway remains: one order of shafts with scalloped capitals, plain tympanum, arch with roll moulding, and hoodmould with worn pellet decoration.* Mixed nave S windows, including a large four-light Perp example. C14 S porch with Dec windows, rebuilt by *J. A. Cossins,* 1902. The lower stage of the W tower is C13, the upper Late Perp. N aisle with Dec or Perp windows, the former mostly of 1867; large raking NE buttress of 1820. The most interesting feature of the church, however, is the chancel, rebuilt in 1624 by Sir John Franklin; it shows just how vague Jacobean Gothic could be. The E window has curious tracery of three stepped trefoil-headed lights incorporating elements of the Franklin arms: carved dolphins in the spandrels, hoodmould with three lions' heads. Date plaque above the priest's doorway, which has a leaf frieze up the very arch. The N and S windows apparently incorporate C14 tracery. Alterations of 1834–6 included inserting a small nave SE window and rebuilding the chancel arch, which copies the mouldings of the four-bay N arcade, but with telltale guttae to the brackets beneath the capitals. The arcade is Late Perp, with octagonal piers and four-centred arches of one bold hollow moulding. Its W half was reinstated at the 1867 restoration, by *W.H. Baker* of Birmingham; he removed a schoolroom of 1842 that had been built partly within the aisle. Further restoration by *Gerald Cogswell,* 1913, exposed the nave roof.

FONT. Elaborate Perp. Octagonal bowl with fleurons in quatrefoils; below, large leafy knobs like pendants. – COMMUNION TABLE. C17. – Other furnishings C19–C20: oak PULPIT and deal PEWS by *Baker*; STALLS, chunky LECTERN, ORGAN and

---

* Also two Norman fragments inside, chancel S wall.

tower SCREEN by *Cogswell*. – STAINED GLASS. Large-scale E
window of 1879 by *Frank Holt* of Warwick; subtler chancel side
windows by *F. Holt & Co.*, 1912. – N aisle E by *Florence Camm*,
1932; not her best. – One nave S with Cheyne heraldry, *c.* 1400.
– MONUMENTS. In the chancel, an anonymous stone tablet of
1651 facing a Grecian one, with draped urn, to W.H. Baldwyn
†1857, by *G. Lewis* of Cheltenham. – Also earlier Baldwyn wall
tablets and floor ledgers. – LYCHGATE. 1931 by *G.H. Wigley*;
solid oak, on a stone plinth.

The VILLAGE CROSS, probably early C15, stands outside the lychgate; a fine example with three steps, base, and shaft with
shield, its top replaced by a sundial. Nearby, WALNUT
THATCH, good C16–C17 timber-framed; similar cottage,
mostly of stone, opposite. The C17–early C18 MIDDLE FARM
further S is entirely of stone, with mullioned windows; its long
SHELTER SHED, probably late C18, survives largely unaltered
behind the smaller house to the N. More good farm buildings
at OLD MANOR FARM a little SW, remodelled 1638 for the
Baldwyn family; originally part stone, part timber-framed, the
latter mostly replaced with chequered brickwork *c.* 1800. Long
timber-framed mid-C17 BARN, rectangular stone DOVECOTE in
the angle with the house, tall brick mid-C19 STABLES behind.

The main part of the village, stretching some distance N along
ELMLEY ROAD, has more worthwhile stone and timber-
framed farmhouses, mostly C17, often thatched, interspersed
with C18 and later brick. The most interesting is first on the E
side: the OLD FARMHOUSE, an expanded L-plan. The N half
of the stem, with three pairs of crucks, is a hall house of
c. 1400, later extended S; horizontally divided and chimney
inserted in the C16–C17, when the narrow-studded N cross-
wing was added. Further N, beyond the plain NATIONAL
SCHOOL of 1876 and later, GRASSMERE COTTAGE and OLD
BEAMS are a nice thatched timber-framed pair, possibly late
C16. N again, facing Cotton's Lane, the MANOR HOUSE of
c. 1700, stone, H-plan, much altered in the C19; fine C18
gatepiers with ball finials.

More stone and timber-framed houses in COTTON'S LANE,
leading W uphill. Two carry dates on their rectangular stone
chimneys: 1642 on the well-restored ORCHARD HOUSE in
Croft Lane, S; 1623 on the enlarged COPPICE COTTAGE, W
end.

Further N in ELMLEY ROAD later brick buildings include SHER-
BOURNE HOUSE, *c.* 1795, three bays and storeys; and the FREE
CHURCH of 1923–4 by *F.W. Anderson* of Birmingham; small,
with stone dressings and free Dec tracery. Contemporary
stained glass by *Pearce & Cutler*.

At the N end, BREDON HILL MIDDLE SCHOOL by *L.C.
Lomas*, 1963–5, the curtain walling of its four-storey classroom
block seeming oddly alien in this rural setting.

On the former Midland Railway branch ½ m. E, only the former
STATION HOUSE, by *George Hunt*, 1864, remains; of Lias with
freestone segment-headed windows (cf. Beckford).

ASTLEY

32 ST PETER. Ralph de Todeni (or Tosny, †1102) founded a Benedictine priory here, attached to the Abbey of St Taurin, near
Rouen; it, like other 'alien' foundations, was suppressed in
1414. Its church survives, lavish despite its small scale. The
nave S wall suggests the mid C12. It is horizontally divided by
a string course and by an eaves corbel frieze with heads; and
vertically by buttresses of semicircular section above, but of
two semicircles with keel moulding between, as in Norman rib-
vaults, below. Three windows are placed in this framework, the
central one a C19 re-creation. S doorway set in the usual projecting piece of wall, here edged with zigzag. Two orders of
shafts, the inner with restored zigzag; scalloped capitals;
chevron also in the arch. The chancel also has Norman
windows, one S, one (blocked) N. The chancel arch has paired
demi-columns, plus one recessed shaft E, one W; decorated
scallop capitals, single-step arch. N arcade also Norman, but
later: circular piers with trumpet-scallop capitals, octagonal
abaci, single-step arches; one Norman head on the easternmost pier. Perp alterations and additions include a few inserted
windows, the fine W tower, and a N chapel. The tower has large
diminishing diagonal buttresses, and renewed battlements and
pinnacles; a refinement is the canting of the E corners of the
upper stage, presumably to disguise the stair-vice, NE. Tall
triple-chamfered arch to the nave, its flat responds and thin
capital-band with concave sides. The N chapel is Late Perp,
with rounded arch to the chancel and altered narrow arch to
the aisle. *Harvey Eginton* rebuilt and widened the aisle in
1837–8, but its windows and much else in the church belong
to a restoration of 1903–4 by the rector, the Rev. *M.B. Buckle*;
he rebuilt the chancel E end and the S porch (restoring the
tower in 1906–7).

Most FITTINGS, especially in the chancel, are of 1903–4. –
C18 COMMUNION RAILS, now in N aisle. – The PULPIT must
be a made-up piece: C18 in form, but with the usual broad
Jacobean blank arches. – FONT. Very odd and certainly not
Norman (as the VCH claims). Octagonal, each side with a big
rising tulip petal; heavily moulded top. Perhaps Late Perp,
though unusual. – STAINED GLASS. E window by *William
Pearce Ltd*, 1904. – It replaced two Norman lights with picto-
rial glass by *Charles Evans & Co.*, 1889, now re-set in the nave
SE windows. Chancel SW of the same time. – The other nave
S, semi-abstract, by *Nicola Hopwood*, 2001.

MONUMENTS. In the N chapel, two similar, brightly painted
monuments of 1577 (according to a contemporary brass
plaque): paired recumbent effigies on tomb-chests, with fluted
pilasters and kneeling children, each named on ribbons. That
61 to Walter Blount †1561 and wife shows him with a book, the
daughters with closely pleated skirts, treated in a exceptionally
Mannerist fashion. – That to Robert Blount †1573 and wife,
with broader balusters and Early Renaissance wreaths filled

with Tudor roses, is prominently signed, w end, by *John Gildon* (or Guldo) of Hereford. – John Winford †1682; provincial tablet with broken segmental pediment, but more up-to-date than the cartouches in the chancel to Samuel Bowater †1696 and Anne Bowater †1687. – Sir Thomas Winford †1702, attributed to *Grinling Gibbons* (GF). Standing white marble monument with large urn in a square recess with looped-up curtains; flanking obelisks with paired cherubs halfway up and eagle on top. – Sarah Winford †1793, by *John Bacon Sen.* (similar to his earlier monument to Mrs Draper at Bristol Cathedral). Benevolence (with pelican) and Sensibility (with flowers), either side of a round pedestal with wreathed urn; both look outwards. – Harriet Winford †1801 and her sister Sarah Freeman †1806, both by *Bacon Jun.*, each with seated pensive female figure by an urn; the details differ just about enough. – Neat war memorial tablet, of blue Hornton stone, designed by *W. Curtis Green, Son & Lloyd*, 1948. – HATCHMENT to Walter Michael Moseley, 1827.

In the churchyard, the base of a medieval CROSS and C18–C19 CHEST TOMBS. – Immediately NW is the OLD RECTORY, brick, three storeys and three wide bays, with shallow-hipped roof. This all looks early C19, but closer inspection shows that there were formerly five narrower bays; probably altered *c.* 1885 by *F.C. Penrose*.

PRIOR'S MILL, on the Dick Brook, ⅓ m. WSW. Small C17 timber-framed water mill, picturesquely set above a very high weir; not improved by C20 alterations.

YARHAMPTON HOUSE, ¾ m. W, is an attractively restored early C17 farmhouse: hall range with gabled wings; gabled dormer above the centre. Mostly close studding below, square panelling above, with flat oriels on brackets, one dated 1610; tall brick chimneys. LITTLE YARHAMPTON provides a modest square-panelled foil.

At ASTLEY TOWN, ½ m. NE, the SCHOOL is by *J.T. Meredith*, 1892–3; brick, with half-timbered gables.* Further E, ASTLEY TOWN HOUSE, *c.* 1600, F-plan, i.e. hall range with small gable adjoining the W cross-wing, and ASTLEY TOWNE, also early C17 timber-framed: hall and cross-wings, the E attractively underbuilt in sandstone.

THE POOL HOUSE, ⅔ m. NE, has a delightful sandstone ashlar façade, Gothick, of *c.* 1760, fronting a mid-C17 house, the character of which reveals itself on the returns: here are cross- or mullioned windows, brick star-stacks, and shaped gables. C18 brick rear addition, NE, with hipped roof. The Gothick façade has three bays and two storeys with moulded cornice; three even ogee gables above, with quatrefoils (with octofoil glazing), and finials. Ogee Venetian windows flank both the ogee-headed first-floor window and the moulded doorway below; this has a curious stepped label, not Gothic but not correctly classical

---

* It replaced an ENDOWED SCHOOL of 1743 (now a house) in an isolated position ½ m. E of the church; detached schoolroom nearby, of 1875.

either, no doubt derived from Batty Langley's *Gothic Architecture* (of 1747). Gothick entrance hall, but other rooms with classical decoration. – Rusticated C18 GATEPIERS, SE, set in a quadrant wall.

ASTLEY HALL, ¾ m. E. Ashlar-faced Tudorbethan country house, rebuilt *c.* 1838 for the Lea family, by *Harvey Eginton*; now a nursing home. Symmetrical, with three-bay centre with two-storey canted bays, surmounted by three shaped gables containing keyed wreaths; lower wings, also with shaped gables. The central porch, of Grafton type (*see* p. 321), is dated 'SLB 1912', for Stanley and Lucy Baldwin; they purchased the house in that year (having lived here since 1902), and remodelled some of it, especially the brick service wing, S. Eginton's plainer garden front, W, of five bays, also has three shaped gables and a central porch-like projection; its large first-floor window lights a viewing balcony at the head of the main staircase. The large tripartite Ionic loggia further S (at the rear of the service wing) must be of *c.* 1912. A convincingly Jacobean plaster ceiling survives in the entrance hall. – LODGE, to the E, also of *c.* 1838, in similar style.

BULL HILL FARM, further E, is early C17, mostly square-panelled framing, hall and cross-wing type; paired gables above the entrance and the service end.

To the N, on the Stourport Road, a MEMORIAL of 1950 to the former Prime Minister Stanley (later first Earl) Baldwin, born (at Bewdley) 1867, died (at Astley Hall) 1947: quadrant wall and stone plinth with attached seats.

The C17 LONGMORE HILL FARM, 1¼ m. NE, has gables flanking the central brick stack (above a lobby entrance). Early C19 stone outbuildings to the E: cowhouse and stable flanking a square pyramid-roofed dovecote.

DUNLEY, a more nucleated settlement, 1 m. N, has two larger houses worth a glance. DUNLEY HALL has a C16–C17 core, hall and cross-wings, with lower C18 N wing; all remodelled in the mid-C19, with bargeboarded gables. OAKHAMPTON, further S, early C19 sub-Italianate, was unsubtly enlarged in similar style in the later C19.

GLASSHAMPTON MONASTERY, ½ m. SSW, now Friary of the Society of St Francis (of Cerne Abbas). Glasshampton, a large rectangular mansion built *c.* 1705 for Thomas Cookes Winford by *John Watson*,[*] was burnt down in 1810. The early C19 brick STABLES, NNE of the house site, remain, converted in 1918 as the monastery of St Mary at the Cross, founded by William Sirr as a Cistercian house within the Church of England. Handsome brick, U-plan, with four pyramid-roofed corner pavilions. The front range has a pedimented centre with clock lantern, linked to the pavilions by five-bay ranges; tripartite central window (formerly doorway), beneath a blank segmental arch. The stable yard is now the monastery garth. Near the

_____

[*] Described as 'architect of Glashampton' on his ledger stone in Astley church.

start of the long drive, a pair of early C19 LODGES, much altered.

The drive meets the B4196 close to GLAZEN BRIDGE, rebuilt 1925. This spans the Dick Brook, an important focus of the mid-C17 iron industry. A short distance W, due N of the lodges, is a single-arched PACKHORSE BRIDGE. Further WSW, at the former head of Sharpley Pool, remnants of a mid-C17 BLAST FURNACE, the earliest surviving English example with round hearth and bosh. On the N bank, ½ m. E of the bridge, is the site of a FORGE; its water wheels were fed by a leat alongside the brook. Further E two flash locks provided access to the Severn. The sites have been excavated, but little remains visible; they are traditionally associated with Andrew Yarranton (cf. Worcester, Introduction p. 669), born at Astley in 1619.

ASTON SOMERVILLE   0030

Transferred from Gloucestershire in 1931.

ST MARY. Mostly C14–C15 in appearance, with Dec-Perp W tower with battlements, pinnacles and lively gargoyles. The chancel, though, with NE lancet and S priest's doorway with plain tympanum, is perhaps as early as *c.* 1200. The tower was also begun in the C13, see the fine double-chamfered arch towards the nave, with semicircular responds and good moulded capitals. Dec nave windows, plus two more, and a trefoil-headed piscina, in the chancel; Perp E window. Both nave and chancel were heightened in the C15. Good chancel roof, with tie- and collar-beams linked by queen-struts; one tier of wind-braces. A nave SE chapel, demolished *c.* 1688, may also have been Perp, judging by the window re-set in its blocked arch; signs of the adjoining rood stair outside. *C. Ford Whitcombe*, in 1908, rebuilt the N porch and chancel arch, provided most of the simple furnishings, and paved the sanctuary in black and white marble, reusing a C19 stone ALTAR. – FONT. A very odd piece, probably post-Reformation despite its Norman-style carving and incised decoration; severely cut down at some stage. The circular plinth could be Norman. – Rectangular PULPIT with reused Jacobean panels. More panels, probably from former box pews, were used to line the sanctuary in 1908. – SCREEN. C15, with pretty Perp tracery; good carving, especially the foliage frieze. – STAINED GLASS. C14 fragments in the nave NW window. – MONUMENTS. Sandstone effigy of a Somerville knight wearing a mail coif and hauberk, perhaps *c.* 1290; very tall but much damaged, now resting on a stone coffin. – Rebecca Parry †1709; good cartouche. – Simple tablets to C19 lords Somerville, and an ornate Renaissance-style one to the Rev. George Head †1893, also commemorated by a flamboyant churchyard TOMB, E of the chancel.

To the N, the former RECTORY, plain stone Tudor of 1861; enlarged by *Waller & Son*, 1914.

The church lies at the SE edge of the mostly C20 village. MANOR FARM is probably of 1867 by *George Hunt*, see the tall sub-classical centre, of yellow brick. In the later C19, large red brick wings were added and various windows inserted.

0060   ASTWOOD BANK
                         Feckenham

Large suburban brick village, expanded in the C19 as an outpost of Redditch's needle- and spring-making industry.

ST MATTHIAS and ST GEORGE, Church Road. By *W.J. Hopkins*, 1883–4, but of his spacious church only the chancel, N vestries (now chapel), and stump of a big S tower were built. Nave, of roughcast brick, added to a reduced scale by *W.G. St J. Cogswell*, 1911. Hopkins's E end is in his typical intricate Dec style; of snecked Bromsgrove stone, but yellow brick with patterned bands inside. Ornate roof; rich foliage carving by *Martyn & Emms*, especially on the hefty chancel arch. The playful tops of the nave's long paired lancets betray its date externally; one might otherwise be reminded of Commissioners' churches of a hundred years before. Two very high W lancets. Narrow passage aisles with three-bay arcades, their piers typical early C20: oblong octagons in section with short main sides and long diagonals or chamfers; Cogswell may have been influenced by W.H. Bidlake of Birmingham. – STAINED GLASS. N chapel E window by *Claude Price*, 1970.
   Neo-Georgian VICARAGE of 1926; purple brick with red trim.
Former BAPTIST CHAPEL, Chapel Road. 1822. Brick. Pedimental gable with corner urns and lunette; two tiers of windows with stepped voussoirs; wide recessed doorway. Originally three bays long, later extended.
(WESLEYAN) METHODIST CHAPEL, Chapel Street. 1863 by *Alfred Smallwood* of Redditch. Red brick with yellow quoins and patterning; arched windows. One nave S window by *Hardman*, 1977. – Schoolroom by *E.A. Day*, 1876; enlarged 1907.
(BOARD) SCHOOLS, SW, by *E.A. Day*, 1876–7 (enlarged 1894). Of brick, with stepped lancets: two large gabled blocks, the W less altered, separated by a pair of teachers' houses.
RIDGEWAY MIDDLE SCHOOL, Evesham Road, S end. By *Frederick Gibberd*, 1957–8. Two storeys, concrete-framed with brick infill, to a broad U-plan. At the entrance, a matching brick caretaker's house (No. 1366).
Of C19 NEEDLE FACTORIES, the notable survivor is the DOUBLE CENTURY WORKS of James Smith & Sons, at the S end of High Street, set round an irregular courtyard. The earliest parts are probably of *c.* 1810–20, especially the integral master's house at the SE corner (facing Chestnut Road). Impressive range to High Street: two storeys of round-arched windows;

8+10 bays, of at least two C19 builds. – Yeomans & Sons' FACTORY, Feckenham Road (corner of Queen Street) made springs; mid-C19, fourteen by nine bays of round-arched windows in two storeys, mostly with yellow or blue heads. – Also of note, the ANCHOR WORKS of Vulco Springs, No. 1154 Evesham Road: *c.* 1840–50, with six-bay front with continuous lintels on brackets.

YEW TREES, No. 1190 Evesham Road. Dated 1769 on its central gabled dormer. Brick, three bays, with later Doric porch.

The outstanding house is TOOKEYS FARM, probably basically C16, at the end of a long drive W of the S end of Evesham Road. Three-bay hall and lower E cross-wing, the latter with square panelling, the former with a tall projecting central N bay with narrow studding, herringbone work above, and decorative concave lozenges in the gable; sandstone stack with three tall brick star-stacks to its r. The hall has an elaborate early C17 plaster ceiling, with strapwork, foliage, vine trails, and winged putti. The S side of the cross-wing, faced in C18–C19 brick, has a two-storeyed E extension, with another chimney with three tall stacks. The house, formerly moated, is said to stand on the site of King John's hunting lodge.

ASTWOOD COURT, ⅞ m. WSW, also occupies an ancient site, within a water-filled moat; the home of the Culpeper family in the C16–C17, entirely encased or rebuilt in brick in the C18. Main SW–NE range, with SE solar wing; this retains more of its framing, including two cusped trusses with scrolled vine paintings.

ASTWOOD FARM, ¼ m. to its SSE, is an attractive C17 house of square-panelled framing, with gabled cross-wings; central lobby-entrance plan.

BADSEY

0040

Large village at the centre of the Vale of Evesham market gardening district.

ST JAMES. A possession of Evesham Abbey until the Dissolution. Of the Norman nave only the N wall remains, largely rebuilt in 1885; the present N window was formerly in the S wall. The jamb of another N window is visible inside. Norman N doorway: lintel with rope frieze, arch with incised zigzag.* Handsome Perp W tower of *c.* 1450, ashlar-faced, with battlements with lively gargoyles and crocketed pinnacles; lofty tower arch, continuously double-hollow-chamfered. Early C14 chancel and N transept, the detail of the former slightly later (with ogee tracery forms); the rounded head of the E window must be the result of repairs after the gable collapsed in 1653. Competent restoration of 1884–5 by *T. G. Jackson*; he added

---

* Other Norman fragments are built into a gatepier of the SW churchyard extension (towards Chapel Street).

the Dec-style S aisle and porch, also a N vestry. Neat four-bay arcade with octagonal piers. His also the chancel arch.

FONT. Plain bowl of 1885, good early C14 octagonal stem: attached shafts with excellent leaf capitals. – PULPIT, with linenfold panels of c. 1529. – COMMUNION RAILS. 1730, with fluted balusters. Matching ALTAR TABLE. – STALLS by *Jackson*, his PEWS altered in 1931. – S DOOR. Probably C14, re-set with its simple doorway in 1885. – PAINTING. The Raising of the Widow's Son, early C17 Flemish, said to be by Rubens's master, *Otto Venius* (or *van Veen*). – ROYAL ARMS. George II. – STAINED GLASS. Minor C15 fragments in the W window. – N transept N, good early work by *Frederick Preedy*, 1854. – Two by *James Powell & Sons*: chancel E 1902, SE 1923. – MONUMENTS. Richard Hoby †1617 and his wife Margaret †1625; quite large, in poor condition. They face each other across a prayer-desk, on which are two bibles (and formerly a skull); above, an hourglass in relief. Kneeling children (originally three), facing W, not E, as they are issue of her former husband. Flat canopy, with obelisks and heraldry, on fluted columns. Possibly by *Samuel Baldwin*. – William Jarrett. Good cartouche of 1685, attributed to *William Stanton* (GF); white marble, rich surround. – Two stone tablets in the N transept: Edward Seward †1772, with urn; Rev. John Rawlins †1784, by *W. Laughton* of Pershore, with obelisk. – War memorial tablet by *W.E. Ellery Anderson*, 1920.

Simple CHURCHYARD CROSS by *T.G. Jackson*, 1910. – To High Street, a Gothic stone WALL and GATEPIERS of 1872.

Several good houses survive in HIGH STREET. First, NW of the church, Nos. 23–25, originally one house of c. 1800. Brick, four bays, the outer ones with shallow two-storey bows; flat door-hood on consoles. Opposite, No. 26, early C18, altered in the early C19. Then SEWARD HOUSE (No. 24), C17, stone, 1+3+2 bays: recessed centre and gabled wings. The windows of the S wing are C17, with concave-moulded mullions, of the N wing mid-C18, with stone architraves and keystones. Centre altered in the early C19.

Further N, No. 18, C17, with central gable and other alterations of 1857, faces No. 11, late C18 brick, with the rusticated lintels typical of the district. Other Georgian houses then form a group with the striking late C16 MANOR HOUSE, on the site of the Seyne House, an early C14 rest house of Evesham Abbey, granted in 1545 to Sir Philip Hoby of Bisham (Berkshire). Lias rubble below, perhaps incorporating earlier masonry; above, elaborate timber framing with lively lozenge or diamond patterns, plus S-scrolls. Three renewed oriels; hipped roof above pronounced coving. U-plan, with longer S wing; the infilled archway suggests a former courtyard house. N wing with large chimney-breast with three diagonal brick stacks. Restored c. 1946.

In HIGH STREET, S of the church, one house stands out: BADSEY HALL, No. 42 (formerly Stone House), of beautiful late C17 ashlar. 1+5+1 bays, the slightly recessed centre flanked by gables with ball finials. Windows (apart from some small round-headed ones) of cross type, already of classical proportions; mostly continuous string courses. The rear, with the entrance, is undistinguished, apart from the huge chimney of the s cross-wing. Staircase with splat balusters at the rear of the N wing.

From the s end of High Street, SCHOOL LANE leads E to the BOARD SCHOOL of 1894–5, by *E.H. Lingen Barker*; red brick, gabled, with sparse yellow bands; very large windows. Additions of 1958. MILL LANE, with some C17 timber-framed cottages, leads s W to the former SILK MILL, dated 1864. Brick, two storeys and ten bays, the central four under a pedimental gable; segment-headed windows.

ALDINGTON. *See* p. 104.

BARNT GREEN 0070

A well-to-do suburb on the Birmingham–Gloucester railway, situated on the wooded s slopes of the Lickey Hills. The station opened in 1846 (with a branch to Redditch from 1859), but development began in earnest in 1889 when Lord Windsor (of Hewell Grange, *see* p. 625) auctioned off housing lots: small ones near the station, larger further w where some substantial houses had already been built. The larger plots carried precise covenants, e.g. each residence was allowed only one lodge. The late C19 houses are mostly in routine sub-Norman Shaw style, brick with half-timbering or tile-hanging. Early C20 examples, Arts and Crafts-influenced, are usually more appealing: long and low, stone or brick, often roughcast. The chief later contribution has been to cram in additional houses, thus eroding the suburb's sylvan character.

Barnt Green, St Andrew.
Original design, drawing

p. 121 St ANDREW, Sandhills Road. 1909–13 by *Arthur S. Dixon*. Brick,
Early Christian basilica-style, simply but subtly detailed; the
structural piers rise artfully above the shallow pantiled roofs.
Broad nave and chancel in one, with lower E apse, low nave
aisles, and large N vestry; the W end, with NW tower, was unfortunately never built. The present W façade, with apsed porch,
is by *Liz Jeavons-Fellows*, 2001. Rendered interior with plain
three-bay arcades and open roofs, highlighted by stencilling
at the E end. Similar stencilling on the sturdy open timber
SCREEN, Italian in style, now one bay E of its original position.
Other fine furnishings are the square marble FONT, and the
patterned clerestory STAINED GLASS by *R.J. Stubington*, especially telling in the more closely windowed chancel. – WAR
MEMORIAL by the *Bromsgrove Guild*, *c.* 1920, now set in a wall
NW of the church. – PARISH CENTRE, at the rear, by *S.T.
Walker & Partners*, 1980, also brick, pantile-roofed.

FRIENDS' MEETING HOUSE, Sandhills Road. By *Marsh &
Jolley* of Birmingham, 1969. Square, brick, with central glazing;
low pyramidal roof, rising again at the corners to form
clerestory windows. Calm interior.

DESCRIPTION

1. The eastern part, around the railway

HEWELL ROAD, E of the railway, is the main street, with shops,
school (of 1926), and pleasant cottage terraces of *c.* 1900.
Further E, in Sandhills Road, Sandhills Lane, Bittell Road and
Bittell Lane, detached or semi-detached houses in simple Arts
and Crafts-style, mostly roughcast brick. The nicest group, in
SANDHILLS ROAD W of the church, is Nos. 14–22, two long
and low pairs flanking a taller brick singleton. The best individual house must be WICKHAM HOUSE (No. 9 Bittell Lane),
probably by *W.A. Harvey c.* 1910; brick, with steep gable.
LONGMEAD, at the beginning of Sandhills Green, is an earlier
ashlar-faced survivor, formerly Sandhills Farmhouse. Dated
1678, still with mullioned windows but now symmetrically
arranged: 3+2+3 lights above, 3+doorway+3 below. C18 porch
with thin engaged Doric columns. Timber-framed end gables
and internal walls.

Two roads connect this E part with the area of ampler houses
further W. CHERRY HILL ROAD is the more northerly. At its E
end, the timber-framed BARNT GREEN HOUSE (now an inn),
p. 45 probably of *c.* 1620–30. This refers to the symmetrical r. part
only: two gables above close studding and moulded bressumers.
The more elaborate l. wing, the tall brick chimneys, and much
else are of *c.* 1880, by *John Cotton* for J.J. Tomson, Lord
Windsor's agent. Remains of an C18 walled garden at the rear.

Large houses begin halfway along Cherry Hill Road, N side.
First, standard brick and half-timbered ones, then the excel-
lent PINFIELD HOUSE by *C.E. Bateman*, 1905–6, for Walter
Goodrick-Clarke. Tall, of brick with warm stone dressings; two

gables with diamond-infill decoration, attached battlemented porch, very tall chimneys.

FIERY HILL ROAD lies further S, its E section, alongside the railway, with modest early C20 housing and much late C20 infill; Nos. 2–20 OAKDENE DRIVE, of 1987 by *Paul Burley* (of *S.T. Walker & Partners*) have startlingly steep roofs. Larger houses begin as the gradient increases (formerly known as Station Road), the best on the S side. No. 30 (WESTFIELD) by *C.E. Bateman*, 1900, is refreshingly simple, gabled and pebbledashed. No. 16 is similar; No. 14, by *Crouch & Butler*, 1899, has rather glib and heavy half-timbering. No. 10, the RED HOUSE, set back in ample grounds, is the most notable: a brick farmhouse of *c.* 1800, remodelled in 1901 by *Bateman* for the shopfitter A.E. Harris. Externally the only sign of this is the recessed Tudor N entrance. Within, however, it is a typical low-ceilinged Arts and Crafts-house, apart from the slightly odd proportions of the rooms. Central living hall, with the staircase rising to one side, and a large framed cartoon by *Henry Payne* of St Augustine converting King Ethelbert. No. 6, 1964 by the Danish architect *A. Monrad-Hansen*, is the best later C20 house in Barnt Green: pale brick, long and low, with higher angle-roofed section, achieving two full storeys on the garden side, next to a sun terrace approached up impressive steps; entrance hall with spiral staircase. Opposite, N side, typical brick houses with half-timbered or tile-hung gables. No. 5 (1898–9), well set back, and No. 3 (1896), are both by *Charles A. Edge*, who did much routine work in Barnt Green and Blackwell.

2. Further north-west

TWATLING ROAD leads NNW, from the W ends of Fiery Hill and Cherry Hill Roads, towards Lickey. At the start, W side, BEACONWOOD (No. 3), large, brick and half-timbered, mid-1880s. Further N, most larger houses were demolished in the late C20, their names commandeered for cul-de-sacs crammed onto their sites. Four survivors deserve mention (all W side). BRIAR WOOD (No. 15) by *J.L. Ball* for J.A. Christie, 1891, is of smooth hard brick, the centre recessed with twin gables, the wings with broader gables to embrace the recessed entrance, l., and staircase, r. Next door, THE CLOCK HOUSE, formerly Twatling Green Farm, a C17 L-plan group of timber-framed buildings, the N the former lobby-entry farmhouse. Remodelled, with central brick link, by *Bateman*, 1912–13; additional work 1920. Further on, No. 27 (MOSS HOUSE) is by *Edwin F. Reynolds*, 1907–8, for W.B. Challen, also severe brick, relieved by diapering; gabled, with two-storey canted bay and prominent chimneys, including a quadrupled group particularly striking from the rear. Lastly MERRIEMONT, 1930–1 by the cinema architect *Harry W. Weedon*: Hollywood Arts and Crafts, flagrantly picturesque. Brick and stone, with timbered gables, fancily leaded flat dormers, and canted rear bay windows. Simpler rendered lodge.

PLYMOUTH ROAD, leading NW from the S end of Twatling Road, begins with more typical houses. The best are by *T. W. F. Newton*: No. 3, 1890, with nicely arranged porch beneath its half-timbered gable; and opposite, Nos. 6 (THE OAKS) and 8 (TANGLEWOOD), a neat mirror image of 1893: No. 6 with tile-hung gable and timbered main range, No. 8 all in reverse. PETERSCOURT, in Plymouth Drive, is a rare example of a house of *c.* 1890 retained as a focus for late C20 development. Further W little of note survives, apart from the typical No. 23, dated 1893, and the atypical No. 25 (THE WHEEL HOUSE), large Deco *moderne* by *Philip Haworth* (of Nelson, Lancs), 1933; rendered, the roof flat apart from a shallow octagonal 'belvedere' with port-hole windows (lighting the staircase).

MEARSE LANE runs across the W end of Plymouth Road, its S section well preserved. MULBERRY HOUSE (originally the Grey House), by *Bateman*, 1900, lies at the end of a very long drive. Mellow brick with ample stone dressings, imposing from the drive partly because of the strong horizontal lines of the service wing, r., with white painted windows. The main part is gabled, with a low stone bay (to the corner living hall) adjoining the front door.

Further S is DESWOOD, built for himself in 1914 by *Harold S. Scott*, also better known as a cinema architect; modest and homely Arts and Crafts: L-plan, brick, gabled. Opposite, THE MEARSE, a greatly expanded C17 cottage. HILLCROFT (No. 15, W side), with slate-hung gables, is an enlarged former lodge, no doubt by *Bateman*. Then, DALE CROSS GRANGE, one of the best and least altered of the Arts and Crafts houses, by *Crouch & Butler*, 1899–1900, for Frank Rabone. The entrance side (with stable range at right angles) has narrow studding relieved by an apposite brick chimney. The garden front, S, is mostly roughcast. Quirky details include the W end gable, of brick, squeezed by two stout chimneys. Inside, a fine living hall, also narrow-studded, its N landing with balustraded oriel; the chimneypiece beneath reuses a C17–C18 Flemish overmantel, with biblical scenes. Another recycled overmantel in the panelled dining room; C18-style plasterwork in the drawing room, E. BREMESGROVE CHASE, opposite, brick and gabled, said to be by *Bateman*, is rather flat, though with nice details; its slate-hung gabled lodge, towards Brookhouse Road, is certainly *Bateman*'s, of 1891.

Other lodges in BROOKHOUSE ROAD, heading back E, heralded substantial houses in spacious grounds. A good survivor is LONG REDE (formerly Bloemfontein) by *Ewen Harper* for himself, 1892; low, spreading, brick, with Queen-Anneish details. Its lodge has a mansard roof.

3. To the south-west

The SW part of Barnt Green, towards the Shepley Hills, also preserves the sylvan atmosphere of the 1880s–90s. LINTHURST ROAD, leading from the W end of Fiery Hill Road S towards

Blackwell (q.v.), retains several large late C19 houses, still within ample grounds. First on the W is SHEPLEY MANOR, built for the brewer Henry Mitchell by *Cossins & Peacock*, 1890, but enlarged in identical style by *Mansell & Mansell*, 1895; brick with half-timbered gables, loosely grouped. The entrance side is entirely of 1895, as is the big lodge (No. 45). Further on, off the E side, LINTHURST COURT, an early example, built as Linthurst Hill for Arthur Ryland, 1867–8; already tile-hung with timbered gables, gawkier but prettier than many of the later 'Old English' houses. Tile-hung lodge. At the end, W side, just before the M42, OSMOTHERLY is of the 1890s by *Martin & Martin*; gabled brick with stone dressings, more restrained, but hardly yet Arts and Crafts.

In PIKE HILL, descending N, and its continuation PUMPHOUSE LANE, a couple of earlier farmhouses survive. In SHEPLEY ROAD, leading back E, the first house, No. 2 (OVERDALE), is probably one of those built for Thomas Worthington in 1886 by *John G. Elgood* of Manchester; its half-timbering has Lancastrian reminiscences, e.g. the coving beneath the gables. No. 4, *c.* 1890, is more routine. No. 6, SHEPLEY GRANGE, by *Essex & Nicol*, 1890–1, for Thomas Walker, is larger, tall and upright, with rather forced picturesque trappings. No. 8 (UPWOOD) dated 'TW 1886', also quite large, must have been Worthington's own house, no doubt again by *Elgood*. Finally, at the junction with Brookhouse Road, STRETTON CROFT, a big, dull, gabled brick house of *c.* 1890.

BAYTON

6070

ST BARTHOLOMEW. Norman, partly rebuilt 1817, thoroughly remodelled in Dec style by *John Oldrid Scott & Son*, 1904–5. The sole remaining Norman detail is the S doorway, with one order of shafts with worn trumpet capitals, plain tympanum, and arch with chevron broken as lozenges round the angle (cf. Chaddesley Corbett).[*] Of the 1817 rebuilding only W tower and nave W wall survive. The former has battlements above a moulded cornice, and openings with key blocks and imposts: two W windows with Y-tracery, one above the other, and round-arched bell-openings. The latter has, high up, two small arched windows formerly lighting a gallery. In 1905 the chancel was all but rebuilt, the nave refenestrated, and a timber S porch added. The frames of the nave NE and SE windows are probably C15. Also mostly of this date the fine nave roof, with cambered tie-beams, braced collars and two tiers of wind-braces. – Full-height timber chancel SCREEN, of 1905 like most other furnishings. Some incorporate earlier woodwork, e.g. CHANCEL STALLS (early C17 linenfold with fish-scale detail) and PULPIT (Jacobean panels). – REREDOS. 1912, carved by

---

[*] Noake noted a figured tympanum which might have cast some light on the relationship between Bayton, Rock, and Chaddesley Corbett.

Florence Mole. – FONT. Drum-shaped, Norman. Bowl with long beaded scrolls, double rope moulding below; short stem with long ribbed leaves (cf. Rock and Linley, Shropshire). – STAINED GLASS. Good E window of 1919, perhaps by *F.G. Christmas*. – MONUMENT. War memorial tablet of 1921 by *Powell & Sons*, with *opus sectile* St George. – HATCHMENT to Edmund Meysey-Wigley, 1821. From the churchyard sweeping views extend W to Shakenhurst Hall (*see* below) and across the Rea valley to Shropshire and the Clee Hills.

BROADMEADOWS FARM, S, is mid-C18. Three-bay S front with central pedimented gable; attached timber-framed stable. CHURCH HOUSE, ESE, is convincing late C20 pastiche, reusing timbers from a Herefordshire barn. OLD SCHOOL COTTAGE to the NE, perhaps of *c.* 1500, has two bays with a full cruck truss visible in its N gable-end; well restored in 1985, but conversion to two cottages has ruined the former SCHOOL of 1810 to its N.

A little further NE, a most attractive group of C17 timber-framed houses at the so-called SQUARE. More good C17 framing, plus C18–C19 brick, around the central road junction to its E.

GLEBE HOUSE, the former vicarage ¼ m. NNW, is of 1822–3 by the Worcester surveyor *William Wood*. Brick, the S front of three bays, plus a later E bay; pedimented Doric porch. Original single-storey bow on the W return.

Of outlying farms, NORGROVESEND FARM, ⅔ m. NNE, is worth mentioning, partly in its own right (early C17 hall and cross-wing plan, with brick-filled timber framing above a sandstone ground floor), but more for the way that Mawley Hall (by *Francis Smith*, *c.* 1728–33) looms up behind, from its bluff further NNW (*see The Buildings of England: Shropshire*).

SHAKENHURST HALL, 1¼ m. WSW, in a beautifully remote landscaped park, has belonged to the Meysey-Wigley family since the mid C14. The present red brick house is mid-C18, much remodelled by *Samuel Knight* of Kidderminster, 1798–9. He heightened the main (E) front to two-and-a-half storeys, with modillion cornice and parapet; three-bay centre with Ionic porch with open pediment, flanked by broad full-height canted bay windows. All windows have prominent keystones. The S bay existed before the remodelling and the room behind it (originally dining room) has good Adamish plasterwork and chimneypiece. The decoration of the large central hall and drawing room, N, is slightly later and more restrained, with reeded doorcases. Behind the drawing room, a mid-C18 dog-leg staircase, of oak. Additional rear accommodation was provided *c.* 1812 by *William Hams* (though his intended colonnade between the front bays was not executed). On the S return, two late C19 single-storey bay windows.

Behind the house, L-plan brick STABLES, probably originally C17, remodelled in the C18, and a brick-walled KITCHEN GARDEN, dated 1804.

LODGE. A substantial early C17 timber-framed house, hall and cross-wing plan, with porch and brick stack at the junction.

At CLOWS TOP, a former coal-mining hamlet 1½ m. SE, a MISSION CHURCH of 1895, with walls and roof of corrugated iron. The interior, lined with deal boarding, retains original furnishings.

BECKFORD

9030

Transferred from Gloucestershire in 1931.

ST JOHN THE BAPTIST. On the site of a Saxon minster. Broad nave with S porch, central tower, and chancel with N vestry. The nave contains excellent Norman work of c. 1160–75, notably the large S doorway, originally in a wall projection (and now sheltered by the much-altered C15 porch). Its decoration is more typical of Gloucestershire than Worcestershire. Two orders of columns plus an outer vertical band of furrowed zigzag; decorated scallop capitals of the folded variety (cf. Eldersfield). The tympanum is supported on two corbels each with two heads, an Italian motif (cf. Ely Cathedral). In the tympanum a cross with, above the arms, a roundel and bird; below, two strange quadrupeds. It may symbolize animal creation adoring the Holy Trinity. Roll moulding above, on further heads; lintel with intersecting circles. The main arch has two rows of frontal chevron. The Norman N doorway, much worn and not in its original state, has two beast-head corbels of Malmesbury type. The tympanum represents the Harrowing of Hell: Christ thrusts his cross into the mouth of the dragon and, with his other hand, holds Adam (?) on a leash (cf. Quenington, Gloucestershire, and Shobdon, Herefordshire). Rope-moulded arch; lintel with honeysuckle frieze. One Norman window survives towards the W end of both N and S walls. The W wall shows blocked traces of Norman fenestration, replaced by a large Perp window. Other windows are late C13 (NE), early C14 (SW) and C15 (SE). Near the last, inside, a jamb shaft with scalloped capital, presumably of another, larger Norman window. C15 pointed wagon roof, with moulded tie-beams. The central tower may have been begun at the same time. Its W arch resembles the doorways, with decorated scallop capitals, including heads, rope-and-pellet abaci, and arch with chevron, furrowed on the soffit. The central shaft, l., has a centaur placed across (again an Italian motif; cf. W doorway, S. Ambrogio, Milan), with beakheads above and below. The base of the inner shaft has a spur bearing a human head. To the N, a C15 blocked recess and the doorway to the rood loft. Other tower arches late C13, with continuous chamfers, tripled to the E, single N and S (though transepts may never have been built); springers for a rib-vault. The tower's second stage is late C13, with two widely spaced lancets each side. It carried a spire, taken down in 1622 and replaced (perhaps in the C18) by the present ashlar-faced upper stages, supported by large stepped buttresses: bell-openings with intersecting tracery, gargoyles, battlements and finials. The chancel is again late C13, with single or paired lancets and an even E triplet with plate-tracery quatrefoils above; C14–C15 SW window, originally lowside. C17–C18 queenpost roof. The N vestry began as an early C15 chantry, remodelled 1686–7, and later further enlarged.

FONT. Octagonal, Perp; bowl with fleurons in quatrefoils. The pretty cover and several other furnishings (including the PULPIT) are by *Ford Whitcombe & Cogswell*, who restored the church in 1911–12. – Mid-C19 PEWS, probably incorporating medieval work; buttressed bench ends with traceried panels, moulded top rails. – CHANCEL SCREEN. 1915, probably also by *Cogswell*. – WALL PAINTINGS. Fragments of C15 black letter text S of the W tower arch; also an inscription above the S doorway. – STAINED GLASS. E window by *Burlison & Grylls*, c. 1901. – By *Hardman* the nave NE and SE, 1898–9; also that by the S door, designed by *Donald B. Taunton*, 1935. – The Norman windows have glass of c. 1840–50, including a possibly Flemish panel. – MONUMENTS. Richard Wakeman †1662; attributed to *Thomas Burman* (GF). Grey and black marble, with strange and elegant vertically halved balusters l. and r.; open segmental pediment with heraldry. – William Wakeman †1836, by *Cooke* of Gloucester; mildly Grecian. – Large CHURCHYARD with a few C17–C18 headstones and chest tombs. – War memorial LYCHGATE. 1920.

The church lies back behind an asphalted remnant of the village green. DALTON HOUSE, by the lychgate, is modest early C18 brick. Opposite, the former SCHOOL of 1863 (enlarged 1898) and gabled ESTATE COTTAGES dated 1864; these, brick with blue trim, belong to extensive village rebuilding carried out for Robert Timbrill by *W.H. Baker* of Birmingham.

BECKFORD HALL, to the NE, stands on the site of an Augustinian priory, founded as a cell of Ste Barbe-en-Auge (Calvados) c. 1128, dissolved by c. 1400. Rebuilt for the Roman Catholic Wakeman family, probably in the early-to-mid C17, and much enlarged in the C19, it became a Salesian theological college from 1936 to 1975. Now subdivided, with housing in the grounds.

The C17 stone house can only be appreciated from the W: a long flat front of seven bays, with continuous dripmoulds and large, renewed, mullioned-and-transomed windows; above, seven even gables, each with a two-light window. Between the gables, elaborate later C17 rainwater heads bearing arms; central porch 1884. The S front, with a battlemented central tower with oriel and Tudor entrance below, flanked by two differing gables, was rebuilt for Hattil Foll by *Prichard & Seddon*, 1858. Its recessed E part stands above a restored stone-vaulted undercroft, perhaps the oratory built by the canons between 1135 and 1153: four bays, with massive buttresses and two C12 round piers, one with cushion capital, the other square with chamfered abacus. In 1884 *John Middleton* of Cheltenham added large rear wings for Capt. H.A. Case, a Roman Catholic convert. The NW (originally containing a billiard room) matches and continues, though is slightly taller than, the main W range. The NE had a ground-floor chapel decorated by *Ion Pace*; Perp-style windows; large figure of a bishop in a canopied niche on the blank N wall.

Also at the rear, L-plan STABLES, part C17, part C19, converted to housing. – Facing the village street, good mid-C18 ashlar GATEPIERS carrying tall fluted urns.

In the village street is more multicoloured brick housing of the 1860s by *W.H. Baker*. Near its E end, next the stone and timber-framed OLD HOUSE, an urban pair of semi-detached villas: tall, gabled, quite spiky, with timber porches. Then, beyond the late C18 ROSE VILLA, a three-cottage terrace dated 1866. Opposite, N, the OLD RECTORY, with tall brick front of *c.* 1800 (earlier at the rear, facing the churchyard); altered by *Baker*, 1866. Set further back, facing the church from the W, the COURT HOUSE, C17 stone, with mullioned windows and two gables; timber-framed service cross-wing, N. Beyond is THE GRANGE (formerly The Towers), large brick, Italianate, built for Robert Timbrill in 1865. Two towers; the NE standard Italianate, the other taller and blunter, with iron balustrade. Large matching SW archway. At the W end of the street, a columnar milepost of 1887, its battlemented top with orb and crown; restored 1953.

In COURT FARM LANE, to the N, a pair of sub-Norman-Shavian cottages, half-timbered above roughcast, with brick chimneys; built for Capt. Case in 1897.

BACK LANE leads S, across the Carrant Brook, to the MANOR HOUSE, stone, early C17, with mullioned windows with hood-moulds, and four gabled dormers; large early C20 additions. Opposite, CRUMPS FARM COTTAGES, a pleasant mix of new build and converted farm buildings by *T.R. Bateman*, 1985. Then BECKFORD HOUSE, of the early 1860s; brick, very Gothic, with ornate patterned-tiled roof with tall clustered chimneys. Elaborate brick patterning also on the chimney-breast next to the recessed S doorway.

Of the RAILWAY STATION, $^3/_8$ m. SE, on the Barnt Green–Ashchurch loop line, opened 1865, there survive the station-master's house and a plain engine shed, both probably by *George Hunt*.

IRON AGE SETTLEMENT. A complex series of rectangular ditched enclosures, discovered by aerial photography in the fields E of the village and N of the Carrant Brook, partially excavated, in advance of gravel quarrying, in the 1970s. Each enclosure probably represented a family nucleus, with round houses, clusters of pits, and smaller internal compounds.

GRAFTON, a hamlet below Bredon Hill 1 m. NE, has a pretty group at its W end by the former LOWER FARM, of mixed stone and timber framing, with thatched roof. Cottage of *c.* 1600 to its S, to a miniature hall and cross-wing plan, with renewed decorative patterning in its E gable-end. C17 timber-framed cottages further W. More attractive farms and cottages

in the lane further E, running uphill from the late C18 MIDDLE
FARM. To its N, a large thatched house, part stone, part timber-
framed, faces MANOR FARM, early C19 with cast-iron porch;
C17 at the rear, with contemporary farm buildings. Then the
thatched NORMAN COTTAGE, incorporating the N, W and E
walls of the nave of a C12 chapel.* Blocked N window; blocked
chancel arch, E, with, inside, shafts with cushion capitals and
rope-moulded abaci, plus a roll-moulded arch.

BELBROUGHTON

A centre of scythe-making until the mid C20, the most prominent reminder of this the chain of mill pools to the N, along the
Belne (or Barnett) Brook.

HOLY TRINITY. Dec-Perp, the Norman origin revealed only by
the renewed S aisle SW window and reconstructed S doorway,
with original fragments in its arch. Tall late C14 W tower, with
battlements and recessed spire with lucarnes. C14 chancel, with
good Dec S windows, restored by *J.M. Derick*, 1847–8 (e.g. the
E window). The round-arched priest's doorway, with continuous roll moulding, seems Late Perp rather than Norman (cf.
the sedilia, below). In 1894–8 *Bodley & Garner* added a new
Dec-style nave and chancel N of the existing ones. Their whole
N wall is irregular, partly because of an unexecuted NE vestry,
partly because they reused existing windows; doorway also
Dec, with depressed ogee arch. They also added a porch to the
much restored S aisle. Inside, the three-bay S arcade is Late
Perp, partly renewed *c.* 1895; concave-sided octagonal piers, cf.
St Mary, Kidderminster. Matching chancel arch. The N arcade,
with more slender piers and continuous double chamfers, is
also partly medieval. Bodley & Garner found it built into the
nave N wall and, rather bizarrely, set their proposed N arcade,
with quatrefoil piers, against the N wall of their new nave.
Another oddity is that the whole rood stair is exposed, S of the
chancel arch. C19 roofs, apart from reused nave tie-beams (one
dated 1654) and the fine chancel roof of 1660: tie- and collar-
beams linked by three straight braces. The chancel has a broad
Dec ogee-headed N recess, perhaps an Easter Sepulchre, and
round-arched triple sedilia, no doubt Late Perp. Good C13 S
aisle piscina, with fillet and trefoiled head.

FONT. Octagonal, standard Perp, with quatrefoils enclosing
flowers. – PULPIT. Jacobean; the usual arched panels, plus a
fine dragon frieze. – LECTERN. Also Jacobean, with fluted Ionic
pilasters and frieze with mermen and an angel. – COMMUNION
RAILS. C17; now in the old chancel flanking the reredos. –
WALL PAINTING. A female saint, perhaps the Virgin, within a
thick red frame, also foliage; S aisle E, N side. – Remnants

---

*Nave S wall and rectangular chancel were excavated in 1926.

around the chancel arch. – ROYAL ARMS. George III, dated 1765. – HATCHMENT to Charles Noel, 1877. – STAINED GLASS. In the old chancel, E window by *Joseph Bell* of Bristol, 1853, and three S by *Kempe*, 1902. – Also by *Kempe*, 1896, four in the S aisle. – N chancel N of 1912, no doubt *Burlison & Grylls*. – One N nave N window has good C15 fragments, including roundels, restored by *A.L. Pike* who added the Arts and Crafts window to its E in 1921; to its W, one by *F.W. Skeat*, 1965. – MONUMENTS. Large tablet, with Doric columns, to the Rev. G.F. Blakeston †1837, by *W. Herbert* of Pimlico.

CHURCHYARD CROSS. Steps and base probably C15; shaft and head by *Bodley*, 1901. – Simple LYCHGATE by the *Bromsgrove Guild*, 1912.

To the S, behind a mid-C18 wall with corner pavilions, is CHURCH HOUSE, late C18 Gothic: three storeys, 1+3+1 bays, roughcast. The first-floor windows have four-centred arches with Y-tracery, set half a storey higher in the projecting centre. Ogee gables containing quatrefoils or trefoils. Opposite, the (BOYS') SCHOOL by *J.A. Chatwin*, 1873–4; vigorous patterned brick, with central stepped gable with chimney. Bold cloakroom apse l. of the porch.

The three-bay OLD RECTORY E of the church, of *c.* 1762, received one-bay wings, half a storey lower, later in the C18. The CHURCH HALL, further N, is the former rectory barn, C17, with large tension braces; converted by *William Weir*, 1912–15, with central timber bay window.

CHURCH HILL, running along N of the church at a lower level, begins with No. 19, neat late C18; Doric porch and tripartite window details of *c.* 1960. The nice brick group at the bend includes the mid-C18 OLD SCHOOLHOUSE, its upper floor added *c.* 1850 (but the Gothick detail again late C20 re-creation); and former C18 almshouses converted to parish workhouse in 1823–4. At the foot of the hill, NW, a good group of mostly C18 houses around the Belne Brook.

HIGH STREET further E has a raised pavement on its NW side, but no buildings to single out. The largest of the scythe mills, NASH'S WORKS, lay further NW, at the end of Forge Lane; only a few late C19 brick buildings remain. Mill pool filled in.

BRADFORD HOUSE, ⅜ m. SSE. Coursed sandstone, H-plan, probably mostly late C17. The S side was perhaps the original front (*see* the remains of the surrounding C17 wall); gables with moulded strings beneath oval openings, tall brick chimneys. NW wing added *c.* 1770, its ground-floor room with good plasterwork and panelling. The Venetian N doorway with steep open pediment may be contemporary. – To the SE, a fine brick STABLE BLOCK of six bays, dated 1772 on an internal beam. The upper floor of the pedimented centre is blind as there is a dovecote behind, with pretty roof cupola.

THE LYDIATE, opposite, is a three-storey five-bay brick house of *c.* 1760, with steep three-bay pediment on consoles, enclosing a keyed oculus; hipped roof. Doorway, with shallow open pediment, probably later C18.

BROOKFIELD, ½ m. WNW. Mid-C18 brick, three bays and storeys, with projecting centre and quoins. Late C19 additions include the SW wing, NE Doric porch, curved dormers, and small rear tower with recessed top stage with ogee roof.

YEW TREE HOUSE, ⅜ m. NNE. Large early C19 stuccoed villa, in its own grounds; three by five bays, roof with bracketed eaves. Altered *c.* 1920 by *W. H. Godwin*, who added the entrance with segmental pediment, pilasters and swags.

BELL HALL, 1 m. E. Rebuilt 1847 for Charles Noel by *Edward Smith* of Oldswinford, probably on the site of the manor house of Belne. Basic Tudor Gothic, brick, with sharp gables including the full-height porch; plainer E service range. Matching LODGES.

By the drive, the rectangular late C12 CHAPEL of Belne, of coursed sandstone blocks. Side windows still Norman, but the E and W now plain three-light mullioned, C16–C17. The doorways are also Norman, the S with weathered arch mouldings and renewed inner order, the N blocked but retaining its hoodmould.

BELL END FARM, further E by the main Stourbridge Road, is probably late C17. Brick, with three shaped gables; matching C19 porch. SE wing, with stone quoins and straight gable, probably early C18.

CASTLE BOURNE, 1½ m. E. Tall, mid-C19; square, rendered and battlemented. Thin octagonal corner turrets as chimneys; S wing with porch. Attached on this side, by a connecting wall with three arches, a late C18 folly castle of two linked round towers; pointed windows below, quatrefoils above. Below the embattled top, blank Maltese-cross loops (cf. Clent Grove, p. 232).

BENGEWORTH *see* EVESHAM

9060

BENTLEY PAUNCEFOOT

Well-wooded landscape, with C19 Hewell Estate farms and cottages.

ST MARY, Lower Bentley. A chapelry of Tardebigge. Simple red brick with minimal black bands, by the estate bailiff *W. Buckley*, 1874–5, for Robert, Lord Windsor. Nave and chancel, with skeletal timber bell-turret, W; Geometrical E window, otherwise lancets. – Good STAINED GLASS by *Alfred L. Pike*, *c.* 1915–20, in the E window and the lancets flanking the chancel arch.

KEYS FARMHOUSE, ¼ m. SSE. Early C17, mostly close-timbered, to a T-plan. The long stem is the hall range, with fireplace bay (with lobby entrance and triple brick stack), hall, and kitchen bay, all of two floors with attic. Solar cross-wing, W, with parlour fireplace dated 1604. Restored 2004. C19 brick farm buildings to the N, converted to housing.

FOSTER'S GREEN FARMHOUSE, ⅝ m. SW, is a good example
of a C17 single-range plan, close-studded with herringbone
brick infill.

The rectangular wet MOAT, ½ m. NE by The Thrift wood, may
be the site of the medieval manor house of the Pauncefoot
family.

At the more nucleated UPPER BENTLEY, several C17 timber-
framed cottages and farms. BENTLEY HOUSE FARM, further
N at Bank's Green, is late C18 brick, three bays with wide
segment-headed windows; long NE wing, lower and earlier,
with square stone piers now built into the ground-floor brickwork. The late C17 ball-finialled GATEPIERS are on this, N, side.

TARDEBIGGE FARM, 1 m. NNW. Hall-type timber-framed house
of *c*. 1600. The central, two-storey, hall part comprises the
'house place', with the fireplace bay at its upper end (with three
brick star-stacks). At this E end, a two-bay gabled cross-wing
is also served by the fireplace structure. The main staircase is
beneath a gabled extension S of the fireplace bay. The lower
(service) end, W, has an ashlar chimney-breast (with diagonal
shafts) of slightly later date. Its W gable, giving the appearance
of a second cross-wing, and separate two-storey gabled
entrance porch, S (now blocked), were added *c*. 1650. A staircase in the porch leads directly to the attic, which seems to
have been used as a separate dwelling, perhaps for the parents
after the next generation had taken over the farm.

BEOLEY

0060

ST LEONARD. On the slope of Beoley Hill, looking SW across the
Arrow valley towards Redditch. Mostly Perp exterior, with
good W tower and N aisle. The former has heavily crocketed
hoodmoulds with grotesque- or headstops to its W doorway
and other openings. The aisle has a moulded four-centred N
doorway with carved spandrels; narrow, heavily detailed niche
above, now hard to see because of the glazed link to the N
vestry (or Tapestry Room), added by *Anthony B. Chatwin*,
1974–5. This is rubble-faced with tile-hung gables. The large,
square N chapel was built by Ralph Sheldon late in the C16:
plain mullioned N windows and a very characteristic round-
arched E window, of five lights. These have straight heads with
two tiers of simplified rectilinear panel tracery above, i.e. an
elementarized Perp conceit.

The interior is older, beginning with the chancel arch of
c. 1140: unmoulded, on the most elementary imposts. Then the
S arcade, early to mid-C13, with double-chamfered arches and
semicircular responds with fillets. Its crude E pier has a round
core with moulded capital and two detached W shafts with
shaft-rings; the octagonal W pier may be a later replacement.
More regular three-bay N arcade, *c*. 1300, with typical quatrefoil piers in two versions, the W with nailhead in its moulded
capital. Lofty Perp tower arch. Both chancel and N (Sheldon)

chapel are approached up five or six steps, reflecting the slope of the hillside and the vaults beneath them. S aisle dormer of 1686, restored 1884–5 by *E.A. Day*; his also the two-light Neo-Norman window above the chancel arch, most roofs, and the timber S porch. *Eginton*'s restoration of 1844–5 was subtler; his the fine PEWS, low, with doors and big poppyheads, panelled stone PULPIT, and 'perspective' chancel FLOOR TILING. – FONT. Round, said to be C12 or C13, but the decoration at least could be C17: four big female heads on the underside, linked by the flowing tresses of their hair, rather like swags. Nice COVER, with gilded dove on the underside, by *Robert Pancheri*, 1948. – SCULPTURE. Small Norman relief of an abbot (perhaps St Leonard), both arms raised; formerly outside. – ALTAR HANGINGS and CARPET by *Rodney Hodge*, 1947–51. – The stone ALTAR of the Sheldon Chapel, late C16, on small Doric columns, is a rarity. – STAINED GLASS. C15 fragments in the N aisle NE and S aisle SE windows. Other S aisle windows by *Hardman*: E 1854, S 1866–8. – E window by *William Pearce Ltd*, 1893. – N chapel NW by *F.W. Skeat*, 1965.

MONUMENTS. An important collection, mostly in the Sheldon Chapel. On the E window sill, a fine C13 coffin lid with relief cross with encircled foliated head. – In the arcading beneath the N windows, tomb-chests with wall achievements to William Sheldon (†1517) and his brother Ralph (†1546), identical except in detail (one Ionic, the other Doric). Both were made in 1600–1, as the strapwork-enriched cartouches betray. – The two principal monuments stand beneath the arches towards the chancel: William Sheldon †1570 and his wife Mary; and Ralph Sheldon †1613 and his wife Anne (†1603).* Both are again the same in type, of stone, with recumbent praying effigies of each couple on elaborate tomb-chests, beneath coffered arched canopies flanked by Composite columns and with top achievements. But details are tellingly different. The earlier has more intricate carving (cherubs in spandrels, trophies behind the columns, obelisks above) but the later is decidedly more affluent, with greater use of colour. – Then a series of large C17 Sheldon wall tablets, all attributed to *Thomas Cartwright I* (GF), mostly with Corinthian pilasters and segmental pediments. In the chapel: Elizabeth †1656 (N wall), and antiquary Ralph †1684 and his wife Henrietta Maria †1663 (both W wall). Elsewhere, Edward †1643 (chancel S) and William †1659 (nave, E wall). – Also in the N chapel, four good C18 Sheldon tablets (dates of death 1720–66). – HATCHMENTS. Four, C18–C19, in the nave and aisles, probably to the Holmes-Hunter family.

CHURCHYARD CROSS. C14–C15 steps and base with blank quatrefoils; C17 stump of a sundial shaft. – The roughcast VICARAGE, SW, was much altered in 1824, see the three-bay S front.

*William started the first English tapestry workshops (at Barcheston, Warwicks., and Bordesley Abbey, p. 550, sending his son Ralph to Flanders to learn the art.

Well-sited WAR MEMORIAL CROSS of c. 1920. Further S, across
the B road, THE MOUNT, a more or less oval earthwork surrounded by a deep ditch, on a spur facing S. Probably Iron
Age, perhaps reused in the medieval period. The Sheldons'
house, Balford Hall, reputedly burnt down in 1643, stood
somewhere N of the church.

BEOLEY HALL, ⅓ m. N. Large, three-storeyed, stuccoed, with
projecting wings; probably early C18. Remodelled, and the E,
entrance, wing rebuilt in 1791, for Thomas Holmes, by *John
Sanders*, Soane's first pupil. This is architecturally far more
ambitious, two-storeyed though to the same height, and with
only three wide bays to the E. Quoins, and balustraded porch
on four Doric columns, beneath a central round-arched recess;
above this, the parapet rises to a dashingly handsome vase and
garland arrangement. Tripartite ground-floor windows either
side, their blank segmental arches with relief medallions of
Pompeian or Wedgwood type. The N return has a similar
window, flanked by niches with urns. The bow windows of the
projecting wings, S side, must also date from c. 1791; originally
they were single-storeyed. Converted to apartments after
almost all the internal decoration had disappeared. Stair of
stick baluster type behind the entrance hall, beneath a round
skylight. – Low stuccoed LODGE and ball-finialled GATEPIERS,
no doubt also by *Sanders*.

Two houses further N, by the Roman Ryknild Street, both built
for the Timmis family, form an interesting contrast. LILLEY
GREEN HALL, 1½ m. N, of c. 1837, is stuccoed and castellated,
with garlands below the cornice; wider centre of the five-bay
W front with battlemented porch with Ionic columns *in antis*.
STORRAGE HOUSE, 1⅛ m. NNW, probably only a few years
later, say c. 1845, is fully Tudor Gothic; gabled with central
porch, all red brick with blue diapering and fish-scale roofs.

At HOLT END, ½ m. E, a banded brick BOARD SCHOOL by *John
Cotton*, 1876, poorly altered, and C17 timber-framed farms and
cottages.

BERROW

ST FAITH. Of Norman origin. The N doorway has one order of
shafts with (renewed) scallop capitals and single-stepped arch.
Good timber N porch, C14–C15, its cambered tie-beams with
arched braces with blank tracery. In the nave N wall, one
renewed C13 lancet and a lowside window (though there has
been much disturbance here). The chancel, rebuilt in the C14,
has Dec side windows but a Late Perp E window. Strong
embattled Perp W tower with higher square stair-turret, NE; its
three-light W window with reticulated tracery is probably re-
set. Arch to the nave of two continuous chamfers. Narrow S
aisle with Tudor-arched windows. Late Perp three-bay S arcade
with octagonal piers with oddly ill-fitting capitals; the narrower

w bay must be yet later. No chancel arch. All much restored
in 1856–8 by *J. W. Hugall*, who provided most of the fittings. –
Norman FONT, tub-shaped, with beaded rope moulding at the
top, plain rope moulding below. – PULPIT. C17. The panels
have centres with simple flowers in roundels. – STAINED
GLASS. E window no doubt by *Wailes*, *c*. 1858. – Chancel N 1873
by *Powells*, designed by *Harry Burrow* (cf. Pendock); chancel S
by *J. A. Crombie*, 1978. – Nave NE, *c*. 1909. – W window by
Hardman, 1897. – MONUMENT. Under the tower, a headless
effigy, probably a C15 civilian with hands at prayer, the l. side
broken off.

CHURCHYARD. Nice group of C17–C19 tombs, NW of the
porch. Also base and shaft of a late medieval CROSS.

The parish, extending NW towards the S end of the Malvern Hills,
consists mostly of scattered farms. The BARN NE of the C18
HOLIDAY'S FARM, ⅝ m. W, now converted to a thatched and
weatherboarded house, has three splendid internal cruck
trusses, probably C14–C15. WHITING ASH FARM nearby
is an attractive late C16 hall and cross-wing house, mostly
close-studded.

BERROW HOUSE, facing the B road, 1¼ m. WNW, is early C19
brick, of three bays and storeys; windows with stepped false
voussoirs, stucco pedimented doorcase. – At the crossroads
further N, RYE COURT FARM is C18–C19 brick (one window
keystone dated 1775), with C17 cross-wing, S, of sturdy square-
panelled framing; herringbone bracing in its gable.

9040   BESFORD

St PETER. The church (or rather its nave) is the only surviving
timber-framed example in Worcestershire; comparison would
have to look to Shropshire (Melverley, Halston). The framing
is in very large squares (nearly 5 ft, 1.5 metres), yet the date
can hardly be later than mid- or late C14; see the ogee-headed
N doorway and W window with quatrefoil in a roundel between
two ogee-headed lights. There are also bold diagonal braces,
especially to support the W bell-turret. S porch also of timber,
probably C15. *Hopkins* rebuilt the bell-turret, with traceried
bell-openings and short pyramid spire, in 1879–81, and copied
the W window for the nave side windows. His also the stone
chancel with typical Geometrical Dec E window, and the N
vestry above a crypt lit by the former E window: a stepped
triplet under one arch. Inside, the nave's wall-posts carry
slightly cambered tie-beams on minimally curved braces;
queen-struts above. Panelled roof mostly of 1889–91. But there
is also the complete ROOD LOFT parapet with a string of quatrefoils enclosing rosettes, still with some original painting;
renewed top cresting. The handsome vine foliage trail below
was no doubt the top of the screen, but only a section nearest
the N end is original. All restored by *Hopkins*, who supplied

new wooden fittings (PEWS, PULPIT etc.). His work was toned down in 1919 by *Harold Brakspear*.*

Plain octagonal FONT (C14?); base by *Brakspear*. – COMMUNION RAIL. Jacobean, with heavy close-set balusters. – Nave PANELLING made up from the C17 pews. – OAK REREDOS (now W end) by *J.H. Williams*, 1896, carved by *Forsyth*. – STAINED GLASS. C14 quarries and Bokleton arms in the W window. – MONUMENTS. Richard Harewell †1576, aged fifteen. Recumbent alabaster effigy within a thin low wooden railing, on a stone tomb-chest; the (much damaged) railing has, very curiously, horizontal reticulation units. On the front of the tomb, a small arched panel with frontal child, flanked by shields; on its W end, a hare, the family emblem. Back wall of timber, with fluted Doric pilasters and panelling with faded heraldry. – Originally nearby, now at the nave W end, another Harewell, probably one of the sons of Edmund and his wife Susan [Colles], of the 1590s: a painted oak triptych with movable wings (cf. Burford, Shropshire, signed by *Melchior Salabossh*, 1588). Heraldry outside, the upper two shields held by large angels; on each 'predella' a set of twelve shields. When opened it reveals a large kneeling figure of a boy, with Resurrection scenes above (and at the top, now gone, Christ in Majesty). In the 'predella', his body in its shroud, flanked by putti, one holding a rose, one blowing bubbles. On the inner wings above were Father Time and a skeleton, now largely destroyed, with long inscription below. Its second part reads: [62]

> Of Harewell's blodde ere conquest made
> Knowne to descende of gentle race,
> And sithence linckt in jugall leage
> With Colles whose birthe and vertues grace,
> An Impe entombed heere dothe lie,
> In tender years berefte of breath;
> Whose hope of future virtuous lyfe
> Was plaine forshewde by lyfe and death.
> A childe he seemde of graver years,
> And childish toies did quyte dispise:
> He sought by yealdinge parents due
> And serving God to clime the skies;
> But prickte with percing plagues of death
> For mercie still to God he cryde.
> Soo lyvde he with the love of men,
> Soe deere in sight of God he dyed.
> Blushe elder sex from Christ to strai
> When suche an impe forshewes the waie.

– Sir Edward Sebright †1679, by *William Stanton*; twisted columns, broken segmental pediment. In the 'predella' two kneeling daughters who died aged two and five. – The HELMET

---

*Planned 1914. He replaced encaustic tiling with stone paving, and, outside, *Hopkins*'s diapered infill rendering with smooth plaster over a steel network.

with tiger *sejant* crest and other funeral armour is said to be that of Sir Edward Sebright †1702. – HATCHMENT to Sir John Sebright, 1794.

To the NW, the modest CHURCH FARM HOUSE of *c.* 1800, its garden surrounded by a fine serpentine brick WALL. The tiny VILLAGE is overshadowed by the late C20 satellite dishes and geodesic domes of the Ministry of Defence TRACKING STATION on the former airfield site (RAF Defford), across the railway to the SW.

BESFORD COURT, ⅜ m. NE. Besford Court has not only a very good timber-framed range of *c.* 1600, but also first-class work of 1912–14 behind, the best of that just pre-modern date in the county. The manor, belonging to the Harewell family from the early C15 and the Sebrights from 1606, was sold by the seventh Earl Beauchamp in 1910 to Major (later Sir) George Noble. He commissioned *A. Randall Wells* in 1912 to design large additions. Wells (1877–1942), one of the most interesting architects of that moment in England, started as clerk of works to Lethaby at Brockhampton church (Herefs.) in 1901–2, built Kempley church (Glos.) for Lord Beauchamp, 1902–3, and, in 1906–7, was 'resident architect' for E.S. Prior at Roker church (Durham). All three are among the best of their years in Europe. At Besford, in 1914, work (having already cost £30,000) was curtailed when Wells eloped with Lady Noble; they married in 1917. Sir George immediately sold out to the Roman Catholics, for whom *Henry T. Sandy* of Stafford finished and adapted Wells's building as a home and school for 'mentally defective' children, opened in 1917. This survived until 1996. The premises were converted to housing in 1999–2001 by *Banks Design Architects* of Bicester, with discreet enabling development around the grounds.

The timber-framed range is approached from the W, through C18 GATEPIERS and past a C17 FARMHOUSE (or lodge) with matching barns. Its flat W FRONT has a slightly projecting gateway with four-centred arch containing the original studded door. Above, a square oriel on coved overhang and gable with trefoiled bargeboards of *c.* 1600. All the rest is of typical close-set vertical studding. Ground-floor windows with transoms and pediments, renewed, probably correctly.* Wells extended the building, N, re-setting the return oriel in his new gable-end; a narrow-studded wing runs E from here. The S side of the front range has two unequal gables, the second larger and particularly decorative. After that the work of 1912–14 begins. It is planned round a courtyard (as no doubt was the C16–C17 house), but is wider and of Cleeve Hill stone, with big Cotswold-tiled roofs with hipped dormers. The end gables are tellingly different, the N well fenestrated, the S largely blank. Wells's long S FRONT is Neo-Tudor and no mistake about it. But the way he organized the façade is admirable: three ground-floor canted bay windows and two first-floor oriels

---

*Behind this range, until 1910, stood a large Georgian house.

interspaced in a carefully chosen rhythm. Blunt parapet; fenestration with mullions and transoms, broken just once, beneath the easternmost oriel, by two pointed cloister-like openings (infilled as tripartite windows in 1926). The E FRONT is more symmetrical, with end and central gables. Beneath the former, two-storey canted bays; beneath the latter the canted apse of the chapel projects, not to Wells's design as only the foundations were ready in 1914. It is in imitation Romanesque, uninspiringly imitative in contrast to the rest. The N FRONT, with some particularly broad mullioned-and-transomed ground-floor windows (originally for the servants' hall and kitchen), was most altered by the school, but has been acceptably restored.

But the real thrill of the house is the INTERIOR. Through the W gateway one enters a straight passage with low cloister-like mullioned openings, l., revealing the timber studding at the rear of the NW range. Then, r., in a bold sweep of Lutyens inspiration, the main staircase curves up in Baroque-like waves to the upper floor. Its lowest part is in two forks, the W with stepped Neo-Norman arch, the E rising immediately from the entrance passage. At the end of the passage the spacious courtyard is reached, with cloister on the ground floor, gallery above. The cloister, groin-vaulted in concrete, has paired round-arched openings with roundel above, a little too conventional a motif. The gallery has large round arches, W side, but on the others, rather uncomfortable Tudor fenestration. A secondary staircase, also curved, in the SE corner (near the external two-arched opening), leads to the impressive former ballroom. This, filling some two-thirds of the upper storey of the S front, has boldly pointed transverse arches, a motif earlier used by Norman Shaw (as at Adcote, Shropshire), but in this case supporting a concrete roof reminiscent of Brockhampton church. Two chimneypieces with blank stone overmantels, presumably incomplete. The concrete-vaulted White Parlour in the SE corner below is also remarkable, almost Soanean in its umbrella-like effect: octagonal, incorporating two bay windows, and with apsed alcoves. The rest of the S range's ground floor comprised billiard room, dining room, and library. The nave of the former chapel in the middle of the E range is covered by very impressive closely placed transverse stone arches, on doubled forward-curving corbels – all this a South French motif. Wells was as remarkable in his choice of patterns as in his treatment of them. The chancel, with a more conventional semi-dome, was completed after Wells's departure, as we have seen.

Some later school buildings have been retained. The earliest is the quadrangular INDUSTRIAL BLOCK, N, by *E. Bower Norris* of Stafford, 1926–7; of painted concrete block (manufactured by the boys on site), with buttresses and high-set mullioned-and-transomed windows. Also by *Sandy & Norris*, 1931–2, the imposing, rusticated concrete ARCH, SE, originally carrying a statue of St Teresa and meant to lead to unexecuted dormitory blocks. To the sw, the former St Teresa's Chapel, now community centre; 1972–3 by *Horsley, Currall & Associates* of Stafford. Square plan with chamfered corners. Rubble walls; pyramidal roof, recessed to provide peripheral top lighting.

7070

BEWDLEY

Bewdley, the most perfect small Georgian town in Worcester-shire, has three great visual blessings: a riverside street, a broad river crossed by a fine bridge, and a short wide main street continuing that bridge and ending in a Georgian church. Higher up, the narrow High Street is also mostly Georgian. Much timber framing also remains, either hidden by Georgian remodelling, or further w (especially at Wyre Hill).

Bewdley (originally Beaulieu), situated at a convenient Severn river crossing, was already important by the C15–C16, with at least three town gates. The first bridge was built in 1446–7, and a charter granted by Edward IV in 1472. Prince Arthur resided for a time at Tickenhill Manor (being married there in 1499, by proxy, to Catherine of Aragon). Leland in 1539 wrote: 'the hole towne gliterithe, being all of new buyldinge.' In the C16–C18 flourishing local industries included cap-making, tanning, horn-working, and the manufacture of brass and pewter. Much of the Severn's carrying trade centred on Bewdley, making it one of the most important inland ports of the West Midlands. Exports included coal from Shropshire and pottery from North Stafford-shire; of imports the most important was European bar iron destined for the Black Country. Trade diminished rapidly from the late C18 when Stourport (q.v.) was chosen as the Severn terminus of the Staffordshire and Worcestershire Canal. The sub-sequent commercial decline contributed to Bewdley's preserva-tion. There is almost no C19 development. Modern traffic congestion has been partly relieved by a southern by-pass, opened 1987 (*V.E. Jones*, County Engineer).

CHURCHES

St Anne, Load Street. w tower of 1695–6, paid for by Salway Winnington, M.P.; the body of the church of 1745–8 by *Thomas Woodward*, assisted by his young nephew *Richard*.[*] The tower is of rougher stone, but there is no clash in style between the two periods (or did the Woodwards modify the tower?) The nave has five round-arched windows each side, with keystones and imposts, divided by broad pilasters; parapet with inter-mittent balustrade. One-bay chancel, its Venetian e window facing down the street. The windows of the tower are also arched, but the difference in date comes out in the different surrounds; quoins, similar balustrade with corner urns. Inside,

---

[*] A stone dislodged in 1950, now re-set inside at the e end of the n aisle, is inscribed 'Ric: Woodward Campden in Glos 1745'.

giant Roman Doric columns carry a straight entablature; plaster tunnel vault in the nave, flat ceilings in the aisles (cf. the Woodwards' earlier churches at Alcester, Warwickshire, and St John the Baptist, Gloucester). Segmental arch to the lower chancel, which has a decorated plaster ceiling and E window with fluted Ionic pilasters; its N and S windows were reduced in size in 1881 (by *J. T. Meredith*).

Some original WOODWORK by *Thomas Cook*, a local joiner who undertook the rebuilding jointly with Woodward: PULPIT with chamfered corners, each main face with discreet inlay; panelled GALLERY, cut back as just a W gallery in 1987. The PEWS were cut down in 1881. – Neo-Norman FONT of *c.* 1890. – Two striking glass and metal CHANDELIERS by *Adrian Tilford*, 1992. – STAINED GLASS. Dreary C19 patterned work: E window 1881 by *Jones & Willis*, aisles 1892 by *William Pearce*. – No MONUMENTS as the church (until 1853) was a chapelry to Ribbesford. Woodward's church replaced a C15–C16 one, of timber, built above secular premises, its chancel flanked by chantry chapels. – Outside, beneath the E window, good, slightly Grecian WAR MEMORIAL by *W.H. Godwin*, 1920.

HOLY FAMILY (R.C.), behind No. 63 High Street. Built *c.* 1778 for Presbyterians; later Unitarian. Restored for Roman Catholics by *Homer, Jennings & Lynch*, 1952–3. An unusual building, brick with moulded stone cornice; oblong, with both ends rounded. In 1952–3 the round-arched windows were accurately renewed, and the open external stair at the entrance end, with roof on thin, widely spaced, wooden columns, infilled in brick for internal access to the curved E gallery. Low NE vestry of *c.* 1800. – FITTINGS of 1953; a canopied reredos replaced the pulpit between the W windows.

BAPTIST CHAPEL, behind No. 61 High Street. Founded *c.* 1649, rebuilt *c.* 1764; brick with round-arched windows. A plain Sunday School of 1925–6 now hides the front. Interior gutted in the late C20.

FRIENDS' MEETING HOUSE, Lower Park. Rebuilt 1706; brick with tiled roof with louvre. Entrances now in the gabled end walls, originally at the centres of the longer sides (with wooden cross-windows). Small late C18 SW wing; C20 additions, NW end. Inside, the SE gallery remains, with open balustraded front and shuttering below. Early C19 benches. Secluded GRAVE-YARD enclosed by a brick wall, perhaps built *c.* 1691.

(WESLEYAN) METHODIST CHAPEL, High Street. Of 1794. Three-bay stuccoed front with two tiers of round-arched windows; central doorway with open pediment. Extended 1850. Subdivided interior.

PERAMBULATIONS

1. Severn Side and Load Street

We start on the BRIDGE, by *Thomas Telford*, 1797–9, built by his usual contractor *John Simpson* for £9,300. Three beautiful

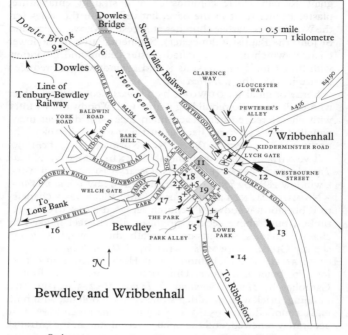

Bewdley and Wribbenhall

1	St Anne	11	Bewdley Bridge
2	Holy Family (R.C.)	12	Bewdley Station
3	Baptist Chapel	13	Bewdley High School
4	Friends' Meeting House	14	Winterdyne
5	(Wesleyan) Methodist Chapel	15	Kateshill House
6	Site of St Andrew, Dowles	16	Wyre Court
7	All Saints, Wribbenhall	17	Tickenhill Manor
8	Site of Christchurch	18	Guildhall
9	Dowles Manor (site of)	19	Silver Jubilee Gardens
10	The Summer House		

segmental arches, of sandstone, with rusticated extradoses; triangular cutwaters with broad pilasters above, substantial stone
balustrade. Small land arches, then slimmer cast-iron
balustrading along both banks, especially the Wribbenhall
side.* About 70 yds s are abutments for the c15 bridge,
destroyed in the great Severn floods of 1795.

From the Bewdley end of the bridge, one should first walk along
5 the river. SEVERN SIDE is a perfect river-bank street, as good
in its minor way as the Brinks at Wisbech (Cambridgeshire).
What makes it so attractive is the direct relationship between
houses and river, without trees and with minimal railing. The
mostly c18 sandstone wharves are preserved for some distance
N and s. The individual houses of SEVERN SIDE NORTH, formerly Coles Quay, are modest, mostly c18 brick, with two

* The bridge is also the starting point for the Wribbenhall perambulation (p. 779).

timber-framed survivors: Nos. 7–10, originally two houses, with square C17 panelling above a brick ground floor; and Nos. 15–16, probably C16. This has five framed bays (the N part, No. 16, refaced in brick), with central chimneystack and lobby entrance. Behind, visible from Dog Lane, an early C17 detached cottage.

Along SEVERN SIDE SOUTH the houses are again mostly brick, but to a grander scale, mostly three storeys, e.g. No. 5 (SARACEN HOUSE), early C18, five bays, and Nos. 6–7 (ALVE-STON HOUSE), late C17, 3+3 bays, with cross-windows and elaborate dentil cornice. By the abutment of the medieval bridge, a BANDSTAND of 1921, unfortunately without its canopy. Nos. 8–9 (THE OLD BANK) are early C19, stuccoed. Then No. 10 (RIVER HOUSE), again fine late C17, five bays, with moulded band courses. Central first-floor window with far-projecting broken pediment; the shell-hood of the doorway, on carved brackets, was renewed after a lorry demolished it in 1974. No. 11 (KIMBERLEY HOUSE) is also late C17; the bay windows with coved cornices may by Victorian. Then a long, plainer stretch, including acceptable, if unexciting, late C20 infill, before No. 26 (now THURSTON COURT). This is late C18 (said to be *c.* 1775), 2+1+2 bays, the recessed centre with doorway with engaged Tuscan columns and pediment (echoing the bigger stone pediments above the projecting parts). No. 27, restored early C17, is of close studding, with slight overhangs and two gables. Finally three modest C18 brick houses and the lower No. 32, incorporating earlier timber framing, and continuing beyond its canted corner into Lax Lane (Perambulation 2).

Now LOAD STREET, leading from the bridge to the church. It is, as has already been said, short and wide, closed at the end by the six-bay side of the largest Georgian house in Bewdley and by the E view of the church, subtly (by chance) out of axis. The S side starts better than the N, with various early to mid-C18 brick houses: No. 1 tall with hipped roof, four bays to the river, three to Load Street; No. 4, with good Gothic overlight above its side passage; No. 5, stuccoed in the early C19, only one-and-a-half bays wide, the single bay with giant blank arch; No. 6 (BOROUGH HOUSE), of five bays with decorated lintels with fluted keystones and canted ground-floor bays.

The N side is spoilt by the rebuilt ANGEL INN, 1938, unnecessarily set back, but redeemed by the fine Nos. 70–71, mid-C18, of four bays, the central two advanced and quoined beneath a pediment; windows with stepped voussoirs, Venetian windows on the upper floors of the outer bays. Plainer C18 houses follow: No. 66 has a good C19 shopfront of Tuscan columns with cast-iron foliage ventilators above the windows; Nos. 64–65 is six-bay early C18, with quoins and large fluted key-stones on the upper floors. The central archway leads to ST GEORGE'S HALL, large, brick, with round-arched windows, built 1901 in connection with the adjoining GEORGE HOTEL. This has a four-bay stuccoed front with ground-floor bow windows, but is gabled at the rear (like the adjoining houses), but here with timber framing exposed. No. 62 has indeed a fine lively timber-framed front, early C17, with the second and third floors jettied on console brackets. The decoration includes concave-sided lozenges and, on the third floor, squares with lobes at the middles of the sides, raised with plain framing in the C18.

Back on the s side, C18 brick houses of varying widths lead up to the GUILDHALL, its good ashlar front of 1808 probably by *John Simpson* of Shrewsbury. Three bays, tall rusticated ground floor filled with wrought-iron gates; giant Doric pilasters above in a 1+2+2+1 rhythm, the central pairs flanking a pedimental projection with heraldry. First-floor courtroom with tall sashed windows. Enlarged at the rear by *Henry Rowe*, 1866. Behind this, now forming Bewdley's Museum, the remarkable SHAMBLES, opened 1802: fifteen bays of segmental brick arches on square brick piers either side of a narrow lane. Its far end is blocked by a similar arch, flanked by three prison cells with rusticated ashlar surrounds and tunnel-vaulted interiors; the single one, l., has a datestone 1802. Further w, also part of the museum but at the rear of No. 17 (*see* below), the well-preserved BRASS FOUNDRY, established by Christopher Bancks in 1697 and belonging to his family until 1828. Its brick buildings, set along the e side of a narrow alley, may be late C18–early C19. Four blocks N–S, alternately two and one storey: office and store, casting shop (with a tapering brick stack at the rear), machine shop, and finishing and adjusting shops (with external forge, SE).

Next to the Guildhall, at Nos. 13–14 Load Street, a fine timber-framed house dated 1636, with gabled wings and recessed gabled centre, all close-studded; two overhangs with moulded bressumers on consoles. In the centre, an undulating early C19 shopfront. Adjoining, at right angles, the six-bay three-and-a-half-storey flank of Nos. 15–18, noted earlier, said to be of 1765. The street front is a fine composition of 3+3+3 bays, the pediment of the projecting centre surmounted by an eagle. The first-floor middle window here has Corinthian pilasters and broken pediment, the window above a Gibbs surround. All others have fluted or enriched keystones, but the half-storey has round-arched windows. Ground floor ruthlessly spoilt; only No. 18 retains its pedimented Tuscan doorcase.

The narrowed street now rises and divides either side of the church. Nos. 19–20, s side, seems five-bay C18 brick, but the side passage, l., reveals an elaborate early C17 timber-framed house, with gables, spurred quadrant bracing, and overhang on carved figure consoles. This must originally (i.e. before Nos. 15–18 were built) have faced e onto an open market area. The BEWDLEY INSTITUTE (Nos. 21–23, formerly the Wheatsheaf Inn) was another substantial framed house, dated 1632 on the less altered r. gable; the rest was rebuilt in 1877–8 by *J.M. Gething*, with feeble half-timbering above brick. The stuccoed early C19 front of Nos. 24–25 also hides C17 framing; its moulded first-floor bressumer is visible behind both shop windows.

N of the church, an almost continuous row of plain C18 frontages, mostly again covering timber framing; this is visible in the side passages (e.g. that called 'No Road', next to Nos. 59–60), at the gabled rears (one still exposing its framing), and often within (especially Nos. 44–48). Of the frontages, No. 55 has an early C18 moulded cornice, No. 54 early C19 stuccoing with pedimented windows. The range curves round towards Dog Lane, with more framing visible in the end gable of No. 43. Houses opposite also conceal framing, visible in the passageway of No. 40. A refronting date is provided by the dismal stucco of Nos. 35–36, which retains a fine downpipe dated 1722 (and an elaborate C17 plaster ceiling on the first floor).

2. High Street and to the south

HIGH STREET (formerly Upper or Over Street) leads SE from Load Street's W end; narrow, but not straight, with shops only at its N end.* No. 1, taking the corner well by stepping out in response to the reduced street width, is followed by a row of other modest Georgian houses and warehouses, terminated by the C17 timber-framed and gabled No. 9. On the W side, after two larger early C18 houses, comes Nos. 68–69 (BAILIFF'S HOUSE), a splendid two-storey-and-attic house, the best timber-framed example in the town; close-studded, with concave-sided lozenge patterns, and three gabled dormers. The doorway, r., with carved arch and spandrels, is dated '1610 TB', for Thomas Bolston.[†] The overhangs are supported on heavy Jacobean console-brackets; original first-floor windows with ovolo-moulded mullions and transoms, planted on the face of the wall frame. Three-bay plan, with a wide gallery at the back for the lateral fireplace and staircase. No. 67 is close-studded. No. 64, five bays with wooden cross-windows, was built as the workhouse in 1736–7. At its rear, an industrial wing extended in the C19 when used as a horn-works. Then, quite far back, Holy Family (R.C.), the former Presbyterian chapel (p. 141).

Opposite, No. 11 (REDTHORNE) also lies back, on its own; built 1775–6 for William Prattinton. He supervised the construction himself, importing building material from Bristol. Five close-set bays, with central doorway with broken pediment on Tuscan columns. At the rear two outer bow windows rise to full height.

A good group continues the W side: No. 63, mid-C18, five bays, and the MANOR HOUSE, in three sections. The first is early C18,[‡] with rusticated even quoins, pronounced string courses

---

*The description assumes that the street runs N–S rather than NW–SE, so that the NE side can be described as E and the SW as W.
[†] Dendrochronology dating in 1969, the first English example, revealed tree-felling dates of 1607.
[‡] A timber doorhead dated 1607, now *ex situ*, must refer to the earlier house.

and small off-centre doorway with high-set segmental pediment. The adjoining four-bay section is mid-C18, then a higher one, probably late C18; dormers added 1935. The parts are tied together by nice iron railings. A passage leads through the stuccoed No. 61 to the disappointing Baptist chapel (p. 141). Nos. 59–60 are remnants of a late C15 timber-framed pair, which had ground-floor halls and, in the inner bays, first-floor solars partly projecting into each hall. Partly encased in brick, with additional early C17 gabled rear wings.

Retracing our steps to consider the E SIDE allows an opportunity to admire how the street focuses on the church tower. After the Methodist chapel (p. 141) comes a long run of modest C18 frontages, often concealing earlier work. Their varied rears can be seen from the pleasant SILVER JUBILEE GARDENS, excellent infill of c. 1980 by P.A.K. Gibbs for Wyre Forest District Council, accessible immediately N of the chapel; Nos. 14–16 clearly hide a substantial C17 L-plan timber-framed house. Variety to the street frontages is provided by No. 24 (SKEY'S HOUSE), of c. 1780, set back, with pedimented Tuscan doorway with fine fanlight. After the stuccoed early C19 Nos. 25–26 is the former GRAMMAR SCHOOL of 1861, by Henry Day; small, Gothic, red brick, partly diapered, with bellcote over the twin doorway.

More plain Georgian houses opposite (W side). The archway adjoining No. 47 gives access to a passage (The Park), leading to the earlier GRAMMAR SCHOOL, timber-framed, and dated 1607 above the spurred quadrant bracing of its rear wing.* The early C18 brick front of Nos. 44–45 completely hides a three-bay house, perhaps late C15, with central hall and solar, S; the framing includes arch-braced tie-beams and curved windbraces. COOKE'S ALMSHOUSES next door, despite its neat foundation plaque of 1693, seem externally of 1860. The rear, however, displays the sandstone walls and two big rectangular brick stacks, each a row of four. No. 42, late C18, set at right angles by the entrance to Park Alley, forms a triangular cobbled space in front of the almshouses. The street then narrows and dips downhill, a telling townscape effect; Nos. 37–41, to an attractively shallow U-plan, step down the slope.

In LAX LANE, leading back to the Severn (and a former ford), brick terraces, N side, face the former NATIONAL SCHOOL of 1829–30, by John Smalman of Quatford (Salop); 2+2+2 bays, with minimal Tudor detail and central gable. Doubled in size to the E, in identical style, by Pritchard & Pritchard, 1912.

LOWER PARK continues High Street. No. 15, E side, the birthplace of Stanley Baldwin in 1867, is mid-C18, five bays, with elaborate wooden doorcase: Ionic columns, segmental pediment on richly carved brackets, enriched rounded architrave. Then Nos. 13–14 (Bank House and former Bank, opened 1810), with pretty embellishments of 1892 by J.H. Webb.

---

* Best seen, together with its brick neighbours of c. 1800, from the pathway at the end of Park Alley (see below).

Opposite, in its own grounds, LOWER PARK HOUSE (the former rectory), also five bays, *c.* 1760, with parapet and pedimented Tuscan doorway. Early C19 additions include the square GATEPIERS. By the road, SE, its pedimented coachhouse. This faces SAYERS ALMSHOUSES, founded 1625, rebuilt 1763 (and restored 1897). Brick with sandstone dressings, 4+4+4 bays; plain parapet, slightly projecting centre. Two dwellings in each section with four-centred doorways and Tudor-arched windows with hoodmoulds. Adjoining, the upright Nos. 6–7, early C18 brick, both doorways within a central passage. Beyond, set well back, the Friends' Meeting House (p. 141); its graveyard deserves a visit.

The end of the town here is marked by an effective bend in the road before it ascends RED HILL. At its foot, W side, is KATESHILL HOUSE, mid-C18, five by four bays; steps curve up to its pedimented Venetian doorway, with engaged Tuscan columns and Gothick glazing. Late C19 canted bay, SW, low curved service wing, NW.

WINTERDYNE, off the E side ¼ m. further S, on a sandstone bluff above the Severn, was built for Sir Edward Winnington in 1758–60; probably altered later in the C18. Stuccoed, three wide bays and three storeys, the entrance front, SW, with single-storey bows flanking a Tuscan portico, distyle *in antis*. Full-height bows also at the side and in the centre of the rear form inside a delightful series of curved rooms. The central one, which also has an apse backing onto the wide entrance hall, has a good Adam-style ceiling. Former LODGE also with semicircular end towards the road.

3. To the south-west and west

The W parts of Bewdley were extensively developed in the C20, beginning with council housing on BARK HILL (Tudor Road, Baldwin Road, York Road) in 1935–7 (*S.J. Rowe*, Borough Surveyor). But much Georgian building survives, as well as several timber-framed buildings, particularly at Wyre Hill; these form a group distinguished by clasped purlin roofs and arch-braced tie-beams.

First SW from St Anne (*see* above) into PARK LANE; the opening was sadly widened *c.* 1968 by the demolition of a timber-framed house, N side. BURLTON'S ALMSHOUSES, S, founded 1645, were plainly rebuilt in 1810; the notable feature is the entrance, a basket-arched recess above a doorway, with even flatter basket arch. PARK HOUSE (No. 15) is early C18, with pedimented doorway. Opposite, the nicely converted SNUFF MILL WAREHOUSE, C18 brick, three storeys, with two gables each end; added lower barn, forming an L-plan. Back on the S side, No. 21 (PARK LODGE), early C18, five bays, the r. two hidden by an early C19 bow.

Then, as the lane becomes very steep, TICKENHILL MANOR, high above on a knoll. It became a royal manor in the C15 and subsequently (with Ludlow) a seat of the Council of the

Marches. Edward IV added a wing in 1473–4 and there was
further rebuilding in 1493 (for Prince Arthur), in 1525 and in
1582. The Crown sold it, with its park, in 1870–3. One range
survives of the large timber-framed C15–C16 house. This was
remodelled, at least externally, when the rest was demolished
c. 1738. Plain brick s front of nine bays and two storeys, with
renewed pedimented Tuscan doorway; a later three-bay wing
projects to the SE. Inside, the main range reveals four late C15
framed bays, their close studding visible in several rooms; plain
roof with trusses with arch-braced collars. It is unclear what
this range represents; it seems to have been floored, so was
perhaps a subsidiary or lower hall, possibly the *longa domus*
'with chambers above and below' built 1473–4. – To the NW,
late C18 STABLES, with central gable; octagonal GAZEBO added
at the rear c. 1980. Nearby LODGE, mid-C19 Tudor Gothic.

Now back to our starting point and W up the curving WELCH
GATE, the main road to Ludlow and the Welsh Marches.
Mostly plain brick houses, occasionally stuccoed, e.g. Nos. 1–2
which turn the corner to Load Street admirably. Timber
framing is occasionally revealed, no doubt more frequently
hidden: see No. 5, N side, where a doorway, l., perhaps *in situ*,
has a decorated head dated 1637. No. 80, s side, at the corner
of the steeply rising Sandy Bank (the original road to Wales)
is part of a four-bay house of c. 1500, its framing visible high
on the E gable; roof trusses with struts to collars, clasped
purlins, and curved wind-braces. Welch Gate was diverted in
1753; it now swings round the late C18 WOOD COLLIERS
ARMS, with a N offshoot towards Bark Hill, all with closely
packed Georgian frontages. The later houses of WINBROOK,
the continuation of Welch Gate, are more strung out, but still
provide an excellent W approach to the town.

From here we should return to SANDY BANK or its even steeper
raised pavement, with vertiginous drop to the roadway below.
It was formerly lined with timber-framed houses; the four-bay
Nos. 38–39, much altered c. 1800, is almost the only survivor.

A long, uneventful C20 climb leads to WYRE HILL, quite a surprise with its raised pavements lined with C18 brick and earlier
timber framing. The traditional explanation for its village-like
feel is that this was the original centre (it is still known as the
'Old Town'), but it seems just as likely that it was a medieval
suburb, in itself an indication of contemporary importance.
The market granted in 1375 was perhaps held here. STILE
COTTAGE (No. 4, s side) is the first of the timber-framed
houses, with three C15–C16 timber-framed bays; C17 SE wing.
No. 5 has taller C17 framing, No. 6 is C18 brick. Timber framing
opposite begins at Nos. 51–52, C17, followed by the BLACK
BOY INN, probably C15–C16. Nos. 12–14, s side, represent a
three-bay late C15 house, with central open hall and cross-
passage, E (at No. 12). No. 15, early C19, has segment-headed
windows. Then, as the road levels out, No. 19, called THE OLD
TOWN HALL, but perhaps another late C15 timber-framed
house with central open hall, much restored. C20 development

then takes over, with only a few earlier survivors. The most striking timber-framed example is the large WYRE COURT, ¼ m. further on. Its centre (optimistically dated 1165!) is probably late C16; lower C17 square-panelled w wing. The higher E range, which also wraps around the rear with gables and a spindly turret, is all applied half-timbering, presumably c. 1860–70.

BEAUCASTLE, 1⅓ m. WSW. A Ruskinian fantasy by *William Doubleday*, 1877, for George Baker, former Lord Mayor of Birmingham. Rock-faced yellow sandstone with smooth pink dressings. Mostly trefoil-headed lancets; brick and half-timbered gables, with oriels, coving and bargeboards. The memorable features are the high, circular, conically roofed turret, and the timber fretwork balcony on the N and E sides, approached by a w stair behind a stepped arcade with carved foliage capitals. Inside, panelling and marble chimneypieces; drawing room with beamed ceiling with fire-brick infill. – Quieter Gothic STABLES opposite the entrance.

Almost facing the gatepiers, on the s side of LONG BANK, a former MISSION CHURCH by *J. T. Meredith*, 1896. Red brick, nave with open timber bell-turret, lower chancel; shoulder-headed lancets, stepped E and W triplets. Now a house.

Further up Long Bank, a short octagonal WATER TOWER, of reinforced concrete with stepped Deco panels; 1933 by *S. J. Rowe*.

BICKMARSH see CLEEVE PRIOR

BIRLINGHAM

9040

ST JAMES. By *Benjamin Ferrey*, 1871–2, apart from the Perp w tower (its middle stage used as a dovecote). It now stands forward beyond the s aisle, which was built on the site of the former nave. Ferrey gave it a higher NW stair-turret with spirelet, using it to picturesque effect in the composition of his w end. His building has competent Geometrical tracery to w and E. Segment-headed imitation Dec windows N and S. Striking interior with four-bay arcades with octagonal piers and arches with alternating red and white voussoirs; chancel arch and most windows are similarly treated. Red banding on the walls. Good cusped and wind-braced roofs. The rebuilding was paid for by the Rev. R.E. Landor (†1869), commemorated by a very large credence of polished Madrepore marble. Other *Ferrey* furnishings include *Godwin*-tiled floors, FONT, and former LECTERN carved by *Theodore Phyffers*: a life-size stone angel holding a Bible. – Oak REREDOS of 1911, probably by *Gerald Cogswell*. – SCULPTURAL FRAGMENTS. Two C12–C13 corbel heads (nave w). – Parish STOCKS. 1789. – STAINED GLASS. Mostly *Hardman*: E 1874, chancel s and s aisle E 1879, w 1880, N aisle w 1891. – s aisle SE by *A. J. Davies*, 1949. – MONUMENTS. Brass plate to Thomas Harewell †1603, with three kneeling figures (s aisle w). – Rev. R.R. Duke †1908; ornate brass plaque by *Jones & Willis*, 1911.

The CHURCHYARD ENTRANCE is the Norman chancel arch from the old church; one order of shafts with single-scalloped capitals, arch with chevron. Much renewed by *Ferrey*. – Good Free Perp CROSS nearby, by *Gerald Cogswell*, 1911.

Opposite, the former SCHOOL (with house), dated 1855; Tudor-style, blue brick with stone dressings. On the small green, a good WAR MEMORIAL CROSS of *c.* 1920.

The OLD RECTORY, a little w, built 1774, with five-bay s front of roughcast brick, was enlarged for Robert Eyres Landor (brother of the poet W.S. Landor); he became rector in 1829 and introduced a number of garden features including a small Perp chapel near the entrance. Large N service range added by *Ferrey*, 1871.

MANOR HOUSE, ⅓ m. S. Late C18 brick, two-and-a-half storeys and three bays; tripartite windows flank the pedimented doorway. At its rear, IVY COTTAGE, C17, timber-framed and thatched. More such cottages further E. Also the PORTER ALMSHOUSES, a two-storeyed brick range of eight dwellings, dated 1824; upper windows all semicircular, small central pediment.

THE COURT HOUSE, ¼ m. N. Of *c.* 1850, perhaps by *Henry Rowe* who was working at the Porters' Mansion (further s, demolished 1929) at this time. Large, rendered, mildly Italianate; bracketed eaves, hipped slate roofs. – C17 timber-framed BARNS and COTTAGES, SW.

BIRTSMORTON

ST PETER AND ST PAUL. Unusually for Worcestershire, almost entirely Dec, but much belongs to a drastic restoration of 1877 by *T.D. Barry & Sons*. The nave and chancel s windows seem original C14 work; the E and transept N and S windows, and timber S porch, are of 1877. W tower *c.* 1400 (restored 1896), meant to be vaulted; tall arch of two continuous chamfers. Dull interior with thin roofs of 1877; foliage carving by *Charles Hill* of Ledbury. – Mostly C19 FITTINGS, though the PEWS may be partly C15–C16. – Mid-C18 COMMUNION TABLE, wrought iron with grey marble top; graceful and very unecclesiastical-looking (cf. St Swithin, Worcester). – C18 COMMANDMENT BOARDS. – Plain C12 FONT, with round bowl and stepped base. – Small ROYAL ARMS of George IV. – EMBROIDERY with Hastings arms, dated 1693; perhaps from a funeral pall. – STAINED GLASS. Chancel N by *Donald Brooke*, 1970. – Good medieval fragments, especially C15 pieces from the E window, reassembled in the chancel SE in 1940: heads, two kneeling donor knights, and a very rare representation of the Baptism of St Christopher. – C14 Ruyhall arms elsewhere. – MONUMENTS. Tomb of *c.* 1500, probably erected by Jane Nanfan in memory of her three husbands: Sir John Nanfan, Sir Renfrey Arundel,

Sir William Houghton. Many kneeling figures in cinquefoil-cusped panels which retain much paint. The bishop must be John Arundel, of Lichfield (†1502); the brass indent in the Purbeck top was perhaps for Sir Richard Nanfan II. Above, carved stone arms dated 1572. – Small tablet to Bridgis Nanfan †1704, signed by *White* of Worcester. – Rear-Admiral William Caldwall †1718: excellent standing monument, of grey marbles, attributed to *Edward Stanton* (GF). He reclines on a tomb-chest, with a finely carved panel of his flagship. Reredos background with Composite columns, inscription flanked by a multitude of nautical instruments, and top with asymmetrical cartouche and military trophies. – HATCHMENT. Richard, Lord Coloony, 1740.

Attractive, secluded CHURCHYARD, with C18–C19 chest and pedestal tombs.

BIRTSMORTON COURT, SW. An eminently picturesque, half-timbered manor house, to a courtyard plan, within a wide moat (with outer moat, E, and large collecting pond, Westminster Pool, W). The architectural history is far from clear. Perhaps of C13 origin, it was bought in 1424–5 by John Nanfan who is said to have demolished most of the earlier house before his death *c.* 1447. Probably remodelled for Giles Nanfan from 1572. Further work in the C18–C20 (including restoration by *F. S. Waller*, 1871–2) provided varied prospects on every side. The segmentally moulded entrance archway, N side, is of stone, and clearly C14; C16 brick battlements, C20 stone bridge. The timber-framed range to its E, with stone base and two projecting stone stacks, may be as old. The E range of the house, destroyed by fire in the C18, was re-created in 1929–30 by *A. Hill Parker & Son*: successful pastiche, of square panelled framing, with gabled cross-wings and its own stone bridge across the moat. The set-back S range is especially picturesque. Its stone E section, formerly a service range, now contains the dining room; then comes the timber-framed hall, with a gabled bay either side of the stone chimneybreast with its tall star-shaped brick stacks. The W range, the solar cross-wing, once had a jettied S gable, but the original roof has gone; externally all is now late C18 brick, with sashed windows and hipped roof.

As one enters the irregular courtyard from the N, the hall lies ahead, with enormous wall-posts, heavy square panelling, and large Elizabethan window. The pointed timber doorway leads into the screens passage. The hall itself, once panelled all round, has a large stone fireplace in its S wall. The screens gallery, supported by circular oak posts, formerly continued across the chimneybreast and round the upper end of the hall. The wall fronting the gallery (with a display of heraldry), and the hall ceiling, are of geometrically moulded plasterwork, apparently renewed in the C20. The trusses, still in medieval tradition, seem never to have been open to the hall. W of the hall is the parlour (or council chamber) with fine panelling with Corinthian pilasters, frieze with dragons, and rich oak overmantel with caryatids and heraldry datable to 1572–80;

contemporary ceiling with geometrical plasterwork, divided into six compartments by plastered beams. A fragment of wall painting upstairs has also been dated (by Clive Rouse) to the 1570s. The structure, plan, and details here thus all point to the time of Giles Nanfan. Less clear is the development of the NE range, now containing the banqueting hall, with an authentic-looking Elizabethan ceiling. Was this perhaps an adaptation by Giles Nanfan of the service range of the C15 house, which may have had its main accommodation in the vanished E range? The present E range, internally remodelled by *S. T. Walker & Partners*, c. 1966, has an elegant Neo-Georgian staircase.

Splendid late C20 GARDENS (including within the C16 walled garden, N) laid out by *Veronica Adams*, with ornamental ironwork by *Mike Roberts*.

Church and Court stand on their own, some distance from the dual centres of the parish. In RYE STREET, 1 m. W, are the OLD RECTORY, big stuccoed mid-C19; HOME FARM, C17 timber-framed, altered 1798; and, attached to an earlier brick house, the former SCHOOL by *G. R. Clarke*, 1860, with W rose window. In BIRTS STREET, 1¼ m. WNW, a former WESLEYAN CHAPEL of 1902 by *William Jones Jun.* of Gloucester, still banded brick, with paired lancets; entrance front with rose window and porch-tower with stone spire. To the W, its altered predecessor of 1844. A little E is PROVIDENCE BUNGALOW, built in the early C20 around two C19 railway carriages, set side-by-side.

Further W, at COOMBE GREEN, a MISSION CHURCH of 1904; corrugated iron, with bellcote.

PUMP HOUSE FARM, on the A-road, ½ m. SE of the church (in Berrow parish), is a good hall and cross-wing house. The main range, with remains of crucks inside, may be C15; narrow-studded N wing, perhaps C16.

BISHAMPTON

ST JAMES. Good Perp W tower, battlemented, with tall C19 corner pinnacles; the rest, nave with S porch and chancel with N vestry, rebuilt by *Preedy*, 1869–70. He reused ancient parts, especially the late C12 doorways. The S has one order of shafts with trumpet-scallop capitals and moulded arch with keeled roll; hoodmould with billet, animal head above the apex. Simpler blocked N doorway, with continuous roll. Also old, two Norman nave windows and, at least in part, a couple of late C13 chancel windows. Typical *Preedy* are the Dec-style E window and muscular S porch. Rendered interior, distinguished only by heavily braced roofs. – FONT. Of cauldron shape; late C12. Decoration of crosses, rosettes, and six-pointed stars; rope moulding below (cf. Bricklehampton). – Other *Preedy* fittings include the stone PULPIT, with canopied figure of St James; iron HOURGLASS STAND, probably C17.

The church stands at the N end of a long village street, mostly C20, but with a number of C17 timber-framed cottages and farms. MANOR FARM, N end W side, is the largest; broad H-plan, its N wing C18–C19.

Opposite, a little S, the two best houses stand next to each other. The MANOR HOUSE is stately and symmetrical, with projecting gabled wings, dated 1629, and tall central gabled dormer, all with original bargeboards. Mostly square-panelled framing with some diagonal and some curved struts at high level. COURT FARM is much older, perhaps C15, originally a cruck hall with solar cross-wing, The latter has C17 square panelling and half-hipped gable, the former a dormer with decorative bracing; the inserted floor of the upper hall bay has richly moulded beams.

Further S, at the Broad Lane corner, a former BAPTIST CHAPEL of 1844; small, brick, gabled. The porch has been removed.

THE LARCHES FARM, 1½ m. SSE. Big early C19 brick house, square, of three bays and storeys, with hipped slate roof; Doric doorway.

BLACKWELL

Lickey and Blackwell

9070

The development of Blackwell (formerly The Linthurst) resembles that of Barnt Green (q.v.), on a more modest scale. Its railway station, closed 1966, stood at the summit of the notorious Lickey Incline (p. 315), the scale of which can be appreciated from the massive sandstone retaining wall alongside Pikes Pool Lane and by the depth of the rusticated bridge across Blackwell Road.

ST CATHERINE. 1939–40 by *H.L. North* of Llanfairfechan, his last major work; roughcast with dark brick plinth, rather Scandinavian-looking. Narrow slit windows with triangular tops, mostly tall and grouped, but a big W wheel window flooding the church with light. Steep roof (now pantiled), echoed by the saddleback tower emerging from above the choir, and continuing, slightly splayed, over the aisles to link up with the roof of the W narthex-cum-baptistery. The impressive interior is predominately white, with sharply pointed three-bay arcades and yet sharper crossing arches. The painted decoration of the sanctuary and S chapel roofs, plus narrow bands across the open nave roof, provide the only colour, apart from small, red hanging candelabra. The large stone FONT and STALLS are original; PEWS added 1958.

Circular PARISH ROOM, NW, linked by a glazed porch and open timber N cloister; by *J.T. Christophers* (*Associated Architects*), 2003. Roughcast to match the church.

Former WESLEYAN CHAPEL, Greenhill. By *John Cotton*, 1881–2, E.E.-style; a memorial to Henry Taylor of Leahyrst (*see* below).

Chancel extended and transepts added 1901. Of grey Bromsgrove sandstone, Cotton's original building enhanced by a little
red banding; timber N porch, good octagonal NE turret with
timber bell-stage and shingled spirelet. Sturdy arch-braced
nave roof; (later) transept arches with two-bay arcades. – Much
late C19 STAINED GLASS by *T.W. Camm* (for *Winfield & Co.*)
or his brothers (*Camm & Co.*). – Chancel N lancet by *Pearce
& Cutler*, 1928. – Fine S transept S window by *Paul Woodroffe*,
1921.* – Good LYCHGATE of 1907. – Former SUNDAY
SCHOOL, E. 1893, enlarged 1906; brick and half-timber.

Modest houses surround St Catherine's church: in STATION
ROAD, S, brick and half-timber by *Charles A. Edge*, 1895–7
(especially Nos. 3 and 11); in LINTHURST NEWTOWN, E.
roughcast and semi-detached by *F.F. Baylis* (Nos. 11–11A, 1912,
and perhaps Nos. 2–4). In ST CATHERINE'S ROAD, N, *Baylis*'s
own house, No. 6 (THE WHITE HOUSE), of 1912, well and
simply detailed (despite the later Doric porch); also
LINTHURST SCHOOL by *John Cotton*, 1884 (enlarged 1893),
brick, with large round-arched windows.

Further N, at the top of DALE HILL, a brick and timbered group
by *Edge*: DALE HEAD, on the corner, 1898–9; the earlier IVY
COTTAGE (No. 2), given nice bay windows in 1889; and APES-
DALE HOUSE (No. 4), *Edge*'s own, of 1891, with later square
tower.

To the NW, off Spirehouse Lane, the larger LINTHURST HOUSE,
by *Cossins, Peacock & Bewlay*, 1905–6, for Barrow Cadbury;
roughcast, with Neo-Georgian detail and big square stair-
tower with open wavy-roofed top stage. In 1921–2 *Peacock &
Bewlay* expanded the house as Cropwood Open Air School,
now part of Hunters Hill School. Roughcast LODGE, incorporating elements of the earlier house (by *Osborn & Reading*,
1880).

More larger houses in GREENHILL, the narrow lane descending
SW from Blackwell. WADDERTON (formerly Holly Hill House,
now a conference centre) is of 1870–1, its sharp gables based
on a *retardataire* design by *Edmund Axten*; much altered by
Dallas & Lloyd, 1919. HILL HOUSE, S side, built as a 'speculative' lodge by *John Cotton*, 1874–5 (enlarged 1881), has his
typical chunky Gothic detail. LEAHYRST, lying back here, by
Cotton, 1878, for Henry Taylor, received its own tile-hung lodge
(now Coppice Gates) in 1901. The diapered brick house has
twin gables, the l. above a very fancy Decorated triple window
(with good Aesthetic-style glass, lighting the spacious staircase
hall); timber porch (and billiard room) added 1886. The duller
UPLANDS, N side, 1868, much enlarged by *Cotton*, 1879, was
tactfully extended by *C.E. Bateman*, 1911, with an angled porch
into his new hall. Now a children's home. Next downhill,
SPRING VILLA (No. 34), a quirky brick confection begun
1871. BURCOT GRANGE, N side, the largest house, is by *J.A.*

---

*The excellent chancel WALL PAINTINGS by *Bernard Sleigh*, 1913, are now at
Methodist Central Hall, Westminster.

Cossins & Peacock, 1890, for H. Follett Osler. Floridly half-timbered, with nice details: timber-arcaded porch, oriel windows,
decorative plaster panels. Now a retirement home, but the interior well preserved, with fine panelling and joinery, Jacobethan
ceilings, and spacious staircase with good stained glass. Then
a couple of altered CI7–CI8 farmhouses.

At the bottom, the East Worcestershire Waterworks Co.'s
ENGINE HOUSE, a strong design of 1924 by the engineer *Fred
J. Dixon*; big round-arched windows, fine Deco lettering. The
original waterworks buildings of 1882 (engineer: *S. W. Yockney*)
are further S, with a half-timbered cottage by *Edge*, 1883, facing
Alcester Road.

BURCOT, an earlier settlement along Alcester Road (B4096),
retains some attractive houses. At the entrance to Greenhill,
the brick OLD HOUSE, dated 1734, faces BURCOT FARM,
much altered early CI8. Further W, a CI7–CI8 sandstone
cottage (No. 352), and BURCOT HOUSE, early CI9 stucco,
mildly Tudor but a Doric porch. At the far W end, THE
MOUNT (Nos. 309–315), a neat group by *Edge*, 1891–2.

BLACKWELL COURT, ½ m. SSE, now a scouting centre, was built
for George E. Unite, 1874. Brick, with pyramid-roofed tower,
canted bays, and bargeboards. Large NE addition of 1921, with
broadly mullioned-and-transomed windows.

BLAKEDOWN   8070
Churchill and Blakedown

ST JAMES. A chapel of ease to Hagley. By *Street*, 1860, but of his
simple nave-and-chancel building only the uncoursed Hagley

Blakedown, St James.
Drawing, as in 1862

sandstone walls remain, with a chamfered N doorway. Big
timber bell-turret by *F. Smalman Smith*, 1866, rebuilt in more
or less the same form in 1915 by *T. Grazebrook*. He added the
S aisle and vestry in 1905. Street's S windows were reused and
the arcade given a bold circular pier (but four-centred arches).
The plate-traceried E and W windows were replaced with fancy
Dec examples in 1936–7 by *E.B. Hoare* (*Hoare & Wheeler*). Also
theirs, most FURNISHINGS: lavish PEWS, SCREENS, and huge
Perp REREDOS, of stone. – STALLS, 1898. – FONT and PULPIT,
1905. – LECTERN by *Pancheri & Hack*, 1954. – STAINED
GLASS. E window 1891, the backgrounds removed in 1937,
when *James Hogan* (of *Powell & Sons*) provided the W window
and that by the font.

Former SCHOOL, SE, by *Grazebrook*, 1884, plain brick;
enlarged 1894.

HARBOROUGH HALL, ¼ m. NE. Timber-framed, three bays and
two storeys plus gabled dormers, the centre a projecting full-
height porch; built 1635 for William and Anne Penn (according to a dated keystone, now lost). Lobby-entrance plan: large
central brick stack serving both the hall (N) and parlour (S).
Good plaster ceilings especially in the N front bedroom: four
compartments with patterns of thin ribs between beams with
sturdy vine trails. A lower, probably earlier, N range (now
dining room) links to a half-timbered billiard room added
c. 1920–5, when the house was much restored. Partly rebuilt
in brick and stuccoed in 1954 by *Harry Bloomer & Son* for
Birmingham Corporation, as a convalescent home for single
mothers.

Of Blakedown's C19 iron foundries the best reminder is the string
of MILL PONDS along Wannerton Brook at the village's SW
end; SPRINGBROOK FORGE, of *c.* 1840, between Swan and
Forge Pools, retains its overshot iron waterwheel and other
machinery. *Brunel*'s Oxford, Worcester & Wolverhampton
Railway arrived in 1852; his timber VIADUCT (across Churchill
Lane) was replaced in 1882 by a blue brick one by *Kellett &
Bentley*.

On the E and S outskirts (cf. Broome), large mid-C20 houses,
especially in NEW WOOD LANE, ⅝ m. SW. The first here,
No. 2 (originally Blakedown Rough), is of 1934 by *S.N. Cooke*
of Birmingham; roughcast, three storeys, with flat roof, one
narrow rounded bay, and other mild Deco detail.

WANNERTON FARM, ¾ m. W. Built for Lord Ward in 1856;
roughcast, with stone dressings and bargeboarded gabled
dormers.

PARK HALL, 1⅛ m. WSW. Large, brick, of various dates. The earliest part, SW, is early C18, probably for Thomas Foley II; three
bays, with broad full-height bow windows flanking a pedimented Doric doorcase. This leads to a good contemporary
staircase, with three slender balusters to each tread. The house
was more than doubled in size, perhaps *c.* 1833. The additions
included a (now central) three-storey canted projection E of
the original building, leading into a wide new entrance hall,

and a further three-bay range, E. NE wing *c.* 1900. – Gabled LODGE dated 1902.

BOCKLETON

Remote country on the Herefordshire boundary.

ST MICHAEL. C17 or early C18 W tower, late C12 nave, and mid-C13 chancel with a N chapel originally built *c.* 1560 for the Barneby family. The battlemented tower has a broad W window with Y-tracery, round opening above, and paired-lancet bell-openings. Of the Norman nave most buttresses survive, plus the N and S doorways of *c.* 1160–70, with (enlarged?) windows either side. Both doorways are set in the usual Worcestershire frontispiece (or projecting section of wall, cf. Stoulton, Eastham etc.). The elaborate N doorway has two orders of shafts with decorated scallop capitals and arch with two thick rolls with smaller twisted rope mouldings between. Label with wide crenellation motif and narrow lozenge chain. The frontispiece is framed by billet or zigzag mouldings, with fluting and rosettes in the spandrels. Blind arcading above, its capitals also with scallops plus some heads, the arches with billet. The S doorway is almost as richly decorated, but differs in detail. Mid-C13 easternmost nave windows, contemporary with the chancel which has two-light S windows with pointed-trefoiled heads and chamfered priest's doorway, all with hoodmoulds. The showy Dec E window belongs to *Woodyer*'s restoration of 1861–2. Cruder N chapel remodelling by *Henry Curzon*, 1867, with bald trefoil-headed W doorway; but its three-bay roof, with tie-beams beneath paired arched openings, may be partly of 1560. Otherwise the interior is *Woodyer*'s, with two-bay arcade between chancel and chapel, and typical FURNISHINGS: full-height Dec-style SCREEN, of timber with matching PULPIT; carved stone REREDOS; round FONT with trefoiled arcade and carved heads. *Minton* tiles throughout.

STAINED GLASS. Good E window by *Kempe*, 1906. – In the nave NE, a discoloured Virgin and Child, presumably medieval. MONUMENTS. Round-arched recess with thick roll moulding, nave NE, probably C16. Plain tomb-chest within; back wall with blank shields. – Richard Barneby †1597 and his wife Mary †1574; large, sandstone, dated 1594, and almost certainly by the Dutchman *Gerard Holleman*.* Elaborate recumbent effigies, a helmet with lion's crest between their heads; his feet on a lion, hers on a startled eagle. Tomb chest with heraldic shields between caryatids. Larger caryatids carry tapering fluted pilasters and obelisks to frame the back wall, its inscription panel flanked by five sons and four daughters. The top heraldry is set, oddly enough, into a broken pediment of two

---

* Alias *Garrett Hollyman*; in July 1594 he left Kyre Park (p. 422), where he had been making chimneypieces, to go to 'Mr Barnebies'.

double curves; on them recline a boy blowing bubbles and Father Time, both naked. – Charles Baldwyn †1706. Of grey marbles, without effigy; predominant 'reredos', gadrooned base with cherubs. – William Wolstenhulme Prescott †1865; signed *Thomas Woolner*, 1867. Recumbent white marble effigy, on a stone tomb-chest with relief of the young gentleman holding the hand of an ailing older man; Prescott died of fever contracted while tending his dying gamekeeper. Above, brass TABLET with alabaster frame to his mother Arabella †1886.

Two LYCHGATES, the NE perhaps built from the oak timbers of a former C15 porch, the NW also with old timbers. A building outline, visible in dry weather between them, is said to be that of the foundations of the Saxon predecessor church.

BOCKLETON (COURT) FARM, W, was the manor house: early C17, altered in the C19. H-plan, mostly roughcast. Central range with chimney (with C19 brick stacks) towards the N end, forming a lobby-entry plan; N wing with some exposed framing, taller S wing. On the main range's upper floor, a mid-C17 fireplace, with demi-figures and carved frieze; panelled room, SW, with plastered compartment ceiling.

BOCKLETON COURT, ⅝m. NW; now a Birmingham City Council study centre. By *Henry Curzon*, 1866–9, for Arabella Prescott, widow of a London banker. Mildly Jacobethan, brick with stone dressings. Long E front, the lower service range to the N. The distinguishing feature is the tower above the entrance, more Gothic than the rest, its top stage with sculptural decoration and blind quatrefoil parapet with gargoyles; quadripartite vault of grey and yellow stone within the porch. One gabled range either side, the N with big mullioned-and-transomed window lighting the billiard room; then a further gabled recession with the huge staircase window. Short S return with full-height canted bay, SW. Flat W front with gables over the drawing room and recessed library, plus a pair above the dining room. The service range here is nicely terminated by a further gable for the servants' hall. Well-preserved INTERIOR, exhibiting typical planning for a small Victorian country house. Its centre is a fine hall, entered from the SE. Three-bay E arcade into the billiard room; two-bay N arcade to the open-well oak staircase (with Aesthetic stained glass). Ornate Gothic chimneypiece, painted hunting frieze (by *J.H. Wallis* of Chiswick Mall), and colonnaded W and E galleries beneath an impressive lantern roof. Other rooms have simple Jacobean ceilings and, apart from the dining room, early C19 white marble chimneypieces brought from the Prescotts' former home, Clarence Lodge, Roehampton, London. That in the drawing room has caryatids, that in the library Egyptian figures; here also (and in the lobby) a painted Grecian frieze by *E.T. Parris*, 1841, again from Roehampton. A central corridor leads N from the hall, through the altered service range.

Adjoining the latter, the SERVICE COURTYARD, with the laundry on its N side. Then the STABLE YARD, with clock tower above the carriage entrance. These form a most attractive

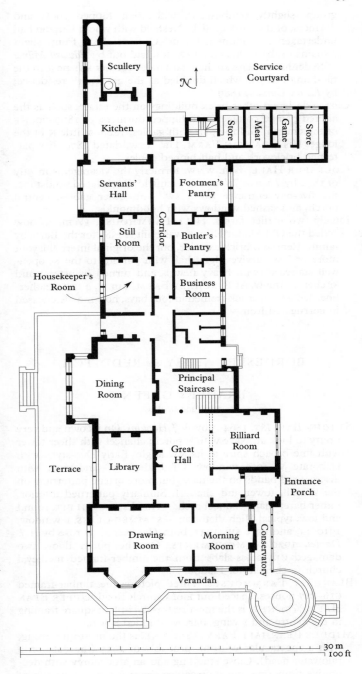

Bockleton Court.
Ground-floor plan

group, slightly reminiscent, with their hipped roofs and dormers, of the work of W.E. Nesfield with whom Curzon had undertaken a Continental tour. Outside the S front, slight remains of the FORMAL GARDENS, laid out by *Edward Milner* of Sydenham. – The kitchen garden lay further ESE next to the tile-hung LODGE, which doubled as the gardener's residence; by *Henry Curzon*, 1889.

Curzon designed other brick buildings on the estate, such as the altered pair of cottages with hipped dormers, of 1869–70, NE of the church, and the pair with gables, 1868, a little N of the lodge. His GRAFTON FARM, 1 m. WSW, dated 1870, has patterned brickwork and half-hipped gables.

COCKSPUR HALL, 7/8 m. WNW, formerly the vicarage, is mostly of 1842 by *Thomas Johnson* of Lichfield. Rock-faced sandstone, the five-bay entrance front, SW, with outer gables, central porch, and sashed windows with hoodmoulds.

Finally two earlier farms. HILL FARMHOUSE, 1¼ m. N, now called the Old Manor House, was built *c.* 1583 for the Barneby family. Renewed brick exterior, but the original internal layout more or less survives: long hall with parlour to the N, open-well staircase (with heavy newels and turned balusters) and kitchen to the w. At BIRCHLEY FARM, 2 m. N, a C15 weather-boarded BARN, cruck-framed in four bays; now mostly encased in corrugated iron.

BORDESLEY ABBEY *see* REDDITCH

9060

BRADLEY GREEN
Stock and Bradley

ST JOHN BAPTIST. 1864–5 by *W.J. Hopkins*. On its own and very pretty to look at. Nave with N porch; chancel with sheer tower with fine broach spire at its NW angle. Early Dec-style, with elaborate W rose window. Of Inkberrow sandstone, with discreet red bands on the nave, but more ornate patterning on the W wall, tower and chancel. Similarly patterned interior, rather bare; sharp chancel arch. – Good stone PULPIT, round and low; typical High Victorian. – STAINED GLASS. E window, 1910–13, and nave SW, 1937, both *Hardman*. – W rose by *A.J. Davies*, 1920. – MONUMENTS. On the porch floor, two damaged C14 cross-slabs from the timber-framed medieval church (a chapelry of Fladbury).

BEANHALL FARMHOUSES. Three picturesque timber-framed C16–C17 houses, spaced out E of Church Road. UPPER BEAN HALL, ¾ m. NNE, is the most restored: H-plan; square framing in the centre and S wing, narrow-studded N wing.

MIDDLE BEANHALL FARM, ½ m. NNE, is the most interesting, with a spectacular W front, probably of 1635 (the date on a rainwater head). Close studding and an attic storey with decorative timbering and four gables above a continuous run of

five-light mullioned windows, now blocked. These only lit a
low attic, but clearly attempt to copy the fashionable long
gallery (cf. Mere Hall, Hanbury). Rear stone chimney with tall
brick star-stacks with joint cap. Inside, first floor, two rooms
with C17 panelling, in one also an arcaded chimneypiece with
carved frieze. The S part of the house, beyond the herringbone-
braced porch, is older, probably *c.* 1500, of upper-floor-hall
type. Its S end was a smoke bay, later incorporated into the
kitchen.

LOWER BEANHALL FARM, ¼ m. NE, dated 1564, has narrow
studding on the ground floor, square panelling above, separated by tiled weatherings. Windows of four and five lights on
the W side; large square chimney with three brick star-stacks.
Mid-C18 brick addition, S.

PRIEST BRIDGE HOUSE, ¼ m. SE, was the Stock and Bradley
Board School, by *E.A. Day*, 1874. Brick, with half-hipped roofs
and steep pyramidal bellcote.

At STOCK GREEN, 1¼ m. SW, a diminutive three-bay BAPTIST
CHAPEL, opened 1846; entirely domestic, attached to a
cottage. Porch rebuilt 1988.

BRANSFORD

ST JOHN BAPTIST. A chapelry of Leigh, in an isolated situation
¾ m. S of the modern village. Small, nave and chancel in one;
carefully restored in 1956–7 by *Robert Potter*,[*] who, however,
altered the form of the square timbered W bell-turret, and
removed a SW dormer. The church is early C13, with a SW
lancet, much rebuilt in the C14; see the ogee-arched S doorway
and the window to its E. Altered in the C15; C16–C17 timber S
porch. The chancel E and S walls were mostly rebuilt in brick
in 1812; each has one large, entirely domestic-looking window.
Homely interior, with fine single-framed C14 wagon roof; two
tie-beams, the E supporting two vertical struts (in lieu of a
chancel arch). The bell-turret part of the nave is separated by
a C17 wall of square-panelled framing; two (blocked) wood-
mullioned openings flank the doorway to the nave. Some
original supports of the turret survive, with diagonal braces. –
Good C17 COMMUNION RAIL; sturdy, with moulded balusters. – PULPIT, with C17 arched panels. – PEWS. Probably of
1869. – WALL PAINTINGS were found in 1957; only one small
square N of the sanctuary is exposed. – STAINED GLASS. Nave
N, with small-scale scenes, by *Florence, Robert & Walter Camm*,
1940.

GILBERT'S FARM, ⅓ m. NE. Cruck-framed hall range with E
cross-wing; *c.* 1500, later floored. The walls are mostly C19
brick, but framing is exposed at the rear, N. Here also a single-
bay, two-storey range, added *c.* 1625.

---

[*] In succession to his former partner, *W.H. Randoll Blacking*.

BRANSFORD BRIDGE, across the Teme, 1⅛ m. NNE. Rebuilt 1924, using Hennebique's ferro-concrete system, by *C.F. Gettings*, County Surveyor; segmental arch with pierced spandrels. The first bridge was built in 1338 by Prior Wulfstan de Braunsford, also Bishop of Worcester.

BREDICOT

9050

ST JAMES. Tiny church of *c*. 1300 in the Old Rectory garden; much restored in 1843, probably by *Perkins*.* Nave and chancel in one; bellcote, timber S porch. All windows have renewed Y-tracery apart from the E. of three intersecting lights. N and S doorways with roll mouldings. Inside, an ogee trefoiled piscina, but otherwise the atmosphere of 1843 prevails: typical three-bay roof, PEWS with tall poppyheads, stone trefoil-panelled PULPIT, wooden ALTAR RAILS, simple STAINED GLASS (apart from the nave S window of *c*. 1900, no doubt *Clayton & Bell*). – Octagonal C14 FONT, with tall cusped panels, perhaps re-cut. – C14–C15 TILES in the porch.

The OLD RECTORY was rebuilt in 1817 by *William Bowen*, surveyor, of Worcester. Brick, tall T-plan, with hipped roof; three-bay, three-storey entrance front.

Church and rectory are linked to the small village by two original stone segmental-arched BRIDGES across the deep cutting of the Birmingham–Gloucester railway, opened 1840. Its largest house is BREDICOT COURT, early C17 timber-framed, enlarged in the C18, further altered *c*. 1840 for the Chamberlain family (of the Worcester porcelain factory).

BREDON

9030

An important medieval manor belonging to the Bishops of Worcester.

ST GILES. Impressive and varied, with central tower; on the site of a Saxon minster, high above the Avon. Long Norman nave, with later aisles stopping well short of the W end. The N aisle has Dec windows. The S is a fine C13 chapel, heavily buttressed, with high-pitched roof: four pairs of S lancets with trefoiled heads, similar W pair with blocked quatrefoil above, slightly stepped E triplet. The plain Norman corbel table must have been reused. On the N side of the nave this remains complete, above the aisle. The lower two stages of the tower also have trefoiled lancets, but the two-light bell-openings are early C14, perhaps as early as 1300; battlements, slim recessed spire. Low N vestry by *Ninian Comper*, 1913–14. The large chancel was probably rebuilt *c*. 1300–10, see the early bar tracery of the two-light side windows. Renewed E window. Pellet frieze with good

---

* He designed the National School, ½ m. S, now demolished, in 1841–2.

heads; blocked lowside window, SE; recess with ballflower on
a N buttress, also trefoil-headed. Fine Norman NW porch, its
entrance of two orders, the inner a continuous keeled roll, the
outer with keeled shafts with reeded foliage capitals; arch with
diagonally set zigzag that seems to open and shut; chevron
hoodmould. Matching string course above. At the top, a gabled
chamber, probably added later (accessible only from inside, by
ladder). The porch vault (a rarity for parish churches) has diagonal ribs, of two rolls with hollow between, on keeled corner
shafts with decorated trumpet-scallop capitals. The inner
doorway also has a continuous inner order, then shafts with
foliage capitals; arch with frontal chevron. One Norman nave
window W of the porch, both N and S. The S doorway is similar
to the N, but its capitals have decorated trumpet capitals; arch
with a band of lozenges enclosing rosettes connected by
straight lines; hoodmould with beast-stops (one re-set inside,
S arcade, W end). Similar W doorway, with renewed hood; five-
light Perp window above. The W front is flanked by clasping
buttresses rising to square turrets with pyramidal tops, no
doubt influenced by Tewkesbury Abbey nearby.

Inside, the three doorways have, oddly enough, segmental
arches with continuous rolls; N and S have hoodmoulds
forming part of the string course, the W a billet hood, at higher
level. To the same build belongs the W arch of the tower. Continuous outer order, then again keeled shafts with trumpet
capitals; pointed arch with point-to-point chevron meeting at
a thin roll moulding. All this Norman (or Transitional) work
must be of c. 1180–90 at the earliest.* Next followed the S aisle
(or Mitton Chapel); its two-bay arcade has sturdy quatrefoil

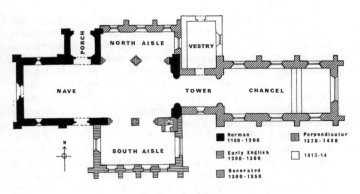

Bredon, St Giles.
Plan

*Willis, in 1863, attributed it to the master of the W bays of Worcester Cathedral,
no doubt the source for many features of common Worcestershire occurrence, especially continuous mouldings alternating with normal arch orders on shafts, and
advanced varieties of zigzag, set diagonally or enfolding a roll.

piers and arches of one chamfered and one rounded step (not
unlike the doorways). That looks early C13, but the beautiful
windows can hardly be earlier than *c.* 1250. The E window and
pairs of S lancets have detached Lias shafts. In its S wall, a large
trefoil-headed piscina and three plain tomb recesses. The two-
bay N arcade seems Perp, despite the Dec windows: piers with
a core of eight polygonal shafts, triple-chamfered arches. Spacious chancel all very early C14; the chancel arch corresponds,
as does the trefoiled piscina and triple-stepped sedilia.

FONT. Plain, octagonal, C15; Jacobean COVER, with nice
scrolls up the edges. – COMMUNION RAILS. Also C17; long
pendants between the balusters. – Most other FURNISHINGS
are early C20 Perp: LECTERN 1923, ORGAN CASE 1926, both
by *Harold Brakspear*; PULPIT 1939, by *A.J.J. Ayres.* – Large
ROYAL ARMS. George III. – TILES. In the chancel, an extremely
interesting early C14 set. Those on the risers of the three altar
steps, entirely heraldic, are probably in their original positions.
They include the arms of England and France, as well as those
of many prominent local families: Berkeley, Mortimer,
Hastings, Beauchamp, Clare; also Bishop Trillek (1344–60),
formerly rector of Bredon. The rearranged tiles on the treads
include a very worn series with inscriptions of the months. –
Nave and aisle floors have a charming perspective chequer
pattern, from *Eginton*'s restoration of *c.* 1843. – STAINED
GLASS. In four chancel side windows excellent grisaille foliage
trails, early C14, with heraldic shields in the tracery lights. The
NW also has two very fine small panels of St Mary of Egypt
and St Mary Magdalene. – E window by *Heaton, Butler &*
Bayne, 1885, with Renaissance detail. – Two heraldic windows
beneath the tower are by *Comper*, 1914. – In the S aisle E, five
C14 shields from Hadzor.

MONUMENTS. In the chancel N wall a renewed C14 tomb
recess, with crockets and pinnacles, moulding of large ballflower, and cusped and sub-cusped arch. Within, the original
blue-stone tomb remains, but on it sits a heavy coped slab with
apparently more ballflower (much weathered), perhaps a
churchyard memorial. – Opposite, an extremely fine effigial
slab with crucifix with lopped-off branches; above the arms,
head-and-shoulder busts of a husband and wife, beneath
crocketed gables; early to mid-C14. – To its r., a tomb recess,
said to be to William Reed †1357: depressed cusped arch,
fleuron frieze along the straight top; on its underside, Christ
in Glory. It contains three late C14 effigies: husband (with cloak
over his l. shoulder, sword between his legs), wife (her feet on
a bedesman), and child. – In the S aisle recesses, three C13
tombs, probably all *in situ*. The most interesting, the narrower
E, has a shield from which issue two arms holding a heart, i.e.
no doubt a heart-burial. The other two have coffin lids with
crosses, the central one of unusual form (cf. Overbury). – The
aisle is dominated by the superb alabaster monument, probably by *Samuel Baldwin*, of John Reed and his wife Catherine
(daughter of Sir Fulke Greville), both †1611. Their finely

29

carved effigies rest on a gadrooned sarcophagus, between black
Composite columns, with coffered arch above; rear inscription
with strapwork. Outside the columns, lower square-topped
side-pieces surmounted by obelisks, for the kneeling children.
Balustraded superstructure with standing putti and more
obelisks; yet higher centre with heraldry. – Tablets include
Charles Parsons †1732, by *Michael Sidnell* of Bristol (s aisle),
and the Rev. Prideaux Sutton †1748, by *T. Ricketts* of Gloucester (chancel E), both of grey marbles. – On the chancel floor,
C17–C18 ledgers, that to Bishop Prideaux, †1650, with brass
inscription, mitre, and corner shields. – Nearby, a bronze wall
plaque of 1914, with the bishop's profile.

Large CHURCHYARD. Small obelisk, NW, to Seth M. Wilkes
†1871, by *Wood* of Bristol. – s of the nave, three medieval monuments. One, a coped coffin lid, now sits on top of a medieval
tomb-chest of large stone blocks, with crosses on the ends and
at the middle of the sides. The other coffin lid has a C13 relief
cross. – LYCHGATE by *Francis B. Andrews & Son*, 1929.

Around the church, an exceptional group of buildings. The OLD
RECTORY, to the N beyond an C18 brick wall, is a C15 stone
house, originally a central hall with big gabled wings. The original roofs survive, of four bays above the centre, with cusped
wind-braces and two rows of collars, the lower arch-braced.
Two small weathered equestrian figures on the roof ridge are
said to represent Cromwell and Charles II. Tall gabled ashlar
porch to the former screens passage, N, with moulded round
arch flanked by Ionic pilasters; probably late C16, though the
cartouche of arms above is dated 1683. The wings, partly brick,
have canted bays probably added in 1771 by *Anthony Keck*. The
house was much enlarged in the 1880s,* but again reduced in
size *c.* 1957 by *M. W. Jones*; his, the rather weak Neo-Cotswold
centre. Some C17 panelling within.

Tall rusticated GATEPIERS with enriched ball finials adjoin
large C18 STABLES, brick with tall stone plinth; raised pyramid-
roofed centre, with blocked archway. The l. half was converted
to parish rooms in 1912, the r. to a dwelling in the 1950s.

PRIOR'S GARDEN to the E, also once part of the rectory, is
now a separate timber-framed cottage with a large C17–C18
brick addition. At the cottage's NE angle, a reconstructed
stone porch, two-storeyed and gabled, with C14–C15 Y-cusped
window above the flat-arched entrance.

NE of the rectory, across Dock Lane, the OLD MANSION, late
C17 brick, with ample stone dressings; three gabled dormers
and renewed mullioned windows. The gabled stone porch must
be entirely C19. C18 brick outbuildings.

BREDON MANOR, W of the church in ample grounds with walled
gardens, is of ashlar, probably late C18, though the singularly
uncouth detail implies an earlier date. W front of 1+3+1 bays,
the centre projecting beneath a three-bay segmental or rather

---

* The then rector, H.G. Cavendish Browne, a relative of the dukes of Portland, kept
eighteen rooms heated and employed fifteen servants.

basket-arched pedimental gable; the central tripartite window and the doorway with elemental Tuscan columns both have a pediment of the same shape. The entrance hall leads to a serpentine staircase. High up on the s return, two horizontal oval windows. The N extension hides an earlier wing, perhaps C16. Alterations by *Charles Armstrong* of Warwick, 1909–10. – Early C19 S LODGE, its gateposts apparently formed from inverted cannon barrels.

To the E of the lodge, at the s end of CHURCH WALK, a MILESTONE of 1808, an obelisk on a high plinth.

W of the manor house, to the rear of the early C19 MANOR FARM, is the splendid MANORIAL BARN built *c.* 1340–50 for the Bishops of Worcester; of coursed oolite rubble with ashlar dressings, 134 ft (41 metres) long by 44 ft (13.5 metres) wide, beneath an enormous steeply pitched stone-slated roof. The barn, given to the National Trust in 1951, was much damaged by fire in 1980; subsequent reconstruction, by *F.W.B. Charles*, reused many original oak timbers. On the E side, two large porches with timber-framed gables, the s one including a remarkable upper solar for the reeve, approached by an external stone stair; it contains a fireplace (its chimney with pierced octagonal flue with pyramidal cap), garderobe in the NW re-entrant angle, and gallery overlooking the middlestead. N and S gable-ends of the barn have differing patterns of slit openings, the W side an impressively regular flat front (without porches). Within, the barn is aisled in nine bays, the only aisled example in the county, and quite unlike those of lowland England. Long arched braces rise from the aisle-posts to high-set tie-beams. These main frames were reared singly from s to N, hence the horizontal strainer-beams connecting the posts some 6 ft (1.8 metres) below the tie-beams are tenoned into the N faces of the braces. The aisle-posts are also arch-braced longitudinally, with apexes abutting the middle purlin; one tier of wind-braces above.

CHURCH STREET, leading E from the lychgate, is uncommonly enjoyable. Near the W end, a mix of early C19 brick and C17 thatched timber-framing, including the FOX AND HOUNDS INN, with good matching rear wing by *L. W. Barnard & Partners*, 1937. Then HANCOCK'S ENDOWED SCHOOL, competent Gothic, stone with trefoiled lancets, by *Harvey Eginton*, 1845; feeble additions of 1931. Opposite, set back by the thatched LONG FURLONG, a former WESLEYAN CHAPEL of 1871, milder Gothic, rendered. At the E end, REED ALMSHOUSES, of 1696, display modest brickwork to Church Street, but have to the s a shallow open courtyard, stone-faced, with Tudor-arched doorways to the (originally) eight dwellings; mullioned windows, mostly with continuous dripmoulds, gabled dormers. The square brick chimneys must date from 1871, when *Bodley & Garner* added the piquant LAUNDRY as a focus for the courtyard: square pavilion, pyramidal roof with pretty wooden louvre, tall chimney to one side. – More pleasant C17–C18 houses in TEWKESBURY ROAD, more or less parallel to the s of Church Street.

CONIGREE (formerly Heatherdale), ¼ m. NNE. An early Modern house set high above tacky later development facing the Avon; designed for himself by *Geoffrey Boumphrey*, 1935–7, with *F.R.S. Yorke* as consultant architect. Cream-washed brick, with large rectangular windows to enjoy the splendid view; flat-roofed, with SE sun-terrace. Entirely horizontal emphasis; only the chimneys provide any vertical accent. The NW end was altered in the 1960s, when a second sun-terrace and integral garage were incorporated into the body of the house. Inside, the reinforced concrete and steel staircase survives.   *p. 88*

WESTMANCOTE, 1¼ m. ENE. A stone-built hamlet straggling up the angle of Bredon Hill. At the SW end, a former BAPTIST CHAPEL of 1878 by *Capel N. Tripp* of Gloucester, partly reusing stone from the earlier chapel of 1771; tall Gothic, with broad side lancets and E plate tracery. The former burial ground lies beyond the rather stark OLD MANSE, late C18, five bays with hipped roof.

A nice group where the road widens further uphill includes a thatched rubble cottage, and C18 farm (GREEN HAYES) with good C18–C19 outbuildings. C17 farms in FARM LANE, to the N.

KINSHAM, a compact hamlet 1¼ m. SE, also has a BAPTIST CHAPEL, of *c.* 1871, built for seceders from the Seventh-Day Baptists at Natton near Ashchurch (*see The Buildings of England: Gloucestershire 2*); brindled brick, three bays, with broad round-arched windows flanking the doorway; hipped slate roof.

Further S, TRUEBLUE FARM, coursed rubble, three wide bays with continuous dripmould; four-centred central doorway with Jacobean carved frieze, leaf spandrels, and cambered hood on brackets. The gable-ends retain original mullioned-and-transomed windows. Garden wall with Tudor-arched gateway dated '1662 WT'. The C17–C18 MANOR FARM, diagonally opposite, is part brick, part stone, plus a little timber framing; earlier brick S range with another four-centred doorway. Brick boundary wall with gatepiers with stone ball finials.

At BREDON'S HARDWICK, 1¼ m. SSW, more C17–C18 farms, and HARDWICK HOUSE, a small, oddly detailed, mid-C19 country house. Tudorish, but with Frenchy detail; steep gables with bracketed eaves. Contemporary lodges.

BREDON HILL   *9030*
Kemerton

The best-known landscape feature of SE Worcestershire, a large hump-backed Cotswold outlier rising to 962 ft (298 metres).

The well-preserved PROMONTORY HILL FORT, also known as Kemerton Camp, on its N spur, was excavated by T.C. Hencken, 1935–7. He suggested two construction periods: the first, with inner rampart of glacis construction with deep outer   *3* ditch and single off-centre entrance, perhaps early CI B.C.; the second, enclosed by an outer rampart doubling the defended area to some 17 acres (7 ha.), about a hundred years later. This latter rampart, also with outer ditch, has a stone revetment and inturned entrances either end. An alternative interpretation is that the outer was the original rampart, of *c.* 300 B.C. Occupation came to a sudden, violent end, possibly in the early CI A.D., when the Belgic peoples were expanding into the area. Bodies of over sixty defenders, many brutally hacked, were found in the ditch adjacent to the inner entrance.

PARSONS' FOLLY, a stone tower at the SW end of the inner rampart, probably built *c.* 1765 as a summer house for John Parsons of Kemerton Court. Square, not particularly high, with chamfered plinth; one plain square opening each side. Now disfigured by telecommunications equipment.

BREDON'S NORTON

₉₀₃₀

ST GILES. A chapelry of Bredon; long and low, with unbuttressed W tower. Chancel and nave are mostly by *Preedy*: the former, with renewed C14 tracery, of 1877, the latter, with paired or single lancets, 1883. Only the nave NE lancet is C13. Another, W wall, was soon covered by the tower, which has a C15–C16 embattled upper stage. Re-set Late Norman S doorway: continuous roll-moulded inner order, thin outer shafts with scalloped capitals (cf. Bredon). The C19 porch entrance has slightly earlier Norman forms (decorated scallop, furrowed chevron, lobed hoodmould), probably from the former N doorway, all re-cut 1883. Early C13 chancel arch of three moulded orders, the inner with broad fillet; capitals with stiff-leaf perversely growing horizontally. Sturdy C19 arch-braced roofs, of Baltic fir. – FONT. Plain, heptagonal, perhaps C15, severely scraped. – Oak PULPIT and PEWS by *Preedy*. – ORGAN. By *John Snetzler*, *c.* 1760. – STAINED GLASS. E by *Hardman*, 1891. – Nave NW by *Gerald Paxton*, 2000. – MONUMENT. Large tablet to William Hancocke †1719 and his wife Mary †1685, perhaps erected *c.* 1693; black and white marble, Composite columns, broken segmental pediment.

Attractive VILLAGE, part stone, part brick, with several C17 timber-framed and thatched cottages. The stone SCHOOL (now village hall), SW of the church, said to be of 1876, looks earlier; plain Tudor with W bellcote and porch. To W and NW, extensive mid-C19 farm buildings of BROOKSIDE FARM, stone with brick trim. BROOKSIDE HOUSE, rendered early C19, has a C17 gabled S wing.

BREDON'S NORTON MANOR, ⅛ m. ESE. The earliest part must be the long stone central range, gabled with two-storey dormers and some original mullioned windows; gabled porch. Remodelled 1585 when Thomas and Margaret Copley added the tall timber-framed N wing (restored 2000). Their initials are high up on the broad stone N chimney-breast, and (with the date) on the four-centred fireplace of the first-floor great chamber. Stone S wing, mostly C19. – Handsome ARCHWAY to the front garden, also dated 1585. Moulded round arch, fluted frieze above, gable on pilasters starting in an unstructural manner from a kind of trefoil (cf. Woollas Hall, p. 279). – LODGE of *c.* 1840, inflated *c.* 1900. – Further N, a large C16–C17 BARN (now housing); stone and timber-framed, thatched roof, half-hipped end gables.

NORTON PARK, ¼ m. E. Built for Frances Penelope Martin, elder daughter of Robert Martin of Overbury (q.v.), perhaps by *G. S. Repton*; cf. Dumbleton Hall, Glos. Dated 1830, but said not to have been completed until 1839. Large Tudor Gothic country house, of good ashlar, already Victorian in layout and stylistic detail: large mullioned-and-transomed windows, gabled dormers with ball finials, lower S service wing, grouped diagonal chimneys. Closer inspection reveals the detailing to be very flat, especially the gabled rectangular bay window (to the library) adjoining the shallow porch, E front. The two-storey (drawing room) bay with ball-finialled parapet on the garden front, W, has scarcely greater depth, nor the projecting W and N oriels. – Contemporary STABLES, SE, later enlarged. – Cotswold-style LODGE dated 1867.

CROSS COTTAGES, on the B4080, ⅔ m. SSW. An unusual group dated 1839; cruciform plan, gabled and roughcast. – NORTON COTTAGES, on the same road (⅓ m. WNW) are more conventional Gothick of 1820.

BRETFORTON

0040

The most attractive of the Vale of Evesham villages, its buildings a mix of Cotswold or Lias stone, brick, and timber and plaster, with some thatch. The manor belonged to Evesham Abbey from the early C8.

ST LEONARD. Long late C13 chancel, the detail consistent with a re-consecration of 1295 (cf. Honeybourne): cusped side lancets apart from the N and S sanctuary windows, with cusped Y-tracery; renewed E window of three stepped cusped lancets.[*] The same motifs in the S transept S and W windows, and the N aisle W. Dec N transept N window. All other openings in the short aisles and transepts are Perp; also the battlemented W tower. The interior is much older. Both arcades are late C12–early C13, the S probably ten or twenty years earlier than the N. Both have pointed arches and round piers with round abaci, but the S capitals are excessively high trumpet scallops and the arches have a single step only. The N arches have a step and a chamfer, the flatter capitals, decorated trumpets. The W pier here has four heads, and the E a lively dragon devouring a human, no doubt St Margaret being swallowed and

[*] On the central S buttress, a good pair of MASS DIALS.

regurgitated; the dragon's tail sprouts into leaves (cf. the font at Elmley Castle). Style and choice of subject point to inspiration from the s transept and nave of Wells Cathedral, work of c. 1210–15. Nailhead decoration on the E respond. The original N aisle roof pitch is still visible. The W end presents a puzzle. The s arcade's W pier was originally a respond. Its W half and the half-arch connecting it with the tower are probably of 1847. But on the N side the three-bay arcade is complete. Where then was the W wall? It must have been in agreement with the N side, with, on the s, a piece of the s wall of the preceding aisleless nave left standing, with its SW respond set a little further E. Also of 1847, when *Solomon Hunt* restored the church, the shallow N and S porches and all roofs. No chancel arch, though steps to the rood loft remain.

FONT. Plain Norman, with cover dated 1721. – PULPIT. 1895. – REREDOS by the *Campden Guild*, 1911–12. – STALLS brought from Stratford-upon-Avon in 1898, so probably by *Bodley & Garner*, 1890. – PEWS of c. 1871 (from St Peter, Bengeworth). – The Ashwin FAMILY PEW, s transept, is made up from Jacobean pieces; leaf panels and blank arches separated by atlantes, similar to that in the Manor (*see* below). Door panel dated 1615. – Early C19 DECALOGUE and CREED, the latter now at the W end. – ROYAL ARMS. 1814. – STAINED GLASS. C15 bits in the aisles and N transept. – Stiff E window by *Preedy*, 1857. – Small s transept W by *Paul Woodroffe*, 1941. – The rest all by *A.L. Moore*, 1894–1902, except the chancel NE, by *Jones & Willis*, 1891, and chancel NW, by *T.F. Curtis, Ward & Hughes*, 1899.

In the CHURCHYARD, headstones of c. 1800 with Resurrection ovals, especially two s of the chancel: Sarah Ford †1797 (by *Samuel Hobday*), and its eroded neighbour (by *Thomas Laughton*), with Christ emerging from a sarcophagus. – Opposite the s porch, a neat square TOILET/BOILER ROOM, stone, with hipped roof, by *David Duckham*, 2004–5. Nearby, in the CHURCHYARD WALL of 1847, a s gateway, to the Manor, with Jacobean ball finials and flowing Dec tracery (where from?). Small rectangular windows further W, said to have formed part of the village lock-up.

SCHOOL, N, dated 1876. Tudor Gothic, stone, with pretty wooden bell-turret. Later brick additions behind.

THE CROSS, a square SE of the church, now mostly under tarmac, is surrounded by a good C17–early C19 mix. At its s corner, the FLEECE INN, owned by the National Trust. Of square-panelled framing, probably in origin an early C15 open hall with floored N service wing (with living chamber above). The hall was floored in the C16, the building enlarged in the C17–C18. Good pub interior, restored after a fire in 2004. Further SW, MANOR FARM, late C17, stone; gables and mullioned windows.

MAIN STREET, running SE–NW, is the village spine. To the SE, past UPPER END HOUSE (No. 73), large, part C17 stone, part narrow studding, it soon reaches UPPER END, a cul-de-sac with two more large farms. BRETFORTON HOUSE, late C18, is quite sophisticated: three bays, brick with ample stone dressings, with four Venetian windows with rusticated voussoirs; large C18–C19 barns. TOP FARM, probably late C16, is best seen from the S, where gabled projections form a U-plan: brewhouse, r., taller wing dated 1649, l., plus further C18 additions.

In Main Street, NW of the church, stone gabled COTTAGES, dated 1605, restored 1877, their garden entrance with reused crocketed finial. The same dates may apply to BRETFORTON MANOR. Its stone frontages seem entirely 1870s remodelling for W.H. Ashwin; lively entrance façade with gabled dormers with ball finials and canted and battlemented two-storey bay. Entrance hall behind, lined with vigorous Jacobean panelling. In the gardens an excellent collection of buildings, probably mostly C18: timber-framed and thatched CIDER HOUSE (retaining its press), rectangular stone DOVECOTE dated 1743, and, in a line further N, timber AVIARY and APIARY, the village STOCKS beneath a rustic canopy, and a similar SUMMER-HOUSE overlooking the churchyard (inside, a re-set medieval corbel head).

BRETFORTON HALL, almost opposite, is charming three-bay Gothick, probably of c. 1800. Stuccoed, with ogee-headed windows with Y-tracery; convex porch with ogee arches on fluted Roman Doric columns. Similar E return and octagonal embattled tower, NE, with lancets and semicircular angle buttresses. The porch leads into an elongated entrance hall, with restrained Gothick stair, the upper landing supported on a nodding ogee arch. At the plainer Gothic rear, a ballroom with conventional mid-C19 plaster decoration. In the garden, the original E window of the church, now in fragments.

Further NW, another notable group stands at the angle with the B4035, centred on the Neo-Cotswold VILLAGE HALL, of 1920 by *Guy Dawber*. To its N, a thatched group of c. 1700 (Nos. 1–3 Shop Lane), timber-framed and brick. To its W, the former HOME FARM (No. 41 Main Street), late C17, ashlar, three bays, with two-light mullioned windows and platband. Immediately adjoining, almost the same in height, its Lias rubble DOVECOTE. Then a lower BARN, part rubble, part square framing. Thatched rubble cottages, Nos. 33–35, complete this fine C17 group. Further attractive cottages and houses stretch further W along Main Street.

BRETFORTON GRANGE, ½ m. WNW, an expanded L-plan house of Lias with ashlar dressings, was an important grange of Evesham Abbey. Its main N–S range, probably early C14, was no doubt an open hall above an undercroft. This survives, tunnel-vaulted, with three single-chamfered round transverse arches. Of the hall, one NW window, two trefoiled lights under a straight head, remains. It was otherwise subdivided and given mullioned windows in the C17. The attic, with braced collar roof with vertical ashlar pieces, was converted to a theatre in 1979 by *Patrick Burton*, reached by an external stone stair, NE. Lower SW service wing, and projecting S wing dated 1635 on its door hood; the gabled angle turret contains a C17 baluster stair. – To the N, a very long C15 BARN, timber-framed and weatherboarded, with Lias plinth; two gabled porches either side. Originally eleven bays, with tie-beam and braced collar roof, the two W bays replaced by a brick cartshed c. 1800. Further C19 barns to the E. All restored and converted to a theatre complex, 1987–90. – Further NE, a rectangular DOVECOTE, probably also C15, rendered Lias, with tiled gambrel roof; 800 nest holes inside.

The OLD VICARAGE, ¼ m. SE, of 1846–7, is probably by *Solomon Hunt*. Brick, with wide eaves; double pile, each end expressed as a pair of pediments, all four pierced by solid chimneys. Central round-arched doorway on the SE end.

₉₀₄₀
BRICKLEHAMPTON

ST MICHAEL. A chapelry of St Andrew, Pershore. Mostly by *Henry Woodyer*, who rebuilt the chancel (with N vestry) in 1875, and restored the remainder, 1876–7. The timber S porch is his and, mostly, the meagre W tower with saddleback roof. Much of the nave is medieval. Late C12 S doorway, its arch with chevron set diagonally in the inner order, frontally in the outer; shafts with trumpet-scallop capitals decorated with small sprouting leaves (cf. Bredon). To its E, a blocked lancet and late C13 trefoil-cusped one. C19 windows vary from lancets to Dec-style. Nave roof partly medieval, also sedilia and trefoiled piscina. – Woodyer's REREDOS and polygonal PULPIT are both stone, relatively plain. – FONT. Norman; large tapering bowl, its only carving two crosses and two rosettes (cf. South Littleton and Bishampton). – STAINED GLASS. E window by *Hardman*, 1877. – Chancel side lancets, 1887, and tower W, 1898, all by *Kempe*. – Poor nave NE by *Jones & Willis*, 1915; two other windows probably by *William Pearce Ltd*, c. 1900–5. – MONUMENTS. Some good tablets, especially Francis Palmer †1715, with fine lettering. – LYCHGATE. 1914.

CHURCH HOUSE, SW, is mostly timber-framed, c. 1600; gabled E cross-wing with brick chimneystack.

BRICKLEHAMPTON HALL, ¼ m. SW. By *S. W. Daukes*, 1848, for the Pershore solicitor, Francis Woodward; an excellent example of a small ashlar-faced Italianate country house. The asymmetrically placed tower, with open Tuscan-arcaded top stage, is particularly characteristic. It stands at the NW corner, its ground floor serving as an outer hall, with bow-fronted breakfast room, E. The rest of the L-plan N front was service accommodation. The show front faces the garden, S; of nine bays, with quoins: ground-floor windows round-arched, the first-floor with eared architraves. A full-height bow (to the library) occupies the three central bays; the flanking drawing and dining rooms have similar single-storey bows on their returns. Additions by *Daukes*, 1866, included a billiard room, SE, now overshadowed by a plain block of 1985 for nursing home use.

Inside, the hall forms a W–E spine containing the top-lit stair-case, with French-looking iron balustrades and blind-arcaded walls.

STABLES, at right angles to the N front, no doubt also by *Daukes*; brick, stone quoins, three pedimental gables, pretty cupola. Further E, the KITCHEN GARDEN, its cemented wall with blind arcading. The Long Walk to its S leads to an Italianate SUMMERHOUSE. – Matching LODGES, also one or two ESTATE COTTAGES.

BROADHEATH
(or Lower Broadheath)

Mostly outer suburban Worcester, its two parts separated by a rough common.

CHRIST CHURCH. 1903–4 by *C.F. Whitcombe*, his only new church in the county. Of Holt sandstone; Free Perp style with raking buttresses. Not large, though with narrow S aisle, S porch, and W tower. This, with its pierced battlements and crocketed pinnacles, seems rather top-heavy; the unusual fen-estration of the lowest stage reflects its varying uses: vestry below, musicians' gallery above. Gilded galleon weathervane of 1920. The S porch also provides access to the tower and its undercroft. Four-bay S arcade with octagonal piers, meant to be cut into quatrefoil form (see the uncompleted E pier); matching chancel arch. Good wagon roofs. – Oak FITTINGS by *Whitcombe*, in his usual Perp style, but the striking COM-MUNION RAILS (1910) and REREDOS (1908) have organic plant forms verging on Art Nouveau. – Plain octagonal FONT, 1903, with tall COVER carved by *R. Haughton*. – STAINED GLASS. *Whitcombe* also designed the E window, 1904, and sanc-tuary N, 1908; cf. Feckenham. – Nave NW by *Powell & Sons*, 1911. – S aisle windows by *Camm & Co.*, 1942, and *Jones & Willis*, 1926. – Simple LYCHGATE, *c.* 1905.

The earlier CHURCH, to the NW, a plain Tudor Gothic brick rectangle by *Harvey Eginton*, 1836, now forms part of the SCHOOL. This is mostly of 1872–3 by *Henry Rowe*: banded brick, the end windows stepped triplets.

The OLD VICARAGE, a little N, built 1909–10, may also be by *C.F. Whitcombe*. Schizophrenic façades, the S with two unequal half-timbered gables, the W of brick, with canted bays linked by a timber balcony. Patterned parapets.

Former COUNTESS OF HUNTINGDON'S CHAPEL, ¼ m. SE. Dated 1825. Red brick, round-arched windows; three bays long. Entrance front with gabled parapet and later C19 porch.

PEACHLEY MANOR, ⅜ m. ENE. Tall, narrow, brick, mostly early C19; three bays and storeys, rusticated lintels, central Doric doorway.

TEMPLE LAUGHERNE HOUSE, 1 m. ESE; mid-C19 brick, gabled Tudor Gothic, with large windows and tall star-shaped chimneys.

LOWER TEMPLE LAUGHERNE, 1⅜ m. SE, even closer to Worcester, is a rectangular red brick farmhouse of *c.* 1680; two storeys beneath a big hipped roof.

Beyond the common, 1 m. S, is the ELGAR BIRTHPLACE MUSEUM: the modest mid-C19 cottage where the composer was born, plus a low-key brick exhibition centre of 2000, discreetly sited to its N.

BROAD MARSTON *see* PEBWORTH

BROADWAS

ST MARY MAGDALENE. By the Teme. Sandstone nave and chancel of *c.* 1200, the former with a couple of inserted Perp windows and a fine S chantry chapel added in the mid C14. Of *c.* 1200, the small, deeply splayed lancets, especially handsome on the renewed N side, with a doorway of simple round-arched Norman form. The pointed S doorway, of three orders, has lively mouldings of rolls and fillets, and shafts with (eroded) capitals with waterleaf and heads. The nave was later extended W to enclose a timber-framed bell-turret, but the present square pyramid-roofed turret, together with the attractive W wall, timber S porch, and Dec-style E and SW windows of the chancel, belong to the restoration of 1881–5 by *Charles Hodgson Fowler* of Durham, younger brother of the rector. The ashlar S chantry chapel can be closely dated: dedicated 1340, complete by 1344. It has a separate steeply gabled roof and good flowing Dec tracery; the pair of cusped E lancets with small mouchette wheel above are specially attractive. String course beneath the windows, continuing across the stepped buttresses (gabled with blind cusped tracery). Within, the chapel is separated from the nave E end by a two-bay arcade with quatrefoil piers: moulded capitals, sunk quadrant arch mouldings. E lancets with moulded rere-arches; two S windows with hoodmoulds on headstops. Ogee-headed piscina (also a simpler trefoiled piscina in the chancel). The bell-turret space is divided from the nave by renewed timbering, with C17 balcony RAILING (probably from former communion rails). All the roofs by *Hodgson Fowler.* No chancel arch.

FONT. Octagonal bowl, round stem with multi-scalloped top; *c.* 1200, much renewed. – In the NW corner of the nave, some plain C17 BENCHES with moulded top rails. – PULPIT. Dated 1632. Rather bold carved decoration including scroll patterns; contemporary tester with pendants, set high up. – TILES. The chancel floor has an excellent C15–C16 display, reassembled by *Fowler*; much heraldry, with some sixteen-tile patterns in the sanctuary, including Berkeley arms. – Blocky ORGAN CASE of 1978 (by *Trevor Tipple & Peter Hughes*). – STAINED GLASS. Three typical windows by *Burlison & Grylls*: E 1898, S chapel 1911–12. – Chancel NW by *Chapel Studios*, 1974; NE, with C15–C16 fragments from Fowler's own collection, installed 1950. – MONUMENTS. Henry Roberts †1761 and family; by *W. Stephens c.* 1800. Of white marble, with draped urn in an aedicule with fluted pilasters and open pediment. – Also tablets by *J. Stephens* and early C18 ledgers.

In the CHURCHYARD, the base and stump of a C15 cross, restored 1900; the base has a niche, S, for the pyx or a lamp (cf. Severn Stoke). – Nearby, a neat group of three early C19 CHEST TOMBS, with Grecian detail.

BROADWAS COURT, NW. Early C19 brick. Rambling rear towards the church, but an upright, formal N front of five bays and two-and-a-half storeys. This has segment-headed windows, moulded eaves cornice, and rusticated stone porch with fluted Doric pilasters and small pediment.

Church Lane meets the A44 opposite THE CEDARS, large, brick, with pierced bargeboards and segment-headed windows, probably by *Henry Rowe, c.* 1880 (cf. Grimley Vicarage). To its W, STONE FARM, probably a C15 cruck hall house refronted in brick in the C19. Fine late C16 gabled cross-wing, W, of square-panelled framing; to its side a big sandstone chimney-breast and an odd little projection, jettied on brackets, not apparently a porch. The C19 brick hop kiln attached to the W end, and C17 weatherboarded BARN and STABLE complete a most attractive group.

The VILLAGE straggles E along the main road to the SCHOOL, S side, by *Perkins,* 1862–3; banded brick with nice plate-traceried window, plus house of 1869, now submerged by the usual C20 additions. By BROOK FARM, C16–C17 with gabled W cross-wing, the road turns NE. In the by-passed section here, more interesting farms. BUTTS FARM has a two-bay cruck-framed centre flanked by C17 square-panelled wings, the W slightly jettied, the E to an L-plan; C20 additions. Behind BUTTS BANK HOUSE, early C19 brick, further uphill, is a weatherboarded BARN on a sandstone plinth, once Butts Bank Farm (and formerly attached). This is probably a remnant of a C14 cruck-built LONGHOUSE. The present house must have replaced its solar bay and half the upper hall bay; the two lower or 'animal' bays remain, plus a further bay, probably C15.

BROADWAY

Broadway is the show village of England. Pevsner, writing in 1968, thought it deserved its fame, at least when its delights were not being swamped by tourists. He added: 'There is only one thing to be said against it. Everybody over the years has been so full of good will, so tactful, so conformist to its beauties that the result has become almost too good to be true. Broadway is by no means lacking in variety. Not only are Tudor, Stuart, and Georgian happily mixed, but the early C20 also has contributed, not in the modern idiom, but by the efforts of architects of sensibility and some individuality. A walk through Broadway should be taken seriously and done at leisure.' His assessment remains valid; judiciously sited car parks and a by-pass (opened 1998) have prevented too much further smothering of its attractions.

A glance at the map shows how Worcestershire has plundered Broadway from Gloucestershire, no doubt because it was a possession of Pershore Abbey from at least the late c10. A permanent market, established 1251 (perhaps also borough status), must have lapsed by the c15. The Dissolution apparently brought greater prosperity. In 1660 the mapmaker John Ogilby described Broadway as 'a well-built town of five furlongs length affording several good inns . . .' Its strategic position on the Worcester–London road, at the foot of Fish Hill, the steep Cotswold escarpment, led to increasing importance in the coaching era, but by the mid c19 it had become a rural backwater. 'Rediscovery' began in 1885, when Broadway became something of an artists' colony for illustrators working for *Harper's Magazine* of New York: the Americans Edwin Abbey and Frank D. Millet, and the Englishman Alfred Parsons. They were soon joined by John Singer Sargent, then by Edmund Gosse and Henry James. Of the 'architects of sensibility' the earliest to arrive was *Guy Dawber*, who described Broadway in *The Builder* of 1888; then, early in the c20, *C.E. Bateman* of Birmingham (at first working in the Evesham office of *G.H. Hunt*) and the ubiquitous London-based Scot *A.N. Prentice*. The railway arrived in 1904, the year S.B. Russell bought the fine but neglected Lygon Arms hotel. By *c.* 1907 he had begun a sideline selling and repairing antiques, a business expanded into a major furniture-making concern by his eldest son (*Sir*) *Gordon Russell* (1892–1980). The youngest son Dick (*R.D. Russell*), who trained as an architect, carried out design work for both family businesses. The stories of the hotel and the development of tourism, and of the furniture workshops (closed 2000) are closely interwoven for most of the c20.

CHURCHES

ST EADBURGHA. Beautifully sited ¾ m. s, in a fold between the Broadway and Buckland hills. Externally mostly Perp: cruciform, with fine central tower with battlements and pinnacles. Blocked openings in the N transept and s aisle relate to former c17–c18 galleries. Much of the interior, however, is of *c.* 1200. Three-bay nave arcades with round piers with trumpet-scallop or moulded capitals, round abaci, slightly pointed arches with double step or one step and one chamfer. Of this Late Norman building, once one watches for it, two W buttresses and the stump of the middle E buttress also tell; so the Norman church extended to its present length. The crossing is confusing, as the tower was built into the nave. The piers of its fourth bay were preserved, also the E responds, though their capitals were crowned with battlements (perhaps for supporting images). The tower's W and E arches are c14, and not too late, with their beautifully sheer continuous double chamfers. But the plain imposts of the chancel arch of *c.* 1200 also seem to survive, just W of the E arch, adapted as supports for the vanished rood loft. The inner chamfers of the narrower N and s arches die into their imposts. Beneath the tower, a vault of eight ribs radiates from the moulded circular bell-opening (cf. Hampton, p. 294), Perp like the upper parts. Perp also most of the chancel windows; the three-light sw has odd rather thin tracery, perhaps early C19, but its deep inner splay has a convincingly Perp roll moulding. Earlier evidence includes a blocked N door (replaced by a C17 one close to the NE corner); blocked C13 S lancet, plus remnant of another; and the trefoiled piscina with continuous roll mouldings. The S transept must be late C13, see the renewed S window with three stepped trefoiled lights; C16 E window. Both transepts were extensively restored in 1865, when the lead roof of the nave was replaced with Cotswold stone tiles, its arcade plinths cut down from square to circular, and plain floor tiles inserted. The C15 arch-braced nave roof, with pretty wall-plate with fleurons, was stabilized in 1916 by *C.E. Bateman*, with the insertion of two tie-beams. The chancel was restored in 1890.

COMMUNION RAIL. Sturdy Jacobean, with knobs and narrowly spaced balusters; contemporary ALTAR TABLE. – STALLS, under the tower, those at the rear supporting PAR-CLOSE SCREENS; all probably made up from C15–C16 benches. – Present PEWS *c.* 1840, from St Michael (*see* below). – PULPIT. C15, wood, with Perp panels; stone base by *Harold Brakspear*, 1927. – Circular ALMS BOX nearby, perhaps C16. – FONT. A plain truncated cone, presumably Norman; plinth with reused C15 TILES. – By the N door a tall hexagonal stem (for a font?) with slender attached shafts with moulded capitals; probably late C13. – ROYAL ARMS. Charles I; dated 1641. – STAINED GLASS. C15 fragments in several windows, mostly quarries and borders. Medieval shield in the E window, small damaged head of Christ in the W; here also C17 Sambach arms. MONUMENTS. Two parts of a late C13 (?) priest's effigy, now lying in a medieval stone coffin in the S transept. Nearby, a C13 coffin lid with relief cross. – Brass to Antony Daston †1572. The stolen central figure in armour has been renewed. The original was a palimpsest, its underside part of a Flemish brass, of which another section is at Westerham (Kent). – Walter Savage. Small tablet of 1640, still entirely Jacobean; Composite columns and strapwork. – William Taylor †1741, signed *Samuel Chandler*. Large marble tablet with columns and open segmental pediment with cartouche of arms; in the frieze, two cherubs holding a crown. – The Rev. David Davies †1819, by *W. Clemson* of Broadway; pretty, black slate with gold lettering (nave W). – Thomas Phillips †1818; black and white marble tomb-chest of 1820, with Ionic corner demi-columns.

Large CHURCHYARD with many C17–C18 chest tombs and headstones. – The new CEMETERY ⅛ m. s has a LYCHGATE by *Gordon Russell*, 1931.

ST MICHAEL, Church Street. 1839–40 by *Harvey Eginton*, on the site of a chapel of 1608.* A fine church in convincing E.E. style, solidly built of local ashlar. Nave with aisles, deep chancel, and

---

* Its bell-cupola is now at Fresden near Highworth, Wiltshire.

w tower with angle buttresses, paired-lancet bell-openings and
solid parapet with pinnacles like little broach spires. Aisle w
windows with authentic-looking bar tracery; side lancets and
stepped buttresses more typical of *c.* 1840. The porches-cum-
vestries at the aisle e ends are a surprise. The chancel lancets
and stepped e triplet are enriched with nook-shafts. Inside,
five-bay nave arcades with circular piers with four attached
shafts; lancet clerestory. Plaster quadripartite rib vaults, on tall
wall-shafts with stiff-leaf capitals. The aisle ceilings are flat, as
there were originally n and s galleries (removed 1918); the w
gallery survives. Window mouldings are decidedly flatter inside
than out. Restored and re-seated in 1890.

Carved stone REREDOS, 1874; stone ALTAR TABLE of 1840.
– Perp-style SCREEN (1921) and CHOIR STALLS (1926). –
PULPIT. A sumptuous early C17 piece with tester, over-restored
in 1920; probably from the chapel of 1608, though for many
years at St Eadburgha. Blank arches with elaborate carving
beneath dragon panels. – FONT. 1840, typically thin; engraved
slate plinth by *Bryant Fedden*, 1964. – STAINED GLASS.
Chancel e by *Clayton & Bell*, 1901; side windows by *J.E.
Nuttgens* 1959. His also two by the font, 1966. – Other aisle
windows by *Burlison & Grylls*, 1922–35.

ST SAVIOUR (R.C.), Leamington Road. Built 1828–9 for
Benedictines, see the arched side windows. The Passionists
took over in 1850, remodelling the church with double bellcote
above the sanctuary and unsubtle Neo-Norman façade. –
Large stone and marble ALTAR of 1900. Wall decoration of this
date, removed 1935, was partly replaced with oak panelling
incorporating STALLS. – PEWS probably of 1850–1. The
original MONASTERY at the rear, begun 1830, is plain Late
Georgian: six bays, double-pile. Much enlarged, at right angles
to the church, in 1909 by *Curran & Sons* of Warrington: two
storeys of tall mullioned windows, E.E.-style doorway.

ST JOSEPH'S COTTAGE (No. 26), SE, the schoolteacher's
house, is by *C.F. Hansom*, 1855; Tudor-style, twin gables. Less
sophisticated SCHOOL, s, of 1851.

CONGREGATIONAL CHAPEL (now United Reformed), High
Street. Set back behind its former graveyard. 1842–3 by *J. &
R. Varden*, drastically altered by *Peter W. Neale*, 1961. He reduced
the height, eliminating windows from the n entrance front;
shallow pedimental gable. Inside only the altered PULPIT of
1842–3 remains. – STAINED GLASS. Two re-set windows of
c. 1902–7 by *F. Holt & Co.*

MANSE (No. 77), to the NE, of 1897. Gabled Cotswold
revival.

(WESLEYAN) METHODIST CHAPEL, High Street. Of 1811, with
the original doorway (now blocked) in the centre of the long
w wall. Remodelled *c.* 1860: windows made round-arched, new
entrance (with porch) on the steeply gabled s front.

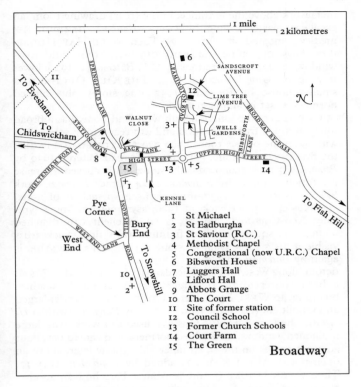

1 mile
2 kilometres

To Evesham
To Chidswickham
11
SPRINGFIELD LANE
STATION ROAD
WALNUT CLOSE
7
8
9
15
1
Pye Corner
SNOWSHILL ROAD
West End
WEST END LANE
Bury End
To Snowshill
KENNEL LANE
BACK LANE
HIGH STREET
13
3
4
5
(UPPER) HIGH STREET
14
LEAMINGTON ROAD
SANDSCROFT AVENUE
6
12
LIME TREE AVENUE
WELLS GARDENS
BIBSWORTH LANE
BROADWAY BY-PASS
CHELTENHAM ROAD
N
To Fish Hill
10
2

1   St Michael
2   St Eadburgha
3   St Saviour (R.C.)
4   Methodist Chapel
5   Congregational (now U.R.C.) Chapel
6   Bibsworth House
7   Luggers Hall
8   Lifford Hall
9   Abbots Grange
10   The Court
11   Site of former station
12   Council School
13   Former Church Schools
14   Court Farm
15   The Green

Broadway

PERAMBULATIONS

The essential perambulation (3a and 3b) starts from the Green,
at the w end of the broad, gently curving High Street (from
which the settlement takes it name). Before embarking on the
High Street, however, it may be as well to examine Bury End
(near the old church), and Church Street between the new
church and the green, plus the few interesting buildings to its
NW.

1. Bury End (and West End)

THE COURT, N of St Eadburgha, incorporates the late C16 gatehouse of Broadway Court (on the E side of Snowshill Road,
demolished 1773). Moulded round archway with imposts and
small roundels above with crests and the quartered arms of
Sheldon; all beneath a gabled five-light mullioned-and-
transomed window. Simpler archway inside. The adjoining
block (presumably porter's lodging) is contemporary, but the
rest of the gabled house was added in 1898 by *E. Guy Dawber
& Whitwell*; stone with some half-timbering. Portcullis-like

metalwork above the entrance; in the (rear) drawing room, an excellent plaster ceiling by *George Bankart*. GAZEBO, NE; medieval moated site further N. Then MILL HAY HOUSE, three bays, C17 stone rear, early C19 brick front with cross-windows and other alterations by *C.E. Bateman*, *c.* 1920; lower N wing by *Guy Pemberton*, 1934. THE OLD ORCHARD, a smaller house by *Bateman*, 1932, one storey plus hipped dormers, is set in ample grounds.

PYE CORNER, at the junction with West End Lane, has a broad four-bay stone front of *c.* 1800 and C17 rear wings; square bay window at the side, *c.* 1900. Then two THATCHED COTTAGES: the first C17, part stone, part timber-framed (altered 1930 by *Pemberton*); the second, mostly stone, with curved staircase projection, entirely by *Bateman*, 1924. Other *Bateman* work follows: Nos. 45–47, 1937, utilitarian semi-detached, of stone, and Nos. 41–43, set back, of 1936, asymmetrical, more typically Neo-Cotswold. No. 39 is an excellent C16 thatched cottage, of square-panelled framing, with fine cruck truss visible in its S gable wall; its stone N part, MEADOWSIDE, is again by *Bateman*, 1936.

A detour along West End Lane leads, past PYE CORNER FARM, a barn converted by *Bateman*, 1923, with much weather-boarding, to WEST END. Here, COPGROVE is C17, enlarged and rebuilt end-on to the lane in 1910 by *Bateman* (with *G.H. Hunt*). The long S front is mostly reused C17 work, with large mullioned windows, two gabled dormers, and canted bay. Four adjacent gables on the N, entrance side, the W later, above an open porch. Music Room, E, added by *Pemberton*, 1911–12. Then WYCK HOUSE (formerly Manor Farmhouse), another broad stone front of *c.* 1800, with some tripartite windows.

2. South and north-west of the green

A fresh start can be made in CHURCH STREET, S of St Michael. The prominent AUSTIN HOUSE of *c.* 1700, ashlar, five bays, is set back behind fine tall panelled gatepiers with ball finials. Long side wing, SE, between a bow window of 1865, with Jaco-bethan detail, and a plainer one from additions of *c.* 1990 by *Peter Yiangou Associates*. Alterations of 1898 by *Dawber* included a new garden layout.

Facing the church, a stone thatched late C17 cottage, and an odd pair of *c.* 1900 with straight-sided bays and roughcast gables projected to be flush with their fronts. Then BANNITS (formerly the Bakers' Arms), early C17 L-plan, with gables and mullioned windows. N wing, mostly roughcast, by *Bateman*, 1912–13.

Opposite, No. 16 (KYLSANT HOUSE) is also C17, much altered 1874; excellent re-set early C17 doorway with fluted engaged Ionic columns and delightful swan-neck pediment carved with a thick garland. Further N, past the early C19 CROWN AND TRUMPET INN, No. 4 was formerly two cottages of *c.* 1700, one stone, one timber-framed, both thatched.

ABBOT'S GRANGE, set back, W side, once a summer residence of the Abbots of Pershore, is archaeologically the most important house in Broadway: C14, with C16–C17 alterations and good early C20 wings, one N, two to the W. The early C14 core is L-shaped, with an extension S beyond the L to where one chamfered jamb of the original gateway survives. The (N) stem of the L is the hall (originally with service range to its N), the short cross-wing the solar, or abbot's study, with his chapel (or oratory) projecting slightly further E from the angle between hall and solar. The former has two E windows of two trefoiled lights with transoms, the southernmost, with ogee heads, in a skew position to admit light in spite of the chapel wing. The first-floor chapel has a fine E window of two lights with a reticulation unit but no transom, and ogee-headed side lancets; small chamber beneath with original rectangular windows E and S. The two-light transomed E window of the solar is simpler, so as not to compete with that of the chapel. The S extension was much altered in the C16–C17, but its S end wall still shows C14 work. On the W front the most prominent window is that of the solar, here flush with the hall but with a tall gable; also two lights with transom, but a reticulation unit in the head beneath a two-centred arch. The hall has two differing W windows, each of two lights with transoms and ogee head, both entirely renewed.

The hall is entered near its N end, its main entrance from the W (now with renewed porch). The three service doorways from the screens passage are preserved, the E two ogee-headed, the W wider with three-centred head. At the high-table end, S, another ogee-headed doorway leads to the (renewed) staircase. Roof with arched braces to collar-beams, and one tier of windbraces. From the chapel there is a circular window, originally

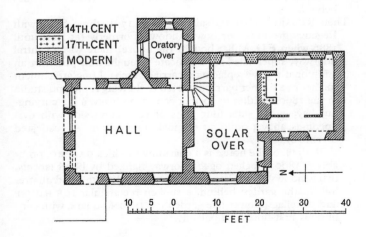

Broadway, Abbot's Grange.
Plan of medieval extent

quatrefoiled. A much narrower squint, deeply splayed, spies into the hall from the solar (with similar wind-braced roof). The solar screen, with one-light Dec tracery divisions, is not *in situ*. Room S of the solar with good C16–C17 panelling.

In 1885, after Abbot's Grange had suffered years of decay as a parish workhouse and lock-up, Edwin Abbey and F.D. Millet began a series of minor alterations. In 1907–8, the medieval range was extended N, no doubt by *A.N. Prentice*, to include a studio for Millet (†1912), with huge six-light E window with three transoms. *Prentice*, in 1912–13, subdivided its interior and added a SW servants' wing, with perfunctory half-timbering. In 1933 *Bateman* added a NW wing with broadly canted two-storey S bay window with battered chimney above, and W entrance with fat circular columns, leading to a garden hall; barrel-vaulted day nursery above.

At the N end of Church Street two contrasting houses face the Green. THE HOUSE ON THE GREEN, late C18, 3+1 bays, is not too formal. FARNHAM HOUSE, *c.* 1660, is almost symmetrical, with continuous dripmoulds and two high gabled dormers with horizontal blank ovals; central doorway of *c.* 1900. Paired diagonally set chimneys with lozenge friezes, S. Attached, N, a former barn, the longer return front with many triangular ventilation holes.

Now, before examining the High Street, briefly NW along STATION ROAD. First, N side, COTSWOLD COTTAGE by *Norman Jewson*, 1930, a late example of Cotswold Arts and Crafts. Opposite, LIFFORD HALL, 1915–17 by *A.N. Prentice*, again Neo-Cotswold, with a well-considered rhythm of gables and larger mullioned windows; blank NW end (for the stage). The former TELEPHONE EXCHANGE, beyond a simple C18 terrace, is Neo-Cotswold too, as late as 1950; its more functional successor, by *Badger, Harrison & Cross c.* 1980, lies behind.

Then RUSSELL HOUSE, said to be of 1791, three bays, with Regency ground-floor bow windows. Formerly (at least until 1886 when F.D. Millet bought the house) there was a central doorway, superseded by a delicate wrought-iron porch in an additional r. bay (replacing a carriage arch). Long attachment further r., a former barn converted to drawing room and studio in the 1890s. Within its former central archway, a big curving-out bay; either side, four pairs of ventilation slits with oval openings above, quite an original composition. – Rusticated GATEPIERS.

To the l. of the house is a charming Gothick GAZEBO, probably *c.* 1800; blocked ogee doorway flanked by blind lancets, two windows above, beneath a shaped gable with blind quatrefoil. In the garden behind, a sunken rectangular ICE HOUSE and castellated tower-like garden PAVILION, square, with continuous first-floor iron balcony.*

---

*Station Road continues to the site of the former STATION, opened 1904; a brick engine shed, the station house, and cottages of 1904–11 remain.

In SPRINGFIELD LANE leading N from the Green is LUGGERS HALL, by *Prentice*, 1911, for the artist and garden expert Alfred Parsons (†1920). Straightened Z-plan, gabled with hipped dormers, a lantern (above the domed open-well staircase), and other odd Regency-style detail. Main porch with segmental canopy; garden entrance, S, with porch with fluted columns and balustrade. This led to the studio, which has a large, strangely bald, tripartite N window.

3a. The High Street

The HIGH STREET is exceptionally long, longer than the main street of many a small town (say Evesham or Pershore), and its appearance changes all the time. There are grass verges all the way along, some prettily kept front gardens, and a scatter-ing of trees, especially on the GREEN. We can start here, at its E end, with the excellent WAR MEMORIAL by *F.L. Griggs*, 4 *c*. 1922; tall shaft surmounted by a Latin cross within a lozenge. To its SW, BROADWAY HOTEL, the only major building with prominent black-and-white work, the timber-framed r. wing, C14–C15 in origin; stone recessed centre and l. wing, C17. Then modest buildings pierced by a well-planned shopping passage, by *Patrick J. Burton*, 1985–6, leading to a discreet car park. CROFT VILLA, rectangular, hipped-roofed, of *c*. 1820–30, is unusual for Broadway.

The N side begins with the SWAN HOTEL, tactfully reconstructed in 1938 by *F.W.B. & F.R.S.Yorke*. A varied mix leads up to No. 20, formerly Gordon Russell's furniture showrooms. Early C18, of three bays with cross-windows; datestone 1588 (?), on the W chimney, presumably *ex situ*. Hipped-roofed porch by *Bateman*, 1916, with oval side windows on both storeys. The adjoining house, higher but also three bays, is late C18, of beau-tiful simplicity, with central round-arched doorway. The Cotswold wing, r., has mullioned windows beneath a gable, bearing the surprisingly late date 1687. Round the corner, a gabled overhanging upper floor with narrow studding, imported from a C15 house in Worcester. THE RUSSELLS, tra-ditional-style housing by the *Lapworth Partnership* of Birming-ham, 2004–5, has replaced all the C20 buildings of Gordon Russell Ltd, apart from the former DRAWING OFFICE of 1925 by *Leslie Mansfield*, along Back Lane: long cranked plan, rubble with hipped tile roof, now forming the N side of a small shop-ping square.*

Then comes the early C17 LYGON ARMS, formerly the White Hart. Lord Torrington in 1787 saw in it 'all the marks of having been a manor house', and so can we, though early C20 internal amendments have made the evidence difficult to interpret. By far the best and largest Cotswold-type house in the village,

---

*Further N, only one pair remains of twelve semi-detached workers' cottages of 1922–3 by *Bateman* or *Mansfield*, stone and thatched; the rest were destroyed by fire in 1934.

even if less monumental than Tudor House (p. 185), it became
an inn, or at least partly served as one, at a remarkably early
date. Broad recessed centre, two projecting wings. These have
gables, the centre two two-storey dormers. Grouped diagonal
chimneys. Several windows were renewed in the early C20. In
the W wing, they are mullioned-and-transomed; in the centre
and E wing, mostly of the cross-type, paired, under linked
hoodmoulds. Door surround with tapering Ionic pilasters,
strapwork frieze and top, and date 1620 with the names of John
and Ursula Treavis. It leads into a passage with (probably) the
former hall to its W, with large fireplace with wooden lintel. In
its SW corner (between centre and W wing), a small Tudor-
arched doorway, apparently C16, probably re-set; its original
position was perhaps further S in the same wall, facing the main
entrance. The doorway leads to a parlour, with early C16 chimneypiece from Merton Abbey; moulded four-centred arch with
bird and foliage in the spandrels. In the small room E of the
entrance passage, probably the pantry, a large fireplace (with
fireback dated 1671). Beyond this the former kitchen, now
Small Dining Room, with small-scale panelling from Babington Hall, Derby. The Cromwell Room above, once the Great
Chamber, has an ornamental early C17 plaster frieze and
ceiling, and striking Jacobean stone chimneypiece: much strapwork, with Corinthian capitals.

Sydney Russell bought the Lygon Arms in 1904, at the dawn
of the age of motor tourism. To the E of its façade, in 1909–10,
C.E. Bateman added a large single-storey dining room. It fits
in outstandingly well, in scale and its display of different
motifs: one canted bay window with ball finials, one square
and gabled, plus a projecting entrance, r. Inside, a barrel-
vaulted ceiling with plasterwork by the *Birmingham Guild*;
heraldic signs painted by the Rev. *E.E. Dorling*. To the W, the
C17 No. 28 was also much altered for the hotel in 1922, and
connected by a high-level timber bridge. Beneath it, one enters
a courtyard with a chestnut tree. Long gabled ranges either
side, that on the W by *Bateman*, 1919–22, including former
garages, lengthened (with additional garages and small clock
tower) in 1926 by *Leslie Mansfield*. The E Kitchen Wing, also
Bateman, 1910–11, was extended in 1960–1 by *Russell, Hodgson
& Leigh* (who had added the low Russell Room in 1957). This
extension, the Garden Wing, showed just how such a modern
addition could be done; stone ground floor, above two projecting brick storeys with wood slatting stressing the verticals
of the window bays. Further E, forming a smaller courtyard,
the Orchard Wing by *Russell & Hodgson*, 1968, stone, roughcast, with boxy oriels, its style perhaps best described as Arts
and Crafts Brutalist. In Back Lane, W of Mansfield's 1926
range, his contemporary apsidal Power House; opposite, a
delightful thatched building for staff accommodation, brick,
part weatherboarded, of 1920, and the stone laundry, *c.* 1915,
both by *Bateman*.

Back to the HIGH STREET and its s side. First the former POST OFFICE by *E. Guy Dawber & Whitwell*, 1899, nice and subdued, with bowed two-storey oriel, and ST PATRICK'S, C17, stone with gables, much redone. Then LLOYDS BANK (originally Capital and Counties) by *G.H. Hunt*, 1914–15, with two gables, conforming, yet not effacing its function.

Kennel Lane leads s here, past a pyramid-roofed dovecote, to the NORTH COTSWOLD HUNT STABLES of 1867, by *George Hunt*; brick, plain, with cupola and three projecting gables facing the white-painted Huntsman's Lodge.

The s side continues with a C17–C18 range, one house (No. 45) near its centre rising to three storeys plus gable. At No. 47, an alleyway leads to the former BRITISH SCHOOL, originally a Congregational chapel of 1798, mostly rebuilt 1811. Tall ogee-headed central doorway (with Gothick-traceried reveal); much else was reconstructed *c.* 1995. No. 49 is C17 stone and thatched, the lower E part showing signs of earlier cruck construction. HSBC BANK (formerly Midland), 1922–3 by *Woolfall & Eccles* of Liverpool, is more wilful than Lloyds, with a single asymmetrical gabled dormer.

On the N side, after the Lygon Arms, No. 32, modest late C17, is spoilt by a shocking C20 shop. The unprepossessing No. 34, mostly roughcast, must represent a C14 hall-and-solar house, see the tiny solar window of two pointed trefoiled lights in the w return. BARN CLOSE, early to mid-C17, H-plan, has gabled wings that do not project equally. The w also extends at the rear to include a former barn, with roof truss dated 1637; the higher E wing has a chimney dated 1657. Then PICTON HOUSE, dignified Georgian, eight bays, behind an undulating mid-C20 wall; big gatepiers with ball finials. Closer inspection reveals a more complicated history. The middle five bays, with central doorway with moulded and lugged architrave, must be *c.* 1700, probably originally with cross-windows; the later C18 added two plainer bays l., and one r. above an archway. Gabled rear wing. A path beneath the archway leads to BELL YARD, a pretty row of cottages, one keystone dated 1811. YEW TREE HOUSE (No. 44), mostly C17, is much altered.

BROAD CLOSE (No. 48), further up facing open country, is more elaborate; of 1806, perhaps altered *c.* 1825. Three bays, the centre projecting beneath a thin open pediment. Doorway with pediment on Tuscan columns, flanked by shallow timber bows; tripartite first-floor windows. Lower bay, w, with similar windows. Behind this a low rear wing, C15–C16, with small quatrefoil openings and three cruck trusses. HUNTER'S LODGE, set back, seems mid-C19, with its starved gables; rear wing, NE, by *Guy Pemberton*, 1903, with applied half-timbering.

The s side, after the unexpected rural break, continues with the monumental TUDOR HOUSE, dated 1659–60; symmetrical, of three bays and storeys, the top one reaching into the gabled ball-finialled dormers. Canted projecting two-storey centre with parapet; doorway to the screens passage at the w end, not

in the middle, still with cambered head. The six-light concave-
moulded mullioned windows have continuous drip-courses, no
longer individual hoodmoulds. Grouped diagonal chimneys.
Restored in 1907–8 by *C.E. Mallows*, who converted the lower
attached farm building, w, to a service wing; this has a Voy-
seyish garage archway (and flat-roofed rear dormers). No. 67,
adjoining E, has four bays of sashed windows, the l. above a
carriageway with keystone dated 1774. Then the former
CHURCH SCHOOLS, a welcome gaffe in a street of such perfection. Vigorous Victorian Gothic by *George Hunt*, 1868–9,
incorporating earlier work by him, 1856–7; plate or Dec
tracery, porch, fine octagonal corner turret. Cast-iron bracket
clock added 1887. No. 69, early C19, with C16 cross-gabled w
range, was converted as St Eadburgha's Bindery for Katie
Adams by *Ernest Barnsley*, 1907. Then No. 71, early C19, with
upright mullioned windows, and No. 73 (LITTLE GABLES),
mid-C17, its mullioned windows with continuous dripmould.
Blocked C17 doorway, l.; present doorway 1920.

Worth noting on the N side: No. 58, its C17 gable end-on to
the street; No. 62, mid-C18, with upright broad-mullioned
windows; and the Methodist Chapel (p. 178). PRIOR'S
MANSE, at the corner of Leamington Road, is an important
C14 stone-built survival, said to have housed the Abbot of Pershore's steward; a large attached barn was demolished in 1877.
Hall range with gabled solar cross-wing, w; the E service range
was extended N as a second gabled cross-wing in the C17. Well
restored 1958. The early C14 doorway to the cross-passage
(recessed centre, E) has sunk-quadrant moulding and keeled
hoodmould. Blocked chamfered doorway in the return of the
solar wing. All windows are C17 mullioned. The hall range, containing at least three cruck-trusses and some curved wind-
braces, was probably horizontally subdivided in the 1680s
(re-cut inscription on the fireplace).

The fine large GABLE HOUSE, set back in its garden, s side,
facing Leamington Road, is probably early C17. Four-bay main
range with small gabled dormers containing blind round-
headed lancets; projecting w cross-wing with four-light king-
mullioned window beneath a larger gable. Tall rear wing, SE.

3b. The upper High Street

The upper part of the High Street has fewer major buildings, but
is delightfully free of through traffic since the opening of the
by-pass. The highlights lie at the far E end.

First, s side, the modest Congregational chapel (p. 178), discreetly set back. It faces No. 70, neat later C18; ashlar, five bays,
timber door hood on brackets. The three-bay Nos. 74–76 are
early C19, with good stone doorcase with Tuscan columns and
open pediment. No. 78, also early C19, has tripartite upper
windows and a nice pair of bowed shopfronts. After that an
attractive but uneventful stretch; thin timber-framing appears
on the W elevation of No. 100 (INGLENOOK).

The s side is equally pleasant and uneventful. Georgian buildings worth highlighting are No. 87 (standing back), symmetrical, with early C19 wrought-iron porch; Nos. 89–91, a random
agglomeration with some stone tile-hanging and carriage
entrance, clearly a former inn; and No. 105 (LEEDS HOUSE),
early C19, three bays, with two neat ground-floor bow windows
and pretty porch, all timber, mostly C20 renewal.

Back on the n side, the picturesque gable-end of MILESTONE
COTTAGE (No. 112) is late C17, partly restored in 1913 by *Guy
Pemberton*. The MILESTONE stands outside the mid-C18
MILESTONE HOUSE (No. 122). Then (opposite No. 111,
ashlar-faced four-bay late C18, with Tuscan doorcase) the n
side opens out somewhat with poor mid-C20 Cotswold imitation, initiated by the former POLICE STATION of 1937, probably by *A. V. Rowe* (now Peel House). Nos. 128–138 successfully
restore the streetline. No. 140 (BANKSIDE), C17 L-plan, incorporates earlier fabric; see the small C15 trefoil-headed window,
probably *ex situ*, and timber framing on the much disturbed e
side. FENCOTE HOUSE (No. 144) is by *Bateman*, 1936, but
unexciting.

The unusual BARN HOUSE (No. 152) lies back at an angle.
Three-bay centre dated 1703, with two storeys of upright mullioned windows and continuous dripmould; wings with gabled
dormers by *A. N. Prentice*, c. 1908. A curved single-storey link,
with three-light mullioned window flanked by ovals, leads to
the converted barn, with a large window of five Tudor-arched
lights and two transoms, beneath a half-hipped gable. Barn and
link are probably by *Guy Pemberton*.

Almost opposite, HAWSTED HOUSE (No. 143), early C18, three
bays, much enlarged in 1919 by *Prentice*, who added a link to
his rear hipped-roof range. Then ORCHARD FARM COTTAGE,
dated 1722 (actually an addition at right angles to an existing
cottage); symmetrical façade with confined (former) central
doorway, and still two-light mullioned windows with individual hoodmoulds.

On the n side ORCHARD CLOSE of c. 1860 is followed by TOP
FARM, now Knap House and East House; the latter is
C17–early C18, the former (with canted bay window) of 1910
by *G. H. Hunt* for T.E. Wells, the inventor of Quaker Oats. He
joined his new house to the existing one by a slightly pointed
archway, an attractive idea. East House has two gabled bays:
the e with individual hoodmoulds; the w with continuous dripmould, perhaps as late as the incised date 1759. Pyramid-
roofed GAZEBO and battlemented WALL, its merlons pierced
by small slits: a fine boundary to the High Street. At the rear
former STABLES. Further up Bibsworth Lane, half-timbered
COTTAGES, presumably all by *Hunt*.

ORCHARD FARM (No. 149), s side, is an early C17 L-plan farmhouse greatly expanded by *Prentice* for Lady Maud Bowes-
Lyon c. 1905. The original main range faces the road, with
four-centred doorway with leaves in the spandrels and hoodmould on large lozenge stops; diagonally set chimneys. Gabled

cross-wing, w, with two gabled dormers on its w side. Prentice extended this by converting an attached barn into a spacious music room, the asymmetrical fenestration on its s
elevation balancing the bold sw chimney-breast. He also
extended the street front to the E with a low kitchen wing
(no doubt providing the latticing for most of the windows).
No. 153, dated 1718, of three bays, is symmetrical apart from
its squeezed-in doorway; upright mullioned windows again,
hoods only on the ground floor.

Finally COURT FARM, actually two farmhouses altered and
linked by *Prentice* as a single dwelling for Antonio de Navarro
and Mary Anderson, *c.* 1899. The original Court Farmhouse,
w, is early C17, gabled L-plan, absorbing a former farm
building on its w flank. The former Bell Farmhouse, E, has two
unequal C17 gables and larger mullioned windows. Evidence
for a cruck-framed late C14 hall within, vertically subdivided
with fine C16 moulded beams with defaced angel-stops. Prentice's buttressed single-storey link has a canted bay adjoining
Court Farmhouse and gabled two-storey central projection.
Parallel rear range with large music room with canted ceiling
(and oak chimneypiece imported from Hereford); the gabled
central projection here contains an upper chapel with dormers
with stained glass by *Paul Woodroffe*. Large GARDEN at the rear,
begun 1896, to a design by *Alfred Parsons*.

Opposite, terminating the N side, the modest late C18 PIKE
COTTAGE, with only a single-storey canted bay to monitor the
former traffic on Fish Hill.

4. Leamington Road

A postscript, with early C20 housing. Opposite the R.C. complex
(p. 178), simple early C19 villas, then an attractive example of
philanthropic housing of 1907–8, by *G.H. Hunt* for T.E. Wells
(cf. Top Farm, above). Four almost identical terraces, Nos.
17–27 and Nos. 45–51 Leamington Road, intersected by Nos.
1–7 and Nos. 2–8 WELLS GARDENS. Stone ground floors with
mullioned windows, roughcast with gabled dormers above;
green slate roofs. The adjoining Evesham RDC housing,
mostly *c.* 1929 by their surveyor *R.J. Atkinson*, forms a telling,
dreary contrast.

Good COUNCIL SCHOOL, at the corner of Lime Tree Avenue,
of 1913–14 by *C.E. Bateman* (with *G.H. Hunt*). Roughcast
Tudor Renaissance, with gables and large windows, broadly
mullioned and transomed; mottled green slate roof.

SANDSCROFT AVENUE further N leads to earlier, more appealing Evesham RDC housing, a well-laid-out development by
Dicks & Waldron, begun 1912; mostly terraces of four, brick
painted white, with little gables and stone-trimmed windows.

N again, BIBSWORTH HOUSE, a small country house of 1903 for
H.G. Clegg by *Guy Dawber*; the façade shows him at his most
Lutyensesque. E-plan, of very neatly coursed rubble with
deeply raked joints; stone-slated roof with diagonal brick

chimneys. Fine central two-storey porch with Jacobean finials, rounded entrance with voussoirs of alternating stone and brick-tile. This leads into a corridor hall linking the well-lit parlour, s, to the kitchen, N. Also at this end, an entrance to the stables, with attached cottage. The garden front, E, is more varied, with roughcast and weatherboarding. – Rectangular LODGE, with a little brick patterning in the gables.

OUTER BROADWAY

FARNCOMBE HOUSE, 1¼ m. ENE of St Michael. Built for Sir John Cotterell, 1780. The castellated centre of the W front has two full-height bow windows flanking the doorway; further N, 3+1 bays, the last again castellated. Behind the three bays the former ballroom, with excellent Ionic fireplace with carving of Britannia. Much enlarged to the s and rear in the late C19 for the Chadwick family; mullioned-and-transomed windows, square battlemented SW tower. Further altered c. 1930 as a hotel, and after 1964 for Group 4; now Cotswold Conference Centre. – Terraced GARDENS, with superb views.

The former FISH INN at the top of Fish Hill, 1½ m. E, curiously barbaric and said to be of 1771, was originally a summerhouse on the Farncombe estate; Lord Torrington called it 'the most extraordinary gaze-about house in the world'. Square with, on the NW front, a double flight of steps leading to a rusticated Venetian window; blind balustrade below, triglyph frieze above, the metopes simply rubble. Pyramid roof, with square stone sundial finial. Acceptable C19 addition; awful C20 ones.

BROADWAY TOWER, a prominent folly 1⅓ m. ESE on Beacon Hill, the second highest point of the Cotswolds, was built for the sixth Earl of Coventry on his Spring Hill estate (see The Buildings of England: Gloucestershire 1). The 'Saxon Hexagon Tower', by James Wyatt, designed 1794, built 1797–9, has three higher round turrets rising from alternate corners; the detail is of course Norman rather than Saxon. Three storeys above a battered base (its only opening, the moulded doorway). The second floor was the most important, with moulded two-light windows with nook-shafts and corbelled balconies with parapets formed of intersecting arches. Simple oculus windows on the third floor; battlements above with bold gargoyles. The tower housed the private printing press of Sir Thomas Phillips (see below) from 1822 to 1862 and in 1866 was restored for Cormell Price, friend of William Morris and Burne-Jones.

MIDDLE HILL, 1½ m. SE. William Taylor's house of c. 1725, rebuilt for George Savage c. 1779, probably by Anthony Keck, was bought in 1793 by Thomas Phillips; his son, the bibliophile Sir Thomas Phillips (1792–1872), kept his huge collection of books here. The ashlar-faced house is typical of Keck. Former entrance front, SE, of 2+1+2 bays, the projecting centre wider and pedimented; tripartite entrance below, with panelled pilasters, palm-leaf capitals, and fluted frieze with paterae. The present entrance front, NW, also 2+1+2 bays, is plainer; porch

95

with three round arches perhaps by *G.M. Hills c.* 1872. At the centre of the sw return, a full-height bow, enjoying spectacular views across the North Cotswolds. The NE return was reconstructed by *Peter Yiangou Associates c.* 1985–90, following the demolition (in 1977) of large late C19 additions by *Guy Dawber*. This last faces, uphill, to a fine octagonal STABLE BLOCK dated 1886 (apparently begun 1874), and a square POWER HOUSE with hipped roof with cupola. – Tall gabled late C19 LODGE at the end of the long former w drive, opposite St Eadburgha.

DOR KNAP, 1⅛ m. SE. A row of four early C18 cottages, nicely adapted as a single house in the early C20; further Neo-Cotswold alterations and additions, 1987. Two C20 E wings, one with mullioned corner windows, one with an oval in the gable, form a small entrance courtyard.

KITE'S NEST FARM, 1⅓ m. SSE. An interesting house, of two contrasting parallel ranges. The earlier N front, dated 1677 on the w return gable, is symmetrical, of three bays; blank centre, except for the four-centred doorway, flanked by two storeys of mullioned windows with hoodmoulds, plus gabled dormers.* The only break in symmetry is that on the ground floor the hall window, l., has six (rather than four) lights. On the taller s front all five windows are of cross-type, with continuous dripmoulds; between the two gables, a small incongruous segmental one. The date of this range, *c.* 1700 or later, is confirmed by the wide open-well stair with closed string and twisted balusters.

BROMSGROVE

Bromsgrove's splendid church, on its ancient hilltop site, gives an indication of its importance as the medieval market town; its size may also reflect the extent of its parish, which stretched as

---

*The date 1879 beneath the E gable may refer to alterations to these dormers.

far NE as Kings Norton (now within Birmingham). The town, granted a market charter in 1199 and a borough by 1295, lay to the E, developing in decidedly linear fashion along the former Roman road (or Saltway) leading N from Droitwich. 'The towne of Bremisgreve is all of a maner in one very longe strete, stondynge on a playne grownde,' wrote Leland in the 1530s, adding that it 'standyth somewhat by clothinge'. By the C17–C18 its prosperity depended rather on the home production of wrought-iron nails, an industry mostly carried out in alleys and courtyards opening off the High Street; the outlines of a few can still be traced. In 1778 nearly a thousand were employed in this trade. James Dugdale, in 1819, called Bromsgrove 'a large and dirty place, full of shops and manufacturers of needles, nails, sheeting and other coarse linen'. The hand-made nail industry declined later in the C19, in the face of industrialized manufacture elsewhere in the West Midlands. In 1898 the town's economy received a boost from the founding, by Walter Gilbert, of the Bromsgrove Guild of Applied Arts, which developed into a thriving enterprise, attracting craftsmen from across Europe; it closed in 1966. Of local architects, the most notable was *John Cotton* (1844–1934), a native of the town who also opened a Birmingham office, retiring early, in the 1890s.

CHURCHES

ST JOHN BAPTIST. Of red sandstone, its spire dominating views for miles around. Mostly Perp, with battlements and pinnacles, including the fine clerestory; thoroughly restored in 1857–8 by *G.G. Scott*. Closer inspection reveals significant earlier fabric. Of the Late Norman church there remains the reused arch of the S doorway, with double roll moulding. The chancel was rebuilt in the mid C13, its E window with five stepped lights; the priest's doorway is Scott's, the S windows early C14 insertions. Of this date also the N vestry, renewed by Scott; canted outer N choir vestry added by *A.H. Parker*, 1908–9. The S aisle has an E window with late C13 intersecting tracery, but otherwise seems entirely Perp, the most curious feature the square bay window, no doubt for a funerary monument (cf. Spetchley). This is flanked by pointed windows (one blocked), but 42 further W are very tall, straight-headed ones; similar window above the contemporary S porch (with deep, slightly projecting, battlemented parapet). So there are at least two phases of Perp work here. Signs of a blocked lancet N of the aisle's four-light W window suggest an explanation: that the pre-Perp aisle was narrower and that there was also a S transept (with late C13 E chapel), remodelled separately. The N aisle is simpler. Its W part is of *c.* 1300, with doorway with depressed two-centred arch flanked by windows with stepped cusped lights. The wall was heightened when the E half, including a chantry chapel endowed in 1478 by Eleanor Stafford, was added; only the easternmost (square-headed) windows here are original, the others are Scott's. The W tower may also have been begun *c.* 1300; its w doorway seems of that date, the C19 N and S windows are probably accurate copies. But the splendid upper parts are of course Perp, beginning with the five-light W window; above, three ogee niches with weathered figures of SS Peter, John the Baptist, and Paul. Two-light bell-openings, continued by rich blank arcading; ornately panelled and battlemented parapet, tall corner pinnacles. Behind rises the ribbed octagonal spire; lucarnes at the base, some decoration higher up, top renewed 1892. Within, the lofty tower arch has fine continuous mouldings.

The INTERIOR clarifies the historical development. Parts of the E respond of the N arcade and the respond of the first pier seem Norman, despite Scott's alterations; the slightly higher arch suggests the remnant of a N transept. Mid-C13 chancel arch, with demi-quatrefoil responds, finely moulded arch, and capitals with a little nailhead. The narrow triple-stepped arch, chancel SW, now filled by the organ, must have led to the chapel E of the S transept, for which the trefoiled piscina, S, provides more evidence. The three W bays of the N arcade are also mid-C13: quatrefoil piers, moulded capitals, double-chamfered arches. Scott linked them to the E bay by a narrow trefoiled arch. The S arcade, however, is consistently Late Perp, four bays, with piers and arches of fine complicated section. Splendid Perp arch from chancel to N chantry chapel, deeply panelled with a kind of Gothic coffering with bosses; the w doorway led to the rood loft. A hollow four-centred moulding with fleurons against the chapel's E wall is all that remains of its original roof. Other roofs by *Scott*, except that of the nave, which is Late Perp, renewed by *Harold Brakspear*, 1925. The steeper pitch of its predecessor can be seen above both chancel and tower arches.

Scott's FURNISHINGS include an Ancaster stone REREDOS, and oak STALLS and PEWS. – ROYAL ARMS. Early C19. – Perp-style FONT. 1847, carved by *Irving* of Leicester. – LECTERNS. One, of oak, with baluster stem, is C17; the other, a brass eagle, of 1862. – Early C20 fittings by the *Bromsgrove Guild* include the mosaic-paved CHANCEL FLOOR, designed by *Walter Gilbert*, 1907, and the carved oak ALTAR, 1911. – Perp-style PULPIT by *J.A. Swan*, 1945–6, carved by *Pancheri & Hack*. – ORGAN SCREEN by *Robert Pancheri*, 1969–70, with scenes of local history. – STATUE of St John Baptist above the porch entrance, also by *Pancheri*, 1973.

STAINED GLASS. A varied collection. Superb E window by *Lavers & Barraud*, 1861. Their former S chapel E window, of 1867, was spoiled when re-set in 1950, without its backgrounds, at the N aisle w. – *Clayton & Bell*'s chancel S windows, of 1859, received similar treatment. Their contemporary N chapel E was treated more sensitively when *Hardman* re-set it in the nave S clerestory, in 1909. – Pictorial W window of 1870 by *J.B. Capronnier* of Brussels; tower S by *Lavers, Barraud & Westlake*, 1882. – By *Ward & Hughes*, the S aisle bay, 1883, and one of 1885, N aisle, commemorating *Henry Hughes* himself (who died here in 1883). – N chapel N of 1892, probably by *Wyndham Hughes*, from the E window of Bromsgrove School Old Chapel. – N aisle NW by *Heaton, Butler & Bayne*, 1912, designed by *Amy Walford*; by the same no doubt, the adjoining window. – S aisle W by *Powell & Sons*, 1913–14. – S porch W by *P.E. Lemmon*, 1958.

MONUMENTS. On a N aisle window sill, a hollow stone cube, crudely carved; apparently C12–C13, said to be for a heart burial. – Within the S aisle bay, a fine C13 coffin slab with raised foliated cross, and two defaced C14–C15 effigies, one female, the other a man praying. – N chapel. Humphrey Stafford of Grafton †1450 and his wife Eleanor; excellent alabaster effigies, probably from the Chellaston (Derby) workshop. He wears splendidly detailed armour, she a mitred head-dress. Renewed tomb-chest, no doubt originally beneath the arch to the chancel. – Sir John Talbot, also of Grafton Manor (p. 321), †1550, flanked by his two wives: Margaret with pedimented head-dress, Elizabeth with close-fitting cap. Also alabaster, also excellent (possibly by *Richard Royley* of Burton-on-Trent). The tomb-chest's N and E sides have richly cusped quatrefoils with heraldry, separated by twisted colonnettes. Two early C17 brass plaques nearby commemorate Sir John's daughters. – Chancel. Fine alabaster effigy of Lady Elizabeth Talbot of Grafton, †1490, the tomb-chest with cusped panelling and two standing deacons holding shields. – The quatrefoil panels forming a sedilia, chancel S, are reused from the Stafford monument. – George Lyttelton †1600. Painted alabaster. He leans stiffly on his elbow, dressed in sergeant-at-law robes. High gadrooned base; flat back arch with strapwork cartouche, flanked by Composite columns (S aisle SW). – John Hall, Bishop of Bristol, †1710; attributed to *William Townesend* of Oxford (GF). Large, with segmental top; flaming urn above a roundel with three putto heads. Wooden replicas of his crozier and staff (chancel). – Minor tablets include Christopher Bell †1690, a nice cartouche (N aisle); and Benjamin Maund, the botanist, †1864, by *Herbert Harvey*, 1927, with portrait roundel (chancel). – Boer War memorial by *Amy Walford*, 1904–5, beaten brass (S aisle). – First World War memorial by *Richard R. Goulden*, 1920; large bronze panel (N aisle).

Large CHURCHYARD, encircled by limes planted *c.* 1790; sandstone wall of 1815. Simple LYCHGATE, SE, dated 1656, at the top of the long, informal flight of steps from the town. – N of the vestry, a hopelessly defaced EFFIGY, head on tasselled cushion; said to be William Chance †1768. – Of HEADSTONES the most remarkable are a pair, some distance N of the nave, to the 'engineers' (i.e. railwaymen) Thomas Scaife and Joseph Rutherford. They died in 1840 when the boiler of an experimental engine exploded. Each has an oval medallion of a locomotive and the gravestone to Scaife, a bank-engine driver, the following poem (signed *Pratt*):

My engine now is cold and still
No water does my boiler fill;
My coke affords its flame no more,
My days of usefulness are o'er.
My wheels deny their wonted speed,
No more my guiding hands they heed;
My whistle too has lost its tone,
Its shrill and thrilling sounds are gone;
My valves are now thrown open wide,
My flanges all refuse to guide.
My clacks also, though once so strong,
Refuse to aid the busy throng.
No more I feel each urging breath,
My steam is now condens'd in death.
Life's railway o'er, each station's past,
In death I'm stopp'd and rest at last.
Farewell, dear friends, and cease to weep,
In Christ I'm SAFE, in Him I sleep.

ALL SAINTS, Birmingham Road. By *John Cotton*, 1872–4; NW
tower added 1887–8. Large, rock-faced, with transepts and
polygonal apse. Mostly Geometrical tracery, particularly striking the large W window and the N transept, doubled with the
organ chamber. The S transept has plate tracery, hinting at a
hypothetical building history. Well-detailed tower: slit lancets
on the middle stage, the bell-openings much larger trefoiled
and gabled lancet pairs. Spire never built. Interior of buff-
yellow brick with blue and red patterns. Five-bay arcades, with
alternate round and octagonal piers, not taking account of
the transepts. A second arch W of the chancel arch marks off
the crossing. High arch-braced roofs. Good carving by *John
Roddis*. – *Cotton*'s FURNISHINGS include a large carved FONT,
round stone PULPIT and low SCREEN (both with red and
yellow brick patterning), STALLS, and carved and painted
stone REREDOS. – ROOD BEAM and chancel PANELLING by
Maurice W. Jones, 1937–8, made by the *Bromsgrove Guild*. –
ORGAN by *Tamburini*, 1980–1, the elm case designed by *A.B.
Chatwin*. – STAINED GLASS. By *Hardman*, the apse windows,
1897, and two in the N aisle, 1898–1903. These flank another,
of 1989, designed by *A.S. Clarke*, who also designed the aisle
NE, made by *A.J. Davies*, 1950. – N transept N by the *Camms*,
1956. – S transept S, 1927, and one in the S aisle, 1932, both by
A.E. Lemmon, both very good. – Two other S aisle windows by
Samuel Evans, 1912, and *Jones & Willis*, 1901.
  LYCHGATE. 1923, with large obelisk WAR MEMORIAL
nearby. – SUNDAY SCHOOL, across Burcot Lane, by *E.A. Day*,
1882; brick, lancet style.
ST PETER (R.C.), Rock Hill. 1858–60 by *Gilbert R. Blount*. Sandstone with ashlar dressings; aisleless nave with N porch, wide
polygonal apse with NE vestry. Dec tracery, Geometrical to
ogee. A stepped triple bellcote provides a dramatic crown to
the ornate, boldly handled W front with its rose window. Broad

interior, little altered. High arch- and wind-braced roof, the
chancel emphasized by tripled wall-shafts. w gallery. – Elaborate wrought-iron CHANCEL SCREEN of c. 1863, with polygonal stone PULPIT carved by *Boulton*, 1866. – The most
important fitting is the HIGH ALTAR, designed by *Pugin* for
the chapel at Alton Towers, and completed in 1839; given to
Bromsgrove, 1860. Gilt oak reredos with nodding ogee
canopies and *ex dono* paintings of John Talbot, sixteenth
Earl of Shrewsbury (born at Grafton Manor, p. 321) and his
Countess, Maria Theresa. Below, finely painted enamel
plaques of the Life of Christ. The gilt-bronze altar front is a
little earlier. – Painted and inset STATIONS OF THE CROSS by
A. de Beule of Ghent, 1910; of the same date, the carved foliage
corbels. – Painted TRIPTYCH (nave SW) by *A.E. Lemmon*, 1936.
– STAINED GLASS. Two apse windows of c. 1862, probably by
O'Connor. – Nave SE of 1947 by *A.E. Lemmon*; probably also
the SW, c. 1920.

SCHOOL, NE. Brick, mostly by *Cotton*, 1886; enlarged by
Sandy & Norris, 1931.

BAPTIST CHURCH, New Road. 1990, by *Trinity Road Developments Ltd* (replacing *George Bidlake*'s Gothic chapel of 1866–7).
Low, brick, with hipped pantiled roof, and curved N end with
cylindrical semi-glazed NW tower with open metal spire. –
Former SUNDAY SCHOOL of 1888 at the rear.

CONGREGATIONAL CHAPEL (now United Reformed), Chapel
Street. Of 1832. Stuccoed, four bays, with over-tall windows
with outer architraves and panels below. W front (facing
Windsor Street) with fluted Doric porch, beneath a squat
gallery window. On the N side, sandstone remnants of the
earlier chapel, dated 1693. Interior renovated and E organ
chamber added by *Cotton*, 1887–8. – STAINED GLASS. Roundel
portraying A.J. Davies, by *Hardman*, 1968.

Former SUNDAY SCHOOL, across Chapel Street. A nice
single-storey building, dated 1852. E-plan, the central porch
and projecting wings with pedimental gables. Red brick,
arched windows with blue brick heads and iron glazing bars.

Former EBENEZER METHODIST CHURCH, Broad Street. By
F.W. Anderson, 1933. Quite large, brick with artificial stone
dressings, the front a kind of Deco Gothic, like a suburban
cinema. Round-arched side windows, lavishly buttressed on
the N, but quite plain, S, towards the brick Sidemoor School
(of 1884). Much small-scale STAINED GLASS, by *A.J. Davies*.

Former HEPHZIBAH CHAPEL (Primitive Methodist), Birmingham Road. Of 1861; builder *Philip Bowater*. Red brick, yellow
and blue trim; round-arched windows, full-width pediment.

METHODIST CHURCH, Stratford Road. By *Donald Cornfield*,
1981–3;* low, brick, with a glass-fibre spike. Splayed W
entrance to lower vestibule. Later extended. One re-set window
by *A.E. Lemmon*, c. 1956.

---

*Replacing the Gothic Wesleyan Chapel in New Road, by *F.J. Yates*, 1883;
demolished 1984.

CEMETERY, Church Lane. By *C.H. Cooke*, 1857. Lodge replaced *c.* 1960, so that only an oak LYCHGATE survives, at the Church Street junction. Good, already muscular, central Gothic CROSS to John Adams †1859, by *W. Prosser*, Scott's clerk of works at the church.

PUBLIC BUILDINGS

BROMSGROVE DISTRICT COUNCIL OFFICES, Burcot Lane. Bland brick front range by *Temple Cox Duncan Associates*, 1986; canted bay, l., for the councillors. The rest was the former Shenstone Training College by the County Architect, *L.C. Lomas*, 1962–4; assorted, rather feeble buildings, still of Georgian proportions.

COUNTY BUILDINGS, Windsor Street. 1968 by *Worcestershire County Council Architects' Dept*. Long brick front towards Windsor Street containing the Fire Station, with offices above; central open access to the rear yard. Taller, rather cubic N end, with the concrete-faced and glazed entrance. Behind, the L-plan Library, set back from Stratford Road. Later accommodation block, S end.

POLICE STATION, The Crescent. By *Henry Rowe*, 1890. Severely plain brick, including the former Magistrates' Court. Split-roofed E addition, *c.* 1980.

DOLPHIN CENTRE, School Drive. By *Jackson & Edmonds*, 1964–6. The usual incoherent mix deemed appropriate for later C20 leisure centres. Tile-hung front, above purple brick, for the swimming pools. Later corrugated sports hall at the rear.

PRINCESS OF WALES COMMUNITY HOSPITAL, Stourbridge Road. By the *Hospital Design Partnership*, 1989–91. Huge expanded cross-plan; brick, narrow green-glazed upper storey, hipped pantiled roof. – In the grounds (of the demolished Workhouse Hospital), the best building is BROOK HAVEN, the mental health unit, by *Abbey Hanson Rowe*, 1994–5: red and blue brick, triple-cross plan, with pyramid-capped roof-lights.

BARNSLEY HALL HOSPITAL, Barnsley Hall Road, off Stourbridge Road. The Second Worcestershire County Lunatic Asylum; by the mental hospital specialist *G.T. Hine*, 1903–7. Brick, terracotta trim. Only the entrance range and chapel survive, incorporated into a housing development; the landmark water tower was demolished. Entrance building symmetrical, with shaped gables and polygonal cupola. Aisled CHAPEL, quite large, free Perp style; tall flèche above the chancel arch.

Former UNION WORKHOUSE, Birmingham Road. By *Bateman & Drury*, 1837–8. Only the entrance range remains (now offices). Utilitarian Late Georgian, brick, with channelled stucco ground floor and stuccoed parapet. Nine bays, with thin three-bay pediment above the humble doorway; projections and recessions add a simple rhythm. The rest followed a square plan, not the more usual cruciform one.

MARKET HALL, St John Street. 1994 by *Keith Richardson* of *Bromsgrove District Council*. Large square plan, red brick with cream band; hipped roof, clerestory lighting. The front, with big timber pediment, projects slightly on thin iron columns.

Former DRILL HALL, Recreation Road. By *A. V. Rowe*, 1914. Central round-arched gateway, with gable flanked by canted battlemented projections. Neo-Georgian brick wings, three bays and two storeys, hipped roofs. A good building, its future uncertain.

Educational buildings

BROMSGROVE SCHOOL, Worcester Road. Of C15–C16 origin, re- *p. 198* founded by Sir Thomas Cookes (cf. Tardebigge) in 1693. His building (now COOKES HOUSE), probably built 1695, lies back from Worcester Road behind rusticated brick gatepiers by *John Cotton*, 1876–7. Of 1+2+1 bays and two storeys, brick with stone quoins; slightly projecting centre, the doorway with big segmental pediment on carved consoles. Third (dormitory) storey added 1859. Rear wing mostly by *Joseph Bateman*, 1832, with later wooden porch.

The school extends much further E than this road frontage suggests. C19 expansion firstly created a tight quadrangle to the SE. On its E side, the former CHAPEL by *Henry Day*, 1850, small, yellow brick, with trefoiled lancets. Bolder chancel added by *Hopkins*, 1867, with buttresses supporting two internal transverse arches. Stained glass of 1889–91, probably by *Wyndham Hughes*. Set back, NE, is BIG SCHOOL, a large hall above smaller rooms, by *Cotton*, 1882–3. Red brick, Queen Anne school-board style with two shaped gables; a chimney on the SW one originally provided piquant asymmetry. Next door, the L-plan MILLINGTON LABORATORY, by *Lewis Sheppard & Son*, 1898. On the quadrangle's S side, a gabled classroom block of 1844–5 was absorbed, in 1893, by *Sheppard*'s extensive LYTTELTON HOUSE, set round three sides of a courtyard; severe gabled brick, with stone mullioned-and-transomed windows. *Arthur Bartlett* (cf. Dodford) completed the courtyard to the S in 1913–15, including the Headmaster's House, SE; he uses similar elements to Sheppard, but with far more subtlety and sensitivity.

Subsequent growth is grouped loosely around the large Gordon Green, its extent established by three buildings by *John Bilson* of Hull. The first, GORDON HOUSE, N side, a gabled residential block of 1898–1904, is well-proportioned. The second, KYTELESS, S side, a large classroom block of 1913–14, of harsher Leicestershire red brick, has broader mullioned-and-transomed windows. In 1926–8 ROUTH HALL, the most attractive of the three with its central cupola, was added on the E side.

The finest building is the MEMORIAL CHAPEL, SE corner, by *Sir Giles G. Scott*, 1928–31; W end completed by his successor firm only in 1960. Pale brick, steep roof, prominent

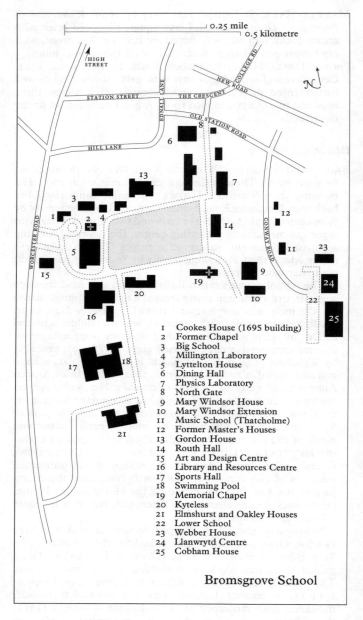

— 0.25 mile
— 0.5 kilometre

HIGH STREET

NEW COLLEGE RD

STATION STREET

THE CRESCENT

EDNALL LANE

OLD STATION ROAD

HILL LANE

N

WORCESTER ROAD

CONWAY ROAD

1   Cookes House (1695 building)
2   Former Chapel
3   Big School
4   Millington Laboratory
5   Lyttelton House
6   Dining Hall
7   Physics Laboratory
8   North Gate
9   Mary Windsor House
10 Mary Windsor Extension
11 Music School (Thatcholme)
12 Former Master's Houses
13 Gordon House
14 Routh Hall
15 Art and Design Centre
16 Library and Resources Centre
17 Sports Hall
18 Swimming Pool
19 Memorial Chapel
20 Kyteless
21 Elmshurst and Oakley Houses
22 Lower School
23 Webber House
24 Llanwrytd Centre
25 Cobham House

Bromsgrove School

buttresses, simple trefoiled windows above a sloping plinth. The E end with narrow transepts has conventional Dec tracery; later W window also Dec, above a narthex. The exterior generally is nothing like as bold as Scott's earlier Charterhouse Chapel (Surrey). The interior is a surprise, dominated by its soaring oak roof, of open collar-beam construction like a medieval tithe barn; the straight braces begin low down, almost at window-sill level. The short transepts provide galleries above low two-bay arcades, the N carrying the organ. Deep W gallery. Routine FITTINGS, the choir brought out into the nave within low stone walls. Fine limed-oak REREDOS by *Scott*, 1930, carved by *Pancheri*: Christ seated beneath open Dec tracery. It is set forward of the E wall, partly obscuring excellent STAINED GLASS by *Herbert Hendrie* in the E window: small scenes in Arts and Crafts mode. Two re-set windows in the narthex, the NW by *A.L. Moore & Son*, c. 1915.

Late C20 buildings by *Graham Winteringham* (of *S.T. Walker & Partners*) in chunky modern style include some in the NE corner, amongst uneventful earlier C20 buildings: DINING HALL 1964, PHYSICS LABORATORY 1968–9. External access here is via the NORTH GATE in Old Station Road, with gates by *C.E. Bateman* and gabled brick lodge by *A.V. Rowe*, 1927–8.

MARY WINDSOR HOUSE, SE of the chapel, a girls' boarding house by *Clifford Tee & Gale*, 1980–1, brick, three-storeyed, with some tile-hanging and hipped roof, is rather lumpish. Its detached S extension, a sixth-form house by *Associated Architects* (project architect *Adam Wardle*), 2001–2, forms a complete contrast: a sleek white rectangle with such Modernist devices as split stairs, pierced projecting wall, and curved lower NE addition. S front, towards the playing fields, mostly weatherboarded. Other work by *Associated Architects* includes the E wing of Kyteless, 1996, Postmodern Arts and Crafts, and the large LIBRARY AND RESOURCES CENTRE of 1994 (project architect *Richard Slawson*) at the SW corner of Gordon Green. Large butterfly plan façade, behind a slightly sunk courtyard; at the rear rises the reading room, with clerestory-lit rotunda. Their ART AND DESIGN CENTRE of 1999–2000 (project architect *J.T. Christophers*) lies further W; brick, with monopitch roofs and much glazing, including brises-soleil. To Worcester Road, a curved wall of sandstone, with incised inscription and little boxy windows.

Finally, S, beyond the Sports Hall (1979) and Swimming Pool (1984–5), ELMSHURST and OAKLEY HOUSES, by *S.T. Walker & Partners*, 1976 (project architect *Peter Noyes-Lewis*); U-plan brick, with angled roofs.

LOWER SCHOOL, Conway Road. Its main building, COBHAM HOUSE, 1958–9 by *Cassidy, Farrington & Dennys* of London, brick, three storeyed, is placed crosswise over a single-storey range to form a porte cochère on pilotis; enlarged 1978. To its N, the LLANWRYTD CENTRE, by *Associated Architects*, 1992, weatherboarded, with big sloping roof; and WEBBER HOUSE, a plain brick boarding house of 1974 by *S.T. Walker*

& Partners. – Further N, the MUSIC SCHOOL, built as a private house, Thatchholme, for Philip Brazier by *C.E. Bateman*, 1929; huge thatched roof replaced after a fire. Then, two brick Neo-Georgian masters' houses by *R. Thompson*, 1930.

NORTH EAST WORCESTERSHIRE COLLEGE, School Drive. *Yorke, Rosenberg & Mardall's* concrete-framed buildings of 1957–9 (extended 1964–70) were mostly replaced in 2005–6 by slick new buildings by *D5 Architects*; two-storeyed, mostly corrugated-clad, with much glazing including a prominent clerestory. – To the N, ARTRIX, an arts centre by *Glenn Howells Architects*, 2004–5: a cuboid of purple-grey brick, with mini-malist glazing, only broken by the PVC-clad fly tower.

NORTH BROMSGROVE HIGH SCHOOL, School Drive. By *Yorke, Rosenberg & Mardall*, 1961; enlarged 1971. Of three storeys, concrete-framed with brick infill. Massive H-plan, the broader centre higher, of redder brick; diluted by entrance additions of 2000.

SOUTH BROMSGROVE HIGH SCHOOL, Charford Road. By *Richard Sheppard, Robson & Partners*, 1968, extended 1981. A strong friendly design, set back behind a former mill pond. Dark brick with window bands with a varied rhythm of mullions. Three-storey classroom block with broad timber eaves band, its upper floor (with four larger rooms) cantilevering out towards the lower buildings. Future uncertain.

Former HIGH SCHOOL, Stourbridge Road; now Parkside Middle School. 1909–12 by *G.H. Gadd*, with *A.V. Rowe*, County Architect. Wrenian Baroque, two-storeyed, brick with ample stone dressings. Symmetrical, with gabled wings and centrepiece of channelled stone with a steep pediment for the doorway and a segmental one high above. Wooden cupola. Boundary wall with ball finials.

BOARD SCHOOLS. The Bromsgrove School Board was formed in 1875. Its first school, LICKEY END, by *Cotton*, 1875–7, has lost its angle bell-tower and been spoilt by later additions. Red brick with blue bands; projecting end gables with stepped lancets, iron-topped boundary wall to School Lane. STOUR-BRIDGE ROAD SCHOOL, 1879–80 by *Day & Yates*, is better preserved. Brick, symmetrical, still Gothic; pointed stone window heads with circular plate tracery. *See also* Dodford.

PERAMBULATIONS

1a. Around the church

To the NE, the former CHURCH SCHOOLS (now RMC House), by *William Lea* of Beoley, 1833. Brick, Late Classical; two storeys and seven bays, windows with eared and moulded architraves. Classrooms and teacher's residence added in keeping, 1871.

To the N, the town CEMETERY (p. 196). To the NW, flanking the junction of Church Lane with Kidderminster Road, are RYDAL MOUNT, large mid-C19 stuccoed, with battlemented

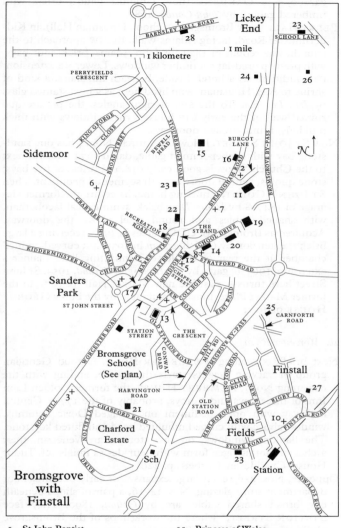

Bromsgrove
with
Finstall

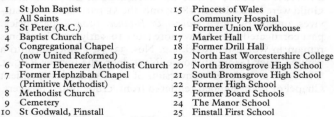

1	St John Baptist	15	Princess of Wales
2	All Saints		Community Hospital
3	St Peter (R.C.)	16	Former Union Workhouse
4	Baptist Church	17	Market Hall
5	Congregational Chapel	18	Former Drill Hall
	(now United Reformed)	19	North East Worcestershire College
6	Former Ebenezer Methodist Church	20	North Bromsgrove High School
7	Former Hephzibah Chapel	21	South Bromsgrove High School
	(Primitive Methodist)	22	Former High School
8	Methodist Church	23	Former Board Schools
9	Cemetery	24	The Manor School
10	St Godwald, Finstall	25	Finstall First School
11	Bromsgrove District Council Offices	26	Crab Mill
12	County Buildings	27	Rigby Hall
13	Police Station	28	Former Barnsley Hall Hospital
14	Dolphin Centre		

gazebo, and OAKDENE (now Unionist Club); brick, with timbered gables, by *John Cotton*, 1887.

PERRY HALL (now Bromsgrove School: Housman Hall), in Kidderminster Road, facing Adams Walk, the SW approach to the church, was rebuilt in 1824 for John Adams; brick, four bays, with pretty paired-lancet timber windows. Lower NE extension; C20 additions as a hotel. Inside, beneath the stairs, a kind of shrine to A.E. Housman, who lived here as a boy; stained glass by *P.E. Lemmon*. To the SW, at right angles, the picturesque ruined wall of the early C17 house: cross-windows with thick mullions, round-arched doorways.

Now ST JOHN STREET, below the church. No. 14 has one sandstone bay with timber-framed gable, dated 1674. No. 10, next to the Church Steps, is good early C18, red brick, of five bays; stone quoins, central doorway with segmental pediment. Then ST JOHN'S COURT, a nursing home, its centre the former vicarage of 1847–8 by *Henry Day*; brick, symmetrical Jacobethan, with shaped gables and round oriel above the doorway. Acquired as Bromsgrove UDC offices in 1928, receiving a large brick N extension by *C.E. Bateman* in 1939–40; curved council chamber at the rear of the lower connecting link. Plainer S extension, 1965–6; gates by the *Bromsgrove Guild*, 1953. St John Street here turns E, past the new Market Hall (p. 197), to the former Market Place, mostly obliterated by the bulky GEORGE HOUSE of 1964.

1b. Worcester Road

Next briefly SW along WORCESTER ROAD. A good Georgian group of varying heights starts the E side, ending with the charming No. 7, KEMBREY HOUSE, the former Golden Lion Inn; of three bays and storeys, probably of the 1770s. Central doorway with open pediment on engaged Doric columns, window above with curved moulded head and fluted keystone. The flanking windows, on two storeys, are Venetian, their arches of Gothic ogee form with fleur-de-lys finials (cf. Tudor House, Chaddesley Corbett, p. 220).

Opposite, Nos. 4–6 retain large expanses of early C20 first-floor department store glazing. Nos. 14–16, a pair of shops beneath one broad shared gable, are by *Cotton*, 1890. They face STATION STREET,* where the workshops of the Bromsgrove Guild were located from 1899; only the SE part, at the top, survives, mostly by *Ewen Harper & Brother*, 1904–8, part brick, part corrugated iron. A few more late C19–early C20 shopfronts remain in Worcester Road, e.g. Nos. 33–35, E side, set into a painted brick Georgian house. Next door, the former REGAL CINEMA, a thorough conversion of 1934 of an Independent Chapel of 1786; stepped rendered front, crude fluted pilasters.

---

* On its S corner stood the late C15 merchant's house, demolished 1962, re-erected at the Avoncroft Museum, p. 608.

Further S, YE OLDE BLACK CROSS (No. 70, W side), the only surviving timber-framed building in the street; partly early C17, the N cross-wing gable with simple framing, the main range with dormer with some decorative patterning. Nos. 87–89, E side, an C18 brick pair, have a more attractive return towards the original building of Bromsgrove School (p. 197).

2a. The south end of High Street and into New Road

Bromsgrove's HIGH STREET runs NE (here for convenience assumed to be N), from the former Market Place. Some Georgian houses remain, their ground floors mostly with routine C20 shopfronts; far more have been replaced by C20 buildings, hardly any rising above the mediocre.

The W side begins with No. 1, c. 1600, timber-framed, restored by *F.W.B. Charles*, 1962; façade with two jettied gables, concave-sided lozenges, and fleur-de-lys motifs. Originally four gables; two (and part of the third) were destroyed when the tall MANCHESTER HOUSE was built to the N, in 1897. Nos. 7–9 are standard five-bay three-storey Georgian brick, with quoins; Nos. 11–13 are by *John Cotton*, 1871, with tall central gable. Nos. 25–27 make a more consistent C18 display, with Nos. 29–31, the same elements but given uplift by its parapet with upturned ends.

C18 houses on the E side, after the narrow MARKET PLACE POST OFFICE, with timber oriel, by *Cotton c.* 1866, are stuccoed or painted. Then the GOLDEN CROSS HOTEL by *Watson & Johnson* of Birmingham, 1932, five bays, stuccoed, with mildly Deco detail, continued in the little-altered interior. Nos. 22–24 are grander Georgian, of six bays; two storeys above the shops with four giant Doric pilasters, above the cornice a separate attic storey with plainer pilasters.

Now into New Road, especially for Nos. 1–3, originally the HOP POLE INN, standing in the High Street where New Road now starts. Re-erected here as a bank by *Hopkins* in 1866–7; restored and altered, also reduced in height. But the composition of jettied gables, small–large–small, is original, so are the concave lozenges and fleur-de-lys motifs. The date WB 1572 (for William Brooke) is also original, so here is a very early case of such lavish decoration. Hopkins renewed the bargeboards with their running animals, adding the gabled porch, canted W bay window, and projecting E wing for the bank manager's residence.

NEW ROAD, cut through 1864–5, was a quicker route from town to railway station (opened 1840, p. 315). It soon filled with detached or semi-detached villas, almost all replaced by anodyne late C20 blocks of flats. The first of these, S side, on the site of two of *Cotton*'s best buildings, the Institute and School of Science and Art, 1893–5, and Cottage Hospital, 1890–1, incorporate various fragments, especially the Hospital's entrance bay. Of surviving villas, the best is NEWLANDS (No. 27), N side, by *E.A. Day*, 1866: severe brick with hipped roof, but varying this earlier villa type with studied asymmetry and heavy detailing. (For New Road further E, *see* p. 205).

The better-preserved COLLEGE ROAD, leading N, was built up later, the E side mostly from *c.* 1900. Best here is No. 26 (GEORGIAN HOUSE), good austere Neo-Georgian by *Ewen Harper & Brother*, 1909.

Modest late C19 development in THE CRESCENT, to the S, its curve enhanced by VICTORIA VILLAS (Nos. 4–10), two pairs by *Cotton*, 1876. Further on, the Police Station (p. 196) and then, to the S, the lodge and gates to Bromsgrove School (p. 199).

2b. The north part of High Street

Now back to HIGH STREET, pedestrianized since 1982. Amongst the usual commercial ill-assortment, more Georgian fronts can be picked out; occasionally, e.g. at No. 49, hiding earlier timber framing. The C18 RED LION (No. 73, W side) even retains part of its ground floor, with central doorway with segmental pediment; brick, five widely spaced bays, moulded string courses breaking forward over the keystones.

Further on, good houses on both sides. Nos. 108–110, E, are tall, much restored late C16, with close studding and two gables; second-floor jetty on moulded brackets, renewed flat oriels above. Early C19 shop window and reeded doorcase at No. 110. No. 112 next door (LLOYDS TSB), six-bay Late Georgian, has even quoins, segment-headed bolection-moulded windows with carved keystones, and shallow heavy Doric porch. Opposite, No. 89, dated 1699, only two bays with quoins and pedimented dormers; and Nos. 91–93, early C18, six narrow bays, with dentil cornice and dormers. In the street stands a bronze statue of A.E. Housman, scholar and poet, by *Kenneth Potts*, 1983; ribbed concrete plinth.

A parade of shops leads E to Windsor Street, with Congregational chapel (p. 195) and County Buildings (p. 196). On the hillside high above the latter, THE MOUNT, early C19 with stuccoed S front with two-storey bow windows; enlarged by *Cotton*, 1874.

Again back to HIGH STREET and No. 120, mid-C18 painted brick, five bays, with giant fluted angle pilasters alternately blocked, and shallow central pediment. Segmental-headed windows, the middle one with fluted keystone and pilasters widening out into a curve at the bottom. Then Nos. 126–130, good Gothic of 1851, built for Dr George Horton; blue brick with yellow diapering, three gables with pierced bargeboards, the central one taller with stone oriel. Five gabled dormers at the rear. Opposite, outside the POST OFFICE of 1937, is a Bromsgrove Guild memorial, a fibreglass copy (by *Terry Simons*, 1983) of *Louis Weingartner*'s Dryad with Boar.

3. Further north-east, along Birmingham Road

THE STRAND, a widening of the High Street as it meets Stratford Road, remains a well-enclosed space despite heavy through traffic. On its E side, set at an angle, are Nos. 2–4, the former Empress Theatre, stuccoed, mostly by *H. W. Simister*, 1921–2, and Nos. 6–12, C18 painted brick. On the w, a low brick range (its rear partly timber-framed) includes the late C18 QUEEN'S HEAD, remodelled by *G.H. Gadd*, 1907. STRAND HOUSE, N, between the former Stourbridge and Birmingham roads, of *c.* 1701, was converted and enlarged as the parish workhouse in 1723; later a tannery. At the start of the present STOURBRIDGE ROAD, the former High School (p. 200).

In BIRMINGHAM ROAD, leading NE, the most notable building is No. 28 (DAVENAL HOUSE). Mid-C18, five bays and three storeys, with deep parapet ramped up at the ends and centre; pedimented doorway with Doric pilasters, against a rusticated surround. Its former coachhouse is now the Bromsgrove Museum. There follows assorted C18–C19 pairs and terraces; the former Hephzibah Chapel (p. 195); a good brick house (No. 94) with terracotta trim and timbered gables, built for himself *c.* 1880–90 by the builder *Joseph Tilt*; and a shopping arcade dated 1922. At the end, facing All Saints (p. 194), the mid-C18 CRAB MILL INN (restored early 1950s); similar to No. 7 Worcester Road, but with normal un-ogeed Venetian windows on its two lower floors, flanking the pedimented doorway. The parapet ramps down over the centre bay. SE of All Saints is the Council House (p. 196). Further along Birmingham Road is the former Union Workhouse (p. 196).

OUTER BROMSGROVE

A few outlying items, following a more or less clockwise direction.

East

The THOMAS WHITE COTTAGE HOMES, near the SE end of NEW ROAD (cf. p. 203), are three semi-detached gabled pairs of 1885–6. In EAST ROAD, Stoney Hill, further NE, is ELMSHURST, by *John Cotton*, 1874–5, for William Holyoake: large, banded brick, tall and gabled. For New Road E and SE of the by-pass, *see* Finstall.

A little S, at No. 80 Old Station Road, hemmed in by housing immediately E of Bromsgrove School playing fields, is the late C17 BROOM HOUSE. Sandstone, two bays and storeys of cross-windows, the string-course rising above as hoodmoulds; close-studded gable-end. Earlier E range, lower and timber-framed. Further E, approached from Harvington Road, the C17 timber-framed former farm buildings.

South

WORCESTER ROAD, SW of the centre, with straggling early to mid-C19 development, soon becomes ROCK HILL, where most of Bromsgrove's sandstone quarries were situated. At the

junction with Charford Road, CHARFORD LODGE is stuccoed
early C19, three by three bays; blocky W porch, good incised N
doorcase. Above, S, rises St Peter (R.C., p. 194). 1 m. further
WSW, approached via Grafton Lane off the Worcester road, is
Grafton Manor (p. 321).

In Charford Road, the excellent South Bromsgrove High School
(p. 200). The CHARFORD ESTATE, to the S, begun 1950,
probably by *J.E. Seabright*, was the largest erected by
Bromsgrove UDC. Brick semi-detached pairs or terraces of
four, spaciously laid out round a circular spine (LYTTELTON
DRIVE), varied with occasional longer terraces or three-storey
flats. Pleasant, low brick PRIMARY SCHOOL, E end, by *L.C.
Lomas*, 1954–5.

West

On the S side of KIDDERMINSTER ROAD, beyond the municipal
SANDERS PARK, is DENMARK HOUSE (No. 33), a large villa
built for Benjamin Sanders in the 1820s; painted brick, with
attractive two-storeyed wooden verandas on both garden
fronts. Much further out, by the M5, the HANOVER INTER-
NATIONAL HOTEL, a huge white-rendered confection of
c. 1980–90.

MONSIEURS HALL, Monsieurs Hall Lane, 1¼ m. WNW. C17,
much restored. Tall sandstone block with timbered gable; high
rectangular brick chimney with frieze of small blank arches just
below the cap. Lower rendered N range, partly timber-framed.
The stone block has mullioned windows, S, facing nice
gatepiers with ball finials and a yard with large sandstone
BARN.

North

Along STOURBRIDGE ROAD, mixed C19 housing and the Board
School (p. 200). Further N, the Princess of Wales Hospital
(p. 196). In BEWELL HEAD, W, a simple pair of early C19 brick
nailers' cottages (Nos. 57–59), a rare survival. Close to the M42
are remnants of Barnsley Hall Hospital (p. 196).

SIDEMOOR, further W, consists mostly of early C20 Bromsgrove
UDC housing, its spine being Broad Street (with the former
Ebenezer Methodist Church, p. 195). The most consistent
UDC housing is around KING GEORGE CLOSE, mid-1930s by
Robert Thompson of Catshill, a spacious layout of severe brick
houses in twos or fours; one relieving darker brick band, hipped
pantiled roofs. PERRYFIELDS CRESCENT, by *Thompson*, 1936,
has friendlier pairs, with roughcast gables.

In BIRMINGHAM ROAD, N of the former Workhouse (p. 196), is
the former TOWNSEND MILL, on the Spadesbourne Brook;
C18 brick, retaining some machinery and part of its mill pond.
Further on, near the by-pass, THE MOUNT SCHOOL, built as
All Saints Vicarage by *J.A. Chatwin*, 1876–7; large unsubtle
brick, with half-timbered gables.

At LICKEY END, in the angle of roads s of the M42 junction, the former FOREST HOTEL, large, mid to late C19; roughcast, pierced bargeboards, canted bay windows with iron cresting.

CROWS MILL, ⅛ m. s of School Lane (with the Board School, p. 200), is another c18 mill on the Spadesbourne Brook, sandstone and brick, but with an earlier L-plan house: timber-framed and thatched, of cruck construction, probably c15.

BROOME

9070

Transferred from Staffordshire in 1844. Compact brick village, with a couple of timber-framed survivors.

St PETER. A medieval chapelry to Clent. Rebuilt 1780. Red brick with stone dressings, once no doubt an uncommonly charming little Georgian church. w tower with circular openings; tower arch with imposts and keystone. Nave only two bays, with large round-arched windows. The chancel, however, rebuilt in 1861, is too long, though in keeping and apparently reusing the original E window. N vestry added by *M. W. Jones*, 1936–7. Inside, the architect of 1861 could not resist adding foliage capitals to the E window and similar sandstone shafts to the chancel arch. Further restored and re-seated by *Hopkins*, 1879.

FONT. Norman. Small round bowl with diminutive intersecting arcading of beaded arches; narrow foliage band above. The top of the sturdy circular stem is also c12, with big grotesque heads, the rest renewed. – Oak REREDOS by *Francis B. Andrews & Son*, 1931–2; barley-twist ALTAR RAILS, *c.* 1913. – STAINED GLASS. Chancel windows by *Hardman*: E 1870, two s 1878. – MONUMENTS. Anne Hill †1804, by *Flaxman*. Young woman in profile, seated on the ground reading the Bible. Grey obelisk behind; beautifully spaced and lettered inscription. – In the NE corner of the CHURCHYARD, a good Gothic tomb to the Bourne family, *c.* 1860.

CHURCH HOUSE, NE, is said to be of 1826, by *Swift & Dudley* of Birmingham. Italianate, with shallow hipped slate roof on bracketed cornice; enlarged *c.* 1840–50. N porch with rounded oriel added by *T. Grazebrook, c.* 1900.

The former SCHOOL to its s, dated 1889, and the SCHOOL HOUSE further s (of 1839, remodelled 1890) both have unexpectedly classical detailing. Opposite the latter a striking pair of Gothic banded brick cottages, *c.* 1860–70.

The OLD RECTORY, a little WNW, probably *c.* 1820, has three bays with hipped roof; central pedimented Doric doorway flanked by broad single-storey bows. – C17 timber-framed BARN.

BROOME HOUSE, in fine grounds SSE of the church, has two worthwhile but contrasting stone façades, probably of *c.* 1760–70 encasing an earlier house. The E, of redder sandstone with three widely spaced bays, has a lively semi-Gothick skyline. Taller outer bays, square with battlements; round-arched ground-floor windows, but tripartite Gothick and Y-tracery above. Recessed centre with big ogee gable containing a quatrefoil; below, a small battlemented porch, with blocked ogee-arched doorway. The entrance front, s, is largely Palladian; five bays, the central three projecting beneath a pediment, and two-and-a-half storeys, with plain giant angle pilasters. The columns of the semicircular central porch have capitals already reeded in the Adam way; Venetian and Diocletian windows above. Pevsner thought the semi-Gothick front earlier, by a decade or so. Andor Gomme suggests they are contemporary, possibly by *William & David Hiorn* of Warwick. Interior altered in the late C19, with large panelled entrance-cum-staircase hall. Converted to a nursing home *c.* 1979, with low N additions.

Former STABLES, E, also late C18; brick with stone dressings. Small pediment above the entrance, hipped roof with cupola. – Large LAKE, s of the entrance front.

RED HALL FARM, ⅓ m. SE. Also Gothick in a style akin to the E front of Broome House, presumably remodelled as an eye-catcher *c.* 1760–70. Roughcast, three bays, H-plan; curved outer gables with quatrefoils, two tiers of tripartite windows below. On the return front, Y-tracery with ogee finials.

THICKNALL FARM, ½ m. N, is upright late C18; brick, segment-headed windows, hipped roof.

Large Birmingham suburban houses on the w outskirts of the parish. At HACKMAN'S GATE, ⅔ m. WSW, the earliest is MARYKNOWLE of 1904: prominently sited, roughcast white, with weatherboarded gable-ends. Further w is BLAKEDOWN HOUSE, brick, 1932; elephantine butterfly plan.

At YIELDINGTREE, ⅔ m. SSW, the neat C18 MANOR HOUSE has five bays with segment-headed windows, and central one-bay pediment with circular opening.

BROUGHTON HACKETT

ST LEONARD. Small; nave and chancel in one, weatherboarded w turret with pyramid roof. The nave is C14, with Dec w window. A clear break in the N wall's Lias stonework suggests the chancel may be later. Much restored by *Perkins*, 1843; he rebuilt the s wall, with its upright porch, and probably the Perp-style E window. Simple plastered interior. – STAINED GLASS. E window by *Francis W. Skeat*, 1971.

The OLD RECTORY, SW, also by *Perkins*, is prominently dated 1845; brick, with diapering. Tudor-style, with two gables, a star-shaped chimney set back between them. Much enlarged at the rear.

The mostly C20 village retains some C17 timber-framed cottages and the brick MANOR FARM, of *c.* 1800; its former HOP KILNS form a nice punctuation mark at the E end.

CHURCHILL MILL, on the Bow Brook ½ m. SSE. The Blue Lias rubble walls and exceptionally large size of this mill, built *c.* 1620, probably saved it from demolition in the late C18, when most of Worcestershire's water mills were rebuilt. It was altered internally but the main structure, with its great s chimneystack with two diagonal brick shafts, survived. Two iron water wheels remain *in situ.* Converted for themselves by *F.W.B. & Mary Charles* in the early 1960s.

BUSHLEY

8030

ST PETER. Rebuilt by *Edward Blore*, 1842–3, for the Rev. Canon E.C. Dowdeswell. Of Lias with Cotswold stone dressings. w tower with broach spire, aisleless nave, shallow transepts; *G.G. Scott* replaced the short chancel with a demonstratively higher one, in 1856–7. To him Blore's Gothic, following the Commissioners' early C19 conventions, must have been distasteful. Its details are mostly Perp, with pleasantly naïve carving; battlements, pinnacles, and the spire's flying buttresses were all removed *c.* 1958. Scott's chancel is of course Middle Pointed; E window with Dec butterfly tracery and ballflower, pierced quatrefoil parapet, crocketed pinnacles. Chancel arch with rich foliage corbels (carved by *Forsyth*); arch-braced roof. The s organ chamber was converted into a chapel in 1908–9 by *Anthony Wilson* of London; his also the fine w ORGAN GALLERY. – Oak REREDOS, with painted scenes by *George Ostrehan.* – Stone PULPIT. 1853. – Other furnishings all designed by Scott: low iron SCREEN (made by *Skidmore*), lavish chancel TILING, free-standing timber SEDILIA, STALLS and PEWS. – The FONT may incorporate an ancient bowl. – STAINED GLASS. By *Warrington & Son*, 1862–3, the chancel E and NW, and nave N central windows. – All others in the nave and the N transept N by *George Rogers*, 1850–3. – By *Hardman*, chancel SE (1876) and NE (1894), also the s transept s (1888). – Small s chapel window by *Paul Woodroffe*, 1909.

MONUMENTS. Brass to Thomas Payne †1500 and his wife Ursula. Only the 25-in. (63-cm.) figures remain, the rest lost or renewed. – Roberts Freeman †1651; brass plate, with good lettering. – Other tablets, all Dowdeswells. Roger †1633,* already post-Jacobean and classical, has columns and steep broken pediment. – Judith †1666, attributed to *Jasper Latham* (GF), just a flaming urn on a column; William †1683, opposite, has an identical 'pillar'. – Richard †1673; twisted columns, broken pediment with reclining allegories. – Elizabeth †1706; Ionic columns, but more rustic. – Standing monument of 1777 by *John Hickey* to William Dowdeswell †1775, Chancellor of the Exchequer 1765–6. Fulsome epitaph composed by Edmund Burke; above, fine relief of a grieving woman, with small portrait roundel, seated at the plinth of a garlanded urn. – Brass to the Rev. E.C. Dowdeswell †1849, by *Hardman*.

---

*He acquired Pull Court, *see* below, in 1628.

The former VICARAGE (now Wellingtonia House), NW, is an attractive Jacobethan remodelling by *Richard Armstrong*, 1850–2; brick, stepped gables, latticed windows, angle porch. Equally picturesque, the OLD SCHOOL of 1855, NE, probably again by *Armstrong*; half-timbered with latticed windows and bargeboards, attached to a close-studded former farmhouse of *c.* 1600.

CHURCH END otherwise consists of timber-framed or brick estate cottages, many prettified in the mid C19. The brick SHEPHERD'S PEACE, at the crossroads, has a finely carved C15 bressummer on its side wall, reputedly from Payne's Place (*see* below). TUDOR COTTAGE, W, mostly C16 close studding with brick-nogging, has an earlier, lower rear wing, with full-cruck truss exposed at its N gable-end.

PAYNE'S PLACE, ¼ m. further WSW in Stokes Lane, probably built in the late C15 for Thomas Payne, is all close-studded, with brick infill. Long hall range, with E cross-wing, perhaps later. C19 porch at the angle; brick extension, W. The entrance front must have been the present rear, S, where the gabled wing is jettied, with richly carved bargeboards. Part of the originally open hall roof remains visible upstairs: moulded wall-plate beams, chamfered arched braces to the collar-truss; wind-braces now plastered over. In the cross-wing parlour, part of a painted frieze with text commemorating the marriage of Anthony and Margaret Stratford, 1577.

At BUSHLEY GREEN, a separate settlement ¾ m. WNW, more timber-framed cottages and brick farms; also SARN HILL GRANGE, a larger brick and half-timbered house by *Richard Armstrong Jun.*, 1888.

PULL COURT (now Bredon School), 1⅓ m. NW. Rebuilt for Canon Dowdeswell by *Blore*, 1834–9: a large, competent, highly monumental mansion, his first in Elizabethan or Jacobean style. *Richard Armstrong* was clerk of works. Mostly limestone ashlar, with large mullioned-and-transomed windows. Shaped gables are the predominant feature; balustraded parapets and many finials have been removed. The N front, partly coursed Lias, is approached through an entrance court: rather low stone screen of narrow arched openings on

Bushley, Pull Court.
Drawing

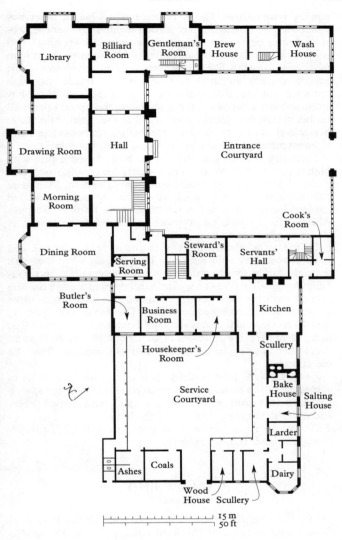

Bushley, Pull Court.
Ground-floor plan

square piers; imposing central gateway of Neoclassical solid-
ity, with raised centre. Short projecting wings, the same height
as the house, extend as lower service ranges to the screen wall.
Ashlar frontispiece flanked by tall square angle turrets with
ogee stone caps; lofty three-transomed three-light windows
either side of the small elaborate doorway. The other fronts are

p. 210

equally symmetrical. The w return has full-height outer bay windows. The broad five-bay garden front, s, has canted two-storey outer bays (now without their strapwork cresting), and projecting one-bay centre again flanked by square turrets with ogee caps, looking like a gatehouse. Compact service court (much altered) attached to the E return. Inside, the high entrance hall has ashlar walls and a flat timber roof; three-bay stone arcades either side, the E screening the grand open-well timber staircase, Jacobean-style like the stone fireplace; heraldic glass of 1908–9. Good Jacobethan timber ceilings and chimneypieces in the reception rooms along the s front.

Early C19 STABLES, E. Brick, nine bays; raised centre with high round arch, recessed corner shafts (originally stuccoed), stone platbands. Hipped roof with timber cupola. Many late C20 additions for the school, mostly set in the three walled gardens beyond. Further E, GATES of 1750 from Tewkesbury Abbey, with ornamental ironwork and overthrow; restored by *Armstrong Jun.*, 1897.

Of the terraced GARDENS, to s and w, only outlines and parts of boundary walls remain. – The landscaping of the PARK is partly earlier, attributed, without documentation, to *Capability Brown*. – THE STALLS, ⅓ m. s, is apparently a C17 timber-framed barn (or deer house), remodelled *c.* 1860–70 as three picturesque half-timbered cottages. – The PAVILION, ¾ m. SE, now Moss Green House, is similarly ornamental work of 1864; in its shrubbery, NW, remains of an artificial RUIN, built as an eyecatcher in 1843, incorporating two C14 windows from the old church.

PARK LODGE, near Bushley Green, is of brick, *c.* 1860, in gabled Jacobean style. On the main road, 1 m. further ssw, a Lias LODGE, presumably by *Blore, c.* 1840, with shaped gables and other detail matching that of the house.

For MYTHE BRIDGE, across the Severn, 1 m. ESE, *see The Buildings of England: Gloucestershire 2.*

8040

CALLOW END
Powick

ST JAMES. A chapel of ease to Powick, built for the sixth Earl Beauchamp in 1888, by the local builder *Charles Bishop*. No architect was employed. The Diocesan Architectural Society noted at the time that it was 'without any architectural pretensions'. Brick, quite small, with louvre-like bell-turret, domestic N windows, and two small two-light w windows in free Perp style. s addition 1980. – STAINED GLASS by *Camm & Co.*, 1962, from the demolished Powick Asylum chapel.

Brick SCHOOL, N, by *Preedy*, 1870–1, much altered; only the two bold chimneys and the timber N window, of five lights, look original.

To the s, CALLOW END CLUB, 1908; single-storey, gabled and weatherboarded.

STANBROOK ABBEY. In 1838 the Benedictine nunnery for English ladies, founded at Cambrai in 1623, expelled from France (1795) and installed at Abbot's Salford (Warks.) from 1807, moved to Callow End. The nuns took over Stanbrook Hall, which *Charles Day* doubled in size for them, from 1835; his chapel wing survives. In 1869–71, *E.W. Pugin* provided a new church further N, and, from 1878, his successors *P.P. Pugin & C.W. Pugin* planned ambitious ranges around three sides of an enclosed courtyard N of their brother's church. Only the E and N ranges were built. The future of the buildings is uncertain at the time of writing.

E.W. *Pugin*'s CHURCH is a good example of his work. Red brick, with stone dressings and Seddon's patent Roman roof tiles. Quite large: choir (in the unaisled nave) and sanctuary, plus an extern chapel (for the laity), SE. Geometrical Dec windows. Pugin intended a W bell-turret but the chaplain, Dom Laurence Shepherd, insisted on a high, narrow W tower, with taller round stair-turret, NW, all of red and white striped brick in the Sienese-Ruskinian way. This is the most striking external feature. Stone-faced interior, with closely set transverse ribs rising from wall piers (a typical E.W. Pugin feature). Windows recessed between each pier, with the choir stalls set back into them; these, of New Zealand satinwood, were made by *Morley* of Ramsgate. Fine stone carving by *R.L. Boulton*;[*] *Minton* tiled floors; organ case by *Farmer & Brindley*. Sanctuary drastically reordered in 1971 by *Anthony Thompson* (of *Peter Falconer & Partners*); Pugin's fine reredos of 1878, his iron screen, and the last of the wall paintings by *Clayton & Bell*, were all removed. The long Holy Thorn Chapel, S, was added by *P.P. Pugin*, 1885; he also modified the W end (for the abbatial throne). – STAINED GLASS. Mostly *Hardman*, 1871–5, their W window 1913. – Extern chapel E by *Lavers & Westlake*, 1901. – Holy Thorn Chapel windows by *J.N. Pearce*, c. 1885–6. – MONUMENTS. Recumbent effigies of Dom Shepherd †1885, by *P.P. Pugin*, carved by *Boulton*; and of Abbess Gertrude d'Aurillac Dubois †1897, by *Dame Beatrice Brown* of Stanbrook Abbey, marble and alabaster.

The NE SACRISTY by *Pugin & Pugin*, 1898–1900, links the church to the high E range of their MONASTERY, built, together with the start of the N range, in 1878–80. Trefoiled lancets are the dominant theme, with gabled attic dormers. Unfinished square tower above the main doorway; large gabled projection to its N. The remainder of the N range, added 1895–8, is similar, but with mansard roof with timber dormers, and Perp Tudor detail at the W end (for the refectory). Both ranges have internal cloister-like corridors, with cells on the upper floors instead of a dormitory. The finest cloister, the *Via Crucis*, runs W from the church, with excellent stone Stations of the Cross carved

---

[*] Boulton, wrote Pugin in 1870, 'can do angels to perfection, but his foliage carving is certainly not stone carving.'

by *Boulton* in 1871. Other linking corridors, brick and much inferior, by *Martin Fisher* of Bath, 1963–4.

Another corridor by *E. W. Pugin* runs s from the church's E end to the surviving E wing of the mid-C18 STANBROOK HALL (later presbytery); relocated Tuscan doorway, good staircase within. The larger part, facing N and duplicated for the Abbey by *Charles Day* in 1835–8, was demolished in 1898, but Day's W wing, with CHAPEL, chapter room and school survives. The chapel has large round-arched W windows, in Nonconformist style. Most interesting interior, later a library: coved nave ceiling, but the sanctuary top-lit by a small glass dome in Baroque-inspired fashion.

Further s, two octagonal brick LODGES of 1849, perhaps by *Henry Day*, with depressed Y-tracery. The present entrance, from the N, passes a modest stuccoed house of 1865, much enlarged as a retreat house by *Anthony Thompson*, 1986.

The sprawling VILLAGE retains some timber framing, especially in BEAUCHAMP LANE, running E from Pole Elm. This begins with a former CONGREGATIONAL CHAPEL, by *G. Johnson* of Worcester, 1864, and ends at BEAUCHAMP COURT, on the site of the manor house of the Beauchamps of Powick; early C19, roughcast, three storeys and five bays, the central three beneath a pediment.

Further N is WHEATFIELD, a substantial Italianate villa, prob-ably mostly of 1836 by *Thomas Prosser*, for William Wall. Stuc-coed, with five-bay s front: central porch of paired Doric columns, outer bays emphasized by straight quoins and first-floor iron balconies. Asymmetrical return to the main road, some windows with shell tympana.

PRIOR'S COURT, off Lower Ferry Lane, at the s end, is a pic-turesque C16 house, round a small courtyard (only 16 by 12 ft, 5 by 4 metres). Irregular timber framing, partly with brick infilling, partly plastered. Restored 1898–9. Triple gabled N front, with cross-gabled porch on baluster-like Tuscan columns, of oak; door with two large oval panels. Most ground-floor rooms open directly from the court. The principal entrance, at the centre of the s range, leads into a cross-passage, partly open to the hall, W, within which rises a C17 staircase, with closed string and turned balusters. Parlour, E, with no doubt great chamber above, these rooms served by a fine brick chimney with two star-plan stacks. The adjoining narrow brick-built section, SE corner, must have been added in the C17 to provide a closet for the great chamber. Kitchen wing added to the service range, W, *c.* 1789.

THE COURT, Kent's Green, ½ m. W of Stanbrook Abbey, is early C19 stuccoed; five bays with central stone porch of Ionic fluted columns between antae.

CASTLEMORTON

ST GREGORY. A chapelry of Longdon until 1880. Of C12 origin, see the chancel N windows, some reused beaded cable

moulding above the E window, and the Norman nave doorways, both with scallop capitals and arch with furrowed frontal
chevron (cf. Earl's Croome). The N doorway has an Agnus Dei
tympanum; the clumsily re-set S doorway a (later?) head at the
apex. S transept *c.* 1300: S window with cusped intersecting
tracery, trefoiled pointed E lancets with twin-arched hoodmould on large headstops, and piscina with acute ogee arch;
hipped roof of 1908. Most other windows Dec or Perp. The
nave N wall has an ogee-headed lancet with low transom, and
a three-light Perp window, flanked inside by handsome
canopied niches with angels above; this looks too grand for the
church and may be imported, perhaps from Little Malvern
Priory. Close-studded N porch, C15–C16. Embattled W tower,
reputedly *c.* 1387, with diagonal W buttresses with ogee image
niches. The recessed stone spire is probably of *c.* 1683, when
much else was done to remedy Civil War damage. The three-
and-a-half-bay S arcade must then have been re-assembled,
jumbled up, and partly replaced. The octagonal piers may also
be of *c.* 1387, but the round W pier belongs to an earlier arcade.
There is no reason, though, to assume that the blocked openings above belong to a C12–C13 clerestory; their function seems
purely to support the two huge beams inserted to stabilize the
S aisle. All thoroughly restored in 1879–80 by *Ewan Christian*,
who faithfully rebuilt the chancel N wall. – PEWS and STALLS
also of this date. – Oak REREDOS and ALTAR by *Richard
Haughton*, 1900. – COMMUNION RAIL. With flat openwork
balusters, a very late occurrence considering the inscribed
dates 1683 and 1684. – S transept ALTAR. 1908, painted 1918.
– Three FONTS. That in use has a Perp stem and C17 bowl with
acanthus leaves. The original bowl, half-broken, is now in the
S transept, on a plain octagonal stem. The third, an C18 baluster font, has flat foliage on its base and bowl. – STAINED
GLASS. C15 borders and tracery fragments, chancel SE. – E
window (1900) and S transept E (1929), both *Hardman*. –
MONUMENT. Richard Cocks †1821, by *Sidney Gregg* of
Ledbury. Mourning woman, with inversed torch, leaning on
an urn. Competent work, as is Gregg's Grecian tablet nearby
to Francis Cross †1838. – Several nice earlier tablets.

WAR MEMORIAL CROSS, to the NW, by *W.D. Caröe*, 1921.
Modest buildings around the church. FOLLIOTT HOUSE, formerly Church Farm, E, of brick, is dated 1785. The rendered
OLD VICARAGE, to the N, must be *c.* 1800, with hipped roof
and later bay windows. TROY CHIMNEYS, W, mostly C17
timber-framed, incorporates earlier cruck trusses in its N–S
range. To the S, the former brick SCHOOL, 1849 and later,
poorly adapted as a house.

Further S, the well-preserved earthworks of the CASTLE,
with its bailey to the N and high oval motte, S. It was probably
built by the Folliotts *c.* 1140, i.e. in Stephen's reign; the village
was formerly known as Morton Folliott.

Larger houses further WNW begin with ROUGH CHASE, early
C18, three-bay brick; timber-framed C16–C17 wing with cruck
truss exposed in its W gable, reused or a late example? Almost

opposite, FRISBY HOUSE also has cruck remnants within; W wing added 1901, the whole converted to a thatched, half-timbered, H-plan confection in 1924. The OLD ALMSHOUSE, further W, was also 'period restored' as a house, by *Reginald Craft*, 1961–2; previously there was a forest of chimneystacks, probably of 1869. The C14–C15 core survives, with a relatively large two-bay cruck hall (formerly with spere-truss), and smaller cross-wing, W. The three N gables facing the road (the easternmost cased in brick), are probably all basically mid to late C16.

BANNUT TREE HOUSE (originally Walnut Tree Farm), ⅔ m.
WNW. Dated 1890, the first medium-size country house by *C.F.A. Voysey*; L-plan, with short E service wing, for R.H. Cazalet, at a cost of only £1,120. It stands behind a restored cottage (with modern date 1576), which surely influenced Voysey's choice of style. His house is already of white roughcast with green-painted woodwork (now black), and already with great emphasis on horizontals, mullioned windows, and big roofs, their almost detached gutters on thin curved brackets. But the main (garden) front, S, has four even gables with half-timbering, a motif Voysey later more or less discarded. The upper floor is jettied out, though this is disguised by the picturesquely detailed chimney, l., by typically sloping buttresses, by the projecting garden porch, and also by the nice solution of the r. corner, where the ground-floor window bay is polygonal but the floor above juts out at a right angle. End gables again half-timbered; E front of the service wing with more pronounced horizontal emphasis. On the N entrance front the tiled roof sweeps down to low eaves, with a large roughcast gable in the angle; broadly gabled porch on sloping piers. The plan is simple: a corridor along the entrance side at both levels, with the stick-balustraded staircase, E end; three reception rooms along the S front. Most original fittings survive. – Opposite the entrance front, forming an open courtyard, the contemporary stable block, rectangular and also decidedly horizontal. Typical rear buttresses continue as a boundary wall towards the C16–C17 cottage. Minor alterations by *Voysey*, 1894, when he laid out the garden.

HILL END COURT, 1 m. E. Four-square, brick, early C19, with hipped roof; Greek Doric porch in front of the well-detailed round-arched doorway.

CATSHILL

Dreary suburban village, a former outpost of Bromsgrove nail-making.

CHRIST CHURCH, Stourbridge Road. Of red ashlar, badly weathered. Nave and W tower by *Harvey Eginton*, 1837–8, E end rebuilt by *J.A. Chatwin*, 1887. The nave is typical Commissioners' work, with long lancets and thin buttresses;

sturdier tower with paired bell-openings, but gauche corner pinnacles. Chatwin reused the stepped E triplet of the original short chancel, re-setting as his S chapel S window. His own work is more severe, especially the plate tracery of the high-set E window. The nave has standard 1830s roof trusses, and W gallery on thin iron columns, screened off in 1977 (by *Snell & Thompson*) to provide upper and lower rooms. An unusual feature of the E end is that the entrance arches to S chapel and N vestry are set diagonally forward from the chancel arch. Chapel reordered by *G.E.S. Streatfeild*, 1936. – Most FITTINGS by *Chatwin*, though the plain octagonal FONT, with quatrefoil stem, must be Eginton's. – Good ORGAN CASE of 1897, green-painted and gilded. – Oak PULPIT by *C. F. Whitcombe*, 1903, free Perp; from St John Baptist, Bromsgrove. – STAINED GLASS. Chancel N and S by *Burlison & Grylls*, 1889. – By *Hardman*, the E window, 1897, and two S chapel lancets, 1887. – The chapel E is fine Arts and Crafts work by *Karl Parsons*, 1931. – Nave SW by *P.E. Lemmon*, 1958.

BAPTIST CHURCH, Barley Mow Lane. Rebuilt by *Trinity Road Developments Ltd*, 1990. Red brick, low and spreading, with pantiled roof; hexagonal central space with roof-light, crowned by an openwork metal spire.

METHODIST CHURCH, Golden Cross Lane. By *Donald Cornfield*, 1968. Paler brick, with gabled chancel, nave and tower, all stepping up slightly, the last with a glass-fibre spike.

Former WESLEYAN CHAPEL, Barley Mow Lane. 1859. Small, brick, lancet style. Now County Library.

SCHOOLS. Three, providing a summary of C20 County Council design. CATSHILL FIRST SCHOOL, Gibb Lane, by *A. V. Rowe*, 1913–14, long, low, and roughcast, has brick pilasters and sharp, classically detailed gables. – The MIDDLE SCHOOL, Meadow Road, 1937–9 by *Rowe*, is plain Neo-Georgian brick; central hall flanked by higher hipped-roofed classroom blocks. – Next door, CHADSGROVE SCHOOL, 1976, for physically handicapped children; low, flat-roofed, crisply detailed.

Former GOLDEN CROSS HOTEL, Birmingham Road, Marlbrook. Large half-timbered road house by *J.H. Hawkes & McFarlane*, 1938; bargeboarded gables, tiled roof with hipped dormers, tall chimneys.

LYDIATE ASH HOUSE, No. 61 Halesowen Road, 1⅛ m. NE, close to the M5 interchange. Early C18, five bays, of patterned brick with stone quoins (cf. Chadwich Manor, p. 585). Segment-headed upper-floor windows, but those below blocked and replaced with two very wide sashes. – Stone gatepiers with ball finials.

CHADDESLEY CORBETT

8070

ST CASSIAN. An important village church, probably on the site of a Saxon minster. The dominating W steeple is by *James Rose*, 1778–9; battlemented tower with Y-traceried bell-openings and

similar W window beneath a large blank quatrefoil (typical late
C18 motifs); recessed spire with quatrefoil bands. Closer attention, however, will no doubt focus on the brilliant chancel, the
most spectacular Dec piece in any Worcestershire parish
church. E window of five lights, with many ogees, but also trefoils, reticulation units flanked by reversed ogee-ended triangles and, at the top, a large roundel with four split-cusped
trefoils. This last motif also in a S window; in another a bold
mouchette wheel, in the third cusped and sub-cusped trefoils.
Boldly stepped and gabled buttresses; ogee-headed priest's
door. No N windows as the chancel was rebuilt against an existing chapel of c. 1280, see the Y-tracery of its three N windows
and the three stepped lancets under one blank arch of its E
window (above the low vestry); buttresses probably C16. The S
aisle, with Dec W window and crocketed ogee-headed tomb
recess, S, was mostly rebuilt in the early C16; embattled
parapet, three-light Late Perp windows. Its Dec E window is a
renewal by *William Butterfield* who restored the church in
1863–4 (and again 1878–9). The N aisle windows are all his,
but the re-set Norman N doorway prepares for the interior; it
has one order of shafts with scalloped capitals and arch with
chevron forming lozenges at the angle. Butterfield also filled
Rose's W doorway with a window, opening up a new entrance
in the tower S wall.

So to the INTERIOR, where both arcades are Norman,
impressive but teasing. The N is clearly of two periods. Its three
E bays are convincingly mid-Norman: strong, relatively high,
round piers; round multi-scalloped capitals, with bits of decoration; square abaci; single-step round arches. The W pier was
the original W respond. Then a further W bay was added and at
the same time the S arcade built; this covers the same E–W distance in only three bays. Yet capitals and other details, as far as
they are not renewed, are identical. What happened then? To
venture a possible explanation, one must first look at tower arch
and chancel arch. The tower arch (now difficult to see clearly)
is doubled, in the sense that the modest round C18 arch stands
behind an earlier one, with three thin chamfers. This indicates
a previous W tower. The earlier arch is hard to date. The VCH
makes it C14, but it could be C15 or even later. The double-
chamfered chancel arch, tallying more or less in its details, is
clearly a makeshift affair. Might it not be then that, when the
church received its earlier tower, the S arcade piers and
responds were re-spaced to the new length required and a new,
Norman-looking, NW bay provided by using the responds of
the chancel arch? The VCH's explanation, that the S arcade and
the W bay of the N followed the rest of the N arcade before the
end of the C12, must in any case be excluded. Such widely
spaced single-step (pointed) arches are out of the question.

Splendid, elaborately cusped nave roof by *Butterfield*, also the
quieter wagon roof of the chancel. This is otherwise of course
Dec, with ogee-headed sedilia and piscina, the thickly moulded
arches of the former on prominent heads. Opposite, an ogee-

headed aumbry, with crockets, finial and headstops. The adjoining vestry doorway, round-arched with continuous mouldings, may be contemporary. Flanking the E window, large crocketed ogee image niches, on green-man corbels. The interior of the N chapel has been altered. The W arch to the aisle and similar triple responds of the two-bay S arcade tell of the late C13 date, but the central pier and arches of the latter must be C14 rebuilding; the pier is octagonal, the arches have a hollow chamfer moulding.

The E ends of both chancel and N chapel were reordered in the 1960s, with fittings by *R.B. Martin*. – Several Butterfield FURNISHINGS survive, notably the typical low PEWS and timber PULPIT. – FONT. A superb piece, probably *c.* 1160–70, an outlier of the Herefordshire school (cf. Norman fonts at Eardisley and Castle Frome). Of goblet shape, with short stem and tapering base, and decorated all over; on the base, two-strand interlace; on the stem, thick plaiting. The (partly renewed) bowl has a main band of five serpentine dragons, their tails wildly but not tightly twisted. This motif, of Anglo-Saxon derivation, presumably represents the evil forces over which Baptism can triumph; but the carver was clearly intent on enjoying himself. At the top another band of interlace, more tightly woven. – SCULPTURE. In the inner W wall of the tower a fragment of a mid-C12 tympanum: Christ in Majesty within a beaded mandorla; drapery and ornamental detail are both very close to the tympanum at Pedmore (Stourbridge). – Gothic ORGAN CASE. 1817, enlarged 1884, on a W gallery by *F.L. Randle*, 1972. – STAINED GLASS. Colourful E window by *George Rogers*, 1865–6, probably his best. – Chancel S, *c.* 1912, no doubt *Clayton & Bell*. – N aisle, from E: first, clearly *Burlison & Grylls*, *c.* 1880; second, *A.J. Davies*, 1927; third, *Hardman*, 1905. – The S aisle E and W, by *Walter Camm*, 1947–8, incorporate C14–C15 fragments.

MONUMENTS. Limestone effigy of a (probably) Corbett knight, *c.* 1325; cross-legged, wearing a mail coif, in the act of drawing his sword. Frieze of flowers along the chamfer of the tapering slab. – Sandstone priest's effigy, in eucharistic vestments, C14–C15. – Brass to Thomas Forest †1511 and wife Margaret; 37-in. (94 cm.) figures; children below, Evangelist symbols at the corners of the border inscription. – Elizabeth Holt †1647. Still entirely Jacobean, with black Composite columns and much strapwork. – Humphrey Pakington of Harvington Hall (p. 366) †1631, probably by *Edward Marshall*, but not earlier than *c.* 1646; a fine piece, already classical. Black and white marble, Ionic columns, broken pediment with impressive heraldry, but many still somewhat restless details. – Flanking tablets to his daughters: Dame Anne Audley †1642, a smaller, simpler version, also attributed to *Edward Marshall* (GF); and Lady Mary Yate †1696, a telling contrast, grey and white marble, very restrained.

In the CHURCHYARD, pedestal and chest tombs including one (E of the S aisle) to the architect James Rose †1796. Also steps and base of a C15 CROSS; shaft and gabled head added 1904. – LYCHGATE by *W. Bassett Smith*, 1889.

LODGE FARM, to the SW. The Georgian front hides a C16–C17 timber-framed house, of which the narrow-studded NW wing is visible. Late C17 SW wing.

The VILLAGE STREET is one of the most attractive in the county. First, at the SE corner opposite the church, set back in its own grounds, is HUNTERS RIDE, the vicarage by *Henry Day*, 1856–7; gabled brick with blue brick patterning. Then the former POLICE STATION by *Henry Rowe*, 1863, three bays with hipped roof but a round-arched stone doorway for added severity; and CHARITY HOUSE, a three-cottage terrace dated 1812. SPENCER HOUSE, at the Fold Lane corner, minimal brick Tudor Gothic of 1848, was built as teacher's house and girls' school. After CHURCH VIEW, an early C19 terrace, comes the TALBOT INN, its long impressive timber-framed frontage on a sandstone plinth. Two separate units of *c.* 1650, both perhaps built for the inn; ground floors all close-studded, but the upper storey of the larger S unit has (later?) square panelling. Porches mostly of 1931.

Opposite, LYCHGATE HOUSE, Early Georgian, three bays, with lively details. Odd parapet starting gablewise; panelled keystones; flat door canopy on carved consoles. Behind, facing the churchyard, the brick ENDOWED SCHOOL of 1809, with five large Gothic-glazed windows, arranged symmetrically around two pointed doorways. The BOYS' SCHOOL, N of Lychgate House, brick with timbered gables, is by *J. T. Meredith*, 1894. C20 additions. Then SADDLERS COTTAGE, late C16, encased in C18 brick, followed by a C17–C18 timber-framed range.

Back on the E side is the misnamed TUDOR HOUSE; stuccoed, with two-storey canted bays with Venetian windows broken round them, and two big ogee gables. Central doorway with classical pediment, but blank doorways and windows in the end bays again ogee-headed. The date may be *c.* 1760–70, the architect probably *James Rose*, apparently the owner.* Adjoining, N, a two-bay brick house of 1785, for the schoolmaster. Then BEAM'S END, *c.* 1730, timber-framed with central gable, and further C16–C17 timber framing, punctuated by two brick houses: the POST OFFICE (No. 13), *c.* 1760–70, and GEORGIAN HOUSE, some ten or twenty years earlier.

The best timber-framed group is BATCH COTTAGES, near the end, E side. The farthest was a typical late C16 yeoman house with cross-wing. Altered in the early C18 and later three cottages, the hall bays are now reunited as one house (No. 1). The square-framed early C18 row S of the cross-wing (No. 3) contains a cruck, quite unsuspected from outside. The end is HARKAWAY HOUSE, the workhouse of 1795, rebuilt in the 1960s retaining its external form.

---

*No. 7 Worcester Road, Bromsgrove (the former Golden Lion) is similar.

BROCKENCOTE HALL, ⅓ m. SW, stands on the site of an elaborate baronial mansion built by *J. G. Bland*, 1882 for the carpet
manufacturer Henry Willis. Largely destroyed by fire in the
1920s, and rebuilt in an almost equally grand neo-William-
and-Mary style; cement-rendered, not quite symmetrical, with
high hipped roofs. The porch with fluted Ionic columns may
be reused work of *c.* 1760. Large SW hotel addition in similar
style, 1992–3.

Late C19 outbuildings include a brick and timber LODGE.
Opposite it, the matching VILLAGE HALL of 1894, enlarged by
Clist & Chandler, 2000. To the W, at right angles to the main
road, the DELABERE ALMSHOUSES, built 1637 for poor
widows; sandstone ashlar with five round-headed doorways
and four-light mullioned windows, narrow brick upper floor
with dormers. Restored by *M. W. Jones*, 1955.

At BLUNTINGTON, ⅝ m. NNE, a PRIMITIVE METHODIST
CHAPEL of 1873, builder *Thomas Baylis*, lancet style, red brick
with yellow trim; and BLUNTINGTON FARM, solid square C17
timber framing.

DRAYTON, a brick hamlet on the Barnett Brook, 1¾ m. NNE,
has at its centre a mid-C19 scythe-grinding MILL (cf. Belbroughton): two storeys and fourteen bays, with very large mill
pool to its E. DRAYTON HOUSE of *c.* 1720, half-facing this
from the NW, is exceptionally handsome. Two storeys, seven by
three bays, brick with stone trim; straight-headed windows
with prominent keystones, heavily detailed doorway, quoins,
hipped roof with dormers. Good closed-string staircase with
turned balusters. Tall contemporary DOVECOTE. GROVE
FARM, at the hamlet's SW entrance, is a mid-C18 version of
Drayton House, reduced to five bays; fluted keystones,
doorway with Doric pilasters and pediment.

On BARROW HILL, 1½ m. NE, a large tree-capped circular
mound, perhaps a Bronze Age bowl barrow.

SION HOUSE, Hillpool, 1¾ m. N. Five-bay brick, with lower
wings. Early C19, mostly rebuilt from 1995 (by *Geoff Sidaway*)
as Neo-Georgian pastiche.

CHARLTON

ST JOHN EVANGELIST. 1872. Goodhart-Rendel wrote: 'Old
barn bedevilled by a Mr Workman, Esquire, with Mr Forsyth
of Worcester as his aid.' *Henry Workman*, who had recently
acquired the estate, was indeed 'his own architect', according
to a contemporary account; elsewhere, the sculptor *William
Forsyth* is called 'designer and builder'. The resited barn,
forming nave and chancel in one, was given a W porch (and
bellcote, since removed). High Victorian details; wide Dec nave
lancets, plate tracery for the sanctuary. Interior little altered:
tie-beam and cross-braced roof, *Godwin* tiles, round stone
PULPIT. – STAINED GLASS. Three sanctuary windows by *Ward
& Hughes*, 1872.

Former SUNDAY SCHOOL, N. 1879; brick, central chimney with bellcote.

CHARLTON HOUSE, W, the home of the Dingleys (or Dineleys; cf. Cropthorne), was demolished *c.* 1960. All that remains is its large stone DOVECOTE, rectangular, C17–C18, now a focus for housing built on the site.

Opposite, two C17 thatched and timber-framed cottages. More further SW, around the GREEN (picturesquely traversed by the Merry Brook).

CURSUS, I m. NW. Aerial photography revealed a long, ditched, rectangular enclosure orientated N–S, with a circle placed symmetrically over its S end.

0030

CHILDSWICKHAM

Transferred from Gloucestershire in 1931.

ST MARY. In origin Norman and cruciform, the S transept demolished 1805–6. Nave rebuilt in unsatisfactory Perp style by *George Hunt*, 1870–1; most of the chancel is of 1874 by *H. Linaker* of Frodsham (Cheshire). Fine W tower, begun in the C14 (see the Dec W doorway and N and S ogee-headed lancets), completed in the C15: slightly protruding battlements, recessed corner pinnacles, ribbed spire with lucarnes at its foot. C14 sanctus bellcote on the nave E gable. The tower hides the original Norman W wall, with doorway of *c.* 1130–40: one order of columns, single-scallop or cushion capitals, arch with fat roll moulding; above, blocked by the organ, the former two-light W window. N transept, with plain Norman arch and enlarged E window, mostly rebuilt in the late C13; two-light N window with quatrefoil in plate tracery. Chancel partly Perp: wide chancel arch and former E window, replaced by a crude Geometrical specimen in 1874 and resited at the chancel SW; blocked N arch for a proposed organ chamber. Surprisingly, however, the chancel retains evidence for an early C13 rib-vaulting scheme. The central shafts survive, tripled with the middle ones keeled, with close trumpet-scallop capitals. They are linked by a string course to single shafts in the E corners, also keeled, and sprouting small leaves.* Two crocketed and pinnacled C14–C15 image niches are reused near the E end of the nave walls. Plain W gallery, 1991, and Gothic N vestry, 1994, both by *Healing & Overbury*.

FONT. Octagonal, in two tiers; the elemental fleurs-de-lys and diamond patterns suggest a date in the early 1660s. – Other FURNISHINGS of 1871–4, the PULPIT perhaps reusing some Perp tracery panels. – ROYAL ARMS. George III. – STAINED GLASS. E window 1874, no doubt by *Wailes*. – C14–C15 fragments, re-set in the chancel S in 1962. – Nave SE,

---

*These can be compared with some at Abbey Dore (Herefs.), the triple shafts and their capitals with Pershore Abbey chancel.

1977, and two lancets under the tower, 1979, by *Eric Fraser*, executed by *Joseph Bell & Son* of Bristol. – MONUMENTS. William Perrin †1797, good tablet with fluted pilasters and putto heads. Nearby in the N transept, two identical ones with flower borders to other Perrins (Thomas †1786, William †1820). – Thomas Fisher †1830, by *W. Edwards* of Didbrook; neat, with urn.

An attractive village, with an intricate plan. The church lies at its SE corner. To its NW, the OLD MILL, late C19 brick, opposite the C17 MILL COTTAGE, one of several that are timber-framed and thatched. Then a small green with a CROSS, probably early C15: high base and tapering shaft, now capped by a late C18 urn. It is surrounded by a delightful group of stone and brick houses. THE CROSS HOUSE, S, dated 1711, is no longer in the C17 tradition; three symmetrically set sash windows, apparently original, though the date is early for a Worcestershire village (cf. Queen Anne House, below). THE OLD COTTAGE, to its W, dated 1751, hides a possibly C16 cruck frame. The stone front of the OLD MANOR HOUSE, NW, *c.* 1700, also hides timber framing, visible at the rear.

Vicarage Lane leads back E to the OLD VICARAGE, mostly *c.* 1861 and 1879; roughcast, mullioned windows, pretty barge-boarded gables.

More good houses in the mostly C19 NEW STREET, a little NW. The OLD POST OFFICE, the E half of a stone pair of *c.* 1800, has a C17 E bay of banded limestone and Lias, with small four-light mullioned window, early C15, with trefoil-headed lights; octagonal gable-end chimney above also late medieval, though reduced in height. Nos. 21–23, further E, are also partly of *c.* 1800, but the latter incorporates a fine C15–C16 house, with narrow-studded E cross-wing with jettied first floor.

In ATKINSON STREET, the E continuation of New Street, ATKINSON HOUSE, heavily braced timber framing on a stone base, was well restored by *F.W.B. Charles.* Jettied solar cross-wing, W, C14–C15; hall range partly rebuilt in stone, perhaps in the C16. One first-floor stud on the E return of the wing is pierced by a tiny two-light trefoiled window. Then, QUEEN ANNE HOUSE, dated 1711, stone, symmetrical, three bays, still with mullioned windows; continuous dripmould.

At the NW corner of the village is the brick CHILDSWICKHAM INN, of 1897. A little to its S, CHILDSWICKHAM HOUSE has a symmetrical stone ground floor with cross-windows and continuous dripmould; Jacobean-looking ball-finialled central doorway, dated 1698. Restored by *T.D. Baker* of Kidderminster, 1866, with brick upper floor and hipped roof.

A large stone building excavated in 2001 about ⅓ m. N of the church was probably a C3–C4 ROMAN VILLA; finds included box-flue heating tiles and painted wall plaster, also the remains of several barns and a stone-lined well. The only other known Worcestershire villa was excavated at Bays Meadow, Droitwich, *c.* 1970.

CHURCH HONEYBOURNE *see* HONEYBOURNE

8070   CHURCHILL
                      ½ m. N of Blakedown

Also known, after its medieval hundred, as Churchill in Halfshire.

ST JAMES. Rebuilt by *Hopkins*, 1867–8. Of Hagley Park sandstone, Early Dec style, with nave, chancel and NE tower; this
has an attached spiky vestry, E, and blunt parapet of pierced
quatrefoils (the intended broach spire was never built). Also
typical Hopkins, the flat Geometrical tracery, the broad patterned stonework band beneath the richer chancel windows,
and the timber S porch. Tall interior with high-set chancel arch.
Immediately E of this, on either side, a recessed sedile with
steeply gabled canopy. They served the matching square stone
PULPIT and READING DESK, replaced by carved oak ones by
the *Bromsgrove Guild*, 1930. – Most other 1868 furnishings
survive; stone REREDOS, carved by *Luscombe & Son* of Exeter,
added 1889. – STAINED GLASS. Good E window by *Clayton
& Bell*, 1877. – Nave NE 1889, by *Frederick Drake* of Exeter;
nave SE 1895. – To the NW, a solemn Arts and Crafts war
memorial window of 1920 by *A.J. Davies*.
The church faces a pleasant village group of farm and other
buildings, brick and timber-framed, all much restored.
CHURCHILL COURT, SW, was rebuilt in stockbroker Tudor,
c. 1970. Further uphill, W, CHURCHILL OLD FARM, *c.* 1800,
imposing brick with mostly tripartite windows, has stylish patterned brick farm buildings of *c.* 1860 by *J.H. Chamberlain*,
converted to housing 1985.
A secondary nucleus by the crossroads ⅓ m. NE includes the
former RECTORY, white-painted brick of 1812 by *John White*
of Stourbridge, the Hollington stone WAR MEMORIAL by
Haughton Bros, 1920, and former SCHOOL by *T. Grazebrook*,
1895, brick with stone dressings. Its predecessor of 1797 stands
to the N, a three-bay cottage with sweet bargeboarded additions of 1871; now the village hall. Further E, the square
VILLAGE POUND of 1862, brick with sandstone coping.
  Just S of the crossroads, a lane leads to CHURCHILL FORGE,
the former spade and shovel works of the Bache family, an
important industrial survival. Large mill pool with opposite (S
of the C20 house), low brick buildings of *c.* 1800. Of the two
larger buildings, the N, L-plan with truncated stack, retains an
overshot water wheel, of oak and cast iron, also its drive-belt
system and drop hammer; the S has a narrower high-breast iron
wheel which drove the furnace blower. The premises were
worked in conjunction with Stakenbridge Forge a little
upstream.
ISMERE HOUSE, I m. W. Built for John Smith *c.* 1775; three
storeys, double-pile plan, brick with stone dressings. Entrance
front, S, of three wide bays, the projecting centre with pediment; good pedimented Doric doorcase, windows with eared

moulded architraves, modillion cornice. Plainer rear façade of five bays (cf. Wolverley House, p. 666). Two-storey service wing, NW. – Contemporary brick BARNS further W.

At PARR'S FARM, by the Stourbridge Road ⅓ m. NE, a good C18 brick BARN, with 'hit-and-miss' ventilation holes. Further on, CHURCHILL PUMPING STATION, 1954, for the South Staffordshire Water Works Co.; brick, five bays of tall windows, flat concrete roof. The drive is flanked by pairs of contemporary houses.

CHURCHILL

½ m. S of Broughton Hackett

Also known as Churchill in Oswaldstow. Mostly scattered timber-framed cottages and farms.

ST MICHAEL. Vested in the Churches Conservation Trust since 1999. Nave and chancel; small slate-hung W bell-turret. Basically C14 (with earlier fragments inside), thoroughly restored by *C. Ford Whitcombe*, 1904–11; he largely rebuilt the nave, including W window and timber S porch, and altered the chancel, already restored 1866. Nave roof mostly medieval, stabilized with steel ties by *John Goom* for the CCT. Ceiled chancel roof. Odd blocked opening in the chancel N wall, a concave-sided lozenge in a chamfered four-arched recess. – C17 ALTAR TABLE and chancel PANELLING. – COMMUNION RAIL. Also C17; vertically symmetrical balusters, carved top rail with ball finials. – FONT. Plain octagonal, probably C15; simple C18 cover. – Plain late C17 PULPIT. – SCULPTURE. Fine lion *couchant*, in two pieces, from the bottom corner of a gable. What date? – STAINED GLASS. C14 Wysham shield, E window. – Victorian ROYAL ARMS. – MONUMENTS. Good cartouche to Thomas Barker †1688; painted heraldry at the top, skull with bats' wings below. – Simon Barker †1717 and his wife Olive †1741; stone tablet, segmental pediment.

To the NE, the MOATED SITE of the medieval manor house.

Former RECTORY, W. Modest early C19, three-bay brick with hipped roof; later (?) one-bay stuccoed wings; gabled rear.

CHURCHILL FARM, ⅛ m. N. Late C18 brick, with segment-headed windows. Longer parallel rear range, late C17, with shaped end gables. C19 farm buildings.

CHURCHILL MILL. *See* Broughton Hackett.

CHURCHILL WOOD FARM, ⅝ m. NW. Long brick house with timber-framed dormers; late C17, renewed *c.* 1800. Adjoining, a tall square brick DOVECOTE, with timbered cross-gables, combined with an L-plan barn.

CHURCH LENCH

ALL SAINTS. The W tower, with rectangular openings, battlements and large pinnacles, is probably early C16. Norman nave, the re-set s doorway with one order of shafts with foliated capitals (all much renewed) and roll-moulded arch; plainer N doorway. Nave and s aisle windows are all CI4–CI5, the Perp central N window with its own gable reaching up into the clerestory (with thinner walls). Inside, the two w bays of the arcade are CI4, with paired continuous hollows. The E bay has a later four-centred arch, probably replacing an earlier chapel; image niche in its E respond, with nodding ogee canopy. Low chancel arch, also four-centred, with contemporary rood stair, N. Dec chancel all but rebuilt by *Frederick Preedy*, 1852–4; he restored and reroofed the rest in 1857–8, also providing a s porch. Further restoration, by *J.A. Chatwin*, 1887–8, added the N vestry.

Preedy's FURNISHINGS include painted stone PULPIT, wooden eagle LECTERN (made by *Rattee & Kett*), and carved octagonal FONT with tall oak cover. His tiled REREDOS was replaced by one of oak by *Chatwin*, carved by *Robert Bridgeman*. – Also of 1887–8 the WALL PAINTING above the chancel arch: Christ in Glory, still High Victorian. – Heavy CI9 brass CANDLESTICKS, in an imitation Limoges-Romanesque. – EMBROIDERY. Early CI6 cope of blue velvet, the orphreys with saints split vertically and used as a border. – STAINED GLASS. All by *Preedy*, those in the chancel, 1853–4, his most important early commission. Nave N central and s aisle E and SE windows of 1858, the rest 1866. – Good CI5 fragments in the N doorway tympanum.

Also by *Preedy*, the CHURCHYARD CROSS of 1867, shaft and head now lying loose by the porch, and no doubt the LYCHGATE. His brick SCHOOL, opposite, of 1864, has long bands of edifying stone inscriptions (cf. Quinton, Warks.); bellcote beneath the E gable; attached house.

The VILLAGE, in a fine elevated situation on the brow of the Lench Hills, has a few CI7 timber-framed houses and CI9 estate cottages (cf. Rous Lench). Also notable, TWO ROOFS, in Evesham Road, 1962 by *Robert Harvey* of Stratford-upon-Avon, in his typically Frank Lloyd Wright-inspired idiom; the shallow-pitched roofs are those of the brick and timber house, and the open garage in front.

OLD RECTORY, Ab Lench Road. 1842–3 by *Thomas Smith* of Hertford; Tudor Gothic, brick with yellow trim, pretty bargeboards. Extended s by *A.B. Rowe*, 1886; largely spoilt by further additions, *c.* 1934.

Three outlying hamlets also display some timber framing, the best at ATCH LENCH, ⅔ m. ESE. Here a good group of thatched cottages, the largest two containing CI5–CI6 crucks: at MANOR FARM COTTAGES, s side, originally separate cottages, with later infill, one spindly pair can be seen in the w gable-end; at the other, N side, crucks are only visible inside. A smaller cottage has a massive w gable stack, of Lias. Further E, opposite the brick CI8–CI9 MANOR HOUSE, a former BAPTIST CHAPEL of 1829. Red brick, the gabled s entrance front with two tiers of segment-headed windows and central round-arched doorway; two arched side windows, plus a blank bay (for vestry and first-floor schoolroom), N end, all under one slate roof. The schoolroom had two shuttered openings into the chapel. Some fittings (S end gallery, small polygonal pulpit) survived conversion to a house in 2005–6.

The largest house at AB LENCH, ¾ m. WNW, EASTER HILL HOUSE, gabled brick Tudor, is dated 1866, with initials of C.H. Rouse Boughton (cf. Rous Lench).

SHERIFF'S LENCH, 1⅓ m. SSW, has a roughcast C18 MANOR HOUSE, with extensive early C19 brick farm buildings, showing a fine rhythm of gables and round-arched recesses; all now housing. Further E, an estate cottage of 1871, brick and half-timber, again with edifying text.

CLAINES

A large parish, more properly called North Claines, immediately N of Worcester; the church now lies just within the city boundary.

ST JOHN BAPTIST. Perp throughout, with battlemented W tower, aisled nave, and chancel with slightly later chapels. Mostly straight-topped windows with ogee-headed lights. S chapel more ornate than the rest, with quatrefoiled parapet and pinnacles, the windows probably re-set from the chancel S wall. The overall effect is almost like post-Reformation Gothic. So the best part of the church architecturally is the outer N aisle (again with re-set windows), especially its N porch and vestry: a free Perp paraphrase by *Aston Webb*, 1886–7. The S porch is perhaps by *G.G. Scott*, c. 1867; re-set dole cupboards flank its W window. The tall Perp nave arcades, of four quite narrow bays, have sturdy octagonal piers with coarse capitals and two-centred, single-chamfered arches. Matching chancel and tower arches. Similar two-bay S chapel arcade. The N chapel's is slightly more ornate; its octagonal pier has two small mouldings in the diagonals, one hollow, one with sunk quadrant, and arches to match. Remains of the rood stair, N chapel, W end. Only the chancel's plain corbel tables, visible from within the chapels, tell of the C13 church (*see* below). Webb's outer N arcade is deliberately low-key: quatrefoil piers, four-centred arches.

Almost all FURNISHINGS are by *Webb*, 1886–7, notably the splendid marble mosaic chancel FLOOR in the form of a Jesse tree. – In the N porch, C15 TILES and a C13–C14 FONT bowl (or stoup). – ARCHITECTURAL FRAGMENTS, under the tower. Early C13, including most of a pier, with capital and base. – Good STAINED GLASS, mostly *Burlison & Grylls*, from 1889. – The exceptions are three windows by *Powell & Sons* (S chapel SE 1906, SW 1915; S aisle SE 1919), and two in the N chapel: E by *Clayton & Bell* c. 1865, N by *M.C. Farrar Bell*, 1981. – MONUMENTS. John Porter †1577, a lawyer. Recumbent stone effigy; tomb-chest with pilasters separating panels with shell arches.

The trefoil shapes below are reconstruction of 1887. – Many
worthwhile tablets. Mary Porter †1668; pediment with reclining female allegories, angel's head at the foot. – Some good
cartouches with lively surrounds: John Carpenter †1696
(chancel); Henry Wynne †1693 and George Porter †1709 (N
aisle). – Several by *W. Stephens*, e.g. William Thomas †1803,
cherub weeping by a draped urn (N aisle). – Sir Harry
Wakeman †1831 by *Peter Hollins*; white marble, bust on top of
a draped sarcophagus. – Mary Wigley †1846, by *Thomas
Denman*; Grecian, with reversed torches (S chapel).

In the CHURCHYARD, early C19 chest tombs and, W of the
tower, a larger Gothic one to the Dyson Perrins family, *c.* 1855.
– Portland stone WAR MEMORIAL, ESE, by *Sir Reginald Blomfield*, 1920, a reduced version of his Cross of Sacrifice.

LYCHGATE, S, by *R. Haughton*, 1919. Near this, THE MUG
HOUSE INN, probably a C16 church house in origin; it incorporates two reused crucks.

Around the church, something of a village atmosphere remains.
To the W, CHURCH HOUSE, mid-C18 brick, five bays; beyond
that, a C17 farm. To the NE, the CHURCH INSTITUTE by *Lewis
Sheppard*, 1891, brick with timbered gables. Then, up Church
Bank, the SCHOOL by *Eginton*, 1840–1; steeply gabled Tudor
Gothic house to the road, the schoolrooms behind altered and
enlarged. Further N, the former VICARAGE of 1859–60, by
Henry Rowe, plain Tudor Gothic, brick and gabled.

A number of well-to-do C18–C19 houses betray the proximity of
Worcester, the best collection at BEVERE, ¾ m. WNW. First, in
Bevere Lane, two similar stuccoed villas of *c.* 1830, with
shallow hipped roofs. Then larger C18 houses around the sylvan
BEVERE GREEN. BEECHWOOD HOUSE (formerly The Firs),
E side, is plain five-bay late C18 brick, with pedimented Doric
doorcase; large garden surrounded by pretty Gothick iron railings. BEVERE HOUSE, in its own small park to the N, is more
special, built *c.* 1765 by *Anthony Keck* for Dr T. R. Nash, the
county historian. Rendered, 1+3+1 bays, the centre projecting
beneath a pediment. Porch of four Ionic columns, Venetian
window over, Diocletian one above that. Other windows have
shouldered and moulded architraves. Wide entrance hall with
open-well staircase with three turned balusters per tread. The
drive crosses a bridge with pretty C18 railing. Late C19 brick
LODGE; rusticated GATEPIERS. The early C19 Tudor Gothic
LODGE further W announces the mostly roughcast BEVERE
MANOR. Flanking its mid-C18 five-bay S front are early C19
wings ending in shallow full-height bows, their windows tripartite with Doric columns. The early C19 W front faces
towards Bevere Island in the Severn.*

At HAWFORD, ¾ m. NNW, either side of the Kidderminster road,
two more brick houses, both again of five bays, quite plain

---

*This is linked to the E bank by a surprisingly sturdy BRIDGE of 1844, presumably
built in connection with the nearby lock and weir; segmental iron arch, blue engineering brick abutments.

except for the doorway – a standard English product for the prosperous middle class, if ever there was one. KINGS HAWFORD (formerly Hawford Lodge), W side, *c.* 1800, painted apart from the brick voussoirs with stone keystones, has a door pediment on carved brackets; the architect *Charles Day* lived here. HAWFORD HOUSE, E, is larger, probably *c.* 1840, with four-column Doric N porch.

Next to the mid-C19 HAWFORD GRANGE, ½ m. further N, a fine, tall C16 DOVECOTE. Square-plan, all close-set studding above a sandstone plinth; cross-gables, gabled lantern. Inside, a few timber nesting boxes survive, high up on the W and N walls. Restored by the National Trust, 1973–6.

MILDENHAM MILL, 1¼ m. N between the Droitwich Canal and the River Salwarpe, is brick, C18–C19, three storeys with scattered fenestration; it retains its timber hoist and most machinery: an undershot wheel each end and four pairs of millstones inside. Nearby mill house part C17 timber-framed, part early C19 brick. The mill had its own wharf on the Canal, here crossed by a brick BRIDGE of *c.* 1771, adjoining a contemporary LOCK.

JACOBS, ¼ m. S, is an attractive brick house, with steep tiled roof on plain round wooden pillars, built *c.* 1997 for himself around an existing cottage by *Richard J. Slawson* (formerly of *Associated Architects*); garage wing, with open archway towards the lane, added 2002.

At PORTER'S MILL, 1¼ m. NNE, another picturesque spot by the Salwarpe and Droitwich Canal, the brick MILL (now a house) is probably of *c.* 1861. MILL HALL, to its E, was probably built for John Porter (†1577), though a panel in the jettied W gable-end bears the date 1503. Irregular square panelling, with a fine group of five star-topped chimneys; late C17 staircase with twisted balusters, S of the stack. Over the hall fireplace, plaster royal arms flanked by the ER monogram and Tudor roses. The first-floor room, E, presumably the great chamber, has beams with plaster vine-trellis patterns. The best room is the jettied one in the W attic (above the kitchen end) with panelling and assorted plaster motifs, all quite simply done, probably early C17.

FERNHILL HEATH, 1 m. E on the Droitwich road, is now the main centre of population. At its E end (in Hindlip parish), two pairs of Victorian Hindlip estate houses, and HINDLIP SCHOOL, built as a mission room in 1879 by *R.B. Morgan* of Birmingham; brick, chunky Gothic, with attractive dormers. Opposite, FERNHILL HEATH HOUSE, once the dower house to Hindlip Hall (p. 375), is three-bay late C18, with hipped roof and wrought-iron porch. Off the W end, N side, some larger C19 houses, especially OAKFIELD (now the River School), cement-faced with plain giant pilasters and portico with paired Tuscan columns; probably *c.* 1840.

Finally, in Hindlip Road, S of the A449 link road, ROSE PLACE, an excellent ashlar-faced villa of *c.* 1820–30; 2+1+2 bays, rusticated ground floor, first-floor windows with straight architraves, except that above the doorway which is pedimented. Entrance hall with two Ionic columns.

0040

CLEEVE PRIOR

An attractive village, mostly of Lias, on a prominent ridge above the Avon. It belonged to the Priors and Chapter of Worcester Cathedral from 872.

ST ANDREW. W tower, nave and chancel, plus originally N and S transepts; the N was demolished, probably in the C18, when the S was rebuilt as a low brick structure (now roughcast). E.E. nave, with S doorway and N and S lancets, but the simple N doorway is Late Norman; there cannot be much difference in their dates. The S transept arch on elementary imposts might just be coeval. Early C14 chancel, much redone in 1863 by *Ewan Christian*; medieval the NW and SW windows, priest's door, and most of the chancel arch. The fine tower is probably mid- to late C14: tall arch to the nave with continuous broad hollow and sunk quadrant mouldings. Several openings, especially to the stair-vice, have crocketed ogee gables; two-light Dec bell-openings. Tower (and nave) were restored in 1906 by *C.F. Whitcombe*; his no doubt the Perp W window. Top renewed 1961. – FONT. Plain, octagonal, probably C14. – PEWS. Mostly 1906; a few C14–C15 survivors at the W end. – Bold TOWER SCREEN by *F.S. Coleridge*, 1984; bronze tinted glass in a black anodized aluminium frame. – Massive dug-out CHEST, elm, 8 ft (2.5 metres) long; possibly C14. – STAINED GLASS. Colourful sanctuary windows by *Preedy*: E and S 1869, N probably *c.* 1863. – Chancel NW by *Paul Woodroffe*, 1934; SW by *Hardman*, 1897. – Good nave N lancet by *Benjamin J. Warren* of Birmingham, 1927.

Outside, beneath an ancient yew S of the nave, enjoyable rows of C18–early C19 HEADSTONES, many no doubt by the local *Laughton* family of masons.

At the SW corner of the churchyard, a former SCHOOL of *c.* 1800, with pointed brick windows. CHURCH CROFT, to its S, formerly Home Farm, is mid-C18, with a big hipped roof; the OLD VICARAGE, to its E, of 1737, later rendered. This faces MAIN STREET, with an attractive C17–C18 Lias assortment on its E side. The street then doubles back (past the small Gothic CHURCH SCHOOL of 1858, by *George Hunt*) to a triangular GREEN, W of the church. Another good Lias selection on its N side; to the SE, a timber-framed and thatched cottage, and stone VILLAGE HALL by *H.E. Dicks*, 1919–20, enlarged 2000.

Main Street, continuing for some distance NW, is nicely terminated by the mid-C18 PRIOR HOUSE (formerly Top Farm); brick, three storeys, at right angles to the road. UPPER HOUSE, in Nightingale Lane, a little NW, also brick, is probably slightly earlier.

CLEEVE PRIOR MANOR, ⅛ m. NNE. A very fine late C16 house, to an expanded T-plan, built for the Bushell family. The short-

ish stem, or s range, has a splendid two-storey E porch. Round
arch flanked by medallions with projecting frontal busts;
above, also slightly projecting on three carved brackets, a pair
of cross-windows. Mask frieze below, shouldered gable above
with ball finials and small figure of a boy on the apex. All
windows have broad mullions or mullions and transoms, very
finely detailed; the largest is the five-light ground-floor window
on the E gable-end of the long N range. Large chimneystacks
with C19 brick shafts. The date 1709 on the chimney-breast at
the rear of the s range may refer to substantial alterations; the
E porch now leads into an early C18 hall. Several panelled
rooms; one bedroom has a good late C16 fireplace, *ex situ*,
apparently severely reduced in size. The house was much
restored in the 1950s, and subdivided *c.* 1990, together with its
C17–C18 FARM BUILDINGS. Next to the fish pond, NE, a splendid circular stone DOVECOTE, presumably medieval; stone-
tiled conical roof, notably bulging base.

CLEEVE HOUSE, ½ m. WNW off Mill Lane, high above the Avon,
   is by *C.E. Bateman*, 1933, for William Heaton. Arts and Crafts
   Cotswold style, of coursed limestone rubble; cranked plan,
   with big hipped stone roof with dormers.
BICKMARSH HALL, 1⅓ m. ENE. Large, H-plan. Low C16 centre
   timber-framed, above a Lias ground floor. Higher wings of
   Lias, with ashlar dressings. The E is early C17, four storeys, with
   mullioned windows and gables; big chimneystack balanced
   by a pair of gables on its E front. Matching W wing, lower,
   mid-C19.

CLENT

9070

The Clent Hills, rising to 997 ft (315 metres), a bulwark between
the Black Country and NE Worcestershire, provide some of the
best walking country in the Birmingham area. At the top of Clent
Hill are the mock Druidical FOUR STONES, probably set up in
the mid C18 by George, first Lord Lyttelton (cf. Hagley); further
EARTHWORKS nearer the summit. The village below exudes an
atmosphere of prosperity, its roads happily intricate and confusing. Transferred from Staffordshire in 1844.

ST LEONARD. Much is Late Perp: W tower with diagonal buttresses and battlements, its arch towards the nave with characteristic mouldings and respond capitals; part of the s aisle
   fabric; and the chancel. This has an E window with ogee
   hoodmould and transom at the arch springing; also a large,
   ogee-arched, s priest's doorway, with, on its inner E jamb, the
   inscription: Juxta hunc lapidem jacet corpus Johannis Cleye.
   Good wagon roof. In 1864–5 *Kirk & Parry* (of Sleaford, Lincs.)
   rebuilt the nave and N aisle in Dec style, adding the N vestry
   and s porch. Their N arcade is in C13 style. But they renewed
   and raised the late C12 three-bay s arcade, see the trumpet-
   scallop capitals of the round piers, especially the less-restored
   W respond, rebuilding its single-stepped arches. Chancel,

raised five steps above the Amphlett family vault, entirely refurnished by *Harvey & Wicks*, 1956. – Neo-Norman FONT of 1864–5. – STAINED GLASS. W window. 1866, 'of French design'. – N aisle N, *c.* 1868. – S aisle: W by *Lavers & Westlake*, 1897; SW by *Heaton, Butler & Bayne*, 1885; SE by *A.J. Davies*, 1920. – Two others are by probably *Clayton & Bell*, *c.* 1866–70. – MONUMENTS. Several good tablets. Chancel S: John Amphlett †1705; twisted columns, broken segmental pediment. – Cartouche under the tower to John Cox, also †1705; opposite, William Waldron †1764, with fluted Corinthian pilasters. – Chancel N. Thomas Liell †1807, by *Sir Richard Westmacott*, with broken column; Rev. Adolphus Perkins †1855, by *J. Stephens*, draped Grecian. – LYCHGATE. 1874.

The OLD VICARAGE, SW, is mostly early C19 stuccoed. Further W, the former SCHOOL, built by John Amphlett, with attached house, in 1705; enlarged to a T-plan, with pretty bargeboards and patterned tiled roofs, in 1847.

A second SCHOOL (for infants), S of the church, was built in 1863 for the Durant family by *W.J. Allsop Jun.* of Stourbridge; equally pretty Tudor Gothic, yellow brick, bargeboards, open bellcote. The detail is less altered on the detached house.

The Durants lived at CLENT HALL, further uphill, SSE: three-bay stuccoed, early to mid-C19, with moulded segment-headed windows. The core is earlier, though the fine Tudorbethan plaster ceiling in the main room looks like C19 renewal. Gardens laid out *c.* 1875 by *Sir Joseph Hooker*, director of Kew Gardens.

At LOWER CLENT, ½ m. WNW, was the large CLENT HOUSE, rebuilt for Joseph Amphlett in the early C18; demolished 1936. STABLES dated 1709 remain, converted to a house in 1955. Of plum Flemish-bond brick, eleven bays, with quoins and prominent acanthus keystones; three-bay centre with steep pediment and open cupola. WALLED GARDEN, E; square brick DOVE-COTE, W. Further NW, in Woodman Lane, the neat brick CLENT HOUSE FARM, dated 1760.

Another large C18 house was CLENT GROVE, ½ m. NW, rebuilt 1863, in stone, sub-Italianate style; now submerged by additions as a children's home. Off its drive, a little E of the lodge, a late C18 brick FOLLY TOWER; linked round towers, formerly battlemented, pointed Gothick windows, also some in the form of quatrefoils or Maltese-cross loops. It resembles the folly at Castle Bourne (p. 132).

ADAM'S HILL, leading NE, provides the main access for visitors to the Clent Hills.

From the church, Church Avenue, with the nice ALFRED ROBERTS MEMORIAL HALL (by *Tom Grazebrook*, 1906), leads SW to HOLY CROSS, a further nucleus at the junction of five roads. Here the brick late C18 HOLY CROSS HOUSE faces the rendered BELL AND CROSS INN, which unusually retains its multi-room layout. Further W, in HOLY CROSS GREEN, past half-hipped houses of 1872–3 carrying the Amphlett camel emblem, is ST OSWALD AND ST WULSTAN (R.C.), converted from a C17–C18 barn by *R.L.B. Moore*, 1926–7; deliberately rustic interior.

CLENT GRANGE, ¼ m. SE of Holy Cross, is a good unaltered Italianate villa by *Henry Day*, 1855–6. Brick, ample stone dressings, four bays, hipped roof, solid tripartite porch; all details much thicker than a decade or two earlier.

FIELD HOUSE, 1⅛ m. W, now a nursing home. A fine three-by-three-bay brick house of *c.* 1750, altered 1919–21 by *Forbes & Tate* for Ernest Vaughan. Entrance front, S, with two-storey canted bays flanking an Ionic stone pedimented porch, and low SW extension with paired Doric columns, all *c.* 1921; the mid C18 is only represented here by the giant angle pilasters with urn finials, upper Venetian windows, and parapet with central pediment on consoles. The less-altered E front, also with central pediment, has four giant pilasters and all windows Venetian, apart from tripartite ground-floor ones. Interior, with wide entrance hall and spacious well stair, W, mostly by *Forbes & Tate*. Their large NW ballroom, of 1929, has a central bow facing a formal garden with rectangular pool, laid out by *Gertrude Jekyll*; enlarged brick SUMMERHOUSE, with pyramidal roof. Altered STABLES, N, retaining a quirky ogee-roofed late C19 cupola.

   LODGES to SE and, less altered, SW, are both dated 1870, with monograms of the Roberts family. Already Queen Anne-ish, with hipped roofs with central chimneys.

WALTON HOUSE, ½ m. S, is trim late C18 brick. WALTON FARM nearby, probably slightly earlier, has segment-headed windows, sandstone quoins and hipped roof; contemporary farm buildings, E.

MOOR HALL, on a moated site ⅓ m. further ESE (in Belbroughton parish), also three-bay brick, is dated 1680 above its central pilastered doorway; mid-C19 windows with cambered heads. Moat bridge and walls also late C17; large brick BARN and STABLES perhaps of *c.* 1700.

CLIFTON UPON TEME   7060

ST KENELM. C13–C14, sandstone with tufa dressings; much restored by *Harvey Eginton* (1843) and *James Cranston* (1851–3). The best C13 feature is the W tower: lancets (some blocked) on its lower two stages; paired lancet bell-openings, E, the others plain mullioned, probably *c.* 1668. The present form of the broach spire (last reshingled 1968) is due to *Cranston*. Tower arch, mostly tufa, with two continuous chamfers. The chancel has a tufa NW lancet, but its other windows were renewed in Dec style by *Eginton* (and again 1968). S aisle, added in the early C14, with similarly renewed windows: reticulated, E, Y-tracery, W. Three-bay S arcade with short octagonal piers, restored moulded capitals and double-chamfered arches. Ogee-headed *piscina*. *Cranston* designed the entertaining tracery of the nave N windows, exposed the nave and chancel roofs, and added the NE vestry and the oak Dec-style porch, S. – His also the deal PEWS and chancel floor TILING (the sanctuary floor may be of 1843). – His stone PULPIT was replaced by a free Perp timber one, *c.* 1910. – Most chancel FITTINGS of the 1930s. – FONT. Hexagonal tapering bowl, perhaps C13, much renewed. – ROYAL ARMS. Charles II; dated 1660. Restored 1971.

STAINED GLASS. Excellent S aisle E window by *Preedy*, 1862, with early C14 heraldry in the traceries. – Chancel side lancets by *George Rogers*, *c.* 1848–9. – E window by *A. L. Moore & Co.*, 1882, better than their later work, of which the S aisle SW, *c.* 1887, may be an example. – MONUMENTS. Effigy of a cross-legged knight, feet on a lion; probably Sir John de Wysham †1332. The upper r. tip of his shield is supported by a small squirrel, now headless; perhaps from the 'Westminster Workshop', cf. two in the Temple Church, London. – For the tablet to Elizabeth Jefferys †1688, the contract of 1689 between her husband Henry and *Grinling Gibbons* exists. Yet it is nothing special, nor would be even if top and bottom were in their original state. Hanging draperies flank the inscription; cherubs' heads above, flowers and leaves below. – The better-preserved tablet nearby to Jane Jefferys, Henry's adopted heir, †1718, is a near copy, said to be by *Thomas White*. – Simple Grecian tablet to the Ingram family by *Westmacott*, 1798. – Tiny coped tomb in the sanctuary to Emma Prothero, the vicar's infant daughter, †1849. – Good C17–C18 ledger stones, the best at the nave E end: William Jefferys †1658 and wife †1664. – In the CHURCHYARD, a medieval CROSS, almost entirely renewed *c.* 1861 by *W. J. Hopkins*; also early C19 CHEST TOMBS, one near the porch, to James Strickland †1819, signed *W. Milton*.

The OLD VICARAGE, a little E, is by *John Collins* of Leominster, 1840. Tudor Gothic, sandstone; two S gables, a third on the E return with porch below, all with pretty pierced bargeboards.

Opposite the church, S, the brick OLD SMITHY, dated 1874. From here the VILLAGE STREET curves NW, past the green. Its close-built nature is unusual in this part of Worcestershire and may owe its origin to the charter for a free borough granted by Henry III in 1270 to Roger de Mortimer, though nothing further is heard of the associated market and fair. The cessation of military activities against the Welsh may have rendered further development unnecessary. The LION INN, on the green's NE side, C18 brick round an earlier core, is said to have been used as the court house. Plain sandstone SCHOOL of 1844, to the SW. The houses along the street are an attractive mix of timber framing, brick, and occasional sandstone. The OLD HOUSE, once the vicarage, has a brick front of *c.* 1700, three bays with central pediment; the timber-framed POST OFFICE opposite carries the date 1721. At the end, the late C18 MANOR HOUSE, also three bays, with tripartite outer windows.

WOODMANTON FARM, ¾ m. SSE. A moated medieval site. Sir John de Wysham was given licence to crenellate in 1332. The

HOUSE, a neat brick villa of *c.* 1827, has three bays, stuccoed doorcase with incised Soanean ornament, plain angle pilasters, and hipped slate roof. Attached, SW, a sandstone building with raking buttresses, which turns a right angle to end with the base of a circular NW tower projecting into the moat, all presumably of C14 origin. More remarkably, the three-bay brick range attached to the house's NE corner encases a timber-framed C14 CHAPEL. This was floored in the C16–C17, when the ground floor became the kitchen, its big fireplace and chimneystack built into the E end. A timber N window (now internal) survives, two lights with ogee-trefoiled heads. Also the chapel's lofty wagon roof, more or less complete over two bays, one of the few examples of a rafter roof with curved ashlar pieces originally supported by a wholly timber-framed substructure. This necessitated an enormously broad wall-plate, in two sections, both heavily moulded. Curved braces to the collar, massive tie-beam, renewed curved braces.

HOMME (or HAM) CASTLE FARM, 1¼ m. E, commands a splendid site above the Teme valley, S of the motte and bailey of a Norman CASTLE (first mentioned 1207). Rebuilt in brick after a fire of 1887, it stands on the platform of the house of the Jefferys family (which carried dates 1677 and 1680). The rubble and brick terracing of the platform is particularly prominent to E and S (where it is doubled above the former fish ponds); hipped-roofed pavilion above the road, W side. Most notable is the N side where an amazing C16–C17 basement about 100 ft (31 metres) long is preserved, its brick tunnel vault pierced by slit-openings, N side. An early C18 brick COACHHOUSE stands above its W end, with the remnant of a long sandstone and timber C17 BARN further W. Nearer the house, a square rubble PUMP HOUSE, now roofless.

Good gabled C17 FARMHOUSES include NOAK FARM, 1⅓ m. SE, with an attractive LODGE on the B4204, and HAM FARM, 1⅞ m. SE. Also HAM BRIDGE HOUSE, just W of the BRIDGE across the Teme, rebuilt by *J.H. Garrett*, 1908: three brick arches, sturdy cast-iron balustrade.

A rectangular EARTHWORK of Roman date, on the Herefordshire boundary 1⅜ m. NW, shows three periods of occupation, though whether civil or military is uncertain.

COFTON HACKETT

Close to the Birmingham boundary but also to the Lickey Hills. Church and Hall linger in a secluded semi-rural setting despite the proximity of the mainline railway.

ST MICHAEL. A former chapelry of Northfield (Birmingham). Much rebuilt 1860–1: the nave, in Perp style, by *Henry Day*, the chancel, Dec, by *Dudley Male* of London. Medieval fabric includes the priest's door, chancel S, and parts of two Perp nave N windows. The double W bellcote, with three pinnacles, may be *c.* 1500, the arch-braced timber s porch, with finely moulded cornice, C14–C15. C19 interior little altered; good chancel arch. N organ chamber added by *T. Plevins* of Birmingham, 1890. – Decent timber furnishings by *Male*: STALLS, PULPIT, LECTERN. – Oak REREDOS by the *Bromsgrove Guild*, 1937. – STAINED GLASS. E window *c.* 1849. – Chancel SW lancet by *Kempe*, 1881. – Nave: NE by *William Holland*, 1865; NW by *Hugh Easton*, 1946 (designed 1939); SE, *c.* 1862. – MONUMENTS. Very fine incised alabaster slab to William Leycester †1508; in armour, feet on a greyhound, flanked by wives Eleanor †1514 and Anne, whose date of death remained blank. Heraldry above, two small children below. – William Babington †1625 (and wife †1671); simple tablet with good lettering. – At the W end, four tablets, quite illuminating as a sequence. Margaret Skinner †1651, is already entirely architectural, with columns and broken pediment. The others to Jolliffes of Cofton Hall: Thomas †1693 and Benjamin †1719 are similar, with drapes and cherubs; Thomas †1758, plainer, with garlanded urn.

Large CHURCHYARD with C18 headstones and iron-railed C19 chest tombs. – C15 CROSS, with two steps and square base with shields in quatrefoils.

COFTON HALL, ¼ m. SW. The medieval manor passed, *c.* 1316, from the Hacketts to the Leycester family, who retained it until 1525. In 1645 Thomas Jolliffe set the house on fire to prevent it falling into Parliamentarian hands. There have been many excavations, including interesting discoveries of medieval stone structures, but the results have never been published.

The larger, brick part of the present house is late C18, perhaps partly by *George Byfield*.* Plain stuccoed entrance front, SE, six irregular bays and three storeys; Doric porch, parapet with moulded cornice. But to its l. are two short parallel gabled ranges, mostly sandstone, lower and clearly earlier; they were restored in the mid C20, but surviving Gothick detail suggests remodelling of *c.* 1800. The front range hides one of the finest late medieval halls in Worcestershire, 38 ft (12 metres) long by 21 ft (6.5 metres) wide, originally no doubt with timber-framed walls. The surviving roof has nine boldly moulded pseudo-hammerbeam trusses, with gently cusped, solid spandrel-brackets from wall-post to hammerbeam. Shorter arched braces from hammerbeam to cambered collar; moulded cornice, two moulded purlins. Each collar, also moulded, with pentagonal boss, is surmounted by a row of plain and slender vertical struts; the hexagonal louvre opening also remains, off-centre. The whole effect, though splendid, seems overdone, almost claustrophobic, suggesting perhaps local imitation of a high-status roof elsewhere; the date may be mid to late C15. The solar block presumably stood on the site of the present house.

53

*He prepared two modish schemes for Robert Biddulph in 1796, one Neoclassical, one Gothick. These were not executed, though there was apparently a tetrastyle Corinthian portico, moved to Hewell Grange *c.* 1816, p. 628.

Some 100 yds N, by Cofton Church Lane, extensive brick farm buildings, now housing. The main range to the S, towards the house, contained the STABLES, refronted in sandstone ashlar in the late C18, perhaps by *Byfield*; slightly projecting centre with pediment and pilasters, short matching r. wing.

TOWER HOUSE, ¼ m. E. Mid-C19 brick, square with battlements and higher attached round turret. Later C19 addition.

The OLD VICARAGE, ½ m. WSW (No. 10 Cofton Church Lane) is by *John Cotton*, 1882; brick, quite large, with pedimental gables. Doorway with steep open pediment, brick decoration including thin pilaster strips.

CONDERTON

9030

Attractive stone-built hamlet on the S side of Bredon Hill, part of the Overbury estate.

The MANOR HOUSE, NE of the Yew Tree Inn, is late C17, H-plan, of coursed rubble with hipped tiled roof; two storeys, originally seven bays, the recessed central three filled with a low classical entrance *c.* 1960. Discreet N bay and service wing added by *Norman Shaw*, 1888; also his, some panelling and the staircase with twisted balusters, S range. – Former STABLES, N, probably also by *Shaw*. – GARDENS laid out by *Brenda Colvin*, 1932–6. By the SW gates, a thatched stone cottage restored by *Ernest Newton c.* 1909.

To its S, a farmhouse dated 1675, now CROSS COTTAGES, shows how the Jacobean type became classical by gradual symmetrization; each mullioned window here still has its own hoodmould. CONDERTON CHASE further S, part stone, 1830s, part brick *c.* 1860, has a rectangular stone C18 DOVECOTE, with renewed lantern.

To the W, on the Overbury road, DARKES HOUSE by *Ernest Newton*, 1908, with near-central front door with cambered hood; above, a circular stair window and small half-timbered gabled dormer. Nearly opposite, N, MANOR FARM, three bays with cast-iron porch, probably of 1832 (datestone at the rear); minor alterations by *Newton*, 1910. Then CONDERTON COTTAGES (Nos. 65–67), an excellent terrace of three by *Newton*, 1909–10; symmetrical, the outer bays with projecting gables, but all three doorways, round-arched with circular stair windows above, in the long recessed centre; also four weatherboarded dormers.

CONDERTON CAMP (formerly known as Danes Camp), ⅞ m. NNE. An elongated, roughly triangular Iron Age hill-fort, on a steep-sided spur with strong natural defences. The first earthwork, perhaps C6–C5 B.C., a comparatively slight univallate structure, enclosed the whole of the spur, some five acres. Entrances on the S and in the middle of the N side. The defended area was later reduced to two acres by the construction of a stone-faced rampart across the spur's S end.

Excavation in 1958–9 revealed that occupation during this phase was probably permanent; the interior contained a series of storage pits, also circular huts with stone footings.

COOKHILL

Inkberrow

0050

St Paul. By *Preedy*, 1875–6; coursed rock-faced Inkberrow sandstone, white Bath ashlar bands. Not small. Nave with paired lancets and good Geometrical w window, also a w bellcote and s porch; chancel with trefoiled lancets, the stepped e triplet with filleted nook-shafts inside. Broad interior, most of its c19 furnishings removed or reordered. – STAINED GLASS. e by *Hardman*, 1919. – Fine w window of 1932–3 by *Sidney H. Meteyard*, Arts and Crafts Pre-Raphaelite. – Nave n: one by *Donald Brooke*, 1962; one by *Pearce & Cutler*, 1921.

Former BOARD SCHOOL, se. By *E.A. Day*, 1876; enlarged 1891. Red brick, with blue banding, half-hipped gables, and attached house. Now all housing.

BAPTIST CHAPEL, ½ m. s. Of 1841. Long brick rectangle; the chapel fills w part, with two Gothick n windows and porch added *c*. 1920, the minister's house the e part, but facing s. Also this side, a gabled schoolroom, probably late c19, reusing the chapel's s windows. Within the chapel, an e gallery, lit by a skylight.

COOKHILL PRIORY, 1 m. s. This was a Cistercian nunnery, probably in existence by the late c12, refounded 1260 by Isabella, wife of William Beauchamp, Earl of Warwick. It was apparently never well off. All that remains is a fragment of the later medieval church: parts of the chancel e and n walls. The site was granted in 1542 to Sir Nicholas Fortescue, Groom Porter to Henry VIII. Capt. John Fortescue partly rebuilt the house in 1763, on part of the site of the nuns' quarters (and, in 1783, adapted the medieval fragment as a chapel). The w front, brick with ashlar dressings, appears oddly irregular, as Fortescue only built the central doorway, with fluted Doric pilasters and segmental pediment, and the wide canted bay window, l. The three bays to the r. were added in keeping in 1907. Spacious Edwardian entrance hall, with fine staircase, no doubt reusing some of the c18 turned balusters; also good chimneypieces and doorcases. The longer rear range, timber-framed, probably c16, mostly clad in brick, contains the dining room with heavy-beamed ceiling.

The CHAPEL adjoining to the n is rendered and crenellated. Two n windows with Y-tracery; above the w doorway, a large quatrefoiled roundel, all characteristic of late c18 Gothicism. Most surviving medieval detail is internal, notably the lower part of the very large blocked surround of the e window. In the n wall, the e respond of a n chapel arcade; details, including a shaft and broad wave moulding, are c14 or early c15. The n chapel piscina, with ogee trefoiled arch, has been revealed outside. A late C18 communion rail survives, as well as Fortescue wall tablets and ledger stones.

Extensive medieval earthworks around the house, especially several fish ponds, w. To the E, close to The Ridgeway, a restored octagonal brick GAZEBO, two storeys with pyramidal roof; also built for Capt. Fortescue.

THE RIDGEWAY forms the spine of Cookhill and, more or less, the boundary with Warwickshire. Several timber-framed and thatched C17 cottages; at NEW END, ⅝m. N, a good group (Nos. 164–170) is hidden behind an unsightly garage.

The best timber-framed house is DRAGON FARM at Edgiock, 1 m. NW. C16–C17, T-plan; square-panelled stem mostly rebuilt in brick, N cross-wing with narrow studding, curved tension braces, and W overhang. Big ashlar chimneystack at its E end; panel with two dragons in relief above the fireplace, dated 1614.

EDGIOCK MANOR (formerly Manor Farm), ½ m. further N, is mid-C18, brick with stone dressings, three wide bays of segment-headed windows. Timber-framed STABLES and BARN to the S, renewed as housing.

COOKLEY
Wolverley and Cookley

8080

ST PETER. 1848–9 by *Edward Smith* of Oldswinford;* red and blue brindled brick with stone dressings, E.E.-Dec style. Thin battlemented W tower, nave with quatrefoil clerestory, aisles, N porch. Chancel doubled in length, exceptionally tactfully, by *J. T. Meredith*, 1874–5; he also added a S chapel and N vestry (adjoining his organ chamber of 1872). Good five-bay C13-style nave arcades, with round cast-iron piers and double-chamfered arches. Meredith provided a matching two-bay arcade between chancel and chapel, the latter boldly refurnished by *John Greaves Smith*, 1999. – Several FITTINGS of 1849 survive, including a basic octagonal FONT and fine set of BOX PEWS with flat poppyheads: Georgian trying to become archaeologically correct; also STAINED GLASS by *Wailes*. – Plain wooden PULPIT by *Meredith*.

SCHOOL, N, also by *Smith*, 1849; brick, gabled, with bellcote. Later enlarged. Master's house by *Henry Edmonds*, 1928.

The C19–C20 VILLAGE stands high above the River Stour. This is accompanied by the Staffordshire and Worcestershire Canal, which passes through a TUNNEL, with segmental-headed entrance portals, far beneath Bridge Street; built 1769–70, only 65 yds (59 metres) long (but the longest on the canal). Nearby were the IRONWORKS founded by John Knight *c.* 1650 (later with their own barge arm); closed 1887, reopened to manufacture pressed wheels in 1904. A few C19 buildings remain, but the premises were otherwise reconstructed in 1935 by *Pritchard, Godwin & Clist* who added streamlined single-storey

* Funds proved insufficient to build a stone church by *Perkins*, 1847–8.

offices, in 1937, facing the road. – The OLD BLUE BALL, Nos.
18–20 Caunsall Road, ¼ m. further NE, restored square panelling with three gabled dormers, was built c. 1465 remodelled
c. 1582 (according to dendrodating).

AUSTCLIFFE FARM, ½ m. NE. Late C16 timber-framed, with
gabled dormers. Also much restored, but a good display of
close studding and herringbone framing. A little W, a lane leads
NE, past the late C18 brick AUSTCLIFFE HOUSE FARM (and
mobile homes) to a secluded spot beneath the sandstone cliff
where canal and river run side by side; the former is crossed
by a typical brick BRIDGE, the latter by a narrow cast-iron
FOOTBRIDGE, possibly c. 1795.

LEA CASTLE, ½ m. S, demolished c. 1945, was a large irregular
pile built for John Knight c. 1812–16, almost certainly by the
'architectural antiquary' *John Carter*. Only battlemented two-
storeyed brick lodges remain, plus much of the park wall (to
the S along the B4189; to the NW, picturesquely facing the canal
across Lea Lane). The finer NE LODGES flank a tripartite
entrance, its wider central part four-centred and castellated.
The simpler S LODGES facing Sion Hill, Kidderminster, are
somewhat altered. Both pairs may be as late as c. 1840–50.

LEA CASTLE CENTRE, ⅞ m. SE. Begun as 'a colony for mental
defectives' in 1947 by *J.M. Sheppard & Partners*. Low pale brick
units (clinics, workshops, housing) dispersed in a rural setting;
many additions, 1966.

₈₀₃₀   CORSE LAWN
                    Eldersfield

An extended linear hamlet, set back behind wide common verges
along the B4211 (and the Gloucestershire boundary). The
largest building is CORSE LAWN HOUSE; late C18 brick, five
bays, greatly expanded in matching style c. 2002, as a hotel, by
Trevor Hewett (of *Hook Mason Ltd*). Stone SCHOOL, further
NE, by *Norman Shaw*, 1871–2, with large casement windows;
SW porch with vesica-shaped window above the moulded
Gothic entrance. Adapted as a mission chapel by *A.W. Allard*
of Tewkesbury, 1883, with E.E.-style chancel at the N end
(following 'by permission' Shaw's original plan). Large SE
additions, c. 1970.

Also thatched timber-framed cottages, one in Linkend Road of
cruck construction, and C17 farmhouses. SWINLEY COURT,
¾ m. N, also has a good collection of C17 farm buildings,
including barn, stable, and cider house.

₇₀₅₀   COTHERIDGE

ST LEONARD. All white-plastered, except the late C20 weatherboarding of the upper stages of the remarkable timber-framed
S tower. On the lowest (porch) stage, the pointed S doorway is

flanked by solid tongued and grooved boarding of wide oak planks (4 in. (10 cm.) thick), perhaps C14–C15; C17 W window with ten chamfered mullions. Within the porch, massive cruck-like braces N and S. Its thick plank ceiling conceals the fact that these braces intersect on the second stage and are supplemented by two more long pairs crossing higher up. The church, probably of sandstone, is Norman; nave and chancel with flat buttresses, augmented by C14–C15 corner buttresses and a C17 raking one, N, of brick. Most nave windows have cambered heads, probably C18 (i.e. later than the known restoration date of 1684), no doubt enlargements of Norman openings. A three-light Perp window, nave SE, gave additional light to the former rood. Chancel with renewed Dec-Perp windows. Brick N chapel, c. 1620, with straight-headed E window of sandstone: three round-arched lights with hoodmould. The interior is also plastered, the barrel-vaulted nave ceiling a reconstruction* after the original collapsed in 1947. Of Norman details there remain a deeply splayed S window (blocked by the tower) and the chancel arch. This has one order of beaded and spiral-fluted shafts, with decorated scallop capitals like folded material; arch with chevron. Large flanking C18–early C19 openings: round-arched, N, four-centred, S. Good chancel roof, perhaps C14, with tie-beam, kingpost flanked by curved braces, and two bays of wind-braces. Wide round-arched C17 entrance to the plain N chapel.

COMMUNION RAIL, perhaps c. 1684; tall, narrowly set balusters. C17 sanctuary panelling. – Two pairs of BOX PEWS, chancel W. – The chancel floor TILES are C15, with elephants, and Berkeley and other heraldry. – Excellent PULPIT, perhaps also c. 1684, hexagonal, with oblong and arched panels; back panel, frilly tester with pendant knobs. – COMMANDMENT BOARDS, c. 1800. – Mid-C19 carved hexagonal FONT. – STAINED GLASS. E window by *Preedy*, 1872. – Chancel SE, 1879, probably *Clayton & Bell*. – Other windows have *Powell*'s stamped quarries, early 1870s. – In the N chapel E, a late C17 oval with mantled Berkeley heraldry. – MONUMENTS. Two Gothic tablets to the Berkeley family, c. 1869–75; also Thomas Berkeley †1669, of slate, probably once part of a larger monument, to which the finely carved marble urn, now in the S porch, belonged.

COTHERIDGE COURT, a little W (now subdivided). In essence, late C16, with close studding and carved bargeboards. The present E façade, red brick with stone dressings, is a thin veneer of 1770 (replacing the former gabled front). Of 1+5+1 bays, the centre recessed, with fenestration looking if anything earlier than 1770; doorway with pediment enclosing the Berkeley arms. The wings have ground-floor Venetian windows. Above these, stepped tripartite ones, so coarsely detailed that they must be post-Georgian; the early 1870s is the most likely date, also for the crowning balustrade. S wing also of 1770, and

---

* By *M. W. Jones*, completed by *J. Homery Folkes*, 1961.

somewhat broader than the E front. Its contains a late C18 staircase and fine drawing room with Adam-style ceiling, doorcases and chimneypiece. The principal staircase, rear centre, is late C16, with square tapering balusters around a (probably reduced) open well. Late C16 panelling in the N wing.

COW HONEYBOURNE see HONEYBOURNE

8040

CROOME D'ABITOT

The D'Abitots, originally from St Jean d'Abbetot (Normandy), owned the manor from the C12 until 1592, when the lawyer (Sir) Thomas Coventry bought it. His son Thomas, Lord Keeper of the Great Seal, was created Baron Coventry in 1628. In 1697 his grandson, the fifth Baron, was created first Earl of Coventry and Viscount Deerhurst (*see* p. 284). The present appearance of the estate is mostly due to George William, sixth Earl, who remodelled the house, laid out the grounds, and rebuilt the church on a hillside well away from the house. *Lancelot 'Capability' Brown* was both the Earl's architect and his landscape designer, no doubt introduced to him by *Sanderson Miller*. The latter was an important source of advice and inspiration to his friend Lord Coventry. He wrote to Miller in 1752: 'Whatever merits it [Croome] may in future time boast it will be ungrateful not to acknowledge you as the primary Author . . . It was owing to your assurances that nature had been more liberal to me than I apprehended . . .'

St Mary Magdalene. Vested in the Churches Conservation Trust since 1975. Built 1759–63, almost certainly by *Lancelot Brown*; *Robert Adam* was responsible for the interior and furnishings. The church, as originally planned by Brown, 1758, was to be classical, with tetrasyle portico. As built it is medievalizing: one of the most serious of the early Gothic Revival outside, one of the most elegant within. With its W tower and large E window it must have looked perfectly convincing from the house as well as the road. Of smooth ashlar (mason *Robert Newman* of Whittington, Glos.), with Y-cusped and intersecting-cusped tracery; ogee-canopied niches on the end walls of the square nave (apart from NE, where there is a discreet doorway for the tenantry). The chancel is long for an age that liked its chancels short, and might have satisfied the Ecclesiologists (were it not for the monuments choking it within). The tower's top stage would also do credit to a progressive architect of the 1830s, though the quatrefoil openings of the narrow middle stage are of course Gothick, also the high W porch beneath the tower with its stone vault of twelve radiating ribs. *Adam*'s interior is pure Georgian Gothic. Three-bay arcades with quatrefoil piers, rather too wide for the entablature they support. The delicate ceilings, moulded by *Joseph Rose*, are flat over the aisles, coved like a flattened tunnel vault above the nave; delightfully dainty stucco centres and borders. The black-and-white floor mirrors their layout. Chancel ceiling with one fine central oval. Chancel arch, tower arch, and aisle windows all have crocketed ogee hoodmoulds. Ogee-headed panels with Commandments and Creed on the chancel arch reveals.

Adam's FITTINGS are Gothick, the hexagonal PULPIT, carved by *John Hobcroft*, especially playful, done with the greatest delicacy, especially the pierced brackets for the tester. – His mahogany FONT however, carved by *Sefferin Alken*, is classical, exquisite in shape and detail. – COMMUNION RAIL. Pretty, in the Chippendale way. – PEWS altered and rearranged, but the panelling of the ends probably original (cf. the body of the pulpit). – Also noteworthy, the W DOOR and iron PORCH GATES. – *Adam* designed stained glass for the E window, apparently never executed.

MONUMENTS. Thomas, first Baron Coventry †1639, probably by *Nicholas Stone*. Large, white and black marble. He reclines beneath a big richly panelled segmental arch, resting on pairs of side columns, Mannerist Ionic with garlanded capitals. In front, the bag for the Great Seal and his mace; either side, seated figures of Justice (holding the Seal) and Prudence. Large angels recline on top. Excellent quality, iconographically very progressive. – Mary, wife of his eldest son Thomas, †1634, attributed to *Stone* (by Adam White). Standing black and white monument; twisted Corinthian columns, broken segmental pediment. Reclining effigy, stiff but delicately carved. She holds a baby; two more tiny sons kneel at her feet. – Opposite, her husband, the second Baron †1661, attributed to *Joshua Marshall* (GF); almost identical, the effigy even more stiff and awkward. – John, fourth Baron †1687, by *Grinling Gibbons* (contract 1690); large, of Italian marble. The top garlands are worthy of him, also the exquisitely fluted Corinthian pilasters flanking the wide reredos. Dull figure carving. He reclines on a sarcophagus, flanked by Hope and Faith, and turns the upper part of his body awkwardly to the E, where Faith, now seeming to block his view, once held out his heavenly crown. – Hon. Henry Coventry †1686; long attributed to *William Kidwell*, more recently to *William Stanton* (GF). Originally at St Martin-in-the-Fields, London. Very large tablet with white allegorical caryatids; swan-neck pediment with urn. – George William, sixth Earl †1809, by *John Bacon Jun*. Kneeling woman bent over the pedestal of a draped urn. Fine carving, in the style established by Bacon's father. – Neo-Grecian tablets by *J. Stephens* include George William, seventh Earl †1831, and George William, eighth Earl †1843, whose HATCHMENT is on the N aisle E wall. – A similar Grecian style (by *C. F. Brown*) still prevailed for George William, ninth Earl, †1930.*

66

---

*In the shrubbery S of the churchyard, a domed brick ICE HOUSE, originally with a thatched conical roof 18 ft high.

CROOME COURT

The core is of the early 1640s, the central section a broad U-plan
with hipped roof and three pairs of arched chimneys (probably an early C18 amendment). Remodelled for the sixth Earl
in 1751–2 by *Lancelot Brown*, a curious choice as he had until
then been exclusively a landscape gardener. He was thirty-five
when introduced to the Earl by *Sanderson Miller*, who may have
had some hand in the original design or at least its broad outlines; his Hagley Hall (p. 335), 1754–60, is remarkably similar.
Brown's team was more or less the same as that employed on
the church: bricklayer *William Eltonhead*, mason *Robert
Newman*, carpenter *John Hobcroft*, slate roofing supervised by
Henry Holland (father of the architect, later Brown's partner).
After 1760 *Robert Adam* was largely responsible for the interior; he continued to work here until shortly before his death
in 1792.

The EXTERIOR, of warm-coloured Bath ashlar, is a cool
composition, correctly Palladian or Jonesian. Eleven-bay
entrance front, N, with basement, *piano nobile*, and upper floor
with balustrade; low square angle eminences carry pyramidal
roofs – the motif of Jones's Wilton, of Houghton Hall, Norfolk
(of the 1720s), and of Hagley. The angle pavilions and three-
bay centre have quoins, the latter also a pediment (with
heraldic cartouche by *Adam*). The only other enrichments are
the spacious two-armed open staircase (cf. Lord Burlington's
Chiswick House), the Doric doorway with segmental pediment, and the pediments of the *piano nobile* windows beneath
the eminences. The garden side, S, is grander, with pedimented
tetrastyle portico of unfluted Ionic columns, approached by a
broad flight of steps with later *Coade*-stone sphinxes. Venetian
windows on the *piano nobile* beneath the eminences; tripartite
openings in their basements. Short W return, just the two eminences squeezing a two-storey canted bay: that is all.

The INTERIOR is no longer what it was. Significant parts
were removed when it came into institutional use after the
Second World War, some re-created since re-conversion to a
private house. *Brown* was responsible for the most of the sober
rooms on the *piano nobile*, with finely carved straight-topped
doorcases on fluted columns, deeply moulded cornices, and
elaborate, mostly Rococo-style, chimneypieces. His best rooms
are the Entrance Hall, with rear screen of four fluted Doric
columns fronting a cross-corridor (a reflection of the mid-C17
layout); and behind, at the centre of the S front, the gold, white
and green Saloon: coved ceiling with three plain panels by
Francesco Vassalli, doorway with broken pediment flanked by
fluted Ionic chimneypieces. The cross-corridor leads E to the
main staircase: not showy, of stone, cantilevered, with iron
balustrade. *Adam* designed three splendid rooms after 1760,
his *pièce de résistance* the Tapestry Room, bodily removed to
the Metropolitan Museum, New York. Of the Library, c. 1763,

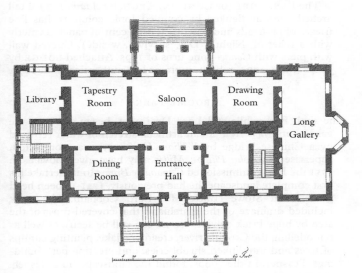

Croome Court.
South elevation and ground plan

SE corner, the delicate ceiling and chimneypiece (by *John Wildsmith*) survive; the mahogany bookcases have gone to the Victoria and Albert Museum. Much more remains of the Long Gallery, 1761–6, along the W return (cf. Hagley). Ceiling with elongated lozenges and octagons (as at Syon House, London) and other plasterwork by *Joseph Rose*; splendid white marble chimneypiece with life-size nymph caryatids, carved by *Joseph* 93 *Wilton*.

Attached to the house, E, an L-plan brick service wing, its upper floor converted to a private suite for Lord Coventry by *James Wyatt*, 1799. Then the STABLES, a large quadrangle open to the S, a rebuilding by *Brown*★ of ranges by *Francis Smith*,

★ *Sanderson Miller* also 'drew stables' in 1750.

1716–19; brick with pedimented entrance arches (all three stone-faced within). Beyond, the very large walled KITCHEN GARDEN.

Behind the garden, a little ESE, is the Home Shrubbery with, on a slight eminence surrounded by cedars of Lebanon, the ROTUNDA by *Brown*, 1754–7, formerly approached by a sinuous path flanked by urns and termini busts. Circular, of Bath stone, with entablature and shallow dome; six pedimented openings beneath panels with festoon carving. The dome is coffered inside; the walls have delicate Rococo plasterwork by *Vassalli*, 1761.

The PERSHORE (or LONDON) ARCH, by *Adam*, 1779, a tall arched gateway flanked by coupled Ionic columns, has fine friezes of ox-heads and paterae. Raised central panel, formerly with a relief of 'Night' ('Day' survives, W side). Curved wall with piers with *Coade*-stone urns of 1795. Attached LODGE by *James Wyatt*, 1794, rebuilt, more or less authentically, in 1877.

CROOME PARK

The sixth Earl, while still Lord Deerhurst, began work on the gardens in 1747. By 1748 an artificial stretch of water (crossed by a Chinese bridge by *William Halfpenny*) was completed, supervised by *John Phipps*; *Miller* may have given advice. In 1751 the Earl commissioned *Capability Brown* to undertake his first complete landscape; he had previously, 1741–9, been head gardener at Stowe (Bucks) for Lord Cobham. The work included drainage of the marshland that covered most of the area by huge brick culverts (some can still be seen), as well as remodelling the Croome river, creating a lake, planting clumps of trees and interlinked shrubberies, and erecting park buildings. Pevsner, in the 1960s, found the landscape 'in a desperate state of neglect'. Its main focus, the Pleasure Grounds N and W of the house, was taken over by the National Trust in 1996; its conservation programme has made it possible to again appreciate this important early example of Brown's remarkable skill. The original buildings, by *Brown* or *Adam* (from 1760), were altered or supplemented after 1792 by *James Wyatt*, so that attribution is not always straightforward. This description deals firstly with the Pleasure Grounds, then the distant eyecatchers, some visible from the church (*see* above), the best place to start.

The CHURCH is reached from the present National Trust entrance*, former Second World War hospital buildings attached to RAF Defford, through a Wilderness replanted in 1999 to an 1824 plan by *J.C. Loudon*. Itself a major landscape feature, it formed the E tip of the view from the house, answered, some distance W, beyond the replanted Evergreen Shrubbery, by *Robert Adam*'s superb TEMPLE GREENHOUSE,

p. 57

* N of this were an Arboretum, and Flower or Botanic Garden.

his first commission here: designed 1760, completed 1763. Of Painswick limestone, really just a temple façade with little space behind; six Doric columns, metope frieze, long pediment with very crisp carving (by *Sefferin Alken*) of a basket and flowers. Gigantic sashed windows were lowered when required from behind the columns. Recessed either side is just one closed bay, originally with niches for statues; cornucopia panels by *Alken* above; screens of paired columns inside. So here, viewed from the house, was a classical foil to contrast with church's Gothic. The HA-HA (of 1764) faces inwards, ensuring uninterrupted views back to the house; the landscape was meant to be enjoyed equally from this direction. Nearby, the remains of a PRIVY of 1765 and *Coade*-stone statue, THE DRUID, by *Wyatt*, 1796. Then comes the DRY ARCH BRIDGE, a tunnel beneath the carriage drive; by *Brown*, remodelled by *Wyatt* with vermiculated *Coade*-stone façades and keystones with heads of river gods, one dated 1797. An iron BRIDGE of *c.* 1972, replacing a ferry, crosses the Croome river, to the lake. At its NW corner, beyond a *Coade*-stone monument of 1797 to Brown, stands his GROTTO, its curved rocky front with roughly arched openings; begun 1765, and by the 1780s decorated with numerous crystals, fossils, shells and corals. Renewed statue of Sabrina, reclining; the water pouring from her urn was lit at night by a lamp, the iron hook for which remains. Nearby, the PUNCH-BOWL GATES by *Wyatt*, 1793–4, a pair of arches on broad piers with *Coade* festoons above; each carries an elegant, shallow, oval urn. The lake has two islands, the further one reached by two delicate wrought-iron BRIDGES, rebuilt 1806. On this, the TEMPLE PAVILION, a summerhouse of 1776–8, probably by *Adam*; Corinthian distyle *in antis*, finely carved frieze. *Coade* plaques inside, two with griffins and tripods, the third representing the Aldobrandini Wedding, flanked by roundels of shepherds. Beyond, at the lake's S tip, remnants of *Brown*'s BOATHOUSE; this probably had a banqueting room above the dock. Finally, on the lake's E bank, a large elegant URN on a circular plinth, typical *Wyatt*.

Now the eyecatchers outside the present grounds. On Knight's Hill, 1⅜ m. WSW, against the backdrop of the Malvern Hills, is the PANORAMA TOWER by *Wyatt*, 1801, based on an *Adam* design; built 1805–12. Round, the lower part with four groups of Tuscan columns *in antis*, solid walls between lightened by niches beneath blank panels. Intermittent balustrade, recessed drum with shallow dome. In the Old Park, 1⅓ m. NW, near Pirton Pool (a huge medieval fish pond partly landscaped by *Brown c.* 1763), is PIRTON TOWER, a Gothic ruin by *Wyatt c.* 1801: a length of ashlar wall, partly ivy-covered, with circular tower off-centre, against a belt of trees. Beyond the tip of the Croome river, 1 m. S, is the PARK SEAT (or OWL'S NEST), by *Adam*, 1766, simplified in execution 1770–2: a large alcove, its archway on Tuscan columns *in antis*, flanked by giant attached columns with acanthus capitals supporting a pediment. Inside, plaster apses l. and r. Superb view of the house and park.

For Dunstall Castle and the Tower on Baughton Hill yet further s, *see* pp. 275–6. Broadway Tower (p. 189) is also a far-distant eyecatcher, 15m. SE.

HIGH GREEN, ¾ m. w, the Coventry estate village of the 1780s, by *Brown*, is modest but formally planned; brick hipped-roofed houses, some detached, some paired, all more or less identical. Larger houses either end (a farmhouse, w, a former inn, E); one gabled interloper of 1870.

Beyond, cut off by the M5 motorway, is *Wyatt*'s WORCESTER LODGE of 1801, the former w approach, just gatepiers and separate two-storey ashlar lodge (rebuilt 1879); window and pedimented doorway, both with engaged Tuscan columns.

⅓ m. further s was the MENAGERIE, for which *Adam* designed an ambitious, unexecuted scheme in 1780. He had to settle for adding an ashlar w front to the KEEPER'S HOUSE. This survives within the C19 brick kennels enclosure. Projecting pedimented centre over a recessed arch, with oculus above, large tripartite window below; from this, visitors viewed the animals. Balustraded archways set back either side, the N one blind.

CROPTHORNE

ST MICHAEL. Tall narrow nave, perhaps of Saxon origin; see the long-and-short quoins at clerestory level and the former roof-line visible inside (nave w end). Unbuttressed Norman w tower with small windows, one in each shallow mid-buttress; cf. Fladbury. Battlemented Perp top; tall transomed two-light bell-openings. Clerestory also Perp, the N side renewed in the C18. Most other windows are late C14. *Jethro A. Cossins* rebuilt the chancel in 1893–4, reusing existing material including a C13 N lancet. Chamfered nave N doorway perhaps also C13. Similar s doorway, but with sunk moulding. The s porch, once two-storeyed, was rebuilt in the C16 and again in 1968. Within, Norman four-bay nave arcades with round piers, very flat capitals, square abaci, and single-step arches; the s arcade, with slightly broader capitals and bases, seems a little later, perhaps *c.* 1150. Pointed tower arch with two slight chamfers and nail-head hoodmould; that is C13, representing a later heightening and widening. But the chancel arch is again Norman, or at least its scalloped capitals are; the pointed arch with two slight chamfers must belong to the C13 remodelling. – Stone Perp-style REREDOS by *R.L. Boulton & Sons*, 1909. Nearby, a C13 PILLAR PISCINA. – STALLS by *Cossins*, with naïve carvings by *Louise & Minnie Holland* added 1910. – The PEWS, with traceried bench ends, are partly C15, much renewed. – Fine Comper-style s aisle REREDOS, by *W.E. Ellery Anderson*, 1931–2. – FONT. Perp-style, *c.* 1850. – WALL PAINTING, discovered above the N arcade in 1911. At least three layers, the earliest late C14, overpainted with a C15 St Christopher; now indecipherable. – CROSS-HEAD. The best Anglo-Saxon piece in the county. Large, of oolite, the arms double-cusped or lobed. On the front animated birds in bold trails with a griffin at the foot; cable-mould border; pellets at the base. The rear is similar but with lion-like creatures in the arms. The sides, surprisingly enough, all have close Greek key decoration. The date is supposed to be as early as *c.* 825–50. – STAINED GLASS. E window, *c.* 1894. – Chancel N and tower W lancets probably contemporary.

MONUMENTS. In the N aisle, an early C14 tomb recess, with flattened ogee arch, ballflower moulding, and carved heads. Beneath it, the slightly coped, coffin-shaped slab of a priest, with incised cross, its stem flanked by a hand raised in blessing and a chalice; perhaps *c.* 1200. – Francis Dingley †1624 and his wife Elizabeth (Bigg), possibly by *Samuel Baldwin*. Two painted recumbent effigies (he in armour), nineteen children kneeling small against the high tomb-chest; three who died in infancy are poignantly shown in their cradles. Back wall with inscription, strapwork pilasters, and heraldry. – Edward Dingley †1646 and his wife Joyce, perhaps also by *Baldwin* but much more accomplished. Standing monument, with kneeling husband and wife facing each other across a prayer-desk. Paired black Composite columns l. and r.; straight top with heraldry. Seven children, again kneeling small against the tomb-chest, though the boy who died young is here raised on a pedestal. – Minor tablets to later Dingleys (*see* p. 222) include a matching stone pair to Francis †1786 and Samuel †1801. – Eleanor Browne †1756; nicely gilded drapery (chancel).

In the churchyard a C14–C15 CROSS with complete base and shaft; converted to a war memorial *c.* 1920.

CROPTHORNE COURT, NW, mostly *c.* 1830–40, on the site of the medieval manor house; stuccoed, tripartite windows with shutters, shallow hipped roof.

The VILLAGE STREET is especially pretty. It runs SW from the church, parallel to but high above the Avon, and consists mostly of scattered houses in gardens. The first house, NW side, is THE MANOR, early C18, painted brick, six bays with Ionic pedimented doorway, and hipped roof. But much of the nicest work is black and white, for example the next two, fine early C17 timber-framed and thatched cottages.

Further on, another good group begins with CROPTHORNE HOUSE, the former vicarage: tall, red brick, by *Thomas Johnson*, 1789. Opposite, SE, a particularly picturesque thatched farmhouse; then, NW side, HOLLAND HOUSE, the largest in the street. Its L-plan core, C17 timber-framed and thatched, was remodelled and enlarged in 1891–3. The very pretty garden front has a gable dated 1904, facing a sunken garden following a design by *Lutyens*, 1900. Street front extended N and NW wing added by the Lancashire architect *Q.M. Bluhm*, *c.* 1913–20. Now a retreat and conference centre, with large NW accommodation block, with chapel at the S end, both brick, by *M.W. Jones*, 1963–4. THE POUND HOUSE, SE side, is another good C16–C17 example; gabled and jettied N cross-wing, S hall range.

More thatched cottages in MIDDLE LANE, s, and in
KENNEL BANK, leading N; the latter make a charming group,
with stone and brick additions.

Finally downhill, where the street turns s as Brook Lane, the
C17 BROOK FARM COTTAGE, mostly roughcast but a good
decorative timber display in its N gable, and PATTY'S FARM-
HOUSE. This is larger, H-plan: timber-framed centre and N
wing; roughcast s wing above stone ground floor with mullioned windows, one dated 1609.

CROPTHORNE MILL, ⅝ m. NNW. *See* Fladbury.

9050   CROWLE

ST JOHN BAPTIST. Rebuilt by *Preedy*, 1881–2; snecked coursed
rubble, ashlar dressings. C14 Dec window parts were reused,
especially in the s transept. In 1885 *Lewis Sheppard* rebuilt the
Late Perp w tower, more or less in facsimile; an image niche
high up on the E face is original, also much of the tower arch,
with big hollow mouldings and matching capital bands. The
heavy timber N porch is authentic C14, with arcades of ogee-
trefoiled openings either side and arch-braced entrance; above
it, a fine Annunciation carving, apparently resting on the head
of King David. Panelled ceiling with good bosses and more
figure carving.

FONT. Octagonal, Perp; trefoil-cusped panels on the bowl,
big fleurons beneath, alternating tracery patterns on the stem.
– LECTERN. An extraordinary piece, of Much Wenlock marble
(similar to Purbeck), expelled to the churchyard until restored
by *Harvey Eginton*, 1841; first described in 1851. The stem, five
polished marble shafts, must be entirely of 1841, the capitals
and much foliage drastically re-cut. The plain sloping top
surface, however, is old, but what else is? The central figure
seems the most trustworthy (apart from its patched chin): a
kneeling man, kneeling dead-frontally on nothing, grasping
symmetrical vine tendrils either side; beneath his feet and at
the sides, inversed lions' heads. It is tellingly Romanesque, with
distinct Italian affinities,* but is no doubt English of *c.* 1200
or a little later; foliage reminiscent of the Wells s transept. The
lectern at Norton (p. 502), found at Evesham Abbey, is a companion piece; a very similar lectern, though without a figure,
was excavated at Wenlock Priory, Shropshire. – Most other
FITTINGS are by Preedy, though some encaustic chancel tiling
is from an earlier restoration, 1840–1. – Good Perp CHANCEL
SCREENS by *C.F. Whitcombe*, 1905–6. – STAINED GLASS.
Excellent E window, 1882, no doubt *Burlison & Grylls*. – In the
N vestry W, good C15 fragments. – MONUMENTS. A few tablets
under the tower, the best, with draped urn, to Robert Smith
†1799, signed *Jos. Stephens Jun*.

---

* For the motifs one ought to compare the ambo of S. Ambrogio in Milan, *c.* 1100.
The foliage is much like that of the Trivulzio Candlestick, in Milan Cathedral, in
its turn claimed as English work of *c.* 1200.

At CROWLE COURT FARM, NW, the moat of the medieval manor belonging to the Priors of Worcester; within it, a brick house of *c.* 1900. But a ruined stone building to its NW, small and square, was probably a C16 detached KITCHEN, with large W fireplace. Outside the moat, SW, a Lias rubble BARN, of seven bays, now converted to housing. Much rebuilt in brick, after the S end lay derelict for many years, but the roof, of 30-ft (9-metre) span, survives over the four N bays; dendro-dating gave *c.* 1355 for the N arch-braced collar truss, but also several C16 dates.

The expanded VILLAGE retains several timber-framed buildings, some thatched. Most seem C17, though three are visibly of earlier cruck construction: CHURCH COTTAGE, at the start of the lane to the church; CROWLE COTTAGE, further N on the W side of Church Road; and WOODSTOCK COTTAGE, School Lane, E end. The SCHOOL (with attached house) is by *Hopkins*, 1861–4; brick with half-hipped roofs, and good Gothic detail. Ornamental banding on the schoolroom, repeated on an addition of 1912. Opposite, set back, the brick VICARAGE of 1884 by *Henry Rowe & Son* (with large early C20 addition); to its W, the low STABLE BLOCK of the previous house, *c.* 1800, with central pedimental gable.

LOWER CROWLE, ⅔ m. ENE, consists of three large C16–C17 farmhouses, much rebuilt in the C19, all with good timber-framed farm buildings. The most imposing, COMMANDERY FARM, has a gabled E front of mid-C19 brick, but the N gable-end has exposed C17 framing.

FROXMERE COURT, formerly The Priory, 1 m. E. Probably of *c.* 1836, an early example of a C19 Tudorbethan country house, notably picturesque. Diapered brick, with rubbly Lias quoins; asymmetrical, with gables, hoodmoulds, some latticed windows. The most notable feature is the trio of tall, cylindrical, patterned brick chimneys on the gable adjoining the four-centred porch, which has a canted and battlemented stone oriel. Side chimney with more orthodox star-shaped stacks. Bay windows at the rear, where the service wing, NE, is Lias-faced. Inside, especially on the upper floor, high-vaulted plaster ceilings.

CROWN EAST AND RUSHWICK

St THOMAS, Crown East. Small, brick with limestone dressings and slate roof, probably by *Hopkins c.* 1860–5. Picturesque Dec style, with varied windows, timber S porch surmounted by an open bell-turret with steep shingled spirelet, and large dormer nearby with pierced bargeboards. Originally a private chapel in the grounds of Crown East Court, re-erected here 1876, with little alteration apart from a slight lengthening of the nave. Quite ornate roofs within. – Costly timber FURNISHINGS, all with lavish tracery, the VESTRY DOOR also with large dragon knocker. – FONT. Neo-Norman, the round bowl said to come from St Cuthbert, Lower Wick (p. 776). If so, entirely re-cut, with the most unlikely subjects (cf. Hindlip). – STAINED GLASS. E window signed *Lavers, Westlake & Barraud*, 1882.

Former NATIONAL SCHOOL, N, of 1878; brick, with yellow and blue patterning.

CROWN EAST COURT (later Aymestrey Court), ¼ m. S. Large country house, probably rebuilt *c.* 1856 for the Rochdale banker and freemason *Albert Hudson Royds* (perhaps to his own designs). Steeply gabled Tudor Gothic, quite plain; mottled brick, large stone windows. The low S porch leads into a spacious entrance hall, with stone chimneypiece with large owls, and rear staircase of Imperial type, but with simple pierced Gothic timber balustrades. Canted bay, for the drawing room, on the E return. Matching W extension with lower service wing, for H. Bramwell, by *Haddon Bros*, 1873–4. – Fine PARK with lakes and views S to the Malvern Hills. – NE LODGE, probably *c.* 1874. – Plainer LODGE and FARM BUILDINGS of *c.* 1856, NW.

RUSHWICK, ¾ m. SE, is mundane C20, but UPPER WICK, ½ m. further SE, has some good houses. Timber-framed ones include UPPER WICK FARM, C17, partly rebuilt in brick, but with full-height gabled rear stair-turret, W. Three of *c.* 1800 reflect the proximity of Worcester. STANFIELD HOUSE, N of Upper Wick Farm, is brick, five bays (the two N apparently later), its wide Tuscan doorway masked by a thin Doric porch. The MANOR HOUSE, further W, also has five bays, plus lower wings; central pedimented pilaster doorcase.

WICK EPISCOPI, a country seat of the Bishops of Worcester until 1558, stands apart, ¼ m. ESE of Upper Wick; partly late C17, remodelled *c.* 1790 for Thomas Bund, probably by *George Byfield*.[*] Six-bay N front, stuccoed, with Tuscan porch. Wide entrance hall, the earlier staircase with three slim turned balusters per tread. Large room behind the three E bays with excellent Adamish plasterwork. Stables and coachhouses, W, added *c.* 1828.

DEFFORD

ST JAMES. Much is by *Horatio Richard Snelgrove* of Cirencester (who later worked in G.G. Scott's office); he rebuilt the chancel and restored the W end, 1865, and repaired the roofs, 1875. The nave is medieval, with inserted C17 windows; timber-framed S porch rebuilt 1977. The best part is the timber-framed upper part of the W tower, quite closely set studding with short broach spire; stone lower part with Dec window; all renewed by *Francis B. Andrews*, 1903. A notable but small female head is used as the keystone of the S doorway: a queen of the lineage of the *Portail royal* at Chartres, perhaps late C12. There are few

---

[*] *Byfield*'s pupil *John Phillips* exhibited 'two intended new fronts' at the Royal Academy in 1790.

successors of that type in England, the Rochester W portal
chiefly; so the little head, perhaps a label stop, assumes importance. The nave has a heavily ceiled roof, with one moulded
tie-beam; chancel arch, 1865. Re-seated 1887. – Late Georgian
WEST GALLERY. – Oak REREDOS by *R. Haughton*, 1911. –
STAINED GLASS. Gaudy E window of 1899, probably by
William Pearce Ltd.

CANNON HOUSE, S, is the former vicarage of 1866–7, also
by *Snelgrove*; red brick with blue patterning, bargeboarded
dormers. WHITE HOUSE, immediately E, consists of cruck hall
and gabled cross-wing, the cruck frame visible in the W gable-
end. Otherwise much rebuilt in brick, coated in roughcast.
Further E, NOAKE'S COURT, a thatched cruck house, one of
the best-looking externally as the almost straight crucks stand
out beyond the plaster of the lower gable wall, E. Three bays
with central hall, as usual with fireplace and first floor inserted;
the roof of the W bay has been lowered.

In Croome Road, ⅓ m. NNE, past a Beauchamp estate lodge of
1885, the former NATIONAL SCHOOL by *W.J. Hopkins*, 1872;
raw brick, much altered, apart from the attached house with
alternating stone and blue brick voussoirs.

DODDENHAM

ST MARY, Knightsford Bridge. Now redundant. 1854–5 by
A.E. Perkins, one of his most attractive churches, built to
replace both the parish church at Knightwick (p. 420) and
its chapel (*see* below), so set halfway between them. Of local
stone, laid crazy-paving fashion, with banded tiled roof. Nave
with N porch, chancel with N vestry with its own porch set
diagonally. Geometrical Dec style. The best feature is the tall
stone bell-turret rising from a central W buttress, then turning
octagonal, with eight small gables over trefoiled lancets,
and sharp stone spirelet. Carving by Moyson of Birmingham.
– Plain Norman tub FONT, on a round base; from Knightwick. – STAINED GLASS. E and W windows by *Clayton &*
Bell, 1914. – Central nave S by *Christopher Whall*, 1918; very
good.

Opposite, N, the former CHURCH SCHOOLS, a strong design of
1888 by *Henry Rowe & Son*; red brick with yellow banding, the
schoolroom still E.E.-style with steep bellcote, the attached
house domesticated by a little half-timbering in its gables.
Immediately NE, stepping uphill, three pairs of ALMSHOUSES,
to an L-plan; dated 1889 and, like the schools, paid for by
J.F. Greswolde-Williams. Also brick with yellow bands, two-
storeyed rear, single-storeyed to the road with timber-arched
verandas. The painted brick house beyond, of 1892, was built
for the district nurse.

W of the church, the H-plan TALBOT INN, part C17 but mostly
C18 and later brick. It stood at the approach to KNIGHTS-
FORD BRIDGE, the C19 brick abutments and flood arches of

which now support a crass tubular steel footbridge. The present elegant BRIDGE carrying the A44 across the Teme, a little SE, is of 1956–8 by *W.R. Thomson*, County Surveyor; segmental concrete arch on elongated brick piers with rounded ends. Neat cubic river-flow MEASUREMENT STATION nearby: brick, on a concrete plinth.

The lane beside the Talbot leads NNW to ANKERDINE FARM, in origin a four-bay cruck hall house (the two upper bays rebuilt in the C17); C16 S cross-wing, mostly reconstructed, but with a large brick chimneystack on its E gable.

The WHITE HOUSE, near the summit of Ankerdine Hill, ⅝ m. NNE, by *J.H. Williams c.* 1895, is Voysey-inspired; roughcast, timbered gables, battered chimneys, and bulgy oriels to enjoy the splendid views. – TOWER COTTAGE, downhill, is of the same date (reputedly to accommodate servants); its oblong water tower has a half-timbered top stage with pyramidal roof.

DODDENHAM HALL, 1 m. E. Early C18 brick, seven bays, with Doric porch and hipped roof, is surrounded by C19 farm buildings, all converted to housing. The Norman chapel, St Andrew, of which nothing remains, stood a little W.

DODDERHILL

An extensive medieval parish, its S end, with the church, now part of Droitwich.

ST AUGUSTINE. A very interesting church, originally cruciform, on the site of the Roman fort overlooking Droitwich (q.v.), and possibly of a Saxon minster. What remains, outside and in, is surprising, its history much obscured by patching because of subsidence, by partial demolition after the Civil War, and by dubious C19 restoration. The mighty four-stage S tower, rebuilt on the site of the medieval S transept in 1708, dominates the exterior; the tooling betrays its date. The central tower was dismantled in the C17, when the nave also disappeared. Much of the material of the demolished tower must have been stored and reused; the two-light bell-openings are clearly late medieval, as is a tiny light for the stair-vice, high up, S side. The long E and W lancets may be C13 survivors of the S transept, their particularly deep splays perhaps the result of thickening the walls to carry the tower. N transept also medieval, partly rebuilt in brick from *c.* 1803, with tracery (Perp N, Dec W) renewed by *John Shilvock*, 1848. He filled the former arch to the nave with flowing tracery in 1850. The similar tracery in the ambitious Dec chancel may also be untrustworthy; it would be very progressive for 1322, the date when new altars were dedicated. N wall again C19 brick, now obscured by a neat, minimally Tudor, meeting room added in 1998–9 by *Patrick J. Burton*. In the chancel S wall C14 piscina and sedilia, low-high-low (an unusual composition), with ogee trefoiled arches, and also, SW, a blocked shafted low side

window. But the greatest surprise inside is that the late C12–
early C13 crossing survives intact; a consecration date of 1220
is recorded. Tripled responds to all sides, with keeled shafts
and decorated trumpet-scallop capitals; also one early stiff-leaf
capital, NW (cf. St Andrew, Droitwich). Pointed arches, of
three orders, the outer a continuous half-roll. In the NW
corner, the access to the former tower (and later rood?) stairs.
But how is the medieval-looking quadruple-chamfered arch S
of the S crossing arch to be explained? Its southernmost
chamfer is strengthening work of 1848, so it must be assumed
that the others filled a similar function for the 1708 rebuilding. Roofs throughout also of 1848, as is the S vestry.

Further restoration by *Lewis Sheppard*, 1889–90 (paid for by
John Corbett), provided most furnishings, including the round
PULPIT, openwork wrought iron (by *Letheren & Sons* of
Cheltenham) on a stone base, and the octagonal FONT, carved
by *H.H. Martyn & Co.* – REREDOS (now at the W end). Of
1905; painted scenes with Renaissance surround. – ARCHI-
TECTURAL FRAGMENTS. A couple of Norman pieces, cur-
rently in the piscina. – STAINED GLASS. Nearly all by *Samuel
Evans* of West Smethwick, 1890–1; five windows in his usual
semi-pictorial style. – The exceptions the chancel SE, by *T.F.
Curtis, Ward & Hughes*, 1904, and N transept W, by *Pearce &
Cutler*, 1921. – MONUMENTS. Of that to Gerrard Dannet (of
Elmbridge) †1615, only a fragment remains: four children
kneeling beneath their initials. – Later tablets: Dorothy Hol-
beche †1771, by *Richard Squire*; Capt. Richard Norbury †1800,
by *W. Stephens*.

In the CHURCHYARD, late C18–early C19 tombs, a few still
with iron railings.

HILL COURT, now a school, a little N of the church. Large stuccoed villa, mostly of *c.* 1840; six-bay W front with thin fluted
Doric porch, five-bay S front with central staircase window. The
other sides, of painted brick, must survive from the C18 house.
Ionic columns in the entrance hall. – Additions for the school
include a large block, with turret, by *Jonathan Gale* of Rye
(Sussex), *c.* 2000.

CHÂTEAU IMPNEY, in ample grounds ⅝ m. ENE. The palace of 109
John Corbett (1817–1901), the salt-king of Stoke Prior and
Droitwich, now a hotel. How self-assured Corbett must have
been to build thus: a compact, towering chateau in the highest-
pitched Louis XIII style that his architect *Auguste Tronquois* of
Paris could dream up; designed from 1869, built 1873–5. The
contribution of the executive architect, *Richard Phené Spiers*,
should not be underestimated; he was one of the very few contemporary London architects with Beaux Arts training. Why
Corbett opted for such a French-style building is not entirely
clear. His wife (*née* Anna Eliza O'Meara), the elder daughter
of the Secretary of the Diplomatic Corps in Paris, was certainly
brought up in France; more relevant may have been his desire
to cock a snook at his political rival, Sir John Pakington of
Westwood House (p. 653).

The house, of Fareham brick with ample Bath stone dressings, has a splendid garden façade, SW, nearly but not quite symmetrical: the full-height canted l. bay (to the dining room) has a small adjunct for ancillary rooms, unlike its counterpart, r. (the former library); the drawing room filled the centre. Much carved stone decoration, enlivened by alternating brick and stone voussoirs, and ironwork balconies and balustrades. Very steep pavilion roofs with three tiers of dormers: the upper small and circular, the middle large, of wood, the lower even larger, of stone with extravagant pediments. The entrance side (SE) has a tall polygonal corner stair-tower with steeply pointed roof, but its deep porte cochère (by *J.R. Nichols*, 1893) has been replaced by a bland curving hotel entrance of 1972; other additions at the rear, NE, obliterated Nichols's contemporary iron conservatory (and much else). The unaltered NW return has a smaller, slightly tapering round turret, for the backstairs. The interior is not in its original state though the basic layout is clear, with a corridor leading NW from the entrance hall, with receptions rooms off its SW side. The panelling is not particularly French, the plaster ceilings rather more so. The best-preserved interior is the spacious Jacobethan well staircase, behind columns NE of the hall; very good stained glass by *James Powell & Sons*, 1879, with figures of Chaucer, Shakespeare and Spenser, designed by *Harry Burrow*.

Fine terraced GARDENS with balustraded parapets descend from the SW front, their focal point an ornate, octagonal, cast-iron FOUNTAIN. The grounds further SW retain much of their original layout, with a statue of Flora and differing, tellingly sited iron footbridges crossing the River Salwarpe. RAVENS-CREST (formerly The Chalet), a little S of the house, dated 1891, still has the regulation circular turret with conical roof. This repeats that of the S LODGE, *c.*1875, formerly with a very French-looking pair of rusticated gatepiers. The N LODGE, by *John Cotton*, 1882, is entirely Old English, half-timbering above brick, the style of Corbett's Droitwich spa buildings.

DODFORD

HOLY TRINITY AND ST MARY. Built 1907–8, largely at the expense of the Rev. W.G. Whinfield; one of the best churches of its date in the county. The architect, *Arthur E. Bartlett* of London, a pupil of Sir Reginald Blomfield, briefly opened a Bromsgrove office after receiving the commission. Roughcast brick, with sandstone dressings, the details mostly Arts and Crafts Dec-Perp. The exterior is an excellent composition: aisleless, quite large, with a long two-bay S transept, the outer bay the base of a bold tower, with strong angle buttresses, broad two-light bell-openings, and battlements interrupted by sharp N and S gables. The most striking element, the fanciful S rose window of the bottom stage, is quite rectilinear but with centre medallion of flowing tracery. The bell-openings above develop into a large Celtic cross. The church itself has broad seven-light W and E windows, and again prominent buttresses, except for the narrow, battlemented S chapel, with just slender pilasters. Nave S and tower doorways are connected by a dog-leg brick and timber passageway, forming a small cloister. An open-air pulpit, in the tower W wall, approached from its stair-vice, faces the paved courtyard. The only external sculpture is the Good Shepherd, of lead, in the nave W gable above the low polygonal baptistry, by *Louis Weingartner* of the *Bromsgrove Guild*, and relief carvings above the cloister entrances, by *Charles Beacon*.

Light, spacious interior, on the model of Norman Shaw's St Margaret, Ilkley, West Yorkshire. Massive pointed diaphragm arches cross the nave, with a similar, slightly moulded arch dividing off the chancel. Most other arches, e.g. the two-bay arcade to the S chapel, are without mouldings. The chapel is rib-vaulted, other roofs are quite plain, of timber. But it is the carved embellishments that take the eye, mostly by the *Broms-grove Guild*, interesting transitional work between their early individualistic phase and later architectural reticence. On the soffits of the diaphragm and chancel arches, square plaster panels of fruit, flowers and birds, by *Charles Bonnet* and *Leopold Weisz*; wall plate also carved with fruits, one of the first Guild jobs by the Italian *Celestino Pancheri*. He probably also exe-cuted most of the carving of *Bartlett*'s original FURNISHINGS, notably the fine musician's N GALLERY, PULPIT (with some inlay), and COMMUNION RAILS. The ROOD BEAM, supporting a splendid beaten copper and enamelled cross by *Amy Walford*, is by *H.H. Martyn & Co.* of Cheltenham, and the LECTERN (and probably PEW CARVINGS) by *Richard Haughton* of Worcester. Throughout classical and Gothic details are freely mixed, in Ninian Comper fashion. Equally remarkable is that later fittings are entirely in keeping: REREDOS of 1972–3 by *Robert Pancheri* (Celestino's son) and sinuous iron handrails by the local blacksmith *John Gale*. Only the ORGAN CASE, 1936 by *J.A. Swan*, is perhaps too conventionally Gothic (though again carved by *Pancheri*). – STAINED GLASS. By *A.J. Davies* (with *Joseph Sanders*); mildly Art Nouveau, mostly just leading patterns with a few quarries with symbols and occasional splashes of colour, especially in the S rose.

The former VICARAGE, higher up, NW, is also by *Bartlett*, 1907–8; butterfly plan, very varied in outline and surfaces. The wings are gabled and pebbledashed, but the central pivot, a polygonal four-storey tower, is hard red brick, with, at the top, a balcony enjoying a splendid view. Timber porch with text and cherubs, no doubt carved by the *Bromsgrove Guild*.

DODFORD PRIORY, ¼ m. N. Founded for Augustinian canons by Henry II *c.* 1184; Premonstratensian from 1464, when granted to Halesowen Abbey. The present house, approached picturesquely through the central bay of a C19 brick barn, is mostly C16–C17; L-plan, the main sandstone range with renewed windows, the shorter NE wing timber-framed. The rear of the main range reveals its earlier origin; at the SE corner, broad angle buttresses; at the W end, a narrow pointed, chamfered doorway. In between, a large stone chimney-breast with three diagonal brick shafts; a smaller chimney rises from the roof to its l., another with two star stacks on the wing.

CHARTIST SETTLEMENT. Great Dodford, the Dodford Priory estate, was bought early in 1848 by Feargus O'Connor to build the fifth (and last) village for his National Cooperative Land Company.* The company, which aimed to provide smallholdings for working people who would thereby also obtain the right to vote, was dissolved in 1851; the Dodford estate, still incomplete, was sold in 1850. Some forty cottages were ready by 1849, all to a standard design created (probably by *Henry Cullingham*) for the other estates: single-storey, here brick on sandstone bases, three bays, the centre projecting beneath a pedimental gable with trefoil-shaped ventilator. Inside, a central kitchen was flanked by sitting room, l., bedroom, r., with small open yard with well and outbuildings at the rear. The plots were each of four acres, larger than the earlier estates as O'Connor thought the soil here more suitable for grazing and plough crops rather than market gardening; in the end, growing strawberries proved the salvation. The cottages are mostly ranged along the straight Victoria Road and the curving Woodland Road further W, both very narrow, with a few more at the N end of Priory Road. Some ten or eleven survive in more or less original form; one, ROSE DENE, near the central crossroads, was also restored internally by the National Trust, 2000–1. Nearly opposite this, a two-storey house, GREAT MEADOW, perhaps for O'Connor's agent. PRIORY COTTAGE, with pretty bargeboards, S of the Priory in the uncompleted Rose Lane, also seems contemporary. Off the NE end of Priory Road, a modest BAPTIST CHAPEL of 1865, with two pointed windows each side; Sunday School extension, E, 1926.

At LITTLE DODFORD, ⅛ m. S, is DODFORD LODGE, a gabled brick farmhouse of 1881 by *John Cotton*. Further S, the former BOARD SCHOOL, by *F.J.Yates* of Bromsgrove, 1876–7, minimal Gothic with banding and saddleback bell-turret; its detached house, added by *Cotton*, 1882, resembles Dodford Lodge.

WOODCOTE MANOR HOUSE, by the Kidderminster road ⅝ m. WSW, is early C19, stuccoed and upright; three bays and storeys with Doric porch. Ornate cast-iron porch at the rear. Opposite, a large early C19 brick BARN.

FOCKBURY FARMHOUSE, ⅝ m. E, by *Cotton*, 1887, has wide segment-headed windows, and half-timbered gables. He also restored FOCKBURY MILL FARM, ½ m. further E, by the M5; part C17, sandstone with mullioned windows and timbered gables, part brick, 1758. Long C17 timber-framed BARN.

*Previous estates were at Heronsgate, Chorleywood, Herts.; Lowbands, Redmarley D'Abitôt, and Snig's End, Corse, both Glos.; and Charterville, Minster Lovell, Oxon.

DORMSTON

ST NICHOLAS. What will be remembered is the timber-framed W tower, probably *c.* 1450; three stages of close-set studding, with saddleback roof. Within, heavy cross-bracing, plus a curiously crude later N strut, with double curve. Of heavy timbers also the S porch, perhaps mid-C14, contemporary with the nave's two-light Dec windows. Nave and porch restored by *C.C. Rolfe* of Oxford, 1899; chancel mostly rebuilt by *C.F. Whitcombe*, 1903–5. – COMMUNION RAILS. C17; tall tapering balusters. – SCULPTURE. Remains of a Crucifixion, from a churchyard cross; also part of a trefoiled window head. – The Arts and Crafts Gothic PULPIT and LECTERN must be by *Rolfe*. – Plain octagonal FONT, C14–C15. – Six late medieval BENCHES, nave W. – WALL PAINTING, nave N wall, now indecipherable. – STAINED GLASS. Minor C14 fragments in the nave S windows, including the Lovell arms. – Chancel S by *Jim Budd*, 1996. – WAR MEMORIAL by *W.W. Harris* of Worcester, 1920, a pleasantly naïve oak triptych. – Large SUNDIAL, nave S wall; dated 1841, signed *Thomas Davis*, sciagrapher, of Inkberrow.

DORMSTON MANOR, formerly Bag End Farm, ¼ m. SE. Probably *c.* 1600; partly timber-framed with brick infill, to an expanded L-plan with two sets of triple star-stacks. The W wing looks the least altered: close studding on the ground floor, square panelling above. The S front has mostly been rebuilt, but the original internal layout survives, with lobby-entry in front of the staircase, quite small with imposing tapering newel posts. The rooms either side have panelling and good wooden chimneypieces, the E with fluted pilasters and a little strapwork; the W has two tiers of small Ionic columns. – S approach picturesquely flanked by two timber-framed DOVECOTES, the SW with pyramidal roof, the SE, set behind a small stable, cross-gabled. Other good C17–C19 farm buildings, E and NE.

MOAT FARMHOUSE, ⅓ m. SW. A remarkable timber-framed house, dated 1663; high, all square panelling, with three large gabled dormers along the (W) front and one gable to each short side. It is one of the few to have retained its tiled weatherings, bracketed from the wall framing at first-floor level and beneath the gables. Central staircase; central stack with three brick star-shafts. The plan clearly derives from medieval solar wings, but the central hall has become a single-storey projection at the back, in other words the kitchen (later enlarged). The moat survives to the N.

Weatherboarded BARN, S. To the W, a timber-framed DOVECOTE, the same date as the house, also with a weatherboard. The original four-gabled roof was replaced by a pyramidal one with gabled lantern, probably in the early C19. Inside, some 720 timber nesting boxes, all, except on the W wall, rebuilt 1972–4.

DOVERDALE

ST MARY. Almost entirely by *Preedy*, 1858–9; Dec-style chancel, nave with S vestry, timber W turret with leaded broach spirelet. Medieval, probably C14, fabric only in the nave, which has renewed C17 windows. Most of Preedy's FURNISHINGS survive, with reused C17 PANELLING as a nave dado. – STAINED GLASS. C15 Virgin, nave NW, much restored. – Nave SW, *c.* 1850–60. – Excellent E window by *Hardman*, 1859–60. – Sanctuary N and S, *c.* 1896, no doubt *Clayton & Bell.*

EARTHWORKS W of the church reveal the site of the medieval settlement.

DOVERDALE MANOR, ¾ m. NNE, the rectory from 1791 to 1918, is mostly *c.* 1710. Five-bay, three-storey front of red brick with painted stone dressings; windows with prominent fluted keystones. Central tripartite doorway with segmental pediment, probably *c.* 1810; also, the broad two-storey bow on the S return. Fine early C18 staircase with three balusters to the tread (twisted-columnar-twisted), and carved tread ends; cf. Ombersley Court. The staircase window, N, has early C19 stained glass with Gothick tracery. – Early C19 GATEPIERS. – In the grounds, S, a derelict ICE HOUSE.

DOWLES
Upper Arley

Dowles (in Shropshire until 1895), cf. Bewdley town map, p. 142, has lost its most important buildings: the church and manor house. ST ANDREW, largely of 1789, altered 1882, stood S of the confluence of Dowles Brook and the Severn; demolished 1956. Its churchyard remains, hidden in a copse, near the ruins of the brick parish room of 1883. The small exceptionally complete DOWLES MANOR, standing in perfect seclusion in a dip surrounded by a wood, immediately N of Dowles Brook and W of the B4194, suffered a yet more grievous fate. Probably built *c.* 1622 (though dated 1560), restored by *W.H. Bidlake*, 1908–15, it was partially destroyed by fire in 1982, and subsequently all but replaced by an illegal new house, since demolished. What little remains lies beneath corrugated iron roofs, awaiting possible reconstruction.*

Crossing the Severn just N of the Dowles Brook, the impressive remains of DOWLES BRIDGE, built for the Tenbury & Bewdley Railway, 1863–4; engineer *William Clarke*. Its four piers stand to full height, the outer two linked to curving rock-faced abut-

---

* It contained a central hall flanked by kitchen wing, W, and solar, E, both cross-gabled; sandstone ground floor, close-studding above. Inside much of the framing must always have been exposed, for the amazingly preserved decorative wall paintings took the posts into consideration. These had survived in the hall and room above, and in both lower and upper rooms of the E wing: grey and red, largely arabesques, very boldly done, also in one upper room a gentleman and a lady. In the kitchen was a wooden Elizabethan overmantel from a house at Bewdley.

ments; blue brick with grey rock-faced quoins, of tapering rectangular form, with rounded triangular cutwaters. Above each
pier rise two others, thinner, of ashlar; these flanked the lattice-
girder deck (dismantled 1966).

Two C17 timber-framed houses worth noting are PAINSMORE,
facing the Severn N of the bridge, with end gable with decorative quadrant bracing; and QUAINTWAYS, above the B road
towards Bewdley, with mostly narrow studding.

DRAKES BROUGHTON   9040

ST BARNABAS. A neat compact early work by *W.J. Hopkins*,
1856–7. Nave and chancel in one, slender SW tower with open
timber top and weatherboarded broach spire (renewed 1978).
Coursed Lias with Bath dressings, the details mostly Dec,
especially the larger windows. Timber S porch. Inside, patterned brickwork, now sadly painted white. High roofs, sturdier above the chancel, given further prominence by good leaf
capitals. SE vestry by *Hopkins*, 1897–8. – Of original fittings,
only the big carved octagonal FONT and simple PEWS remain.
– STAINED GLASS. E window by *A.J. Davies*, 1951. – Chancel
NE by *Hardman*, 1867.

Simple brick SCHOOL opposite, by *S.W. Daukes*, 1867–8,
submerged by later extensions – a fate symptomatic of that of
the village itself.

CALDEWELL, ⅞ m. WNW. An early C19 country-house version
of the late C18 Pershore town-type (e.g. No. 37 High Street).
Brick, three bays, with two-storey canted bays flanking the
doorway; above these, Diocletian windows, in the centre a
round window above an arched one. Much altered in the late
C19: gabled porch, central staircase hall, large rear extensions.
Brick LODGE dated 1888.

The best C17 timber-framed group is at WINDMILL HILL, 1 m.
NW (in Stoulton parish): three thatched cottages along the W
end of Windmill Lane, leading to the large WINDMILL HILL
FARM, of square panelling with brick infill.

At the NW end of WADBOROUGH, Broughton's sister village
1¾ m. WSW, one of *Daukes*'s brick two-storey LEVEL CROSS-
ING LODGES for the Birmingham & Gloucester Railway
c. 1840; much altered but a rare survival. Large C18 brick farms
are dotted around the wide, open landscape, the neatest HER-
MITAGE FARM, further NW, five-bay brick, with square stone
DOVECOTE; the C18–C19 WADBOROUGH PARK FARM, on a
medieval moated site, is now a dramatic ruin.

DROITWICH   8060

Salt has been the centre of interest at Droitwich from at least the
Iron Age and Roman periods. The *salinae* appear in Domesday
Book as a royal possession producing an annual thousand tons

of salt, from five brine wells. The town achieved borough status
by 1155–6, confirmed by King John's charter, 1215, which gave
the burgesses the *vill cum salsis et salinis*. A Hospital of St Mary
was founded in 1285, N of the bridge over the Salwarpe (on which
stood a small chapel), and an Augustinian priory in 1331, in the
W part of the town. But Droitwich remained small; Leland
(*c.* 1535), Torrington (1781), and *The Beauties of England* (early
C19) are unanimous in calling it dirty. The six-mile Droitwich
Canal, from the Severn at Hawford, was surveyed by *James
Brindley* in 1767, opened in 1771; it ran close by the main salt-
producing area. By 1772 annual production was about 15,000
tons. Yet in 1826 the town consisted only of the Friar Street–High
Street axis, St Andrew's Street, and the street N to the bridge.
The railway arrived in 1847; the canal was extended in 1853 to
join the Worcester and Birmingham Canal at Hanbury (p. 352).
Peak salt production (120,000 tons) was achieved in 1872, but
the industry then gradually relocated to Stoke Prior, the last
Droitwich works closing in 1922.

The medicinal value of brine immersion is said to have been
discovered during the cholera epidemic of 1832. The first brine
baths were built off Queen Street in 1836. That the spa flourished
as the salt industry declined was due to John Corbett (of Chateau
Impney, p. 255), owner of the Stoke Prior Salt Works (p. 607). At
Droitwich he remodelled the Raven Hotel (from 1879), and built
the Salters' Hall (1879), St Andrew's Brine Baths (1887) and
Worcestershire Hotel (1891); the Corbett style is brick with half-
timbered upper parts. The spa flourished until the late 1930s (cf.
Norbury House Hotel and the Lido), but rapidly declined after
the Second World War, when Droitwich was already being
suggested to receive 'overspill' population from Birmingham.
Largely to avoid designation as a New Town, a joint Droitwich
Development Committee (involving the County and Borough
Councils) was established in 1964 and *Gwilym Rhys* (formerly at
Bracknell New Town) appointed chief planner and architect; he
was succeeded by *M.F.B. Ashdown*. Droitwich Town Development disbanded in 1978. Its legacy has been extensive new
housing, an inner ring road and leafy W by-pass, but very little
of architectural interest. Even less excusable has been the fate of
Droitwich's timber-framed buildings, too readily demolished
because of the threat of subsidence, and the equally distressing
loss of most of those associated with the late C19 spa.

CHURCHES

St Andrew, St Andrew's Street. The finest parts are the early
C13 chancel arch and N tower, the latter with S arch at right
angles to the chancel arch and considerably narrower E and W
arches; two N lancets with nook-shafts. Upper stages removed
by *Harold Brakspear*, 1926–7, because of the fear of subsidence.
The arches have crocketed capitals with uncommonly many
heads, and moulded arches with fillets. Only the chancel
arch S respond still has trumpet scallops (cf. St Augustine,

Dodderhill). Also C13 the nave W buttresses. Most of the rest is early C14, probably rebuilt after fire in 1290. Three-bay nave arcades and two-bay S chapel arcade, with octagonal piers and double-chamfered arches (though the moulded capitals differ). S aisle and chapel have Dec windows; the arch between rests on excellent busts of a king and mason (?). Blocked Dec chancel side windows, plus a C13 N lancet now looking into the short N chapel E of the tower (perhaps adapted for this position when the chapel was rebuilt); this has an excellent four-light E window, probably late C14. Chancel E wall rebuilt by *Brakspear* in 1928. Good chancel roof; plain S clerestory, probably C16 Perp. Nave W wall with an early C19 window of three wide stepped lancets. N aisle rebuilt, Perp style, by *Ford Whitcombe & Cogswell*, 1910–11.

Oak REREDOS by *Brakspear*. – FONT. Probably Jacobean. Square stem with lozenges; goblet bowl with other elementary geometrical motifs (cf. St Peter, below). Sweet C17 COVER, with turned balusters. – PEWS. 1893–4. – Eight C17–C18 BELLS from the demolished tower. – STAINED GLASS. E window by *Pearce & Cutler*, 1928. – N chapel E with heraldic bits of *c*. 1800; S aisle SE, with C17 oval shield with many quarterings. – MONUMENTS. Several tablets, the largest to Capt. Coningesby Norbury †1734, with military trophies. – Also nave E, Thomas Hopwood †1758 by *Richard Squire*, with obelisk; John Taylor †1794 by *W. Paty*, oval with urn. – S chapel: John Browne †1791, by *Truman* of Worcester; Adamish Grecian.

ST AUGUSTINE, Church Road. *See* Dodderhill.

ST NICHOLAS, Ombersley Road. 1867–9 by *John Smith* of Droitwich, who added the N aisle and vestry, 1872–3 (the latter altered by *Lewis Sheppard*, 1892). Snecked Hadley sandstone, the SW tower without its intended spire. Plate to Dec window tracery. French Early Gothic capitals to the chancel arch; those of the nave arcades remain uncarved. – Stone PULPIT and FONT, carved by *William Forsyth*. – CHANCEL FITTINGS by *Sprague & Evans*, 1923. – STAINED GLASS. Good E and chancel side windows by *Preedy*, 1869. – MONUMENT. G.E. Penrice McConnel †1886, aged 14; by *F.J. Williamson* of Esher (a favourite of Queen Victoria); Sicilian marble, with free-standing angel by a white rock.

ST PETER DE WITTON, St Peter's Church Lane, ½ m. SSE of the old town, once quite separate from it. It belonged to an Augustinian priory, founded *c*. 1130–40, which moved to Studley (Warwickshire) some ten years later. Norman chancel with three small N windows. The chancel arch Norman too, though renewed; plain stepped arch with, as responds, coupled shafts with decorated scallop capitals. Of the early C13 the (former) S aisle and S transept, with an originally combined three-bay arcade with round piers and double-chamfered arches; S aisle demolished, with only traces remaining of its two bays. Capitals of early stiff-leaf type, the aisle arcade survivor also with heads (cf. St Andrew). Late C13 S transept SE window of three stepped lights. A riddle is the two blocked arches in the transept w wall. One would connect them with the s aisle, but the aisle cannot have had the width of both. Was there a chapel s of the aisle? Dec N transept, its N window with reticulated tracery. Dec windows also in the nave. Perp w tower with a tall arch of two continuous sunk quadrant mouldings. Late Perp the timber-framed clerestory and handsome low-pitch roof; also a good boss of Christ, s transept. The clerestory was partly faced in brick, probably c. 1780, and a s porch, of Broseley brick, added 1825. *P.C. Hardwick* restored the church in 1853, adding a s vestry, inserting the Dec-style E window, and re-roofing the chancel. In 1890–1 *Lewis Sheppard* enlarged the vestry, added the Neo-Norman triplet above the chancel arch, and provided tiling and other furnishings. Unsightly NW parish room of 1972–3 (by *Neville Williams* of Droitwich).

FONT. Jacobean, with square stem and goblet bowl; elementary geometrical motifs inspired by Norman work (cf. St Andrew). – Stone PULPIT by *Snow* of Droitwich, no doubt to *Hardwick*'s design. – CHOIR STALLS. 1916. – C15 TILES in the s vestry. Those formerly by the font are to be re-set in a display case. – STAINED GLASS. s transept E, with characteristic early C14 yellows and greens: parts of a Crucifixus and decorative motifs including birds; also C13 heraldry. Re-set by *Paul Woodroffe*, 1936. – Of 1853, the E window by *Preedy*, and three chancel N by *William Holland*. – Tower W and nave N by *O'Connor*, c. 1868. – Nave s by *Kempe*, 1876. – s transept s window by *Burlison & Grylls*, 1884. – N transept: E *Alexander Gibbs*, 1886; N *Hardman*, 1958. – MONUMENTS. Under the tower remains of tablets to John and Isabel Wythe, 1548, and their son Robert †1586. – George Wylde, sergeant-at-law, †1616, perhaps by *Samuel Baldwin*. In his red judge's robes, lying on his side. Inscription with strapwork surround, within a shallow arch flanked by Composite columns. – Richard Nash †1690. Naïve and engaging tablet, with two allegorical girls and two trumpet–blowing cherubs on the broken pediment. – Charles Fortescue †1736 and family, pedimented, with fluted Ionic pilasters; by *Thomas Scheemakers*, 1779. – Several early C19 tablets by *J. Stephens*. – Bronze plaque to Edward Winslow, a Pilgrim Father, †1655, by the *Bromsgrove Guild*, 1945. – Outside the s transept, a C13 coffin lid with relief cross. – LYCHGATE by *J. Arnold Crush*, 1914.

SACRED HEART AND ST CATHERINE (R.C.), Worcester Road, Witton. 1919–21 by *F. Barry Peacock* (*Peacock & Bewlay*). An Early Christian basilica; of brick, with pantiled roofs. Quite large, with aisles, apsed sanctuary flanked by apsed chapels, narthex with baptistery, and (ritual) SW campanile of Lombardic inspiration; a standard type of its date. The interior should not be missed. It has the usual seven-bay arcades with Byzantine capitals, but is transformed by glittering mosaic filling every surface above the cool green, blue or grey marble dados. The mosaics, designed by *Gabriel Joseph Pippet* of Solihull, were executed mostly by *Maurice Josey*, 1922–32; their (often naïve) story-telling follows Renaissance rather

than Byzantine precedent. At the E end, Christ with arms out-
stretched, beneath the Resurrection; Te Deum on the w wall.
Episodes from the Life of the Virgin above the N arcade, the
Life of St Richard de Wyche above the S. Figures and roundels
of prophets, saints and apostles elsewhere. Lady Chapel, N,
with scenes of St Francis and St Theodore. Those in St
Catherine's Chapel, S, are particularly fine, especially its
vaulted ceiling. S aisle chapel added 1938, N aisle chapel completed 1963 (with inferior mosaics by *Hardman*). Much carved
stone and marble, all designed and executed by *Pippet* (†1962);
this includes two external tympana, ALTAR, FONT (of 1948,
now in the sanctuary, reordered 1970), and wooden STATIONS
OF THE CROSS. The sculptural inspiration is mostly from Eric
Gill, via the Birmingham Arts and Crafts school. – Matching
PARISH HALL by *ALP Architects* of Cirencester, 2000.

BAPTIST CHURCH, Ombersley Street East. 1905–6 by *Francis B.
Andrews*. Brick; fancy Perp, with small louvre. Five-light
window above the shallow narthex, three-light aisle windows;
raking buttresses. Broad interior with chancel-like baptistery.
Schoolroom beyond. – STAINED GLASS. Two by *Donald
Brooke*, c. 1963.

METHODIST CHURCH, Birmingham Road. By *G.R. Acton*,
1937–8. Brick, arched windows; stumpy tower over the sanctuary, flanked by vestries. Enlarged 1962.

Former WESLEYAN CHAPEL, Nine Foot Way; now a hall. By *John
Smith*, 1860; rebuilt, because of subsidence, 1887. Red and
yellow brick, lancet-style; only the N porch, with foliage capitals and frieze, looks original.

CEMETERY, Worcester Road. Dec-style mortuary chapel with w
porch, by *John Smith*, 1867; purple brick, stone dressings. It
stands on the site of the medieval St Mary de Witton. This
explains the fine C13–C14 COFFIN LID outside the N doorway;
heavy relief cross, foliage on the head and stem.

PUBLIC BUILDINGS

TOWN HALL, St Andrew's Street. Humble, stuccoed, not
detached, set on a curve. The three S bays are the original
1825–6 building. The ground floor was then open, with Tuscan
columns *in antis*; round-arched window above. Remodelled
and extended by *Henry Rowe*, 1867. He provided the N curve,
continuing it into Friar Street as the POLICE STATION;
painted brick, tripartite windows.

COUNTY OFFICES, Ombersley Street East. By *A. V. Rowe*, 1934,
for Droitwich RDC. Brick, five-bay Neo-Georgian; oversized
segmental pediment above the central first-floor window.

POLICE STATION AND MAGISTRATES' COURT, Ombersley
Street East. A complementary pair of 1975–7 by *Iain Paul* of
Hereford & Worcester County Council; brick with projecting
roughcast upper floors, beneath sloping metallic roofs.

FIRE STATION AND TRAINING CENTRE, Saltway. Also by the
County Architects' Dept, 1976–7. Orange brick, angled slate

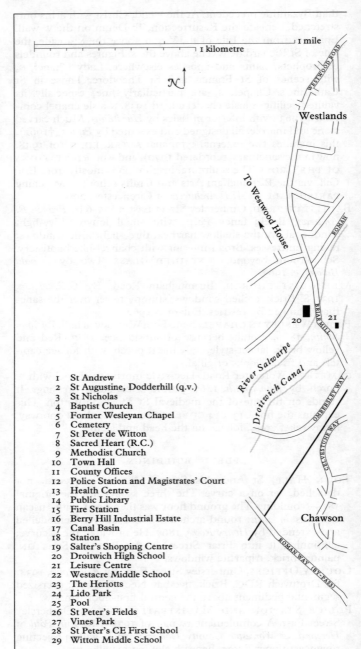

1 kilometre

1 mile

N

Westlands

To Westwood House

ROMAN

BRIAR MILL

River Salwarpe

Droitwich Canal

OMBERSLEY WAY

CHLYESTUNE WAY

ROMAN WAY (BY-PASS)

Chawson

20

21

1	St Andrew
2	St Augustine, Dodderhill (q.v.)
3	St Nicholas
4	Baptist Church
5	Former Wesleyan Chapel
6	Cemetery
7	St Peter de Witton
8	Sacred Heart (R.C.)
9	Methodist Church
10	Town Hall
11	County Offices
12	Police Station and Magistrates' Court
13	Health Centre
14	Public Library
15	Fire Station
16	Berry Hill Industrial Estate
17	Canal Basin
18	Station
19	Salter's Shopping Centre
20	Droitwich High School
21	Leisure Centre
22	Westacre Middle School
23	The Heriotts
24	Lido Park
25	Pool
26	St Peter's Fields
27	Vines Park
28	St Peter's CE First School
29	Witton Middle School

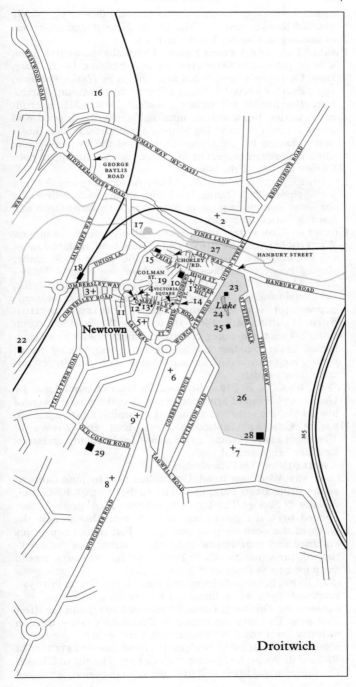

WESTWOOD ROAD

ROMAN WAY (BY-PASS)

KIDDERMINSTER ROAD

BROMSGROVE ROAD

16

GEORGE BAYLIS ROAD

WAY

SALWARPE WAY

2

17

VINES LANE

HANBURY STREET

27

UNION LA.

FRIAR ST.

SALT WAY

15

CHORLEY RD.

18

OMBERSLEY WAY

COLMAN ST.

HANBURY ROAD

QUEEN STREET

3

19

10

HIGH ST.

TOWER HILL

OMBERSLEY ROAD

4

VICTORIA SQUARE

23

14

OMBERSLEY ST. E.

ST PETERS WALK

Lake

11

12 13

SALT WAY

ST ANDREWS ST

24

5

Newtown

25

22

WORCESTER ROAD

THE HOLLOWAY

6

26

STALLS FARM ROAD

CORBETT AVENUE

LYTTLETON ROAD

9

OLD COACH ROAD

M5

29

28

ZIGWELL ROAD

7

8

WORCESTER ROAD

Droitwich

roofs, the garages at right angles to the office wing. Nicely detailed low-key rear, to Friar Street. Neat staggered terrace of housing in Chorley Road, further E.

PUBLIC LIBRARY, Victoria Square. Originally the Salters' Hall, a large gabled, half-timbered Corbett building by *H. Fagg*, 1879. Completely remodelled as a cinema by *Hurley Robinson*, 1933. Further altered 1982, as a library, by the County Architect, *Alan Meikle*; job architect *Andrew Shephard*. Indeterminate exterior, brick with minimal half-timbering, hipped roof above a coved cornice; big lean-to W entrance. Inside, this is neatly framed by the Deco surround of the former screen; more decoration preserved at cornice level. The upper floor follows the line of the balcony.

LEISURE CENTRE, Briar Mill. 1984 by *Badger, Harrison & Cross*, for Wychavon DC. Orange brick with angled roofs, relieved by the lower swimming pool, of blue brick with orange trim and festively varied fenestration.

COUNTY COUNCIL SCHOOLS. Three typical examples. WITTON MIDDLE SCHOOL, Old Coach Road, by *L.C. Lomas*, 1954–6, built as a Secondary Modern, is mostly brick; timber slatting between the floors of the classroom wing. – WEST-ACRE MIDDLE SCHOOL, off Briar Mill, 1968–9, also brick, has curtain walling, with the white timber-slatted eaves bands popular for schools at this date. – DROITWICH HIGH SCHOOL, Briar Mill, 1969–71, uses the Scola construction system. Two three-storey classroom blocks linked by a wide-spread lower building containing concourse, dining room, theatre etc.; mostly dark curtain walling, with prominent concrete floor bands.

ST PETER'S C. OF E. FIRST SCHOOL, St Peter's Church Lane. By *Godwin & Cowper* of Stourport, 1982. A striking assemblage of inward-sloping walls like truncated pyramids, all shingle-clad.

HEALTH CENTRE, Ombersley Street East. By *Hereford & Worcester County Council*, 1978; *Alan Meikle*, county architect. Low-key brick, angled roofs.

SPA BUILDINGS. *See* Perambulation.

LIDO PARK, Worcester Road. Established 1895 by John Corbett, as the Brine Baths Park; brick and timber LODGE by *Cossins, Peacock & Bewlay*. The LIDO, by *Thomas H. Mawson & Son*, opened 1935, is a good example of its type, though here the water of the open-air pool was brine. Flat-roofed two-storey entrance and refreshment building, rendered like the brick-topped surrounding walls. St Peter's Fields, given 1951, extend the park S to St Peter de Witton (p. 263).

VINES PARK, between Saltway and Vines Lane. Begun in 1930s, reopened 1984 as a linear park extending alongside and between the Droitwich Canal (abandoned 1939) and the River Salwarpe. This was the centre of Droitwich's salt extraction industry until 1922. A disused lock survives near the E end, also some rebuilt swing bridges. Portland stone STATUE of St Richard de Wyche by *Boulton & Sons*, 1935. The site of Upwich Pit, the principal brine well from the Roman period, is marked by a reconstruction of its form as rebuilt 1264–5, with timber beams overlapping at the corners; excavated 1983–4. Further w, the former Canal Basin.

PERAMBULATIONS

1. Old Droitwich

We start at St Andrew (p. 262), the centre of old Droitwich, opposite the modest Town Hall (p. 265). Friar Street and High Street formed the main w–e thoroughfare; St Andrew's Street leads s to the c19–c20 centre (Perambulation 2).

1a. To the west along Friar Street

FRIAR STREET begins with pleasant Georgian houses either side, the narrower Nos. 56–58 perhaps concealing earlier timber framing; Nos. 105–107, n side, with early c19 Gothick windows, were Dr Rickett's 'asylum' for brine treatment. Then, s, vehicular access to the shopping centre (p. 271). The scale of the street, however, was already exploded in 1935 by the huge NORBURY HOUSE HOTEL (now flats), dull between-the-wars semi-modern by *Stanley Hall, Easton & Robertson*. Brick, H-plan, with gables, steep tiled roofs, and mild Deco detail, especially the metal balconies, s, above a sunken garden.

Visible timber framing begins opposite with Nos. 79–81, late c16, jettied, with moulded bressummer on renewed brackets. Adjoining, the roughcast OLD COCK INN, licensed 1712, incorporating in its gabled e part a window from the ruined St Nicholas*: of four lights, with early c14 decorated Y-tracery. Behind it, an c18 assembly room with plaster figures and arms. There are also two medieval corbel heads (plus another, smaller, inside). The simpler Gothic windows with segmental heads are probably c18 revivalism.

Then more minor brick houses, both sides. The HOP POLE INN (No. 40), s, roughcast early c18, has six bays with fluted key-stones; c17 gables at the rear, now brick-faced. Next PRIORY HOUSE (Nos. 36–38), the largest timber-framed building here (since the destruction in 1962 of the more valuable Chorley House, at No. 89). Front range *c.* 1650, with decorative timbering above narrow studding, all over-restored *c.* 1900. Brick gable-end chimneys, the e retaining its original rectangular shaft with ornamental brickwork of recessed squares and lozenges. The square-panelled rear wings are earlier; the service wing, se, has been altered, but the late c15 solar wing, sw, although truncated by one bay, still retains its upper great chamber with fine collar truss and wind-braces, well renewed in 1973.

---

*This stood on the opposite side further wnw, its site obliterated by the ring road; the tower survived until *c.* 1830.

Opposite, the rear of the Fire Station (pp. 267–8), suitably scaled down. The street ends at an uninviting underpass beneath Saltway, the inner ring road.

1b. High Street and further east

The STAR AND GARTER, facing the N flank of St Andrew across a slight widening of HIGH STREET, is early C19 stuccoed, with raised parapet (formerly with contemporary lettering). It and No. 17 next door conceal timber framing. This becomes visible at Nos. 21–23, with much-renewed narrow studding.

Opposite, S, a good stretch of mid-C18 houses: Nos. 2–8 each of four or five bays (No. 4 with early C19 shopfront), Nos. 10–12 narrower but higher. Between the two ranges, TOWER HILL ascends to a plain brick brine PUMP HOUSE, of the 1890s but not used until 1921, the date of the surviving machinery; it still serves the Droitwich Spa Hospital (p. 272).

Back on the N side, the late C18 Nos. 27–29 have a good Doric doorcase. Then, either side, modest, probably earlier, houses, though their tendency to lean is mostly due to underground brine pumping rather than concealed timber framing. The stuccoed front of Nos. 31–35, however, hides an outstanding survivor. No. 31, at right angles to the road, is the three-bay solar wing of a house of *c.* 1400, its current doorway on the site of the original passage entrance; Nos. 33–35, the former hall, part rubble, part timber-framed, was probably rebuilt in the C17. The solar is a perfect example of medieval carpentry, uniquely rich in its timber moulding, with heavy first-floor beams. An open collar-truss divides the two bays of the original great chamber; the third bay, N, was an antechamber. Wall framing with large curved braces in the upper storey; roof heavily framed, with cusped wind-braces between two tiers of purlins. C15–C16 stone fireplace in the chamber W wall. The ramshackle rear, including the timber-framed stair-tower behind the solar wing, is visible from Gurney's Lane, now a small shopping square created 1977–8, with remnants of another brine PUMP HOUSE, of *c.* 1850: part of the brick furnace and a resited pressure regulating vessel.

Little else worth recording in High Street, except minor timber framing. Its most notable feature is the undulating roadway, which sank markedly *c.* 1900 (perversely because of pumping the underground brine to Stoke Prior). The best that can be said of the C19–C20 rebuilding is that it preserved the streetline.

Turn S briefly into WORCESTER ROAD. On its E side, in extensive grounds, THE HERIOTTS, a brick villa of *c.* 1840–50, hugely expanded in the same style *c.* 1900 as the Park Hotel; big cast-iron porte cochère. Now an old people's home. Beyond its lake, S, is the Lido Park (p. 268).

Back N into QUEEN STREET, where No. 9, the former ROYAL EXCHANGE HOTEL, was blandly reconstructed *c.* 1998 (by *Clist & Chandler*): stuccoed, with close-studded stair-tower at the rear. It is now the only reminder that the first spa buildings were nearby.* Further N, beyond the bridge, VINES PARK (p. 268), dominated from its hill by St Augustine (p. 254).

Now E into HANBURY STREET, past the BARLEY MOW, by *H.E. Dicks*, 1938, then S, by a square brick TOLL HOUSE of *c.* 1800, into THE HOLLOWAY. Here is the COVENTRY HOSPITAL, a fine two-storey group of almshouses built before 1686: brick, sandstone dressings, behind a raised pavement. Three-bay projecting centre with plaque and small pediment. Lower fourteen-bay S range, 'modernized' 1934 when *A. V. Rowe* replaced the matching N wing with a suburban substitute. Parallel at the rear, a raw brick, gabled Tudor range by *Lewis Sheppard*, 1901–2.

OLD SCHOOL HOUSE beyond is all that remains of *John Smith*'s modest St Peter's National School, 1857. Yet further S, in St Peter's Walk, the former ST JOHN'S HOSPITAL, 1891–2 by *John Douglas* (*Douglas & Fordham* of Chester), built to provide brine-bath treatment for the poor. Brick, terracotta trim, gables with ball finials, mullioned-and-transomed windows with fancy Gothic heads. Converted to housing by *Pentan Partnership* of Cardiff, 2003. (The Holloway leads on to St Peter (p. 263), ⅓ m. further S, whence a return to the town centre could be made through the Lido Park; *see* also Outer Droitwich, p. 273).

2. The C19 and C20 town centre

Starting again from St Andrew (p. 262), ST ANDREW'S STREET leads S, uphill. One or two minor Georgian buildings survive. Most of the W side has been sacrificed for access to the large SALTERS SHOPPING CENTRE, by *T.P. Bennett & Son*, 1974–6, aggressively detailed but with reasonably welcoming open areas, meant to be alleviated by colourful decorative panels, in tile (by *Threlfall*) or cast concrete (by *Joyce & Henry Collins*).

At the top is VICTORIA SQUARE, now mostly filled by the Public Library (p. 268). To its N, LLOYDS BANK by *J.A. Chatwin*, 1892; L-plan, with angled corner with battlemented oriel, ribbed brick gables, and Gothic windows. Between them, an attractive cast bronze statue, Saltworkers, by *John McKenna*, 1998.

Opposite, across St Andrew's Street, the timber-framed RAVEN HOTEL; late C16 centre, narrow-studded with three gabled dormers, lower two-gabled N range, both with C18 sash windows. Originally St Andrew's Manor House, it was bought by John Corbett, 1879, and converted to a hotel by *John Cotton*, who in 1883 added the porch and altered the higher mid-C19 N and S wings; extensive later additions (e.g. by *Hurley Robinson*, 1935), with far less convincing half-timbered work. Entrance hall with some Jacobean panelling; above the C19 iron-balustraded stair, good heraldic stained glass, with various

---

*Namely the Royal Brine Baths, forming a single stuccoed composition of 1836 with the five-bay Royal Hotel.

C16–C17 dates, re-set here *c.* 1825, no doubt from the old Exchequer House (next the town hall).

Corbett made Victoria Square the centre of his late C19 spa town, but painfully little remains. S of the Raven was the larger Worcestershire Hotel (by *J.R. Nichols*, 1889–91), replaced by *Wimpey* Neo-vernacular flats, 2003–4. Diagonally SW, across Victoria Square, were St Andrew's Brine Baths (mostly by *Cotton*, 1887). Of these all that survives is the anodyne front range, 1933–5, probably by *Thomas H. Mawson & Son* of Lancaster, built for electro-medical facilities; now called ST RICHARD'S HOUSE, used as a heritage centre. Brick, with mullioned-and-transomed windows; half-timbered upper floor with gables. It continues in the same style, as shops, along the S side of Ombersley Street East. Behind, replacing the C19 baths, the large DROITWICH SPA HOSPITAL AND BRINE BATHS, a disappointingly safe design of 1984–5 by *Associated Architects*; partner-in-charge *Richard J. Slawson*, project architect *Michael A. Pitkin*: long, low cross-plan, pale brick, pantiled roofs ending in gambrels. Nearby in ST ANDREW'S ROAD, mid-C19 Italianate brick villas and the larger RAVENSTONE, by *Lewis Sheppard*, 1892, for Dr H.S. Jones, with big half-timbered gables; enlarged as a nursing home in 1986–9.

OMBERSLEY STREET EAST, N side, has semi-public brick buildings. NAT WEST BANK, *c.* 1905, and the POST OFFICE by *John Rutherford* (of the Board of Works), 1907, have contrasting pedimented entrances. The former has ample stone dressings and Edwardian features such as blocked paired columns and vermiculated voussoirs; the latter, with big stepped keystones, eared architraves and hipped roof, is the more coherent design. Then the Baptist Church (p. 265).

Opposite, the modest Health Centre (p. 268), then the Police Station and Magistrates' Court (p. 265). The rest is unexciting Neo-Georgian, including the County Offices (p. 265), and two ranges of shops with green pantiled roofs by *Philip B. Herbert* of Birmingham, 1935–6. In COLMAN ROAD, leading N to the ring road, COVERCROFT DAY CARE CENTRE, a Postmodern rectangle by *Mark Humphries Architects* of Droitwich, 1985; striped red and yellow brick, broad end pediments, and central corridor with bulbous clerestory.

OUTER DROITWICH

There is little to note. This clockwise account includes a few earlier survivors amongst the extensive late C20 housing, itself requiring minimal comment. (For the NE part of the town and Chateau Impney, *see* Dodderhill.)

The main N–S artery is WORCESTER ROAD. Off it, E, to the S of the Lido Park (p. 268), the former CORBETT TRUSTEES ESTATE OFFICE (No. 1 Corbett Avenue), a good building of 1906; brick, one half-timbered gable, one with terracotta trim, rounded door hood. Nearby, in LYTTELTON ROAD, detached houses of 1910, sub-Voysey style, roughcast, with a little narrow studding. Further up CORBETT AVENUE, five large brick and half-timbered ones, built for Corbett, 1895, probably by *Cossins & Peacock*.

In WORCESTER ROAD, to the S, one or two villas remain. THE HOLLIES, by the roundabout, is Italianate with small tower, typical of *c.* 1840. Nearly opposite, hidden above the road, the small cemetery (p. 265), then the CASTLE INN by *Cotton*, 1881, for John Corbett; the usual brick and half-timber, much enlarged.

St Andrew's Drive, W side, N of the Methodist Church (p. 265), leads to ST ANDREW'S HOUSE, three-storey early C19 stuccoed, with two full-height bows; now a hotel.

TAGWELL ROAD leads E to extensive late C20 housing (where the most prominent edifice is a high, mid-C20, concrete WATER TOWER), but also to the S end of The Holloway, off which is ST PETER'S CHURCH LANE. At its corner the striking St Peter's First School (p. 268), then an unexpected village group: the church (p. 263) with, to its E, ST PETER'S MANOR, the home of the Nash family; three-storeyed, with three by two even gabled dormers, all close-studded. The porch carries the date 1618, convincing though added when the house was restored in 1867. In the dining room to its l., panelling and a chimneypiece with stuccoed overmantel with strapwork and inscription and excessively upward-tapering pilasters. Brick DOVECOTE at the rear; much-restored C17 timber-framed BARN, E.

Back to WORCESTER ROAD, where Sacred Heart and St Catherine (p. 264) lies a little S of OLD COACH ROAD. This leads W, past Corbett Estate late C19 semi-detached pairs to Witton Middle School (p. 268). Then on, as Celvestune Way, to CHAWSON, a housing area of 1964–8, planned by *Jackson & Edmonds* for the *Droitwich Development Committee*; good views (for example to Westwood House, p. 653), plenty of green space, and some attempt to segregate vehicles from pedestrians. To the N, around STALLS FARM ROAD, COUNCIL HOUSING of 1945–50 by *G.L. Robinson*, Borough Surveyor; mostly semi-detached brick, also Airey concrete-faced houses, again quite well laid out. Further N at NEWTOWN, minor development of the 1880s, including a smart group in OMBERSLEY ROAD (Nos. 5–17), facing St Nicholas (p. 263).

BRIAR MILL leads N from Ombersley Way, past schools and the Leisure Centre (p. 268) to WESTLANDS (originally Boycott), a large *Development Committee* housing area of 1967–72 beyond the by-pass, near the edge of Westwood Park; project architect *H. Noble*, with *Norman & Dawbarn* of Wolverhampton. Mixed development of two or three storeys, with much tile-hanging, laid out on Radburn principles to separate vehicles from pedestrians. Culs de sac lead inward from an outer spine (Westwood Road), footpaths run along the centre, where the small shopping precinct now looks decidedly shabby.

Most of the rest of the town's N sector is given over to industrial development. Despite *Development Committee* planning, it is the usual rag-bag. Something more coherent was attempted in GEORGE BAYLIS ROAD, off Kidderminster Road. This, Phase I of the BERRY HILL INDUSTRIAL ESTATE, is a cluster of factory units of 1968–71 by *G. Rhys*, architect-in-charge *C. Mercer*; brick, corrugated roofs with angled clerestories.

The Roman SALINAE, named after the salt springs, was a *vicus* (or industrial settlement) rather than a town. An early FORT at Dodderhill was replaced *c.* A.D. 60 by a more permanent structure on the site of St Augustine (p. 254), implying military control over the salt production. A large VILLA at Bays Meadow to the W, in use from the mid C2 until destroyed by fire *c.* 300, may have been for a civilian administrator; winged corridor plan, 130 ft (40 metres) long, with several rooms with underfloor heating, mosaic floors, and painted plaster walls. The site was protected, from the late C3, by a rampart which partly survives. Its replacement, occupied until the C5, may have been a converted barn. Roman material has also been found S of the bridge over the Salwarpe, and near the W end of Friar Street.

8040

EARL'S CROOME

p. 22 ST NICHOLAS. Norman, much altered. Embraced tower, nave W end, rebuilt 1832 by *E. Blakeway Smith*; lower two stages Neo-Norman, the upper Dec-style and battlemented. A drawing in the Prattinton collection records the richly decorated former W front, with two tiers of blind arcading above a later W doorway. Two good Norman doorways survive, each with one order of shafts covered all over with flat incised zigzag, and arches with roll moulding and furrowed chevron (cf. Malvern Priory). Only the capitals differ. The nave S doorway has decorated scallops; the N a plain block capital, W, and an E capital with furled foliage wandering onto the adjacent wall (cf. the much later Leigh). Short chancel structurally Norman, but only the N window remains in its original state. The late C13 E window, a broad trefoiled lancet, still has its Norman form within; above it externally a Norman string course and small gable window, richly decorated. The chancel arch matches the nave doorways: the same shafts, but with scalloped bases, similar arches; N capital with entwined leaf decoration, S with close interlace trail. Flanking the capitals, carved panels (cf. Ribbesford and Rock): a plain ring-knot, N, a triquetra, S. The imposts have remarkably classical leaf trails; the lion rampant, S, should be noted. The chancel SW lancet is early C13, in a deep splay, apparently contemporary. Assorted later windows: a Dec one N of the tower, with pierced trefoiled rerearch and re-cut dogtooth; Perp nave SE, with panel tracery and original painting in its head. Others either C16–C17 (chancel SE, with timber tracery; nave NW and SW, both made up to imitate plate tracery, apparently within Norman splays), or inserted at the restoration of 1869 by *G.R. Clarke*. Roofs, N vestry and W gallery all belong to this latter date.

PEWS and FONT also 1869. – Encaustic chancel FLOOR TILING. 1875. – PULPIT and READING DESK reuse linenfold and Jacobean friezes. – The S DOOR retains early medieval ironwork. – STAINED GLASS. Excellent E window, 1864, and nave SE, 1861, both no doubt *Lavers & Barraud*. – Nave NE by the same firm, 1874. – The other nave S window, *c.* 1876, clearly by *Heaton, Butler & Bayne*. – Minor medieval to early C19 fragments elsewhere. – MONUMENTS. Plain tablet to Thomas Jeffery †1650. – The carved heraldry opposite commemorates him or another Jeffery. – Simple LYCHGATE. 1902.

Former RECTORY, N. Brick, rebuilt 1707, but the three-bay N front must be late C18; open-pedimented doorway flanked by shallow canted two-storey bays.

EARL'S CROOME COURT, W, bought by the Jeffery family in the mid C16, now the seat of the Earls of Coventry, turns its back to the church. The present entrance front is approached by a long drive from the Worcester road. Timber-framed, probably early C17, with much C19 restoration. Centre with a large gabled dormer, gabled cross-wings. Mostly closely set studs, in the centre also concave-sided lozenges; five-light windows with ovolo-moulded mullions and transoms. S front now rendered; three identical gables with moulded bargeboards, square C19 hoodmoulds. The rear, E, of painted brick, has only two outer gables. C19 brick chimneys. – Long timber-framed C17–C18 BARN, SE. – Then, a late C19 LODGE, opposite the rectory.

In the village further N, the former SCHOOL, 1855 (enlarged 1892), plain brick with bargeboards and fish-scale roofs; Coventry estate housing (dated 1906 and 1879); and much mid-C20 Upton RDC housing.

In WORCESTER ROAD, opposite the drive to the Court, three pleasant late C18 houses; HAZELDENE, of three storeys, has shallow curved bows flanking the centre.

At DUNSTALL COMMON, 1 m. NNE, DUNSTALL HOUSE, of C16–C17 square-panelled framing, with a fine tall brick chimney with paired round-arched panels, rising from the E roof slope. Also a pair of Lias-built estate cottages dated 1874.

DUNSTALL CASTLE, further E, is a sham Norman ruin built 1766–7, of Lias, an eyecatcher for Croome Court (p. 244); almost certainly by *Robert Adam*, an early and unexpected example of his castle style. Open triangular plan with central round tower with large round-arched doorway high up; ruined top with machicolation. Linked to a similar E tower by a wall containing an unrealistically high, double-layered archway. To the W, a shorter stretch, with shallow gable above a large ruinated window with Bath ashlar trefoil-cusping (rather like plate tracery), linking to a thinner square tower. Some billet-like mouldings, but classically moulded string courses.

At BAUGHTON, ½ m. E (in Hill Croome parish), timber-framed cottages and farms, and the C16–C17 BAUGHTON COURT (with modern date 1520; old drawings show 1632). L-plan, with later extensions. Hall range mostly close-set studding, with dormer gable; (later?) w cross-wing, square-panelled, with lateral Lias chimney with three star-shaped brick stacks. Simple plaster ceiling decoration on the first floor of the hall range. Rock-faced C18 SUMMERHOUSE, NW, square with pyramidal roof; early C17 timber-framed BARN, SE.

On Baughton Hill, ¾ m. further E, overlooking the M5, an early C19 cottage in the form of an octagonal TOWER, also built as an eyecatcher from Croome Court. Rendered brick, pointed doorway, two storeys of pointed windows with Y-tracery (blank on two faces), pyramidal slate roof.

6060

EASTHAM

ST PETER AND ST PAUL. Norman, of tufa from Southstone Rock (p. 602), the chancel apparently doubled in length in the C14. Squat brick w tower, by *William Knight* of Kidderminster, 1830, with large lancet bell-openings, battlements, and tufa pinnacles. Drastic later C19 restoration (chancel 1864; nave by *H. Hardwicke Langston*, 1889–90) has further obscured the Norman work, though much of interest survives, notably the s doorway, set in a slight projection between slender pilaster buttresses; above it, four intersecting blank arches on shafts with block capitals. The doorway has one order of shafts, also with block capitals, continued as a roll moulding in the arch. Here also, an inner order of two bands of thin saltire crosses (perhaps also an outer one, now eroded). All this resembles Martley, Knighton and Stockton. Stockton has another motif of Eastham: small carved panels with figures. At Eastham there are four, all sandstone, probably re-set: two within (*see* below), two, very weathered, outside. Randomly placed E of the doorway, these represent Sagittarius and, now almost indecipherable, Leo. The pointed N doorway, with continuous keeled roll, is probably early C14; above, an original Norman window. Also Norman the flat nave buttresses and apparently those of the chancel, including two on the E wall. This is windowless, apart from a small sexfoil of 1864 in the gable. Does this represent the Norman arrangement, and how much Norman work was reused when the chancel was extended E? Its w half has enlarged Norman windows; the two-light NE and SE windows are early C14, as is the nave SE. Other nave windows, Neo-Norman and Dec, are of 1890. One final external oddity is the tiny Norman-looking window in the chancel NW pilaster buttress, lighting the C15–C16 rood stair. C19 restoration has spoilt the interior; crude vestry of 1864 halfway along the chancel N wall, large Neo-Norman chancel arch of 1890. The bases of the original chancel arch, some 2–3 ft (60–90 cm.) narrower, are visible beneath the present chancel floor level.

FONT. Large Norman bowl, cauldron-shaped; wide fillet at the top, rope moulding at the base. Stem renewed. – SCULPTURAL FRAGMENTS. The two Norman panels (nave E wall) are

an Agnus Dei roundel and two affronted beasts with single
head. They perhaps flanked the original chancel arch. – Most
other furnishings are made up from C17 woodwork. REREDOS
with arched panels and six figures, perhaps from an overmantel or bedhead. More such pieces, plus a good head roundel
of c. 1535, line the sedilia. STALLS, DESKS and PULPIT similarly made up. The LECTERN has a large baluster stem on four
lions' feet. – PAINTING, above the s door. Christ Crucified,
perhaps C18; poorly restored. – DECALOGUE, in an ogee
frame; probably early C19. – ROYAL ARMS. George III; dated
1779. – STAINED GLASS. Four chancel windows by *Hardman*,
1864. – Nave NE, 1936 by *E.R. Phillips* (of *Fouracre & Son*,
Plymouth); nave NW, c. 1889, probably *Lavers & Westlake*. –
MONUMENTS. Several tablets, the naïve ones by far the best:
Edward Soly †1690, with inscription cartouche beneath an
oval with mantled heraldry; Samuel Whitcombe †1749, brass
plate in painted stone frame. – All that remains of the C14
CHURCHYARD CROSS, to the s, is its large octagonal base.

EASTHAM COURT FARM, E. Early C17, of square-panelled
framing infilled with brick. Central hall with projecting wings,
each with narrower gabled bay on its inner side; the E wing
contains the oak staircase and panelled parlour. Brick chimneys, the E stack of tufa. C19 casement windows, finialled
bargeboards. – The timber-framed COTTAGE, SW of the
church, was probably the original rectory.

EASTHAM BRIDGE, across the Teme, ¼ m. NNE. Of 1793; three
elliptical brick arches, the central one larger, with roundels in
the spandrels. Partly rebuilt for the County Council by *J.H.
Garrett*, 1898.

ROBIN'S END, the former rectory, ½ m. SSE. Of 1735; brick, five
bays, with central projecting two-storey porch. Lower C19
service wing, E. *Maurice Chesterton*, 1929–30, provided a
matching W wing, creating an impressively flat, symmetrical
garden front, S, of 2+5+2 bays. Fine early C18 open-well staircase: three balusters per tread, one fluted, one twisted, one
turned.

OLD FARM, ⅔ m. S. A good example of square-panelled framing,
c. 1600; hall and gabled W cross-wing, the latter with rubble
stack with brick shafts. The larger HILLWOOD FARM, 1 m.
SSE, probably late C16 (altered 1882), has central hall (with
truncated chimney) and N parlour cross-wing, all of brick-filled
framing; projecting service wing, S, of rubble.

EASTHAM GRANGE, 1⅛ m. ESE. By *Walter J. Tapper*, 1910–11. A
good, if not highly personal design. Large, brick, free Tudor in
the Hampstead Garden Suburb way; upper storey and gables
all tile-hung. The main S front has one big straight gable, W
(the service end), balanced by a half-hipped E gable; recessed
centre with hipped dormers. Matching stables at the rear.

LOWERHOUSE FARMHOUSE, 1¼ m. ESE. A nice early C18 composition. Brick, seven bays, the middle three breaking forward
beneath a big shaped gable into which rises a round-headed
window; below, one normal segment-arched window flanked

by two very narrow ones, Queen Anne fashion. Straight-headed windows in the wings. Inside, a good oak staircase, and parlour with bold panelling and giant spiral pilasters flanking the fireplace. – Good farm buildings, including HOP KILNS.

PUDDLEFORD FARM, 1¾ m. ESE. Of *c.* 1600, mostly close stud-ding with brick infilling. T-plan, the S cross-bar with central projecting porch with overhang on coved cornice and shaped brackets; row of four brick chimneys behind, forming a lobby entrance. Lower W wing, two C19 hop kilns at its rear.

EASTINGTON HALL *see* LONGDON

ECKINGTON

HOLY TRINITY. The W end, with its battlemented Perp SW tower with lively gargoyles, faces the main street. The W doorway, relocated from the nave N wall in 1831, is latest Norman. Two orders, the shafts with early stiff-leaf capitals. Inner arch with lozenges broken round the angle; outer with the motif of crenellation with reversed and interlocked trian-gular merlons, also floral motifs (cf. Bredon and Netherton). Large (renewed) Perp window above, but originally lancets; one with billet hoodmould remains (another visible within, lighting the stair-vice). Three-bay S arcade also latest Norman: round piers with base spurs and typical scalloped capitals, single-step arches. The S aisle's late C13 E window shows that it was originally much narrower; Geometrical S windows, *c.* 1869. The tower was built into the aisle's W end: Perp W window, N and E arches with typical mouldings. Early C14 chancel, its E window three stepped ogee-trefoiled lancets. The fine nave roof is basically Perp; moulded rafters and purlins, bosses, and arched braces to collars, elaborately carved with foliage and dragons. Sturdy S aisle roof by *F.B. Andrews & Son*, 1928.

C19 work began with the addition of the brick N aisle by *Richard Hope* of Pershore, 1831; lancets with cast-iron tracery. Its W end, competent Perp, of stone, was built as vestry-cum-schoolroom, 1836. The medieval W part of the nave N wall survives. Restoration in 1886–7, by the Tewkesbury builder *Thomas Collins*, provided a Neo-Norman N arcade meant to match that on the S, and an even less subtle chancel arch. N organ chamber of 1908, reusing two Dec windows.

FONT. Plain round bowl on four clustered shafts, C13–C14. – ALTAR TABLE. Dated 1663. – Small primitive CHEST, of elm. – ROYAL ARMS. Probably George I. – Assorted C19–C20 fur-nishings, the best the chunky CHANCEL STALLS by *Walter & Florence Camm*, 1925, made by *Bridgeman & Sons* of Lichfield. – STAINED GLASS. C14–C15 fragments in the heads of the chancel N and SW windows. – Three windows by the *Camms*: E 1924, S aisle E 1928, chancel SW 1936. – Chancel SE by

E. Stanley Watkins, 1923. – Chancel N and N aisle N by *J.E. Nuttgens*, 1969. – MONUMENTS. John Hanford †1616 and wife Anne, probably by *Samuel Baldwin*. Elaborate standing monument, unpainted stone, their large kneeling figures facing one another across a prayer desk. Shallow arch, inscription with a little strapwork, single Composite columns, straight top with achievement. Thirteen children kneel against the high base. – Tablets: Rev. Christianus Kenrick †1711; moulded oval frame. Flock Kenrick †1746, by *Richard Squire*; pedimented, of grey marble.

At the N end of the main street, the VILLAGE CROSS, with medieval stepped base and shaft, heightened and given a gabled cross-head by *Hopkins*, 1897.

Many C16–C17 timber-framed cottages and farmhouses in the side streets. BOON STREET, W, has several thatched examples. In the winding MANOR ROAD, further W, an earlier cruck-framed one (S end), also the MANOR HOUSE of *c.* 1800; brick, L-plan, with good fluted Doric doorcase.

More such cottages to the E, with larger houses in JARVIS STREET, including ELM HOUSE, painted brick of six bays, its sundial dated 1728, but three gables at the rear. At the N end, HOPE CHAPEL (Baptist), 1840, brick with broad lancets; off its S end, the SCHOOL by *Hopkins*, 1869, submerged in mid-C20 additions. Off PASS STREET, further E, the former VICARAGE, mostly by *John Blizard* of Pershore, 1812; canted bay window and rear service wing added by *Henry Rowe*, 1866.

The remains of a ROMAN building (perhaps a villa) were discovered 200 yds N of the village in 1838, when the Birmingham–Gloucester railway was under construction.

ECKINGTON BRIDGE, ½ m. N. Rebuilt 1729–30 by the Worcester masons *Robert Taylor* and *Thomas Wilkinson*; narrow, of Ombersley stone, with six irregular arches and stepped-up parapet. Foundations of the C15–C16 (mostly timber) bridge were reused, including no doubt the pointed cutwaters either side. – To the NW, a square Type 26 PILLBOX, *c.* 1940, of concrete poured between pre-cast concrete sheets.

WOOLLAS HALL, 1⅔ m. ESE on the slope of Bredon Hill. High-gabled ashlar house, built for John Hanford, 1611. Irregular N front with projecting three-storey porch, off-centre. The pilasters flanking its round-arched entrance start halfway up from flat trefoil shapes (cf. Bredon's Norton Manor, p. 169); big canted oriel on the second floor. To its r., the two hall windows, each of four tall lights with two transoms; above, similar but shorter windows beneath gabled dormers. To its l., a bigger, higher gable; below this, a full-height canted and castellated bay window with different floor heights. The whole façade is framed by screen walls in the form of two sides of a shaped gable. Early C18 W additions. The interior is now subdivided. The hall has a screen with Ionic pilasters, ribbed plaster ceiling, modest C18 chimneypiece beneath the Hanford arms, and remains of a heraldic glazing scheme of 1867 by *Thomas Baillie & Co.* In the former dining room l. of the

p. 49

screens passage, a fine wooden chimneypiece with tall engaged columns and overmantel with the usual blank arches. Early C18 well stair at the rear: two balusters per tread, carved tread ends.

The various outbuildings behind may incorporate remnants of an earlier house. There is also an early C17 BREWHOUSE. – STABLES of the same date, NE, with symmetrical front with three gabled dormers.

Nearby was the medieval village of WOOLLASHILL and, ½ m. ESE, just E of St Catherine's Well, was ST CATHERINE'S CHAPEL, probably mid-C13 in origin; later a dwelling, demolished c. 1895. Excavations, 1927–30, disclosed a long rectangular plan.

At NAFFORD about 1 m. E, aerial photography revealed three rectangular ditched ENCLOSURES, and a large double-ditched CIRCLE; probably Bronze Age.

7030   ELDERSFIELD

Extensive parish on the Gloucestershire boundary, partly open marshy common, with outbreaks of irregular hills. On the most prominent, ½ m. NW of the church, is GADBURY BANK, an approximately oval Iron Age hill-fort, nine acres within a single rampart, above steep wooded slopes.

ST JOHN BAPTIST. Sturdy W tower, mostly C14, with Dec bell-openings, diagonal buttresses, low battlements, and C15 recessed spire. The middle stage has a small trefoiled niche flanked by blank quatrefoils; similar niche on the SW buttress, with an early C14 standing figure of a knight. Three-light Perp W window. The church is of Norman origin. Above the S doorway, remains of its predecessor of c. 1160–80: one shaft with scallop capital like folded material (cf. Beckford), part of the arch with chevron decoration, hood with beaded interlace. Contemporary chancel arch: engaged quarter-shafts with similar capitals, plain imposts with incised zigzag, renewed hood with billet. Chancel and nave were rebuilt in C13, see the renewed lancets. N aisle added in the early C14; restored four-bay arcade with quatrefoil piers and double-chamfered arches. Perp the S transeptal chapel, with good early C15 E window; and the chancel NW window, its delicate tracery only visible within. Much restored by G.R. Clarke, 1852–4, and again by F.S. Waller & Son, 1876; they rebuilt the nave S wall, and nave and chancel roofs. Timber S porch by Healing & Overbury, 1925.

FONT. Perp, octagonal; shields in re-cut cusped panels. – PEWS. Mostly by Clarke, incorporating C16 work with linen-fold panelling. – PULPIT. Simple Jacobean, the book-rest (and that of the C19 lectern) made up from carved fragments from a C15 SCREEN. – STAINED GLASS. In nave and chancel S windows, good coats of arms of 1629, originally in the S chapel S window. This now has glass of 1868, no doubt by Lavers & Barraud. – Chancel E c. 1918, Percy Bacon style; SE by Camm

& Co., 1906. – N aisle: NE window by *Powell & Sons*, 1878, to a *Henry Holiday* design; NW by *Roy Coomber*, 2002. – MONU-MENTS. Tablets include Anne Turton †1661, with broken ped-iment and good stone carving; and Henry Brown (†1684) and family, with black Ionic columns, probably *c.* 1700.

In the CHURCHYARD, good C18 headstones and a surpris-ing number of early C18 chest tombs, especially four with scrolled ends S of the chancel, and a later one, square pedestal type, S of the transept. – By the SE gate, a massive coped grave-slab: cross in circle at the head, incised cross at the foot; C12 or earlier.

The church stands alone, apart from ELDERSFIELD COURT and its farm buildings, restored by *Waller & Son*, 1873–4. The house is *c.* 1700, brick, three by three bays; continuous brick string courses, the lower stepping over the central doorway, so that the central first-floor window must also be raised. To the E, behind a pond, its C17 timber-framed rectangular DOVECOTE. Then, S to N along the churchyard's E side, the C19 stone POUND, and converted timber-framed BARNS, the E cruck-framed.

Further E, the OLD VICARAGE by *G.R. Clarke*, 1861–2; tall, stone, minimally Gothic. *Clarke*'s former SCHOOL of 1859, on its own ⅛ m. further ESE, is more appealing. Schoolroom with five stepped trefoil-headed lancets, attached house with simpler notched mullioned windows and hipped roof; their doorways side by side.

Many timber-framed farmhouses. PIGEON HOUSE FARM, on a moated site ⅔ m. E, is distinguished by its fine tall brick DOVE-COTE, dated 1705: square, cross-gabled. HARDWICK FARM, 1½ m. NE, formerly Hardwick Court, is also partly moated; hall range rebuilt 1618, with medieval E cross-wing, all mostly encased in C19 brick. The wing retains its massive stack and fine three-bay roof, perhaps late C14, with cambered tie-beams, intermediate collars, cusped wind-braces, cusped knee-braces, and principals forming quatrefoils.

Early farms of cruck construction include COLE'S FARM, ⅓ m. NW, its crucks visible in the SW gable end. Remains of crucks also at VINE FARM, ¾ m. SW, an attractive house with three unequal gables; hall-range and N cross-wing may be C15, with S cross-wing and short parallel bay to its N added in the C17.

Most intriguing is THE RED HOUSE, ¾ m. SSW at Pillow's Green, on the outskirts of Staunton (Glos.), said to be of 1647, exceptionally of brick. The gabled W (former entrance) front is irregular, with parlour wing, S, staircase N of that, and less-projecting kitchen wing, N end. The five-bay S return is symmetrical (emphasized by an inserted early C19 central doorway), as is the wide E front, of 1+3+1 bays, the outer gabled. The consistently applied brickwork patterning is entirely unexpected: plain full-height pilasters (rather like flat buttresses); cambered heads, also Gothic-looking, on the ground floor; shouldered heads with keystones over the first-floor windows. This may all be a distant reflection of C17 London Mannerism, but its quirkiness sticks in the memory.

Interior layout, with timber partitioning, also far from routine; the staircase, with closed string and turned balusters, seems almost too big for its setting. – Stone BARN, N, dated 1826.

ELMBRIDGE

ST MARY. A chapelry of Dodderhill until 1877; mostly rebuilt by *John Smith* of Droitwich, 1870–2. Chancel and nave in one, with double W bellcote; continuous N chapel and aisle. Snecked sandstone, E.E. style, apart from the E window with Geometrical tracery and alternating red and white voussoirs. The notable medieval survival is the Late Norman S doorway (reset beneath a C19 gable); two orders of shafts with shapeless capitals, arch with frontal chevron and lozenges broken round a step in the moulding. Hoodmould with a kind of trapezoid ornament, unique in Worcestershire. Early C13 N arcade of three wide bays. Only the round piers and E respond are medieval, with very simple moulded capitals, perhaps even contemporary with the doorway. Segmental arches of 1872, as are PEWS and FONT (carved by *William Forsyth*). Chancel refurnished by the *Bromsgrove Guild*, 1937–8, altered by *Pancheri & Son*, 1961–2. – COMMUNION RAILS (N chapel). Jacobean with flat cut-out balusters, surrounding an C18 ALTAR TABLE. – STAINED GLASS. E and chancel S windows by *Ward & Hughes*, 1872. – N chapel E by *Herbert W. Bryans*, 1906. – N aisle N by *Hardman*, 1920. – MONUMENTS. Tablet to Edmund Purshull †1650, probably *c.* 1675; garlands at the top, side volutes, skull with bat's wings below. – Nicely lettered brass to the Dannet family, by *John Barber*, 1779. – George Penrice †1827 and family; Gothic, by *Forsyth*, 1872.

MANOR HOUSE FARM, Elmbridge Green, ⅔ m. NNW. By *Thomas and Joseph Bateman*, *c.* 1826, for George Penrice; brick, three bays and storeys, fluted Doric porch. Behind it, W, the former FARMHOUSE by *W.G. Newton*, 1921, modest Neo-Georgian; altered and enlarged.

BADGE COURT, 1⅓ m. NNE (in Upton Warren parish). C16, restored by *F.W.B. Charles*, 1977. Central range mostly stone below, brick above; unequally projecting wings, all close-studded with big diagonal braces. Dendro-dating suggests the centre and jettied S (parlour) wing may be early C16, with the N wing and adjoining gabled porch added or rebuilt *c.* 1579. At the back, two timber-framed gables and, asymmetrically in the recessed centre, the hall chimney-breast with three fine tall diagonal brick stacks. The manor belonged to the Cokeseys before passing to the Wintour family in the late C16.

PURSHALL HALL, 1½ m. N. Large, brick-built, mostly early C17. Characteristic porch with round-arched entrance, two-light mullioned window to the room above, gable with ball finials; this and the adjoining bay have vertical and horizontal brick bands. The two S bays, with brick band course, may be *c.* 1700, the N bay later C18. Hipped roof overall. On the rear, W, front, the N two-thirds project slightly, with six tall, narrow first-floor windows. At the start of the set-back portion, the hall chimney with stone base and three diagonal shafts. Inside, the early C17 timber frame of hall and S cross-wing survives. Signs also of an original four-bay cruck house: one cruck remains, buried in a later partition. The house became a Roman Catholic stronghold especially after it was bought by John Baynham, 1750.

PURSHULL GREEN, ½ m. further NNW. A scattered hamlet alongside a wide, ragged green, ending in a large pond; one or two C17 cottages.

ELMLEY CASTLE

9040

Elmley Castle is named after the CASTLE on the flank of Bredon Hill, within the E portion of an Iron Age hill-fort, ½ m. SSW of the village; first constructed in the late C11 by Robert D'Abitôt, later the stronghold of the Beauchamps. By the early C14 however, when Warwick had become their principal seat, Elmley was neglected. Despite various C14–C15 repairs, Leland in the 1540s saw only 'one Tower and that partly broken', with stone being carted away for repairs to Pershore Bridge. Extensive outer bailey; pear-shaped inner bailey with high ramparts and deep ditches, the keep probably near the N end. Still visible are foundations of the N section of the curtain wall and perhaps part of the rectangular keep (or its forebuilding).

ST MARY. The main village street runs straight towards the middle of the N aisle; the treatment of the church shows that this must always have been so. Transept, N aisle, and N porch are all C15–C16, embattled, the windows flanking the porch (but also the aisle W window) given specially pretty tracery. Simpler transept N window, and one of five lights to the E, now blocked. Porch entrance with two continuous rolls, likely to be C13, re-set. Unbuttressed W tower, not high; its two lower stages are also C13, the battlemented top stage C15. The chancel, though with C14–C15 tracery, must be the oldest part, its herringbone masonry probably of before 1100. This being so, the interior poses a problem. The N arcade is a straightforward, plain C15 job, except that its E arch, the transept arch, points to a somewhat earlier date. But the S arcade consists of two E bays separated by an octagonal C14 pier, then no piers at all, just two C14 arches connecting square chunks of wall. Such an arrangement usually indicates the cutting through of earlier walling of an aisleless church. If this is so here, we would have to assume a church of Saxon proportions: long chancel, long nave, made yet longer by the C13 tower. The VCH's dating of the square piers as C14 does not satisfy in any case. Or can the piers be connected with early C17 rebuilding (a date 1629 was formerly visible on the S wall outside)? The aisle E end, with a C14 piscina, was remodelled in the C15; *Preedy* rebuilt much of the rest during his extensive restoration in 1878. He also replaced the E window. The chancel otherwise was restored by *Ewan Christian*, 1863–4; his, the rather florid chancel arch.

FONT. Octagonal, *c.* 1500, the bowl with various heraldic shields. The base, probably early C13, has four fully carved, very menacing dragons, their writhing tails showing a tendency to develop stiff-leaf tips (cf. Bretforton, pp. 169–70). – PEWS. Mostly C16; plain bench ends, straight moulded tops. – The former STALLS, S aisle E end, also probably C16, are reinforced by four C17–C18 balusters. – SCULPTURAL FRAGMENTS. In the N porch, Norman architectural bits; also a small stone carved with a rabbit, another with a pig. – STAINED GLASS. C15–C16 fragments, mostly heraldic, in the N transept N and S aisle SE windows. – Good chancel E by *James Powell & Sons*, 1878, designed by *Henry Holiday*; patterned N and S windows, 1863. – Also by *Powells*, designed by *Ada Currey*, the S aisle E window, 1897.

MONUMENTS. Two in the N transept are amongst the best of their dates in the county. That to William Savage (†1616), his son Giles †1631 and the latter's wife Katherine (†1674), is probably of *c.* 1631, by *Samuel Baldwin*. The three recumbent effigies, she holding her swaddled baby in her arms, show alabaster carving of superb quality. By their feet supporters, two lions and a stag's head, its neck pierced by an arrow; then four small kneeling children. No large superstructure, just two back plates with heraldry. – Thomas, first Earl of Coventry †1699. Intended for Croome D'Abitot church, but refused admission by the second Earl on account of the dubious ancestry of his stepmother, who later married Thomas Savage of Elmley Castle. The monument, of white, grey and black marble, signed by *William Stanton*, dates from shortly after 1700. Reclining bewigged effigy, his l. hand indicating his coronet. Canopy of four Ionic columns with depressed rounded arch with vestigial pediment; on its curves, two small seated allegorical figures; elaborate heraldry. Two large angels with gilded wings stand outside the columns. – Nearby, a C13–C14 coffin slab with stepped relief cross. – Chancel. Tablet of 1668 to an unknown lady (E.G.), with broken pediment. – S aisle W. Thomas Vale †1769 by *William Laughton* of Cleeve Prior; stone, pedimented.

In the CHURCHYARD, two curious SUNDIALS, mid- to late C16. The taller, a square pillar, has the arms of Savage, N, and very odd geometrical patterning, a kind of gross Chippendale fretwork; C19 finial. The other, further E, more faceted, once carried a ball finial. Their various dials indicated the time in any part of the world. Both restored 1971. They must have come from the garden of the C16–C18 mansion (THE PARK HOUSE), to the W; demolished 1960, its site now a housing estate.

CHURCH HOUSE, the former vicarage, ENE, by *James Rowley* of Walsall, 1875–6, is gabled, of banded brick, quite plain.

MAIN STREET has few highlights but is most attractive with its unbroken row of houses, W side, of timber framing, brick and stone, and its row of trees on the E. The slight widening at the church end may reflect a short-lived market, for which a charter was granted in 1254. The first house, E side, largely C16, formerly the VILLAGE HALL, has a stone ground floor connected with the existence here in the C14 of a Chantry and College of St Mary; upper floor timber-framed, with slightly projecting early C20 windows. The stone OLD COTTAGE adjoining, mostly refaced in brick, originated as the rectory of the college warden. Its close-studded end gable faces THE CLOISTERS, C17 L-plan, across the very narrow Kersoe Lane.

Opposite, a good timber-framed group includes several C17 thatched cottages, which continue along HILL LANE, running W. Amongst them, the OLD VICARAGE of 1711, rubble, five bays with wooden cross-windows.

At the N end of Main Street, a C14–C15 VILLAGE CROSS, with stepped base, tapering shaft and renewed head (probably of 1648). Nearby, SE, the SCHOOL, also by *J. Rowley*, 1868–9, paid for by Lady Pakington; orange brick with stone dressings, Tudorish with nice bargeboards. More good C17 cottages in MILL LANE, leading SE, and in the Bricklehampton road, further N.

ELMLEY LOVETT

ST MICHAEL. By *John Mills* of Worcester, 1837–40, except for the C14 W tower, with battlements and recessed spire with roll-moulded angles; renewed Dec W window (plus another, S, now inside). Mills reused much medieval walling material; some stones on the nave N wall still bear traces of wall painting. His ashlar-faced church has lancets, stepped buttresses, and battlements. Broad nave with W porches embracing the tower, much narrower chancel with stepped E triplet. Seven-bay nave roof typical of its date: tie-beams with upright braces, plus decorative ogees. Chancel altered 1877–9. – PULPIT and FONT. 1884. The earlier font also survives. – Large ORGAN by *W.J. Bird & Son* of Smethwick, 1902. – ALTAR TABLE by *Braithwaite & Son* of Worcester, 1937; Jacobean style. – ROYAL ARMS. George III. – HATCHMENT. Rev. R.T. Forester, 1867. – STAINED GLASS. Colourful E window by *Cox & Son*, 1868–9. – MONUMENTS. Several Gothic tablets, the largest, to the Townsend family, by *Moysen* of Birmingham, c. 1842.

In the CHURCHYARD, a C15 CROSS on three steps; base with big angle spurs, late C19 shaft and head. – Square LYCHGATE. 1924.

The church stands alone, apart from CHURCH COTTAGE, the former school, by the lychgate; early C17, stone with mullioned windows, timber-framed end gables. Mounds to W and S indicate the site of the medieval village; Elmley Court, large C17 timber-framed, demolished c. 1890, stood to the SE.

RECTORY, a little W, by *Maurice Jones & Graham*, 1950; brick, shaped end gables.

The present small VILLAGE lies ⅓ m. ESE. The early C18 OLD
RECTORY, brick, five bays, with quoins and modillion cornice,
has a doorway with apsed hood on carved brackets; pedimented tablet above, instead of a middle window. Lower E
wing early C19, when the S façade was stuccoed. Set back
opposite, STONE HOUSE, an unusual farmhouse of *c.* 1640,
sandstone ashlar, originally three bays and two storeys with
attic, all beneath one roof. Some mullioned-and-transomed
windows survive, plus one large stack on each side. The
impressive kitchen, with 8 ft- (2.5-metre) wide lateral fireplace,
was altered in the 1960s when a large SW extension was added.
Further E, UPTON FARM, *c.* 1870, good stone Gothic, its angle
porch with foliated pier.
At CUTNALL GREEN, 1 m. SE, the Tudor Gothic SCHOOL by
T.D. Baker, 1862–3, enlarged 1872, further extended by *A.H.
Parker*, 1914; mostly swamped by later C20 additions. The best
earlier survivor is MOAT HOUSE, at the W end of School Lane.
Brick, *c.* 1700, four bays with stone quoins and hipped roof;
three rear gables light the attic. Contemporary staircase and
panelling, especially in the dining room, l., its fireplace flanked
by alcoves with fluted pilasters and painted shell heads.

EVESHAM

Evesham has many attractions: the River Avon, which it has
wisely made the most of by tree-planted walks along the stretch
that matters most; its abbey precinct, entirely unexpected in what
it does and does not present; and streets with good houses, a few
of them of a high order. The town lies within a loop of the river,
at the centre of a rich agricultural area. Its medieval development
was closely dependent on the abbey, but its plan has some
unusual features, with two apparently distinct market areas. The
larger, Merstow Green, immediately W of the abbey's great
gateway, must be the earlier. The current, smaller market place

perhaps resulted from the establishment of a 'new borough' in the C12, its regular grid of streets within the L formed by High Street and Bridge Street. At the E end of the latter was the only medieval bridge, leading to Bengeworth (which had a C12 castle of the Beauchamp family). Most town buildings must have been timber-framed; Leland, in the C16, noted that it was 'meetly large and well builded with timber'. The charter of 1604–5 incorporated Bengeworth into the borough. Trade was boosted by the Avon improvements carried out by *William Sandys* of Fladbury, 1635–9, rendering it navigable for the 43½ miles from Tewkesbury to Stratford; the latter was linked by canal to Birmingham in 1816. The railway (*Brunel*'s Oxford, Worcester & Wolverhampton) arrived in 1852, then, in 1864, the Midland's Barnt Green to Ashchurch loop line. For a period Evesham had its own architectural dynasty. *George Hunt* (1826–1917), son of *Solomon Hunt* (†1868), built up an extensive local practice; his son, *George Henry* (1851–1915), kept an Evesham office as well as one in London in partnership with Thomas Verity. C20 expansion included the absorption of Hampton, S and W of the river, into the borough in 1933, and from 1989–90, following the building of an eastern by-pass, extensive residential and business development to the SE.

THE ABBEY PRECINCT

Evesham Abbey was founded *c.* 701 by St Ecgwin, Bishop of Worcester. His church collapsed *c.* 960 and was rebuilt thereafter. Whether this is the same building as that said to have been entirely built between *c.* 1045 and the consecration in 1054, we do not know. Another rebuilding took place after the Conquest, mostly under Abbots Walter (1077–1104) and Reginald Foliot (1130–49). Of the early phase was the E, of the later the W parts. Excavations begun by Edward Rudge in 1811 revealed the plan of the Early Norman crossing and transepts (with E apses) and of the Late Norman nave with large round piers. The E parts, badly damaged when the central tower fell, were remodelled with square ends in the time of Thomas of Marlborough (1207–36); a narrow Lady Chapel, E, was added under Abbot John de Brokehampton (1282–1316). From *c.* 1320 the central tower was surmounted by a spire. The *Chronicle of Evesham* furnishes many more dates, but visible remains are scarce (apart from the early C16 Bell Tower and the two parish churches). All that can now be seen is as follows.

Of the ABBEY CHURCH almost nothing, just a lump of the N transept a little S of the Bell Tower, with the base of the N respond of the arch to the N aisle. Hidden in the cutting, S, is the base of the central tower's NW compound pier. The nave extended *c.* 157 ft (48 metres) to the W, the line of its N aisle N wall just behind the existing wall to the parish cemetery. The outline of the transepts and E end, extending *c.* 79 ft (24 metres) (into Abbey Park, p. 299) is marked out on the ground,

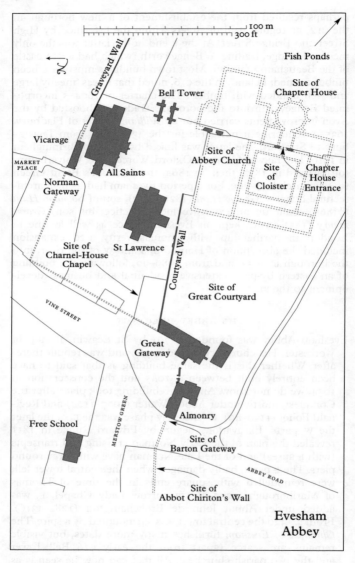

100 m
300 ft

Fish Ponds

Graveyard Wall

Bell Tower

Site of Chapter House

Vicarage

Site of Abbey Church

MARKET PLACE

Norman Gateway

All Saints

Site of Cloister

Chapter House Entrance

Courtyard Wall

St Lawrence

Site of Charnel-House Chapel

VINE STREET

Site of Great Courtyard

Great Gateway

MERSTOW GREEN

Free School

Almonry

Site of Barton Gateway

ABBEY ROAD

Site of Abbot Chiriton's Wall

Evesham Abbey

with a monument of 1965 to Simon de Montfort more or less
on the site of the High Altar.

Of the CLAUSTRAL BUILDINGS S of the church all that remains
is the very fine entrance arch to the CHAPTER HOUSE, from
the E walk of the cloisters (their site now used as allotments).

Twin niches either side, each with a little vault, the arch itself without its lowest voussoirs; fine mouldings separate two orders of canopied figures, the inner standing, the outer seated and rather better preserved. The style suggests *c.* 1290. The archway led, via a passage beneath the monks' dormitory, to the decagonal chapter house, also now marked out. This, begun *c.* 1296, completed by 1317, was vaulted without a centre pier.

Much more substantial is Abbot Lichfield's BELL TOWER, a free-standing campanile or clocher such as many medieval English cathedrals used to possess, although Evesham's is exceptionally late. Clement Lichfield became abbot in 1513, his tower was completed *c.* 1525–30; a most lavish piece, 110 ft (34 metres) high, pierced by an archway. Outer and inner sides are panelled all over, including the faces of the set-back buttresses. The gate arch as well as the main four-light windows and paired two-light bell-openings have crocketed ogee gables; reticulated motifs also reminiscent of the Dec style. The N and S sides in contrast are absolutely closed to the bell-stage. Battlements with trefoil-headed openwork panelling and pinnacles. Beneath the archway, springers presumably for a fan vault, probably never executed, and soon to be superseded by the inserted polygonal stair-turret, NW.

The Bell Tower separated the inner precinct from the parish cemetery (with its two churches, pp. 291–4), between which and the town Abbot Reginald erected a WALL. A short stretch survives N of All Saints' chancel, with, further w, the NORMAN GATEWAY (or Cemetery Gate). Its upper parts are C15–C16, gabled, with close studding, continuing onto the adjoining VICARAGE, its first-floor overhang on a moulded bressummer (and inside a little painted decoration). The lower part of the gateway is stone, Abbot Reginald's C12 work, though the details look even earlier than *c.* 1130. Single order of columns with block (or single-scalloped) capitals; inside, blank arcading on thin triple shafts. Vicarage and gateway (restored by *R.A. Briggs*, 1899) form a picturesque group immediately N of All Saints. To the S of St Lawrence is the C14–C15 COURTYARD WALL; its E end may have abutted on the Abbey Church's N porch. In the wall, a double-chamfered four-centred arch, two chimney-breasts of a building that faced the Great Courtyard, one with part of its octagonal flue, and a blocked two-light cusped window.

The remains of the GREAT GATEWAY, erected *c.* 1320–30 by Abbot William de Chiriton, lie further w, embedded in a beautiful L-plan house of 1711 facing Merstow Green (p. 301). Of two storeys, with hipped roof above a modillion cornice. Its two doorways, with fluted attached columns, are Late Georgian. Excellent early C18 railings and iron gates, with overthrow. The rear, E, front has seven flat bays with moulded cornice; pedimented Tuscan porch, apparently mid-C18. The projecting wing lies on the line of the gateway passage, the only visible signs of which are a small blocked side doorway close to the NE return, and the outline of the main arch (and one impost) on the rear wall; here also various other blocked openings, difficult to interpret. Within the wing, a fine staircase of *c.* 1711, three balusters per tread; at the N end of the house, a good panelled room. An adjoining building, S, has against its S wall the remains of a vaulted passage or room, probably early C14, with thin vaulting shafts and springers; beyond this, the so-called STABLES, with a C14–C15 doorway and window. All converted to housing by *Eastabrook Associates*, 2006.

Finally, W of and at right angles to the Great Gateway, beyond a renewed archway that probably led into its courtyard, is the ALMONRY, now a museum,* but itself a most interesting house. The core, visible externally as the deeply recessed centre of the W front, is a C14 first-floor hall of four bays, to which C15–C16 stone-built N and S wings were added. The latter was mostly rebuilt and extended W in C17 timber framing. The former, altered in the C17, forms the gabled and buttressed E part of the present N front, with a high four-light mullioned window. The low stone section at the W end of this N range was the C14 kitchen, apparently originally detached, with massive N chimney-breast. These two parts were probably joined in the later C16 (see the lower part of the stone S wall of the N range, with its two-light Tudor-arched window and blocked doorways). The N wall, however, was rebuilt in narrow-studded framing in the C17, the kitchen end with gabled overhang with carved bargeboards and oriel window; overhang brackets with leaf decoration. Inside, the first-floor hall retains the two W bays of its C14 arch-braced roof: cusping along the upper edge of the collar-beams, wind-braces, and parts of a pierced quatrefoil frieze above the wall-plate. *In situ* on the W wall of the original S wing, an excellent chimneypiece with five big trefoil-cusped quatrefoils on its lintel. Four contain emblems, which together with the pomegranate and rose foliage spandrels of the moulded four-centred opening, point to *c.* 1500 (when Clement Lichfield was prior). N of the chimneypiece (i.e. in the W wall of the stone ground floor of the C14 hall), the re-set head of a four-light trefoil-cusped window head, vaulted on its underside, quatrefoil frieze above.

Irregular masonry on the outer W wall of the kitchen block probably indicates the site of the Barton Gateway. This was built by Abbot William de Chiriton (1316–44), together with a long WALL which ran over 600 yds W to the Avon. Part, still some 10 ft (3 metres) high, remains on the S side of Boat Lane, close to the Hampton Ferry.

---

*Its collections include: a remarkable C15 canopied stone lantern, with crocketed ogee arches and spirelet; the impressive abbot's chair, probably *c.* 1335–40; a doorway with fine C14 ironwork; the original wooden quarter-jacks from the Bell Tower clock; and *Preedy's* carved octagonal font from his Workhouse Chapel, 1879–80.

CHURCHES

Church of England

The town centre churches, both Blue Lias with ashlar dressings, must be considered first. The curious thing about them is that they both stand within the Abbey precincts (*see* above). This has never been fully explained: All Saints seems to have been the parish church for E part of the town, St Lawrence for the w. The latter was more closely connected with the abbey, physically in fact to its church by a 'very great and curious walk'. Abbeys in any case liked a church in their immediate neighbourhood, to get rid of parish duties; St Margaret, Westminster is a good example.

ALL SAINTS. The battlemented church appears Perp throughout but is of Norman origin, heavily restored by *Preedy*, 1874–6.* The w doorway of a towerless nave, *c.* 1200, is preserved: round arch with slight chamfer, imposts not of the most elementary kind. N transept added in the early C14, with continuously double-chamfered arch to the nave and five-light N window with intersecting tracery, both renewed by *Preedy*. He rebuilt the chancel in Geometrical Dec style, retaining only the upper part of the C14 chancel arch, and a double-layered trefoil-cusped doorway as the entrance to his new N vestry (outer choir vestry added by *R.A. Briggs*, 1897). The rest is Perp, the w tower with tall recessed spire, preceded by a lavish Late Perp w porch. Dating is easier from within. Both three-bay nave arcades are similar in design, but the much lower N clearly comes first, probably quite early C15. The piers have four flat canted projections separated by hollows, the arches echo that arrangement; two capitals have a little foliage. Matching arch between the N aisle and the (existing) N transept. The aisle was almost entirely rebuilt in 1874–6, but one N window, if it can be relied on, still has tracery of flowing form. The higher s arcade is of a piece with the arch to the s transept, as wide as its facing Dec counterpart. The matching Late Perp windows of the s aisle and transept retain noticeable Dec reminiscences. Blocked transept w window, proving that it predates the Lichfield Chapel, the climax of the church, built by Abbot Clement Lichfield when he was still prior, probably *c.* 1505–10; he was buried here in 1546. Panelled arch to the s aisle, splendid fan vault of two square bays, the pendant boss 39 above the entrance initialled C.L.P[rior]. Below the windows, friezes of big trefoil-cusped quatrefoils with central foliage lozenges. The chapel's exterior is of ashlar, with fleuron eaves frieze, openwork trefoiled parapet, and (formerly) tall pinnacles. The w porch was also no doubt built by Lichfield early in the C16. Again ashlar, with similar eaves frieze, openwork parapet and pinnacles, but also all-over panelling. Four-centred N and s entrances (respectively towards the Norman Gate and the Abbey); to the w, only a five-light straight-headed

*The original scheme was drawn up in 1872 by *T.D. Barry & Sons*.

window. Flat wooden ceiling with moulded ribs and central boss of the Wounds of Christ.

FONT. Octagonal, Perp; fleurons in quatrefoils on the bowl, in cinquefoiled panels on the stem. Nice COVER of 1909. – *Preedy*'s FURNISHINGS include the alabaster REREDOS, carved by *Boulton & Sons*, *Godwin* encaustic floor tiling, PEWS, and the stone and marble PULPIT. This has a TESTER by *F. Bligh Bond*, who renewed the STALLS, adding a tall canopied one for the vicar, and also provided a SCREEN and triptych REREDOS for the Lichfield Chapel, all 1911–12. – Fine ROOD SCREEN by *C. Ford Whitcombe*, 1904–5, with low Arts and Crafts metal gates made by *Blunt & Wray* of London. – SCULPTURE. Under the tower, a fine small late C13 or C14 seated figure of Moses. Also two bosses from the Abbey: a Pelican in Piety and angel with the abbey arms. Another, a bearded head, on the sill of the chancel SW lancet. – By *P. Lindsey Clark*, statues of the Virgin and Child (W porch, 1946) and St Christopher (N arcade W pier, 1948–9).

STAINED GLASS. The only medieval piece is a C14 Christ in Majesty in the tracery of the N aisle NE window. – Much good C19–C20 glass. All in the chancel, and the N transept E, are by *Preedy*, 1875–6. – N transept N, typical *Capronnier*, dated 1882. – S transept E *Heaton, Butler & Bayne*, c. 1880. – S transept S, a splendidly colourful composition by *Henry Holiday*, 1882–3, for *Powell & Sons*. – Also by *Powells*, the Lichfield Chapel windows, of 1882–3, the S aisle SE, 1884 (again to *Holiday*'s cartoons), and S aisle SW, 1900. – By *Percy Bacon Bros*, the N aisle NE, N aisle NW, and two high up, nave W end, all 1909–10. – The rest by *Shrigley & Hunt*: two above the chancel arch and S aisle W of 1899, N aisle N central 1906, N aisle W 1908–9.

MONUMENTS. Elizabeth Baylies †1754, attributed to *Sir Henry Cheere* (GF). Fine standing monument of coloured marbles: inscription panel curved in plan, putto with anchor at the foot, wreathed urn in front of an obelisk (N transept). – Perhaps also by *Cheere*, the tablet to William Baylies †1760 (S aisle). – Many other tablets, including a good collection of late C17–early C18 cartouches, on the S transept E wall and above the nave N arcade. – Also here, Mary Bulstrode †1715, small, but with portrait roundel beneath draped baldacchino. – Elizabeth and Anne Cave †1728, by *Richard Squire* (nave W); fluted pilasters, broken segmental pediment. – Ann Bodledge †1781, by *Leonard Mole* (N aisle), quite severe plain pilasters. – Thomas Dunn †1777, by *W. Stephens* (S aisle), is more stylish: grey and brown marbles, with draped urn.

ST LAWRENCE. Vested in the Churches Conservation Trust since 1979. Entirely Perp, though much of its conformity results from restoration by *Harvey Eginton*, 1836–7. Perp W tower with chamfered corners between set-back buttresses, and W doorway with trefoil-traceried spandrels beneath a broad four-light window; battlements, pinnacles, and short, not at all happy spire. At the foot of the tower, N side, a defaced small relief of the Crucifixion. Perp also the spectacular E end. The aisles have separate gabled roofs (the S amended by *Eginton* to match the N*), but not much in the way of features. The chancel, however, has a six-light window surrounded by panelling which even extends across the diagonal buttresses; these have battlements with tiny flying buttresses at the set-offs. Instead of a transom the window has a very odd undulating tracery arrangement, repeated on the equally tall, narrow two-light N and S windows (one each side). The S aisle is Perp (with trefoil-headed openwork battlements renewed in 1836–7); the N aisle is mostly by *Eginton*; the Perp N arcade was demolished *c.* 1737. From the middle of the S side projects the ashlar Chantry of St Clement, probably built for Abbot Clement Lichfield *c.* 1505–10 (cf. All Saints), though it could be as late as *c.* 1530; five-light E and S windows, the latter transomed, openwork battlements above a fleuron frieze. Its W wall is blank, with disturbed masonry; the 'very great and curious walk' to the Abbey may have adjoined here.

Inside, the Perp arcades are identical: of four bays plus three similar chancel-chapel bays, separated by the (altered) stretch of wall where the rood screen stood. In fact the N arcade is a careful copy by *Eginton*. The completeness of the scheme is enhanced by his four-centred ribbed and panelled roof, running from tower arch to E window. Piers with four thin shafts, hollows in the diagonals set between raised ledges; panelling above, two small two-light clerestory windows per bay. The S chantry chapel, accentuated by its large windows, is rich inside, with panelled arch and fan vault with central pendant. Elaborate niches flank the E window, its sill higher than the S window's because of a former reredos. Trefoiled panelling below the S window. (Renewed) tierceron star vault beneath the tower, its arch to the nave again panelled. *Eginton* gave the interior a central twin pulpit and reading desk, with chancel seating facing towards them. *Carpenter & Ingelow*, in 1892, established a proper Ecclesiological chancel, with stepped, encaustic tiled floors, and new seating throughout. Wooden PULPIT of 1906, with canopied figures of apostles, by *C.F. Whitcombe*, who also provided PARCLOSE SCREENS in 1911. Eginton's are the stone REREDOS and TOWER SCREEN (supporting his ORGAN CASE of 1840, moved to the N aisle in 1892). His FONT, in the S chapel, is a copy of its ejected Perp predecessor, now returned to the S aisle; octagonal bowl with paired quatrefoils, stem with two-light tracery patterns. – ALTAR TABLE. Dated 1610. – C19 PARISH BIER, from Pebworth. – SCULPTURE. Two square panels, one (N aisle) with lion's head, the other (S aisle) with the abbey arms; they seem to have formed part of a monument to Thomas Newbold, abbot 1491–1513. – STAINED GLASS. E window by *Willement*, 1862, N and S sanctuary by *Alexander Gibbs*, 1864, all three with colourful pictorial scenes. – N chapel E window by *Preedy*, 1862. – S

---

*To achieve this, he removed most of the crypt beneath the S chapel; also his the chimney, copied from that on the courtyard wall opposite, p. 289.

chapel E by *Michael O'Connor*, 1847; S chapel S by *A.L.Wilkinson*, 1957. – In the N aisle, from the E, three by *Geoffrey Webb*, 1938–44, then a similar one by *F.W. Skeat*, 1956. – The S aisle SW is also by *Skeat*, 1959, the other S aisle S window by *Paul Woodroffe*, 1934. – S chantry: S by *Hardman*, 1864; E (much inferior) by *S. Evans & Co.*, 1932. – Only one MONUMENT, a draped urn to J.H. Beaufoy †1836, by *Lewis* of Cheltenham.

ST ANDREW, Pershore Road, Hampton. A Perp village church, the plan, aisleless nave, central tower and chancel, perhaps reflecting its Norman predecessor. Nave and tower are of *c.* 1400, with continuous plinth and side windows with straight-sided arches. The tower's upper stages, crowned with battlements, gargoyles and pinnacles, are slightly narrower, resting within on four continuous concave-moulded arches, doubled to W and E; high bases with large spurs, vault with eight ribs radiating from a large circle. Polygonal stair-vice, NE, doubling as the rood stair. The chancel is probably a remodelling of that erected *c.* 1300, under Abbot John de Brokehampton; E wall refaced 1900. The S porch is slightly later Perp, with stone roof on three chamfered transverse arches (cf. Honeybourne); four-centred entrances, the outer with pierced trefoil spandrels, the S doorway with leaf spandrels. *C.F. Whitcombe* restored the church in 1903–4, adding a short N transept and N vestry-cum-organ chamber, with double-chamfered arch to the chancel.

FONT. Plain Norman, tub-shaped. – ARCHITECTURAL FRAGMENTS. Pieces of Norman chevron built into the nave walls, mostly inside. – Jacobean-style PULPIT by *John Clackson* of Worcester, 1893. – STAINED GLASS. E window 1859, N vestry E *c.* 1858, and tower S, *c.* 1873, all *Ward & Hughes*. – Chancel SE by *Hardman*, 1902, also the nave SW, 1982. – W window by *Burlison & Grylls*, 1891. – Nave SE *c.* 1899, no doubt *William Pearce Ltd*. – Nave NE by *Ray Bradley*, 1988; NW by *Nicola Hopwood*, 1998. – MONUMENT. Benjamin Scarlett †1739, by *Richard Squire*; architectural tablet, of grey marbles.

C14–C15 CHURCHYARD CROSS: three steps, octagonal base with quatrefoils and fleurons. *A.M. Durrant* (a pupil of Whitcombe) renewed the shaft in 1912, and added the LYCHGATE. – CHEST TOMB to John Martin †1714, with scroll ends and jolly carving of winged cherubs and skulls. – VICARAGE, N. Plain brick Gothic, 1881.

ST PETER, Port Street, Bengeworth. 1871–2 by *T.D. Barry & Sons* of Liverpool. It cost only £4,500, yet is large, with aisles, transepts and prominent SW steeple with broach spire. Blue Lias with ashlar dressings, Dec-style, the larger windows with complicated but graceless tracery. Inside, piers of polished Westmorland granite, with stunted foliage capitals. NW vestry by *C.E. Bateman* and *G.H. Hunt*, 1912–13, much enlarged by *Patrick J. Burton*, 1991–2. – Of original furnishings only the carved stone REREDOS and PULPIT remain. – C14–C15 FONT brought from the old church (*see* p. 307) in 1917. – CHOIR STALLS. 1926 by *Sprague & Evans*. – ROOD, on a high-set beam, by *Alec Miller* of Campden, 1934. – STAINED GLASS. An interesting if unexciting collection. By *W.H. Constable* of Cambridge, 1872, the E, N transept E, and N aisle W windows; also chancel NE, 1878. – Chancel NW by *J. Wippell & Co. Ltd*, 1921. – W window, *c.* 1904, and S aisle W, 1913, by *T.F. Curtis, Ward & Hughes.* – By *A.E. Lemmon* of Bromsgrove, 1937, the N aisle NE and S aisle SE, plus another in the S aisle, of 1954. – The other N aisle N window clearly by *Burlison & Grylls*, 1894.

MONUMENTS. All from the old church. Thomas Watson †1561. Quite small, but typical of the elegant classical detail of some of the earliest Elizabethan work: two short, fluted Ionic columns, fine foliage frieze, pediment with a skull; strapwork panel. – John Deacle †1709, attributed to *Francis Bird* (GF). Impressive standing monument, of grey marbles. He reclines on a bulging sarcophagus, pointing towards the inscription on a piece of drapery; back wall with fluted Composite pilasters and broken segmental pediment with heraldry. – The Rev. Thomas Beale †1805; neat oval tablet by *Bryan & Wood* of Gloucester (N aisle).

Other denominations

ST MARY AND ST EGWIN (R.C.), High Street. 1912 by *Sebastian Pugin Powell* (*Pugin & Pugin*). Large, of rock-faced Lias; SW tower with blunt parapet, nave with narrow aisles and shallow transepts, chancel with polygonal apse and short chapels. Dec-Perp windows, mostly beneath gables. Inside, tall four-bay arcades with octagonal piers; W choir gallery. – Elaborate wooden REREDOS, with paintings by *Hardman*. – STAINED GLASS. Apse and chapel E windows by *Paul Woodroffe c.* 1924–5. – By *Hardman*, N chapel N, 1928, and S chapel S, 1931.

Tudorish brick SCHOOL, SE, of 1900, and plain hipped-roofed PRESBYTERY, SW, 1903, both by *G.H. Hunt*.

BAPTIST CHAPEL, Cowl Street. Of 1788; demolished 1979. The rendered brick schoolroom of 1870–1 then became the chapel, surrounded by new housing.

FRIENDS' MEETING HOUSE. Secluded, with its burial ground, behind No. 28 Cowl Street (stuccoed, early C19, with two gables). Rebuilt 1892–4, on a site acquired in 1676. Roughcast, half-hipped end gables, domestic windows. Inside, three main beams on thin quatrefoil iron columns; re-set early C19 panelling and benches.

METHODIST CHURCH, Bridge Street. 1906–7 by *Frederic Foster* of Coventry, in the free Gothic typical of Nonconformists at that date. Large, brick with stone dressings. Twin ogee-headed buttressed doorways beneath a six-light Perp window, surmounted by blind flowing tracery; flanking polygonal buttresses with battlements and gargoyles. Polygonal leaded nave flèche. Interior with hammerbeam roof to the four-bay nave and shallow transepts; mildly Art Nouveau stained glass. Restored 2000–1 by *David Robotham Ltd* of Warwick.

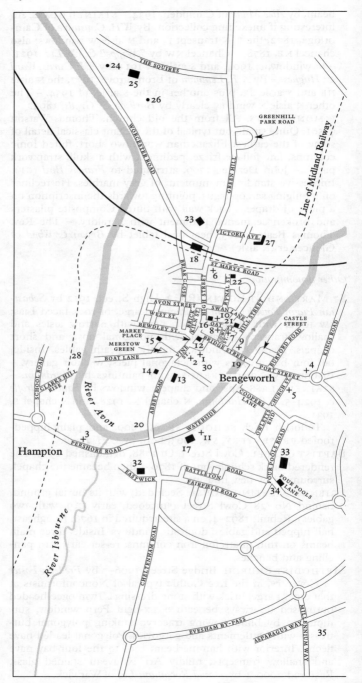

• 24
■ 25
• 26

THE SQUIRES

WORCESTER ROAD

GREENHILL PARK ROAD

GREEN HILL

GREENHILL

Line of Midland Railway

◆ 23

VICTORIA AVE. ◆ 27

■ 18

BRIAR CLOSE

ST MARYS ROAD

+ 6

RYNAL ST

22 ■

AVON STREET

SWAN LANE

HIGH STREET

MILL STREET

CASTLE STREET

WEST ST.
BEWDLEY ST.
BRICK KILN ST.
FLINT ST.

■ 16
OAT ST.
8 + ■ 7
+
■ 10
21 ■
9 +

KINGS ROAD

MARKET PLACE
◆ 15
MERSTOW GREEN
BOAT LANE
VINE ST.

■ 12
+ 2 + 1
30

BRIDGE STREET

19

PORT STREET

FULFORD ROAD

+ 4

Bengeworth

+ 5

28

School Road

Clarks Hill Rise

River Avon

■ 14
■ 13

ABBEY ROAD

20

+ 3

PERSHORE ROAD

Hampton

WATERSIDE

+ 11
■ 17

COOPERS LANE

OWLETTS END

CHURCH ROAD

FOUR POOLS ROAD

■ 33

FOUR POOLS LANE

■ 34

■ 32
EASTWICK

BATTLETON ROAD

FAIRFIELD ROAD

River Isbourne

EVESHAM BY-PASS

ASPARAGUS WAY

35

MILLENNIUM WAY

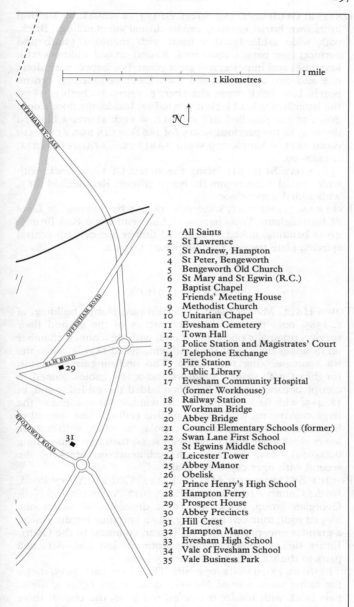

1 mile
1 kilometres

N

1 All Saints
2 St Lawrence
3 St Andrew, Hampton
4 St Peter, Bengeworth
5 Bengeworth Old Church
6 St Mary and St Egwin (R.C.)
7 Baptist Chapel
8 Friends' Meeting House
9 Methodist Church
10 Unitarian Chapel
11 Evesham Cemetery
12 Town Hall
13 Police Station and Magistrates' Court
14 Telephone Exchange
15 Fire Station
16 Public Library
17 Evesham Community Hospital (former Workhouse)
18 Railway Station
19 Workman Bridge
20 Abbey Bridge
21 Council Elementary Schools (former)
22 Swan Lane First School
23 St Egwins Middle School
24 Leicester Tower
25 Abbey Manor
26 Obelisk
27 Prince Henry's High School
28 Hampton Ferry
29 Prospect House
30 Abbey Precincts
31 Hill Crest
32 Hampton Manor
33 Evesham High School
34 Vale of Evesham School
35 Vale Business Park

Evesham

UNITARIAN CHAPEL, Oat Street. Of 1737; a remarkable survival in its own burial ground, amidst dismal surroundings. Brick, with wide ashlar-faced s front with moulded plinth and cornice; four bays, hipped roof. Round-arched windows with keystones and imposts; two giant pilasters – between windows one and two and three and four. Later pedimented central porch. Low brick organ chamber, E, vestry, W, both of 1875, the latter beneath a blocked W window. Inside, the floor slopes down to the panelled C18 PULPIT, W end; above, a blocked doorway to the previous vestry (of 1862). – C18 BOX PEWS, cut down 1875. – Simple C19 WALL TABLETS. – STAINED GLASS, c. 1888–99.

SUNDAY SCHOOL, facing the street. Of 1759; brick, with wide central archway into the burial ground. Remodelled 1862, with added upper floor.

EVESHAM CEMETERY, Waterside. 1874–5 by *Sansome & Lunn* of Birmingham. Two chapels, of Lias with some Red Bromsgrove banding, linked by a gabled timber arcade with central spirelet; plate tracery. Contemporary LODGE.

PUBLIC BUILDINGS

TOWN HALL, Market Place. Of Sir Edward Hoby's building, of c. 1585, only the round-headed arches of the ground floor survive, originally open. The s end, with the council chamber on its upper floor, is of 1728. All remodelled 1833–4, when the NE staircase wing was added. The undistinguished result, roughcast with sashed windows and a few gables, gained in conspicuousness when *G.H. Hunt* added the gabled N end, in 1884–5, with its large canted oriel window (at one end of the large courtroom, with good panelled ceiling); and the rather Scandinavian-looking timber cupola, in 1887, with square lower clock stage with corner balusters, then two diminishing octagonal ones, the first with pediments on brackets, the second with ogee cap with finial.

POLICE STATION AND MAGISTRATES' COURT, Abbey Road. By the County Architect, *A.V. Rowe*, 1937. A symmetrical Neo-Georgian group, brick with stone dressings, all under one hipped roof; fourteen bays long, plain entrance for the Police, a grander one, pedimented on Tuscan columns, to the Court. Either side, a three-bay house; four modest semi-detached pairs to the NE, facing Little Abbey Lane.

TELEPHONE EXCHANGE, opposite. The earlier part, 1935, shows the rather more refined Neo-Georgian of the *Office of Works*; pale brick with redder dressings, five bays, the central three with round-arched windows with shell-like tympana. The large concrete-framed s extension of 1958 is equally typical of its date.

FIRE STATION, Merstow Green. 1967 by *Worcestershire County Council*. Brick, slate infill below the windows; flat-roofed and cubic.

PUBLIC LIBRARY, Oat Street. 1989–90 by *Iain Paul* of *Hereford & Worcester County Council*. Brick, with much glass; its large monopitch slate roof seems to lean against the rear wall of the former cinema (p. 304). Surprisingly spacious interior.

EVESHAM COMMUNITY HOSPITAL, Waterside. The site of the WORKHOUSE (by *John Plowman Jun.* of Oxford, 1836–7). One drab brick outbuilding survives, probably the Infirmary added by *George Hunt*, 1869–70. Also the stone UNION CHAPEL, bold Dec style by *Preedy*, 1879–80. Its interior, now a pharmacy, has a sturdy arch-braced roof; good contemporary *Preedy* stained glass in the chancel. The remainder is a dispiriting C20 rag-bag. Only the WATERSIDE DAY HOSPITAL of 1979 has any presence; brick, L-plan, slightly sunk, with projecting upper floor with glazing bands, split end gables, and rooftop brick water tank.

ABBEY PARK. A fine site sloping down to the Avon. Next to the Abbey remains (*see* above), the WAR MEMORIAL by *Harold E. Dicks*, 1921, a curved stone wall with central bronze figure of an infantryman (by *Henry Poole*). Below, beyond early C20 paddling pools on the Abbey fish ponds site, a ferro-concrete BANDSTAND of 1910 by *H.S. Harvey*, Borough Surveyor; octagonal, shallow dome on thin square piers.

RAILWAY STATION. Opened 1852; rebuilt 1896 in standard GWR form: low platform buildings, red and blue brick, overhanging roofs. Across the forecourt, the former Midland Railway station by *George Hunt*, 1864; also low, red brick, projecting end bays with tripartite round-arched windows.

AVON BRIDGES. The elegant WORKMAN BRIDGE, 1854–6 by the engineer *James Samuel*, on the site of the medieval one, was named after the then mayor. Of coursed Lias; three shallow segmental arches with rusticated ashlar voussoirs, modillion cornice, open balustraded parapet. – The ABBEY BRIDGE, 1925–8 by the County Surveyor, *C.F. Gittings* (succeeded by *B.C. Hammond*), is a period piece of 'Feathercrete' (ferro-concrete) construction. Of bowstring form, intersected by the road deck, preceded by a long N causeway on a double row of thin concrete supports; contemporary iron railings, concrete piers topped with thin obelisks.

Educational Buildings

For pre-C20 schools, *see* pp. 301–2 and 306–7.

EVESHAM HIGH SCHOOL, Four Pools Road. 1951–2 by *Richard Sheppard & Partners*; extended 1974. Good original building, two storeys, of varied outline. Slightly recessed ground floor of light engineering brick, wood slatting above; hall with shallow gable and glazed end wall. Many later additions.

Further S, facing Four Pools Lane, the VALE OF EVESHAM SPECIAL SCHOOL, a watered-down version by *Worcestershire County Council Architects Dept*, 1969; orange brick, weatherboarded upper floor.

PRINCE HENRY'S HIGH SCHOOL, Victoria Avenue. By *Buckland & Farmer*, 1909–10. Two storeys, red brick with blue trim and stone dressings, in mild Wrenaissance style. To the NE, 1950s additions, then the ARTS CENTRE of 1978–9 by *Hereford & Worcester County Council* (project architects *Stephen Taylor* and *Bob Anderson*): auditorium of sheer dark brick, lower foyer of black-tinted glass.

ST EGWIN'S C. OF E. MIDDLE SCHOOL, Worcester Road. 1975–6; *Alan Meikle*, County Architect. Compact, two-storeyed; brick, interspaced with curtain walling, the upper floors projecting like oriels.

COUNCIL ELEMENTARY SCHOOLS, Chapel Street (the site of the Wesleyan Chapel of 1808); now County offices. By *Alfred B. Rowe*, 1909–10, brick, two storeys, with roughcast gables. Single-storey Infant School, NE, added by *A. V. Rowe*, 1912–13, rather more Neo-Georgian.

The replacement SWAN LANE FIRST SCHOOL, Rynal Street, N end, is of 1989–91 by *C.M. Brain* (*Hereford & Worcester County Council*). Two-tone brick, parallel classroom ranges separated by central hall and courtyards, all beneath a top-lit, wide-span roof. Inside, the upper floors continue each end as a balcony around the hall.

PERAMBULATIONS

The three perambulations follow the main streets, all three radiating from the Market Place. This, like the narrow Bridge Street, E, is now pedestrianized. High Street (leading N) and Vine Street (S) are wider, with informal groups of trees, an amenity much diminished by car parking.

1. The Market Place and to its south

Adjoining the Norman Gateway (p. 289), NW, is WALKER HALL, a fine early C16 house restored by *C.F. Whitcombe*, 1906; built during the abbacy of Thomas Newbold (1491–1513), his monogram on the N gable. Close-studded with overhang, canted ground-floor oriel, doorway with rose and leaf spandrels; first floor with C18 horizontal-sliding sashes. Nos. 6 and 8 opposite, timber-framed, mostly roughcast (separated by the C18 brick No. 7), are perhaps also of C16 origin; No. 8's narrow-studded and jettied gable picturesquely abuts the Gateway.

The E side of the MARKET PLACE is dominated by the former FREE LIBRARY and PUBLIC HALL, rebuilt 1908–9 by *G.H. Hunt*; dignified Neo-Georgian, brick with stone dressings. Ground floor with round-arched windows and big Doric porch on fluted columns, now leading into the Riverside Shopping Centre (p. 302); first-floor windows (to the unaltered hall) with pediments and blind balustrades. To the N, the JOURNAL BUILDINGS, a tall Norman-Shavian range of shops with offices above (continuing into Bridge Street), also by *Hunt*,

1898; brick, first-floor oriels, roughcast top floor with half-timbered gables, some rising to two storeys.

The remarkable ROUND HOUSE, now NatWest bank, fills the N 54 side; formerly known as the Booth Hall, though probably never a booth (or market) hall, perhaps originally an inn. An exceptionally complete late C15 timber-framed building, restored in 1964–5 more or less to its pre-C19 form (except that it no longer leans precariously to the W); close-studded, three storeys with double overhang, the attic storey with two gables to N and S. The overhangs, originally supported on brackets, are reinforced by wooden posts, W and E, the former rising through two storeys. Mostly oriel windows, reproductions of C19 replacements.

On the Market Place's W side, the Town Hall (p. 298). The s side has mixed C20 brick buildings. At the E end, the former POST OFFICE, 1925–6 by the *Office of Works*, with giant Ionic angle pilasters and parapet urns. At the W, the former MAIDEN'S HEAD inn, 1936; nicely curved corner with prominent chimney towards Vine Street, its fine brickwork unfortunately covered by paint *c.* 1990.

VINE STREET begins, opposite the Town Hall, with KING CHARLES COURT, a former inn, its entrance unfortunately widened; C18, five bays, stuccoed, with finely carved modillion cornice. Small blocked lancet in the rubble N return (to Bewdley Street). No. 2, the former Falcon Hotel, later C18, is also stuccoed; four bays, windows with moulded architraves, giant Ionic corner pilasters. No. 3, late C18 brick, has channelled lintels. Then the ROYAL OAK, gabled C16–C17, but now mostly C20 black-and-white work. Most of the remainder of the W side has modest, mostly stuccoed frontages, interrupted by the late C19 brick archway to VINE MEWS (No. 15). At the end, YE OLDE RED HOUSE, genuine C16–C17 close studding, with first-floor overhang particularly to the s end gable.

The humbler E side opens out to the Abbey precincts (p. 287), with All Saints and St Lawrence (pp. 291–4) framing the Bell Tower. Further precinct buildings, the Great Gateway and Almonry, close the view, s, around two sides of a fragment of Merstow Green; resited here, the town STOCKS, under a 1920s Cotswold stone roof, and two milestones, the taller, *c.* 1730, from Greenhill (p. 305).

The larger part of MERSTOW GREEN, stretching W, is no longer green, but a car park. The N side begins with stuccoed C19 fronts, then the early C16 GRAMMAR SCHOOL, or at least its stone porch, with the Abbey arms and inscription: 'Orate pro anima Clementis abbatis'; he died in 1546. Flat arch with foliage frieze, head or figure stops, more foliage above, roses on the square hoodmould. Battlements replaced the porch's gable when the schoolroom was all but rebuilt in 1828–9. Now grimly cement-faced as a working men's club, as is the former master's house, w, of 1707. Set back here, the TRUMPET INN by *J.R. Wilkins* of Oxford, 1928, feebly half-timbered. But

No. 14 adjoining is authentic C16 close studding, with two overhangs, each above coving; C17 wing behind. Nos. 15–19, brick, *c.* 1800, step back rhythmically, but only to more car parking and the Fire Station, NW corner (p. 298).

The W side of Merstow Green, with neat early C19 brick houses stretching back into terraces behind, is enlivened by the former NATIONAL SCHOOL of 1843–4; symmetrical Tudor Gothic, two-storeyed, the gabled centre with an oriel above a four-centred mullioned window retaining its latticing. Single-storey brick boys' school, N, by *C. Hugh Slatter*, 1885. On the S side, only the brick garden wall survives of the plain Gothic VICARAGE (by *Alfred Espley* of Evesham, 1873).

ABBEY ROAD, the S continuation of Vine Street, was created only in 1928, as access to the new Abbey Bridge. In it just the Police Station and Magistrates' Court, and Telephone Exchange (p. 298). So back to the Market Place.

2. East of the Market Place

BRIDGE STREET, predominately Georgian brick, provides the best sense of enclosure in the town centre. The N side starts, however, with late C20 pastiche, successful in form but not detail: No. 1 (Cheltenham & Gloucester Building Society) with rounded corner, by *Phillips Phillips Architects*, 1990–1; No. 3 with ground-floor arcade, by *Jellicoe, Coleridge & Wynn*, 1975. The half-timbered No. 5 by *Bromley & Watkins* of Nottingham, 1915–16, for Messrs Boots, fortunately retains the alley through to High Street; Ipswich-style first-floor oriels (to the former lending library). C18 houses begin with Nos. 8–18, S side, with polygonal glazing bars on the upper floors. Nos. 20–22, early C18, have three bays with segment-headed windows, moulded keystones, straight quoins, and top balustrade.

Opposite, No. 21, with, on the upper floors, three very shallow bows, their three-light sash windows with thin dividing columns.

Then No. 32 (HSBC BANK), S, of five bays, perhaps mid-C18, the best Georgian house not least because of its well-restored ground floor, with two doorways with segmental pediments. Windows above with alternating pediments, all without bases; excellent rainwater heads and downpipes, panelled parapet above a modillion cornice. Discreet renewal follows, before the large gabled entrance, with wide pseudo-stone arch on columns, to the RIVERSIDE SHOPPING CENTRE; by *Farrell & Clark*, 1988–9. The shopping arcade, mostly top-lit, its L-plan pivoting around an octagonal centre, is neatly tucked in between the rear of Bridge Street and the Abbey Precincts; here, an inoffensive brick and artificial stone front, punctuated by small stair-towers.

Bridge Street, N side, opposite, has a good late C18 group flanking the narrow Cowl Street: Nos. 37–41, of seven bays, and No. 43, of four, with fluted keystones, quoins, and modillion cornice.

In COWL STREET, remnants of the humble brick cottages that formerly filled the back streets, often encasing earlier timber framing; also the Baptist chapel and Friends' Meeting House (p. 295). Nos. 18–19, at the far NE end, are an almost complete C16–C17 house, narrow-studded, with jettied upper floor; gabled S cross-wing, roughcast, with good carved bargeboards.

Back to Bridge Street's S side, with the CROWN HOTEL (No. 58) at the start of the descent to the river. The street range has gone, so that the inner courtyard, the 'inn', is now exposed; perhaps C16, altered in the C18–C19, all now rendered. The long side wings end in gables with overhangs on big volute brackets; canted oriels below. Beneath the l. one, a stone Tudor-arched doorway. The rear range has an archway through; its first-floor sliding sashes probably infill the original open gallery.

More C16–C17 timber-framed remnants behind No. 64, Bridge Court, its side wall with probably medieval buttressing.

Then Workman Bridge (p. 299), splendidly flanked by the Methodist church (p. 295), N side, and AVON BRIDGE HOUSE (Nos. 66–68), built c. 1864–5 for himself by *George Hunt*, architect, builder and surveyor. Free Italianate, five bays, ashlar-faced with channelled ground floor; balustraded Doric porch, moulded windows with blind balustrades, dormers with curved roofs. An extra set-back bay, W, with rusticated entrance, was presumably Hunt's office.

Across the bridge is Bengeworth (*see* p. 306). A little to its N, approached via Mill Street, is EVESHAM LOCK, in origin part of the Avon improvements of 1635–9. Restored 1962, with steep slate-roofed lock-keeper's house on sloping piloti. Nearby, the four-storeyed EVESHAM MILL, early C19 brick, much renewed as housing.

3. North of the Market Place

HIGH STREET, attractive as a whole if not rich in individual houses, begins, W side, with MANCHESTER HOUSE, Neo-Georgian of 1932, curving round the corner to Bewdley Street. A varied mix leads up to LLOYDS BANK, its N part, originally with twin canted oriels, built for the Worcester City and County Bank, 1863; doubled in size by *P.B. Chatwin*, 1926–7, further watered down by *Pemberton & Bateman*, 1966.

At this point the street widens as the E side receives the Alley from Bridge Street (*see* p. 302), its N end flanked by C17 timber framing and C18 brick. The dominant buildings are a contrasting C19 pair: Nos. 28–34, c. 1890, tall, brick with stone dressings, three shaped gables with chequerboard infill, and ANCHOR HOUSE (No. 36), some twenty years earlier, more vigorously detailed, but stuccoed; upper floor nearly all plate glass, a rare survival of a popular late C19 scheme for department stores. A stuccoed late C18 group follows, with fluted keystones and quoins, ending at No. 50, BARCLAYS BANK, its ground floor reconstructed in 1921.

The w side also has mostly stuccoed C18 houses, before DRESDEN HOUSE (No. 51), the best in Evesham, built for Robert Cookes, dated 1692 on a lead rainwater head (itself an outstanding piece). Of russet brick, five bays and three storeys, with stone quoins, fine modillion cornice, and plain sashed windows, except the middle one with broken pediment rising from the moulded band course; below, the doorway has gloriously big iron brackets, issuing from the forecourt railings. The rear, visible from Brick Kiln Street, has outer bays projecting to full height and a coved cornice.* Wide entrance hall leading to a closed-string staircase with twisted balusters; good panelled rooms.

Back on the E side, the Oat Street corner is marked by the former CLIFTON CINEMA, its front bland rebuilding of 1959; behind, in redder brick, the taller auditorium by *Satchwell & Roberts*, 1923 (remodelled 1938), bearing its former name 'The Scala'. (At its rear, the Public Library, p. 299, and Unitarian chapel, p. 298.) The low stuccoed Nos. 58–60 is C16–C17 (with traces of wall paintings inside on the upper floor). No. 62, late C18 brick, has a nice doorcase, its carriage archway well used as the entrance to a small shopping arcade. No. 64, with Venetian windows on the upper floors, is probably also late C18, though now stuccoed. No. 66 (OLD SWANNE INNE, formerly Star Hotel) is good early C18, stuccoed, five bays, with Venetian doorway and one-bay ball-finialled pediment on the parapet above; projecting two-bay N wing, with quoins. Across Swan Lane, the former CROSS KEYS HOTEL by *H.E. Dicks*, 1938–9, nice townscape, feeble detailing.

In SWAN LANE, some distance E at the corner of Rynal Street, a long brick terrace of *c.* 1820, with Gothick windows and four-centred doorways; end houses slightly raised and completely without Gothick detail. Further E, a former Infant School of 1831 with battlements and pinnacles; other detail obliterated as a Masonic Hall. It was succeeded by the Council Schools, a little SE (p. 300).

The N part of HIGH STREET, only slightly less wide, has fewer C17–C18 houses. No. 85, W side, late C18, with pedimented doorway flanked by two-storey canted bays, adjoins the brick and slate POST OFFICE, by *W.T. Powell* of the *Ministry of Works*, 1960. No. 93 (ALMSWOOD), *c.* 1700, is roughcast, with gables flanking a recessed centre with balcony above the cambered doorway; windows now sashed.

Opposite, a contrasting stuccoed pair. No. 86 reveals C17 framing on its gable end; No. 88, typical early C19, has four bays, with moulded architraves, giant fluted Ionic corner pilasters, and blocky porch with incised ornament.

High Street then becomes domestic and Victorian, with pleasant brick terraces either side. Nos. 90–104 (East Terrace) by *George Hunt, c.* 1870–80, has plain outer gables and two shaped ones

---

*Further S in Brick Kiln Street, Sladden & Collier's late C19 BREWERY, banded brick with square corner tower, well converted to flats.

at the centre. Nos. 106–116 (Leicester Gables) by *G.H. Hunt*, 1890, is more sophisticated; white and red brick, bay windows, two hipped dormers in the centre, two tall half-timbered gables either end. The R.C. church follows (p. 295). Opposite, Nos. 103–113 (North Terrace), *c.* 1880, enlivened by canted bays with wooden balconies (beneath gables). Beyond Queens Road, two late C19 singletons, again probably by *G.H. Hunt*; the more northerly is the finer, with projecting half-timbered gable above one of its canted bays.

The end is the railway station (p. 299). Facing its approach, formerly sandwiched between the GWR and Midland lines, is the RAILWAY HOTEL of *c.* 1850–60: five bays, three storeys, stuccoed, ground floor rusticated with round-arched windows.

Artisan housing fills the streets w of High Street. Their spine is BRIAR CLOSE, with plain late C19 brick terraces all along its E side, probably mostly by *George Hunt*, whose COTTAGE HOSPITAL (1877–9) occupied part of the w side. All that remains is the former NURSES' HOME, 1912–13 (probably by *G.H. Hunt*); gables flank its recessed centre, with pretty rounded oriel. Additions by *C.E. Bateman*, 1926–7.

More brick terraces in AVON STREET. Nos. 13–43, N side, have a central gable labelled 'Evesham Artisans and Labourers Dwellings Co. Ltd. 1881. *A. Espley*, mayor'. Later terraces further s, succeeded by council housing, w, mostly *c.* 1925–35 (Borough Surveyor, *Jerrold Abbott*).

OUTER EVESHAM

1. North

Ribbon development along GREENHILL, the main Birmingham Road, probably began *c.* 1820–30. Surviving stuccoed villas, E side, are No. 66 (Greenhill School), in its own grounds, and No. 70, by the roadside, its three bays articulated by arches on lanky pilasters. Later stuccoed examples (No. 46, Greenhill House, *c.* 1850) were superseded by raw brick Gothic (No. 74, Fernbank House, *c.* 1860–70), then by sub-Norman Shaw houses, especially around GREENHILL PARK ROAD. The largest, THE DRIFT (now Greenhill Park), by *Gant & Slatter* of Hastings, 1891–2, has tile-hanging as well as half-timbered gables. Others are by *G.H. Hunt*, *c.* 1885.

ABBEY MANOR, 1¼ m. NNW. Gothick, of three storeys, ashlar-faced, but stuccoed at the rear; built for Edward Rudge, 1816–17. The flat, castellated s front is largely of this date. Five widely spaced bays, the outer ones projecting with diagonal buttresses and corner pinnacles; shallow central porch. Gothic additions *c.* 1840 included the low conservatory prolonging the s front to the E, and a NW extension. The former, of stone, has seven bays of depressed Y-tracery, the central three recessed. The NW extension has a deep, asymmetrically set porch, with pierced battlements and pinnacles, its Dec-Perp detail imitated from the remains of Evesham Abbey; embattled two-storey canted bay nearby, to the former library. The interior (now sub-divided) was renewed by *G.H. Hunt*, after being gutted by fire in 1894, but the NW porch still houses part of Rudge's remarkable collection of sculptural fragments from the Abbey. These include four large feathered-angel gargoyles, a Norman shaft with scalloped capital, and C14–C15 niches and bosses.

In the GARDENS, a little SE, more Abbey fragments, laid out as an Antiquarium. Particularly notable, the lower parts and bases of four massive nave piers. Also two smaller Norman shafts and pieces of C14–C15 tracery and niches. A stone OBELISK nearby, erected by Rudge in 1845, commemorates the Battle of Evesham, 1265.

LEICESTER TOWER, a stone folly W of the house, was erected by Rudge, 1842, to the memory of Simon de Montfort. Octagonal, of five stages, most with lancets in raised surrounds. Top stage with Y-tracery, its battlements on corbel brackets with grotesque heads at the angles.

2. East of the Avon: Bengeworth

The spine of BENGEWORTH is Port Street, an outer High Street continuing Bridge Street (*see* pp. 302–3) across the river. After the Workman Bridge was rebuilt (p. 299), the wharf, SE, was replaced by WORKMAN GARDENS (opened 1864, with whalebone arch presented in 1906). WATERSIDE has pleasant early C19 terraces ending at the NORTHWICK HOTEL, altered 1863 by *Henry Day*; three storeys, 3+1+3 bays, the centre pedimented, most detail early C20.

PORT STREET, connecting bridge and once separate village uphill, begins with BRIDGE HOUSE, subdued mid-C19 French Renaissance but a good start. Otherwise, mostly C18–early C19 frontages preserving the modest streetline. No. 14, set back, S side, is the former DEACLE'S CHARITY SCHOOL of 1736, its lower part hideously disfigured by shopfronts; only one round-arched window survives (now a doorway). The upper storey retains its five square windows, eared at each corner; modillion cornice, hipped roof. The scale of the N side is decisively broken by the REGAL CINEMA, by *Hurley Robinson*, 1932. Four storeys, brick with artificial Guildstone trim, breaking out into sub-Egyptian lotus ornament above the rounded corner entrance (to Burford Road). The small foyer and its steel staircase are little altered; most of the auditorium's decoration and light fittings also survive.

The more interesting houses of Port Street are nearer the upper end. Nos. 58–64, S side, an ashlar-faced early C19 terrace of 3+5+3 bays, has very curious wilful detailing of the ground floor. There are wooden posts but, instead of capitals, oblong fluted boxes; equally odd cornice. Opposite, a former BANK, *c.* 1920–5, mildly Grecian, and No. 63, late C18 brick, three storeys, with flat Venetian windows.

The street becomes broader where the late C18 TALBOT INN fills the once wider entrance to Church Street (probably the

remnant of a former marketplace or green). The stuccoed
SWAN INN is slightly later. Then, s side, No. 82, dated 1772,
stuccoed with paired sashed windows, and Nos. 84–86, two
brick cottages with wrought-iron porches with canopied
hoods. The end, opposite St Peter (p. 294), is LANSDOWNE, a
handsome stuccoed villa with giant Ionic fluted angle pilasters
and Doric porch; built for Henry Burlingham, as late as
c. 1850, by *George Hunt*. Brick STABLES nearer the road;
pedimented end pavilions, rebuilt centre.

Back to CHURCH STREET where, in its former churchyard surrounded by cottage terraces, there is a fragment of the OLD
CHURCH (demolished 1870). This was the lowest stage of the
C14 W tower, also serving as a porch; diagonal buttresses,
entrance with continuous double chamfers, slight remains of
vault springers within. Opposite, Nos. 32–34, part of the
former manor house (restored 1975 by *Patrick J. Burton*): two
gabled C18–C19 stuccoed bays with attached Lias range with
massive lateral chimney; in the end wall, a segment-headed
doorway with C15–C16 door. Inside, late C15 moulded beams
and, at the rear, part of a blocked Norman arch with zigzag
moulding. On the s side of the churchyard, the former
NATIONAL SCHOOLS (and master's house), brick Tudor
Gothic of 1841 (porch added 1914).

Church Street leads to COOPERS LANE, with more remnants of
the old village. DURCOTT HOUSE, at the corner of Owletts
End, rubble, mostly C19–C20, has a blocked C16 window in its
N gable. Further W, THE COTTAGE, C17, mostly stone: E gable
with tall C19 iron-casement windows, lower W range with large
mullioned-and-transomed one, with ovolo mouldings. Then, in
its own grounds, the roughcast EVESHAM HOTEL, the former
Mansion House. Originally C16–C17, remodelled probably
c. 1735 for Benjamin Seward; enlarged for Thomas Beale
Cooper, 1810–12. Five-bay entrance front, E, with unequal
gabled wings; central three-bay gable, pedimented doorcase
with Tuscan columns. Shallow early C19 bow at the rear. Inside,
early C18 panelling and staircase. Extensive C20 additions in
keeping.

Opposite, FAIRWATER, a handsome sub-Lutyens house, built
c. 1900 for Dr L.F. Leslie. Gabled and pebbledashed, with
wooden mullioned-and-transomed windows; Cotswold stone
roof with slightly battered chimneys.

N and NE of Port Street is much brick artisan housing, begun in
the 1890s. Near the end of ELM ROAD, opposite Offenham
Road, PROSPECT HOUSE, brick, *c.* 1820, has a semicircular
Tuscan porch with wrought-iron balustrade flanked by shallow
bow windows.*

BROADWAY ROAD leading SE has larger early-to-mid-C20
houses. At its end, HILL CREST (originally Holly Mount),
stuccoed Italianate, large and crude, probably by *G. H. Hunt*,
c. 1874, for G.H. Garrard; matching LODGE.

---

* The composer Muzio Clementi died here in 1832.

3. South and west of the Avon

Towards the sw end of WATERSIDE, at Little Hampton, the Evesham Cemetery (p. 298) and Community Hospital (p. 299).

At the former village of HAMPTON (or Great Hampton), further w, are St Andrew (p. 294), a few C17 timber-framed cottages, especially at its former centre around School Road, ¼ m. NW, and one or two larger C18–C19 houses. HAMPTON HOUSE, now approached from Clarks Hill Rise, is late C18 (probably with C16 core); stone-faced, three storeys, 6+1 bays, parapet with ball finials. Now flats.

Off Cheltenham Road, in Eastwick, is HAMPTON MANOR, an excellently preserved house of c. 1705. Brick, five by four bays, with segment-headed windows, modillion cornice, and hipped roof with pedimented dormers. Inside, good panelled rooms and fine open-string staircase, three balusters per tread.

FAIRFIELD, E of Cheltenham Road, has council housing of c. 1950–5 by *Pemberton & Bateman*; pleasant tree-lined roads of brick semi-detached houses. BATTLETON ROAD, to its N, pivots around a square green, with small church-cum-hall (ST RICHARD), also by *T.R. Bateman*, 1955. Further E, at the s end of Four Pools Road, a large schools complex (*see* p. 299).

Much further s, off Evesham by-pass, is the messy VALE BUSI-NESS PARK. Its best building, EVESHAM TECHNOLOGY, corner of Asparagus and Millennium Ways, is by *Rod Robinson Associates* of Hereford, 1997–8. Concrete-framed, with shallow-vaulted central spine; two-storey offices, E, with grey-glass curtain walling, production area, w, clad in ribbed silver aluminium. The reception area, N end, is a glazed drum with dome-like roof. PRIMAFRUIT, by *Peter Barnsley Associates Ltd* of Broadway, c. 1999, at the end of Millennium Way, is in contrast Arts and Crafts- rather than High Tech-inspired. Its office part has chequerboard grey and white patterning, with close-latticed first-floor glazing strip (with triangular oriel), influenced no doubt by C.R. Mackintosh; projecting upswept roof.

FAIRFIELD
Belbroughton

ST MARK. By *Benjamin Ferrey*, 1853–4; opened 1857. Snecked sandstone, with patterned tiled roof. Nave and chancel in one, with s porch and w bellcote. Below the latter, five shafted lancets, the central one wider and blind. Otherwise the nave has plate tracery, the chancel lancets, the E end three stepped below a large rose. Inside, each lancet pair is linked by an arcade with central shaft well detached from the wall. Tall arch-braced roof. – Most furnishings survive, notably the sexfoil-shaped FONT and polygonal stone PULPIT, the latter re-set adjoining a low stone WALL (meant to carry a wrought-iron screen) by *Webb & Gray*, 1938. – COMMUNION RAILS, c. 1916. – STAINED GLASS. E window 1949 by *F.M. Baker* (for *G. Maile & Sons*).

FAIRFIELD HOUSE, ⅛m. NNW of the church. Narrow-studded below, square timber framing above; apparently typically Tudor, but the central porch carries the remarkably late date, 1669. Lobby-entry; good brick chimney with arcaded top. Rendered S wing, c. 1835. Brick farm buildings (one dated 1712) mask the house from the village street. All now housing.

FAIRFIELD COURT, ½m. NNW. A most attractive house, formerly moated. The main part, early C17 lobby-entry plan, is of brick, with sandstone ground floor and ample dressings. Three bays, the projecting centre with full-height porch; three-light windows, mullioned above, plus transoms below. Jettied and gabled cross-wing, E, mostly of C16 close studding. Brick star-plan chimneys, the wing's lateral stack with a huge stone chimney-breast. C18 dairy wing, W side. – Mid-C19 BARNS.

Further N, at STONEYBRIDGE on the A491, an early brick C19 TOLL HOUSE, single-storey with canted centre.

PRIMITIVE METHODIST CHAPEL, Fairfield Road, Bournheath, ⅞m. SSW. Opened 1837; stuccoed, pointed windows. Later altered.

FAR FOREST

Rock

HOLY TRINITY. 1843–4 by *A.E. Perkins*; originally a chapelry of Bewdley, the site given by the Crown. Of coursed sandstone rubble, lancet-style, with buttresses. Nave with W bellcote and porch, shallow transepts, lower chancel with stepped E triplet (repeated on the vestry, S, added by *Lewis Sheppard*, 1889). Four equal crossing arches, plainly chamfered, give the interior a simple dignity. Original W gallery. Chancel restored 1891. – Perp-style PULPIT. 1894. – STAINED GLASS. Good E window, 1859, probably *Clayton & Bell*. – N transept N, patterned glass of 1871–4. – All other windows by *Goddard & Gibbs*, 1955–66, designed by *A.E. Buss*.

The VICARAGE, W, by *Maurice Jones & James Snell*, 1969, a brick cube with tile-hung first floor and hipped roof, forms an unexpected contrast.

Former VICARAGE, N, probably also by *Perkins*, c. 1845; simple Tudor Gothic, with rear additions by *A.E. Lloyd Oswell*, 1900. Nearby, the former SCHOOL of 1829; plain house and schoolroom, the latter doubled in length c. 1849.

LEA MEMORIAL SCHOOL, ¼m. SSE. By *Meredith & Pritchard*, 1902–3. Large, brick, with broad tripartite windows, half-timbered gables and tall open bell-turret. Matching school house.

At CALLOW HILL 1¼m. SE, a brick WESLEYAN CHAPEL built 1864, by *Shinston* of Rock. Nicely reactionary, with round-arched windows, W lunette to light the shallow gallery, and hipped slate roof. Attached early C20 schoolroom.

FECKENHAM

An attractive village, of brick and timber framing. It stood at the heart of the royal Feckenham Forest, disafforested 1629, when much had already been hewn away for the fires of the Droitwich salt-makers. There was a royal hunting lodge, probably nearer Hanbury, much used in the C12–C13, and, in the village, a manor house (incorporating the forest prison), sold to the Abbot of Evesham in 1356; its large moated earthwork remains. A market and fair, established 1237, had died out by the late C18 when Feckenham had become a centre for the manufacture of needles, pins and fish-hooks, an industry later superseded by that of nearby Redditch.

St John Baptist. Square Perp w tower, an earlier origin suggested by the (blocked) pointed bell-opening, E, and tall, continuously double-chamfered tower arch. The rest is much renewed. *Butterfield* rebuilt the chancel, 1852–3, reusing medieval features: two differing Norman N windows, a C13 s lancet and three-light intersecting window of *c.* 1300, and two opposing lowside Perp windows, w end. N aisle windows also Perp, no doubt representing a widening. Broad nave almost entirely by *Henry Day*, 1866–7; his the s wall with Geometrical tracery, s porch, and arch-braced roof on stone angel corbels. The four-bay N arcade, with round piers and octagonal abaci, is probably *c.* 1240–50; the capital of the w pier has wind-blown stiff-leaf, plus one carved head. Double-chamfered arches, with heavy PAINTING of geometrical motifs including perspective effects, based on original patterns in the easternmost arch, especially its N side. The repainting is of 1903–4, when there was further restoration by *C.F. Whitcombe*, who removed a N aisle gallery.

REREDOS by *J.B. Surman*, 1954; other chancel FITTINGS by *Butterfield*. – PEWS by *Whitcombe*. – N aisle REREDOS by *Pancheri & Son*, 1971. – Bulky VESTRY SCREEN, w end, by *Conrad S. Rowberry*, 1987–8. – Large ROYAL ARMS, probably George I. – C17–C18 CHARITY BOARDS. – WAFER TONGS. C15–C16, displayed on the s chancel sill. – STAINED GLASS. Excellent E window by *Lavers & Barraud*, 1862. – By *Hardman*, the chancel SE, 1906, and tower W, 1874. – N aisle E, designed by *Whitcombe*, made by *O'Neill* of London, 1904. – MONUMENTS. Robert Boulton Waldron †1823. Large tablet, with a young woman, her child on her arm, leaning on a Grecian altar with reversed torches. – Black marble inscription beneath to Sir Martyn Culpeper †1604, from his large effigy tomb, dismantled 1853. – Other good tablets: Christopher Smith †1724, with columns and swan-neck pediment; John Boulton and family, 1781, with fluted pilasters and drapery. – Also two by *J. Stephens*.

In the CHURCHYARD, s, the steps and base of a C15 CROSS, renewed 1881, and a WAR MEMORIAL CROSS of 1920 by the *Bromsgrove Guild*.

PERAMBULATION

The church lies N of THE SQUARE, an elongated green with
modest C17–early C19 houses. The OLD VICARAGE, NE, gabled
brick, is mostly c. 1840–50; the OLD COURT HOUSE, further
W, is an early C17 timber-framed cottage. MILL LANE leads
NW, past the former EBENEZER CHAPEL, multi-coloured
brick, 1861, to the OLD SCHOOL HOUSE, also timber-framed,
built as a free grammar school c. 1611; roughcast and given
pretty Gothic fenestration in 1848. The medieval manor house
(*see* above) stood a little to its S.

HIGH STREET, running along The Square's E side, has good
Georgian houses, interspersed with timber-framed survivors.
First, a good early C19 group: Nos. 44–46, a tall brick pair with
pedimented doorways, and No. 42, the OLD NEEDLE MILL,
stuccoed, with central pediment, six bays articulated by large
round arches. To its S, the stately OLD HOUSE, three bays and
storeys, with central doorway and upper window again surrounded by a giant arch. Tripartite ground-floor windows;
porch with fluted columns and frieze with paterae and urns.
Quadrant walls, mostly C20, with gatepiers with large ball
finials.

Opposite, W, the best house is No. 41, mid-C18, four bays, with
quoins, stepped voussoirs, and pedimented doorhood on consoles. No. 39 masks a four-bay timber-framed house of
c. 1600, aligned W–E (best seen from the S). Timber framing
appears on the E side at No. 16 (Forest Cottage), early C17, to
a long L-plan, and Nos. 12–14, probably early C16, narrow-
studded on a high brick plinth. No. 10, late C18 with two canted
bays, contrasts with No. 8 (The Little House), earlier and
lower, with quoins, bow windows and pedimental gable.
Beyond, a pathway leads to ST JOHN FISHER AND ST
THOMAS MORE (R.C.), by the *Rev. F. Askew*, 1935; brick with
pantiled roof. Finally, W side, three well-detailed pairs of Feckenham RDC cottages by *J. J. Johnson* of Redditch, 1926–7.

The B4090 runs across the S end of High Street. More good
houses in DROITWICH ROAD, W. A run of timber framing,
encased in brick, ends with No. 12 (The Old Black Boy), its
square panelling exposed. The TUDOR HOUSE (No. 20) has
grander timber framing of c. 1600: three-bay hall range with
gabled E cross-wing, on a high sandstone plinth; renewed after
C19 subdivision into three needlemakers' tenements. No. 22,
Chesterfield House, with segment-headed windows and
shallow matching porch on thin columns, was probably the
home farmhouse to the MANOR HOUSE next door, set back
behind its high garden wall. Rebuilt for the Throckmorton
family c. 1730, of five bays and two storeys, it is of brick with
stone keystones, strings and quoins; solid doorcase with projecting open pediment on engaged Doric columns, hipped roof
with dormers above a wooden bracket cornice. At the rear,
brick gables surviving from the house of c. 1600, also Jacobean
chimneypieces in the SE and NW rooms. The SW room has C18

panelling; dog-leg staircase also of this date. Further on, next to Bow Brook Bridge, *c.* 1800, brick with elliptical arch, is the Brook House, originally part of a needle mill; early C19, mostly stuccoed, two ranges with an angled link with cast-iron porch.

Little to note in Alcester Road, to the E, apart from The Priory, early C19 battlemented brick encasing C17 framing. Further E, in Moors Lane, is Manor Farm, *c.* 1500: T-shaped, of the type with a lower-end gabled cross-wing, originally entered from the screens passage. The two-bay hall was originally open to the roof. At the upper end, N, a very small ground-floor parlour; jettied first-floor chamber above. Originally close-studded throughout, but the ground floor of the cross-wing underbuilt in brick in the mid C19, with a chimney inserted into the screens passage.

Dunstall Court, ¼ m. N. Brick, Jacobethan, *c.* 1840, with symmetrical, triple-gabled S front; outer bays with square bay windows, higher pinnacled centre with oriel above the tripartite entrance.

The brick school in Swansbrook Lane, ⅓ m. NE, by *Henry Day*, 1857–9, has an unusually symmetrical plan for its date. S front with four gables, the central pair teachers' houses, with schoolrooms for boys and girls either side; smaller classrooms at right angles to the rear. Windows mostly Dec with ogee heads, the main ones stepped triplets under thin black relieving arches.

Shurnock Court, 1¼ m. ESE. A large, complex, timber-framed manor house, on a moated site, with modern date 1606; a rebuilding of a medieval predecessor, a possession of Worcester Cathedral Priory, leased to the Egiock family from the early C17. Three-bay hall range aligned W–E; brick chimney with four star-shaped C19 stacks at the junction of the central and E (service) bays. Large chimney also centre rear, with row of four similar stacks. Two-bay NW cross-wing, with C16 close studding, especially its central porch; lateral stone chimney-breast with two original star-stacks. Two further rear N service wings: the E, a single bay, now forming the main entrance; the central one, lower, of four bays, encloses the N lateral chimney.

More notable timber-framed houses in the N part of the extensive parish. At Ham Green, 1¼ m. NNE, first Brickhouse Farm, typical of *c.* 1600. Two-and-a-half-bay hall range, close-studded on the ground floor, its S passage bay filled by an inserted chimney with four brick stacks; two-bay cross-wing, extended W by an attached C18 L-plan cider mill and a further C19 brick addition with re-set datestone, 1601, in the gable. To its S, joined by a short brick wall, a C17 timber-framed privy. – To the NW, an early C17 four-bay barn and single-bay stable. A little W, three good hall-and-cross-wing houses, all of C17 square-panelled framing. The Little Manor has mixed brick and rendered infill, Cruise Hill Farm entirely brick. Further uphill, The Mount, with rendered infill and plank weatherings; weatherboarded stable by the road. The late C16 Lower Berrow Farm has again the same plan, obscured by later brick encasing, but its cross-wing still makes a splendid show of close studding.

The restored CROSS LANES FARMHOUSE, 1¾ m. N, *c.* 1620, has a two-bay hall range and ornate two-bay cross-wing, E. Close-studded ground floor, square panelling with straight diagonal braces above. The fireplaces of the cross-wing are placed centrally, beneath three conjoined brick star-stacks. There is also a small gabled projection N of the hall, and low service wing, W, with two tall diagonal brick stacks above the kitchen fireplace.

On the S side of LOVE LYNE, Callow Hill, 2 m. NNE on the outskirts of Redditch, are three more splendid timber-framed houses. First (from the W), WHITE HOUSE FARM, probably early C17, to a standard T-plan, but the hall range extended on both N and S fronts. The N now has one very large gable, perhaps *c.* 1650; the S a hipped-roofed staircase structure, probably the same date as the hall, plus a second gable sandwiched between stair and E cross-wing. Framing of small square panelling throughout, the solar wing retaining its shallow first-floor jetty, on consoles, on both E and S walls. In the N wall of the hall range, a sandstone fireplace nearly 10 ft (3 metres) wide. – Long weather-boarded range of C17 farm buildings, NW.

LANE HOUSE FARMHOUSE, probably *c.* 1590 (though with modern date, 1550), retains exceptionally many original features. Close-studded framing throughout, the timbers surviving in untreated condition, with (restored) tiled weatherings on brackets at storey height. Two-bay hall range, with splendidly built three-bay solar cross-wing, E, jettied at the gables; original five-light dormer window at the centre of its E side, complete with mullions and transom. Other original windows with heavy mullions are built in with the structure. A brick addition of *c.* 1710, across the N front of the hall range, has

Feckenham, Lane House Farm.
South elevation

gable-ends with ball finials and ashlar copings; central entrance with doorhood on consoles, several original mullioned windows with fixed glazing in rectangular cames. Two staircases: the earlier, at the SW angle of cross-wing and hall, is spiral, of solid oak, constructed like a masonry stair; the later, at the E end of the brick extension, has turned balusters. Good oak panelling in the hall part.

Then, LOVELYNE FARM, c. 1600, with two-bay hall and w cross-wing; mostly square framing, with close studding at the front of the wing. – To its W, a timber-framed GRANARY, square, on staddle stones.

LOWER GRINSTY FARM, 2⅝ m. NNE, next to the Redditch Golf Club of 1972, is an early C17 farm group, described in an inventory of 1617 as consisting of a 'hall-house' and a number of rooms in 'a fore-chamber of the house'. This fore-chamber, a separate square-panelled T-plan farmhouse, has three equal-sized rooms on each floor. The Hall House (still so named), SE, only one-and-a-half bays, the E half-bay 'chamber' lower, may be the first house on the site, even if no earlier than c. 1550; or was it a detached kitchen? – Early C17 farm buildings, N.

CALLOW PARK, to the E, a small estate of the 1980s, contains two larger brick houses, at right angles: CALLOW COURT, by *Associated Architects c.* 1975, meant to form part of a larger development. Long and low, with strips of clerestory glazing.

NORGROVE COURT. *See* p. 500.

9060

FINSTALL

p. 201

A medieval chapelry of Stoke Prior. Its centre shifted w to Aston Fields after the railway arrived there in 1840, and became even more closely linked with Bromsgrove when New Road opened in 1865.

ST GODWALD, Finstall Road, Aston Fields. 1883–4 by *John Cotton*. Dull exterior of snecked sandstone, in the style of c. 1300. Chancel and nave, with broad S transept and S porch intended to carry a pyramidal-roofed tower; N transept also never built. S organ chamber and N vestries added by *Philip Green*, 1923–4. The interior, mostly faced in yellow brick, is more interesting, with good, uncompleted carving; spacious crossing with sharp brick arch to the nave, two-bay arcade to the S transept. – Stone and marble REREDOS by *Jones & Willis*, 1897 (embellished 1924). – Oak ORGAN CASE. 1899. – PULPIT by *Philip Green*, 1900. – Also of this date, the chunky Gothic FONT. – Clipsham stone MEMORIAL to the Normandy landings, carved by *Robert Pancheri*, 1946. – STAINED GLASS. E window 1883–4, designed by *Temple Moore*, made by *Burlison & Grylls*; also theirs no doubt the chancel S. – S transept S by *A.E. Lemmon*, 1937. – Nave SE by his son *P.E. Lemmon*, 1964.

Of 1897, the attached PARISH ROOM, NE, and former VIC-ARAGE, NW, by *Lewis Sheppard & Son*; brick, big hipped roof, tall chimneys, but still basically Gothic. The earlier church, rebuilt 1772–3, to the E immediately beyond the railway bridge, was demolished in 1969–71.

Of BROMSGROVE STATION, opened 1840, no buildings remain. Immediately to its N begins the LICKEY INCLINE, one of the most dramatic railway features of the Midlands, which took the Birmingham & Gloucester from the Severn plain straight up the Lickey Hills onto the Birmingham plateau. It rises nearly 400 ft within two miles, an average gradient of 1 in 37. Engineer: Capt. *W.S. Moorsom*.

At the head of the station approach, the vaguely Jacobethan DRAGOON HOTEL (now Ladybird Inn) of 1905. Nearby, modest brick housing, in pairs or short terraces, the best unfailingly by *Cotton*, of the 1880s (such as Nos. 26–40 Stoke Road). The former BOARD SCHOOL, Stoke Road, is also by *Cotton*, 1881–2. Brick, with short gabled wings with tripartite Gothic windows, the centre horribly infilled; patterned tiled roof. Infants School at the rear added by *Cotton*, 1886.

More expensive houses further N, around NEW ROAD. The best, ELMSDALE (No. 94, corner of Clive Road), probably by *F.J. Yates* for himself *c.* 1880, has pierced timber gables and Gothic window heads with inset ceramic roundels. It marks the entrance to the WARWICK HALL ESTATE, with several good late C19–early C20 houses, especially in WELLINGTON ROAD and MARLBOROUGH AVENUE. Here, No. 6 (Redlands) was built for himself by the Bromsgrove architect *G.H. Gadd*. The C16–C17 timber-framed WARWICK HALL is a surprising survivor, marooned in housing off Old Station Road: narrow-studded ground floor, with square panelling above, dwarfed by half-timbered additions.

FINSTALL FIRST SCHOOL, Carnforth Road. 1992 by *R.W. Cheney* and *K. Wilkin* of *Hereford & Worcester County Council*. The usual low brick building with jokey Postmodern features, but the entrance given presence by a glazed gable next to a stunted pyramid-roofed turret, set back from an incurving brick gateway.

ST GODWALDS (now Primrose Hospice), ⅓ m. SSE. By *Payne & Talbot*, 1869, for the Rev. J.H. Bainbrigge. Gritty brick Gothic, with patterned window heads, canted bays, and eccentric gables. Much enlarged 2003.

RIGBY HALL, Rigby Lane, ⅛ m. NE. Large stuccoed villa, built 1838 for George Ellins; mostly remodelled in the late C19. Porch, with Doric columns *in antis* between bay windows, the capitals with sunk disc motifs. Mansard roof. Within, a spacious staircase hall and good Jacobean-style plaster ceilings.

FINSTALL PARK, ½ m. ENE, off Walnut Lane. The Neo-Grecian house of *c.* 1830 was destroyed by fire in the 1970s (and replaced by C20 buildings). The grim brick service range of 1884 survives, plus earlier stone outbuildings. Much of the fine park also remains, a significant landscape feature S of Finstall Road.

FLADBURY

ST JOHN BAPTIST. Probably on the site of a Saxon minster. The lowest part of the w tower is Norman, with windows set in mid-buttresses (cf. Cropthorne). When heightening was begun, its walls were strengthened by an inner facing, with tall pointed rere-arches framing the Norman window embrasures. The arch towards the nave, with three slight chamfers, shows that this was already done by the C13. The Perp-looking top stage, with bell-openings with cusped Y-tracery, battlements and pinnacles, is of 1750–2 by *Thomas Woodward* of Chipping Campden, assisted by his nephew *Richard*.* The rest of the church was rebuilt *c.* 1340, its exterior not of special interest, except for the splendid rib-vaulted porch. The single-chamfered ribs stand on slender corner shafts with early C14-looking capitals; upper storey removed, probably in the C17. Dec nave arcades of four bays with the routine octagonal piers and double-chamfered arches. Coved nave ceiling clearly Georgian; its lower pitch necessitated raising the clerestory walls in brick. Chancel and N vestry mostly by *Frederick Preedy*, 1864–5; the vestry doorway, however, seems C14, and outside, chancel N wall, is a Dec piscina, presumably for a sacristy. In 1871 *Preedy* restored the nave, rebuilt the chancel arch, and added a s organ chamber.

Most FURNISHINGS by *Preedy*: PEWS and stone PULPIT of 1871; splendid alabaster and tiled REREDOS, executed by *Boulton*, 1865. – FONT, *c.* 1848; CHOIR STALLS, 1931, with fronts of 1914. – TOWER SCREEN. 1953, incorporating panels from the w gallery of 1783. – Many C15 TILES with the usual patterns, in the blocked N doorway and tall narrow opening E of the s door. – STAINED GLASS. An excellent early C14 Virgin and Child from the same cartoon as Warndon (p. 649); now set in a light box within a cross (s aisle E). – In the chancel NW, six fine C14 heraldic shields. – Ten windows are by *Preedy*, spanning almost his complete career from *c.* 1854 to *c.* 1882 (compare the two adjoining N aisle NE windows). Several commemorate his family, resident here from *c.* 1840. Most striking is the unusually pictorial E window, 1865. – One s aisle s, of 1883, in Westlake style, is probably by *F.A. Oldaker*. – Two N aisle NW by *Heaton, Butler & Bayne*, *c.* 1901–2.

MONUMENTS. Under the tower an exceptionally large tomb-chest of Purbeck marble, five by two bays with cusped quatrefoils in panels; on it, two excellent brasses 4 ft (1.2 metres) long, representing John Throckmorton (Under-Treasurer of England) †1445, in fine armour, and wife Eleanor, dressed as a widow. – Other BRASSES. Edward Peytoo †1488, in armour, 2 ft 3 in. (68 cm.); his wife's figure is modern (nave w end). – Thomas Mordon, priest, †1458; demi-figure, 19 in. (48 cm.) (chancel s). – William Plewme, priest, †1504; 12 in.

---

* A stone with *Richard Woodward*'s name and the date 1750 was found when the tower was repaired, 1983–4; cf. Bewdley.

Fladbury church, brass to John Throckmorton †1445,
and his wife Eleanor.

(30 cm.) (chancel N). – Bishop William Lloyd †1717, the contract with *James Withenbury* of Worcester of 1718. Imposing
standing monument with fluted Corinthian pilasters and side
volutes with elaborate flowers and foliage; at the top, his frontal
demi-figure. The arrangement is not as it originally was. –
Many TABLETS. Elizabetha Charlett †1746, by *Thomas Ricketts*
of Gloucester, with bust. – Four by *W. Stephens*, notably Arthur
Charlett †1779, brown and white marbles. – George Perrott of
Craycombe House †1806. Big, dignified tablet with straight-
sided sarcophagus. Adjoining tablet with draped urn to his wife
Jane †1835, by *J. Stephens*. – Rev. Martin Stafford Smith †1834,
by *Reeves & Son* of Bath; Grecian. – HATCHMENTS. George
Perrott, 1806; George Wigley Perrott, 1831. – Outside, nave SE
wall, the upper part of a very thick sandstone cross slab, probably C13.

THE MONASTERY, to the w. Early C18 brick, four wide bays with segment-headed windows. The hipped roof must have been raised, probably by *Preedy c.* 1860–70; see the top frieze with chevron diapering in blue brick.

CHURCH SCHOOL, NW, by *Preedy*, 1864–5; Dec-style school-room and house, the former with slight banding and rear infant room of 1873. C20 additions. Further N, the PARISH ROOM, 1905, and RECTORY, 1952; Neo-Georgian with hipped roof.

Opposite, a couple of good houses. WHITE HOUSE, early C19 stuccoed, has giant pilasters; s end with two-storeyed canted bay, the other three first-floor windows with blank arches filled with shells. Then THE MANOR, brick, early C18, of five bays, the central bay projecting with steep pediment; plain giant angle pilasters, urns above, three on the pediment. Altered, with matching s wing, early in the C20. Then a large timber-framed C17 BARN, now a house, and thatched C17 cottage.

The fine rectory of *c.* 1713, s of the church, was destroyed by fire in 1968. By the small green opposite, OLD FLADBURY STORES, large early C17 timber-framed, with gabled s wing and long N range.

FLADBURY MILL at the s end of the village, mostly C18 brick, has two earlier gabled wings by the Avon, retaining some machinery. It forms a picturesque group with CROPTHORNE MILL, across the weir by Fladbury Lock, also brick, irregularly gabled; *c.* 1800, enlarged *c.* 1860, pretty oriels added 1906.

JUBILEE BRIDGE, ⅓ m. further SE, was rebuilt in 1933, *B.C. Hammond*, County Surveyor; three steel spans, the centre wider.

94 CRAYCOMBE HOUSE, ¾ m. NNE. By *George Byfield*, 1790–1, for George Perrott of the East India Company. Ashlar-faced, little more than a villa in size: two storeys, five by three bays. Refined reticent detail; no window mouldings at all. Ground-floor windows in blank arches, with paterae in the spandrels, of *Coade* stone like all the external detail. Three urns top the s façade, the middle one larger; two more at the ends of the return fronts. The only other ornamented piece is the doorway: tripartite, with Corinthian pilasters, garlands in the frieze, and a lunette with fan glazing filling the rest of the central blank arch. The motif was taken up on the E return with two more tripartite windows, the first obscured by a later blocky bay window. Between them a large *Coade* urn in a niche, particularly crisply carved, with the date 1791 and inscription: Solus vivat que jucunde. Subsidiary w doorway at the junction with the short rear service wing, reduced by *Guy Dawber*, 1933, from a large addition made for the Duc d'Aumale *c.* 1863.

Elegant INTERIOR, most rooms with hardly more decoration than fine friezes and matching fireplaces. The wide entrance hall, with bucrania frieze, leads to a cantilevered stone staircase with thin iron balustrade, beneath a round domed skylight. On the walls of the afternoon room, SW, rectangular and circular panels with plaster frames, also a hop-bine frieze;

that of the music room, SE, includes Perrott's double-punning crest, parrots grasping pears. In the small library, NW, a frieze with heads and pine chimneypiece with the Nine Worthies. In the dining room, NE, a serving recess behind two Ionic columns.

Outbuildings also 1790–1. The STABLES, W, hidden by C19 additions, have again five round blank arches, with circular openings in the spandrels. In the wood, NE, a five-bay ORANGERY, ashlar, with round-arched windows. Further N, the KITCHEN GARDEN, its brick wall following an elegant U-plan.

FLYFORD FLAVELL

9050

ST PETER. Battlemented Perp W tower; large W window with hoodmould on diamond stops. The rest was rebuilt by *Hopkins*, 1882–3, for William Laslett of Abberton Hall; Dec style, of Inkberrow stone, with open timber S porch. Old parts were reused or heeded in the nave, notably the blocked Norman N doorway and small trefoiled lancet nearby. Austere interior, the chancel well-detailed: triple E window with detached shafts, curved piscina, SE corner. – Perp SCREEN, incorporating one or two medieval fragments. – FONT. Perp octagonal bowl, plain; three small motifs (roses flanking a fleur-de-lys) against the hollow-chamfered underside. – LECTERN. The lower part of the black and gilded stem, with winged griffins at the base, seems early C19; was the top added later? – BENCHES. Two plain Jacobean ones (nave NW). – TILES. Under the tower, a good C15 display, several in sets of sixteen with heraldry. – STAINED GLASS. C15 bits, much restored, nave SE.

In the VILLAGE, a few C17 timber-framed cottages, and nice mid-C19 pub, the BOOT INN: red and yellow chequered brick, heavy lintels, hipped roof; former stables at right angles.

FRANCHE *see* KIDDERMINSTER

FRANKLEY

9080

ST LEONARD. In an isolated setting, though close to the Birmingham city boundary. Of C13 origin, but the masonry of nave and chancel probably C15–C16. Good Perp E window, its four-centred hoodmould with winged grotesques (cf. Romsley); other windows are renewed Perp. Short W tower built into the nave 1750–1, using stone from the ruined manor house* and following either the advice or designs of *Sanderson Miller*; parapet, corner obelisk pinnacles. *Preedy*, in 1873,

---

*W of the church, the home of the Lytteltons until they moved to Hagley (p. 335), mostly destroyed 1645.

rebuilt most of the chancel and added the S porch. Of 1931–2 by *C.E. Bateman* (after a severe fire) are the tall NE vestry and top of the tower. The nice tripartite arrangement of the supporting Alveley-stone tower arches is his, its wider central arch with headstops of George V and Queen Mary. Perp wagon roofs to nave and chancel, the latter with added arch-braced tie-beams. Chancel arch by *Preedy*. – FONT. Octagonal bowl, *c.* 1661, with raised triangular pattern; gadrooned stem, 1967. – PULPIT. C17; good grotesque carving. – STAINED GLASS. E window by *Swaine Bourne*, 1876. – Chancel SE, heraldic, *c.* 1840. – Nave SE, *c.* 1857, no doubt *Wailes*.

CHURCHYARD CROSS. Octagonal step and base, probably C15, but the Saxon shaft and head entirely of 1915, by *Henry Hoare* of Hasbury (Halesowen). – To the E of the church, signs of the deserted medieval village.

The view NE of the church is across Bartley Reservoir (completed 1930), towards high Birmingham blocks of flats. The semicircular FRANKLEY RESERVOIR, E, completed 1904, was the terminus of the Birmingham water supply brought by aqueduct from the Elan Valley (cf. Trimpley); octagonal inspection turrets, brick with stone quoins. Engineers: *James Mansergh & Sons*.

At the small C20 village of FRANKLEY GREEN, ½ m. W, the former RECTORY, at the crossroads, by *J.H. Chamberlain*, 1860, Gothic, brick with blue banding; and former SCHOOL further W, also brick, far more basic, by one *C. Wyatt*, 1864–5.

9050

GRAFTON FLYFORD

ST JOHN BAPTIST. Prominently sited. C14–C15 W tower, of two builds judging by the differing stone colours; Perp W window, Dec bell-openings, battlements, and unusual pyramidal stone stump for a spire. Chancel and nave, with S porch and shallow NE chapel (now organ chamber), are almost entirely by *Hopkins*, 1874–5. As usual he reused old features, especially the C14 nave and chancel N windows, the former with good Dec tracery. Most other windows in Perp style. In the chancel, a C13–C14 piscina and cusped sedile (?), reset in unlikely juxtaposition. – Simple PULPIT, with Perp traceried panels. – PAINTED BOARDS. Two, square, quite large, with emblems of St John and St Mark; probably C16. The full set of four formed a ceilure noted by Prattinton *c.* 1812. – STAINED GLASS. C15 fragments in the W window and, in poor condition, in the chancel. – MONUMENTS. Unornamented marble tablet, with finely lettered inscription to the Rev. Robert Stonell †1645. – Restored C19 HATCHMENT.

The medieval village lay N of the church. Nearby now are only the C17 CHURCH FARM, timber-framed with central brick chimney; the brick SCHOOL, mostly of 1875, adapted as a village hall 1995; and the OLD RECTORY, plain gabled brick by *Lewis Sheppard*, 1877.

RECTORY FARM, ⅓ m. N. The plain C18 brick exterior conceals remnants of a C14 base-cruck hall, though little more survives than the smoke-blackened central truss with its short crown-post and vestiges of the rafter roof. At right angles, NE, originally all but detached, a three-bay solar wing, medieval but later than the hall: heavily moulded timbers and four-centred doorhead. – The small cruck-framed BARN, NW, has collapsed. Straggling VILLAGE, yet further N, with several restored C17 cottages and farms.

HILL COURT, 1 m. NNW. Large and picturesque, timber-framed with brick infill and star-shaped stacks. C16 hall range, slightly jettied, structurally independent N service wing, and larger cross-wing, S, of c. 1630. Restored by *G.C. Gadd*, 1935–6. The wing has regular but slender subsidiary studding (perhaps intended for rendering), a lateral stone chimney-breast with three stacks, and two S gables. Within it, high ceilings with fine plasterwork in both parlour (lit by a timber six-light ovolo-moulded transomed E window) and great chamber above: narrow-rib quatrefoils and Greek crosses enclosing floral motifs.* – To the E, a square timber-framed C17 DOVECOTE and small BARNS.

By the main road, ¼ m. SW, the brick GRAFTON MILL, c. 1800, small, three storeys, with detached cottage, and the three-bay HUMBLEBEE HALL, late C18.

LIBBERY, ¾ m. WSW, is an attractive hamlet of C16–C17 timber framing.

GRAFTON MANOR
Dodford with Grafton

Now a hotel. The manor belonged to the Staffords from 1372 until 1485, when Henry VII gave it to Sir Gilbert Talbot, whose descendants became Earls of Shrewsbury. John Talbot rebuilt Grafton in 1567–9 (with further work in 1576). Much of his brick house, two main ranges at right angles, survives, but only the W remained habitable after a severe fire in 1710. The rest lay in ruins, despite partial restoration in 1809, until rebuilt by *David Brandon*, 1861.

On the entrance side, the E front of the W range and almost all the N range are in *Brandon*'s mild plain Jacobethan, with parapet of linked circles. At the NE end, however, remain the late C16 porch and short adjoining cross-wing with crow-stepped gable, advanced and memorable work of their date. *p. 48* The porch, dated 1567, is ashlar-faced (mason *Stephen Merryman*), its round entrance flanked by coupled fluted Doric 59 columns with triglyph frieze. On the upper floor three fluted pilasters frame tall slender cross-windows, beneath a scrolled Vitruvian frieze and pediment with roundel. The cross-wing,

---

*Claire Gapper has shown that these mostly use the same moulds as at the Long Gallery at Aston Hall, Birmingham.

r., has diapered brickwork and fine five-light s window, with roll-moulded mullions and fluted band as transom; frieze and pediment (containing the Talbot dog) above. The inscription in the frieze reads: 'Plenti and grase bi in this plase. Whyle everi man is plesed in his degree, there is both pease and uniti. Salaman saith there is none accorde when everi man would bi a lorde'. The window lights an upper parlour, restored by *Brandon*, with quatrefoil plaster ceiling and stone fireplace with strapwork and large c16 plaster coat of arms. The N front of the cross-wing may be older: partly ashlar-faced, various blocked windows (and originally a straight gable). The N end of the w wing has Georgian windows. Most of its w side is again progressive c16 work, diapered brick, with a fine rhythm of crowstepped gabled dormers alternating, not quite regularly, with tall pairs of star-shaped stacks.

This w front overlooks important remains of an Elizabethan terraced GARDEN, laid out by *John Braye* from 1569. It contains a stone-lined FISH STEW, and descends, between stone-capped brick walls, to a lake, on the bank of which is a circular stone DOVECOTE, probably earlier, now in ruins.

The c15 sandstone CHAPEL, nave and chancel in one with w bellcote, linked to the house, sw, remained roofless from 1710 until restored by Charles, fifteenth Earl of Shrewsbury, in 1809. Its Perp windows probably represent what was there before; early c19 battlemented s porch. Inside, a nice tunnel-vaulted plaster ceiling with ribs and bosses, and contemporary Gothick FURNISHINGS, including BENCHES, wrought-iron COMMUNION RAILS, and pretty WEST GALLERY with balustrade and three ogee arches on thin quatrefoil columns. The STAINED GLASS, also mostly early c19, incorporates small grisaille figures of apostles and, in the nave N window, two c16 shields and c16–c17 Netherlandish roundels. – At right angles to the sw, a restored c16 brick BARN (now a house), forming a small courtyard with the chapel. This is entered though an arch with stepped gable, quite a Puginian effect.*

PRIEST'S HOUSE, E of Grafton Court. Brick, five bays, early c19.

GREAT COMBERTON

St MICHAEL. There is one mystery about this church. The three-stage w tower is Perp, embraced by narrow side attachments making it as wide as the nave; the base moulding of the tower goes round them. Inside they form shallow compartments (the N smaller because of the tower stair), open to the tower in shapeless pointed arches, on imposts that look Early Norman. The arch to the nave, higher and equally shapeless, also has such imposts. Is all this accident, implying only that the tower

---

* *Pugin* in fact made designs for furnishing the chapel in 1850, presumably unexecuted; cf. St Peter (R.C.), Bromsgrove.

was built into the nave, its inner buttressing never tidied up?
The solution does not entirely satisfy. The lower parts of the
nave walls are probably Norman, the upper parts C14, supporting a massive cradle roof. Straight-headed Dec windows
renewed by *G. G. Scott*, 1861–2. He also rebuilt the Dec chancel
'to its original design'; re-set C14 piscina, N priest's doorway
with good headstops. Tall chancel arch and N vestry by *John
Cotton*, 1885. S organ chamber 1890. – FONT. Perp, octagonal;
blank shields in quatrefoils. – PULPIT and STALLS by *Scott*, the
latter reusing Jacobean panels. – BENCHES. Mostly C16, with
absolutely plain, straight-topped ends. – STAINED GLASS.
Almost entirely by *Clayton & Bell*: chancel 1890s, nave
c. 1900–10. – Tower S by *Reginald Bell*, 1936. – Chancel NW,
semi-abstract, by *Nicola Hopwood*, 2000.
The VILLAGE retains many C16–C17 timber-framed cottages and
farms, mostly thatched. The best group, NW of the church, continues N along the main road.

GREAT MALVERN *see* MALVERN

GREAT WITLEY   7060

Witley Court and the attached parish church are unforgettable:
the latter, set at a slightly higher level, stately, self-assured,
unshowy, the house enormous and ruinated. The church,
planned by Thomas, first Lord Foley, built by his widow, was
consecrated in 1735. Witley Court owes its present appearance to
the first Earl of Dudley, for whom *S. W. Daukes*, in 1854–60, converted the house into a palace of regal grandeur; but also to a
devastating fire of 1937. It began as a Jacobean house, bought by
Thomas Foley in 1655; his grandson, created Lord Foley in 1711,
died in 1732. The church, being his conception in the first place,
should be looked at first.

ST MICHAEL was built, in 1733–5, in place of a medieval church
a little further W. Its architect is unknown, but may have been
James Gibbs (*see* below) whom Lord Foley would have known,
as a New Churches Commissioner. The building, originally
exposed brick with stone dressings, is more or less a plain rectangle, topped by a balustrade with urns. Very shallow chancel
with Venetian E window beneath a pediment. Other windows
round-arched, with keystones and pilasters with sunk panels,
mostly beneath moulded blank arches. Five side bays, the easternmost shallow transeptal projections marked by quoins; the
W (entrance) bay also has quoins. Three-bay W front, its projecting centre with pedimented Doric porch. Square tower
above, supporting an open, quite substantial, octagonal cupola
with gilded dome. In 1861 *S. W. Daukes* faced the whole building with cream-coloured Bath ashlar, matching his remodelling of Witley Court.

78   Enter and you are transported into a different climate, for
here is the most Italian ecclesiastical space in Georgian
England. This came about in the following improbable way.
Between 1713 and *c.* 1720, James Brydges, Duke of Chandos,
built for himself the palatial mansion of Canons near Stanmore
(Middlesex); its chapel, of 1716–21, was designed by *Gibbs*. The
second Lord Foley may have bought the chapel's ceiling paintings immediately after Chandos's death in 1744, for they did
not appear amongst the list of contents sold off in 1747 (prior
to the house's demolition), when he acquired the stained glass.
In 1747 *Gibbs* himself was appointed to embellish the interior
at Great Witley for these newly acquired items, designing new
decorative ceiling surrounds in Roman taste. The interior is all
white and gold. The walls have panels, their style just pre-
Rococo; the gently coved ceiling (suspended beneath the original flat one) has triangular penetrations above the windows.
Either side of the ORGAN CASE, also from the Canons chapel,
are round-arched openings to small box-like galleries. An interesting feature of the ceiling is that what seems to be stucco is
in fact papier mâché, a material recently introduced by Henry
Clay of Birmingham, but here the work of *Thomas Bromwich* of
London. The CEILING PAINTINGS, on canvas, are by the
Venetian *Antonio Bellucci*. Three main scenes: the Ascension in
an elongated central quatrefoil, with circular Nativity (w),
Deposition (E). In addition there are twenty medallions, ten
with grouped cherubs, ten with single cherubs holding Passion
symbols. Bellucci, born 1654, was nearly thirty years older than
Piazzetta, over twenty years older than Pellegrini, and five years
older even than Sebastiano Ricci; Pellegrini painted at Castle
Howard and Kimbolton in 1708–13, Ricci in various places in
England *c.* 1709–16. Bellucci arrived only in 1716 and, though
the oldest of the Italian invaders of England, his style already
approaches that of Piazzetta. The colouring is still sombre, not
as blissfully light as Pellegrini's and sometimes Ricci's, but his
figures already have Rococo proportions, and his compositions
boldly precipitous recession.
    The STAINED GLASS windows, the best early C18 set in
England, are by *Joshua Price*, one of the leading glaziers of the
time; most are signed and dated 1719, the two w windows are
of 1721. Painted in enamels, they are based on oil sketches by
Francesco Sleter, who painted at Canons (though at the time of
the sale they were said to be have been designed by *Sebastiano
Ricci*). Apart from Moses and the Golden Calf, NW, they
portray the life of Christ, purely pictorially, without any consideration of the natural prerequisites of stained glass. Lower
bands of foliage were added in 1747, to fit the larger Witley
openings. – The WOODWORK belongs to *Daukes*'s restoration,
1861. It complements the C18 work admirably, an interesting
attempt to marry the Italian Baroque with English church
traditions. Thus the PEWS (made by *Hindley & Son*) have
poppyheads, though of acanthus foliage, and the ambo-like
LECTERN has more than a touch of the Norman. But the

PULPIT, mostly carved by *William Forsyth*, is in Baroque style, with reused C18 wrought-iron stair railing.* – Also of 1861, the black-and-white marble FLOOR; superb FONT, carved by *James Forsyth*: of white marble, very chaste, with round bowl on three kneeling angels; and brass and iron ALTAR RAILS. – The REREDOS has early C18 carving, plus mosaic panels of 1913 by *Salviati & Co.*

MONUMENTS. Thomas Foley †1677, from the previous church; attributed to *Jasper Latham* (GF). Black and grey marbles, with Composite columns and curly broken pediment with heraldic cartouche in front of a segmental one, with urn. – Thomas, first Lord Foley †1732, by *J.M. Rysbrack*, 1735, probably not completed until some years later. One of the tallest funerary monuments in England, its grey marble base alone some 6 ft (1.8 metres) high. Dark grey sarcophagus and obelisk, the rest white. On the former, the reclining figure of the deceased, turning with a telling gesture towards the onlooker. By him his seated widow Mary (†1735) nursing a baby. Two older children stand either side, two more higher up flank a large urn, all set on a base draped with beautifully carved damask. The arrangement of these minor figures is not as successful as on the original drawing (at the Victoria and Albert Museum).

WITLEY COURT is now in the care of English Heritage. Stripped and abandoned after the fire of 1937, it remains a supremely splendid shell; consolidation began in 1972. What survives looks entirely mid-C19 at first, but much earlier work was kept when this rebuilding took place. The Russell family rebuilt their medieval house here *c.* 1610–20, in brick, to an H-plan with two long N wings; in their re-entrant angles were the two N towers that are still a prominent feature. The estate was sold in 1655 to Thomas Foley, son of a Stourbridge industrialist. His son, also Thomas, carried out much work on the house (called 'fair new-built' in 1695), as did Thomas III, first Lord Foley; this included the infilling of the central recession of the S front, *c.* 1725–30. Thomas IV, the second Lord, added Palladian-style service wings to the N (perhaps by *Henry Flitcroft*, who designed a keeper's lodge before 1762); nothing of this survives. Thomas VII employed *John Nash* from *c.* 1806 for further ambitious additions, including massive N and S porticos. In 1837 the estate was acquired for William, eleventh Lord Ward (created first Earl of Dudley in 1860), then still a minor but already one of the richest men in England, his wealth based on Black Country mining and industry. He at first let the house, but in 1854–60 it was transformed to its present dimensions by *Samuel Whitfield Daukes*, who had already rebuilt Abberley Hall nearby. Daukes cased the whole exterior in Bath stone (to match Nash's porticoes) and refashioned the interiors in lavish French Renaissance style (almost all destroyed in 1937).

*The Canons pulpit is at Fawley, Bucks.

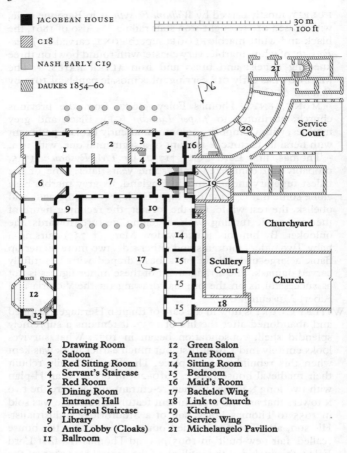

Great Witley, Witley Court.
Plan

Legend	
■	JACOBEAN HOUSE
▨	C18
▨	NASH EARLY C19
▨	DAUKES 1854–60

30 m
100 ft

1	Drawing Room	12	Green Salon
2	Saloon	13	Ante Room
3	Red Sitting Room	14	Sitting Room
4	Servant's Staircase	15	Bedroom
5	Red Room	16	Maid's Room
6	Dining Room	17	Bachelor Wing
7	Entrance Hall	18	Link to Church
8	Principal Staircase	19	Kitchen
9	Library	20	Service Wing
10	Ante Lobby (Cloaks)	21	Michelangelo Pavilion
11	Ballroom		

The N (ENTRANCE) FRONT retains the long wings and the two four-storey re-entrant towers of the Russells' early C17 house. *Nash*'s portico of *c.* 1806 projects between the towers, its six unfluted Ionic columns rising through two storeys and topped by a deep cornice with balustrade. But what one gasps at is not what was taken over by Lord Ward, but what *Daukes* made of it. His building is Early Victorian, handled with great assurance, not High Victorian. The consistent Italianate detailing is remarkable, with much foliage carving, quoins, rusticated basements, balustraded parapets, and occasional balconies. Daukes evidently intended to keep in harmony with the chapel. Hence, though the scale is colossal and the principal features grand, the rest is very restrained. The motif of the main windows, for example, round arches and surrounding blank arches, is inspired directly by the chapel.* The two-and-a-half-storey wings project six bays, again topped by balustrades. Their ends have two-storey canted bay windows (of early C18 origin, though no one would guess). The ruined upper floor of the W wing contained a picture gallery, part of the family's processional route to the church, via a three-bay NW link.

Since the house is ruined, it may be more rewarding to look at the INTERIORS before examining the two garden façades. Behind the N portico ran the long ENTRANCE HALL. Something of its C19 plaster panelling remains, made of *carton pierre* (an enhanced form of papier mâché) and also some of the iron supports for its all-round first-floor balcony. A surprise is one broadly mullioned early C17 cross-window, S, exposed by the fire. (Beneath the hall, the remains of a C13–C14 rib-vaulted undercroft.) To the W was an imperial staircase, replacing the early C17 staircases in the N towers (the shadow of one remains in the NW tower). At the E end of the hall was the DINING ROOM, an elongated octagon (behind a canted bay) originally created by Nash. The long E wing contained the lavish BALLROOM with, at its end, separated by a screen of which the riveted iron girder remains, the entrance to the GREEN SALON, another bay-windowed octagon, created by Daukes. To the S of the hall were sitting rooms either side of a central SALOON, with tripartite bowed end. The main DRAWING ROOM, E, has another girder (originally above Ionic columns), marking the position of the exterior wall of the early C17 house.

Having examined this internal skeleton, we can now look at the E FRONT, a plain façade of five bays plus two outer canted bay windows, with a rather unsatisfactory additional N bay, of C18 origin. The S FRONT however, raised above flights of steps, is splendid, with the second giant portico by *Nash* as its centre; this, probably later than the N portico, has eight giant unfluted Ionic columns (plus two at the sides). The refaced flat C18 bow of the saloon appears centrally within it, and behind the centre rises higher than the plainer three bays either side, which repeat the detailing of the N front wings; top balustrade throughout. W of the S façade is a boldly curved seven-bay wing, built by Daukes to mask the service courtyard; his use here, for the ground-floor servants' quarters, of the oblong openings previously only seen at attic level, produces a happy staccato effect. Moreover, the wing ends in a splendid pavilion whose giant paired pilasters and Corinthian columns set into the ground-floor openings derive from Michelangelo (e.g. the Capitoline Museum) or Bernini; fine tessellated floor and niches within. Beyond lies the CONSERVATORY, an Italian villa-like structure of thirteen (5+3+5) by five bays, with round

108

---

* This might explain *The Builder*'s comment, when the designs were exhibited at the Royal Academy in 1855, that 'the details are a little commonplace'.

arches on thin columns, Quattrocento rather than C16–C17 Italian; now of course without its great glass roof. To the w of the service yard, the STABLE COURT has an open cupola like that on the church, and beyond this an outer court with pedimented coachhouses.

The TERRACES and GARDENS of 1854–60 were laid out by *W.A. Nesfield*; their formality complements Daukes's Italianate architecture. At the base of the steps below the s front are four plinths, originally carrying sculptures of lions. The gardens slope down to *Nesfield*'s remarkable PERSEUS and ANDROMEDA FOUNTAIN, carved in Portland stone in 1858–60 by *James Forsyth* (with his brother *William*). It displays all the Baroque abandon which Daukes kept away from. Perseus is mounted on a prancing horse, 26 ft (8 metres) high, thrusting his lance into the sea monster's mouth (from which the main jet of the fountain issues). Big icicled base of shells alternating with scaly dolphins and, either side in the big quatrefoil pool, renewed cupids riding dolphins. Beyond, a cross-terrace is terminated by two elaborate stone pavilions with attached columns and Hindu-looking domed roofs. The ground then rises again to a semicircular parterre, bordered by balustrades and plinths, with formerly magnificent iron gates of 1862 at the summit. In front of the E façade was a smaller formal garden focussed on the FLORA FOUNTAIN, again mostly by *James Forsyth*. Her small, now fragmentary figure stands on a plinth of bulrushes, shells and intertwined dolphins; surrounding it, four fine large tritons, who blew jets of water from their conch-shells, the famous Bernini motif. Balustrading, renewed 1998–9, continues round the N front of the house (and also the adjoining churchyard).

To the N of the house much survives of the mid-C18 landscaping, perhaps modified in the early C19 by *Humphry Repton* for Thomas Foley VII, as well as by *Nesfield*. The main element is FRONT POOL, created, by a massive dam, to become the largest of a chain of lakes along the valley of the Shrawley Brook. It has two boathouses, a renewed rustic one of *c.* 1900, SW, and a tunnel-like opening on the N bank. The area to the E has been reclaimed as a woodland garden by English Heritage. The late C18 WILDERNESS GARDEN, closer to the A443, has also been re-created, to the designs of *Colvin & Moggridge*, 2003.

To the w of the church is a long Italianate range of housing for the gardeners. The RED HOUSE, ½ m. WNW, originally the kennels by *G.S. Repton*, *c.* 1828, consists of four brick octagons grouped round a larger fifth; much altered in the C20. The WORCESTER and STOURPORT LODGES, by *Henry Rowe & Son*, 1884, are in a more fulsome Italianate style, each to a T-plan, with two Ionic quadrant porches and channelled rustication.

HILLHAMPTON HOUSE, ½ m. NE. Early C17 E-plan, of sandstone ashlar, the w front remodelled with sashed windows in the C18–early C19. Central porch of two-and-a-half storeys with hipped roof; round-arched doorway with moulded imposts. Moulded string courses continue onto the less altered N and S sides. The latter has big buttresses, mullioned-and-transomed windows, and chimneystack with tripled brick shafts. On the first floor, a good plaster ceiling with geometrical patterns. Many C19–C20 additions.

The main nucleus of the parish, about 1 m. WNW of Witley Court, begins with the replacement church of ST MICHAEL, built as a mortuary chapel in 1882 by *J.P. St Aubyn* (now a scout hall). Brick, nave and apsed chancel in one, early Dec-style. Extended W, reusing the large W window and bellcote, in 1895 by *William Cooke*, the Earl's clerk of works; SW vestry added 1897. Sturdy arch-braced roofs.

The OLD RECTORY, ¼ m. N at Redmarley, is early C19, three storeys and 2+1+2 bays, with central pediment above a tripartite window; other first-floor windows also stone-framed. Central doorway with attached Doric columns flanked by later C19 canted bays. Facing the lake in the grounds is ALLONBY HOUSE, built 1965, with pediment on four Doric columns.

The former SCHOOL, W of the church, was built in 1844 for Queen Adelaide, who rented Witley Court in 1843–6. Pretty bargeboarded gables for the school and attached house, each with its own gabled porch; square hoodmoulds, fish-scale roofs, spiral-fluted chimneys. The present SCHOOL by *W.H. Birch* of Worcester, 1895, with half-timbered upper parts and open bellcote, stands back opposite.

The imposing HUNDRED HOUSE HOTEL, ½ m. further NW at the Stourport Road junction, was built for Lord Foley *c.* 1790; four bays and two-and-a-half storeys, with segment-headed windows and hipped roof. Big two-storey tripartite bow windows flank the Doric porch. Beyond it, two pairs of pretty ESTATE COTTAGES of *c.* 1840–50, red and blue brick, with latticed windows and pierced bargeboards.

Several good C17–C18 outlying farmhouses, particularly on the slopes of Walsgrove and Woodbury Hills, at the W end of the parish. The most interesting is HOME FARM, 1⅛ m. W, on a moated site: a largely intact timber-framed manor house of *c.* 1500, now almost entirely cased in C17–C18 brick. Hall range with three-bay solar cross-wing, NW; its upper chamber was open to the roof, with knee-braced main trusses, tie-beams with continuous mouldings, and shallow arch-braced intermediates providing footings for pairs of wind-braces. – The mostly C18 brick outbuildings, SW, include a cruck-framed BARN.

WITLEY MANOR, 1 m. WSW, seems to be an L-plan conglomeration of early C17 timber-framed cottages. – On the Martley road, ¾ m. S, an early C19 TOLL HOUSE, painted brick, with the usual three-sided front; lancets with Y-tracery.

On WOODBURY HILL is an IRON AGE hill-fort; univallate, roughly kidney-shaped in plan following the crest of the hill, and enclosing some 26 acres. The best-preserved portion of the rampart is on the NW. Entrance gaps occur on the NW and NE, the latter inturned.

GRIMLEY

ST BARTHOLOMEW. Norman nave with early C13 chancel, altered in the C14–C15; all much obscured by extensive C19 restoration. Of the Norman nave the S wall survives, with one pilaster buttress stump and narrow blocked window above; three inserted Dec windows. The Norman S doorway has one order of shafts with (renewed) trumpet-scallop capitals and arch with heavy roll moulding, set in the usual piece of projecting wall. A Neo-Norman porch all but hides this, linked to an external stone staircase to the gallery with sloping arcade of intersecting Norman arches, both added by *Harvey Eginton*, 1845–6. He also rebuilt the four-stage W tower in Perp style, its true date revealed by the bell-openings and carved heads and gargoyles. The chancel was mostly rebuilt by *Ewan Christian*, 1863–4, though the small side lancets no doubt repeat what was there; E wall C15, with Perp three-light window. Finally, in 1885–6, *Henry Rowe & Son* restored the nave and added the large N aisle (and NE vestry). The Dec-style N windows were no doubt re-set from the nave N wall, already been rebuilt by Christian. Three-bay N arcade, with high, wide, hollow-chamfered arches, on round piers with moulded capitals.

FONT. Plain, octagonal, C14–C15. – Other FITTINGS by *Christian* (chancel) or by *Rowe & Son* (nave and aisle); they rebuilt Eginton's WEST GALLERY, on elaborate pierced brackets, and added the carved stone and marble PULPIT. – Rather pale ROYAL ARMS of George III, dated 1817. – STAINED GLASS. Good E window by *Clayton & Bell*, 1864. – The Annunciation in the nave S window and the St John and God the Father, N aisle N, are basically C15, extensively restored in the C19. – MONUMENTS. Martha Farmer †1781, by *Stephens & Bott*; urn with palm frond. – Margaret Price †1800, by *W. Stephens*; putto by a draped urn. – Mary Bourne †1812, by *J. Stephens*; paired urns with weeping willow. – Large pedimented marble tablet of the 1830s to the Griffiths family of Thorngrove. – The HATCHMENTS above the gallery are also to Richard Griffiths †1830 and his widow Elizabeth †1836.

Attractive CHURCHYARD with remains of a C15–C16 CROSS, and early C19 TOMBS, the largest, a Neo-Grecian chest, again to Richard Griffiths.

Little else to note in the VILLAGE, apart from the SCHOOL of 1834 (a brick cottage by the church gate), and its replacement opposite, designed by the donor *Samuel Baker* in 1856, with many C20 additions. The best house, THE DALLOWS, S end, is mid-C18 brick, with a timber-framed rear wing.

The OLD VICARAGE, ½ m. WSW, by *Henry Rowe*, 1879, is brick, gabled, with wide segment-headed windows with minimal stone enrichment.

THORNGROVE, on higher ground 1 m. WSW. A curious design, probably the result of remodelling for Richard Griffiths, *c.* 1815–20, round a late C18 core. Ashlar-faced, the E front of two storeys and 3+1+2 bays. The single bay projects with an underdeveloped pediment and porch with paired Ionic columns. The giant angle pilasters and parapet are also oddly thin. Three further bays to the N, with elongated ground-floor windows, were probably added c. 1840. The S return has two not quite matching canted bay windows, plus a rounded bow. This has on the ground floor an ogee-headed opening flanked by pointed ones, all with early to mid-C19 stained glass. Entrance hall, with Ionic columns (S), leading to a spacious, top-lit, open-well stair with cast-iron balustrade, probably also c. 1840. The ballroom, in the N extension, has a fine painted and stuccoed ceiling of about the same date. The rich ceiling decoration of the drawing room, behind the middle canted bay, seems even later, together with its elaborate walnut chimney-piece with paired Corinthian columns. Napoleon's brother, Lucien Bonaparte, Prince of Canino, lived here from 1811 to 1814, as did, later in the C19, the African explorer, Sir Samuel White Baker (†1893).

Round the corner, N, a long brick SERVICE RANGE, two-storeyed, and formerly containing stables and coach and cider houses. It is articulated by an irregular pattern of blind pointed openings, and two pediments containing keyed oculi.

Fine PARK, with long curving drive from the Worcester road, crossing the serpentine lake by a three-arched stone BRIDGE. This has a pretty projecting cast-iron parapet dated 'RG 1819'; at the centre of each side, a big wheel like a ship's helm, and lamp-holders. – Former LODGE of c. 1840–50, red and blue brick with bargeboards.

Ditches in the grounds belonging to a ROMAN FORT have been partly excavated.

The parish extends some distance further W, its main nucleus at SINTON GREEN, 1¼ m. W of the church. SINTON COURT, E end, is dated 1838. Brick with stone dressings, in accomplished Tudor Gothic; symmetrical S front with three gables, projecting centre with porch, canted corners, and oriel. *Eginton* seems the most likely architect, especially considering the refined detailing of the staircase; excellently preserved drawing room to its W. Later C19 estate cottages nearby.

Of outlying farms the most attractive is OLD HILL, on a prominent site 1⅜ m. WNW. Late C16, mostly square-panelled framing, to a hall and cross-wings plan (best seen from the S). The N side has three gables, the added jettied central one with a lateral stone chimney with a pair of diagonal brick stacks. Similar stack, W side.

GUARLFORD

8040

ST MARY. 1843–4 by *Thomas Bellamy* of London. Of Malvern rubble, laid crazy-paving fashion, with ashlar dressings. The plan, nave with W porch and short chancel, is still of the Commissioners' type, but the stonework and details such as the very tall lancets and stepped buttresses point forward to a bolder age. Three graduated E lancets. W wall, originally windowless, partly rebuilt, with a thinner triplet, in 1906. S vestry enlarged by *Preedy*, 1877. Good interior with high arch-braced roof. – Original fittings include the FONT, with octofoil bowl on shafted stem, and stone ALTAR. – Carved oak PULPIT. 1906. – STAINED GLASS. Varied Victorian. Mid-C19 the nave NE, clearly *Wailes*, and the next W, both N and S, by *George Rogers*. – The second S (to a 'beloved child' †1849) is by *Lavers & Barraud*, 1868. – Most others by *Alexander Gibbs & Co.*: two, almost opposite in the nave, of 1884; the E of 1892. – W window *c.* 1906, no doubt *Burlison & Grylls*.

OLD RECTORY, a little SW, also *c.* 1844, still Georgian classical: three bays with Doric porch.

RHYDD COURT, 1½ m. E. Of *c.* 1800, enlarged by *Richard Ingleman c.* 1820, much rebuilt for Sir E.A.H. Lechmere by *David Brandon*, 1863–4. Partially destroyed by fire in 1922; adapted as a County Council special school in 1950–1. Long rambling fronts, brick with stone trim, in indeterminate Jacobethan classical: porte cochère, NE; large canted bay windows, S. The large timbered gables are post-1922. Full-height early C19 bow on the E return, overlooking the Severn. The rebuilt staircase in the large top-lit entrance hall retains a Late Georgian feel. In the central reception room, E, C17 panelling and fine wooden overmantel with paired arched panels and columns, no doubt from Severn End (p. 354).

Early C19 STABLES to the W. – Attached to their rear, the CHAPEL of 1864 by *C.F. Hansom*, completed during his illness (1865–6) by *Norman Shaw*. Of snecked sandstone; nave with timber SW porch, and apsed sanctuary, in conventional Dec style, but the pitched roof has gone and the interior is gutted. Some carving by *Earp* remains as well as *Shaw*'s mosaic REREDOS. – STAINED GLASS. Six good windows by *Clayton & Bell*, *c.* 1865–70.

Much of the early C19 PARK survives. – Gabled stone LODGE, *c.* 1864.

HADLEY *see* OMBERSLEY

HADZOR

HADZOR HALL (formerly Hadzor House) stands in a fine landscaped park. Its core is of 1779, by *John Yenn* for Richard Amphlett, but the present stuccoed appearance is mostly what *Matthew Habershon* made of it from 1827, for the banker J.H. Galton. The entrance front, W, seven bays and two-and-a-half storeys, with slightly projecting centre with three-bay pediment, is basically Yenn's; Habershon added the portico of four Greek Doric columns, and perhaps the moulded window cornices. The extra N bay is a remnant of *P.C. Hardwick*'s service range, 1859. Five-bay garden front, S, with higher projecting three-bay centre with giant upper Ionic pilasters. Habershon was apparently superseded *c.* 1835 by *Alexander Roos*.* He probably extended the S range, single-storey with end bow, and added a high-level colonnade at the rear of the W block, and tall square tower with round-arched openings and small dome with urns. Roos was certainly responsible for the interior: inner hall with open-well staircase with ornate cast-iron balustrade (and Grecian plaster plaque, high up); drawing room, SW, with elaborate Raphaelesque grotesque ceiling, designed 1835; and fine plaster ceilings in the library and saloon, S range, restored 2005–6.

In front of the house, big square GATEPIERS, with attached classical archway to the garden, S, separated from the house by a (renewed) balustraded terrace. This approach and the formal Italianate layout of the GARDENS are again by *Roos.* Their main surviving feature is the Potsdam-like DELL POOL SHRINE; cast-iron frame (with timber infill) including pediment and fluted corner columns; lattice-glazed round-arched side openings, rear apse. Roos's similar conservatory has been demolished, though parts of its ironwork survive at the time of writing.

ST JOHN THE BAPTIST (closed 1978) stands behind Hadzor Hall, E. Nave and chancel are basically Dec, probably restored by *Matthew Habershon*, 1835, when he added the tight little oblong W tower: oddly detailed, with battlemented corner turrets. C14 work includes most of the masonry (especially the lower courses, see the blocked lowside window, chancel SW), and much of the varied Dec tracery and pretty eaves frieze of square fleurons, interrupted by the foliated finials of the ogee hoodmoulds. Interior with big headstops, and nice cusped roofs by *R.C. Hussey*, 1846–7. *Habershon's* high WEST GALLERY survives. – STAINED GLASS. E window 1863, probably by *Holland & Son* of Warwick. – The rest by *Hardman*: two chancel S 1860, chancel N 1902, nave S 1896 and 1900.[†] – MONUMENTS. Against the nave N wall, a cusped tomb recess beneath an enormous crocketed gable with blind Dec tracery and niches; probably essentially C14. Below, a pink marble tomb (perhaps by *G.E. Street*) to John Howard Galton †1862, in Rome. – Several grey marble tablets to Amphletts, those to William †1768, by *Richard Squire*, and his mother Sara †1729, opposite, almost identical.

Beyond the church, NE, are *Roos's* STABLES, 1842–3: brick, Italianate, with distinctive blind-arcaded tower; absorbed, together with his CHIMNEY HOUSE, NW, into overweening enabling development of 2004.

ST RICHARD DE WYCHE AND ST HUBERT (R.C.), Hadzor Lane. By *C.A. Buckler*, 1878, for T.H. Galton. Small, brick,

---

* Italian-born, but a pupil of Schinkel in Berlin; *see* Richard Garnier, 'Alexander Roos *c.* 1810–81', in the *Georgian Group Journal* 15, 2005/6.
[†] Their three nave N windows of 1868 incorporated an Annunciation and Visitation, *c.* 1340, now at the Ely Stained Glass Museum.

with grouped lancets; nave and chancel in one, W bellcote, S porch. Simple interior with W gallery. – STAINED GLASS. E window, 1950s. – Unusually pictorial nave S, Christ preaching, probably Glasgow School work, *c.* 1900. – Plain gabled brick PRESBYTERY.

COURT FARM, in Hadzor Lane a little S, is also by *Habershon*, *c.* 1830. Brick, Tudor-style, with windows with hoodmoulds and end pilaster-buttresses; gabled porch with the Galton arms. – To its N, a more or less contemporary brick DOVECOTE, tall and four-square, with lancets flanked by blind cross-loops; pyramid roof with pretty timber louvre with bargeboarded gables.

Further SE, a matching COTTAGE, then late C16 timber-framed houses with brick infill, probably also altered by *Habershon*. THREE WELLS, L-plan, with C19 chimneys, has, at the end of its garden, a charming little WASHHOUSE with latticed windows and octofoil chimney. THE OLD MANOR, four bays with lobby-entry, has a large chimney, N end, with row of four octagonal shafts.

HAGLEY

9080

ST JOHN BAPTIST. The typical estate church, in a parkland setting close to the Hall, away from the (present) village; generous in dimensions, smooth in architecture. Essentially by *G.E. Street*, who could be so much more forceful and blunt (as at St John, Stourbridge), but of medieval origin. The S aisle retains C13–C14 fabric: the masonry of its E end, the E window tracery (renewed 1983), piscina, and E part of the S arcade with its octagonal piers. The N aisle, with matching arcade and E window (reset, W end, by Street), had already been added in 1827–8 by *Rickman & Hutchinson*. In 1856–8 *Street* rebuilt the chancel,[*] with N vestry, and remodelled nave and aisles, adding an extra W bay and S porch. His fine W tower with broach spire, all of redder sandstone, is of 1864–5. Details throughout are Middle Pointed, late C13–early C14. – FURNISHINGS mostly by *Street*: octagonal panelled FONT, round stone and marble PULPIT, low PEWS, typical STALLS with spiky heads, later stone and alabaster REREDOS. – Fine wrought-iron SCREEN by *Sir T.G. Jackson*, 1917. – Early C18 FONT, under the tower; oval gadrooned bowl, square stem with the Lyttelton arms. – S aisle LADY CHAPEL furnished by *Guy Pemberton*, 1924. – Reset in its E wall, a small CARVING of a lion, *c.* 1150, perhaps from a tympanum; cf. the seven re-set Norman corbels, including beakheads, beneath the E eaves of the porch.

Good STAINED GLASS, the two best by *Henry Holiday*: central S aisle, influenced by Morris & Co., executed by *James Powell & Sons*, 1876; S aisle E, much more monumental but also a little showier, made by *Lowndes & Drury*, 1907–8. – By

[*] Previously rebuilt by *Sanderson Miller*, 1754–6.

G.J. Baguley, the s aisle sw window, 1876. – By *Kempe* (or his firm): s aisle se 1899, chancel e 1900, n aisle central 1897, and n aisle w 1918. – By *C.C. Powell*, still in Kempe style, the n aisle nw, *c.* 1917. – By *Clayton & Bell*, 1879, the chancel sw and no doubt tower w window. – By *Hardman*, n aisle ne 1866 and s aisle w 1984.

MONUMENTS. In the n aisle, a c13 coffin lid with specially rich foliated cross, its foot thrust into a dragon's mouth; set in a gabled and arched recess, only very partially medieval. – 'Luciae' it says on the urn to the wife of the first Lord Lyttelton, †1747, below a delicate relief of a reclining woman; next to it sits a sturdy putto with inversed torch. Carving by *Roubiliac*, the design by *Charles Frederick*. Inscription tablet opposite, tower n wall.* – Sybella Lady Lyttelton †1900; painted terracotta plaque probably by *Lionel Cust*, 1906.

In the CHURCHYARD, s of the chancel, chest tomb to Meriel Lyttelton †1630, with attached columns and round-arched panels. – Good LYCHGATE by *Street*, 1876.

HAGLEY HALL

The Lytteltons (from Frankley, p. 319) acquired the estate in 1564; their timber-framed house (demolished 1758) stood nw of the church. George, first Lord Lyttelton, who began the park and garden ornaments in the 1740s (*see* below), inherited in 1751 and immediately consulted the gentleman architect *Sanderson Miller* about a new house (or perhaps remodelling the existing one); this was no doubt intended to be Rococo Gothic, a style Miller pioneered. Lady Lyttelton, apparently unhappy with a Gothic house, prevailed on her friend Thomas Barrett Lennard (of Belhus, Essex) to obtain designs from *John Chute* (of The Vyne, Hants.) in 1752. His designs, in Roman p. 336 Renaissance style, were eventually sent to Miller, who was asked to 'transfer some of the beauties of them into your plan' and produce a classical house. The present Hagley Hall was thus built by *Miller*, 1754–60, assisted by *Thomas Prowse* of Axbridge and of Wicken (Northants.). The latter probably suggested employing the London architect *John Sanderson* as professional draughtsman; Sanderson was perhaps also responsible for much of the interior decoration. *James Lovell* probably executed most of the chimneypieces, *Robert Bromfield*. *Francesco Vassalli*, perhaps assisted by his brother *Giovanni*, may have undertaken much of the plasterwork; *Robert Moore* of Warwick seems also to have been involved.

Miller's house, decidedly in the Anglo-Palladian tradition, was probably immediately inspired by Croome Court, by Lancelot Brown, 1751–2 (though Miller seems to have been involved there as well, p. 244); the ultimate source for both was no doubt Houghton Hall in Norfolk, of the 1720s. It is of the type with four projecting corner pavilions, square eminences 88

---

* Other monuments, including one by *Soane*, were destroyed in 1858.

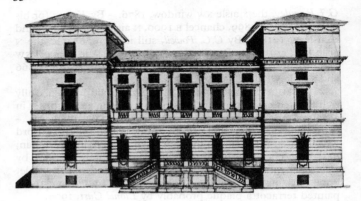

Hagley Hall, unrealised design by John Chute.
Elevation

with low pyramid roofs, a type initiated by Inigo Jones at Wilton. Although Hagley follows this established early C18 formula, its plan no longer comprises a ceremonial centre with private apartments in both wings. It is rather an early example of a plan based on two overlapping circuits: a private section in one half (here the W), grouped round one staircase, a public section in the other, round a second staircase. The plan here was adaptable enough, because of its central hall and relatively modest saloon, to be used just by the family when on their own.

88   EXTERIOR. The house, of pinkish brown sandstone, sits up neatly on its spacious lawn. Entrance front, SW, of eleven bays, with large open staircase in two arms leading to the main doorway. Below the landing in front of the doorway, a deep recess leading to the basement (service) entrance. The whole of the basement is of even ashlar rustication. *Piano nobile* above with windows with blind balustrades, then a half-storey with square windows; the corner pavilions have an additional storey, and windows emphasized with pediments or ears. Moulded cornice with balustraded parapet. The three-bay centre projects beneath a pediment, its doorway also with pediment, on unfluted Ionic columns. To NW and SE there are five bays, to the NE (facing the church) again eleven. Here also a three-bay pediment, but, instead of the pedimented doorway, a pedimented window. On the lawn in front, a spirally fluted urn in memory of William Shenstone (cf. p. 339).

The INTERIOR, seriously damaged by fire late in 1925, was meticulously restored by Messrs *Howard*, 1926–7.* The entrance hall or WHITE HALL has niches with statues and very

---

* The decoration of Saloon, Library, and Crimson Drawing Room was almost completely destroyed; other state rooms were less affected.

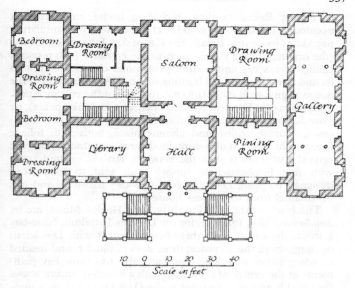

Hagley Hall.
Plan of principal storey as built

pretty Rococo plasterwork. Chimneypiece by *James Lovell* with Herculean atlantes, lintel with lion and knotted clubs, and large urns. Above, a fine rustic relief of Pan presenting a fleece to Diana, based on a lost painting by Carlo Maratta; signed by the stuccadore *Francesco Vassalli*. Opposite, a large medallion of Cybele in a frame of fruit and flowers, flanked by busts of Rubens and Van Dyck (by *Rysbrack*, 1746). In the back wall, a lower tunnel-vaulted recess receives cross-corridors from either side. The vault is coffered, with, at the rear, an elaborate double shell cartouche. The corridors lead to top-lit w (private) and E (public) STAIRCASES, the E largely original, the W mostly reconstructed after the fire. Behind the entrance hall is the Dining Room (formerly SALOON and start of the public 89 circuit) with splendid Rococo ceiling of cherubs in clouds (restored from photographs); garlands and trophies on the walls. The trophies represent Music, Gardening, Drama, Literature, Painting, and Archery. Beautiful stucco frames to the mirrors between the windows. Chimneypiece of Siena and white marbles, with Ionic columns. The DRAWING ROOM, E, was designed to display the splendid Soho tapestries (of 1725), acquired 1752. Again fine Rococo decoration, the ceiling with central painted oval of Flora and corner medallions of the Seasons, by the painter and architect *James Stuart*. More intimate chimneypiece, again Siena and white marbles. The GALLERY runs all along the SE side. Screens with fluted Corinthian columns mark off both ends (beneath the corner pavilions); Rococo ceiling, including ho-ho birds, turning decidedly *chinois*; cf. the wooden chimneypiece with miniature pagoda as its centre. Finally the CRIMSON DRAWING ROOM (the original dining room), next to the entrance hall; restored ceiling with vines and cornucopiae, stone chimneypiece with frontal termini and small hunting scene. The private half of the house begins with the LIBRARY, to the l. of the entrance hall. Small busts (of Dryden, Milton, Spenser and Shakespeare), by *Peter Scheemakers*, are set in the open pediments of the bookcases; simpler ceiling and chimneypiece, both with foliage friezes. This section also contained three apartments, but the central NW room is now the BARREL ROOM, created 1926, with fine Jacobean-style tunnel vault said to have been designed by *John, Lord Lyttelton*; C16–C17 panelling and oak overmantel from the former house.

The brick STABLES a little NW, now Hagley Mews, are by *Sanderson Miller*, 1749–51, for Sir Thomas Lyttelton. Nine-bay E front, the centre with three-bay pediment with Diocletian opening above the entrance; three bays of blind round-headed arcading either side. The courtyard also has three-bay pediments at the centre of each side, with a wooden lantern above the coachhouse, w. – Further N, the OLD DAIRY (now a summerhouse), of 1752, a small pedimented ashlar temple, Tuscan tetrastyle, then the former WALLED GARDEN; at the centre of its N side, a three-bay pedimented brick ORANGERY (now a house). – W LODGE and GATEPIERS, Neo-Georgian brick, by *J. Homery Folkes*, 1953–4.

THE PARK. Hagley, one of the most famous C18 gardens, was praised at an early date by James Thomson (*The Seasons*, 1744); and Horace Walpole was particularly enthusiastic after his visit in 1753. Park and gardens were exceptionally rich in garden ornaments. A number survive, though mostly in poor condition. The only ones still clearly visible from the Hall are the Obelisk (*see* below), and the PRINCE OF WALES'S COLUMN, on a hillside NE of the church; some 50 ft (15 metres) high, with free Composite capital, supporting a statue of Prince Frederick (to whom George Lyttelton was secretary) in Roman garb. Perhaps by *Henry Keene* (assisting Miller in 1749).

The most intriguing park building, the TEMPLE of THESEUS, nearly ½ m. NNE, high above the Birmingham Road, commands splendid views w, along the valley which Lord Lyttelton called his 'Vale of Tempe'. It is by *James Stuart*, 'Athenian Stuart', who, while in Rome with Nicholas Revett in 1748, planned to visit Athens to record its ancient buildings. The two indeed set off, with support from Charles Watson-Wentworth, later second Marquis of Rockingham, in 1751, returning in 1755. The first volume of their *Antiquities of Athens* (by then supported by the Society of Dilettanti) came out only in 1762 and did not contain the so-called Theseion. But they had measured it and as early as 1758–9 Stuart designed a miniature copy for Hagley (little more than the portico in fact), not completed until 1761–2; cf. the Doric Temple,

Shugborough, Staffs, probably also by *Stuart*.* The temple, originally coloured white, has six fluted Doric columns with metope frieze and pediment, but is sadly lacking in depth; the proportions of the columns are Vitruvian rather than Greek. However, even if the majesty of the order does not lend itself entirely to the smallness of the copy and the picturesque setting, it is a remarkably early example of a baseless Greek Doric order on the Athenian model. Now again in poor condition, with collapsed ceiling. – The uncommonly slender OBELISK, of *c.* 1760, stands further N on the slopes of Wychbury Hill (*see* below), a prominent landmark despite losing its tip.

The largest park ornament, the CASTLE, ⅝ m. E, is oblong in plan with four corner turrets. Only one, NE, rises to full height, with battlements, pseudo-machicolations, and matching higher stair-turret; top-floor room with domed ceiling with Gothick decoration. To its W, a stretch of wall complete with three Y-traceried windows and central doorway with three heraldic shields. The rest was left deliberately ruinous, a typical *Sanderson Mille*r piece, built as early as 1747–8; he is said to have reused stone from Halesowen Abbey. Horace Walpole certainly saw in it 'the true rust of the Barons' Wars'. – At the head of the valley ¼ m. N of the tower, the contemporary ROTUNDA by *John Pitt* of Encombe (Dorset), 1748–9, with eight Ionic columns, but its stone dome now almost entirely gone. Its planning is mentioned in a letter of 1747 by William Shenstone, who built similar garden attractions at The Leasowes near Halesowen. Further W in the valley, back towards the Hall, were ponds with a cascade and Palladian Bridge (by *Thomas Pitt, first Lord Camelford, c.* 1763). Other former garden furnishings included a hermitage, grotto, and statue of Venus.

OTHER HAGLEY BUILDINGS

The VILLAGE retains only one or two late C18 houses. LYTTELTON PLACE, off Park Road further W, is a neat Bromsgrove RDC group of eight semi-detached pairs, 1919–20; T-plan layout, with roughcast and gabled brick houses, all nicely detailed.

More remains on the N side of Birmingham Road, beginning (W end) with ROCKINGHAM HALL, a C17 house reconstructed by *Miller*, 1751, for Admiral Tom Smith, Lord Lyttelton's illegitimate half-brother; altered in the C19, now flats. White-rendered, with gables flanking Miller's square castellated tower, one l., three r.; central Gothick porch. Two rooms have Jacobean ceilings. Former mid-C18 STABLES, W, six bays, with two-bay pediment. Then a few early C19 houses, including LYTTELTON TERRACE, mostly linked pairs.

At the top of the hill, s side, near a pretty stone LODGE of *c.* 1840, is the OLD RECTORY, by *Edward Smith* of Oldswin-

* He may have designed an earlier Doric portico at The Grove, near Watford, Herts.; *see Georgian Group Journal 14,* 2004.

ford, 1849. Tudor Gothic, brick with some diapering; a two-storey canted bay faces s towards the Clent Hills.

WASSELL GROVE, 1⅓ m. NE, a large classical villa by *Charles Edge*, 1831, was demolished in the 1950s; a roughcast LODGE survives, very similar to that near the Old Rectory. WASSELL GROVE FARM must also be of *c.* 1831; upright brick, three bays and storeys, with doorway and flanking windows in arched recesses. Excellent cast-iron railings.

WYCHBURY HILL CAMP, ⅔ m. N. An Iron Age fort, strategically sited at 704 ft (214.5 metres), commanding a fine view of the Stour valley; roughly heart-shaped in plan, univallate except on the s, where a more gentle approach necessitated the construction of a second bank and ditch. SW and SE entrances. Trial excavation in the C19 produced a bronze terret (from a chariot).

WEST HAGLEY

West Hagley developed after the arrival of the Oxford, Worcester & Wolverhampton Railway, 1852. The present STATION, a GWR rebuilding of 1884, has a standard brick platform building and roofed U-plan FOOTBRIDGE, iron and timber on cast-iron lotus columns, now a rare survival.

ST SAVIOUR. By *Tom Grazebrook* of Stourbridge, 1907–8; uninspired Perp, of rock-faced Hasbury sandstone. Nave, chancel and s vestry, with bellcote; a hall by *J. Homery Folkes*, 1971–2, stands on the site of the unbuilt N aisle. – Fittings include a ROOD BEAM (1911), Perp-style PULPIT and STALLS (1924), angel LECTERN (by *Pancheri & Son*, 1959), and deep W GALLERY (by *David Mills*, 1979–80). – STAINED GLASS. Chancel SE window by *Powell & Sons*, 1920. – E, W, and two chancel N all by *F. W. Skeat*, 1961–5.

HAGLEY PRIMARY SCHOOL, Park Road. A standard job of 1939, with striking addition by *Associated Architects*, 2004. Mostly red brick, beneath a pitched butterfly roof; two-storey verandas front the twelve glazed classrooms, W and S; deep cutaway, supported on a timber column, at the 'prow'. Angled roof-light stacks provide natural ventilation.

The best houses are in BRAKE LANE, W of the railway, beyond a PUMPING STATION of 1958, and a large complex of C20 high schools. HAYBRIDGE HIGH SCHOOL has sleek white-rendered additions by *Nicholas Hare Architects*, 2005–7. THE BRAKE, corner of Sweetpool Lane, a small group of houses round a green, by *John F. Phillips & Associates*, 1965, is nicely varied; split-level roofs with clerestory bands. Further W, SOUTH BANK (formerly New Place), large cemented-brick classical by *A. T. Butler* of Dudley, *c.* 1920; wide balustraded Tuscan porch flanked by single-storey bow windows. Matching LODGE. Some distance N, reached by the lane opposite The Brake, is THE BIRCHES, a large villa of *c.* 1839 for the Stourbridge banker, Thomas Bate; stuccoed, outer pedimental gables on plain paired pilasters, slightly recessed centre, doorway with fluted Doric columns *in antis*.

HALLOW

8050

ST PHILIP AND ST JAMES. 1867–9 by *W.J. Hopkins*, his most important church, large and townish. Of red Holt sandstone with Bath dressings, with deep S porch and three-stage W tower (completed 1879), crowned in 1900 by a commanding broach spire with corner pinnacles and lucarnes. The style is of *c.* 1300, but with the fanciful tracery patterns that Hopkins liked: see the W windows and especially the alternating round clerestory windows. A notable exterior feature is the pierced flying buttresses, springing from pinnacled aisle buttresses. They support moulded stone diaphragm arches impressively high up across the nave, resting on long shafts with moulded capitals, standing on foliage corbels. The weight is further supported inside by stone arches across the aisles, their inner spandrels with pierced tracery. Four-bay arcades with sturdy round piers with foliage capitals. Higher chancel arch, trefoiled in form with more pierced cusping, on big foliage corbels. Ornate chancel roof: steep trefoiled arched braces, pierced spandrels, elaborately arcaded wall-plate. – *Hopkins*'s fittings are largely complete, the most prominent the huge shrine-like REREDOS of alabaster and marble, carved in 1872 by *R.L. Boulton* of Cheltenham. Triple gabled canopy, elaborately vaulted and cusped, sheltering a Crucifixion with almost detached figures. – Boulton's stone PULPIT is rather less appealing. – Striking octagonal FONT, executed by *William Forsyth*; again richly carved, with strips of green marble inlaid with lilies of the valley. – STAINED GLASS. E window by *Clayton & Bell*, 1897; sanctuary S by *Hardman*, 1878. – S chapel E by *A.J. Davies*, 1936.

MONUMENTS. Many tablets from the earlier church. Under the tower: Edward Hall †1616, kneeling figure between Corinthian columns, straight top with cartouche of arms; and Edward Bull †1700, two black columns, outer garlands, weeping putti and heraldry above, skulls below. – Nave W end: Anne Bull †1680, with open pediment and gadrooned base, probably London work; and Robert Harrison †1820, sarcophagus type, a little more exotic than usual, signed *Peschiera* of Genoa. – S aisle: John Pardoe †1680, stone tablet with carved fruit and flowers, putto head at the top. – John Evett †1657, gristly cartouche of *c.* 1678. – Richard Harrison †1795, by *W. Stephens*, plain urn with coat of arms. – Large bronze war memorial plaque by the *Bromsgrove Guild*, 1920.

Outside the porch, a plain FONT, octagonal bowl with tall stem, no doubt *c.* 1830, from the previous church. – Square timber LYCHGATE by *Henry Rowe & Son*, 1922.

Large suburban VILLAGE, stretching N along the A443, with a few early C19 brick villas and some timber-framed cottages. The small wedge-shaped GREEN, S end, provides some variety with its various half-timbering of 1904–5. CHURCH LANE leads E to the site of the earlier church, a rather forlorn cemetery with ledgers within the railed-off space of the medieval chancel. The church, otherwise rebuilt 1829–30 by *James &*

Edward Lucy, was demolished in 1869. A little s is Hallow Park, *see* below.

The SCHOOL, near the N end, by *Hopkins*, 1856–7, is one of his best early buildings. Brick with vigorous blue brick patterning and good Geometrical Dec tracery. Two parallel schoolrooms, for boys and girls, the former along the street, with square bell-tower above the porch, its top with open wooden tracery and tall pyramidal cap; classroom set at right angles beyond. The half-hipped N gable of the girls' schoolroom has been crudely rebuilt; other C20 additions are reasonably discreet.

Further NW, in Moseley Road, a former CONGREGATIONAL CHAPEL of 1832; plain brick, square-headed windows, pedimental gable, later C19 porch.

HALLOW PARK, ¼ m. E, began as a medieval deer park of the Priors of Worcester; Nash (1781) illustrates a substantial C18 mansion high above the river. The present house, of 1914 by *Hubert C. Corlette* (former partner of Sir Charles Nicholson), is Neo-Georgian, two-storeyed, of white-plastered brick; grey Delabole slate hipped roof, gabled dormers behind a balustraded parapet. Eight very tall, sentinel-like chimneys, symmetrically arranged (said to be have been necessitated by the height of neighbouring trees). The entrance front, N, has recessions between the outer pairs of bays and the centre, its tripartite stone porch with attached Doric columns. Spacious oak-panelled entrance hall, a dog-leg staircase with twisted balusters opening off its E side. The garden front is simpler, with projecting three-bay centre for the morning room, flanked by dining and drawing rooms. Lower W service range.

PARKFIELD, ½ m. SSE, close to the Worcester City boundary, was built *c.* 1870 (as Bohun Court) for Charles Wheeley Lea; by *W.J. Hopkins*, his only substantial country house, with huge bay windows, massive entrance tower, and prominently banded roofs. The present house, innocuous brick and half-timbering, replaced it in 1932. Of Hopkins's work there survive the long, low brick wall to the road; the S LODGE with timbered gables, pierced bargeboards, fish-scale roofs, and typically chunky gatepiers; terracing on the garden side of the house; and several features in the grounds including a cast-iron *Coalbrookdale* FOUNTAIN surmounted by a (renewed) putto riding a swan; large polygonal basin with water-lily decoration. Also two remarkable timber-framed GARDEN PAVILIONS of *c.* 1870. The more northerly, an elongated octagon with tripartite opening facing across the Severn valley, has lavish tiling on the floor but also all over the interior and most exterior walls. The other, intended as a games pavilion, a regular octagon with tiled gablets and spiky central finial, has even more lavish exterior and interior tiling, including three large blue and white panels signed by *W.B. Simpson & Sons*; they depict archery, croquet and badminton.

Opposite the later N LODGE, a pair of cottages dated 1878, their brick and sparse half-timbering showing Hopkins struggling towards the Queen Anne style (cf. his vicarage at

Tibberton, p. 637). The WALLED GARDEN across Parkfield Lane retains a three-bay early C19 house with Doric porch.

GREENSTREET FARM, 1¾ m. WNW. C17, remodelled c. 1850; modest stuccoed front with iron veranda. But the central first-floor room has an elaborate plaster ceiling of c. 1660–70 and Jacobean overmantel with arched panels above tapering composite columns. Remains of an ornamental canal E of the house.

HAMPTON see EVESHAM

HAMPTON LOVETT 8060

ST MARY AND ALL SAINTS. Nave and chancel are basically Norman: N doorway with one order of columns with single-scalloped capitals and roll-moulded arch, flanked by flat buttresses; Norman chancel S buttress, with probably the stump of another, W end. Battlemented S tower Dec: entrance with two continuous chamfers, inner doorway also with continuous mouldings. Dec windows were also introduced into the nave, and the chancel given a new arch and E window. Perp chancel S windows, probably c. 1414, when the N (Westwood) chapel was added. This has a moulded four-centred arch to the chancel and similar N windows, probably re-set in 1561 when the Pakingtons enlarged the chapel; five-light E window with Tudor-arched heads. *Perkins* restored the church in 1858–9. He renewed the W end and roofs, inserted an arch between nave and chapel, and added a N vestry.

His FURNISHINGS include encaustic tiled floors and the diapered stone PULPIT. Plain FONT also C19, on a C14 stem. – Some BENCHES in the N chapel have C15 traceried panels, probably from a screen. – CHOIR STALLS. 1904 by *R.B. Ward*. – Good carved oak SCREENS by *Lorimer & Matthew* of Edinburgh, 1937; also the canopied figure of a saint (chancel S) and panelling flanking the stone REREDOS (1893). – Fine ALTAR TABLE, c. 1600 with bulbous legs. – SCULPTURE. White marble Pietà, probably C19 Italian, given 1928. – STAINED GLASS. In the nave N window, heraldic glass of 1561 from the N chapel. – By *Hardman*, the E and chancel SE, both 1859, chancel SW 1892, and chapel E 1882. – N chapel N windows by *Walter & Florence Camm*, 1928–37. – By *William Pearce Ltd*: nave SE 1912, W c. 1917. – MONUMENTS. Sir John Pakington †1551. Still entirely Perp: tomb-chest with cusped quatrefoils, recess with panelled wall, depressed arch, heavy top cresting. The detail is almost entirely of 1858–9 (when it was discovered behind the 1727 monument). – Dr Henry Hammond, Bishop Designate of Worcester, †1660; signed *Joshua Marshall*, 1661. Large black and white tablet with Corinthian columns; demonstratively learned inscription, mixed Latin and Greek, characterizing him as errorum malleus, veritatis hyperaspistes etc. – Sir John

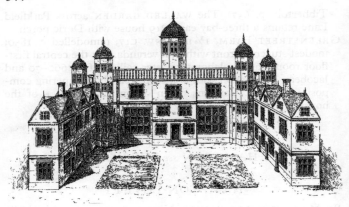

Hampton Lovett, Manor House.
Etching after a C17 painting

Pakington †1727; one of only two signed monuments by the elder *Joseph Rose*. Good effigy, reclining on a high gadrooned base; reredos background with pilasters and segmental pediment. – Two Pakington tablets by *Joseph Stephens*, one Grecian *c*. 1843, one Gothic *c*. 1846. – Brass to Lady Diana Pakington †1877, by *Hardman*.

In the CHURCHYARD, a high Gothic CROSS to Augusta Lady Pakington †1848, by *P.C. Hardwick*, 1849. – To the SW, remains of the large vault of the Lords Doverdale, 1937. – Timber LYCHGATE, probably 1858–9.

The church's setting is still rural, despite the proximity of Droitwich industrial estates. Across the railway, E, was the site of the Pakingtons' early C16 manor house (before they moved to Westwood House, p. 653). On the hill, N, the former RECTORY, brick, *c*. 1800, with hipped roof. In the lane to the W, a plain brick PARISH ROOM by *Lewis Sheppard & Son*, 1896, and Pakington estate cottages of *c*. 1860 by *John Smith* of Droitwich, partly suburbanized.

9060

HANBURY

ST MARY. Quite large, in an isolated elevated setting, with extensive views S; probably on the site of a Saxon minster (and Iron Age hill-fort). All sandstone, the E end by *G.E. Street*, 1860–1, the rest much rebuilt by *Thomas Johnson*, 1792–5, notably the battlemented W tower with diagonal buttresses with tall trefoiled panels. W doorway with deep-moulded ogee arch, large circular N and S windows; on the upper stages, Y-tracery and more round windows. The nave has two pedimented S dormers, the aisles mostly wide pointed windows, alternating with square-headed ones on the heavily buttressed N side. But much of the fabric is medieval, see the double-chamfered window heads, and blocked s doorway with continuous sunk quadrant moulding. The interior is nonetheless a complete surprise, with fully medieval four-bay arcades, the s not later than *c.* 1210; round piers, round moulded capitals, double-chamfered arches, one capital still with large trumpet scallops. N arcade Perp, not very good: octagonal piers, crude capitals, quite steeply pointed arches. Walls and ceilings are plastered but some C13 detail remains: shafts and moulded rere-arch of the s aisle w window, triple-chamfered upper part of the tower arch. *Street*'s chancel is flanked by organ chamber and vestry, N, and Vernon Chapel, s. His E.E. external detail is perhaps rather over-dimensioned on the N side, but the double-gabled s chapel is boldly asymmetrical, its doorway balanced by the vigorous trefoiled founder's-type MONUMENT to Thomas Bowater Vernon †1859. Inside, a lavish display of polished marbles and large foliated capitals; two-bay s arcade linked to a two-bay N–S one dividing the chapel into the two parts. Boldly painted roofs, encaustic-tiled floors.

FURNISHINGS by *Street* include the alabaster Last Supper REREDOS, STALLS, iron PARCLOSE SCREENS, round timber PULPIT with stone base, and quatrefoil-shaped FONT. – Fine green-stencilled and gilded ORGAN CASE by *F.H. Sutton*, 1881. – Of 1792–5, the BOX PEWS, cut down 1880 (apart from the NE and SE family pews), and pretty WEST GALLERY: Gothick, with curved corners, on thin wooden shafts; ROYAL ARMS carved by *Celestino Pancheri*, 1954. – Baroque brass CHANDELIER also given 1795. – Late C18 DOLE CUPBOARD (N aisle SE). – ALTAR TABLE, s chapel, from St Helen, Worcester; C17, cf. Spetchley (p. 597). – SCULPTURE. Two original plaster moulds (Nativity and Resurrection) for the reredos at *Sir Giles Scott*'s Liverpool Cathedral; by *Walter Gilbert*, 1924, modelled by *Louis Weingartner.*★ – STAINED GLASS. Excellent chancel E and s windows by *Clayton & Bell*, 1861. – By *Hardman*, the organ chamber N, 1871–2, s chapel E, 1903, unusually pictorial, and chancel N, 1908. – s chapel SW by *J.C.N. Bewsey*, 1922.

MONUMENTS. Nearly all Vernons. In the chancel, the Rev. Richard V. †1627 and his wife Frances. He kneels in front of her, both facing E. Recess with fluted Corinthian pilasters, straight top. – s chapel. Several good tablets: Edward V. †1666, open pediment with reclining figures; Rev. John V. †1681, twisted columns; Richard V. †1678, erected 1697, swan-neck pediment, gadrooned base. – Rev. George V. †1732, urn and drapery. – Of standing monuments, the largest and best is to Thomas V., builder of Hanbury Hall, †1721, signed *Edward Stanton* and *Christopher Horsnaile*. Grey, pink and white marbles. His reclining effigy, wearing lawyer's robes and wig, is flanked rather too closely by seated figures of Justice (now

83

★An early C16 German limewood relief of the Adoration of the Magi, about 3 ft (0.9 metres) high, is in store at Hanbury Hall.

without her scales) and Learning. The 'reredos' has Composite columns, and curtains looped up to reveal the long Latin inscription; open pediment with urns and heraldry. – Bowater V. †1735; probably *c.* 1740, traditionally ascribed to *Roubiliac*, but more probably from *Sir Henry Cheere*'s workshop. He stands pensively, one elbow on an exquisitely carved pedestal, a book in his other hand, a posture taken from Guelfi's Craggs of 1727 in Westminster Abbey; obelisk background. In front, a putto holds a medallion portrait of Bowater's wife. – Thomas V. †1771, attributed to *Richard Hayward* (GF). Mourning female leaning on an urn; tall plinth, excellent lettering. Adamish. – Thomas Tayler V., by *Chantrey*, 1837. Grecian, white marble. Kneeling woman in profile with two children, the sentiment quite convincing. – Other tablets: John Bearcroft †1723, by *W. Stephens & Co.*, sarcophagus-shaped, *c.* 1800, almost identical to one at Spetchley (S aisle); Ann Burslem †1796, by *W. Paty* of Bristol, delicate draped urn (organ chamber).

Large CHURCHYARD with C18–early C19 table tombs and headstones; also a headstone to Henry Parry †1847, with naïve scene of a railway accident. – Nice cast-iron RAILINGS and GATES W of the church, presumably *c.* 1795.

SCHOOL, ¼ m. S. By *Street*, 1858–9. Large schoolroom and attached house, brick, with patterned door- and window heads; sadly altered.

Opposite, the base and stump of a medieval CROSS, perhaps C14.

Former RECTORY, ¼ m. ENE (visible from the churchyard). By *David Brandon*, 1861–2. Brick, gabled, banded tiled roof, tall chimneys; open timber porch on the entrance front, E. Contemporary STABLES, N.

By the entrance to the long drive, RECTORY GATE COTTAGE, C17 timber-framed, hall-and-cross-wing plan. Contemporary farm and cottage nearby.

HANBURY HALL

The hall, ¾ m. SW, has belonged to the National Trust since 1953. Edward Vernon, son of the rector, bought the estate in 1631. His grandson Thomas Vernon, later an eminent barrister, inherited in 1679, and may have begun a gradual rebuilding almost immediately. The datestone 1701 on the main S front is C19 but may repeat an original date recording completion. The house is a child of the Wren age, a late example of the E-plan double-pile type instigated by Sir Roger Pratt at his short-lived Clarendon House, Piccadilly (1664–7), also imitated for example at Belton House, Lincs (1684–6). Its architect is unknown. Three early drawings of the S front survive at the house; one by the otherwise unknown *John Chatterton*, another by the mason *James Withenbury* of Worcester (cf. Fladbury, p. 317), the third by *William Rudhall* of Henley-in-Arden. Rudhall may be the most likely candidate; his name recurs in 1718 in connection with a chimneypiece. However, his design does not particularly resemble the present elevation,* but it does show precise knowledge of the vanished Thoresby Hall (Notts.), remodelled 1685–7; the present centrepiece also takes Thoresby as its model. This Nottinghamshire house was formerly attributed to *William Talman*, whom Pevsner suggested as architect of Hanbury; this now seems most unlikely. His suggestion that Rudhall was only the builder is more tenable. A probable local influence (though on a grander scale) is Robert Hooke's Ragley Hall (Warwicks.), built 1679–83; perhaps Rudhall worked there as a young man. The most obvious resemblance to Ragley is the plan: four corner pavilions, each containing an 'apartment' on the upper floor. The highlight of Hanbury's interior, the painted staircase by *Thornhill*, is probably of *c.* 1710. Thornhill rose to fame in 1708 73 when commissioned to paint the great hall of Greenwich Hospital, but Vernon may have employed him here on the strength of his work at Stoke Edith Park (Herefs.), 1705, for his friend Thomas Foley.

EXTERIOR. The approach is from the S (actually SSE), through a welcoming FORECOURT of 1856 by *R. W. Billings*. This, despite its roguish detail, provides a splendid prelude, with brick wall, gatepiers, and two Moorish corner pavilions with fanciful ogee roofs (and internal detail). As regards the substantial house itself, one is struck by the perfect Englishness of the picture; it could be in no other country. Brick with stone dressings, including quoins and elegantly moulded windows, shallow hipped roof with triangular-pedimented dormers, alternating with segmental ones for extra emphasis. The S FRONT, of two 71 storeys and 3+recessed 5+3 bays, is handsomely articulated: projecting three-bay wings, centre with three-bay frontispiece with rather tightly placed giant Corinthian columns on high pedestals, its pediment with keyed oval opening. The middle-window has a stone surround with volutes and carved foliage decoration; the inscribed date 1701 comes as no surprise. Early C19 porch with Corinthian columns, open octagonal cupola rebuilt 1809. The return elevations are composed like the front, but differ in detail. The E SIDE is probably a little earlier, with a 3+4+2 rhythm (2+5+2, before the SE projection was widened in the late C18). The S bay of its recessed centre, formerly a subsidiary doorway, has a bolection surround with broken segmental pediment and pretty carved decoration. The later W SIDE, slightly more severe, is long and even, of 2+7+2 bays. The REAR FRONT, N, probably the earliest, is more haphazard, exaggerated by small mid-C19 balustraded additions inserted into the angles with the wings. A mostly C19 service range, NW, linking the Long Gallery (*see* below), was demolished *c.* 1962.

INTERIOR. The spacious ENTRANCE HALL opens, l., directly, without any screen, to the large, square, open-well staircase.

---

*Its columned centre is only one bay wide, with segmental pediment and more decoration.

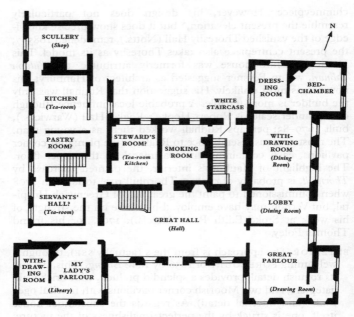

Hanbury Hall.
Reconstructed ground-floor plan of *c.* 1701

The hall has grained pine panelling, round-arched doorways (those on the more important E side with fluted Corinthian half-columns), and ceiling painted with *trompe l'œil* domes and corner panels of the Seasons. Above the bolection-moulded black marble fireplace, an arched recess with Thomas Vernon's bust. STAIRCASE with prettily decorated fluted balusters, two per tread, carved tread ends, and fine parquetry on the landings; a wall shadow remains from an original wooden dado. Walls and ceiling now painted all over, in the fashion of *c.* 1700, with large figure scenes in Baroque style. Comparable English staircases are at Hampton Court, Burley-on-the-Hill (Rutland), and Drayton and Boughton (both Northants.). The Hanbury staircase, signed by *Sir James Thornhill*, must according to topical allusion date from *c.* 1710. A flying figure of Mercury, also painted, connects walls and ceiling in the Baroque way; he points to a portrait print of Dr Henry Sacheverell which the Furies are about to burn. Sacheverell's trial took place in 1710. The ceiling depicts an assembly of the Gods. The wall scenes, flanked by fluted Composite pilasters painted in perspective, portray the story of Achilles: his mother Thetis at the forge of Hephaestus (N), Achilles choosing the spear (W), Ajax and Ulysses contending for the armour of the dead Achilles (E landing). Below and on the window wall, monochrome episodes and military trophies. The quality of the painting is quite high, although it cannot of course compare with the exuberance of most Italian and some German work; but it is as high, perhaps a little higher than the best of Verrio, one of Thornhill's foreign competitors.

The E RANGE originally formed the 'State Apartment', with Great Parlour (now Drawing Room), Lobby, Great Withdrawing Room, and Best Bedchamber and Dressing Room. The DRAWING ROOM is now entirely of *c.* 1776, when it was enlarged, probably by *Anthony Keck*, to incorporate a former E closet; narrow plaster frieze, central rose, green and white marble chimneypiece. The DINING ROOM, an amalgamation of *c.* 1830, probably by *Matthew Habershon*, preserves the separate painted ceilings, again by *Thornhill*, of lobby and withdrawing room, the former, portraying Boreas, the North Wind, abducting Oreithyia, almost monochrome; the latter apparently depicts Apollo with his chariot taking leave of Clymene. The panels have good plaster foliage surrounds, oak, laurel and acanthus, that of the former lobby probably added *c.* 1830. The original chimneypiece (resited) and its overmantel are embellished with exquisite Rococo wood carving of *c.* 1760; broken pediment with ho-ho birds. Behind the hall, N, the PARLOUR was probably Thomas Vernon's office; late C17 panelling, black marble chimneypiece. The LIBRARY, SW, probably by *Keck*, also combines two original rooms; delicate Adamish ceiling, another crisp green and white chimneypiece. The rest of the W range may have been the original service wing. – On the upper floor, a central corridor (with Gothic wallpaper of *c.* 1830–40) leads to a doorway with broken segmental pediment and pierced urn; similar doorway re-set nearby. The 'apartments' are mostly altered, but the HERCULES APARTMENT, NW, survives largely in its original form; panelled throughout, the bedchamber with bolection fireplace with diamond-shaped panel above, the dressing room with pretty corner chimneypiece with Doric pilasters and overmantel like a section of an ogee dome. Its closet is now a bathroom. BACK STAIRCASE inserted 1988, within the C19 NW-angle addition.

The detached LONG GALLERY, to the NW, now linked only by a high wall, formed Thomas Vernon's own working apartment (its N bay formerly divided off as a closet), with his study to the E; later a picture gallery. Brick, seven bays, with hipped roof; tripartite mid-C19 loggia, S end. Panelled inside to shoulder height, with central bolection chimneypiece and overmantel made up from C17–C18 woodwork, some ecclesiastical. A second wooden overmantel (or bedhead), said to have come from Tickenhill Manor (p. 147–8), is displayed at the N end: Jacobean, with coarse caryatids dividing three deeply moulded arched panels, the Prince of Wales's feathers in the centre; friezes with fruit, flowers and strapwork. The study has reused Jacobean panelling. Beneath the Long Gallery, a simple tiled DAIRY with cheese room. NE of the house, forming the other range of the rear courtyard, the much-altered C18–C19 STABLES, 3+1+3 bays, with hipped roof,

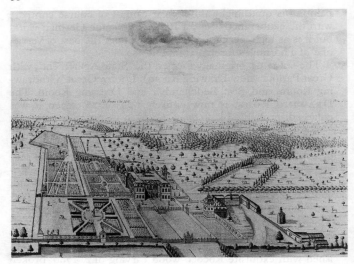

Hanbury Hall.
Bird's-eye view by Joseph Dougharty, 1732

and lower N extension; then, NE, a square mid-C19 GAME
LARDER with pyramidal roof.

GROUNDS. Dutch-style FORMAL GARDENS by *George London*,
depicted in Dougharty's view of 1732, were swept away later
in the C18. The National Trust began their re-creation, to a
plan by *Paul Edwards*, in 1993, using, for economy, hedges
instead of low brick walls, and timber for other structures. SW
of the house is the Grove, with the Bowling Green and its
rusticated ogee-roofed pavilions beyond. To the W, a Sunken
Parterre with tall rusticated piers, with Fruit Garden, N,
adjoining the Long Gallery, and Wilderness, W. – Further NW,
on its own, forming a separate picture facing a wide expanse
of lawn, is the ORANGERY, probably *c.* 1745–50, perhaps by
Francis Smith. Nine bays long, its projecting three-bay centre
with pediment carved with a beautiful basket of fruit, foliage
and garlands; tall windows, parapet with urn, pineapple finials.
At its rear, a mushroom house of 1860. The path beyond, from
the late C18 WALLED GARDEN further W to the rear of the
house, passes though a narrow mid-C19 vaulted TUNNEL, constructed so that the servants might remain invisible. – The
CEDAR WALK, leading N, with fine views of the Deer Park, E,
beyond its ha-ha, was all that survived of London's layout.
Mid-C18 ICE HOUSE, off its N end, uncommonly well-
preserved: circular, with domed brick vault beneath a grassy
mound. The narrow entrance passage slopes down from the
pit to a sump by the doorway; hatch opposite for shovelling in
the ice. Nearby a small cottage, and two pools plus a freezing
pool.

LODGE, SSE. Early C19, three bays, two storeys; hipped roof
with central chimney.

THE MOORLANDS, N of the lodge, is timber-framed, dated 1615.
The W entrance front, with tall projecting porch between large
gables, is mostly remodelling of 1879, but the N front makes a
fine display of decorative timbering: herringbone struts, close-
set studding, and three attic gables with concave quatrefoils,
the storeys divided by continuous runs of five-light mullioned
windows.

BECKS FARM, further NE, has a small late C18 house, with
large granary, C17 timber-framed stable, and another house
dated 1856 (probably by *John Smith*).

OTHER BUILDINGS

The timber-framed and brick PUMPHOUSE FARM, ¾ m. S, is
mostly hidden by its C18–C19 farm buildings. The best,
however, lies isolated on a hill to the S: a sweet early C17 timber-
framed DOVECOTE, with gabled roof and lantern.

VILLAGE HALL, Carters Hill, ¾ m. SE. By *W.H. Bidlake*, 1891.
Brick, with diapering at the N and S gable-ends; freely detailed
S window.

At WOOLMERE GREEN, a little S, the main nucleus of this large
scattered parish, is the VERNON ARMS; late C18, three bays
with small central pediment with Gothick window, and W addition curving nicely along the road. Further SW, the former ST
MARK'S MISSION CHURCH, mid-C19 brick, with stepped E
and W lancets.

MERE HALL, 1⅔ m. S. A fine, large, timber-framed manor house,
traditionally a possession of the Bearcroft family from the C14
(which accounts for the date 1337, later inscribed on the
central bressummer). Central hall with large gabled cross-   58
wings, all closely studded, with large diagonal struts, dendro-
dated to *c.* 1611. The hall range's second storey is jettied, with
herringbone struts and five delightful little gables with
concave-sided lozenges and finials; below, a continuous run of
five five-light ovolo-mullioned windows, clearly attempting to
reproduce the appearance of a long gallery at attic level (cf.
Middle Beanhall Farm, p. 160). The two-storey porch, off-
centre W, was superseded *c.* 1691 by an open central one, with
thin barleytwist Corinthian columns and open pediment.
Pretty fretted central lantern, of about the same date. The E
cross-wing was also slightly raised in the later C17. The delicate Gothick glazing in most windows looks early C19, but predates 1828 when *Matthew Habershon* carried out substantial
alterations for E.H. Bearcroft, adding a large SW service wing
of painted brick. At the rear of the central range, a stone
chimney with four star-shaped stacks, now enclosed by early
C19 additions; lateral chimneys to both wings. Inside, much
C17 panelling, the best in the dining room (W wing), which also
has a fine wooden chimneypiece with arches and caryatids.

Very attractive FORECOURT of *c.* 1700, its brick walls topped with iron railings. Two square corner pavilions have ogee fish-scaled roofs; open rear sides with timber arches with pendants.

BECKNOR MANOR (formerly Broughton Court), on a moated site ¼ m. SE of Mere Hall, was later used as its dower house. Central hall, rebuilt in brick with prominent chimney in the C18; timber-framed gabled wings, probably late C16, all but the E service wing much renewed in the late C20.

The brick SCHOOL at Broughton Green, further S, by *Street*, 1858–9, was adapted as a chapel by *Hopkins*, 1872. Derelict by the 1990s, since converted to a house.

Many outlying C17–C18 farmhouses, the most attractive probably PARK HALL FARM, 2¼ m. SE, *c.* 1600, mostly close-studded with brick infill. Narrow central range, with lobby entrance and row of diagonal star-stacks; gabled cross-wings.

HANBURY WHARF, 2 m. WSW, developed where the Droitwich Junction Canal, built 1852–3, met the Worcester and Birmingham Canal. The former has a distinctive flight of three LOCKS with intermediate holding pools, probably the last deep canal locks constructed; of blue engineering brick, with integral steps and water-conserving side ponds. Restored *c.* 2002.

8040   HANLEY CASTLE

Of the CASTLE, ¼ m. S, only the wide dry moat (dug *c.* 1324) round a D-shaped platform remains. Built by King John, 1207–12, as a hunting lodge for Malvern Chase, it passed to the Clares, Earls of Gloucester, then to the Despencers, and later the Beauchamps, Earls of Warwick. Much rebuilt in the C14–C15, dismantled in the C16. One tower (of at least six) survived until 1795 when its stone was used to repair Upton bridge.

ST MARY. Norman nave, with renewed S doorway with one order of shafts with scalloped capitals; roll-moulded arch. Remodelled in the early C14, when the wide N aisle was added; this has N windows with cusped Y-tracery (the NE of 1902), and doorway with sunk quadrant mouldings; the DOOR is probably contemporary. Other windows all early Dec style. In 1674 Sir Nicholas Lechmere (*see* below), rebuilt the whole E end, in brick with sandstone dressings: sturdy central tower with battlements and plain-mullioned bell-openings, chancel, long N chapel. The chapel's C17 windows survive, three-lighters with transoms, straight heads, and hoodmoulds, interesting posthumous essays in the Gothic: E window with (incorrectly flattened) ogee arches below Tudor-arched panel tracery, N windows with paired Tudor-arched heads to each light. *G.E. Street*, in 1858, replaced the chancel windows with crisp Geometrical specimens of his own, and renewed most others, especially the two large W windows (*see* the late C17 hoodmould above the nave W window). His also the porches, the N of timber, the S of stone. Early C14 four-bay N arcade with round and octagonal piers, moulded capitals, and double-chamfered arches. The E end arches are also double-chamfered, but the broad mouldings of their capitals, continued as string courses, prove they are late C17. Chapel roof with collar-beams supported by long straight braces.

FITTINGS mostly by *Street*: PEWS and STALLS with his characteristic spreading foliage heads, splendid tall REREDOS of alabaster, stone and marble. – The chapel's W SCREEN is his low timber chancel screen, heightened 1912. – ALTAR RAILS of 1898. – COMMUNION RAIL, N chapel. Early C18; close-set balusters, alternately columnar and twisted. – FONT. Perp; octagonal bowl with paired quatrefoils. – Prettily painted BENEFACTION BOARDS of 1715–80. – STAINED GLASS. Two notable windows of Street's time, 1859–60, the E by *Hardman*, the nave W a superb Last Judgement by *Clayton & Bell*, one of their finest works. – Also theirs the more subdued N aisle W, 1870, the aisle NW, and chancel S. – Also by *Hardman*, two nave SE windows, 1861–2. – Nave SW, probably *Heaton, Butler & Bayne*, c. 1870. – N aisle NE by *H.W. Bryans*, 1902. – N aisle central by *Lavers & Barraud*, 1860, designed by *G.R. Clarke*. – MONUMENTS. The N chapel has C18 Lechmere ledger stones. Also Winifred Lechmere, C17 oval slate tablet with small frontally kneeling figure; and Col. William Dingly †1653, cartouche with large cherubs. – Nave: Rev. A.B. Lechmere †1878. Large alabaster tablet with sgraffito scene of St Peter kneeling before Christ.

Outside, SW of the S porch, a finely carved coped tomb to Sir E.H. Lechmere †1856, by *G.R. Clarke*. – Good WAR MEMORIAL, c. 1920, with carved cross-head on a tall, partly medieval, shaft.

The setting of the church is most attractive. To its E, the earlier buildings of the school (*see* below); to the N, the ALMSHOUSES, painted C18 brick, with upper floor of C19 half-timbering. The triangular open space, NE, perhaps the site of the market recorded in the early C13, has a fine central cedar tree. On its W side, the THREE KINGS, a cruck-framed hall now encased in C19 brick, with large close-studded C16 cross-wing; unspoilt pub interior. CHURCH END otherwise consists of timber-framed cottages, the earliest, GLEBE COTTAGE, to a small hall-and-cross-wing plan, set well back, interspersed with modest brick houses.

The earliest surviving building of the GRAMMAR SCHOOL, a late medieval foundation, stands at its NW corner; probably late C16, close-studded, with broad N gable with traceried bargeboards. To the churchyard, three gables, the outer two painted brick. Then the schoolroom, rebuilt 1733; carved stone plaque with heraldry and Latin inscription. In 1868 *William Chick* of Hereford added a long brick Tudorbethan range, set W–E, with open bellcote; gabled entrance wing by *A.B. Rowe*, 1909. Later C20 additions, with, NE, a house of c. 1600 with mid-C19 E front, adapted as a sixth-form centre, c. 1997, by *Wheatley Taylor Stainburn Lines*.

SEVERN END, ⅔ m. NE. The timber-framed mansion, probably originally built for Richard Lechmere in the late C15, much rebuilt in the C16–C17, was one of the most spectacular in the county until consumed by fire in 1896; little other than later C17 brick walls were left standing. Immediate rebuilding by *Lewis Sheppard & Son* created an almost exact replica. The W front, timber-framed with traditional box framing, partly close-studded, probably reproduces the C16 forms accurately; the three-gabled top storey of the broad projecting centre may represent a C17 improvement. Short wings with single broad gables with diagonal braces, the S extended as the service end (encased in brick until 1896). The centre of the E front, with livelier framing, closely represents what had been there before, except that its N bay had been of brick. The timber decoration, with concave-side lozenges and keyed-in ovals both horizontal and vertical, must be of *c.* 1668, when Sir Nicholas Lechmere apparently turned the house round, making this the entrance side. Was the Elizabethan-looking doorway, with stubby Ionic columns on high pedestals and shallow segmental arch, relocated from the W front? It is flanked by large brick chimneystacks (with paired star-stacks). The diapered N one is probably C16; the other, judging by the odd disposition of the fireplaces within, must have been added by Sir Nicholas for effect. Of his activity on this E side the two long brick wings of 1673, built by *John Avenant*, are also telling. They are brick, with three Dutch gables on the inner sides, the central one crowned with a segmental pediment, the outer with steep tri-angular ones; near the E corners, small stone doorways with steep Mannerist triangular pediments. The interiors of the N wing, the least damaged by fire, are conservative for their date; the dog-leg staircase survives, and the plaster ceiling of the former drawing room, divided by moulded beams into sixteen panels with foliage and angel's heads. Others interiors all *c.* 1897–8, with good panelling and plaster ceilings, the best in the new drawing room.*

Entrance COURTYARD with low brick walls; gatepiers with a lion and talbot.

To the S, the WALLED GARDEN of 1656–62, its E side a raised walk. At its SW corner, a square PAVILION of 1661 (restored 1861) above a two-bay arched loggia; steep hipped roof. A fine avenue of limes leads to the centre of the W front; formerly there were three radiating avenues, first planted 1641–50.

To the N lies an impressive array of farm buildings, all of Sir Nicholas's time. The earliest, a large BARN of square-panelled framing, was mostly rebuilt in 1658. The others are of red brick. Immediately N of the house, set N–S, the STABLE of 1670, with cider mill and press (N end). Another BARN is set W–E; L-plan with attached cottage. E of this, the BREWHOUSE, 1681, its

---

*In the house is the LECHMERE STONE, probably C9–C10, a small Byzantine-influenced headstone with rounded top. On one side, a standing figure of Christ holding a book; on the other, an encircled cross-head with baluster shaft.

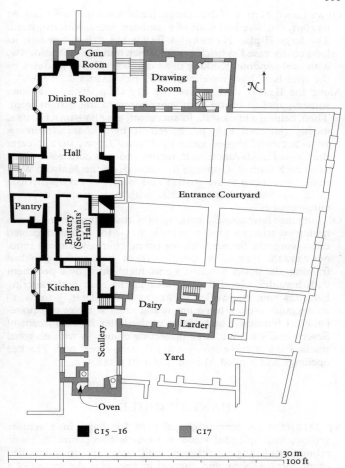

■ C15–16   ▨ C17

```
|------------------------------| 30 m
                              | 100 ft
```

Hanley Castle, Severn End.
Plan, before the fire of 1896

hipped roof supported by kingpost trusses as well as more traditional arched braces. Further N, an oblong DOVECOTE of 1677, with two louvres, a complete set of nesting boxes, and the original potence (or rotating ladder).

The LODGE, on the B-road, SW, by *Lewis Sheppard*, c. 1898–9, is brick and half-timbered, L-plan, with oak Tuscan porch. Good GATEPIERS with the Lechmere carved stone Pelicans.

The parish (*see also* Hanley Swan) is rich in enjoyable houses. There are two further nuclei, as well as many outlying farmhouses, mostly C17 or earlier.

QUAY LANE, ¼ m. E of the church, leads down to the Severn. At its start, the base and shaft of a medieval cross, with C19 head. The large H-plan HERBERT'S FARM has C16–C17 wings, its long centre cased in brick c. 1748. Brick mid-C18 GAZEBO, NW, with oval windows flanking the S doorway. The C17 houses by the river both have warehouse-like brick BARNS.

Along the B4211, ¼ m. N, first the C17 OLD VICARAGE, long square-panelled centre with short wings to the garden front. Then, behind a brick wall, its successor, now PYNDAR HOUSE: mostly rendered C18, partly rebuilt by *Richard Armstrong*, 1851–2, central shaped gable by *Michael Tapper*, 1922. Nearer the Cross Hands junction, attractive C16–C17 cottages, at least two cruck-framed. Opposite the second, on the Malvern Wells road, a small C19 PUMP HOUSE and former PARISH SCHOOL, by *Lewis Sheppard*, 1893; brick, with nice central bellcote-cum-chimney.

Of outlying farmhouses, two, N of Cross Hands, are worth noting. WHITTEMERE, E side, is C15–C16, hall and gabled cross-wing, the former with big lateral chimney; altered 1790. MEREVALE FARM, W side, c. 1600, has square-panelled framing, the upper window, S end, highlighted by a pediment with heraldry. Good dog-leg stair at the rear, with tapering balusters and strapwork. GILBERTS END FARM, ⅝ m. W, to an irregular L-plan, has a low N and taller W range of square-panelled framing. The W front of the latter is reminiscent of Severn End's E front: large projecting chimneys with diagonal stacks flank a three-storey central stair-tower, with blocked openings and hipped M-roof. Later C17 BARN, E.

6060
HANLEY CHILD

ST MICHAEL. A former chapelry of Eastham, in a remote setting, with splendid views W towards Shropshire. A rustic rebuilding of 1805–7, sandstone with some tufa; brick dentilled eaves cornice. Nave and chancel in one, plus the stump of a thin W tower; this fell in 1864 and was given a gabled tiled roof (continuing that of the body of church) and simple W bellcote. Broad lancet windows, with Y-tracery in the E. Large raking buttress at the centre of the N wall. Rendered interior with plastered ceiling. – Contemporary COMMUNION RAILS with close-set balusters and fluted posts; sanctuary dado panelling brought from Kyre Park (p. 422) in 1932. – Most other FITTINGS probably of 1872, when the church was 'modernized'.

COURT FARM, a little ESE, forms an attractive group. H-plan house, mostly C17 timber-framed; S cross-wing of C19 rubble, but its attached malthouse, W, again of C17 framing. To the NE, a seven-bay barn, to the SE a stable block, both mostly rubble but basically C17, with weatherboarded ends.

HANLEY SWAN

St Gabriel. By *Sir George Gilbert Scott*, 1871–3, paid for by Samuel Martin, a retired Liverpool merchant. Rock-faced Cradley stone with Bath dressings; aisles, timber NW porch, NE tower with typical Scott broach spire. Late C13 style with plate tracery, the clerestory windows circular and cinquefoiled. The best feature is the E window, of five steeply stepped lancets. Routine interior: four-bay arcades with octagonal piers, taller chancel arch. Good nave roof, the centre raised. Nicely detailed chancel piscina. – Most of Scott's furnishings survive, with *Godwin*-tiled floors. – Notable REREDOS, given by Sir E.A.H. Lechmere of Rhydd Court (p. 332), who also donated the site. Of alabaster and mosaic, by *Powell & Sons*, 1873, with figure panels by *Clayton & Bell*; enjoyable patterned tiling either side, aesthetic foliage above geometrical patterns. – Oak vestry SCREENS, N aisle E. Typically intricate Perp by *C.F. Whitcombe*, 1907. – STAINED GLASS. E window 1877 by *J.A. Forrest* of Liverpool; rather good. – Chancel SE by *Kempe*, 1885. – S aisle E by *A.L. Moore*, 1901. – N aisle W by *Tom Denny*, 1986, a semi-abstract landscape, boldly coloured.

Our Lady and St Alphonsus (R.C.), Blackmore Park; *see* below.

In the village, E of the green with its pond, several C19 villas, reflecting the proximity of Malvern Wells. Brummell Court, *c*. 1850, N side, has fluted pilasters and broad canted bay windows; Ladywell, S, *c*. 1820, brick, three storeys, has a good pedimented doorcase with paterae, swags, and winged head.

School, ¼ m. SSE. A school-cum-chapel by *J.W. Hugall*, 1862. Of Malvern stone, E.E.-style, the S gable with good sharp bell-cote, roguishly off-centre. N sanctuary apse removed 1895. Large C20 additions.

Hanley Hall, ⅝ m. SE. C16–C17 timber-framed; reputedly the house of the chief forester of Malvern Chase. H-plan, the earliest part probably the three-storey E cross-wing, with close studding. Two-storey hall range and W wing, mostly square-panelled, probably early C17; the odd, lower gabled addition in front of the E wing may be contemporary. N front of the W wing rebuilt in brick, with canted bay; the room behind has good decoration of *c*. 1840. In the SW room, C17 panelling and a fine plaster ceiling with thin moulded ribs forming intersecting quatrefoils containing various sparse motifs. Later oak over-mantel with fluted Corinthian pilasters, the stone fireplace still with its four-centred arch. – C17 outbuildings, N.

Blackmore Park, ¾ m N, was rebuilt in uninspired Jacobethan style by *David Brandon*, 1861–3, for J.V. Gandolfi, a London silk merchant who inherited from the staunchly recusant Hornyold family in 1859. A private chapel, added by *A.E. Purdie*, 1877–8, survived when the house was gutted by fire and rebuilt by *Brandon*, 1881–2. All demolished 1925. Only LODGES remain, the N one of brick, dated 1884, the S earlier,

picturesquely half-timbered.* Between them stands the fine
Puginian R.C. church.

OUR LADY AND ST ALPHONSUS (R.C.), by *Charles F. Hansom*,
1844–6, is remarkably stately, without the pinch of poverty that
mars so much Roman Catholic architecture in England before
1850. Paid for by J.V. Gandolfi, who arranged for the Redemp-
torists to run the mission, only their second foundation in
England. Of Cradley rubble with Forest of Dean dressings.
Chancel, nave and aisles under one continuous slate roof,
double bellcote over the chancel arch; organ chamber off the
N aisle, sacristy N of the chancel. The nave is E.E., modelled
on St Giles, Skelton, near York, the chancel Dec, with flowing
tracery; the junction is treated in such a way that it should look
real history, an early example of this aspect of historicism.†
Striking W front, the tall single nave lancet flanked by buttresses; oculus above, smaller lancets for the aisles. Elaborate
SW porch, deep and stone-vaulted; wrought-iron gates by *Pugin*
(made by *Hardman*), doorway with much dogtooth. Inside, the
four-bay arcades are Dec rather than E.E., with quatrefoil piers
with fillets. Nave and chancel both have stone rib vaults, the
latter with painted decoration.

Lavish original FITTINGS. Every window has STAINED
GLASS by *Wailes* (not all figurative), all floors tiling by *Minton*,
to designs by *A.W.N. Pugin* (who also designed plate and
candlesticks). – Carved octagonal FONT. – In the aisle E bays,
side chapels with carved stone altars and wooden screens, the
N also with a gabled tomb recess intended for the founder. –
Two *coronae lucis* by *Hardman*. – Timber ROOD SCREEN. – Rich
stone ALTAR and REREDOS, the latter with ogee arcading,
angels in the spandrels. – MONUMENTS. Five brasses by
Hardman: Charles Filica †1849, to a *Pugin* diamond-shaped
design; Mary Teresa Fitzherbert †1852; Valentine Browne, third
Earl of Kenmare, †1853; T.C. Hornyold †1859; T.C. Gandolfi
Hornyold †1906, more thinly engraved. – Outside, the
CHURCHYARD CROSS (now incomplete) and simple timber
LYCHGATE are also by *C.F. Hansom*.

Hansom's PRESBYTERY, built as the Redemptorist
monastery, is connected by a roofed covered way. Also of
Cradley rubble and especially Puginian, with steep gables or
gabled dormers and thin timber bellcote.

HANLEY WILLIAM

6060

The main nucleus, at BROADHEATH on the Worcester–Tenbury
road, is mostly C19–C20, apart from the C17 FOX INN. The
church stands apart, ½ m. NE.

---

* A larger brick LODGE, 1½ m. W, on the B4208, is dated 1874.
† W.B. Ullathorne, Hansom's early patron at Coventry, and from 1846 Vicar
Apostolic at Clifton, suggested aspects of the design.

ALL SAINTS. Of red sandstone with some tufa. Norman nave
and chancel, the former lengthened in the early C13; partly
rebuilt by *Henry Day*, 1866–7, his the weatherboarded w bell-
turret with shingled broach spire. Timber s porch, 1904. Of the
Norman church the unmoulded chancel arch survives, with
the plainest chamfered imposts, partly cut away for a former
screen; also a chancel N window and part of the nave s
doorway, re-set. C13 are the nave NW and SW lancets, N and S
doorways, and probably the chancel s doorway (no doubt also
moved). Other windows, tall stepped, E, trefoiled lancets elsewhere, are of 1866–7. – FONT. Plain round bowl, C12–C13. –
SCULPTURAL FRAGMENT. Above the s doorway, a rectangular
Norman panel of the Agnus Dei. – C19 PULPIT, a five-sided
concave screen cut from a single piece of oak, with Jacobethan
carving. – Other fittings made up from C17 woodwork, the
READING DESK with panels perhaps from the former pulpit. –
STAINED GLASS. E window by *Hardman*, 1867. – MONUMENT.
Anne Newport †1717, John Newport †1760, the latter signed
by *Richard Squire*; similar tablets with plain pilasters and
heraldry. – Large Grecian tablet, white marble, to J.W.N.
Charlett †1838, by *J. Stephens*. – Rev. Rice Mark †1811, by *John
Soward*; Grecian but simpler.

The C18 HANLEY COURT, ½ m. further NE, was demolished
in 1931. The STABLE COURTYARD, which adjoined the NW
end, remains. This belongs to alterations for Col. Wakeman
Newport by *Andrew Maund* of Bromyard, 1802–8. Main front,
SW, with rusticated archway beneath a high gable and hexagonal timber cupola; low five-bay wings each side, their centres
also with gables above rusticated doorways (now blocked). The
SE range was the mansion's service wing, with the servants'
hall, N end, marked by a pediment; blank round arch below,
with Diocletian lunette over a tripartite sash window. The
hipped-roofed NE range contained the larder. – Some distance
SW, the C18 KITCHEN GARDEN, its curved brick wall rising, E,
into a wide false shaped gable to shelter the gardener's cottage.

The surviving layout of the GROUNDS seems to follow a
scheme of 1786 by *John Davenport*. Also two lodges of *c.* 1800.
CHURCH LODGE, E of the church, of rubble, is round with
shallow conical slate roof with broad eaves; low attached
cottage. SOUTH LODGE, ⅝ m. S, altered and rendered, retains
an octagonal tower with Y-traceried windows beneath oculi.

HARPLEY
Lower Sapey

6060

ST BARTHOLOMEW. By *Frederick R. Kempson* of Hereford,
1876–7, replacing the old church at Lower Sapey (p. 438).
Rock-faced with ashlar dressings; chancel with N vestry, nave
with S porch and broad twin bellcote on a flat W projection.
Thoughtfully designed, not at all run-of-the-mill. The nave has
grouped lancets, arranged in a different rhythm N from S. More

elaborate chancel, the E window with bar tracery; shafts of red sandstone inside. The group of three trefoil-headed lancets, S, is balanced by triple sedilia; double piscina opposite. Crisp carving by *Robert Clarke*. – FONT. Tub-shaped bowl, from Lower Sapey, perhaps C13. – Other fittings by *Kempson*, notably complete; *Godwin* encaustic floor tiles (also used as dadoes in the porch). – STAINED GLASS. Nice E window by *Hardman*, 1925.

OLD RECTORY, a little S, mostly *c.* 1845–50; roughcast, gabled wings with wavy bargeboards, cross-windows with square hoodmoulds. Small SE addition, in keeping, by *Aston Webb*, 1880. – C17 weatherboarded BARN, S.

8070

HARTLEBURY

Large parish with attractive village centre; to its NW, Hartlebury Castle, a see house of the Bishops of Worcester from the early medieval period.

ST JAMES. Of sandstone, by *Thomas Rickman*, apart from the W tower built for Bishop Sandys, 1567, and medieval parts at the E end. *Rickman* rebuilt the chancel in 1825, and designed the rest of the large, competent church (cf. Ombersley) in 1832–3; built 1836–7 (with *William Knight* as clerk of works). High two-storey W porch. Nave and aisles under one roof, long three-light windows alternating (also across) between Geometrical and reticulated tracery; small rose windows at the E and W ends, the latter above cathedral-like doorways. Spacious interior, with four-bay nave arcades with thin Perp-style quatrefoil piers, lightly detailed galleries recessed between them; quadripartite plaster vaults with ridge ribs. Chancel chapels also of 1836–7, except for the N chapel's Perp E window (now within the vestry) and its two-bay arcade of *c.* 1300, with quatrefoil piers and double-chamfered arches (copied by Rickman, S). Chancel restored by *Preedy*, 1878, e.g. STALLS and TILING. – He also renewed the FONT, 1882: half the bowl is C12, the rest by *Martyn & Emms*. – *A.E. Perkins* altered *Rickman*'s large hexagonal stone PULPIT in 1866. – PEWS by *J.A. Chatwin & Son*, 1908, their ends carved with arms of the Bishops of Worcester from 680. – BISHOP'S THRONE by the *Bromsgrove Guild*, 1925. – Large ROYAL ARMS, probably George I. – STAINED GLASS. E window by *Burlison & Grylls*, 1883. – S chapel E by *Hardman*, 1875. – Two fine early C19 HATCHMENTS, Bishop Hurd and John Baker, in the ringing chamber. – MONUMENTS. Chancel. Edwyn Eyre †1707, gilded and painted cartouche; John Baker †1814, with broad urn, and the Rev. Samuel Picart †1835, draped altar, both by *J. Stephens*. – Beneath the tower. E.J. Gibbons †1900, by *F. Wheeler*, copper plaque.

In the CHURCHYARD, a large MEMORIAL CROSS to Gibbons by *E.P. Warren*, 1901, now without its shaft; the base copies the C15 one at Ombersley. – Also early C19 CHEST

TOMBS. The best group, N, includes one to Bishop Hurd
†1808, by *George Perry*; Gothic, with mitre and crozier on top.
Facing the churchyard, THE GABLES, the former grammar
school of 1702. Painted brick, five bays (plus another of the
late C18); pedimented Doric doorway with triglyph frieze.
Gables at the rear. To its S, approached from Quarry Bank (past
the upright early C19 usher's house), the OLD GRAMMAR
SCHOOL, single-storey, of 1794; four bays, with Y-tracery. The
larger replacement, now HARTLEBURY SCHOOL, further up
Quarry Bank, is by *S. S. Reay* of Bath, 1910–11; rock-faced
stone, gabled Tudor style.

Further uphill, W side, two contrasting C20 houses. THE
PLECK, 1912, probably by *E. P. Warren*, is Neo-Georgian: large,
roughcast, hipped roof of green Cumberland slate. PLECK
ORCHARD next door, by *Malcolm Booth* (of *Associated Architects*), 1980–1, is low and reticent, brick, with much glazing,
and pantiled roof; square plan, with small central courtyard.

The OLD RECTORY, Inn Lane, NNE of the church. Built 1700
for the Rev. James Stillingfleet, Bishop Stillingfleet's son, a
good, large example of its date; brick, ashlar window surrounds
and flat quoins. Seven bays, the central three projecting;
doorway with ribbed hood. Hipped roof with pedimented
dormers; modillion cornice.

Set back opposite the W end of Inn Lane, the CHURCH SCHOOL
of 1878 by *E.A. Day*; brick, Gothic, with stepped lancets.
Detached house. Large addition of 1958. PARK COTTAGE,
further N, is C17 timber-framed, with brick infill; lobby
entrance, fine central brick chimneystack, quadrupled star-
plan.

THE TALBOT, facing the far E end of Inn Lane, is T-plan, the
painted brick stem of *c.* 1800; gabled early C17 N range, timber-
framed and jettied. Large chimneystack in the angle, with
paired star-plan shafts.

HARTLEBURY CASTLE

Hartlebury Castle is a deliciously peaceful sight. Of its military
past hardly anything remains visible. Bishop Walter de Cantelupe
began work *c.* 1255, Bishop Giffard obtained licence to complete
it in 1268. The wide moat, still filled with water to the W, survives, also the base of the NW tower. Much of the fabric, great
hall with solar to its S and S wing beyond, is later medieval,
probably of the time of Bishop Wakefield (1375–95). Bishop
Carpenter (1444–76) built a fine gatehouse in the 1460s, but no
trace remains. After the Civil War the castle was left to decay.
Rebuilding by *Thomas Wood* of Oxford, begun *c.* 1675 for Bishop
Fleetwood, completed just before he died in 1683, resulted in a
comfortably stretching-out red sandstone building, with low
centre and higher L-plan wings. Alterations continued into the
late C18. There is a spacious turfed forecourt, with circular drive
introduced in the mid C18, when battlements were added to the
two late C17 entrance lodges, square, of brick. Further N are the

coachhouse and stables, with hipped roofs and cupolas, built for
Bishop Hough (1719–23).*

69 The embattled centre of the symmetrical late C17 E FRONT has
a tall, pretty Gothick lantern, added *c.* 1750; the wings have the
hipped roofs with dormers characteristic of their date. The
central range contains the great hall of *c.* 1395, but what one
sees now are three large pointed windows with Gothick glazing
bars, an alteration for Bishop Johnson (1759–74), possibly by
Stiff Leadbetter, either side of Bishop Fleetwood's central
porch. This has a heavily moulded door surround with lugs top
and bottom and big semicircular pediment with his arms and
ball finials. Windows of the wings also of Bishop Johnson's
time, those of the ground floor Gothic to match the centre.
The brick SERVICE WING, N now houses the Worcestershire
County Museum (opened 1966).

The S WING forms the bishop's private residence. Entrance hall
with C18 overmantel (from the Saloon), with landscape by *Zuc-
carelli;* behind, the grand staircase with turned balusters,
typical of *c.* 1680. The buttressed CHAPEL, structurally late
C14, fills the projecting part of the wing. Its Y-traceried
windows and broad stepped E triplet belong to a remarkable
remodelling of 1748–50, carried out for Bishop Maddox by
Henry Keene, his earliest major work in Gothic style. Inside, an
extremely pretty plaster fan vault (modelled on Henry VII's
Chapel at Westminster Abbey), and splendid Gothick FUR-
NISHINGS, with many ogees: stalls and panelling, fretwork
entrance door to the ante-chapel, charming bishop's throne,
and tripartite W screen (particularly indebted to Batty
Langley's *Ancient Architecture Restored and Improved* of 1742).
C18 heraldic STAINED GLASS in the heads of the side windows
by *John Rowell* of Reading; E window by *William Pearce Ltd,*
1898. Long irregular W FRONT, with battlements and buttresses, partly late C17, partly C18; small mid-C18 canted bay,
S end. The ample two-storey bow was introduced by Bishop
Hurd (of the *Letters on Chivalry and Romance*), when he
installed the new library, 1782, above the late C17 long gallery
(now subdivided).

The STATE ROOMS are now approached through the Museum,
part of internal adjustments by *Marshall Sisson,* 1962–3. The
principal room of the low centre, the HALL, retains evidence
of the late C14 great hall, especially its five-bay roof with thin
double-hollow-chamfered timbers. It consists of jointed crucks
(combined wall-posts and principal rafters) with elementary
arched braces supporting the collar-beams; raking struts
above, largely obscured by the later plaster ceiling. The
medieval entrance would have been at the N end; the present
porch, SE, must have replaced a bay window, with perhaps
another opposite (an arrangement reflected by big opposing

* Bishop Yeatman-Biggs adapted the stable block, now museum offices, in 1905, as
a college for clergy.

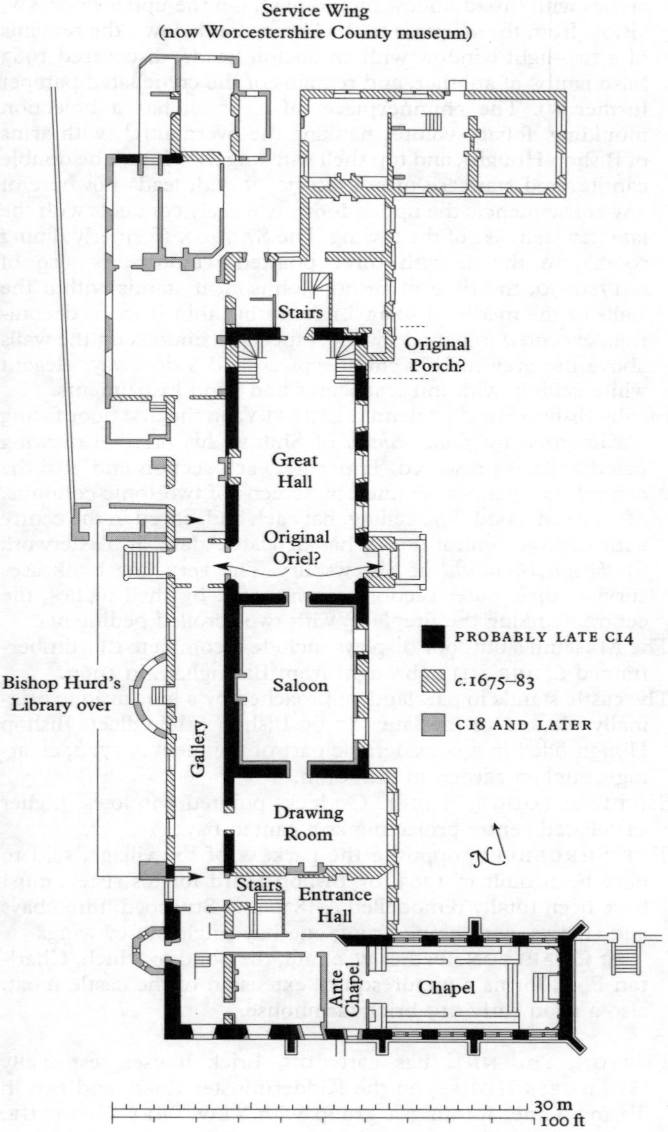

Service Wing
(now Worcestershire County museum)

Stairs

Original Porch?

Great Hall

Original Oriel?

Bishop Hurd's Library over

Gallery

Saloon

Drawing Room

Stairs

Entrance Hall

N

Ante Chapel

Chapel

■ PROBABLY LATE C14

▨ c.1675–83

▨ C18 AND LATER

30 m
100 ft

Hartlebury Castle.
Ground-floor plan

arches with broad hollow mouldings). On the upper floor, sw, visible from the staircase to the library (*see* below), the remains of a two-light window with cinquefoil heads, discovered 1963 (also jambs of another, and remains of the crenellated parapet further N). The chimneypiece, of *c.* 1720, has a bolection moulding, foliage volutes flanking the overmantel (with arms of Bishop Hough), and top shell with angels' wings. The double cantilevered staircase of *c.* 1760–70, N end, leads nowhere of any consequence; the upper doorway merely connects with the late C17 staircase of the N wing. The SALOON (formerly dining room), to the S, with three pointed windows, is also of *c.* 1760–70, the time of Bishop Johnson; it stands within the walls of the medieval solar. Light, rather thin Rococo decoration, executed in papier mâché, especially sinuous on the walls above the grey marble chimneypiece and S doorway; elegant white ceiling, with musical scores and wind instruments.

97 Finally Bishop Hurd's splendid LIBRARY, on the first floor facing W, designed by *James Smith* of Shifnal; his original drawing dated 1782 is preserved. Tripartite, each section and also the central bow window defined by screens of two Ionic columns, of marbled wood. The ceiling, flat each end, coved in the centre with shallow central dome, has delicate Adamish plasterwork by *Joseph Bromfield* of Shrewsbury. The very fine bookcases survive, their outer sections surmounted by shell niches, the centre, flanking the fireplace, with two scrolled pediments.

The Museum's outdoor displays include a complete C17 timber-framed CIDER MILL, brought from Birlingham in 1969.

The castle stands in parkland, approached by a lime avenue originally planted in the late C17 by Bishop Stillingfleet. Bishop Hough filled in a considerable part of the moat *c.* 1720, creating a sunken garden to the south.

Sandstone LODGE, *c.* 1781. Gothick, pointed windows, higher castellated centre projecting as a canted bay.

THE SHRUBBERY, opposite the park, W of the village, said to have been built in 1783, by Bishop Hurd for his sister, must have been totally remodelled *c.* 1830–40. Stuccoed, three bays and storeys, with hipped roof; one-bay single-storey wings.

At CHARLTON, further W, a mill, the pond to which, Charlton Pool, forms a picturesque S extension of the castle moat; also a good early C19 brick farmhouse.

TORTON, 1 m. NNE, has early C19 brick houses, especially GOLDNESS HOUSE, on the Kidderminster Road, and two in Torton Lane, forming a group with YEW TREE COTTAGE: L-plan, the earlier wing with three cruck trusses.

WHITLENGE HOUSE, 1¼ m. ENE. By *Thomas Bateman* of Birmingham, 1826–8, for the Rev. Thomas Taylor, the Bishop's secretary. Brick, four bays, with thin Doric porch, and full-height end bow (to the drawing room); nice internal detailing.

Beyond the railway, E of the village, are various scattered premises of the RAF 25 MAINTENANCE UNIT, established 1938; the largest, now a trading estate, has pale brick administrative buildings, in typical low-key Neo-Georgian.

The late C18 WARESLEY HOUSE, ¾ m. SSE in its own park (severely curtailed by mid-to-late C20 housing), was built for John Baker. Brick with stone dressings, three storeys, 2+3+2 bays, the projecting centre with pediment with oculus opening. Rounded Doric porch, Venetian and Diocletian windows above; other windows have stepped voussoirs. Entrance hall altered c. 1912.

WARESLEY GREEN FARMHOUSE, to its SW on the main road, is good early C18 brick; three bays with hipped roof, quoins and pedimented doorway.

WARESLEY MANOR, ENE in Manor Lane, is half late C18, half C17: lower, timber-framed with jettied N end gable. This must have had a lobby entry until a gabled C19 wing replaced the porch.

YEW TREE HOUSE, at Norchard ⅔ m. further S, is an unusual house of sandstone ashlar, dated 'RH 1754'. Three wide bays, windows with fluted keystones, quoins, and rather basic doorway with plain pilasters and moulded cornice.

At CROSSWAY GREEN, 1½ m. S, the MITRE OAK INN, a half-timbered road house of 1935–6, and a chapel of ease, ST MARY, Bishop's Wood, built by *Thomas Vale*, 1882, for Bishop Philpott; his arms appear in the E window (by *Swaine Bourne*). Timber-frame construction, with iron stays to a brick plinth; nave and chancel in one, with W bellcote, S porch and N vestry. Most internal fittings survive, including a cedar-wood FONT. Memorial LYCHGATE by *Vale*, 1892.

TITTON, 1 m. SW, has two good houses. PANSINGTON, high above the Stourport Road, retains a complete late C17 timber-framed farmhouse behind its late C18 front. Square panelling with diagonal bracing; central hall with projecting wings. Timber-framed and brick barns. CLARELAND, S of the main road, a neat brick villa of 1814, has three bays with central Tuscan porch.

At LINCOMB, ½ m. further SSW, two more early C19 brick houses, a C17 timber-framed T-plan farmhouse (GROVE FARM), and LINCOMB HALL, mostly rebuilt for the Lingen family in 1874: brick, with two gables above two-storey bay windows. The large LINCOMB LOCK, completed 1843, was part of the Severn improvement scheme begun in 1835; chief engineer *Sir William Corbett*, supervising engineer *Edward Leader Williams*.

HARVINGTON

Chaddesley Corbett

8070

ST MARY (R.C.). Built 1825 for Sir George Throckmorton. Nave and chancel in one, of sandstone ashlar; three N windows with Y-tracery, castellated W porch. E window (intersecting tracery), SE vestry and outer W porch added 1854–5, probably by *C.F. Hansom*. Simple segmental plaster ceiling; W gallery. Sanctuary panelled 1953. – FONT. Round bowl, cylindrical

stem; perhaps 1854–5. – STAINED GLASS. By *Hardman*, the E
window of 1893, extended 1953, and the NE, 1920. – SHRINE
to St John Wall, with bronze plaque by *Faith Tolkien*, 1987. –
ORGAN. Built by *H.C. Lincoln*, 1819, for St Austin, Stafford.

Adjoining the nave, S, the upright PRIEST'S HOUSE of 1838,
brick, three bays and storeys, set within the brick WALL of the
Elizabethan Great Garden.

HARVINGTON HALL

A picturesque, irregular, L-plan Elizabethan house, of brick with
sandstone dressings. It is scarcely apparent that the brick largely conceals an H-plan C14–C15 building, timber-framed above a sandstone
base. John Pakington, a lawyer, bought this house in 1529. His
nephew, another John (1523–78),* or more probably the latter's son,
Humphrey (1555–1631), a recusant, carried out the brick refacing,
enlarging the house around a courtyard. The most likely date is *c.*
1580, with further work *c.* 1600. On Humphrey's death the house
came to his daughter Lady Mary Yate, then, 1696, to the Throckmortons, also Catholics; they demolished, probably *c.* 1701, its N and
W ranges. It was donated, in dilapidated condition, to the Roman
Catholic Archdiocese of Birmingham in 1923. *George Drysdale* began
long-term repairs in 1930–1; further restoration from 1985.

67 EXTERIOR. The moated house is approached from the E. The
lower, central part of the E range represents the medieval solar
wing, with a splendidly tall brick chimney of *c.* 1500 just S of
the gateway. The tower-like N end, its brick in Flemish bond,
is probably mostly of *c.* 1756: two oval windows, E, the lower
blocked. The equally tall S end is late C16, with gables, four-
light mullioned windows, and bold S chimney-breast with two
diagonal brick stacks. This forms the E end of the gabled Elizabethan S range, as varied as can be pictured, with details
matching the SE tower. The most important room here, marked
by the four-light mullioned-and-transomed window in the
rectangular projecting E bay of the central recess, is the first-
floor Great Chamber. The corresponding bay, beyond a further
tall narrow recess, houses a newel stair. The late C16 kitchen
wing, SW, projects yet more boldly forward, to the edge of the
moat, with attached garderobe at its SW corner. There is a
C16–C17 bridge here but we must return to the E bridge to
enter the now reduced courtyard.

The striking feature of the COURTYARD front of the S range
is the curious giant basket arch carrying the gables; probably
an alteration of 1701 (see the rainwater head), but no doubt
determined by the sandstone plinths of the medieval hall, with
projecting bays for its dais end and for the porch. There are
now only modest facing doors in the returns of each projection. The largest Elizabethan windows again light the great
chamber: four-light mullioned-and-transomed in the E bay,
six-light in the recess. The W end was altered and patched in

*A date 1576 was formerly scratched on a second-floor window.

sandstone after the removal of the w range, which may have contained the great hall, perhaps with long gallery above. Nothing can be determined of the n range; the blocked ground-floor arches of the NE tower suggest some form of loggia.

The INTERIOR is most notable for its numerous priest holes, the finest surviving series in England, and its wall paintings. Humphrey Pakington was in constant trouble for his religion from 1585, but the most ingenious hiding-places are probably c. 1600, set around the stair well then under construction.

FIRST FLOOR

1 South Room
2 Mermaid Passage
3 Great Chamber
4 Lady Yate's Bedroom
5 Withdrawing Room

GROUND FLOOR

6 Brew House
7 Great Kitchen
8 Dairy
9 Buttery
10 Parlour
11 Gateway

0 5 10 20 30 40 50 60
Feet

Harvington Hall.
Ground- and first-floor plans

Nicholas Owen, an Oxford carpenter who specialized in such covert work, was probably responsible. The wall paintings, also partly of *c.* 1600, partly slightly earlier, are by far the best of their age in the county. They have nothing of the clumsy naïvety of most Elizabethan decoration; their stylistic source probably lies in Flanders.

The rooms are described according to the recommended public route. First the Elizabethan BUTTERY (now shop), on the site of the medieval hall, with some timber framing exposed; then the PARLOUR (now tearoom), the medieval solar, its fine ceiling of moulded beams inserted *c.* 1500. Stairs lead up to LADY YATE'S BEDROOM, SE tower, first floor; this, with good Elizabethan panelling (and SE garderobe), is the innermost of a suite of three. The WITHDRAWING ROOM, in the solar wing, has more good panelling and a tunnel-vaulted plaster ceiling. The doorway l. of the fireplace opens onto a passage to the room above the gateway; below the passage floor, a hiding-place 8½ ft (2.6 metres) down and only 4 ft by 2 ft (1.2 by 0.6 metres) in size. The third room of the suite is the GREAT CHAMBER. Renewed panelling, with chimney-piece added 1996 (carved by *Michael Ford* of Bromsgrove); stained glass of the 1930s by *Hardman*.* The door in the SW corner, with prettily decorated panels, leads to the rear MERMAID PASSAGE, with the best-preserved earlier paintings. Here, and on the nearby newel staircase, exquisite arabesques with lush foliage and elegant nudes, some children, some women, including a mermaid with leaf tails (above the doorway to the South Room); black tempera, the nudes coloured pink. Before ascending the newel stair, a detour NW to see the ingenious priest hole in DR DODD'S LIBRARY, a small room lit by a large Georgian window. The panelling at the rear of the book cupboard recess opposite this could be removed to reveal a wall-stud which pivoted into the priest hole (best seen from the newel stair).

At the top of the stair, the SMALL CHAPEL, with walls painted with vertical chains of drops of blood and water. The NURSERY, above the E end of the Great Chamber, with windows in three directions, no doubt provided an excellent lookout; more stained glass by *Hardman*, 1951. To the SE, on the tower's second floor, is the CHAPEL, probably a replacement for the small chapel, its walls (and originally ceiling) painted with a late C17 pattern of vines, lilies and pomegranates; a trap-door, l. of the altar, concealed vestments and other 'Massing stuff'. In the N–S PASSAGE, W of the newel stair, considerable remains of a painted series of the Nine Worthies, probably *c.* 1600. Here again at least some figures display remarkable ease and delicacy, especially young David slaying Goliath. Three rooms further W, with remains of simpler painting schemes, were used as priests' lodgings, with further

---

* Except that in the NE bay, dated 1911, originally at *J. T. Hardman*'s own house, No. 24 Westfield Road, Edgbaston, Birmingham.

hiding-places in the roof space; the brick fireplace in the N room is entirely false. The top two of five steps down to the great staircase lift to access another priest hole, from which there is said to have been a spyhole into the Great Chamber below. The GREAT STAIRCASE itself, made by *William Fowkes* of Droitwich, 1936–47, replaced that of *c.* 1600, removed by the Throckmortons in 1910 to Coughton Court, Warwickshire. Its walls are stippled red, black and yellow, with shadow balusters (cf. Knole, Kent). Finally, on the ground floor, the KITCHEN range, SW corner. Above the bread oven next to the main fireplace, one more priest hole entered through a trap-door in the floor of the garderobe off the South Room above; presumably obsolete by *c.* 1600, when it was pierced for the pulley cord which runs in a brick shaft behind to drive the kitchen spit.

The house occupies less than a quarter of the area within the square moat. Also on the approximately triangular island, a C17–C18 MALTHOUSE, timber-framed with sandstone ground floor, and a brick building with high stone plinth, perhaps originally STABLES. Sir Robert Throckmorton converted its upper floor into a R.C. CHAPEL in 1743. The interior, badly damaged by fire in 1823, later used as a school, was restored 1986–7. It is divided into three parts by Venetian-like arches, the easternmost with an early C19 altar and C18 communion rails from Upton upon Severn.

The only other buildings close to church and Hall are HARV-INGTON HALL FARM, mostly brick, *c.* 1700, and its restored timber-framed BARNS. – In the VILLAGE, ⅓ m. NW, the two best houses almost face each other across the Stourbridge Road: STEPPE FARM, C16, with close-studded gabled wings, much rebuilt in the C18–C19, and RED HOUSE FARM, neat C18 three-bay brick, with hipped roof.

WINTERFOLD HOUSE, ⅜ m. SSW, now a school, was probably mostly rebuilt for William Wheeler *c.* 1800. Brick, three storeys, 2+1+2 bays, with modillion cornice and parapet; slightly advanced centre, with arched recess above the projecting Ionic porch. Spacious entrance hall with fluted Doric columns; round circular stair with pretty cast-iron balustrade.

BELLINGTON FARMHOUSE, 1½ m. NNE. Gabled and close-studded, the centre probably late C15 (with partly sandstone kitchen at the rear), the S cross-wing early C17. Original doorway (now blocked) replaced by one, N end; early C18 staircase.

HARVINGTON

near Evesham

0040

ST JAMES. Norman W tower, with small, deeply splayed W window; two-light bell-openings divided by polygonal shafts. Nave and chancel are early C14, the former with cusped Dec Y-tracery, the latter with ogee trefoil-headed lancets, all beneath continuous dripmoulds. Those above the chancel windows are very oddly truncated by short straight tops above the ogee curves. The flowing tracery of the E window, apparently copying the nave N at nearby Salford Priors (Warwicks), belongs to the major restoration of 1853–5 by *Frederick Preedy*. He also added the broach spire (originally shingled, clad in copper by *Andrews & Son*, 1949) and small S vestry; nave vestry by *Maurice Jones*, 1960. Inside, the tower arch, pointed with two slight chamfers, is C13; above it, the roof-line of the earlier nave, very high for its width. In the chancel, an ogee-headed piscina with some ballflower, and remnants of niches flanking the E window. Simpler nave piscina, near the continuously double-chamfered chancel arch. – Norman tub FONT. – PEWS. 1853. – Remains of the back rails of BENCHES of 1582, with incised texts. – STALLS and ORGAN by *C.F. Whitcombe*, 1904–6. – STAINED GLASS. E window by *Preedy*, 1855, less than subtle. – Nave NE by *Shrigley & Hunt*, 1923; SE by *A.L. Moore*, 1896. – MONUMENTS. Thomas Feriman, rector, †1619, stone tablet with corpulent columns. The small strapwork 'predella' is continued below by the handsome tablet (with strapwork surround) to Thomas Jun., also rector, who died soon afterwards. – Mary Ramell †1786; coloured marbles.

MANOR FARM, SE. T-plan, timber-framed on a stone base. S cross-range late C15, partly narrow-studded; the stem mostly early C15, of cruck construction. C17 gables at the junction. – To the N, a stone DOVECOTE, now derelict.

Two probably C16 thatched cottages, NW of the church, also contain crucks, an almost complete pair visible in the E wall of the second. Picturesque black-and-white houses continue S along the main street, most C17, some thatched.

In VILLAGE STREET, leading N, a more varied mix. The brick OLD RECTORY, set back, W side, mostly by *Solomon Hunt*, 1849–50, is minimal Tudor Gothic. In the garden, remnants of the C14 E window of the church. On the E side, C18 brick houses, nicely converted brick barns, and more timber-framed thatched cottages, the N one with an exposed cruck.

Further N (in Station Road) the SCHOOL, originally by *Solomon Hunt*, 1848–9, painted brick, with Perp-style window, and a small brick BAPTIST CHAPEL, 1886.

By the NEW LOCK of 1982, on the river Avon ⅞ m. SE, a memorial to Robert Aickman, pioneer of waterways preservation; bronze portrait roundel, in a curved yellow brick wall with seat, by *Walter Thomson* (of *Associated Architects*), 1983. Derelict early C19 brick MILL nearby, retaining much machinery. The C18 MILL HOUSE further N has been swamped by C20 hotel additions.

HEADLESS CROSS see REDDITCH

HEIGHTINGTON
Rock

7070

Scattered hamlet, in beautifully hilly country s of the Wyre Forest.

St Giles. Nave and chancel in one, small timber w bell-turret. Of the medieval chapel, only the rubble N and S walls survive; one early C13 N chancel lancet, opposite a three-light C15 window. Nave s windows and the E lancet of 1892–3. Early C19 brick porch, sw. The w end, probably also the two squared N windows, is of 1736, when the medieval nave was curtailed. Perhaps also contemporary the unpretentious roof, with tie-beams and braced kingposts, and west gallery, its front with thinly turned balusters. Whitewashed walls, but traces of wall paintings which seem to belong to a significant early C13 scheme. – stained glass. Nice nave s lancet, c. 1902. – Chancel s by A.E. Buss (for Goddard & Gibbs), 1963–4.

Heightington House, ¼ m. wnw, a neat three-bay brick villa of c. 1830, has a good fluted Doric porch. Nearby, Elford's Farm, C17, square-panelled framing, with off-centre gable, porch to its l.; central brick stack with lobby-entry.

Of outlying farms the most picturesque is Deasland Farm, ¾ m. nnw. Timber-framed, probably C15, remodelled 1611 when the pretty porch was added (plus an extra s bay). Ground floor with brick infill, the upper, clearly heightened, with rendering; gabled dormer with C17 oriel, startlingly undulating roof. Lobby-entry, the sturdy central brick stack flanked inside by cruck trusses.

Worsley House, in a remote situation 1¼ m. sw, is also late C15, close-studded with curved tension braces, ground floor underbuilt in brick. Enlarged N and w, with square-panelled framing, in the C16–C17. The C15 roof has collar- and tie-beam trusses, with curved wind-braces. Later farm buildings, of rubble with brick dressings.

HEWELL GRANGE see TARDEBIGGE

HILL AND MOOR

9040

St Thomas, Lower Moor. 1868–9 by Preedy. Simple brick chapel of ease (to Fladbury); nave and chancel in one, single or paired trefoil-headed lancets, stepped triplets w and E. w porch 1922–3, by Williams & Smith of Worcester. – stained glass by F.W. Skeat: E 1952, nave sw 1954.

Lower Moor retains several modest C17 timber-framed cottages. The Old Chestnut Tree, a remnant of a larger framed house, is probably late C16, much restored c. 1900; gabled and jettied w wing with carved bargeboards, former hall

with tall gabled dormer. Rebuilt E wing. Further E, the early
C19 MANOR FARM, stuccoed, three storeys and bays, with
large semicircular windows on its top floor.

At HILL, ¾ m. NE, are HILL COURT, large, restored, cruciform-
plan with projecting gables, of 1681 (according to the weathervane), and HILL HOUSE, dated 1713, brick, stone dressings,
five by three bays, with hipped roof. Further E, the site of a
deserted MEDIEVAL VILLAGE.

HILL CROOME

8040

ST MARY. On a hillside, looking W to the Malverns. Small, of
C13 origin. Blunt W tower, unbuttressed, with W lancet, rectangular bell-openings, and saddleback roof. *Prothero & Phillott*
restored the nave and chancel in 1907, rebuilding the timber S
porch. C13 S and (fragmentary) N doorways; nave windows all
apparently C16–C17. Chancel E window *c.* 1300, with simple
bar tracery; plain mullioned side windows. Inside, diagonally
across the SE corner, a remarkably large PISCINA, perhaps also
c. 1300. Is it imported, or does it indicate the intention of an
apse? Timber-framed tympanum between nave and chancel;
roofs 1907, with reused tie-beams. – COMMUNION RAIL. C17;
tall close-set balusters. – PULPIT. Late C17, simply panelled;
the more ornate tester looks earlier. – PEWS. Partly C16. –
FONT. Renewed C12 tub bowl; cover 1981 (replacing a humble
C17 one, banished to the tower). – Also under the tower, a large
CHARITY BOARD, 1848. – STAINED GLASS. E window 1860,
probably by *Joseph Bell* of Bristol.

GLEBE FARM, SW, formerly the rectory. Timber-framed, L-plan:
E cross-wing C16–C17, hall range said to be of C14 origin, much
rebuilt in brick. Further alterations by *Thomas Collins*, 1870. –
Fine DOVECOTE, to its SW, of cruck construction, probably
early C15; restored 1972–3. Large pair of cruck blades on its E
front, side walls with mirrored tension braces. The W wall (with
120 nesting holes) was rebuilt in brick in the C17. Small
wooden turret.

The MOAT nearby belonged to the manor house, long since
demolished.

BAUGHTON, 1⅛ m. NNW. *See* Earl's Croome.

HIMBLETON

9050

ST MARY MAGDALENE. One of the most worthwhile smaller
medieval churches in the district, sensibly restored by *Ewan
Christian*, 1893–4. Norman in origin: late C12 S doorway, one
capital with waterleaf. The doorway was modified in the C14
when the timber porch was added. Also C14 the S transept
(Shell Chapel), with good two-light Dec S window.* Chancel

---

* Above the SE buttress, a well-preserved MASS DIAL.

mid-C13, though only the E window, three closely-spaced stepped lancets, tells of this date. Apart from the SW window, inserted 1893–4, its side windows, as well as others in the church, are plainly mullioned, probably C17. Nave W end probably also of this date, perhaps too the large, square bell-turret. Its present attractive form, oak-shingled with timber-framed top with pyramidal roof, is due to *Christian*. Early C16 N aisle, with windows with Tudor-arched lights; spacious NW vestry added by *C. F. Whitcombe*, 1906. Inside, the three-bay N arcade is also latest medieval: short octagonal piers, broad capitals, double-chamfered arches. Nice Perp wagon roofs over nave and chancel, the former with wall-plates with fleurons, heads, and intertwined reptiles. No chancel arch. The C14 transept arch, continuously double-chamfered, retains traces of painting.

FONT. C12, table-top type, with later chamfered underside. The only decoration, one small medallion with the Agnus Dei, may also be later; flat C17 cover. – An C18 baluster FONT is now in pieces in the S transept. – Good PEWS by *Ford Whitcombe*, 1907. – Other fittings mostly by *Christian*. – SOUTH DOOR. Sturdily cross-battened, with quatrefoil infill; probably late C14. – ROYAL ARMS. Elizabeth I; painted, mostly in red outline, above the E window; dragon supporter instead of a unicorn. – STAINED GLASS. Notable medieval remains, plus fine later glass. In the E window, a C13 figure of St Mary Magdalene, plus a few leaf quarries; the rest is outstanding imitation of the style of *c.* 1300 by *George Ostrehan*, 1904. – Also his, 1901, much of the Crucifixion, S transept E; most of the figures of Mary and John and parts of the donors below are C15. – More good C15 fragments, chancel NW: heads, St Anne teaching Mary, fine border with crowns and stags' heads. – The N aisle NE window has most interesting early C16 remains with Renaissance detail, including St Catherine, parts of St George and the Dragon, and heraldry and emblems connected with the Wintour family of Huddington (p. 384). – N aisle E by *Kempe*, 1907. – Chancel SE and S transept S windows by *Geoffrey Webb*, both *c.* 1910. – MONUMENTS. S transept. Simple tablets to Philip Fincher †1755, by *John Laughton*, and Eleanor Payton †1812, by *E. Truman*; also an iron ledger, *c.* 1700, to the Finchers of Shell Manor.

Attractive LYCHGATE of 1931, copying details from the S porch.

The early C17 CHURCH FARM, SE, timber-framed, of four bays, has a central two-bay hall divided from the parlour, N, by a large chimney with six brick stacks; N gable, facing the churchyard, with some decorative bracing. Charming contemporary DOVECOTE, to the SE. COURT FARM, W of the church, probably late C16, is taller and gabled, with C19 additions; weatherboarded BARNS. More timber framing in the village street further S. Facing its end, the BROOK HOUSE, also timber-framed, probably late C16, with brick star chimneys, much altered and extended S in 1932–3. Of this date, the small N

porch with Ionic demi-columns, and the brick lodges and
gatepiers. By the latter, the octagonal base of a medieval
PREACHING CROSS.

Brick SCHOOL, with attached house, ¼ m. SSE, by *Hopkins*, 1873;
poor C20 additions. Further E, *Hopkins's* former VICARAGE,
1870–1, brick, gabled, less altered. The tree-lined drive to its N
leads to HIMBLETON MANOR, mostly of 1868; large, brick,
gabled, surprisingly plain.

Outlying hamlets, with large C16–C17 timber-framed farm- or
manor houses: SALEWAY, 1½ m. WNW, with square dovecote;
DUNHAMPSTEAD, 2 m. WNW (by the Worcester and Birmingham Canal), on a formerly moated site.

The most rewarding hamlet is SHELL, ¾ m. NNE, with notable
timber-framed buildings either side of the Bow Brook. By the
ford, a PACKHORSE BRIDGE, C17 or earlier; two round arches,
only 5 ft (1.5 metres) wide between the parapets.

SHELL MANOR, to its NW, mostly close-studded, H-plan
with two end gables, was restored by *F. W. B. Charles*, 1961–2.
It began, *c.* 1450, as a hall and cross-wing house. The classic
medieval solar wing, NW, survives, its ground-floor parlour (or
cellar) with heavy flat joists grooved for a wattle ceiling; splendid open arch-braced roof over the two-bay upper chamber
and single-bay antechamber. Remarkable lateral stack, probably early C16, with brick cappings with gablets at the angles
and two huge diagonal brick shafts. Inside, shaped doorheads
and stone fireplaces. The present central hall and service wing,
SE, both *c.* 1600, conform to the medieval cross-passage plan.
The porch has a jettied upper storey, the service wing (two
bays, extended at the rear in the C17–C18) decorative timbering and lateral Lias stack. Similar stack at the rear of the hall.
Both have three star-shaped brick shafts, though each serves
only two fireplaces. – Brick GATEPIERS with stone ball finials.
– Long C17 weatherboarded BARN, SE, with higher C19 brick
GRANARY, N end.

The thatched SHELL COTTAGE, E of the ford, is a diminutive C15 hall house, a rare survival, though with later inserted
fireplace and first floor. Shallow triangular doorheads (just discernible) mark the screens passage; the framing shows traces
of the mullions of tall hall windows. Central roof truss, purlins,
and rafters are heavily smoke-blackened. Solar and service
bays were both in the form of outshuts. The former survives,
together with its doorheads from the hall; a C20 brick wing has
sadly replaced the latter.

Further NE, the C19 Lias and brick MILL, and SHELL MILL
FARM, probably late C16: narrow studding infilled with brick,
stone chimney with two star-stacks.

At EARL'S COMMON, ¾ m. ENE, the MOLE HOLE, a C17
thatched cottage with good crisp extension by *Conrad S.
Rowberry*, 1972–4, for himself. ASHCOURT, in Stoney Lane, a
bungalow by *David Clarke*, 1988, with shallow slate roof and
projecting timber gable on wooden pillars, is well above the
usual standard.

HINDLIP

Hindlip now means the Headquarters of the West Mercia Constabulary. They took over Hindlip Hall in 1946, later making it the centre of a campus, and using the nearby parish church as a police memorial chapel.

ST JAMES. Nave and chancel originally Dec, almost entirely rebuilt by *Hopkins*, 1863–4. *Lewis Sheppard*, 1887–8, added a continuous s aisle and chapel, as well as a larger N vestry, all smooth ashlar, Dec style; three E gables, the chancel's slightly projecting. Small C14 windows survive only in the nave N wall and s aisle (re-set). Perp w tower, its w window and doorway of 1863–4; C17 upper stage with mullioned bell-openings and low battlements. Good Perp tower arch. The interior otherwise is of 1887–8: three-bay s arcade with quatrefoil piers, rich two-bay arcades flanking the chancel. – Sheppard's lavish FURNISHINGS include mosaic-tiled floors by *de Grellor* of London, expensive oak carving mostly by *Martyn* of Cheltenham (especially SEDILIA and long row of sixteen SEATS, s aisle s wall, all with misericords), and brass-work by *Singer* of Frome, notably the elaborate chancel SCREEN with marble and onyx plinth. The oddest fitting is the Neo-Norman FONT, with deliberately archaic carved figures, tightly set in Romanesque arcading (cf. Crown East). – Large Caen-stone REREDOS mostly of 1864, the Last Supper carved by *J. Roddis*. – TILES. Many of the C15, tower N and s walls. – STAINED GLASS. All by *Hardman* and of 1876–8 (chancel E, vestry, s chapel, nave NE, s aisle central and w) or 1887–9, apart from the nave NW, 1905. – MONUMENTS. John Habington †1582, wooden panel with many shields of arms; renewed 1778 and 1864. – Two large Gothic marble tablets by *M. W. Johnson*: Thomas Anthony, third Viscount Southwell, †1860; his wife Jane †1853. – Elizabeth Allsopp, Dowager Lady Hindlip, †1906, by *James Powell & Sons*, 1908; mosaics of Christ, with Phoebe and Dorcas.

In the CHURCHYARD, N, a large Gothic chest tomb, white and pink marble, to Henry Allsopp, first Baron Hindlip, †1887, carved by *William Forsyth*.

CHURCH COTTAGE, the former rectory, w of the church, said to be *c.* 1490; square-panelled timber framing, extended by a wing of 1683.

HINDLIP HALL. The large brick house completed for John Habington, 1572, was demolished *c.* 1818. Its successor, built for the third Viscount Southwell, pale brick with ashlar dressings, has a N front of two-and-a-half storeys and 1+3+1 bays: projecting centre with pediment, portico of four unfluted Ionic columns, plain giant pilasters. Outer service wings (kitchen, E, stables, w) of one-and-a-half storeys; three bays articulated by blind arches, originally linked to the house by quadrants. In 1864 the brewery magnate Henry Allsopp replaced these with balustraded three-bay, two-storey wings, in line with the house. Large entrance hall with Ionic columns to the rear; open-well staircase with wrought-iron balustrade, w. On the garden side, s, the morning room is flanked by drawing and dining rooms, each with single-storey canted bay. Here the centre has a raised parapet with Grecian detail, the outer wings pediments. Reconstruction after a fire in 1967 (by *L. C. Lomas*) included cladding the roof in copper, and adding a plain two-storey sw wing sporting a huge radio mast.

Buildings added 1991–4 for West Mercia Constabulary form a campus, all light-coloured brick, all by *Hereford & Worcester County Council* under *R. W. Cheney*; project architect *Andrew Shephard*. E of the Hall, the FIREARMS SCHOOL, gabled, with corrugated metallic roof. To the w, the POLICE TRAINING SCHOOL, a successful group of three ranges round a well-landscaped quadrangle, open towards the church. Varied two-storey buildings, articulated by piers or pilasters: E, the SCHOOL itself, with partly projecting upper floor; S, LECTURE THEATRE and RESTAURANT, with much recessed glazing (and minimalist rear garden with fine view over Worcester); w, the SPORTS HALL, sheer brick. W of the church, a RESIDENTIAL BLOCK, then the long HQ CRIME & DISORDER, both with corrugated metallic roofs, the latter's split level with clerestory glazing. Opposite, the smaller TRAFFIC & OPERATIONS BUILDING, entirely corrugated-clad.

The LODGE, ½ m. NW on the A38, must also be *c.* 1818: stuccoed, many plain pilasters, shallow hipped roof; big ashlar GATEPIERS.

Late C19 brick estate buildings. COURT FARM, ¼ m. WSW, is an interesting early attempt at Queen Anne, probably *c.* 1879 (the date on the nearby cottages): segment-headed windows, hipped roof, square bay set at an angle across the NE corner. One of three pairs of estate cottages ¼ m. further w carries the date 1876, when there was a spate of these throughout the parish. Nearby, THE MANOR, the rectory of 1841, by *D. R. Hill* of Birmingham for the Rev. John Webster; squared-off, embryonic Tudor.

CUMMIN'S FARMHOUSE, ⅜ m. SE. Gabled late C19 brick, N side, mostly C17, S, with partly C16 timber-framed cross-wing, E, with fine interior decoration. Its front parlour has an elaborate plaster ceiling of *c.* 1660, divided into compartments by stuccoed beams. Bold central oval wreath, deep frieze with foliage and cartouches for painted arms; above the (renewed) chimneypiece, a scrolled segmental pediment, with swags of fruit and flowers flanked by small symbolic figures. Contemporary open-well rear staircase with dumb-bell balusters. Plainer cross-beamed plaster ceiling on the upper floor; on the landing, a plaster panel with lion rampant, dated 1615.

Near the C18–C19 brick OFFERTON FARM, 1 m. ESE, a series of LOCKS on the Worcester and Birmingham Canal (opened 1815), ending in an original one close up against the brick BRIDGE No. 24.

WORCESTER RUGBY GROUND, 1 m. SE, close to the M5. Mostly by *McConaghy Architects*, 1996: training area and grandstand with elegantly curving aluminium roofs, supported from steel stanchions.

HINTON ON THE GREEN

A possession of St Peter's Abbey, Gloucester, until the Dissolution. The parish was transferred from Gloucestershire only in 1931.

ST PETER. Lias, with ashlar dressings. Norman nave with good N and S doorways, the former largely unaltered; one order of shafts, capitals with scalloped decoration like folded material (cf. Beckford), roll-moulded arch. The N doorway retains its tympanum, with crudely incised trellis pattern. Dec and Perp nave windows, the former perhaps dating from a consecration of 1315; the latter, both of four lights, belong to a remodelling that also added battlements with gargoyles. Excellent Dec-Perp W tower, with diagonal buttresses and battlements with gargoyles and pinnacles; tower arch with broad hollow mouldings. Rood stair and piscina, nave SE. *Preedy* restored the nave and tower in 1862–3, renewing tracery and adding the S porch. The medieval chancel had been demolished by the C17. Its blocked Perp arch was reopened when the present chancel was added, 1894–5, to designs by *J.D. Sedding*; Perp-style windows, only the five-light E showing his more personal interpretation.

FONT. Octagonal, Perp, the bowl with fleurons in quatrefoils. – Other FITTINGS mostly by *Preedy* (nave) or *Sedding* (chancel), the latter a good ensemble with *Godwin* encaustic floor tiles. – LECTERN and LITANY DESK by *J. Wippell & Co. Ltd*, 1936; they added the matching wooden PULPIT, on the round base of *Preedy*'s stone predecessor, in 1948. – A few medieval TILE FRAGMENTS. – STAINED GLASS. Fine E window by *Christopher Whall*, a war memorial of 1920–1. – Chancel N and S by *Heaton, Butler & Bayne*, 1916–17. – MONUMENTS. Large incised alabaster slab to William Halford, former Abbot of Bordesley (p. 550), †1490. A youthful figure, perhaps wearing academic dress; the diagonally set crozier may indicate retirement. Canopy and roundels with Evangelists' symbols.

MANOR FARM, SW. The existing house represents the SE wing of a large manor house, probably early C17, much rebuilt *c.* 1670 after Civil War damage. Main range demolished early in the C19, when the wing was remodelled as a farmhouse, still in C17 style with gables and ovolo-mullioned windows; the W front is entirely, the S front largely of this date. Late Georgian well stair. – The unusual early C17 GATEWAY (SE of the church) consists of two rectangular gabled dovecotes linked by a pair of high classical arches; these have double-hollow mouldings, continuous apart from imposts and keystone.

OLD RECTORY, NE, by *J.A. Chatwin*, 1874–5. Red brick on a stone plinth, ample blue brick patterning, especially in the gables, patterned tiled roof; bay window, half-timbered W porch.

Former SCHOOL, WNW of the church, similar but simpler, also by *Chatwin*, 1882.

The STATION HOUSE, ½ m. WNW, by *George Hunt*, 1864, on the former Barnt Green–Ashchurch loop line, survives; Lias, with freestone segment-headed windows (cf. Ashton under Hill).

HOLDFAST *see* QUEENHILL

HOLLYBUSH
Berrow

ALL SAINTS. 1869 by *Frederick Preedy*; of rock-faced sandstone. The finest thing is the position, on its own against the Malvern Hills. Nave and chancel in one, the latter tactfully increased to two bays in 1929 (by *Nicholson & Clarke* of Hereford). W bell-cote above a cinquefoiled rose; SW porch. Plate tracery elsewhere; especially forceful the stepped E window. Heavy arch-braced roofs, nave and chancel separated by cinquefoil cusping on foliage corbels. Elaborately carved piscina. – Fittings mostly original, the alabaster and marble REREDOS slightly later. – STAINED GLASS. Good E window by *Preedy*, 1869.

The OLD VICARAGE, a little SSE. Of 1920, roughcast brick, with slate roof.

The MANOR HOUSE, uphill ½ m. W, is mid-C18, brick, two storeys and three bays, with projecting centre. Doorway with open pediment on brackets, small window either side, boldly detailed Venetian window above. In the entrance hall, a good open-well staircase. Attached timber-framed cottage.

THE LODGE, on the lane to Chase End, a thatched *cottage orné* of rock-faced Malvern stone at the start of the long drive to Bromesberrow Place (remodelled by *George Basevi*, *c.* 1825; *see The Buildings of England: Gloucestershire 2*). The drive crosses Whiteleaved Oak by a low, tunnel-like bridge.

HOLT

Church and castle stand almost on their own, ¾ m. ESE of Holt Heath, the nucleus of the parish since the opening of the bridge across the Severn in 1828.

p. 22   ST MARTIN. One of the most impressive Norman village churches in the county, and except for Rock the most profusely decorated. The evidence, however, is obscured by vigorous Neo-Norman work of 1858–9. Norman nave and chancel, the latter extended in the C13–C14, long Dec S chapel, Perp W tower. The fine Norman S doorway, in a full-height wall projection, has two orders of shafts carrying fantastical capitals: l., a dragon biting its tail and crowned man grasping a foliage trail that issues from his mouth; r., intertwined tendrils and toothy monster-head. Imposts with interlaced trails, arch with elaborate stepped chevron. To the W, a decorated Norman string course interrupted by a lavish window that seems entirely of 1858–9, adopting motifs from the Norman work. Simpler N doorway, also with finely carved capitals: l., the fable of the fox and crane, both drinking from a barrel; r., leaf and volute decoration. Arch with chevron, one order at right angles to the other. The Norman string course, of beaded cable moulding, survives along most of the nave N wall; two original Norman openings stand on it. The elaborate window further E, however, again interrupting the string course, is of 1859. The original extent of the Norman chancel is shown by its string course, a crenellation frieze. Its two N windows were lengthened in the C13–C14; blocked lowside lancet, NW, partly obscured by the plain vestry of 1858–9. The chancel lengthening provided, surprisingly, an extra Norman-style lancet each side; the E window is simple Dec. S chapel with more elaborate Dec windows, three-light E, three S of two lights. Blocked lowside lancets, one S, one W (next to the S doorway); also a blocked four-centred doorway. Finally the W tower, perhaps C14 in origin, but with a Perp W window and slightly projecting bell-stage which is late C15, with four-centred bell-openings, battlements and short crocketed pinnacles.

Inside, the original chancel arch is preserved. Two orders, the inner, larger demi-shafts with capitals with grimacing heads above scallops (l.) or volute-type foliage (r.), the outer with trails or decorated scallops. Arch with elaborate chevron, a beast's head at the apex; its inner order, with incised soffit, reads as a kind of crenellation with sparse triangular merlons. The hoodmould has ribbed chain-links, a pellet at the centre of each, and grotesque headstops. Neil Stratford proposed c. 1160–75 for all this Norman work, comparing it with Herefordshire (for example Bromyard and Upper Sapey), but not the so-called Herefordshire School. The carving of the N vestry arch is of course Neo-Norman of 1858–9, probably executed by *Mary Sale*, the rector's wife (cf. Little Witley). C13 trefoil-headed piscina with fillet. The S chapel has a two-bay arcade to the nave, a wider single arch to the chancel. Both were clearly cut through the Norman wall, on which their short demi-octagonal responds rest. Rather coarse details, with round double-chamfered arches; the octagonal free-standing pier has a round capital. If this is indeed all C14, it, together with the Norman-style chancel windows, is a notable case of 'keeping in keeping'.

FONT. Norman, cauldron-shaped, on an earlier base with incised zigzag. Short, thick, round stem with spiral fluting like the nave piers at Durham. Beaded cable moulding beneath the bowl, which has six big monster-heads with a chain of symmetrical trails issuing from their mouths. Deeply drilled eyes, probably for inserted 'jewels'. – Neo-Norman stone PULPIT carved by *Mary Sale*, with strong reminiscences of Ravenna. Her matching lectern was removed in the 1970s. The *Building News*, 1858, commented: 'We refuse to criticize [them], as they are the work of a lady and it is pleasing to find them taking an interest in these matters.' – MOSAIC of 1859, above the chancel arch: the Good Shepherd, copied from the Mausoleum of Galla Placidia at Ravenna. – The REREDOS mosaics have angels after Fra Angelico, signed '*F. Novo*, Venezia. 1886'. – Brass ALTAR RAILS, Neo-Norman style, 1877. – CHOIR

STALLS. 1897. – TILES. A good patch, chancel S side, with heraldry and quatrefoiled inscriptions, including the date 1456. – More late C15 tiles in the S chapel, several patterns of sixteen by the arch to the chancel. – STAINED GLASS. E window by *Herbert W. Bryans*, 1897, still entirely in Kempe style. – One N window has fragments from Nuremberg (inserted 1906), including a C17–C18 panel of the Transfiguration in deep yellow stain; other lancets with *Powell*'s quarries, 1858–9. – In the S chapel, the C14 E window traceries have the Scull and Talbot arms, the SE window much of a fine mid-C15 Annunciation, also with Scull arms above. – MONUMENTS. Clumsily repainted effigy of a Beauchamp lady, her feet on a lion; early to mid-C14 (rather than C15 as inscribed on the plain York stone tomb-chest of 1938). Tabard and helmet above. – On the chapel W wall, a richly detailed tablet to Mercy Bromley †1704; twisted columns, seated putti outside them, rays, clouds and putto heads above the inscription. – Other good tablets: Henry Bromley †1670, erected 1683, with Ionic columns and broken curly pediment (S chapel); Sir Henry Bromley †1615, with short columns, strapwork below, allegorical figures and heraldic cartouche above (chancel). – Also C18 black ledgers, mostly with heraldry.

Neo-Norman stone LYCHGATE, presumably of 1858–9. Pevsner thought the shafts may have been reused Norman work; their odd capitals have a kind of convex scallop reminiscent of beakhead. C18 paintings show a S porch but no lychgate, so recycling is certainly possible.

HOLT CASTLE, to the E. In 1086 Holt was held by Urse D'Abitôt who built a castle here. After his death it passed to the Beauchamp family and by c. 1600 belonged to the Bromleys, who sold it, c. 1760, to Thomas, second Lord Foley (cf. Great Witley). The oldest surviving part is the sturdy square tower, built c. 1385 by John Beauchamp (who was executed in 1388); it is unclear whether this was built as part of a larger building. Battlemented, of four stages, the upper three with small two-light Dec W windows. On its S side, a chamber lit by three narrow rectangular windows; a fourth, SW, lit a former spiral stair. On the N, a straight staircase rises within the thickness of the wall. Four-centred W entrance added in the C15, in connection with an L-plan hall and solar block built behind the tower, E. The entrance hall, within the tower, has two bays of rib vaulting, with ridge as well as diagonal ribs; circular murder holes at their intersections. This must have led into a screens passage at the hall's N end. The most prominent feature of the hall now is its large central C16 chimney-breast with three tall brick stacks. The solar block projected to the NE; upper floor now subdivided, but part of the C15 roof survives. Early in the C18 the whole interior was remodelled, with a drawing room and spacious staircase infilling the area E of the hall. The dog-leg staircase has two turned balusters per tread, an elegant moulded handrail, and panelled dado; ceiling with floral stucco decoration. The medieval hall retained its open proportions

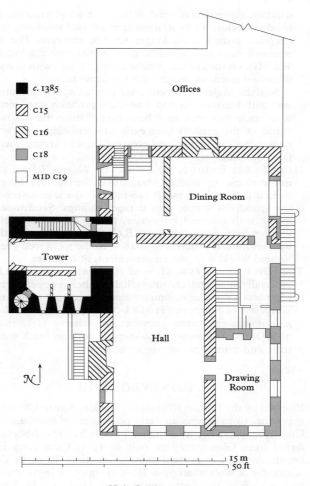

Holt Castle.
Plan of principal floor

Legend:
- ■ c. 1385
- ▨ C15
- ◩ C16
- ▦ C18
- □ MID C19

Offices

Dining Room

Tower

Hall

Drawing Room

N

15 m
50 ft

but was encased in excellent fielded panelling, as was the room on the lower floor of the solar wing. In the C19, perhaps in 1868, a large double-pile service range was built N of the solar wing, so that the tower now appears more or less central to the w entrance front. This range, also battlemented, has four bays and two storeys of upright mullioned windows. Its roof-line is lower than the C15 block (though inside the floor is at a higher level). Two gables to the N return, with a short battlemented stretch between. The garden front, E, is at a lower level, but stands high above the Severn. Its battlements are interrupted near the centre by a gable with C16 four-light mullioned window, expressing the end of the solar wing; tripartite sashed windows below. To its N, upright mullioned windows, to the S, irregular sashed ones, longer for the staircase. The garden entrance steps have wrought-iron railings with the initials WB and MB. S return of five regular early C18 bays with two storeys of sashed windows, again with battlements.

At right angles to the entrance front, SW, is a tall sandstone wall with battlements and wall-walk, probably C15, continued W in brick; this must have been part of the outer defences. To E and SE the gardens have early C18 retaining walls and terracing; the S terracing may preserve the C16 arrangement. C19 farm buildings, N.

HOLT FLEET BRIDGE, ½ m. NNW. By *Thomas Telford*, 1826–7, ironwork cast by *William Hazledine* of Shrewsbury. Single segmental iron arch of 150-ft (46-metres) span; cross-bracing in the spandrels, simple iron parapet railings. Sandstone abutments with battered buttresses, two flood arches each side. Cruder in appearance since *B.C. Hammond*'s strengthening with reinforced concrete in 1928. – To the NE, a well-preserved Second World War gun emplacement, of concrete.

The HOLT FLEET INN, SE, is of 1937; brick with stone bands, especially on the tall chimneys; half-timbered upper parts. Holt Fleet was a popular stopping point for pleasure steamers from Worcester or Stourport. HOLT LOCK, upstream, W, belongs to *E.L. Williams*'s Severn improvement scheme of *c.* 1840 (cf. p. 365). Contemporary lock-keeper's cottage, brick with blue trim, and central two-storey canted bay.

HONEYBOURNE

Bisected by the Roman Ryknild (or Buckle) Street. Church Honeybourne, to its E, was an early possession of Evesham Abbey; Cow Honeybourne, W, a manor of Winchcombe Abbey, transferred from Gloucestershire only in 1931. Until 1969 Honeybourne was an important railway junction: Brunel's Oxford, Worcester & Wolverhampton Railway, opened 1853, was joined by a branch to Stratford-upon-Avon in 1859, then by a through line to Cheltenham, 1906.

ST EGWIN, Church Honeybourne. A dedication in 1295 may indicate the date of the chancel (cf. Bretforton); side windows with cusped lancets, E window a stepped group of three, recessed under one chamfered arch. The nave is a little later; its NE window has Dec tracery, the NW Y-tracery (perhaps an amendment connected with the insertion of a W gallery in 1826). A short S aisle was demolished in the late C17, its blocked arcade now filled with two C19 Dec windows. Plain W tower carrying a fine ribbed Dec spire, quite a personal job. Its corner pinnacles and octagonal spire start in the main directions flush with the tower, in the diagonals behind the pinnacles. Three tiers of lucarnes, the lowest right at the foot; there are eight altogether: large, of two lights, with Dec tracery under steep gables. Massive sloping four-stage buttress, NW, added *c.* 1700. Perp s porch with stone roof on four transverse stone arches (cf. Hampton, p. 294). Entrance with spandrels pierced with quatrefoils, its hoodmould on large round stops. The three-light Perp window to the w has the same (cf. the E window at Pebworth). The nave roof was also raised at about this date and given a s clerestory. Roof of shallow pitch, with moulded tie-beams on angel corbels and good foliage-carved spandrels. The chancel has very satisfying internal proportions; chamfered rere-arches, continuous filleted string-course. The chancel arch, roof and fittings are by *Ewan Christian,* 1865. Re-set C14 piscina with crocketed head.

FONT. C19 Perp; the plain bowl of its predecessor lies under the chancel arch. – PULPIT, from Cow Honeybourne. Reassembled panels of *c.* 1600, quite lavishly decorated. – C19 poppyhead PEWS, from the same source, fitted with doors from the former pews of 1826. – STAINED GLASS. Chancel s, two large figures of Faith and Hope, *c.* 1897, from the demolished Unitarian Chapel in Gloucester, re-set here 1970. – MONUMENTS. William Bennett †1825, by *T. Davis* of Inkberrow; tablet with urn.

The OLD VICARAGE, w, is pleasant if rather reactionary Tudor Gothic of 1870.

CHURCH (dedication unknown), Cow Honeybourne. Rebuilt, apart from the Late Perp w tower, by *Hopkins,* 1861–2; converted to housing, with nave dormers, *c.* 1978. The yellow ashlar tower has gargoyles, battlements, and one remaining corner pinnacle. Hopkins's nave, N porch and chancel, Lias with ashlar dressings, have his typical Late Dec tracery. The transomed three-light Perp N chancel window, an oddity in his *œuvre,* probably represents the renewal of an existing feature; parts of the E wall also seem medieval.

COW HONEYBOURNE retains a pleasant village nucleus. The MANOR HOUSE, sw of the church, narrow Late Georgian, has an upright brick s front with stone dressings and Doric porch. Probably of 1831, the date on the down-pipe of one of the two low rear wings. Impressive stick baluster staircase. To the N, a small green with, E side, GREEN FARM, a good C17 Cotswold farmhouse with central gable. HIGH STREET, running across the N side of the green, has more C17 houses, with, immediately w, the former WESLEYAN CHAPEL of 1864, purple brick lancet-style (builder *Benjamin Sharp* of Paxford, Glos.). Further NE, the THATCHED TAVERN, C16–C17 timber-framed, its NE gable end with a thin cruck-truss. The former MANOR FARM opposite, also C17, stone, L-plan, has several inserted C18 windows, but more of mullioned type at the rear, towards SCHOOL STREET, plus a datestone 1627. The BOARD SCHOOL of 1896, brick with half-timbered gables and some Queen Anne touches, incorporates an earlier building of *c.* 1860, its cross-windows with latticed glazing. Opposite, THE GABLES (No. 61), again C17, with bands of Cotswold and Lias stone; three gabled dormers, a little attractive plasterwork inside. Further on, where School Street doubles back towards High Street, a few more C17–C18 houses.

HONEYBOURNE AIRFIELD, 1 m. s, built 1940–1, now an industrial estate. Most of its wartime buildings survive, including one Type J HANGAR (with curved roof) and four of T2 type, two of them a linked pair.

HUDDINGTON

ST JAMES. Close to Huddington Court. C12–C16, well restored by *C.F. Whitcombe*, 1900, with some interesting fittings. Norman nave, with plain s doorway and NW window; most others are C14, the more ornate Dec one, NE, of 1900. Small timber-framed bell-turret. Short s aisle also probably C14, altered in the C17, partially rebuilt 1900. Good Perp timber N porch, its entrance and the N doorway with flattened ogee arches. Stately Late Perp chancel: side windows with straight heads and panel tracery, E window of three stepped lights with stepped panel tracery above stepped transoms. Defaced image niches inside, blank shields above. Contemporary chancel arch. The two-bay s arcade has handsome piers, cruciform with hollowed re-entrant angles and demi-shafts attached to the ends; moulded capitals, moulded arches. *Whitcombe* reopened the w bay, formerly blocked. Good nave wagon roof. – COMMUNION RAIL. Mid-C17; vertically symmetrical balusters. – STALLS. The s side is early C16, *in situ*, with a form of linenfold and steep bench ends. N side renewed, with standard linenfold. – Dado chancel PANELLING made up from former box pews, also parts of a C14 screen with spyholes (cf. Shelsley Walsh). – SCREEN. C17–C18; widely spaced Jacobean balusters above a dado matching the simply panelled C18 PULPIT. – Plain BENCHES, some C16–C17. – Plain octagonal FONT; late C14. – TILES. A good C15 display on the s aisle w wall, mostly sixteen-tile quatrefoil patterns. – Late medieval CHEST, decoratively carved. – ROYAL ARMS. George III; late C18. – STAINED GLASS. Chancel. E window. Early C16 Crucifixion with the Virgin and St John, said to come from Cornwall; well restored by *Geoffrey Webb*, 1933. – In the side traceries, early C16 glass with emblems of the Wintour family. – s aisle. A jumble of old fragments in the s window; heraldic shields in the w, the best dated 1584. – Nave NW, 1900. – MONUMENTS. Brass inscription plate to Dom Adrian Fortescue †1653; early C20 classical wooden frame. – Sir George Wintour †1658, and his wife Dame Mary †1696; very good tablet, white and black marble, with Corinthian columns and heraldry.

HUDDINGTON COURT. A close-studded T-plan manor house, set within a moat. It does not conform to the usual hall and cross-wing plan, and must have formed part of a much larger house; the present main range was perhaps its solar wing.*
The manor came to the Wintour family in the mid C15,

* Prattinton, 1811, reported that the 'Great Part of the Court House has been pulled down lately, amongst other Parts the Gate House.'

remaining in their hands until 1658, despite their involvement
in the Gunpowder Plot (for which three Wintour sons were
executed). Restored 1919–23, after years of decline as a farmhouse, by Hubert Edmondson, with assistance from the artist
and antiquary *Oliver Baker* (and probably also from *W. A.
Harvey*).

Seen from the E, it is the most picturesque house in Worces-   55
tershire. In the angle between the main range and rear S stem
is a deliciously fanciful chimney of the kind familiar from
Hampton Court and other houses of the time of Henry VIII.
This, however, is probably late C15; tall stone base and two
twisted and moulded brick shafts with trefoiled panels below.
The rear wing, three unequal bays, probably predates the large
tall E–W range, of six bays and two storeys plus attics, dendro-
dated to *c.* 1493. The central N porch, with thin Ionic demi-
columns, was perhaps added *c.* 1584 (the date on heraldic
stained glass in the upper W room); the former entrance was
probably one bay further E. Most windows project slightly,
oriel-wise, as was the tradition; the only original one seems to
be that with plastered coving below, first floor, E of the porch.
Imported rainwater heads, one of 1742, plus a large trough W
of the porch, dated 1714. Two-storey bay window on the E
return added *c.* 1920.

The present entrance leads into a wide hall with a late C16
open-well staircase. Richly moulded ceiling beams and arched
doorheads throughout. The outstanding room, the Great
Parlour, fills the three E bays of the first floor. It has a canted
ceiling and moulded stone fireplace with spectacular early C14
stone frieze, probably from the preceding house; four quatrefoils enclose suspended heraldic shields, held by a bird's head,
dog, hooded man, and hare. The quatrefoils are studded
with embryonic ballflower; bigger, fully carved ballflowers in
between. Two priest holes at attic level, fully convincing
and really safe, are probably of *c.* 1584, by *Nicholas Owen* (cf.
Harvington Hall, p. 368).

The house is approached across the moat by a C16 brick
bridge, through brick GATEPIERS with stone lion finials; late
C18 gates, imported from Yorkshire. In the garden, two timber-
framed C17 DOVECOTES, the NE from Abbots Morton, the NW
probably from Broughton Hackett; by the W brick bridge, a
sweet timber-framed PRIVY. To the N the moat is crossed by
an elliptical cast-iron FOOTBRIDGE, from Eardiston (p. 429);
large pierced spandrels, decorative balustrade, inscribed
'Stourport Foundry 1827'. Ornate late C18 iron GATES, SW,
also from Yorkshire. To the S, a large, rectangular, Grecian
ORANGERY from Strensham Court; ashlar, probably *c.* 1824,
with widely spaced tetrastyle Tuscan portico, N side.

At the start of the short village street, N of the gates to Court and
church, is PRIEST'S COTTAGE, an exceptionally well-
preserved cruck example, probably late C15. Three full cruck
frames, the outer two visible in the end walls; the W porch
towards the N end marks the former through-passage. The

additional SW porch probably represents early subdivision into two cottages, with inserted floors.

At SALE GREEN, a larger hamlet 1 m. NNW, a brick PRIMITIVE METHODIST CHAPEL of 1893, windows still round-arched; and SALE GREEN FARM (now Aulseter House), timber-framed, late C16, H-plan, its diapered brick SW front, with gables and timber porch, by *John Cotton*, 1880.

INKBERROW

ST PETER. Mostly Perp: early C15, the nave and battlemented W tower, with four-light window above the finely moulded W doorway; later C15, the fine N aisle with panel tracery, battlements, crocketed pinnacles and gargoyles. Ornate porch with ogee arch and large grotesque gargoyles, reconstructed by *Ewan Christian*, 1887–8. He also rebuilt most of the chancel and part of the S transept; its S window, a stepped trefoiled triplet with raised surround, is of 1784. Heavy Late Perp N arcade: four bays, octagonal piers, double-chamfered arches. N chapel yet later, with very shallow four-centred arch to the chancel; no arch between aisle and chapel. Tall tower arch, continuously double-chamfered. S transept arch probably C14. Roofs all of 1887–8.

FONT. Large square bowl of *c*. 1200. Beneath it a kind of large elaborate dogtooth; on each side three medallions with rosettes or crosses, also the Agnus Dei and fleurs-de-lys. The top surface retains part of a Lombardic inscription, a rare survival. – PULPIT. Probably of 1840–1; thin Gothic panelling. – CHANCEL FURNISHINGS typical of *Christian*. – VESTRY SCREEN by *Pancheri & Son*, 1970; nicely stylized carving. – By the same, the ENGLISH ALTAR, N chapel, 1968, with C16 TABLE. – STAINED GLASS. Late C15 fragments, especially N aisle W: SS Catherine and Margaret (?), with musical angels, all yellow stain. – Chancel SE by *William Pearce Ltd*, 1899; SW by *A.K. Nicholson*, 1920. – MONUMENTS. John Savage of Edgiock (p. 239) †1631; probably by *Samuel Baldwin*. Alabaster recumbent effigy wearing armour, damaged kneeling children against his tomb-chest. Black composite columns, flat canopy with achievement flanked by obelisks. Its soffit has, instead of Renaissance coffering, Gothic quatrefoiled panels with trefoiled sub-cusping, an interesting case of Gothic Survival (cf. the Sandys monument, Wickhamford). Restored 1988. – Retardaire tablets: Frances Sheldon †1690, Corinthian columns, segmental pediment; John Gower †1769, big curved pediment with heraldry.

Detached PARISH ROOM, S, by *Bartosch & Stokes* of Cheltenham, 1994–5. – Good LYCHGATE by *Harold Brakspear*, 1919.

The rectangular wet MOAT, ⅛ m. ENE, probably marks the site of the C12–C13 castle, or rather fortified manor house. This was derelict by 1392.

The OLD VICARAGE, NW of the church, rebuilt by *Lewis Belling* of Worcester, 1837, incorporates part of the parsonage of 1762; brick, Tudor Gothic, straight-headed windows, bargeboarded gables. Later C19 battlements and canted bay window.

Pretty triangular GREEN further W with C17 timber-framed inn and C18–C19 brick houses. In HIGH STREET, along its W side, a similar mix and a former BAPTIST CHAPEL (Bethesda), of 1861, brick, round-arched windows. More timber-framed houses in PEPPER STREET, leading SE, especially THE ROCK, L-plan, with gables.

At STONEPITS, further W, a former stone windmill, *c.* 1840, converted to a house with gabled wings, 1906; extra battlemented storey added 1924. STONEPITS COTTAGE to its S, thatched stone and render, is successful pastiche by *T.R. Bateman*, apparently of 1954. The square, folly-like, castellated TOWER, of salmon brick, on the hillside to the E, was erected as a telecom transmitter in 1996.

(BOARD) SCHOOL, N end, by *E.A. Day*, 1876; rock-faced Tudor, the detached house little altered, the school all but overwhelmed by low C20 brick additions.

STOCKWOOD LANE opposite leads W to STONEHOUSE FARM, C17 and exceptionally for this district entirely of sandstone ashlar; broad U-plan, with gables and mullioned windows.

Many other attractive houses, farms and cottages throughout the extensive hilly parish, either of C17 timber framing or C18 brick. STEP HILL FARM, at Morton Underhill, 1¼ m. NNW, is late C18 brick, of three bays and storeys, with attached timber-framed barn, facing a pond, with two larger weatherboarded BARNS further S.

MORTON HALL, 1⅓ m. NNE, near Holberrow Green.* Said to be of *c.* 1781. Five bays and two-and-a-half storeys, the ground floor ashlar-faced; tall parapet, stone quoins, windows with straight rubbed brick heads and horizontally set oblong glazing. Stone porch with pairs of Doric columns, flanked by urns. Lower l. wing, probably early C19. – The C19 MORTON HALL FARM, SW, has a large weatherboarded C17 BARN.

At BOUTS, 1¼ m. NE, several C17 (or earlier) timber-framed farms and cottages, some later faced in brick.

The two main farms at KNIGHTON, 1⅜ m. ESE, are mostly C18, with attractive outbuildings. The early C18 GREAT KNIGHTON FARM has quoins and moulded cornice; the plainer late C18 BARRELS MANOR FARM has a central round-arched doorway and window, with earlier timber-framed rear wing.

THORN FARM, 1 m. SSW, is probably C16, part timber-framed, part ashlar; H-plan, the hall-range set N–S, with inserted, high-set, Elizabethan ceiling.

* At Holberrow Green, the remnant of a second WINDMILL, late C18 brick, domesticated 1979–80.

IPSLEY *see* REDDITCH

9030

KEMERTON

Transferred from Gloucestershire in 1931.

ST NICHOLAS. Rebuilt, apart from the W tower, by *R.C. Carpenter*, 1846–9, one of the rare major churches by this favourite of the Cambridge Camden (later Ecclesiological) Society; built for the Rev. Thomas Thorp, Archdeacon of Bristol, president of the Society 1839–59. The early C13 tower, which Carpenter intended to replace with a broach-spired steeple, was remodelled in the early C16 when the battlemented top stage was added; restored by *William White*, 1879. C13 tower arch of two slight chamfers. Carpenter's church is of fine ashlar, in early C14 Dec style: nave, S aisle (with timber S porch) and chancel of 1846–7, N aisle 1849. The S aisle tracery patterns are surprisingly wilful, especially its E window. N aisle quieter. Chancel with ballflower frieze; tall N vestry with pointed cinquefoil window. Four-bay arcades with filleted quatrefoil piers and finely moulded capitals and arches; matching chancel arch, high arch-braced nave roof. The boarded and canted chancel roof is painted, as were originally the chancel walls (remnants on sedilia and piscina).

Carpenter's FURNISHINGS are gratifyingly complete. Most notable, the standing octagonal FONT, richly arcaded, the ornate wooden SCREEN with returned stalls, and splendid iron and brass nave CORONA (made by *Hardman*). – STAINED GLASS. Of 1847, by *Willement*, the E and S aisle windows. – Good chancel side windows by *Hardman*, 1852–4, also one in the N aisle, 1883; the E and NE windows here are by *Clayton & Bell*, 1880–1. – Tower W by *William Pearce Ltd*, 1903–12. – REREDOS. Painted by *Miss G.M. Hopton*, 1912, using Florentine quattrocento models. – C14 PISCINA, loose in the S aisle. – MONUMENT. Chancel recess with incised portrait slab, with Italian marble inlay, to the Rev. Thomas Thorp †1877. – Outside, a large angel by *L. Croce*, to his successor the Rev. J.J. Mercier †1901.

Some distance N, *Carpenter*'s former SCHOOL of 1845, mostly grouped lancets, somewhat altered: schoolroom with E.E. doorway, hipped-roofed master's house.

ST BENET (R.C.), E end of the village. A notable small-scale Puginian group of 1842–3, by *M.E. Hadfield* (of *Weightman & Hadfield* of Sheffield), entered through an arched gateway. The ashlar church, with sanctus bellcote and (ritual) NW porch, is in Dec style. Largely unaltered interior, open roofs with arched Gothic bracing; chancel arch on semi-octagonal responds. – Contemporary FONT and stone PULPIT. – Gabled stone REREDOS, 1853–5. – Timber W GALLERY. 1896. – STAINED GLASS. The N chancel lancet has a C16 roundel and six C17 Netherlandish panels, said to come from Woollas Hall (p. 279). More old glass in the porch. – Other windows mostly

Hardman: nave NE 1854, SE 1858, another nave S 1885, E window 1898. – MONUMENTS. Three brasses of kneeling females, all by *Hardman*, 1848–50.

Adjoining PRESBYTERY, Tudor Gothic style. – Matching SCHOOL, NW, by *Thomas Collins*, 1850, with attached teacher's house; enlarged 1905.

Several good houses to the S of St Nicholas. First, SE, is UPPER COURT, stone, *c.* 1760–70, seven bays, the central three deeply recessed; hipped roof. The r. projection has a two-storey rounded bow, probably added *c.* 1840. Spacious staircase hall, perhaps an early C20 amendment. Close to the churchyard, the former STABLES: five bays, central archway beneath a pediment. To the NE, facing a lake created *c.* 1960 from a former mill pond, a rectangular mid-C18 DOVECOTE. TheVILLA, next the rusticated gatepiers, is neat three-bay C18; rusticated, pedimented doorcase. Immediately S, the OLD RECTORY, L-plan, roughcast, said to be of 1678. The five-bay N wing looks early C18, with sashed windows and handsome central shell-hood on carved brackets; the E wing probably incorporates C16 fabric.

KEMERTON COURT (formerly Lower Court), further SW, is of C17 origin. Undistinguished rear (to the lane), but an impressive W front of *c.* 1720–30, built for John Parsons, perhaps by *Thomas White* of Worcester. Nine bays, with recessed five-bay centre, its middle bay again projecting with the pedimented Doric doorcase; above this a round-arched window, then the moulded cornice shaped to form a segmental pediment, then an attic gable oculus. The broad parapet sweeps up at each section, divided by plain giant pilasters supporting ball finials. Other windows have moulded architraves with dropped keystones. Large central W room (incorporating the former hall) with fine early C18 panelling, giant fluted pilasters flanking the S fireplace. Behind, a good open-well stair with panelled dado, again with fluted pilasters. Several later doorways no doubt resulted from internal reordering, after the road was diverted to the rear of the house in 1825.

The OLD MANOR, S again, is early to mid-C17, timber-framed; L-plan: three-bay hall range, formerly with lobby-entry, two-bay N cross-wing with stone base. Further on, attractive C17 thatched cottages, rubble or timber-framed.

On the main W–E road less of interest. THE GRANGE, late C18, has two tall storeys and three bays, quoins, and pedimented central door with tall round-arched staircase window above.

At UPPER KEMERTON, more thatched cottages and a former WESLEYAN CHAPEL of 1819; stone, hipped roof, two three-light S windows with arched heads. Brick entrance-cum-schoolroom added by *Thomas Collins*, 1885. Larger houses uphill. THE PRIORY, mostly *c.* 1800, ashlar, 3+1 bays, with a fine C16–C17 timber-framed, thatched cottage in its grounds; NORTHWOOD, brick with half-timbered gables, built *c.* 1886 for the Rev. J.J. Mercier; and MERECOMBE by *Ernest Newton*, 1910, for E.H. Barnes: stone, with gables flanking a two-storey bow.

BELL'S CASTLE, at the top of Merecombe Hill. An elaborate
Gothic folly built between 1825 and 1838 for Edmund Bell,
reputed ex-pirate and smuggler. Of 2+2+1 bays, the outer parts
unequal three-storey towers with battlements sweeping up to
corner pinnacles; high basement with Tudor-arched windows.
Other windows pointed, Y-tracery on the ground floor. Pinnacled and embattled porch leading up eleven steps into the E
tower. To the W, at an angle, a shorter tower, an earlier folly
perhaps of c. 1810. C17 cottage range, E, alongside the lane,
expanded for the Martin family (cf. Overbury) by *Ernest
Newton*, 1904–10 (and later by *Sir Herbert Baker*).

8040   KEMPSEY

Large village, the first S from Worcester on the Tewkesbury road.
The bishops of Worcester had a palace here, close to the church,
from the Saxon period; demolished before 1695.

ST MARY. Probably on the site of a Saxon minster. The earliest
surviving evidence is Norman: flat buttresses at the angles of
the nave, one NE by the N transept, and two, less broad, at the
W corners. At the S aisle W end, a lancet of c. 1200. So the
church was then already quite large. The grand chancel is of
c. 1250–60, of Lias with sandstone dressings: beautiful E
window with five stepped lancets under one blank moulded
arch; pairs of lancets each side, also under blank arches; contemporary priest's doorway. The whole is reminiscent of the
eastern arm of Worcester Cathedral. Aisle and transept walls
are mostly of red sandstone ashlar, a rebuilding of c. 1400, with
three-light early Perp windows. S aisle and transept, partially
with C13 rubble walling, were restored by *John Collingwood*,
1800,* see his large transomed five-light Perp window, S
transept S. The five-light N transept N, somewhat earlier in style
with a common central light, was renewed by *Ewan Christian*,
1864–5; his also, the N aisle W window, N porch, and SE vestry.
Later Perp W tower, of grey sandstone, with diagonal buttresses
and embattled parapet with crocketed corner pinnacles. Two-
light openings in the two upper stages; deeply recessed four-
light W window, hoodmould on crouching animal stops. Arch
to the nave with flat panelled jambs and soffit.

The three-bay nave arcades are of c. 1300, the N perhaps a
little later. They are similar but differ in several ways: quatrefoil piers (with fillets), but a convex rounded shape in the diagonals, S, a projecting diagonal spur, N; the S arches have two
hollow chamfers, the N normal chamfers. Generally the S
arcade mouldings are much finer, the arches and responds of
alternate green and white stone. This arcade clearly takes the
existing S transept into account. Embedded in the transept
walls here, traces of filleted shafts of two C13 windows, one E,

---

*He replaced *Thomas Johnson*, consulted in 1799.

one W; trefoil-headed piscina. The N transept piscina has a Dec ogee arch. The internal effect of the mid-C13 chancel was enhanced by *Christian*'s high rebuilding of the chancel arch, its large grey marble corbel shafts with deeply carved foliage capitals. The side windows have concave reveals and plain hoods, the E window a stepped hood and tall outer shafts with moulded capitals and shaft-rings. Trefoiled piscina, with rebate for a shelf, but also three moulded brackets, one foliated. Stepped sedilia also with cusped arches, beneath a continuous hoodmould with headstops; in the spandrels, foliage carving, plus a leopard's head and fleur-de-lys, apparently emblems of Walter de Cantelupe, Bishop 1237–66. All roofs are of 1864–5, that of the nave to a bold trefoil form.

FITTINGS by *Christian* include the fine stone PULPIT: round, pierced trefoil frieze at the top. – FONT, octagonal with Gothic lettering, of 1852. – STAINED GLASS. One chancel window each side with four very good medieval saints or bishops; all from the N transept N window, re-set here 1865. The larger upper figures, beneath canopies, are C14, the lower ones probably late C13. – E window by *Edward Frampton*, 1890–2, quite effective; Last Supper at the bottom added by *Hardman*, 1958. – Chancel NE by *Wailes*, c. 1868; NW by *Hardman*, 1872. – Chancel SE, c. 1871, no doubt *Heaton, Butler & Bayne*. – Also theirs the S aisle window, c. 1898.

MONUMENTS. Sir Edmund Wylde †1620, perhaps by *Samuel Baldwin*; restored by *Elsie Matley Moore*, 1952. Recumbent armed effigy beneath shallow arch; strapwork-enriched inscription. Fluted Composite columns either side, base with diamond-rusticated round arches; his two sons kneel in front. At the top, a pedimented achievement and the unusual motif of balustrading; above this, Wylde's helm and sword. – Mrs Elizabeth Eaton †1790, by *William Stephens*; remarkably good. Standing monument with large urn, in front of a grey obelisk, on a brown and white sarcophagus; on this, a fine oval relief of the mother with her children. – Other tablets by the prolific Stephens family include two by *J. Stephens*: Thomas Farley †1821, solid Grecian with stern bust on top (chancel); Samuel Salisbury †1853, with draped urn (S transept). – Other good tablets. W.H. Derrington †1836, by *Lewis* of Cheltenham, draped broken column (S transept); Thomas Hyde †1858, by *W. Perks*, dignified Grecian (N transept); and Louisa Temple †1837, by *H. Hopper* of London, also Grecian, with draped urn and willow (tower). – Next to this, Rt Hon. Sir Richard Temple, a former Governor of Bombay, †1902; stiff bronze bust with moustaches and a goatee, by *Adolphus Rost*, 1904.

CHURCHYARD. The CROSS, made up 1865, reuses a medieval base dug up from beneath the E end of the S arcade. – LYCHGATE, NE, of 1868, facing a ford across Hatfield Brook, with brick pedestrian BRIDGE of 1792.

The church lies within the S part of a quadrangular earthwork, perhaps of Iron Age origin, enclosing about four acres (now mostly obliterated). A probable ROMAN MILESTONE, inscribed to Constantine (early C4), was found, to the NW, in 1818.

In CHURCH STREET, to the NE, a nice pair of thatched and timber-framed cottages of c. 1700, then the former BAPTIST CHAPEL, 1866–7 by the Worcester builder *J.H. Higgs*; Gothic, brick with stone dressings. On the SW corner of the crossroads with the main road is IVY HOUSE, three-bay brick, c. 1800, with segment-headed windows. MELBURY HOUSE, to the NE, stuccoed, c. 1830–40, has pretty Gothick detail: Tudor-arched frieze, pilasters with tracery panels, four-centred windows with hoodmoulds. More Georgian brick houses in OLD ROAD NORTH, straight ahead: PARK HOUSE, with good pedimented doorway; EASTERN LODGE, larger, of five bays, with panelled or fluted keystones; and, set back after the road turns N, the MANOR HOUSE, with another good doorcase.

On WORCESTER ROAD, some distance N, the SCHOOL by *John J. Cole*, 1848–9. Brick, gabled, with four-centred windows of three lights, with transoms and rounded cinquefoiled heads; simpler attached master's house. Spoilt by later additions (e.g. by *Hopkins*, 1872) and conversion to a community centre, 1980.

More good brick or stuccoed houses survive amongst the C20 development along Worcester Road, S of the crossroads.* The TALBOT INN has two-storey bows with tripartite windows and a pedimented Tuscan doorway. Of early C19 stuccoed villas, the best is the OLD VICARAGE, set back, E side; plain corner pilasters, shuttered windows, and a two-storey cast-iron veranda right across the two-bay front. COLNE HOUSE (No. 65), opposite, has giant pilasters rising from its first-floor balcony to the big cornice and blocking course; one-storey wings. Then a nice brick group: No. 63, three bays, and WEST ROYD, of four, with amply rounded S end.

Beyond the S end of the village are DRAYCOTT HOUSE (No. 27), late C18 (with fluted keystones), much altered by *A. William West*, 1895; and opposite, E, DRAYCOTT LODGE, c. 1800, three bays and storeys, painted brick.

NAPLETON HOUSE, ¾ m. ESE. Late Georgian, thoroughly overhauled by *Yeates & Jones*, 1878, with bay windows, blocky porch, and an extra storey.

CLERKENLEAP FARM, 1⅜ m. N. C16–C17 timber-framed, remodelled in Tudor style c. 1840: brick, three gables with bargeboards.

BAYNHAM FARM, 1⅛ m. S, has a contrasting three-bay classical house of c. 1840, with thin Tuscan porch; good array of brick hop kilns at the rear.

THE NASH, 1¼ m. SE. An interesting brick house with crow-stepped gables, mostly c. 1600, but according to the VCH a

---

*On the N side of Squires Walk was the late C18 KEMPSEY HOUSE, enlarged for the Rev. A. Boucher by *E.A. Day*, 1879–83. The only significant remains are the pair of semi-detached COTTAGES in Old Road South, ¼ m. further S; brick, gabled, heavy-handed Queen Anne.

compound of three formerly independent half-timbered blocks; much altered in the C19–C20. Striking s front, symmetrical, with two pairs of large stepped gables either side of and progressively set back from the narrow two-storey central porch; this, gabled with three tall pinnacles and vaulted within, is probably of 1831. The mullioned-and-transomed windows are all renewals of *c*. 1926 for Mrs Dunn (who purchased the house from the Temple family, owners from *c*. 1738). Similar gables on the w return, but the two stone bay windows here, one square, one canted, as well as the renewed windows, are by *W.A. Forsyth*, 1905. The oldest part externally seems to be the rear NW (containing the parlour, *see* below), probably mid-C16; brickwork with blue-brick diapering, chimney-breasts rising boldly between its two pairs of stepped gables. The similar gables and Tudor windows, NE, beyond the central staircase recession, are probably again of 1831. Other grouped diagonal chimneys, very tall, also C19.

The s porch leads into a wide entrance hall, remodelled by *Forsyth*, 1905 (with carving by *Sprague & Evans*): linenfold panelling, inglenook with re-set C17 overmantel with caryatids, richly plastered ceiling, the decoration continuing across the (reused) beams. The rear staircase must be of *c*. 1700–10, with its slim balusters, twisted but columnar (alternately stone and wood), carved tread ends, and undulating underside; elaborate stone vault above, with pendant bosses, of 1905. The former dining room, w, has a delightfully intricate plaster ceiling of *c*. 1600, with bands of vine, rose, oak and thistle, generally in ogee-shaped forms arranged almost like reticulation units (cf. Madresfield Court); oak panelling with fluted Ionic pilasters, renewed frieze of large Tudor roses and Prince of Wales' feathers. The bedroom above, formerly linked by a direct stair, so presumably the great chamber, has a similar plaster ceiling and oak panelling; chimneypiece with fluted Ionic pilasters supporting columns decorated with strapwork, but the painted plaster overmantel dated 1598 has disappeared. (The roof structure above has curved tie-beams and wind-braces.) The rear part (with the oldest-looking brickwork outside) displays much close studding within. In the partly panelled parlour, an exceptionally fine wooden overmantel with tapering pilasters, caryatids, and arched panels with very rich architectural inlay (showing men standing beneath pavilion-like structures). Part of the cellar beneath this side of the house has brick octagonal piers supporting brick vaults. The E half of the house was much enlarged in 1831 and later, as a service range, with further outbuildings beyond.

KENSWICK

7050

Small civil parish with neither church nor village.

KENSWICK MANOR. On a formerly moated medieval site, its chapel of St John the Baptist (with timber-framed chancel) demolished *c.* 1860. The present house, perhaps of C17 origin, is rendered, three bays and storeys, with tripartite windows of *c.* 1800. Much remodelled for Rear-Admiral Richard Britten, 1893, with gabled timbered dormers, tall brick chimneys, and two canted bays at the side. In the dining room, NE, C17 panelling and an elaborate overmantel from Wichenford Court (p. 658). – Half-timbered LODGE dated 1897.

WOODHALL FARM, ⅝m. WSW, C17 timber-framed, H-plan, somewhat altered, on a formerly moated site. THE KEDGES, ¾ m. WNW, also of altered C17 framing, has three N gables, a separate small house, and extensive weatherboarded farm buildings, NW, all now housing.

In 736 King Aethelbald of Mercia granted land to Earl Cyniberht for the foundation of a minster, presumably the predecessor of the present parish church, established on its elevated site above the River Stour by the C12. The medieval parish was extensive, reaching W to the Severn; the parts outside the town were known as Kidderminster Foreign. The town achieved borough status by the early C13, when, no doubt partly because of the fast-flowing Stour, it had become an important cloth-making centre. Its specialities were bombazine and 'Kidderminster Stuff', a coarse woollen fabric often used as floor covering. Carpet-weaving, introduced *c.* 1735, soon became the staple trade; by 1772 there were eleven master carpet-weavers. The Staffordshire and Worcestershire Canal, constructed 1766–71, provided easy access to the Severn at Stourport, further stimulating the trade. There were three hundred carpet looms in 1784; between 1801 and 1851 the population rose from 6,110 to 20,852. Thereafter, despite the arrival of the Oxford, Worcester & Wolverhampton Railway in

1852, there was something of a decline, largely because Kidderminster was slow to accept power looms. They only really began to replace handlooms after 1856 when Stour Vale Mills opened (p. 413); subsequent recovery was gradual. The population by 1881 was 24,270, then continued to rise steadily. Even at its prime, the carpet industry remained one of relatively small family businesses.

Most of the C19–early C20 mills and other buildings were the work of local architects, notably *T.D. Baker* (1830–80); the prolific, often inventive *J.T. Meredith* (1840–98), whose practice continued into the C20 as *Pritchard, Godwin & Clist*; and *J.M. Gething* (1830–1919), *Gething & Son* from 1899, later *Gething & Rolley*. *J.G. Bland* of Birmingham (1828/9–98) was also extensively employed. The industry declined in the late C20, but the surviving C19 mill buildings, together with the churches, provide most of the architectural interest in a town otherwise uncommonly lacking in visual pleasures. An exception is Church Street, largely Georgian, originally rising to the open space in front of the splendid parish church. The municipal authorities decided to absorb that very open space into a new ring road, of 1967–73, completely cutting Church Street off from the church, a crying-out crime against the town. The road's s extension has the slight compensation of a retaining wall with concrete shuttering designed by *William Mitchell*, 1975–6; the NW extension, 1983, wreaked further havoc, especially around Mill Street. The centre has suffered further indignities, many of the buildings mentioned in the first edition (1968) having been demolished.

CHURCHES

1. Church of England

ST MARY AND ALL SAINTS. The largest parish church in Worcestershire (215 ft (66 metres) long), a very varied building of red sandstone. Much is Victorian, most of what is older belongs to the years either side of *c.* 1500.

A consecration in 1315 probably refers to the present chancel, though its Dec tracery and wavy parapet are all renewal of 1847–9, by *Harvey Eginton*, who added the matching s chapel. The mighty SW tower, probably late C15 (preceding the present nave), was richly refaced by *J.A. Chatwin*, 1893–5. Of three stages, with strong diagonal buttresses and panelled parapet with corner pinnacles; a spire was intended. Bell-openings of two lights with transom, repeated blind either side. Below, s, three stepped image niches; on the ground floor, s and w, five-light windows with transoms. The s window, reinstated by *Chatwin*, is partly filled by a Perp doorway with traceried spandrels, removed (by *Eginton*) from a porch against the w bay of the s aisle. Chatwin also refaced the nave w wall, with renewed eight-light Perp window, and the fine clerestory, raising its octagonal rood-stair turret; both are essentially early C16. Each clerestory bay has two slender straight-topped two-

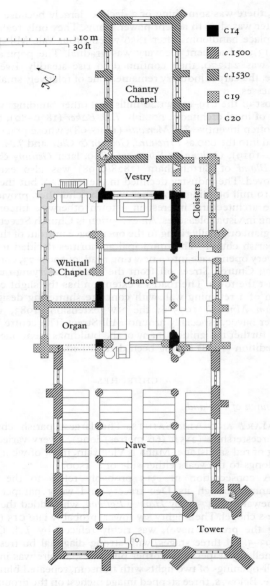

10 m
30 ft

c14
c.1500
c.1530
c19
c20

Chantry
Chapel

Vestry

Cloisters

Whittall
Chapel

Chancel

Organ

Nave

Tower

Kidderminster, St Mary and All Saints.
Plan

light windows; tall panelled and battlemented parapet. The chantry chapel, E of the chancel (now Parish Hall), rebuilt by the London mercer Simon Rice *c.* 1530, is a separate building like that of Long Melford, Suffolk (though less subtly handled); it became a grammar school after the Dissolution. Three bays of plain three-light cinquefoil-headed windows; octagonal NW turret. No connection originally with the chancel, but a separate SW doorway (cf. Long Melford), with traceried spandrels. A late C18 vestry inserted between chancel and chantry* was Victorianized in 1887–8 when *W.J. Hopkins* added a Dec-style cloister linking it to the S chapel. Also his, the N transeptal organ chamber, 1870–2. The Dec-style Whittall Chapel to its E was added by *Sir Giles Gilbert Scott*, 1921–2. This N aspect, however, is spoilt by brick service additions (by *Hubert Clist*, 1966–7) to the former chantry chapel.

The INTERIOR also appears to be thoroughly Victorian. But the nave arcades are of *c.* 1500 or soon after, with concave-sided octagonal piers, moulded capitals, and four-centred arches; four bays, S, an irregular six, N, a curiously curved NE respond ensuring parity with the SE one (behind which is the rood stair). Flat panelled nave roof by *Eginton*, 1849; aisle roofs, 1901. Lierne vault under the tower reinstated by *Chatwin*; high moulded N and E arches. Attached to the tower, towards the S aisle, an odd corbelled-out feature, perhaps connected with an upper chamber above the former porch. Eginton also designed the fine wind-braced chancel roof, based on the Guesten Hall (p. 698); three-bay arcade to his S chapel. To the N, *Giles Scott's* Whittall Chapel, 1921–2, has a splendidly subtle three-bay interior with finely moulded rere- and cross-arches; carved and gilt oak REREDOS, portraying Christ as prophet. Scott added the matching ORGAN CASE and painted CEILING in 1927–8. The notable internal feature of the former chantry chapel is its traceried tie-beam roof, of five bays; probably largely restoration by *Hopkins*, 1867, boldly painted 1946.

The FURNISHINGS in the body of the church are mostly C19 or belong to a re-ordering of 1989–90, in the manner of George Pace, by *Ronald G. Sims*: the central altar with iron *corona*, similar font canopy (1991–2), organ case, and nave light fittings. The major C19 contributor was *Hopkins*; his are the brass LECTERN, stone PULPIT and FONT, all 1872–4, and huge alabaster REREDOS, 1880, lavishly carved by *Boulton & Sons* of Cheltenham. – Oak SCREEN, N of the sanctuary, by *Julian Clist*, 1946, with carving by *Robert Pancheri*. – ROYAL ARMS. George III, dated 1787. – STAINED GLASS. A notable C19–C20 assortment. By *O'Connor*, 1848–50, the colourful E and W windows, and all four in the S chapel. – By *Hardman* the fine blue and red angels in the nave clerestory, 1894–7, the S aisle SW, 1902, and chancel S, 1947 (designed by *Donald B. Taunton*). – Two

---

* Probably in 1786 when *James Rose* of Bewdley carried out extensive work.

other s aisle windows by *Samuel Evans*, 1892. – By *Powell &
Sons*: three in the N aisle 1917–18, three in the Whittall Chapel
1927, and tower s, 1921. – Tower W and N aisle W windows by
William Pearce Ltd, 1904–6. – Finally, above the N aisle N
doorway, one of 1889 by *Wyndham Hughes*, formerly a designer
for Kempe's studios.

MONUMENTS. Fine brass to Matilda (Harcourt) and her
two husbands: Sir John Phelip †1415 and Walter Cookesey
†1407 (N aisle E). 5-ft (1.5-metre) figures, the men in armour,
the lady's sleeves reaching the ground; three concave-sided
gables above. Re-set on a slate base in 1977. – Lady Joyce
Beauchamp †1473 (s aisle E). Tall tomb-chest, with four frontal
angels bearing shields. The widow's effigy lies behind close-set
buttresses, rising from the chest to carry a big canopy with four
decapitated statues (Gabriel, the Virgin, the Trinity, St John the
Baptist) beneath little vaulted canopies; the underside of the
main canopy is a panelled lierne vault. – Below, good stone
ledger to Sir Ralph Clare †1670; against the rood stair, HATCH-
MENT to Henry Gorges †1658. – Chancel N. Sir Hugh Cokesey
†1445 and wife. Restored alabaster effigies on a panelled and
cusped tomb-chest, in a big projecting recess with four-centred
arch; heavy top cresting with heraldry and angels. His armour,
including sallet with raised visor, can be dated *c.* 1450–60. Gar-
ishly repainted 1954, as was the nearby monument to Sir
Thomas Blount †1568 and wife Margery †1595 (perhaps by
Richard Parker of Burton-on-Trent). Also recumbent alabaster
effigies, he on a lower tomb-chest, she in the round-arched
recess; back wall with row of four small children and an infant,
heraldry above. – Sir Edward Blount †1630. Only the three
alabaster effigies remain, on a renewed tomb-chest; he reclines
stiffly on his elbow facing his two wives (chancel s). – A few
minor tablets: Henry Toye †1713, a good cartouche; Jacob
Turner †1820, with mourning female (both s chapel); Ann
Turner †1856, by *T. Gaffin*, with seated figure of Faith (chancel
N). – War memorial (N aisle) by *Sir Giles Scott*, 1921; green
Forest of Dean stone, flatly Gothic, with crowned angel.

Outside, a large CHURCHYARD CROSS by *A. W. Blomfield*,
1876–7. The base and tall shaft of its medieval predecessor were
resited a little E. – Attractive C18-style CHURCHYARD GATES;
four rusticated piers, renewed wrought ironwork.

HOLY INNOCENTS, Stourport Road, Foley Park. 1937–8 by *W.E.
Ellery Anderson* of Cheltenham. Coleford brick, pantiled roofs,
Early Christian style; nave with very narrow aisles, chancel
with N chapel and s vestry. W end never finished. Calm white-
rendered interior, the arcade arches without mouldings; simple
tie-beam roofs. – Perp-style FONT of 1866 by *William Forsyth*
(from Areley Kings). – STAINED GLASS. By *A.L. Wilkinson*,
1938, the E and two s aisle windows; the third is by *Arthur
S. Walker* for *G. Maile & Sons*, 1953. – N chapel E also by
Wilkinson, 1948.

The PARSONAGE (No. 9 Sutton Park Road), roughcast
Regency style, 1926, may also be by *Ellery Anderson*.

Kidderminster, St Mary, brass to Matilda (Harcourt) and her two husbands, Sir John Phelip †1415 and Walter Cookesey †1407

St Barnabas, Wolverley Road, Franche. By *Martin & Chamberlain*, 1870–1. Red brick, minimal stone dressings; crisp foliage-enriched Geometrical tracery, nicely distinguished between nave and chancel. Crude little square tower (originally with spire) above the s porch, perhaps early C20. Good interior, well lit by three w windows; exposed brick, some painted and encaustic tile decoration in the chancel. Reordered *c.* 1986. – STAINED GLASS. Excellent Arts and Crafts e window of 1925, possibly by *Benjamin J. Warren*. – Chancel sw by *Walter Camm*, 1954. – Nave se by *Jane Gray*, 1987. – Nave sw 1949 by *A.S. Walker* (for *Maile & Sons*).

SCHOOL opposite, by *J.T. Meredith*, 1874, also Geometrical Dec; house added 1887.

St Cecilia, Hoo Road, Hoo Brook. Former Infant School of 1872, the church added *c.* 1995 by *David R. Mills* of Hagley; brick, picturesque traditional in style, square sanctuary with cupola, much lower nave.

St George, Coventry Street. 1821–4 by *Francis Goodwin;** *William Knight* was clerk of works. A stately Commissioners' church, similar to Goodwin's contemporary St Peter, Ashton-under-Lyne, Lancs., faced in Bath ashlar; Perp style, cost over £19,000. Very tall w tower, four stages, with angle buttresses, battlements and polygonal pinnacles. Paired bell-openings filled with an unglazed diagonal tracery grid, cast iron like all the tracery in the church. On the first stage, three carved round openings for clocks; the faces, again cast iron, but never installed, survive in the ringing chamber. High, ornate w doorway, with ogee crocketed gable; deep recessed porch. Six Perp side windows, of three lights with solid battlemented transoms; stepped buttresses; hoodmoulds with good carved head-stops. Flatly projecting chancel flanked by tall polygonal pinnacles, a rose window high up in the e wall; low canted vestry below, later enlarged, N. The ogee doorways in the nave w bays led to high-set galleries on thin cast-iron columns, beneath a plaster vault. The interior, burnt out 1922, was reconstructed to a new design by *Sir Giles G. Scott*, 1923–5; soaring six-bay arcades of Bath stone with thin, minimally Perp, piers; plain tie-beam roofs, w gallery only. – *Scott*'s FURNISHINGS, *c.* 1927, are quite modest, the STALLS and PEWS of western hemlock. – Not by him, the Perp FONT and wooden eagle LECTERN, 1936. – STAINED GLASS. Patterned glass in the e rose by *Norgrove Studios*, 1986. – s aisle e by *Florence & Walter Camm*, 1928.

Large CHURCH HALL, NW, by *H.W. Rolley*, 1979.

St James, Jerusalem Walk, Horse Fair; now Salvation Army. 1872–3 by *John Davis* of Birmingham. Small; nave, chancel, and N vestry with tall polygonal bell-turret. Red brick with notched decoration, simple early Dec stone tracery. Interior altered, but the foliated corbel shafts of the chancel arch survive. – Tiled REREDOS, again with foliage capitals, now

---

* *Thomas Rickman* and *Thomas Lee Jun.* also submitted designs.

hidden, as is the E window's STAINED GLASS, a Crucifixion by *Heaton, Butler & Bayne*, 1900.

ST JOHN BAPTIST, Bewdley Road. Of *George Alexander*'s Neo-Norman church of 1842–3, only the blue brick SW (former W) tower remains; atrociously inaccurate detailing, especially the ribbed spire with lucarnes.* It had a wide nave, short transepts, and rounded apse. In 1892–4 *J.A. Chatwin* sliced off its N part, attaching a large new nave with N aisle, and chancel with wide polygonal apse and N vestry, all of smooth Alveley sandstone; the windows have lancets or Geometrical tracery. In 1902–4 *J.A. Chatwin & Son* returned to replace the rest with a new outer S aisle, three-sided-apsed S chapel, and large porch (replacing the former S transept). Again very red sandstone, but battlemented, with somewhat richer Dec-Perp tracery. Impressively high interior, exposed yellow brick with red brick patterning. Tall nave arcades with quatrefoil piers and moulded arches; the more modest outer S arcade has octagonal piers. Clumsily reordered in 1972 by *Burman Goodall & Partners*, who partitioned off the lower parts of the outer aisles and nave W end.

Chatwin's FURNISHINGS, and later ones by the *Bromsgrove Guild* (1948–54), have been partly dispersed. – Neo-Norman FONT and stone PULPIT, the latter of 1868, with Dec stone canopy added 1898, when the chancel arch corbels were carved. – S chapel with excellent Perp-style SCREEN by *W.E. Ellery Anderson*, 1931, and Neo-Norman REREDOS of 1880, carved with the Last Supper. – STAINED GLASS. Much by *Powell & Sons*: E 1911–12, flanked by two of 1919–22; nave W 1927–8; two, particularly good, in the subdivided N aisle, the easternmost 1896, the other 1947. – Pictorial N clerestory window by *John Davies* of Shrewsbury, 1881, from the earlier church, as are two in the S clerestory and the S chapel SE, *c.* 1859, probably by *O'Connor*. – S window here by *A.L. & C.E. Moore*, 1927, apse windows by *Heaton, Butler & Bayne*, 1925. – Small outer S aisle window by *Walter Camm*, 1958.

Blue brick BOUNDARY WALL to Bewdley Road, 1842–3, with Neo-Norman gateway. – In Brook Street, W, the former GIRLS' SCHOOL of 1884; brick, lancets.

ST OSWALD, Broadwaters Drive. The church by *Maurice W. Jones*, 1964, with a hyperbolic paraboloid roof, was demolished because of structural instability in 1981. A plain hall added to its NE, by *Michael E. John*, 1970, now serves as the church.

2. Roman Catholic

ST AMBROSE, Birmingham Road. By *G.R. Blount*, 1857–8. Brick, stone and blue brick dressings; Geometrical Dec tracery. SW tower completed, with buttressed and pinnacled spire, by *Joseph Pritchard*, 1901; niche with statue of St Ambrose, 1897.

---

*A Commissioners' church, like St George, but built under the second parliamentary grant.

Plain interior, typical Blount, the four-bay arcades with double-chamfered arches dying into octagonal piers; two-light clerestory windows above the spandrels. Arch-braced roofs, panelled and painted at the E end. – Ornate stone and marble REREDOS. – Stone PULPIT, with mosaic panels added *c.* 1916. – STAINED GLASS. Monochrome E window by *Camm Bros*, 1874. – By *Hardman*, the S chapel E 1877, N aisle W 1901, and three of 1913–22 (N aisle, second E; S aisle, the two easternmost). – By *Camm & Co.* the N chapel E, 1892. – The adjoining RECTORY is a five-bay stuccoed villa of *c.* 1830.

Further E, HOLY TRINITY CONVENT, founded by Trinitarian Sisters. About 1903 they purchased Elderslie, built by *J.M. Gething*, 1874, for William Adam; red and yellow brick, two-storey bays flanking a hipped-roofed tower. *Pritchard & Pritchard*, in 1909–10, added the main three-storey school building in a slightly purer classical style. Dull mid-C20 additions; behind these, a forceful brick and concrete wing by *Michael Godwin*, 1969, ending in an assembly hall raised above the swimming pool.

OUR LADY AND ST PIUS X, Canterbury Road, Habberley. By *Sandy & Norris* of Stafford, 1966–70. Pale brick with blue trim, mildly Early Christian. Nave and chancel in one, tall straight-headed mullioned windows, pantiled roof, Italianate NW tower. Plain plastered interior with squared-off arcades.

OUR LADY OF OSTRA BRAMA (Polish Church), Pitt Street, Broadwaters. Opened 1963. Brick with wide lancets, an onion-domed turret at the E end of the pantiled roof. Pleasant white-washed interior, with painted E wall.

3. *Nonconformist*

Kidderminster has a strong tradition of Nonconformity, largely derived from the C17 Presbyterian preaching of Richard Baxter, and now best represented by two large C19 churches (Congregational and Unitarian) standing close together in the town centre.

BAPTIST CHURCH, Marlpool Place, Franche Road. 1970–1 by *Denys Hinton & Partners*; a squat brick complex, the church with angled clerestory lighting. (It replaced a Gothic chapel in Church Street, by *George Bidlake*, 1867–8.)

BAXTER CONGREGATIONAL CHURCH (now United Reformed), Bull Ring. Rebuilt 1884–5 by *F.W. Tarring*.* Large, of rock-faced Alveley sandstone with ashlar dressings; aisled nave, chancel, and commanding SW tower and spire, the latter also rock-faced, with steep lucarnes and heavy pinnacles. Geometrical tracery, the main window, S, of 2+1+2 lights; triple gabled doorways below, with foliated shafts. Facing the Stour, W, four cross-gables with similar tracery above trefoil-headed triplets.

---

*The Presbyterian Old Meeting House, of 1693, had previously been rebuilt twice on this site, in 1753 and 1824.

Inside, four-bay nave arcades: cast-iron columns supporting timber arches with pierced spandrels; galleries on three sides. Chancel arch with foliated corbel shafts. – Stone REREDOS. – COMMUNION TABLE, C17, from the parish church. – STAINED GLASS. Chancel window by *Ward & Hughes*, 1885. – NAVE: two NE by *James Powell & Sons*, 1921–2; two NW, of excellent quality, by *R. Anning Bell*, 1926.

At the rear, the brick SUNDAY SCHOOL of 1864, with stuccoed round-arched doorway, SW, leading to stairs to the first-floor schoolroom: five bays of round-arched windows, tripled to E and W; simple hammerbeam roof.

FORMER COUNTESS OF HUNTINGDON'S CHAPEL, Park Street. 1895–6 by *H.E. Lavender*; brick with Gothic stone details, dowdily altered.

MILTON HALL BAPTIST CHURCH, Lorne Street. By *Ingall & Son*, 1890. Brick, the gabled façade with Geometrical tracery; outer porches, above the S one a tower with octagonal spired turret. Sunday Schoolrooms along the flanks.

PRIMITIVE METHODIST CHAPEL, Chapel Hill, Broadwaters. 1859, brick, round-arched windows. Later additions.

SALVATION ARMY, Horse Fair; see p. 400.

TRINITY METHODIST CHURCH, Churchfields. 1975 by *W.H.C. Cripps* of Oxford; brick, with granite aggregate panels.* The aisled and clerestoried church is set N–S, with canted entrance end; attached W tower, its gabled roof capped by a spike. Large ancillary buildings, further W.

UNITARIAN CHURCH (New Meeting), Church Street. Built for Presbyterians 1782; brick, Perp-style chancel and N vestry added by *J.M. Gething*, 1879. Remodelled, with fancy rock-faced Gothic façade, by *Payne & Talbot* of Birmingham, 1883; quite different from anything Anglican. Buttressed with pedimental gable (without its open parapet and pinnacles since 1955). Central doorway flanked by two smaller ones, all with crocketed ogee gables; windows similarly treated, including the cusped intersecting pair above the doorways. Inside, four-centred chancel arch with boldly foliated triple shafts. Galleries on three sides, mostly 1879, modified when the nave roof was rebuilt in 1883. – Beneath the chancel arch, Baxter's octagonal PULPIT, from the parish church, dated 1621. Very rich Jacobean work: gadrooned base, blank arcade with foliage carving, tester with painted star on its soffit. – Sanctuary TILING by *Maw & Co.*, 1883. – PEWS. 1870. – STAINED GLASS. By *Hardman*, the E window, 1890, and three under the N gallery, 1903–13. – Beneath the S gallery: two, SE, of 1897, no doubt *Heaton, Butler & Bayne*; two, SW, by *William Pearce*, one a very pictorial Sower, *c.* 1887, the other, almost as odd, *c.* 1903.

HALL, N, by *C.A. Downton*, 1907; brick, with depressed wooden Y-tracery, its rock-faced front matching the chapel's.

---

*It replaced three earlier chapels, all demolished: two were Wesleyan (Mill Street, 1803, enlarged 1821; Birmingham Road, 1905), the third Primitive Methodist (George Street, 1901–2).

Of the SCHOOLS, S, only the ogee-arched staircase doorway of 1883, remains. Two pairs of contemporary gatepiers.

4. Cemetery

CEMETERY, Park Lane. The CHAPEL in the earlier part, in the angle with Castle Road, is probably of 1843; stuccoed, a pedimented portico of four Roman Doric columns either end. The CHAPEL in the larger undulating section, W, by *J.T. Meredith*, 1876–8, is Geometrical Dec, brick with stone dressings; apsed chancel, S tower with octagonal bell-stage and spire, three-bay cloister S of the nave. Contemporary LODGE to Park Lane, SE.

PUBLIC BUILDINGS

TOWN HALL, Vicar Street. The present complex consists of two complementary buildings, both brick with ample Hollington stone dressings; well restored by *S.T. Walker & Partners*, 1979. The CORN EXCHANGE AND PUBLIC ROOMS, S, by *Bidlake & Lovatt* of Wolverhampton, 1853–4, are a controlled piece of work, despite their curious details.* Three-bay front with giant Corinthian pilasters, paired at the ends, triple-layered in the centre. Channelled ground floor with central round-arched doorway, flanked by tripartite windows with odd lotus capitals. Brick first floor with stone balconies; heavy cornice, small central pediment containing the town arms. Italianate tower, set back from the corner. The fine seven-bay main hall has equally odd details; pilasters with fluted capitals and side volutes, apsed W end, with matching organ case.

The MUNICIPAL BUILDINGS, N, by *J.T. Meredith*, 1875–6, are decidedly wilder; *The Builder* called the style Free Italian, Pevsner 'really indescribedly debased'. Three bays (plus Frenchy N tower), again with pilasters, channelled ground floor, and heavy cornice and parapet with inset iron grilles. Round-arched entrance beneath the tower, ornately carved window with stone balcony above; projecting wrought-iron clock, truncated pyramid roof. Inside, an enormous iron stair, top-lit, with the oddest balustrade, ascends to the first floor, with council chamber at the rear.

An arched carriageway links the two buildings; above it, a colourful stained glass window by *Antoine Acket*, 1959, depicting local dignitaries and professions.

COUNTY COURT, Comberton Hill. By *Stephen Loughe* of *HBG Design Ltd*, 2001. Large, quite bland. Brick, much glazing; large two-storey windows with broad architraves of reconstituted stone, glazed entrance at a slight angle.

POLICE STATION, Mason Road. By the County Architect *L.C. Lomas*, 1954–5, and astonishingly reactionary. Large, Neo-Georgian, brick with Hollington stone dressings; slightly

---

* Compare their contemporary town halls at Bilston, Staffs, and Pontypool, Gwent.

higher main entrance, E end, with giant Composite columns *in antis* (and fancy door made by the *Bromsgrove Guild*). – Further E, along Mason Road and into Cedar Drive, semi-detached police houses in the same buff brick.

FIRE STATION, Castle Road. By the Borough Engineer, *Joseph Hawcroft*, 1929, plain brick. Later C20 additions.

PUBLIC LIBRARY, Exchange Street. 1996–7 by *David Millis* and *Duncan Bicknell* of *Hereford & Worcester County Council*. A red and yellow brick oblong, three storeys with two-storey rounded bays on the shorter sides; projecting grey roof, narrow clerestory band. Spacious top-lit staircase.*

FOREST GLADES LEISURE CENTRE, Bromsgrove Street. By *Graham Luxford* of *Wyre Forest District Architects Dept*, 1983–5. Large, in two disparate parts: the N the white-clad curved-roofed sports hall, the rest beneath a plethora of dimpled roofs.

INFIRMARY, Mill Street; now housing. By *J.G. Bland*, 1870–1. Good, symmetrical, High Victorian Gothic; brick with some blue patterning, stone dressings. Taller administrative block, with hipped roof and gable above the main entrance, flanked by long ward wings terminated by smaller projecting gables; nice display of chimneys and wooden roof ventilators. Set back above a Gothic revetment wall topped with iron railings. At the rear the staircase hall projects, the stairs with cast-iron balustrade; stained glass by *Gibbs & Howard*, 1888. Side wings extended back in 1886 and 1902–3. Here also the plainer detached Isolation Ward by *Meredith*, 1888, and a small Dec mortuary chapel, 1908. To the SE, on Mill Street, a large detached block by *Pritchard & Godwin*, 1925–6, still respecting the Gothic ethos.

KIDDERMINSTER HOSPITAL, Bewdley Road. A sprawling conglomeration mostly by *Leonard J. Multon & Partners*, on the site of the Union Workhouse (by *Knight & Nettleship*, 1837–8); of C19 buildings only the chunky brick lodge, 1874, survives, facing Sutton Road. Behind it, the long D-Block (Psychology) of 1979; plum brick, two storeys, reasonably stylish. The five storeys of C-Block, 1971–2, rise behind, faced with cast-iron concrete panels. To the NE, E-Block, lumpen two-tone brick of 1995 (by the *Hospital Design Partnership* of Leeds); new entrances and interior re-ordered, with a crisp atrium, by *MAAP Architects*, 2003–4. Adjoining, the plainer, higher B-Block, 1985. Brook House, an eight-storey brick accommodation tower set back towards Franchise Street, is again of 1971–2.

WATERWORKS, Pump Street. 1905. A small brick pumping station, with terracotta trim; shaped gables either end. The original building by *T.D. Baker*, 1872, is impounded within the council depot opposite.

RAILWAY STATIONS, Comberton Hill. A miserable late C20 building replaces the 1863 half-timbered GWR station. Nearby a large late C19 GOODS SHED, brick with blank round arches.

---

*It replaced a white brick Italianate complex by *J.M. Gething*: School of Art 1878–9, School of Science 1885–6, Free Library 1891–2.

The Station Approach is enlivened by the terminus of the Severn Valley Railway, called Kidderminster Town, effective pastiche of 1986; single storey brick, with short Frenchy end towers, based on the 1890 GWR design, by *J. E. Danks*, for Ross-on-Wye (Herefs.).

Educational Buildings

KIDDERMINSTER COLLEGE, Market Street. By *Nigel Skelton* of *GVA Grimley*, 2002–3. Large, tri-tone brick and render, four storeys, beneath an ungainly curved metallic roof.

Former KING CHARLES I GRAMMAR SCHOOL, Bewdley Road (now Register Office). Tudor Gothic, of Trimpley stone, built 1848 (possibly by *Eginton*). Buttressed four-bay schoolroom, its Dec tracery mostly replaced by Y-tracery; slightly project-ing E end (with war memorial stained glass by *Powell & Sons*, 1921). Projecting porch, SW: four-centred moulded doorway, canted oriel above (for the master's study); round battlemented stair-turret. Matching NW lecture room, 1901, and E classroom range, 1907–8, both by *Joseph Pritchard*. – To the W, the former LIBRARY BLOCK (now Blakebrook School), by *W.H. Godwin*, 1936; Dec style, of rock-faced Hollington stone.

The present KING CHARLES I HIGH SCHOOL, Chester Road South, was built as the High School for Girls, by *Pritchard & Pritchard*, 1912–13. Brick, stone dressings, Elizabethan Tudor style; gabled wings, recessed battlemented centre with five three-light windows for the hall, central cupola. Behind, various crowded additions, the largest by *L.C. Lomas*, from c. 1960. Further back, HILLGROVE HOUSE (now school offices), brick, c. 1800–20. Five-bay W front, the central three with pediment; porch with paired Tuscan columns, segment-headed windows with reeded stone heads and keystones. S side doubled in length c. 1860–70.

OTHER SECONDARY SCHOOLS. Two by *Pritchard, Godwin & Clist*, both brick with hipped pantiled roofs, and typical of their date. BAXTER COLLEGE (formerly Harry Cheshire School), Habberley Road, 1938–40 (rebuilt after war damage, 1947), has a two-storey main block with carved figures above the door; long classroom wings. Their SLADEN C. OF E. SCHOOL, Hurcott Road, 1939–40, is similar but more modest, with a wooden octagonal turret instead of sculpture. SION HILL SCHOOL, Sion Hill, a particularly good example of 1957–8 by *Sir Frederick Gibberd*, has a tidy two-storey concrete frame, infilled with brick or curtain walling; a square concrete water tower on stilts provides vertical emphasis.

ELEMENTARY SCHOOLS. Few C19 church schools survive (*see* also pp. 400–1). ST MARY'S INFANT SCHOOL, Broad Street, by *T.D. Baker*, 1870–3, has grouped, oddly triangular-headed lancets; converted to a community centre (with the loss of its bellcote) c. 1985. ST GEORGE'S INFANT SCHOOL, Leswell Street, by *Meredith & Pritchard*, 1899–1900, is brick, gabled, with plain terracotta trim.

Kidderminster School Board, formed 1871, built five schools. Of COVENTRY STREET by *Meredith*, 1872–3, in 'Early Geometrical style', only a fragment remains (in Radford Avenue). Two others survive. LEA STREET by *J.M. Gething*, 1882–3, U-plan, with turrets with wooden spirelets in the inner angles and large segment-headed windows; and FOLEY PARK, Northumberland Avenue, by *Meredith*, 1894–5: gabled, terra-cotta trim, narrower grouped windows, spired bell-turret.

Typical late C20 schools are ST JOHN'S, Blakebrook, begun by *L.C. Lomas*, 1963, low, with slightly angled roofs; and ST OSWALD'S C. OF E., Sion Avenue, Broadwaters, a spreading affair of 1995 by *Hereford & Worcester Property Services*: orange brick with dark blue trim, pantiled roof with inserted glazing.

PERAMBULATIONS

Kidderminster is a frustrating town to perambulate, partly because of the obtrusive ring road, partly because of its apparently continuous redevelopment. The inner area described here lies (mostly) between the ring road and the Staffordshire and Worcestershire Canal. The first walk covers what remains of the historic town centre, the second looks at the main area of surviving C19 carpet mills.

1. The town centre, from parish church to Town Hall

St Mary and All Saints (p. 395) is the obvious starting point. Outside its gates, a small paved square, now only facing roaring traffic, with the town's WAR MEMORIAL: by *W.H. Godwin*, 1922, with bronze Angel of Peace holding a child by *Alfred Drury*. Below, SW, a STATUE of the C17 Puritan divine Richard Baxter, his right arm raised, by *Thomas Brock*, 1875; high granite plinth.*

Nearby, where the Canal crosses the Stour on a three-arched aqueduct, was KIDDERMINSTER WHARF; a lock and timber post-crane survive, otherwise all has been municipally tidied away. Fine view of the church on its sandstone knoll.

Now s, by the pedestrian subway, to CHURCH STREET, the most worthwhile in the town. It has handsome Georgian brick houses on both sides, several with pretty doorcases. The E side begins with Nos. 22–23, late C18, three storeys with stepped lintels, pedimented doorways with fluted pilasters; Nos. 24–25 are lower. The W side commences with No. 12, square-panelled framing, *c.* 1600; bracketed overhang, two restored shallow-canted oriels on each floor, higher gabled bay at the rear. Nos. 7–11, all three storeys, were taken over *c.* 1879 by the carpet manufacturers Tomkinson & Adam. Their offices were at the taller Nos. 5–6, early C19, with three-bay pedimental gable; pilastered central doorway opening onto the stairs, tripartite windows above. The arcaded shopfront of the five-bay No. 4

*It stood in the Bull Ring until 1967.

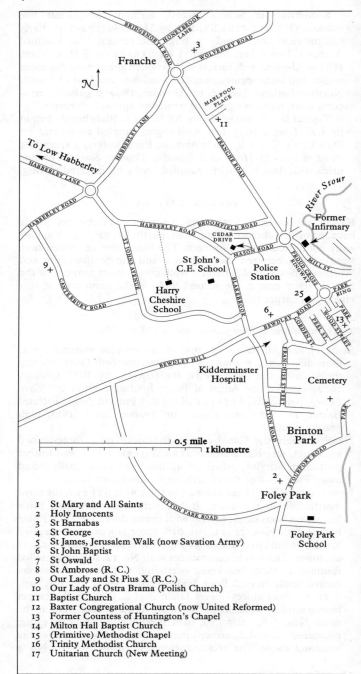

Franche

𝒩

To Low Habberley

River Stour

Former Infirmary

St John's C.E. School

Police Station

Harry Cheshire School

Kidderminster Hospital

Cemetery

Brinton Park

Foley Park

Foley Park School

0.5 mile
1 kilometre

1 St Mary and All Saints
2 Holy Innocents
3 St Barnabas
4 St George
5 St James, Jerusalem Walk (now Savation Army)
6 St John Baptist
7 St Oswald
8 St Ambrose (R. C.)
9 Our Lady and St Pius X (R.C.)
10 Our Lady of Ostra Brama (Polish Church)
11 Baptist Church
12 Baxter Congregational Church (now United Reformed)
13 Former Countess of Huntington's Chapel
14 Milton Hall Baptist Church
15 (Primitive) Methodist Chapel
16 Trinity Methodist Church
17 Unitarian Church (New Meeting)

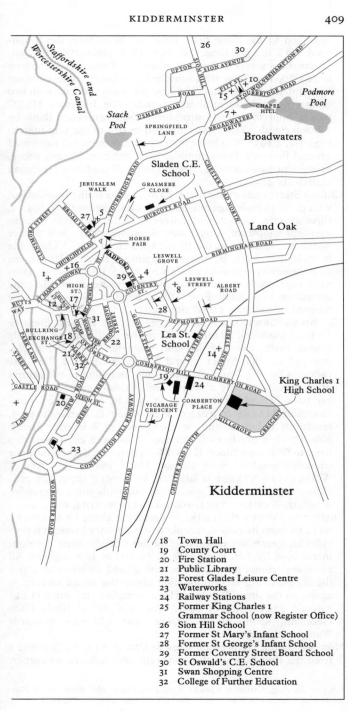

18 Town Hall
19 County Court
20 Fire Station
21 Public Library
22 Forest Glades Leisure Centre
23 Waterworks
24 Railway Stations
25 Former King Charles I
   Grammar School (now Register Office)
26 Sion Hill School
27 Former St Mary's Infant School
28 Former St George's Infant School
29 Former Coventry Street Board School
30 St Oswald's C.E. School
31 Swan Shopping Centre
32 College of Further Education

belonged to the same firm. Back on the W side, the rough-rendered No. 27, c. 1800, then Nos. 28–30, mid-C18, with pedimented doorcases and round-arched yard entrances. The best is No. 30, four bays with enriched key blocks; fine doorway with fluted Ionic columns and fanlight, good staircase with two balusters per tread and carved ends. The Italianate HSBC BANK, built for the Stourbridge & Kidderminster Bank by *Thomas Smith*, 1856–7, was doubled in size to the S, in matching style, c. 1957. Red brick with stone dressings, tall rusticated ground-floor windows, moulded segment-headed ones above, prominent eaves cornice. Beyond, set well back, the Unitarian church (p. 403).

Church Street ends at the BULL RING, now a traffic roundabout with pre-C20 buildings only on its N side. The mid-C19 No. 13, three storeys with curved corner to Church Street, has an excellent shopfront; longer side elevation ending in a former warehouse. Further W, the Baxter Church (p. 402).* The S side is cudgelled down by the overbearing CROWN HOUSE, an eight-storey concrete-faced slab by *Harry W. Weedon & Partners*, 1971, built to house various government agencies; the encircling two-storey Post Office podium is meant to be relieved by its black fluted ribbing.

The SWAN CENTRE, a shopping precinct by *Bernard Engle & Partners*, 1968–70, fills the E side of the Bull Ring; of friendly orange brick, two-storeyed and staggered this side, single-storeyed to High Street, S, and Worcester Street, E. Tent-like canopies by *The Design Solution*, 1999, here and in the central open square, provide a festival feel. Massive ribbed-concrete car park behind. HIGH STREET, S side, has a quiet Neo-Georgian MARKS & SPENCER by *Albert E. Batzer*, 1932–3, sensitively enlarged, and, at the corner of Worcester Street, Nos. 17–18, a five-bay C18 survivor. This has a good early C19 front to Worcester Street (Nos. 83–84), stuccoed, the first-floor tripartite windows with Roman Doric shafts. The rest of WORCESTER STREET is late C20, its curving street line providing a good sense of enclosure, but with some aggressive detailing: WOOLWORTHS, 1969; LITTLEWOODS, 1973.

Further N, TOWER BUILDINGS, stretching along BLACKWELL STREET from its curving corner with Coventry Street (E), provides an interesting example of earlier C20 shopping development: 1934 by *J.H. Hawkes & McFarlane* of Birmingham. All rusticated stone, three storeys, with glazed showrooms above the shops, living accommodation above the dentil cornice. N again, on the site of Rowland Hill's birthplace, the brick TELEPHONE EXCHANGE of 1937, reticent *Office of Works* Neo-Georgian, spoilt by monstrous rear additions (towards Waterloo Street).

Now we should retrace our steps to VICAR STREET (leading S from the Bull Ring), with a more city-like scale. At its corner,

---

*Across the river, CHURCH STREET SURGERY, Lower Mill Street, lively Postmodern, red brick with blue trim, by the *Gould Singleton Partnership*, 1992.

BOOTS (Nos. 25–26 High Street), with quirky Egyptian classical detail, built for Burtons by *Harry Wilson* of Leeds, 1928. Then LLOYDS TSB, originally Worcester City & County Bank, by *H. & E.A. Day*, 1868–9. Good Italianate, grey brick with stone dressings; seven windows, round-arched with blind balustrades on the upper floor, above a Greek key band. Rounded Ionic N entrance; top-lit banking hall. Nos. 17–20, W side, are vigorous multicoloured brick by *J.G. Bland*, 1872, built as offices and showrooms for Barton & Sons; two upper storeys with round-arched windows. Opposite, ROWLAND HILL SHOPPING CENTRE by *Barratt, Shaw & Wheeler*, 1978–80, smaller but more aggressive than the Swan Centre, with much canted progression and recession.

Almost opposite, before the Town Hall (p. 404), a pedestrian way leads across the Stour to WEAVERS WHARF, infill retail development of 2003–4 by *Lyons, Sleeman & Hoare*. All pretty uninspiring until one reaches its centrepiece, the former SLINGFIELD MILLS, the most imposing in the town, built 1864 as a worsted spinning mill for Thomas Lea, by *Lockwood & Mawson* of Bradford. A huge rectangular block with end pediments, best seen from the canal side: over twenty bays long, five bays wide, of red Staffordshire brick vigorously patterned in blue and yellow (especially striking on the wide eaves cornices); round-arched windows on the ground floor, slightly pointed on the upper three. Near each corner, pyramid-roofed stair-turrets, the NW supplemented by a smaller pediment. This faces the detached boiler house from which rises a majestic tapering square chimney, of equally vibrant brickwork; still 180 ft (55 metres) high, despite the removal of its top in 1981.

2. Further south, around New Road and Green Street

We can start from the Town Hall (p. 404). Outside it, a small square with STATUE of Sir Rowland Hill by *Thomas Brock*, 1881, on a round granite plinth. Opposite, at the angle of Exchange and Oxford Streets, is BARCLAYS BANK (formerly Midland Counties); red brick, ashlar ground floor, corner entrance with granite columns beneath an iron-crested rounded oriel. Of 1874–5 by *J.T. Meredith*, whose offices were in the lower extension along Exchange Street. Then, across the Stour, with curved corner to Market Street, the former POST OFFICE by *J.M. Gething*, 1881. This faces the Library (p. 405), adjoining which, E, in MARKET STREET, is Kidderminster College (p. 406). Market Street is named after the CATTLE MARKET, the Jacobean-gabled entrance lodge of which, by *J.H. Moore*, 1871, survives at the corner with New Road (with one cast-iron gatepier).

EXCHANGE STREET, W side, opposite the Library, is filled by the impressively large premises of BRINTONS LTD, of 1876, demonstrating what the offices of the leading C19 carpet manufacturers were like. Brick with stone dressings, seven by nine bays, with curved corner entrance; by *Meredith*, whose

successors *Pritchard & Godwin* added a matching fifteen bays
in 1926. Brinton's factories formerly covered an extensive area
to the SW, now mostly occupied by an enormous car park. All
that remains is the PIANO BUILDING, a plain brick wool warehouse of 1868, at the N end, perhaps also by *Meredith*; five
storeys, sixteen bays, the S front blind because of demolished
later additions. Its N side, curving along an alley called The
Sling, faces Slingfield Mills (*see* above). Restored and extended
by *Garnett Netherwood Architects* of Leeds, 2006, as part of the
Weavers Wharf development. Across the car park, S, a large
TESCO supermarket by the *Saunders Partnership*, 2001, with
slickly glazed front and brick side walls with sharply angled
dormers. Its S front reuses the fine long façade of Brinton's
Castle Road block, by *Pritchard & Godwin*, 1924–9; brick and
reconstituted stone, two storeys divided by mildly Deco metal
panels.

On the S side of CASTLE ROAD, a great surprise, an octagonal
medieval tower, the sole remnant of CALDWALL CASTLE:
more probably a C14 upper floor hall house, with the tower at
its centre. The rest, rebuilt *c.* 1690 as Caldwall Hall, was demolished in 1961. Of red and grey sandstone, perhaps built for the
Cokesey family *c.* 1347. Three storeys, the lowest, since the creation of Castle Road in 1901, appearing as a substantial basement; embattled parapet, restored 1934. Windows mostly
C17–C18, except the small openings in the NW stair-turret,
compatible with a mid-C14 date. Inside, the basement has
sixteen radial ribs, a worn lion boss at their centre; eight single-
chamfered main ribs alternate with lesser ones, slightly hollow-
chamfered. W of the tower, the former SWIMMING BATHS, by
the Borough Engineer *Joseph Hawcroft*, 1932. To its E, his Fire
Station (p. 405).

MORTON'S WORKS, further E at the corner of New Road and
Dixon Street, extending back to Green Street, are the
most completely surviving of the C19 carpet factories. Mildly
Gothic, brick with some blue banding, by *J. G. Bland*, 1869–70;
matching later extensions. The main office block (now
Paddington House), of twenty bays and three storeys, has a
pyramid-roofed NW corner tower. The premises continue along
Dixon Street with two-storey yarn and pattern stores, a gabled
lodge giving access to the large courtyard. On the S side of this,
three-storey stores and winding and finishing rooms; on the E,
towards Green Street, two large dye houses, their lantern roofs
with louvred ventilators, followed by ranges of two-storey
warehouses. The gabled north-lit weaving sheds are ranged all
along the E side of NEW ROAD, seven bays originally, extended
by four, 1878, and eight more later. Opposite, surrounded by
C20 clutter, the plain CASTLE SPINNING MILLS, by *Meredith*,
1877, for Edward Broome, mostly rebuilt after fire damage by
Pritchard & Godwin, 1928: seventeen bays, three storeys of
segment-headed windows, stair-tower centrally at the N end.

Now GREEN STREET, from its S end (by the Waterworks,
p. 405). Its S half gives the best impression of Kidderminster's

later C19 industry, with the rear premises of Morton's Works, w side, and those of the VICTORIA CARPET COMPANY, E. Their main building, built 1869 for William Green by *T.D. Baker*, has fifteen bays and three storeys of round-arched windows, in a paired rhythm apart from the three-bay pedimented centre. Blue brick with white Stourbridge brick trim, including rusticated pilasters and zigzag string courses. Poor S extension of the 1920s, much better one, N, *c.* 1890. Then, with a stylish curving corner to Dixon Street, a fine streamlined office wing, in matching brick but with extensive glazing, by *C.F. Lawley Harrod* of Birmingham, 1937–8. All converted to offices by *FJ Architects* of Wakefield, 2001, the weaving sheds demolished for rear car parking.*

Further N, more carpet factories on the E side. The CHLIDEMA WORKS, built for Winnall & Fawcett, 1872, are quite plain, brick with stone dressings; originally eight three-storey bays, much enlarged to the s after 1887. Then, beyond the Stour, the attractive STOUR VALE MILLS (now Woodward, Grosvenor Ltd) by *Bland*, 1855–6, also known as Lord Ward's Shed; built to provide manufacturers with rentable space for power-loom weaving. Two-storey front, red brick with yellow dressings, 9+3+9 bays, the centre pedimented above the former entrance. Enlarged to the N *c.* 1900. The weaving sheds survive at the rear.

Green Street meets the E end of OXFORD STREET at Worcester Cross, with a good gabled Gothic canopied FOUNTAIN by *J.T. Meredith*, 1876. Octagonal with an arcade of red granite shafts, two-stage pyramidal roof with animal gargoyles; carving by *William Forsyth*. It is overlooked by the former WORCESTER CROSS CARPET FACTORY OFFICES of Willis & Co.; of 1878–9 by *J.G. Bland*, an interesting contrast with his earlier buildings. Impressive, rather lanky Queen Anne façade, of brick, eleven bays and three storeys with three Flemish gables. Lower W wing. To its W, in the tail-end of WORCESTER STREET, the brick BOAR'S HEAD, 1888. This faces Nos. 50–51, a semi-detached mottled brick pair, *c.* 1800–20, a rare survival for Kidderminster; each three-storey house has only one bay, plus doorway.

Little to note in the NE sector of the town centre, approached up PROSPECT HILL. Most of BROMSGROVE STREET is a wasteland, with only the Leisure Centre (p. 405); HEALTH CENTRE, two plain linked red brick boxes by *Worcestershire County Council Architects Dept*, *c.* 1972; and YOUTH CENTRE by *S.N. Cooke & Partners*, 1969–70, darker brick.

OUTER KIDDERMINSTER

To the W, the Canal divides inner from outer Kidderminster. In other directions the ring road must form the boundary, though

---

*Dixon Street led E to LONG MEADOW MILLS, the carpet factory of H.J. Dixon & Co., originally by *J.G. Bland*, 1853–4.

it cuts off areas that really belong with the inner town. In these directions (especially NE, E and SE) it is best to follow the course of the three main roads.

1. West and north-west

MILL STREET, just S of the Stour, an important nucleus of the early carpet industry, has been left a demoralized backwater by the ring road. The TOWN MILLS, dated 1881, built as Goodwin's steam-driven flour mill, are probably by *J.M. Gething*; brick, four storeys, with Dutch gable. Next door, the IDEAL BUILDING by *R.O.Warder* of Birmingham, 1935, for the Ideal Benefit Society; three-storeyed flats with inset balconies, above shops and offices. To the NW, the former Infirmary (p. 405).

The only carpet industry remains in this area are in PARK LANE. At its N end, W side, is Richard Smith's ROCKWORKS of 1884, three storeys with segment-headed windows; sawtooth-gabled N extension, 1927. Tunnels reach back into the sandstone bedrock.* Opposite, remnants of the late C19 PARK WHARF FACTORY, by *Gething*, backing onto the canal.

No. 40, further S, near Castle Road, a purple brick house of *c.* 1840, was presumably also built in connection with the canal; three bays, central pedimented doorway. At the S end, by the cemetery lodge, are two startling late 1890s terraces (Nos. 102–113), perhaps by *Meredith*, said to have been for carpet designers; red brick ground floors, yellow brick above with red trim and terracotta panels of thistles and sunflowers. The end houses have four-storey towers with gabled half-timbered tops.

The streets between the Cemetery (p. 404) and Bewdley Road are filled with late C19 terraces, for the skilled carpet workers. Many in PARK STREET, WOOD STREET, PEEL STREET and COBDEN STREET have 1880–90s datestones, with some brick or terracotta decoration. A Neo-Georgian EMPLOYMENT EXCHANGE, by the *Office of Works*, 1934, is conveniently situated in Castle Road.

In BEWDLEY ROAD, between the former Grammar School (p. 406) and St John Baptist (p. 401), is WOODFIELD HOUSE, an unexpected survivor of 1784; five bays, three storeys, pedimented Doric porch. To the SW rises the bulk of Kidderminster Hospital (p. 405); opposite, behind a small green, SUMMER PLACE, a pleasant terrace dated 1822; thirteen single-bay brick houses with stepped voussoirs and round-arched doorways.

BLAKEBROOK, to the N, has detached or semi-detached villas of the 1820s, brick or stucco. The latter, often with Doric door-cases, make the best display, especially two large pairs (Nos. 16–19) near the NE end, probably by *William Knight*, who built the pair opposite (Nos. 13–14) before 1827. The Police Station

---

* Kidderminster carpet weaving is said to have begun on Mount Skipet, to the NW, in 1735.

(p. 404) closes the view N. Further NE, off Franche Road, were large late C19 houses. COOMBE HOUSE (formerly Oakden), Broomfield Road, is a rare survivor, mostly by *J.M. Gething*, 1893; brick, L-plan, with terracotta-clad entrance beneath an odd octagonal tower, its bulbous top with iron cresting.

To the w of Blakebrook, in spacious grounds, is a complex of schools (p. 406–7). The town ends in this direction with the large HABBERLEY ESTATE, varied roughcast council houses mostly of 1956–9 (*J.G. Stewart*, Borough Surveyor); its spine is CANTERBURY ROAD, with the R.C. church of Our Lady and St Pius X (p. 402).

HIGH HABBERLEY, further NW, a large three-bay villa of *c*. 1840–50, is submerged amongst late C20 nursing home additions; of false ashlar, with plain pilasters, wide eaves frieze, and projecting Ionic porch.

LOW HABBERLEY remains a separate hamlet, stretching from the half-timbered FOUNTAIN INN, *c*. 1900, to LOW HABBERLEY FARMHOUSE, of *c*. 1773: brick, four bays, with segment-headed windows. On the hillside, w, THE WOODLANDS, a large unexciting house of *c*. 1880 for the carpet manufacturer, Edward Hughes; brick and half-timber, H-plan, with varied gables.

FRANCHE, I m. NW, was also a separate hamlet until the mid C20. Rural houses still at the start of BRIDGNORTH ROAD (w of St Barnabas, p. 400): Nos. 4–6, C18 brick; one or two earlier ones in Honeybrook Terrace opposite. HONEYBROOK HOUSE, Honeybrook Lane, further N, is a rare surviving early C19 carpet manufacturer's country residence, built for George Talbot *c*. 1824; roughcast, two storeys and four by three bays, much enlarged in matching style as a nursing home.

2. North-east

The tail end of BLACKWELL STREET, NE of the ring road, has a few late C18–early C19 survivors, the best one facing NW from the end of Union Street (actually No. 25 Silver Street): three bays, pedimented Tuscan doorway. Then HORSE FAIR, now nearly all in poor condition, including the late C18 No. 5, taller brick, with fine doorcase with attached Doric columns and open pediment; it faces the OLD PEACOCK, *c*. 1820, stuccoed, with embattled parapet, its central section carrying the boldly lettered name of the inn. Further NE, Nos. 20–22 Horse Fair are a short pebbledashed terrace of C18 worsted weavers' cottages, their attic workshops lit by rectangular windows; a rare survival. Nos. 20–21 may be late C18 adaptions, No. 22 was perhaps purpose-built for industrial use in the mid C18. To the NW, the former St Mary's Infant School (p. 406); to the NE, the former St James (p. 400).

CHURCHFIELDS leads back SW to St Mary (p. 395), past TOMKINSON'S CARPET WORKS. Central three-storey warehouse dated 1902, flanked by ranges of gabled weaving sheds; further late C19 factory buildings behind. Curtain-walled office block, facing Clensmore Street, by *S.N. Cooke & Partners*, 1965.

The area NE of Horse Fair is dominated by three twelve-storey tower blocks, rising from the oddly named GRASMERE CLOSE, off Hurcott Road. Of 1963–7 by *Miall Rhys-Davies* (in conjunction with *J.G. Stewart*) and faced in red brick, they are the earliest example of prefabricated Bison concrete wall-frame construction. In HURCOTT ROAD and the streets off it further E, much housing of *c.* 1900.

STOURBRIDGE ROAD continues NE towards Broadwaters. In a small park, off Springfield Lane, is the STACK POOL, the site of the Broadwaters Iron and Tinplate Works, demolished 1893, apart from one tapering brick chimney, 78 ft (24 metres) high, rising from its edge. Ponds and sluices further upstream (W of the larger Podmore Pool) are utilized as focal points for the attractive elongated green at the centre of BROADWATERS, enhanced by stone bridges, *c.* 1987.

From Broadwaters, SION HILL leads N. On its W side, around UPTON and USMERE ROADS, a large council estate begun in 1933–4 by *Joseph Hawcroft*, Borough Engineer; nicely varied roughcast houses in fours or pairs, with hipped roofs, their underlying brick revealed as quoins. Further N is Sion Hill School (p. 406). Sion Hill leads on to Wolverley and Cookley (qq.v.).

3. East

The E part of COVENTRY STREET, ENE from the ring road, is dominated by the splendid tower of St George (p. 400). It soon becomes BIRMINGHAM ROAD, with occasional good groups of brick mid-to-late C19 houses and one or two stuccoed early C19 survivors. The first, No. 1 (Elderfield), opposite St Ambrose (p. 401), four bays and three storeys, has plain giant pilasters, paired on the W return (formerly with an entrance veranda). Further on, S side, THE SHRUBBERY has seven bays, the lower storey channelled; projecting central porch with coupled Ionic columns.

In the streets S of Birmingham Road, amongst mid to late C19 brick housing, a surprise survivor, the ashlar-faced LESWELL HOUSE (No. 4 Leswell Grove), built *c.* 1825–30 for Henry Woodward; modest, three bays with projecting porch with fluted Doric columns, but originally in spacious grounds. Also worth seeking out, Nos. 10–18 ALBERT ROAD, a lavish artisan terrace of *c.* 1900; brick with much terracotta trim, including paired gabled door hoods and dormers with mullioned windows.

At LAND OAK, where Birmingham Road crosses Chester Road North, is THE MILESTONE, a simple road house with weatherboarded upper floor, by *Henry Rowe & Son*, 1931. Opposite, LAND OAK HOUSE, detached brick, *c.* 1880, by *J.M. Gething*, well-preserved. Further out, the GREENHILL CARPET WORKS of W. & R.R. Adam, one of the first to be built out-of-town, by *Pritchard & Godwin*, 1928; office block in stripped classical style, with mild Deco touches.

HURCOTT, an attractive hamlet outside the town, depended entirely on its large paper mill, almost completely destroyed by fire in 1974; a datestone 1857 presumably refers to a rebuilding. The large mill pool remains, plus various C19 terraces, the MILL HOUSE, *c.* 1800 with Tudor overlay, and its mid-C19 coachhouse. HURCOTT HALL, E, is a gabled brick farmhouse built for Lord Ward, 1855.

4. South-east

COMBERTON HILL climbs up ESE from ring road to railway station (p. 405). A few late C19 commercial buildings, N side. On the S, the County Court (p. 404), set back in Comberton Place, the entrance to the former CATTLE MARKET, by the Borough Surveyor *J.G. Stewart*, 1957–9; most buildings remain, including enclosed pens with undulating reinforced concrete roofs. Further S, off Hoo Road, is the OLD VIC-ARAGE (No. 23 Vicarage Crescent), a stuccoed villa of *c.* 1830–40, with projecting Doric porch and hipped slate roof.★

Further E in COMBERTON ROAD, a few more stuccoed or brick early-to-mid C19 villas, mostly semi-detached, with one or two larger examples beyond Chester Road: No. 25, with Doric side entrance; also Hillgrove House (*see* p. 406).

In HILLGROVE CRESCENT, S, late C19 houses, including No. 54, OAKHILL, built for the carpet designer F.J. Mayers by *C.F.A. Voysey*, 1899. Typically roughcast, with sloping buttresses, irregular green-painted casement windows, and tiled roof. Asymmetrical entrance front, the main, more or less central gable with round-headed doorway; projecting gabled wing, l. The garden front is even more characteristic, its r. half with two canted bays (for dining and drawing rooms), the roof sweeping down low between them. The l. half is plainer, with a tall chimney as punctuation mark. Inside, a standard Voysey staircase doubling back above the front door; otherwise mostly altered. No. 51, opposite, roughcast, quite small, with hipped roof, may also be by *Voysey*, perhaps built for the coachman.

5. South

HOO BROOK, between Worcester and Chester Roads, is domi-nated by two tower blocks of 1965–6, by *Mason Richards & Partners* (with *J.G. Stewart*); of dark brick, the infill of one painted blue, the other green. Each block is staggered, one part of twelve storeys, the other ten, but seeming lower because of the slope. They had to be substantially strengthened in the early 1970s. Matching lower blocks. Despite their crude detail-ing, they provide a foil to the imposing HOO BROOK VIADUCT, E, built 1883–5 (replacing *Brunel*'s timber viaduct

★ Originally St Mary's vicarage, but St George's from 1888 to 1933.

of 1847–52); twenty high, relatively narrow arches, purple and blue engineering brick with stone dressings.

AMADA (UK) LTD, at the corner of Spennels Valley and Heronswood Roads, is the best of Kidderminster's late C20 factories. 1986 by *Glazzard Architects Co-operative*; project architect *Malcolm Leech*. Much glossy black glazing, relieved by exposed lattice trusses, facing an attractive marshy pool.

SPENNELLS further E, extensively developed for housing from the 1980s, retains two large pools from the Hoobrook mills.

6. South-west

On the NW side of STOURPORT ROAD is the pleasant BRINTON PARK, created from Sutton Common in 1887. Near the Sutton Road entrance, a MEMORIAL to Richard Eve by *Joseph Pritchard*, 1902. Square, 29 ft (9 metres) high; canted corners with columns, balustrade, and octagonal top, all encrusted in glazed brown, green and yellow *Doulton* tiles. Various inscriptions, drinking fountains with fish, and portrait medallion signed *J. Broad*. Nearby, a concrete BANDSTAND by *J. Hawcroft*, 1934, with vaulted semi-dome roof. Further SW, at Foley Park, are Holy Innocents (p. 398) and the former Board School in Northumberland Avenue, set in an area of 1880s–90s housing. The SUTTON ARMS, Sutton Park Road, by *A. T. Butler* of Dudley, 1933–4, is large and quite varied, of brick, with mullioned and transomed windows and hipped slate roof with dormers; projecting half-hipped wing.

The dreariness of Stourport Road further S is only relieved by the tall twin concrete SILOS of the former British Sugar beet factory. The huge BIRCHEN COPPICE council estate, to its W, begun 1946 (*J. G. Stewart*, Borough Surveyor), is scarcely more appealing; dull brick houses, in pairs or short terraces.

KINGTON

ST JAMES. Small, opposite modest C18 brick farms with C17 outbuildings. Timber-framed W bell-turret, its stone ground stage as wide as the nave, with square trefoil-headed openings N and S; probably C15. The framed structure, resting on large beams across the stonework, narrows the width to a normal two-stage turret with saddleback roof; all close-studded, perhaps contemporary with the stone base, which was clearly built to carry such a turret. Nave and chancel of C13 origin, the former widened, S, in the C16. Much restored 1881 by *W. J. Hopkins*, who rebuilt the chancel: the E window is his, others are assorted medieval, reused; the aumbries were oddly re-set between the chancel side windows. Pierced wooden arch in lieu of a chancel arch. Three of the nave windows are also his; the fourth, NW, is a widened lancet. – FONT. Big plain octagonal bowl, perhaps C13. – SCREEN. Part of the dado now serves as a rectors' board (nave S). – Painted stone panel from the

REREDOS, 1890, loose under the turret. – Iron-bound dug-out CHEST, perhaps C16. – Timber GABLE CROSS, on the chancel NE window sill; probably C19. – STAINED GLASS. Two colourful windows by *John Petts* of Abergavenny: nave NW 1987, SW 1988.

KNIGHTON ON TEME

6060

ST MICHAEL. A chapelry of Lindridge until 1843. Mostly C12, of sandstone. Early in the C13 the nave was lengthened w and the chancel perhaps partly rebuilt, both incorporating significant amounts of tufa. Nave again extended probably soon afterwards, see the two w lancets, to enclose a timber-framed bell-turret; its supporting framework of massive cross-braced oak timbers has been dendro-dated to the early C13 (cf. Mamble). The present shingled turret, simplified and rather blunt, is by *Godwin & Greenway*, 1959. Norman are the flat buttresses of the nave, and the s doorway with plain blank four-bay arcading above, all projecting as usual. The doorway has one order of shafts with block capitals, with thin ribs down the angles (cf. Stockton), and roll-moulded arch; this is flanked by a double rope moulding and double band of thin saltire crosses. Impressive chancel arch, similarly detailed. Either side, two-light Norman openings, probably blank from the start, their sills at the height of the springing of the arch; they also have block capitals, with plain tympana. What was their function? The Norman work, Neil Stratford suggested, was probably executed by the same masons who worked at Eastham, Martley, and Stockton (qq.v.). In the nave N wall, early C13 lancets flank the tall inner Norman doorway; two-light nave NE and SE windows of *c.* 1300, probably inserted to light the rood. Perp the SW window and good nave roof, with moulded tie-beams, purlins, and arched braces to collars; painted ceilure, E end. A timber-framed wall with square panels divides the W end from the tower space (providing additional support for the bell-turret); its ogee-headed doorway suggests a C14 date. Chancel mostly reconstructed by *Lewis Sheppard & Son*, 1902–3; it has two N lancets, a pair of enlarged Norman E windows, and two-light SE window like those in the nave. *Weaver & Adye* of Devizes restored the nave in 1884–5; theirs, the PEWS and PULPIT. – Panels from C18 BOX PEWS line the long narrow vestry (beneath the bell-turret). – FONT. Round bowl on baluster stem, C17–C18. – COMMUNION RAILS. C18. – STAINED GLASS. C14 fragments in the nave NE window, otherwise by *Florence & Walter Camm*, 1956. – Nave SE by *Joseph Bell & Son*, 1885. – The two E are by *Hardman*, 1903. – MONUMENT. Small stone tablet to John Cecill †1697, big heraldry above.

In the CHURCHYARD, S, a CROSS with three square steps, base, and part of the shaft; probably C14, see the small pinnacled ogee niche, w.

The church stands alone, apart from the mid-C18 CHURCH FARM; a little NW, the OLD RECTORY, gabled brick, perhaps c. 1843 (altered 1868). Then, at the crossroads, contrasting large, timber-framed houses. HILLTOP FARM, S, hall with big S cross-wing, of square panelling infilled with brick, is partly hidden from the road by outbuildings. MAES COURT, N, with pristine white infill, originally H-plan, with lobby entrance, c. 1630, received a third gable when an adjoining barn was incorporated.

Former SCHOOL, ⅜ m. ESE. By *Henry Rowe*, 1872–5; school with attached house, mildly banded brick. Enlarged 1911.

NEWNHAM BRIDGE, ¾ m. SE, became the centre of the parish in 1864 with the arrival of the Tenbury & Bewdley Railway (partly following the course of the aborted Leominster Canal, p. 487). The plain brick STATION by *William Clarke*, now a garden centre, survives intact. Further E, in the sharp angle of the Bewdley and Worcester roads, the patterned brick TALBOT INN, High Gothic, c. 1865–70, perhaps by *F.R. Kempson*. Ornate central stone doorway; chamfered angles either side emphasized by high, tight windows bisected by a detached quatrefoil shaft with foliage capital; small half-hipped gables. To its S, the prominent WHITE HOUSE, c. 1800, red brick, three bays, with hipped roof. S again, NEWNHAM COURT, stuccoed, c. 1820–30, U-plan. Narrow E front with two Doric columns *in antis*, matching loggia above with cast-iron balustrade; doorway with moulded jambs surmounted by Soanean urns.

At BICKLEY, 1 m. NE, is GREAT HOUSE, c. 1600, to a lobby-entrance plan, remodelled for Edward Milward, 1709. Symmetrical SW front with projecting wings with shaped gables. The recessed centre has a segment-headed doorway with upper pilasters, cornice and urns, all moulded brick; cogged brick string courses. These also on the SE wing (still with thick stone-mullioned windows) but not on the NW, which must be later; its broad sash window is probably c. 1816. The return side of the latter, and the whole rear elevation, reveal the timber framing, square panels with brick infilling. Brick outbuildings.

BICKLEY HOUSE, further S, mid-C18 brick, has an impressive array of MODEL FARM BUILDINGS dated 1863, arranged round a square comprising four yards. Most prominent, the big square dovecote at the centre of the E side, and hop kilns and malthouse, SE corner.

ASTON COURT, ⅞ m. WSW. C17–C18, mostly remodelled 1850. Brick, U-plan, the gabled wings with giant pilasters with big coving and plaster garlands, plus elaborately pierced bargeboards. Doric doorway.

KNIGHTWICK

ST MARY. Rebuilt as a mortuary chapel, 1879, paid for by J.F. Greswolde-Williams. It reused stone from the chancel of the medieval church, otherwise demolished c. 1856; cf. Doddenham. A minimal job: nave and chancel in one, gauche Dec-style windows, patterned tiled roof, basic timber bell-turret. Rendered interior, the boarded roof with pseudo-hammer-beam arched braces; stridently tiled floor. – FONT. Part of a round Norman bowl, with closely set chevron; originally at St Andrew, Doddenham. – MONUMENTS. A few tablets, two mildly Grecian, c. 1839–46, signed by *J. Wood* of Worcester. – CHURCHYARD with beautiful views, and early C19 headstones and chest tombs, that to Joseph Southall †1838 signed *J. Milton* (cf. Clifton upon Teme).

The OLD RECTORY, SE, is late C18; five bays, brick, with dentilled eaves cornice and hipped roof. Moulded plaster key blocks, the round-arched middle window more elaborate. Central doorway masked by a glazed porch added by *Aston Webb*, 1880; earlier C19 canted bay window to its l. Timber-framed cottage attached at the rear.

KNIGHTWICK MANOR, ½ m. WSW. Early C18, brick, of two storeys and 2+3+2 bays; plain giant pilasters at the corners and main bay divisions. Hipped roof. Within, late C17 carved oak chimneypieces in both hall and parlour, S; the latter also has Jacobean panelling, moulded compartment ceiling, and an early C18 pedimented aedicule with fluted Ionic columns, four nude children painted on its rear wall. The house stands on the sandstone cellars of an earlier building, within a small park.

By the W approach to the former Knightsford Bridge (p. 253), ½ m. NE, are WOODFORD HOUSE, late C18 brick, three bays and storeys, and the former FLYING HORSE INN, C17 timber-framed, remodelled in the early C19.

By the A44 at Sapey Bridge, the Herefordshire boundary, ⅝ m. further W, MONKS ORCHARD is early C17 timber-framed, with lower, earlier E range; attractive C18–C19 outbuildings: stone and timber, E, brick with hop kiln, W.

KYRE

6060

On the Herefordshire boundary; also known as Kyre Wyard (the seat of the Wyards), and Kyre Magna or Great Kyre.

ST MARY. Norman one nave N and the internal head of the chancel N window; apse foundations were discovered in 1992–4. The Norman chancel arch was cut away in 1833–4. Remodelled in the early C14, and Dec S aisle chapel added: tall three-light E window with reticulation, two S windows with cusped Y-tracery; trefoiled piscina. A single arch with two continuous chamfers (partially blocked) opens into it from the centre of the nave S wall. Chancel E window also reticulated. All roofs single-framed, of C14 ashlared collar type. The bell-turret formerly stood above the nave W end, supported by the surviving C17 tie-beam truss. Replaced c. 1700 by the existing turret, though its present form, weatherboarded with copper-clad broach spire, must be C19. Timber W porch and NW cloister link to Kyre Park, dated 1893–4.

FONT. Small round bowl with short stem, probably C13. – Caen stone and marble PULPIT by *Jones & Willis*, 1893. – COMMUNION RAIL. Mid-C18; close-set balusters. – PEWS. Quite upright, made up from C18 woodwork; matching dado. – The PARISH BIER, dated 1682, stands in place of the s chapel altar. Hexagonal TABLE nearby, probably the tester of an C18 pulpit. – WALL PAINTINGS. In the w splay of the chapel sw window, a female saint of *c.* 1400 (perhaps St Mary Magdalene); beautifully done, against a delicate quatrefoil-latticed background. Fragments in the E splay and on the chapel w wall. – STAINED GLASS. E window and three in the s chapel by *E.R. Suffling*, 1897–8, in his peculiarly heavily painted style. – MONUMENTS. Edward Pytts †1672, attributed to *William Stanton* (GF). Tablet of grey, black and white marbles, with oval inscription surrounded by a wreath; composite columns, broken segmental pediment with heraldry, garlands at the foot. – Catherine Pytts †1702. Similar materials and elements, but darker in tone; black twisted columns. – Jonathan Pytts †1807, by *W. Stephens & Co.*, with large straight-sided sarcophagus. – Annabella Pytts †1832, by *J. Stephens*, flat draped urn. Below, large plain tablet to Edmund Pytts †1781. – Lady Harman †1967, by *John Skelton*; good cartouche with painted heraldry. – Two small HATCHMENTS: Jonathan Pytts, 1807; Harriet Childe, 1849.

KYRE PARK

In institutional use from 1950 until 1994, when it again became a private house. Large, of medieval origin, extended in the C16–C17, much altered and enlarged 1753–6, and again in 1938–40. The thick walls of the broad w wing belong to a rectangular medieval stone building, probably a C14 fortified house, perhaps with square corner towers (cf. Acton Burnell, Shropshire). Sir Edward Pytts bought it in 1586 and set about remodelling and enlarging, from 1588. He kept a close record: a plan was obtained from *John Symonds* of London, *John Chaunce* of Bromsgrove was appointed 'cheiff mason', and chimneypieces were obtained, in 1592–4, from *Gerard Holleman* (cf. Bockleton). A second phase began in 1611, with *John Bentley* of Oxford providing the design; *Chaunce* carried on as surveyor, under the direction of Pytts himself (after his death, in 1618, of his son James). The main addition, a large hall range at right angles to the C14 building, was demolished in the C19–C20. In 1753–6 *William and David Hiorn* of Warwick remodelled the medieval wing and added a new main s front, for Edmund Pytts; this forms the most substantial element of the present building. Plans by *T.F. Pritchard*, 1776, including a matching E wing, were rejected as too ambitious, but interior decoration continued into the 1780s. Further alterations by *Henry Curzon*, 1880–90, for E.G. Baldwyn-Childe, were swept away in 1938–40 when the present E wing was added and the main N front rebuilt for Sir Patrick

Duncan, sixth Earl of Clarendon, probably by his friend *Sir Herbert Baker.*

EXTERIOR. Seen from the S, the house consists of the medieval W wing, of which only stone walling, with quoins, survives; the recessed brick main S front, of two-and-a-half storeys; and the Neo-Georgian E wing, dated 1940, to the same height, with several round-arched windows and parapet with ball finials. The main range, largely by the Hiorns, 1753–6, has seven bays, with central stone doorcase with tapering Doric pilasters, bolection frieze and segmental pediment; half-storey above the modillion cornice added 1938–40. The rendered S wall of the medieval wing is also of the 1750s: two Venetian windows, E, one above the other, with Diocletian window above the cornice, then a canted bay rising to full height. Five-bay W front, the central three projecting beneath a pediment, entirely faced in brick; tall ground-floor windows with eared architraves, stepped keystones. Similar, shorter windows in the flanking bays, their stonework with much brick patching. The wing's N front has another full-height canted bay, and Venetian first-floor window (lighting the main staircase). The rest of the N elevation is of 1938–40: projecting centre with brick quoins and open pediment, free Neo-Georgian porch with curved hood on Composite columns. The E wing again projects; beyond it, low brick additions of 1950.

Little remains within, apart from the grand open-well staircase of 1753–6, white-painted deal, three thin balusters per tread, with carved tread ends; the landing has the Hiorns' typical Chinese fret frieze. Suggestions of the fine C18 plasterwork, mostly by *George Roberts*, survive here (also with fret frieze) and in some adjoining rooms. A resited subsidiary staircase to the E, with flat cut-out balusters, is the only survivor of the C16–C17 house.

The splendid GROUNDS, ascribed by family tradition to *Capability Brown* but probably by *John Davenport*, c. 1770–80, with a chain of four lakes in U-formation W of the house, are gradually being re-created. To the E is a fine, large, buttressed brick BARN, with circular DOVECOTE, probably C16, to its NE; this, of rendered rubble, formerly S of the house, was re-erected in its present position in 1752. Of this date perhaps the dormers in its conical tiled roof. Inside, 600 nesting holes in ten double tiers with stone ledges; also a working potence. The BARN is of 1618 by *William Harrison*, bricklayer of Alvechurch: ten bays with stepped gable ends; short SW and SE wings also with stepped gables; stone-mullioned windows. Interesting roof construction, mostly doubled tie-beams with raking struts to the collars. Beyond the church, SE, the *Hiorns'* STABLES, 1753, remodelled for staff accommodation in 1950. Then, across the road, the large C18 brick-walled KITCHEN GARDEN, with gabled cottage, NW corner.

Mid-C18 LODGE on the Bromyard road, ⅓ m. NNE, facing a disused drive: three bays, upper Venetian-type windows, projecting centre with pediment. Further N, the former DEER-PARK, its large elongated lake of late C16 origin.

ALMSHOUSES, ⅛ m. SW. Founded for eight widows in 1716 by the will of Anne Pytts. Brick, broad U-plan, projecting wings with steep gables, centre with timber pediment; wooden cross-windows on the ground floor. It could all be c. 1675.

PARSONAGE FARM, once the rectory, ¼ m. WSW. Early C14, cruck-framed, in three bays, with additional C17 gabled S bay. The N cruck frame is visible in the gable end. There are said to have been two more bays, destroyed by fire and replaced by the detached C17 square-framed kitchen block, immediately NW. Large weatherboarded C17 BARN, NE.

PIGEON HOUSE FARM, ⅝ m. WSW. Also partly of cruck construction, much altered in the C17. Hall (with central cruck-truss) and W cross-wing; C19 sandstone extensions, E, attached sandstone barn, W.

KYRE GRANGE, ½ m. NNW. Small gabled sandstone house, c. 1840–50, converted to the rectory by *Henry Curzon*, 1867; his the entrance range, S, with recessed Gothic doorway.

LEIGH

Leigh – pronounced Lye – is a very large parish (including Bransford, q.v.), which stretches S from the river Teme to the outskirts of Malvern.

ST EDBURGA. One of the most important churches in its district; the dedication reveals that it belonged to Pershore Abbey. Nave and chancel are Early Norman (perhaps earlier). The unmistakable chancel buttresses are, quite exceptionally, stepped in section. Two more clasp the nave NE bay. Further W, high up, a niche (cf. Rock) with shafts with cushion capitals, roll-moulded arch, and chip-carved label; until 1970 it housed a figure of Christ (*see* below). The chancel arch, of two orders, has single-scallop capitals, almost as elementary. The arch must be later, but what was the purpose of the roll mouldings up the E angles of the nave (also one bay W, N side) – did they support some kind of ceilure over the rood? S arcade Late Norman, probably shortly before c. 1200: four bays, the W rather narrower, sturdy round piers with decorated scallop capitals, square abaci, single-step pointed arches. The paired attached shafts of the E and W responds already have crocket capitals. Between the chancel and S chapel is a double-chamfered arch which cannot be earlier than c. 1200: shafts with fillets, foliage capitals as well as trumpet scallops. This E end of the S aisle may have originated as a transeptal chapel; its E wall has a pair of lancets under one internal arch (but divided by a buttress outside). In the late C13 long side lancets were inserted in the chancel, all cusped except the NW. Similar cusped lancet, S aisle W wall. Two-light nave N windows of c. 1300, which must also be the date the S aisle was widened to correspond with the chapel (if the forms of its C19 windows can be trusted). The s aisle s wall, with its large ogee-trefoiled tomb recess, was rebuilt in 1855, as was the chancel E, with its ornate five-light Dec-style window. Four-square Dec w tower, with diagonal buttresses and battlements; double-chamfered arch to the nave. Renewed Perp w window. By the w doorway, an odd C13 STOUP, probably not *in situ*: finely moulded bowl on a grotesque. The timber w porch is probably C15.

FONT. Round, Norman style, with scallops and chevron band; probably a C19 copy. – TILES. C15, in patterns of four, just within the s door. – Perp SCREEN, between s aisle and chapel, with broad one-light divisions and deep top friezes. How much is of 1855, when it was repainted by the curate, the Rev. *Edward Bradley* (the author Cuthbert Bede)? – SCULPTURE. The large figure of Christ, about 4 ft (1.2 metres) high, cross-staff in his l. hand, his r. raised in blessing, is a fine and important piece; dated to *c.* 1100 by the VCH, and by Charles Avery of the Victoria and Albert Museum (in 1970, when re-set on the chapel E wall). It could be even earlier.* Good COMMUNION RAILS, mid to late C17. – Elizabethan ALTAR TABLE, with bulbous legs. – Of 1855 the carved stone REREDOS, PEWS and PULPIT, the last, timber, with big carved Ascension; boldly crocketted stone base. – STAINED GLASS. Late C19 E window by *Heaton, Butler & Bayne.* – Chancel lancets by *Francis Barnett* of Leith, three N of 1866, two s earlier; also one nave N, *c.* 1861. – Nave NE, *c.* 1850, and tower w window, 1858, must be by *George Rogers.* – s aisle: one by *Hardman*, 1870; also various medieval bits, including a good C15 head.

MONUMENTS. Edmund Colles †1606 (chancel s), 'a grave and learned justice of the shire'. Recumbent effigy (until the C19 wearing a real leather skull cap); big tomb-chest over-crowded with atlantes, caryatids, close strapwork, and shields. Large back panel also with ornate strapwork. The quality is not very good. – Opposite, William Colles †1615 and wife Mary †1602. Stiff kneeling figures, both facing E, as do all twelve of their dutiful-looking children below. Square pillars, segmental arch, top achievement. – Walter Devereux (†1649) and wife Elizabeth, erected 1640. Of alabaster. Two recumbent effigies, she beneath a shallow back arch; tomb-chest with six kneeling children. Flat canopy with four Ionic front columns. – Above, no doubt by the same sculptor, their son Essex Devereux †1639 and wife Anne, kneeling figures facing each other across a prayer-desk. Their daughter sits precariously on the ledge in front. Composite columns, achievement above. – Good smaller tablets: George Freke †1639 (in the same drowning accident as Essex Devereux), slate and alabaster; John Baker †1706, a nice cartouche; several by *W. Stephens.*

CHURCHYARD CROSS. C14 base, with ogee-headed s recess; C19 shaft and cross.

*Pevsner dated it *c.* 1220, partly because of the French-looking drapery, partly because the head as well as the arms, carved from separate pieces of stone, were then incorrectly adjusted.

LEIGH COURT, N, probably rebuilt in the early C17 for Sir Walter Devereux, but poorly remodelled in the C19; brick, crow-stepped gables. More interesting, the two narrowly spaced LODGES to its SE: square, with continuous stone entablatures and big shaped gables each side.

The great early C14 timber-framed BARN, to the W, built for Pershore Abbey, now in the care of English Heritage, is not only the largest cruck building in England (and thus probably anywhere), but also the longest medieval barn in the county: over 140 ft (43 metres) long, 34 ft (10.5 metres) wide, nearly 33 ft (10 metres) high. Exterior partly weather-boarded, partly exposed framing infilled with brick (or wattling, N side). Huge tiled roof (perhaps originally thatched) sweeping down low on the S side, between two wagon porches, also of cruck construction. Inside, the eleven cruck trusses stand practically as first built. Each cruck must have been made from the stem of a single oak tree, rather than halved in mirror-image as was more usual. They support arch-braces to a collar-beam, with extra struts in the spandrels. Their tops are joined by a yoke, carrying the ridge directly or by means of a short vertical post. Two tiers of curved wind-braces. The gable trusses have base crucks, i.e. reaching only to collar-beam level, so the end roofs are half-hipped. F.W.B. Charles showed that the cruck frames were reared in pairs, together with their two-bay purlins, from W to E. Radiocarbon dating, while not conclusive, suggested c. 1325. Restored by *Michael Peach* in 1987–8, see the rebuilt sandstone stone plinths; the entire barn was structurally underpinned with concrete and stainless steel stanchions and bars.

To the S, a long open-sided range, probably a C17 HAY BARN. Further W, C19 brick farm buildings: square DOVECOTE with pyramidal roof, and round hop kilns, all poorly converted to housing.

Scattered VILLAGE, with a few timber-framed cottages. By the bridge over the Leigh Brook, N side, the OLD RECTORY, late C17 painted brick, with central two-storey gabled porch. The largest house, set back, S, is BROOKLANDS; by *William Oakley* of London, 1878, for G.B. Essex. Hard red brick with terracotta panels of fruit and flowers, tile-hung projecting gables over the two-storey outer bays.

More large houses at BROCKAMIN, ¾ m. W, notably the excellent GREAT HOUSE, of brick, early C18. S front of five bays, the segment-headed windows with carved keystones. Angle quoins and quoins for the central bay, the latter of even length, all with broken dentilled cornices. Parapet, with blank panels again segment-headed, rising in the middle to a curve like an open segmental pediment. Round-arched mid window with Gothick glazing above the pedimented doorway (an early C19 replacement). Earlier gables at the rear. Early C19 open-well staircase.

At LEIGH SINTON, 1⅝ m. S, along the Worcester-Hereford road, some framed cottages (including one with visible remains of a cruck hall), C18–C19 brick farmhouses, and prominent

hop kilns. On the w side of the B4503, to the s, a former
COUNTESS OF HUNTINGDON'S CHAPEL, dated 1831. Long
brick E front, with three round-arched windows, two doorways
in between; hipped slate roof. Attached two-storey manse, set
back, sw.*

On a low-lying site, probably once marshy, NW of Castle Green
Farm, ¾ m. N of Leigh Sinton, are earthworks of a large
MOTTE, with probable remains of a round BAILEY to its s. The
VCH suggested it may have been built for Henry de Pem-
bridge, active in the Barons' War (1263–7).

SHERRIDGE HOUSE, off Sherridge Lane, ½ m. NW, has a plain
early C18 SE front, 1+4+1 bays, two-and-a-half storeys, with an
early C19 portico of five Doric columns. On the E return, two
full-height canted bays; on the w, Venetian windows, one above
the other. – The early C19 SHERRIDGE LODGE, further N, has
a stuccoed front of three wide bays, divided by plain pilasters,
paired at the ends; thin Doric porch.

At SMITH END GREEN, on the corner of Sherridge Lane, a
former WESLEYAN CHAPEL of 1839, with round-arched
windows, reasonably altered as a house.

ASHCROFT HOUSE, Sandlin, 2 m. sw of Leigh church, is a three-
bay stuccoed Regency villa; full-width iron Gothick veranda,
lower wings, set back, each with an upper oculus window.

HOPTON COURT, 1¾ m. wsw. Also early C19, much larger, of
unpainted stucco. Five-bay, three-storey centre, two-bay two-
storey wings. Giant pilasters, two for each wing, four for the
centre, two flanking the Greek Doric porch: this, of limestone,
has two fluted columns between unfluted antae.

LICKEY

9070

The Lickey Hills provide the nearest hill-walking to Birmingham.
From 1889 they gradually became communal property, though
much, especially at Barnt Green (q.v.), continued to be developed for well-to-do houses. There are two ranges, Bilberry and
Cofton Hills, E, Rednal and Beacon Hills, N and w (the latter
with the highest elevation, 955 ft (301 metres). The village, properly called The Lickey (or Bromsgrove Lickey), stands at the head
of the valley in between.

HOLY TRINITY. By *Henry Day*, 1855–6. Snecked sandstone,
E.E.-style; chancel, nave with double bellcote on its E gable,
narrow lean-to aisles, s porch. w window of five stepped
lancets, narrow clerestory with trefoil openings. The E window
has three trefoiled lancets. Whitened interior, with thin roofs;
sturdier five-bay arcades of round piers and double-chamfered
arches. In 1893–4, *Alfred Reading* of Birmingham widened the
chancel arch and opened N and s arches for organ chamber

---

* A ROMAN TILE KILN found at Leigh Sinton, datable to the C2, made roof tiles,
bricks, and flue tiles.

and vestry. The S vestry, built 1898, was enlarged in 1970. –
FONT and PEWS. 1856. – PULPIT and STALLS. 1894. – Oak
sanctuary PANELLING of 1930; matching REREDOS added
1975. – STAINED GLASS. E window by *T.W. Camm*, 1870. –
Sanctuary N, 1900, S 1903, both *Hardman*. – S aisle: two SE by
J.B. Capronnier, 1884, SW by *J.E. Nuttgens*, 1979. – Two fine N
aisle windows: NE by *M. Farrar Bell*, 1972; the other by *R.J.
Stubington*, 1934, intricate Arts and Crafts.
   CEMETERY, S, with hipped-roofed LYCHGATE by *A.
Edgerton Leeson*, 1912.
   Former SCHOOL, SW, also by *Henry Day*, 1854, spoiled by
later additions. Across Old Birmingham Road, behind the WAR
MEMORIAL, 1920 by the *Bromsgrove Guild*, and chunky sand-
stone DRINKING FOUNTAIN, 1906, the PARISH HALL by
Harold S. Scott, 1935–6; brick, quite modern in style.
Further W, off Monument Lane, a tall OBELISK erected 1834 by
J.A. Hansom to commemorate Other Archer, sixth Earl of Ply-
mouth. Some 90 ft (28 metres) high, of white Anglesey marble;
plinth, on three steps, quite high, slightly battered.
On BEACON HILL, ⅝ m. NW, a low OUTLOOK TOWER like a
small castellated folly; 'crazy-paving' stone work, reconstructed
in its present form *c.* 1989. Remarkable views across
Birmingham.
Nearby two good houses (with lodges) by *Cossins, Peacock &
Bewlay*. HEANOR, on the brow of Beacon Hill road, for
Edward Cadbury, 1904–5, enlarged 1914–15, is brick, to a but-
terfly (or rather X) plan; central hall range with narrow-
studded gable, loggia with balcony above on the garden side.
The altered, roughcast BEACONWOOD, ¼ m. SW, for George
Cadbury, 1904–5, also had angled wings, SW, towards the
splendid view, both sadly truncated.
ROSE HILL descends steeply N from the church, past the early
C19 OLD ROSE AND CROWN INN, unexcitingly rebuilt as a
private house (with landscaped gardens) in 1880. At the
bottom, in REDNAL, the former BILBERRY HILL TEA
ROOMS, built for Barrow Cadbury, 1904, again by *Cossins,
Peacock & Bewlay*. Roughcast, broad H-plan, differing bay
windows or oriels in each gabled wing; long, low centre with
smaller gable and curved dormers.
Nearby in Lickey Road, on the Birmingham boundary, the
former WAITING ROOM of the Bristol Road tram terminus,
opened 1924; low, rendered, with green slate roof. Tram rails
remain on its E side.
LICKEY GRANGE, ¾ m. SW. Built 1880 for Joseph Rowlands;
large, brick, gabled, mildly Gothic, with two-storey canted
bays. In the hall, Pre-Raphaelitish wall paintings. Bought
c. 1908 by Sir Herbert Austin, founder of the Austin Motors;
now, with its former lodge, part of an 'exclusive' housing
development.

LINDRIDGE

Extensive parish on the N bank of the Teme, in beautiful hop-growing country; many C19–C20 oast houses, their kilns capped with the characteristic cowls.

ST LAWRENCE. Rebuilt 1860–1 by *Thomas Nicholson* of Hereford. Large, of partly snecked sandstone, with ashlar dressings; Dec style, the details Geometrical to ogee. Proud SW steeple above the porch, three stages plus broach spire with lucarnes. S aisle with two cross-gables, answering the spire. Unaltered interior, ashlar-faced; two-bay S arcade and chancel arch with good foliage carving. – FURNISHINGS include *Godwin*-tiled floors and an alabaster FONT. – CHOIR STALLS added 1878. – Colourful patterned STAINED GLASS by *Chance & Co.*, c. 1861. – MONUMENTS. Four brass plaques, S aisle, with Penell heraldry, c. 1623–66. – Arthur Onslow, Dean of Worcester, †1817. For its date very fanciful in the details, e.g. the Empire forms of the elaborate sarcophagus; fancy obelisk, with rays and angel on a cloud.

Former VICARAGE (now The Priory), NE, by *Richard Morton* of Worcester, 1788; brick five-bay façade, the wider centre projecting with Doric-pilastered doorcase. Earlier work behind. SCHOOL, S, by *J. T. Meredith*, 1894–5, also brick, the large tripartite windows edged in yellow; timbered gables. Matching house.

The main nucleus is EARDISTON, 1¼ m. ESE. At its W end, EARDISTON HOUSE, large, rambling, stuccoed, probably mostly c. 1825–30 for Sir William Smith. N entrance front, of 4+1+4 bays, with plain giant pilasters and minimal Grecian detail: projecting centre with Doric porch, flanking ranges each with a pediment. Additions for George Wallace by *E.A. Day*, 1869,* no doubt included the large E service range; timber staircase, with encaustic tiled floor, of the same time. Otherwise subdivided.

To the NE, in Dumbleton Lane, EARDISTON PLACE, early C17 timber-framed, T-plan, prettified c. 1840–50 with pierced bargeboards and tall brick chimneys.

Further E, on the S side of Tenbury Road, a nice early C19 group: No. 41, plain brick; Nos. 42–43, sandstone, four bays with two storeys of brick-trimmed, Y-traceried windows, central embattled gabled porch – were these almshouses? Then, in Mill Lane, MOOR FARM, on a formerly moated site. Mid-C18 brick, H-plan; now the offices of a hop-processing works.

At FRITH COMMON, 1 m. ENE, a plain WESLEYAN CHAPEL, 1811. Sandstone rubble, hipped tiled roof, two pointed W windows; entrance at the E end.

LOWER DODDENHILL FARM, 1 m. WNW, is typical of the district. Farmhouse to hall and cross-wing plan, early C17 timber

* *William Burn* made unexecuted plans, apparently for a new Jacobethan house for Wallace, 1867.

framing in the side and rear walls; gabled front of mid-C18 brick with segment-headed windows. Good C19 brick out-buildings: malthouse with three hop kilns, NW, farmyard, NE, with barn, stable and cowhouse.

9040

LITTLE COMBERTON

ST PETER. Norman (severely restored by *William White*, 1886), with stately Early Perp W tower, ashlar-faced, with diagonal buttresses, battlements and pinnacles; four-centred arch to the nave. Three Norman windows in the nave N wall, the west-ernmost with rope motif in its head, all 'reinstated' in 1886; the pair flanking the doorway, with deep internal splays, make a convincing display, despite their alternating red and white voussoirs. The doorway has a very strange tympanum with equal-armed cross and bulgy whorls, four l., four r. Stone and timber porch dated 1639; various Dec windows. The chancel, higher than the nave, is mostly Perp, paid for by the Savage family of Elmley Castle, their initials on the N window's hood-mould; half-timbered W gable of 1886. *White*'s best external display is on the S side, with gables to both his chapel (with typical S window and doorway) and transeptal aisle. He also remodelled the nave S wall, rebuilt 1836, reusing its windows. Interior mostly Victorian, with forceful arcades and arches of red and white banding to the narrow N chapel, and linked S chapel and aisle.

FURNISHINGS also mostly *White*'s, with much *Godwin* floor tiling. Either side of the altar, good displays of C15 TILES. – Elaborate oak REREDOS by *Richard Haughton*, 1900. – Fragment of a Norman PILLAR PISCINA on the W window sill. – STAINED GLASS. Various fragments: C15 heads (nave SW), early C19 heraldry (S aisle S). – E window 1848, perhaps by *Clutterbuck*. – Of 1886–8 the chancel and nave N windows, by *James Powell & Sons*; those above the chancel arch are by *William Pearce*. – MONUMENTS. Thomas Shekell †1809 and wife Elizabeth †1826, probably by *Lewis* of Cheltenham (cf. Pebworth); angel mourning over an urn. – Brass by *Gawthorp & Sons* to Major W.H. Abell †1914, at Mons: a silvery angel presents a wreath to the dead soldier.

Former RECTORY of 1853, SE, beyond a duckpond. Brick, still Late Classical; shallow hipped roof, Grecian stone doorway, large service wing.

To the N, the C17 OLD (MANOR) HOUSE, of square-panelled framing, with two unequally projecting gables. NASH'S FARM-HOUSE, further N, has a tall centre and gabled wing with fine display of mostly narrow studding, C16–C17; also, a good cir-cular DOVECOTE, stone with conical roof, perhaps also C16. Then the SCHOOL (now Village Hall), 1840, plain stone Tudor, with half-timbered W porch of 1890–1; formerly by the church-yard, re-erected here 1898–9. Much enlarged 2006.

The later MANOR HOUSE, W of the church, is early C18 brick, mostly painted, with hipped roof above modillion cornice;

Worcester Cathedral, from the NW, across the Severn; tower completed
1374 (p. 672)

Abbots Morton village, with C17 cottages (p. 103)
Bredon Hill, from the NW, showing the Iron Age hill-fort (and Parsons'
Folly, *c.* 1765) (p. 167)
Broadway village, from the green; war memorial by F.L. Griggs, *c.* 1922
(p. 183)
Bewdley, Severn Side South, from Wribbenhall; bridge by Thomas
Telford, 1797–9 (pp. 141–2)

2	4
3	5

6	8
7	9

10. Malvern, Great Malvern Priory, from the w; nave arcades early C12, the rest C15 (p. 448)

11. Pershore Abbey, s transept, c. 1100 (war memorial by Alfred Drury, 1920–1) (p. 525)

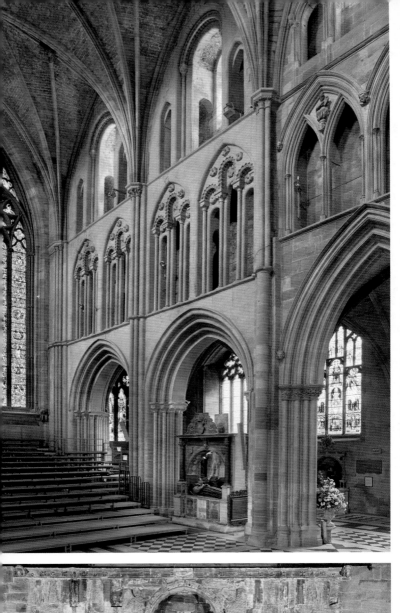

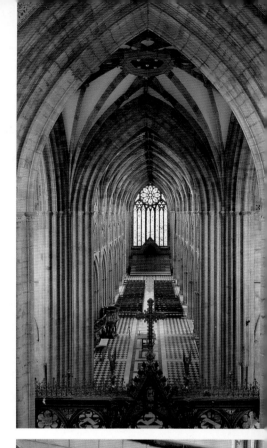

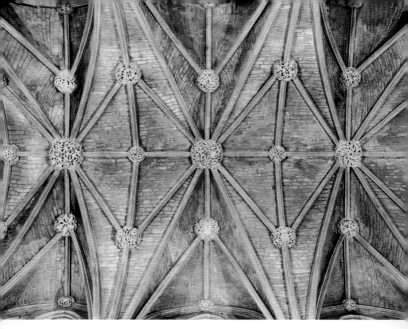

23. Pershore Abbey, chancel, consecrated 1239, vault late C13 (p. 527)
24. Pershore Abbey, chancel vault, probably *c.* 1290–1300 (p. 528)
25. Pershore Abbey, chancel vault boss, probably *c.* 1290–1300 (p. 528)

23 | 24
    | 25

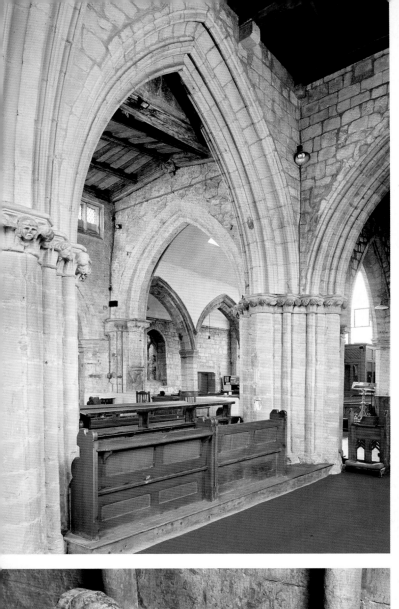

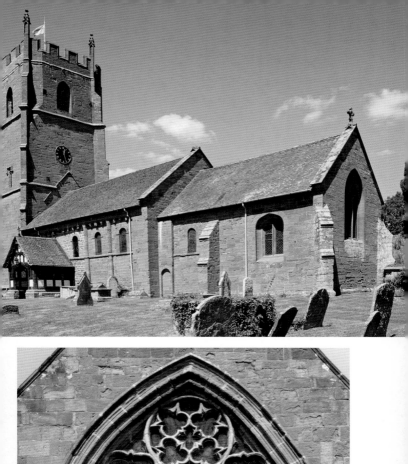

$$\begin{array}{c|c} & 35 \\ 34 & 36 \\ & 37 \end{array}$$

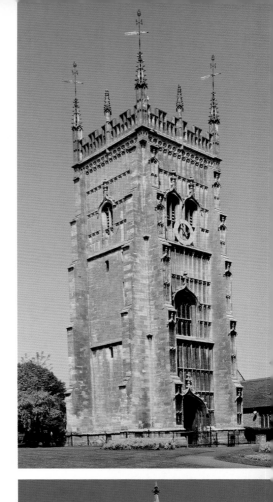

42	44
43	45

MEMORIA SACRVM

Heere lyeth the body of Brackley Paddington Esq. who departed this life the 2 day of Avgvst 1615 hee was borne of Iohn Paddington of Compteß Covrte Esq. and married Abigall daughter of Henry Bromley in the covnty of Glarem Esq. by whome hee had fovre Mary & Anne, Mary married Sr. Iohn Vice of Bvckland in y covnty of Bvcke K. & baronett Anne married Sr. Henry Askeley of Bretherton in y covnty of Essex K. of Baron... ...

In memory of you who did dispise
Vayne pompe though in y self both rich & wise
And ride not home with knowledge did pofes
The rarest Mixture of all scienses,
That those who truly studied you might knowe
The truths which best of bookes did vnto shew
Fayre I your Lovd wee three Nvrfees send
To testify that love which nere shall end
For to your vertues ender it I and
Till I be bedded heere with you in dvst
From whence I hope wee shall in glory rise
And yet Svrmovnt whats worne by mortall Eyes
And thus noe tyme nor death shall vs annove
But wee shall triumphe in Eternall ioye.

MANSVETE et CONSTANTER

MANDAVIT   ANGLIS

67 | 69
68 | 70

| 74 | 76 |
| 75 | 77 |

Hanbury, St
Mary,
monument to
Thomas Vernon
†1721, by
Edward Stanton
and Christopher
Horsnaile, detail
(p. 345)
Powick, St Peter,
monument to
Mary Russell
†1786, by
Thomas
Scheemakers,
1787, detail
(p. 543)
Worcester
Cathedral,
monument to
Richard Solly
†1803, by John
Bacon Jun.,
1804, detail
(p. 695)
Worcester
Cathedral,
monument to
Bishop Hough
†1743, by L.F.
Roubiliac,
1744–7 (p. 692)
Worcester
Cathedral,
monument to
Charlotte Digby,
by Francis
Chantrey,
1823–5 (p. 687)

83 | 86
84 | 87
85

93 | 95
94 | 96

97	100
98	101
99	102

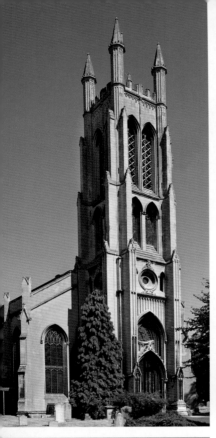

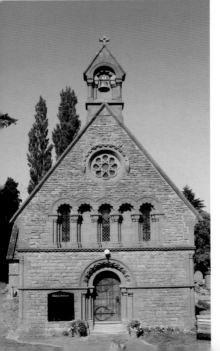

103. Kidderminster, St George, 1821–4
  by Francis Goodwin (p. 400)
104. Ombersley, St Andrew, 1825–9,
  by Thomas Rickman (p. 507)
105. Trimpley, Holy Trinity, 1844,
  by Harvey Eginton (p. 637)
106. Abberley Hall, clock tower, 1883–
  by J.P. St Aubyn (p. 101)

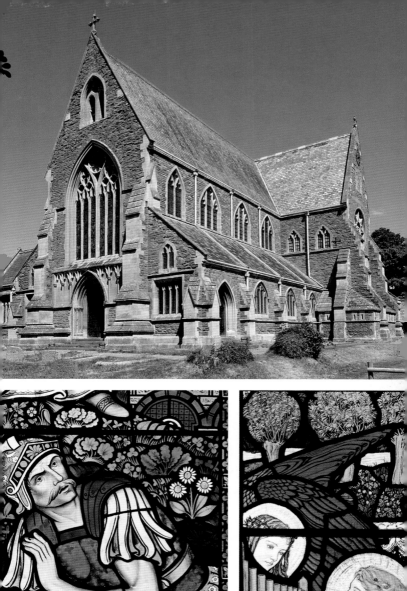

121	123
122	124

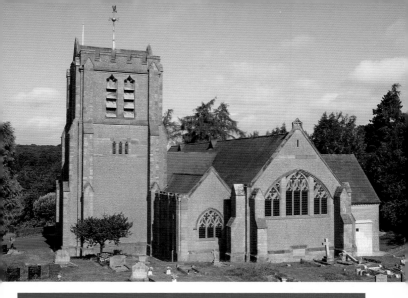

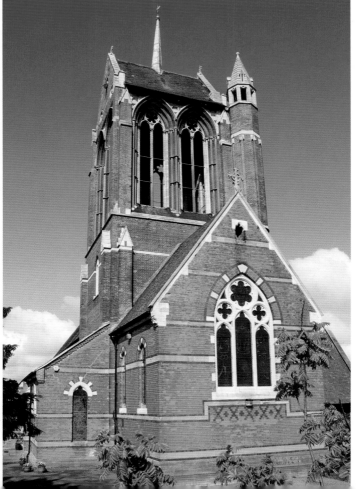

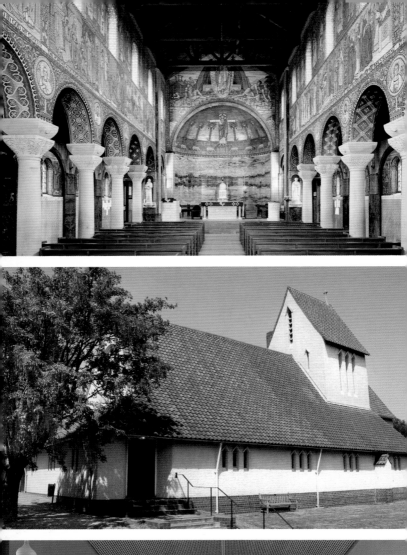

stuccoed s wing, *c.* 1840, facing the garden, with pierced barge-boards and bow windows. Rectangular C17 stone DOVECOTE, w; large brick and half-timbered BARN, N. Further N, flanking the narrow MANOR LANE, a fine group of C17 timber-framed and thatched COTTAGES.

LITTLE MALVERN

ST GILES. The church of a Benedictine priory, probably founded *c.* 1127, perhaps refounded 1171; it was dependent on Worcester Cathedral Priory. Only the Dec to Perp chancel and central tower remain, most impressive viewed from the E, against the backdrop of the Malvern Hills.

The chancel was flanked by two-bay late C15 chapels, now in ruins, as are the transepts probably rebuilt at the same time. Each side, above the chapels, two three-light clerestory windows; the sanctuary projects beyond, its transomed E window of six lights. Tall transomed three-light N and S windows, their reticulated heads no doubt reusing Dec material. This late C15 work is of 1480–2, when John Alcock was Bishop. The tower's lowest stage is apparently Dec (*see* below); the upper two are Perp, probably mid- rather than late C15. Middle stage with just two quatrefoil openings; top stage with full-height narrow panelling around the two-light bell-openings. Later hipped tiled roof. Little survives further W. The late C12 respond by the present entrance, W of the N transept, claimed as the E respond of a nave N arcade, is more probably re-set from an aisle doorway: thin triple shafts, the central one keeled, with common multi-scallop capital; a smaller trumpet-scallop capital behind suggests a second order. Small four-centred doorway opposite, from nave SE to the former cloister, Perp though set in Norman walling. The vanished nave seems to have stretched as far W as the entrance into Little Malvern Court (*see* below).

One enters now into a small narthex (by *Graham & Bellamy*, 1964), then E through a plain timber plank-and-muntin screen into the lofty space beneath the tower. Its E and W arches are probably Dec, though the lower blocked N and S arches have similar sunk wave mouldings. Two-light Dec window in the blocking of the S arch. Broad four-centred arches, also blocked, from the chancel into the chapels, are presumably Perp; capitals with blank scrolls, once no doubt with painted inscriptions. Blocked squints from chapels to High Altar. A three-light Perp N window here was originally the chapel's E window. Flanking the altar, two blocked openings which no doubt led to a sacristy. The flat mid-C19 plaster ceiling incorporates foliage bosses from the C15 roof, which collapsed; the quatrefoil frieze against the E wall shows its shallow pitch.*

REREDOS, now hidden. Stone, mid-C19, with Lord's Prayer, Decalogue, and Creed. – TILES. C15, on the sanctuary floor,

* *Walter Tapper* prepared unexecuted restoration plans in 1910.

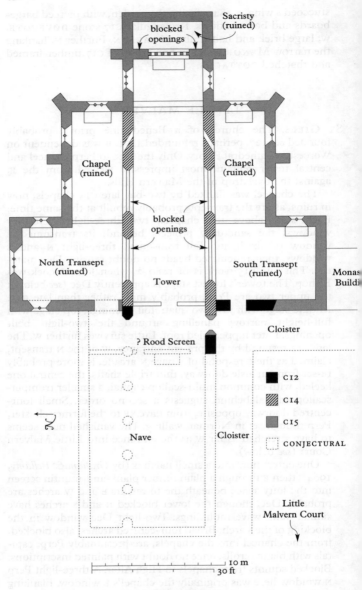

Little Malvern Priory.
Original plan of church

Legend:
- C12
- C14
- C15
- CONJECTURAL

Labels on plan:
- Sacristy (ruined)
- blocked openings
- Chapel (ruined)
- Chapel (ruined)
- blocked openings
- North Transept (ruined)
- South Transept (ruined)
- Tower
- Monas[tic] Buildi[ng]
- Cloister
- ? Rood Screen
- Cloister
- Nave
- Little Malvern Court

10 m
30 ft

with heraldry and inscriptions; one is dated 1456. More on the shelf of the blocked N chapel arch. – PILLAR PISCINA. A made-up piece: double-handled C12 bowl, probably a stoup, on an imported column. – STALLS. Five each side, their misericords chopped off. The carving of the arm-rests remains: heads, angels with shields, two pigs feeding from the same trough. – SCREEN. C14–C15; broad one-light divisions. The foliage bands above, the lower a fine vine trail, belonged to the ROOD BEAM. – FONT, apparently the reused base and stump of an octagonal Perp pier. – SCULPTURE. Above the W doorway, a wooden carving of a man, 16 in. (41 cm.) long, resting on his elbow, legs crossed; probably C14. Where from? – Many ARCHITECTURAL FRAGMENTS: a late C12 trumpet capital; twin plain capitals of c. 1200, perhaps from the cloister; parts of an elaborately canopied Perp niche. – STAINED GLASS. In the E window *in situ* fragments of considerable interest. Of 1480–2, probably by the *Twygge-Wodshawe* workshop, including well-preserved kneeling figures: Edward V, then Prince of Wales; a headless figure, probably his younger brother Richard;* and their mother Queen Elizabeth, with three daughters. Above, part of one figure survives, perhaps St Egwin. In the traceries, royal arms, those of Bishop Alcock, and other fragments. – In the tracery light of a N window, a contemporary figure of God the Father, probably from a Coronation of the Virgin. – MONUMENT. Two long sides of a Perp tomb-chest, each with five cinquefoiled panels containing blank shields and two elegant little female figures. The head of a lady, c. 1390, with jewelled head-dress (found 1976, now displayed in the narthex), probably belonged to it. – Also displayed, a knight's head and other fragments. – Two BRASSES to the Berington family, both designed by *Pugin* for *Hardman*, 1847. – Seven Berington HATCHMENTS, late C18 to late C20.

LITTLE MALVERN COURT came into the possession of the recusant Russell family (cf. Strensham) after the Dissolution, passing early in the C18 to the Berington family who still own it. A complex house round a small central courtyard, immediately SW of the church, incorporating significant remains of the former priory cloisters in its E range, notably the refectory or prior's hall. Its E front, part rubble, part timber-framed, has this hall at first-floor level above a basement; renewed windows (the N c. 1800) either side of a projecting stack. From the SE corner projects a small gabled C16–C17 wing, three storeys, the upper two close-studded; the middle storey was the porch, formerly approached up steps, leading into the screens passage (*see* below). The S (service) end of this E range, with renewed square-panelled framing, adjoins (SW) a big square three-storey block of local stone, perhaps medieval in origin, remodelled c. 1600. At its SW corner, an attached round tower with conical cap, formerly a garderobe, now containing a spiral

* Bishop Alcock, later founder of Jesus College, Cambridge, was their tutor.

staircase; the weathervane dated 1856 indicates rebuilding of the upper part. Ovolo-moulded mullioned-and-transomed windows, of timber, on its w side. A second spiral stair in the diagonally opposite corner of this block links with the hall in the E range. The other fenestration of the tower block, with the remainder of the s range and s part of the w front, of Lias with ashlar dressings, belongs to rebuilding by *Joseph Hansom & Son*, 1859–60, for Charles Berington. Various Tudor Gothic or bay windows, including one to the drawing room; lower dining room and vestibule projection along the w front. High gables unfortunately removed in the 1960s. The rest of the w range is of C15–C16 close studding, with broad NW gable. The N range, poorly refronted in brick in the early C19, may include stonework from the nave s wall of the church. The timber framing at first-floor level, of a very wide span, with richly moulded floor beams, no doubt incorporates remains of the prior's private accommodation, including his great chamber, which was at least partly remodelled in the C15.

An external C19 stone stair, NE, leads up to the prior's hall. Its splendid, smoke-blackened roof was exposed during work in 1964–7 (planned by *F.W.B Charles*, executed by *Ivan Bellamy*). Probably early C14, completely intact: four-bay double-purlin roof, cinquefoil-cusped wind-braces to each purlin, arch-braced collar-trusses with trefoil openings above. An extra bay for the screens passage, s, is separated by a spere-truss; this, with quatrefoil and dagger tracery in the spandrels between tie-beam, knee-braces, and aisle-posts, may be slightly earlier. On the passage's s side, ogee-headed openings to buttery and pantry. The whole arrangement seems thoroughly domestic though on the grandest scale. The stone side walls presumably survive, at least in part, from an earlier monastic hall; the w wall has remains of the tall shafted jamb of a window or doorway: C13, perhaps later C12.* From 1791 until the 1960s, the hall, with its roof hidden, served as a chapel. The wooden REREDOS, a late C19 compilation by *Hardman*, has some excellent carving, especially a crowded Crucifixion scene of the Antwerp school, *c*. 1500. An earlier chapel tucked away above the porch, and generally the contrived planning of concealed stairs and small rooms in this part emphasizes that the house was a recusant stronghold.

On the site of the cloisters N walk, the weathered base and shaft of a medieval CROSS, resited 1993 from a position s of the house.

Splendid GARDENS redesigned in 1983–8 by *Michael Balston*, in conjunction with *Arabella Lennox-Boyd*. Small compartments in the Arts and Crafts mode close to the house; a chain of descending lakes further s, presumably remnants of the fish ponds. Timber-framed former STABLES, N, by the main road, partly rebuilt 1857.

---

* A similar jamb, plus other medieval stonework, can be seen on the s front chimney, between the timber range and stone tower block.

St Wulstan (R.C.), Wells Road, ⅓ m. N. By *Benjamin Bucknall*, 1861–2, on a dramatically sloping site. Malvern rubble with ashlar dressings. Aisleless nave with NE Lady Chapel; the large apsed chancel, raised above an undercroft, was never built. Bold Geometrical tracery, the chapel with three sharp N gables; W doorway beneath a very large rose. The piquant SW baptistery, hexagonal with pyramidal tiled roof, was probably added *c.* 1866; SE sacristies. Wide nave with arch-braced collar roof on thin wall-shafts. Recessed windows, tall blocked chancel arch. High three-bay arcade to the stone-vaulted chapel. Baptistery also vaulted, with painted and stencilled decoration, patterned glass, and tiled floor; small FONT dated 1866. – Stone and tile REREDOS in the chapel. – Later C19 pitch-pine WEST GALLERY. – Polished grey marble ALTAR. 1962. – STAINED GLASS. Three, chapel N, by *Hardman*, 1882–92.

In the S corner of the churchyard, a simple headstone to Lady Elgar †1920 and Sir Edward Elgar †1934, contrasting with the ornate memorial crosses nearby.

KIRKLANDS, SW, the former presbytery, dated 1845, intended as a Benedictine priory, is very tall, of stone, Tudor Gothic style, with two storeys plus gabled attics; higher at the rear.

LITTLE WITLEY

7060

St Michael. A chapelry of Holt until 1904. Rebuilt by *Perkins*, 1867, on the lower sandstone courses of the C13 church. E.E.-style chancel, its rounded apse with three tight E lancets. Nave with Y- or plate tracery, the N doorway early C13, reused: pointed, with continuous roll moulding. Timber S porch. Octagonal stone bell-turret with pyramidal spirelet, the diagonals open lancets; the narrower solid sides have tripled foliated shafts, the W on a far-projecting bracket, like a bit of machicolation. Pleasant unaltered interior, with distinctive stone carving executed in 1867 by *Mary Sale*, the rector's wife (cf. Holt), a pupil of the watercolourist David Cox. Most remarkable the capitals of the chancel arch, with lush and free foliage, and large birds. The chancel altogether is more richly adorned than the nave. – Contemporary FITTINGS: round FONT, carved with arum lilies by Mrs Sale; ornate stone PULPIT with open arcading. – C18 baluster FONT, from Great Witley. – ARMS of Queen Adelaide (cf. p. 329), painted by *J.M. Mabey*, 1853. – STAINED GLASS. Patterned chancel windows, 1867. – Nave W 1953, by *A.E. & P.E. Lemmon* of Bromsgrove.

Former SCHOOL, a little ENE. Dated 1874. Sandstone, gabled Tudor Gothic, small, with attached house; mullioned-and-transomed windows, oriels, dormers, also a canted bay. Reactionary but very pretty. – C17 COTTAGES nearby.

8030

LONGDON

St Mary. Early C14 w tower, of Lias. Tall Y-traceried bell-openings, with transom (cf. Upton upon Severn); recessed ribbed spire with corner pinnacles, rebuilt 1826. Arch to the nave with three chamfers dying into the imposts. Three-bay nave by *William Marshall* of Bourton-on-the-Water (Glos.), 1786–7. Its s side, false ashlar stucco with stone dressings and quoins, has large round-arched windows flanking a projection with a slightly lower Venetian one. Parapet with tiny central pediment. N side of exposed brick, its central projection with just one small window that once lit the pulpit. Inside, these central bays are flanked by Ionic demi-columns. Small (internal) dome above, flat ceiling otherwise. Neo-Norman apsed chancel,* N vestry and s porch, of 1870–1 by the vicar, the Rev. *A.C. Lefroy* (following plans of 1868 by *Arthur Blomfield*); he also intended to rebuild the nave. The detail is not particularly convincing.

Neo-Norman FONT, c. 1870. – PULPIT, a charming late C18 piece, with a little inlay, thin back wall, and small concave-sided tester (perhaps the original base; the present one is C19). – CHANDELIER. Brass, Baroque type, given 1789. The chancel chandelier was its former upper tier. – Modest tiled REREDOS by *Powell & Sons*, 1870. Above it stood the pyrographic Crucifixion PAINTING, on Spanish chestnut, by the Rev. *W. Calvert* (now in the nave). Replaced by a new window, 1946, with STAINED GLASS by *James Hogan*, for *Powells.* – Other apse and chancel windows by *Heaton, Butler & Bayne*, 1870. – w window by *M.C. Farrar Bell*, 1972; his also the wrought-iron TOWER SCREEN. – MONUMENTS. Brass to William Brugge †1523 and wife Alice, good 3-ft (0.9-metre) figures; at his feet a lion, by hers her pet dog. – Thomas Parker †1751, by *W. Stephens*, probably c. 1790; straight-sided sarcophagus against an obelisk, quite elegant as Stephens so often was. – Two chancel tablets (1811 and 1864) by his son and grandson, both signed *J. Stephens*.

SCHOOL, by the w gate. 1848–9, of Lias; Tudor Gothic, with attached house. Enlarged by *Henry Gorst*, 1969. – Simple VICARAGE of c. 1800, to the s, remodelled and roughcast by *R.J. Withers*, 1867.

MANOR FARM, NE. Mid-C18, three bays, brick, with quoins and platbands of iron slag; projecting centre with pediment. All five windows and the doorway are Venetian. C17 timber framing at the rear.

MOAT HOUSE, s. T-plan, the short stem a hall range, probably C15, with cross-passage, E; the separate stone building, w, may be the remains of a (detached?) service end. Three-bay cross-wing, E, c. 1600, jettied with moulded bressummers both ends; close-studded ground floor, lively diagonal timbering with double-curved struts above. C17 porch with crude wooden Ionic demi-columns. The moat survives.

---

*The late C18 chancel was also apsed.

CHAMBERS COURT, ½ m. SE. Small Jacobethan country house by *Richard Armstrong*, 1845–7, for E.G. Stone. Of Lias, encasing a brick house of *c.* 1750. Five bays, projecting centre with gable and side pinnacles; gabled return, S, continued by a well-preserved stone conservatory.

PARSONAGE FARM, Birtsmorton Lane, ½ m. S. The oldest part is the N–S hall range, its service end, N, rebuilt in the C17. Behind this survive the central truss and upper-end frame of a two-bay cruck hall; brick chimney built into the lower bay, blocking the former cross-passage. Two-bay late C17 range, E; C19 W wing, of Lias.

LONGDON HALL, ⅞ m. SSE. Large, altered C16–C17 (said to be of 1589), mostly of heavy square framing; central hall range, gabled cross-wings. These are paired on the E front, with a fine late C17 open-well oak staircase with twisted balusters in the inner N wing. The slightly richer W front (altered 1968–9) has single gabled cross-wings; centre with continuous moulded jetty, interrupted by the large hall chimneystack. Blocked four-centred doorway to its r., marking the former screens passage. C17 panelling in the NW wing. The house, formerly known as the White House, belonged to the Parker family until 1901. – C17 timber-framed outbuildings.

Many C16–C17 timber-framed farms and cottages throughout the large parish. Several (interspersed with Georgian brick) line the B-road at BUCKBURY, 1¼ m. SSE, the best BUCKBURY HOUSE, the former manor house. Small, T-plan; S cross-wing with close studding below, large tension braces above.

EASTINGTON HALL, Longdon Heath, 1½ m. NNW. A splendid large timber-framed house, the result of four or more distinct phases. The core is a superb late C13 hall with E cross-wing, remodelled *c.* 1500, probably for William Brugge (or Bridges); he may have added the long, originally detached, W solar range. These two were linked either in the C17 or *c.* 1870, and in 1914–15 the whole doubled in size, in convincing half-timbered style, to a broad U-plan, for Mlle Gabrielle de Montgeon.

The core, perhaps *c.* 1280, is at the centre of the N, entrance, front, the hall masked by its big lateral brick chimney-breast. The cross-wing has an ornate close-studded front of *c.* 1500, jettied on traceried brackets: hipped-roofed two-storey porch, projecting bargeboarded gable to its l. This has an oriel above, flanked by Tudor-arched struts with carved pendants, and bay window below. Exceptionally rich oak and rose carving, also little figures, notably full-length ones to the E, and on the dragon beam of the porch, NW corner; spandrels of its four-centred entrance carved with grotesque faces. The huge Gothic inner door, into the through-passage, reveals the late C13 origin, though the spere-truss and screen here are of *c.* 1500. The hall is probably the earliest base-cruck example in the county, with two huge trusses with collar-beams (and scissor-braced roof above). The ground-floor room of the cross-wing has moulded beams and a C15 stone fireplace, its moulded jambs ending in carved heads. Splendid roof in the chamber above, with tie-beams and cinquefoiled wind-braces.

Externally most of the rest is of 1914–15, apart from the close studding of the solar range of *c.* 1500 (perhaps built as lodgings) visible on its W side, with another fine brick chimney-stack with two star-shafts. The work of 1914–15, also mostly close-studded, above a Lias ground floor, has further elaborate carving and vine-trail bargeboards, especially to the S, set round three sides of a square; open loggia below the projecting centre (and to its W). The drawing room, in the E range, has a good Neo-Jacobean plaster ceiling; fine staircase in the same style. NW of the house, now attached, a former C17 BARN, over-prettified in the 1980s. – To the NE, a circular Lias DOVE-COTE with conical roof, perhaps C15–C16.

LODGE COTTAGES. Mid-C19; red brick, blue trim, latticed windows.

LOWER MOOR *see* HILL AND MOOR

LOWER SAPEY

ST BARTHOLOMEW. In a remote, secluded setting on the Here-fordshire boundary, above a tributary of the Sapey Brook. Formerly a chapelry of Clifton upon Teme, replaced, 1877, by Harpley (p. 359). Then a farm building until the 1970s; vested p. 22 in the Churches Conservation Trust 1994. Nave and chancel, sandstone with some tufa, formerly rendered (recently renewed, E and N sides). Norman W and E openings (the latter only visible within), also one nave S, one chancel N. The S doorway, perhaps slightly later, has two orders, the outer with engaged shafts with scallop capitals, the inner plain, its blank tympanum cut into by a segmental arch; chamfered hood-mould. Later windows: a large lancet (nave SE), good C14 two-lighter (chancel S), and early C19 ones in the E and nave N walls; also a rectangular opening of indeterminate date, low down, nave W. Timber S porch, C14–C15, with bargeboards, arch-braced entrance, and curved wind-braces; original N DOOR. Interior without furnishings apart from the renewed W gallery. A simple early C19 plastered tympanum replaced the Norman chancel arch. Elliptical ceiled roofs with tie-beams, the trusses above dendro-dated *c.* 1465–90. The W tie-beam supports oak framing for an internal double bellcote, a rare survival. Plastered walls with traces of PAINTINGS, notably a royal arms, nave N, probably C17, the lion's hindquarters still legible. Double aumbry below the chancel N window; single aumbry and piscina remains, S.

To the W, CHURCH HOUSE FARM, C17, square-panelled framing; facing the church, a central gable, gabled stair-turret, and lower gabled N wing. – Renewed rubble OUTBUILDINGS: cider house and granary, W; cowhouse, SW.

At HOPE MILL on the Sapey Brook ⅛ m. NE, a C17 timber-framed cottage with attached early C19 brick mill retaining an overshot waterwheel dated 1853.

HOPE FARMHOUSE, ¼ m. N. Attractively rebuilt in sandstone, *c.* 1830–40; three storeys of square-headed windows with hood-moulds, central recessed Tudor doorway, three gables with bargeboards and finials. – C18 framed BARNS.

LOWER WICK *see* OUTER WORCESTER, p. 776

LULSLEY

7050

Secluded, scattered village, within a bend S of the River Teme.

ST GILES. Rebuilt, slightly W of its medieval predecessor (a chapelry of Suckley), by *Henry Rowe & Son*, 1892–3, for J.F. Greswolde-Williams; closed 1972, now a house. Unaltered exterior, local sandstone with red Alveley dressings. Chancel with N vestry; nave with open W bell-turret and S porch, both timber. Good Geometrical to Dec tracery. Inside, a false hammerbeam nave roof; chancel arch with polished granite corbel shafts. – STAINED GLASS. E window by *Heaton, Butler & Bayne*, 1899.* – Typical *Rowe* LYCHGATE, 1892–3: square, timber, sprocketed hipped roof.

LULSLEY COURT, ¼ m. N. Hall range with gabled cross-wings. C16 centre and W service wing, of square-panelled framing. The projecting E solar cross-wing was given a parallel outer range in the C17, all close-studded; the outer range is jettied from a bressummer with billet decoration on console brackets. Windows, bargeboards and finials are all C19. Tall brick chimneys: tripled stacks above the lower end of the hall, a cluster of four, solar end.

COLLES PLACE, at the S end of the drive, is probably early C17; square-panelled framing, hall-and-cross-wing plan with baffle entry, the wing underbuilt in sandstone.

UPPER COURT, further E, of emaciated C18–C19 narrow studding (no doubt intended for rendering), is built above a sandstone terrace; large segmentally arched entry to the cellar. Small moated site at the rear of the farmstead, SE.

KNIGHTWICK STATION, ½ m. SW. Of 1874, plain brick with segment-headed windows. Enlarged as a house, but a rare survivor of the Worcester to Bromyard railway (completed 1877); engineer: *W.B. Lewis*.

MADRESFIELD

8040

ST MARY. 1866–7 by *Frederick Preedy*. Aisleless nave, S porch, chancel with N vestry. Of snecked grey Cradley sandstone with

---

* Pre-C19 FITTINGS are at Alfrick, p. 105.

prominent bands of red Alveley ashlar. NW tower with elaborate recessed spire, not originally intended but also complete by 1867. Windows late C13–early C14 in style, some, notably the E and W, reused from the previous church by *E. W. Pugin*, 1852–3 (SW of Madresfield Court, *see* below). Inside, the chancel arch has red marble shafts, the chancel windows green shafts and heavily cusped rere-arches. Good arch-braced roofs, the nave with bold corbels portraying Doctors of the Church, carved by *Boulton*. – Octagonal FONT, and fussy PULPIT and diapered REREDOS, of Caen stone, by *E. W. Pugin*, the last with added painting by *Preedy* and carved figures by *Boulton*. – Paintings by *Preedy* also on his oak CHANCEL SCREEN and ORGAN CASE, both carved by *Earp*. – Small gadrooned C18 FONT bowl, used as a piscina in the N vestry. – WALL PAINTINGS. Last Judgement, above the chancel arch, by *Clayton & Bell*, 1894. Angels and stencilling on the chancel E wall presumably earlier. – STAINED GLASS. Excellent E window by *Henry A. Payne*, 1908, an Arts and Crafts depiction of the Heavenly Jerusalem. – W by *Lavers & Barraud*, 1867. – Others all by *Heaton, Butler & Bayne*: chancel 1878; three in the nave 1894–6, the fourth, NW, *c.* 1901. – MONUMENTS. Unassuming C18–C19 tablets to the earls Beauchamp. – Against the nave W wall, an extraordinary memorial of 1904 by Lady *Feodora Gleichen*, to Edward Lygon and Richard Somerset; both died during the Boer War. Stiff Arts and Crafts, with three bronze figures (Obedience, Fortitude and Loyalty) beneath gold mosaic canopies, on shafts of lapis lazuli; bronze reliefs between, showing figures shepherded by angels. – Carved Crucifixion, exterior E wall, a memorial to the Rev. George Munn †1906.

The CHURCHYARD began as the parish cemetery, by *John Norton*, 1857; his the LYCHGATE and damaged memorial CROSS, to the E. – Stepped WELL-HEAD, SW of the porch, sandstone with fine wrought-iron canopy, by *Preedy*, 1866. – Also his, the plain TOMB-CHEST to Henry, fifth Earl †1866, SE of the chancel.

SCHOOL, W, also by *Preedy*, 1868. Brick, long schoolroom, small attached house; scalloped bargeboards, ogee-headed timber windows. Poor C20 additions.

Beauchamp ESTATE COTTAGES line the village street, the gabled one N of the church perhaps by *Preedy*. The rest, plainer brick pairs mostly with prominent central chimneys, are probably by *Haddon Bros*, 1869–71. At the N end, the excellent NORTH LODGE by *Norman Shaw*, 1871–2; picturesque half-timbered, two storeys, with cleverly varied gables and high central starplan chimney. Opposite it, the early C19 HAYWOOD FARM, with C17–C18 outbuildings. Further on, round the bend, a good C17 timber-framed pair (Byeways and Lavender Cottage): three bays with dormers, then two gabled cross-ranges, the NW probably earlier.

MADRESFIELD GRANGE, ½ m. N. 1905–6. Roughcast over brick, big hipped green slate roof. Garden front with gables above oriels, linked by a timber balcony; entrance front with timber porch and staircase window (with Art Nouveau glass).

The OLD RECTORY, ¼ m. WSW, by *John Norton*, 1857, is mild Gothic, of painted brick; tall brick star chimneys either end, gabled porch, NE, with pierced bargeboards.

MADRESFIELD COURT

Madresfield Court, ¼ m. E, has belonged to the Lygon family since the mid C15; William Lygon became the first Earl Beauchamp in 1815. The brick mansion stands in a perfect moat, quite wide, the masonry of its walling indicating an early date, possibly C13. By 1451 it had developed into a substantial manor house, to a courtyard plan with gatehouse, no doubt represented by the present entrance range, S side. William Lygon rebuilt the house from 1584; the datestone 1593 above the entry, a relic of this, was originally at the rear. The earliest datable features, notably this entrance range, are indeed Elizabethan. Other parts, including a three-by-four-bay NE wing by *George Byfield*, 1799, were largely rebuilt during a thorough remodelling begun by *P.C. Hardwick* for the fifth Earl in 1863; only completed for the sixth Earl *c.* 1890.* The younger Hardwick was hardly an exemplar of architectural discipline and the variety of his work here is not totally successful. Interiors are also mostly his, supplemented by some outstanding early C20 Arts and Crafts work, carried out for the seventh Earl.

EXTERIOR. The C16 S ENTRANCE FRONT, approached by a brick bridge across the moat, sets the tone for the very large and varied house. It has stepped gables, the central two of four bays projecting as a gate tower. The unusual height results from an extra storey added by Hardwick, 1885; the canted-back wing, SW, shows the original height. Matching SE wing removed by Hardwick and replaced by a canted bay (for the billiard room, now library). The side of the chapel, built 1866–7, follows. Its blank E front forms one end of the loosely composed E FRONT, externally the best of Hardwick's work. It follows the footprint of the earlier house, with the long gallery on its upper floor. Heights nowhere tally, symmetry is shunned, gabled projections and recessions follow each other bewilderingly. Parts have a decidedly Germanic feel, notably the large projecting canted bay with three sharp timbered gables. A high timber bell-turret of 1875, two tiers plus spirelet, signified completion of the exterior; it provides an excellent vertical accent, especially for the distant views against the fine backdrop of the Malvern Hills. The surprisingly deep NE WING (1866–7, replacing that of 1799) is standard Jacobethan, with shaped gables and projecting bays. The Jacobean styling becomes yet plainer along the

* In a paper read to the Worcester Diocesan Archaeological Society, 1881, the sixth Earl claimed: 'It was found necessary, for the most part, to substitute reconstruction for repair.'

N FRONT, the service range. This was probably completed by
J.S. Alder, *c.* 1890, though a covered wooden bridge of 1870
already linked it to outbuildings N of the moat, including game
larder and brewhouse. The whole W FRONT, hard up against
the moat, mostly containing servants' accommodation, is
severely plain: two storeys of Georgian-looking sashed
windows above a high, buttressed, stone plinth, of medieval
appearance.

INTERIOR. The order here follows the guided public route (omit-
ting any description of the notable art objects and furniture).
Some major rooms are on the grand scale, though this is not
immediately obvious. The entrance hall leads into a sombre
claustrophobic passage around the INNER COURTYARD, which
is in contrast perhaps the happiest product of the Victorian
rebuilding. Here the half-timbering has Germanic infill panels
decorated with red sgraffito patterns, particularly on the high
rear gables of the entrance range; this contrasts effectively with

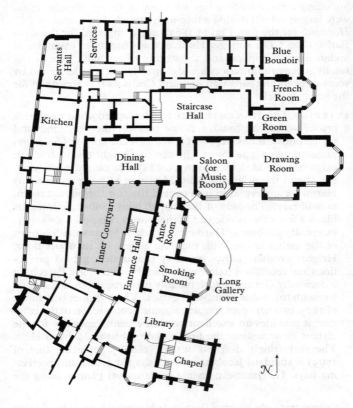

Madresfield Court.
Ground-floor plan

the lower ranges: an open first-floor gallery, W; dining room, N, with vast Perp-style windows. Hardwick installed a glazed roof over this courtyard, but *Preedy* (probably assisted by *Alder*) removed it in 1887; the pavement has an inlaid marble maze dated 1888.

The LIBRARY, E of the entrance hall, is an august space as remodelled and expanded by *C.R. Ashbee*, with fine woodwork by his *Guild of Handicraft*: low-relief carvings of 1902–3 on the doors by *Alec Miller*, who, with *Will Hart*, executed the Tree of Life and Tree of Knowledge on the bookcase ends. Chimneypiece by *Sidney Barnsley*, 1908. The CHAPEL beyond also has exceptionally complete Arts-and-Crafts decoration, contemporary but wholly different in feeling. Begun in 1902 by Birmingham Group craftsmen for Countess Beauchamp, as a wedding present for the seventh Earl, but work continued until 1923; the delightful tempera wall paintings, latest Pre-Raphaelite, by *Henry Payne*, assisted by *Richard Stubington*, *J.N. Sanders* and *Henry Rushbury*, therefore include the Earl and Countess as donors as well as all their seven children. Stained glass also by *Payne*'s team, as is the decoration of the roof, W gallery and organ case above. The gallery has inset ornamental glass quarries, especially pretty, by *Bertram Lamplugh*. The Perp-ish altar triptych, by *W.H. Bidlake*, 1902–3, has paintings by *Charles Gere*, who also designed the frontal (worked by the rector's daughters). Hanging lamps by *A.S. Dixon*; candlesticks and crucifix by *A.J. Gaskin* and his wife *Georgie*. Will Hart, in a letter to Ashbee, compared this kaleidoscopic decoration to 'a barber's pole or an ice cream barrow'.

The chapel gallery provides access to the LONG GALLERY (of 1863) along the upper floor of the E range. Hardwick retained its form from the C16 house, throwing out a new bay at its centre, and re-creating all the decoration including the intricate plaster ceiling. Wooden chimneypiece, with caryatids and arched panels, dated 1610, from Stonehouse Farm, Kempley (Glos.). Parallel to the W (facing the courtyard), the Victorian NEW GALLERY, with heraldic glass (probably by *Hardman*, 1897). Then comes the dramatic STAIRCASE HALL, a creation of the seventh Earl *c.* 1913 (though the basic layout differs little from that shown in ground plans of 1898 by *H. Percy Adams*). *Randall Wells* submitted a design for a new hall *c.* 1908, and was still involved, with *Ernest Gimson*, in 1912, when he was dismissed, perhaps because of the 'scandal' at Besford Court, p. 138. The room, lit solely by three circular domed skylights, has a remarkable balcony on three sides, plus W staircase, of ebony woodwork: heraldic beasts on the newels, twisted balusters of crystal. Large chimneypiece of alabaster, red porphyry and green serpentine, a wedding gift in 1902 from the Countess's brother, the Duke of Westminster; it could well be by *Alfred Waterhouse* (cf. Eaton Hall, Cheshire). Back on the ground floor, NE wing, SALOON and DRAWING ROOM have varying plaster ceilings and marble chimneypieces by

Hardwick. In the ANTE-ROOM a stone overmantel by *J. S. Alder*, 1890, with a word square commemorating Frederick, sixth Earl. Finally the DINING ROOM, again by Hardwick, 1863, on the site of the medieval Great Hall; its minstrels' gallery, said to be a relic of this, is of wrought iron, entirely C19. Large Perp-traceried windows (as noticed before); false hammerbeam roof. Much C17 panelling from a farmhouse at Newland; chimneypiece flanked by Ionic marble columns. Early C20 stained glass in the W window, no doubt by *Henry Payne*. (The room above the S entrance has an original plaster frieze and ceiling in three panels. Another bedroom nearby has a shallow-pitched ceiling with plaster vine, rose and acorn ornament in ogival patterns, cf. The Nash, Kempsey, p. 392.)

GROUNDS. The ROSE GARDEN, within the moat at the house's SE angle, has a stone well-head with elaborate iron canopy, perhaps 1867–8, (cf. St Mary, above). Beyond it, E, an architectural YEW GARDEN, with brick and terracotta walling. CAESARS' LAWN, NE, on the site of the bowling green, has a N border of yew with alcoves containing busts of emperors. S of the house a pair of L-shaped ponds form a kind of outer moat. To the SW, the site of the medieval church, rebuilt 1852–3 (*see* p. 440), is marked by a large Celtic memorial cross to Frederick, sixth Earl †1891; built into its base, a C12 tympanum, with scalloped and chip-carved decoration.

The main part of the wooded grounds is set round a triangle of drives. Poplar Avenue (with a yew MAZE of 1893, to the N) leads NW to a TEMPLE, made up from an early C19 lodge, standing beside a large pond: four Tuscan columns, without their pediment. Oak Avenue leads back NE, past clipped yew hedges that once surrounded FORMAL GARDENS laid out by *Thomas Mawson*, 1903–9. Near where it meets Cedar Avenue (planted 1866–8, leading back S to the house), a resited STATUE of Mercury (by *C. Giddings*) on a tall plinth. Further NW, across the Madresfield Brook, a splendid ROCK GARDEN and GROTTO by *James Pulham & Son*, 1878–9; quite extensive, on two levels, using the substantial blocks of artificial stone they patented (of rubble cased in cement).

A little S of the house is the STABLE BLOCK of *c.* 1800, U-plan, two storeys, with wooden Y-traceried windows. To its E, Tulip Tree Avenue leads S to LODGE COTTAGES, by *C.F.A. Voysey*, *c.* 1901, a charming symmetrical pair either side of a round archway, each with one narrow gabled bay. Unusually for Voysey, they are of brick with stone dressings, but the completely flush surrounds of the long horizontal runs of broad-mullioned windows are unmistakable. Nearby, the early C19 HOME FARM has an octagonal timbered dairy dated 1889 at its rear; also a brick arch with C17 wrought-iron gates (said to come from Worcester Cathedral's N porch), stables of 1856, and smithy of 1924. To its SE, a notable circular brick DOVECOTE, restored or rebuilt by *Norman Shaw*, 1872. Conical roof with curiously tall château-like dormer of stone, with two-light mul-

lioned window, rows of flight-holes above, and pinnacled gable.
LODGES. For *Shaw*'s NORTH LODGE, see p. 440. – The
SOUTH LODGE, dated 1875, probably by *Hardwick*, is also pic-
turesquely half-timbered, but far less sophisticated: fancy
bargeboards, open porch with twisted balusters. – On the
B4424, at the end of the mile-long Gloucester Drive, the EAST
LODGE of 1926; brick, half-timbered gable above coving, four
brick piers with wrought-iron gates.

MALVERN

The town climbs up and around the two highest and most
northerly of the superb Malvern Hills: Worcestershire Beacon
(1,395ft, 425 metres) and North Hill (1,303ft, 397 metres).
Walking and driving are much as in the small towns on the banks
of the North Italian lakes. This account deals mainly with Great
Malvern (*see* Perambulations), but also includes North Malvern,
Malvern Link, the eastern suburbs, and The Wyche (*see* Outer
Malvern). Malvern Wells and West Malvern have separate entries.
Great Malvern began as a village outside the priory; the
priory church became the parish church after the Dissolution.

Development started in the late C18, long after the discovery of the medicinal waters of Malvern Wells (q.v.) in the C16. Some prosperity followed Dr Wall's publication, of 1757, on the purity of the waters; in 1796 the first guide for visitors came out. The town began to grow from c. 1810, partly as a rustic retreat from Cheltenham. Several hotels were established, and Circulating Library, Pump Room and Baths were built in 1819–23. In 1830 Princess Victoria spent some time in Malvern. In 1842 Dr James Wilson (soon followed by his friend, later rival, Dr James Gully) created a sensation by introducing the German type of hydropathic treatment. Great Malvern became an English equivalent of Graefenberg, the town where Vincent Priessnitz established his world-famous water cure; Kelly's *Directory*, 1850, noted: 'Hydropathy has taken possession of Malvern and peopled its houses.' The Malvern Improvement Act received assent in 1851, its twelve commissioners being replaced by a Local Board in 1867; the railway arrived in 1859–60. Population figures highlight these stages of growth: 819 in 1809, 2,768 in 1841, 7,600 in 1871. By c. 1900 the spa had declined in importance, but Malvern remained a desirable place to live, with cultural and educational facilities, for retired people or for Birmingham and Worcester commuters.

Wide and sweeping roads, with mostly gentle inclines and much planting, are the uniting factor in Malvern's development. Early C19 stuccoed villas began to be superseded by more extravert Tudor or Gothic houses in the 1840s; of these Great Malvern retains an exceptional variety. The sale of the Mason estate in 1846 began the development around Abbey and Priory roads, s of the town centre. The founding of Malvern College in 1862 stimulated growth further s. The area N of Church Street, for example Graham Road, belonged like much else in Malvern to Lady Emily Foley (of Stoke Edith Park, Herefs.), who was reluctant to release building plots much before c. 1858, then only gradually. Of local architects, *E. W. Elmslie*, elected a town commissioner in 1855, was especially busy. His partners and successors, the brothers *George C.* and *Henry Haddon*, were yet busier, the latter running their Malvern office c. 1863–93 (with George based in Hereford). Of London architects, only *S. S. Teulon* made a notable domestic contribution.

PREHISTORIC REMAINS. Two Iron Age hill-forts stand near the s end of the Malvern range, on Midsummer and Hollybush Hills (*see The Buildings of England: Herefordshire*). The two highest N hills, in Worcestershire, are notable for their lack of prehistoric features; they were perhaps considered too sacred for such use. The SHIRE DITCH, along the crest of the hills, reputedly created c. 1287 as a boundary by Gilbert de Clare, Earl of Gloucester, is probably of late Bronze Age origin. Evidence for Roman activity in the area is provided by the discovery of numerous sites of pottery kilns, especially around North Malvern and Leigh Sinton (cf. p. 427).

GREAT MALVERN PRIORY

The Benedictine priory, dedicated to St Mary and St Michael and dependant on Westminster Abbey, was founded *c.* 1085; the story of a pre-Conquest foundation by St Werstan must be medieval fabrication. The cruciform Norman church, perhaps completed by *c.* 1120, probably had an E apse (possibly three). An eastern Lady Chapel, added later in the C12, was apparently enlarged in the C14. Rebuilding began in the early C15. The new chancel and its chapels, perhaps also the crossing, were presumably finished by 1460 when the Bishop of Worcester consecrated seven altars; the tower, transepts, and W end, all reusing Norman fabric in their lower parts, may not have been complete until the 1480s. This Perp work, clearly modelled on Gloucester (especially the tower), is especially valuable historically; monastic churches in the late Middle Ages rarely rebuilt so sweepingly. An exceptional quantity of C15 stained glass also survives, plus a unique collection of wall tiles. At the Dissolution, the church, apart from Lady Chapel and S transept, was saved when the parish purchased it, in 1541, to replace their own small church (St Thomas of Canterbury, at the NW corner of the priory churchyard). Little money, however, was available for its upkeep. After *C. H. Tatham* surveyed for repairs in 1802, almost nothing was done. The Rev. Henry Card began refurbishment in 1816, but Pugin, in 1833, found the fabric 'in dreadful repair.' Further work after 1836–7, by *Henry Rowe*, was followed by a major restoration by *George Gilbert Scott*, 1860–2, with fittings completed by 1864. Of monastic buildings only the gatehouse remains.

Exterior

The exterior is entirely of the most ornate Perp; a great variety
   of sandstones, buff, red and green, plus some cream limestone,
   give a somewhat mottled effect. Norman evidence is not
   wholly absent but the inquisitive student will need to seek it
   out (*see* below). The Perp building reads as follows: relatively
   short aisled nave with two-storey NW porch, central tower, N
   transept, chancel with N and S chapels. The impressive CROSS-
   ING TOWER dominates; only two stages, but with a strong vertical thrust. The two lower stages are panelled, with diagonal
   buttresses; the top stage has paired two-light bell-openings
   under steep ogee-crocketed arches with more panelling above.
   Openwork battlements and square pinnacles, on the Gloucester pattern. The CHANCEL, as an entirely new structure, has
   wider bays than the nave; plain battlements, simply chamfered
   plinths. Its chapel (or aisle) windows have four lights (two plus
   two); similar clerestory windows, but taller, with transoms.
   Giant E window of eight lights (four plus four), all again
   inspired by what Gloucester had done a hundred years before.
   At the foot of the E window, the rough junction with the former
   Lady Chapel has a low, wide depressed arch, probably (as at
   Gloucester) only the entrance to a passage. A fragment of tiled

41

pavement shows its floor level; on the N wall some weathered heads of cusping survive. Present doorway and steps inserted 1861. Something of the former crypt also remains: two trumpet-scallop, i.e. Late Norman, capitals, mysteriously not at the same level. The N one (now buried) and the heavy chamfered rib it carries are *in situ*; the S one must be re-set. The N TRANSEPT, lower than nave and chancel, probably repeats the Norman height; no main E window, one three-light transomed, W, but a six-light N window, divided three plus three. Parapets taller than on the chancel: plain, E side, panelled, N, pierced, W. NAVE and AISLES have three-light windows, the clerestory again taller, with transoms; panelled battlements, pierced and with pinnacles above the clerestory. A further difference from the chancel is that plinths are now moulded. NW PORCH rebuilt, correctly, by *W.J. Hopkins*, 1894. Its whole façade is panelled, more busily above than below. Image niches above the entrance and on the diagonal buttresses; panelled battlements with pinnacles. Fine iron GATES probably by *Skidmore*, *c*. 1862. Inside, an uninspiring lierne star vault. The nave W front can hardly be seen, as it is jammed up against rising ground and the Abbey Hotel.

To study the S SIDE closely one must enter the hotel car park and garden. The chancel S side is the same as the N, but without battlements. Against the SE stump of the S transept, part of a renewed Perp reveal belonging to its E window. The S side of the nave S aisle had of course the cloister against it. The rough masonry here also betrays the steep pitch of the original aisle roof. Three Perp windows inserted 1841. The doorway from its E end into the former cloister is Norman, with two conjoined orders of shafts with cushion capitals, all detail decayed or renewed. The small cloister doorway in the W bay is plain four-centred Perp. Next to it, a similar but narrower blocked opening, perhaps a night stair from the prior's lodging. No other signs of the claustral buildings.

Interior

10   The NAVE at once reveals its Norman date – a surprise despite what we have seen outside. Six-bay arcades, their short round piers about 5 ft (1.5 metres) in diameter, with round, heavily and bulgily detailed capitals, like the naves at Gloucester and Tewkesbury; double-step arches. The N arcade E respond has unfinished scallop decoration. The simpler bases of the two E bays indicate the position of the pulpitum. Norman work ends abruptly a few feet above the arcade, i.e. below a former Norman triforium or gallery, but the high Perp clerestory is very effective above this massive substructure. Perp W window apparently of immense size, nine lights arranged 3+3+3, but everything below its transom is blank, as are the outer lights – a subtle use of blind panelling we shall see elsewhere. The rebate at the arch height of the clerestory windows perhaps indicates an intention to vault. The present ceilings, largely by

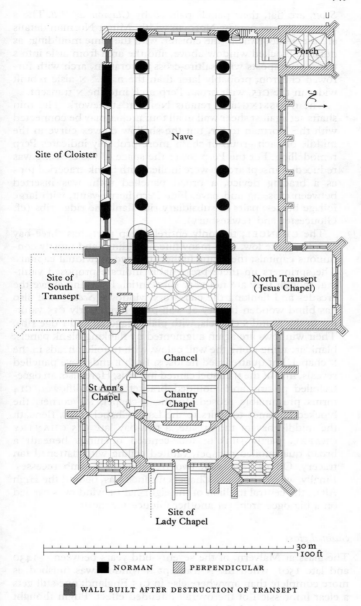

```
|————————————————————————| 30 m
|————————————————————————| 100 ft
```

■ NORMAN   ▨ PERPENDICULAR

▨ WALL BUILT AFTER DESTRUCTION OF TRANSEPT

Malvern, Great Malvern Priory.
Plan of church

Scott, are flat, their panels painted by *Clayton & Bell*. The S aisle retains its narrow Norman width. Minor Norman details are the SE doorway to the cloister, with the same mouldings as outside, blocked window above, and the arch from aisle into S transept; imposts with saltire-cross decoration, arch with furrowed chevron, probably later than the nave.* N aisle rebuilt wider in the C15, with broad Perp arch into the N transept.

The CROSSING also retains Norman stonework. The thin shafts set against sheer wall in all four arches may be connected with the Norman tower, but the shallow convex curve in the middle of each group of shafts more probably indicates Perp remodelling. For the Perp tower the space of the crossing was reduced: transept arches were infilled with blank-traceried tops as a bracing device, a broad panelled soffit was inserted between crossing and nave. Fine Perp lierne-vault, with large foliage bosses; pairs of subsidiary ribs flank the ridge ribs (cf. Gloucester and Tewkesbury).

The CHANCEL, the only entirely Perp part, has three-bay arcades, quite low, with many fine mouldings and mostly continuous capitals; the shafts higher up have individual capitals. The springers up there presumably indicate proposed vaulting, though they are not very substantial. Panelling above the arcades and flanking the clerestory windows. *Scott*'s roof also has blind wooden tracery at wall-plate level. Early C15 vaulting in the N and S chapels, with plain diagonal and ridge ribs. Their windows are again augmented by flanking blank panels; blank arcading along the wall below, with trefoiled heads in the N chapel, but quatrefoiled heads, S. Both E ends have panelled reveals, that of the N chapel canted inwards. Here also, an ogee-trefoiled piscina and moulded bracket on a ballflower, C14 forms presumably reused. In the S chapel, NE corner, the blocked entrance to stairs to the Lady Chapel crypt. Beneath the middle bay of the arcade, a two-bay late C15 CHANTRY CHAPEL, partly sunken: four-centred openings beneath a broad quatrefoiled parapet, vaulted ceiling with flattened fan tracery. On its rear wall, two trefoil-cusped tomb recesses. Finally, where the Lady Chapel entrance was, behind the High Altar, the central mullion of the eight-light E window is carried on a big ogee arch, yet another Gloucester motif.

Stained glass

The glass at Malvern, of the seventy-odd years between *c.* 1430 and late 1501, when the N transept N window was finished, is more complete than anywhere else in C15 England; one still gets a clear impression of the overall intended effect. Pugin thought it 'truly magnificent'. It is certainly light, not obscuring as C13 glass had been. Of darker colours blue and red are fully represented, though not in large areas, but less green. Instead there is

---

* Neil Stratford compares this with Beckford, Bredon's Norton, Castlemorton, Earl's Croome, Eldersfield, Pendock, and Queenhill, *c.* 1150–75.

much yellow and white. The E and W windows, those in the S chapel, and several clerestory and aisle windows survive in excellent condition; others contain at least fragments. *Kempe & Co.* began major restoration in 1910. There are also good C19 windows, plus two of the early C21. Descriptions in the detailed list below always begin with the easternmost window in any sequence.

E WINDOW. Of *c.* 1430, similar to the St William window at York Minster (by *John Thornton* of Coventry or his workshop). The upper three tiers have Passion scenes, beginning with the Entry into Jerusalem and Last Supper. At the centre, the Nailing to the Cross and Crucifixion. Many inserted figures and other fragments (e.g. a fine group of five musical angels, below the transom, r.). Lowest tier with kneeling donors, from clerestory windows; names include Besford, Harewell, Lygon, and Lyttelton. *In situ* in the traceries, the twelve Apostles; above them, Annunciation and Coronation of the Virgin.

CHANCEL N CLERESTORY. First: the early life of the Virgin. Below the transom, the Annunciation to Joachim up to her Presentation; above, Annunciation and Presentation in the Temple. – Second: six saintly Bishops (with local associations), Virgin and Child, St Anne teaching Mary. – Third: the Founders' Window. Above, the Legend of St Werstan: his vision, the consecration of his chapel, Edward the Confessor granting the charter, Werstan's martyrdom. Below, the Benedictine foundation, with the Donations of St Wulfstan, William the Conqueror, Osbert Fitzpons, and the earls of Gloucester and Hereford. Heads of saints in the spandrels.

CHANCEL S CLERESTORY. Nearly all the original glass has gone; the first window had Nativity scenes, the other two an Apostles Creed. The present figures come mostly from the nave N clerestory. First: below, St Andrew, Angels with Fathers of the Church, St Peter; above, Passion shields, more Orders of Angels. – Second: above, St James the Greater, St Catherine (*in situ*), St Giles (?), another St James; below, angels and a fine Crucifixion, across three lights. – Third: above, arms of Richard, Duke of Gloucester, fragmentary Archangel, remains of a St Edmund, an Apostle; below, four of the Nine Orders of Angels.

S CHAPEL. E window, Crucifixion, by *Kempe*, 1898. – The S windows have easily read Old Testament stories, *c.* 1480–90, in three tiers, from the nave S clerestory (where there were seventy-two such scenes). First: Genesis, from the Creation to the Expulsion and Adam delving and Eve spinning. – Second: Noah and the Ark; the Tower of Babel; scenes of Abraham and Isaac. – Third: the continuation of the preceding, with the Journey to Mount Moriah, then the Sacrifice of Isaac and two Isaac scenes, then two Joseph scenes, the Finding of Moses, the Manna, Golden Calf, and the Doom of the Idolaters.

N CHAPEL. Good E window, Adoration of the Magi, by *Clayton & Bell*, 1862. – Two N windows have fine semi-abstract glass by *Thomas Denny*, 2003–4, with his typical ethereal figures, extending into the traceries where C15 fragments remain. (The first window had the four Latin Doctors, the second the Seven Sacraments.) – Third window, originally with the Apostles' Creed, now with fragments; those in the traceries, *in situ*, include the Coronation of the Virgin and scenes from her life.

N TRANSEPT. N WINDOW. Given by Henry VII, 1501; darker in tone than the C15 windows, probably by the *Richard Twygge-Thomas Wodshawe* workshop. In the four central lights, the Joys of Mary, eleven scenes representing the Magnificat. Well preserved, below the transom, Jesus in the Temple, Marriage at Cana, Visitation, Nativity; Ascension above, and, in a vesica awkwardly off-centre, the Coronation of the Virgin. In the outer lights were the Four Archangels; only Michael and Uriel remain. Saints and angels in the traceries. Kneeling at the bottom, Sir Reginald Bray, Arthur Prince of Wales (†1502), Henry VII. – W WINDOW. St Paul, St John Evangelist, St John Baptist, from the nave N clerestory. Below the transom, *in situ*, the Last Supper, almost complete. – E CLERESTORY. Hope, Faith and Charity, 1846, clearly by *George Rogers*.

N AISLE. First, Freemasons' window by *Shrigley & Hunt*, c. 1906. – In the second are collected what remained of all five N aisle windows: four rows of Gospel scenes. The Annunciation, top l., is nearly perfect. Others portray the Visitation, Nativity, Adoration of the Magi, Presentation, Temptation, Pool at Bethesda, Healing the Sick, Healing the Deaf and Dumb Man, Cleansing the Leper and Healing the Centurion's Servant, Marriage of Joachim and Anne, Annunciation to Anne. Saints in the traceries. – The next two have glass designed by *T.W. Camm*, for *R.W. Winfield & Co.*: of 1887–8 (a period piece celebrating 'The Jubilee of the Nations') and 1898.

NAVE. W WINDOW. Originally with the Last Judgement (cf. Fairford); below were the Virgin and six Virgin Martyrs, also arms of Richard, Duke of Gloucester, and Anne [Neville], i.e. 1472–83. Now there are below five Bishops, the Virgin and Child and Mary Salome; second tier: Joachim, a Bishop, Angels, St Catherine, St Anne teaching the Virgin; top tier: St Anne and the Virgin, St Catherine, St Laurence, St George, St Christopher, St Margaret, the Virgin. The large figures are from the nave N clerestory. – The N and S CLERESTORIES have a remarkable display of early C19 heraldry, mostly of subscribers to Dr Card's restoration, from a N aisle NE window of 1820 (probably by *W.R. Eginton*). Re-set here 1842, probably by *Rogers*. He also provided three S AISLE windows, 1849; only the traceries remain.

Furnishings and monuments

CHANCEL. REREDOS. By *A.W. Blomfield*, 1883–4, made by *Powell & Sons*. Mosaic, with *opus sectile* Adoration. Set into a medieval stone screen wall, with doorways either side into an apsidal sacristy, perhaps reflecting the Norman E end. – TILES. The chancel screen walls are faced with mid- to late C15 tiles (mostly re-set by *Scott*), the best collection in England; Malvern was of course a major tile-making centre. Some 1,300 survive, in a hundred different designs, rectangular ones originally for walls, square ones for the floor. The colours, pink, golden-brown, and lavender, are delightful. The best displays are at each end of the altar screen, on its curved ambulatory rear wall, and on the wall beneath the central arch of the N chancel arcade, chapel side. The ambulatory has large rectangular tiles below, with the date 1453, square ones above, many with crowned Ms (for the Virgin). The astonishing group in the N chapel includes rectangular tiles dated 1457/8, with IHS symbols or pinnacles, and six rows of smaller square tiles with very varied patterns: inscriptions, intricate four-tile sets, royal arms, other heraldry (Stafford knots, double-headed eagles etc.), and pelicans and religious emblems; also one with the name *Whillar*, perhaps the tiler. Beneath the dado, five more rows of square tiles from the sanctuary steps: more crowned Ms, Instruments of the Passion. – The *Minton* sanctuary TILING of 1860–2 seems gaudy in comparison. – STALLS. Two tiers of six, both N and S; the three easternmost are C19. The superstructure is missing, but the MISERICORDS survive (plus carved figures on the arms). They comprise two series, all with supporters: a late C14 set of mythological and domestic scenes, and most of a mid-C15 Labours of the Months (cf. Ripple). N side, front row (from W): January, April, three rats hanging a cat, June, September, a basilisk. Back row: a lion, October, drunkards? (upside down), intertwined grotesques, February, March. S side, front row: a mummer's mask, long-haired man, December, angel playing a cittern, a wyvern, May. Behind:

Malvern, Great Malvern Priory, tile designs

addorsed grotesques, merman and mermaid, sick man with his wife and doctor, a figure driving away a demon. – SCREENS. Behind the stalls, with one-light divisions, very restored. More ornate C19 screen in the S arcade E bay. – Fine ORGAN CASE, Jacobean Renaissance style, by *W.D. Caröe*, 1931–2. – From *Scott*'s restoration survive the big oblong PULPIT and CHOIR STALLS, carved in oak by *Boulton*, 1864. – Good brass eagle LECTERN, *c.* 1877.

MONUMENTS. Worn mid-C13 effigy of a knight, limestone, very flatly carved. One of the earliest surviving military effigies in England, it is the only one shown holding a war-hammer (double-ended pick) and target (round shield). He seems to be lying to attention, legs and feet rigidly parallel, head on a square pillow. – John Knotsford †1589 and wife Jane †1582, probably by *Samuel Baldwin*, *c.* 1615. Excellent carved alabaster effigies, on a tomb-chest, pairs of daughters on each side. The eldest daughter Anne [Savage], who gave the monument, kneels, the same size as her parents, at their feet, facing the altar. No superstructure. – In the ambulatory, many tablets, the best two, with draped urns, by *W. Stephens*, *c.* 1800–2.

S CHAPEL. Good Jacobean ALTAR TABLE, STATUES by *Pancheri & Son*, 1976, and PEWS by *T.G. Jackson*, 1902. – MONUMENTS. Within the sunken chantry (*see* p. 450) are two inscribed coffin lids, the larger, slightly coped, to Prior Walcher †1135, re-cut. The other, C13, to Prior William de Wykewane, has, in two rows either side, indents for a separate letter inlay brass Lombardic inscription.* – Thomas Woodyatt †1841, by *Peter Hollins*. Seated woman in profile, looking towards heaven; draped urn with profile medallion.

N TRANSEPT. MONUMENTS. Sophia Thompson †1838, also by *Hollins*, superbly carved. She reclines on a couch, looking up in Baroque fashion towards the unseen call; the head, covering and legs of the couch are realistically detailed. Gunnis thought it 'as fine as anything executed by Chantrey'. – Tablet to John Dandridge and family, by *Sir Richard Westmacott*, *c.* 1830, with beautiful figure of a resting pilgrim, a Westmacott staple. – Emily Elizabeth Wilmot †1900, good brass by *James Forsyth*. – Gen. Sir William Campbell †1918, by *W.D. Caröe*; Hoptonwood stone.

NAVE AND AISLES. FONT. Plain round Norman bowl; stem and base 1839. – Very fine BANNER by *J.N. Comper*, 1910, in the blocked cloister doorway; worked at St Mary's Convent Embroidery School, Wantage. – MONUMENTS. S aisle. Large war memorial by *W.D. Caröe*, 1923; Beer stone, fluted Ionic columns. – Nave w end. Sir H.E.F. Lambert †1872, by Sir *Gilbert Scott*, 1873. Large Perp arch, straight crested top, double-layered cusping; small brass inscription. – Many tablets in the N aisle, the best two, with draped urns, by *W. Stephens*, *c.* 1802, and by *T. King* of Bath, *c.* 1827.

---

* Here also many architectural fragments, including bosses, and remains of paired shafts, probably from the cloister.

Precincts

Attractive CHURCHYARD: fine trees, good tombs, a C15 CROSS with octagonal steps and tall shaft (renewed 1896), and six late C19 LAMP-POSTS.*

All MONASTIC BUILDINGS to the S have disappeared. The cloister seems to have been rebuilt in the early C13, see the paired bases and crocket capitals of shafts, now in the Gatehouse museum and S chapel chantry. Also displayed in the former, window-heads from the timber-framed GUESTEN HALL, *c.* 1400, which stood beyond the SW corner of the cloister until 1841.

The broad late C15 GATEHOUSE, all that now remains standing, W, in Abbey Road, is now visually separate. Its N façade (towards the town) is elaborately panelled; bigger motifs below, daintier above, just as on the N porch. Small oriel above the four-centred archway. Entirely refaced by *Nevinson & Newton*, 1891; they added the panelled parapet and small W extension (containing a good stone and iron staircase). The S front, rebuilt further S in brick in the C16, has three timber-framed gables with mid-C19 bargeboards. Affixed to the E gable, sixty-four C15 tiles, mostly very weathered. Within is now the town museum.

OTHER CHURCHES

I. Church of England

ALL SAINTS, Wells Road, The Wyche. 1902–3 by *A. Troyte Griffith* (of *Nevinson & Newton*). Built against the hillside; rock-faced, ashlar and Hereford brick dressings. Nave and chancel with N vestry and curved E apse (its niche with stone St George by the *Bromsgrove Guild*, 1934). Mostly lancets, but the true date revealed by the SW porch and oak bellcote with copper flèche above the chancel arch. Good brick-faced interior, windows recessed within large relieving arches; arch-braced roof, wide moulded stone chancel arch. – Small FONT. 1877, from the earlier church. – Low stone and brick SCREEN; timber PULPIT from Emmanuel church (p. 460). – Oak ALTAR. 1911, from Malvern Wells. – Oak REREDOS designed by *Griffith*, 1905, with fine painted panels, on mahogany, by *Henry A. Payne*. – Excellent STAINED GLASS also by *Payne*: apse 1903–4, chancel S 1905, nave S 1918, nave N 1937 (probably executed by his son, *Edward Payne*).

SCHOOL, N, also Malvern stone, early Dec style; by *Haddon Bros*, 1877, built as a school-chapel, with E apse. Later additions in keeping. – Uphill, the roughcast WYCHE INSTITUTE by *Griffith*, 1906, completed 1915.

ASCENSION, Somers Park Avenue. By *Walter J. Tapper*, 1902–3, his first church, clearly inspired by Bodley, and one of the best

---

* Generally Malvern's gas lamp-posts are a delight; a remarkable number, by various makers, survive throughout the district.

of its date in the county. Unassuming exterior: rendered walls, ample yellow Guiting stone dressings, green Collyweston slate roofs. All windows lancets, set quite high up: paired in the nave, triplets E and W. Nave and chancel of equal height, though the latter seems taller as its lancets are set higher; square-cut bell-cote above the chancel arch. Distinctive W tower, small, cross-gabled, broader N–S; Ascension, W face, carved by *Farmer & Brindley*. Fine interior, rendered with ashlar dressings. Four-bay nave with pointed plaster tunnel vault, the stone cross-ribs on tall wall shafts; clerestory wall-passage behind detached shafts. Baptistery beneath the tower. The chancel is richer, with quadripartite rib vault (plastered brick), and clerestory wall passage of stepped triplets; vestries beneath. – Original fur-nishings, notably the high gilded metal SCREEN by *W. Bain-bridge Reynolds*. – Other metalwork also his, including the COVER to the black marble FONT (with slightly Art Nouveau detail). – Oberammergau hanging ROOD. – TRIPTYCH painted by *Sister Catherine Ruth* (of All Saints Community, Margaret Street, London). – Painted PANEL of St Christopher, designed by *Temple Moore*, 1917. – STAINED GLASS. E and small baptis-tery window by *Victor Milner*, 1903. – Lower attached HALL, E, conforming to the original design.

CHRIST CHURCH, Avenue Road. 1874–5 by *T.D. Barry & Sons* of Liverpool. Large, grey rock-faced sandstone, with lofty W steeple; deeply broached spire with lucarnes. Dec-style, with restlessly varied tracery, the only unexpected details the sharply spired turret at the S chapel's SW corner, and cross-gable behind the S porch (lighting the font). Spacious, rather dull interior: six-bay arcades with alternating round and octag-onal piers with foliage capitals, paired clerestory windows above, scissor-braced roof. Tall chancel arch with tripled shafts. – Original FITTINGS mostly survive, notably the lavishly carved FONT. – ORGAN. 1884, nicely decorated 1896. – Oak ALTAR and RAILS by *J. Wippell & Co.*, 1929. – PAINTINGS. Annunciation by *A. Ratti* of Rome, 1858; 'Follow Me' by *Jessy Darbyshire*, 1955. – STAINED GLASS. E window by *Kempe*, 1895. – S chapel E by *Clayton & Bell*, 1887. – Three by *Hardman*: S chapel S 1934, S aisle 1897, N aisle 1913.

PARISH HALL, NE, by *Mervyn J. Mason*, 1988; brown brick, gabled windows and dormers. – Its predecessor, behind, facing Barnard's Green Road, is by *E.E. Baldwin*, 1905; rock-faced Tudor, with hipped dormers and nice louvre.

HOLY TRINITY, Worcester Road, Link Top. By *S.W. Daukes*, 1850–1. Quite large, with aisles, S porch, and octagonal NE turret with pyramidal cap; of Malvern stone, late C13 style, plate to Geometrical tracery. *Haddon Bros* widened the N aisle in 1872–3; *William Henman*, 1896–7, added its N vestry and inserted nave dormers. Daukes's clerestory had only small trefoil openings. Low five-bay arcades with round piers; high arch-braced roof. E window with foliated marble shafts. *Henman* renewed most fittings (oak PEWS, PULPIT and STALLS), 1908–9, altering the chancel arch. Chancel decoration, with painted figures and stencilling, by *W. Forsyth*, completed 1901. – Octagonal FONT. 1851. – STAINED GLASS. E window by *Kempe*, 1902. – Two chancel S *Ward & Hughes*, 1873. – W window by *O'Connor*, 1858. – Three in the S aisle by *Powell & Sons*: E 1896, the others 1903. – Tall WAR MEMORIAL CROSS, S of the chancel, by *Bernard Miller* of Liverpool, 1919–20.

TRINITY HALL, NE, by *H. Percy Smith*, 1910–11; roughcast above brick, gabled projections, buttresses rising into the roof, small domed louvre.

ST ANDREW, Churchdown Road, Malvern Common. By *Lewis Sheppard*, 1885, built as a chapelry of Christ Church and memorial to Edward Chance. Of 'crazy-paving' stone; trefoil-headed lancets, the central light of the stepped W triplet set between the buttresses of a chunky bellcote. NE vestry enlarged 1897; attached brick HALL, E, 1980. Pleasant interior, with mostly contemporary fittings. – Big square carved FONT by *Preedy c.* 1877, from St Mary Magdalene, Worcester.* – TABLET to Major E.F. Calthrop †1915, with good lettering (said to be by *Eric Gill*) and bronze portrait. – STAINED GLASS. All 1890–1: E (and chancel SW) no doubt *Burlison & Grylls*. – The others by *Heaton, Butler & Bayne*, apart from the nave SW, signed *J. Jennings*.

ST MATTHIAS, Church Road, Malvern Link. Large, of red rock-faced granite, mostly 1880–1 by *F.W. Hunt* of London, who added the broad SW tower, 1898–9. The original E.E.-style church by *Eginton*, 1844–5, received a new S aisle and tower by *G.G. Scott* in 1858–60, and N organ chamber by *Haddon Bros*, 1873. Hunt rebuilt everything to a larger scale, apart from Scott's S aisle. This explains the varied fenestration: lancets to the N, following Eginton's, and in the clerestory (alternating twins and triplets); two-light plate-traceried windows in the S aisle (the four E bays Scott's); Geometrical tracery E and W, entirely by Hunt. Seven-bay nave arcades with alternating round and octagonal piers; high roof with kingposts. Two W bays divided off as a parish room, 1992, with tent-like roof, by the *Snell Taylor Partnership*. N aisle E chapel refitted by *Leslie T. Moore*, 1934. – Other FITTINGS mostly by *Hunt*: Dec-style CHANCEL SCREEN made by *Robinson* of Bayswater, its dado painted, 1920–2, with figures of saints copied from Ranworth, Norfolk, by *Sister Annabel* of the Community of the Holy Name (*see* below); painted REREDOS by *Kempe*, dismantled, part in the S aisle, part in the parish room. – Octofoil FONT, no doubt by *Eginton*. – War memorial SCREEN, W, by *Michael Tapper*, 1948. – STAINED GLASS. By *Kempe* the E window, 1881, chancel N and S, 1883, and N aisle W, 1884. – By *Burlison & Grylls* the striking W windows, 1906, and S aisle W, 1911. – S aisle: SE by *Clayton & Bell*, 1877; four by *Mayer & Co.*, 1891–6.

---

* It replaced a FONT found in Northumberland, inscribed 1724: round stem, stoup-like bowl; now expelled outside.

– CHURCHYARD CROSS, S, by *A.H. Skipworth*, 1909, Arts and Crafts style.

SCHOOL, SW. Brick, 1862, enlarged by *Hunt*, 1878–9. – CHURCH INSTITUTE, S, in Hampden Road, by *Lewis Sheppard*, 1893; brick, gabled, wooden tracery.

ST PETER, Cowleigh Bank. By *Street* 1863–6, a chapelry to West Malvern; crazy-paving granite, ashlar dressings. Chancel, aisled nave, sharp NE bellcote. Plate-to-Geometrical tracery; odd clerestory windows: half quatrefoils under round arches. Splendid interior. Five-bay arcades with round piers with boldly simplified, deliberately primeval capitals. Their blunt arches have only a slight chamfer; above, the buff sandstone ashlar changes to rock-faced blue stone. Boarded nave roof with tall kingposts on tie-beams. Chamfered chancel arch with basic stringcourse capitals. – Street's fittings were altered in 1924. His round FONT remains, also his PULPIT, a semicircular railing of alternate pink and green marble shafts, attached to a low stone screen. – STAINED GLASS. Mostly by *Clayton & Bell*: excellent E window, 1866, the rest 1870s–80s, the W as late as 1908. – Two S aisle exceptions: central window 1910, probably *Burlison & Grylls*; SW *c.* 1876, probably *Mayer & Co*.

The SCHOOL, S, by *Henry Haddon*, 1885–6, was rebuilt after a fire (*see* p. 467).

CONVENT OF THE HOLY NAME (now Christian Conference Centre), Ranelagh Road, Malvern Link. The Convent, an Anglican order founded by the Rev. George Herbert at Vauxhall, South London, established the Diocesan Penitentiary for Fallen Women here in 1879. The whole community followed in 1887, eventually taking over four remarkable brick houses, pioneering examples of the Queen Anne style, built, for Father Herbert and others, 1868–9, by *G.F. Bodley* (assisted, during his illness, by *Philip Webb*). Later additions, mostly in keeping, have confused the original forms, but their general character, relaxed and unassuming, survives:* hipped roofs with dormers, sashed windows with louvred shutters, projecting weatherboarded bays, other occasional asymmetrical touches, also a few Venetian windows. Within, simple fireplaces, plaster cornices, stick-balustered staircases. SALVATION HOUSE, W, Herbert's own house, only absorbed in 1924, has four N gables with apex chimneys. Opposite, MANNA HOUSE (extended by *Lewis Sheppard & Son*, 1901), at right angles to HARVEST HOUSE (much enlarged as the refectory, 1896–7), formed the convent's entrance court. SANCTUARY HOUSE, further N, the first acquired, forms a second courtyard with the chapel.

The splendid CHAPEL by *Bucknall & Comper*, 1891–3, is linked to the houses by a low narrow cloister. William Bucknall was largely responsible for the structure, based on Bodley's St Augustine, Pendlebury (Lancs.), 1871–4. Large, brick, rectangular, seven bays, with crocketed SE turret and tall late

---

* Bodley's pupil E.P. Warren thought they possessed a charm 'like that of Jane Austen's heroines'.

c13-style windows high up: four-light elaborately intersecting E window (shafted within), cusped Y-tracery to the sides, blank w wall. High interior, painted white 1927. Windows in deep moulded arched recesses, between wall-shafts rising to support the cross-braces of the ribbed and panelled wagon roof; its two E bays are painted and gilded. – Many of *Ninian Comper*'s FUR-NISHINGS (on which he worked until 1947) are also gilded; much was damaged when the Convent stood redundant in the 1990s. – Fine gilt stone REREDOS, 1906 (now covered): seven figures under crocketed ogee arches, ogee-headed sacristy doorways either side. – WEST GALLERY, above a screen; pret-tily Perp, painted white. – Simpler oak STALLS. – STAINED GLASS also by *Comper*, in his pale refined style: E window 1927, sanctuary SE 1925, fragments of two others.

Further N the former laundry; a brick accommodation block by *Forbes & Tate*, 1922–3, broad half-H-plan with cross-windows and hipped roof; and Nos. 1–4, a gabled Gothic terrace, c. 1867, later an orphanage. All now flats.

2. Roman Catholic

OUR LADY AND ST EDMUND (former), College Road; closed 1996, now St Edmund Hall, belonging to Malvern College. By *Peter Paul Pugin* (*Pugin & Pugin*), 1904–5. Rock-faced Cradley stone, green Tilberthwaite slate roofs; large Dec/Perp windows. Chancel (with E rose), nave, wide N aisle with E chapel, lower side chapels. Good interior, retaining a fine set of carved stone STATIONS OF THE CROSS. – STAINED GLASS. All *Hardman*, 1907–11.

The adjoining MONASTERY, founded for Douai Bene-dictines, 1891, occupied TOWNSHEND HOUSE, Dr R.B. Grindrod's hydropathic establishment, built 1850, enlarged by *E.C. Allflett*, 1862; snecked stone, severely plain. Sold to the College in 1918, now its Music School.

ST JOSEPH, Newtown Road. 1876 by *T.R. Donnelly* of Coventry. Nave and chancel in one, sharp central flèche; attached SE presbytery. Of Malvern stone, late c13 style. Much enlarged by *John D. Holmes*, 1997–8; he added aisles with timber arcades connecting to the existing arch-braced roof, also a W narthex, and parish rooms, S. – Large timber REREDOS, c. 1883. – STAINED GLASS. E window, 1887, and chancel N, 1889, by *Hardman*; also one, 1918, now re-set S aisle SW, with half of a good window of c. 1924 by *Arthur A. Orr*. – Others by *Goddard & Gibbs*, 1948.

3. Nonconformist

BAPTIST CHURCH, Abbey Road. 1893–4 by *Ingall & Son* of Birmingham. Quite large, on a steeply sloping site; brick, the more visible parts clad in rock-faced sandstone. Dec-style, with pseudo-transepts, apsed E end, and ritual SW tower with oddly stunted recessed spire (a reduction of the original scheme).

Spacious unaltered interior, without galleries; boarded roof on arched braces, more complicated in the apse. Large immersion pool with curved stone wall in front of the E dais.

COUNTESS OF HUNTINGDON'S FREE CHURCH (now United Reformed), Worcester Road, Malvern Link. 1903–4 by *H.E. Lavender* of Walsall. Rock-faced Perp; pinnacled NE tower of three diminishing stages, two-bay porch. Yellow brick sides, red terracotta trim. – Low mildly Deco HALL, E, by *Harold S. Scott*, 1932.

The previous CHAPEL stands further NE in Worcester Road, opposite Spring Lane: 1837, rebuilt 1861–2. Rendered Neo-Norman; grossly elongated pairs or triplets, with foliated shafts; pedimental gable with crude Lombardic frieze. – At its rear, the former BRITISH SCHOOL by *W.M. Teulon*, 1844–5; gabled brick, greatly altered.

EMMANUEL (Countess of Huntingdon's Connexion), Wells Road; now a gym. By *Henry Haddon* (*Haddon Bros.*), 1873–4, replacing a church of 1827. Snecked ashlar, with much alternating colouring. Vigorous Neo-Romanesque with Gothic detailing (Pevsner thought it 'architecturally poor stuff'). Broad Lombardic-gabled façade, gabled porch, stepped NW tower with leaded spire. Two-light side windows with Venetian tracery. Wide tie-beam roof, round-arched trusses above. W gallery.

FRIENDS' MEETING HOUSE, Orchard Road. 1937–8 by *J.R. Armstrong* of the Bournville Village Trust. Pale brick, with big hipped pantiled roof coming forward over the projecting porch. Venetian-type window, S end.

HOLLY MOUNT CONGREGATIONAL CHURCH (now United Reformed), Queens Drive. 1875–6 by *James Tait* of Leicester. Rock-faced Cradley stone, Geometrical to Dec. Commanding ritual NW steeple, quirkily detailed: elongated single bell-openings with ogee hoodmoulds, broach spire with acutely gabled lucarnes. Built into the slope; schoolroom below, E (ritual N) side. Small transepts with sexfoil windows, aisles with four-bay arcades with octagonal piers; no galleries, big arch-braced roof. Carving by *Forsyth*. Aesthetic STAINED GLASS, with sunflowers, in the E window.

METHODIST CHURCH, Somers Park Avenue. 1935–6 by *Stanley A. Griffiths* of Stourbridge. Widely gabled Deco brick; diagonal porches, S (ritual W) end, flanking a curved vestibule, beneath a lunette. Round-arched side windows.

Former SCHOOL-CHAPEL, W, by *T.W. Holds*, 1907; basic Gothic.

(WESLEYAN) METHODIST CHURCH, Lansdowne Crescent. By *John Tarring*, 1865–6, replacing a chapel of 1840. Rock-faced Geometrical; shallow transepts, lower chancel, big square NW tower with battlements and pinnacles, all sitting upright upon a schoolroom undercroft. Tall iron pillars within, some with foliage capitals; roofs lowered, galleries removed. Floral STAINED GLASS in the E window.

4. Cemetery

CEMETERY, Wilton Road. By *W.H. Knight* of Cheltenham, 1860–1. His chapels, linked by an archway with tower and spire above, make a fine group. They are Dec style, of a darker stone than the tower, staggered so that the central archway opens to three sides. The Anglican chapel, E, is more ornate, with gabled dormers; behind it, a detached MORTUARY by *A.C. Baker*, 1887. The tower has pierced bell-openings, the broached spire sharp lucarnes. Neat LODGE also by *Knight*, 1861; impressive GATEPIERS by *Haddon Bros*, 1873–4. – The Victorian part of the cemetery is well preserved, with many memorial crosses. One, by *C.B. Birch*, to Jenny Lind, 'the Swedish nightingale', †1887, stands E of the chapels, near a gargantuan flat tomb-slab to the Speer family, with relief cross and corner angels, on stumpy piers; no doubt by *Henry Haddon*, *c.* 1878.

PUBLIC BUILDINGS

COUNCIL HOUSE, Priory Park; *see* p. 474.

FIRE STATION, Worcester Road, Malvern Link. By *Hereford & Worcester County Property Dept*, *c.* 1984; project architects *David Mills* and *Stephen Taylor*. A triangular prism, brick end walls with circular openings, main sloping façades clad in grey weathered zinc. Detached brick tower with monopitch roof.

PUBLIC LIBRARY, Graham Road. 1905–6 by *Henry A. Crouch* (who trained in Australia and later worked in India). Symmetrical, brick with stone dressings, free William-and-Mary style. Two-storey centre with giant Ionic pilasters, big cartouche, and narrow segmental pediment; single-storey wings, the S originally a hall. Nicely detailed interior: clerestoried centre with wide aisles, Ionic columns, segmental ceilings with good plasterwork. Rear additions by *M.W. Jones*, 1937, and by *Worcestershire County Council Property Services*, 2005.

In front, WAR MEMORIAL by *Sir Aston Webb & Son*, 1921–3; large bronze angel with upright wings, holding up the Torch of Truth, by *Richard R. Goulden*.

WINTER GARDENS (now Malvern Theatres), Grange Road. By *John Johnson*, 1884–5; of his work only the entrance survives: indeterminate in style, the porch vaguely Italian Gothic, flanked by cast-iron verandas, otherwise flimsy mixed Renaissance. In 1927–8 *A.V. Rowe* added a new concert hall, S (extended 1951), and altered most of the rest, converting the assembly rooms, N, into a theatre (re-fitted by *Deacon & Gude* of Bedford, 1948–9). On the entrance side all is masked by further reconstruction by the *Renton Howard Wood Levin Partnership*, 1997–8, their crudely patterned fly-tower the predominant element. The rear to Priory Park shows the C20 phases more clearly: *Rowe*'s hall of Neo-Georgian brick; *RHWL*'s work all white, with broadly gabled centre and much glass, awkwardly buttressed, approached up wide steps. Inside, they created a spacious two-level foyer right across the building, and converted the concert hall to a single-rake auditorium.

Attractive GARDENS with octagonal CI9 BANDSTAND, its ironwork by *W. Macfarlane & Co.* of Glasgow (re-erected here *c.* 1984); elongated lake (Swan Pool) of the 1820s, crossed by a timber bridge and narrower stone one.

On the E periphery, facing Priory Road, MALVERN SPLASH, swimming pool and leisure complex of 1989, by *Charles Smith* of Boston Spa (with *Abbey Hanson Rowe Partnership*); square glazing panels in red-painted frame, curved brick wall and pyramid-roofed tower flanking the entrance, NE.

COMMUNITY HOSPITAL, Lansdowne Crescent. By *William Henman*, 1909–11, for C.W. Dyson Perrins. Rock-faced Cradley stone, Tudor-style. Tall gabled centre with green slate roofs and chamfered chimneys, lower ward blocks either side. Angled porch, with nice green Art Nouveau tiling inside. Spoilt by additions.

The former RURAL HOSPITAL by *Henry Haddon*, 1868, survives in Hospital Bank, off Newtown Road. Red, yellow and blue brick, with bands and alternating voussoirs. Taller centre with high-set gabled timber door hood; wings with gabled dormers.

GREAT MALVERN STATION, Avenue Road. 1860–2 by *E.W. Elmslie* (*Elmslie, Franey & Haddon*). Long low front of rock-faced Malvern stone with ashlar dressings; French Gothic style. Very varied, with gables, timber dormers, paired chimneys, and segment-headed doorways with alternating stone voussoirs and foliated shafts; quatrefoil roof cresting and, formerly, a tall spired turret above the main entrance. The façade towards the up platform has many more such openings, also projections for refreshment and waiting rooms (both with coloured glass windows). Deep platform awnings both sides, with elaborately pierced ironwork, their cast-iron columns with extraordinary foliage capitals by *William Forsyth*, boldly three-dimensional, vividly coloured; *The Builder*, 1863, noted how he had 'cleverly introduced the foliage of the plants of the neighbourhood'. The station lies in a cutting, the segmental stone arch and pierced parapet of the Avenue Road bridge forming an attractive feature at its N end, also by *Elmslie*, as is the station approach, spaciously set around an elongated green; stone bases for fluted iron lamp standards, only two of which remain. A partly surviving covered way from the down platform led to Elmslie's Imperial Hotel (*see* Malvern Girls' College, p. 466).

120

EDUCATIONAL BUILDINGS

MALVERN COLLEGE, College Road. Founded as a Proprietary College, on the model of Cheltenham, in 1862. It was a good time for founding public schools; Malvern started ambitiously in scale and architectural worth. A competition late in 1862 was won by *Charles F. Hansom*, fresh from his success at Clifton College, Bristol; his building (apart from the chapel, S) was erected 1863–5. Large and impressive, of local Cradley stone

Malvern College.
Original design by C.F. Hansom

with banded slate roofs, Dec-to-Early Tudor style, but the
details not particularly distinguished. Towards the road, w,
behind the original wall (with SW LODGE), stands a fine central
gatehouse, connected by low battlemented ranges to gabled
end bays. The GATEHOUSE was clearly based on Lupton's
tower at Eton; tall octagonal corner turrets, two-storey canted
oriel above the entrance. Gabled wings with six-light Here-
fordshire-type Dec windows to their large upper schoolrooms
(classical, N, modern, S), steep dormers to the sides. On the E
front these wings, projecting to form an open courtyard, are
terminated by slightly lower, square, pyramid-roofed blocks,
with stair-turrets at their inner angles. Both fronts are entirely
symmetrical. Like Clifton, but unlike earlier schools, the whole
building is given over to teaching; boarders were to be accommodated in separate houses nearby (*see* below). At the middle
of the open E side, the WAR MEMORIAL by *Sir Aston Webb &
Son*, 1922; bronze St George by *Alfred Drury*.

The large CHAPEL, immediately S, is by *Sir Arthur W.
Blomfield*, 1897–9. Rather fussy exterior, of Milton-under-
Wychwood stone, with tall Perp windows, pinnacles, and flying
buttresses across the low S aisle, widened by *C.J. Blomfield*,
1908. High interior with impressive tie- and collar-beam roof.
Distinctive S arcade with low, paired, four-centred arches; big
four-centred diaphragm arches across the aisle. Ornate sedilia,
1902. – Large figured stone REREDOS by *Reginald Blomfield*,
c. 1910. – Huge ORGAN, 1900, on the W gallery. – STAINED
GLASS. Nearly all *Kempe & Co.*: sanctuary and ante-chapel
1902–3, nave S 1903–9, nave N 1914–21 (with two interlopers
of 1935–6: by *Comper*, W, by *Burlison & Grylls*, E). – S aisle, two
SE by Kempe, 1903–4, the rest probably by *Clayton & Bell*,
1875, from the temporary chapel in the main building's S wing.

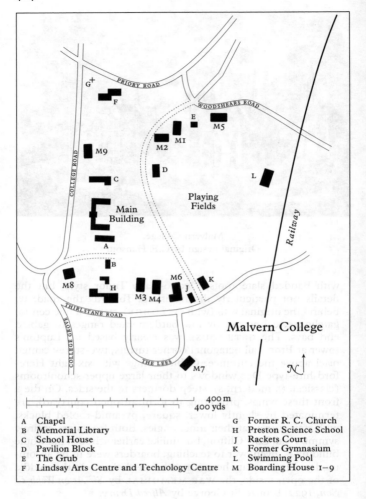

A Chapel
B Memorial Library
C School House
D Pavilion Block
E The Grub
F Lindsay Arts Centre and Technology Centre

G Former R. C. Church
H Preston Science School
J Rackets Court
K Former Gymnasium
L Swimming Pool
M Boarding House 1–9

Malvern College

– WAR MEMORIALS. Of 1922, simply set into oak panelling N
of the sanctuary. – Of 1950 (ante-chapel) by *P.W. Hubbard*,
carved by *H.H. Martyn*; Portland stone, with Hopton Wood
stone panels.

The excellent MEMORIAL LIBRARY, set N–S, to the S of the
chapel, by *Maurice Webb* (*Sir Aston Webb & Son*), 1923–4, is of
Leckhampton ashlar, with Gothic detail handled lightly and
imaginatively. N front with giant segmental arch, with three big
fleurons, dying into the chamfers; it encloses a three-light
window with two transoms, above a pretty portal with square

hoodmould on squirrel and pelican stops. Long sides with three five-light windows with two transoms and round-arched lights, between canted stair projections. The first-floor reading room, approached by a delightful wood-panelled staircase, is now the staff common room. White tunnel-vaulted ceiling, with wooden Composite pillars marking off the entrance part and far end, with the s window above a fireplace; chubby stone figures of the Zodiac. Stone carving by *Walter Gilbert*; woodwork by *Robert Bridgeman & Sons*.

Other College buildings extend along the N and s sides of the splendid playing fields.* First along the N perimeter. Immediately N of the main building is SCHOOL HOUSE, the headmaster's house by *C.F. Hansom*, 1864–5. Stone and Gothic like the school, with gables, tower, and canted oriels; enlarged, E, as a boarding house, 1875–6, by *Haddon Bros*, who intended a far higher NE tower. To its E, the PAVILION BLOCK, also by *Haddon Bros.*, 1876–7, expanded as a cricket pavilion by *Charles A. Edge*, 1894; three sharp dormers, curved balcony, open turret. Further N, towards Woodshears Road, HOUSES Nos. 1 and 2, by *Hansom*, 1864–5, gabled, red brick with blue diapering, mostly Tudor detail. Then, by the N gate (of 1915), THE GRUB, low traditional brick, by *Howard Robertson*, 1927. HOUSE No. 5, further E, by *Nevinson & Newton*, 1894, is still Tudor brick, with some patterning and open timber turret. The former SWIMMING BATHS, E of the playing fields, also by *Nevinson & Newton*, 1891–2, brick above a rubble plinth, have decorative half-timbered gables and another nice open turret with ogee leaded roof. In the NW angle of Priory and College roads, the LINDSAY ARTS CENTRE by *Hammett & Norton*, 1973–4; concrete-framed, brick infill. Attached TECHNOLOGY CENTRE by *David Duckham*, 1992–4, similar, with long runs of intersecting triangular roof lights.

Now along the s side, backing onto Thirlstane Road. s of the Memorial Library is the PRESTON SCIENCE SCHOOL by *P.W. Hubbard* (*George Hubbard & Son*), 1937–8, brick with concrete infill, 4+3+4 bays to the E; L-plan w extension, brick and weatherboarded, by *Hammett & Norton*, 1957–65. To its E, BOARDING HOUSES Nos. 3 and 4, by *W.J. Hopkins*, 1866–8, brick, decidedly forbidding. Varied gables, side stair-towers, variegated window heads, and steep stone dormers provide character; attractive patterned brick gatepiers, N. Then HOUSE No. 6 by *Haddon Bros*, 1871, red brick, irregular and gabled; ornate top floor, hipped-roofed angle tower. Later extended (like most other houses). Flanking the s entrance, two brick buildings by *Henman & Cooper*, 1904–5: the RACKETS COURTS (partly of 1881) have some close-set timbering; the large GYMNASIUM (now theatre), Tudor with pyramid-roofed N angle towers, incorporates a fives court and gabled s LODGE.

MALVERN GIRLS' COLLEGE, Avenue Road. Founded 1893. In 1919, as a sign of its coming into its own, it purchased the

*It has also absorbed several nearby houses, *see* Perambulation 3.

enormous IMPERIAL HOTEL, close to Great Malvern railway station; L-plan, built by *E. W. Elmslie*, 1860–1, for £18,000. Red brick with stone dressings, four storeys above a basement, with big, somewhat French hipped roofs with steep bargeboarded dormers; segment-headed windows, mostly paired, with grey and cream voussoirs and carved foliage sills, some with stone balconies. Eminently Gothic, especially towards the w, entrance, end; above the round-arched doorway, a round three-storey oriel, with Dec windows and candlesnuffer top, on a huge foliage corbel. An extra bay, w, was tactfully added by *Peacock & Bewlay*, 1927–8. E of the entrance rises a big square tower (containing a fine iron-balustraded staircase) with tall Loire-type window; top stage, with tripartite openings and pyramidal roof, unfortunately removed. A full-height canted bay marks the E end of this s front. Other fronts slightly more utilitarian. To the road, four fine round GATEPIERS, with griffins and foliage on the octagonal bases of the (now removed) lanterns. Further E, the SCIENCE CENTRE by *Heath Avery Architects*, 1998–2001, Postmodern brick, its canted corner bays trying to reflect the hotel's.

In 1932–4 *E.C. Bewlay* added a large two-storey brick wing at the rear of the former hotel, along Barnards Green Road. This follows Elmslie's style, reusing a porte cochère, w, from Blackmore Park (p. 357); the spacious ground-floor York Hall and Library above have tall square piers, the latter also a round oriel each end from Bohun Court (p. 342) and imported panelling. More panelling in the small CHAPEL nearby, with large alabaster reredos of the Annunciation, early work by *David Wynne*, 1959. Further E, a severe square classroom block, also partly by *Bewlay*, 1929–30, on the site of the hotel's brine baths (by *Haddon Bros*, 1876). Then THE BENHAMS, the former Christ Church VICARAGE (by *Henry Haddon*, 1879–80), extended as a boarding house by *George Hubbard & Son*, 1937–8; large, L-plan, Neo-Georgian.

Across the railway, w, two good C20 buildings in ample grounds. At the N end of Imperial Road, HATFIELD, a middle-school house of 1963–4 by *T.H.B. Burrough* (with *Maurice W. Jones*), workmanlike concrete framing, with brick and curtain wall infill, and many polygonal projections and recessions.[*] Butterfly-plan entrance with central concrete porch; small lobby with spiral concrete staircase. Further S, the EDINBURGH DOME by *Godwin & Cowper*, 1977–8, a reinforced concrete Parashell sports hall, i.e. inflated during construction; consultant engineers *Oscar Faber & Partners*. Large windows at ground level, flanked by supporting sloping piers, their base shoes attractively set in a moat-like pond. Exterior clad in copper *c.* 1985; concrete exposed within.

MALVERN HILLS COLLEGE, Albert Road North. By *A. V. Rowe*, 1927–8, built as a school of art. Long two-storey brick front,

---

[*]Pevsner noted the resemblance to 'The Beehives' at St John's College, Oxford, 1958–60; Burrough was unaware of this building when he produced the designs.

Neo-Georgian; narrow pedimented centre with Doric doorway, wider projections with tripartite windows formerly marking the ends either side. Enlarged by *Rowe*, 1936.

Former LYTTELTON GRAMMAR SCHOOL, Church Street; *see* p. 473.

THE CHASE HIGH SCHOOL, Geraldine Road. Spreading Secondary Modern by *L.C. Lomas*, County Architect, 1951–3; brick, with Dutch-inspired patterning. Broad U-plan, part single-, part two-storeyed with angle tower; wings with rounded ends, doubled for the larger NW wing. Additions in keeping.

PRIMARY SCHOOLS. Gabled brick former NATIONAL SCHOOL, Manby Road, by *Elmslie*, 1857–8; above the entrance, an octagonal tower with steep pyramidal roof and open timber turret. Attached house, E, Tudor Gothic; the school part, W, more decidedly Dec. W end masked by an addition by *A.T. Griffith*, 1914. – SOMERS PARK SCHOOL (formerly Malvern Link Council School), Somers Park Avenue. 1908–9 by *Pritchard & Pritchard*; detached Infant School behind, later C20 extensions. Gabled, tripartite windows with fancy stone lintels, attractive round-arched entrances, domed louvre. – Of later schools the best is NORTHLEIGH C. OF E. PRIMARY, St Peter's Road (next to St Peter, p. 458), by *Kirsten Conquest* (*Oxford Design Partnership*), 1990–1. Postmodern coloured brick, to a curving plan; all-over slate roof sweeping low over the entrance, varied fenestration.

GREAT MALVERN: PERAMBULATIONS

Systematic perambulation of Great Malvern is not easy, even if one is happy to negotiate some steep climbs. There are substantial rewards, however, especially for devotees of the C19. Perambulations 1a and 1b follow the N–S axis below (and briefly onto) the Hills, where development was concentrated before 1850. Perambulation 2 deals with the W–E axis. Perambulation 3 offers a circular route through the S part of the town, the area of the most extensive mid to late C19 development.

1a. North, along Worcester Road, returning via Graham Road

We start at the N end of ABBEY ROAD, by the Priory Gatehouse (p. 455). A former butcher's shop, Nos. 23–25, NE, perhaps by *John Deykes c.* 1830, provides an excellent foil. Gothick, battlemented gables, pinnacles, canted bay above the iron balcony; later C19 tiling round the shopfront. By the steps and C19 gates into the Priory churchyard, LYTTELTON HOUSE, mid-C19 stuccoed; attached shop with doorway with foliated columns. The POST OFFICE, *Office of Works* Neo-Georgian, dated 1935, replaced the Georgian vicarage; its range, along Church Street, *c.* 1895, with large windows and coved cornice, is on the site of the medieval parish church.

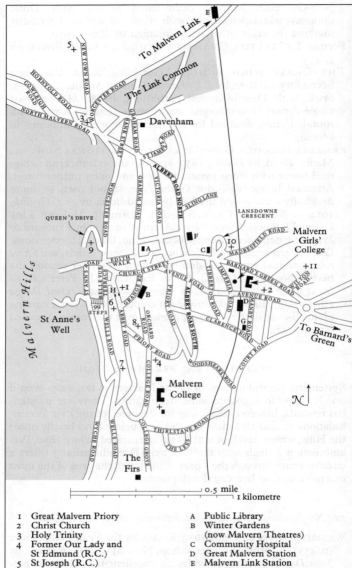

To Malvern Link

The Link Common

Davenham

NEW TOWN ROAD

HORNYOLD ROAD

COWLEIGH ROAD

NORTH MALVERN ROAD

WORCESTER ROAD

GRAHAM ROAD

BANK STREET

ST JAMES ROAD

ALBERT ROAD NORTH

VICTORIA ROAD

GRAHAM ROAD

SLING LANE

LANSDOWNE CRESCENT

QUEEN'S DRIVE

5 +

3 +

9 +

Malvern Hills

St Anne's Well

99 STEPS

ST ANNE'S ROAD

EDITH WALK

CHURCH STREET

GRANGE ROAD

AVENUE ROAD

TIBBERTON ROAD

MADRESFIELD ROAD

BARNARD'S GREEN ROAD

IMPERIAL ROAD

WELLS ROAD

ABBEY ROAD

PRIORY ROAD

ALBERT ROAD SOUTH

ORCHARD ROAD

PRIORY ROAD

COLLEGE ROAD

CLARENCE ROAD

WOODSHEARS ROAD

COURT ROAD

MANBY ROAD

AVENUE ROAD

WELLS ROAD

COLLEGE ROAD

THIRLSTANE ROAD

COLLEGE GROVE

THE LEES

Malvern Girls' College

Malvern College

The Firs

A

F

C

10

D

G

B

H + I

6 +

8 +

7 +

4 +

2

+ 11

N

| 0.5 mile |
| 1 kilometre |

1 Great Malvern Priory
2 Christ Church
3 Holy Trinity
4 Former Our Lady and
   St Edmund (R.C.)
5 St Joseph (R.C.)
6 Baptist Church
7 Former Emmanuel Church
8 Friends' Meeting House
9 Holly Mount Congregational Church
   (now United Reformed)
10 (Wesleyan) Methodist Church
11 Cemetery

A Public Library
B Winter Gardens
   (now Malvern Theatres)
C Community Hospital
D Great Malvern Station
E Malvern Link Station
F Malvern Hills College
G Former National School
H Priory Gatehouse (now Museum)

Great Malvern

Above, BELLE VUE TERRACE, three-storeyed, forms a sloping
square, Belle Vue Island, with Abbey Road. Here, two water
sculptures by *Rose Garrard*: the ENIGMA FOUNTAIN, 2000,
four standing stones, with life-size bronze statue of Elgar
leaning on the railing; and MALVHINA SPOUT, 1998, a Seces-
sionist female head. Also, a small medieval CROSS, with
renewed head. MOUNT PLEASANT, *c.* 1790, now a hotel, at
the S end of the Terrace, is red brick, three plus two bays, the
latter canted back; broad tripartite pedimented doorway,
Venetian windows above, others all paired. Full-height bow to
the S; five-bay detached ORANGERY, further W. Next, LLOYDS
BANK, dignified ashlar-faced Italianate by *J.A. Chatwin*, 1892;
ground floor round-arched, pedimented first-floor windows,
with continuous iron balcony, channelled top floor, finely
carved friezes. Originally six bays, increased very tactfully to
nine, 1929–30. It replaced the Crown Hotel, renamed Grae-
fenburg House when Dr James Wilson established his water-
cure treatment here in 1842. The former BELLE VUE HOTEL
(Nos. 34–44), plain stuccoed, *c.* 1816, probably by *John Deykes*,
has six bays, a couple of windows retaining their individual iron
balconies. Then two stone-faced mid-C19 interlopers, the first
with overpowering dormers, before more plain stucco at Nos.
12–18. Belle Vue Terrace ends with the UNICORN INN, roughcast C16, much altered, but timber framing still visible in its N
gable.

Meanwhile, E side, at the top of CHURCH STREET, two well-
sited buildings, the first, 1877, no doubt by *Haddon Bros*: timbered gables, tiled lintels. The HSBC by *J.A. Gotch* (*Gotch &
Saunders*), 1920–1, is of channelled ashlar, with pediment
and big arched windows; good compartmented plaster ceiling
within.

WORCESTER ROAD begins with the best early C19 group in
Malvern. First, the former LIBRARY and ASSEMBLY ROOMS
by *John Deykes*, 1818–21 (adapted for Barclays Bank by *Guy
Pemberton*, 1930); stuccoed, three-storeyed, with telling full-
height S bow: ground floor with attached Ionic columns à la
Nash, broad tripartite windows above. Attached, facing Edith
Walk, a later lodging house. The W front has channelled ground
floor, plain pilasters and pediment; simpler N section. Then the
former PUMP ROOM and BATHS, also by *Deykes*, 1822–3.
Three bays, with Greek Doric columns *in antis* between round-
arched rusticated entrances; wreathed frieze and balustrade
above. A later steep gable ill fits this classical composition.
Three-storey N extension with the same details; round-arched
upper windows. The FOLEY ARMS HOTEL by *Samuel Deykes*,
1810, completes the group; wings added 1812 and 1817 form
a seven-bay front with projections. Enlarged by *S.W. Daukes*,
1863, retaining the Regency character. Fine cast-iron name-
plate; big iron veranda across the two lower floors of the four
central bays, with large attached royal arms. Bow windows at
the rear.

This fine group is now overshadowed by later stuccoed buildings opposite, w, especially BEAUCHAMP TERRACE (Nos. 11–17), c. 1856, perhaps by *James Shipway*, with pedimented first-floor windows. Then Nos. 19–29, probably by *Henry Day*, c. 1860, yet higher because of its narrow attic storey; brick, turning Italianate, 2+6+2 well-composed bays. QUEEN'S DRIVE opens up to reveal the striking Holly Mount Congregational Church (p. 460), followed by BRAY'S DEPARTMENT STORE, large debased classical, with rounded s end; still stuccoed, probably 1860s. This shopping area, known as The Promenade, ends at Nos. 41–43, by *Henry Haddon*, 1891. A great contrast, though equally tall. Brick with three gables with terracotta sunflower decoration; contemporary shopfronts.

Meanwhile, a long chain of early C19 villas has begun on the E side, most, especially the earlier ones, probably by *Samuel* or *John Deykes*. The first three (one hidden by white-tiled early C20 shops) are of 1807–8, No. 28, Foley House, with fine pedimented doorway with very large fanlight. No. 32 (Burford House), 1816–17, has a Greek Doric portico; No. 34, Bredon House, c. 1824, particularly blocky, a two-bay centre with matching porch, and lower wings. Then a semi-detached pair, Nos. 36–38, 1821–2. No. 40, Sidney House, c. 1827, with windows in recesses and timber portico, retains its carriage house. No. 44, Montreal House, c. 1830, has giant fluted pilasters, paired at the rounded corners, yet Tudor hoodmoulds. The contemporary No. 46, Oriel House, has gone Gothick, its trefoiled pilasters and crocketed pinnacles comparable with Nos. 23–25 Abbey Road; doorway with ogee hood, head corbels sprouting foliage. At No. 50, Worfield House, the fluted Doric columns look more convincingly Greek. No. 52 has cast-iron veranda and fluted pilasters with acanthus capitals; No. 54, Aucott House, a fine wide doorway with iron trellis porch; No. 58, Sidmouth House, again has paired pilasters at the rounded corners, here with wreathed capitals, and solid Doric portico. All have stunning rear views, and face w to the greenery of the hillside. Here, hidden in the trees, is HOLLY MOUNT, a larger stuccoed house where Princess Victoria stayed in 1830; mostly rebuilt later in the C19, and enlarged by *Mackmurdo, Hornblower & Walters* of London, 1892, but keeping entirely to a debased version of the stuccoed style.

BANK STREET continues downhill, N, with more minor villas, then a modest C18 to mid-C19 mix: No. 17, Late Georgian brick, has three bays and storeys; No. 34 is a C17 timber-framed cottage. It emerges at the sw corner of The Link Common. Just to the E here, in finely landscaped grounds, is the very large DAVENHAM (No. 148 Graham Road), now a home for the elderly. The original gabled stone house, by *E. W. Elmslie*, 1859, was much expanded in elaborate C15 Loire style for C.W. Dyson Perrins by *William Henman*, c. 1900–2 and, after a fire, in 1904–5. Elmslie's core is recognizable on the entrance front, though much altered by Henman, who added the long dining-room wing (with broad canted bay window), SW, and further ranges, NW, including an octagonal room between billiard room and top-lit picture gallery. Several panelled ceilings of 1859 remain, but most decoration is Edwardian: very fine open-well timber staircase, much stained glass by *H. W. Lonsdale*. Outside, in the angle of main range and dining-room wing, a very fine bronze well-head, Byzantine/Italianate, with upright lion. – Extensive C20 additions in the grounds, incorporating the STABLE BLOCK, *c.* 1900, with tall balconied spirelet. – Large apsed LODGE also by *Henman*, with curved, splendidly ornamental, wrought-iron GATES, almost Art Nouveau in style, by the *Bromsgrove Guild*.

We can return s along GRAHAM ROAD, which begins with minor early C19 Tudor Gothic houses, outliers of development round The Link Common. In ST JAMES ROAD, E, big mid-to-late C19 stuccoed houses. To the SE, in ALBERT and VICTORIA ROADS, a few larger late C19 Gothic ones, now mostly hemmed in by C20 infill. WOODGATE, the first encountered, perhaps by *Nevinson & Newton c.* 1880, displays a typical mix: crazy-paving stone, ashlar dressings, thinly half-timbered gables, three canted bays to the E (the N one by *Henman*, 1897).*

The s part of GRAHAM ROAD mixes Gothic villas and stuccoed sub-classical (much of it C20 pastiche). More of the latter, E side; especially well preserved, No. 98 (Stokefield), probably *c.* 1840, with tented iron verandas. Of Gothic examples, w side, the gaunt No. 71 (Granta Lodge) is probably by *A. E. Perkins*, 1868; the tall gabled No. 59 (Kensington House) may be by *W. H. Knight* of Cheltenham. Best is the picturesque COTFORD HOTEL, said to be of 1851; Dec details, pierced bargeboards, even a timber-framed gable. Further on, stucco dominates even this w side. An interesting stretch begins with two good examples of *c.* 1850: No. 35 (Buckingham House) and No. 33 (Clanmere), each with bracketed eaves, wrought-iron honeysuckle balconies, and inset fluted Ionic porches. No. 29 (Belford House) is the Italianate villa type turned into snecked stone; No. 25 (Uplands), of 1854, again fully Gothic, has bargeboarded gables and Dec bay window. Then the stuccoed MONTROSE HOTEL, *c.* 1840, five bays, pedimented first-floor windows. Opposite the Library (p. 461), some three-bay villas of *c.* 1830, notably No. 19, with window shutters and tented porch on thin fluted columns. The large WAITROSE supermarket, by the *Hancock Ward Company*, *c.* 1999, looms up on the hillside above, gabled and white-rendered in a forlorn attempt to appear inconspicuous. Edith Walk, along its s side, leads back up to Worcester Road.

* Also worth a look: LANGHOLME, Albert Road North, w side, by *Henry Haddon*, 1894, rock-faced, patterned roof, gables chequered red and yellow; and LORNE LODGE, Sling Lane, patterned brick, *c.* 1870–80, no doubt also *Haddon*.

1b. Up to St Ann's Well, then south along Wells Road

From the Unicorn Inn (p. 469), ST ANN'S ROAD climbs steeply uphill. Minor early C19 stucco is followed by HOLLYMOUNT COTTAGE, mostly by *E.E. Baldwin*, 1903; then, after a turn S, KENSINGTON COTTAGE, mid-C19 Gothick with window shutters (enlarged 1907), and the former ALDWYN TOWER HOTEL,* by *Henry Day*, *c.* 1850. Gabled Italianate, red brick with stucco trim, tall tower with arcading above Venetian windows. Further on a winding path ascends, even more steeply, to ST ANN'S WELL; many C19 clients would have approached it on the back of a donkey. A two-bay rubble cottage of 1813, with Y-traceried round-arched windows and wide rectangular doorway, contains the marble water fountain (renewed by *W. Forsyth*, 1892); taller octagonal wing, *c.* 1860, crazy-paving stone with purple brick dressings, overhanging pyramidal roof. Outside, an ornamental pool by *Rose Garrard*, 2005. From back in St Ann's Road, we can descend by the ninety-nine steps forking E by BELLO SGUARDO, a stuccoed villa of 1833 with two full-height tripartite bow windows (altered by *J.H. Strudwick & Son*, 1893). C15 tiles discovered nearby probably mark the site of the medieval St Michael's Hermitage.

We emerge at the N end of WELLS ROAD, which can now be explored; for the Abbey Hotel below, *see* p. 479. Buildings are again all on the E side, facing the hillside. First WARWICK HOUSE, the long rambling premises of Cox & Painter Ltd, a department store established 1833, now housing. An over-expanded mid-C19 gabled section, then a narrow, vigorously Gothic part by *G.C.Haddon*, 1867–8, with foliated columns and decorated iron beam, followed by lower, plainer, late C19 sections. Steps lead down to the Baptist Church (p. 459), on the site of Hay Well. This was the reason for the establishment here of the (former) TUDOR HOTEL, another water-cure centre, founded 1842 by Dr James Gully. Two separate buildings, the first, HOLYROOD HOUSE, stuccoed Tudor Gothic, *c.* 1840; four bays, the outer projecting with gables, pinnacles, and square bay windows, their storeys divided by cusped quatrefoil friezes with fleurons. First-floor veranda on the N return and at the rear. TUDOR HOUSE is mostly of 1852, for Gully, by *S.S. Teulon*, red brick, in lively Jacobethan style; shaped gables, square bay windows, rusticated doorway, tall chimneys. Splendid rear façade, the central chimney flanked by canted bays on robustly carved brackets; beyond these, either side, tall pinnacles and higher ogee-roofed viewing towers. Complicated arrangement of brick terraces below. Tudor House, for gentleman clients, was connected to Holyrood House, for ladies, by the so-called Bridge of Sighs (for the use of medical staff only). Then earlier houses: Nos. 21–23, stuccoed semi-detached, four bays sharing a two-bay pediment, and the larger MELTON

p. 473

* Advertised as the 'highest boarding house in Malvern; 600 ft above sea level'.

Malvern, Tudor House, Abbey Road.
Original drawing by S.S. Teulon

LODGE (No. 29), *c.* 1818, in large grounds; also stuccoed, with iron verandas, projecting gabled centre, and wide eaves on brackets. Altered by *G.C. Haddon*, 1867–8, and again by *Nevinson & Newton*, 1894, who added the tripartite stone porch. Coachhouse by the road, NW. Further on, Emmanuel Church (p. 460) is preceded by a contemporary brick pair (Nos. 37–39), no doubt also by *Haddon Bros*. Beyond, two large houses of *c.* 1850, now belonging to Malvern College: SOUTHLANDS, bleak Tudor Gothic, stuccoed and gabled; CHERBOURG, Italianate, five bays, the central three with conjoined windows.

2. To the east: Church Street and Avenue Road

CHURCH STREET begins, w end, with routine C19–C20 shops; on the s side, a stone wall of 1889 (formerly with iron cresting) separates off the Priory churchyard. To its E, the former LYTTELTON GRAMMAR SCHOOL, rebuilt by *Henry Haddon*, 1887–9. Symmetrical, rock-faced, two gables with Dec tracery flanking the first-floor schoolroom; square clock tower, N, formerly with big open top with half-hipped roof. Caretaker's house at the rear, forming a narrow courtyard with LYTTELTON WELL, a pale brick ecumenical centre by *Bartosch & Stokes*, 1993. Early C19 stuccoed survivors include Nos. 18–22, rising to four storeys (with one slightly Art Nouveau shopfront). Between, stairs ascend to CECILIA HALL, *c.* 1860, the earliest surviving concert hall in Malvern (now a dance studio); interior with Corinthian pilasters, coved cornice, and cast-iron gallery. WOOLWORTHS has a jazzy Deco first floor, an in-house job of 1935–6.

The crossroads with Graham and Grange roads has four prominent buildings, three with rounded corners. The former
BEAUCHAMP HOTEL, NW, *c.* 1845, is stuccoed with tripartite
corner window; enlarged by *Elmslie, Franey & Haddon*,
1865, and again by *G.C. Haddon*, 1883. Opposite, NE, THE
EXCHANGE, *c.* 1905, red brick with terracotta details, including first-floor oriels; iron balconies, some original shopfronts,
especially No. 4 Graham Road. The stone-faced NATWEST
BANK, SW, 1930–1 by *F.C.R. Palmer*, has paired Ionic columns
and narrow first floor. Instead of a curved corner, the former
MALVERN CLUB, SE, Italianate, snecked sandstone, by *Henry
Haddon*, 1869, has a jutting square bay with pediment; blocky
ashlar N porch.

In GRANGE ROAD, S, two good villas. PRIOR'S CROFT, W side,
c. 1851, perhaps by *Elmslie*, is picturesque Gothic, white-rendered and gabled, the S part set back beyond a boldly buttressed tower with higher SW stair-turret; multi-cusped ogee
doorway, triangular oriel. THE GRANGE, E side, behind a car
park, irregular Tudor of *c.* 1830, has flat-topped gables, an oriel,
grouped brick chimneys, and, to the garden, a big square bay
with semicircular projection.

Back to CHURCH STREET. Stucco houses of *c.* 1835, N side,
perhaps by *Richard Varden* (who produced designs for Edward
Foley at about this date): Nos. 119–121, with nice round-
arched doorway; No. 125 (Holland House), a neat villa with
rusticated ground floor and Greek Doric porch. Two very
large, rendered Italianate houses of *c.* 1840–50, with groups of
round-arched windows, follow: GROSVENOR HOUSE and
PORTLAND HOUSE, the latter almost doubled in size, as a
hotel, by *Albert C. Baker*, 1907.

Opposite, more of a mix: No. 36 (Highlea), snecked stone Italianate with Doric porch; No. 38 (Chartwell House), a late
hipped-roofed villa, with fancy brackets and other overloaded
detail; and ROCKCLIFFE, *Henry Haddon*'s own house, 1872.
As asymmetrical as possible, of irregular rubble, with assorted
Gothic windows, mostly beneath pointed tympana of multi-
coloured stone or tile; side porch and tripartite window with
odd tented roof, resting on large iron brackets.

Set back from the corner with Priory Road, is the largest and
best of Malvern's Victorian Gothic houses, PRIORY PARK
MANSION (now Malvern Hills District Council House), by
Henry Haddon (of *Haddon Bros*), 1874–80, for A.M. Speer, a
South American merchant. Stone, mostly in elaborate Perp
style, the entrance front, W, particularly asymmetrical. Shallow
lavish porch more or less central, projecting tall gabled dormer
above, with flushwork, piquant small dormer to its l., steep
slate roof with rows of brick chimneys. A gabled S wing projects, with more flushwork; set back, N, the four-storey stair-
tower with open parapet and higher spired turret. Lavish
carving, especially grotesques, by *Forsyth*. N service wing, of
brick (stone-faced towards Priory Road, E). Garden front, S,
with two-stage canted bay at its centre, but any thought of sym-

metry soon dispelled by the large polygonal oriel projecting on a big hexagonal shaft at the SE corner. Slightly quieter E front with well-preserved conservatory, NE. Within, a broad hall runs N–S across the house, from staircase to large central S bay; oblong opening to the floor above, so that the circulation is repeated around a balcony on the bedroom floor. Fine tiled or marquetry floors, excellent carved woodwork, especially beasts on the dog-leg staircase, all again by *Forsyth*; enjoyable, richly coloured stained glass, no doubt by *Heaton, Butler & Bayne*, on the staircase and elsewhere. The house replaced The Priory, Tudor Gothic, 1833–4, probably by *Harvey Eginton*, the home of Dr James Gully 1847–73.

Back in CHURCH STREET, stuccoed Italianate houses soon give way to rock-faced Gothic ones, two of *c.* 1890 (Nos. 137 and 141, N side, with coved cornices) already edging towards Queen Anne; No. 62 Albert Road North is similar. Probably all by *A.C. Baker*, as is SUMMERSIDE, 1884, at the corner of Albert Road North, with pyramid-roofed tower with triangular oriel; an early home of the Girls' College, for which *George Hubbard & Son* added large brick Neo-Georgian additions, S, 1937.* The OLD VICARAGE (Oriel House), at the Tibberton Road corner, with timbered gables, is dated 1880. In TIBBERTON ROAD, W side, TIBBERTON GRANGE is dated 1872; large houses opposite by *Baker*, 1885–6.

Church Street ends with a final Italianate outbreak at LANSDOWNE CRESCENT, off the N side: three stuccoed terraces, *c.* 1851–2, on a slight curve, each of four houses, probably built as lodgings. Paired doorways approached up steps, tripartite windows, projecting eaves on brackets, bay windows on the returns. Further terraces may have been intended around the small central green, but instead the Methodist Church (p. 460) and Community Hospital (p. 462) moved in. The humble brick LANSDOWNE TERRACE further E, off Madresfield Road, may be contemporary. It faces the railway, across which are LANSDOWNE HOUSE and ROW, a disciplined reconstituted-stone group, flats and a terrace, the latter with pantiled roof, by *Raymond Hall* of London, 1977–8.

Now back and S, via Imperial Road, with its C20 outliers of Malvern Girls' College, E side (p. 466), to Great Malvern Railway Station (p. 462). The main premises of the Girls' College, the former Imperial Hotel, stand proudly to its NE. Christ Church (p. 456) is further E in Avenue Road.

We can return W along AVENUE ROAD, which linked Station and Hotel to the town centre. Several good Gothic villas, beginning with BATSFORD, at the Imperial Road corner, by *Haddon Bros*, 1869–70, for H.T. Speer; angled timber porch and other quirky details, steep gables with pierced ogee-trefoiled bargeboards, tall patterned brick chimneys. Later examples by

121

---

*The College also colonized the roughcast IVYDENE, further S, giving it half-timbered gables, 1903, and THE MOUNT opposite, Italianate with raised pedimented centre.

Henry Haddon opposite (PRIORY HOLME 1885, THORNBURY 1888, MARCHWOOD 1887), more in Tibberton Road, S, e.g. FRANCHE, 1889; opposite this, LAWNSIDE LEA, a crisp stuccoed classical villa, with rusticated ground-floor and Doric porch. Then beyond Tibberton Road, two good earlier rock-faced ones, LINDFIELD and ENDERLEY, probably by *Elmslie*, 1861–2; both have irregular gables and trefoiled bargeboards, the latter also an angled porch. LAWNSIDE, in spacious grounds at the angle of Avenue and Albert roads, is the largest stuccoed house, rambling and formless (including matching additions by *Elmslie*, 1884). On the opposite corner, SW, THE GROVE, a fine rock-faced villa dated 1867, no doubt by *Elmslie, Franey & Haddon*. Timbered gables, banded brick chimneys, ornate Gothic doorway, round gatepiers like those at the Imperial Hotel; at the rear, S, a big round bay window-cum-garden entrance. Further along this side of Albert Road, S, a good brick pair, perhaps again by *Elmslie*, 1861–2, with black patterning and Dec detail, a change from all this from rock facing. The last house in The Avenue, No. 1, N side, is also red brick, *c.* 1880, gabled, quite plain.

3. South: Priory Road, College Road, Abbey Road

PRIORY ROAD begins with Priory Park Mansion (p. 474). The late C19 No. 10, S, was probably its gardener's cottage: single-storeyed, timbered gables, patterned tiled roof with central chimney. Then No. 14 (Spa Cottage), the former chalybeate well and pump room of *c.* 1840: painted brick, with lean-to timber pentice across the E front. Later gables. Next door, hidden behind its hedge, No. 16 (Oakdale), the Spa Villa; irregular stuccoed Gothic, with big canted bay with pointed windows, battlements, and octagonal turret behind; later additions. Both back onto Swan Pool, in Priory Park (p. 462). Nos. 17–19 opposite are a brick semi-detached pair by *William Lunn*, 1894. Larger late C19 houses begin with two of Malvern 'crazy paving', probably *c.* 1860–70. DARESBURY (No. 27), E side, has irregular recessions, patterned brick tympana, and very nice round gatepiers; PORTSWOOD, W, crowstepped gables, oriels, turrets and a good array of brick chimneys.

A brief diversion into WOODSHEARS ROAD, SE, leads to the gabled brick No. 3 (The Chantry), a severe Butterfieldian essay, *c.* 1860, no doubt by *W.J. Hopkins*; its studied asymmetry, tall square chimneys, and severe brick patterning are a welcome antidote to the usual excesses of Malvern Gothic. ORWELL LODGE beyond reminds us that overblown Italianate is also inescapable here. Further down is Malvern College's N entrance and its No. 5 boarding house (p. 465).

Back to PRIORY ROAD, which now curves SW past two good mid-C19 brick Jacobean houses. The exhuberant No. 36 (St Ronans) has a round central oriel, square projection, r., with triangular centre rising into a steep spirelet, and rear tower with double ogee cap. No. 40 contents itself with shaped gables and strapwork. Then stuccoed development of *c.* 1850 takes over, mostly of the tall Tudor Gothic type.* This continues N into ORCHARD ROAD, the corner marked by a fine LETTER BOX of early type, *c.* 1857, in the form of a Doric pillar; here also the Friends' Meeting House (p. 460). Further NW in Priory Road, good earlier stuccoed houses, perhaps *c.* 1846, especially No. 37 (Southfield House), at the College Road corner. Projecting gabled centre above the doorway with elaborate carved brackets, flanked by sweet little bow windows; Ionic first-floor pilasters along the sides. Round-headed gatepiers. The Gothic No. 52 has quoins, gables with small inset figures, battlemented gabled porch, and four-centred hood on heads.

Now s down COLLEGE ROAD, originally Radnor Road. Its E side starts with the former R.C. church (p. 459). Opposite, RADNOR LODGE, snecked-stone Tudor Gothic, with fancy pierced bargeboards; and No. 10 (Royds Lodge), single-storey Tudor by *Teulon*, 1851, formerly the bath house of the demolished Hardwicke House on the hill above (*see* p. 478). ROSLIN HOUSE, E side, large Italianate, with quoins and timber lean-to porch on huge brackets, was much extended in roughcast *c.* 1903 as the College's No. 9 boarding house. Then Malvern College itself (p. 462). Beyond, RADNOR HOUSE, big stuccoed sub-classical; open-pedimented Doric doorway, paired chimneys with Vanbrughian arches. Altered by *Elmslie*, 1882, much enlarged by *Henman & Cooper*, 1907–8, as the College's House No. 8.

Thirlstane Road leads s to COLLEGE GROVE. On its E side, a nice group of four houses by *Nevinson & Newton*, 1885; Malvern stone, two with tile-hanging, all with gables, dormers, and hipped roofs. No. 1 is the best, a nice restrained design, with pretty oriel; No. 3 (Eastry) was Edward Nevinson's own house. At the end, in extensive grounds, THE FIRS, originally a lodging house for visitors, now another Malvern College possession. Lodge with paired round-arched windows and hipped roof.† The house itself is of *c.* 1825. Ashlar façade, 2+3+2 bays, the centre projecting beneath a shallow pediment, with infilled porch with attached Ionic columns; moulded architraves and cornice, rusticated ground floor. Enlarged by *J.A. Chatwin*, *c.* 1890–5.

It is worth following THIRLSTANE ROAD further E, along the College's s edge, to THE LEES, a large uncompleted crescent of 1886. The tall houses, mostly semi-detached, brick or stone, are nothing special; layout and planting are remarkably generous. No. 7, of 1887, was extended *c.* 1892 as the College's No. 7 boarding house. The two largest houses, NW, by *A.C. Baker*, 1892, are more elaborate.

Back to COLLEGE ROAD, which now turns uphill, N. THE NOOK (now Headmaster's House), rock-faced Gothic, is probably by *Elmslie c.* 1862, with very fancy gatepiers. Next door,

---

* The grid-like bay windows of No. 42 belong to its conversion to the vicarage, by *Haddon*, 1880.
† There is also a rustic thatched lodge, NW, off Wells Road.

ASHFIELD, a fine large C19 Italianate stone house, more classically composed than most; grouped round-arched windows, pedimented porch on paired Ionic columns, non-matching wings with quoins and balustrades. Rock-faced STABLE BLOCK by *Douglas & Fordham* of Chester, 1891, with Staffordshire blue brick dressings; clock turret with leaded ogee cap.

The SW tip of ABBEY ROAD has two more large houses in extensive grounds, both mid-C19, stone-faced, now belonging to Malvern College. HAMPTON HOUSE, SE side, good Italianate, perhaps by *Elmslie*, is set well back beyond its lodge of 1896 (and MARGARET PRIOR HALL by *Godwin & Cowper*, 1980, concrete block with much glass). The plainer, more irregular ELLERSLIE opposite, *c.* 1855, the water-cure establishment of Dr Edward Johnson, is swamped by C20 prep-school additions; nice LODGE, with timber balcony, by *Nevinson & Newton*, 1897. Nos. 67–69 at the summit, SE side, are an enormous semi-detached, stuccoed Italianate pair, probably of *c.* 1860–70; mostly paired windows, tall channelled porches.

Now NE along ABBEY ROAD, curving above MALVERNBURY, a large sub-Voysey house by *A. Hill Parker*, 1907; roughcast, canted bays and corners, green slate roof with battered chimneys. The E front, with three canted bays and two broad gables with green tile-hanging, overlooks spacious gardens.

Further on, E side, HARDWICKE HOUSE, a severe block of flats of *c.* 1965, replaced *S.S. Teulon*'s 1851 house of that name, the establishment of Dr J.L. Marsden; five storeys, alternatingly brick with projections, and obscured glazing. Then No. 53 (Elmsdale), also built for Marsden, *c.* 1853, no doubt by *Teulon*; austere, coursed rubble, with crowstepped gables, two-storey balustraded porch, excellent N tower with broached tiled spirelet and attached round bartizan. No. 51 (Sutherland) is mid-C19 stuccoed classical, of three bays. No. 49 (Walmer Lodge), with the same dimensions, adds no end of elaborate detail. Wide outer bays with pediments and giant fluted columns with flat acanthus capitals; also bracket-ed eaves, hoodmoulds, fluted Doric porch with wrought-iron balcony. No. 47 (Southbank), also early 1850s, perhaps by *Teulon*, provides a splendid Gothic riposte; red brick, with blue diapering, Tudor-arched windows, irregular gables, large NE tower with stepped battlements and higher stair-turret.

Further down, still on the E side, is MALVERN HOUSE (No. 35), built for Dr James Wilson, 1859; red brick Jacobean, tall outer shaped gables above canted bay windows, tripartite round-arched porch. PARK VIEW (No. 33), at the Grange Road corner, was Wilson's main hydropathic establishment, built, at a cost of £18,000, in 1845 (when it was appropriately named Priessnitz House); still classical, the five-bay centre of its long three-storeyed front emphasized by giant Ionic pilasters and heavy projecting porch with Greek Doric columns *in antis*. Wings, seven bays N, five S, mostly by *Healing & Overbury*, 1930. The taller rear façade of the central part has two wide full-height bows.

Opposite, w side, we are back with tall Tudorish houses of c. 1846–50, stuccoed and gabled, interrupted by the Baptist Church (p. 459); looming above are Holyrood and Tudor houses (p. 472). The last house, Nos. 2–4 (The Gatehouse), earlier C19 stuccoed, has balconettes and pedimented doorcases.

Finally, E side, immediately s of the Priory Gatehouse (p. 455), the ABBEY HOTEL by *S. W. Daukes*, 1848–9, its Jacobean style imitating the C17 Abbey House it replaced. Of stone, mostly hidden by Virginia creeper, three-storeyed, with oriels, strapwork balustrades, battlements, and shaped gables; Jacobethan timber staircase within. Semi-octagonal projection, r., added soon afterwards. The restless Gothic half-timbered wing next the gatehouse is probably c. 1870–80. Extensive C20 additions.

OUTER MALVERN

1. North Malvern, including Link Top, Cowleigh and Newtown

Holy Trinity (p. 456) occupies a fine island site at LINK TOP, above the w end of the Link Common. Early to mid-C19 houses nearby: THE VAULTS, No. 102 Worcester Road, opposite Trinity Hall, is three bays, stuccoed, with nice doorcase. Altered former POLICE STATION, s, by *Henry Rowe*, 1860; single-storey brick, stuccoed quoins, doorway with rusticated pilasters, heavily bracketed eaves. (Demolition proposed 2007.) At the start of NORTH MALVERN ROAD, Nos. 1–3, pretty early C19 cottages; lower centre, taller thatched end bays with intersecting tracery. Further up, by the C19 pound, the former STOCKS and WHIPPING POST.

The core of NORTH MALVERN lies WNW, beneath the impressive scars of North Malvern and Tank quarries. The former BOYS' NATIONAL SCHOOL by *Henry Haddon*, 1886, is no longer Gothic; brick, broad gables with terracotta decoration, short tower, detached house. It supplemented the MORRIS SCHOOL of 1836 further on, Malvern stone, with large moulded round-arched windows flanking a similar doorway; almost identical extension, of 1838, obscured by a gabled addition of 1912. Early to mid-C19 stuccoed or brick houses nearby, Continuing into BELVOIR BANK; on the corner, the larger four-bay NORTH MALVERN HOUSE.

Opposite, on a stone base of 1835, the battlemented brick WATER TOWER rebuilt by Malvern UDC, 1901, probably by their surveyor *H. P. Maybury*; thin, of four diminishing stages, the upper two with clock and orange terracotta trim.

COWLEIGH ROAD, to the N, an older, lower route, begins with a Brethren GOSPEL HALL, 1894, with attached house. Then larger houses of the usual Malvern types, the best No. 18, c. 1870, with small tower between asymmetrical gables. In HORNYOLD ROAD, leading back E from the crossroads with Belvoir Bank, big late C19 semi-detached pairs. Further w, ST NICHOLAS HOUSE, Neo-Victorian flats by *Martin Booth*, 1988, utilizing a few original 'features'. Almost as large, the

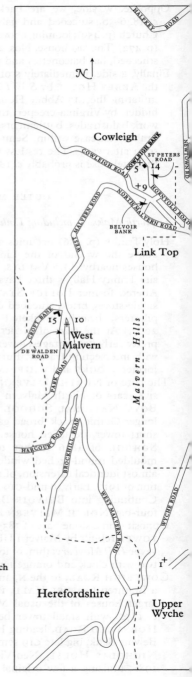

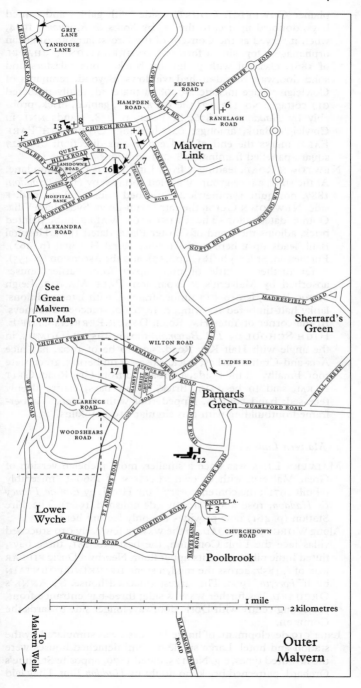

GRIT LANE
TANHOUSE LANE
LEIGH SINTON ROAD
YATES HAY ROAD
LOWER HOWSELL RD.
WORCESTER ROAD
REGENCY ROAD
HAMPDEN ROAD
+6
RANELAGH ROAD
+2
13 +8
SOMERS PARK AVE.
CHURCH ROAD
HOWSELL RD
QUEST HILLS ROAD
LANSDOWNE
ALBERT PARK RD
+4
11
+7
16
ROAD
SOMERS ROAD
PICKERSLEIGH AVE.
Malvern Link
HOSPITAL BANK
WORCESTER ROAD
PICKERSLEIGH ROAD
ALEXANDRA ROAD
NORTH END LANE
TOWNSEND WAY
MADRESFIELD ROAD
See Great Malvern Town Map
Sherrard's Green
CHURCH STREET
WILTON ROAD
BARNARDS GREEN
PICKERSLEIGH ROAD
LYDES RD
HALL GREEN
17
MANBY RD
CHRIST CHURCH
AVENUE RD
CHURCH ROAD
COURT ROAD
GERALDINE ROAD
Barnards Green
WELLS ROAD
CLARENCE ROAD
GUARLFORD ROAD
WOODSHEARS ROAD
Lower Wyche
ST ANDREWS ROAD
12
POOLBROOK ROAD
PEACHFIELD ROAD
LONGRIDGE ROAD
KNOLL LA.
+3
CHURCHDOWN ROAD
HAYES BANK ROAD
Poolbrook
1 mile
2 kilometres
To Malvern Wells
BLACKMORE PARK ROAD
Outer Malvern

plainer COWLEIGH COURT, s side, with gables and canted
bays, doubled in size, to the SE, by *Scoles & Raymond*, 1914,
when it served as the Convent of the Cross; later an Anglican
orphanage. Opposite, a former CONGREGATIONAL CHAPEL
of 1861, classical with pediment; brick, stone pilasters and
solid doorway, round-arched windows. Beyond, remnants of
Cowleigh village include No. 98, a thatched, thinly timbered
C17 cottage. No. 112 was the VICARAGE, gabled, brick, probably by *Haddon*, *c.* 1876; St Peter, p. 458, stands NNE in
Cowleigh Bank, amongst C20 housing. COWLEIGH PARK
FARM marks the end of Malvern in this direction: C16–C17
square-panelled framing; C18–C19 additions.

NEWTOWN ROAD, leading N from Link Top, is more mundane.
At the start, a nice group of gabled cottages by *Henry Haddon*,
1887, not quite symmetrical. Stuccoed houses follow, and, E
side, NEWTOWN CLUB, the rather run-down Sydenham Villa:
Gothic dated 1862. The PRINCE OF WALES pub, painted
brick, adjoins the s end of Gloster Place, dated 1863. Hospital
Bank leads up E here to the former Rural Hospital (p. 462).
Further on, St Joseph (R.C., p. 459), and the Ascension (p. 455).

Yet further N little of note, apart from earlier houses
absorbed by Malvern's N expansion. PALE MANOR, Leigh
Sinton Road, is C16–C17 timber-framed, with later additions:
lanky half-timbered NE wing, *c.* 1850–60, stuccoed chimneys.
At the corner of Yates Hay Road, DYSON PERRINS C. OF E.
HIGH SCHOOL by *T.R. Bateman*, mostly 1957–9. DOMUS, in
the angle with Half Key Road, said to be of 1902, has nice
Arts-and-Crafts touches; brick, close-set timbering, green slate
roof. Finally, off the E side, approached from Grit Road, GRIT
FARM, said to be 1719. Brick, 2+1+2 bays, centre deeply
recessed; band courses, hipped roof with dormers. Timber-
framed outbuilding with two circular C19 hop kilns.

2. Malvern Link

MALVERN LINK was once a smaller, more plebeian version of
Great Malvern, with its own STATION of 1860–1 (miserably
rebuilt 1971); the contemporary Link Hotel, by *Elmslie, Franey
& Haddon*, rose above it, NW (demolished 1967). The Fire
Station (p. 461) now provides the only feature here.

Along WORCESTER ROAD, to the WSW, a few early C19 stuccoed
villas face the Link Common, the best No. 181, three bays,
fluted Ionic pilasters on its upper floor. Nearby a Doric PILLAR
BOX of *c.* 1857; across the road, a stone DRINKING FOUNTAIN
by *W. Forsyth*, 1900. The largest stuccoed house, ST ANNE'S
ORCHARD, lies further WSW, s side: three-bay entrance front,
projecting centre with Doric doorway; longer side towards the
Common.

Later C19 development, of limited success, was stimulated by the
station and hotel. Large single or semi-detached houses were
the favoured types, e.g. No. 125, dated 1879, opposite St Anne's
Orchard, patterned brick, no doubt by *Haddon Bros*. They laid

out the ALBERT PARK ESTATE to the N in 1875. Modest houses in ALEXANDRA ROAD, more interesting ones in SOMERS ROAD, leading back E. At its W end, semi-detached brick pairs of 1886–91 by *Henry Haddon* (Nos. 5–11); opposite, S, No. 8 (The Skilts) by *William Henman*, 1891: terracotta trim, canted bay with finial, big stone doorway. Further on, earlier Italianate brick pairs, especially Raglan House and Link Tower Lodge, with end towers, set on the diagonal at the Albert Park Road corner; probably by *Henry Day*, enlarged by his nephew *E.A. Day*, 1874. OVERDALE, dated 1899, above the corner with Lansdowne Road, yellow brick with red trim and chequer-board gables in Henry Haddon's style, is by his successor *E.E. Baldwin*.

In WORCESTER ROAD, E of the station, the Common ends at the corner of Pickersleigh Road, overlooked by a neat early C19 villa, LINK LODGE, with full-height angle bow. Then, opposite the United Reformed Church (p. 460), a brief urban feel with a couple of good late C19 houses with timbered gables and COLSTON BUILDINGS (Nos. 217–231), a three-storey brick shopping parade of 1896–9, with timber oriels and yellow terracotta balustraded parapet; Hampden Road leads N to St Matthias (p. 457). The rest of the shopping area is mostly scrappy C20. In RICHMOND ROAD, N, a short brick terrace, *c.* 1858, and contemporary villas. More villas in Worcester Road NE, the best, N side, No. 285 (Sunny Lodge), *c.* 1833, with timber veranda, and the earlier No. 303 (Rose Garth), an unusual design: roughcast, wide eaves, outer full-height semi-circular bows with conical roofs. Further on, opposite brick outbuildings of TOWNSEND HOUSE, a farm of *c.* 1800, the earlier Countess of Huntingdon's Chapel (p. 460).

Before this, LOWER HOWSELL ROAD, leading N, has various earlier survivors amongst C20 housing (including, around Regency Road, a flat-roofed concrete-faced Malvern UDC group, *c.* 1945, by their surveyor *C.C. Judson*). SUMMER-FIELD, the largest, stuccoed, *c.* 1839, has a good four-bay E front: first-floor fluted pilasters with wreath capitals, Doric porch. Much expanded by *Lewis Sheppard & Son*, 1902–3, later a school. Opposite, W, No. 79, a C17 thatched cottage. Timber-framed remnants further N include Nos. 132–136, larger, with unequal gables, its N hall range rebuilt in brick. C18 brick farms also remain, on the way to Leigh Sinton (p. 426).

At the NE end of Worcester Road, ISOBEL HARRISON GARDENS, *c.* 1951–2, a generously laid out group of single-storey housing for the elderly; hipped pantile-roofed centre. Opposite, S, in Ranelagh Road, the former Convent (p. 458).

3. The eastern fringes: Barnard's Green, Pickersleigh, Poolbrook

The shopping area of BARNARD'S GREEN ROAD is the nucleus of the E suburbs. At its W end, a thirties-looking BUS SHELTER with small clock tower, a war memorial of *c.* 1950. Nearby, a large stone 'Hand of Peace' by *Rose Garrard*, 1999. In WILTON

ROAD, NW, amidst small-scale housing of *c.* 1880–95, is the
cemetery (p. 461). To the NE is GREAT MALVERN PRIMARY
SCHOOL by *A. V. Rowe*, 1916; brick, symmetrical front to Lydes
Road, its higher centre with open pediment. Otherwise mostly
monotonous C20 estates. Earlier rural survivors provide some
relief. The best, PICKERSLEIGH COURT, some distance N in
Pickersleigh Road, timber-framed, originally *c.* 1500, is quite
large. Two-storey W end, its two gables with renewed weatherings; brick star-stacks. Longer single-storey E range, with four-
light transomed windows and dormers, linking to an early C19
painted brick wing.

More timber framing in COURT ROAD, SW: three C17 cottages,
two thatched. Here is also some good Birmingham Arts and
Crafts work. First, at the corner of Christ Church Road
(No. 26 there), CHALFONT HOUSE by *Marcus O. Type*, 1905,
brick, roughcast and half-timbering, with hipped roof.*
Further on, at the SW corner with Woodshears Road, a nice
group by *Crouch & Butler*: a semi-detached pair and singleton,
1898–9, plus another pair, S, 1905. These are also brick or
roughcast, with close studding, but their Arts-and-Crafts
detailing is rather starchily applied. Further on, the former
FOUNTAIN INN by *A. Hill Parker*, 1898; roughcast brick, terracotta trim, wide porch on timber columns.

On the W side of BARNARD'S GREEN, Barnard's Green House
(No. 10), late C18, stuccoed, has three wide bays with segment-
headed windows and pedimented Tuscan porch; at the rear, a
hipped-roofed wing and gables dated 1635. Here the road
forks, but attractively wide verges, remnants of Malvern Chase,
continue to E and S. Several C17 or Georgian survivors line
GUARLFORD ROAD, leading E. No. 170, the last, S side, is C17
timber-framed, lobby-entrance plan, with wood-mullioned
windows on console brackets; gabled W cross-wing.

MOAT COURT, Sherrards Green, ½ m. N, on the site of a C14
moated grange of Malvern Priory, is C17–C18 brick, with C19
oast house and C17 dovecote.

POOLBROOK ROAD leads S to Malvern Common. Near St
Andrew (p. 457), a few houses to note. THE KNOLL, imme-
diately E, is large half-timbered, of 1893. LITTLEWOOD
HOUSE, NW, late C17, has square-panelled framing and pretty
early C19 windows. Further S, side by side in HAYES BANK
ROAD, are PEACHFIELD HOUSE, for Apphia, Lady Lyttelton,
1822–3, three-bay stuccoed with giant angle pilasters, and
HAYES BANK, a little later, with projecting central gable. The
Common here was formerly laid out as a golf course. Its stone
CLUBHOUSE by *Lewis Sheppard*, 1883, survives at the SW tip of
Longridge Road. Further W, at the St Andrew's Road corner,
another Doric LETTER BOX of *c.* 1857. This part of Malvern is
overshadowed by the sprawling MALVERN TECHNOLOGY
CENTRE, an upgrading (by *Design Works Services Ltd*, from

*At the corner of Manby and Clarence roads, the former National School, p. 467.

c. 2000) of the government's Radar Research Station, established 1942, with dull permanent buildings from 1955.

4. South: The Wyche

A fine stretch of common separates The Wyche from Great Malvern. UPPER WYCHE clinging to the hillside, has typical late C19 Malvern villas along and above Wells Road, s of All Saints (p. 455). EATON GABLES (No. 4 Eaton Road), by *T. Tayler Smith* of London, 1874–5, rock-faced with brick trim, is worth singling out as it attempts to break away from strict adherence to Gothic, with big half-hipped gables and tall ribbed brick chimney. Further uphill, C19 housing for quarry workers. Nearer the crest, a few more large houses off WYCHE ROAD, climbing up to the Wyche cutting.* The most prominent are No. 25 (Wych Crest), by *Haddon Bros*, 1876–7, brick, with three gables containing Venetian windows; and No. 43 (Stonycroft), *c.* 1900, probably by *Albert C. Baker*, cement-faced semi-classical, with balustraded parapet, but a polygonal SE turret.

At LOWER WYCHE, along PEACHFIELD ROAD, s side, facing the Common, large houses of *c.* 1900, the best two roughcast in the Voysey way, with canted bays. No. 20 (Greyroofs) by *A. Troyte Griffith*, 1909, has large mullioned-and-transomed windows and big hipped roof of green slate; brick chimneys. No. 26 (Northwood), built for himself by *G. Lewis Sheppard*, 1903, has a central gable with fleur-de-lys or other floral emblems; roughcast chimneys.

MALVERN WELLS

7040

The medicinal waters of Malvern Wells were appreciated from at least the C16. The Holy Well, according to *Newe Metamorphosis*, was already held in 'wondrous fame' in 1612–13. Yet neither Celia Fiennes nor Defoe mentions Malvern. Commercial exploitation began after Dr John Wall's publication on the purity of the waters, in 1757 (*see* p. 446). From the early C19, especially after 1842, development was overshadowed by that at Great Malvern, 2¼ m. N.

ST PETER. 1835–6 by *R. W. Jearrad* of Cheltenham; now housing. Grey stone with slate roofs: nave, transepts, shallow chancel. Wide lancets between thin buttresses, the principal windows stepped triplets, all emphatically pre-Ecclesiological in style. Pinnacles, paired E–W, flank the W end, above the round-arched doorway. – The WEST GALLERY survives. – STAINED GLASS. Excellent E window by *Heaton, Butler & Bayne*, 1865; lively composition, strong warm colours. – Nave SE by *Morris & Co.*, 1897 (a *Burne-Jones* design); adjoining window by *Hardman*, 1887.

---

*The railway traverses the Hills through a tunnel of 1860–1, 1,567yds (1,433 metres) long, engineer *Stephen Ballard*; renewed 1926.

THE DELL HOUSE below the church, E, early C19 stuccoed, with hoodmoulds and good plaster ceilings, was converted *c.* 1860 as a vicarage for the *Rev. Francis Hopkinson.** He may have designed the oddly detailed front and chunky tower, and certainly carved the ornate Neo-Norman FONT, 1866, now in the lobby; the church had a matching octagonal pulpit. Resited near the entrance, a timber SUMMERHOUSE by *Hopkinson*, with painted lettering, heraldry and map. Opposite, SEVERN LODGE, 1875 for J. Severn Walker, probably by *W.J. Hopkins* or *George Truefitt.*[†] Rock-faced, brick trim, unusual details: above the porch, a huge timber Dec window lighting the staircase; SE turret with steep conical roof.

Further E in Green Lane, the CEMETERY by *E.A. Day*, 1890. Rock-faced Geometrical-style chapel, with apse; deep W porch, also a large N one. – Unusual headstone to Malcolm Hillier Crew †1934, NNW, with bronze portrait and figures of St Francis, a wolf and lamb; by *L.S. Merrifield*.

NW of the church, a Queen Victoria JUBILEE FOUNTAIN, 1887, sandstone, two tiers, the upper with Ionic pilasters. Nearby, in Grundy's Lane, the former FIRE STATION, *c.* 1890, red terracotta with crazy-paving stone gable. WELLS ROAD forms the main N–S axis. Most of its houses, N, are stuccoed early C19. No. 194, W side, has quoins and timber veranda; No. 190 (Hill Mount) behind, gables with pretty bargeboards. A path here leads steeply up to the Holy Well (*see* below). By the roadside stands the splendid WAR MEMORIAL by *C.F.A. Voysey*, 1919; high polygonal base (with typical lettering) and tall shaft, both concave-sided; capital with Byzantine foliage, pelican on top. Houses are then mostly on the E side, at first classical (No. 187 with pedimented doorway and large N addition of 1889; Nos. 181–183 with rustication and Doric porch). Then a good Tudor Gothic group of the 1840s, still stuccoed, with gables and hoodmoulds, before the altered HORNYOLD ARMS. High up, W side, the former ESSINGTON'S HOTEL, plain, four storeys, three bays. Further N, a contrasting roughcast pair: No. 110 (The Ruby), late C18, with wide bow window, and No. 108 (Cob Nash), a simple *Voysey* cottage of 1919 (converted from a coachhouse), with his usual broad-mullioned windows; hipped slate roof. On the hillside above, HIGHFIELD, large, stone, *c.* 1850–60; gabled, Jacobethan windows.

HOLY WELL ROAD, climbing back SW, has an outstanding set of C19 Malvern LAMP-POSTS. At its start, the stone GOTHIC COTTAGE, *c.* 1860. Halfway up, THE WELLS HOUSE, an C18 hotel, painted brick, seven bays and three storeys, with five-bay N extension; later a prep school. At the top, a small square focused on the HOLY WELL, rebuilt 1843; restored 1974. Stuccoed, red brick trim; two-storeyed, round-arched openings, Neo-Norman doorway giving access to the drinking fountain. Bracketed gables, central timber lantern. The brick ROCK

---

* Replaced by a large stone VICARAGE in Hanley Road, NE, 1877.
[†] Both executors of Severn Walker's will, 1875.

HOUSE, at right angles, S, of 1812, provided further accommodation for visitors: three bays and storeys, pedimented doorcase flanked by windows in round-arched recesses.

Now WELLS ROAD S of the church, starting with the CHURCH INSTITUTE by *Albert C. Baker*, 1898–9; stone, Perp doorways, three half-timbered gables. BREDON HOUSE, a Gothic villa of *c.* 1870, stone with red and blue brick patterning, is followed by two tall late C19 Gothic ranges, with good contemporary shopfronts; perhaps all by *Haddon Bros*. Opposite, W, No. 214 (White Lodge), stuccoed, early C19; three bays divided by plain pilasters, S bow.

The same pattern continues further S; stuccoed villas (with later infill) on the higher W side, mostly large late C19 rock-faced ones below the road, E. The largest early C19 example is No. 254 (The Belvedere), four bays with Doric porch, full-height SE bow with tripartite windows. Opposite, two larger Gothic houses have been absorbed by THE ABBEY COLLEGE, formerly Abbey Girls' School (established here 1909). Graham House has straight and half-hipped gables, banded fish-scale roofs, and brick chimneys. The Abbey, dated 'JD 1872', a striking octagonal stair-turret with open timber top, between outer gables; more severe gabled façade with large bay windows towards the view, E. Later school buildings by *Troyte Griffith*. He added a CHAPEL lower down in the terraced grounds in 1913, of Frazzi terracotta slabs, roughcast, with domestic windows and open arch-braced roofs; and, at the S end of the main range, a hall, rock-faced with brick dressings, in 1924, extending it E as a library, 1937–8. He also enlarged the central mid-C19 stuccoed building, in stone and brick, 1929.

No. 262 (Bernard Lodge), opposite the College, with two gables and central stone drainpipe, looks like work of *c.* 1860 by *Benjamin Bucknall* (cf. p. 435). The final stuccoed villa is No. 268 (Roseville), three bays with Doric porch. Beyond the college, E side, the parish SCHOOL by *C. W. Stephens*, 1885, paid for by Eliza Warrington of The Belvedere. Rock-faced, almost symmetrical, an unusual Free Gothic and Renaissance mix: outer gables with large round openings (the S originally the house), high pedimented dormers linked by round arches, ogee window heads.

SHERBORNE TOWER, Hanley Road, ⅜ m. E. Typical Italianate, of the 1840s; brick, stone quoins, square tower, Jacobethan porch.

MAMBLE

6070

Upland rural parish on the Shropshire boundary, with scattered C17 or Georgian farms. It formed part of the West Worcestershire coalfield, the last mine closing in 1972. The Leominster Canal, begun 1791 (engineer: *Thomas Dadford Jun.*), intended to join the Severn at Stourport, reached the Wharf House at Marlbrook (Salop), about 1½ m. WSW of Mamble, in 1794. The project, however, was abandoned after the Southnett Tunnel collapsed a year later.

ST JOHN BAPTIST. Chancel and nave with s aisle, mostly c. 1200; timber bell-turret within the nave w end. The turret itself, partly c. 1600, is now shingled, with splayed-foot broach spire. The supporting framework within has a splendid system of scissor-braced members, dendro-dated to the early C13, contemporary with the deeply splayed lancets in the nave w and NW walls. Renewed lancets in the chancel. Three-bay s arcade with round piers, plainly moulded capitals, arches of one step and one chamfer. It is linked by a string course to the chancel arch, which has capitals with broad flat leaves, but already fillets down the demi-shafts; moulded arch of much variety, hoodmould on headstops. So this may have been the last piece completed. Most other windows are early C14, all renewed in 1880 by *Arthur Blomfield*, who added a SE vestry and provided new roofs. The s aisle, probably built as a chantry chapel, has a C14 tomb recess with flatly crocketed ogee arch; ogee-trefoiled piscina. C17 timber-framed s porch, with brick infill. The red brick N (Blount) chapel, its lower courses c. 1560 with blue brick diapering, the upper parts C18, has been shamefully neglected. Now roofless, the tops of its walls crudely levelled off c. 2000. Blocked four-centred arch to the chancel.

Most FURNISHINGS and encaustic FLOOR TILING, 1880. – Small stone and marble PULPIT by *Jones & Willis*, 1881. – C13 FONT. Round bowl and stem, the latter with a moulding like a shaft-ring. – Timber-framed SCREEN between nave and 'tower space', C16–C17, its lower part with plain mullioned openings. – STAINED GLASS. In the E window a memorable early C14 panel of the Crucifixion; red lattice and blue diapered background. – Two rather gaudy nave N windows by *Henry G. Murray*, 1909. – Two s aisle s by *Kempe & Co.*, 1917–20; a third, s vestry E, 1929. – MONUMENTS. Sandstone effigy of a (Mortimer?) knight, probably c. 1330–40, a slender cross-legged figure wearing a deep kettle hat, his feet on a lion. Exceptionally both arms lie alongside the body, the r. hand on his sword (attached by a guard-chain), the l. resting on his belt-strap, i.e. he has no shield. – Brasses to Sir John Blount †1510 (in armour) and wife Katherine (in widow's dress); 3-ft (0.9-metre) figures. – Simple C15 tomb-chest with quatrefoils. – The standing monument, N chapel NE corner, to Thomas Blount †1561 and later members of his family, has all but disappeared;* one fluted column remains on the back wall, its strapwork-panelled tomb-chest a shapeless brick hulk. On it, instead of the customary effigy, lay a recumbent skeleton, its head on a half-rolled-up mat; this survives, much damaged, in the s aisle recess. – Early C19 tablets, the best Richard Watkins †1805, with urn and branch. That, with draped urn, to Charles Watkins Meysey †1774 and wife Anna Maria †1808 is signed by *R. Blore & Son*. – Two good ledger stones, c. 1736–8.

*As have two fine Blount tablets, c. 1760–70, both probably by *T.F. Pritchard*.

The early C19 brick terrace to the s, Church Cottage and Church
House, conceals a C15 hall house, with three pairs of full
crucks. The open hall was floored in the C17, with large sandstone and brick chimney inserted w of the central bay. Further
E, facing a small green, the SUN AND SLIPPER, mostly early
C17 timber-framed, now entirely rendered; central two-storey
gabled s porch.

SODINGTON HALL, ½ m. SE, on the moated platform of the
house of the Blounts, demolished 1807, is neat and modest
early C19: brick, three bays and storeys, hipped roof. Central
doorway with open pediment on fluted pilasters; hall with
open-well oak staircase with wreathed moulded handrail.

MARTIN HUSSINGTREE   8060

ST MICHAEL. Nave and chancel in one, restored by *Albert
Hartshorne* of London, 1883; he rebuilt the bell-turret and
added a narrow s aisle. Nave w wall possibly Norman, w
window enlarged 1898–9. The chancel has an early C13 N
lancet, stepped late C13 E window (the date 1625 on a reused
corbel above must refer to repairs), and Late Perp s window
with squared tracery lights. Also Perp the nave N wall and
timber N porch (much renewed). Hartshorne repeated the
Perp windows; his three-bay arcade, surprisingly of timber, has
thin paired octagonal pillars. – Some fittings from a restoration by *Preedy*, 1857–8: plain FONT, timber PULPIT, patterned
STAINED GLASS in the E window. w window by *Hardman*,
1899. – MONUMENTS. Several tablets, the best to Thomas
Tomkyns †1675; pilasters with skulls, steep open pediment. –
Also worth noting an ultra-conservative mid-C19 cartouche,
with foliage border, to the Williams family, by *W. Perks* of
Worcester.

The OLD RECTORY, NNE, neat early C18, has Flemish bond
brickwork with very fine joints; five bays, two storeys, hipped
roof. Later three-bay E wing, in keeping.

MARTIN COURT, w, C17 brick, has some unusual details. N front
with central projecting wing with massive stepped chimney-
breast, flanked on both floors by (renewed) cross-windows.
The recessed part, E, must have been the hall, the E wing, with
two lateral chimneys, the kitchen; further w wing added later.
Three-gabled rear, well restored 1956, with inexplicably wide
segmental archway. What was its purpose?

MARTIN HALL FARM, at the corner of Drury Lane ½ m. NE, is
C16; narrow studding on its s cross-wing, w side of its main
hall range jettied. E front refaced in C18–C19 brick; large chimneystack with four clustered diagonal shafts near the junction
with the wing. At its rear a mid-C17 open-well stair with twisted
balusters. Good wind-braced roofs.

HILL HOUSE opposite, probably C17, is also of hall and cross-
wing type, plus a C19 service wing, N, but the timber framing
is hidden by early C19 brick and stucco.

7050

MARTLEY

Not a large village, but of local importance. A royal manor until 1196; in more recent times the centre of a Poor Law Union (formerly with a workhouse by *Sampson Kempthorne*, 1837–8) and, until 1974, of a rural district council.

St Peter. Large, aisleless, of Norman origin. Mid-C15 w tower of very red sandstone, with stepped diagonal buttresses, battlements, and renewed pinnacles. Large three-light Perp w window (restored 1876); tall double-chamfered arch to the nave. The Norman church was built of alternate bands of light red and grey sandstone; these remain intact at the top of the nave walls. Of other detail there survive the flat buttresses (or their stumps), parts of the chamfered string course, and two almost identical nave doorways, both in slight wall projections; one order of columns, shafts with cushion capitals with angle ribs, blocks outside them decorated with small saltire crosses. Arch with a roll between two square mouldings, the inner with similar saltire crosses, the outer with pattern of small lozenges. The date is probably before 1150. Chancel largely rebuilt in the early C13, see the two small, deeply splayed N lancets. N vestry added 1875. Shortly before 1315 a chantry was established within the s side of the chancel. The two-light Dec windows flanking the priest's doorway belonged to it; the doorway, three-centred with continuous roll, must then have been remodelled. Chancel SE window probably slightly earlier. Also early C14, the E window, three lights with cusped intersecting tracery. Two-light Dec windows throughout the nave, mostly renewed. Large Dec-style timber s porch, 1884. The attractive interior owes much to sensitive restoration in 1909, by *Sir Charles Nicholson* (*Nicholson & Corlette*). He exposed the single-framed roofs, also early C14, with probably later tie-beams; only a timber-framed C17 tympanum divides nave and chancel. Damaged C14 piscina with one fine headstop (of a priest?). But what was the large blocked opening near the rood stair, nave SE corner?

Oak PEWS, STALLS, open Dec-style ROOD SCREEN with attached PULPIT, green-and-red-painted ORGAN CASE, all by *Nicholson*, 1909. – TOWER SCREEN by *Nicholson & Rushton*, 1949. – Octagonal FONT. 1875. – Two Jacobean HOUSELING TABLES, with turned baluster legs. – Re-set across the sanctuary, a line of C15 TILES. – Large figure of Christ, carved in cedar by *Leslie Punter*, 1976. – C18 CHARITY BOARDS. – Mid-C19 DECALOGUE above the s door. – Large ROYAL ARMS. George I, dated 1720, painted on boards. – Important WALL PAINTINGS, beginning with extensive mid-C13 masonry patterns in the chancel. Each 'stone' contains a stalked and petalled flower; ornamental borders frame the windows. On the E wall, at dado level beneath a lozenge border, a drapery pattern containing in its top loops a frieze of fabulous C13 or C14 beasts. Above, l., a large canopy, probably C15. – The fine Annunciation, chancel s, is probably mid-C14, connected with the chantry; elegant figures of Mary and Gabriel in red outline, both barefoot, a female donor below. – Paintings on the nave N wall also largely C14, the main scene too decayed to interpret with certainty. Said to be either St Martin on horseback or the Entry into Jerusalem, but more probably the tormenting of Christ. To its E a Crucifixion or Deposition (with unexplained figures including a king and two women). Further E, a fragment of Doubting Thomas (or perhaps the Harrowing of Hell). – STAINED GLASS. Three by *Kempe & Co.*: nave N 1912, S 1909 and 1916. – Nave SW (originally E) by *George Rogers*, 1849, designed by *Preedy*. – Tower W window by *Tom Denny*, 1999, a semi-abstract forest scene; brilliant swirling colours, orange, yellow, blue, and violet. – MONUMENTS. Large stone coffin; (restored) coped lid with incised cross-shaft. – Good alabaster knight, probably Sir Hugh Mortimer †1460; straight-legged, in elaborate armour with Yorkist collar, head on his helm, feet on a lion. Renewed stone base; the front of the tomb-chest is at the former rectory (*see* below). – Good tablets include Robert and Henry Vernon †1724, grey marble with fluted pilasters; Henry Meade †1824, by *R. Westmacott*, simple Grecian; and George Nash †1840, by *J. Stephens*, plain draped sarcophagus. – Good C18 LEDGER STONES, mostly with Nash heraldry.

THE OLD HALL, NE, the former rectory, is an attractive, but quite informal and unassuming house of mellow brick, apparently mostly late C17. This, however, encases an early C14 timber-framed hall, with much altered cross-wings: service wing, S, three-bay solar, N. The latter, probably C15, was originally detached, though standing only five feet away from the hall gable. The whole may be the earliest post-and-truss frame of any domestic building in Worcestershire. The garden front,

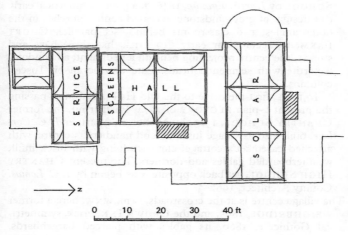

0   10   20   30   40 ft

Martley, former rectory.
Development plan

w, best reveals the form of the medieval house: recessed central hall, s service wing behind a large C17 gabled brick porch with toothed string, N solar wing concealed by an ample bow of *c.* 1800 and extended N by a low C17–C19 service range. Pierced bargeboards of the s wing probably *c.* 1840; twin gables s, with sashed windows and single-storey canted bay of stone, centrally placed.

The entrance front, E, yet more rambling, has various C18–C19 additions, including the rather thin porch. This forms the entrance to the original screens passage, with spere-truss and gallery. Three flattened ogee-headed arches open off its s side. Much mid-C15 painting has been revealed in the SE room, perhaps a winter parlour: heads, black-letter inscriptions, chevron on the undersides of beams. Here also (formerly above the hall fireplace) the front slab of the alabaster TOMB of *c.* 1460 in the church; six frontally placed angels holding painted shields, beneath crocketed ogee-cinquefoiled arches. The alabaster is coated with a sandstone-looking film. The hall was floored in the C16, and a straight open staircase, with turned balusters, built into the gap between it and the solar range. The original hall roof, of the usual two bays, survives. Its tie-beams and knee-braces are enormous, the trusses of very remarkable forms. The swept braces of the central truss resemble a giant cusped arch interrupted by the tie-beam; the spere-truss is hardly less odd, a bite out of the tie-beam completing a Gothic arch defined by the knee-braces. What remains of principal rafters and purlins is extremely light by contrast. The roof pitch is nearly 60 degrees; the present roof was built over the original trusses without destroying them.

The footpath N of the church meets the main road at cast-iron GATES of 1897, flanked by stone urns of 1778, removed from the church tower in 1909.* Adjoining, the former NATIONAL SCHOOL by *Harvey Eginton*, 1846–7, a good symmetrical early C14 design, of grey sandstone; recessed centre, porches in the outer angles, two classrooms behind, set parallel. COURT FARM, w, rectangular early C19 brick, has three bays and storeys, the centre projecting beneath a pediment; all windows tripartite with segmental heads. Late C20 porch on Tuscan columns.

To the E, first the drive to the Old Hall (*see* above), passing the present L-plan RECTORY of 1974. Further on, the former CHANTRY SCHOOL, 1913, by Nicholson's partner *H.C. Corlette*, built also as village institute and handicrafts centre, with attached caretaker's cottage; close studding with brick infill, weatherboarded gables and dormers. The present CHANTRY HIGH SCHOOL, set back opposite, was begun by *L.C. Lomas*, County Architect, 1962–3.

The village centre is at the crossroads, ¼ m. WNW; here a former WEIGHBRIDGE, 1895, and the CROWN INN, brick, symmetrical Gothic, *c.* 1860, its gables with pierced bargeboards.

---

* The other two are in the garden of the former rectory.

Further sw, hemmed in at the corner of Jury Lane, is THE JEWRY, early C17; square-panelled framing, T-plan, tall narrow porch in the angle.

BARBERS FARM, beyond the E end of the village, has a good late C18 brick front, five bays and three storeys; large canted bay on the W return.

LAUGHERN HOUSE, ⅝ m. ESE, lost amid enabling development of *c*. 2000. Late C18 brick, L-plan, two-and-a-half storeys. Five-bay entrance front distinguished by an ashlar-faced central bay: lofty pedimented doorcase on four attached Doric columns, tripartite window with two thin Ionic columns above, top pediment. Ground-floor windows with moulded stone frames and straight entablatures. Several doorcases with broken pediments within. At the rear, much-renewed C16–C17 timber framing.

THE NOAK, ½ m. NW. Of two parts, both brick with stone dressings. The front range, symmetrical Tudor Gothic, was built for John Nash, 1853, with gabled wings flanking a narrower recessed gabled centre; canted oriel above the tripartite recessed entrance, which has four-centred arches and blind quatrefoil frieze. Wings with canted ground-floor bays, windows with square hoodmoulds above. At the rear, the early C17 house is also of three storeys, the narrower top one with coped parapet; cross- or single windows, linked by dripmoulds stepping up over them, two-storeyed canted bays faced in stone. C17–C19 outbuildings.

Extensive parish, with superb scenery along its W edge, overlooking the Teme valley. Many good FARMHOUSES; only a few can be mentioned here. The earliest may be TOMKINS FARM, ⅔ m. SE, its plain roughcast exterior hiding a cruck-framed structure, probably C15. Other notable timber-framed examples include UPPER HOLLING FARM, ⅞ m. S, probably C16, brick-infilled, with frilly mid-C19 bargeboards, and early C19 L-plan farm buildings; and BROOK COURT, 1⅛ m. NNE, early C17, to an E-plan, with wobbly square-panelled framing. PUDFORD FARM, 1⅓ m. NW, has exceptionally a sandstone W front, with irregular mullioned windows, partly masked by outbuildings. The best-looking brick farmhouses are probably THE TEE, ⅞ m. WNW, five bays, early C17; HAMBRIDGE FARM, 1⅛ m. WNW, three bays, later C18; and HILL TOP FARM, at Horsham, 1⅝ m. SW, probably of the 1820s: large and square, three bays divided by plain giant pilasters, fluted Doric porch. LOWER HILL TOP FARM, almost opposite, also early C19, has good attached outbuildings including two well-preserved hop kilns.

On BERROW HILL, 1 m. SW, is an elongated, waisted HILL-FORT, probably early to middle Iron Age; its rampart follows the contours of the hill. There may have been a surrounding ditch, with the entrance on a very steep slope near the SE corner.

MIDDLE LITTLETON
North and Middle Littleton

St Nicholas. Severely restored by *Preedy*, 1871–5; he rebuilt the nave N wall and most of the chancel. Lancets here, one (s) in the nave plus its simply chamfered doorways, and the W tower's lowest stage all suggest an early C13 origin. Chancel E window of stepped trefoiled lancets, a late C13 form. Of the C14 the N transept, with ogee-headed piscina, and ample S porch, originally two-storeyed. Most of the tower is good Perp, with battlements, gargoyles, corner pinnacles; also one nave S window. Ambitious battlemented early C16 S chapel with three-light windows, straight-headed, cinquefoil-cusped; Thomas Smith (†1532) endowed it as a chantry (his brass is lost). Inside the C19 predominates, with encaustic floor tiling and heavy arch-braced roofs. The tower arch, with huge leaf spandrels and crenellated top (cf. Offenham), might be a re-set Perp doorway; it sits comfortably, however, between lancet-like recesses. – REREDOS. By *Preedy*, 1876; gabled, foliated marble shafts, painted metal panels. – FONT. Norman, round; tapering bowl with one band of thin decorated lozenges (cf. Suckley). – PULPIT. Hexagonal; Perp panels. – PEWS. A complete C15–C16 set, much renewed; moulded straight tops, traceried bench ends. – C14–C15 TILES on the N transept floor and beneath the chancel NE lancet. – Solid C15–C16 CHEST with one surviving rose-decorated finial.

CHURCHYARD CROSS. C15: three steps, base and shaft; cross-head by *Preedy*, 1871. – Also no doubt his, the attractively gawky LYCHGATE.

MANOR HOUSE, W. Beautiful, reposeful mid-C17, with short gabled wings; of Blue Lias stone with Cotswold dressings. Three-light windows in each of the three gables, four-light with king mullions below. Central Tudor-arched doorway and two flanking three-light windows connected by a continuous string course, instead of hoodmoulds. This continues round the E return, but does not appear at all on the W wing, implying that the latter may be earlier despite the apparent symmetry; it stretches back quite far, ending in a hipped N gable. At the rear the recessed centre has one large ground-floor window, of six lights. Some inserted C18 sashes.

Behind the manor house is the great TITHE BARN of Evesham Abbey, no doubt the 'very fine' grange built at Littleton towards the end of the abbacy of John de Brokehampton (1282–1316). Of thinly coursed Lias with Cotswold stone dressings and stone tiled roof; eleven bays, with straight buttresses, long ventilating loops (widely splayed inside), and many putlog holes. Originally two large S wagon porches stood opposite much shallower N ones; only the W pair, front and rear, survive. The SW porch gable and main E gable have striking clover-leaf finials, copied on the others when *F.W.B. Charles* restored the barn for the National Trust, 1976–8. The porch has a rounded double-chamfered entrance; small pointed doorway in its W return. Magnificent interior, 136 ft (42

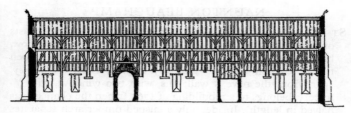

Middle Littleton, tithe barn.
Section

metres) long, 32 ft (10 metres) wide, some 40 ft (12 metres) high. The framing consists of one aisled bay each end and, dividing the nine intermediate bays, eight base-cruck trusses carrying doubled-collar and tie-beam trusses.* Triple purlin roof with two tiers of wind-braces throughout; the lower tier springs from the cruck blades and rises to the roof-plate, the upper from the upper principal rafters to the top purlins. Altogether a remarkable achievement of medieval carpentry, especially considering the indifferent quality of the available timber. None of the four end aisle-posts, for example, are single timbers; all are scissor-scarfed at about two-thirds height. – Low attached C19 farm buildings at both ends, the SE with a well-preserved cider press.

Former NATIONAL SCHOOL, further w, by *George Hunt*, 1872–3; polychromatic brick, still proclaimed on the attached house and main schoolroom, hidden by rendering on the altered classroom (and large addition of 1894).

Most of MIDDLE LITTLETON consists of Evesham RDC housing by their surveyor *R. J. Atkinson*. A group of concrete slab-faced 'Airey' houses of 1948 (in Manor Road) is particularly prominent. At the w end of School Lane, six brick terraces of four, 1914, rather more attractive. – ASH GROVE, NE of the church, by *Robert Harvey* of Stratford-upon-Avon, 1964, to a square plan, is rendered above a coursed rubble plinth; broad hipped roof, chains instead of down-pipes.

The centre of NORTH LITTLETON, built around an elongated hexagon, has C17–C19 Lias houses, and occasional C16–C17 timber framing. The best group, s end of WEST SIDE, flanks the early C18 POST OFFICE: brick, stone dressings, hipped roof. WALNUT HOUSE, further N, altered mid-C17, has a two-light cusped C14–C15 window re-set in its s gable-end. In the garden, a circular medieval DOVECOTE with conical roof, containing nearly 200 nest holes. In EAST SIDE, behind the C17–C19 OLD FARM, a large C17 BARN (now housing), perhaps incorporates timbers from a tithe barn built here by Abbot John Ombersley (1367–79).

---

*Early C20 aisle-posts and cross-beams were replaced in 1976 by thin stainless-steel rods.

NAUNTON BEAUCHAMP

ST BARTHOLOMEW. Two-stage Perp w tower; damaged beasts on the first offset of its diagonal buttresses, large w window, blunt parapet. Perp-style nave and chancel in one, with open timber s porch, all 1896–7 by *W.J. Hopkins & A.B. Pinckney*, apart from the nave N wall; this, with two windows with Y-tracery, belongs to a rebuilding of 1767 (when the chancel was halved in length). Inside, only a cusped timber arch separates nave and chancel. – FONT. Massive octagonal bowl, perhaps C14. – PULPIT. Probably *c.* 1600, with angle balusters; moulded panels, loose cornucopia and leaf motifs above, the usual blank arches below. – COMMUNION RAILS. C17; tall, close-set balusters. – A couple of C16 BENCHES, nave w end, with crude linenfold and moulded top rails. – Under the tower, C17 panelling with heraldry, from the Littleton FAMILY PEW. – Brass eagle LECTERN by *Jones & Willis*, 1896–7. – MONUMENTS. Humphrey Littleton †1624; small tablet with pretty strapwork surround and long inscription.* – Contrasting adjoining tablets: one *c.* 1821 Grecian, by *J. Stephens*, the other a decorated oval, *c.* 1747. – Outside, E of the chancel, good chest tomb to John Hunt †1826, within cast-iron railings.

Attractive VILLAGE with C17 timber framed houses. The OLD RECTORY (altered *c.* 1730), s of the church, and two at the E end, OLD HOUSE and THE ELMS, all have regular square panels, the last enlarged in Tudor style *c.* 1840.

NAUNTON HOUSE, ½ m. ESE. Late C18 brick farmhouse, five bays and three storeys, surrounded by small-scale C17 timber-framed farm buildings.

NAUNTON COURT, ¼ m. WSW. Large timber-framed L-plan farmhouse, two storeys plus attics, on a formerly moated site. The s wing, partly stone, must survive from the house of the Littletons (or Lytteltons), *c.* 1600. It has an ambitious two-storey canted bay, E, the lower floor with transom, the upper without; moulded string course, ornamental cresting. The lower room, with beams with fine plaster vine-leaf decoration, was no doubt the parlour, the upper probably the great chamber. The hall must have been in main N range, all thoroughly remodelled, presumably in the C17: mostly narrow studding, half-hipped N gable.

SEAFORD GRANGE, 1⅛ m. SSW. Gabled Tudor Gothic, built for himself *c.* 1850 by *Richard Varden*, who, because of failing eyesight, gave up architecture and engineering to pioneer large-scale fruit farming; diapered brick, grouped lancets, rows of square chimneys.

NETHERTON
¾ m. NE of Elmley Castle

Brick hamlet, with some C17 timber-framing. A medieval chapelry of Cropthorne.

*His tomb, erected *c.* 1590, is at Kings Norton, Birmingham.

The ruined Norman CHAPEL, immediately E of Netherton Farmhouse, was probably disused by the C14; converted to a house in the C16–C17, used as a barn by 1738. Nave and chancel walls survive to eaves level, with an extensive gap, N side. Late Norman N doorway, its surviving shaft (E) keeled, with grotesque-head capital. Arch with typically late complicated motifs, the outer order with deeply undercut zigzag forming lozenges containing flowers, the inner elongated hexagons broken round an angle (cf. Eckington). Internal arch with two triangular crenellation chains, one, upside down, interlocking with the other. S doorway with earlier Norman tympanum (re-set in the early C20), a splendid winged dragon with insect-like body and long tail with forked tip.* Norman windows W of both doorways, the N one, with continuous roll moulding, the best preserved. C17 chimney at the W gable, serving fireplaces on two levels. Chancel probably early C13, see one small S lancet. Late C13 E window, a broader lancet with trefoiled head. Various C16–C17 openings. The double bellcote above the chancel arch collapsed c. 1907, bringing down the whole wall. Ruins consolidated 1920.

NETHERTON FARM, rebuilt 1828, is brick, its higher gabled W wing perhaps incorporating earlier fabric. An outbuilding N of the chapel has a small re-set Norman window, with continuous roll. Large mid-C19 farm buildings, N, to a U-plan, the long N barn with central gable and roof turret; partly infilled in the 1920s, when two brick silos were also added, NW.

NEWLAND

7040

The BEAUCHAMP ALMSHOUSES (or Beauchamp Community) form a most attractive group along the S side of Newland Common. Founded 'for twenty-four decayed agricultural labourers' through the bequests of John, third Earl Beauchamp of Madresfield Court (†1853) and his first wife Charlotte (†1846), but the stone church (also meant for parish use) and adjoining brick quadrangle were not built until 1861–4; architect *P.C. Hardwick* (cf. Madresfield). Later additions have not spoiled the open S aspect but have slightly impaired the N front. Here the steeple rising from behind the church is eclipsed by the imposing brick tower above the entrance, rather too high and broad for it; the rest appears somewhat confused behind its modernizing adjustments of 1963–4, despite the fine array of brick chimneys.

ST LEONARD, *Hardwick*'s church, consecrated 1864, lies at the NE corner. Of snecked Bisley limestone, comprising nave with N porch (for parishioners) and long chancel with S aisle and vestry. Beyond this, the square (vaulted) lowest stage of the steeple serves as a SE lobby for the almspeople. Above, it is immediately broached to a tall octagon with elongated Dec

---

*Perhaps C12, second quarter; cf. tympana at Egloskerry, Cornwall, and Wynford Eagle, Dorset (Neil Stratford).

bell-openings, capped by a short crocketed spire. Windows in Geometrical Dec-style, rose windows at the nave w end and at each end of the chancel aisle (also two s dormers, with half-timbered gables). Overwhelmingly elaborate interior, completely covered by wall paintings and with rich stained glass; James Skinner, first vicar and warden 1861–77, and his successor George Cosby White, were much involved in working out the overall scheme. The most remarkable architectural feature, the four-bay arcade between chancel and aisle, is early French Gothic in style, with alternate pairs of light and dark marble columns; foliage capitals of alabaster. This separated the female pensioners, in the aisle, from the men, who sat behind the choir stalls. Chancel arch and windows with foliated shafts, floors with *Godwin* encaustic tiles, open timber roofs, gilt and stencilled. In the nave w wall a romantic canted oriel, gabled as if it were part of a castle, connects with the infirmary on the upper floor of the adjoining matron's house.

Elaborate FURNISHINGS including the REREDOS, with Crucifixion scene in high relief by *Boulton* (not painted until 1928); fine SEDILIA with crocketed gables, a memorial to Skinner †1881; and stone CHANCEL SCREEN, with sunk panels of the Virtues and iron cresting and gates, linked to the round marble PULPIT. – FONT. Cylindrical bowl, *c.* 1200, with top band of chip-carved stars, originally in the church of St Thomas adjoining Great Malvern Priory; marble base by *Hardwick*. – The first of the WALL PAINTINGS, the Last Judgement above the chancel arch, was executed by *Preedy*, 1865. Later largely renewed by *Clayton & Bell*, whose work covering the rest of the interior, utilizing Thomas Gambier Parry's 'spirit fresco' technique, continued into the 1880s. Their paintings are in red outline with some green and blue; more extensive blocks of solid colour in the chancel. Large biblical scenes at upper level, smaller scenes or single figures below, 'stoning' or marbling to dado height. – STAINED GLASS. E window by *Hardman*, 1863–4. – w rose by *Lavers & Barraud*, *c.* 1864. – The rest all by *Clayton & Bell*: chancel again 1864, nave completed 1869. – BRASS, chancel aisle, to the founder, John, third Earl Beauchamp, by *Hardman*, 1853; richly enamelled heraldry. Originally in Madresfield church.

The church has its own LYCHGATE, N, built with timber from the C14 church; here also an early C20 memorial CROSS. The ALMSHOUSES are best seen from the s, where they form a large, picturesque open quadrangle. The church's spire marks the NE corner, answered almost immediately w (beyond the matron's, now chaplain's, house) by the lofty oblong GATE-TOWER, dated 1882, apparently built to Hardwick's original design exhibited at the Royal Academy, 1861; the gateway at first had a low hipped cap. A far more effective foil here than on the N front, it is of redder brick with some terracotta; blind trefoiled parapet, recessed half-timbered top with steep French pavilion roof. The rest of the N RANGE and all the W RANGE,

extending generously round these two sides of the turfed quadrangle, comprise the original almshouses of 1862–3. Trefoiled
windows of three lights, half-timbered gables, wide arched
entrances to each block of four dwellings, the stairs to each
upper two lit by quirky pyramid-roofed dormers. Nicely varied
brick chimneys, many twisted.

The E RANGE has a low brick corridor or cloister of 1876,
linking the church to the large warden's lodge, SE corner. On
its E side, first a small CHAPEL of square-panelled framing,
with tension braces, built as a mortuary by W.J. Hopkins, 1865,
reusing timbers from the C14 church (see below); two- or three-
light trefoiled windows, stained glass again by Clayton & Bell.
To its S, also projecting E, the LIBRARY of 1910, probably by
C.F. Whitcombe; high-set mullioned windows, good plaster
compartment ceiling. The cloister leads to the BOARDROOM,
with reticulated three-light windows, W and E, five-bay false
hammerbeam roof, and stone fireplace with foliage carving, its
moulded overmantel enclosing the founder's portrait. This
forms the N wing of the WARDEN'S LODGE, the first part completed, in 1863, with gables, canted bay windows with top
trefoil friezes, timber oriels, and tall patterned brick chimneys.
Beyond the E range lies PYNDAR COURT, housing by the
Mason Richards Partnership, 1986–7, a watered-down version of
the C19 buildings. To its S, reached by a footpath along its E
side, lies the burial ground that surrounded the medieval
timber-framed church, demolished 1864–5; a massive CROSS
of 1866, no doubt by Hardwick, marks the site of the altar.

At its centre of the open S SIDE of the quadrangle, in axis
with the gatehouse, stand wrought-iron GATES, bought 1871
for Madresfield Court, said to be part of the C18 choir gates
of Cologne Cathedral; openwork iron piers, scrolled overthrow.

Hardwick's ranges continue W of the quadrangle, with two
more blocks of four. Then the LYGON ALMSHOUSES, an
extension of 1889 with similar central arched entrance and trefoiled five-light windows. Further W, the ST BARNABAS
CLERGY HOUSES, two detached blocks of 1900 and 1908,
each with four gables; plainer, with flat bay windows.

THE GRANGE, to the E, is early C19 brick, three bays, the pedimented doorway with fluted pilasters and frieze; similar rear
doorway. Lower E wing. BENLAKE, further SE, must be a little
later: brick, two-storey bows with tripartite windows divided
by fluted pilasters, central pedimented doorway with engaged
fluted Doric columns.

Former CHURCH SCHOOL, ⅛ m. N. By F.W. Hunt, 1879, small
schoolroom with attached house; brick, tile-hung gables.

NORGROVE COURT

Feckenham

0060

An intriguing complicated house, subdivided in the early C19,
restored for the Sinclair family in the 1970s by James Reid and

Norgrove Court.
Drawing of south front, c. 1913

John Bucknall. The first view of the S FRONT, dated 1649 on an eaves bracket, suggests a progressive house of this Commonwealth date (notably so for Worcestershire), presumably built for William Cookes, High Sheriff in 1651. English bond brick, with sandstone dressings; two storeys of cross-windows beneath a big hipped roof, its 2+4+2 bays reflecting the layout of rooms behind. But from the middle rises a bold hexagonal chimney, instead of a cupola. And there are other oddities: firstly the lack of an entrance; secondly, the rhythm of windows is really 2+1+2+1+2, the single axes given elongated French upper windows. Their wooden balconies, as well as the four dormers, are of the 1970s (when the roof was rebuilt to one overall span). Disturbances in the brickwork imply there may have been doorways under the original balconies; an early C19 drawing shows one beneath the l. balcony, probably a garden entrance. This may mark the site of the screens passage of an earlier house, the wings of which are suggested by the closer spacing of the outer window pairs. The E RETURN, of five bays, is again symmetrical; plain central entrance, the two lower N bays blank because of a former single-storey wing. The fenestration of the N FRONT, though, is amazingly chaotic: windows of all shapes and sizes, at varying heights, some parts set above cellars. The tallest opening is a staircase window (above a C17 doorway, perhaps from the E front). Yet the brickwork perpetuates the regularity of S and E sides, emphasized by the autocratic hipped roof. An estate plan of 1591 shows this front as a broad U-plan. An explanation for all these anomalies may be that the centre of such a (timber-framed?) late medieval house was infilled, c. 1600, with a new staircase and high-level parlour, the whole being then encased or rebuilt in brick. In that case work in 1649 would have been limited to the provision of the massive hipped roof, hence the unusual position of the datestone, and the discreet regularization of the rest (albeit with limited success on the less conspicuous N front).

The INTERIOR provides further enlightenment. The staircase has splat balusters and solid newels with openwork tops, clearly *c*. 1600, probably re-set in the early C19. Also of *c*. 1600 two fine overmantels in the first-floor rooms, E side, the SE with splendid broad strapwork with caryatids, based on the titlepage of Vredeman de Vries's *Caryatidum*, 1565. Another fireplace, in the corner of the panelled parlour (now reached from the staircase, W side, at mezzanine level), has a geometrical overmantel in high relief. The hall behind the central four bays of the S front presumably follows the footprint of the late medieval great hall, horizontally subdivided *c*. 1600 to provide a first-floor great parlour. The odd arrangement of the NW part of the house, only accessible by its own modest entrance, confirms the pre-1649 origins. A very large fireplace at lower level indicates that this was its kitchen. Several (blocked) segment-headed doorways suggest that the mezzanine parlour in the infilled section was approached by an internal stair from the hall, the main staircase providing the processional route from hall to great chamber (and the rooms to its E).

NORTH CLAINES *see* CLAINES

NORTH PIDDLE 9050

Small village with timber-framed farms, scattered along a square of lanes.

ST MICHAEL. Rebuilt 1875–6 by *Henry Rowe*. Small, well-proportioned; coursed rubble, ashlar dressings, features mostly Middle Pointed, i.e. style of *c*. 1300. Buttressed chancel, the nave unbuttressed apart from the W end, with forceful plate tracery beneath a bellcote. Open timber N porch. S vestry enlarged 1893. Brick-faced interior, painted white; good roofs: high scissor-braced to the nave, the chancel arch-braced. Moulded chancel arch on pink marble foliated corbel shafts. – Original furnishings, including panelled stone PULPIT. – Plain octagonal FONT, perhaps C14. – The chancel PISCINA is a reused C13–C14 bust corbel. – Six C15 TILES, nave W end. – STAINED GLASS. Excellent E window, no doubt *Burlison & Grylls*, *c*. 1880.

NORTON AND LENCHWICK 0040

ST EGWIN, Norton. A possession of Evesham Abbey from the early C8. Of coursed Lias with oolite dressings. Part of the nave N wall may be all that remains of the church consecrated (or re-dedicated) in 1295. C14 N transept: large N window with unusual Dec tracery (cf. Dumbleton, Glos.), good pointed wagon roof. Perp chancel, its windows with very large lozenge-shaped hoodmould stops. Nave in similar Perp style, almost entirely rebuilt 1843–4, when the S porch was added. Four-light Perp N window, with round hoodmould stops, from Bengeworth (p. 307). Later Perp W tower with battlements and pinnacles; splays at its E corners allow light to two small nave W windows. Modest tower arch. Further restored, and large NW vestry added, by *C.F.Whitcombe*, 1905–6.

FONT. Octagonal, Perp, quatrefoils on bowl and stem. –
LECTERN. A splendid, mysterious piece, dug up in 1813 in Evesham Abbey churchyard, described in *Archaeologia* the year after; installed here, on a shaft by *William Forsyth*, 1865. Of Wenlock marble, in this as in the whole programme and details of the carving a companion to that at Crowle (p. 250). Seated caryatid-like figure of a bishop as its centre, rich leaf scrolls either side; at the back, two faun-like heads. The main figure and its function are Italian-looking, reminiscent of ambones, such as that of S. Ambrogio, Milan, *c.* 1100, but the foliage is English. It may be the *lectricium capituli* made for Abbot Adam (1161–89), and if so belongs to his last years. – PULPIT. Jacobean. Separate back panel with low, broad, blank arch, Jacobean too, but different; another has bold reticulation, probably early Gothic Revival. – PEWS. 1906. – Sanctuary refurnished 1887; crudely Gothic SEDILIA, imported PANELLING with early C16 linenfold. – ROYAL ARMS. George III. – STAINED GLASS. Chancel E and SE by *Clayton & Bell*, 1870–1. – Chancel SW also 1871, but by *George Rogers* (also probably chancel N, *c.* 1840–50). – These two, like the nave SE by *Preedy*, *c.* 1855, sadly lost their backgrounds in the mid C20. – Two other nave S windows: by *Burlison & Grylls*, 1890; by *Henry Payne*, 1906, splendid Arts and Crafts. – Fine TABLET accompanying the latter, to Mary Beatrice Boulter †1902, by *Eric Gill*.*

MONUMENTS. Thomas Bigg †1581 and wife Maudlen, sister of Sir Philip Hoby of Bisham (Berks.); finely detailed. Recumbent stone effigies, hands at prayer. Gadrooned tomb-chest with strapwork piers; six kneeling children, each partly in profile, partly frontal. – Sir Thomas Bigg †1613 and wife Ursula; probably by *Samuel Baldwin*. Large kneeling effigies facing across a prayer-desk, beneath a panelled arch flanked by black Composite columns. Nine children kneel against the high base. – Sir Thomas Bigg †1621, probably also by *Baldwin*. Recumbent alabaster effigy. Four Composite columns of black touch support a flat canopy with shield and emblems. – Two sets of funerary armour and four banners above this and the late C16 monument are C17 memorials to the Craven family (who bought the estate from the Biggs, 1625); HATCHMENT

---

*Nearby tablet to her parents by Gill's nephew, *John Skelton*, 1948; one in the porch by another Gill pupil, *Joseph Cribb*.

to Sir William Craven, 1655. – Elizabeth Craven †1687; nice stone cartouche.

In the CHURCHYARD, W, two headstones by *Eric Gill*: Hannah Boulter †1909, low with crucifix, in his early Expressionist style; Rev. W.C. Boulter †1912, tall, slender, more sentimental. – LYCHGATE. 1919. Churchyard entrance made up in 1871 from the nave N doorway (replaced by the Bengeworth window). Unusual Perp arch, a cusped half-hexagon (cf. the rebuilt nave S doorway); hoodmould on big heads.

In CHURCH LANE, NE, a good collection of C17 timber-framed and thatched cottages. Larger black-and-white houses in EVESHAM ROAD, further N. Nos. 51–54, L-plan, have a probably C15 S range, with curved bracing, prettily adapted as a school in the mid C19; late C17 N wing. Nos. 47–51 also seem to be C15, close-studded, enlarged in the C17. Nos. 41–43, C17 U-plan, have a flat front to the road, the later N section higher. More C17 thatched cottages before the road turns E. Here NORTON FARM, mid-C18 brick, three bays, centre with narrow pediment; former GRANARY, contemporary but timber-framed, on staddle stones.

Former NATIONAL SCHOOL, ¼ m. SSW, beyond 1920s council housing. 1872–3 by *George Hunt*; brick, Gothic, bellcote between schoolroom and house.

LENCHWICK, ½ m. WSW, mostly C20, has some C16–C17 timber-framed survivors along its main street, between the early C19 MANOR FARM, of stone, N end, and the mid-C18 BLACK MONK FARM, austere brick, S. TYTHE BARN COTTAGES, W side, are a good conversion by *Pemberton & Bateman*, 1976.

WOOD NORTON HALL, 1½ m. WSW. The estate was bought in 1872 by the Duc d'Aumale (fourth son of King Louis Philippe of France), who lived here from 1857, employing *George Hunt* to adapt an existing house (with detached chapel, 1865, now demolished). In 1896–7 his great nephew (and heir to his claim to the French throne) the Duc d'Orléans built a large new house to the S, costing £100,000. Designed by *G.H. Hunt*, it is gabled and vaguely Jacobethan, brick with freestone dressings, some half-timbering with pargeted panels. The entrance front, E, is quite picturesque, with applied French details, including a splendidly carved stone coat of arms beneath the N gable (stepped with large polygonal pinnacles). Long asymmetrical garden front, S, rather dull; fine views across the Avon. Inside, most rooms are lined with expensive carved oak, with ubiquitous fleurs-de-lys; upper floor restored after a fire in 1940. The house was converted to a hotel in 1994 by *Norman Lucy*, staff architect to the BBC, which bought the estate in 1939, later developing a conference centre in the grounds, E, with large residential blocks: 1955, *c.* 1975–80, and 1984.

Plain brick N LODGE, no doubt by *George Hunt*. More picturesque S LODGE by *G.H. Hunt*, 1898, with splendid C18-style wrought-iron gates from Orleans House, Twickenham, probably made for the Duc d'Aumale by *J. Starkie Gardner, c.* 1864.

Overthrow renewed after removal of the royal arms during the Second World War.

CURSUS, about ¾ m. ENE. The site, visible only from the air, lies in a field adjacent to the former Evesham–Harvington railway.

8050

NORTON-JUXTA-KEMPSEY

ST JAMES. Quite large, Lias with sandstone dressings, the first impression Victorian, resulting from restoration by *W.J. Hopkins* (with *Ewan Christian*), 1874–5. Nave and chancel, however, are Norman. In the nave N wall, a small Norman window and plain blocked doorway; larger round-arched window further W, probably later, perhaps representing an extension soon after *c.* 1200. The Norman S doorway also remains, renewed and re-set: one order of shafts with scalloped capitals, roll-moulded arch. Norman masonry may also survive in the chancel, see the quoins; side windows simple C14, reused when *Christian* rebuilt the chancel for the Ecclesiastical Commissioners. *Hopkins* was generally responsible for the restoration, adding a N chancel vestry and Dec-style S aisle, with timber porch. His also the top stage of the W tower, with pierced quatrefoil parapet; lower part probably late C14, with small Perp W window. Inside the Victorian style, or rather *a* Victorian style, is dominant, the tone set by Hopkins's characteristic four-bay S arcade, its round piers with gargantuan moulded capitals; good S aisle roof. Sharply pointed chancel arch.

Plain octagonal FONT, perhaps C13, cut down from a round Norman one. – Good Bath stone PULPIT, Dec-Perp wine-glass style, by the *Bromsgrove Guild*, 1929. – REREDOS, carved stone and mosaic, *c.* 1880. – ORGAN. 1912 by *Nicholson & Co.* – STAINED GLASS. E window by *Hardman*, 1877. – Chancel S by *Shrigley & Hunt, c.* 1906. – S aisle E *Kempe & Co.*, 1908. – The nave NW has a C17 Netherlandish panel, probably Joseph in the well, amongst early to mid-C19 glass. – MONUMENTS. Thomas Brewer †1810; grieving woman hunched over a pedestal. – Several by *J. Stephens*: Benjamin Hooke †1848, large draped Grecian sarcophagus; Thomas Hooke †1864, Gothic. – In the CHURCHYARD, chest tombs of *c.* 1800 and a very large Carrara marble cross to Emily Childers †1875, by *E.J. Physick*, 1877.

The OLD VICARAGE, W, is also by *Hopkins*, 1875–6. Red brick, stone dressings, steep gables, big tiled roof; Gothic detail, round timber oriel where the NE service range adjoins.

The parish is mostly C20 Worcester suburban. A few scattered C17–C18 farmhouses remain. The neatest, NEWLANDS FARM, NW of the church beyond the M5, is late C18 brick, three bays, two-and-a-half storeys, the outer windows of the main floors tripartite with rusticated lintels.

NORTON BARRACKS, a little further W, 1875–6 by *Major H.C. Seddon*, Assistant Director of Works (Barracks), the base of the

Worcestershire Regiment until 1962. Long, almost symmetrical entrance range, red brick with stone bands and dressings, converted to apartments when Neo-vernacular housing replaced the rest, c. 1994. Keep-like central gatehouse with square corner turrets, battlemented with false machicolations; fire-proof, with cantilevered dog-leg stairs with cast-iron balusters and jack-arch ceilings, it contained the armoury and guard house. Flanking wings, ending in stepped gables, housed offices and officers' quarters.* Assorted windows, their lintels with notable stop-chamfered undersides. Good boundary wall with iron railings, extending E, then N in plainer style. At the rear (where the entrance range has two severe battlemented porches), an attractive cricket green with small brick PAVILION, again with stepped gables.

At LITTLEWORTH, ¾ m SSE, a WESLEYAN CHAPEL of 1881, small, brick, round-arched windows; builder: *William Patrick* of Worcester.

ODDINGLEY 9050

St JAMES. Small Lias church, C15, mostly tactfully rebuilt by *R.C. Hussey*, 1860–1,† for J.H. Galton of Hadzor (p. 332). C17 W tower, with paired bell-openings and plain pointed arch to the nave. It probably truncated the nave doorways (four-centred S, blocked N), now hard up against it; the Perp W window must be the nave W window re-set. Transept end window traceries, if restored accurately, imply a C14 date. All other windows are in C15 Perp style. Renewed timber S porch. The interior retains its medieval atmosphere, despite the ruthless stripping of nave and transept walls, and thorough rebuilding of the chancel. Moulded wooden arch to the S transept, with small opening, E, no doubt for the rood-loft stair (now giving access to the C19 pulpit). – Octagonal FONT. C15, re-cut; against the underside, alternating roses and fetterlocks. – PEWS. Plainly moulded top rails; basically C17. – Iron HOUR-GLASS STAND, now attached to the front bench. – COMMUNION RAIL, again C17; tall, narrowly spaced balusters. – STAINED GLASS. The E window has a complete late C15 ensemble, albeit reassembled, probably by the *Twygge-Wodshawe* Malvern workshop: St Katherine, two bishops (the upper wrongly labelled St Martin), composite female saint; kneeling donors with *Orate* inscriptions below, then two kneeling priests. – Chancel N: St Mary (restored) and God the Father, from a Coronation of the Virgin; other C15 fragments opposite. – Sweet little BRASS (from Hadzor) to R.C. Galton †1866, by *Hardman*; his wife and children kneel before his body.

48

---

* Three gabled brick terraces, ⅓ m. SSW, by *J.H. Williams*, 1886–7, provided further married quarters.

† 1851, according to *Kelly's Directory*.

The church, delightfully secluded, is reached by a lime avenue, at the rear of the brick mid-C19 CHURCH FARM. Nearby otherwise, only the early C17 timber-framed OLD FARM-HOUSE, SE, the Worcester and Birmingham Canal, and railway. In the VILLAGE, ½ m. NW, POUND FARM is C17 timber-framed, L-plan. Opposite, FARTHING PIECE, a C17 cottage with a pair of fine brick chimneys, late C15, no doubt reused: spiral-fluted, concave octagonal caps.

Former SCHOOL, I m. N next to C20 houses. Plain brick school-room and attached house, by *John Smith* of Droitwich, for J.H. Galton, 1855.

0040

OFFENHAM

A possession of Evesham Abbey from the early C8. Now a market-gardening centre with acres of greenhouses.

ST MARY AND ST MILBURGH. Rebuilt 1860–1 by *Frederick Preedy*,[*] apart from the C15 W tower, with battlements, gargoyles, and tall pinnacles. Preedy's church, chancel, nave, N aisle and S porch, has plate or bar tracery and patterned tiled roofs; fanciful foliage carving on the E window and N aisle E rose. Quite an elaborate interior: further foliage carving (by *Earp*), much polished Blue Lias and red Devonshire marble. Four-bay N arcade with circular polished Lias piers with moulded capitals, alternating with ashlar ones, octagonal and foliated. Delightful C15 tower arch like an over-sized doorway (or is it re-set?): two-centred, large leaves in the spandrels, square hoodmould with fleuron frieze (cf. Middle Littleton). – FONT. Octagonal, Perp; large bowl with fleurons in quatrefoils. – Other furnishings by *Preedy*, notably the alabaster REREDOS, and PULPIT with heavy open parapet with polished Lias and red marble columns. – Fine STAINED GLASS by *Preedy*: E and two N aisle N windows, 1861, N aisle E rose, 1864, tower W lancet, 1868.

Attractive village centre, to a T-plan, centred on a very tall, striped and tapering MAYPOLE (last renewed 1987). The stem, MAIN STREET, has the church, W, and a fine display of thatched timber framing further N, E side: MILBURGH HOUSE, C16–C17, L-plan, much restored; THE MALT HOUSE, C17 with charming C19 bargeboards; then a long row of seven C17–C18 cottages. Another good C17 thatched group frames the maypole. In Gibbs Lane, NE, the contrasting AVONCROFT FARM, with flat late C18 façade of roughcast brick, three bays and storeys.

Church Street, NW, begins with THE PRIORY, Lias, C17 with central gable, much remodelled in the early C19 when pretty Gothick glazing was fixed to the window frames (rather than the sashes); rectangular C18 DOVECOTE. Then, at the angle with Court Lane, the OLD MANOR, U-plan, part C17 timber-

---

[*] Preedy was born in the village in 1820.

framed (with big diamond-plan stone chimney), mostly rebuilt in late C18 brick. It faces THE GRANGE, also of C17 origin, rebuilt in the C18–C19, with stuccoed front; good cross-gabled DOVECOTE, *c.* 1700.

Court Lane leads to COURT FARM, on the site of the grange, a favoured later medieval residence of the Abbot of Evesham. C18, Lias, three rear gables, but a fine S façade of Cotswold ashlar, three broad bays, two storeys, with modillion cornice and hipped roof; the central rear gable is dated 1767. Notable Jacobean overmantel in the SW room: carved oak, with figures and arms of the Haselwood family.

More nice cottages further S in Church Street; the most interesting, LONGTHATCH, reveals its C14–C15 cruck construction inside.

Former PAROCHIAL SCHOOL, ¼ m. SSW in the angle of Boat and Ferry Lanes. 1846, small, painted brick; Tudor Gothic, central gable.

OMBERSLEY

8060

ST ANDREW. An early example of a C19 estate church, large, well built, close to the grounds of Ombersley Court, but also with easy access from the village. By *Thomas Rickman*, 1825–9, costing about £18,000, some two-thirds contributed by Mary Sandys, Dowager Marchioness of Downshire. Dec style, flowing tracery, the aisle windows of three lights, the E of four. Stately W tower with recessed spire connected by thin flying buttresses to the parapet pinnacles (the type of Louth, Lincs.). Flanking the tower, entrance lobbies to the galleries. Battlemented chancel (not too short) and clerestory. The chancel W bay is flanked by transeptal vestries, with boldly crocketed ogee inner arches. Spacious, high interior. Thin four-bay nave arcades of Perp type, rather dull, the piers with cast-iron cores. The galleries have plain wooden fronts, kept inside the aisles, N and S. Quadripartite plaster rib vaults to nave and chancel. – Most of Rickman's FURNISHINGS remain, a rare example of a relatively untouched pre-ritualist Anglican interior. They include Gothic PANELS (Decalogue, Creed, and Lord's Prayer) flanking the E window, PULPIT, BOX PEWS (the Sandys family pew, S aisle E end, complete with Gothic fireplace), ORGAN CASE, and full set of mostly patterned STAINED GLASS by *Thomas Gray & Son.* – Also, N aisle, a tall, fully Gothic iron stove made by *Robert Howden.* – ROYAL ARMS. Probably George I. – Large Elizabethan ALTAR TABLE (N aisle). – Restoration by *Lewis Sheppard*, 1888, provided encaustic tiling, supplementary furnishings, and big, square, carved FONT (now under the tower). *J. Homery Folkes* coloured the ceiling, 1957.

CHURCHYARD WALL of *c.* 1829, with iron railings towards the street. Timber LYCHGATE by *A. Hill Parker & Son*, 1925. Stark WAR MEMORIAL CROSS, *c.* 1920, by *Ben Davis* of Worcester.

104

The medieval church, of almost equal size, lay to the s. The chancel, rather its E two-thirds, survives, converted by *Rickman* into the SANDYS MAUSOLEUM. He built a new w wall, refaced the E wall, and provided battlements all round. Side walls late C13: small trefoil-cusped lancets, deeply moulded beneath continuous dripmoulds; internal shafts with moulded capitals, one with dogtooth. Fine contemporary piscina and triple sedilia, again pointed trefoiled arches; two good headstops. – MONUMENTS. Four notable tablets. Samuel Sandys †1685, by *William Bird* of Oxford; cartouche with weeping putti. – Samuel Sandys †1701; black barley-twist Corinthian columns. – Martin Sandys †1753 and wife Elizabeth †1760; grey and white marbles. – Edwin Lord Sandys †1797, by *Nollekens*; bust on top against a grey obelisk. – Two HATCHMENTS, the larger to the Dowager Marchioness, 1836.

Outside, early C19 CHEST TOMBS. – C15 CROSS, NE, four steps and base with quatrefoils and angle spurs; C19 shaft, square C17–C18 top with ball finial.

OMBERSLEY COURT, to the sw. Built 1723–6 by *Francis Smith* of Warwick for Samuel, first Lord Sandys, Speaker of the House of Lords. His house, brick with stone dressings, was refaced in smooth sober ashlar, 1812–14, for the Marchioness of Downshire, by *John Webb* of Lichfield.* Seven-bay entrance front (E), two-and-a-half storeys, the central three bays projecting; portico (by Webb) with four pairs of unfluted Ionic columns. The other sides also have 2+3+2 bays, but hardly any pronounced emphases. The garden front (w), with simple central doorway with finely carved brackets, is extended N by a large dining room, three bays and two storeys, again by Webb.

The glory of the house is its INTERIOR (mostly completed by 1730), to Smith's standard plan of eight rooms per floor, arranged 3+2+3, the staircases filling the centres of the sides. He employed many of his usual craftsmen: *Thomas Eborall*, joiner; *Joshua Needham*, plasterer; *John Wilkes* for door furniture. Two-storey ENTRANCE HALL, with rear balcony passage connecting the upper rooms; the lower part has fluted Ionic pilasters and blank niches. Noble ceiling, probably mostly c. 1814, with simply distributed panels. Entirely by Smith, the three principal rooms along the w front, all with dark wood panelling punctuated by pilasters of different orders and details: in the DRAWING ROOM, sw, they are Borromini-inspired Corinthian; fine door surrounds and overdoors 72 (perhaps by *Edward Poynton*). In the SALOON, behind the hall, a marble chimneypiece with lintel with young head flanked by garlands. GREAT STAIR also by *Smith*'s team, each step with three balusters: twisted–columnar–twisted; tread ends carved with scrolls, wonderfully wavy underside. Contemporary

---

* *John Nash* made plans in 1808 for sweeping alterations to the façades, with Ionic portico, E, and colonnade, w. Smith's house was linked by quadrant colonnades to three-bay pavilions. Webb, working here until 1821, replaced these with a large N office wing, demolished in the 1960s.

plaster ceiling. Service staircase, with small skylit dome and simple handrail, by Webb, as is the detail of the LIBRARY, S of the entrance hall, and the room to its N. On the first floor a room with painted Chinese silk panels and drapes over the doors, rather in Brighton-Pavilion taste. On the second floor one with a *Dufour* wallpaper of Constantinople, datable *c.* 1816.

Large STABLES, N, round a two-storeyed ashlar-faced quadrangle, by *Webb c.* 1813; entrance side, 3+1+3 bays, the centre with high round arch beneath a pediment. Contemporary walled KITCHEN GARDEN further W. The N entrance, facing Holt Fleet Road, has short solid GATEPIERS.

Webb, a pupil of William Eames ('élève of the great Brown'), was also responsible for landscaping the fine PARK. The ICE HOUSE, SW of the house, a particularly good example, is probably late C18; sandstone and brick, domed and egg-shaped.

Former MAIN LODGE on the Worcester Road, ⅔ m. SSE, probably *c.* 1820. A modest pair of segmental-arched gateways with oval paterae flanking wrought-iron gates. Dwelling with canted end and Doric porch, enlarged in the C20.

Especially rewarding VILLAGE. The main street, WORCESTER ROAD, runs S–N. At its S end, W side, two sets of pretty midC19 black-and-white cottages.* The first pair, PARK COTTAGES, dated 1841, are particularly picturesque: balustraded end porches, pinnacled gables, fish-scale roofs; said to be the former Bewdley Pewterers' House (from Pewterers' Alley, p. 780), re-erected here by Lord Sandys. PARK VILLAS are a more regular group of three. Opposite, the CROWN AND SANDYS ARMS, fancifully refronted *c.* 1700; whitewashed brick, the S part with two by two bays of shaped gables, the N with five similar ones. Then the KING'S ARMS, timber-framed, long T-plan: S range C16–C17, N cross-wing probably late C15, jettied, with close-set studding. In its ground-floor room a ceiling with moulded beams interspersed with individual plaster motifs (mermaid, rose etc.).

The lane alongside leads up to the former WORKHOUSE, 1827; brick, two storeys, three bays, the outer with segmental relieving arches.

Back in Worcester Road, W side, much square-panelled C16–C17 framing, the best group at the corner of CHURCH LANE, a reversed U-plan: l. wing with gabled dormer, the r. apparently earlier. It faces LLOYDS CHARITY SCHOOL, 1729, brick, with hipped roof; L-plan, with renewed shaped gable towards the old church. Further N, the approach to the new church.

On the E side, after more C16–C17 timber framing, some hidden by stucco, two groups of Sandys estate housing, perhaps *c.* 1830–40: Tudor-style, hoodmoulds, gables with quatrefoils. Then a castellated four-bay brick pair, mid-C19, more consciously Gothic. Lying back, the former VICARAGE, late

---

* At the corner of Sinton Lane ¼ m. further S, a C19 brick SMITHY, its horseshoe-shaped entrance outlined in black (cf. Tibberton).

C18, three bays, tall and thin; Ionic doorway with open pediment, flanked by two-storey canted bays probably added *c.* 1840. Good staircase.

By the roundabout turn W into Holt Fleet Road for some modest early C19 brick villas, and THE DOWER HOUSE, early C17, long hall range with gabled E cross-wing; big rectangular brick stack near their junction. All square-panelled framing, with diagonal first-floor bracing; renewed windows. Inside, a modest but pretty plaster hall ceiling with stray motifs; two stone chimneypieces with similar carved decoration. Rusticated gatepiers with ball finials.

Back to the main street for two good cruck houses. First, SW corner, CRESSWELLS, its S gable with thin decorative mid-C19 timberwork, and only the upper part of the cruck blades discernible. Framing of the E side also restored, its square panelling bearing little resemblance to the original wall frame; decorative brick chimneys. The crucks are wholly visible in the N gable, also inside. Floored throughout and subdivided, but originally an open-roofed, two-bay hall with solar and service bay each end: the typical four-bay cruck house to which any date pre-1450 might be given. The other house, THATCHED COTTAGE, further N, E side, now consists of the two-bay C15 hall and N service cross-wing of two bays; solar bay, S, demolished *c.* 1900. Mostly square panelling, probably *c.* 1600, but the full cruck frame visible in the S gable; big stepped brick chimney, E side. As at Cresswells, the great central cruck arch dividing upper from lower bay of the hall survives. Only one bay of the service cross-wing was floored; the other may have been for keeping livestock.

More early C19 brick houses, larger than in Holt Fleet Road; the set-back WELLINGTON HOUSE has two-and-a-half storeys, with hipped roof. Then ALBION HOUSE, roughcast brick, its middle bay treated as a full-height blank arch; probably *c.* 1840–50, badly altered.

ENDOWED SCHOOL, ENE on the Droitwich Road, by *Henry Rowe*, 1875–6. Gothic, red brick, yellow patterning, sharp bellcote. Later additions.

The OLD PARSONAGE, Parsonage Lane, ¾ m. WNW, is an odd-looking brick farmhouse. Early C18 two-bay centre with pedimented doorway, taller three-storey wings: the W, probably early C19, has cambered tripartite windows, the E a full-height early C20 canted bay. – Good C18 brick BARN, W.

WHITNEYS FARM, a little E, early C17 L-plan, has square-panelled framing, later heightened, an E gable, and good brick stacks.

The extensive Ombersley parish includes a number of hamlets, most with timber-framed cottages and farmhouses, and often boundary walls of sandstone blocks. Only a selection can be mentioned here.

UPHAMPTON, the largest, 1 m. NW, has especially many C17 cottages; at least one, THE HINKS, is of earlier cruck construction. W of this, PIPESTYLE HOUSE, a timber-framed farm group, *c.* 1600: square-panelled house with gabled cross-wing and hall range (w wall of brick, 1766); cider mill, s, partly weatherboarded.

NORTHAMPTON, 1½ m. NNW, is more scattered. The largest house, in fine parkland, is WOODFIELD HOUSE, late C18 brick, three bays and storeys, with broad Ionic porch; lower two-bay wings. – Further N, EDEN FARMHOUSE, late C17, whitewashed brick, a two-storey gabled porch with pediment implanted below the gable; modillion string course. Opposite, forming a fine group, YEW TREE HOUSE, square-panelled, *c.* 1600, much remodelled *c.* 1840; its central bedroom has early C18 painted decoration of birds amid foliage. Long weatherboarded BARN, S.

TYTCHNEY GABLES, 1¾ m. NW, big square-panelled late C16, has a hall range with particularly large gabled cross-wing, w, with additional side gable to the lane.

Timber framing at SYTCHAMPTON, 1½ m. N, includes SYTCHAMPTON FARM, C15 cruck-framed, and PARDOE'S FARM, the usual early C17 hall and cross-wing. On the main road, E, another LLOYDS CHARITY SCHOOL, rebuilt 1826 by *John Witney* (Rickman's carpenter at St Andrew); three-bay brick with pilasters, centre with full-height blank arch beneath a gable. Later C19 rear additions. – Further N at DUNHAMP-TON, HALFWAY HOUSE, a large roadside inn by *Collier & Keyte* of Birmingham, 1938–9; painted brick, non-matching end gables, three hipped dormers in between.

At HADLEY, 1 m. E of Ombersley, the large CROSS HOUSE, mostly late C16–early C17 square-panelled framing, has six gables to the s, some no doubt mid-C19 as is much of the N front. The added date 1537 perhaps applies to the NE wing, next to the timber-framed stable block. Nearby, CROSS COTTAGE, cruck-framed, extended in C17–C18 brick, all now thatched. – More C16–C17 farmhouses in the E part of the hamlet, ending at a mid-C19 MILL with patterned brickwork; most original machinery remains, including the undershot wheel.

HAYE LANE FARM, ⅔ m. WNW of Hadley. Brick Tudor Gothic, dated 1834.

ORLETON

Stanford with Orleton

6060

ST JOHN BAPTIST. Rebuilt 1816–17; surveyor *George Albot* of Sodington (p. 489). Converted to a house *c.* 1972. Small red brick chapel of ease to Eastham: nave and w tower, thin, quite tall, with lancet bell-openings and battlements. Two pointed-arched s windows, broader E window, their fenestration renewed more or less to the original forms: Y-tracery s, three-light intersecting E (originally cast-iron tracery). N wall formerly blank.

ORLETON COURT, ⅛ m. E. Mostly mid-C18, H-plan, 1+3+1 bays,

brick, hipped roofs. SE return, facing down the Teme, with smart five-bay front, its central bay projecting with pediment above tripartite window and pedimented doorway. – Large contemporary brick BARN and STABLES, NW.

ORLETON HOUSE, ¼ m. W. Rebuilt in 1858 for Thomas Davis. Neat Jacobean, red brick, blue diapering, quoins; shaped gables, canted bays, banded roof. Square pyramidal tower with open bellcote, closest to the detached N service range.

9030

OVERBURY

Below the S slope of Bredon Hill; one of the most attractive, best-maintained villages in Worcestershire. Stone houses of all periods from the C17–C20 mingle with a sprinkling of C18–C19 brick and late C19 half-timbering. The estate belonged to the Martin banking family from the C18. After c. 1875 Robert Martin (†1898) and Richard Biddulph Martin (†1916) employed *Richard Norman Shaw*, then his pupil *Ernest Newton*, to carry out exceptionally sympathetic additions and improvements; a comparison of their work is most instructive. The estate then came to Robert Holland-Martin (†1944), closely involved with C.R. Ashbee's Guild of Handicraft.

ST FAITH. A possession of Worcester Cathedral Priory from 875. Dominating Perp central tower, with gargoyles, battlements and pinnacles; the rather florid bell-openings may be C17 alteration. Closer inspection should begin inside, with the Norman nave. Four-bay arcades with round piers, many-scalloped capitals, square abaci, single-stepped arches. Capitals and bases a little later N than S; the N hoodmould is plain (on re-set heads), the S scallop-decorated. Norman clerestory windows, now opening only into the aisles, above the spandrels not the apexes of the arches. Renewed S doorway, of three orders, the outer two with tall scallop or volute capitals on keeled shafts, the inner with shafts without necking, a West Country peculiarity of the end of the C12 (cf. Wells and St Davids); much-moulded arch. W window restored C13, a stepped triplet with internal shafts. The aisles, widened in the mid C14, have Dec windows, those on the S renewed 1850 by *Jacques & Son* of Gloucester, who rebuilt the porch. Sturdy Late Perp tower arches, their responds sitting very oddly on inverted Norman capitals, no doubt relics of the Norman central tower; Perp N and S windows. Tower vault of 1879–80, when *Norman Shaw* carried out general restoration. The finest piece of architecture is the E.E. chancel. It has two lancets N and S, shafted outside and in, with stiff-leaf capitals, finely moulded surrounds and, inside, fillets. Two-bay rib vault, the ribs and vaulting shafts again with fillets and stiff-leaf, also some heads; each bay has a figured boss: the Virgin crowned, E, a serpent with female head, W, presumably representing Eve. Roof-space above the vault used as a dovecote. Two red-painted consecration crosses remain. The eight-light E window is of course a Perp insertion, slightly modified by *Shaw*.

FONT. Norman bowl, of steep goblet shape. Two standing figures, one with pastoral staff in each hand, the other holding a church. Third panel with large symmetrical scroll pattern, comparable to the Gloucestershire lead fonts and the stone font at Coleshill (Warwickshire); the fourth, with dove and cross, seems entirely C17–C18, when much else was re-cut. The original parts may be mid-C12 or earlier. Dec octagonal stem, with ballflower. – PULPIT, with parts of the C15 screen. – CHOIR STALLS by *Shaw*, who renewed the PEWS, which incorporate C15 moulded rails, traceried bench ends, and other carving. – N aisle ALTAR by *Sir Edward Maufe*, 1938. – Oak VESTRY SCREEN, N aisle W, by *J. Howard Leech* of Burford, 1959. – STAINED GLASS. S aisle SE by *Heaton, Butler & Bayne*, 1880. – Others by *Burlison & Grylls*: chancel N and S 1881, E 1885, nave W 1893, aisle E windows *c.* 1897. – MONUMENTS. Parts of two C13 coffin slabs, one with incised chalice, the other with unusual cross with circular terminals (cf. Bredon). – Small tablet to Sir Richard Biddulph Martin, Bt, by *Nelson Dawson*, 1917; bronze and green marble.

War memorial LYCHGATE, above a stream, by *Sir Herbert Baker*, 1921. Heavy timbers, stone memorial block inside; carving by *Alec Miller*. – The CHURCHYARD has C17–C18 chest tombs. Memorial garden, SW, with timber arcade of 1964 by *Sir William Holford*.

OVERBURY COURT, NW. Large ashlar house, rebuilt, after a major fire, in 1739–43, perhaps by the younger *William Smith*. S front of seven bays, the three-bay centre projecting; rusticated quoins of even length. Windows with moulded architraves, the middle one slightly emphasized by ears and enriched keystone. Attic storey above the cornice perhaps added later in the C18 and the pediment raised; below it, three short segment-headed windows. Pedimented doorway on engaged Ionic columns; late C19 plinths. The five-bay W return has a doorway with Gibbs surround, and similar attic; large round-arched porch added by *Sir Herbert Baker c.* 1925. E return with central porch-like projection; this, rising to a proper third floor with one large round-arched window, was added by *Ernest Newton c.* 1910 to incorporate a lift shaft. *Shaw* carried out minor alterations in 1887, and further work, 1897–1900, including the chimneys and N entrance with domed vestibule. *Victor Heal* demolished his NW wing *c.* 1959, replacing it by a smaller NE version. Inside, the former entrance hall leads to an excellent mid-C18 staircase: three turned balusters per tread, carved tread ends; late C19 armorial stained glass by *Heaton, Butler & Bayne*.

The early C18 COACHHOUSE (now Estate Office), to the N, is a little more rustic, but all the more lovable for that. Five bays, slender wooden cross-windows, mid-gable above a rusticated doorway. Hipped slate roof with square turret with open octagonal lantern. – Rectangular GAME LARDER, SE, probably by *Shaw*. – Certainly his, the elaborate wrought-iron GATES nearby, dated 1887; tall GATEPIERS with ball finials, flanking segmental arches for pedestrians.

The formal C19 GARDENS were simplified by *Guy Dawber*, 1923; his pyramid-roofed GAZEBO, SE corner, is said to be a reconstructed C18 building from Burford. Further rearrangement by *Russell Page*, 1968. – Large PARK, of mid-C18 origin, extending W and N, divided from the gardens by two artificial pools and a cascade.

VILLAGE PERAMBULATION. The plan of the village is more or less a reversed T, the base the main street, the stem one of scarcely less importance ascending Bredon Hill. The W end of the former, S of church and Court, is a good place to start. At the corner of the lane leading to the estate yard is GARDENS HOUSE, late C18 originally, its E front, with two-storey wooden canted bay windows flanking the doorway, a typically subtle remodelling by *Ernest Newton*, 1908. Also his the attractive gateway piercing the long garden wall.* The next two houses also received the *Newton* treatment: BARON HOUSE, late C18 with pedimented Doric doorcase, was given a short E wing, 1904–5, the early C19 HOME FARM (Nos. 43–44) more substantial additions in 1905.

On the N side, behind a HORSE POND no doubt smartened up by *Newton*, the large BERKELEY HOUSE, plain mid-C18, ashlar with hipped roof. BERKELEY COTTAGES, *c.* 1639, with three gabled dormers, were altered and given a rear wing by *Newton*. The former small gateway, dated 1639, now stands opposite, at the corner of the grounds of the OLD VICARAGE; this, set well back, an interloper of 1877–8 by *William (Bassett-)Smith*, brick with stone dressings, has tall gables and chimneys.

Then a flurry of buildings by *Norman Shaw*, starting with the former POST OFFICE AND STORES, 1879; stone ground floor, projecting half-timbered upper floor with gable with decorative circles; additions by *Newton*, 1905. The pretty BUS SHELTER was a roadside fountain of 1878–9, apparently designed by *Newton* when in Shaw's office. Nos. 45–47, and Nos. 48–49 round the corner in School Lane, are pairs of stone cottages, both dated 1875, probably also by *Shaw*. More notable, his fine ashlar SCHOOL, 1875–7: Tudorish, mullioned-and-transomed windows, projecting gabled wing, fine tall bellcote rising from the W end. The T-plan SCHOOL HOUSE next door is by *Newton*, 1908, its low-key Cotswold Tudor detail forming an interesting comparison with Shaw's work.

The village's E end is marked by PIKE COTTAGE, an early C19 toll house with canted bay; opposite, the brick-faced former STAR INN. Yet further E, a stone-built STABLE and HAY BARN, an unaltered group probably by *Newton c.* 1902, a rare example of Arts and Crafts farm building.

Now back and to the N, uphill. CHURCH ROW opens W towards the gatepiers of Overbury Court. Nos. 2–8, N side, a row of

---

*At the estate yard, a former ENGINE AND DYNAMO HOUSE by *Norman Shaw*, 1898, with half-hipped gable-ends. Further SSW, ROBIN'S MILL, C19; large L-plan brick extension by *Newton*, 1912.

stone cottages converted from an C18 malthouse, have lean-to door hoods on wooden brackets, probably by *Shaw c.* 1877–8. Certainly of this date, the house opposite, COURT LODGE, its upper floor of close-set timbering similar to the Post Office. Past WHITCOMBE, *c.* 1820, with pedimented doorway, to the VILLAGE HALL, 1895–6, *Shaw*'s best building in the village. Ashlar, Neo-Tudor, large mullioned-and-transomed windows, but a heavy English Baroque porch with curved gable and round-arched doorway of alternating rustication; three big flat-roofed canted dormers provide lantern lighting. Behind, NW, the C18 LAUNDRY COTTAGE shows clear signs of alteration by *Newton*.

The late C18 GABLE ROW, E side, also has *Shaw*'s lean-to door-hoods. Further N, THE NORLANDS, large late C18, of stone, three bays with quoins; tall round-arched central staircase window. The inevitable *Newton* addition, S, 1902; he also heightened the C17 rear wings.

There follows a stretch with houses on the W side only, behind a raised pavement. RED HOUSE, the best Georgian house in the village, brick with stone quoins, of three bays and storeys, has six rather flat Venetian windows. *Newton*'s additions here, 1901–10, include a hipped-roofed NW wing. SUNNY BANK COTTAGE is humbler C18, again with central round-arched staircase window (and *Newton* addition, 1902). The stuccoed mid-C18 NINDFIELD has a similar, even longer central window flanked by three-storey canted bays; altered and enlarged by *Newton*, 1913.

Uphill, with houses again on both sides, the best group by *Ernest Newton*, all of stone. First, the L-plan PARK LODGE, 1902–3. To its N, DORMAY COTTAGES, 1902–4, an attractive terrace of three, at right angles to the street; square-headed recessed entrances, one on the E end, weatherboarded dormers. Rear with three gables flanked by catslides. Opposite, PARK VIEW, 1914, small but with ample wood-mullioned glazing; and MILLBANK (once Cogsbill's Cottage), also 1914: big projecting gable to the road, entrance cleverly tucked into its angle with the main range.

As the steepness of the hill increases, buildings become brick and more utilitarian, early to mid-C19, including remnants of former mills. The OLD BREWHOUSE has a *Newton*-looking shell-hood; the one larger stone house here, the early C19 SILVER RILL, in splendid grounds, additions by *Shaw*, 1891, and *Newton*, 1910–14, partly demolished. At the top, SILK MILL COTTAGES, stone, rebuilt by *Newton*, 1907.

A final group by *Newton* in PIGEON LANE, leading E from the Old Brewhouse: YEW TREE COTTAGE (No. 34), of 1905, with nicely corbelled-out corner; YEW TREE HOUSE (No. 35), 1906, plainer, L-plan; also no doubt the earlier remodelling of the modest Nos. 36–39.

PEBWORTH

The most easterly parish in Worcestershire, transferred from Gloucestershire in 1931.

ST PETER, on a mound at the W end of the village. Mostly Perp. The S aisle is called 'new' in the will of Edmund Martin, 1528; much else may also be of *c.* 1500. Some late C13 trefoil-headed lancets (also the chancel piscina) and one Dec nave N window provide the only earlier evidence. Battlemented W tower with very tall Perp window, its collapsed tracery partly infilled in the C18–C19. High double-chamfered arch to the nave; similar chancel arch. Three-bay S arcade, the piers of typical Late Perp section: octagonal with small hollow in the middle of the diagonals. The arches correspond, but with a deeper recess between their two chamfers. Internal walls limewashed. Nave wagon roof ceiled, with thin moulded ribs; four attractive C19 dormers pierce its S side. Part of the rood stair remains, also canopied Perp niches: aisle SE corner, and S of the chancel arch.

FONT. Perp, octagonal, with fleurons in quatrefoils; short stem with attached priest's step. – PULPIT. Jacobean: blank arches, arabesque top panels. Base and steps 1931. – COMMUNION RAIL. Late C17, deprived of half its balusters. – Nice PEWS. 1860. – N DOOR, *c.* 1500, with contemporary ironwork. – WALL PAINTINGS. C16–17 texts, nave N, and above the tower arch, accompanied by a large angel. – STAINED GLASS. Two C15 female saints in the E window tracery. – MONUMENTS. Chancel. Eroded effigy of a C14 priest, brought in from the churchyard; and floor slab of another priest (Thomas Viliett †1380, according to the *Little Guide*), hidden by the organ. – Good tablets. Robert Martin †1629, large, with round arch, Composite columns, and strapwork. – Robert Martin †1720, by *Edward Woodward* of Campden; stone, panelled pilasters, segmental pediment, urn above, two putto heads below. – Ann Shekell †1811, by *Lewis* of Gloucester; pretty, sub-Adam, coloured marbles with draped urn. – Thomas Shekell †1852, the usual mourning female leaning on a pedestal; one of several by *Lewis* of Cheltenham.

Former VICARAGE (now Hill House), a little SW. Rather severe Neo-Georgian by *Harold Stratton Davis* of Gloucester, 1926; roughcast, some brick trim, hipped roof.

Several pleasant houses in FRONT STREET, leading downhill, SE. First, facing the churchyard, PEBWORTH HOUSE, originally C16 timber-framed, much enlarged in brick in the early to mid C19;* restored *c.* 1981 by *Michael Reardon* (gardens landscaped by *Alison Higgins*). Then the OLD VICARAGE, modest C17–C18, roughcast, and THE KNOLL, part late C17 with mullioned windows, part 1713 with mullioned-and-transomed. Further on, BANK HOUSE, dated 1705; banded Lias, with platband and blank horizontal ovals, still mullioned windows. The long NORTON CLOSE was much rebuilt in 1912. Opposite, a former

---

*Datestones on the early C19 part, 1766 and 1779, must be re-set.

WESLEYAN CHAPEL of 1840; yellow brick, iron Gothick glazing, hipped roof. To the NE, the SCHOOL of 1903–4 by *Harvey Bros* of Evesham; brick, large half-timbered central gable.

MANOR FARMHOUSE, Long Marston Road, further E. Refined façade, *c.* 1820–30, three bays and storeys, cement-rendered with ashlar dressings; moulded architraves, fluted Doric porch flanked by shallow bows with tripartite windows in reeded frames. – BARN dated 1720; the DOVECOTE and rusticated GATEPIERS with ball finials are probably contemporary.

More attractive houses in FRIDAY STREET, running N–S yet further E, a mix of timber framing, brick, and Lias and Cotswold stone; the C17 COURT FARM displays all four. At the S end, a fine row of five C17 thatched cottages.

BROAD MARSTON, ⅞ m. ESE, has some interesting houses. BROAD MARSTON MANOR, probably remodelled *c.* 1622 when Sir Thomas Bennett bought it from the Bushell family, is Cotswold stone, three storeys, without gables; four-centred doorway, mullioned windows with hoodmoulds: of four lights S end, of three at the N (service) end. Small medieval window of two cusped lights on the S return. Mostly timber-framed within. – Fine large weatherboarded BARN, N, the three W bays, of cruck and braced-collar construction, perhaps C14–C15; the five E bays are C18, with tie-beams and queen-struts. Rectangular stone DOVECOTE, SW, C17–C18.

Priory Lane, with four neat timber-framed thatched C17 cottages, leads to THE PRIORY, mostly C17, but of three distinct builds. The W range, said to be of 1654, has a rendered N front with C19 porch, but symmetrical rear elevation of Cotswold stone: mullioned windows flanking the Tudor-arched doorway, continuous dripmould, two shallow gables above a parapet. Earlier W wing, mostly Lias, set N–S. Higher E range, double-pile C17–C18 with mixed fenestration, largely rebuilt by *Sir Lancelot Keay & Partners*, 1970; notable C17 open-well staircase, SW corner, with moulded rail and pyramid-capped newels.

CHAPEL HOUSE, at the SE end of the hamlet, was the former C16 chapel of ease. Only the shell remains, converted to cottages probably *c.* 1800; diagonal SW and SE buttresses, blocked Tudor S doorway. – To the E was a medieval burial ground.

PENDOCK   7030

CHURCH. Vested in the Churches Conservation Trust since 1987. Nave and chancel of *c.* 1170. N doorway with one order of shafts with decorated scallop capitals (including small crosses), arch with furrowed zigzag (cf. Malvern Priory), hoodmould with pellets (cf. Queenhill). Chancel arch also Norman, though the arch itself has been rebuilt: similar shafts and capitals, incised imposts, the S with zigzag (cf. Eldersfield). Triangular-headed piscina. All windows C14, most renewed in 1873 when *G. R. Clarke* restored the church and added the N vestry. Less-altered w tower with Dec two-light w window with pretty tracery; low pyramidal roof. Arch to the nave with Perp-type mouldings. Perp also no doubt, the remains of the rood stair: its upper doorway inside; outside, small blocked windows high up in nave s and e walls to light the loft. Timber n porch, probably c16. Homely interior, walls and roofs plastered; small fragment of foliage WALL PAINTING, nave e wall. – Simple round Norman FONT; later base. – SCREEN. The c14–c15 dado with blank tracery panels remains, the n side differing from the s. – COMMUNION RAIL. Sturdy Jacobean; carved top rail. – PEWS. Some c16, with linenfold panelling. – Medieval N DOOR. – c18 DECALOGUE and CREED; COMMANDMENT BOARDS, 1851. – STAINED GLASS. e window c. 1847, probably *Powells*. – By the same firm, indicating the arrival of Aesthetic precepts, the s chancel, 1874 (designed by *Harry Burrow*), and nave sw, 1880 (by *Charles Hardgrave*). – w window by *Charles Hean*, 1888; nave nw by *Hardman*, 1905. – MONUMENT. Sir Joseph Hooker, the botanist, †1911. Bronze tablet of 1918, signed *HH*; portrait roundel, copper, by *F. Bowcher*, 1898.

The church stands alone, with the M50 motorway to its s. Extensive earthworks, n, mark the site of the medieval village.

PRIOR'S COURT, ⅛ m. ene. Late c17, brick, H-shaped, the wings gabled; good chimneys with arched panels; windows apparently renewed *c.* 1840–50. In the entrance hall a plaster overmantel with two large wreaths; dog-leg staircase, with turned balusters, in its own tall gabled projection, sw.

The c18 OLD RECTORY, ¼ m. nw, has a three-bay w front of sandstone rubble, meant to be rendered as is proved by the irregular brick surrounds of the windows and doorcase inserted 1804. Doric side porch and conservatory added 2005–6.

The parish centre is at CROMER GREEN, 2 m. wsw, with its own wooden church, THE REDEEMER, by *W.J. Hopkins*, 1888; weatherboarded, reinforced later by diagonal struts. w bellturret, sw porch, and e and w windows have Dec quatrefoil detail typical of Hopkins. Unspoilt interior. – A little se, a former WESLEYAN CHAPEL dated 1824; red brick, hipped slate roof.

The outstanding house is FISHER'S PLACE, at the ne end, a Baronial Arts and Crafts confection built for G.O. Fisher, 1909–10; to the road, half-timbered and gabled, but behind much higher, mostly red brick with thin black bands. The w front has in addition small gables of snecked stone, with tall tower above the entrance: lavishly carved heraldic doorway, deep battlemented parapet with brick and stone flushwork. To the e, a full-height, rendered, canted bay; further heraldry above. Now subdivided; much stained glass within.

PENSAX

Upland parish, a chapelry of Lindridge until 1843. Formerly part of the West Worcestershire coalfield (cf. Mamble).

ST JAMES. Rebuilt in ashlar, 1832–3, by *Thomas Jones* of Chester, who specialized in Perp-style churches (especially in North Wales). Wide three-bay unaisled nave, as usual in the 1830s, the buttresses along the sides also fitting this date. Otherwise the degree of exactitude in the Perp detailing is exceptional, far beyond anyone else in 1832, apart perhaps from Rickman. The battlemented w tower is particularly substantial, despite the loss of its pinnacles; its three-light w window as well as those of the nave have surrounds no late Victorian could have improved on. Their real date is betrayed by the grotesque head-stops of their hoodmoulds, too big, perhaps too characterful, for late C19 tastes. *George Vialls* added the present chancel, with N vestry, 1890–1; rock-faced purple sandstone, freeish Dec-Perp. Nave interior, originally with w gallery, a little bleak despite its pleasant if flimsy hammerbeam-style roof. – Only the simple FONT of 1832–3 survives. – PEWS of 1891. – Most chancel fittings of 1910, probably all by the *Bromsgrove Guild*: oak REREDOS with inset paintings, ALTAR RAILS, low stone SCREEN topped with dense wrought ironwork, SANCTUARY LAMPS. – More memorable, the Free Style timber PULPIT and matching LECTERN, probably by *Charles Spooner*, 1897. – STAINED GLASS. Excellent E and chancel N windows by *Christopher Whall*, 1899. – Two chancel s by *Heaton, Butler & Bayne*, 1891–7, feeble in comparison. – In the CHURCHYARD, sw, the base and stump of a C15 CROSS.

PENSAX COURT, a little E, rendered brick, probably *c.* 1840, is a pretty sight from the s, with cambered windows, three steep gables with pierced scalloped bargeboards, large brick chimneys, and thin central octagonal clock tower with domed roof. Three ground-floor canted bays must be of 1882, the date on the low brick and half-timbered E wing. Exposed brickwork at the rear, N, apparently partly C18. Also here, a large Y-traceried window lighting the open-well staircase (with cast-iron balustrade).

To the N, late C19 STABLES and other outbuildings, amongst late C20 housing. Good-sized lake, s. Across the road, w, a large walled KITCHEN GARDEN; the path to the church leads alongside its buttressed N side.

Former NATIONAL SCHOOL, Pensax Common, sw, below the church. 1871–3 by *John B. Smith* of Bewdley; brick, plain, adjoining gables for schoolroom and house.

The OLD VICARAGE, ½ m. NNE, by *A.E. Perkins*, 1855–6, is gabled Tudor Gothic, little altered. Brick, black bands, yellow borders to the windows, banded tiled roofs.

At MENITHWOOD ⅞ m. WNW, a former MISSION CHURCH (now Old Chapel Hall), probably built as a school *c.* 1820. Stone, brick trim, three round-arched windows with wooden Y-tracery; slate roof, small timber clock turret.

CLAYWOOD HOUSE, ⅓ m. further SSW (just within Lindridge parish), has an unusual s front of *c.* 1830; brick, two storeys and three bays, centre recessed beneath a full-height segmental arch. Within this a balcony above the wide doorway, with fluted Doric columns and Y-traceried fanlight. In the central hall, a large spiral geometrical staircase with wreathed moulded handrail.

9050

PEOPLETON

St Nicholas. Nave and chancel, the former with a low brick w tower of 1840 built into it (replacing a timber bell-turret). Much restored by *C.F. Whitcombe*, 1908; his the timber N porch and large sw vestry projecting beyond the nave w wall. Perp nave windows. The chancel has two renewed lancets, C16–C17 sub-Perp sanctuary windows, and a Dec-style E window, presumably from the earlier restoration of 1855. Inside, finely moulded Perp-style chancel arch of 1908; nave and chancel with good C15 wagon roofs. The beautifully carved beam, nave w end, with the most delicate leaf frieze and carved spandrels, belonged to the former ROOD SCREEN. – FONT. C14–C15; plain octagonal bowl, moulded stem. – FURNISHINGS mostly by *Ford Whitcombe*; his black-and-white-tiled sanctuary has dado panelling from an early C19 w gallery. – A few C15 TILES, NE corner. – PULPIT. 1919. – COMMUNION RAILS. Probably mid-C17, with sturdy balusters; the wide central opening is filled by three housling benches by *Robert Pancheri*, 1971. – VESTRY DOOR. Solidly cross-battened, said to be c. 1540. – STAINED GLASS. E window, 1889, and nave N, 1890, by *Cox, Sons, Buckley & Co.*; still pictorial. – Chancel NE by *A.J. Davies*, 1941. – MONUMENTS. Good tablets. Mark Dineley †1682, a gristly stone cartouche, designed with gusto. – Three, mildly Grecian, by *J. Stephens*, c. 1844–8.

Former SCHOOL, SE, 1871. Brick, with stone Dec windows. Now a house.

A good village group to the NW: three C17 timber-framed cottages, the larger PERRY MILL FARMHOUSE, and, set back in its own grounds, BOWBROOK HOUSE (now a school), stuccoed, c. 1840–50, with wing added 1905.

Further N, a couple of early C19 brick farmhouses, and the WHITE HOUSE, the most notable timber-framed building here, mostly cased in C19 brick. F.W.B. Charles considered that it contained more original internal timbers than any similar house in the county. The N part is a cruck-built hall, with half-hipped N gable-end; instead of the normal four bays under one roof, with hipped gables either end, there is a solar cross-wing, s, in place of the upper bay. The cruck part, its three full cruck frames clearly visible inside, could be C14, the cross-wing C15.

NORCHARD HOUSE, ⅓ m. NE. Brick, its central part Queen Anne, with five narrowly set bays: windows with moulded architraves, quoins, hipped roof; later Roman Doric porch with fluted columns, the capitals decorated with swags. Lower one-bay wings also Late Georgian, their windows with rusticated voussoirs. Older brickwork at the rear. – Nearby, an attractive timber-framed cottage.

WOLVERTON HALL, Lower Wolverton, ½ m. WNW (in Stoulton parish), belonged to the Acton family from 1585. Early C18 brick, three storeys, absolutely plain apart from stone quoins and stone keystones linked to narrow stone platbands; tall parapet hiding the shallow hipped roof. Seven bays, S; six, E, with moulded doorcase with large segmental pediment. The present entrance side, W, three bays, with lower attached service wing, has a substantial later Georgian doorway, with Tuscan columns and open pediment. Interior much restored c. 1963, with wide, plain, early C18 staircase. – Brick outbuilding, SW, five wide bays with hipped roof, dated 1714. – C17 timber-framed BARN, W.

PERSHORE

9040

Pershore has two main attractions: the pleasant little town itself, mostly of Georgian brick; and its medieval abbey church, a fragment but one of outstanding architectural interest. The town, on a gravel terrace above the Avon where the flood plain is at its narrowest, received a charter in the early C9 from King Coenwulf of Mercia. The abbey, founded in the late C7, had some two-thirds of its lands confiscated by the Mercian nobility c. 976, four years after Benedictine rule was introduced; these were mostly given by King Edward the Confessor to his favoured Westminster Abbey in 1065. The ownership of the town was thus divided between the two abbeys (Westminster's half being mostly to the s); each had its own parish church: St Andrew for Westminster, the abbey nave for Pershore. Broad Street, astride the two parishes, served as a marketplace. Westminster's part was a borough by 1086, Pershore Abbey's by the late C12; the market remained under monastic control. Decline was already apparent by the C15. After the Dissolution, the town continued to provide a local market, its industries ranging from wool-stapling to glovemaking. By the late C18 it had clearly become fashionable, partly

no doubt because it was the first coach-stop on the route from
Worcester to London. Later, market gardening and fruit growing
(especially plums) flourished, stimulated by the arrival of the
railway in 1852–3, though the station lay some distance N of the
town. Specifically Victorian display is largely absent. The best C19
work is by *Samuel Whitfield Daukes* (1811–80), whose family came
from Pershore, though he practised elsewhere (Gloucester from
c. 1834, London from 1848). For the C20, *Darbourne & Darke*'s
redevelopment and infill of the S part of the town centre, 1973–7,
is a model of its kind.

ABBEY CHURCH OF THE HOLY CROSS
AND ST EDBURGA

Pershore Abbey was founded *c.* 689 by Oswald, nephew of King
Ethelred of Mercia; re-founded by King Edgar, 972, when Bishop
Oswald of Worcester introduced the Benedictine rule. A new
church was built by 1020, probably following a fire in 1002; foundations terminating in an E apse, excavated when a new chancel
floor was laid in 1996, belonged to this church (or perhaps that
of *c.* 972). The dates of Norman rebuilding are unknown. From
the close resemblance to work at Gloucester and Tewkesbury,
also in other details to Worcester and Hereford Cathedrals, it
must have been begun shortly before *c.* 1100.* There are also no
fixed dates for the C13 rebuilding of the E arm. Most of it must
be subsequent to a fire of 1223, but the E end, especially the new
Lady Chapel, had probably already been begun; all was presumably complete at a consecration in 1239. Another fire, 1287–8,
caused grave damage, apparently bringing down the central
tower; the chancel vault must be of after that date, probably not
much after. Rebuilding of the tower seems to have been completed by *c.* 1327; a petition of that date (for the appropriation of
St Andrew's church), claiming that the nave and claustral buildings were still in ruins, makes no mention of the tower. The abbey
was dissolved in 1539–40; nave and Lady Chapel were then
pulled down, the remainder acquired for parochial use. In 1686,
after the N transept collapsed, a huge raking NE buttress was built
to support the tower. The present E apse is by *Harvey Eginton*,
1845–7; *G. G. Scott* carried out general restoration, mostly 1861–4.
Further work by *Sir Harold Brakspear*, 1912–14, included shoring
up the tower from the W.

The church, mainly of local limestone, was originally some 325
ft (100 metres) long (Tewkesbury was also *c.* 325 ft, Norman
Gloucester *c.* 365 ft (112 metres)). Less than half remains: the
stump of the nave, the crossing, S transept, and chancel (with its
C19 E apse). Yet this truncated remnant displays significant work
from three or four major campaigns, all at the vanguard of architectural development. Surviving evidence suggests that Norman
Pershore may have been a rare example of a West Country church
with high stone vaults throughout. The fine early C13 work of the

---

* A suggested re-entry of the monks in 1102 seems unrecorded before the early C20.

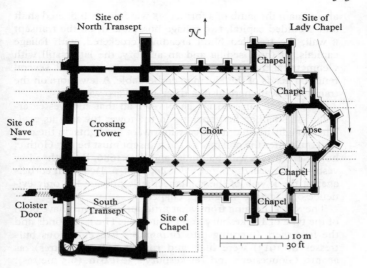

Pershore Abbey.
Plan of church

E arm is of two distinct periods, the first highly innovative with a unique ground plan, the second rather more conservative, but with a strong vertical élan uniting triforium and clerestory. Finally there is beautiful late C13–early C14 work, particularly the early lierne vault of the chancel and the noble crossing tower. 24

Exterior

Examination of the Norman building should start with the SOUTH TRANSEPT. Major medieval buildings were nearly always started at the E end, but as the Romanesque chancel has disappeared, as well as most of the N transept, the S transept contains the earliest surviving work. Its S wall shows, at the very foot, the bases of two shafts of blank arcading of the former SLYPE; then the roughly blocked place where the night-stair within the transept would, by a doorway, have led into the DORMITORY, its roof-line still clearly visible. Above, three widely spaced C13 lancets, renewed by *Scott*. Finally, in the gable, on a beaded spiral string course, intersecting blank arcading with block or single-scalloped capitals and arches with lateral chevrons on the soffits. The gable can hardly be older than the second quarter of the C12. The transept E wall has one shafted Norman window, with roll moulding and decorated scallop capitals, and the blocked opening of a former E chapel. This was replaced soon after 1288 by one two bays square. What survives of its shafts and vaulting springers is elegant and slender, with fine mouldings and capitals. There also remain the jamb of a former NE window, with filleted shaft and moulded capital, two foliage bosses, and, on the transept E wall, the trefoiled blind arcading, crocketed, with foliage capitals, of three sedilia and an aumbry, the latter still with Geometrical tracery. At the top of the transept E wall, several renewed heads of the Norman corbel table. A few more on the transept W wall; here also, a three-light Perp window.

Of the Norman NORTH TRANSEPT all that survives externally is a small arched opening in the tower towards its roof. The straight-headed trefoiled window, of five lights, in the new wall built after the collapse of the transept must be C17 Gothic; huge NE buttress with ball finial and date 1686. Beneath, a low vestry by *Francis B. Andrews & Son*, 1935–6. Two plain corbels against the N wall of the N chancel aisle provide the only evidence of a former N transept chapel.

The NAVE, judging from what little survives, must have been of the type of Tewkesbury and Gloucester. The E responds and the first piers (merging into *Brakspear*'s two enormous buttresses of 1913) were high and round: 25 ft (8 metres), as against Gloucester's and Tewkesbury's 30 ft 6 in. (9.5 metres). Their naves were begun *c.* 1110–20; can one assume *c.* 1120 for Pershore? The piers have bulgy, simply moulded capitals and round abaci (as at Tewkesbury and Gloucester). There could have been only a narrow triforium (rather than gallery) above. Of these upper parts all that can be seen, more clearly from the N side, is the jamb-shaft of the E end of blind arcading which must have incorporated the clerestory windows. Malcolm Thurlby suggested, from close examination at high level, that the nave may have had a rib rather than barrel vault;[*] shallow-pitched roof-line against the tower. The present W doorway and window above, in the blocking of the crossing's W arch, are of 1866. The Norman aisles were of course very high, as the blocked transept arches show; shafts again with block or one-scallop capitals. The aisles were vaulted, see the E springers, no doubt with groin vaults. The elegant SE doorway to the former cloister must be late C13: richly moulded arch, jambs with filleted shafts, naturalistic foliage on one set of capitals, rather late examples of waterholding bases. Above, a contemporary window jamb. The nave arcades, probably of nine bays, are partly indicated by small trees W of the crossing; wrought-iron gates, of 1964, are probably sited just beyond the W wall.

Now the C13 CHANCEL. Its aisles and clerestory have lancet windows, with continuous dripmoulds, N side, of the building period between the 1223 fire and the 1239 consecration. The N aisle NE window is different, three stepped lancets under one arch, comparable to the E arm of Worcester Cathedral (begun 1224). Plain E.E.-type corbel table beneath the battlements, but the flying buttresses belong with the rebuilding of the high vault after 1288. The E end is notable for the strange

---

[*] *Transactions of the Worcestershire Archaeological Society*, Third Series 15, 1996.

combination of an (originally) straight-ended Lady Chapel of
three bays flanked by single-bay chapels with additional N and   p. 523
S chapels like a minor second transept. The English, ever since
Canterbury, had liked that kind of plan; at Pershore it clashes
with the high chancel ending in a three-sided apse. *Eginton*'s
low apse, 1845–7, is a rather starved, though properly detailed,
replacement for the Lady Chapel. The two E chapels alongside
it have the earliest C13 details seen so far. Their flat buttresses
have nook-shafts, with fillets and trumpet-scallop capitals; that
cannot be much later than *c.* 1210–20. The N and S transept-
like chapels have different buttresses of proper C13 type, with
set-offs, but the continuation of the plinth mouldings from the
NE chapel onto the N chapel E wall proves they were planned
at the same time. The N chapel has a renewed Perp E window,
the S chapel is entirely by *Scott*. He also contributed the E
window of the SE chapel, based on its stepped S window
which belonged to remodelling of *c.* 1300. Two S chancel aisle
windows are similar but slightly later, with more ogee detail.
This post-1288 remodelling may have been connected with St
Edburga's shrine, if this stood in the SE chapel (the demolished
chapel in the angle of S aisle and transept is perhaps another
candidate).

The CROSSING TOWER, a beautiful piece of the early C14,
has polygonal buttresses, each containing a stair-vice; tall
pinnacles by *Scott*, 1869–71. Two two-light windows each side
with very curious tracery: a broad top trefoil into which the
pointed-trefoiled heads of the two lights stick up (cf. Madley,
Herefordshire, *c.* 1318); no ogees yet. The embattled string
course above with its ballflower frieze suggests a date
c. 1320–30. More embryonic ballflower beneath the plain
parapet. Bell-openings also two of two lights, with blind two-
light windows either side. All have tracery with ogee reticulation units and gables with pinnacles above, very similar to the
tower of Salisbury Cathedral. Low, copper-covered, pyramidal
roof.

Interior

The present entrance, through the N transept vestry, emerges
immediately beneath the crossing tower, exhilaratingly open to
the ceiling; it is even more difficult to divert one's eyes from
the splendid C13 chancel. Detailed inspection, however, should   23
begin in the SOUTH TRANSEPT, where it is evident that, just
as at Gloucester and Tewkesbury, the system of elevation dif-
fered in the Norman chancel from that in the nave. The nave,   11
as we have seen, had high piers and high narrow aisles. The
arches into the chancel aisle show a perfectly normal height,
which in Norman terms means enough space for a gallery of
normal height. The arches are simple, with just one roll moulding; so are the capitals, just one or more scallops. The blocked
opening to the E chapel or apse follows in the E wall. Its N
capital looks even more ancient, a vestigial volute, a type of

c. 1100. Beneath the S, of block type, a C13 trefoil-plan piscina, with nailhead. S of the blocked opening is the shafted window, detailed as outside. Below it begins blank arcading, continuing round the S wall. All shafts are missing, but the arches have thinly incised zigzag with flat beading. Above the aisle arch is the blocked gallery arch;* above the chapel arch, the blocked arch of an upper apse at gallery level (again as at Tewkesbury). Then a low triforium wall passage again continuing onto the S wall; shafts mostly with block capitals. The upper part of the wall poses a problem. Above the triforium level is another row of small single openings with short shafts and wall passage. This does not appear to have been a clerestory (though external evidence is confusing). Jean Bony, in 1937, suggested that this upper triforium may have been followed by a clerestory yet higher up: a four-tier elevation such as had also been postulated for Tewkesbury. However, as at Tewkesbury, it is now generally accepted that the Pershore Norman transept had a three-tier elevation, with barrel vault above. A break in the masonry is visible on the E wall immediately above the upper triforium; the outline of such a vault can indeed be made out high up on the circular SW stair-turret. The upper triforium wall passage continues onto the S wall with a larger two-bay opening; this has spiral and zigzag shafts, and capital with beaded interlace spreading round the angles. The E wall passage also has slightly later capitals than the stages below (though one shaft still has a volute). This tallies with the chevron arches in the gable outside. The three-bay vault has ridge ribs, one pair of tiercerons towards the E and W walls, and large bosses: mostly foliage as in the chancel, also two heads, one crowned. One shield, against the SW turret, refers to Abbot William Newnton (1413–57) but the vault is earlier, probably *c.* 1320 (see the large ballflowers at the junction of the transverse ribs with the wall arches). It probably belongs to the end of the post-1288 campaign. The limited evidence in the NORTH TRANSEPT fits the above interpretation. Against the N crossing arch are further indications of a barrel vault. Arch to the N chancel aisle with capital with beaded interlace, N, remains of a volute, S.

The CROSSING arches rest on elongated piers, with responds of paired demi-shafts, once more as at Tewkesbury and Gloucester. Of capitals one, SW pier, has lively human busts and beaded interlace, another, SE, is scalloped, with trefoil-leaf patterns (cf. the font), two heads, and more beaded interlace; others are mostly plain blocks. Single-stepped arches. The early C14 work above has a glorious grille of window openings and blank panelling, a presage of the Gloucester Perp tracery panelling. Window openings with double tracery, one layer to the outside, one inside. All beautifully complemented by *Scott*'s amazing ringing-stage of 1862–4, miraculously

---

*Its E face shows it had two sub-arches. The chancel gallery must have been reached, from the transept's SW stair-turret, along the S and E wall passages.

supported by flying timbers, one of his happiest inventions. Ornate two-light w window, also of course by *Scott*.

The CHANCEL is of four bays plus the canted bay which, with the entrance arch to the former Lady Chapel, forms the three-sided apse. The piers are almost as exuberantly subdivided as at Wells Cathedral. There, in work begun in the 1180s, they have twenty-four shafts in eight groups, at Pershore there are mostly sixteen in eight groups, with bolder singles in the diagonals, and triplets (with axial fillet) in the main directions. Arches subdivided accordingly. Capitals of the richest stiff-leaf of *c.* 1230, much richer than the shafts in the w bays of the chancel aisles which are closer to the tighter stiff-leaf or crocket type (which we shall see in the surviving bay of the slightly earlier Lady Chapel). Above the arches, hoodmoulds on stiff-leaf sprays. In the spandrels the vaulting shafts start. They end in lush stiff-leaf, but end very low compared with the upper system of openings. This is of a peculiar, very characteristic kind. Clerestory lancets set very high up, but with the internal wall passage at a much lower level. From that level rises a stepped tripartite shafting of clusters of shafts with stiff-leaf capitals tying the lancets in with the passage. It is a pulling together of what used to be gallery or triforium with the clerestory, resulting in a two-tier instead of three-tier elevation. In this Pershore follows St David's Cathedral (*c.* 1180–93) and Llanthony Abbey (begun *c.* 1190). That far the chancel represents what existed at the consecration in 1239.

The former LADY CHAPEL and the arrangements connected with it seem, as we have noted from the exterior, to predate the 1223 fire. Inside, the apse part and the remaining w bay of the Lady Chapel have exuberant Purbeck-type marble shafting in profusion. Similar details in the three-light N aisle window. The fire may have dictated that work begun *c.* 1220 beyond the E end of the Norman church had to be continued in a more sober style.* The entry arch from apse to Lady Chapel is higher than the others. A certain muddle appears in the shafts, especially above the s entry pier, where sprays of foliage disguise the end of the s arcade mouldings; this could have resulted from work begun from the w after 1223 having to join up with what already existed. A date of *c.* 1220 is perhaps confirmed for this E end when one looks at the tripartite arcading above, here of course blank. The shafts are gathered together by big round capitals; the outer ones have foliage, but the inner are late trumpet scallops, almost as if pleated, the so-called cornucopia (or piecrust) variety. This also occurs with stiff-leaf and moulded capitals, well into the c13, at Bretforton (q.v.), Slimbridge (Glos.), and Wells Cathedral, nave w end. Such capitals, consistent with the external detail of the flanking chapels, are surely impossible much after *c.* 1230. In the first bay of the Lady Chapel the early c13 work,

---

* Roger Stalley and Malcolm Thurlby speculate that the first early c13 master mason at Pershore may have moved on to work on the Worcester Cathedral E arm, 1224–32.

with its stepped sharply pointed lancets, can easily be distinguished from the competent E.E. style of *Eginton*'s apse.

The AISLES have quadripartite rib vaults, as have the chapels, except the SE; its vault has ridge ribs with large central foliage boss and foliated shafts on head corbels, remodelling consistent with the inserted windows, *c.* 1300, which belong to the same campaign as the post-1288 chancel vault. In the S chancel aisle W bay, the former entry to the chapel (or ?sacristy) is evident, with the same details as outside. Opposite, beneath a trap-door under the S arcade W bay, are the footings of the Late Saxon church.

24 The extremely beautiful CHANCEL VAULT is historically very important; it is of shortly after the fire of 1288, certainly not later than the first decade of the C14. It is remarkable how perfectly it blends with the chancel's early C13 work. The historic interest of the vault is this. It consists of transverse arches, diagonal ribs, ridge ribs, one pair of tiercerons to N and S, but in addition lierne ribs (possibly their first surviving usage), forming a kind of scissors movement: open-closed-open-closed, all along. Such scissor liernes also appear in the crypt of St Stephen's Chapel in the Palace of Westminster, 1292–7. At Pershore the design may have been triggered by the complication of vaulting the space above the High Altar in the three-sided apse; this in turn may have inspired the lost vault of Tewkesbury's eastern Lady Chapel and consequently the stunning vaulting above the High Altar there). Pershore must be as early as anywhere in this enrichment of rib vaulting with 25 a view to creating delightful confusion. Beautiful large bosses, still naturalistic, with occasional heads (cf. Exeter Cathedral, *c.* 1280–1300), not yet of the bubbled-foliage type of the C14.

Furnishings

FONT. Norman, much weathered. Round bowl, with tapering sides, with Christ and the Apostles under beaded intersecting arches, also trefoil-leaf patterns. At the top of the shaft (added by *Brakspear*, 1920), trumpet-scallop capitals. Dating is not easy. The beaded interlace and trefoil-leaf, comparable to that mostly at high level in crossing and transepts, suggests the second quarter of the C12; the trumpet-scallop capitals make a later date more probable. COVER by *Claude E.A. Andrews*, 1951. – REREDOS, in the blocked arch of the S transept E chapel. Perp, with blank trefoiled and sub-cusped arcading, and foliage frieze as on timber rood screens. – SCREEN. N transept E. A fragment, of timber, inscribed: MC bis bino triplex et addere quarto/Anno Willelmis dni Newnton fect Abbas; also a king's head with H.VI. anno XII, and abbot's head with W.N. anno XXII. All this means 1435. – LECTERN. Brass eagle by *Hart & Son*, 1868. – TILES, SE chapel. C15. – PEWS and STALLS (now S transept) by *Scott*. – STALLS and ALTAR TABLE in the apse are by *George G. Pace*, 1961–2. – CURIOSUM. Parchment inspeximus, 1453, granting royal privileges to the abbot (S transept NE). – WALL PAINTINGS. Traces of a large figure, SE crossing pier, N side. – On the W wall, the memorial to Dr Williamson, designed by *Scott*, executed by *Clayton & Bell*, 1866. – Also theirs, faded painting above the Lady Chapel arch. – STAINED GLASS. By *Clayton & Bell*, the apse and W windows, 1866; S aisle SW and four in the clerestory, 1871–2; N aisle NW, 1877. – By *Lavers, Barraud & Westlake*, N aisle central, 1870, and NE chapel E, 1879. – By *Hardman*, two large historical S aisle windows of 1870, and S chapel S, 1874. – By *Mayer & Co.*, S chapel E, 1879, and N aisle NE, 1898. – SE chapel E window by *Kempe*, 1888.

Monuments

All S transept, unless otherwise stated. – Knight, *c.* 1280–1300, perhaps of the Harley family; cross-legged (minus his feet), in chain-mail and surcoat, with sword and shield. The hunter's horn in his ungloved r. hand and the three buckles of his chest-plate are rare features. He rests on the lid of an earlier stone coffin.* – C15 abbot, perhaps Edmund Hert (1456–79), his head on his mitre; much eroded. Low C14 tomb-chest with quatrefoils. – Thomas Haselwood †1624. Large standing monument, long and low, with recumbent effigy; large kneeling figures of his widow Elizabeth at his head, his son Francis by his feet. Three Composite columns support a straight top with heraldry; strapwork decoration. – Fulke Haselwood †1595 and wife Dorothy †1625. Round arch between Composite columns, their kneeling figures missing; heraldry above. Kneeling children against the tomb-chest (N transept). – War memorial by *Alfred Drury*, 1920–1; winged bronze figure of Immortality, Portland stone pedestal. – Many tablets. William Cradock †1782, with broken pediment, has his hatchment above. – So has the Rev. William Probyn †1825, by *J. Stephens*. Nicer tablet, with draped urn, to his wife Mary †1802, by *Bryan & Wood*. – S aisle. John Bedford †1840 and son †1854; Gothic, by *Peter Hollins*, the son's hatchment in the N transept.

Precincts

The basic layout of the monastic buildings, S of the church as usual, was revealed by excavations in 1929–30; nothing remains above ground. The Norman chapter house seems to have been round (cf. Worcester Cathedral), its diameter about 36 ft (11 metres). It did not project beyond the E range of the cloister, and its ceiling must have been flat, as the dormitory lay above (cf. Haughmond Abbey, Salop). The cloister garth was only some 70 ft (21.5 metres) square.

The present churchyard, with many trees, merges to S and W into Abbey Park, the grounds of the demolished Abbey House (battlemented Tudor Gothic, *c.* 1840). Several chest

*Another heavy stone coffin, with coped lid, in the N transept.

tombs, *c.* 1800; also an early C17 one, a little N of the E end. C15 CROSS, S, with octagonal base and part of the shaft, from Wyre Piddle (p. 783).

OTHER CHURCHES

ST ANDREW (now Parish Centre), facing the E end of the Abbey church. Originally built for Westminster Abbey tenants (*see* p. 521). Nave N arcade probably of *c.* 1190; five bays, rather thin round piers with round trumpet-scallop capitals, single-chamfered arches. The aisle is otherwise C14, and what remains of the medieval chancel may also be of this date; Dec nave W window with reticulated tracery. Wide S aisle added in the early C15, with good Perp tower at its W end: four-centred bell-openings with ogee tops, battlements, gargoyles and other grotesque carvings; four-centred tower arch with concave mouldings and capital bands. Against its NE angle, the W respond of the S arcade, replaced later in the C15 by the present one further N, making the nave rather narrow. This four-bay arcade, with octagonal piers with castellated capitals, was much renewed by *Aston Webb* who restored the church in 1887. Much other detail must be his, see the gabled Perp window lighting the chapel in the N aisle E bay; the crocketed image niche in its E reveal is at least partly C15. Late Perp wagon roofs. Poor brick S porch, *c.* 1800. S aisle crudely subdivided for parish use by *Neil Macfadyen*, 1971–2. – SCULPTURE. In the N aisle E wall, inside, a headless Saxon figure, with close diagonal draperies, holding a strap; probably C9–C10 (cf. Breedon-on-the-Hill, Leics.). – ROYAL ARMS. George II. – STAINED GLASS. Two N aisle windows by *William Pearce Ltd*, 1899 and *c.* 1908. – Outside, S of the S aisle, the former FONT; Late Norman, with square bowl, triple-scalloped below, circular stem. – Large CHURCHYARD, S, with early C19 chest tombs.

VICARAGE, NE. 1827 by *Thomas Lewis*, builder, of St Pancras, London; altered 1848, for example the two canted bay windows at the side. Stuccoed three-bay front with recessed central entrance; shallow hipped slate roof.

HOLY REDEEMER (R.C.), Priest Lane. 1958–9 by *Hugh Bankart* of Bath. Traditional buttressed brick exterior, with mullioned stone windows and shallow-gabled, pantiled roof; flat-roofed W narthex. The interior is more progressive, at least liturgically. Almost square in plan, with broadly curved roof; only the small NE and SE chapels provide separately enclosed spaces. – Some FURNISHINGS by pupils of Eric Gill: FONT by *John Skelton*, stone ALTARS by *Joseph Cribb*. – STATIONS OF THE CROSS by *Rosamund Fletcher* of Oxford, sub-Gill in spirit. – CROSS behind the High Altar (and other metalwork) by *Michael Murray*. – STAINED GLASS. Round chapel windows by *Philip Brown*. – *Dalle-de-verre* W window by *Dom Charles Norris* of Buckfast Abbey, *c.* 1985. – Attached PRESBYTERY, 1966.

Neat pale brick SCHOOL, further S, by *Pinckheard & Partners* of Oxford, 1966–7.

BAPTIST CHAPEL, Broad Street. The brick chapel by *S.W. Daukes*, 1839–40, is hidden from the street by ancillary buildings: two-storeyed schoolrooms by *Ingall & Son*, 1888, free Tudor Gothic, brick with stone dressings; and the earlier school and manse, 1866–8, of vigorously patterned brickwork. The chapel, reached through a central passage, has four bays of Y-traceried windows in recessed Gothic frames. Flat panelled ceiling on corbels. Refitted in the 1980s; the original three-sided gallery remains, its trefoil-panelled front on thin quatrefoil iron columns. Unusually the baptistery stands at the opposite end from the pulpit.

CEMETERY, Defford Road. By *S.W. Daukes*, 1874–5. Brick LODGE, with notched window heads. CHAPELS of coursed Lias, with heavy plate tracery, linked by the usual high-gabled central archway, but the stone-spired turret is set asymmetrically above the buttressed SE vestry of the Anglican (N) chapel. Nonconformist chapel with slightly lower roof-line.

PUBLIC BUILDINGS

WYCHAVON CIVIC CENTRE, Queen Elizabeth Drive. 1990–1 by *C. Roger Ainley*, Wychavon District Chief Architect. A rambling conglomeration of sub-vernacular styles. Pink brick core, its high round-arched entrance leading through to the civic suite, flanked by square meeting rooms: both have pyramidal roofs, partly glazed, S, with heavy octagonal skylight, N. Two-storey office wings either side, occasional leaded bay windows. Big addition with half-hipped roofs N of the entrance. Attractively paved courtyards to the rear, by the pedestrian entrance from High Street.

PUBLIC LIBRARY, Church Street. 1974–5 by *Darbourne & Darke* (principal architect *Graham Hussey*); part of their town centre redevelopment (*see* pp. 537–8). Orange brick, variously pitched roofs of artificial slate, patches of full-height glazing; square central clerestory. Inside, the structural steel frame supports a narrow all-round gallery. – Across a garden court, facing Lower Priest Lane, the same practice's HEALTH CENTRE, 1975–6; small entrance courtyard, irregular street front.

COTTAGE HOSPITAL, Defford Road. 1895 by *J.H. Williams*; plain brick, gabled. Later additions, the S wing by *Claude E.A. Andrews*, 1937. – The ABBOTSWOOD MEDICAL CENTRE, S, is by the *Gould Singleton Partnership*, 1991–2; plum brick, orange trim, shallow-hipped pantiled roof. – A little N, two pairs of semi-detached ALMSHOUSES, the earlier, S, dated 1913; low, brick, outer half-timbered gables.

Former UNION WORKHOUSE, Station Road. By *Sampson Kempthorne*, 1836. Only the plain brick entrance range remains,* flanked by additions by *George Hunt*: lancet-style chapel, 1871, N, with inserted late C20 roundels; projecting

---

*The main part behind followed Kempthorne's usual square cross plan.

wing, 1891, s, with large canted bay to the former boardroom. Converted to sheltered housing 1974.

PERSHORE COLLEGE (OF HORTICULTURE). *See* Wick.

PERSHORE HIGH SCHOOL, Station Road. By *A. V. Rowe*, 1930–1, rendered, with hipped pantiled roof; central hall, with three large windows, two-storey classroom wings. Extensive additions, especially 1961–2 (entrance block) and 1971–8.

RAILWAY STATION, 1⅓ m. N. Opened 1853; no buildings remain. At the head of the station approach, the former COVENTRY ARMS HOTEL; brick, three bays, recessed centre with triple-arcaded entrance, hipped roof.

PERSHORE BRIDGES. In three sections, the two N probably still partly medieval: a timber bridge, first mentioned 1290, was later rebuilt in stone, traditionally in 1413. N part with three segmental arches with cutwaters. The main bridge, with upstream cutwaters only, has five small arches and one large middle one, widened *c.* 1635 for William Sandys's Avon improvements, again rebuilt after Civil War damage. Much brick patching and renewal, see the NW arch dated 1820. S part probably mostly by *Thomas Fulljames*, 1840.

The current ferro-concrete bridge is by the county surveyor, *C. F. Gittings*, 1925–6; three segmental arches, the central one very wide, all slightly skewed. Four circular flood openings on the town side. Solid concrete parapets.

PERAMBULATIONS

1. Broad Street

The best place to start is BROAD STREET, a little SSW of the Abbey, short and wide like a market square; now inevitably a car park, until 1836–7 the centre had houses and a shambles. Mostly uneventful Late Georgian, the best displays either end. Nos. 7–11, NW corner, a good group of three, *c.* 1810, are each of three bays and storeys, with channelled voussoirs and pedimented doorways (leading to stick-balustered stairs). The central house is emphasized by a small central pediment, and canted bays flanking a taller doorcase with Doric columns. No. 21 (now Lloyds TSB) is similar. The Baptist chapel (p. 531), dominating the SW corner, is followed by modest early C19 frontages: No. 4 stuccoed with even quoins and two-storey bay; No. 12 nicely combining bow window and reeded doorway.

Nos. 1–5, originally one house, also *c.* 1810, fills the short W end: three storeys, three wide bays, lower two-storey wings. Central Venetian doorway flanked by single-storey bay windows; round-arched window above, flanked by Venetian ones (with brick mullions and pretty keystones). The outer second-floor windows are tripartite. The irregular wings repeat the Venetian prejudice.

DEFFORD ROAD, s, starts with more houses with nice doorcases, especially No. 3, late C18: enriched Doric pilasters with oval

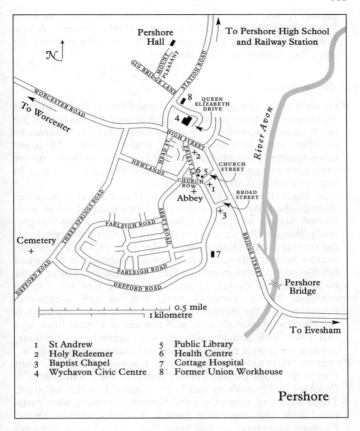

Pershore
Hall

To Pershore High School
and Railway Station

𝒩

To Worcester

WORCESTER ROAD

MOUNT PLEASANT

GIG BRIDGE LANE

STATION ROAD

QUEEN
ELIZABETH
DRIVE

8

4

HIGH STREET

PRIEST STREET

HEAD STREET

NEWLANDS

2

6 5

CHURCH
STREET

CHURCH
ROW

1

Abbey

BROAD
STREET

3

River Avon

Cemetery

THREE SPRINGS ROAD

DEFFORD ROAD

FARLEIGH ROAD

ABBEY ROAD

FARLEIGH ROAD

DEFFORD ROAD

BRIDGE STREET

7

Pershore
Bridge

0.5 mile
1 kilometre

To Evesham

1   St Andrew
2   Holy Redeemer
3   Baptist Chapel
4   Wychavon Civic Centre

5   Public Library
6   Health Centre
7   Cottage Hospital
8   Former Union Workhouse

Pershore

rosettes, Gothick fanlight, open dentilled pediment. Its side
elevation, two bays with tripartite windows on both floors,
adjoins the higher hipped-roofed PRESTON HOUSE, and this
in turn PERSHORE HOUSE, c. 1830: stuccoed, three broad
bays, lower one-bay wings. Ground floor breaking forward, tripartite windows flanking its wide doorway; first floor with
louvred shutters, bracketed eaves. Both these houses have
drives curving back from Defford Road, the latter with
wrought-iron gates with openwork piers of linked circles.

Back to BROAD STREET. Its E end opens onto the main N–S road
through the town, here with some good façades (p. 534).
Higher buildings mark the E ends of Broad Street, plain stuccoed NE, more varied SE: the rendered Nos. 24–28, mid-C18
with segment-headed windows, then former THREE TUNS
HOTEL, ashlar-faced, probably c. 1830. Longer side towards

Broad Street, with fine wrought-iron first-floor veranda
fronting wide sashed windows; three-bay front towards Bridge
Street, its big porch with square piers now sadly without the
three barrels that sat on its flat roof.

2. *Bridge Street*

BRIDGE STREET, by far the best Georgian street in Pershore, is
also one of the most complete in the county. All the houses are
brick (unless otherwise stated); relatively few, in contrast to
Bewdley, seem to conceal earlier timber framing. Most are
three-storeyed, several have two-storey bay windows. As we
shall have to retrace our steps, we can examine each side in
turn, beginning with the E side, N end.

E SIDE. No. 1 (BRIDGE HOUSE), facing Broad Street, is plain but
distinguished late C18, four bays, the l. one wider above the segmental carriage arch; pedimented Doric doorway with fanlight.
No. 3 (Barclays Bank), also late C18 but grander, has seven bays,
the central one projecting with an elaborate tripartite doorway:
narrow central pilasters with rosettes, repeated on the broad
brick outer pilasters, grandiose fanlight exaggerated by an outer
band of linked circles. Inside, a charming Gothick dog-leg
staircase. No. 5, restored 1973, was an C18 warehouse,
converted to a fire station 1902. No. 7 (BEDFORD HOUSE), is
stuccoed two-bay early C19, with rusticated ground floor, and
first floor with delicate wrought-iron veranda on brackets;
upper storeys with panelled pilasters. Contemporary interior.

PERROTT HOUSE (No. 17) is the finest in Pershore, built
c. 1770 for Judge George Perrott, Baron of the Exchequer; *T.F.
Pritchard* of Shrewsbury has been suggested as the architect.
Three bays and storeys, central Venetian doorway with rusticated arch and decorative glazing, Venetian window above.
Flanking two-storey canted bays, their ground-floor windows
also Venetian (bent round). All the second-storey windows are
tripartite. One-bay central pediment; even quoins. All these are
typical county motifs, but the Adamish interior decoration
(well restored after fire in 1998) is exceptional, leading to spec-
ulation that the judge employed London designers and craftsmen. The entrance hall runs through the centre of the house,
with wings projecting to either side at the (rendered) rear. The
front room, l., has extremely delicate stucco work: central
ceiling roundel of a reclining female figure, painted, plus busts
in the main directions, hunting scenes in the angles. Behind
this, the delightful dog-leg staircase, with restrained panelling
and glazed skylight. The rear room has splendid panels of
musical instruments or thyrsi with grapevine foliage. Oval
mirror above the grey marble fireplace; fluted Venetian window
with acanthus decoration. – Low COACHHOUSE, N, with
basket-arched carriage entrance and upper lunette windows.
The long garden stretches down to the Avon (as do most on
this side of Bridge Street); fine wrought-iron railings and
gateway facing the river.

Next door, No. 19 (WESTERN HOUSE), dated 'ID 1825' on a brick above the cellar grille. Three bays, doorway with open pediment on engaged Doric columns, l., nicely adjoining the roll-moulded elliptical carriage arch. Much contemporary detail inside. Nos. 21 and 23 (THE STAR INN) incorporate earlier timber-framed structures; No. 25 (THE BRANDY CASK), stuccoed, with broad later C19 bay, has basket-arched windows with cable-moulded surrounds. Then three houses of c. 1800 with further variations on the theme of Doric columns for doorways: No. 27, pedimented with fine triglyph frieze; No. 29, taller columns, with fluted capitals and triglyph frieze, but no pediment; No. 31, as above but severely undecorated. Plainer houses follow but the doorways continue to provide interest: that at Nos. 35–37 has Soanean incisions and Y-fanlight. Even the modestly stuccoed No. 51 has a notable doorway, round-arched and fluted, with paterae. At No. 55 the late C18 Venetian window theme reappears, their rusticated arches highlighted by alternate black and white painting. Finally, after a former warehouse, long and low, later used as a Friends' Meeting Room, the three-bay MILL HOUSE, again c. 1800, at right angles to the street, facing S. The large mill, gutted by fire in 1976, was unfortunately replaced by housing c. 2000. At least the open countryside of the Avon flood plain follows immediately; Pershore Bridges (p. 532) are a little further S.

Now back along the W SIDE, beginning, slightly further S, with the TOLL HOUSE, a late example of 1857: gabled brick, flat castellated bays, wavy bargeboards. The footpath alongside leads to the long crinkle-crankle brick WALL of the former Manor House garden (now filled with late C20 housing). The MANOR HOUSE, back in Bridge Street, is stuccoed Tudor Gothic, with bargeboarded gables, bay windows, and castel-lated porch with Dec-traceried upper window; quoins and square hoodmoulds to the road. Probably by *S. W. Daukes*, c. 1840–50.

Then continuous Georgian brick houses, the most worthwhile at this end, in contrast to the E side. The first, No. 74, modest enough, three bays with rusticated lintels masking C17 timber framing, has an ostentatious mid-C18 doorway with fluted columns with swag capitals supporting an oversailing wooden hood on heavily carved brackets; it leads straight into the main room, with Adam-style fireplace. Nos. 70–72 are semi-detached later C18; each house has only one bay with windows with stepped lintels and iron balconies, plus outer doorway with attenuated Doric columns and inward-curving moulded hoods. Then, the OLD MALTHOUSE, a former warehouse, and Nos. 66–68, with good later C18 Doric doorcases with pedi-ments.

No. 60 (STANHOPE HOUSE), a notable example of c. 1770–80, 96 was built for George Perrott, nephew of the judge (cf. Cray-combe House, p. 318). Open-pedimented Doric doorcase, approached by a curving double flight of steps; two-storey bay windows either side. The narrow second floor has outer tri-partite windows. Good interior: central dog-leg staircase with grooved balusters, panelled room with Adamish fireplace. To its l., the former STABLE BLOCK, a fine five-bay composition, the centre projecting with pediment; round-arched ground-floor windows. Nos. 56–58, another good semi-detached pair of *c.* 1800, have three bays altogether, the central window blind above a double doorway with three Doric columns; quoins, rusticated window lintels, parapet with three blocked roundels. The w side continues with mostly Late Georgian houses. No. 48 (GOTHIC HOUSE) has a mid-C19 stone Gothic doorway, tall, with hoodmould, and matching canted bay window. Nos. 42 and 44 (FERN HOUSE) have doorways with fluted pilasters, but completely differing detail; compare the doorcase of No. 36. The remainder are uneventful. Some hide vestigial timber framing, visible from the passageway at No. 28, which has a rear WOOL BARN, early C19, brick, three storeys. In Masons Way, the passage between Nos. 22 and 24, a timber-framed C17 cottage with jettied upper floor. Several houses clearly once served as shops; No. 10 was, from 1841 to 1864, the town's police station, with courtroom on the upper floor.

3a. High Street

HIGH STREET, the N continuation of Bridge Street, contains less of interest, though it remains basically Georgian despite later shopfronts. At the start, facing Broad Street, are Nos. 1–3, rendered early C19; pretty first-floor wrought-iron verandas in front of shuttered windows, more or less original shopfronts below. No. 5 (HSBC bank) is fine Early Georgian brick, with rusticated ground floor: five bays, three storeys, segment-headed windows with decorated (mostly floral) keystones, even quoins. Good staircase, each tread with one turned, one twisted baluster. Then the ANGEL INN, refronted 1922: rendered, two-storey bow windows flanking the entrance. In the rear bar, a tall decorative plaster panel with female figure and remains of the date 1575 (found between timber studs). At No. 11, a late C18 doorway with fluted pilasters and Gothick fanlight.

Opposite, late C18 brick frontages with windows with rusticated voussoirs. The largest, No. 8, three storeys and five bays, with stuccoed and channelled ground floor, was converted to an arts centre by *McMorran & Gatehouse*, 2004; theirs the tented iron balcony and large rear auditorium.

Back on the E side, No. 19, four bays, has a pedimented doorway with Doric columns with fluted capitals and enriched fanlight; a rounded rusticated carriage entrance opens onto a courtyard, with C18–C19 wool barn closing the rear, E, side. Then Nos. 21–23, three bays with central double doorway of *c.* 1800: three Adamish columns with combined triglyph frieze. Beneath runs a medieval tunnel-vaulted cellar. The part below No. 21 contains, on the s wall, a large beautiful piscina, pointed-cinque-foiled with fillets, late C13, apparently *in situ*; so this must have been a chapel of some kind, approached from the floor above by a stone spiral stair, which partly survives. Steps down from the street are probably post-medieval. No. 25 has a timber-framed carriage arch, labelled Lunns Yard; Nos. 31–33, lower, brick-faced, also conceal C16–C17 timber framing. The three-bay No. 35 has another good doorway. Then No. 37, formerly Pershore RDC offices; late C18, three wide bays, three storeys, the same provincial type we have met before. Slightly project-ing centre with doorway with open pediment on unfluted Ionic columns, two-storey canted bays either side; above them, Diocletian windows. Mostly C19 rear wing. Formerly the home of the Wilson family, whose tannery lay at the rear.

Opposite, the TOWN HALL, built as a Post Office, 1932; typical *Office of Works* Neo-Georgian, five bays, the stone ground-floor with three round-arched windows flanked by doorways with rusticated voussoirs. Rear extension by *McMorran & Gate-house*, 2002, its long side with timber-framed glazing; this faces a new crinkle-crankle brick wall, creating a passageway to the Abbey. At No. 40, another pleasant pedimented doorcase.

After No. 45, five-bay stuccoed with heavy doorway, the scale begins to decrease, with more buildings concealing earlier timber framing behind their brick fronts. The rendered chapel-like No. 57 (Pershore Working Mens Club), dated 1847, was built as the British School; tall square-hooded windows flank-ing the doorway, shaped parapet. Opposite, occasional door-ways to note, now plainer (No. 66), and several canted bay windows, now single-storeyed (No. 74 and Nos. 80–82).

After the intrusive garage (incorporating 1871 brick buildings of the Atlas agricultural machinery works), High Street turns W, its houses reducing to cottage scale, mostly still with early C19 brick frontages. No. 102, a former smithy, shows timber framing at the rear. This makes a rare street appearance at No. 103A on the opposite, now N, side. Then one or two detached early C19 villas (No. 115, set back) before the pathway to Wychavon Civic Centre (p. 531). On the S side, after Priest Lane (leading back to Holy Redeemer R.C., p. 530), the former POLICE STATION by *Henry Rowe*, 1865–6; three-bay centre with segment-headed windows and hipped roof, lower wings. No. 184 is a final three-bay Georgian house, with pedimented doorway.

3b. South of High Street: Head Street, Newlands etc.

We can return to the Abbey along HEAD STREET, leading S from the W end of High Street. No. 63, NE corner, is early C19 stuc-coed; almost opposite, a restored C17–C18 timber-framed barn. Then all is C20, apart from the plain ST AGATHA'S MISSION HALL (by *William Lunn*, 1895). On the W side, standard council houses of the 1930s. The E side has a long and a short terrace, with neat garden walls, all orange brick, part of a size-able housing redevelopment by *Darbourne & Darke*, immacu-lately stitched into the existing urban fabric; begun 1973 for

Pershore RDC, mostly completed by 1977 for Wychavon DC.
128   The best part is a charming low-key green, E of Head Street,
reached from The Mews (alongside the Mission Hall) by a passageway with houses above. The green, with informal planting,
is surrounded by an irregular mix of semi-detached houses and
short terraces, plus bungalows in little walled enclosures; all
have shallow-pitched roofs. Pathways lead through E, via
parking lots, to Priest Lane, and S, across smaller linear green
spaces to Newlands.

NEWLANDS, a wide, straight, closely built-up street, must have
been a medieval development by the Abbey; its E end focuses
on the church tower. First briefly W, past the stuccoed mid-
C19 VICTORIA HOTEL. One C17 framed house (Nos. 39–41)
survives, the rest are C18–C19 brick. ROLAND RUTTER
COURT is a well-designed brick group of sheltered housing,
built 1977 for the Royal British Legion Housing Association;
mostly two-storeyed, rising higher above the entrance on four
concrete piers. Street front articulated by full-height bay
windows; two well-planted courtyards behind, with instead
intervals of full-height glazing. No. 101 (AMERIE COURT),
further W, an early C19 farmhouse, has three wide bays, stuccoed and rusticated, with quoins; earlier rear gabled range.
Small timber-framed barn.

Now back E, where more timber framing survives, amongst late
C18–early C19 brick. The gabled roughcast No. 58 has an odd
doorway, with pilasters with bulbous capitals and wavy frieze,
perhaps of 1836 (the date above the rear archway from Head
Street). No. 19, S side, is the best brick house, mid-to-late C18:
three bays, rusticated lintels, canted ground-floor bays flanking the doorway. The largest timber-framed one, the so-called
ALMONRY, c. 1600, at the SE end, has narrow ground-floor
studding, with square panelling above. Well restored 1973,
retaining just the original entrance which had the hall to its W,
with parlour beyond. If this was the site of Pershore Abbey's
almonry, the main Abbey gateway must have stood nearby.
Opposite, *Darbourne & Darke*'s housing reappears. In Abbey
Road, S of the Almonry, another group by them: ALMONRY
CLOSE, 1977–8, brick housing for the elderly, arranged cres-
cent-wise with rhythmically broken roof-lines; it faces Abbey
Park.

Finally, along CHURCH ROW, N of the Abbey churchyard:
modest stuccoed early C19 terraces (probably hiding earlier
timber framing); the former Black Horse Inn (No. 3), early C19
brick with thin Doric porch; and the much larger WHITE
HORSE HOTEL, brick, c. 1900, with swan-neck pedimented
doorway on stubby Ionic columns. Behind it, the Health
Centre and Library, by *Darbourne & Darke* (p. 531).

OUTER PERSHORE

Of the swathes of C20 housing N and S of the town, the plain
brick RDC scheme, begun c. 1950 around ABBEY ROAD and

FARLEIGH ROAD, is perhaps worth a mention for respecting the extensive green space of Abbey Park, s of the town centre. Along DEFFORD ROAD, a little sw of the Cemetery (p. 531), three interesting houses, all by *Violet Morris* for Harry Blyth, a market gardener and fellow member of the Agapemonite (abode of love) sect of Spaxton, Somerset.* All roughcast in Voysey fashion, especially the first, TYDDESLEY LODGE, 1919, closest to the road, with tile-hung central dormer and end gables. Then, set well back, BENEDICTS, 1926, with two differing tile-hung gables against a steep hipped roof. THE SPINNEY, 1938, also with tile-hung gables, is more altered.

To the N, off Station Road, approached through late C20 housing in Gig Bridge Lane and Mount Pleasant, is PERSHORE HALL, a spiky Tudor Gothic country house by *S. W. Daukes*, 1862, for Edward Humphries, owner of the Atlas Works (p. 537). Diapered brick, battlemented, with polygonal stone corner pinnacles. The tower-like centre of the five-bay SE front has doubled pinnacles, with triangular oriel above the altered doorway; windows with square hoodmoulds, those of the ground floor with headstops and central carved panels; diminishing two-storey bay windows on the returns. NE and SW fronts with central gables with pierced quatrefoil parapets; rear service range. In the staircase hall, NE, doubled tripartite arcades of quatrefoil piers with foliage capitals; stone stairs with matching quatrefoil newels and decorative wrought-iron balustrades. Fine view E across the Avon valley.

Also in STATION ROAD, the former Workhouse, with Wychavon Civic Centre behind; much further N, Pershore High School and the Railway Station (*see* pp. 531–2).

PINVIN

9040

Mostly C20, apart from terraces of the 1880s near Pershore railway station; scattered timber-framed survivors elsewhere. Yet at the village centre is a large rough green, with the small medieval church on its N edge.

ST NICHOLAS. A chapelry of Pershore Abbey. Heavily roughcast chancel: Dec E window, small square N and s openings, perhaps C17–C18. Norman nave, restored and extended w by *Hopkins*, 1884–5, with odd w bellcote, triangular in plan with crocketed pinnacles; Perp-style windows of 1884–5, except the restored SE. Plain Norman s doorway, continuously stepped but the two steps rounded (cf. Worcester Cathedral). One deeply splayed Norman N window also survives; Hopkins replaced the Norman chancel arch. Architectural fragments built into the C17–C18 porch include heads and, above the entrance, a fine

---

*Violet's father, *Joseph Morris* of Reading, with his son Frank, designed the Agapemonite church, the 'Ark of the Covenant', at Upper Clapton, East London, 1893–5.

E.E. stiff-leaf capital. Good N vestry by *Francis B. Andrews*, 1907.

FONT. Late Norman bowl, octagonal, each face with two elongated round-arched panels; C19 stem. – Other fittings mostly by *Hopkins*; the PULPIT incorporates the legs of a C17 communion table. – *Godwin* chancel floor TILES, with a C15 patch in the SE corner. – WALL PAINTINGS. Nave S wall, either side of the Perp SE window. Two substantial areas, discovered 1855, each with at least three layers. The E section, conserved by the *Perry Lithgow Partnership*, 1992, is the most eloquent: notable remains, in two tiers, of a cycle of *c*. 1300 or earlier.
35 Of the upper tier, only the lowest parts remain: Annunciation and Visitation, with good drapery round the legs. Lower scenes much better preserved. They show the Adoration of the Magi, Crucifixion, Resurrection, and part of the Ascension. Overlaying the last, a large C15 figure, probably St Roch, an angel pointing to his plague sore; tree above, upper border with churches and dragon. The third layer, C16–C17 texts, is scarcely visible here, but takes over in the W section, its only other discernible element a large C15 figure, perhaps St Christopher. – STAINED GLASS. E window by *F. W. Skeat*, 1965; mid-C19 glass in its traceries probably by *George Rogers* (cf. the small N and S windows).

8040   PIRTON

ST PETER. The splendid timber-framed NW tower first catches the eye, the only one in Worcestershire with aisles like such Essex towers as Margaretting. Close-set studding, of four stages, with big diagonal braces; internally, especially between its nave and aisles, scissor-braces of formidable scantling. The VCH calls the tower early C16; its timbering, with great cruck forms as braces, and proportions suggest an earlier date, perhaps C14. Norman nave, Dec chancel, but in origin a
p. 23 Norman three-cell church. Restored S doorway of two orders, one with shafts with bulgy scallop capitals, continuous abacus with angular Ss in relief; arch with frontal chevron. The doorway is set in a wall projection, a common motif in the county (cf. Stoulton). Norman S windows altered, but those on the N side (with deep internal splays) survive, partly hidden by the tower; also remains of pilaster buttresses. It is clear from the changing thickness of the walls and the sloping plinth that the E part of the nave was once a central tower, its broad SW stair-vice later converted to a rood stair. Inside this is confirmed by surviving footings of the tower's W wall, including the base of its N respond, clearly of three orders, two with shafts with base spurs. Its E arch, the present wide chancel arch, is single-stepped, of two orders, the outer again with shafts with spurred bases and scalloped capitals. At the apex a carved figure upside down, presumably St Peter. C14 chancel, the E window with renewed reticulated tracery; side windows partly

rebuilt in brick, perhaps in the C16. Trefoil-headed lowside window, SW, discovered by *Hopkins* when he restored the church, 1882–3; he rebuilt the nave W wall with its Dec-style window.

Both N and S DOORS retain original hinges decorated with trefoil-tipped Cs, probably *c.* 1160–80. Much of the carpentry is also original, especially the N door. – SCULPTURE. Norman corbel head above the S doorway. – Re-set over the N doorway, a small, finely preserved, Anglo-Saxon MASS DIAL; markings round the rim may be original lettering. – The church's most remarkable possession, the C13 PIRTON STONE, found built into the chancel arch in 1871, is now at the Ashmolean Museum, Oxford; a replica is displayed. The original, of fine-grained limestone, only 4¾ by 3½ in. (12 by 9 cm.), was probably a die for stamping tin ampullae or pilgrim badges.* – Plain FONT, perhaps C12; shallow round bowl, octagonal stem. Around its base a collection of C14–C15 TILES, some heraldic. – PULPIT. C17; the usual round-arched panels. – COMMUNION RAIL. C18, with close-set balusters. – PEWS. Part C16–C17, much renewed. – STAINED GLASS. E, probably also the lowside window, by *William Pearce Ltd*, 1909. – S of the nave, the base and stump of the medieval CHURCHYARD CROSS.

The church stands on its own, apart from the mid-C19 GREEN-HILL HOUSE, tall, L-plan, coursed Lias; fine views W to the Malvern Hills. The parish has scattered C17 timber-framed farms and cottages; the VILLAGE, ½ m. NW, is largely C20. Here, the former NATIONAL SCHOOL, brick, *c.* 1840–50, with small Tudor schoolroom and higher attached house. A little S, PIRTON GRANGE, the former rectory, with neat early C18 five-bay W front, with moulded keystones. Much enlarged, E, in similar style, by *J.B. Clacy*, 1848; C20 care home additions.

PIRTON COURT, ½ m. WSW, formerly moated. A fragment of the early C17 timber-framed house of the Folliott family, probably its W parlour wing. It now forms the NW wing of an L-plan house remodelled for Viscount Deerhurst (eldest son of the ninth Earl of Coventry), probably at the time of his marriage in 1894. Until the late 1960s the C17 wing had specially jolly decorative timberwork, mostly quadrant studding; this, lost when the projecting square bay collapsed, has been rebuilt in much plainer fashion. Stout lateral stone chimney with brick stacks; alongside, a lower restored range, brick and Lias, with narrow timber upper storey, which must have faced the moat. In the front room, a big juicy chimneypiece, probably late C17, its semicircular pediment filled by a shell; said to come from

---

* It is roughly elliptical, showing Christ crucified, with the Virgin and St John. Their figures are fragmented by raised parts of the stone, left uncarved; four such areas give the rest the shape of a cross. The style of the Crucifixion, reminiscent of metal work, has C11–C12 affinities; the frame has simple Norman motifs. However, the figure of a bishop and model of a church, at the top, are without any doubt Gothic and C13, perhaps representing Canterbury Cathedral. Presumably the carver copied existing models.

Croome Court (p. 244). In the smaller room behind, a
Jacobean plaster ceiling with thin ribs and simple decorative
motifs. The late C19 additions are of standard half-timbering
above brick and stone; nice stair-tower with hipped gambrel
roof with spike.

Further NE, a long timber-framed C17 BARN; brick infill with
diamond-pattern ventilators. – Opposite, a pair of Coventry
estate COTTAGES dated 1904.

8050

POWICK

p. 23 St Peter. A large church, large already by *c.* 1200, see Late
Norman windows in the transepts: N transept W and E, S
transept E; also the S respond of the arch from S aisle to transept
with filleted shaft and scalloped capital. So by then there were
transepts and at least a S aisle. The transepts, at least the S
transept, seem to have had E chapels (or recesses, cf. Ripple).
On the S transept E wall are the roll-moulded jambs of a mysterious arch, presumably for a chapel; the present segmental
arch spans a doorway of 1850. Chancel lengthened in the early
C13. Its E wall has a triplet of stepped lancets, widely spaced
(shafted inside, with shaft-rings and good stiff-leaf capitals);
the N wall, E end, has two close-set lancets beneath continuous
hoodmoulds, plus chamfered doorway. In the later C13 the N
transept received its E window of rather uncouth plate tracery:
three pointed-trefoiled lancets beneath a big barbed trefoil;
within, it is clear this lit an altar. C14 Dec the remaining
chancel windows and those of both aisles; good S aisle
doorway, now blocked, with two continuous sunk quadrant
mouldings. Perp transept end windows, of five lights (N), of
four (S), beneath straight-sided arches. S transept partly early
C19, with Y-traceried E and W windows. Late Perp W tower,
with diagonal buttresses and battlements with blank trefoils;
arch to the nave with partly panelled jambs. Inside, nave and
transepts are predominately Perp, especially the four-bay
arcades and slightly lower transept arches: octagonal piers and
responds, two wave mouldings to each diagonal side, moulded
capitals, double-chamfered arches. Aisle roofs with C15
moulded beams. All much restored by *Eginton*, 1841–5; his
W doorway, PEWS, and most timber SCREENS. The stone arch
beneath the tower, the chancel arch, and most of the rather
quirky chancel fittings are by *J.B. Clacy* of Reading, 1849–50.
His big square reading desk, of oak, was heightened as a
PULPIT by *Hopkins*, who carried out further work, especially
to the nave, in 1896–7.

FONT. Octagonal, Perp: bowl with fleurons in quatrefoils,
stem with trefoiled panels. – Large C18 ROYAL ARMS. – Fine
late C18 ORGAN CASE, by *George Pike England*. – STAINED
GLASS. An excellent Victorian collection, the best the colourful sanctuary windows by *Lavers & Barraud*, *c.* 1862; theirs also
the S transept E lancet. – By *George Rogers*, the S chancel central,

1867, and tower window, 1854. – By *Hardman*: chancel NW and N aisle central, both 1878, N transept E, 1875, and S aisle W, 1883. – N aisle W, 1905, no doubt by *Clayton & Bell*. – Two others, of the 1870s, are also noteworthy. – Early C19 fragments in the S transept W windows.

MONUMENTS. Mary Russell †1786, signed by *Thomas Scheemakers*, 1787, his best independent monument. Reclining female figure, one breast bare, elbow on an urn. On the sar- 84 cophagus a delightful oval of the young mother teaching her child music, flanked by still-lifes of musical instruments. High base with fluted pilasters. – Above, Sir Daniel Tyas †1673, good rustic tablet of 1678 with two standing allegorical figures, two more reclining on top. – Another rustic tablet nearby to William Cookes †1672; black Ionic columns. – Good C18 tablets include Ann Case †1765 by *Richard Squire*, fluted pilasters; Rev. James Giles †1792, by *W. Stephens*, draped urn; and three of painted wood. – Elaborate brass to Major-Gen. John Hinde †1881, by *Hart, Son, Peard & Co*. – Charles Barry Domvile †1936, by *Cecil Thomas*; Hoptonwood stone, finely carved heraldry.

In the CHURCHYARD, a little SSE, large Gothic chest tomb to John Wheeley Lea †1874, no doubt by *Hopkins*; stone and marble, trefoiled arcades opening out as angle buttresses, carved scenes of charity. – Good LYCHGATE, 1912.

The church stands apart, at the end of a drive, E of the VILLAGE. This, on the main Worcester-Malvern road, is largely spoilt. CROSS HOUSE, C16–C17 timber-framed, much renewed, serves as a traffic island. To its SW, the OLD RECTORY, *c*. 1800, stuccoed, five bays, with Doric porch.* To its E, a brick terrace beginning with the RED LION ends with C17 framing (Nos. 42–43), square-panelled with gabled and jettied cross-wing. Then an overgrown drive, with large mid-C19 Swiss-chalet-style LODGE (now Virginia House): decorative weatherboarding, gables on projecting brackets. The drive leads to THE TERRACE, a substantial, quite secluded, mid-to-late C18 brick house; two storeys, 1+3+1 bays (plus another, set back). The central three, projecting beneath a pediment with lunette, have ground-floor windows in blank arches; tripartite doorway. Square blocky porch, its frieze with paterae and corner urns. It may be early C19, perhaps as late as 1845 when *Jones & Clark* of Birmingham added the pretty curving conservatory round the corner, W: iron and copper, largely unaltered.

In KING'S END LANE, N, a pleasant group begins with DAY-BROOK HOUSE, brick, very early C18. Stuccoed houses lead uphill to the OLD VICARAGE: three brick gables of *c*. 1700, with canted bay on the NE end; five bays with hipped roof to the garden, SE. THE HERMITAGE, late C18 brick, has three bays, the outer wider with tripartite windows, but all with depressed ogee heads.

---

* The architect *J. P. St Aubyn* was born here in 1815.

QUEENSBURY HOUSE, Ham Hill, ½ m. NW, is an early C19 hunting lodge. Rendered brick, elaborate *cottage orné* style, square, each side with a large steep gable with pierced bargeboards; Tudor Gothic windows with hoodmoulds. Similar service block, set at a lower level. Vaulted ceilings within. Originally thatched, it belonged to the Marquess of Queensberry in the C19; Lord Alfred Douglas was born here.

On the Malvern road, to the WSW, is the SCHOOL by *Preedy*, 1870–1, restrained Gothic, red brick with yellow bands, the attached house better preserved. Then, approached by Hospital Lane, the site of the enormous CITY AND COUNTY LUNATIC ASYLUM, 1848–52, by *Hamilton & Medland* of Gloucester; Italianate, of brick with ample stone dressings. All that remains are an outlier, BREDON HOUSE, and some distance further WSW, the tall ADMINISTRATIVE BLOCK, three by five bays, its hipped roof with central chimney. This formed the centre of an extensive range 560 ft (172 metres) long, facing open country to the S. More should have been preserved. Now late C20 housing occupies the site, the surviving block hemmed in by Neo-Georgian units that manage to be simpering and regimented at the same time.

POWICK BRIDGES, ⅝ m. N. *See* p. 777.

CALLOW END, 1 m. S, q.v.

8030

QUEENHILL

ST NICHOLAS. A chapelry of Ripple until 1880. Norman nave, C13 chancel, early C14 W tower. The top of the tower, with saddleback roof, is by *G.G. Scott*; he partially restored the church, 1854–5, adding the timber S porch. Further restoration by *J.D. Sedding*, 1891–2. The nave, mostly rebuilt in the C14, retains its (altered) S doorway, *c.* 1170: one order of shafts with scallop capitals, arch with both furrowed zigzag and frontal chevron, pellet hoodmould; cf. Pendock. Inside, nave N, an upside-down head of a Norman window, chip-carved, with two six-rayed stars. Ceiled nave roof with tie-beams. The C13 chancel has large side lancets, double-chamfered, with oversized Late Perp E window; good roof and fittings by *Sedding*. – He restored the C15 SCREEN, one-light Perp divisions with ogee crocketed tops, and C17 PULPIT. This, and its tester, have a top band of C15 vine foliage, perhaps from a rood beam. – Neo-Norman FONT; C12 base with cable moulding. – STAINED GLASS. E window by *Edward Frampton*, 1892, with over-scaled figures; Pevsner thought it 'ghastly'. – In the nave NE, excellent mid-C14 fragments, including St Anne teaching the Virgin. – In the NW, Royal Arms of before 1340. – MONUMENTS. Incised slab to Henry Field †1584 and two wives; good lettering below. – Nice tablets to Major-Gen. John Barnes †1810, by *Lewis* of Gloucester; Thomas Barnes †1821, by *Osborn* of Bath; and Lt-Col. W.E. Herford †1845, by *Lewis* of Cheltenham. – HATCHMENT to William Tennant, 1848.

CHURCHYARD CROSS. Three steps, base, and half the shaft medieval; upper part with crucifix by *H.A. Prothero*, 1904, carved by *Boulton*.

The church stands SE of the small village, above the M50,* beside the N drive to Pull Court (p. 210). At the head of the drive, CEDAR BANK, a large former lodge, *c.* 1852, no doubt by *Richard Armstrong*; brick, *Rundbogenstil*, Jacobethan gables.

Timber-framed MANOR HOUSE, further N, its jettied N cross-wing with C16 close studding, and diagonal bracing in the gable; it apparently incorporates a former two-bay hall. Altered centre, smaller C17 S cross-wing.

GREEN FARMHOUSE, a little NW, brick, *c.* 1700, has 2+2+2 bays, with slightly recessed centre and hipped roof. Sashed windows in the wings; wooden cross-windows in the centre, with elementary shell-hood above the doorway.

HOLDFAST, NW, is a separate, even smaller, civil parish. HOLDFAST HALL, a brick villa, *c.* 1830, has a large C17 timber-framed rear wing. HOLDFAST MANOR, also brick, larger, *c.* 1700, has 1+5+1 bays, the outer ones projecting; hipped roof, wooden cross-windows, later pedimented porch. HOLDFAST POST is probably C16, with C17 W cross-wing. The main range (close-studded, N side) is cruck-framed, with two full crucks visible in the E gable.

REDDITCH

0060

*A little further E, this crosses the Severn via QUEENHILL BRIDGE, by *Sir Alexander Gibb & Partners*, 1960–2.

Redditch, named after Batchley Brook, alias the Red Ditch, began as a settlement in the shadow of Bordesley Abbey (p. 550), established in the marshy valley of the River Arrow *c.* 1138. After the Dissolution, its gatehouse chapel continued in use until replaced, 1806–7, by a chapel on the hill, sw, where the main nucleus of settlement had developed (now Church Green). Needle-making was the principal occupation of the district by *c.* 1700. Nash says over 2,000 were employed in the trade in 1787, some 400 in Redditch alone, which superseded Studley and Alcester (Warwickshire) as the main centre of production during the c19. The Worcester and Birmingham Canal at Tardebigge, three miles away, opened in 1807 (to Birmingham) and 1815 (to Worcester), provided further stimulation. By *c.* 1850–60 Redditch had become the national centre of the needle industry, with fish-hook manufacture (from the late c18) and spring-making (begun *c.* 1873) as ancillary trades. By this date the population was about 6,700, increasing (with the incorporation of outer districts, especially Headless Cross) to 11,295 in 1897, 19,281 in 1931, 28,400 in 1949. By 1964, Redditch had become a wide-reaching-out town, with 35,000 inhabitants, but one of limited architectural character.

It was designated a New Town in 1964, largely to receive over-spill from Birmingham (only thirteen miles away). Like other 'second generation' New Towns (Runcorn, Skelmersdale, Washington, Telford), this was to be grafted onto an existing settlement (or settlements). *Hugh Wilson* (*Wilson & Womersley*) drew up a master plan, 1964–6, for a target population of 70,000, eventually rising to 90,000.* *Michael Brown* was landscape consultant. In 1965 *Redditch Development Corporation* appointed *Brian Bunch* Chief Architect and Planning Officer (succeeded by his deputy *Graham Reddie*, 1979). The master plan proposed self-contained neighbourhoods, like the 'beads of a necklace', each of up to 10,000 inhabitants, some based on existing communities (Headless Cross, Crabbs Cross, Batchley, Webheath), some expanding other c20 housing areas, especially se around Studley Road (Greenlands), with a new 'bead' further s at Woodrow. Most new development was to be e of the Arrow valley, the three 'beads' of Matchborough, Winyates, and Church Hill, the valley itself retained as a linear 'green belt' (and safeguard against flood risk). A good network of roads was essential and has certainly been achieved. Landscaping, with *Roy Winter* as chief landscape architect, has also been a success, with over three million new trees planted. The architects' department operated as three multi-disciplinary teams, each under an assistant chief. A number of their housing schemes and some 'bead centres' are worthy of note, especially in the new areas e of the Arrow; others are dull, some (e.g. Woodrow South) positively unattractive. Other good buildings (notably the Public Library, p. 552) were designed by private architects. The Development Corporation was wound up in 1985, its architects' department having already been

* In 2001 it was 78,807, including Feckenham and Astwood Bank.

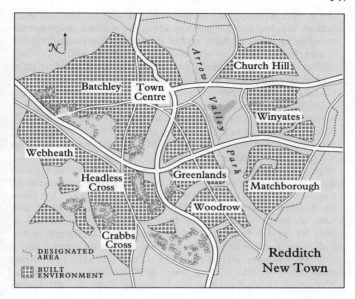

Redditch, New Town area development.
Plan

downgraded to 'technical services' in a Government cost-cutting measure of 1981.

THE CENTRAL AREA

This section covers Church Green, the traditional hub, and surrounding areas, more or less the extent of the early C20 town. Only a few industrial premises remain, divorced from the town centre by the Redditch Ringway, the inner ring road (completed 1984). Also included here, the district to the NE around Bordesley Abbey (*see* below).

Churches

ST STEPHEN, Church Green. By *Henry Woodyer*, 1853–5.* Large, of Tardebigge sandstone, Dec style, but without his usual eloquent radicalism; some tracery displays typical eccentricity. Chunky NW tower with tall broach spire, its best feature the recessed N doorway (now disused); elongated sanctus bellcote on the nave E gable. E end altered and parapets added by *Temple Moore*, 1893–4. Inside, five-bay arcades, so widely spaced that the octagonal piers appear weak. Quirky sanctuary S window, its cusped rere-arch on corbel shafts. Moore's remodelling of

---

* Replacing the chapel of 1806–7, which reused stone from Bordesley Abbey gatehouse chapel.

the E end is more satisfactory. He rebuilt the chancel arch higher, one bay further W, expanding the N and S chapels with two-bay arcades; all have arches dying into their responds (or round piers). His also the chancel clerestory and three-bay timber vault with diagonal and ridge ribs, plus the fine nave and aisle roofs. Two W bays were screened off, 1976–7 (by *Charles Brown*), as parish rooms.

By *Woodyer* the subdued stone REREDOS, plain PEWS, and octagonal FONT, of red Devonshire marble; COVER by *Leslie T. Moore*, 1925. – STALLS by *Preedy* (from St Mary Magdalene, Worcester). – PULPIT by *Temple Moore*, who heightened the wrought-iron CHAPEL SCREENS by *Hardman, Powell & Co.*, 1890. – On the NE vestry floor, a large area of medieval TILING from Bordesley Abbey, mostly foliage arranged in patterns of four. – STAINED GLASS. In the chancel by *Hardman*, 1855 (also the tower W lancet, 1857). – By *Preedy*, S chapel SE, 1866, and nave W, 1870. – S chapel SW by *Clayton & Bell*, c. 1875. – N aisle NE by *J.B. Capronnier* of Brussels, 1880; strikingly pictorial. – By *Burlison & Grylls*, 1889–90, the N aisle central and S aisle SW windows. – By *Kempe & Co.*, two others in the S aisle, 1910–21. – N aisle NW by *Jones & Willis*, 1913. – BRASS to Nathaniel Mugg †1712, good lettering; from the gatehouse chapel.

Outside, S, an early C14 VAULT SPRINGER from the Abbey, with ballflower and moulded ribs. – WAR MEMORIAL CROSS by *G.E. Sprague*, 1922, Portland stone.

ST GEORGE, St George's Road. 1875–6 by *Preedy*. Snecked Hewell sandstone with Bath stone dressings and bands; late C13 style, uninspired Geometrical plate tracery. Clerestoried nave with stocky bellcote on its E gable. N aisle (and large brick N vestry) added by *H.R. Lloyd*, 1898. Matching S porch by *F.B. Osborn*, 1904. Both four-bay arcades are Preedy's: round piers with alternating capitals, moulded, with blocks intended to be carved with stiff-leaf. High arch-braced roofs. – Original FITTINGS include a carved stone PULPIT. – FONT reset in a SW baptistery by *C.F. Whitcombe*, 1908. His also the SCREEN, now W end. – Huge ORGAN imported in 1964 from the Queen's College chapel, Oxford. – STAINED GLASS. E window by *William Pearce Ltd*, 1895. – Excellent S aisle SE, bold Arts and Crafts, by *Alfred L. Pike*, 1920. – S aisle E and W by *T.W. Camm*, c. 1901–8. – Attached, N, a brick HALL by the *Snell Taylor Partnership*, 1991–2.

Neo-Georgian VICARAGE, E, by *E.J. Williams* of Leicester, 1929. Brick, raised centre with ball finials, doorway with segmental pediment, hipped slate roof.

OUR LADY OF MOUNT CARMEL (R.C.), Beoley Road. 1833–4 by *Thomas Rickman*, his only R.C. church, but with little indication of how archaeologically convincing he could be (cf. Ombersley and Hartlebury). Sandstone ashlar, entirely of the contemporary Commissioners' type. No aisles, but transepts; square-ended chancel. Battlemented W tower, its ground floor a high open porch. Mostly Perp detail: nave with square-headed cusped windows, chancel with Perp E window but sexfoil side windows. Rather bare interior, the nave with deep W gallery, four-centred E arch flanked by narrower openings, and broad tie-beam roof; transepts and chancel are enlivened by plaster quasi-vaulting with thin ribs and large bosses. – STATIONS OF THE CROSS. Large, plaster; probably late C19 Belgian. – STAINED GLASS. E window by *Hardman*, 1862. – S transept S probably *Lavers & Westlake*, *c.* 1908.* – Attached PRESBYTERY, brick, terracotta dressings, Tudor transomed windows; *c.* 1900, masked from Beoley Road by an ugly C20 vestry. – Plain brick SCHOOLROOM, probably also *c.* 1900.

BAPTIST CHAPEL, Easemore Road. 1922–3 by *Wills & Son* of Derby (replacing one of 1897–8 by *John Wills*, in Ipsley Street, p. 557). Leicestershire brick, Bath stone dressings; Perp style, with large window above paired doorways, adjoining a stunted stair-tower (for the W gallery). Wide interior: two-bay arcade to a shallow NE choir transept; E baptistery flanked by recesses, the S filled by a landscape painting by *H. Lindsey Ruff*, 1942. – Smaller SUNDAY SCHOOL, in matching style, linked by a corridor, forming an attractive U-plan group.

EMMANUEL CHURCH. An ecumenical centre, opened 1978, on the top floor of the Kingfisher Shopping Centre, at its Evesham Street entrance.† Surprisingly pleasant interior, with angled clerestory lighting. – Re-set one-light window by *Nora Yoxall & Elsie Whitford*, 1935.

Former PRIMITIVE METHODIST CHAPEL, Ipsley Street. 1890 by *M.J. Butcher* of Birmingham. Brick, paired lancets, canted E apse (for the pulpit). Front poorly rebuilt.

Former UNITED METHODIST CHURCH, Mount Pleasant. By *H.R. Lloyd*, 1899. Brick, stone dressings, some banding, raised above a basement. Simple Tudor style; gabled narthex with inset angled porches.

CEMETERY, Cemetery Road. Fine sloping site, with CHAPEL, 1854–5, an early work by *W.J. Hopkins*. Red brick, blue trim, stone dressings. Dec E window, side lancets, bold W front with sexfoil above the moulded doorway.

To the NE, in the angle with Plymouth Road, a Portland stone WAR MEMORIAL by the *Bromsgrove Guild*, 1927: a rusticated stone arch, enclosing a bronze lamp; bronze wreath on the front, Roman military emblems at the sides.

CREMATORIUM, Bordesley Lane. An excellent example, on an elevated site, by *Richard Twentyman* (*Twentyman, Percy & Partners*), 1971–3; planned as early as 1955. Brick, copper roofs. Curving memorial corridor, its E wall fully glazed, leading to the chapel, also with its own flat-roofed porte cochère. Reverential interior, with angled timber-slatted roof, curving white

---

*PROCESSIONAL CROSS, probably from Bordesley Abbey, *c.* 1500, 18 in. (46 cm.) high; roundels at the ends of the arms with Evangelists' symbols, mounted on blue enamel. The Virgin and St John at the foot apparently come from a different cross.
†It replaced the Congregational CHAPEL, Evesham Street, 1825, and Wesleyan CHAPEL, Bate's Hill, by *John Robinson*, 1842–3.

roughcast side walls, and glazed E wall behind the catafalque (with view across the Arrow valley). – Small detached OFFICE in matching style. – The large ABBEY CEMETERY, N, has a good classical entrance of the 1930s: stone piers, cast-iron gates.

BORDESLEY ABBEY

A Cistercian house, founded c. 1138 by Waleran de Beaumont as a daughter house of Garendon (Leics.); refounded by Queen Matilda, 1142. In 1332, it was a sizeable establishment, with thirty-four monks, plus lay brothers. At the Dissolution, 1538, the buildings were demolished, the remaining walls and foundations soon buried. J.M.Woodward excavated the site in 1864; an ongoing archaeological programme, begun 1969, has been continued by Redditch Borough Council. The chancel (or presbytery), S transept, and half the nave are now exposed. Because the site lay undisturbed, the church retained a sequence of seven floor levels. Equally remarkably, the whole of the large abbey site is still pasture, with a complex set of earthworks. This has allowed unusually detailed studies of the structure and surroundings.

The plan of the original CHURCH, completed in the 1150s, of green sandstone probably from Inkberrow,* was of standard Cistercian type, similar to Boxley (Kent) and Kirkstall (Yorks): square-ended chancel and transepts, both with three square-ended E chapels. The two-bay CHANCEL has a sedilia recess, S, and early C13 strengthening with clasping E buttresses (an early sign of structural instability). The CROSSING piers had flat rectangular responds with angle shafts with bell-shaped bases, best seen on the SE pier. Settlement necessitated much later rebuilding. The NW pier was replaced c. 1260–80, and again rebuilt after it collapsed, c. 1330, hence its clusters of three massive Dec shafts. The SW pier was altered to match on both occasions. S crossing arch, into the transept, considerably narrowed c. 1300, with filleted main shafts and four smaller shafts between. The mid-C12 layout is least altered in the S TRANSEPT; its three E chapels remain, their entrance arches also with inset shafts. Floor tiling survives at the N chapel's E end; the other two, blocked off in the C15–C16, have C20 bases marking their altar positions. On the transept W side, the base of the night stair, in remarkable condition: probably originally timber, rebuilt in stone in the early C13 (remains of arcading against its E side). Arch to the S aisle with the same mid-C12 base details, also altered soon after c. 1200. The rectangular room S of the transept must have been a vestry and book store. The N transept remains buried at the time of writing, but four NAVE bays are exposed. The first pair of piers had a rectangular E face, echoing the crossing piers, but a semicircular W

---

* Later work is mostly red sandstone, probably from Tardebigge.

face (cf. Buildwas, Salop). The second pair was octagonal. The evidence for both bays is obscured by partial C13–C14 blocking of their arches to support choir stalls. The third pair was round, see the exposed base, s side; the N bay has Perp infilling. The fourth pair seems also to have been round, as were perhaps the four or five to its w. A rise in ground level marks the nave's w end; Woodward claimed he found the doorway. The nave was apparently remodelled and its upper parts rebuilt in the early C15. – Three floor recesses for stone coffins.

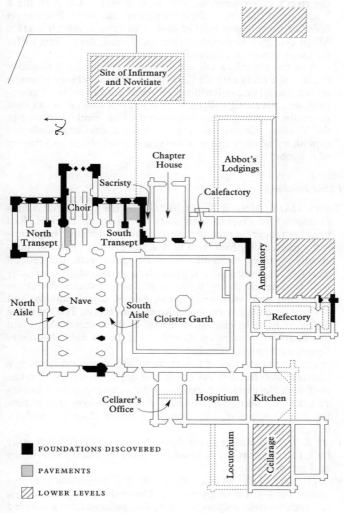

Redditch, Bordesley Abbey.
Plan (after J. M. Woodward)

Of the CLAUSTRAL BUILDINGS little detail can be given. Woodward's plan reconstructs them to the usual Cistercian scheme (apart from showing an unlikely intrusion of the S transept into the cloister walk). The CLOISTER, its square depression clearly visible, was rebuilt in the early C15. Two rectangular hollows were probably undercrofts. – More can be said of the extensive Abbey GROUNDS. The original meandering of the River Arrow, re-routed by the monks, can be seen E of the church. By the 1170s they had created fish ponds, partly surviving beyond it, NE, and built a boundary bank alongside the river's new course, as well as to W and E. Close to the E boundary is the site of their triangular mill pond. Excavation revealed the mill was built of timber, in 1174–6, rebuilt c. 1187. Much evidence of metalworking was found, the earliest so far for water power in England.

W of the church, a tall redwood tree (planted 1864) marks the site of ST STEPHEN'S CHAPEL, S of the gatehouse; remodelled c. 1300, used as Redditch's church until 1806. In its graveyard, an interesting collection of small C18 GRAVE MARKERS, no doubt recycling stone found on the site. Finds displayed in the Visitors' Centre (p. 559) include a mid-C12 scalloped capital, a fine early C14 roof boss, and small shafts and tracery of c. 1400.*

Public buildings

TOWN HALL, Alcester Street. 1981–2 by the *Cassidy & Ashton Partnership* of Preston; engineers *Ove Arup & Partners*. Red brick, overbearing metallic roofs, chunkily detailed; huge butterfly plan, rising from two to five storeys, the centre emphasized by canted tower-like bays. Polygonal attached council chamber, SE, only one storey but given a particularly unwieldly roof (hiding clerestory lighting) in compensation. Attractive open courtyard with brick steps, ramps, low fountains, and octagonal, pyramid-roofed information kiosk. The building overstays its welcome by extending, as three-storey shops and offices above a covered walkway, along the SW side of Alcester Street, aggressively detailed.

POLICE STATION, Grove Street. 1979. Brick ground floor, two concrete-slab faced floors above, the upper projecting. Orange roof with dormers. – Next door, the contemporary MAGISTRATES' COURT, overhauled by *HBG Design*, 2003; now far more appealing, the roughcast upper floor relieved by brises-soleil.

FIRE STATION, Birmingham Road. A severely cubic brick essay by *L.C. Lomas*, 1962; flat roofs for both the main three-storey and garage blocks.

PUBLIC LIBRARY, Market Place. By the *John Madin Design Group*, 1974–5, a strongly modelled brick design. Three storeys, the top one windowless. Rectangular pillars allow a covered walkway along the street, becoming free-standing at the SE,

* *See* also St Stephen, p. 548, for a C14 vault springer, and the reused tiles in its vestry.

entrance, end; here the top floor cants out above two square oriels. Within, an access ramp like a narrow sloping open court-yard, and further spatial delights: views in from the NW stairs, out from windows in unexpected locations.

The former LIBRARY, Church Green West, built as a Literary and Scientific Institute by *G.H. Cox* of Birmingham, 1885, is brick, Gothic, with gables above first-floor windows; Geometrical tracery, steep pyramidal turret.

Former SMALLWOOD HOSPITAL, Church Green West, by *William Henman*, 1894–5. Symmetrical brick, the centre with carved stone gable and Jacobethan porch with obelisk pinnacles; good iron weathervane. Nicely varied fenestration. Later additions in keeping either side. Long three-storeyed health centre and office range at the rear, *c.* 1968 for *Worcestershire County Council*; concrete-framed, faced in yellow brick, continuous window bands.

NORTH EAST WORCESTERSHIRE COLLEGE, Peakman Street. By *D5 Architects* of Birmingham, 2003–4. Two ranges either side of a large open courtyard beneath a sloping glazed roof, linked by a high-level glazed bridge, N end. The long E range is also mostly glazed, with stepped profile, E, but a crisp, sheer, three-storey surface to the courtyard; open balcony access inside. Descending layers, NE. The W range, also three-storeyed, by *Richard Sheppard & Partners*, 1960 (extended 1973), was upgraded, 2003–4, with brises-soleils etc.

TRINITY HIGH SCHOOL, off Grove Street. By *H.W. Simister* of Birmingham, 1930–2. Fine symmetrical Neo-Georgian show front, E, only facing the playing field: dark red brick with lighter dressings, two storeys, parapet, pantiled roof. Nearly thirty bays long, with three projections, the central entrance bay with quoins, ball finials, and pretty timber cupola. Assembly hall behind, set W–E, flanked by internal courtyards. Later C20 additions include a standard three-storey classroom block, 1956–8, nearest Grove Road.

BIRCHENSALE MIDDLE SCHOOL, Bridley Moor Road. By *Richard Sheppard & Partners*, 1958–9; two-storey classroom blocks, brick with timber cladding and curtain walling. New entrance and other large additions by *ECD Architects*, 2001.

HOLYOAKES FIELD FIRST SCHOOL, Bridge Street/Cedar Road. By *A.V. Rowe*, 1913. Long and low, brick and roughcast, sashed windows, round-arched entrances with stone voussoirs. Higher hall with gabled roof and three-light mullioned W window. – Also by *Rowe*, 1913, the former COOKERY CENTRE, South Street; two large roughcast gables, doorway with big segmental stone pediment.

CENTRAL AREA DESCRIPTIONS

1. The town centre

A perambulation of the centre, hemmed in by the ring road, consists mostly of a walk round CHURCH GREEN. At its SW corner, St Stephen (p. 547), its churchyard, with a few C19

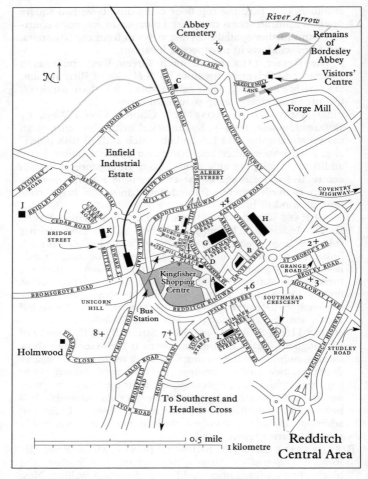

Redditch Central Area

---

1   St Stephen
2   St George
3   Our Lady of Mount Carmel (R. C.)
4   Baptist Chapel
5   Emmanuel Church (Ecumenical Centre)
6   Former Primitive Methodist Chapel
7   Former United Methodist Church
8   Cemetery
9   Crematorium

A   Town Hall
B   Police Station and Magistrates' Court
C   Fire Station
D   Public Library
E   Former Public Library
F   Former Smallwood Hospital
G   North East Worcestershire College
H   Trinity High School
J   Birchensale Middle School
K   Holyoakes Field First School
L   Smallwood Almshouses

---

chest tombs, filling more than half of the green. At the N apex,
a BANDSTAND, originally 1898, and an engaging cast-iron
FOUNTAIN, 1883, made by the *Coalbrookdale Company*, the
design suggested by the donor R.S. Bartleet. Some 12 ft
(4 metres) high, originally coloured, now drab white, with

acanthus, and four large cranes amongst lilies and bulrushes; at the top a maiden, designed by Mr *Wills*.

CHURCH GREEN EAST has the best run of buildings, beginning, N end, with a mid-C19 brick terrace (Nos. 3–5) and contemporary singleton, No. 6 (Beech House): three bays, Doric porch. Late Georgian frontages follow: short brick and stuccoed terraces, and No. 13, taller with giant pilasters. At No. 19 LLOYDS TSB (originally Gloucestershire Bank), an upstanding Renaissance palazzo of 1867; four bays, three storeys, rusticated and vermiculated ground floor with Doric porch. Near the S end, two good brick houses: No. 20 (Webb House), with modern date 1774, has rusticated ground floor and pedimented central first-floor window; No. 24 (NatWest Bank), central doorway with open pediment on fluted pilasters.

Opposite, the LIBRARY (p. 552), at the E end of MARKET PLACE, running along the Green's S side: assorted C19–C20 buildings, of no special merit. Behind looms the KINGFISHER SHOPPING CENTRE, filling the whole S part of the centre, fed by traffic from the Ringway straight into its four multi-storey car parks and cavernous service area. By the *Redditch Development Corporation*, 1970–5, almost doubled in size *c.* 1981; deputy chief architect *Graham Reddie*, project architect *Ian Downs* (succeeded by *Trevor Etherington*), engineers *Ove Arup & Partners*. Enlarged and remodelled 2002–5 by the *Seymour Harris Partnership*. The exterior, of mixed materials but no particular character, is scarcely visible from Market Place. Here, two discreet entrances, the E (Market Walk) remodelled 2002, the W reusing the stump of Evesham Street. This leads into Worcester Square, enhanced by exotic palm trees (renewed 2005). The shopping arcades, set round an oblong, with E–W branch to the bus station (rebuilt 2002), across the Ringway at lower level, are too long and narrow, though relieved by other, smaller, internal squares. Evesham Square, SW, is circular, lit by a dome. Milward Square, SE, has a high glazed roof on iron columns, with, at upper level, twelve colourful semi-abstract mosaics by *Eduardo Paolozzi*, 1983.

Back to Church Green. UNICORN HILL, to the W, is dominated by the former DANILO CINEMA by *Ernest S. Roberts*, 1936–7; brick, Deco inset of stepped windows and canopy. At the corner of BATE'S HILL, blue brick gatepiers with big terracotta caps mark the entrance to the demolished Wesleyan Chapel (cf. p. 549); perhaps of 1889, when *C. G. Huins* enlarged the surviving MANSE.

CHURCH GREEN WEST is mixed C19–C20. HSBC BANK by *Whinney, Son & Austen Hall*, 1964, is decidedly horizontal. Flanking Church Road, the former REDDITCH BENEFIT BUILDING SOCIETY, 1922, and Old Library (with Smallwood Hospital, N, *see* p. 553). In CHURCH ROAD, another former cinema, more altered, the GAUMONT PALACE by *W.T. Benslyn*, 1931. Opposite, Nos. 7–11, early C19 stuccoed: five bays, quoins, big key blocks, pilastered doorway; and former POST OFFICE, 1888. This has four bays, the central two recessed:

round-arched ground-floor windows, doorway partly stone with foliated columns. Refurbished as the County Court in 1990 by *Douglas Hickman* (*John Madin Design Group*). At the end, uncomfortably close to the Ringway, a former EMPLOY-MENT EXCHANGE, 1930, in the quiet brick Neo-Georgian of the *Office of Works*.

The N continuation of Church Green, PROSPECT HILL, has one good brick survivor of *c.* 1800, No. 7 (The Red House): 2+1+2 bays, three storeys, rubbed window heads. Projecting centre with pedimented doorway on engaged Doric columns; immediately inside, an open-well staircase with stick balusters. Opposite, large office blocks. The first, ST STEPHEN'S HOUSE by *Edmund Kirby & Sons*, 1980, has some character; four storeys, red brick, modulated by pilasters and rows of canted bays along the top floor. GROSVENOR HOUSE by the same practice, 1972–3, is taller, paler and blander. For Prospect Hill further N, *see* p. 558.

Now into EASEMORE ROAD, NE. Near the start, N side, the former UNIONIST CLUB (now Masonic Hall) by *John Johnson*, 1908. Severely plain gabled brick, but grouping well with the Baptist Chapel (p. 549). Further E, streets of dour brick terraced housing, *c.* 1900. The former CHURCH INSTITUTE, 1910, at the corner of Archer Road, also gabled, has a roughcast upper floor with some half-timbering. Further E, Trinity High School (p. 553). To the S, North East Worcestershire College (p. 553) dominates a sea of car parks.

Finally ALCESTER STREET, leading SE from Church Green, almost entirely C20. Beyond the library, MARKET GATEWAY has a display of eight upstanding giant needles, stainless steel, with threads in their eyes, by *Eric Klein Velderman*, 2006; they point the way to the MARKET, tucked beneath the Kingfisher Centre, a curved wall with steel roofs. Beyond the Town Hall (p. 552) takes over. Opposite it, a rare survival, the PALACE THEATRE, 1913, by *Bertie Crewe*, better known for his city theatres. Stuccoed front, 2+5+2 bays, the centre with channelled ground floor and giant upper pilasters with Ionic capitals after the Temple at Bassae. Crewe's intimate Neoclassical auditorium is intact; curved balcony, one large box either side with Ionic pilasters and pediment. Restored 2005–6 by *Sansome Hall Architects* of Milton Keynes, who added the glazed foyer and staircase with curved roofs, SE.

2. South of the town centre

To the SE, hemmed in by new town highways are St George and Our Lady of Mount Carmel (R.C.), p. 548. Between them, in Grange Road, GRANGE WORKS, formerly Hewell Works, the well-preserved mid-C19 factory of Joseph Warner, which mostly produced fish-hooks. Three-storeys, 6+2+5 bays, brick, with fine rhythm of round-arched windows with yellow brick heads. A lower five-bay section, S, links to the owner's house, at right angles, facing Beoley Road; ground-floor bays, pedimented doorway. Also in BEOLEY ROAD, remnants of C19 housing, mostly with bay windows with attached shafts.

IPSLEY STREET, the E–W spine S of Redditch Ringway, is dominated by MILLSBOROUGH HOUSE, the works of Herbert Terry & Sons, established 1855, and producing springs. Classical main building of 1912, probably by *F.W.B. Yorke*, its five wide bays articulated by pilasters; broad doorway with segmental hood on paired columns. Good iron railings, continuing into Lodge Road in front of the plainer factory. Large brick extension, continuing along Millsborough Road, E, 1930–2 by *Yorke*, assisted by his son *F.R.S. Yorke*: Deco details including chevron and hexagonal windows. Within the warehouse section, next to the 1912 building, the shell of the former Baptist Chapel (*see* p. 549), commandeered during the First World War. Across Lodge Road, the former WARWICK ARMS HOTEL, *c.* 1890, large, with straight and curved gables, pyramidal turret, and varied roofs. Opposite, the former Primitive Methodist Chapel (p. 549). Scant remains of other industry; part of the ELECTRICITY WORKS, in Summer Street, has a broad gable dated 1898.

Long runs of late C19 housing line LODGE ROAD, MARSDEN ROAD and MOUNT STREET. The last is distinguished by the SMALLWOOD ALMSHOUSES, N side, by *C.G. Huins*, 1896–7, for ten married couples. Two storeys, brick, some half-timbering. Gabled projections: one central, with Jacobethan inscription; the other, E end, with half-timbered balcony above open-balustraded porch.*

Ipsley Street leads up SW to MOUNT PLEASANT, the former main route S, lined with mostly complete late C19 housing (probably partly by *E.A. Day*, *c.* 1882): quite tall, gables with nice brick eaves detailing or half-timbering. At its N end, the former PLOUGH AND HARROW HOTEL, rendered mid-C19 classical; and the United Methodist Church (p. 549) facing the BLACK HORSE, a lower earlier pub: C18 brick, timber-framed core. Further S, the WOODLAND COTTAGE inn, also C18, reconstructed by *F.W.B. Yorke*, 1933, and CRESCENT NEEDLE MILLS, *c.* 1900, respecting the height and style of the surrounding terraces; now housing

Further out, off POOL BANK, is SOUTHCREST, a Neo-Georgian brick mansion by *F.W.B. Yorke*, 1921, for Charles Terry; now a hotel. Entrance front with central canted bay, its ends with rusticated even quoins, above which the parapet sweeps up; segmental doorway, disfigured by the hotel canopy. Large dull 1970s additions. Much of the extensive grounds remains, now Southcrest Wood.† In SOUTHCREST GARDENS, W, three-storey flats by *Mason Richards & Partners*, 1970–2; brick, stone bands, timber balconies, flat roofs. At the corner of Evesham

---

* At the S end of Millsborough Road, SOUTHMEAD CRESCENT, attractive UDC housing by *Arthur J. Dickinson*, *c.* 1926; rendered semi-detached pairs, brick trim.
† At the far SE end, reached from Ashperton Close, a small artificial lake, with stone boat-house, formerly with classical pavilion above, by *Yorke*, 1948.

Road, *Yorke*'s nice Neo-Georgian LODGE of 1930, silver grey brick, red trim.

3. South-west and west of the town centre

To the SW, beyond the Cemetery (p. 549), is HOLMWOOD, a very large vicarage built for Canon Horace Newton, 1892–3, by *Temple Moore*. Roughcast, big green slate roof, hipped except for the four-storey entrance front, NE. Here, three Cotswoldy gables and scattered fenestration; above the round-arched doorway, a large transomed window lights the full-height panelled staircase hall. Quieter regular garden front, SW, only two storeys, with six bays of cross-windows. The entrance faces U-plan stables, at a lower level. Housing, approached via Purshall Close, fills the grounds. Further S, around IVOR ROAD, some nice minor early C20 houses, detached or semi-detached, e.g. Nos. 22–28 by *F.W.B. Yorke*, 1913. Others may be by *F.F. Baylis*.

On the N side of BROMSGROVE ROAD, the main route W, a good sequence of early to mid-C19 three-bay villas, the first two, the earliest, in poor condition, particularly that next to the railway station.* This, with good Doric porch, belonged to the Ivy Needle Works of Abel Morrall Ltd, established 1845; part of the derelict factory survives behind. The following villas, *c.* 1840–50, are brick, apart from the stuccoed owner's house (with good solid porch) adjoining ASHLEIGH WORKS, at the corner of Britten Street. This, an interesting early C20 needle factory, three storeys, with big industrial windows and weaving-shed-type roofs, still feels the need to disply vestigial pediments and pilasters to the main road.

The villa sequence continues with No. 38 (now Trades and Labour Club), stuccoed with black quoins, canted bays, and veranda porch. The remainder are brick, the best, No. 44, with excellent wrought-iron veranda, but also vermiculated quoins, even some terracotta detail, so probably *c.* 1860–70.

In Britten and Edward streets, N, more vestiges of C19–early C20 industry. In Bridge Street, a former Council School, 1913 (p. 553).

4. North of the town centre

At the N end of PROSPECT HILL are BRITISH MILLS, the largest early C19 steam-powered needle mill, built 1840 for Samuel Thomas. His stuccoed house (No. 80) has three-by-three bays, the centre breaking forward with Greek Doric porch; channelled ground floor, parapet rising to central pseudo-pediment. Attached factory in matching style, behind a cobbled forecourt: main range of 1+2+1 bays, with central archway, six-bay S wing at right angles. Then, along Prospect Hill, a slightly later six-bay range, still stuccoed, with archway, pilastered doorway, round-arched windows; square open

---

* The railway, of 1859, was extended to Evesham, 1868; curtailed on this site, 1972.

cupola with ogee roof. At the corner of Albert Street, a taller domestic brick block, c. 1850, 1+3 bays, impressively plain, with good round-arched doorway. Later C19 additions around tiny courtyards behind, and along Albert Street; here, two two-storey ranges with round-arched windows, red brick, blue and yellow trim.

CLIVE ROAD has the impressive three-storey range of WINDSOR MILLS (formerly Excelsior Works), c. 1870; red brick, 6+4+1+4 bays, articulated by plain pilasters; round-arched windows with blue and yellow heads, paired in the six-bay part and above the segment-headed archway. The stuccoed BRUNSWICK HOUSE, at the Birmingham Road corner, is presumably contemporary. Further SW, above the road, S side (actually Mill Street), PROSPECT WORKS, later Redditch Spring Co., a plain C19 three-storey factory with attached house, overshadowed by housing, 2005–6.

The RAILWAY INN, by the bridge in Hewell Road, 1938 by *Cecil E.M. Fillmore* of Birmingham for Mitchell & Butlers, is a nice example of Brewer's Picturesque: brick and render, with limited displays of half-timbering. To the W, in Cedar Park Road (off Cedar Road), THE CEDARS, a farmhouse remodelled 1840, in Tudor Gothic style, for the fishing-tackle manufacturer, Samuel Allcock. Snecked sandstone, hoodmoulds with headstops, gables with pierced scalloped bargeboards. C20 nursing home extensions.

Further NW in HEWELL ROAD, remnants of the ROYAL ENFIELD CYCLE FACTORY. The main range, S, 1907, has been demolished; a N section, probably c. 1920 (now Trenton Engineering), remains: three bays with two storeys of segment-headed windows, plus two broad gabled ranges with wide stepped round-arched triplets. Also two severe brick frontages, one built for Terry & Sons, with groups of three rectangular openings; the other, with big oblong stair-tower, Royal Enfield's former mess-room, by *F.W.B. Yorke*, 1943. Most of the site now forms an industrial estate. Finally, along the N side of WINDSOR ROAD, the large factory of HIGH DUTY ALLOYS LTD (now Mettis Aerospace), mostly by *Col. A.L. Abbott* of London, 1939; corrugated clad buildings of varying sizes, with a plethora of circular ventilators along the roof ridges.

5. North-east, around Bordesley Abbey

The remains of Bordesley Abbey lie (p. 550) E of the Crematorium (p. 549). The Abbey and Forge Mill Needle Museum share a VISITORS' CENTRE, at the end of Needle Mill Lane: a relocated barn, with overtly picturesque additions by *Roger P. Dudley & Associates*, 1992: four wings with timber arcades, attached round structure like a market cross, NE.

FORGE MILL (restored for the *Development Corporation* by *Nigel Lomas*, c. 1982), was converted to needle scouring c. 1730. The W range, said to be the oldest surviving needle-scouring mill, was altered c. 1828 when the taller E range, also with segment-

headed windows, was added. Between them, a Belgian overshot water wheel of 1912. Against the rear two-storey range,
now housing a display of the scouring process, a lean-to bar-
relling (i.e. drying) shop and small stone-crushing mill. Against
the front of the five-bay three-storey E range, low walls mark
the site of an ancillary steam engine and chimney installed
c. 1871. The long mill pond, of bottle type, was fed from the
Batchley Brook. Former MILL HOUSE, W, mid-C19, diapered
brick.

OUTER DISTRICTS, WEST OF THE RIVER ARROW

1. West

Batchley

The largest C20 housing area in Redditch, before the New Town.
After the Second World War, the UDC commissioned a redevelopment plan from *Sir Patrick Abercrombie*, in conjunction
with *Clough Williams-Ellis* and later *Lionel Brett*; Batchley was
partly a result of this. The approach, BATCHLEY ROAD, is
lined with dull brick housing by *A. J. Dickinson*, 1933–5, alternating hipped and gabled semi-detached pairs. The centre,
generously laid out c. 1950, has a parade of shops and hipped-
roofed pub, The Brockhill, 1955, facing a large well-planted
open space, with lake, crossed by a low stone footbridge. In
OAK TREE AVENUE, along its N side, a more attractive style
of UDC house by *Frederick Hill*, c. 1947, also found elsewhere:
again semi-detached, with concrete-mullioned windows and
canted bays. Two schools with low spreading plans typical of
the later C20. BATCHLEY FIRST SCHOOL, Cherry Tree Walk,
by *Robinson & Kay* of Stourbridge, 1949–50, of red brick, has
large concrete-framed windows, and blocky hall and entrance
range towards the rear. PITCHER OAK SPECIAL SCHOOL,
Willow Way, 1975, has the timber eaves bands then still fashionable for schools.

BROCKHILL, further N, is emphatically post-New Town,
mostly c. 2000; winding roads on rising ground, packed with
builders' all-sorts housing.

Webheath

A former hamlet of Tardebigge, absorbed by Redditch's post-
New Town expansion.

ST PHILIP, Church Road. By *Preedy*, 1869–70, for Baroness
Windsor of Hewell Grange. Snecked sandstone, late C13 Geometrical bar tracery. Wide nave with SW porch, E bellcote;
chancel with N vestry (extended by *John M. Collier* of Redditch,
1954). Ashlar-faced interior; good arch-braced roofs, foliage
corbels in the chancel. – Good original fittings include an
octagonal FONT on green Irish marble shafts, and striking

REREDOS made by *Burke & Co.*: bands of alabaster and marble (some said to come from Ancient Rome), with mosaic angels. – Perp-style oak SCREEN by *James A. Swan*, 1933. – STAINED GLASS. E window by *Preedy*, 1870; nave SE by *J.B. Capronnier* of Brussels, 1871, in his typically French, quite un-English style.

At the SE end of CHURCH ROAD, Nos. 22–36 are four pairs of Bromsgrove RDC houses, 1933, painted brick with boarded dormers; only notable as an early work of the later Modernist *F.R.S. Yorke.*

FOXLYDIATE ARMS, Birchfield Road (NW end). By *S.N. Cooke*, 1938. Large, brick, hipped roof, but also two projections with ornately shaped gables.

2. South and south-west

Headless Cross

A C19 suburb, greatly expanded by the mid C20. Originally Headley's Cross.

ST LUKE, Evesham Road. Neo-Norman by *Harvey Eginton*, 1843; sandstone ashlar, 'liberally carved'. Much rebuilt and enlarged in matching style by *Preedy*, 1867–8. He added aisles and rebuilt the chancel, with E apse. Of Eginton's church, the nave S wall and porch, also some windows, were reused; only the centre of his W front, with wheel window and bellcote, is *in situ*. Gabled W doorway by Preedy, all of whose carving was executed by *Boulton*. Particularly lavish chancel, with carved corbel table and buttresses flanked by full-height nook-shafts. N vestry added by *C.F. Whitcombe*, 1905. Fine unaltered interior. Four-bay arcades in early E.E.-style, the banded piers alternatingly round and octagonal, with foliage capitals of Canterbury–Oakham type; pointed arches, high kingpost roof. Neo-Norman chancel and apse, with stone barrel-vault on wall-shafts. Ornate painted decoration by *Preedy*, including figures, and a reredos on tin panels. – His FITTINGS are also boldly Norman: square carved FONT and stone PULPIT and ALTAR, all with attached red marble shafts, the last also with *Salviati* mosaics. – STAINED GLASS. Again by *Preedy*: W wheel window 1861, others 1867–70, apart from a S aisle S, 1875. – One N lancet by *Capronnier*, 1876.

(WESLEYAN) METHODIST CHURCH, Evesham Road. By *Ewen Harper*, 1896–7. Red brick, stone dressings, Tudor Perp style, with aisles, clerestory and chancel; notable (ritual) SW tower with openwork stone spire (a Harper speciality). Good interior: three-bay arcades with ribbed iron columns, W gallery with ramped seating. – STAINED GLASS. One N aisle N, *c.* 1955; one S aisle S by *T.H. Yates* of Smethwick, *c.* 1900. – Attached SUNDAY SCHOOL, 1867. – Future uncertain.

Former PRIMITIVE METHODIST CHAPEL, Middle Piece Drive/Chapel Street. By *Alfred Smallwood*, 1867–8; brick, lancets with white brick heads, set in recesses.

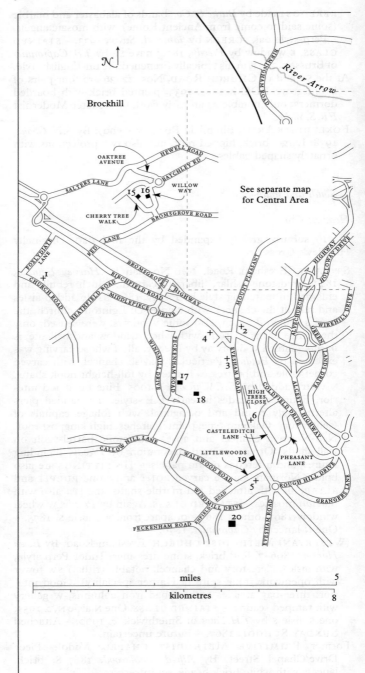

Brockhill

See separate map
for Central Area

miles 5

kilometres 8

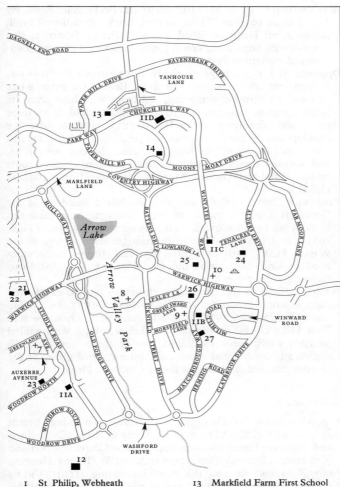

1	St Philip, Webheath	13	Markfield Farm First School
2	St Luke, Headless Cross	14	Moons Moat First School
3	Methodist Church	15	Batchley First School
4	Former Primitive Methodist Chapel	16	Pitcher Oak Special School
5	St Peter, Crabbs Cross	17	Walkwood CE Middle School
6	Jesus Christ of Latter Day Saints	18	Vaynor First School
7	St John, Greenlands	19	Harry Taylor First School
8	St Peter, Ipsley	20	St Augustine's R.C. School
9	Christ Church, Matchborough	21	Woodfield School
10	St Gregory (R.C.), Winyates	22	Oak Hill School
11A	Woodrow Centre	23	Dingleside Middle School
11B	Matchborough Centre	24	Ten Acres First School
11C	Winyates Centre	25	Ipsley CE Middle School
11D	Church Hill Centre	26	Arrow Vale High School
12	Alexandra Hospital	27	Matchborough First School

Outer Redditch

WALKWOOD C. OF E. MIDDLE SCHOOL, Feckenham Road. By
L.C. Lomas, 1958–60. Three storeys, brick, curtain-wall infill.
Below it, off Tennyson Road, VAYNOR FIRST SCHOOL, also
c. 1960, with large additions *c.* 1990, including a pleasant two-
storeyed curtain-walled block.

Opposite St Luke, a huge unwieldy TELEPHONE EXCHANGE,
c. 1970, and brick terraces of 1874–80. Behind the latter, a late
C19 WATER TOWER, octagonal, red brick with blue trim. Its
larger concrete replacement, 1973, stands sentinel, like a huge
mushroom, further S, above HIGHFIELD HOUSE, an office
development by the *Development Corporation*, *c.* 1980; job architect *Gerald Farquhar*. Two long, staggered, three-storey blocks,
with window bands and ribbed brick patterning; hipped roofs
on paired red metal braces. More effective seen from Coldfield
Drive, E.

ROOKERY CLOSE, off the late C19 Birchfield Road, W of the
Green, is a neat example of New Town housing: nineteen
houses, set round a quad, with mature trees; by *David Page*,
1975.* In EVESHAM ROAD, the best secular building is the
WHITE HART, early C19, three bays and storeys; brick, stuccoed ground floor, tripartite first-floor windows. Mid-C19
former stables behind.

Further S, beyond the Methodist church, a varied, excellently
sited housing group for the GUINNESS TRUST, by *Phillips
Cutler Phillips Troy*, 1978. It mostly runs along Guinness and
Four Oaks closes, simply detailed brick groups, with gabled
pantiled roofs, some catsliding; two or three storeys, at all
angles, with occasional courtyards. Fine stepped group at the
SE end; interesting frontages above Coldfield Drive.

Oakenshaw

A good example of *Development Corporation* housing, begun
c. 1979, off Coldfield Drive, along a ring of roads (Castleditch
and Pheasant lanes) surrounding reclaimed derelict woodland
(Oakenshaw Spinney); landscape architect *Roy Winter*. Housing
mostly in culs de sac, the most interesting HIGH TREES
CLOSE, completed 1982; job architects *Gerald Farquhar* and *Jed
Bayley*. At the start, staggered brick terraces with square,
hipped-roofed, tower-like emphases. Further up the steep site,
stepped-back pairs of flats or maisonettes in four tiers, with
ample concrete-framed front terraces, presumably inspired by
Camden Council's Alexandra Road, North London (1969–78).
Eight similar pairs remained unexecuted. Staggered terraces are
used to good effect elsewhere within the exceptionally generous
landscaping. COMMUNITY CENTRE and PUB (The Duck
Pond) in the same simple, unfussy brick style.

The smaller, later development at OAKENSHAW SOUTH, beyond
Rough Hill Drive, similarly arranged along Grangers Lane, is

---

*In Rectory Road, NW, the former Burial Ground, with good timber LYCHGATE,
1861.

much duller; its design ethos is less rigorous and has consequently become incoherent.

Crabbs Cross

St Peter, Littlewoods. Simple brick mission church by *G.C. Huins*, 1896; big lancets, pantiled roof, low canted e apse. Bare interior.

Jesus Christ of Latter-day Saints, Evesham Road, n end. Mostly 1983–4, by *John Porter & Associates*. The standard Mormon plan, two-tone brick, with gabled roof reaching low over n ancillary rooms; thin nw tower.

Harry Taylor First School, Evesham Road. The large red brick core, built for Feckenham School Board, 1876–7, by *E.A. Day* (cf. Astwood Bank), is best seen from the s, where, however, all windows have been altered. Originally of stone, they mostly survive, n side: stepped groups of five lancets, circles in the spandrels. n additions by *Frederick Hill*, 1962.

Late c19 brick terraces line Evesham Road. At their n end, the quirky brick No. 347 (The Castle, formerly Gothic House) has gables and odd detailing: notching, sunk diamonds, patterns made up of the ends of circular drainpipes, especially on the square se tower. Further s, the Fleece Hotel by *G.C. Huins*, 1897; canted bays, square-patterned half-timbered gables.

Hunt End

St Augustine's R.C. High School, Stonepits Lane. By *Brian Rush & Associates*, 1972–3. Two-storeyed, of satisfying dark red brick; long glazing bands. Small nw tower, supporting a water tank. At the sw, a striking entrance range by *Astam GBC* of Gloucester, 1999: splayed corners, glazed projections, curved roofs.

In Enfield Road, brick council housing of the 1930s is all that remains to indicate the site of the Enfield Cycle Works opposite (now an industrial estate).

Further s, in open country, Upper Hunt End Farm, c17, hall and cross-wing plan, the former rebuilt in brick, the latter with square-panelled framing. To the w, in Feckenham Road, Chapel House Farm, probably c. 1840–50, three wide bays to the s, big shallow lunettes in the gable-ends. Within the former moat, se, a brick barn with stone dressings (now Moat House), perhaps the wing of an early c17 brick mansion. Two-light brick-mullioned windows flank a semicircular arch with keystone, all beneath a continuous hoodmould; larger square-headed archway, s end.

Walkwood and Callow Hill

Walkwood has a rather incoherent mix of private and *Development Corporation* housing, the best of the latter around

LIGHTOAK CLOSE, Walkwood Road, w end (just E of Windmill Drive): loosely grouped short terraces round small
squares, by *Bhupendra Arora* and *Mike Potter*, 1980–1.
CALLOW HILL, a long finger of private development begun
c. 1984, stretches in a valley far to the w. Yet Denys Hinton,
chairman of the Development Corporation 1978–85, com-
mended it, no doubt because it followed their favoured principle of a long winding road, here FOXHOLES LANE, with culs
de sac and much open space.
For the fine C16–C17 houses in Love Lyne further s, *see* p. 313.

3. South-east

One of the least inspiring areas of Redditch, mostly a mix of
UDC or early New Town housing and industrial development,
some, at least in the N part, judiciously hidden by planting.
The redeeming feature, the ARROW VALLEY PARK, created
1971–2, fills the river's meadow lands, with a large L-shaped
lake, N end, and another, smaller, s, *c.* 1983; landscape architect *Roy Winter*. Further N, hidden in Marlfield Lane (off Holloway Drive), the C18 BEOLEY MILL, adapted for needle
scouring: brick, three storeys, nine irregular bays of segment-
headed windows. Large mill pond. The mill house, with gabled
cross-wings, has a C16–C17 timber-framed core.

Lakeside

In STUDLEY ROAD, the spine leading SE, the most prominent
building is WOODFIELD MIDDLE SCHOOL by *L.C. Lomas*,
1952–3, concrete-framed: hall and entrance, s, two-storey
classroom ranges, N. Vigorously streamlined by the *David
Hutchinson Partnership* of Bath, 2001, with green infill panels
and blue-framed windows.* Opposite, at No. 99 Studley Road,
a C17 timber-framed hall and cross-wing farmhouse, with
much original fabric.

Greenlands

ST JOHN, Greenlands Avenue. By *Peter Brocklesby* (*Trinity Road
Developments Ltd*), 1990. Brick, hexagonal plan, the pantiled
roof supporting a tall open metallic spire (above a roof-light).
Laminated timber roof within. Oblong vestibule, E, next to the
earlier Church Hall.
GREENLANDS contains much Redditch UDC housing,
c. 1955–60, but also the *Development Corporation*'s first major
scheme, HILLSIDE, a promising start, built 1967–9; job architect *Michael C. Reardon*, landscape architect *Tarsem Flora*. It
lies beyond the w end of Greenlands Avenue, its access roads
GRANHILL CLOSE, off Oakenshaw Road, and DOWLERS

---

*Off Wirehall Drive, w, is OAK HILL FIRST SCHOOL, by *Lomas c.* 1956, overhauled with PVC cladding and curving roofs *c.* 2002 by *Johnson Blight & Dees.*

HILL CRESCENT, off Auxerre Avenue. Two types of simply detailed terraces, some with garages, hug the natural contours of a steeply sloping site, allowing all main rooms fine s views. N sides mostly with sloping roofs, and small entrance courtyards facing footpaths.

Woodrow

The *Development Corporation*'s first completely new housing area, and a grave disappointment. WOODROW NORTH, begun 1968–9, has some architectural presence, though its terraces ranged in straight ranks in closes off the SE side appear far too regimented, despite some staggering and mixing of materials: tile-hanging and weatherboarding, later given up for plain brick. DINGLESIDE MIDDLE SCHOOL, N, by *Worcestershire County Council*, 1970, is purple-red brick, with much glazing.

The WOODROW CENTRE, Studley Road, 1969–70, job architect *Iliffe Simey*, is poorly sited facing grim industrial estates. Two small shopping courtyards, divided by archways with two storeys of housing above; fussily mixed materials, not helping its down-at-heel appearance. FREDERICK EARY HOUSE, s, brick sheltered housing by *Oxford Architects' Partnership*, 1977, three storeys with some monopitched roofs, has aged more gracefully.

WOODROW SOUTH, N of Woodrow Drive, c. 1970, the first use in Redditch of culs de sac off a circular spine, is extremely unappealing. Radburn principles of traffic separation are nullified by the parsimonious allowance of pedestrian space and by using dire roughcast prefabricated housing units. The one privately built cul de sac, GRAFTON CLOSE by *Walker Homes Ltd*, 1971, seems almost joyous by comparison, despite its hackneyed rhythm of steep gables with balconies.

The ALEXANDRA HOSPITAL, in Quinney's Lane, s, a latecomer of 1984–6, is little better; by the *Hospital Design Partnership*, project architect *Jim Richardson*. Brick, two-storeyed, large, industrial-looking; central spine plan with higher lift towers and projecting wings to N and s. Large bronze plaque of a naked family, signed *JT* 1986, by the entrance. HILL CREST, the mental health unit to the NE, by *Abbey Hanson Rowe*, 1992–4, is more uplifting, with hipped and pyramidal roofs.

OUTER DISTRICTS, EAST OF THE RIVER ARROW

The eastern districts of Redditch stand all but independent of the rest, linked only by four roads (and some footbridges). The area, mostly Ipsley parish, was transferred from Warwickshire in 1931. Its church and remnants of the village are dealt with first. Then follow the three New Town districts: s to N, Matchborough, Winyates, Church Hill. Each has approximately the same layout, with housing either side of a local centre, and adjacent industrial areas separated by deep shelter-belt tree planting. The three centres (described first in each case) are connected by a through route, for buses only. Access by car is more convoluted; a good street map is essential.

Ipsley

St Peter, Ipsley Church Lane. Mostly by *Preedy*, 1866–7; he restored the nave and rebuilt the chancel. Good Perp w tower, with three-light w window, and battlements. The nave formerly had aisles, both demolished 1785; their blocked arcade arches remain partly visible. The interior reveals more detail. The s arcade, late C13 judging from its w respond (with carved head of a lady flanked by foliage), had alternating octagonal and round piers; double-chamfered arches. The N arcade was C14;* octagonal piers, double hollow-chamfered arches. Dec-style windows, chancel arch, sturdy roofs, and most fittings, all by *Preedy*. – FONT. Big heptagonal bowl (cf. Warndon); early C14, ballflower up the edges, crenellation round the rim. – PULPIT. Very fine, ornate Jacobean, from Eastnor (Herefs.); large arches with strapwork and other decoration. – SCULPTURE. Small wooden plaque of the Sacrifice of Isaac, probably early C17 Netherlandish. – STAINED GLASS. E window by *Clayton & Bell*, 1887. – Chancel SE by *Preedy*, 1867. – Nave NE by *Hardman*, 1899. – MONUMENTS. Either side of the altar, an incised alabaster slab, each showing one couple, the men with their feet on a greyhound. The better-preserved N pair are Nicholas Huband †1553 and wife Dorothy †1558; border inscription, fourteen children at the base. The s pair are Sir John †1583 and wife Mary †1557. Both may be *c*. 1560. – Good tablet to Anne Huband †1672; Corinthian columns, volutes, swan-neck pediment.

Attached, N, large brick HALL and meeting rooms, 1993–5, by *Peter J. Williams* & *Peter Brocklesby* (*Trinity Road Developments Ltd*); glazed link to the church with angled NW porch. Doors with engraved glass by *Roy Coomber*.

IPSLEY COURT, the late C16 house of the Huband family, large with shaped gables, stood N of the church; mostly demolished after fire, 1724. Two long, parallel, L-plan ranges (flanking its E approach) remain, renewed and incorporated into a large office block, 1980–1. Probably late C17, restored for Dr Walter Landor in the mid C18; substantial, in English bond brickwork, with platbands and hipped roofs on wide bracketed eaves. The N, a barn since the mid C18, has large opposing round-headed archways; the s has a canted E end, rendered, with sashed windows. In the brick wall that later connected their w ends, a small re-set Tudor doorway, SW. The office block, now THE LAW SOCIETY, is by the *Alec French Partnership*, brick, in contextual traditional style; T-plan, the stem thrusting forward between the surviving ranges.

W of the church, the extensive GKN CORPORATE CENTRE by the *Harry Weedon Partnership*, 1972–3. Three-storey main part,

---

* There was a dedication in 1348.

broad U-plan, upper floors concrete-faced, ground floor brick; long two-storey w range. – Much further w, by the Arrow, the OLD MILL HOUSE, early C17, hall and cross-wing plan, square panelled framing. The mill (for needles) was demolished 1965.

More timber framing in IPSLEY LANE, E, notably the OLD RECTORY, now a hotel. Timber-framed H-plan core, behind a pretty cemented front, probably *c.* 1812. Three wide bays with gables with parapets, urns and central griffin; wings with quoins, recessed centre with pedimented Doric doorway. Round-arched windows with keystones, fluted pilaster frames, Gothick glazing. – Former stables, NW, C17 timber-framed: central gable, pretty octagonal cupola.

Matchborough

CHRIST CHURCH, Matchborough Way. By *Thomas White Associates* of Redditch, 1988. Brick, broad end gables with cruciform windows, five triangular dormers either side. – The CHURCH CENTRE, s, of 1973, was the original church; big split-level angled roofs, with clerestory.

N of the church, the large ARROW VALE HIGH SCHOOL, opened 1976; two-storeyed, concrete panels above brick. Many later additions.

BLACKTHORN COURT, s, is a group of fourteen flats round a courtyard, by *Burman, Goodall & Partners*, 1975; pale brick, wood-tiled upper floors, some with monopitch roofs. The former FRIENDS' MEETING HOUSE, square with raised circular clerestoried centre, belonged to the same development.

Opposite, MATCHBOROUGH CENTRE, *c.* 1972, job architect *Mike Rodgers*, oddly a sunken paved area; single-storey shops behind arcades on three sides, three-storey housing above, N side. Car parks N and s; open space, with pond, NE.

Further s, MATCHBOROUGH FIRST SCHOOL, 2002–3 by *David Hayward* of *Worcestershire Property Services*, has the large, low, spreading plan typical of its date; blue-trimmed, shallow-gabled, metallic roofs with angled clerestories.

Housing at MATCHBOROUGH WEST was begun *c.* 1970. The best groups, by *Mason Richards & Partners*, 1972–3, have mono-pitched roofs, the taller fronts tile-hung, set round small squares (e.g. Polesworth and Quinton closes), off GREEN SWARD and MORSEFIELD LANES. Each sub-district was provided with a first school and separate COMMUNITY MEETING ROOM, that in Ilmington Close, by *Brian Bunch*, 1971, brick and hexagonal. – Housing at MATCHBOROUGH EAST is laid out round a peripheral circular road, with culs de sacs off: some roughcast, but mostly more attractive tile-hung brick. Good MEETING ROOM in Dilwyn Close, 1974, job architect *Iliffe Simey*; pale brick, two-storeyed, rounded corners.

Matchborough's industrial area, WASHFORD, to the s, is dominated by the huge HALFORDS in Icknield Street Drive; by *Harper Fairley Associates*, 1971. Four-storeyed, concrete-faced offices; brick distribution centre behind. – At the N end of

HEMING ROAD, ENE, very long examples of the *Development Corporation*'s advance (i.e. speculative) factory units; corrugated upper floors, above brick.

Winyates

A competition, of 1972, for designs for a master plan for Winyates was won by the *Mason Richards Partnership*. Work began *c.* 1974.

WINYATES CENTRE (job architect *Mike Rodgers*) is given far greater presence than Matchborough's: a narrow, elongated square, almost surrounded by three-storey flats above shops, some with balcony access; pub at an angle, NW. Later HEALTH CENTRE, SW, its projecting upper floor tile-hung. Across Winyates Way, a CRAFT CENTRE by *Graham Reddie*, 1976–7, a low courtyard of converted farm buildings.

ST GREGORY (R.C.), Winyates Way, further S, by *Brian Rush*, *c.* 1975, low, brick, has hipped pantiled roof and feeble attached spirelet. – Opposite, in Yardley Close (Lowlands Lane, E end), THE QUANTOCKS, a compact group of twenty-one single-storey houses for the elderly, by *Brian Bunch*, 1975; brick, timber-slatted fronts and porches, set round a well-planted quadrangle. Nearby, IPSLEY C.E. MIDDLE SCHOOL, with good two-storey addition, 1981, facing Lowlands Lane, by *Sheppard, Robson & Partners*.

Typical WINYATES WEST housing can be seen from Lowlands Lane. Roughcast, stepping uphill, N, in WINFORTON CLOSE; strangely upright semi-detached pairs, with monopitch roofs, in closes to the S (PEMBRIDGE and SUTTON CLOSES). – WINYATES EAST follows the pattern of quiet brick closes off a circular spine, here much more informal. TEN ACRES FIRST SCHOOL, Quibery Close, 1975, low brick with higher central hall, was built to incorporate the Community Meeting Room.

WINYATES GREEN further E is mostly later private housing. Off the E side of its spine, Far Moor Lane, an interesting survivor, LOWER HOUSE. Its core, *c.* 1600, has three framed bays aligned E–W: central chimney bay (with three low diagonal stacks), S return (service end), N return to upper E end. This E end has a symmetrical cement-faced Tudor Gothic front of *c.* 1830–40; three wide bays, central gable above the porch, parapets with diagonal pinnacles, latticed windows with hood-moulds. Further alterations *c.* 1910.

Finally, NW, by the Arrow Valley Lake, a COUNTRYSIDE CENTRE by *Online Architects* of Wolverhampton, 2001; split-roofed, weatherboarded, with balcony (for the cafeteria) facing the lake, rather like a yacht club.

Church Hill

The last, largest, and least coherent of the three 'beads' or districts E of the Arrow. Later private housing has diluted the overall concept.

CHURCH HILL CENTRE has one staggered row of shops of 1977, with metallic roofs behind arcades, NE side, with hyperactively designed pub, the BOOK AND CANDLE (1978 by *C. W. Lea* of *Ansells Architects Dept*), S end. These face a sunken amphitheatre, formerly with pond, above which rises three-storey flats, KNOWLE CLOSE, built by the *Development Corporation* for the YMCA, 1977–8; paired balconies, monopitch roofs becoming angled skylights. Also belonging to the YMCA, GORDON ANSTIS HOUSE by *Nicol Thomas Ltd*, 1993, NE, banded brick, L-plan. The church centre, ST ANDREW (Methodist), in Church Hill Way further W, is routine brick, by *Handsworth Associates*, 1983–4.

Housing at CHURCH HILL SOUTH began *c.* 1974. An extensive *Development Corporation* group, completed 1978, runs E of the centre along LOXLEY CLOSE, with culs de sac to its S; job architects *Bhupendra Arora* and *Ron Skidmore*. Brick, mostly short terraces, Radburn-type traffic segregation. At its W end, MENDIP HOUSE, sheltered accommodation, partly tile-hung, and a COMMUNITY CENTRE by *Brian Rush & Associates* (built as St John Fisher R.C. Primary School). In GREYSTONE and HERONFIELD CLOSES, S, good housing by *Manning, Clamp & Partners*, 1978, staggered groups with weatherboarded end gables and pantiled roofs. Further S, to the W of RICKYARD LANE, closes of weatherboarded terraces, nicely opened up by first-floor flats on stilts (for car-ports). MOONS MOAT FIRST SCHOOL, Cleeve Close, opened 1977, is of spreading brick type, with pantiled roof. MOON'S MOAT itself, a C14 moated site, can be reached from the end of Barnwood Close, part of duller housing E of Rickyard Lane.

Housing off Tanhouse Lane in CHURCH HILL NORTH typifies the last phase of the *Development Corporation*. SANDHURST CLOSE, off the E side, completed 1979, job architects *Michael Pearson* and *Tom White*, pursues a winding circuit, excessively narrow to lessen car speeds, but almost claustrophobic; very plain brick houses in compact squares or closes. UPPERFIELD CLOSE, off the W side, job architect *John Nutting*, follows the same principles, with an even more rustic winding spine road. REDSTONE CLOSE, further N (leading to MARKFIELD FARM FIRST SCHOOL, 1978), marks the return of upper-floor half-timbering.

MOON'S MOAT industrial area, to the E, has more groups of *Development Corporation* advance factories (especially in Thornhill Road); also much larger premises designed by them for specific clients.

Earlier survivors: PAPERMILL FARM, Brooklands Lane, off the W side of Papermill Drive, is C19, with C17 barn and stable, N. BEOLEY PAPER MILL, SE, which produced 'blue' needle wrapping papers, a large brick and timbered C17–C19 complex, was converted to housing by *Cross & Craig Associates* of Solihull, 1988.

RIBBESFORD

St Leonard. The mother church of Bewdley, Norman in origin, enlarged in the C15; sandstone, aisled, quite large. N aisle, chancel, and half-timbered W bell-turret are mostly by *Frederick Preedy*, 1878–9, rebuilding after the church was struck by lightning in 1877. Ruskin disapproved, proposing instead that 'the dear old ruin grow grey by Severn's side in peace'. The W part of the N aisle retains Norman walling. Fine N doorway (sheltered by a pretty timber balustraded porch dated 1633), related to work of the Herefordshire School. One order of shafts with very involved capitals with beaded interlace, flanked by similarly carved panels (cf. Rock); the l. panel has instead a large bird attacking a smaller one, plus two fish. Abaci with chequer or zigzag patterns, arch with heavy roll moulding. The tympanum portrays a Kilpeck-like archer (accompanied by his dog?) firing at a plump bird-like monster. Blocked s doorway *ex situ*, badly mauled; also one order of columns, the capitals poorly preserved, again flanking panels. Late C15 s aisle, with plain three-light stepped windows with cusped heads. Inside, surprisingly, its five-bay arcade is of timber, the only case in the county, the arches simply curved braces, the piers octagonal with rudimentary moulded capitals. The stone N arcade gives a lopsided effect. It has octagonal piers with four-centred arches, the two wider W bays basically C15, the two E by *Preedy*. His also the arch-braced roofs. – SCULPTURAL FRAGMENTS show that the Norman church was elaborately decorated. Carved stones are reused as external lintels to the chancel side windows. Within, a length of Norman point-to-point chevron is displayed in the rood-stair doorway, s aisle. Further fragments in the blocked s doorway include two pieces of a cylindrical shaft with three-strand plaiting (cf. Kilpeck, w window), and incised Norman window heads. Other pieces may have come from the Norman N arcade, chancel arch, or s doorway.

Most FURNISHINGS of 1878–9. PULPIT and low SCREEN have applied tracery panels from the C15 rood screen, including lively small-scale carvings. – The LECTERN incorporates Jacobean arabesque work. – Oak REREDOS and ALTAR, carved by *Robert Clarke* of Hereford, 1906. – FONT. By *Thomas Gordon*, 1886; diapered square bowl, carved by *Martyn & Emms*. – STAINED GLASS. The s aisle w window has important C15 fragments: a complete St George spearing the Dragon, various coats of arms. – Excellent nave w by *Morris & Co.*, 1877, designed by *Burne-Jones*; given by Alfred Baldwin (cf. Wilden). – E window by *Powell & Sons*, 1925–6, supervised by *Sir Giles Scott*; chancel N 1894, s 1883, both *Hardman*. – s chapel E by *Heaton, Butler & Bayne*, 1898. – One colourful N aisle N, of 1870. – MONUMENTS. At the N aisle w end, three cross-slabs. Two, with stiff-leaf foliage, must be C13, one of these with large Mortimer shield set across the shaft. Third slab probably *c.* 1400. – Of wall tablets, the earliest two are in the s aisle: John Tiler †1626, simple painted stone; above, John

Soley †1604 and wife Margaret †1639, already classical, with columns and broken pediment. – Many tablets to Bewdley residents, e.g. John Prattinton †1732, by *T. King* of Bath, with flaming urn (N aisle). – Capt. Francis Winnington-Ingram †1843. Brass in C15 style, with figure beneath a pinnacled and crocketed canopy (S aisle).

Large CHURCHYARD sloping uphill, with, especially at the top, several early C19 chest and pedestal tombs.

Opposite the church, NE, a long T-plan farm building, of sandstone, formerly belonging to the C19 HOME FARM. The N section, cross-bar with barn and N half of the stem with cowhouse, is probably mid-C18. The earlier S end, presumably stables, has two basket-arched doorways flanked by horizontal oval windows; between them, an eroded tablet with arms, said to be of the Herbert family. Probably *c.* 1650–75.

RIBBESFORD HOUSE, a little S, presents a puzzle. Its exterior, cement-rendered with Jacobethan Gothic detail, almost entirely *c.* 1830, conceals older features. It stands within the infilled moat of the medieval house of the de Ribbesford family; the moat had a stone revetment, the edge of the enclosed platform still visible on the SE sides. Documentary evidence suggests rebuilding *c.* 1535 (called by Leland a 'goodly manour place'); the general plan, including the two turrets facing SW, may belong to this phase. There was further work in 1669. Francis Ingram purchased the estate in 1787, then demolished the larger part of the house. The surviving main range presumably represents one side of a quadrangle, but further research is needed.

The approach is from the NE, through C19 octagonal gatepiers with open Jacobean finials. The cemented front has gabled dormers and mostly cross-windows; short gabled wing, l., with square two-storey bay window with wavy battlements. Big square full-height porch, with similar top, flanked by obelisks; doorway with engaged fluted Doric columns and feeble metope frieze. A long brick service wing extending forward from the r. end of this front seems mostly mid-C19, the angle masked by a lower, probably later block. The rear (SW) front is more eloquent, its centre, with Doric loggia and canted oriel, flanked by the tall octagonal turrets already mentioned; originally (at least in the C18) these were far less regular, but the whole remains reminiscent of a grand Jacobethan gatehouse. Gabled centre with gables either side; further l., an additional range, now also C19 in appearance, perhaps originally *c.* 1790. An early C19 entrance corridor runs through the main range, with curving stair with cast-iron balusters at the rear; the ceiling retains C16 moulded beams.

RIPPLE

8030

ST MARY. An important medieval possession of Worcester Cathedral Priory, probably on the site of a Saxon minster:

p. 23

137 ft (42 metres) long, with aisles, transepts and crossing tower. The present building must have been begun late in the C12; most is of that date or the first decades of the C13. Chancel replaced in the late C13. The oldest parts may be the transepts and start of the crossing; here the angle shafts indicating the intention to vault are distinguished from the other shafts of the crossing by not being keeled. Pointed single-step crossing arches, N and S. Both transepts have a Norman W window (the S transept's now blocked) and both a contemporary altar recess against their windowless E wall, with round roll-moulded arch on big imposts (those of the S recess hacked off). W and E crossing arches are more decidedly Transitional, their pointed arches with steps and keeled rolls. The capitals of the crossing go from trumpet scallops to crockets and very early stiff-leaf, corresponding to capitals in Worcester Cathedral (the two nave W bays, and transepts). The round arches with continuous roll mouldings, from the transepts into the nave aisles, of alternating green and white stone, are also reminiscent of Norman work at Worcester.

The NAVE has six-bay arcades with quatrefoil piers with very odd capitals, of the most elementary trumpet-scallop shape; possibly they were meant to be crocket capitals but were never carved. Semicircular responds, the W ones with three attached shafts with the same capitals. But the arcades as a whole have a suspiciously re-cut look. Clerestory with small lancets above the spandrels, not the arch apexes; C15 two-light NE window, inserted to light a rood screen. Small lancets also in the aisles; the two-light replacements here, especially S side, are probably C19. The plain corbel table outside is also E.E., as are the three nave doorways, the N one still with round arch, deeply roll-moulded. All have mature stiff-leaf capitals, probably c. 1230, those of the N and S doorways specially attractively arranged. The leaf sprays of their middle shafts spread out to cover the shafts either side, which therefore have no capitals at all. W doorway also with three orders of shafts but here the central one has no capital, the stiff-leaf overlapping it from either side. Hoodmould with reused Norman beast-heads stops, of Malmesbury type, frequent in Gloucestershire, also found in Worcestershire at Bredon; perhaps they come from the original chancel. Perp W window, with traces of the former arrangement of lancets either side. The N PORCH must also be a Perp addition; within, vault springers imply at least the planning of an upper floor. The present upper storey is C18, perhaps c. 1797. Entrance with hoodmould of Norman billet, again perhaps from the original chancel; the pointed arch includes a continuous roll moulding.

The lower stage of the CROSSING TOWER has small Norman openings. Above was formerly a spire, finally removed in 1713 when *Thomas Wilkinson* raised the tower some fifteen feet; Perp-like bell-openings presumably of this date. Further heightened 1797, when the balustraded parapet was added or re-set.

The late C13 CHANCEL has three-light windows, of red sandstone, stepped pointed-trefoiled lights beneath single arches. The W triplets are blocked; the other two, S side, have plate tracery with pointed quatrefoils in their spandrels. NE and SE windows of one trefoiled light only, with encircled trefoil in the head. Round-arched priest's doorway, N, curious for the late C13; was it in deference to the earlier building? The Perp E window matches the nave W; inside, Lias shafts with moulded capitals survive from the former E window (or windows). Side windows with moulded rere-arches; continuous hoodmould. Roof rebuilt by *Henry Rowe*, 1890. The transept N and S windows, also of three stepped trefoiled lights, seem of rather later vintage, perhaps C15–C16 or even C17–C18.

FURNISHINGS. Notable STALLS, probably C15, with an outstanding set of sixteen MISERICORDS. Twelve form a series of Labours of the Months, delightfully lively scenes flanked by leaf sprays. January to June are on the S side (E to W); July to December, N side (W to E). Interlopers at the centres of each side: the sun, S, moon, N. Another sun misericord against the low screen, also a figure of the Water Carrier. The SCREEN has much applied carving, from the C15 rood screen, especially shields with HV monograms. Here also two highly traceried STALL ENDS, with poppyheads. – COMMUNION RAILS. Simple, C17, balusters widely spaced. – Tiled REREDOS (now hidden), wooden fret-carved PULPIT, and PEWS, all standard C19. – Splendid brass LECTERN, 1883, presumably by *Hardman*. – FONT, *c*. 1300, so drastically renewed in 1851 as to seem Victorian: octagonal bowl, each face with paired blank pointed-trefoiled arches. – ROYAL ARMS. George I; 1716. – STAINED GLASS. Chancel S: mid-C15 fragments reset from the E window, including excellent heads. – E window by *Herbert W. Bryans*, 1909, much livelier than the nave W, of 1885 by *Kempe*. – N aisle, from E: 1st *c*. 1888, no doubt by *Lavers, Barraud & Westlake*, 2nd by *George Rogers*, 1875. – S aisle: 1st by *J.A. Crombie* (*John Baker Ltd*), 1990, 2nd by *Hardman*, 1871. – MONUMENTS. Tablets in the chancel window splays, the best, the Rev. John Holte †1734, of grey marble, by *Thomas White*.

CHURCHYARD CROSS, NNW of the porch. C14–C15: two steps, two-stage base with rebated corners, part of the shaft.

The OLD RECTORY, NE, was built in 1726 for the Rev. John Holte. A very handsome brick house, five by six bays, with hipped roof; straight rubbed-brick heads with panelled keystones, stone quoins. Central W doorway, with eared architrave and pediment. A low gabled N wing, of stone, is said to be C15.

RIPPLE HALL, to the WSW, reached by a drive further W. Refined brick, perhaps by *Anthony Keck*, *c*. 1780–90, its S front of two storeys and 2+1+2 bays; Adamish tripartite doorway beneath very wide fanlight, partly masked by a C20 wrought-iron porch. Both return elevations are filled by curved bows. Spacious central hall, its staircase with stick balusters; flanking reception rooms with delicate plaster ceilings. Earlier four-bay rear wing, NW, rendered, with doorcase of *c*. 1700: open scrolled pediment enclosing the Dormer arms. Further rear additions, NE, by *Prothero & Phillott*, 1906–7. – Theirs also the roughcast LODGE.

THE CROSS, W of the church, is a diminutive triangular open space with medieval CROSS: two steps, base, tall intact shaft broached from square to octagonal. Surrounding C17–C18 cottages, timber-framed (Nos. 1–2, a subdivided hall house with jettied cross-wing) or painted brick, including former ALMSHOUSES of 1701, again with Dormer heraldry. MANOR FARM, set back from the S apex, is C16–C17 L-plan, also framed, with jettied gable. Its late C18 brick BARN lies further W, beyond the C19 OLD FORGE.

At the W end of the village, the former RAILWAY STATION (on the Tewkesbury to Malvern line), a well-preserved example of 1864. Red brick, yellow banding and diapering, especially on the taller station-master's house; half-hipped or straight gables with pierced bargeboards, steep slate roofs with trefoiled dormers.

UCKINGHALL, Ripple's sister village ½ m. WNW, with timber-framed cottages and later C18 brick farms, has much less C20 development. At its centre, another medieval CROSS, a weathered base and shaft stump.

Former SCHOOL, ⅜ m. NNW. Of 1844–5, brick, with attached house; two-light pointed windows, brick hoodmoulds, gables with bargeboards. C20 N extension.

The parish extends some distance N, with large hamlets at NAUNTON and RYALL, both largely C20, but with C16–C17 timber-framed cottages and farms. The best is RYALL FARM, big-boned, L-plan, with massive triple brick stack; C18 hipped roofs. RYALL HILL, at the end of Ryall Lane, mostly mid-C19 Tudor brick, has gables with prettily pierced bargeboards.

6060

ROCHFORD

The main settlement, Upper Rochford, lies along the Tenbury to Worcester road, its largest building, ROCHFORD HOUSE, a rendered mid-C19 villa, in its own small park. The church is at Lower Rochford, ½ m. N., behind the C17–C19 Church Farm, right by the Teme and its grassy banks.

p. 22 ST MICHAEL. Norman nave and chancel, altered in the early C14; heavily restored by *Henry Curzon*, 1864–5. He extended the nave W, with weatherboarded bell-turret with shingled spirelet, added a timber S porch, and inserted E and W windows with plate tracery. Two Norman nave windows, one N, one S; also one chancel N. More important, the elaborate though very coarse N doorway, set in the typically projecting section of wall, and now badly weathered. Two orders: shafts with summary volute capitals, imposts with zigzag plait and interlace, arches with frontal chevron. Tympanum with flatly carved, spread-out Tree of Life, beneath arched border of rosettes, cable moulding below; the only example in Worcestershire of this familiar motif, also found at High Ercall, Shropshire, and at Dymock and Kempley, both Gloucestershire. The Norman chancel arch has moulded imposts and also two orders of frontal chevron. This Late Norman motif appears at Peterborough as early as *c.* 1130–5, and at Shobdon (Herefs.) between 1131 and 1148. At Kempley the tympanum is probably *c.* 1140, contemporary with its famous chancel frescoes. Rochford may therefore be of *c.* 1150. The present s doorway is early C14, with continuous hollow-chamfered moulding; contemporary chancel SE window, matching piscina below.

Most FURNISHINGS by *Curzon.* He presented the notable FONT himself: square, with chamfered corners and small carved scene, on dark marble shafts. – ALTAR of 1930, with carved riddel posts by *Herbert Read* of Exeter. – ORGAN. A charming piece of *c.* 1800, with brass inlay, crowned with foliage and gilded double-headed eagle. – ROYAL ARMS. Probably George I. – STAINED GLASS. In the E window, early glass by *Morris & Co.*, 1865. Small panel of the Adoration of the Child plus two angels, all set in ample transparent patterned quarries; three more angels in the traceries. Cartooned by *Burne-Jones* (apart from the flanking angels, which are by *Morris* himself), their style as yet unaffected by the stylized conventions he was later to follow. The work is fresh and naïve, equal in quality to anything of that time in England or abroad. – Small window by the font, also 1865, by *Heaton, Butler & Bayne*, an interesting comparison. – W window, 1885, and nave SE, *c.* 1875, by *Ward & Hughes.* – The nave SW, by *F. W. Cole*, 1952, carries, confusingly enough, the mark of *William Morris (Westminster) Studios.* – MONUMENTS. A couple of rustic tablets, especially Mary Taylor †1758, with fluted Corinthian pilasters.

Near the church, C17 timber-framed cottages and farms. OLD HALL, S, dated 1704, is mostly of *c.* 1840–50; sandstone rubble, H-plan, pretty bargeboarded gables.

ROCK

ST PETER AND ST PAUL. The most significant Norman village church in the county, probably of *c.* 1160–70, with large four-bay nave and two-bay chancel. Of sandstone ashlar, singularly grandly detailed; like Ribbesford, almost certainly work of the Herefordshire School. One approaches from the N, where the nave has a projecting portal with three orders of columns, plus zigzag band on the outer jambs (cf. Astley). Capitals with decorated scallops, apart from the inner ones which are complete masks (cf. Holt and several places in Herefordshire); abaci with foliage trails (cf. Rowlstone, Herefs.); arch with frontal chevron, crenellation, lobes with pellets, and thin rolls with a kind of radiating three-ray motif. Plain tympanum, billet hood-mould. Nave and chancel have of course flat buttresses; corbel tables decorated mostly with heads (some similar to Kilpeck). All windows, placed high up above a chamfered string course, are shafted outside as well as in. Moreover, to the E of each of the two easternmost nave N windows is a blank window, apparently blank from the beginning. Rhythmically this is not at all satisfactory; why was it done? The capitals of the shafts have plain blocks or scallops (in one window they have almost become upright fluted leaves). The chancel arch is a *tour de force* (called by Neil Stratford 'by far the finest example of Norman decorative sculpture in the county'). Responds with one major and three minor shafts: two W, one E. N capitals with entwined trails, several with heads; those on the S have yet more ornate carving: a pliant fertility figure, centaur shooting a stag, a lion (plus heads and birds), and boat with cross-like mast. Square flanking panels with interlace carving (cf. Ribbesford); decorated abaci and bases. Arches mostly frontal chevron; hoodmould with lobes with pellets.*

Later than Norman, the following elements. The chancel was extended in the C13–C14; lean-to N vestry with E and W lancets. The three-light E window has reticulated tracery, Dec (though renewed). Also Dec, a tall (lowside?) window replacing the Norman chancel NW, and another inserted below the nave NE (probably to light a nave altar). Single-framed nave roof, probably also C14, with sturdy later tie-beams. Chancel roof, with arch-braced collars and wind-braces, perhaps also C14, again with later (C16?) strengthening, see the central truss with tie-beam and three struts. The W tower (together with S aisle and chapel) is of *c.* 1510 (*see below*). It is typically Late Perp, broad, of four stages, with diagonal buttresses, battlements, and very large four-light W window with plain tracery. Lofty arch towards the nave, its broad polygonal responds with concave sides. This late Perp motif is taken up by the four-bay nave arcade and by the two-bay chapel arcade: octagonal piers, those of the aisle quite tall, of the chapel short and stubby; four-centred double-chamfered arches, notably sharply pointed in the nave. The windows are not as tellingly Late Perp; most are rather Dec in style (perhaps reused or C19 insertions). Both aisle and chapel have battlements, also four-centred doorways. *Preedy* comprehensively restored the church in 1859–61; *Martin B. Buckle* restored the tower, 1881.

FONT. Norman, coeval with the church (and similar to Bayton nearby); cauldron-shaped, with nine medallions filled with stylized rosettes, connected by clasps. Base by *Preedy*. – His also most other FURNISHINGS: brass eagle LECTERN, chancel STALLS and PARCLOSE SCREENS, encaustic TILING, stone carved REREDOS. – Polygonal PULPIT, added 1869; banded stone with quatrefoils and red inlay. – The S chapel ALTAR is a medieval MENSA; late C20 stone base. –

* George Zarnecki attributed the Rock carving to the Aston master; he later worked in Herefordshire at Shobdon and Kilpeck. Neil Stratford suggested the N doorway might be later than the chancel arch, done locally after the master left.

ARCHITECTURAL FRAGMENTS. Norman bits built into the interior nave N wall, their motifs matching the N doorway; probably from a former S doorway. – At the W end, a medieval dug-out CHEST; STOCKS (of 1782); and WHIPPING POST (of 1773). – STAINED GLASS. E window by *Lavers & Westlake*, 1894. – Two chancel N and one S chapel S by *Preedy*, 1861, their style very close to Alexander Gibbs, i.e. showing strong Butterfield influence. – S aisle SE by *Camm Bros.*, 1870. – MONUMENTS. S chapel. Incised slab to Richard Smith, 'quondam rector huius ecclesiae' †1554 (or †1560, according to his will); still Gothic, with depressed ogee canopy above the figure. Perhaps by *Richard Parker* of Burton-on-Trent. – Big tomb-chest with shields in large quatrefoils, some with traces of heraldic paint. On top, a sharply incised quadruple canopy, crocketed and pinnacled; there may have been painted figures beneath. Nash records the former inscription to Thomas Conyngsby (†1498) which mentions his son Sir Humphrey 'who built this isle and steeple of the church AD 1510'; a rare case of dated Perp in Worcestershire.

CHURCH HOUSE, N, was once the parsonage; C17 timber-framed, L-plan. Replaced by a mid-C18 brick RECTORY ½ m. NNW: five bays, hipped roof, C19 veranda.

The large square MOATED PLATFORM SE of the church marks the site of the manor house of the Tosny family. Another moated site, BOWER COURT, ⅓ m. SE, belonged to the Coningsbys; the house, of C15–C16 origin, brick and timber-framed, with arch- and wind-braced hall, was much renewed *c.* 1978.

ROMSLEY

ST KENELM, 1¼ m. NW of the village, in an entirely rural setting in the Clent Hills, despite the proximity of Birmingham; a chapelry of Halesowen until 1841. According to a disproved legend St Kenelm, the boy king of Mercia, was murdered here after the death of his father Kenulf in 821. In the crypt below the E end (now a boiler house, containing nothing ancient) was the holy spring, said to have risen from the spot where he was killed; the blocked segmental arch, chancel S, led to the stairway down. The spring now rises in a C20 enclosure, downhill, to the E.

Nave and chancel in one, C12, of red sandstone, but the charming, slender late C15 W tower, with its elaborate SW Midlands Perp detailing, is grey. It stands forward from the Norman W wall (with blocked doorway) on two buttresses connected high up by a four-centred arch. Many big winged grotesques: at the W and E angles, on all hoodmoulds, also on the contemporary buttresses at the nave W corners. One-light bell-openings with crocketed ogee canopies, flanked by similar blind windows; also at this level, buttress niches. Parapet with panelled battlements, tall crocketed pinnacles. Timber S porch also Late Perp, its side walls rebuilt in brick: four-centred entrance, spandrels with tracery and spiky leaves, gable with coved jetty. Norman s doorway, perhaps *c.* 1170, with two orders of renewed shafts with cushion capitals; naïve but impressive tympanum of Christ seated, wearing a crown, within an oval glory held by two flying angels.* His ribbed draperies are no doubt inspired by the Herefordshire School (cf. especially Shobdon); the composition of the tympanum is standard Romanesque. But the broad border of very loose interlace, which close inspection reveals as intertwined serpents with biting jaws, is still in the Anglo-Saxon tradition (perhaps inspired by the Chaddesley Corbett font, p. 219). Inner arch moulding with beakheads, the only complete example in the county; the outer moulding has a stylized version of the same motif, the heads having become oblong beaded flaps. The arches are red, the tympanum browner sandstone. Most of the fabric is C12, with chamfered eaves cornices (w end) and flat Norman buttresses. The e end, with large stepped diagonal buttresses, was rebuilt in the C14; windows, where not restored in the C19, also of this date. By the n chancel lancet, faint traces of its Norman predecessor.

The church was restored by *R.C. Hussey*, 1845–6. Most internal detail, especially the high-braced roof, is his; also the FURNISHINGS: Perp-style FONT, polygonal stone PULPIT, PEWS. – PANELLING and carved wooden REREDOS of the Last Supper added 1900. – Deep WEST GALLERY, 1758, reconstructed 1846. – WALL PAINTINGS. By the chancel n window one figure with curly hair, probably early C14. Nothing is now visible of a later C14 cycle of the life of Kenelm; partial tracings, by Hussey, survive at the Victoria and Albert Museum. – SCULPTURE. Outside, high up, nave SE, a small figure of a saint, crude and flat; head corbel above. Both probably C12. – STAINED glass. e window, given by W.E. Gladstone, 1846; perhaps by *Wailes.* – Nave N by *Walter Camm*, 1913–15, with charming intricate scenes of the Kenelm legend. – Nave s by *Morris & Co.*, 1908, with *Burne-Jones* figures of Peace and Faith.

Excellent LYCHGATE by *Harold Brakspear*, 1919; sandstone walls, timber roof.

KENELMSTOWE, which grew up round Kenelm's shrine, has entirely disappeared. The only building nearby now is CHAPEL FARM, SE; banded brick, dated 1868.

ST KENELM'S HALL, ¼ m. SE, a typical house by *John Cotton*, 1884, is gabled, but not quite Gothic; brick, blue patterning.

The present VILLAGE developed beside the Bromsgrove–Dudley turnpike road (now B4551). Roughcast MISSION ROOM of 1925–6 (now church hall), a remodelling of the small National School by *W. Westmacott*, 1849–53.

---

* Neil Stratford suggested that the ring round Christ's raised r. hand may be a misunderstood rendering of an orb.

ROMSLEY HILL GRANGE, 1 m. SSW of the village, was built as
Romsley Hill Home for Consumptives; by *F.W. Martin*,
1911–13, for the Birmingham Hospital Saturday Fund. Huge
butterfly plan, facing S; white pebbledash over purple brick.
Central gable, formerly above an open balcony, three gables in
each wing. Well-detailed rear, N, with hipped roofs, tall chimneys, some half-timbering. Matching gabled LODGE. Closed
1980, now housing.

HUNNINGTON, N of Romsley village, has a few scattered
C18–early C19 farms. The most prominent building is the
former BLUE BIRD TOFFEE FACTORY, built for Harry
Vincent Ltd, 1925–7. Long brick two-storey front, centre
emphasized with stone Doric columns *in antis*. Set back, S, the
large single-storey CANTEEN and ASSEMBLY ROOMS, with
central pedimental gable flanked by open arcades; thin turret.
Across the road, the former VILLAGE SHOP; big hipped
roof with dormers. Further S, a small contemporary MODEL
VILLAGE for the workers: slightly varied semi-detached brick
houses, mostly with hipped roofs, in The Close, and extending N and S along Bromsgrove Road. – Adjoining the shop,
access to the former HUNNINGTON STATION, on the Halesowen to Northfield (Birmingham) branch line, opened 1883,
closed 1964; platform building and attached station house,
brick with segment-headed windows, now all residential.

ROUS LENCH   0050

The Rous family held Rous Lench from 1382 until 1721. It then
came to the Rouse Boughtons, who sold it, in 1876, to the Rev.
W.K.W. Chafy Chafy (†1916). Both he and his predecessor,
Sir Charles Henry Rouse Boughton, built zealously on the
estate.

ST PETER. Norman nave, N aisle and chancel, restored and
enlarged by *Preedy*, 1884–5; his Neo-Norman bellcote replaced
a timber W bell-turret (supported within the nave). C12
Norman work includes the two scallop capitals of the N
doorway and much of the S doorway. This has one order of
spiral-fluted shafts with interlaced capitals; arch with frontal
chevron. Above, framed by renewed shafts with leaf decoration   12
and moulded arch with chevron, an outstanding relief of Christ
seated and blessing, his almond-shaped glory cusped at the
sides; probably *c.* 1140–50, cf. the Prior's Door, Ely Cathedral.* Three-bay N arcade also Late Norman: sturdy round
piers, round capitals with many scallops, arches single-stepped
or without any step. Matching chancel arch of 1884–5; the
arrangement for the late medieval rood stair sits uncomfortably with it. Chancel rebuilt or lengthened in the late C13. Its

---

*Neil Stratford suggested Northamptonshire as a source common to both, basing
his view on comparisons with ornamental detail at Castor, of *c.* 1120.

former E window, with plate tracery, is now the N aisle W. Nave W window probably early C14. Preedy rebuilt the N aisle and nave S walls, adding a lavish Neo-Norman N mortuary chapel, plus sacristy and vestries. N aisle E apse not completed until 1896, its Italian Romanesque-looking ALTAR CANOPY dramatically lit by skylights.

FONT. C15, octagonal; plain bowl with good mouldings. Spire-like C19 COVER. – PULPITS. Two, both Elizabethan and brought in, set up as *ambones*; almost identical, with panels with two tiers of elaborate blank arches. – *Dr Chafy* designed several of the 1884–5 fittings: probably the wooden SCREEN, fancy mixed Gothic with Renaissance motifs, and Jacobethan CHAIRS and KNEELING DESKS in the chancel, coloured black and gold. – PAINTING. The Feast in the House of Simon the Pharisee; Venetian style, *c*. 1600, inspired by Tintoretto. Or is it a C19 copy? – ARCHITECTURAL FRAGMENTS, NE vestry. An amazing collection, the most important piece an Anglo-Danish stone with two peacocks drinking from a vase or chalice; below, a little man (holding a sickle in his r. hand) offers them grapes from his harvest (?). The surface round the corner is also carved, apparently with interlaced serpents. What was this then? It cannot have been a lintel. Was it part of a pillar? Or a sepulchral slab? – Also, three early window heads: one with fake voussoirs, another rebated for a shutter, the third with intertwined tendrils of pre-Conquest type; and fragments of Norman chevron, shafts, capitals and bases, plus later medieval pieces. – STAINED GLASS. E, probably of 1890, perhaps by *A. L. Moore*. – Contemporary W window. – Of 1884, the N aisle N, by *Clayton & Bell*, and N chapel windows, by *Preedy*. – Chancel SE, abstract blue and yellow, by *Mollie Meager*, 2000.

MONUMENTS. Large broken coffin, the lid with two fragments of an incised cross of unusual type, perhaps C11 or C12. – Other monuments were moved into the N chapel in 1885. Edward Rous †1611 and wife Mary †1580. Big tomb-chest with recumbent effigies, painted black, his feet against a large Saracen's head (the family crest), hers against her pet dog. Four children kneel against the chest. Large back cartouche with strapwork. – Sir John Rous †1645. Tomb-chest with canopy on Doric columns, painted black; straight top with obelisks and armorial achievement. No effigy. – Frances Chaplin †1715 (formerly Lady Rous, sister of the architect Thomas Archer who acted as her executor). Baroque style, not particularly good. She is seated holding her heart, next to an urn with two doves on the top. Corinthian columns support an attic with medallion of Sir Francis Rous held by putti in clouds. Open segmental pediment. Erected 1719, in the style of Francis Bird, but attributed to *Richard Crutcher* (GF). – Two similar tablets, with Ionic columns and segmental pediments, to Sir Thomas Rous †1676 and Sir Edward †1677; attributed to *William Stanton* (GF). – Sir Charles Rouse Boughton †1821, by *J. Stephens*; draped Grecian altar.

The rectangular MOAT, E, marks the site of the medieval manor house.

The VILLAGE GREEN, to the NW, best illustrates the C19 munificence of Sir C.H. Rouse Boughton and Dr Chafy. The prevalent style is C16–C17 (with at least one original cottage), but with red or blue brick as well as half-timbering. Most startling is Dr Chafy's LETTER BOX, sandstone and timber with jettied gable, blown up to the size of a moderate dovecote. The most attractive buildings are the former VILLAGE CLUB with attached house, 1872, and former SCHOOL (also with house), 1864, more original in its treatment of Gothic motifs: steep triangular-headed windows, ornate polychrome brickwork, wavy bargeboards. Nearby, a timber-canopied WELL. Other cottages are dated 1862 and 1890. The circular timber SHELTER in the middle of the green is a sensible addition of 2000.

The OLD RECTORY, in large grounds, SW, must be c. 1830–40. Stuccoed with quoins, three-bay W front with canted bays flanking a Tudor porch; windows with hoodmoulds, balustraded parapet.

PROVIDENCE HOUSE, a little SE. Timber-framed, C17, with gabled NW cross-wing, but so overlain with late C19 detail (tall brick chimneys, decorative half-timbering, even biblical texts) as to appear largely Victorian.

ROUS LENCH COURT, further SE, uphill, a large highly picturesque black-and-white house, again appears largely C19, in this case probably mostly c. 1860. Before the C19 it is said to have consisted of ranges round two courtyards. What remains is no more than the S and W sides of the main (entrance) courtyard. The less-restored gateway range, W (to the road), is probably early C16; near its centre a big stone chimney with tall brick stacks (and, in the upper room, a stone fireplace with carved wooden overmantel dated 1651). The early C17 S range is lavishly embellished with C19 decorative timbering, N and S porches, and fancy chimneys; gabled NE projection entirely C19. Inside, much exposed timberwork and reset panelling. Also imported pieces, notably part of a C14 screen forming a balustrade on the main stair and, in the NE room, a splendid late C16 stone chimneypiece with lion supporters and metope frieze with dramatic masks; this came from Shaw in the North Riding *via* William Randolph Hearst's celebrated collection destined for California.

Outstanding terraced GARDENS with balustraded walls and much topiary, the latter, mostly added for Dr Chafy from 1879, shaped as battlemented towers and gateways; massive circular domed arbour near the centre. Burges, already in 1881, called it 'a perfect Paradise', Miles Hadfield, 1959, 'the finest topiary garden in England'. At the top, near the road, a square brick TOWER 60 ft (18.5 metres) high, with machicolated parapet and higher round stair-turret, like an Italian Palazzo Pubblico. Begun by Dr Chafy, 1881, perhaps to a *Burges* design, to commemorate Richard Baxter (cf. Kidderminster).

At RADFORD, 1 m. NNW, a late C18 brick farmhouse (with large C17 weatherboarded barn), several C17 timber-framed cottages, and another overblown Dr Chafy LETTER BOX, with 'crazy' Malvern stone infill rather than sandstone.

At the E end, RADFORD HEIGHTS, large brick and half-timbered pastiche by *Roger P. Dudley & Associates*, 1989–90: half-hipped gables, open timber porch.

9070

RUBERY

Entirely outer Birmingham, part now within the city boundary, where five high blocks of flats, to a heavy butterfly plan, form the dominant visual accent. Rubery began as ribbon development along the new Birmingham–Worcester road, opened 1831 to avoid the steep climb over the Lickey Hills. The only early-to-mid-C19 survivor is the NEW ROSE AND CROWN, four bays, roughcast, with lintels on consoles. This lies near the E end of New Road (itself by-passed 1962), which otherwise consists mostly of C20 shopping arcades.

ST CHAD, New Road. 1957–9 by *Richard Twentyman* (*Lavender, Twentyman & Percy*).* Mostly brick, with continuous low-pitched copper roof; tall, open, square campanile, attached only by a low porch at the SW angle (actually NW, the church is orientated N–S). Nave side walls with strong concrete window grid all the way along. Attached to the chancel, S side, an octagonal, pyramidal-roofed chapel; on the ritual N, a long low range with vestries and cloakrooms. Narrower sanctuary with blank E wall, simply patterned inside; tall mullioned side windows light the altar. Orderly interior, little altered: traditional FONT with spire-like wooden cover; ORGAN neatly set on galleries either side of the chancel opening.

At the rear, the VICARAGE of 1967, of the same materials.

CONGREGATIONAL CHAPEL, Whetty Lane; now Beacon Church Centre (United Reformed). 1927–8 by *J.R. Armstrong* of the Bournville Village Trust. Brick, round-arched windows, the gabled entrance front well handled: large stepped-back arch, triple-mullioned window above the doorway.

The most interesting housing is in REDNAL HILL LANE, Eachway, a small brick group (Nos. 48–64, SE end), single, in pairs or short terraces, by *H. Bedford Tylor*, 1907–8, reminiscent of his work at Bournville (Birmingham).

WASELEY HILLS HIGH SCHOOL, School Road. By *A. V. Rowe*, c. 1930; brick, Neo-Georgian, two storeys, but three large round-arched windows for the central hall. Good large additions by *Architype*, 2000, nicely linked by a curved entrance; angled split roofs, much prefabricated timber construction including weatherboarding.

---

* Replacing a timber church by *W.J. Hopkins & A.B. Pinckney*, 1895.

CHADWICH MANOR, 1¼ m. SW, in the angle between the M5 and A38. Late C17, red brick with dark headers. Five bays with segment-headed windows, flat stone quoins, the central bay breaking forward with its own quoins; big hipped roof, bracketed cornice. – Tall stone gatepiers with ball finials.

RUSHOCK

8070

ST MICHAEL. Rebuilt by *Roger Eykyn* of Wolverhampton, 1756–8.* Small, of sandstone ashlar: nave, W tower, shallow transepts, chancel. Depressed Y-tracery, pedimental end gables with short square pinnacles. Three-stage battlemented tower, its W side blank, with single lancet bell-openings N and S, and S doorway with ogee-arched hoodmould. This last feature, plus the Y-tracery, led Pevsner to question whether there was further work *c.* 1800, but there is no evidence for this. Restored 1871–2 by *T.D. Baker* of Kidderminster; his the bar-traceried E window and most of the interior, including high heavy roofs and almost all FURNISHINGS: encaustic FLOOR TILES, STALLS projecting into the crossing, tall FONT with recessed ogee panels. – STAINED GLASS. E window by *G.J. Baguley*, 1876. – ROYAL ARMS. George III. 1767, restored 1937.

SCHOOL (now village hall), SW. 1854, brick, round-arched windows; altered and given half-timbered gables, 1899.

COURT FARM, E, on a formerly moated site. Early C18 brick, five bays, good moulded and pedimented stone doorway; quoins to the E corner only, plus many other alterations such as blocked windows. – Contemporary brick farm buildings, especially former STABLES, SW, dated 1746. T-plan (later extended) with stone quoins and N doorway (facing the church), with straight hood on brackets; above, big segment-headed window in a broad surround.

The OLD RECTORY, Church Hill, W side, is early C19, white-painted brick; three-bay front, full-width pediment with large semicircular opening. Enlarged by *John Nettleship*, 1846; his most of the four-bay W return.

Some outlying brick farms of interest. Both LOWBRIDGE FARM, ½ m. E, and LEYLANDS FARM, ¾ m. NE, both Clattercut Lane, W side, are very early C18, the former gabled with solid arcaded chimneystack, the latter with just a central gabled dormer. NEW FARM, ⅜ m. WSW, perhaps *c.* 1720–40, is rather more classical; splendid pair of brick BARNS, to its N, enlivened by perforated openings, and linked into a U-plan by an open cartshed. TUDOR COTTAGE, ⅓ m. S, *c.* 1600, has much close-studded timber framing.

* Eykyn was paid £5 5s. for his 'plan'; Mr Pritchard, perhaps *T.F. Pritchard*, received £2 2s. for 'two plans and an estimate'.

ST MICHAELS
Tenbury

St Michael's Church and College (primarily a model choir school) were founded by the eminent High Anglican musician the Rev. Sir Frederick Arthur Gore Ouseley (1825–89); he purchased the land, 1¾ m. SSW of Tenbury Wells, in 1852, aided by the Rushout family of Burford (Shropshire).

113 ST MICHAEL. By *Henry Woodyer*, 1854–6, costing some £7,000; large, impressively tall, of pink sandstone with Bath ashlar dressings. Clerestoried nave with lean-to aisles, transepts, high polygonal apse; Geometrical Dec-style, of *c.* 1300. Woodyer is immediately recognizable by the steep Delabole slate roofs, all of equal height, and by the steep NW porch entrance, with typically quirky details. Other external flourishes worth noting: the blind-traceried panels of the chancel buttresses, differing rose windows in the transepts, the blank trefoil-headed panelling below these and the nave W window, and the two-tier aisle W windows. Nave arcades, three bays plus a narrower W bay, with round piers of blue-grey Forest of Dean stone; early Gothic foliage capitals. Similar tall arches to the transepts, with clustered responds. Already High Victorian, the arcades to N chapel and S vestry, with their two arches beneath one giant arch, a blank sexfoiled roundel in the spandrel. Timber rib vaults, carried through from W to E, without a chancel arch – an exceptionally early date, no doubt for acoustic reasons; only bands of quatrefoils delineate the choir space beneath the crossing. The painted organ fills the S transept, around which a narrow stone-vaulted processional passageway leads to an outer sacristy. Sanctuary with ornate credence recess, N; triple sedilia, S, cinquefoiled under one crocketed gable (no piscina). Woodyer's clerk of works was *William Chick*; stone carving by *Minchall & White*.

Original FURNISHINGS, with *Minton* encaustic tiled floors throughout. – The polygonal FONT almost fills the N transept: ornate, with green Egyptian marble infill, its COVER a gigantic wooden canopy; cusped ogee recess for the baptism register, former well in the NE corner. – Elaborate wooden REREDOS, its projecting upper section gabled like a shrine, surmounted by tall wrought-iron lily-cross. – Delicate SCREENS, also wrought-iron, painted blue. – CHOIR STALLS tactfully modified in 1923. – Stone PULPIT, with angels in narrow niches. – Tall brass eagle LECTERN. – Upright PEWS: open backs beneath a quatrefoil band. – At the W end, an exceptional low stone SCREEN, with bench along its W side. – Large unsubtle PAINTING of Ouseley by *W.H. Florio Hutchinson*, 1857 (N transept). – STAINED GLASS. All by *Hardman*, apart from the N porch windows (by *Lavers & Westlake*, 1897). – Hardman's nine chancel windows, 1856, are especially memorable; also the great W window, 1857. Other earlier windows are recognizable by their bolder colouring (N chapel E, nave clerestory SW, 1858–9). Later ones are more subdued, from the aisle W

windows (1868) to the three N aisle N (1888). – MONUMENT.
Outside, E of the apse, Ouseley's TOMB by *Aston Webb*, *c*. 1889;
pink granite with white cross.

ST MICHAEL'S COLLEGE, to the S, by *Woodyer*, 1855–6, forms
with the church a three-sided quadrangle open to the W; it cost
nearly £14,000.* Closed 1985, now an international school.
Here Woodyer's idiosyncrasies come out much more strongly.
It consists essentially of one oblong S range, with lower gabled
wing, NE, originally the warden's lodging. A wooden cloister
with trefoil-headed openings, connecting to the SE sacristy, is
continued within the buttressed main range by a enclosed
stone cloister, with four bays of handsome plate-traceried
windows. In the re-entrant angle, a low pyramid-roofed square
tower; in the high slate roof (housing the dormitory), crazily
steep and narrow dormers, particularly characteristic of
Woodyer. NW projection for masters' accommodation, with
chapel (never used as such) on its top floor; fine polygonal W
stair-turret. The main entrance, E end, is an off-centre doorway
with stepped trefoiled lancets above, the central one blind with
statue of St Michael. The long S front also seems odd, but its
irregularity accurately reflects the planning: three buttressed E
bays, with transomed windows and steep gables, for the library
(formerly with notable music collection); four buttressed W
bays with transomed windows lighting the dining hall. This
retains its timber minstrels' gallery, E, with typical panelling.
Some original fittings also in the library.

LODGE, SW, dated 1854; rubble, brick trim, tile-hung upper
floor, half-timbered bay window. Is this *Woodyer* in picturesque
mode?

Former VICARAGE, a little NNE, built 1870. Brick, blue bands
and diapering, especially beneath the eaves; segment-headed
windows, big canted bay. – Plain PARISH SCHOOL, ⅛ m. SW,
now a house, also of 1870 (enlarged 1876).

SALWARPE

8060

ST MICHAEL. Perp W tower, earlier aisled nave, S porch by *Preedy*
c. 1857–8, Dec-style chancel rebuilt 1848 by *George Pickering*
of Durham. The aisles are C14, the less restored N probably
slightly later than the S, with finer flowing Dec tracery. The
puzzling interior has three-bay arcades of *c*. 1200, round piers
with moulded abaci, single-step pointed arches, plus a separate
W bay. The separation is marked by a square pier, S, a broad
oblong one, N. These must belong to former nave walls, the
extra length, N side, perhaps implying a former tower over the
NW bay. On the other hand, the (C14?) springer for a transverse arch across the N aisle may have supported a tower within
the present nave W bay. The responds of this bay seem only

* The original plans also envisaged a W cloister, with tower at the W end of the
church.

slightly later than the arcades, the arches are the same. Perhaps their cutting through caused the tower to become unstable. Another possibility is that the wall fragments represent a pre-Conquest church (*see* below). The present tall tower arch has jambs with paired cinquefoiled panels; four-light Perp w window. Both aisles have a series of plain Dec tomb recesses: three segment-arched s, four slightly pointed N. Above the latter a deep cross-shaped recess about 5 ft 6 in. (1.7 metres) high, probably for a (re-set?) Anglo-Saxon rood. Chancel SEDILIA of two round arches, perhaps *c.* 1530, resited outside the sanctuary in 1848. High chancel arch by *J.A. Chatwin*, who restored the church in 1885, adding N vestry and organ chamber, also several furnishings including PEWS. – Attractive nave floor TILING of 1848; much more elaborate *Godwin* chancel tiling by *W.J. Hopkins*, 1864. – C15 TILES, s aisle w end. – FONT. Shallow octagonal bowl with vine trail; possibly C16, re-cut in the C19. – PARCLOSE SCREENS divide off the E ends of both aisles as chantry chapels, the s basically C14–C15, with nice vine and strawberry friezes, the N mostly by *Maurice W. Jones*, 1936. – Stone and marble REREDOS by *James Powell & Sons*, 1911: alabaster Last Supper carved by *Whiffen*. – STAINED GLASS. Chancel E and N windows by *Hardman*, 1863. – SW by *Preedy*, *c.* 1854; SE by *Wailes*, 1859.

MONUMENTS. Effigy of a priest, chancel N, holding a (broken) chalice. Fine soft folds to his garb. Two angels by his pillows, lion at his feet. Probably late C14 (said to be William Richepot †1401). – Thomas Talbot †1613 and wife Magdalena. Tablet, chancel s, the two kneelers facing each other across a prayer-desk, flanked by Corinthian columns; three kneeling children below. – Tablet, s aisle E, to Olave Talbot †1681; black-and-white marble, twisted Ionic columns. – The altar below is a tomb-chest to the same and her mother Elizabeth †1689. Also black-and-white marble; no effigy, but with two white charity girls against the front, flanking an inscription from Acts 9: 36–9: 'This Woman was full of Good workes & Alms-deeds' etc.

CHURCHYARD CROSS almost entirely by *P.C. Hardwick*, 1853. – Early C19 CHEST TOMBS, one, of *c.* 1833, with good cast-iron railings. – LYCHGATE. 1884.

Former SCHOOL opposite the church; now Church and Lychgate Cottages. C17 W wing, partly timber-framed, but mostly of 1821: brick, two storeys, blocked central doorway, overhanging hipped roof. Gabled E wing, *c.* 1882.

SALWARPE BRIDGE nearby is a fine example of a splayed canal bridge, brick with sandstone parapet, built *c.* 1771 by *James Brindley* across his Droitwich Barge Canal (*see* p. 262). Below the arch, remains of the high-level scaffold-bearers with their hardwood padstones; towpath later edged with blue bull-nosed engineering brick.

SALWARPE HOUSE, W, the former rectory, is mostly by *George Byfield*, 1795. Stuccoed five-bay N front: windows with panelled keystones, tripartite doorway in round-arched recess. The side facing the church, six bays with higher two-bay centre, is extended by a later service wing. Large contemporary brick stables by the lane. – Below, N, beside the river Salwarpe, the OLD MILL HOUSE, probably c. 1785; painted brick, three bays, all openings Gothick with finials, ground-floor windows pseudo-Venetian. The mill was demolished in 1941.

SALWARPE COURT, E of the canal. Spectacularly timber-framed, probably rebuilt for Sir John Talbot c. 1580. All close studding, mostly later infilled with brick-nogging (well restored in the 1980s); many bargeboarded gables. Broad entrance front, SE, with central gabled porch with coved overhang: service range, r., ending in a massive stone chimney-breast with triple brick star-stack; hall, l., its projecting gabled upper bay sharing a bracketed overhang with the larger gable of the solar cross-wing. The solar's short SW return is particularly picturesque, its tall and narrow bay with upper overhang and finely carved bargeboards, r., only slightly balanced by an upper oriel, l. Some surviving pink rendering between the timbers here. The long rambling rear is also picturesque, with a far-projecting range at the service end and less projecting centre with sweet little gable. Mostly renewed interior.

The six-bay COURT BARN further SE, also close-studded, has an arch-braced collar-and-tie-beam roof with large wind-braces; three later lower SE bays. All mostly weatherboarded when converted to housing, c. 1984.

OLD SCHOOL HOUSE, S, the replacement parish school by *John Cotton*, 1882, illustrates how progressive provincial architects had turned away from Gothic by this date. Brick, patterned half-timbered gables, some diapering on the adjoining house. The school has segment-headed windows, the large end one loosely based on Norman Shaw's 'Ipswich' windows, complete with terracotta sunflower above.

CHURCHFIELDS FARM, ¼ m. S, is early C17 timber-framed, to an L-plan. Beside its approach is COOKS HILL, a C15 cruck cottage of four bays with two-bay hall and complete central truss. Greatly altered, the crucks no longer visible externally; inserted first floor, large chimney occupying most of the hall's lower bay. Later wings provide a more or less cruciform plan.

The COPCUT ELM, 1 m. ESE by the A38, a Neo-Georgian brick road house by *Holland W. Hobbiss*, 1937, has been insensitively altered and enlarged.

HIGH PARK, ½ m. N, off the Ombersley road, is of 1793: elegant, five bays, of ashlar. Additions of 1830 (partly demolished) included the two-bay ballroom wing, E, making the S front oddly asymmetrical; the wing's square bay window is balanced by another across the two W bays of the original house. Doric porch (below a large central round-arched window) extended up to the E wing as a balustraded colonnade.

0030

SEDGEBERROW

ST MARY. A good Dec church, consecrated 1331, built for Thomas of Evesham. Excellently restored by *William Butterfield*, 1867–8, for Mary Barber, widow of the former rector. Nave and chancel in one: stepped buttresses, linked hoodmoulds, N porch. Slender W tower, hexagonal for two stages before turning octagonal; simple rectangular openings. Butterfield renewed its tall ribbed spire and the Dec tracery of the two-light side windows, all apparently accurately. E window perhaps later C14, its five stepped lights displaying a Perp variety of reticulated. Chamfered N and S doorways, the latter hidden by a long projecting S vestry, added by *Lewis Sheppard*, 1899–1900. Impressive interior, high, quite wide, with restored continuous arch-braced roof. The nave W wall incorporates earlier fabric; the rectangular opening high up is reminiscent of Saxon work at Deerhurst, Glos. The only division between nave and chancel is a high, wide-open wooden SCREEN (with tall stone plinth), clearly by Butterfield; it repeats a simpler medieval predecessor which was flanked by altars, *see* the remains of a piscina, S side.

Splendid *Butterfield* FURNISHINGS, apart from the FONT, a cup-shaped bowl with round stem and base, probably C13. – Ornate, very successful REREDOS, tripartite, with crocketed and pinnacled canopies, vaulted within. Its back wall consists entirely of geometrical patterns of stone and tile mosaic, enhanced by the tiling of the walls to dado height, and by encaustic floor TILES. Similar canopy above the pillar piscina, which, like the sturdy sedilia, probably incorporates medieval fabric. Also noteworthy the ALTAR, wooden ALTAR RAILS, finely detailed STALLS, elemental wrought-iron CORONA, and, in the nave, low PEWS, wooden PULPIT, compact LECTERN, and chunky FONT COVER. – STAINED GLASS. E window by *Alexander Gibbs*, 1871, to a design by *Mary Barber* (whose book, *Some Drawings of Ancient Embroidery*, was published at Butterfield's suggestion in 1880). – In the tracery of the chancel NW, a good early C14 seated figure of a priest, perhaps Thomas of Evesham.

Deep stone LYCHGATE by *Gerald Cogswell*, 1912–13; Perp style, incorporating medieval fragments. – Outside it, a large WAR MEMORIAL CROSS of 1919, white ashlar with crucifix, by the Evesham monumental masons *W. & H. Gardiner*.

On the site of the manor house of the Priors of Worcester, SW, the COURT HOUSE, part timber-framed, part stone; of late C16 origin, with datestone 1572 above the front door (removed from a former rear chimneystack), drastically restored in the late C20. – Former RECTORY, NE, mostly by *J.L. Randal* of Shrewsbury, 1866; plain brick, with fancy timber porch beneath the central gable.

MAIN STREET leads SW from the church, with several bends. The first two are punctuated by Late Georgian brick farmhouses: HALL FARM, then RED HOUSE. Opposite the latter, the T-plan No. 90 (Orchard Dene): cross-wing C18–C19, stem late C16, altered timber framing, with three original coved dormers. At the next bend, opposite the brick school of 1969, is CHURCH HOUSE, mostly C17; lower floor of rubble, upper of renewed timber framing, thatched roof. The ground floor, NE end, incorporates the remains of a medieval chapel, perhaps the domestic chapel of Thomas of Evesham; two-light late C13 window with pointed-lobed quatrefoil in plate tracery; contemporary cusped lancet on the rear, N, wall.

SEDGEBERROW MILL, NE of the church, astride the little River Isbourne, is, brick, roughcast, mid-C19; iron overshot waterwheel and other machinery virtually intact. Nearby, C17 timber-framed COTTAGES, some thatched.

SEVERN STOKE

ST DENYS. Mostly C14, much restored. Nave N and W walls are Norman: one small window remains, high up NW, plus two nearby buttresses and part of the N string course. Tall N tower begun c. 1300, see the bottom window, N side; the rest is Dec: big diagonal N buttresses, battlements, higher SW stair-turret. Dec also the S aisle and transept, and most windows. The S transept S has a top quatrefoil, which, if reinstated correctly, is interesting as a C13 motif still apparently considered permissible. Perp insertions are the chancel E, probably quite early, and larger nave NE windows. The C14 S porch, rebuilt 1890, was – or at least was intended to be – two-storeyed: two surviving vault springers flank the doorway; inside, a blocked upper doorway. Four-bay S arcade with square piers with semicircular projections, making a quatrefoil form; heavily moulded capitals, typically Dec arches. The arcade takes the S transept into account; the wide arch between aisle and transept conforms. The pair of windows beneath a single arch, transept E wall, is an interesting feature (cf. Leigh). Much restored in 1890 by *Thomas Collins* of Tewkesbury, whose building firm had restored the chancel, 1872–4, to designs by the rector, the *Rev. Henry W. Coventry* (see especially its steep roof).

FONT. Octagonal, quatrefoils on the bowl; C14–C15, probably re-cut. – A few mid-C15 TILES in the blocked nave N doorway. – ARCHITECTURAL FRAGMENTS. An odd recess E of this, with part of a re-set Norman arch, contains a respond and shaft perhaps from the Norman N doorway. Other carved fragments built into the walls elsewhere. – Small section of WALL PAINTING, above the PULPIT; this, and the war memorial SCREEN, W, are by *Pancheri & Son*, 1946. – Three READING DESKS with Perp tracery, probably from a former screen. – Carved and painted ALTAR by *R. L. Boulton & Sons*, 1921; their oak REREDOS, 1900, is now in the W vestry. – STAINED GLASS. In two S transept windows, good fragments of early C14 glass, including the Virgin, perhaps from a Coronation scene. – E by *James Powell & Sons*, 1861; two chancel S, 1874, no doubt by

Heaton, Butler & Bayne. – Nave NE window by *A.J. Davies*, 1937. – Minor TABLETS, the best to James Barker †1851, by *George Lewis* of Cheltenham; crisp Grecian, with low, broad urn.

CHURCHYARD CROSS, S of the chancel: chamfered base with niche (for a lantern?) on its S side, and much of the shaft.

Main-road VILLAGE, with C17 timber-framed cottages and brick houses of *c.* 1800; the former RECTORY, opposite the lane to the church, five bays, with doorway with open pediment, canted S bay, and later additions, is now subdivided. Further N a picturesque semi-detached pair of C19 Coventry Estate cottages, brick with half-timbering. The former SCHOOL, N end, is by *A.H. Parker*, 1910, incorporating a good C17 L-plan farmhouse: pretty decorative bracing in one gable-end.

SEVERN BANK HOUSE, ½ m. S, on a fine wooded site above the river. Early C19, stuccoed and battlemented, with C18 core; built as a fishing lodge for the earls of Coventry of Croome Court. From certain angles, it looks like a tower. Two-storey E front, with two broad and flat canted bay windows; full-width cast-iron veranda. Flat porch on the S return. Three-storey W front with pointed windows, including the very large curved central bow. An unexecuted design by *Robert Adam*, 1779–80, was probably for alterations to this front. Instead *Robert Newman* coated it with stucco, 1781–2; it seems by then to have been already castellated. The early C19 work is either of *c.* 1820 or of the early 1840s when the house was let to the Dent glove-making family of Worcester. The house was heightened, and lower N service range added or extended; infilled Greek Doric colonnade of four bays, W side. The first-floor room behind the large W bow has a fine Jacobethan plaster ceiling of *c.* 1840. Early C19 curved and battlemented boundary wall, of Bath stone, with Gothick-panelled piers.

LODGE, at the S end of the village, probably early 1840s. Square, coursed Lias with ashlar dressings. Battlemented, octagonal corner turrets, flat porch; hipped roof with pair of octagonal chimneys.

Of outlying hamlets, CLIFTON, 1½ m. NNW, is least altered: C17 or earlier timber-framed cottages and farms, the latter partly rebuilt in brick, widely spaced round a square of lanes; also C19–C20 Coventry Estate cottages.

7060

SHELSLEY BEAUCHAMP

ALL SAINTS. C14 W tower, of red sandstone, half green with lichens; big diagonal buttresses, later parapet. Perp W window by *James Cranston* of Oxford, who rebuilt the rest, 1846–7, a remarkably competent job. Nave and aisles (under the same roof) in the style of *c.* 1300, chancel in slightly earlier E.E. style, reflecting the respective dates of the medieval church. Three-bay arcades with quatrefoil piers, capitals with dog-tooth, double-chamfered arches. Chancel arch with corbel shafts on hand-held foliage sprays. – Carved stone PULPIT,

STALLS, stone ALTAR TABLE, and arcaded REREDOS, all by *Cranston*; PEWS, 1896. – Medieval are just the plain C12–C13 FONT; the traceried dado of the C14–C15 ROOD SCREEN; and two primitive dug-out CHESTS. – STAINED GLASS. Central light of the E triplet by *Wailes*, 1847; side lights by *Hardman*, 1896, a notable example of 'keeping in keeping'. – MONUMENTS. Two small E.E.-style tablets are worth comparing: E.C. Moore †1847 (s aisle) is crisply carved; R.C. Galton †1866 (chancel), rather over-rich. – In the CHURCHYARD, on the octagonal steps of a C15 CROSS, a bulbous C17 sundial; several late C18–early C19 CHEST TOMBS. – LYCHGATE, *c*. 1887.

CHURCH HOUSE, NW, has a nice rendered front, *c*. 1830–40, with gables and square hoodmoulds. The large C20 brick house, to the N, is unfortunate.

HARBOROUGH BANK, further NW, the former rectory, was built by *James Rose*, 1784–5, probably following a design by *Thomas Johnson*. Red brick, two-and-a-half storeys, five bays, centre breaking forward with pediment; segment-headed windows (on the top floor blind and painted), Tuscan porch.

N again, the former SCHOOL, by *Lewis Sheppard*, 1893–4, brick, semi-Gothic; attached house with half-timbered gables added by his son, 1908.

LOWER HOUSE FARM, ½ m. ESE. A complete brick complex of *c*. 1820–40. Double-pile farmhouse with E gabled cross-wing; attached hop-drying building, NE. Large yard, S, surrounded by barns, stables and pigsties; perforated walls, some lunette windows.

BROCKHILL COURT, ½ m. NW. Early C18 brick, hall range with gabled wings, the S later enlarged. C19 OAST HOUSES at the rear, C18 DOVECOTE, N.

SHELSLEY GRANGE, 1⅛ m. N. Stuccoed with shallow-hipped roof, like an overgrown villa. Built *c*. 1855–6 for R.C. Galton (youngest son of J.H. Galton of Hadzor, q.v.); altered by *Prothero & Phillott* of Cheltenham, 1906. Doric porch with full-height canted bay adjoining; handsome cast-iron and steel staircase.

HILLSIDE FARM, off Camp Lane, 1⅛ m. NNE. Mostly brick, originally a C15–C16 timber-framed hall house with solar cross-wing, the latter mostly rebuilt to a large T-plan with shaped end gable for John Collins, 1678. Tall square-panelled stair-tower at the rear.

SHELSLEY KINGS, a separate civil parish to the N, has two good timber-framed farmhouses. PARD HOUSE FARM, 1¼ m. NW, has a long C15 hall range with later solar cross-wing, W (and service range, E, rebuilt as a stable); in the hall part at least one full cruck truss with collar-beam. At MENEATT FARM, 1½ m. NNW, the modest hall range, mostly rebuilt in brick, retains two cruck trusses; solar wing rebuilt, to a grander T-plan, early in the C17. Tripled brick stacks. THE GREEN, just N of the latter, close to the B4203, is early-to-mid-C18 brick, H-plan with gabled wings; low NE addition dated 1793. Extensive C19 farm buildings.

7060 ## SHELSLEY WALSH

Also known as Little Shelsley. On the Teme's w bank, opposite Shelsley Beauchamp; famous for its motor hill climb.

p. 22 St ANDREW. Mostly local tufa. Nave and chancel in one, with pyramid-roofed timber bell-turret and N porch, both from the distinctively quirky restoration by *George Truefitt*, 1859. Norman nave, C13 chancel, the latter with all windows renewed. The nave retains a tiny s window and its s doorway, with one order of shafts with scallop capitals, uncarved tympanum, and arch with deep frontal chevron. The chancel, slightly wider than the nave, has a remarkable roof: tie- and collar-beams, straight and raking struts, large foiled openings in the top triangle. Much of this must be due to Truefitt; he was certainly responsible for painting the boarded ceiling light blue, with violet stars. Trefoiled piscina, with dogtooth; the sedile is Truefitt's. Simpler C15 nave roof.

C15 SCREEN, plus PARCLOSE SCREENS round the nave SE chantry chapel. All one composition: linenfold dados, one-light divisions with mouchette wheel tracery, very handsome vine-trail frieze and cresting. Above, the original ROOD BEAM, also with vine-trail friezes; C19 crucifix. – TILES, chancel floor. C15, including six sets of sixteen. – *Truefitt's* stone FITTINGS were thrown out in 1908; his wooden ones survive. – PULPIT with linenfold panelling, by *Ninian Comper*, 1908. – Round Norman FONT, restored 1908. – STAINED GLASS. E window by *Wailes*, two nave s by *Lavers & Barraud*, all 1859, under Truefitt's direction. – MONUMENTS. Francis Walsh †1596, tomb-chest without effigy, entirely wood (cf. the Walsh Monument, Stockton on Teme; both have been attributed to *Melchior Salabossh*). Tapering pilasters, panels with the usual blank round arches, enclosing in this case painted shields; moulded top rail with inscription. – Nice tablet to Elizabeth Plampin †1732.

COURT HOUSE, NW, formerly moated. Two ranges, the front one early C18, six bays with hipped roof; central doorway with raised pediment on carved consoles, narrow windows either side. The wider rear range, mostly close-studded, *c.* 1600, was altered *c.* 1870–80; central gable, gabled NW porch, triple diagonal brick stack.

Nearby otherwise, only a couple of C17 cottages and a late C19 LODGE.

Two more C17 cottages stand ⅝ m. SE, by NEW MILL BRIDGE, rebuilt 1931 by *B.C. Hammond*, County Surveyor; stone, with wrought-iron balustrades. This part of the Teme was once an important ironworking area; nothing remains visible.

8060 ## SHRAWLEY

p. 22 St MARY. Norman nave and chancel, the former apparently later, say *c.* 1170–80 as against *c.* 1120–30. The E wall, with two

Neo-Norman windows beneath a large rose, is by *G.E. Street*
who restored the church in 1862. The chancel has flat buttresses and, S side, a zigzag sill frieze, changing to cable moulding across the buttresses. On it three windows, their profiles
small sunk continuous chamfers, the middle one set in a buttress (as on the towers at Cropthorne and Fladbury). Priest's
doorway with segmental head and billet hoodmould. Chancel
N wall with the same pattern of windows, but its sill frieze
entirely cable-moulded. Small brick N vestry, *c.* 1800. The
zigzag frieze continues for a while onto the nave walls, but the
S doorway, with waterleaf capitals and complicated arch decoration (hyphenated chevron and lozenges containing rosettes),
cannot be earlier than 1170–80. The door arch is again segmental; Perp-panelled stoup. (Blocked) nave N doorway with
trumpet-scallop capitals instead, i.e. also Late Norman. Nave
battlements, now lost except at the SW corner, were added in
the C15; also Perp, a large SE window, its tracery removed
c. 1800. Spacious C15–C16 porch, much renewed in brick; four-
centred entrance arch. W tower rebuilt *c.* 1700: diagonal W buttresses, W window with broad-mullioned Y-tracery. By *Street*
are the three-light nave NW window and the Neo-Norman
chancel arch. Good C15 nave roof, with moulded arch braces,
rafters, and purlins.

FURNISHINGS. Complete set of early C19 BOX PEWS. –
Norman FONT, though the trumpet scallops of its bowl look
re-cut; plain C17 cover. – PULPIT also C17; simple incised stars
and foliage. – C18 WEST GALLERY, with balustraded front
(perhaps the former communion rails). – Above, two early C19
HATCHMENTS (to T.S. Vernon, 1825, and a member of the
Severne family), and large ROYAL ARMS: George III, early C19.
– CHANCEL FITTINGS by *Street*. – Painted REREDOS of 1947
by *Walter P. Starmer*. – STAINED GLASS. Good E windows by
James Powell & Sons, 1921, reusing *J.W. Brown*'s cartoons for
Liverpool Cathedral.

C14–C15 CHURCHYARD CROSS: three steps, moulded plinth,
base with big angle spurs. On it, a copper sundial, signed
Samuel Thorpe of Abberley, 1819.

CHURCH COTTAGE, at the churchyard entrance, early C19
brick, is square, with pointed Gothick windows and hipped
slate roof, like a Nonconformist chapel; presumably built as a
school.

Former NATIONAL SCHOOL (now Village Hall), ⅛ m. NNW, on
the B road. By *Street*, 1860. Brick, gabled, some black diapering (except on the attached house); simple wooden tracery.
Discreet later additions.

SHRAWLEY WOOD HOUSE, ½ m. NNW. Early C19 stuccoed, six
bays with panelled pilasters, two storeys of Regency Gothic
windows. A projecting porch, adjoining bay, and various tripartite windows add variety. Pretty iron gates.

At OLIVER'S MOUND, ½ m. further E, was a castle, probably built *c.* 1300 by the Le Poers to guard a Severn crossing.
Excavations, 1928–30, suggested a rectangular court, with

octagonal corner towers and square building in the middle of the E side.

The parish, with no real nucleus, consists mostly of scattered timber-framed cottages and farms. Most seem C17, though several no doubt contain earlier fabric. WOOD FARM COTTAGE, ¾ m. NNE, just E of the early C19 Rose and Crown inn, is a much-restored cruck hall house, with ogee doorheads to its former screens passage.

0040

SOUTH LITTLETON

ST MICHAEL. Norman in origin, with simple S doorway and even plainer N one. One E.E. lancet, nave NW. Of the late C13, the short N transept, and two other windows: nave SW, a broad trefoil-headed lancet, and chancel SE, of two narrow trefoiled lights with quatrefoil above, cut from a single stone. Adjoining the latter, a Perp four-centred priest's doorway linked to its neighbouring window by a fine hoodmould with bold heads. Also Perp, two three-light nave S windows and the battlemented W tower. Timber S porch mostly by *Preedy*, who rebuilt the chancel in his severe restoration of 1883; the Dec tracery of the E window may be trustworthy. Inside, the tower arch reuses an apparently C14 window head (with further use of such material in the ringing chamber). Perp remodelling of the internal chancel S wall includes another big head and a PILLAR PISCINA. Solid arch-braced roofs of 1883. – FONT. Norman round bowl with tapering sides, carved with three rosettes and a cross; band of arrowheads above, rope moulding below. – PULPIT with Perp panels. – Lively wooden eagle LECTERN, probably 1883. – C15–C16 PEWS with moulded tops and traceried bench ends, much supplemented in 1883. – C15 TILES in the transept and, better preserved, at the back of the chancel N aumbry. – Good HATCHMENT to the Rev. Francis Taylor †1722. – STAINED GLASS. C15 fragments, chancel NW. – E window by *T.F. Curtis, Ward & Hughes*, 1903. – Three others by *Hardman*, 1885–91.

CHURCHYARD CROSS: late medieval steps and base, shaft and head 1883. – A few large HEADSTONES characteristic of the district, two by *Francis Ballard*: his own (†1811) immediately S of the tower, and Mary Gibbs †1804, one of an ivy-clad pair SE of the chancel, with decayed Resurrection scene in a quatrefoil.

The brick MANOR HOUSE (formerly Hathaways) opposite the church, behind a good wall with gatepiers, is most attractive. The main, W, part, built for Francis Taylor (†1722), agent to the earls of Coventry, was probably begun *c.* 1712, its completion indicated by the weathervane dated 1721; five by three bays, with wooden cross-windows (probably renewed *c.* 1911), modillion cornice, and steep hipped roof with dormers. On top, a cupola or belvedere flanked by two broad axial blocks, each of two chimneystacks connected by an open arch: quite a Vanbrughian effect, forming a notable skyline. The modest doorway opens into a narrow hall leading to a fine soaring staircase with twisted balusters; early C18 plasterwork in the front room, SW. The E part of the house, mostly *c.* 1588, of Lias, is low and gabled.

VICARAGE, NE, by *John Plowman* of Oxford, 1834, mostly brick, with almost symmetrical garden front, of 1 + 3 + 1 bays. Rambling rear (with porch, 1857) facing two cottages, one of rubble dated 1697, one C17 timber-framed and thatched. Then the rather starchy SOUTH HOUSE, *c.* 1785; double pile, brick with stone dressings, five bays with central pedimented Roman Doric doorcase.

LONG HYDE HOUSE, ⅛ m. SW, built 1838 for the Rev. George Shute, curate, is good Tudor Gothic; brindled brick, gables, diagonally set chimneys.

LONG LARTIN PRISON, 1½ m. ESE. Brick, built by the *PSA*, 1965–71, for maximum security, on the model of Blundeston, Suffolk (1961–3). Two-storey reception building, flat-roofed, rather lame; main block with three-storey T-plan wings of cells, plus two-storey ancillary spur.

SPETCHLEY

The estate belonged to the Spetchleys until 1454, to the Lytteltons until 1544–5, then to the Sheldons. Philip Sheldon sold it in 1606 to Sir Rowland Berkeley, a Worcester wool merchant and clothier. His manor house stood SE of the present mansion, which still belongs to the Berkeley family, Roman Catholics since the C17.

ALL SAINTS. Vested in the Churches Conservation Trust since 1987. Early C14 nave and chancel, much altered in the late C16 and C17. Tower inserted into the nave W end, probably at the latter date: rectangular bell-openings, broad battlements, narrow round-arched entrance with open timber porch. The square bay window, chancel N, late C16, with surprisingly domestic ovolo-moulded mullions and transoms, houses a monument (*see* below). Battlemented Berkeley Chapel, S, built 1614, reusing early C14 windows; only its four-centred W doorway, with fine Berkeley heraldry above, betrays the true date. Within, a wide flat opening to the chancel with simply chamfered responds. C14 chancel arch of two continuous chamfers. Low-key restoration by *Henry Rowe*, 1857, retaining plastered walls and ceilings. – ALTAR TABLE. C17, quite ornate. – Sanctuary PANELLING,* LECTERN and plain PULPIT all seem early C19. – Some C15 TILES in front of the sanctuary steps. – Two solid medieval CHESTS. – STAINED GLASS. By *Hardman* in the S chapel: E 1859, SE 1876, SW 1898; also chancel NW, 1859. – Chancel E window (renewed by *Hopkins*) with *Powell*'s quarries of 1858. – Minor C14–C15 fragments.

---

* Behind the panelling on the E wall are remains of C16–C17 WALL PAINTINGS, with the lower parts of two figures (perhaps Moses and Aaron).

MONUMENTS. An important collection. In the chancel bay, a severe tomb-chest probably intended for John Slade (father-in-law of Philip Sheldon), buried at Hindlip, 1597. Pilasters, eroded heraldry flanked by split-cusped quatrefoils; more heraldry on the bay's side walls. – Between chancel and chapel, Rowland Berkeley †1611 and wife Katherine. Alabaster, of high quality, erected 1614, perhaps by *Samuel Baldwin*. Excellent recumbent effigies, his feet on a bear, hers on her pet dog; tomb-chest with strapwork inscription panels and diagonally projecting corners, with tall obelisks. Thin canopy above with semicircular coffered arch, on two groups of three square fluted Ionic pillars. – Anne Smyth †1638; tablet with black Composite columns (chancel SW). – Sir Robert Berkeley, sergeant-at-law, †1656. Black and white marble. Effigy in full judicial robes, with careful, somewhat pedantic detailing of the fur; panelled tomb-chest, back plate with many shields. – Thomas Berkeley and wife Anne, erected 1693; attributed to *James Hardy* (GF). Standing architectural monument, grey and white marble; broken pediment, gadrooned plinth with good carving. – Robert Berkeley †1694, attributed to *Grinling Gibbons* (GF). Marble, reredos type, with gadrooned sarcophagus flanked by standing mourning putti. Later inscription to his wife Elizabeth, †1708. – Robert Berkeley †1804, by *W. Stephens & Co.*; fine large sarcophagus-shaped tablet, of coloured marbles. His HATCHMENT hangs adjacent.* – Three tablets by *J. Stephens*. – BRASSES. Inscription plate to William Smyth †1658; arms below dated 1611–29 (chancel floor). – Two by *Hardman* (chapel W wall): Robert Berkeley †1845, and his namesake †1874, but erected 1858.

Stone CHURCHYARD WALL, dated 1629 and 1714. Across the main road, the CATHOLIC CEMETERY, 1890, with lychgate; cross with carved lantern head.

SPETCHLEY PARK. The present house, S of the church, is hidden from it by trees. Built 1811–*c*. 1818 for Robert Berkeley by *John Tasker*, a London architect who worked mostly for Roman Catholic clients. It faces away from the church, W and S, towards open country: a dignified, spacious Grecian mansion, of fine smooth Bath ashlar, two storeys beneath a deep entablature with moulded cornice. The shorter ENTRANCE FRONT, W, has a giant portico of four unfluted Ionic columns and deep pediment with the Berkeley arms, flanked by a single bay either side; no ornament except moulded window surrounds, taller on the ground floor, with straight entablatures. The long S FRONT is equally sparing of ornament. Central semicircular projection with giant unfluted Ionic pilasters, three windows either side, then projecting angle accents with plain giant pilasters. These have a pedimented ground-floor tripartite window, with broad oblong moulded tablet (instead of a window) above. Ashlar-faced six-bay service range, N of the entrance front, altered by *E. P. Warren*, 1906. The rear of the

---

*Two other hatchments to Robert Berkeley †1874 and wife Henrietta †1857.

house, round a three-sided courtyard, is all of brick. Impressively lucid PLAN. The three main rooms along the S front – dining room, library (within the central bow), and drawing room – have reticent plaster decoration and simple Grecian fireplaces. Behind, continuing the entrance lobby, a hall screened to W and E by pairs of red scagliola Ionic columns, then the spacious rectangular staircase, with specially fine iron handrail: Venetian window with Ionic detail, N, facing an open first-floor gallery with two widely spaced Corinthian columns, again of red scagliola.

The E wing contains a R.C. CHAPEL, running the whole depth of the house (with vestry, S end). N porch for public access; three blind windows above masking the private gallery. High interior with coved plaster ceiling (and only bedrooms above). The altar wall, S, has a blind Venetian motif, with fluted Ionic columns. Good STAINED GLASS, SE, by *Hardman*, 1861.

STABLES, NE. Plain brick, early C19, broad U-plan; four-bay centre slightly higher with hipped slate roof with cupola, four carriage arches below. The rear bluntly faces the main road, next to the church.

GROUNDS. S of the house, a wide expanse of lawn, part of a fine Reptonian landscaped PARK focussing on the large Garden Pool, with the second larger lake of the Deerpark some distance further S. On the W bank of the Horse Pool, E of the house, a Celtic MEMORIAL CROSS by *Edmund Kirby* of Liverpool to F.C. Berkeley, who died on this spot in 1866; Forest of Dean stone, 7 ft (2.1 metres) high. The splendid GARDENS, further E, were mostly developed from 1891 by *Rose Berkeley* with her sister *Ellen Willmott*. Large brick-walled kitchen garden, N end; set in its S wall, a Doric Bath-stone alcove, facing the Fountain Gardens, with central pool and fountain. Beyond this, the Rose Lawn, then the Cork Lawn set within an angle of the Garden Pool. Between the two lawns, a C19 ROOT HOUSE with conical thatched roof and pebble floor. Copse with tall thin pines along the E boundary. The moat of the earlier house forms the W boundary,* crossed by a pretty wrought-iron FOOTBRIDGE, with ornate spandrels and parapet.

A similar FOOTBRIDGE, but larger, on tall Lias abutments, crosses the main road just W of the church, leading to the wooded park extension.

The main road (A44) bisects the village. On its S side, W of the footbridge, the RED HOUSE, built for the steward by *Harvey Eginton*, 1837; brick, shaped gables. Later C19 W part, with half-timbered jettied porch with carved bargeboards.

On the N side, opposite the rear of the stables, the C19 former FORGE; then HOME FARM, irregular C18 brick, its timber-framed DOVECOTE with hipped roof. Further E, the long low ESTATE OFFICE, with central three-bay pediment with cupola, looking like an early C18 almshouse.

---

*Foundations excavated *c.* 1912, but plans made then were subsequently lost.

Finally, the former R.C. SCHOOL, built for Robert Berkeley, 1840–1, by *A. W. N. Pugin*, his only significant building in the county. H-plan, with teacher's house in the W wing, schoolroom in the centre, with the porch to its r., and classroom in the E wing (no doubt also intended for use as a chapel). Red brick with blue brick ornamental crosses, the only accents a gawky timber bell-turret between schoolroom and classroom, and the three-light Perp S window of the latter. Paired or tripled lancets elsewhere; stone frames to the front, timber to the plainer rear.

STANFORD ON TEME

7060

ST MARY. Built, above the road and grounds of Stanford Court, by *James Rose*, 1768–9, for Sir Edward Winnington, Bt.* Of good ashlar: W tower (now without its pierced battlements), battlemented nave, short transepts and chancel. Cusped Y-tracery, cusped intersecting in the three-light E window. The tower also has the large W and S quatrefoils typical of its date; its W doorway opens into an octagonal vestibule. Flat ceilings, the nave (with central rose) on big coving, chancel and transepts with moulded cornices. Four-centred transept arches; no chancel arch. The interior has lost most of its C18 character, thanks to unsubtle restoration by *Martin B. Buckle*, 1894; his FURNISHINGS include a choir with low stone screen projecting well into the nave. – Good carved oak REREDOS and ALTAR by *Cecil G. Hare*, 1915. – ALTAR TABLE. 1768–9. – STAINED GLASS. Four by *Hardman*: E 1894, S transept S 1901, nave N 1913, nave S 1932; all shamelessly pictorial. Pevsner considered the E window, based on the popular Norwegian painting 'Easter Morn', 'a piece of terrible ham-acting'.

MONUMENTS. Sir Humphrey Salwey †1493 and wife Joyce. Excellent alabaster monument with recumbent effigies, their hands at prayer. He wears fine armour (cf. Martley), his head on his tilting helm, feet against a lion's long tail. She sports a truncated steeple head-dress, with pet dogs at her feet. Busy and pretty tomb-chest with crocketed ogee arches, cusped and pinnacled. They contain kneeling children, an early example of this post-Reformation favourite: six armed sons with shields against the side, another plus a charming group of three daughters (with hats like their mother's) at the W end. – Rt Hon. Thomas Winnington †1746. Standing monument: big grey oval-shaped sarcophagus on large lions' feet, tall pink and grey plinth with side volutes. Bust on top (currently in store). Sculptor unknown (*Roubiliac* has been claimed). – Sir Francis Winnington †1700 and son Salwey; two almost identical tablets, grey marble without figures, flanking the E window. – Dame Mary Winnington †1784; coloured marbles, obelisk background, plus urn. – Other good tablets: the Rev. Thomas

44

---

* The previous church was sacrificed to form the lake in his park, *see* below.

King †1771 (nave s); Anne Winnington †1776, and Sir Edward Winnington †1805 (both s transept). – Two identical brasses, nave w wall, by *Cox & Son*, with kneeling figures of Edith (†1864) and T.E. Winnington (†1869).

OLD RECTORY, wsw, of ashlar, 1772, but only the service wing remains. Former SCHOOL, now village hall, downhill, NE, by *E.A. Day*, 1872–3, brick, with paired lancets and stepped end triplets; good arch-braced roof. The mid-C18 brick HOME FARM, further E, has a full complement of contemporary FARM BUILDINGS, some timber-framed and weatherboarded: granary above cartshed, N, yard to the s with barn, E side, and cowhouse, stables and dairy, SE; square dovecote beyond.

STANFORD COURT, ¼ m. ESE, one of Worcestershire's major country houses, was inherited by the Winnington family from the Salweys in the late C17. Their house, much rebuilt in the early-to-mid C18, enlarged in the 1870s by *E.A. Day*, was burnt down in 1882. The Rev. *M.B. Buckle* rebuilt it, 1886–8, for F.S. Winnington, in 'somewhat similar' style, on the old foundations. Long brick s front, facing the lake, two storeys, 2+6+2 bays, the projecting wings with quoins of even length; a dormered attic storey was not rebuilt. The mid-C18 rear, N, partly ashlar-faced, with central full-height bow window and plain giant pilasters, was least affected by the fire. *Buckle* rearranged the interior, putting the two principal rooms (entrance hall and ballroom, with C18-style ceilings) behind the s front, and staircase hall at the rear (behind the bow window); solid oak staircase, round-arcaded openings on both floors. – Mid-C18 brick STABLES, E, their s front of 7+1+7 bays with pedimented centre, to a U-plan, infilled in the C20 (when the house was used as a timber factory). Either side, further eight-bay service ranges facing E and W, with pedimented two-bay centres.

PARK. The large LAKE, s, was the centre of an extensive park mostly created for Sir Edward Winnington *c.* 1760–70. Much of its basic layout remains, with the church as a *point de vue*, NW. Another, SW (beyond the C18 Noverton Farm), was a classical TEMPLE, now ruined. – Octagonal C18 brick LODGE on the main road, to the N. – Gabled stone LODGE, *c.* 1870–80, no doubt by *E.A. Day*, near the s end of the lake. THE SHRUBBERY, further N, mid-C18, L-plan, stands in the walled kitchen garden.

STANFORD BRIDGE, ¾ m. E. The first timber bridge across the Teme was of 1548. The present bridge, 1971–3 by *W.R. Thomson*, County Surveyor, is the fifth: three slim elongated concrete piers carrying large girders. Its predecessor, N, proudly inscribed 'Rebuilt by the Worcestershire County Council 1905', is now a footbridge. Also concrete, an exceptionally early British example, designed by *L.G. Mouchel*, using Hennebique's patent ferro-concrete system. Its single-span segmental form, with open spandrels, was perhaps influenced by its predecessor, an iron bridge by *John Nash*, 1797; parts of its brick and stone abutments may be remnants of this. Sturdy cast-iron balustrades with ball finials, designed by *J.H. Garrett*, Surveyor of County Bridges. To the NE, a Second World War PILLBOX, unusually of brick.

w of the bridges, the mid-C18 MILL FARM; across the road, its former MILL, mid-C19 painted brick, formerly with open arcades, all much altered. To the E, the BRIDGE INN, mostly early C19, with late C19 brick and half-timbered façade. Higher up, the large, handsome BANK HOUSE, brick, probably *c.* 1840, its garden front overlooking the river; three bays with central Tuscan doorway approached up a curved double flight of steps; all outer windows tripartite, those of the ground floor forming shallow bows. Entrance front, E, of 1+3+1 bays, the pedimented centre projecting; tripartite doorway below.

On SOUTHSTONE ROCK, a large tufa outcrop 1¼ m. SSW, now thickly wooded, was a HERMITAGE, with cells hewn out of the rock, and steps leading up to a chapel of St John the Baptist, belonging to Evesham Abbey. Little remains. The tufa was extensively used in local churches (e.g. Eastham and Shelsley Walsh), also for the restoration of the transept vaults at Worcester Cathedral.

STOCKTON ON TEME

ST ANDREW. Norman nave, *c.* 1130–40, altered in the C14; oak C14 S porch, arch-braced with cusped bargeboards, square weatherboarded bell-turret. Chancel rebuilt in brick, 1718. All much restored by *A.E. Perkins*, 1845–6. He rebuilt the nave N wall, renewed the other C14 windows, and inserted E.E.-style ones into the chancel. The *pièce de résistance* is the Norman S doorway. Two orders, the outer with roll-moulded arch on shafts with block capitals, which have one thin rib up the angle; bases with spurs. Inner arch with two bands of thin saltire crosses. Above, a weathered panel of a large quadruped, said to be a dragon. Contemporary chancel arch: single-scallop capitals, simple chamfered imposts continuing N and S to the nave walls, (renewed) roll-moulded arch. High above, more small carved panels: the Agnus Dei (a roundel), and a lion or wolf.[*] Good C14 tie- and collar-beam nave roof, restored by *P.H. Currey* of Derby, 1898. Central strut flanked by large swept ones; above the collars, V-struts with quatrefoils flanked by trefoils; one tier of wind-braces. Flat chancel ceiling, of sapele wood, 1962.

COMMUNION RAILS. Early C18. – ALTAR TABLE, *c.* 1600. – CHANCEL FLOOR TILING. 1898, with good patch of C15 tiles. – By *Perkins*, the PEWS, with linenfold and simple poppyheads, and matching PULPIT and READING DESK. – STAINED GLASS. E window by *Heaton, Butler & Bayne*, 1892. – Nave SE by *F.G. Christmas* of London, 1924. – Nave W 1966, perhaps by *F.W.*

---

[*] Neil Stratford suggested the same carvers worked at Eastham, Knighton, and Martley.

Cole. – MONUMENTS. Thomas Walsh †1593. Entirely wood (cf. the Walsh monument, Shelsley Walsh), painted grey. High tomb-chest with back wall and flat canopy, all very oddly detailed. The columns or balusters, also used horizontally, are particularly baffling. Blank arches with conspicuous heraldry. – The fine coffin lid nearby was used (until 1933), face down, as the top of its tomb-chest: a cross raguly (i.e. with branch stumps all the way along) flanked by incised chalice and Bible. Lombardic border inscription to Redulphus, 'Ecclesie Rector Stoctone', appointed rector here 1284. – Also smaller slabs, one, perhaps also C13, with encircled cross flanked by lesser ones. – Brass to William Parker †1508, an 18-in. (46-cm.) civilian; now nave E wall, originally on the floor nearby, see the surviving indent, with two wives.

Former RECTORY, NE, gabled brick with tile-hung upper floor; perhaps by *John Douglas*, *c.* 1890. The rear reveals an earlier Tudor Gothic house, *c.* 1840–50. Further E, in Pensax Road, the OLD SCHOOL, half-timbering above brick, dated 1890; built for William Jones of Abberley Hall (p. 100).

The former COURT FARM, S of the church, C18, refronted and extended in the C19, has extensive brick farm buildings now converted to housing: STABLES, NE; large BARN at right angles, with two basket-arched wagon bays and diaper ventilation patterns, dated 1832 on its S gable-end; and C18 GRANARY above stabling, S. Further S, a large group of C19 MALTHOUSE and HOP KILNS, their six roof-ridge cowls forming a prominent landmark.

STOCKTON HOUSE, a little SSW, double-pile brick, *c.* 1698, has elaborately shaped gable-ends; chimneys at the four outer corners. S front remodelled *c.* 1800, tripartite windows flanking a round-arched doorway.

STOKE BLISS

6060

Transferred from Herefordshire in 1897.

ST PETER. Prominently sited on a bank. Mostly by *James Cranston*, 1852–4: chancel, nave with S aisle, sturdily buttressed SW tower with bar-traceried bell-openings above quatrefoils and good shingled broach spire. Nave W and chancel E windows with typically Victorian plate tracery. However, the fabric of the nave N wall, chancel S wall (with two lancets), and most of the S aisle is C13; attractive tall gabled dormer over the two-light aisle SE window probably a little later, introduced to give light to the rood screen as well as the S aisle chapel (with small trefoiled piscina). C13 also the three E bays of the S arcade: round piers, moulded capitals, double-chamfered arches. Matching W bay, as well as chancel arch, 1852–4. Especially typical of Cranston, the internal chancel N window, with good Dec wooden tracery, lighting his organ chamber and vestry.

FONT. Latest Norman; drum-shaped bowl with plain arched panels, the type familiar from Purbeck marble fonts. – SCREEN. Perp, one-light divisions with rose-tipped ogee tracery. – PULPIT. Dated 1631. Octagonal; the usual broad blank decorated arches, upright lozenges below. – READING DESK, dated 1635, also with blank arches, flanked by the small frontal figures familiar from bedheads and overmantels; frieze of addorsed dragons. – Attractive ORGAN CASE, probably early C19. – The PEWS of 1852–4 retain their brass oil lamps on standards. – REREDOS, c. 1864; marble, pink granite and alabaster. – STAINED GLASS. Bold semi-abstract E window by *Roger Fifield*, 1973. – Nave W 1885, no doubt *Ward & Hughes*. – MONUMENTS. Parts of two C13 coffin lids, with relief crosses. – Minor tablets, the best Henry Hyde †1798, nice country work, signed *H. Philpott*. – Also fragments (heraldic cartouche and cherubs) from a grander C17 monument.

Opposite, CHURCH HOUSE FARM, C17 timber-framed, hall and cross-wing plan, the former with big rubble chimneystack.

THE GROVE, 1⅛ m. WNW. Brick, probably late C17; four bays, the middle two projecting beneath a big shaped gable. The quatrefoil within this and the mildly Gothick two-light windows must be c. 1800; matching doorway, approached up eight steps. Tall rear central staircase projection; also a timber-framed wing.

STOKE BLISS AND KYRE NATIONAL SCHOOL (now village hall), 1¼ m. W. By *Henry Curzon*, 1871–2. Sandstone, the attached house with good clustered brick chimney, but renewed windows; large Gothic-arched school entrance.

THE HYDE, 1½ m. WSW. The mid-C19 sandstone exterior, with brick-faced gabled dormers with timber pinnacles, betrays nothing of the splendid medieval timberwork within, one of the earliest intact hall and cross-wing houses in Worcestershire.* The heavily moulded timbers of the base-cruck truss are enormous; both bays of the hall have an intermediate truss of which the lower section of the principal rafters has been cut back. Two tiers of purlins (very slender, an early feature), two of heavily cusped wind-braces; timbers in the spandrel above the base-cruck collar also cusped. Each of the enormous knee-braces had a capital carved in its lower vertical section, the carving continuing into the cruck to conceal the join between the two. Remains of the spere-truss of much lighter construction, but of the same date. F.W.B. Charles thought that this could be as early as the mid C13; the detail suggests rather the early C14, perhaps soon after 1302 when ownership passed from the Mortimers to Limebrook Priory (Herefs.). The solar cross-wing, S, no doubt contemporary, is hardly less interesting. Of three bays but very small, its moulded timbers showing even greater refinement, including two tiers of cinquefoil-cusped wind-braces; beams with remains of decorative

---

*More complete and monumental than the base-cruck hall at Rectory Farm, Grafton Flyford, p. 321.

painting. Re-set above the inner doorway of the porch, the head of a three-light timber window with Dec tracery. This may have belonged to the solar end window, perhaps confirming a date *c.* 1300–20. Dendro-dating suggests the house was floored throughout *c.* 1568, and a large chimney inserted, forming a baffle entry. Most of the service end, N, seems yet later, perhaps C17; attached hop kilns.

Facing the house, E, are four-bay STABLES, with granary above, dendro-dated 1565. Weatherboarded ground floor, with jettied first floor carried round the gable wall supported by attached brackets; widely spaced square-panelled framing. Roof of 28-ft (9-metre) span, with interrupted tie-beam trusses looking rather like braced hammerbeams; much later reinforcement.

GARMSLEY CAMP, 2 m. WSW. A univallate Iron Age hill-fort, of roughly oval plan, enclosing some nine acres; inturned entrances on NE and W sides.

STOKE PRIOR

9060

A possession of Worcester Cathedral Priory from the late C8.

ST MICHAEL. Aisled nave, chancel with W transeptal chapels, the S one forming the base of the tower, the visual climax of the church. Much belongs to the years either side of *c.* 1200, prob-ably built in the following order: N arcade, N chapel, nave S doorway, chancel arch, S chapel. It may be best to examine this work first. The S doorway has two orders, the outer with shafts with plain leaf capitals (including a waterleaf type unique in the county) and round roll-moulded arch. Next the W capital, a reused Anglo-Danish stone with close interlace. Unusual Norman hoodmould, with lobes. To the W, a Norman window; another, much renewed, at the W end of the N aisle. Five-bay N arcade with circular piers with round plainly moulded cap-itals and round abaci; single-step arches. The arch from aisle to N chapel, with simply chamfered imposts, is of the same type; small N window in the chapel, renewed, but probably in its original position. To the chancel, there is a wide double-chamfered arch on tripled attached shafts, with crocket capi-tals, E, capitals with broad leaves, W; all have fillets, the W group continuing into the capitals (cf. the early C13 crypt at Here-ford Cathedral). This is clearly later than the W arch. Renewed chancel arch: shafts with decorated trumpet capitals, double-chamfered arch. The S chapel must be of about the same date. Its N arch, with chamfers flanking a central filleted roll, again has tripled responds with fillets, the larger ones with trumpet capitals, the smaller ones with crockets. Similar arch to the S aisle, one capital scalloped, one moulded, into which the fillets again continue. The windows, at higher level, are lancets, paired to the S. This tower space is continued E by a smaller chapel (probably an afterthought), with small lancet windows and pointed tunnel vault. So Transitional has now given way to E.E. This will be confirmed by examining the exterior of the four-stage tower. On its s side, a narrow doorway with foliated shafts. Above, the pair of lancets is flanked by shorter blank lancets, all shafted, some with shaft-rings; hoodmould with fleurons and headstops. Similar arrangement, E side, but reaching into the blind third stage to clear the lean-to roof of the small E chapel. The bell-openings are lancet triplets, with shafts and continuous rolls. Pointed-trefoiled corbel table above, with several heads. Later recessed spire (shingled since 1895). The tower as a whole is a splendidly self-contained, sturdy piece.

Now the later work. The chancel is basically c13, see the E buttresses and tall NE lancet. So is the restored NE sacristy, with chamfered rib vault beneath an upper room (now inaccessible). Other chancel windows renewed in the early c14, including the five-light E window with reticulated tracery. Beneath the Dec s window, roll-moulded trefoiled piscina and triple sedilia, the latter with grotesque figures as capitals to its octagonal shafts. Similar Dec N chapel N window, beneath its own gable. The battlemented s aisle, with four-centred windows, is of course c15 Perp. The two-bay s arcade, however, is only a little later than the tower, with detail typical of *c.* 1250; pier and responds with round core with four attached shafts, round abaci, deeply moulded arches. Original lean-to roof-line visible above the s chapel arch. Almost everything else belongs to restoration in 1894–5, by *J.L. Pearson* (paid for by John Corbett). His are the s porch, Dec-style N aisle and N vestry, and most roofs, notably the fine oak timber barrel vault over the nave.

FONT. Octagonal, Perp. Base with symmetrically arranged crossed oak leaves, bowl with recessed panels with damaged figures: a baptism scene and angels with shields or censers. – PULPIT by *Pearson*; oak, stone base. – The eagle LECTERN, of Spanish chestnut, probably survives from an earlier restoration by *Eginton*, 1848. – Oak CHOIR STALLS and PARCLOSE SCREENS by *C.F. Whitcombe*, 1906–7. – REREDOS and ALTAR RAILS by *J. Edmund Farrell*, 1948–9, based on a 1939 design by *Eric Gill*; reredos carved by Gill's nephew, *John Skelton*. – STAINED GLASS. In the tower E lancet, medieval fragments (said to be from Malvern Priory). – E window by *Sebastian Evans* for *Chance & Co.*, 1860; strident colouring. – Others by *Chance & Co.*, 1865–6, except chancel NE, by *H.W. Bryans*, 1904, and sacristy E by *Paul Phillips*, 1997. – MONUMENTS. c13 recumbent stone effigy of a priest, much weathered, now upright (s aisle E). – Also two brasses: Henry Smith †1606, kneeling figure, long inscription; and Robert Smith †1609, kneeling frontally with two wives, seventeen children kneeling below.

LYCHGATE, SW. Made up, 1895, from timbers of the c14 s porch.

ALDHAM HOUSE, NE, the former vicarage, is early c18, brick, of five bays; panelled keystones, stone bands and quoins. w wing, *c.* 1875.

CHURCH MILL HOUSE, further NE, early C19 brick with Doric doorcase and bay windows, incorporates a probably C15 cruck-framed hall house as its NE wing. – SE of the church, flanking Stoke Pound Lane, two large brick villas of *c.* 1840, THE MOUNT and SUMMERFIELDS.

At STOKE WHARF, ½ m. SSE, an important transhipment point on the Worcester and Birmingham Canal, various C19 and later industrial development.* By far the best-looking of the latter is HARRIS BRUSH WORKS, further S, by *G.C. Gadd* of Broms-grove, designed 1939, but the brick factory not built until 1947, the office range in 1957–8; streamlined bands of glazing, curved at the corners, raised central entrance with flat concrete roof. Set back, Garden City-style, behind a wide expanse of lawn.

STOKE WORKS, 1 m. SSW, was the most important C19 indus-trial development in the area. Rock salt was discovered here in 1825 and brine pits sunk in 1828. But the saltworks flourished after 1858, when they were taken over by John Corbett, later becoming the principal factory when Droitwich (with Corbett's help) developed as a spa rather than an industrial centre. The works were conveniently sited where canal (cut 1812–13) and railway (opened 1841) converged. Corbett built much model housing for his workers, but almost all that sur-vives, apart from the BOAT AND RAILWAY INN, *c.* 1840–50, is his large SCHOOL (with attached house) of 1871–2, by *Matthew Bohill*, the works' foreman. Pale red brick with blue trim: two-storey house Tudor Gothic with two unequal gables, single-storey school with four bays of round-arched windows either side of the canted double-entrance bay; steep slate roof. The N return, with lancets, originally carried a bellcote. Salt pro-duction ceased in 1972. The brick BAYER OFFICES, NE, by *C.F. Lawley Harrod*, 1929, for The Salt Union Ltd, and their later Polymer Latex Works opposite, are its successors.

In WESTONHALL ROAD, ½ m. E of Stoke Works, three interest-ing farmhouses. The early C18 WESTON HALL FARM, a late timber-framed example, is square-panelled, with brick infill. Then, facing each other, LITTLE ELMS FARM, early C18, brick, with segment-headed windows; and ELMS FARM, early C17, with broadly gabled main range, mostly square-panelled, and early C19 brick NW wing.

SUGARBROOK MANOR, ¾ m. ENE of the church. Complex, mostly timber-framed, its growth best understood from the N side, facing Sugarbrook Lane, where it presents a long T-plan. The stem is probably *c.* 1500, a two-bay hall with one-bay service end, E. The W cross-wing is early C17, when the stone stack with four diamond brick shafts must have been inserted into the open (W) bay of the hall. The wing received its own parlour extension, painted brick with sandstone trim, in the early C18, plus thin wooden Doric porch, NW angle. Good late

---

*Further ENE, a rise of three locks (cf. Astwood, p. 782), prepares for the ascent to the Birmingham plateau, *see* Tardebigge.

C17 stone gatepiers, now without ball finials. – Further NW, TANHOUSE FARM presents a rendered C19–C20 range to Buntsford Hill, but behind is an earlier range with fine NW gable-end dated 1631; narrow studded, with diagonal bracing.

Also worth noting: MEADOWS FARM, 1 m. ESE, timber-framed C17, again a long T-plan, attractively restored; and THE PRIORY, ½ m. WSW, at the end of Brickhouse Lane. Mid to late C17, brick, with gables and tripled stacks either end. Rear elevation, W, with early C19 doorway (leading to a contemporary staircase); E front picturesquely remodelled, with open timber porch, later in the C19.

AVONCROFT MUSEUM OF BUILDINGS, ½ m. NNE, at Stoke Heath, was founded by *F.W.B. Charles*, 1967, in collaboration with Avoncroft College. The latter then occupied STOKE GRANGE, Hanbury Road (now Ottilie Hild School), gabled brick, Tudor Gothic, *c.* 1850, with attractive pyramid-roofed tower; expanded as an adult rural college for George Cadbury, *c.* 1935.

The museum's centre is the NEW GUESTEN HALL, by *Associated Architects*, 1987; brick side walls of post-tensioned diaphragm construction, steep tiled roof, weatherboarded projecting gable-ends. Built, as a concert/meeting hall (with timber N-end gallery), to house the splendid oak ROOF of the Worcester Cathedral Guesten Hall (p. 698), reused by *Hopkins*, 1862–5, as the nave roof of his Holy Trinity, Shrub Hill, Worcester (demolished 1969). At Avoncroft, the eight-bay roof has been re-set to its original (*c.* 34-ft, 10.5-metre) span; the most elegant piece of medieval carpentry in the county, probably of the late 1330s. Trusses with long slender arch-braces to high-set collar-beams; above, open quatrefoils flanked by trefoils. Tripled moulded purlins, delineating a complex pattern of curved wind-braces: cusped, pierced and reversed to form circles. Large stone corbels each end by *Angelo Bordonari*, *c.* 1990, also a series of timber portrait corbels by *Guy Reid*, *c.* 2000. Colourful abstract stained glass in the W clerestory windows by *Alex Beleschenko*, 1996.

The first building re-erected on the site (by *Gunold Greiner*, 1967) was a late C15 MERCHANT'S HOUSE from Worcester Road, Bromsgrove (*see* p. 202), with gabled cross-wing and two-bay hall; the service bay was not rebuilt. A great timber-framed smoke stack, inserted probably *c.* 1550 into the open hall, abuts the screens passage. It is the best place in Worcestershire to experience the effect of a such a hall. Also from Bromsgrove, a small octagonal brick COUNTING HOUSE of 1853, from the Cattle Market, and a C19 NAIL WORKSHOP, from Sidemoor.

Other local buildings include an instructive farm group, supplemented by a three-bay cruck-framed C16 BARN from Cholstrey Court Farm, near Leominster (Herefs.). The Worcestershire buildings are a late C18 timber-framed GRANARY, on round brick piers, from Temple Broughton Farm, Hanbury; early C18 weatherboarded WAGON SHED, also from Hanbury; small late C18 timber-framed STABLE, from

p. 38

Wychbold; and brick PERRY MILL, *c.* 1800, from Hunt End, Redditch. Also a TOLL HOUSE, 1822, from Little Malvern. Other buildings are all from the West Midlands region, apart from the framework of the C14–C15 hall from Plas Cadwgan, North Wales. The early C19 POST MILL from Danzey Green, Warwickshire, can also be singled out, as its sails are visible beyond the museum's precincts.

STONE

ST MARY. A medieval chapelry of Chaddesley Corbett. Rebuilt in grey sandstone ashlar by *William Knight*, 1831–2. Typical of its date: W tower with W entrance, big lancet bell-openings, parapet with heavy pinnacles, and recessed spire; transomed two-light Dec-Perp windows in the buttressed nave. Chancel enlarged by *Prothero & Phillott* of Cheltenham, 1899–1900. Interior, including the W gallery detailing, mostly of this date, also many FURNISHINGS: black-and-white sanctuary tiling, PULPIT, PEWS, large square FONT carved by *William Forsyth*. – Oak REREDOS by *H.H. Martyn & Co.*, 1923. – Most other wood carving, e.g. FONT COVER and LECTERN, by *Pancheri & Son*, 1959–72. – ORGAN CASE by *George Holdich*, 1850. – STAINED GLASS. Medieval and C17 pieces, nave NE. – Under the gallery, heraldic fragments from the E window of 1832. – Its replacement is by *Kempe*, 1900. – Chancel N and two nave windows by *F.W. Skeat*, 1960–7. – MONUMENTS. Brasses to Rev. William Spicer †1656 and wife Ursula †1663, inscription plates with heraldry below. – Benjamin Gibbons †1863, by *Peter Hollins*; the elements still Georgian (draped pedestal, urn, putti heads), but all more naturalistic.

CHURCHYARD. Gothic tomb-chest to Gibbons, NW, also by *Hollins*. – S of the nave, two C18 tombs (Hannah Hill †1788, pedestal with urn, now dismembered), and steps and base of a late medieval CROSS, renewed as a War Memorial *c.* 1919.

The former CHURCH HOUSE (later school and parish room), SE, is H-plan, with centre and N wing of *c.* 1500; later S wing. Timber-framing visible at the rear; E front entirely early C19: painted brick, gables with bargeboards. – Further E, the SCHOOL of 1882 by *J.M. Gething*, half-timbered above brick; rear additions, 1964.

STONE HOUSE, a little N. Distinguished early C18 brick front, 2+3+2 bays, three storeys with parapet and platbands. The core is C17, as shown by brick gables at the rear and the plaster ceiling in the r. front room (with good early C18 panelling). Spacious entrance hall with imported Italian doorway and fireplace, probably part of alterations of *c.* 1900 for Henry Howard by *Prothero & Phillott*, who no doubt provided the Ionic passage to the rear staircase. – Stables, NE, also mostly early C18 brick, with gabled cross-wings and open cupola. – At STONE HOUSE COTTAGE, further E, in the former kitchen garden, an amazing array of towers and other structures, built of reused brick by the owner, *James Arbuthnott*, from *c.* 1980.

STONE MANOR HOTEL, ⅜ m. SE. Large L-plan house of 1926, half-timber and brick, much expanded in matching style as a hotel from 1970. Exposed timberwork inside, much said to come from HMS *Arethusa* (built 1849).

STOULTON

9040

ST EDMUND. Wide Norman nave and chancel; Cotswold stone w tower by *Peacock & Bewlay*, 1936–7, in Free Perp style, replacing a late C18 brick one. Nave and chancel, of Blue Lias rubble with oolite dressings, probably *c.* 1130–40, have original pilaster buttresses and several windows: three out of four chancel side windows, all somewhat altered, plus one blocked, nave SE. Both Norman nave doorways survive, set in the usual shallow projections, here rising to eaves level. The S doorway has a single order, with block capitals (now minus their shafts), roll-moulded arch, and above, two bays of blank arcading with two-scallop capitals (cf. Eastham and Knighton on Teme). Simpler N doorway, with single-stepped arch, but also two-bay blank arcading above. Chancel arch also single-stepped, on the simplest chamfered imposts, continued as string courses to the nave side walls. Three-light windows inserted either side in the early C14, plus a third, chancel SE. C14 roofs, with arched braces forming a depressed arch up to the collar-beams and bold tracery of a quatrefoil over two trefoils above, largely reconstructed when *A. E. Perkins* restored the church, 1848. His also the timber N porch, nave NW and SW windows, and E and W windows, the former set in a brick E wall of 1799, the latter re-set in the tower. Further restoration by *Waller & Son* of Gloucester, 1914–15.

FONT. Norman, round, tub type with tapering sides; wavy top band with pellet decoration. – Oak REREDOS. 1922–3 by *J. Harold Sayner* of Great Missenden; Perp detail, with figures of SS Edmund and Wulfstan. – C17 ALTAR TABLE. – COMMUNION RAILS of 1639, with close-set balusters. – PULPIT and PEWS by *Perkins*, also two large Gothic chancel chairs made up from C14 roof timbers. – Velvet COPE, in a display case in the nave SW vestry; formerly used as an altar cloth. Late C15, embroidered with fleurs-de-lys, conventional foliage, and the Assumption of the Virgin (cf. Othery, Somerset). – STAINED GLASS. E window by *Willam Pearce Ltd*, 1908, from St Helen, Worcester, re-set here by *A. J. Davies*, 1953. – C14 bits, chancel SE. – MONUMENTS. Anne Dineley †1780; obelisk of grey marble. – William Acton †1814, by *Michael Crake* of London; mourning woman leaning on a pedestal, with roundel with initials. His HATCHMENT opposite.* – Good ledgers, *c.* 1700,

---

*The tournament HELMET and SWORD above, said to be Milanese, *c.* 1470, were stolen *c.* 1990.

with heraldry of the Acton and Vincent families of Wolverton Hall. – Oak WAR MEMORIAL tablet by the *Bromsgrove Guild*, *c.* 1920.

The church is at the NE end of a pleasant, short village street. To its N, the OLD VICARAGE, *c.* 1826, somewhat altered; houses of C17 timber framing or early C19 brick, S. Near the SW end, the former SCHOOL, now village hall, of 1876–7 (by Mr *Ness*, Earl Somers's surveyor at Eastnor Castle, Herefs.). MOUNT PLEASANT, facing the Worcester road, larger early C19, is roughcast, with tall hipped roof.

Along the main road, more C17 timber framing. In Froggery Lane, NW, the thatched OLD FORGE, C15–C16, its sturdy cruck construction visible in the SW gable-end.

WOLVERTON HALL, 1½ m. ENE. *See* p. 521.

STOURPORT-ON-SEVERN

The most important, best-preserved town built in England as a consequence of a canal, the Staffordshire and Worcestershire Canal, of 1766–71. Its principal engineer was *James Brindley* (†1772), designer of the first modern English canal, the Bridge-water at Manchester, 1759–61; assisted by *Samuel Simcock* and *Thomas Dadford the Elder*. The canal runs 46 miles from the Trent and Mersey Canal near Wolverhampton to the River Severn, its later stages following the course of the Stour which joined the larger river near the hamlet of Lower Mitton (a medieval chapelry of Kidderminster; hence the relatively remote position of the parish church). The Canal Company began work on its tran-shipment port *c.* 1768, building a large basin, locks and service buildings.

Further trade from Birmingham and the Black Country fol-lowed the opening of the Dudley and Stourbridge canals in 1779; the new town soon eclipsed Bewdley (q.v.) some three miles up-Severn. The Tontine Inn became its unofficial business centre, with neat artisan housing and later industrial development nearby (*see* Perambulation 1). Stourport briefly became 'the resort of people of fashion', the town centre developing N of the port (Perambulation 2). By 1815, when the Birmingham to Worcester Canal was opened, the peak of its prosperity as a port had passed; the Severn Valley Railway, of 1862, further starved it of trade. The town continued to thrive as a Midland holiday resort (with an electric tramway to Kidderminster, 1899–1929). An Urban District Council was established in 1894.

CHURCHES

ST MICHAEL, Church Drive, Lower Mitton. The ambitious Dec-style stone church designed 1875–6 for the Rev. Benjamin Gibbons by *Sir George Gilbert Scott* (†1878) was only begun in 1881 by his son *John Oldrid Scott*. At the consecration, 1910, there was still no W steeple nor chancel, just an impressive

six-bay clerestoried nave, mostly demolished to sill level
1979–80. Its remains form an enclosed garden approach to a
new church by *Adrian Thompson*, on the site of Scott's proposed chancel. Of load-bearing blockwork, square with chamfered corners; pyramidal slate roof, from which separate canted
roofs rise up for entrance lobby and E chapel. In 1988–9
Thompson added a similar, slightly simpler W extension (for a
meeting room) within the E end of Scott's nave. The most
telling remains of the latter are portions of aisle walls to eaves
level, flanking both the N doorway and heavy vaulted S porch
(built 1887); also the rood-loft turret, S aisle E end. Scant
remains of the tower arch bear the date 1892. Much as one
might deplore the loss of such a fine late C19 building, the new
church and its setting can be considered a qualified success.
Interior reordered around a central altar, 2001; furnishings by
Luke Hughes. Matching ORGAN by *William Drake*, 1985. Dec-
style FONT, possibly *c.* 1834.

Scott's church succeeded one of brick by *James Rose*,
1790–2, enlarged by *William Knight*, 1834–5; demolished 1919.
The outline of its late C18 W tower and wide galleried nave and
early C19 transepts and canted apse remains visible near the S
end of the extensive churchyard. – In the CHURCHYARD many
C18–C19 headstones and tombs, several of cast iron: two of
pedestal form to the Baldwin family, one *c.* 1800 topped with
flaming urn, the other *c.* 1861 with pierced finial.

ST WULSTAN AND ST THOMAS OF CANTERBURY (R.C.), Vale
Road. 1972–3 by *H.J. Harper* of Birmingham. Uninspired red
brick rectangle, its angled roof allowing clerestory lighting to
the E end. Glazed vestibule, slit side windows.

BAPTIST CHAPEL, Prospect Road, Upper Mitton. By *Ingall &
Hughes*, 1883. Brick, with lancets, tripled above the gabled
porch, paired at the sides. Similar, grittier SCHOOL at the rear,
of 1896. – Plain MANSE, probably *c.* 1883.

Former CONGREGATIONAL CHAPEL, Mitton Street. 1869–70
by *George Bidlake*. Brick, thin blue bands, stone dressings. Late
C13 style with pseudo-transepts with plate tracery; SW turret
with pyramidal spire (for stairs to the W gallery). Attached two-
storey school behind.

PRIMITIVE METHODIST CHAPEL (now Jehovah's Witnesses),
Lickhill Road. 1855. Red brick, yellow trim; pilasters, large
round-arched windows.

WESLEY METHODIST CHURCH, Parkes Passage off High
Street. The stuccoed N front, 1+2+2 bays, with cornice and
round-arched windows above segment-headed ones, is probably of 1876. It disguises work of two earlier periods. The
gabled centre represents one end of the original chapel of 1788,
set N–S; this was realigned E–W in 1812, with the addition of a
short E chancel and two W bays, the latter now with Doric
porch leading into a stair lobby. W and S sides still expose their
brick; two-storey former manse of 1805 attached to the latter.
Inside, a fine panelled horseshoe gallery of 1812, to W, N and
S. More astonishing, the CHANCEL SCREEN incorporating

pulpit and communion area, all 1894–6 by *Joseph Ward*, a local stonemason. Of alabaster and marble with lavish carving, including biblical scenes, apostles, and various heads including John Wesley; the round pulpit also has green foliated shafts. Metal gates, brass communion rails. – Thin octagonal FONT, perhaps 1812. – STAINED GLASS. Four by *T. W. Camm*'s studio, 1929–47. – Ornate Gothic TABLET to Pearce Baldwin †1863.

The SCHOOL, across Parkes Passage, by *J. J. Baldwin* of Stourport, 1875–6, is brick, with yellow trim; grouped lancet windows, mostly with latticing.

PUBLIC BUILDINGS

WYRE FOREST DISTRICT CIVIC CENTRE, New Road. By *Andrews & Hazzard* of Birmingham for Stourport UDC, 1963–6. Brick, concrete trim, bands of windows. Central office range, with large projecting Civic Hall, w, circular council Chamber with narrow slit windows, E.

COUNTY BUILDINGS, Bewdley Road. 1970–2 by *Worcestershire County Council Architects' Dept.* Orange brick, with continuous window bands, on a large triangular site. The Health Centre, with projecting upper floor, is flanked by the four-storey Police Station, w, curved Library, E, the latter with fashionable concrete fins. Fire Station and former Magistrates' Court at the rear.

SCHOOLS. Two brick church schools survive. UPPER MITTON, Minster Road, 1882, now Emmanuel Church (Assemblies of God), has stepped lancets and gable bellcote. TAN LANE, 1892–3 by *J. T. Meredith*, is symmetrical, with large shaped gables; much enlarged as Stourport First School, 1950–1.

STOURPORT HIGH SCHOOL, Minster Road, begun 1951, *L. C. Lomas*, County Architect, is brick, quite plain; rendered façade of three storeys, tower-like entrance.

LUCY BALDWIN MATERNITY HOSPITAL, off Olive Grove, Bewdley Road. By *Martin & Martin* of Birmingham, 1929, enlarged 1931–5. Very domestic, two storeys, roughcast, big hipped roof.

STOURPORT BRIDGE. The elegant three-arched stone bridge by *T. F. Pritchard*, 1775, destroyed by flood 1794, was replaced by a single-span iron structure of 1806. The present bridge by *Edward Wilson*, 1868–70, incorporates some of their substructure. Again a single iron span, of shallower rise, on five parallel girders; decorative traceried spandrels, parapet of interlaced circles. Spiral stair to the towpath, NW. Either side, stone abutments of three segmental arches, and brick causeways, long and sloping to Bridge Street; TOLL HOUSE on the Areley Kings side.

PERAMBULATIONS

Stourport is a pleasant town, probably more pleasant now that pleasure boats have replaced the canal barges. The first

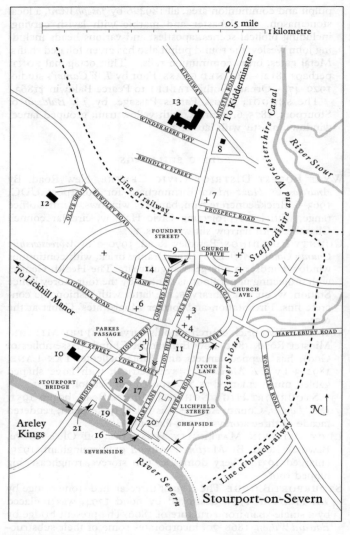

0.5 mile
1 kilometre

To Kidderminster

KINGSWAY

MINSTER ROAD

13

WINDERMERE WAY

BRINDLEY STREET

8

12

OLIVE GROVE

BEWDLEY ROAD

Line of railway

7

PROSPECT ROAD

Staffordshire and Worcestershire Canal

River Stour

FOUNDRY
STREET?

9

CHURCH
DRIVE

1

To Lickhill Manor

LICKHILL ROAD

14

TAN LANE

LOMBARD STREET

2

CHURCH
AVE.

6

VALE ROAD

GILGAL

3

4

MITTON STREET

HARTLEBURY ROAD

PARKES
PASSAGE

HIGH STREET

LION HILL

11

5

STOUR
LANE

River Stour

WORCESTER ROAD

NEW STREET

YORK STREET

10

STOURPORT
BRIDGE

BRIDGE ST

18

17

SEVERN ROAD

15

LICHFIELD
STREET

Areley
Kings

19

20

CHEAPSIDE

MART LANE

21

16

SEVERNSIDE

River Severn

N

Line of branch railway

Stourport-on-Severn

1	St Michael	12	Lucy Baldwin Hospital
2	Site of old Church	13	Stourport High School
3	St Wulstan (R.C.)	14	School
4	Former Congregational Chapel	15	Carpet Works
5	Wesley Methodist Church	16	Tontine Inn
6	Former P.M. Chapel	17	Old Basin
7	Baptist Chapel	18	Clock Basin
8	School (now Emmanuel Church)	19	Lower Basins
9	County Buildings	20	New Basins (now filled in)
10	Civic Centre	21	Engine (or Crown) Basin
11	Drill Hall		

perambulation considers these basins and development nearby. The second deals with the town centre, the third with remnants of the original hamlet, Lower Mitton.

1. The canal basins and to their east

The happiest spot and best place to start is MART LANE, with a good general view, w, of the surviving basins, constructed on a terrace 30 ft (9 metres) above normal river level (to avoid the frequent Severn floods). The nearer, OLD (now UPPER) BASIN, built 1768–71 probably by *Thomas Dadford the Elder*, is linked by a short channel to CLOCK BASIN further w, of 1781–2. Between the two, the former WAREHOUSE for grain 117 and general merchandise (now Yacht Club): late c18, red brick, two storeys, quite long, with central clock turret added 1812. On the sw side of the Upper Basin, THE WHARF, a warehouse of the early 1770s (later maintenance building), painted brick, with large round-arched openings and curved NW corner. Enlarged at the rear in the early c19; the sw part probably always for domestic use. On the basin's s side, originally obscured by a further warehouse, the back of the TONTINE INN,* brick, E-plan with three gabled rear wings, built by the Canal Company, 1772. The front faces a lawn (once a formal garden) at the foot of which is the Severn. The composition here is a terrace of five houses, two-and-a-half storeys, 2+3+2 widely spaced bays, windows with stepped stucco voussoirs. The central inn, with tripartite windows, has a Gothic porch of *c.* 1870. The two houses either side were separate lodgings or offices; two more in each broad four-bay return.

w of the Tontine, between the main basins and river, are the LOWER BASINS, of 1781. The entrance from the Severn through the eastern Lower Basin to the Upper Basin is at an angle through two BARGE LOCKS of 1768–71 (without bridges as the Severn trows had masts). The NARROW LOCKS of 1781, further w (into Clock Basin), specifically for canal boats, consist of two pairs of double locks, each crossed by a brick humpback bridge. By the upper pair, a dry dock with c20 canopy.

Two further basins were constructed E of Mart Lane. The larger NEW BASIN, N, of 1806–10, filled in *c.* 1960, was partially reconstructed in 2006, with proposed surrounding residential development by *Boughton Butler*. Gas works were built on the s basin, of 1810–12, as early as 1866. Near the s end of Mart Lane, E side, the former Tontine STABLES, a painted brick late c18 two-storey range; contemporary house and cottages to their s. The brick-walled path that starts under an archway N of the stables ran between the two early c19 basins; a hump halfway along represents the bridge across the linking channel.

---

*Tontine is a financial scheme by which shareholders receive an equal annuity, but cannot dispose of their shares; eventually the last to remain alive enjoys the whole income.

Now briefly E from the foot of Mart Lane along the towpath, much improved to allow the use of horses, 1802–3; the river wharf wall continues in coursed sandstone for a short distance. In the first section, SEVERNSIDE, backing onto the Tontine stables, an attractively irregular terrace, the part nearer the river late C18: three storeys, brick, pedimented doorways, segment-headed windows. Then the ANGEL HOTEL, three bays of wide sash windows, probably mid-C18, predating the port; the third storey must be late C18. The towpath is then confined by brick walls of the former gas works, and, after a passageway, by the former HOLBROOK'S VINEGAR BREWERY, established 1798, mostly rebuilt (after fire) 1882.*

The passageway between the former gas and vinegar works leads to CHEAPSIDE; remains of a brick terrace, c. 1800, on its N side, namely its W end curving round the corner into SEVERN ROAD. On the W side here, after the exit of the brick-walled path (*see* above), substantial remains of New Basin's sandstone wall, c. 1810, with blocked round archway, S end. Further N, E side, the derelict SEVERN VALLEY CARPET WORKS by *T.D. Baker*, 1868, for T.B. Worth; mildly Deco additions dated 1932, probably by *Sidney Stott* of Oldham.

LICHFIELD STREET leads back W. First, S side, Nos. 16–17, modest two-storey Georgian cottages with nice eared and pedimented doorways; No. 18 has a later doorway. On the N side, a continuous run of little-altered houses of c. 1800: No. 9, with high round-arched and pedimented doorway; Nos. 5–8, a good two-and-a-half-storey terrace with pretty Adamish doorways, the central two paired; No. 4, a larger house with doorway like that of No. 9; Nos. 1–3, with well-preserved shop windows. Another Georgian brick group at the N end of MART LANE, E side (Nos. 2–4), no doubt built by the Canal Company, continued by Nos. 5–6, part of a lower, much longer, early C19 terrace. Of the warehouses that these buildings once faced, only the modest C19 railway warehouse, N end, remains.

A little further N, the Canal enters the Upper Basin via a lock in the angle of YORK STREET and LION HILL. Charming LOCK COTTAGE (now a shop) dated 1854; central gable with finial, matching TOLL HOUSE dated 1853. The balance beams of the lower lock gates are canted back to avoid fouling Wallfield Bridge (rebuilt 1938); complicated overflow sluice nearby. Further N, on the canal's W side, early to mid-C19 remnants of the canal maintenance yard, completing a splendid urban canalscape.

2. The town centre

Set back on the N side of YORK STREET, W of Wallfield Bridge, is OAKLEIGH HOUSE, built for the harbour-master c. 1771 (see the brick rear); stuccoed front range, with bay windows

---

* Further on, across the brick Stour BRIDGE of 1802–3, was a POWER STATION of 1925–6, enlarged in modern style by *Farmer & Dark*, 1947–8; all demolished c. 1985.

and Tuscan porch, *c.* 1840. York Street then assumes a town-centre scale, with three-storey Late Georgian brick houses on both sides. First N, MERCIAN HOUSE (No. 16), the former Police Station, three bays, plaster quoins, and specially nice doorcase: fluted Doric columns, frieze with wreaths, crowned head above the door. The houses opposite, their rears overlooking Clock Basin, were built for wharfingers. Nos. 19–20, 3+2 bays, each part with pedimented doorcase, probably formed a single property. YORK HOUSE (No. 21), built for Aaron York *c.* 1781, has stepped voussoirs, quoins, and fine central Venetian doorway with triglyphs and pediment. Impressive stuccoed rear: rounded bay windows flanking a Tuscan porch, Venetian windows above. Arcaded substructure dated 1787. The rest of York Street is more modest; at its end, the central crossroads of the town.

Straight across into NEW STREET, its N side with a consistent three-storey terrace, *c.* 1800, quite something with its diversity of entrances. It begins with the Hope and Anchor inn, then No. 17 with Doric doorcase, and No. 16 with fine Ionic one. Nos. 9–15 have simpler pedimented doorways with blank tympana; Nos. 7–8 a heavier Doric form, tripartite windows, and flanking late C19 additions. S side mostly rebuilt, respecting the streetline. At its W end, the Wyre Forest Civic Centre (p. 613).

Back to the crossroads and S down BRIDGE STREET. The W side has mostly minor late C18 houses, originally enjoying views over the basins, No. 27 with beaded intersecting fanlight, mildly Gothick. The best doorcase is at No. 13, fluted Doric with steep pediment. Two inns flank the bridge approach: the BRIDGE INN, W, *c.* 1790 with mid-C19 alterations, and YE OLDE CROWN INN, rebuilt by *A. T. & Bertram Butler*, 1936; brick and stucco, pantiled roof. E of the bridge (p. 613), incongruously accompanied by a funfair, is the ENGINE (or CROWN) BASIN, constructed *c.* 1805 partly for town use, but specifically to store water that could be pumped into the main basin system. The pleasant riverside PUBLIC PARK, W of the bridge, is a further sign of Stourport's concern to make itself attractive to visitors.

Now HIGH STREET, the N continuation of Bridge Street. Its E side has continuous three-storey houses of *c.* 1800, nearly all with inserted shopfronts (the late C20 ones unfailingly the crudest). On the W side, the POST OFFICE, 1964, unnecessarily set back, and HSBC (formerly Midland Bank) by *Whinney & Austen Hall*, 1937, with large Venetian window. BARCLAYS BANK, beyond the late C18 Wheatsheaf Inn, is subtler Neo-Georgian, built for Martin's Bank by *E. C. Aldridge* of Liverpool, 1939. The best doorcases, E side, are No. 20, Doric with fluted frieze, flanked by matching early C20 shopfronts with some stained glass, and Nos. 19–19A, pedimented like Nos. 9–15 New Street, with the least-altered ground floor. Nos. 15–17, a six-bay terrace, are followed by the passage to the Wesley Methodist Church (p. 612).

At its N end, High Street curves slightly to another crossroads, dominated by the SWAN HOTEL, *c.* 1840–50: Tuscan porch between two-storey canted bays. To the W, in LICKHILL ROAD, N side, remains of the HAVEN CINEMA, an early example probably of 1912, by *Pritchard & Pritchard*; pedimented lobby and curved-roof auditorium parallel to the street. Beyond, the former Primitive Methodist chapel (p. 612). To the E, MITTON STREET immediately re-crosses the canal, the rebuilt bridge flanked by Nos. 2–2A, three-by-three-bay brick, *c.* 1800, with nicely restored shopfronts, and the BLACK STAR, a rendered canalside pub: low bargeboarded front wing, taller rear dated 1884, its voussoirs with impressed floral motifs. Then the WAR MEMORIAL GARDEN, trimmed with fluted stonework from Witley Court gardens (p. 328); large resited stone plaque by the *Bromsgrove Guild*, 1922.

3. Lower Mitton

A postscript, in defiance of the ferocious one-way traffic system, to reveal what remains of the original hamlet. Opposite the War Memorial Garden, the former Congregational chapel (p. 612), with the R.C. church (p. 612), N, in Vale Road. The former DRILL HALL, S, at the top of Lion Hill, by *Pritchard & Pritchard*, 1911, demolished 2003, was replaced by houses aping the surviving dwelling for the sergeant-instructor: roughcast, with sandstone and brick dressings, purple brick plinth, mullioned-and-transomed windows. In MITTON STREET, further E, pleasant early C19 houses. At the corner of Stour Lane, the only noteworthy pre-canal house, Nos. 40–41, probably early C17; square timber framing, with central brick chimneystack, once nicely detailed. Then the brick ANGLO-AMERICAN MILL, the best of several industrial buildings that clustered around the bridge over the Stour; built by the Baldwins, *c.* 1879, to manufacture cast mottled enamelware: three storeys, mostly paired segment-headed windows, but a tripartite rhythm each end.

At the foot of GILGAL, a good group of *c.* 1800. The best house is No. 19; rendered, canted bays flanking the pedimented doorway, Venetian windows above, Diocletian on the narrower top floor. Gilgal winds back uphill to the canal, separated from the road by a sandstone wall. On its bank, W of Gilgal Bridge, a mid-C19 WAREHOUSE built for Baldwin's Foundry: brindled brick, 6+1+6 bays, two storeys with segment-headed cast-iron windows above an open arcade on iron columns. Its other side, to FOUNDRY STREET, is continued SW by a related early C19 range of houses. The site of the foundry is occupied by County Buildings (p. 613). The parish church, St Michael (p. 611), lies further E.

OUTER STOURPORT

In the angle of Worcester and Hartlebury Roads, E of the town centre, a late C17 gabled brick house, altered in the C18; the date 1671 is formed in the studs of a door. The house became part of the C20 Parsons Chain Co. complex, and in 2001–2 was linked to glossy new OFFICES by *A. Macklin* (of *K3 Consulting Ltd*). The former OLD ANCHOR, Worcester Road, W side, a neat, rendered, Neo-Georgian pub, is by *H.W. Hobbiss*, 1938. Further on, both roads were crossed by RAILWAY BRIDGES carrying a branch line, completed 1949, to the riverside power station (*see* p. 616); that across Hartlebury Road survives.

To the N, in MINSTER ROAD, the Baptist Chapel (p. 612); also schools (p. 613). Off BEWDLEY ROAD, leading NW, the Lucy Baldwin Hospital (p. 613). Nearby, the large BRINTON ARMS, probably by *A.T. & B. Butler*, *c.* 1938: brick, unfortunately painted, gabled Tudorbethan style.

LICKHILL MANOR (now a nursing home), 1⅛ m. W by the Severn. Fine double-pile house of *c.* 1700, seven bays and three storeys; top storey, of different brick, probably early C18. Straight brick window heads, platband between ground and first floors, central door with eared architrave and segmental pediment. The rear elevation, S, probably the original entrance front, is more finely detailed, its doorway with larger segmental pediment on carved consoles. Early C18 dog-leg stair with fluted balusters, just W of the N door, with feeble late C19 armorial glass of the Crane family. Several rooms have good C17–C18 panelling.

WOODGREEN FARMHOUSE, Lickhill Road, N of the drive to Lickhill Manor, is mid-C18 brick; three-storeyed, T-plan.

STRENSHAM

9040

ST JOHN BAPTIST, Lower Strensham. Away from the village, above the Avon; vested in the Churches Conservation Trust since 1991. Architecturally of limited interest, but containing exceptional furnishings and monuments. The exterior is now all lime-rendered, including the hefty Perp W tower, battlemented apart from its blunt oblong stair-turret, SE. Very wide nave with renewed C14 windows. The evidence in the chancel is more confused; its Perp SE window may represent enlargement *c.* 1405, from the bequest of Sir John Russell. Early C19 embattled N vestry. Ceiled nave wagon roof, with three sturdy moulded tie-beams; against the easternmost, a mid-C18 angel ready to take off. Simple C14 chancel arch.

FONT. If Norman, entirely re-cut; circular, plain arcading. – Mid-C16 PEWS, a comprehensive set, the bench ends with linenfold panels between buttresses. Similar PANELLING against the nave walls, still with hat-pegs. – Early C17 FAMILY PEW: Jacobean top frieze. – Plainer two-decker PULPIT, probably *c.* 1700. – WEST GALLERY, decorated with Perp panels containing twenty-two painted apostles and other saints, plus Christ at the centre, from the former rood screen; but from what else? Its dimensions can hardly be reconciled with those of the chancel. Rustic late C15 painting, not helped by 'restoration' in 1875; nonetheless a unique survival for Worcestershire. Woodwork also probably from the screen: big leaf spandrels, posts with elongated canopies with nodding ogee arches. – C15 TILES in the nave, many heraldic. – Above the chancel arch, early C19 ROYAL ARMS, George III, flanked by HATCHMENTS to John Taylor (1848) and James Taylor (1852). – STAINED GLASS. Dark E window by *Cox, Sons, Buckley & Co.*, 1890. – Nave SE by *T.F. Curtis, Ward & Hughes*, 1903. – Far superior chancel SE, by *Florence Camm*, 1926.

MONUMENTS. On the chancel floor, two excellent brasses: Sir Robert Russell, 4 ft 7 in. (1.4 metre) figure in armour, *c.* 1390; and Sir John Russell †1405, a palimpsest, 4 ft 1 in. (1.2 metres) and similar, but beneath a canopy with ogee crocketed gable and flanking pinnacles. – Also chancel brasses to Robert Russell †1502 and wife Elizabeth (3 ft, 0.9 metres); and to Sir John †1556 and wife Edith †1562, kneeling 12½ in. (32-cm.) figures, in a stone frame at the head of a tomb-chest with shields in cusped lozenges. Above, a large plain oval tablet to Sir William Russell †1669. – Sir Thomas Russell †1632 and wife Elizabeth; possibly by *Samuel Baldwin*. Large, painted stone and alabaster, with two well-carved recumbent effigies and delightfully crisp decoration. The tomb-chest is open at the front, revealing the oval-shaped coffin, flanked by the bases of the columns, decorated with strapwork and skulls. The Composite columns carry a straight entablature with globes and central broken segmental pediment with ornate heraldry; arch behind the effigies with ribbonwork spandrels. – Sir Francis Russell †1705, by *Edward Stanton*. Standing marble monument, reredos background of Composite columns and open segmental pediment. He reclines, somewhat twisted, on the tomb-chest. At his head kneels his wife Anne, gesticulating upwards towards putti in clouds holding his coronet, an almost blasphemous composition. – Anne Lady Gyse †1734. Yet taller standing monument, the lady reclining on the sarcophagus, resting from her reading. Restrained back wall of grey marbles, with obelisk and open pediment. – Ann Dansey †1733; tablet with urn and obelisk, attributed to *Thomas White*. – Sir Charles Trubshaw Withers †1804. Brown and white marbles, with stylish urn and two small seated female allegories. – Memorial to Samuel Butler (author of *Hudibras*, born at Strensham, 1612); ornate Gothic tablet by *Robert Ashton Jun.*, *c.* 1830–40. – John Taylor †1848, by *J. Stephens*; draped Grecian altar. – Lt John Walter Taylor †1913; brass by *Gawthorp & Sons*, with standing hussar.

Former brick SCHOOL, N, early C19 Gothick, much altered as a house. – To the SE, the OLD RECTORY, C17 timber-framed with C18 windows; enlarged 1866.

MOAT FARMHOUSE, ½ m. W. Early-to-mid-C18, coursed rubble, H-plan; three-bay centre, two-bay wings, hipped roof. Large quoins perhaps reused from STRENSHAM CASTLE, the site of which lies to the rear. Square moated platform with broad W causeway, surrounded by a rampart (with corners raised in the

Civil War) and outer moat. James Russell acquired the manor in 1298, Sir John Russell received licence to crenellate, 1388. The village may then have stretched from castle to church.

The present village, UPPER STRENSHAM, lies 1 m. SW. At its centre, a routine WAR MEMORIAL CROSS by *Sidney Gambier Parry*, 1919. Facing it, the RUSSELL ALMSHOUSES of 1697, brick, quite humble, centre and two short wings (partly rebuilt 1987). The three restored brick cottages, W, also belonged to the almshouses. Further W, HOME FARMHOUSE, C17, L-plan, timber-framed, and STRENSHAM FARM, brick, dated 1856. Former SCHOOL, to the NE, of 1847 (enlarged at the rear 1893); of coursed Lias, much altered.

The Grecian STRENSHAM COURT, S, built for the banker John Taylor 1824, probably by *George Maddox*, was demolished after fire in 1974; one ashlar GATEPIER remains (at the corner of Court Road), also plain brick STABLES (converted to housing), and, further SE, the brick WALL of the kitchen garden.

BREDON FIELD FARM, 1 m. S, by the M5/M50 interchange. A rare Worcestershire example of a model farm, built 1851. Brick, with gabled Tudorish farmhouse, and extensive double farmyards, the W one later roofed over.

STRENSHAM SERVICES (M5). The large northbound building, by *McColl Design*, 1991–2, is symmetrical, mostly two-tone brick, with central mall leading to the broad circular restaurant. The southbound, by *Roberts Gardner Ltd* of Gloucester, 2002, almost entirely glazed towards the car park, is more wholeheartedly open-plan, with subsidiary facilities pushed to one side.

SUCKLEY

7050

Remote hilly country, a northern continuation of the Malvern Hills, on the boundary with Herefordshire; hop kilns form a conspicuous landscape feature.

ST JOHN THE BAPTIST. By *Hopkins*, 1876–9, in Geometrical Dec style; his most important surviving church after Hallow. Large, of rough-faced elephant-grey Cradley stone, with Bath dressings, replacing a medieval building of almost equal size. Well composed S side, with clerestory of quatrefoil openings, open timber porch, and vertical emphases provided by the pinnacle between aisle and vestry and tall chimney emerging through the roof slope between vestry and chancel. Varied tracery: E window and others purely Geometrical, W window more like *c.* 1300; cusped Y-tracery elsewhere. Sturdy, richly decorated W tower: pairs of two-light bell-openings, pierced quatrefoil parapet with crocketed pinnacles, pyramidal stone-tiled roof with taller such pinnacle as its spire. Starker N side, without an aisle, but with shallow N transept (for children) beneath a dramatic catslide roof. Sober rendered interior. Three-bay S arcade, with round piers with heavily moulded capitals and tall arches. Higher chancel arch on tripled corbel shafts of red Alveley sandstone, the large capitals elaborately carved with foliage, ferns and birds by *Martyn & Emms*. In the chancel a genuine C14 recess with hollow chamfer with ballflower (containing a good heraldic BRASS to Thomas Littleton, rector, †1665). Ogee-trefoiled piscina, at least its ballflowered hoodmould, also C14.

FONT. Mid-C12: tub-shaped bowl with slightly tapering sides, and chain of decorated lozenges (cf. Middle Littleton); later stem of similar size. Nice ogee-shaped COVER, probably C17. – Other FITTINGS mostly by *Hopkins*, his PULPIT incorporating Jacobean blank-arched panels. – Sanctuary re-fitted by *Pancheri & Son*, 1956. – STAINED GLASS. Chancel all by *Kempe*: three of 1898–9, the NW of 1922. – MONUMENTS. Many tablets tidied away beneath the tower, a typical case of such Victorian housekeeping. Several have fine early C18 carving. Good later C18 signed examples include a severe one by *John Broad* of Worcester (Joseph Racster †1777); also two by *W. Stephens*, c. 1766–95, variations on the urn theme.

CHURCHYARD CROSS. C14–C15; three steps, large base with niche on its W side (cf. Broadwas), socket for the lost shaft.

(BOARD) SCHOOL, SW. Of 1875, probably by *E.A. Day* (cf. Alfrick). Quite bold, brick banded in stone and blue brick; schoolroom with stepped end triplet, attached house with gabled dormers.

LOWER COURT, E. Stuccoed, early C19, L-plan; tripartite windows on the lower floor, hipped slate roof with broad eaves. Timber-framed rear wing.

The OLD RECTORY, a little NE, by *A.E. Perkins*, 1850; large, brick, mullioned-and-transomed windows. Shaped gables on the garden side, compact entrance front; straight gables on the other long side. Tall grouped chimneys.

Some distance SSE, beyond new housing, a good VILLAGE HALL of c. 1910, roughcast over brick; sloping buttresses, pretty tracery on the entrance front. Attached house, also roughcast, with some narrow studding.

The WHITE HOUSE, ¾ m. N. Early C18, of whitened brick. Three storeys, with segment-headed windows, modillion eaves cornice and hipped slate roof. Finely moulded doorway with lovely apsidal shell-hood on carved console brackets; within it, foliage scrolls, a basket of flowers, and winged cherub's head.★ The house must have been planned to have 2+3+2 bays, with the doorway in the middle of the projecting centre; an abortive attempt at completion, c. 1765–70, probably by *T.F. Pritchard* of Shrewsbury, resulted only in the present stump of the N wing. Low outer S wing, timber-framed, perhaps C16, later encased in brick. The rear elevation matches the W front, with a simpler shell-hood. Within, a very fine dog-leg staircase of oak: turned balusters, dog-gates, panelled dado; the arched screen, however, must be c. 1765–70, as is the re-fitting of the drawing room, NE. Plasterwork in the overmantel here

★ All but identical to the hood at St Giles' House, Oxford, 1702.

probably by *Joseph Bromfield*, who worked for Pritchard at Gaines nearby (*see* Whitbourne, Herefs.). Much early C18 bolection-moulded panelling and plasterwork survives. On the first floor, a marbled room and richly decorated marquetry closet, its panelling with contrasting veneers; marquetry picture of the house above the door.

Prominent group of C19 brick HOP KILNS, SE.

Opposite, W, HAVENTREE, mostly square-panelled framing. Lower S end, with four bays of cruck construction, probably C15. N part rebuilt higher, as a parlour wing, probably in the C17, with large stone chimney-breast with three brick stacks; single-storey gabled wing, E.

BASTON HALL, Crews Hill, 1⅛ m. NE. Restored framed farmhouse, *c.* 1620, of small square panels, with interesting symmetrical plan: two-storey central porch with baffle entry, hall, r., parlour, l.; small service wing, rear centre.

ROLLS HILL HOP KILNS, ½ m. SSW. A striking brick group of *c.* 1870, converted to housing. Rectangular, with circular kilns with conical roofs at each corner; two more bulge out from the SW side, their tops altered.

UPPER COURT (or Suckley Court), formerly moated, ½ m. WSW. Neat early C18 five-bay brick front; segment-headed windows, paired thin giant pilasters each end.

LOWER TUNDRIDGE FARM, 1 m. ESE. Very large, late timber-framed farmhouse, no earlier than the mid C17; close-studded ground floor, upper floor with square panels. L-plan, with large chimney with four massive brick shafts at the junction (another of C19 date, with three tall slender shafts, at the rear). Three-bay rectangular front block on high sandstone plinth, making four storeys in all: cellar, ground, first, and high attic floor. The main staircase is central. Most of the four- or five-light windows have original ovolo mullions and transoms, projecting beyond the wall face on carved brackets, spoilt in their effect by red-tiled pent-roofs. The design of the chimneystacks, as well as the symmetrical main front, are foretastes of the Early Georgian. From *c.* 1700 houses of identical plan and proportions were built in brick, but their windows became vertically elongated and a central front door was added.

Long BARN of square-panelled framing, S, probably contemporary.

To the SW, across Leigh Brook, UPPER TUNDRIDGE HOUSE, *c.* 1830–40; painted brick, gables with pierced bargeboards, purple brick chimneystacks. Three-bay entrance front with central two-storeyed gabled porch.

TARDEBIGGE
Tutnall and Cobley

9060

ST BARTHOLOMEW. Splendidly sited on a hill. By *Francis Hiorne* of Warwick, 1776–7 (after the tower of the medieval church fell in 1775); *Henry Rowe & Son* replaced his shallow chancel, 1878–9. *Hiorne*'s steeple is not easily forgotten: square W tower, slender needle spire 135 ft (42 metres) high rising from an open, decidedly Baroque, bell-stage with concave walls; pairs of Doric columns jut forward at the angles, supporting urn finials. Pedimented w doorway, Diocletian window above, one-storey attachments either side. The nave has five bays of round-arched windows, the westernmost blind. *Rowe*'s chancel, with semicircular E apse, fits remarkably well, despite its modestly medieval foliated shafts. Wide uneventful interior: flat nave ceiling with central plaster rose; round moulded chancel arch, flat but panelled chancel ceiling.

Of late C18 furnishings, only WEST GALLERY, FAMILY PEW, NE (altered 1926), and small COMMUNION TABLE (nave SE) survive. – PEWS by *Rowe*. – Large square Neo-Norman FONT, 1850, nicely carved. – Excellent Art Nouveau LECTERN by *Amy Walford*, 1907; enriched hammered copper. – Good oak STALLS and canopied PRIEST'S DESK, also 1907, made in workshops at the former village hall (*see* below); matching square PULPIT by *Celestino Pancheri*, 1965. – Other chancel fittings by *Frederick Etchells*, *c.* 1925–30, but the gilt oak REREDOS by *Detmar Blow*. – STAINED GLASS. E window, Ascension, by *Alfred Pike*, the upper half designed by the *Earl of Plymouth*; robust, quite monumental. Completed 1922. – Nave NE by *Amy Walford*, 1894, executed by *Heaton, Butler & Bayne*; good, in the Germanic Renaissance style then considered suitable for Georgian churches.

MONUMENTS. Kneeling headless figure, in armour, with red cloak, from the destroyed tomb of Henry Lord Windsor †1605, so presumably his son Thomas. – Lady Mary Cookes (*née* Windsor) †1694 with husband Sir Thomas (†1701*); attributed to *James Hardy* (GF). Big elaborate tablet, twisted Corinthian columns flanking a large oval with two three-quarter figures in relief; she bares her right breast. Broken pediment with reclining allegories and heraldry. The inscription reads:

> Mary the one Thing Necessary Sought,
> Not what the Rabbies, but what JESUS Taught,
> Soe did our Mary, make't Her Greatest Care,
> T'obey what ye other Mary, once did Heare.
> But Tir'd with th' Eearthly Case, her Soul Inspir'd
> With Love Divine, A Nobler Seat Requir'd;
> Mounted on Cherubs Wings, through Æthers Way
> And Cloath'd with Light of never failing day,
> Sailing by all the Sparkling Orbs of Night
> She Stopp'd at last, where's Intellectuall Light;
> Harke how she Sings, with all th' Celestiall Choire
> Anthems of Praise, in Tune to Davids Lyre.
> Not Taught by Art, Inspir'd from above
> She Chants forth Praises, to the GOD of Love.

---

* Son of William Cookes of Norgrove Court, p. 500; he founded Worcester College, Oxford, and re-founded Bromsgrove School.

Other Archer, Earl of Plymouth †1833 (cf. the Lickey obelisk, p. 428), by *Chantrey*, 1835; the grieving widow sits, in profile, her l. arm against the pedestal carrying his draped urn; book and chalice on the ground in front. – Fine stone WAR MEMORIAL by *Detmar Blow & Billerey*, 1920–1; pediment, black Corinthian columns. – Good ledger by *Etchells*, of Westmorland slate, to Robert George, first Earl of Plymouth (of the second creation) †1923.

s of the church, steps and quatrefoiled base of a C15 CROSS; shaft and head added in memory of Harriet Baroness Windsor †1869.

Brick SCHOOL, sw, dated 1843 on its central gabled house; lower Tudorish schoolrooms each side set in an arc. Sensible later additions. – The OLD VICARAGE, a little SE, mostly by *Thomas Cundy Sen.*, 1815, has five bays, stuccoed, with hipped roof: entrance front, E, with blocky central porch; garden side, s, with central bay. Rear additions, 1868.

Tardebigge, ¼ m. ESE, was the ESTATE VILLAGE to Hewell Grange. The Earl of Plymouth provided the dominant building, the TARDEBIGGE INN by *Francis F. Baylis* of Redditch, 1910–11, as a Village Hall and Institute. Hipped roof with central cupola, big U-plan, N wing with dormered upper storey; oak veranda at the rear. To its s, brick estate cottages of 1856. Opposite, the former sw LODGE, tile-hung with half-timbered gables, by *Goddard & Paget* of Leicester, 1886. It faces their similar, slightly heavier DAIRY LODGE, 1885. Then a long sandstone wall fronting the brick outbuildings of the former home farm, now HEWELL HOUSE, a mid-C19 reworking of a four-cell double-pile brick house, *c.* 1700; central entrance hall, staircase with splat balusters. Low additions by *C.E. Bateman*, late 1930s. Near the road, much further on, *Bodley & Garner*'s WATER TOWER of 1891; sandstone, tile-hung and pyramidal-roofed top stage.

HEWELL GRANGE, further E, now an Open Prison, has been in institutional use since 1946. A former grange of Bordesley Abbey (p. 550), it came to the Windsor family in 1542. The house rebuilt for the second Earl of Plymouth, 1711–12, was altered by *Thomas Cundy Sen.*, 1815–16; its ruined shell survives. *Bodley & Garner* planned additions *c.* 1880, for Robert George, Lord Windsor (Earl of Plymouth from 1905), but instead built a new house, the present lavish Jacobethan one, in 1884–91; the operative partner was *Thomas Garner*. It is one of the most important late C19 country houses in England, perhaps the last Victorian prodigy house (though one of the first to be lit by electricity); already, in 1913, C.R. Ashbee called it, in his journal: 'a noble example of something now I suppose extinct'.

EXTERIOR. A pair of early C19 ashlar-faced Doric LODGES, probably by *Cundy Sen.*, lie rotting by the side of the road, and the present approach is not promising. It passes extensive late C20 housing for prison officers, before reaching the fine avenue

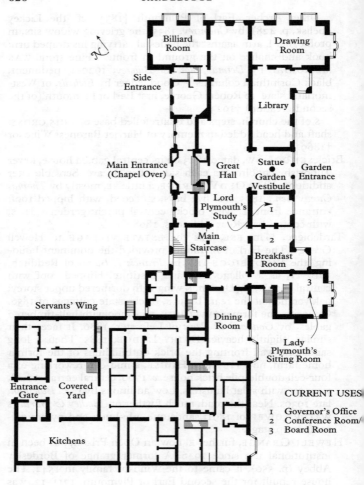

Tardebigge, Hewell Grange.
Ground-floor plan

CURRENT USES

1 Governor's Office
2 Conference Room/
3 Board Room

of limes planted 1906.* The house, however, does not disappoint, a huge mass, sober and dignified, of dark pink Runcorn sandstone, its design based on Montacute (Somerset), with elements added from Charlton Park (Wilts.) or Bramshill (Hants.); much of the decorative detail, carved by *Farmer & Brindley*, is rather Quattrocento or Early French Renaissance. Long ENTRANCE FRONT, NW, three storeys plus attics, with

*This approach also serves BLAKENHURST PRISON, further NE, opened 1993, pink brick with metallic hipped roofs; an anonymous-looking design by the *PSA*, based on their earlier Bullingdon Prison, Oxfordshire.

wings stepping forward, each with a pair of boldly shaped gables. Central two-storey projecting porch with semicircular oriel above the entrance, flanked by paired Composite pilasters. Behind the central shaped gable, a two-stage cupola, set well back. Windows all mullioned and transomed, string courses continuous. From the w end projects, rather too conspicuously, a low but large gabled service wing, with Tudor-arched entrance to its covered yard. The similar GARDEN FRONT, SE, is more impressive in its unbroken symmetry, the service range here set well back. Wings with shaped gables, two-storey bay windows with semicircular projecting centres; in the inner angles, further square bays, rising to four-storey towers with recessed pyramidal roofs. Centre again with large shaped gable, delicate carving, and three-bay ground-floor loggia. Symmetrical RETURN FRONT, NE, with telling central oriel set high up (at the end of a pseudo-long gallery), the effect marred by an ugly fire-escape.

The INTERIOR is far more decidedly Renaissance than the exterior leads one to expect. *Garner*'s original designs, more English and Jacobean, were altered at the instigation of Lord Windsor; the resultant Late Victorian synthesis was originally enhanced by tapestries and paintings. One is received into a prodigious GREAT HALL, filling half the total space of the house: two storeys high, with panelled oak ceiling on large consoles; much Penarth and Italian marble and Derbyshire alabaster. Colonnaded galleries on three sides: on the short sides in one even run, on the long side set in pairs. Below the former, the hall ends with screens of Composite columns of black Frosterley marble, but beyond the tripartite NE screen it continues to the end windows, beneath a ceiling delicately painted (by the Bavarians *Behr & Virsching*) with muses and *grotteschi*. Behind the SW screen, of six columns with raised arched centre, a similar space forms a vestibule to both DINING ROOM (straight ahead, retaining much solemn Jacobethan decoration) and generous STAIRCASE, leading off r.; this has Jacobean detail, but is rather of open-well type of *c.* 1700. It ascends to a first-floor landing filling the area between the staircase and far side of the house. In the garden vestibule opposite the front entrance, lined with canvas hangings painted to resemble tapestries at Schönbrunn (Vienna), an C18 bronze statue of Hermes. Other rooms are insignificant compared to the overwhelming display of the hall. Most retain original stone chimneypieces, either carved locally (for example, in the DRAWING ROOM, by *J. W. Rollins* of Headless Cross, Redditch) or imported from Italy. Several rooms in the SE part have in addition lavish well-preserved decoration: in LORD PLYMOUTH'S STUDY, convincing panelling (much in fact C17), large wooden overmantel, and Jacobethan plaster ceiling; in the delicate BREAKFAST ROOM, an early C18 fireplace with atlantes, from the former house, beneath a late C17-style overmantel, with matching plaster compartment ceiling. Best of all, LADY PLYMOUTH'S SITTING ROOM, entirely

Italian Renaissance (based on the ducal palace at Mantua) with splendid painted maze ceiling, again by *Behr & Virsching*. Above this, LADY PLYMOUTH'S DRESSING ROOM, its frieze (now in poor condition) illustrating Beethoven's Pastoral Symphony, painted on canvas by her mother *Walburga, Lady Paget*. Finally the CHAPEL above the porch, also approached by timber balconies across the bay-window recesses; fine white marble and lapis lazuli paving by *Farmer & Brindley*, barrel-vaulted wooden ceiling by *Detmar Blow & Billerey*, c. 1914, dotted with carved cherubs. Excellent STAINED GLASS: altar window (in the curved oriel) by *Arild Rosencrantz*, c. 1896, a dazzling illustration of Revelations; (ritual) NE with six good late C15 panels, said to be from Bordesley Abbey, restored by *Alfred L. Pike*. His also the (ritual) NW and SW, c. 1920, with scenes of St George and of the history of Bordesley Abbey, designed by the first Earl.

GROUNDS. Semicircular FORECOURT with low arcaded wall, 1902–3, with obelisks and matching gateway. At its centre an 1823 statue of the Fallen Gladiator, signed *William Croggan* of Lambeth (*Coade*'s successor). Elaborate FORMAL GARDENS, SE, were laid out 1900–3 by the gardener *Andrew Pettigrew*;* trimmed hedges survive, also four *Croggan* statues of the 1820s, reused at the centres of each quadrant (now hidden in yew arbours). Central fountain replaced. Further ESE, former brick STABLES, of early C18 form, mostly rebuilt 1815–16. Then the former RIDING SCHOOL, probably also by *Cundy Sen.*, remodelled as an indoor tennis court, 1891 (now gymnasium); stuccoed, with balcony with four Erechtheion-like caryatids guarding the SW entrance front. The Regency-style wrought-iron balcony high up on the sides and rear provided access for opening the upper windows. Of the rest of the GROUNDS, a shadow of their former glory, at least the basic layout remains. The main park feature is a large LAKE further E, probably formed from a chain of fish ponds in the early to mid C18, perhaps following advice from *William Shenstone*. It and the surrounding landscape were partly remodelled by *Capability Brown*, 1768; then by *Humphry Repton*, who produced one of his famous Red Books on Hewell Grange, in 1812.

Between the lake and present house, RUINS of the quadrangular house of 1711–12, probably by *William* or *Francis Smith*. Mostly demolished 1889 (after fire damage caused by a firework display), but three of its outer walls survive. It was eleven bays square, two-storeyed with balustraded parapet, mostly ashlar-faced. Giant Corinthian pilasters flanked the three-bay centres and pairs of outer bays. Some of these survive, also the large pedimented portico, NW, of four-by-two Corinthian columns, added by *Cundy Sen.* for the sixth Earl, 1815–16; said to have been removed from Cofton Hall (p. 236), then also a possession of the Windsor family.

* The garden designer *F. Inigo Thomas* was a pupil in *Garner*'s office at this date.

The parish is crossed by the finest stretch of the WORCESTER AND BIRMINGHAM CANAL: several brick BRIDGES, and a flight of thirty LOCKS (Nos. 29–58) taking the canal from the Severn valley to the Birmingham plateau. Constructed 1812–13, this is the longest such flight in Britain, a total climb of 217 ft (66 metres) in 2½ miles. Each narrow lock, with double-mitred bottom gates and single-leaf top gates, has a rise of some 7 ft (2.1 metres). Above Nos. 50–54, a large storage reservoir; above the well-preserved Nos. 55–57, the tall, brick, former ENGINE HOUSE. The top lock (No. 58), NW of the church, with two-storey cottage remodelled in the mid C19, has a deeper rise of about 12 ft (3.7 metres).* Then, New Wharf depot, with original sandstone WAREHOUSE end-on to the canal, just before the ashlar-faced portal to the 580-yd-long TARDEBIGGE TUNNEL. On the road above, the three-storey PLYMOUTH ARMS (now Plymouth House), late C18, plain brick. The Old Wharf, a little beyond the tunnel, also remains in use. Further on, the slightly longer SHORTWOOD TUNNEL.

In Dusthouse Lane ½ m. WNW, two good C17 farmhouses. THE DUSTHOUSE, much restored, has two high rendered gables and stone ground floor; central baffle entry, three diagonal brick chimneys in a row. STONEHOUSE FARM further w, mostly sandstone with mullioned windows, has a porch with close-studded jettied gable; earlier, square-panelled w cross-wing.

TARDEBIGGE FARM. 1⅝ m. SW. *See* p. 133.

At TUTNALL, ¾ m. NW, early C19 brick houses are dwarfed by the proud early C18 TUTNALL HALL: seven bays, two-and-a-half storeys, brick, of Warwickshire or Shropshire type; giant Tuscan stone pilasters at the angles and flanking the three-bay centre. The pilasters are forceful, but clumsy in the height of their bases and their bulgy friezes, their vigour drained by the loss (probably) of parapet and central pediment (cf. Cound Hall, Shropshire); sash windows with straight rubbed heads, panelled keystones touching the stone platbands or cornice above.

COBLEY, 1½ m. NNE, is more diffuse, with C17 timber-framed cottages at Cobley Hill, and mostly C19 farms along Stoney Lane. CATTESPOOL, the outstanding house, timber-framed, H-plan, *c.* 1640, is one of the few to retain the beautiful natural colours of its materials. Gabled s front with sandstone plinth, close-studded ground floor, square-panelled upper storeys with diagonal bracing. Parlour end, E, with square C19 oriel in its projecting gable; lateral stone stack with brick shafts. The projecting gable of the w service wing extends inwards over a lean-to porch to the cross-passage (divided from the hall by an inserted partition); lower (late C17?) sandstone extension. Inside, hall, parlour, and their chambers have fireplaces with

57

---

*This was the site, 1809–13, of an experimental vertical boat-lift designed by *John Woodhouse*, the then engineer. He succeeded *Thomas Cartwright*, and was replaced, 1811, by *William Crosley*. The complete canal opened December 1815.

stone lintels. Contemporary sandstone garden walls and an
early C18 gabled brick DOVECOTE, NE, complete the picture.

TENBURY WELLS

5060

Small market town close to the Shropshire and Herefordshire
boundaries, at the confluence of the Kyre Brook and Teme. The
first charter for a market and fair was granted to Roger de
Clifford in 1249; the town was a borough by 1455. Tenbury later
also served as a modest coaching town on one of the main roads
to North Wales. Then, in 1839–40, saline springs were discovered
close to The Court (demolished 1966), at the S end of Teme
Street, and a small brick bath house was erected. The present
pump rooms nearby, built 1862, are one of several good buildings by the Birmingham architect *James Cranston* (1821–71). For
a while the little town flourished as 'a spa for middling and
working classes, every convenience at the lowest possible price';
the railway arrived in the early 1860s, on the Shropshire bank of
the Teme. But the town soon sank back into its comfortable tran-
quility, the spa finally closing in 1939.

CHURCHES

ST MARY. Close to the Teme. Mostly by *Henry Woodyer*, 1864–5.
The medieval church was rebuilt 1772–6, after flood damage;
only its W tower, N wall and chancel survived. Woodyer's
restoration, costing over £3,000, swept the late C18 work away,
apart from the tower top with battlemented parapet and
obelisk pinnacles. Otherwise the tower is Late Norman, its twin
bell-openings probably re-set; central shafts with capitals with
flat leaves, S, rather more elaborate, W. Renewed W doorway.
The chancel retains C14 fabric, especially two SW windows.
Woodyer's work displays typically inventive Dec tracery, the S
porch the most distinctive feature. Four-bay nave arcades with
quatrefoil piers; slightly trefoiled chancel arch, good chancel
roof. N organ chamber added by *Henry Curzon*, 1891. Its W
opening, to the N aisle, is entirely in the Woodyer spirit: below,
cusped doorway and window separated by a marble shaft;
above, a three-light reticulated opening.

Woodyer's FURNISHINGS have been diluted; only his FONT
remains unaltered, its tall cover now in the town museum. In
1961–4 *Celestino Pancheri* inserted wooden panelling into the
REREDOS and modified the STALLS. – Low stone CHANCEL
SCREEN and PULPIT, Dec-style, by *Jones & Willis*, 1913–14. –
Full-width WEST GALLERY by *John Collins* of Leominster,
1843. – SCULPTURE. Part of an Anglo-Saxon cross-shaft,
perhaps late C9, with interlace and conventionalized serpents;
small recess perhaps for a relic. – Various ARCHITECTURAL
FRAGMENTS, probably C13, including a stoup. – STAINED
GLASS. E window and two chancel S by *Hardman*, 1864–5. –
Chancel SW c. 1883, no doubt *Ward & Hughes*. – S aisle E

MONUMENTS. *James Powell & Sons*, 1905. On the chancel N wall, an early C14 canopied recess, perhaps used as an Easter Sepulchre: ogee-cusped, pierced trefoil above, gable with pinnacles. The l. pinnacle has a hook-like attachment, perhaps to support the Lenten veil.* Within, a miniature limestone effigy of a late C13 knight, cross-legged, apparently holding his heart; probably a heart-burial. – Much larger sandstone effigy of a knight, *c.* 1300, now in a S aisle recess; legs also crossed (their lower parts missing), shield with Sturmy heraldry. – Thomas Acton †1546 and wife Mary †1564, erected by their daughter Joyce, 1581. Excellent alabaster effigies, richly detailed, tomb-chest with tapering Ionic pilasters; ovals in the panels with kneeling children or heraldry. Inscription tablet above. – William Godson †1822 and wife Margaret †1832, by *Bacon & Manning*, 1843. Large obelisk, with rays emanating from an angel in clouds; below, a woman distraught over a broken column. – Other tablets: one (chancel) with broken pediment, *c.* 1692; Thomas Wall †1814, by *J. Stephens*, with draped urn.

By the church gate, the FIRE ENGINE HOUSE, dated 1858; brick, with bargeboards.

ST MICHAEL, Old Wood, 1¾ m. SSW. *See* p. 586.

BAPTIST CHAPEL, Cross Street. 1854–5 by *G.B. Long* of Whitney (Herefs.). Brick, (former) round-arched windows, the front rendered with pedimental gable. Interior gutted, for commercial use.

(PRIMITIVE) METHODIST CHAPEL, Cross Street. 1893–4 by *W.W. Robinson* of Hereford; red brick, terracotta detailing. Long side to the street with paired lancets; iron railings with sunflowers. – At the rear, the former chapel, 1863, brick, yellow trim; lancets flank the doorway, bigger window above with wooden Y-tracery.

PERAMBULATION

Tenbury has few major buildings, but a stroll through its streets is most agreeable. The essential walk is from N to S, starting from the bridge across the Teme.

The BRIDGE, partly rebuilt and reinforced with concrete by *J.H. Garrett*, the County Surveyor, 1908, with nice cast-iron balustrade (cf. Stanford, pp. 601–2), has six segmental arches, with a change of direction at the centre. Three N arches, with broad heavy ribs on their undersides, basically medieval. The three S (and change of direction) are probably mostly by *Thomas Telford*, 1814.†

* Small rectangular opening above, presumably to a priest's chamber over the medieval vestry.

† Facing the bridge from the Shropshire bank, N, the former SWAN HOTEL, the most important in Tenbury. Partly Late Georgian, with big bow window; large brick addition, W, by *Henry Curzon*, 1866–7, with another bow. Third bow in between by *E.A. Day*, 1886.

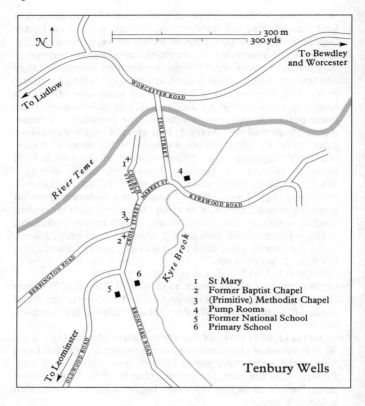

N

300 m
300 yds

To Bewdley
and Worcester

To Ludlow

WORCESTER ROAD

River Teme

TEME STREET

1 +

CHURCH STREET

MARKET ST.

4 ■

KYREWOOD ROAD

3 +

CROSS STREET

BERRINGTON ROAD

2 +

Kyre Brook

6 ■

5 ■

BROMYARD ROAD

OLDWOOD ROAD

To Leominster

1 St Mary
2 Former Baptist Chapel
3 (Primitive) Methodist Chapel
4 Pump Rooms
5 Former National School
6 Primary School

Tenbury Wells

TEME STREET begins, SE of the bridge, with the former UNION
WORKHOUSE, by *George Wilkinson* of Witney (Oxon), 1836–7.
Mildly Tudor, brick, stone dressings. Front range with pro-
jecting gabled porch either side of the central boardroom.
Behind were two courtyards; only the central range (kitchen
and dining room) survives. Converted for use by Tenbury
RDC, 1937. Opposite, the BRIDGE HOTEL, with heavy early
C20 half-timbering, and JUBILEE BUILDING, 1897, brick and
terracotta with timbered gables. Then LLOYDS BANK by
Henry Curzon, 1889 (later enlarged), rendered, with pilasters
with rosettes; further on, the SHIP INN, C17 timber-framed,
refronted with bay windows in the early C19.

The rest of Teme Street, the main shopping street, is mostly
modest brick, late C18–early C19, occasionally rendered, with
spasmodic C17 timber framing. Nos. 51–53, mid-C18 brick, are
followed by the REGAL CINEMA by *Ernest S. Roberts*, 1937.
Tall rendered and pilastered front, central entrance, flanked by
shops, with unaltered foyer with Art Deco pay box; raked auditorium with contemporary Mediterranean scenes painted by
George Legge, a rare survival. Opposite, E, side, one or two nice

shopfronts, No. 44 with fluted Corinthian columns. Also: Nos. 34–36, a brick early C19 pair, with round-arched doorways on reeded pilasters; the POST OFFICE by *W.W. Robinson*, 1894–5, red and yellow brick with terracotta embellishment; and COUNTY LIBRARY by *Hereford & Worcester County Council*, 1990, a neat, brick, hipped-roofed square with chamfered corners.

Back on the W side, the largest house, No. 23, early C18 brick, six bays and three storeys with hipped roof, has its S bay pierced by a vaulted timber passageway. This led to the CORN EXCHANGE, by *James Cranston*, 1858, now in industrial use; its canted end survives, together with most of its trefoiled, transomed windows.

In the final section of the E side, two late C19 buildings catch the eye: No. 18 for its elaborate stuccoed façade; the brick No. 12, built *c.* 1890 for Goodall & Sons, grocers, because of its substantial increase in scale.

At the end, behind the nondescript Crow Hotel (its large brick rear wing built as a boarding house, 1863), and facing the Kyre Brook, *Cranston*'s PUMP ROOMS of 1862, remarkably light-hearted; 'much like Gothicky or Chinesey fair stuff, without seriousness or taste', thought Pevsner. Skimpy half-timbering, canted roofs clad with galvanized iron plates and rolls held together with iron clips, all with fancy Gothic detail, a prefabricated scheme patented by Cranston himself. The solidest part is the big round-arched porch, of banded brick. Assembly Room, W, with pagoda-like tower for the pump, SW corner; ancillary rooms, E, originally with matching attendant's cottage, rebuilt in brick, 1889. Restored 1998–9 by the *Demaus Partnership*.

MARKET STREET, the SW continuation of Teme Street, begins with a large shop building, *c.* 1905, as tall as No. 12 Teme Street, then reverts to the usual scale, apart from the early C17 ROYAL OAK HOTEL, the best display of timber framing in Tenbury; flat façade with square panels decorated top to bottom with cusped concave-sided lozenges. A further outburst of late C19 confidence follows (Nos. 12–14, NW side). Nos. 16–17, facing Market Square, are C17, timber-framed.

The triangular MARKET SQUARE is now largely infilled by the early C19 TAVERN INN, painted brick, and by *Cranston*'s delightful MARKET HOUSE (Butter and Poultry Market), of 1858; oval in form, red brick with blue trim, continuous timber windows with delicate Dec tracery, only interrupted by opposing entrances. Tiled roof on brackets, with upper ventilation stage. The E side of Market Square is all early C19 stucco. On the W, behind attractive cast-iron railings, No. 4, with early C19 front with pedimented Doric doorcase, and Nos. 5–6, an impressive early C18 brick pair, eleven bays altogether. Both doorways are later, with Gothic clustered shafts, engaged at No. 5. On No. 6, they support a flat-roofed porch, leading to a fine panelled entrance hall with closed-string dog-leg staircase; turned balusters, moulded treads.

From Market Square, CHURCH STREET leads N to the church. The OLD RECTORY, E side, a large stuccoed villa by *Harvey Eginton*, 1843–4, has three wide bays to the street, its centre recessed with tripartite windows; narrower three-bay entrance front, S, with big porch on paired Ionic columns. Stained glass above the doorway depicts the earlier parsonage. Then C18 brick cottages all along the E side, with slight kink to negotiate the churchyard, terminated by an C18–C19 MALTHOUSE with attached hop kiln. Opposite, CHURCH HOUSE, neat early C18 brick, behind more nice railings.

Back to Market Square and S into CROSS STREET. Nos. 1–3, E side, have square-panelled framing, *c.* 1600, with first-floor overhang. The rest is all C18–C19 brick, a good long run, nicely varied in height. The mixed W side includes the Methodist chapel and, at the Berrington Road corner, the former Baptist chapel (p. 631).

In BERRINGTON ROAD, the former DRILL HALL (Police Station and Magistrates' Court from 1960) by *H. Percy Smith* of Worcester, 1912; attractive gabled centre, with large arch flanked by canted battlemented entrances, plain Neo-Georgian wings. Opposite, CLARENCE ROW, a good semi-detached pair of 1890, followed by late C19–early C20 houses or terraces, with earlier survivors (for example, some distance further on, No. 68, brick, dated 1681, with adjoining barn).

Back to CROSS STREET, W side, for the KING'S HEAD, square-panelled framing of *c.* 1600, with overhang on brackets. Then CORNWALL HOUSE, fine late C17 brick, with coved cornice and big shaped end gables; two storeys, seven narrow windows, the outer ones blind, the outer ground-floor pairs replaced by early C19 tripartite windows. Central doorway with hooded timber canopy on brackets, leading into the hall with its original staircase; parlour, S. Opposite, set back between Nos. 53 and 55, GOFF'S FREE SCHOOL (now the town museum), dated 1863; small, minimal Gothic, brick, yellow trim. Further on, across the vista, the late C16 PEMBROKE HOUSE INN; timber-framed, with high sandstone rubble plinth, and tall jettied first floor with oriels.

Finally into BROMYARD ROAD. The PRIMARY SCHOOL here is a sprawling C20 expansion of *J. T. Meredith*'s brick Infant School, 1895–6. Opposite, above the road, little altered, the former NATIONAL SCHOOL (now More House) by *James Cranston*, 1855. Brick, some diapering, good Dec tracery; schoolroom with attached house, plus, S, an additional classroom of 1892, no doubt by *Meredith*. High above is THE MOUNT, by *Cranston*, 1861, for the solicitor William Norris (much involved in the C19 development of Tenbury); brick, stone dressings including some notching, one straight gable, one steeply hipped. Its lodge, brick and half-timber, in the angle of Bromyard Road and Cross Street, looks later C19.

p. 84

OUTER TENBURY

KYREWOOD HOUSE, ⅔ m. ESE. Big, square, brick, said to be of
1721. Three storeys and three wide bays to the road; segment-
headed windows, central doorway with open pediment on
engaged Doric columns, low two-storey service wing. Garden
front, N, of five bays, with C19 porch. Fine staircase in an
almost circular hall, with glazed dome and Adamish plasterwork. – Across the road, a large C18–C19 range of brick malthouse and hop kilns. – To the W, extensive farm buildings, all
now housing, then a Victorian LODGE.

Further SE, the WHITE HOUSE, early C19 roughcast, with
hipped overhanging roof; and LOWER KYREWOOD, two large
C17 timber-framed and brick farms.

NEW COURT, ¾ m. SE, off Bromyard Road, a brick villa perhaps
of 1847. Three-bay S front with projecting centre and corner
pilasters; renewed ashlar doorway, big single-storey ashlar bow
to the W return.

SUTTON COURT and SUTTON HOUSE, about 2 m. SE. C18 brick
farmhouses, both L-plan, with earlier cores, timber framing
visible on the rear wing of the latter.

BERRINGTON COURT, 1½ m. WSW. Early C18 brick, five bays,
with segment-headed windows; hipped roof. Inside, C17 panelling from an earlier building, E, linked by a brick wall.

At LOWER BERRINGTON ⅓ m. further on, is LOWER TOWN
FARM, C16–C17, refronted in brick c. 1840; extensive, probably
contemporary, brick and rubble farm buildings. By BROOK
COTTAGE, ENE, a two-bay weatherboarded BARN, its NW bay
with opposed cart entries; inside, three full C14–C15 cruck
trusses, with collars.

THROCKMORTON

9040

CHURCH. A chapelry of Fladbury. Nave with narrow S aisle,
central tower, and chancel; all late C13–early C14. The best-
preserved windows are in the nave, the tall W and the NE, both
of three stepped, cusped lancet lights. Tower and chancel
windows were renewed in 1880 (probably by *Preedy*). Perp
upper stage of the tower, with battlements and pinnacles. S
aisle rebuilt 1894, but the fine medieval arcade survives; five
bays with quatrefoil piers and double-chamfered arches. The
middle arch, oddly, is much lower and narrower than the
others. It corresponds to the S doorway, also with two (continuous) chamfers; similar N doorway, blocked. Small heads re-
set in the arcade spandrels. The nave has a segmental plaster
roof, probably of 1833. Impressive tower space (ceiling raised
1880), again with double-chamfered arches; the unusual
capital blocks of the W arch must have supported the rood loft.
– Small round FONT, of indeterminate date. – Other modest
FITTINGS, mostly 1880.

The church stands in a field, showing clear signs of the
deserted medieval village. – NE, beyond the plain brick

SCHOOL of 1872, a quadrangular wet MOAT, which probably surrounded the Throckmortons' manor house.

THROCKMORTON COURT (formerly Court Farm), ¼ m. SSE. Splendid timber-framed hall and solar, *c.* 1500, L-plan, on a partly moated site. Three-bay hall range, plus wide screens passage (with gallery over, originally divided from the hall by a spere-truss); blocked four-centred doorway. There was in addition a service bay, presumably replaced by a rear extension to the solar wing in the early C17, when the hall part was probably also altered. Though now floored, it retains the almost complete central truss of its two-bay open hall, a collar-truss with the feet of the principals tenoned into post-cappings. These have the appearance of the ends of a sawn-off tie-beam, but their stopped chamfers prove them to be in their original form, a device more frequently found in Shropshire. A six-light timber-mullioned window, now blocked, filled the width of the second, upper bay. The third bay, floored from the beginning, was separated off by a closed tie-beam truss. The positions of the rails of the front wall frame clearly disclose the hall range's original arrangement.

The three-bay solar wing is structurally independent, and remarkable for the cusped timbers of its front and second trusses. In the (renewed) gable they display trefoils the right way up and upside down, with quatrefoil above. The similar central truss of the great chamber, with the extremely refined, shallow mouldings of its brattished tie-beam, plus the lack of structural discipline in the design of the trusses themselves, again points to the late date of *c.* 1500. Moulded stone fireplaces, probably contemporary; the present shaft, octagonal with battlemented top, rising from the big stone chimney-breast, may be a replica of the original, i.e. of a type preceding the great brick shafts of *c.* 1570 onwards.

Between house and road, a large BARN, probably early C17, mostly close-studded; arch-braced collar-and-tie-beam roof.

Most of the W part of the parish is disfigured by the huge, scruffy PERSHORE AIRFIELD, constructed in 1940 for the RAF.

TIBBERTON

ST PETER AD VINCULA. By *W.J. Hopkins*, 1867–8; nave and chancel of coursed Lias, timber S porch, W bell-turret. The nave has paired trefoiled lancets, with four even lancets, W, beneath a small rose; less regular chancel fenestration, with stepped E triplet, repeating that of the medieval church. Bell-turret with short broach spire on splayed weatherboarded base. Brick-faced interior, one of Hopkins's most characteristic, with bands of yellow and black decoration. Also typical the twin AMBOS, square with pierced quatrefoils, beneath the chancel arch. Other furnishings include the rounded stone PULPIT, with some inlaid decoration. – Plain octagonal FONT, probably C13. – C17 ALTAR TABLE, re-set 1902 by *C.F. Whitcombe*,

whose oak Perp REREDOS lies loose at the w end. – STAINED
GLASS. Early C19 trefoil-headed panel, chancel NE. –
MONUMENTS. Three tablets with urns, their differing details
typical of their dates: Ann Brooke †1787, Mary Smith †1804,
Philip Brooke †1817 (Grecian, by *J. Stephens*).

RECTORY FARMHOUSE, SE. Large, timber-framed, early C17,
mostly close-studded below, square-panelled above. Main
range, aligned NW–SE, of two tall storeys plus attic, consisting
of upper bay, narrow fireplace bay with cluster of four diagonal brick shafts on the ridge-line, and house-place bay. The
entrance, on the NE side of the fireplace structure, formerly
had a full-height porch; on the SW side, in the same bay, the
original staircase, only partly surviving. At the lower end, NW,
a two-bay service cross-wing containing the original kitchen.

Between farmhouse and church, a great, contemporary,
seven-bay, weatherboarded BARN; square-panelled framing,
tie- and collar-beam roof with wind-braces. Now converted to
housing. C18–C19 brick STABLES, also converted, surrounded
the fold.

GORDON'S FARM, N, also of hall-and-cross-wing plan: three-bay
hall range of C15 cruck construction, mostly faced in painted
C18 brick, cross-wing perhaps late C16, with C17 rear wing.

OLD VICARAGE, ⅛ m. E. By *Hopkins*, 1884, an interesting
example of a Gothic church architect trying to come to terms
with the Queen Anne style. Brick, tall octagonal chimneys,
canted full-height bay, square oriel on coving, hipped roof.

In the main part of the VILLAGE, ½ m. NNE, leading to the brick
bridge across the Worcester and Birmingham Canal, *Hopkins*'s
plain brick SCHOOL (with attached house) of 1872–4; much
enlarged 2001.

Outlying timber-framed farms include MOOR END FARM, ⅝ m.
SE: C17 hall and cross-wing, with lobby entry below a stack
with three diagonal brick shafts, facing a yard surrounded by
weatherboarded barns. More unusual, RAVENSHILL FARM,
½ m. SSE, late C17, entirely of brick, an early example for this
district: two parallel ranges, chimneys at the gable ends. The
twin-gabled E range was the original entrance side; W range
largely rebuilt in the C19, with segment-headed windows.
Inside, the dividing wall is of Lias rubble.

TRIMPLEY

Kidderminster Foreign

HOLY TRINITY. Vigorous Neo-Norman chapel of ease (to St
Mary, Kidderminster) by *Harvey Eginton*, 1844; coursed sandstone, ashlar dressings. Quite small: nave with W bellcote, 105
apsed chancel with N vestry. Ornate façade, the W doorway
with much chevron; five-bay arcading above, pierced for three
windows, then a rose with odd ropy detail based on St James's
Priory, Bristol. Scalloped nook-shafts at the nave corners, continuous zigzag string course rising as hoods to the side

windows. Further ornate decoration in the chancel and apse, including tripartite buttresses. Inside, tall elaborate chancel arch, and stone-vaulted chancel.

Eginton's Neo-Norman FURNISHINGS are equally bold: deep round FONT, arcaded PULPIT corbelled into the nave NE angle (approached from the vestry), splendid stone LECTERN, no doubt inspired by Crowle (p. 250). – WEST GALLERY on thin iron columns. – STAINED GLASS. In the apse, *c.* 1849. – Nave NE *c.* 1914 by *Pearce & Cutler*. – Nave SE, late Arts and Crafts by *Florence & Walter Camm*, 1952. – Another S lancet by *James Powell & Sons*, 1922. – MONUMENT. Gothic marble tablet to Joseph Chellingworth †1874, by *T. & W. Brown* of Kidderminster.

The churchyard, with fine views N towards Shropshire, may be the site of a chantry chapel founded by Sir John Attwood *c.* 1370.

MYNDHOLM, NE. A standard 1939 house (rendered brick, hipped roof), with striking Modernist NE addition of almost equal size, by *Michael Godwin*, *c.* 1968; shuttered concrete, now painted white, large picture windows on the projecting first floor. Open spiral staircase inside.

TRIMPLEY HOUSE, ⅓ m. SE. Large stuccoed villa, *c.* 1820–30. Three bays and storeys, channelled ground floor with plain Doric porch, hipped roof.

TRIMPLEY RESERVOIR, 1¼ m. W, was constructed by Birmingham Corporation, 1965–70, to process Severn water; landscaping by *Brenda Colvin*. Extended 1982.

Wide PIPELINE BRIDGE across the Severn, ½ m. SE, part of the 73-mile-long aqueduct from the Elan Valley (Powys) to Frankley (p. 320); planned 1891, opened 1904. One segmental decorative steel span of 150 ft (46 metres), rock-faced sandstone and brick abutments; engineers *James Mansergh & Sons*.

UPPER ARLEY

Also known as Arley on Severn; transferred from Staffordshire in 1895.

ST PETER. Of red sandstone, beautifully sited on a hillside looking across the Severn towards Shropshire. Of Norman origin, see the fabric of the nave S wall (with various blocked openings), but mostly early C14. Short nave with three-bay N arcade of quatrefoil piers with thin shafts in the diagonals, moulded capitals, and double-chamfered arches. Chancel arch with somewhat richer detail. Dec N aisle windows. Early C16 clerestory with two large windows each side, a cruder copy of St Mary, Kidderminster; earlier material incorporated within includes two C13 coffin lids, N side, and fragments of Norman ornament high up, SE corner. Contemporary roofs to nave and aisle, the latter extended E as a N chapel, with Tudor-arched three-light N window. Sturdy four-stage W tower probably post-medieval, perhaps late C16; wide, rather crude arch to the nave, diagonal w buttresses, plain parapet with higher SE stair-turret. Its windows (apart from the C19 reticulated w window) are C18, those of the bell-stage perhaps of 1753 (when six were installed). All extensively restored by *Lewis Sheppard*, 1885–6. He rebuilt and extended the chancel in Dec style (with two-bay arcade to the chapel), added the large S vestry, and inserted other Dec windows; S porch also partly rebuilt, retaining its blocky late C18 form. NW vestry added by *Andrew Shenton*, 2005–6.

FURNISHINGS also mostly 1885–6, apart from the carved round FONT of 1848, and survivors from a Gothick restoration, probably of 1791: ALTAR TABLE and COMMUNION RAILS (now N chapel), the latter in two halves projecting on a curve; tall COMMANDMENT PANELS (under the tower). – Doom WALL PAINTING above the chancel arch: large figures of Christ flanked by St Peter (?) and the Virgin; discovered 1884, now almost unrecognizable. – Beneath the chancel N arcade, some medieval TILES. – STAINED GLASS. E window by *Kempe*, 1887. – N chapel E, by *Charles Elliott* of London, 1886, a gaudy contrast. – N chapel N, medievalizing St Clement, amateur work by *Eliza Wilding*, 1925. – Early C19 heraldry in the N aisle traceries, probably by *Francis Eginton*. – MONUMENTS. Fine limestone effigy of a cross-legged knight, Balun *barry dancetty* heraldry on both his shield and ailettes. Traditionally said to represent Sir Walter de Balun (†1288); but the armour suggests *c*. 1340. C19 tomb-chest. – Sir Henry Lyttelton †1693. Large tablet with coved top supporting an urn; still life of skull, trumpet and torch in the draped 'predella'. – Henry Annesley †1818, plain Grecian, by *Chantrey*. – Viscount Valentia †1841, draped urn, by *Joseph Stephens*. – George, second Earl of Mountnorris †1844, is almost identical. – Capt. Robert Woodward †1915. Portrait roundel by *D. Stanton Wise*, 1917; inscription carved into the chancel wall below. – HATCHMENTS of Viscountess Valentia (†1856) and the second Earl.

ARLEY CASTLE, to the N, was a huge castellated pile after remodelling for the second and last Earl of Mountnorris by *R. & J. Varden*, 1843–4; demolished 1962–3, apart from the extreme SE corner. In 1967–8, the long and low ARLEY HOUSE, by *D.H. Blantern Radford* of Birmingham, was built on the S part of its site: reconstituted stone, some weatherboarding, continuous timber balconies, shallow hipped roof. The surviving fragment is chiefly a heavily moulded GATEWAY, asymmetrically flanked by octagonal turret and higher bartizaned lodging. The battlemented symmetrical LODGE to the enclosed gardens, some distance NW, also remains; brick, stone dressings, the wall to its N ending in a matching two-storey gazebo. Splendid park and arboretum, developed for the Woodward family after 1852, and again since 1965.

In the picturesque VILLAGE STREET, descending SE to the former cable ferry across the Severn, are THE GRANGE, early C18 brick, five bays with two top-heavy C19 dormers, and former VICARAGE, mostly mid-C19 decorative half-timbering.

Then ARLEY TOWER, stone, built 1842; small, square, battle-mented, with taller SE stair-turret. By the ferry ramps, the former VALENTIA ARMS HOTEL (now Hafren House), of three distinct parts: symmetrical early C19 house with bay windows, stuccoed C18 centre, former school, again of 1842, sandstone, L-plan, with Tudor openings. An inelegant FOOT-BRIDGE, latticed tubular steel on concrete piers, superseded the ferry in 1972. The street then curves back uphill, NE, to the large NATIONAL SCHOOL, 1859–60 by *F. Smalman Smith*; snecked stone, bargeboards, Dec detail, chunky diagonally set timber bellcote, plainer attached house.

ARLEY STATION, on the Severn Valley Railway (opened 1862), stands on the W bank of the Severn; plain well-preserved plat-form building with attached house, yellow brick, with round-arched windows. The line crosses the river ½ m. SSE by the elegant VICTORIA BRIDGE, dated 1861, designed by *John Fowler*, built by *Brassey & Co.*; segmental, of iron, with pierced spandrels (cast by the *Coalbrookdale Company*), on rock-faced sandstone abutments.

ARLEY COTTAGE, ⅓ m. E. C16, remodelled as a picturesque dower house in the mid C19; rendered, Gothick windows, steep gables with bargeboards.

BRITTLE'S FARM COTTAGES, 2⅓ m. NE. Pretty Tudor Gothic, *c.* 1840–50; purple brick, yellow trim, gabled, with latticed windows and tall chimneys. – On the Staffordshire boundary, ⅔ m. further NE, HIGHTREES FARMHOUSE, C15–C16 timber-framed, both square and close studding, infilled with brick; higher N cross-wing with jettied gable, one stud dated 1611. Extensive C20 restoration.

UPPER WICK see CROWN EAST AND RUSHWICK

UPTON SNODSBURY

ST KENELM. C13 nave, C14 chancel, C15 W tower, early C16 S aisle, all much restored by *Hopkins*, 1873–4. The tall sturdy Perp tower is a landmark, especially since its facing with white lime render in 2001 (by *Stainburn, Taylor*). Diagonal full-height buttresses, plain parapet, tall transomed W window; the W door and rounded SW steps to the stair-vice must be C18 additions. In the nave N wall, three small, widely spaced, E.E. lancets, the E one C19 re-creation. N and S chancel windows have enter-taining early C14 tracery, three stepped trefoiled lights with two cunningly introduced ogee curves; C19 Dec E window (recon-structed 1991–2). Late Perp S aisle with low-pitched roof, its Tudor-arched S doorway protected by Hopkins's open timber porch. Four-bay arcade with four-centred arches, curiously low, on octagonal piers; capitals decorated with shields and roses, and, E pier, a small barrel, probably the rebus of the Lyt-tleton family. Renewed clerestory with broad paired lancets above the apexes of the arches. Original aisle roof, with moulded beams and small carved heads. Lofty Perp tower arch, hollow-chamfered. No chancel arch.

FONT. Octagonal, Late Perp, the bowl with elaborate Signs of the Evangelists and other quatrefoil panels with hatted heads and Tudor rose. – SCREEN. Only the tracery of the cusped single-light divisions is Perp; the rest is of 1874–5 (like most other furnishings). – Oak PULPIT with linenfold panels, by *J. W. Pyment & Sons* of Campden, 1935. – Perp S DOOR, handsomely cross-battened. – WALL PAINTINGS nearby, with remains of Elizabethan texts. – STAINED GLASS. Fragments of early C14 borders, chancel N. – E and nave NE windows by *Francis W. Skeat*, 1968–9; also two, of 1977–80, S aisle. – Other nave lancets, 1912–19. – MONUMENT. The Rev. Henry Green †1805 and wife Penelope †1823; Grecian tablet by *T. Tyley* of Bristol.

CHURCHYARD CROSS. C15; step, chamfered base, fragment of the shaft. – The S porch is approached through arches of yew.

The VILLAGE retains a number of C17 timber-framed cottages and farms, especially SW of the church, around the brick SCHOOL of 1865. – The OLD VICARAGE, N, plain gabled brick, is mostly of 1880, probably by *Lewis Sheppard*.

HALL FARM, formerly Cowsden Hall, ½ m. SSE. Brick, early C19, large and ungainly, distinguished by a full-height bay with three storeys of canted Venetian windows with Gothick glazing; the uppermost reach into the roof. Stone GATEPIERS with big ball finials.

UPTON UPON SEVERN
8040

Upton is a charming little town. First mentioned in 897, it was a chapelry of Ripple until the C13. A timber bridge, which probably replaced the Severn ferry in the C15, was rebuilt in stone in 1605; floods caused this to be rebuilt in 1854 and again, on a new site, in 1940. A market and fair are first recorded in 1415, the borough in 1416–17. The greatest period of prosperity seems to have been the late C18–early C19, induced mostly by the river trade; there were five fairs a year by 1792. Much of the town's Georgian appearance survives, in many cases overlaid on a late medieval townscape with deep burgage plots and narrow frontages. A few timber-framed buildings remain visible, many more are hidden behind Georgian brickwork. These bricks came from an extensive works (now the site of the marina), established on the other side of the Severn in the late C17. The Victorian era brought a few new public buildings; apart from the new parish church, these commissions mostly fell to *George Row Clarke* (1829–1908), a local man with a London practice.

CHURCHES

OLD CHURCH, High Street. Only the W tower remains, red sandstone, with diagonal W buttresses, probably early C14; long, 81

Upton upon Severn, Old Church.
Drawing

slim two-light transomed bell-openings with Y-tracery, arch to
the nave of two continuous chamfers. Renewed Dec w window.
In 1769–70 *Anthony Keck* added the delightful pepper-pot top,
of the greatest possible townscape value to Upton. He capped
the tower with a moulded cornice with corner urns, and on
this set a timber octagonal stage, painted white, with keyed
bull's-eye panels and modillion cornice, supporting a copper-
covered cupola with a little open lantern above; it looks Germanic rather than English. The rest of the medieval church was
replaced in 1756–7 by *John Willoughby*, supervised by *Richard
Squire*: a classical five-bay nave with shortened chancel.
Blomfield at first intended to rebuild it again, but this plan was
abandoned for a new site; the C18 church was demolished in
1937. Fragments of walling remain, especially at the SW corner,
with even quoins and pedimented S doorway with Gibbs surround, much renewed *c.* 1982–3 as a heritage centre. – In the
churchyard, bronze BUST of Admiral Sir William Tennant
†1963, by *Leslie Punter*. – C15–C16 CROSS, with octagonal base
and tall shaft, re-erected here as a war memorial, 1921, after
serving (since the C18) as a sundial at Ham Court.

ST PETER AND ST PAUL, Old Street. 1877–9 by *Arthur W.
Blomfield*. It cost £12,934 5s. 8d., more than half contributed
by G.E. Martin of Ham Court. Large, imposing, of yellow
rock-faced Stanway stone with Bath dressings, Geometrical
Dec style. The slender NW tower, with its landmark broach
spire rising to 183 ft (56 metres), is a fine sight. Four-light W,
five-light E window. Five-bay nave arcades with tall octagonal
piers; paired two-light clerestory windows; good open nave
roof. Chancel roof painted by *Heaton, Butler & Bayne*. The
chancel N side had four open bays, now infilled, to a Lady

Chapel; on the S, the wide opening to the organ chamber and elaborate sedilia and piscina.

Blomfield's fittings include the carved octofoil FONT and Dec-style PULPIT. – Carved stone REREDOS, 1895; chancel floor TILING, 1897. – Iron and bronze ALTAR RAILS by *Nelson Dawson*, 1907.* – From the old church: ORGAN CASE 1812, reconstructed 1910; and small baluster FONT by *Richard Squire*, c. 1757, now in the N chapel (otherwise refitted 1913). – From St Mary Magdalene, Worcester, the wooden SCREEN, W end, typically intricate Perp by *C.F. Whitcombe*, 1907. – CORONA above the nave altar by *Anthony Robinson*, 1987: eight 'spirit figures' in forged mild steel. – STAINED GLASS. W window by *Christopher Whall*, 1905; top-quality Arts and Crafts. – Others by *Heaton, Butler & Bayne*: chancel E 1884, two S 1881; S aisle, 1899; N aisle, 1901–2. – MONUMENTS. Limestone effigy of a Boteler knight, probably c. 1320–40, now without his crossed legs; shield across his shoulder, l., both hands clutching his sword. – Alabaster war memorial tablet above, by *H.H. Martyn & Co.*, 1921. – Good C18–C19 tablets from the old church; also a mid-C17 wooden one, like a hatchment, to Henry Bromley and family. – Tablets with fine lettering to G.E. Martin †1905 and wife by *Eric Gill*, c. 1914.

GOOD SHEPHERD, The Hook, 2 m. W. A chapel of ease by *G.R. Clarke*, 1870. Coursed Charlbury rubble, Bath stone dressings. Nave and chancel under one roof, stone bellcote above the chancel arch. Early Dec style. E window with nicely detailed bar tracery, plate-traceried side windows. S porch with carving of the Good Shepherd. Scissor-braced roofs, good strong chancel arch. – Original FITTINGS include the stone carved PULPIT and FONT. – Stone and marble REREDOS by *Preedy*, 1871. – Oak LECTERN by *R. Hedley*, 1958. – Noteworthy STAINED GLASS, especially the fine Arts and Crafts W window by *Henry Payne*, c. 1906. – Nave NE by *Henry & Edward Payne*, 1938; rather more pallid window, to its W, by the *Camms*, 1950. – By *Heaton, Butler & Bayne*, the E, 1890, and nave SE, 1898.

Timber LYCHGATE, with sloping side roofs, by *John S. Lee*, 1909.

ST JOSEPH (R.C.), School Lane. By *Charles Hansom*, 1850. Simple, brick, Bath stone dressings; nave, S porch, chancel. Only the W end has Gothic detail; domestic side windows. The E bellcote carries twin flues for the small presbytery, E end. NE sacristy, c. 1908. Inside, W gallery, niches with figures of St Joseph and the Virgin flanking the chancel arch, and finely carved stone and marble ALTAR and REREDOS by *A.B. Wall* of Cheltenham, 1907.

BAPTIST CHAPEL, Old Street. Built 1734; extended one bay E, 1863–4. Brick, round-arched windows. W front rendered: arched windows flank the central doorway, with flat canopy on console brackets; two small gables above linked by a parapet. Pleasant interior: panelled W gallery partly original (altered

_____

* Also by him, of the same date, two small delicate brasses.

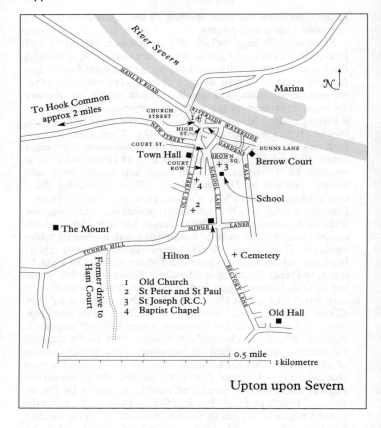

Upton upon Severn

1 Old Church
2 St Peter and St Paul
3 St Joseph (R.C.)
4 Baptist Chapel

0.5 mile

1 kilometre

1903); good set of pews, 1863–4. Vestry, SE, rebuilt and
enlarged as a hall, 2002–3.

CEMETERY, Rectory Road. A Lias ensemble by *G.R. Clarke*,
1865–6. Small LODGE with half-hipped roofs and bargeboards.
Distinctive Dec-style CHAPELS linked by a big square central
tower with tiled pyramid roof: Nonconformist chapel, N, set N-
S, apsed Anglican chapel, S, set W–E. The latter has an arch-
braced roof and good STAINED GLASS: E window probably
Lavers & Barraud, *c.* 1866; two S by *Heaton, Butler & Bayne*,
c. 1870–5. – *Clarke* is buried beneath a small stone cross, SE.

PERAMBULATION

A walk through Upton is most rewarding. We start by the old
church, then take in the riverside, before walking S along the main
spine (High Street, Old Street), with short detours W and E.

CHURCH STREET runs along the S side of the churchyard. At its
W end, a fine brick terrace (Nos. 2–6), *c.* 1720–30, of even

height, yet partly two-storeyed, partly two-and-a-half; pedimented wooden door hoods, parapet with vases. The upper windows of the two-storey part are dummies, as are the attic windows of the rest. Hidden behind, remains of an important late C16 timber-framed building, the town house of the Bromley family of Ham Court, with central hall and separately roofed w range, their roof-lines still visible. No. 2 has a fine C18 interior: hall with squeezed-in staircase and moulded plaster ceiling; two large reception rooms, the lower with contemporary panelling, the upper made grander in the early C19, with two longer windows in its w return wall. Then a plainer late C18 terrace (Nos. 8–14), and good C16–C17 timber-framed house (Nos. 16–18, now Tudor House Museum); close-studded main range, big cross-gabled w wing, through passage between. Restored by *Henry Gorst*, 1975.

w of the church tower, by a white-painted late C18 cottage range, a lane leads down to the river. Alongside, the new BRIDGE by *B.C. Hammond*, County Surveyor, 1938–40: a good steel cantilever design, with very shallow segmental main arch of 200-ft (62-metre) span, rather too solid for this position. The former bridge stood downstream, at the lower end of High Street, which developed s from it.

RIVERSIDE contains early C19 inns and small warehouses, the best of which retains its gabled hoist. The SWAN INN, further E, is a mix of both: C18 house facing E; C17–C18 warehouses. Riverside then becomes WATERSIDE, with two fine Early Georgian houses, of five bays and three storeys (plus basement) with segment-headed windows. WATERSIDE HOUSE, probably of *c.* 1740, has quoins and excellent stone pedimented doorway with Gibbs surround, approached up steps. THE MALTHOUSE, set further back, said to be 1712, has a wide recessed centre with Venetian doorway, Venetian window above, and arched top-floor window. The so-called KING'S STABLE, NE, good mid-C17 brick, has a big shaped end gable above blind arcading. Then smaller later Georgian houses, facing the trees along the river bank.

A detour along the footpath beside The Malthouse leads past a C16–C17 timber-framed house to the NE angle of GARDENS WALK. Here, the best C20 group in Upton, BERROW COURT, retirement houses and flats by the *Sidell Gibson Partnership*, 1980–1; project architect *Giles Downes*. Rendered, tile-hung upper floors, set round three sides of a grassed court.

Retracing our steps, we can return to High Street by DUNN'S LANE, a reminder of the lower end of Upton society. No. 15 is dated 1784. At the centre of the brick front of Nos. 11–12, a C17 timber-framed passage, Lapstone Alley, leads to closely packed C18 cottages, the epicentre of a cholera outbreak in 1832.

HIGH STREET begins with more inns, either side of Dunn's Lane: the STAR, stuccoed, *c.* 1830–40, and the timber-framed and gabled ANCHOR, dated 1601. Its lower N part, hall and cross-wing plan, could be of this date; the taller s part (No. 7) looks C19. Beyond London Lane, a good group: No. 9, with jettied attic storey; No. 11, narrow C18 brick; No. 13, three storeys and three gables of close-studded framing, the date 1603 not original but fitting the evidence. The WHITE LION HOTEL, three bays and storeys, is stuccoed, with mostly tripartite windows; giant fluted pilasters, parapet, deep Doric porch with large lion above. A canted-back wing has the same treatment, plus Venetian window. This all looks c. 1800.

Opposite, w, brick façades: Nos. 2–8, late C18, with bow windows;* No. 12, mid-C18, only one bay, with Venetian window and quoins; No. 18 (Lloyds Bank), early C19, three bays and storeys of tripartite windows with fluted keystones, and three shallow ground-floor bay windows. Beyond, with canted entrance to the New Street corner, an HSBC bank of 1923 (probably by *T.B. Whinney*), also brick.

This main crossroads of the centre is marked by three other good buildings. In High Street, opposite HSBC, the mid-C18 TALBOT HEAD, quite small, two-storey, with projecting pedimented centre with Venetian window; Venetian doorway altered c. 1910. Two long timber-framed rear wings. The start of Old Street is flanked, NW, by Nos. 1–3 New Street, early C18, later stuccoed, with wooden dentil cornice and hipped roof; and, NE, by No. 1 Old Street, perhaps C17, also stuccoed, with Tudorish hoodmoulds, c. 1840.

First W into NEW STREET, relatively short but spacious: mostly C18 houses, the Talbot Head making a fine *point de vue* to the E. On the S side, No. 7 is timber-framed, No. 9, once The Bell inn, C17, has renewed plaster decoration dated 1668. No. 11, substantial late C18, is rather bleak: three storeys with two two-storey canted bays, lower wings, the W with early C19 Tuscan porch leading into a plaster-vaulted passage. Opposite, the stuccoed No. 8, with fine shallow bow-windowed shopfront, c. 1800, flanked by doorways with fluted pilasters; and Nos. 18–20, each with canted bays flanking open-pedimented doorways, all tied together by rusticated quoins and deep parapet with ball finials. The wider No. 18 clearly fronts an earlier house. Beyond, the WESLEYAN CHAPEL dated 1891, round-arched windows but pierced bargeboards; now a garage. On the S side, COLLINGHURST HOUSE, three-storey flats by *T.R. Bateman* c. 1972, and the nicely lettered FIRE ENGINE HOUSE by *Frank Lamb*, 1936, with small practice tower.

Back to the crossroads and across into COURT STREET, where the street pattern is more intricate. Nos. 1–11, of C17 square-panelled framing, was the parish workhouse from 1763.† The OLD COURT HOUSE ahead, of 1863, still has Georgian brick forms, adapted to an awkward triangular site. To its W, COURT ROW, a decided backwater, with remains of the original METHODIST CHAPEL, c. 1770, w, and the stuccoed ROYAL

---

* Another, with original glazing, is displayed in the Heritage Centre.
† The replacement UNION WORKHOUSE by *Sampson Kempthorne*, 1836, SE of the town, was demolished in 1980.

OAK INN, S. Larger houses E and SE of the Old Court House: No. 2 Brown Square, tall three-bay stuccoed, *c.* 1830, with plain giant pilasters; No. 6 School Lane, Tudor, *c.* 1840, also stuccoed. In SCHOOL LANE, St Joseph (R.C., p. 643), and the (NATIONAL) SCHOOL by *G.R. Clarke*, 1858; two-storeyed, gabled brick, rough stone quoins, Dec windows; later additions. Further on, the POLICE STATION, a severe-looking house of *c.* 1800, and low pale-brick LIBRARY, built as its magistrates' court *c.* 1965.

Back to the crossroads and S down OLD STREET, the continuation of High Street. Mostly C18–early C19 brick frontages here, occasionally stuccoed; they mostly follow the widths of the medieval burgage plots, many hiding timber-framed structures. Few call for individual comment. On the W side, slightly set back, the former TOWN HALL, built 1832. Stuccoed, five bays, with four Greek Doric cast-iron columns *in antis* (originally open for a market, with brick-arched cellars and gaol beneath); Doric pilasters above (fronting the Petty Sessions courtroom). Parapet with slightly raised centre. Converted to a War Memorial Hall by *H. Rowe & Son*, 1920–1. No. 16, the Post Office, stuccoed early C19, has Tudor hoodmoulds but a fine reeded and incised doorcase. Opposite, Nos. 11–13, late C18, are the largest brick pair; No. 17 has an early C19 bowed shopfront; Nos. 35–37 are mid-C18 with keystones. Severe late C18 houses flank the narrow entrance to the Baptist chapel (p. 643), the N one (No. 45) its former manse. Then early C17 timber framing appears, before the SOCIAL CLUB, *c.* 1900. At the end, hidden behind St Peter and St Paul (p. 642), the RECTORY, formerly Elmsleigh House, dated 1787 on its S return, with the builder's name, *Ralph Sheward*. Three bays and storeys; two two-storey canted bay windows, lunette windows above. Central doorway with open pediment on console brackets, eared window above with sunflower keystone. Behind the S bay window, surprisingly, is the spacious staircase hall. Adapted as the rectory by *Lewis Sheppard*, 1900, who rebuilt the garden front, E.

A few other houses to note further S, amongst C20 development, mostly post-war Upton RDC housing by *Pemberton & Bateman*.

First, in Minge Lane, HILTON, characterful brick, *c.* 1790, possibly by *Anthony Keck*. Three bays, two-and-a-half storeys, with two-storey bays with iron tent-canopy tops flanking the fine broad-arched doorway with fanlight. This is hidden by a later porch of elaborate wrought iron, with much scrollwork and balcony above; good cast-iron railings and gates. From here RECTORY LANE leads, past the cemetery (p. 644), to SOLEY'S ORCHARD, C16–C17 timber-framed with diagonal brick stacks, once larger. Then on to OLD HALL, the rectory until 1896; big, square, painted brick, with hipped roof, mostly 1826 by *Henry Knight* of Kingston upon Thames, following a design by *Edward Lucy*; later C19 alterations. Coachhouse, S, mostly of 1826.

OUTER UPTON

THE MOUNT, ½ m. SW, above Tunnel Hill, is especially prominent. Probably *c.* 1760–70, white-painted, three bays, with
outer Venetian windows on its lower two floors. On the S side
of Tunnel Hill stands a low brick Tudor LODGE of *c.* 1840, to
HAM COURT, 1 m. further S, built for John Martin by *Anthony
Keck*, 1770–2; demolished 1929. Here remain the large walled
garden and other poignant reminders of the lost seigneurial
landscape: a couple of C17 timber-framed cottages, and the
larger late C16 GLEBE HOUSE, W of the site of the mansion.
Close-studded S front and W return, with renewed herringbone
brick infill; tall diagonal brick chimneys; three rear gables, N,
the outer two extended in C17 brick. C16 stone fireplaces
inside.
Upton parish stretches more than two miles W from the Severn
(cf. Good Shepherd, The Hook, p. 643), with several attractive
Georgian brick farmhouses. YEWLEIGH LODGE, ⅞ m. SW, a
sturdy mid-C18 example, has a fine wooden doorcase with
Corinthian columns, Gothick fanlight, and broken pediment.
From here Yewleigh Lane leads W to DUCKSWICH HOUSE,
large, brick, latter-day Lutyens, by *Curtis Green, Son & Lloyd*,
1953; wide mullioned-and-transomed windows, big stone bows
flanking the broad blocky porch, hipped roof.

9060

UPTON WARREN

ST MICHAEL. The only medieval part is the S tower. Its ground
stage is clearly C14, with Dec S and E windows; fine N arch to
the nave with two continuous quadrant mouldings. The top
stage is a puzzle, with bell-openings of two roll-moulded trefoiled lights and trefoil above in plate tracery; apparently mid-
C13, but surely not of fine enough quality to merit re-setting.
Battlements and recessed spire again seem C14. The rest is all
C18, the nave, with totally bare W wall and side windows with
Y-tracery, of 1798. A rebuilding of the chancel took place in
1724, presumably represented by the masonry of its lower
part;* the finer ashlar above seems contemporary with the
nave. Broad E lancet; blocked square-headed side windows.
Raw N organ chamber, 1923. Inside, plain nave and chancel
ceilings, and simple pointed chancel arch. – Some 1798 fittings
remain, notably the WEST GALLERY, dado PANELLING, and
(probably) thin Perp-style FONT (apparently *Coade* stone). –
PEWS of 1890. – STAINED GLASS. By *W.G. Taylor* (late *O'Connor*), 1880. 'The design', according to *The Guardian*, 'is unique,
having been framed by the donor [Rev. F.J.B. Hooper] from
the frontispiece of his work *The Revelation Expounded*.' Pevsner
thought it 'uncommonly horrible'. – MONUMENTS. Marble

---

* The stone with date 1664 in the S wall perhaps belongs to a former monument.

tablet recording the benefaction of John Sanders, 1670; others, chancel, to former rectors.

CHURCHYARD. Many attractive C17–C18 headstones, NW, of thick sandstone; also chest tombs, with a fine Grecian one to Mary Deakin †1837.

BADGE COURT, 2 m. NW. *See* p. 282.

WARNDON
Worcester

Though now within the city boundary, Warndon, on its formerly moated knoll, remains distinct enough to warrant separate consideration. The view NE from the churchyard is of the M5 motorway junction and its bevy of business parks.

ST NICHOLAS. Nave and chancel in one, basically C12, remodelled in the C15. Earlier foundations, possibly Saxon, were discovered during extensive restoration 1991–2 by *James Snell*, who coated the exterior in white render. Timber-framed W tower with saddleback roof (cf. Dormston and Pirton) of *c.* 1500, three stages, N and S walls all close-studded, as is the W wall's lowest stage; above this, larger panels with curved braces (restored 1909). Late Norman N and S doorways with plain continuous rolls. The N porch, also partly timber, with entrance arch formed by two oak slabs, could be C15, like the two-light, straight-headed side windows with pretty Perp tracery. E window of three stepped lancets under a single arch, a late C13 form, though the mouldings again suggest a C15 date; beneath it, a Norman opening, of uncertain function. Exceptionally for Worcestershire, the interior survives in its pre-Victorian state; rendered walls and ceiled roof, probably remodelled in the C18, remains of a lath-and-plaster tympanum between nave and chancel. At the W end, part of the moulded frame of a C15 window, superseded by the tower.

FONT. C15; heptagonal, low, moulded top and base; C17–C18 cover. – WALL PAINTING. A fragment, with two or three layers, NW end. – BOX PEWS. Early C19, of varying shapes and sizes. Those in the nave encase C15–C16 pews of which the bench ends, some with poppyheads, remain visible; also, S side, the lower part of the ROOD SCREEN. – Early C19 DECALOGUE. – COMMUNION RAIL. Three-sided, with tall close-set balusters; early C17. – On the sanctuary floor, many C14–C15 Malvern TILES. – Low, square STOVE, cast iron, wholly Gothic; probably *c.* 1840. – STAINED GLASS. C15 fragments in the N and S window heads. – In the E window, a beautiful Virgin and Child, *c.* 1330–40, almost identical to but better preserved than that at Fladbury. Good C14 pieces above, an Annunciation, and below, SS Peter and St Paul; also a C15 St Andrew. – CHURCHYARD CROSS, N. Broken octagonal shaft; iron cross-head of 1980.

WARNDON COURT, W. Early C17 brick, perhaps the earliest brick-built farmhouse in the county. Two storeys plus attics, on a Lias plinth, with stone-coped gable-ends; several three-light stone-mullioned windows with moulded lintels, mostly restored by *Nick Joyce c.* 1997. T-shaped plan: two-storey hall range, with W cross-wing. The latter has its own central brick chimney, with four stumpy diagonal stacks emerging above the roof ridge. Another chimney behind the hall part, with three diagonal stacks. Later, lower rear addition. Inside, ceilings with very large oak beams.

Mid-C18 brick STABLES, NE, adjoining the churchyard. Weather-boarded BARNS, *c.* 1700, to NW and SE, supplemented by late C20 replicas.

The OLD PARSONAGE, ⅛ m. E, beyond Parsonage Way, C16–C17, has mostly close studding above square panels. Small SW solar wing; later NE service wing. Imported C17 panelling inside.

WEBHEATH *see* REDDITCH

WELLAND

ST JAMES. By *John West Hugall* of Oxford, 1873–5.* Dour exterior; reddish Malvern rubble laid crazy-paving fashion, Bath stone dressings, Whitland Abbey slates; early C14 style. Aisled nave with SW porch tower with uninspired spire, shingled and broached. Two oddities of the plan are the wide curved passage between S aisle and chancel, and vaulted vestry beneath the latter. Tall four-bay arcades on round piers of banded buff and blue stone; bold early Gothic capitals, probably carved by *Joshua Wall* of Stroud (*Wall & Hook* were the builders). Yet higher chancel arch; lofty arch-braced roofs. – Mostly original FURNISHINGS, the round FONT with deeply cut foliage; good stone, marble and mosaic REREDOS. – STAINED GLASS. By *Hardman* the E window, 1875, and sanctuary N and S, 1877–8. – S aisle, two by *Kempe*: SE 1895; SW 1877, re-set. – N aisle NE by *Henry & Edward Payne*, 1939. – MONUMENTS. Two tablets from the previous church (*see* below): Rev. Thomas Evans †1671, elaborate, with scrolls and broken segmental pediment with heraldry; Edmund Taylor †1802, plain, with urn.

To the W, a good VILLAGE HALL by *McConaghy Architects*, 1992; brown and yellow brick, low hipped roof. Then the stone SCHOOL, 1876, no doubt by *Hugall*, gabled with sharp bellcote, shoulder-arched windows; HOUSE, originally detached, joined by an ugly C20 link.

Hugall's VICARAGE, further WNW, was executed by *W.J. Willcox* of Bath, 1879–80; also gabled, of crazy-paving stone; spacious stair hall with nicely tiled fireplace. Large C20 nursing-home additions.

* Designs by him of 1864–71 were little different, though the upper half of the tower was to be half-timbered.

WOODSIDE FARM, ½ m. NE. C16–C17, timber-framed, with two cross-wings with unequal gables (a lower third added in the C20). The l. wing has close studding, the r. square panelling; both have lateral chimneys.

BROOKEND HOUSE, ½ m. E. Brick, mid-to-late C18, three bays with ground-floor shutters; pedimented Doric doorcase, hipped roof. Rear range dated 1862.

The medieval CHURCH (rebuilt 1672) stood on an elevated site, 1⅛ m. ESE. Its graveyard remains, with crumbling memorials; one good C18 one has paired fluted Doric corner columns and steep pyramidal cap.

The OLD VICARAGE, N, is mostly late C18 brick, with two-storey canted bays flanking the pedimented S doorway; early C17 close-studded cross-wing, W.

The timber-framed WELLAND COURT, S, was completely cased in brick c. 1700. Fine symmetrical W front, c. 1750, 2+1+2 bays, the quoined centre projecting beneath a pediment; stone Venetian window above stone doorway with pediment on brackets. Deep parapet with ball finials.

MARLBANK FARM, ½ m. W. Early C18 brick, seven irregular bays, good keystones, hipped roof; central attic dormer treated as a pediment.

At UPPER WELLAND, 1⅛ m. WNW, two brick chapels of 1886. The WESLEYAN CHAPEL (builders *Thomas Chadney & Son*) has ample yellow and blue trim; round-arched openings on the entrance front, pointed side windows. The GOOD SHEPHERD, an Anglican mission, now a house, carries an E bellcote.

WEST MALVERN
7040

The only Worcestershire parish W of the Malvern Hills, on the steep slopes of North Hill and the Worcestershire Beacon; spectacular views W across Herefordshire.

ST JAMES. 1870–1 by *G.E. Street*; rock-faced, quite large, with aisles and S transeptal tower with transverse saddleback roof (it replaced an E.E.-style church by *Eginton*, 1842–3, which stood to its S). E.E. to Geometrical style, E window with five stepped lancets, always an elevating effect. Interior of snecked Cradley stone; wide two-bay nave arcades, plus narrower bay for the pseudo-transepts. Low W baptistery, with choir vestry beneath, added by *Archibald Gillespie*, 1925–6. N chapel refitted by *W.H. Randoll Blacking*, 1930. – Of Street's fittings, the typical round FONT, PEWS, and STALLS remain. – Brass and wrought-iron COMMUNION RAIL, by *G.G. Scott*, c. 1855, for the High Altar at Westminster Abbey; given by the Abbey, patrons of the living, 1870, central gates added 1938. – Stone, marble and tiled REREDOS by *Harry Hems & Sons*, 1909–12 (altered 1926). – Oak PULPIT with low attached SCREEN, by *L.W. Barnard & Partners*, 1947. – STAINED GLASS. Nearly all by *Hardman*: chancel 1871–2, S transept 1878, otherwise mostly

1881–2. – S aisle SW by *Wailes*, 1871. – Small W trefoil by *Florence & Walter Camm*, 1926.

In the CHURCHYARD, S, the plain 1842–3 FONT; octagonal, with quatrefoil stem. – WAR MEMORIAL. A replica by *A.G. Lewis*, 1921, of the Malvern Priory churchyard cross. – Beyond, the OLD VICARAGE, *c.* 1846, irregular Late Georgian.

Uphill, E, the (NATIONAL) SCHOOL, mostly by *Perkins*, 1872–3, reusing material from Eginton's church. Altered 1962.

ST JAMES'S HOUSE, NW; St James's Girls School since 1902. 'Recently erected' in 1861, spectacularly enlarged to mansion scale 1890–1, at a cost of £100,000, for Lucy, Dowager Lady Howard de Walden.* Three-storeyed above a basement, in a subdued Italianate; rock-faced, ashlar trim, canted bays, windows with fluted pilasters or blocked architraves, balustraded parapet. Equally restrained entrance hall, with top-lit timber staircase behind a modest timber screen. The garden front, W, was made more showy by a two-storey round-arched Doric cloister, leading N, then W to a matching polygonal gazebo. This, now a chapel, has stained glass from the Abbey School, Malvern Wells (p. 487): one by *Hugh Easton*, 1956, two of *c.* 1920. The cloister was mostly replaced by a large contextual wing by *Constantine & Vernon*, 1934–5. Later additions also in keeping.

Splendid late C19 terraces overlook the extensive grounds, with fine specimen trees. At their SW corner a large MODEL FARM, *c.* 1900, all close-studded, a style repeated by other estate buildings in the village.

Extensive C19 STABLING, of crazy-paving stone with ashlar dressings, on the E side of West Malvern Road, also belongs to the school (accessible by a tunnel of 1930); higher six-bay centre, with segment-headed windows and diagonally set turret. Nearby C20 school additions, e.g. Anstruther Hall, 1961–2, of no particular merit.

Further N, beyond the converted Westminster Arms Hotel, the former ST EDWARD'S ORPHANAGE by *F.W. Hunt*, 1881, has also been incorporated. Stone, brick trim, tile-hung upper floors and gables, showing an awareness of Norman Shaw's Old English style surprisingly rare in the Malvern district. Matching N wing by *A. Hill Parker*, 1911, linked by a bridge to the former Clergy House of Rest of 1878. Stone and brick chapel behind, by *Hunt*, 1880: W bellcote above an octofoil rose, E apse, two-bay S arcade; early C20 stained glass.

Few West Malvern houses compare with the C19 villas of Great Malvern. The best is probably MAYNARD HOUSE, Croft Bank, by *Henry Crisp* of Bristol for the Rev. Canon J.H. Pinder, *c.* 1860; crazy-paving granite, big bargeboarded gables projecting on brackets. In PARK ROAD, a flat-roofed house, KANDERSTEG, by *Yeates & Jones*, 1935; rendered, with band courses.

---

* Sister of the fifth Duke of Portland, of Welbeck Abbey (Notts.); building mania was clearly a family passion.

HILLSIDE, above the B4232 further S, stone, with wide windows trimmed in red and yellow brick, was built as a school by *F.W. Hunt*, 1870. Nearby, large houses take advantage of the wide views, especially in HARCOURT ROAD. At its start TANNACHIE, late C19 rock-faced, with sharp gables and brick chimneys, and VERNON LODGE, *c.* 1900, rock-faced below, half-timbering above. Their unremarkable C20 equivalents line BROCKHILL ROAD further S, an unmetalled through-route to Colwall railway station (in Herefordshire), which begins with a pink-rendered, gabled house by *A. Troyte Griffith*, 1924.

WESTWOOD HOUSE   8060

Westwood, founded in the mid C12 as a priory for monks and nuns according to the rule of Fontevrault, later became a normal Benedictine nunnery, its chapel serving as the parish church. After the Dissolution it came to Sir John Pakington of Hampton Lovett (q.v.). His great nephew, also Sir John Pakington (1548–1625), nicknamed Lusty, a favourite of Queen Elizabeth, began a hunting lodge here *c.* 1612; the contract for its carpenters' work, dated October 1612, survives.* A second campaign which probably followed almost immediately added four large diagonal wings; these were presumably completed before Sir John died.

EXTERIOR. The house, brick with red sandstone dressings, lies 68 on an eminence in extensive grounds. The centre, *c.* 1612–17, more or less square in plan, is highly varied in outline, with a passion for full-height canted bay windows, mullioned-and-transomed. The height (indeed the whole scale) is exceptional for a hunting lodge: three storeys to the front, four storeys to the back. The hall fills the façade (SE); behind it were service rooms and staircase; at the rear, kitchen and probably a parlour. All this neatly fitted into the basic square. Such compact plans are rare in Elizabethan and Jacobean architecture; but cf. such hunting lodges as Sherborne, Cranborne and Lulworth (all in Dorset). It is unclear whether all the decoration of this centre block is of *c.* 1612–17, or whether some was added between then and *c.* 1625, after the decision to add the wings was made. Its shaped gables and bold parapets with the Pakingtons' mullets and gerbes (i.e. stars and sheaves) could fit either date. The wings certainly take up such motifs without hesitation.

The wings are in fact the strangest feature of the house, clearly an addition, and attached diagonally to the angles of the compact central block. Were they perhaps enlargements of former (perhaps only intended) angle turrets? The joining was

---

*I am most grateful to Andor Gomme for information about this document (discovered by Sir Howard Colvin), also for much other help with Westwood; cf. his paper in *Architectural History* 44, 2001, and another, forthcoming.

done so well that no change of plan, or break of style, is noticed; the bricks are still laid in English bond. Traditionally, following Nash's statement that they were added after the Civil War when the house at Hampton Lovett was burnt down, they have been dated *c.* 1660–70, i.e. the work of Sir John Pakington III, grandson of the first builder; but this date now only seems valid for work on much of the interior (*see* below). The only feature that distinguishes the wings stylistically from the earlier work is that there is more wall and less window. The sandstone used for dressings is rather redder, and there is much adjustment to the levels of the broad bandcourses.

Another quandary concerns the date of the central porch. This, tripartite, with attached fluted Corinthian columns, and arches arranged à la Arch of Constantine, is probably one of the first British attempts at a serious copy of a Roman arch. Over the side arches are strapwork cartouches, over the middle one, Zeus astride an eagle (now headless). Doorway behind flanked by paired pilasters with raised diamond decoration. Above the porch is a square panel with mantled shield within a circular garland. This all seems more likely to be closer to *c.* 1625 than *c.* 1612.

The pavilion roofs at the ends of the wings, of concave-convex-concave outline, are not original; Kip's engraving in *Britannia Illustrata* (1714) shows plain, steep pyramid roofs. The present fantastic, entirely successful roofs are an alteration of *c.* 1924 by *Sir Reginald Blomfield* for the second Lord Doverdale. The inner sides of each wing have large projecting chimney-breasts. The low two-storey kitchen block between the rear wings, also the ground-floor bay on the end of the N wing, belong to an extensive restoration of *c.* 1840–6, by *Philip Hardwick*, assisted by his son, *P.C. Hardwick*.

The INTERIOR, now subdivided, presents further problems. The porch leads into the GREAT HALL, occupying the whole of this part of the basic square, i.e. about two-fifths of it. It is now entered in its middle, if original an early variation from the traditional entry arrangement. The hall's Jacobean-style plasterwork and other decoration is by the Hardwicks. Behind lies the impressive STAIRCASE, probably of *c.* 1660–70 (when the small outer projection on the NE side was also made). It has an exceptional plan: a short flight runs from the rear of the hall, then turns back 180 degrees to run across the full width of the house, in two flights separated by a landing; these flights are in line, not broken round an angle. The effect, on a limited scale, is comparable to that at Althorp (Northants.). The newel posts are Corinthian columns crowned by large balls, rising much higher that the balustrade. The thick, still vertically symmetrical balusters could be of *c.* 1612–17; the door surrounds with finely carved swan-neck pediments are certainly *c.* 1670. The ceiling is C19, and it must be questioned how much else was due to the Hardwicks. However the original gallery (now subdivided), across the full width of the house above the staircase, has similar column newels, though simpler and Doric.

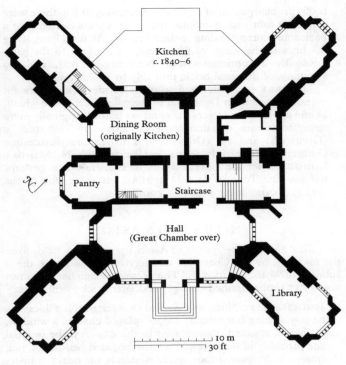

Kitchen
c. 1840–6

Dining Room
(originally Kitchen)

Pantry

Staircase

Hall
(Great Chamber over)

Library

10 m
30 ft

Westwood House.
Plan

The GREAT CHAMBER above the hall, probably always the most spectacular room, has four canted bay windows, two SE, one each to SW and NE. Gorgeous wooden Jacobean chimneypiece, with columns (Corinthian above Ionic), thick vine-trail carving, and dragon frieze. The broad top frieze running all round the room, of broad strapwork with faces and small figures, must be contemporary (or very competent C19 imitation). But the ceiling, equally gorgeous, is certainly of c. 1670 70 or soon after, eminently characteristic of that date in its composition of separate thickly moulded panels as well as in the use of wreaths. Coving with equally lush carving. Contemporary plasterwork in the wings.

OUTBUILDINGS. The GATEHOUSE, facing the SE front, has two lodges with mullioned-and-transomed windows and shaped gables with finials. Round arch between them; above it, open strap decoration with the Pakingtons' mullets and gerbes, also in openwork. Broad wooden cupola on top, its roof of convex-concave outline. It all goes perfectly with the wings of the house. Flanking the spacious forecourt, two tall, square-plan PAVILIONS, with cross-windows and again convex–concave roofs, probably again of *c.* 1620–5. According to Kip there were originally four such pavilions, the other two connected with a back court corresponding to the forecourt. All four, lying along the lines of the wings of the house, were joined to the gatehouse by a continuous wall. Now at the rear, mid-C19 STABLES, of diapered brick, probably by *P.C. Hardwick.*

The PARK is a pale shadow of its former self. A straight avenue leads E from Droitwich to the gatehouse, above which, as one approaches, towers the compact house. Originally more straight avenues radiated from the house. – The main E (Droitwich) and SW (Ombersley) LODGES are picturesque Gothic, probably early 1840s, by *Philip Hardwick.* MIDDLE LODGE, nearer the latter, may be by *P.C. Hardwick*, perhaps too the fine Tudor-style BOATHOUSE, on the S side of the GREAT POOL, at the park's SE corner.

9050

WHITE LADIES ASTON

So called because the manor of Aston Episcopi was held, from the mid C13, by the Cistercian nunnery of Whistones, in the N suburbs of Worcester (p. 728). The present village has a scattering of C17 timber-framed cottages and later brick farmhouses.

ST JOHN BAPTIST. Norman nave and chancel: simple S doorway, the N matching but rebuilt; deeply splayed chancel S window, another N, restored. Remodelled in the C14–C15, the original date probably of the renewed weatherboarded bell-turret: tall, square, with splayed-foot spire; it stands on heavy timbers within the nave W end. *Hopkins*, 1860–1, added the N aisle and vestry, and rebuilt the nave W wall; his three-bay arcade has low alternating piers and flatly pointed arches. His also the timber S porch, 1864. Chancel E wall and depressed, broadly chamfered chancel arch probably both rebuilt by *Henry Rowe & Son, c.* 1925. – Simple FITTINGS mostly of 1861. – Distinctive FONT, twelve-sided, with thin rolls along the angles of the bowl and chamfered underside; perhaps C13–C14. – STAINED GLASS. E lancet by *Hardman*, 1938. – MONUMENTS. Richard Fullwood †1764; odd-looking tablet, obelisk above.

ASTON COURT, ¼ m. ENE. Probably the most attractive of the C18 brick farms, at least for its open setting. Square, three bays of segment-headed windows, hipped roof, behind a wall with gatepiers with acorn finials.

The OLD VICARAGE, ⅛ m. S, is another pleasant C18 house; three bays divided by plain giant pilasters, central doorway recessed behind an elliptical arch.

ASTON HALL FARMHOUSE, S end of the village. Timber-framed, probably early C17, with remarkable brick gable-end chimney; tall, two sunk oblongs at the top above a chain of sunk lozenges (cf. Priory House, Droitwich, p. 629). Long rear service wing, perhaps earlier, cased in C18 brick.

LOW HILL HOUSE, by the main road ⅔ m. WSW. Neat, regular early C17 W front, somewhat renewed. Square-panelled, with three bays of wooden mullioned-and-transomed windows; central jettied and gabled dormer, pert pairs of brick star-stacks either end.

WHITTINGTON

ST PHILIP AND ST JAMES. 1842–4 by *A.E. Perkins*,* of rock-faced Lias with ashlar dressings; fish-scale roofs. Small, little altered. Nave and chancel with plain parapets, buttresses, lancet windows; S porch with overlarge entrance arch. Thin square W tower, with odd octagonal, gabled, ashlar top; SW projection for the gallery stairs, small NW vestry by *Yeates & Jones*, 1890. Inside, the typical thin open nave roof of its date. Chancel with sturdier arch-braced roof, on head corbels; stepped E triplet, with detached shafts with shaft-rings and foliage capitals. – Mostly original FITTINGS: W GALLERY with E.E. blind-arcaded front; BOX PEWS with small poppyheads; Gothic panelled PULPIT and ALTAR on six columns, both of artificial stone; encaustic *Chamberlain* floor TILES; REREDOS with steep crocketed gables and naïvely painted saints. – ROYAL ARMS. George III, dated 1794. – STAINED GLASS. E by *Wailes*, 1850. – Later windows no doubt also by his firm: chancel N and S *c.* 1854, nave NE and SE *c.* 1870–5. – MONUMENTS. Several nice tablets. Francis Best †1795, by *W. Stephens*; urn and willow sprays. – Betty Moule †1811, by *J. Stephens the Elder*; urn and weeping willow. – Rear-Admiral H.B. Powell †1857, by *J. Stephens the Younger*; naval military emblems.

The village centre is surprisingly intricate, despite the proximity of Worcester. WHITTINGTON LODGE, S, early to mid-C19, large and stuccoed L-plan, has a rounded NW end with iron veranda; curved Doric porch on the inner face of this wing. The landscape painter Benjamin Williams Leader lived here, 1862–90. CHURCH FARM, E, painted C18 brick, has a C17 gabled cross-wing; weatherboarded barn, attached oast house. CHURCH TERRACE, further S: three two-bay brick cottages, *c.* 1840–50, their windows of paired four-centred lights with cast-iron glazing bars.

THE ELMS, ⅓ m. NNE. Square three-storey brick villa, *c.* 1820–30; three by two bays, the latter mostly with tripartite windows, the former with fluted Greek Doric porch. Shallow hipped roof, projecting eaves.

CROOKBARROW FARM, ⅓ m. S, picturesquely sited beneath the elliptical Crookbarrow Hill (a natural feature, perhaps modi-fied during the Neolithic period). C17, timber-framed, largely cased in C19 brick, on a formerly moated site. – Pretty dove-cote with lattice-framed gables and open cupola.

---

*Replacing a C14–C15 timber-framed chapel; *Eginton* was initially consulted about rebuilding, 1840.

WHITTINGTON HALL, ⅓ m. w. An Italianate villa by *J.H. Williams*, 1900, for Martyn Smith, in large grounds. Of Stourport yellow brick, with Ionic balustraded stone porch; NE service wing (much extended as offices, 1971–2). Contemporary LODGE. – Further large office ranges added by *SMC Corstorphine & Wright*, 2005.

7060   WICHENFORD

St LAURENCE. C13 chancel, C14 nave and lower part of the w tower. Drastically restored 1861–3 by *Perkins*, who added the tower's slightly recessed upper stage with lucarned broach spire, and s porch and N vestry, all in early Dec style. Dec nave windows much renewed, especially on the N side; side lancets of the chancel in part original. E window by Perkins, also chancel arch and scissor-braced roofs. Trefoiled Dec piscina, nave SE. – Of *Perkins*'s FITTINGS only the stone PULPIT with blank Dec panelling is worth singling out. Chancel fittings mostly replaced in the early-to-mid C20. – ARCHITECTURAL FRAGMENTS. Carved Norman stones discovered in 1861–3 include a capital with toothy grotesque head. Neil Stratford compared them with Rock, *c.* 1160–70. – STAINED GLASS. E window 1863 (designed by *Samuel Evans*), and three chancel lancets, 1866, all made by *Chance & Co.*; the fourth lancet, NE, by *Hardman*, 1892. – Nave NW by *James Powell & Sons*, 1949. – Three others again by *Hardman*, 1899–1902. – MONUMENTS. John Washbourne †1615 and wife Alice. Rather stiff recumbent effigies, of painted oolite, with hands at prayer, on a renewed tomb-chest, against which three children kneel; cartouche of arms on the W wall. Restored 1863, when the superstructure was probably removed. – John and Anthony Washbourne, erected 1631; Anthony (†1570) was the father of John (†1633), father of the John of the other monument. Large standing wooden monument, restored 1863, repainted 2000. Two almost identical knights on shelves, the father below with rather limited headroom. Above and behind, in round-arched recesses divided by fluted Ionic pilasters, kneel John's two wives, Eleanor and Mary. Straight top, much detail with heraldry, but the quality overall not good. How can an old and distinguished family have been satisfied with such a performance? – Several nice tablets, mostly by the *Stephens* family. – Timber LYCHGATE. 1973.

Former RECTORY, E, plain brick, by *William Hemming* of Worcester, 1833; porch and matching rear wing, E, added by *Perkins*, 1867–8.

WICHENFORD COURT, ¼ m. S. Rebuilt *c.* 1710, a perfect example of the type of house customary in the provinces in the late C17–early C18. Brick, two-storeyed, seven by three bays of wooden cross-windows; brick band course, dentilled eaves beneath big hipped roof with small dormers. Nothing more than that. N front with central doorway with flat hood above high-set rectangular fanlight; W return also with pedimented doorway. Roof timbers were mostly reused from the substantial C15–C17 manor house of the Washbourne family that stood on the site (complete with moat, drawbridge and gatehouse). In the E first-floor room, reused early C17 panelling and overmantel with fluted pilasters and open-pedimented panels. Staircase replaced in the mid C20, the cupboard at its head lined with wallpaper of c. 1735, a rare survival.

To the N, a neat, square, C17 timber-framed DOVECOTE (now in the care of the National Trust). Stone plinth, square panelling above with large tension braces; on the E side these are set high up, to allow for the access doorway. Gabled tiled roof with later glazed lantern. Inside, tiers of wooden nesting boxes.

Further N, a large pair of late C17 BARNS, adjoining at right angles; timber-framed (probably also reusing medieval timbers), brick infilling below, split-oak wattle paling above. The barn alongside the road has eight bays with queen- or raking-strut roofs, the four NE ones floored, with stalls for livestock below. SW barn of five bays. At right angles, NE end, a C19 brick GRANARY, of similar size.

The VILLAGE, ⅓ m. N, with former SCHOOL of 1848, brick, quite plain, is almost entirely C20. In contrast the majority of FARMHOUSES in the surrounding pastoral countryside seem C17 in origin, mostly, at least in part, rebuilt in C18–C19 brick. Two little-altered, timber-framed, early C17 examples are WOODEND FARM, 1⅞ m. SSW, irregular, F-plan, on a moated site, and PEGHOUSE FARM, 2⅛ m. SW, to standard hall and cross-wing plan; the latter has the added attraction of a porch incorporating six balusters and other small-scale decoration from *John Gwynn*'s Worcester Bridge (p. 726). Later houses include BURYENDTOWN FARM, ⅞ m. WSW, narrow upstanding early C19, of peach-coloured brick, three bays and storeys, with pedimented doorcase and hipped roof with projecting eaves; contemporary outbuildings. LAUGHERN HILL, 1⅛ m, SW, is also mostly early C19, but large, rambling, and stuccoed.

WICK

9040

ST MARY. A medieval chapelry of St Andrew, Pershore. Of Norman origin, but the exterior almost entirely Victorian: *S. W. Daukes*, 1859–61, rebuilt the N aisle with its timber porch, no doubt also the nave W wall and bellcote; *Henry Woodyer*, 1892–3, remodelled and enlarged the chancel and N vestry, and re-cased the nave S wall, renewing all its C14–C15 windows. Arch-braced nave roof also C14–C15. The three-bay Norman N arcade looks fairly early, and indeed could be if the unmoulded arches were later made pointed; round piers, capitals very elementarily moulded, abaci square. All, however, seems of one build, so perhaps after all it is modest later Norman work. Re-set Norman window, chancel N wall; another nave S, apparently *in situ*. The inner s doorway is also Norman. But is the blocked w arch? It might have been a tower arch, as there is said to have been a former w tower.

Most FURNISHINGS by *Woodyer*, notably the timber SCREEN with typical tracery (and concealed iron strengthening tie). *Daukes* contributed the small canted w gallery and two-thirds of the PEWS. – COMMUNION RAILS. C17; close-set balusters, carved top-rail with knobs. – Norman FONT, much renewed; nice COVER by *J.N. Comper*, 1949. – Gabled CROSS-HEAD with Crucifixion, by *Bodley & Hare*, 1911. – STAINED GLASS. Typical *Kempe* chancel windows: E 1893, two S 1895. – Nave s, from E: 1911 by *William Pearce Ltd*, rather good; 1905 by *Mayer & Co.*; 1999 by *Gerald Paxton*. – N aisle w by *Comper*, 1947–8.

Simple oak LYCHGATE by *Bodley*, 1899. – He planned to restore the medieval CROSS nearby, executed by *C.G. Hare*, 1911; the base was given an extra step, with commemorative lettering, the shaft a carved head (now in the church, *see* above).

OLD VICARAGE, E, by *Aston Webb*, 1888–9; brick, stone dressings. Gabled, Tudor-style, with striking N entrance front, its w half entirely blank. The other half has the recessed doorway; large window above lighting an impressively compact staircase.

The eminently picturesque WYKE MANOR, NW, is entirely evocation, built for the Rev. C.H. Bickerton Hudson by *Cecil G. Hare* (of *Bodley & Hare*), 1923–4. Large, set round a small courtyard (with Georgian core, invisible externally), with all the motifs of genuine Worcestershire timber framing, interspersed with plenty of brick, composed very successfully. s front with two large outer gables with oriels and overhangs, recessed centre with coved cornice and square bay window; this represents the hall which has panelling and ceiling carved by *Bridgeman & Sons*. The E side ends in a small chapel, with Dec-style E window with glass by *Kempe & Co.*, an English Altar, and large alabaster monument to Lt Alban Hudson †1917, his recumbent effigy on a quatrefoiled tomb-chest. A tunnel-vaulted long gallery fills the rest of the N range. – Brick STABLES, w, probably early C19, with pediments and lunette windows.*

In the VILLAGE STREET, w, several timber-framed cottages, some grouped round the former SCHOOL by *Daukes*, 1864; patterned brick, fish-scale roofs, stubby bell-turret, otherwise much altered. OLD SCHOOL COTTAGES are probably C15, with at least three pairs of crucks, one visible in the s gable-end facing the road; side walls with square-panelled framing, later brick range at right angles. RUYHALL'S PLACE, C17, also L-plan, has framing with brick infill and formerly jettied gable to the road. Further w, still N side, the attractive VANDYKE COURT, built for Richard Hudson, 1832; stuccoed, with three-

---

*A scheme of almshouses by *Michael Tapper*, exhibited 1939, was unexecuted: it envisaged an open quadrangle with large chapel.

light Early Tudor-style windows with hoodmoulds, and four bargeboarded gables. Opposite, WICK HOUSE FARM, C17 timber-framed, four bays, extended E by a lower, thatched BARN.*

In the E part of the village street, more timber-framed cottages, some thatched, the best group, C16–C18, at the far E end. Further E, off Owletts Lane, THE GRANGE, modest C18–early C19, given a smart Tudor Gothic s range by *Daukes*, 1853: brick, stone dressings, five bays with windows with squared hoodmoulds, battlements, and central projecting gabled porch. A battlemented wall with four-centred archway completes an impressive approach from the Pershore road.

Three large villas lie along the ridge further S. The first, E, ENDON HALL, probably *c.* 1830, is rendered, four by three bays, with shutters, and rather impure porch of paired Ionic columns. Then LOWER HILL (formerly Bryn Issa), impressive Italianate built for Henry Hudson, 1850, surely again by *Daukes*; only two storeys, all ashlar-faced with quoins, with bracketed cornice. Entrance front, W, with tripled round-arched windows flanking a recessed centre with matching porch below a balustraded balcony. Lower service wing, E. Three assorted LODGES, the central one original.

The third villa, AVONBANK, has been the nucleus of PERSHORE COLLEGE (OF HORTICULTURE) since 1954. Built for Thomas Hudson, 1805, drably altered and enlarged later in the C19. Originally five bays, ashlar, with projecting centre with tripartite window above bald Doric porch; spacious entrance hall with curving rear staircase. The roughcast additions include central attic, higher one-bay wings, and huge rear extensions.

In 1953–5 *Richard Sheppard & Partners* built two straightforward ranges, at right angles with some curtain walling, a little to the E; and, in 1964–6, linked these to the house by a block with narrow horizontal windows, ending in an odd tubular staircase feature cut off diagonally at the top: a Le Corbusier motif, cf. La Tourette near Lyons. Of the same date, set back SE, a four-storey accommodation tower (Hazelwood) with corner features of sudden monopitches, providing the broken skyline then fashionable. All are harmonized by using the same light purple engineering brick, as is the canted SW range, added 1969–71 to complete a welcoming quad, with fine planting. Principal's House, by the entrance, also by *Richard Sheppard & Partners*, 1952–3.

Later college additions are far less coherent. The FRANK PARKINSON CENTRE, W (containing a lecture hall) by *Iain Paul* of *Hereford & Worcester Property Services*, 1985, is of concrete block, with buttresses and busy pantiled roof. The LEARNING RESOURCE CENTRE, a little SE, by *Online Architects* of Wolverhampton, 2003, has a big curving angled roof and higher entrance.

---

*Nearby was the large WICK HOUSE, with notable early C18 hall, demolished in the 1950s.

At PENSHAM, 1½ m. WSW, a couple of C17 timber-framed cottages and the larger OLD HOUSE, T-plan, with square-panelled framing.

WICKHAMFORD

ST JOHN BAPTIST. At the N end of the village, behind the manor house. Ashlar W tower and nave, plain S porch dated 1730, chancel of coursed Lias. This is C13, see the side lancets, altered in the C14: Dec E and SE windows and chancel arch. The nave, also with one Dec N window, was otherwise remodelled *c.* 1640: Gothic Survival S windows (apart from an C18 gallery window) of two blunt trefoil-cusped lights, with hoodmoulds. Similar three-light W window in the tower which was completed in 1686: battlements, short pinnacles, simply chamfered arch on moulded imposts. Thoroughly satisfying interior, full of incident, not demonstratively restored:* stone-flagged floors, plastered walls, queen-strut roofs. Above the chancel arch, the former rood beam with pretty Perp cresting. Above this, a splendid ROYAL ARMS, in red, green and yellow distemper, on panels, dated 1661, but with the monogram of James II; it was probably repainted two or three times during the Stuart period. Beautifully restored 1984 by *Anna Hulbert* (who discovered painting of *c.* 1500 on the rear of the rood beam and truss above). Panelled ceilure probably also *c.* 1500.

Excellent C17–C18 FURNISHINGS, mostly provided by the Sandys family. – On the front of the WEST GALLERY, re-created 1949, three beautifully carved late C17 panels, said to have been brought from a London church in 1841. – Three-decker C18 PULPIT with applied figure carvings from the same source. – BOX PEWS mostly with C16 linenfold panels; that around the pulpit has six panels with ornate Flemish tracery. – C17 GATES to the chancel, which has no stalls, but Jacobean dado panelling of 1921. – COMMUNION RAIL. C18. – Remarkable C17 oak FONT; stem with applied figures of the Evangelists, bowl with winged cherubs; cover with the Sandys griffin. – Under the tower, five wooden panels with tracery, probably from a Perp PULPIT; and CUPBOARD made up from C16 painted panels, probably from Ribbesford House (p. 573). – WALL PAINTING. Virgin and Child, E wall, no detail now recognizable; probably C15 or early C16. – SCULPTURAL FRAGMENT. Behind the Sandys tomb, a Norman arch-head with saltire cross decoration. – STAINED GLASS. E window 1905, designed by *C. F. Whitcombe* (cf. Feckenham). – One nave S by *W. Morris & Co. (Westminster) Ltd*, 1920.

MONUMENTS. Splendid double monument to Sir Samuel Sandys and son Sir Edwyn, both †1626; attributed to *Samuel Baldwin*. Excellent recumbent alabaster effigies on two tomb-

---

Blomfield's restoration, 1899, was either exceptionally low-key or was 'undone' by *G. C. Lees-Milne*, in 1949.

chests, the son (and wife Penelope) a little lower than the father (and wife Mercy); against both, kneeling children. Continuous canopy with five black Corinthian columns carrying four arches; wall arches on alternating pilasters and corbels. Straight tester, underside decorated with panelling of sub-cusped quatrefoils, a remarkable Gothic survival (cf. Inkberrow). Top achievements of mantled arms, obelisks, and allegorical figures. – In the sanctuary, two good late C17 ledger stones, of black marble. – Wall tablet with good lettering to G.C. and Helen Lees-Milne, by *Reynolds Stone*, 1965. – Nice recessed war memorial by *W.E. Ellery Anderson*, 1920.

MANOR HOUSE, S, on the site of a medieval grange of Evesham Abbey: highly picturesque, basically late C16 ensemble, partly stone, partly narrow studding. Main E front, facing the lake (formerly medieval fish pond), with two unequally projecting gabled wings; within the shorter, S, a broad stone fireplace with wooden Jacobean overmantel. Much is early C20, probably by *G.C. Lees-Milne*, including the front of the N wing with two-storey canted bay, and extensive N and W additions, incorporating one of three timber-framed or stone barns.

Circular DOVECOTE, SE, by the lake, medieval, perhaps C13, partly rebuilt in the C16–C17. Mostly Lias rubble, with conical stone-slated roof; inside, central timber post and 300 nesting holes.

The VILLAGE STREET has several timber-framed, thatched cottages, some C17–C18, others early C20 impersonators. ELM FARMHOUSE, H-plan, apparently *c.* 1600, may incorporate an earlier structure at its centre.

MILL HOUSE FARM, ¾ m. SSE. Late C19 brick house, with attached C18 Lias mill, retaining a cast-iron C19 wheel and much of its gearing machinery.

WILDEN
Stourport-on-Severn

The Wilden ironworks, probably of C17 origin, belonged in the C19 to the Baldwins. Enoch Baldwin was succeeded (in 1879) by his nephew Alfred who, in 1866, married Louisa Macdonald, younger sister of Georgiana, wife of Edward Burne-Jones.

ALL SAINTS. By *Hopkins*, 1879–80, for Alfred Baldwin; red brick, blue-black bands, stone dressings, open timber S porch. Nave and chancel in one, with lancets; also some with Geometrical tracery: a gabled window, S, at the junction of nave and chancel, a pair beneath the double W bellcote. Brick also exposed inside, the chancel only distinguished by its more elaborate roof structure. Modest pitch-pine furnishings. – STAINED GLASS, however, renders the interior truly memorable. It is all, quite exceptionally, by *Morris & Co.*, to the designs of *Burne-Jones*, admittedly inserted piecemeal in the early C20 (i.e. after both Morris's and Burne-Jones's deaths), but all the cartoons are of C19 origin; the unity of effect remains prodigious. Backgrounds all of green foliage, apart from the fine W window, 1904. The earliest are the pair of N lancets facing the doorway, 1900, and those of the chancel, 1902; the latest, the large nave SE window, Joshua, 1909, and SW lancet, 1914. – EMBROIDERY. Altar frontal by *William Morris*, with big leaf pattern worked in gold silk and Japanese paper thread by *Georgiana Burne-Jones* and *Edith Macdonald*; exhibited at Birmingham, 1893. – MONUMENT. Alfred Baldwin †1908. Jacobean-style tablet by *Farmer & Brindley*; strapwork surround, profile in relief.

The small CLOCK TURRET, SW, at the entrance to the burial ground, was erected as a memorial to Alfred Baldwin, 1910. Brick SCHOOL, N, 1882, also by *Hopkins*, with substantial late C20 additions. Uphill, NE, the OLD VICARAGE of 1904–5, given by Baldwin, designed by his nephew *Ambrose Poynter Jun.*; Arts and Crafts Neo-Georgian, of local purple-red brick. Weatherboarded gables reflect the influence of Philip Webb.

Baldwin's IRONWORKS lay further N, the site now an industrial estate; the gabled brick office range of 1900–7 survives. WILDEN POOL to its NW, with overgrown sluice gates and water courses, marks the site of the earlier forge.

WILDEN VIADUCT, a little S, of 1859–60, carried the Severn Valley Railway across the Stour and its water meadows; engineer *John Fowler*, assisted by *Henry Bridgeman*. Red sandstone, brick trim; skewed segmental river arch, flanked by smaller round-headed ones.

The core of STOURPORT MANOR HOTEL, ⅓ m. S, submerged by large additions of 1975–6 (by *ABC Designs*), is The Mount: gloomy brick Gothic, with solid bargeboards, built for Enoch Baldwin, probably by *Bidlake & Fleeming*, 1873.

WOLVERLEY

Perhaps the village with the most personal character in the county. Amazingly secluded centre, dominated on the one hand by its early C19 school buildings, themselves a powerful surprise; on the other, by the red church high up on its steep rock, S, approached by steps and winding ramp cut deeply through the red sandstone.

ST JOHN BAPTIST. Rebuilt 1770–2, largely at the expense of Edward Knight of Lea Castle (p. 240). Imposing if not particularly attractive, looking at first rather like an Early Victorian town hall; but it has a strong personality, like the village. Dark red brick, with tall W tower, nave and chancel: all big and blunt. The architect – whoever he was – clearly knew what he wanted. Large round-arched windows, within blank arched recesses, their imposts formed by a plain band course. Battlements on nave and tower,* above dentilled strings and cornices. Chancel altered by *Ewan Christian*, 1882; he capped it

---

* The tower incorporates the core of its medieval predecessor.

with a hipped roof, inserted inner stone surrounds to the side windows, and E triplet of stepped round-headed lights. SE vestry and half-timbered S porch by *J. T. Meredith*, who restored the nave, 1887–9. Inside, five-bay arcades: big square piers carrying plain round arches; instead of capitals and abaci just blocks, the same as outside. Matching chancel arch, slightly stilted. Three nave galleries, N and S added 1813, their silly pierced ironwork panels inserted in 1937.

FONT. Gothic, hexagonal, concave-sided; probably late C17. – Ornately pierced tester from the PULPIT of 1638, now attached to the W gallery. The current pulpit, *c.* 1881, impersonates its style. – Other furnishings mostly late C19. – Simple CHANCEL SCREEN, 1907. – LECTERN by *Pancheri & Son*, 1965. – Large early C18 ROYAL ARMS. – STAINED GLASS. E window *c.* 1844, no doubt by *Wailes*. – Chancel N: two by *Morris & Co.*, designed by *J.H. Dearle*, 1900 and 1906; the third by *Powells*, 1920. – Chancel S: two by *Clayton & Bell*, 1890 and 1916.

MONUMENTS. Alabaster effigy of a knight, probably Sir John Attwood †1391. Legs broken off, but the feet resting on a lion are preserved. His head, with pointed bascinet, rests on a damaged helm with swan's-head crest. – Many worthwhile TABLETS. Chancel: Sarah Hurtle †1771, by *J. Nelson* of Shrewsbury. Coloured marbles, urn against obelisk, flanked by putti; composition, but not the detail, still Rococo. – John Hurtle †1792, also by *Nelson*; pretty, urn before obelisk. – Mary Smith †1804, perhaps again by *Nelson*, the same formula, but more Adamish. – Helen Knight †1801, by *Flaxman*. Quite small. Stiffly reclining female in relief; she has ceased reading, apparently to pray. Gothic frame with quatrefoil spandrels. – Joseph Smith †1840; simple refined Grecian, by *Hollins* of Birmingham. – Lt Col. G.C. Knight †1914, by *J.H.M. Bonnor*, 1916; good lettering with painted arms. – S aisle: Humphrey Bate †1741, by *Edward Truman* of Bewdley; stone, specially pretty carving. – William Hancocks †1844, by *W. Lodge* of Birmingham; Grecian. – N aisle: Rhoda Browne †1808, by *T. King* of Bath; large organic urn. – John Smith †1824, by *Hollins*; Neo-Greek altar, heavily draped. – John Brown †1845, by *M.W. Johnson*, and John Hancocks †1849, both draped urns. – Five HATCHMENTS, 1845–97.

Much of the VILLAGE consists of the buildings of the school founded by William Sebright, a London merchant, in 1620; mostly converted to housing *c.* 1970 (*see* below). The large C17–C18 BURY HALL, S of the church, was rebuilt as the grammar school by *J. T. Meredith*, 1890–1; severe Queen Anne-style, with gables and ogee-capped turret. Earlier cottages and service buildings form a loose quadrangle.

Further S, by the main road, WOLVERLEY POUND, probably early C19, a U-shaped enclosure cut into the bedrock, three deep recesses in its rear wall. ELEMENTARY SCHOOL opposite by *Pritchard & Godwin*, 1926–7; slightly Neo-Georgian, again with gables and turret.

Downhill, N, beyond a wedge-shaped group of Gothic brick cottages dated 1860, the main buildings of SEBRIGHT SCHOOL, mostly of 1829–30, possibly by *Thomas Lee Jun.*, with *William Knight* of Kidderminster as clerk of works;* a spacious brick group, symmetrically laid out. In the centre, alone faced in Bath ashlar, a buttressed Gothic composition with three giant pointed arches, with hoodmoulds with large headstops, above a low ground floor. Two outer staircases ascend to a quatrefoil-balustraded platform, behind the giant Gothic portico, giving access to the first-floor grammar school; large doorway flanked by two huge three-light windows, Perp and transomed. Plain parapet with the endowment date, 1620; octagonal battlemented corner turrets. Either side, at a slightly obtuse angle, two much lower three-bay masters' houses, earlier buildings remodelled with tall parapets, hoodmoulded windows, and central doorways with flat cast-iron canopies beneath little quatrefoils. Then, projecting diagonally, attached only by a battlemented archway, two more buildings not at all Gothic. Both have five bays, big round-arched windows, and slightly projecting gabled centre; giant angle pilasters with urn finials. That on the r., dated 1829, was the boys' elementary school; that on the l., with Doric porch, the former grammar school of 1787, converted in 1829 to the girls' school, later subdivided into two storeys.

Opposite, in its own grounds, the former VICARAGE (now Wolverhill) by *Meredith*, 1886; brick, gabled, mostly plain Queen Anne, still with some Gothic detail.

The N end of the village, uphill again, was also dominated by Sebright School. The large WOLVERLEY HOUSE, incorporated 1948–9, was probably begun *c.* 1749–52 for Edward Knight;† Andor Gomme attributes the design to *William & David Hiorn* of Warwick. Now subdivided as flats. Stately w front, completely flat, brick with stone quoins, seven bays and two-and-a-half storeys plus parapet; conventional doorway with Tuscan columns and pediment. Mostly mid-C20 wings. Much livelier garden front, E: 2+1+2 bays, all windows with stone architraves, those of the pedimented projecting centre Venetian or Diocletian. Short low wings, their inner fronts with three niches.

Good brick outbuildings, s: single-storey STABLE BLOCK with round-arched windows and pedimented three-bay centre; square DOVECOTE, with shaped gables and oculi. – Rusticated GATEPIERS with ball-finials. – Other brick C18–early C19 houses opposite form an attractive enclave.

WOLVERLEY HIGH SCHOOL, further NW, 1930–1 by *Maurice E. Webb* (of *Sir Aston Webb & Son*), was also built for Sebright School. Stripped Neo-Georgian brick, to a loose H-plan. The

---

*In 1829 Mr *Pinches* was paid 5s. a day for seventeen days, including ten 'making drawings for Wolverley School', at Sedgley, Staffordshire (where *Lee* was building several churches). *Knight* received £23 19s. 2d. for 'surveying etc'.
†A stable roof tile dated 1752 was discovered *c.* 1980. Internal work continued into the 1780s, two chimneypieces, now lost, being ordered from *Flaxman* in 1781–2.

entrance front, E, has the only display: richly carved stone doorway with swan-neck pediment, beneath short pyramid-roofed tower. N wing with dining hall, long S wing originally with dormitories. Plain science blocks by *Peter Bosanquet* of Oxford, 1959, form a low-key E courtyard; NW chapel wing by *S. T. Walker & Partners*, 1966, with high angled roof for a clerestory.

WOLVERLEY COURT, ⅓ m. SE, beyond the Staffordshire–Worcestershire Canal, mostly rebuilt to an L-plan *c.* 1820–30, incorporates much fabric of the C16–C17 house of the Attwood family. Early C19 N front, three storeys, 2+1+2 bays, stuccoed, with hipped overhanging roof; Doric porch in the projecting centre, leading into a spacious hall. The other fronts have mullioned-and-transomed windows, notably a large six-light example, E, which must have lit a first-floor great chamber. C16–C17 cellar with large fireplace with bread oven.

Further uphill, ESE, is HEATHFIELD, now a school, stuccoed classical, *c.* 1850–60, with Corinthian side porch and canted N bay windows. Then, with its picturesque gabled lodge almost opposite the S lodges of Lea Castle (p. 240), SION HILL HOUSE, mostly early C19, stuccoed, five bays and three storeys, with plain wooden veranda; re-set C17 panelling inside.

BLAKESHALL HALL, 1¼ m. N. Small country house built for William Hancocks, 1845. Loose Italianate, stuccoed, five bays, two storeys; windows with shaped architraves, raised centre with Doric porch, three-stage balustraded NE tower. Brick rear service wing. – On a wooded knoll in the grounds, a little W, a brick OBELISK erected *c.* 1850 as a memorial to the Presbyterian divine Richard Baxter (1615–91); plinth with decayed inscription. It stands above a circular ICE HOUSE, 8 ft 6 in. (2.6 metres) in diameter, 12 ft (3.7 metres) high, cut into the rock.

Also cut into the rock, various CAVE COTTAGES, probably early C19. The two most visible are in the former quarry in Sladd Lane, Drakelow, ⅞ m. WNW; one retains brick-edged windows, doorway and chimney. A third, a little SE, in the garden of New House. Another, built into Vale's Rock 1⅔ m. N, off Kingsford Lane (now within Kingsford Country Park), is impressive though mostly stripped out.[*]

BODENHAM ARBORETUM, 2 m. NW, opened 1998. The more or less circular EARTH CENTRE, or reception building, by *Roger Dean-Walker*, mostly sunk into the hillside, is covered in grassed earth; of reinforced concrete construction, with bastion-like brick front towards the lake.

---

[*] A later, much larger example of burrowing into the sandstone is the DRAKELOW UNDERGROUND DISPERSAL FACTORY by *Sir Alexander Gibb & Partners*, 1941–2, for the wartime construction of Rover aircraft engines. The site, covering 250,000 sq. ft, is NE of the junction of Sladd and Drakelow lanes.

WORCESTER

INTRODUCTION

The site of Worcester, on the eastern ('English') bank of the River Severn, close to an ancient ford, has been occupied for more than 2,000 years. The first settlement, towards the S end of a sand and gravel terrace near the present cathedral, dates probably from the Late Iron Age, C2–C1 B.C. Excavations in the 1960s revealed the remains of a massive bank and ditch, perhaps constructed in the C1 A.D.

Worcester was a small, though widespread, ROMAN TOWN, with a mixed industrial and agrarian base. Remains of buildings and streets have frequently come to light, though the roads which would be expected to link it with Kingsholm (near Gloucester) and Wroxeter (Salop) remain elusive. There is no certain evidence for a Roman fort. In the early C2 extensive iron-smelting activity began in the present Deansway and Broad Street areas, later extending N to Castle Street and Pitchcroft. Andrew Yarranton in the mid C17 found enough Roman slag remains around the S end of Pitchcroft to be commercially viable for re-smelting. It seems likely that the Romans constructed the first bridge across the Severn here. Suggestions of elegant buildings have been located in the Sidbury area, on the High Street, and around the Butts. Further N at Britannia Square, a circular sandstone structure discovered in the early C19 may have been the remains of a villa, or perhaps a temple. By the early C4, however, the settlement seems to have focused on a defended area no larger than the Iron Age enclosure, though there was still occupation beyond this. The C7 Ravenna Cosmography lists a place called Vertis, 'a place on a sharp bend in a river', usually identified as Roman Worcester.

There is a gap in the history of the town between the late C4 and the early C7. It is probable that the origins of Worcester's importance as a Christian centre lay in this period, with the predecessor of St Helen as its first church. About 628 King Penda of Mercia set up the Anglo-Saxon kingdom of the Hwicce, primarily as a buffer zone against Wessex. In 680 Archbishop Theodore created the see of Worcester as its spiritual centre, building the minster of St Peter on or near the site of the present cathedral (that is, centrally within the Roman defences). The name *Weogornaceaster*, from which Worcester derives, first appears in 691. Some time between 889 and 899, at the request of Bishop Waerferth, Ethelred, Earl of the Mercians, and his wife Aethelflaed issued a charter establishing Worcester as a fortified *burh*. Its N defences lay along the S side of Broad Street, its E perhaps between High Street and The Shambles; to the S it must have included the S end of the river terrace with the minster and related buildings. In 904 Ethelred was given a *haga*, or enclosure, of about eight acres in the NW part of the town, close to the river; this emphasizes the extent of the *burh*, the street pattern of which formed the basis for the medieval town (and the present city). Bishop Oswald completed his new minster of St Mary, on the present cathedral site, in 983, functioning alongside the earlier St Peter until the present building was begun by Wulfstan in 1084.

In about 1069 Urse d'Abitôt, Sheriff of Worcestershire, built a motte and bailey castle in the SW corner of the town to guard the river crossing, annexing a large part of the monks' cemetery as its outer bailey. It was later rebuilt, at least partly, in stone, but declined in importance during the early C13; the land was returned to the monastery, and the castle was all but derelict by the C15. Worcester received its first royal charter in 1189. Documentary evidence for the medieval walls is limited. The line, enclosing some 83 acres, seems to have been completed by the early C13, initially with the gates linked by a bank and palisade, replaced by stone walls over the next 200 years. A section through the surrounding ditch showed it to have been flat-bottomed, water-filled, some 40 ft (12 metres) wide; elsewhere it had a V-shaped profile. The line of the walls to the E can be easily traced, with visible if low stretches alongside City Walls Road; to the N stretches survive S of The Butts. From as early as the C11,

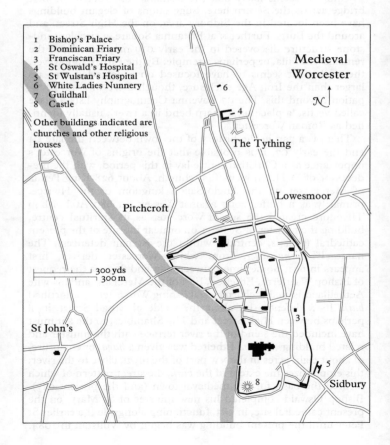

1 Bishop's Palace
2 Dominican Friary
3 Franciscan Friary
4 St Oswald's Hospital
5 St Wulstan's Hospital
6 White Ladies Nunnery
7 Guildhall
8 Castle

Other buildings indicated are churches and other religious houses

Medieval Worcester

N

The Tything

Lowesmoor

Pitchcroft

300 yds
300 m

St John's

Sidbury

suburbs began to spread out E, SE and especially N (the main North Gate was at Foregate); a further suburb emerged at St John's, W of the river, across the bridge (rebuilt in stone *c.* 1313–28).

Worcester's importance in the C13–C14 is shown by the settlement of the Greyfriars and Blackfriars. The Franciscans arrived *c.* 1225–30, with their house in the E part of the city (now Friar Street); the Dominicans came in 1347, their house to the NW, off Broad Street. Nothing of either remains above ground and little more of the Cistercian Whiteladies in the N suburb, Upper Tything (p. 728). Here also was St Oswald's Hospital (rebuilt in the C19). The major survivor is St Wulfstan's Hospital (now the Commandery) in Sidbury, SE. Of eleven medieval churches only three remain (St Helen, St Alban, St John in Bedwardine), the tower of another (St Andrew), plus fragments of four or five others. Generally Worcester's medieval survivals are few. Its late medieval prosperity depended on a great variety of trades and crafts, but by the C15 cloth-making was dominant; Leland wrote *c.* 1540: '. . . noe towne of England, at this present tyme, makes so many cloathes yearly'. By his time the population was probably some 4,000, most living in timber-framed houses. A few precious examples survive, especially in Friar Street.

The late C16 brought a decline, exacerbated by the Civil War, the first and last engagements of which were fought here: in 1642 (at Lower Wick) and 1651. But by the late C17 Worcester was again flourishing, and in the early C18 enjoyed a comfortable affluence: Defoe wrote that 'the people generally [are] esteemed very rich, being full of business'. Much of the city retains a Georgian feel, especially along the main High Street–Foregate Street–Tything axis. Its wealth is reflected by one of the most characteristic features of Worcester, its four C18 churches, three begun by the 1730s. Lord Torrington in 1784, in spite of his usual bickering, calls Worcester 'well built'; as its industries he mentions china, glove-making, and carpet-making.

The coming of the Worcester and Birmingham Canal in 1815 helped to offset its decline as an inland port, leading to an expansion of new industries in the Lowesmoor area, E of the city centre. Architecturally there are the usual feelers of Late Georgian and Early Victorian terraces and villas into the suburbs, plus a few notable early C19 set pieces, especially Britannia and St George's squares.

The C19 saw no great expansion. The arrival of the railway in 1850 caused the industrial area to shift further E to the Shrub Hill area. Worcester's principal C19 architects practised throughout the county, including the *Rowe* dynasty, City Surveyors and/or Architects through three generations: *Henry* (1787–1859), his son *Henry* (1820–1907), and grandson *Alfred Barnett* (1852–1909). The fourth generation is represented by *Alfred Vernon Rowe* (1881–1940), County Architect, who continued in private practice as *Henry Rowe & Son*. Population figures reveal the pattern of C20 growth: 46,000 in 1901; 49,000 in 1931; 73,000 in 1971; 93,353 in 2001.

Little came of an ambitious Beaux Arts-inspired development plan published by *Minoprio & Spencely* in 1946 (which proposed the obliteration *inter alia* of College Street and College Precincts); its only progeny were some street-widening lines (e.g. Angel Street and St Nicholas Street) and the partial inner ring road (City Walls Road). Far more harmful was the 1960s Lych-gate Centre, which erased the medieval street pattern at the SE end of High Street, compounding this by driving the busiest fast-traffic road through a place only a few yards from the cathedral. Worcester, in the C20, was a cathedral city first and foremost, and it remains incomprehensible that this act of self-mutilation should have been permitted. As Pevsner then wrote: 'The crime is the planners', not the architects', and the planners would of course have been powerless without the consent of the City Council.' They at least made amends in the rest of the city centre, operating from 1972 to 1997 the longest-running conservation Town Scheme of any English local authority; particular successes were Britannia Square, Bridge Street, and Friar Street. In addition pedestrianisation schemes have helped to ensure that Worcester, or at least much of its centre, can again be enjoyed as a predominately Georgian red brick city, with good timber-framed enclaves, and an appealing skyline of towers and spires, especially dramatic seen from the railway viaduct, with the Malvern Hills beyond.

CATHEDRAL CHURCH
OF CHRIST AND THE BLESSED VIRGIN MARY

1 Worcester Cathedral from the W, from across the Severn, is a superb sight, the tower one of the noblest of its kind. A view from the E is out of the question; the road and roundabout created in the 1960s have removed all peace. The cathedral stands as in a vice between road and river, only College Green to the S giving any sense of a precinct. The cathedral (with the now vanished Worcester Castle) was built near the S tip of the long ridge of sand and gravel along which the city later developed. The see was founded 680, but it seems likely that there was an earlier ritual building of some kind here. The first cathedral, dedicated to St Peter, stood on the site either of the present nave or of the clois-ters. In 961 Oswald, one of the leading figures in the monastic reform movement, became bishop, and introduced (or reintro-duced) the Benedictine rule; he built a new cathedral dedicated to St Mary, said to have been completed in 983. But St Peter's was 'still standing' in 991 (and its presbytery enlarged *c.* 1040). There must have been two Saxon churches standing close together, either in line or more or less side by side. In the 1050s a bell-tower was added to St Mary's by Wulfstan, then prior. He was appointed bishop in 1062; exceptionally, retained his office after the Norman Conquest; and began the present building in 1084. This must have had transepts with E chapels, and apsed E end with three radiating chapels. The monks re-entered the choir 8 in 1089; a synod took place in the crypt in 1092 (i.e. there was 9 then no chapter house, perhaps completed *c.* 1115).

Worcester from the west in the 1750s.
Engraving

The next relevant date is the fall of a tower, called *nova turris*, in 1175. Probably this was a w tower, thus causing rebuilding at the nave w end, though it is possible it was the crossing tower, excavations here suggesting a possible second tower (between Wulfstan's and the C14 crossing tower). Wulfstan was canonized in 1203, as Oswald had been earlier. In 1216 King John died at Newark, desiring to be buried at Worcester before the Norman High Altar, between St Oswald and St Wulfstan.* Their new shrines were re-dedicated in 1218 in the presence of John's son, Henry III. Then in 1224 under Bishop William de Blois the new E end was begun (*novum opus frontis*, for *frons* could mean E end); it was no doubt well advanced when John was reburied in his new tomb, in 1232. The mason *Alexander*, known to have worked here in the 1230s–40s, may have been responsible for the slightly modified design of the chancel, perhaps not completed until *c.* 1260. Rebuilding of the Norman nave began early in the C14, probably *c.* 1310–20. *William of Shockerwick*, presumably from Shockerwick (Somerset), master mason in 1316, may have been responsible for the N side (most remarkable for conforming closely to the scheme of the C13 E end); the S side was probably built by *c.* 1340–55, the nave as a whole completed *c.* 1380. The name of another mason, *John Clyve*, occurs from *c.* 1376–7, apparently in connection with the cloisters. The N porch is said to be of 1386; other C14–C15 dates will be referred to where appropriate. The most significant pre-Reformation event was the burial here, within a fine late Perp chantry chapel, of Prince Arthur, Henry VIII's elder brother (†1502).

The Priory was dissolved in 1539 and the cathedral lost a significant part of its see to the new diocese of Gloucester. There was also significant Civil War damage. Major repairs were carried

*John's original intention was to be buried at Beaulieu Abbey, Hampshire, which he founded for that purpose in 1204.

out in the early to mid C18; work in the late C18 (by *Thomas Johnson*) included a new E window, previously restored 1660–2, and new W window, both again replaced in the C19. Structural restoration of the E end was begun in the early 1850s by the local man *Abraham Edward Perkins* (a pupil of Rickman), cathedral architect from 1845 until his death in 1873. *Sir Gilbert Scott*, who had been 'occasionally consulted' by the Dean from 1858, designed all the furnishings from 1863 onwards. Scott had nothing to do with the structural restoration; unpublished parts of his *Personal and Professional Recollections* make it clear that he hardly approved of this (and thought Perkins 'very timid'). The resultant smooth exterior has indeed little to recommend it, though Perkins no doubt restored the detail conscientiously, rather too much so in fact as all later detail was comprehensively removed. Both men had to contend with a Joint Restoration Committee (1864–75), a mix of lay and ecclesiastical members.

As at Chester, Lichfield and Carlisle cathedrals, certain sandstones have caused many problems. Worcester's Norman parts include oolitic limestone from the Cotswolds and grey-green Highley sandstone, the latter used also in the W nave bays and in some C14 work; the Highley stone has worn best of all. The webs of the late C12 vaults at the nave W end and the C13 vaults of the eastern arm are filled with local tufa, chosen for its lightness. The exterior, however, is largely of the so-called New Red Sandstones (most frequently Holt stone) which are soft and crumbly and weather badly. There has been incessant refacing, which partly explains the new-looking surfaces and absence of patina. Renewed researches to find a stone that is more lasting while still visually suited to the old work have so far failed. Nevertheless, views of the cathedral during the past three centuries show that its outstanding feature, the central tower, has suffered little alteration to its basic outline. The cathedral is 425 ft (131 metres) long (cf. Salisbury 473 ft, 146 metres, and Lichfield 397 ft, 122 metres).

EXTERIOR

The smooth, rather bland exterior of Worcester Cathedral is, as has already been said, the result of repeated refacings. Its most important feature, the splendid CROSSING TOWER, set almost exactly halfway between W and E ends, seems more authentically medieval, though its detail, essentially as in Hollar's engraving of 1672, was extensively renewed in 1865–7. The rebuilding of the tower was finished in 1374, 'after seventeen years' work'; so it must have been begun *c.* 1357. Of two stages, the lower of seven very slim bays, each with two-light tracery and transom. Only two, the second and sixth, contain windows; the rest are blank. All the bays carry heavily crocketed gables; at the bottom the dividing buttresses terminate in head corbels which climb up the sills of the adjoining rooflines. The upper stage, above a band of quatrefoils, has two two-light bell-openings with transoms, and single bays for

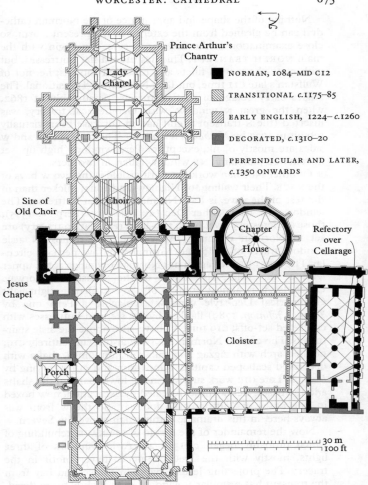

Prince Arthur's
Chantry

Lady
Chapel

■ NORMAN, 1084–MID C12

▨ TRANSITIONAL c.1175–85

▨ EARLY ENGLISH, 1224–c.1260

■ DECORATED, c.1310–20

□ PERPENDICULAR AND LATER,
c.1350 ONWARDS

Site of
Old Choir

Choir

Chapter
House

Refectory
over
Cellarage

Jesus
Chapel

Cloister

Nave

Porch

30 m
100 ft

Worcester Cathedral.
Plan

canopied statuary (mostly C19, by *R.L. Boulton*) either side and
in between; all again have crocketed gables, with blind tracery.
Angle buttresses with attached crocketed pinnacles, C19 crown
with open parapet and crocketed openwork corner pinnacles.
Intermediate pinnacles were removed *c.* 1930, no doubt
improving the general appearance.*

---

* *Lord Grimthorpe*, who designed the clock, claimed, apparently without contradic-
tion, that the parapet and pinnacles were also his.

Nothing of the shape and appearance of the Norman cathedral can be gleaned from the exterior of the present E arm, so
close examination of the exterior, N side, can begin with the
main NORTH TRANSEPT. This has indeed flat buttresses, but
with nook-shafts with fillets and moulded capitals; i.e. not of
Wulfstan's late CII time, but Late Norman or Transitional. The
angles carry octagonal shafted turrets, presumably of 1862,
when the great N window, with Geometrical tracery, was
inserted (the N transept N end had in any case been virtually
rebuilt in 1733 by *Nathaniel Wilkinson*). The transept's E and W
sides are mostly blank, except for Perp windows high up, set
in renewed panelling; NE window taller, in two tiers.

Of other Norman work the most visible is the two W bays of
the NAVE. Their walling, of Highley sandstone, thicker than in
the rest of the nave, is Late Norman, with flat buttresses. The
windows are later, either Dec (*see* below) or Perp (*c.* 1375);
those at clerestory level (with two-light reticulation tracery) are
set in Norman openings. Above the westernmost N aisle
window, traces of a blocked Norman window, perhaps circular. The WEST FRONT again has Norman openings at the upper
level of the aisles, also traces of the N aisle W doorway.
Otherwise it is almost entirely of 1863–5. Ornate eight-light
Geometrical Dec-style window (replacing a Perp one by
Thomas Johnson, 1789) flanked by big stepped buttresses with
crocketed set-offs; C19 turrets above, also above the aisle stair-
turrets. The central Norman doorway also seems entirely C19;
pointed arch with zigzag and thin roll mouldings, shafts with
decorated scalloped capitals, tympanum and other carving by
Boulton. Late C12 work survives in the lower parts of the shafts
and the bases. Below these, revealed by excavation, now boxed
in, the bases of Wulfstan's W doorway. So the W front was
always here, in this dramatic setting high above the Severn.

Now the remainder of the N side of the NAVE, rebuilding of
which probably began *c.* 1310–20. Aisle windows of three
lights, mostly with the Dec five-petal flower motif in the
tracery. The projecting Jesus Chapel in the second bay from
the transept has a similar N window, only slightly more florid.
Clerestory windows Dec too, of three lights but significantly
with four-centred arches, an early example. Two-storey NORTH
PORCH, dated 1386 by Dr Hopkins, renewed 1865–9.* Its
façade is Victorian, with panelled walls and canopied niches
with corny Bath stone statues of Christ and the Apostles by
Hardman; top quatrefoil frieze beneath battlements. Blank
sides, except for plain two-light mullioned windows at high
level. Its interior, of two bays, is vaulted with oblong tierceron
stars on polished marble shafts, carrying sparse knobbly capitals. But the inner portal retains two long thin Norman shafts
with block capitals (plus bases of a second order), part of the
early Norman N portal. At Tewkesbury Abbey such a doorway
is fully preserved, the porch in front of it tunnel-vaulted;

* C17 notebooks of Prebendary Dr Hopkins, presumably based on rolls now lost.

Worcester may have had a similar porch, but no evidence remains. Above the doorway, the reused head of a Dec five-petal window. Of *c.* 1865–70, by *Perkins*, the busy ogee-panelled DOOR and fine iron outer GATES, made by *Skidmore*.

The EAST ARM, begun 1224, should, chronologically, have been considered before the nave. *Perkins's* restoration, *c.* 1855–60, has been blamed for its rather monotonous appearance, but he seems to have reinstated it accurately. Slightly longer than the nave, it consists of four-bay choir, E transept (on the pattern of Canterbury, Lincoln and Salisbury), then three bays of retrochoir with axial chapel projecting only by one narrow bay. Perkins's correct E.E. was guided by the C13 triple lancets of the E transept, long and slender, their upper parts stepped and impressively linked to those below by triple shafts. These he purged of their Perp infill and repeated systematically elsewhere, mostly replacing Perp windows. The effect is certainly very fine, even if the renewed stonework rather dampens enthusiasm. The early C13 buttresses are still flat, the trefoiled corbel table repeats along the whole arm. In the N wall of the N choir aisle triplets alternate with two-light windows with quatrefoil plate tracery; big C18 flying buttress, rebuilt 1861–2. The shorter retrochoir clerestory has single instead of stepped lancets. Perkins's restoration of the E window, 1855–6, where the triplet theme is expanded to five stepped lights (with large gauche trefoil in the gable above), replaced another 'Perp' example by *Thomas Johnson*, 1792.

The S SIDE of the E arm is all but identical to the N. The only major difference is the two-bay chapel at its W end (the S transept's rebuilt E chapel), which received the same systematic stepped lancet treatment as the rest. The main S TRANSEPT is similar to but less restored than the N transept. Its S window is again Victorian, its baldly stepped lancet form betraying an earlier date, 1852, ten years before its N counterpart. Norman side walls again with Perp windows high up, a very tall, impressive S window in the W wall. The NAVE S side can only be seen from the cloister; for the doorways from cloister into the S aisle, *see* p. 696. The very regular upper parts, renewed *c.* 1865, repeat what already existed: ornate late Dec flowing tracery, probably *c.* 1340–50, in the three-light aisle windows, the clerestory windows more Perp, with stylishly steep, straight shanks. Small two-light straight-headed windows in between mark the Library, a room above the S aisle, repaired or newly built *c.* 1376–7 in the former aisle roof, outside the triforium.

INTERIOR

The greatest asset of Worcester Cathedral is the unity of its interior. Although the C13 and the C14 have contributed about evenly, the C14 designers were so conformist that differences of a century or more hardly tell until one begins to study the detail. The fine view E from the nave (enhanced by *Scott's* handsome open screen) takes into account the rise in floor level between cross-arm and eastern arm, allowing for the Norman crypt beneath the choir. At Lichfield or Lincoln or Salisbury there is no such rise; that at Worcester is exceeded by Winchester, even more by Canterbury. Beyond the choir, one can just discern that the floor level sinks again, to that of the nave and crossing. Apart from creating this visual effect, the crypt contains invaluable evidence for the form of Wulfstan's cathedral, begun 1084, so it is here that a chronological tour should commence.

Crypt

Wulfstan's CRYPT, now entered from the S choir aisle E end, by a stair of 1986, contains Early Norman work at its most impressive. It consists of a centre of four E–W vessels, separated by slender limestone pillars, seven bays long plus the *corona* or semicircle of apse pillars. Around this space are square piers some 6½ ft (2 metres) thick (partly infilled between in the early C13). Around these ran an outer ambulatory divided into two vessels; its straight parts (beneath the choir aisles) are now nine bays long, i.e. all that remained after its curved section was destroyed. All the Early Norman pillars, some perhaps reused from an earlier building, have plain capitals, mostly block or single-scallop type; also the rare form of a single-trumpet scallop (a form non-existent either in Germany, whence the block capital was imported, or France). One pillar in the N row of the main vessel has an abacus with double billet enrichment. Vaults are groined, with plain, flat transverse arches. The crypt makes clear that the Norman E end above must have had an apse with ambulatory. Excavations of 1974 at the SE corner revealed further evidence for its plan: part of the crypt ambulatory remains exposed here, plus an irregular pentagonal SE chapel, implying the existence of central and NE chapels. Further excavations, 1986–7, showed that two piers of fine ashlar were inserted in the early C13 so that the ambulatory could be retained when the E arm was rebuilt; the collapse of part of the crypt in 1243 must have led to the decision to curtail and infill it instead. The existence of the expected Norman transept chapels flanking the choir aisles is confirmed by the surviving crypt, S (beneath St John's Chapel), again in two vessels, with matching details. It has a square-ended E.E. continuation (now divided off), with quadripartite rib vault. But this clearly replaced a polygonal (three-sided) Norman apse; from the Norman pillar in the middle of the W side spring three radiating ribs to touch the centre of the E.E. vault and the middles of the two diagonal ribs up to it from the angles. All trace of the N transept chapel has disappeared (as above ground). Originally doorways led down into the crypt from the W ends of the N and S choir aisles. They were replaced, probably in the late C12, by an entrance further S in the S transept, adjoining the present exit (created 1863). The round-arched opening at the W end of the main vessel was probably for a cupboard.

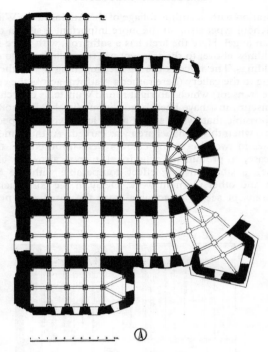

Worcester Cathedral.
Plan of crypt

Transepts

Chronologically we ought next to inspect the transepts, as well
as the extreme W end of the choir. Early Norman evidence here
survives solely in the walling adjoining the crossing tower. The
N side is the most instructive, but little is visible. Here, hidden
by the canopies of the choir stalls, is the start of an arch immediately W of the C13 N arcade, with above it (just visible) part
of a gallery arch W of the later triforium; above again, faint
traces of the Norman clerestory. Behind, at gallery level
towards the aisle roof, a strong semicircular respond with block
capital was discovered built into the wall; this suggests analo-
gies with Gloucester, also that below there may well have been
drum piers as at Gloucester and Tewkesbury. On the S side of
the choir, at the NW corner of its S aisle, a sturdy Norman angle
shaft with block capital, part of the arch to the transept.

Now the SOUTH TRANSEPT where one sees the whole arch
into the transept E chapel; its base is some five feet above the
transept and may never have communicated directly with it, if
access was from the choir aisle. Capitals of cushion type but
with foliage trails, mostly drastically redone. They have profuse

decoration with acanthus foliage of the Anglo-Saxon Winchester School type; also, on the more important E side, a dragon and an angel. Here the arch has a soffit roll, with three square mouldings above; to the transept are two rolls and two square mouldings. The traces of an arched opening above the latter belong to the gallery (here rather a platform across the end bay of the transept) which ran right round Wulfstan's church.* The S transept must have been begun immediately after 1084, but it is possible that, while still at a low level, work stopped until *c.* 1120 when this E chapel arch was carved.† At that time stone courses in two alternating colours were favoured (cf. the SW staircase, a prominent cylindrical turret; also the chapter house), a stone striping effect comparable with the Speyer crypt and other German work. Delay in the construction of the transept seems reasonable from the functional point of

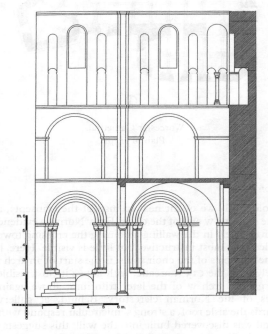

Worcester Cathedral.
South transept, internal elevation, reconstruction

---

*Also visible above the arch into the S chancel aisle, but only on the E side from the roof space.
†Neil Stratford relates the capitals to the early C12 crypt at Canterbury, also to work at Romsey (chancel E bays and S transept), *c.* 1120 or later. George Zarnecki broadly agrees but does not rule out that the capitals could, like Canterbury's, have been carved by *c.* 1100.

view, as completion of the E end would have had priority. The NORTH TRANSEPT also has a few traces of the Norman gallery platform (and of the vaulting which must have supported it in front of the N wall). The arch to the (demolished) Norman E chapel is also there, but all Victorian, without telling details; the arch again has stone in two colours.

What else there is of Norman evidence in the transepts is definitely Late Norman or Transitional, perhaps undertaken in two phases. Whether these can be related to a possible fall of the central tower in 1175 is debatable; they may have been connected with fires that occurred in 1189 and 1202. In any case work on the N transept seems to have predated the S; in addition both transepts were re-vaulted in the late C14, when there were other Perp alterations. For the Late Norman work the SOUTH TRANSEPT again has the more significant details. Firstly a blind opening at gallery level, towards the S end of the E wall, with arch with frontal and diagonal chevron, on keeled shafts with crocket capitals, plus in the outer chamfer large dogtooth. The capitals make a date before c. 1190 impossible.* In the S wall nearby, at lower level, larger openings (now mostly obscured by the organ) with similar details but no dogtooth. In contrast, the W wall at gallery level has the start of blank trefoiled arcading, with double roll moulding and capitals with flat leaves. Such trefoiled heads would be very surprising before 1200 (cf. Lichfield, choir aisles, W bays, c. 1200). The major vaulting shafts of the transept are again keeled; these were, as Willis said in 1863, 'engrafted' into the walls. The corner buttresses outside belong to the same time. The tripartite shafts show clearly that they were intended for rib vaults different from the present ones.† They survive up to their stiff-leaf capitals, but the present vault standing on them dates from c. 1375 and has liernes. At the same time the upper windows were remodelled and given unusual flying ribs linking their main mullions to the transverse ridge ribs of the vault. Especially impressive, the three-tier SW window, four Perp lights, its two lower tiers with openwork cusping. Also notable, the seven-light and five-light stone grilles, with transoms, in the E wall at gallery level, possibly Perp adaptations of early C13 work. The S triplet, as we have seen, is by *Perkins*, 1852. Finally, the arches to choir and nave aisles are late C14 again. The NORTH TRANSEPT differs in many ways. The vaulting shafts, though very similar to those on the S, are not quite the same. Willis is no doubt correct in saying that the remodelling of the transepts c. 1180–90 was done first on the N. The shafts here resemble those of the W bays of the nave (*see* below); those of

---

* These sophisticated varieties of chevron could go with the W bays of the nave, c. 1175–85, but not the stiff-leaf capitals and large dogtooth. In the Canterbury choir of 1174–85 dogtooth and chevron do appear side by side, but in the West Country the earliest occurrence of both motifs together is in the Hereford Cathedral retrochoir, c. 1190–1200.

† Fragments of this vault of c. 1200 remain in the roof space.

the S transept have deeper hollows between the shafts. The vault, *c.* 1375, is simpler than the S one: no liernes, just diagonal and ridge ribs. The Perp wall treatment is also less enterprising, though the same flying ribs link the window mullions to the transverse vault ribs; NE window, only two tiers, again with inner screen. Geometrical N window of 1862. The arch to the chancel aisle (with excellently preserved painting of rose and chevron patterning) is like those in the S transept, but the arch to the nave aisle is somewhat simpler, with plain moulded capitals. On its nave side, at the NE angle of the N aisle, an unexpected survival, another strong early Norman shaft with block capital.

Nave west bays

Next we should examine those two W bays of the NAVE which had promised Norman work outside. Their E piers begin with demi-shafts on a flat surface, again with the green and white stone striping noticed in the S transept. They must be survivors from the vanished Norman nave,* adapted to fit in with the late C12 Transitional work of these two W bays. The adaptation, not without some awkwardness, was to permit a continuation at triforium level with five vaulting shafts (the central one keeled). The W piers have these vaulting shafts from the start. So here is Early *v.* Late Norman. The piers of the arcade arches have a continuous quarter-roll and thin attached shafts, some keeled; capitals mostly decorated scallops but also some foliage. The pointed arches continue the outer quarter-roll, then have keeled rolls before ending (in the innermost order) with steps. The treatment of the TRIFORIUM is highly idiosyncratic. Each bay has two pairs of three stepped round arches, again with continuous quarter-rolls. Attached keeled shafts with trumpet-scallop and crocket capitals support higher arches decorated with chevron, the central one stilted; below these, three large paterae in relief, plus three more in the spandrels above. The whole is set in a pointed arch with continuous quarter-roll. Tripartite stepped CLERESTORY, narrow-pointed, round, narrow-pointed; again continuous quarter-rolls, again chevron (in two varieties) in the central arch. The vaulting shafts, all with foliage capitals (more developed, N side), are arranged for wall arches, transverse arches, and diagonal ribs. The late C14 VAULT contradicts them. In the S aisle the original vault, of double-roll profile, is preserved, the earliest rib vault in the cathedral. The wall-shafts here are as in the nave, their capitals decorated trumpet scallops. The blind Norman windows should also be noted. In the N aisle the vault is Perp, erected after 1352, under Bishop Bryan.

This work at the W end of the Norman nave is neither dated nor closely datable, but (apart from parts of the E piers) is most

---

*And must have been cruciform or compound piers as against the drum piers proposed for the choir.

likely to be of *c.* 1175–85. It is, moreover, difficult to understand why it should differ so markedly from the earlier nave, unless the tower that fell in 1175 was one of a pair of w towers. Among the suggested precedents are Malmesbury Abbey (Wilts.) and Keynsham Abbey (Somerset). The Glastonbury Lady Chapel, datable to 1184–6, has leaf paterae and crocket capitals just like the Worcester w bays.*

The eastern arm

The EASTERN ARM is architecturally the most rewarding part. It is uniform in style, almost a building in itself, with its own transepts to full height, with four bays w and four bays E of these. It is most thrilling in the Lady Chapel bay and in the transepts, where verticalism is unchecked, especially as the latter have no aisles. Unlike other cathedrals with full-height E transepts (Canterbury, Lincoln, Salisbury) this has its High Altar at the E crossing. The sanctuary is raised above the flanking transepts, yet higher than the choir, which stands above the Norman crypt. One descends from the choir aisles to retrochoir and Lady Chapel. The fact that the E crossing piers rise from the latter floor level, even though the E crossing contains the raised sanctuary, increases the sense of verticality. That is further increased by the double tiers of tall lancet windows. The whole *novum opus*, begun 1224, belongs to a more sumptuous period than that preceding it. Purbeck marble was lavished all over it, on the pattern of Canterbury and Lincoln.

Work as usual proceeded from E to w. Ute Engel has identified four PHASES OF CONSTRUCTION. Firstly the Lady Chapel and retrochoir, closely followed by the E crossing and E transepts; irregular stonework on the transept's E walls marks the joint between these phases, probably complete by the death of Bishop William de Blois in 1236. The work started outside the Norman chancel, which only needed to be pulled down when work started on the new choir. To this, the third phase, under Bishop Walter de Cantelupe, belongs only the first bay from the E; work was then halted by the partial collapse of the Norman crypt in 1243. The remainder of the choir, the fourth phase, was probably not finished until *c.* 1255–60.

In the first two phases, the outer walls have blank pointed-trefoiled arcading. Their shafts are Purbeck in the Lady Chapel, freestone otherwise; capitals all leaf crockets. In the spandrels is SCULPTURE: foliage, genre (little animals and monsters), and figure scenes, mostly biblical. The majority are Victorian, by *Boulton*, but some are C13 and well preserved, with thin, agile figures; they must predate the spandrel sculpture in the radiating chapels at Westminster Abbey, begun 1246. The best, starting from the NW corner of the SE transept, include: two Crusaders both fighting lions, a centaur, St

---

*Neil Stratford points to the diagonally set chevron in the triforium arches as a prototype for Bredon and Bricklehampton, qq.v.

19 Michael with scales, the tortures of hell, the jaws of death, a body borne to burial, the Expulsion from Paradise, the dead rising from their graves, Christ enthroned. S aisle: monks building, a devil on a man's shoulders, and various grotesques. Lady Chapel, SE corner: a knight fighting a centaur (across two spandrels). N aisle: a bishop (William of Blois?) offering a model of a cathedral, and the Annunciation, Visitation, and Nativity. NE transept: a monk chastising a novice.

What conveys that irresistible *excelsior* to the Lady Chapel and the transepts is that, though the windows are in two tiers,
20 the Purbeck shafts run up all the way. The RETROCHOIR aisles also have detached Purbeck shafts framing the windows, and are rib-vaulted with small foliage bosses. The responds and E pier of the retrochoir have eight Purbeck and eight subsidiary stone shafts with crocket capitals; W piers slightly simpler, with quatrefoil-form stone cores. Only one N capital shows mature stiff-leaf. Arches with many mouldings. The TRIFORIUM is
22 very odd and very English. It is of gallery proportions, with two layers of arcading. In the front are for each bay two two-light openings with much Purbeck marble, the central shafts with moulded, the clustered outer shafts with foliage capitals; sculpture in the spandrels. The sub-arches grow out of the super-arches in anticipation of what was to be Y-tracery, i.e. the sub-arches have only their inner half-arch entirely to themselves. Behind this detached arcading runs an even blind stone arcade, keeping to its own rhythm; its shafts have moulded capitals, with only small foliage stops above. Tripartite stepped CLERESTORY, with detached Purbeck shafts again with both moulded and foliage capitals. The vaulting shafts in the Lady Chapel rise from the ground, in the retrochoir from the arcade spandrels. They have head corbels here, and foliage capitals first at triforium sill level, then again at clerestory sill. Quadripartite VAULT, with just a longitudinal ridge rib, and with figured bosses. It will be remembered that the E window wall is *Perkins*'s re-creation of the original C13 form; carving in the spandrels by *Boulton*, 1862. In the inner bays of the E transepts triforium, clerestory, and vault are the same. The E crossing piers have to their inner sides four Purbeck and three thinner stone shafts, yet there is no space for shafts for the diagonal vaulting ribs.

The CHOIR W of the E transepts is to all intents and purposes the same. The most obvious differences are that the blank arcading of the aisles ceases and the capitals become richer in their displays of stiff-leaf; most piers are now of the slightly simpler type, the high vault has just foliage bosses. It should also be noticed that the arch soffits differ between the first bay and the three later W bays. In the first (predating the collapse of the crypt) there is an axial roll and fillet here, as in the parts further E. The later three bays have instead a pair of rolls with axial hollow, also one double range of dogtooth in the mouldings above. Many of these later modifications are reminiscent of work at Salisbury. On the choir S side the triforium SCULPTURE includes angels playing musical instruments, the latter restored in the C19. On the N side the triforium carving is of kings and queens, reflecting the tomb of King John below.

Off the S chancel aisle is ST JOHN'S CHAPEL (later used as vestries), on the site of the chapel E of the Norman S transept; two-bay arcade to the aisle, the same details as most of the chancel, two (and a bit) bays of quadripartite vaults. Capitals of the rich type, windows Purbeck-shafted, though the E window is played down for some unknown reason. In the N chancel aisle the two-light windows that alternate with the triplets have cusped rere-arches. At its W end, the pretty Perp ORIEL of the sacrist's lodging (demolished c. 1715); the small doorway below led to it from the aisle.

Crossing

At the main CROSSING the display of Purbeck marble is over. The known date of completion of the tower, 1374, is said to have been seventeen years after it was begun; the Perp piers must therefore be c. 1357. Diamond-shaped in plan, with broad hollows between the shafts; small individual foliage capitals. The arches rise of course to the same height as the nave and chancel vaults. The lowest stage of the tower, not now visible from below, was probably originally intended to be seen; it is surrounded by arcading like Y-tracery with transoms. Unusual lierne vault, intersecting, with some elegant cusping, inserted 1376. Work on the nave vault was going on in 1377, but the crossing piers match the style of the nave S arcade.

Nave and aisles

With the crossing we have anticipated. The first demolitions to replace the Norman nave are recorded in 1309–10; rebuilding must have been well under way by c. 1320. It was not a start from scratch. Apart from the two W bays (see above), we have seen that the N porch contains part of a Norman portal, evidently early, and that the W wall is also early Norman, as is the single shaft surviving at the NE angle of the N aisle. The deep round-arched NICHES along the S aisle wall, completely unmoulded and undecorated, have also been claimed as Norman, but are no doubt C14, meant to hold tombs. C14 work clearly began with the N aisle, said to have been rebuilt by Bishop Cobham (1317–27); the Jesus Chapel, with its more elaborate tracery, was probably meant for his chantry. By 1327 it is likely that the outer wall was completed, as well as the E bays of the aisles with their vaulting, and the chapel. The N ARCADE is of seven bays to the start of the Norman W bays. The piers are very complex, but still start out from the triple vaulting shaft. The centre one has a fillet now. In the diagonals of the piers, 34 two keels. The arches of course are as complex. Capitals treated as one band with thick, knobbly leaves. The TRIFORIUM is based on that of the C13, pared down, without the subtle background arcading; Old Testament figures in its spandrels, partly old but much restored. The CLERESTORY is again stepped tripartite. That is, the nave was designed in a purposely conservative way to carry on from the eastern arm, with a sense of the building as a whole, as at Lichfield. There is, however, a change in the last two bays before the Late Norman W bays are reached; here, at triforium and clerestory levels, are thinner details, similar to though not quite the same as those on the S side,* to which we should now turn.

The S ARCADE is clearly later, tending more towards the Perp style, despite the flowing tracery of the windows which are flanked internally by blank cusped panels. The piers have different bases and thin individual leaf capitals, instead of the band of leaf; the TRIFORIUM also has smaller capitals, the carved figures here entirely by *Boulton*. The vaulting shafts differ too (*see* below). The CLERESTORY, with its sharp triangular heads, is also generally thinner in its forms. So the S side must have gone up after the N, perhaps *c.* 1340–55, reflecting the notable early Perp work at Gloucester. This of course allowed the monastic side to be left alone as long as possible. The E bay of the nave is in its upper details disturbed by internal flying buttresses to support the crossing tower. This must have been done in the later C14, during or soon after the erection of the tower; the straight joints in both N and S elevations show that they are not contemporary with the arcades. Subsequently a thicker buttress was inserted into the second bay, S side.

The vaulting of the nave took place *c.* 1376–80. The VAULT is less elaborate than those of crossing and S transept; it has only diagonal and transverse ribs, and single tiercerons but no liernes. This may, however, have been a compromise (or rather a mid-C14 revision when the S clerestory level was reached), as the springing blocks on the earlier N side made no allowance for the tiercerons. This discrepancy is catered for by inserting tiny ogee arches like fan-vault springers at the base of the vault; similar springers are found in the 1360s–70s in the Tewkesbury transepts as well as the Gloucester N transept. The vault extends W over the two Late Norman bays. Here the infill is mostly tufa, perhaps reused from an earlier vault. The vaults of N aisle and Jesus Chapel as we have seen predate that of the nave. The S aisle has more elaborate lierne vaults, without tiercerons, forming a square grid pattern. Despite these subtle differences, in themselves exemplifying the gradual transition in the West Midlands from Dec to Perp, the overall concern for unity remains remarkable. The overriding consideration at Worcester in the C14 seems to have been to emphasize the antiquity of its cathedral.

*Their headstops, for example, match the others on the N side.

FURNISHINGS

Furnishings are described topographically: from E to W, N before S; fittings, stained glass and monuments are included in each section, usually in that order. It should be added that most of the medieval monuments have been moved at least once (as have some of the later ones).

Lady Chapel and retrochoir

VAULT PAINTING. The E end vaults (chancel aisles excepted) were painted by *Hardman* from c. 1863; here they have musical angels in sexfoils, against scrolly foliage. – STAINED GLASS. Great E window, scenes of the Life of Christ, also by *Hardman*, designed by *J.H. Powell*. Upper lights and central one below, 1859–60, shown at the 1862 Exhibition; the rest 1862–3. – Below, small PAINTING of the Holy Family, by a Flemish follower of Leonardo.

   MONUMENTS. In the Lady Chapel, two effigies of bishops. The finer, SE, of Purbeck marble, has his feet against two big stiff-leaf knops, and stiff-leaf and birds by his head, all in quite high relief; probably William de Blois †1236. The other NE, probably sandstone, noticeably flatter, looks earlier; but it also has wide stiff-leaf by the head. Could it be an inferior copy, perhaps for Walter de Cantelupe †1266? – Good floor brass to the Rev. J.F. St John and widow Frances, by *Hardman*, 1856. – Tablet to Anne Walton †1662, with foliage; attributed to *Jasper Latham* (GF). – Under the N arcade, Charlotte Digby, by *Chantrey*, 1823–5. Seated figure on a couch, gazing heavenward in an attitude of resignation; Gothic detail on the base, its short sides with praying angels in shallow relief. – Lord Lyttelton, chairman of the Joint Restoration Committee, †1876, by *James Forsyth*, 1878. Marble effigy, kneeling angels at each corner, on a rich, heavy alabaster tomb-chest designed by *Gilbert Scott*, with scenes of Christ's Burial and Resurrection. – Opposite, the first Earl of Dudley, the most overwhelming member of the Committee, by *Forsyth*, 1888.* Marble effigy on an alabaster base, livelier than Lyttelton's, with open arcading and marble corner figures. – In a niche behind the High Altar, large mitred figure, of oolite, holding a thick bourdon (staff); tomb-chest decorated with quatrefoils. He probably represents one of the later priors, perhaps Thomas Mildenham †1507. The back of the reredos above is filled by a memorial to Dean John Peel, by *Hardman*, 1876–7; alabaster surface with large incised cross and Evangelist symbols.

Retrochoir north aisle

STAINED GLASS. E window by *Hardman*, 1861; good medallions of the Resurrection. – Below, small PAINTING of the Head of

---

* *Forsyth* also executed the Perseus Fountain at Witley Court, p. 328, for him.

Christ, early C17, attributed to *Tiarini*. – MONUMENTS. A
bishop, probably Thomas de Cobham †1327, of sandstone, his
feet on a lion, damaged angels at his head; originally in the
Jesus Chapel. – Lady, mid-C13, very fine, Purbeck marble, her
dress falling in beautiful symmetrical folds. The feet rest on a
stiff-leaf bracket as if she were standing on a corbel. Around
three sides of the wide slab, an excellent border of pierced
deeply cut stiff-leaf, a curious addition, of limestone. – Cross-
legged knight, in mailed armour, late C13. Good; plain long
shield to his l., his r. hand grasping his sword, its scabbard tip
supported by naturalistic foliage.

North-east transept

Perp stone SCREEN, three-light divisions with dainty quatrefoil
frieze; C15, re-set here, with three new E bays, in 1936 when
the transept became the County War Memorial Chapel. –
STAINED GLASS. W window, First World War memorial, by *J.
Eadie Reid*, 1921, moved from the nave N aisle, 1936. – E,
Second World War memorial, by *Christopher Webb*, 1952.
   MONUMENTS. Against the choir N wall, in a section left
unrestored by Perkins, an arched recess of *c*. 1320, decorated
with ballflower and shields; somewhat later damaged effigy of
a prior or bishop, his feet on two dogs. – To its W, in a big
gabled and moulded recess, a good C15 effigy, with angel supporters, his feet on a lion; remarkably sensitive modelling of
the face. Again, as likely to be a prior as a bishop.

Retrochoir south aisle

STAINED GLASS. E window by *Burlison & Grylls*, 1892. – Central
s by *Hardman*, 1861–2, the Life of Joshua; good portrait brass
below.

South-east transept

TRIPTYCH. Late C15; small alabaster Virgin and Child in centre,
painted wings; on a domestic scale, apparently in its original
housing. – STAINED GLASS. Large s window, Christ as the True
Vine, by *Geoffrey Webb*, 1937. – MONUMENTS. Cross-legged
knight in chain mail, probably *c*. 1320–30; repainted 1805.
Slightly twisting posture, both hands on his sword, shield with
the Harcourt arms; perhaps Sir John de Harcourt †1330. –
Tomb-chest of Sir Gryffyth Ryce †1523. Very like the contemporary tomb-chest of King John and Prince Arthur (*see* below),
its heraldic shields in cusped quatrefoils still pre-Renaissance;
on it, shiny C16-style brasses of Sir Gryffyth and family, by
Hardman, 1863. – The transept's N side is dominated by Prince
Arthur's Chantry (see Choir). Re-set within its substructure,
two effigies, each lying on part of a Purbeck marble tomb-
chest, with six quatrefoils carved with fine seated figures,
angels in the spandrels, all badly decayed. One is a bishop, also

Purbeck, his robes with insets for jewels (cf. King John), a cinquefoiled canopy above his head. Probably *c.* 1290, but perhaps made for Godfrey de Giffard †1302. – The lady to his E, of oolite, with restless drapery, holding a rosary, her feet on her pet dog, could be *c.* 1300; possibly Giffard's sister Matilda d'Evreux †1297.

Choir

Gilbert Scott was first consulted about FURNISHINGS for the restored chancel in 1863; they were installed, all to his designs, in 1867–74. It is the most complete ensemble of his work in any English cathedral; only parts of the stalls, with their mis-ericords, and the pulpit are earlier survivors. Elaborate PAVE-MENT of Devonshire marble and *Godwin* encaustic tiles, with roundels of saints and prophets in the sanctuary, laid by *Poole & Co.*, 1872–3. The vaults, as we have seen, were painted by *Hardman*; more saints in roundels, an array of angels around the boss of Christ in the E crossing. – Opulent gabled REREDOS, made by *Farmer & Brindley*, 1867–8, at a cost of £1,500; stone, alabaster and coloured marbles. Christ in the centre beneath higher gable and tabernacle, flanked by the Evangelists. Further embellished, with much gilding, 1872–4. – Brass COMMUNION RAILS by *Hardman*, 1874. – Of Scott's side SCREENS, that in the first bay (facing Prince Arthur's Chantry, *see* below) is the earliest, of Caen stone and Purbeck marble; the dado incorporates Perp fragments. Then two bays of 1872, mostly oak, followed by the spikily pierced ORGAN CASE (N side, duplicated on the S 1896); and finally, W bays, of elaborate gilt iron, made by *Skidmore*, 1873–4 (Chancel Screen, *see* Crossing, p. 692). – Brass eagle LECTERN by *Hardman*, 1873; three standing bishops below, lions at the base.

The PULPIT is by *Stephen Baldwin*, 1641–2. White stone, wine-glass shape, with six canopied niches containing evange-listic emblems, Tables of Law, the Eye of God etc.; below these, little heraldic cartouches and scrolls. Scott altered it in 1874, adding steps and brass rail. It stood in the nave until moved to the chancel in 1748. Formerly there was an idiosyncratic wooden sounding-board, perhaps C18, with carved drapery held up by disembodied hands (now lost); the carved stone relief from its back support is in the N choir aisle (q.v.).

The BISHOP'S THRONE, ornately carved and canopied, and almost all of the CHOIR STALLS are by *Farmer & Brindley*, 1870–3, again to *Scott*'s design. The stalls, canopied only at the W end, with LIGHTS of *c.* 1965 by *Jack Penton* in George Pace style, contain bits of old work. More importantly they incor-porate, in the upper tier, a fine set of MISERICORDS from the stalls of 1379. Thirty-seven complete scenes, all with support-ers, plus four C19 ones. The medieval scenes, N side, from E are: Temptation of Adam and Eve, their Expulsion, Abraham offering up Isaac, Moses and the Brazen Serpent, Judgment of Solomon, Samson killing the Lion, two men with scrolls, a swineherd striking down acorns, lion and dragon fighting, sow suckling piglets, king hawking, a manticore(?), a sphinx, a basilisk, the Clever Daughter (naked woman on a goat), Adam delving and Eve spinning, a stag beneath a tree, a dragon. S side, from the E: a C19 lion and wyvern fighting; then Abraham leading Isaac, three mowers, three men harvesting, three men reaping, a knight fighting two griffins, huntsman blowing a horn, angel playing a lute, a fine jousting scene, a sower, a woman writing, Presentation of Samuel, a boar, the Circumcision, butcher slaughtering an ox, man bearing foliage (Rogation-tide), angel playing a viol, crowned lion, man playing a flute, an old man stirring a pot. The last, and no doubt others, clearly belong to a series of Labours of the Months; others may be part of a Bestiary series.

MONUMENT. King John †1216. Effigy on a coffin-shaped slab, Purbeck marble, probably c. 1230 (he was reburied in 1232). The earliest surviving royal tomb in England, and one of the finest of C13 monuments; carved in high relief, with realistically modelled head and drapery as good as on any contemporary effigy. His royalty is stressed by the large crown and by the sceptre (now broken off) in his r. hand. The l. hand grips the hilt of his unsheathed sword, the tip of which is bitten by the lion at his feet (with long tail underneath). By his head, two bishops with mitres of Anglo-Saxon type, presumably St Oswald and St Wulfstan, whose shrines may originally have stood to either side. The effigy was originally painted, with insets of semi-precious stones on crown, cuffs, gloves and belt. Tomb-chest of 1529, similar to that in Prince Arthur's Chantry (see below), still without Renaissance detail; shields with royal arms in enriched and cusped quatrefoils.

On the S side of the sanctuary, between the S piers of the E crossing, is PRINCE ARTHUR'S CHANTRY. Arthur, Henry VII's eldest son, died at Ludlow Castle in 1502; work on his chantry chapel started only in 1504. A Late Perp structure with openwork tracery and pierced parapet. To the sanctuary, where there are four sedilia, it begins with an E pinnacle, then has six unusually asymmetrical bays: the E of two lights, the next of three, the third again two, rising higher with pinnacles, then two of three, the second with the depressed ogee-arched entrance (with its original door), then the last blank, of two, again rising higher with pinnacles. The openings have instead of transoms cusped arches, and on them cusped arches reversed. The higher bays and entrance are enriched with panels of canopied niches containing small figures. It is a controlled, not at all haphazard composition.* Interior with flat cusped lierne vault in two bays with two pendants oddly buttressed-out from the E and W ends; royal arms at its centre. Again plenty of small statuary, the heads in many cases spared by the Reformers. The reredos fills the E wall, crowded with figures (principally Christ displaying the five wounds, between

---

* Attached, NE corner, seems to be a fragment of the broad screen on which the shrines of St Oswald and St Wulfstan probably stood.

pairs of kings or saints); densely canopied above. In the w wall, seated figure of Henry VII and a squint. The tomb-chest, without an effigy, stands in the middle; quite simple, decorated only with the royal arms in cusped quatrefoils. From the SE transept, the chantry is even more impressive, as it is one storey higher above a basement (where the two Giffard monuments are incorporated, *see* above, behind open grilles); above them, a broad band with Tudor roses and royal and other arms, an aggressive array of heraldry recalling that at King's College Chapel, Cambridge. The whole composition here is almost symmetrical, the raised centre and blank end bays with five tiers of small statuary.

Choir north aisle

Wrought-iron GATES each end, of 1872. – SCULPTURE (on a window sill). Canopied stone relief of the New Jerusalem, from the chancel pulpit of 1641–2 (*see* above). – STAINED GLASS. 2nd from E, 1906 by *James Powell & Sons*, designed by *William Aikman*; very good. – 4th from E by *Hardman*, 1899.

MONUMENTS. At the E end, bronze plaque of 1913, with portrait roundel, to William, second Duke of Hamilton, †1651 of wounds received at the Battle of Worcester. – W end. Bishop Isaac Maddox †1759, by *Prince Hoare* of Bath; probably his best work, though very staid, perhaps in deliberate contrast to Bishop Hough's monument of 1744–7 (N transept). Large, of grey, black and white marbles. Effulgent inscription; obelisk above, with sarcophagus with relief of the Good Samaritan. On the r., a decently draped female with upturned torch. – Randolph Marriott †1807, by *T. King* of Bath. Pretty tablet with tomb and weeping willow.

Choir south aisle

Oak SCREEN to St John's Chapel, S, 1894–5. – STAINED GLASS. The kneeling prince in the aisle SE window, a copy of a late C15 representation at Little Malvern Priory, is said to be early C19. – St John's Chapel: E by *Hardman*, 1896. – SE by *Hardman*, 1876, SW probably *Clayton & Bell*, 1883, both without their backgrounds.

MONUMENTS. Margaret Rae †1770, by *J. F. Moore*, with his usual excellent use of coloured marbles. Standing monument, inscription flanked by urns, above a sarcophagus with curly top on which perch two putti. Against the obelisk, portrait medallion flanked by palm fronds. – William Burslem †1820, by *R. Westmacott Jun.* Tablet with seated angel in profile, Bible and chalice.

Crypt

WALL PAINTINGS. In the SE chapel, false jointing, double-lined in red, with flowers on curving stalks; probably early C13. Nearby, the soffits of the transverse vault arches are painted orange.* – In the crypt beneath St John's Chapel, two painted lunettes, now all but indecipherable; the W has traces of two figures, the E of a trefoil shape. Probably also early C13. – DOOR, between the crypt 'nave' and the N ambulatory, with Jacobean arched panels. – SCULPTURE. Pietà by *Glynn Williams*, 1991. – MONUMENTS. Many C17–C18 LEDGERS, of black marble. – Also a slab with indents for a C15 priest, discs (Evangelists) at the corners, tabernacle (?) above. – In the closed-off N part of the crypt, two large medieval stone coffins. Further W, two female effigies of *c.* 1300: one very worn; the other, in higher relief, of unusual quality, may represent Isabella, Countess of Clifford, †1301 (widow of Roger de Clifford †1282).

Main crossing

Magnificent SCREEN by *Gilbert Scott*, the first designs 1864, executed by *Francis Skidmore* of Coventry, 1872–3. Of metalwork, oak and marble, of his Lichfield-Hereford type, open, with much cusping and gabled centre, a notable centrepiece to his complete set of furnishings. It replaced a cemented Gothic screen of 1818 (with many misericords fixed to its cornice); this in turn replaced one of 1556, modified 1613, the core of which may have been the original, altered pulpitum of 1381.

North transept

ORGAN CASE. Small, late C17, by *Bernard Schmidt* (*Father Smith*); repaired by *Samuel Green*, 1774. – STAINED GLASS. Great N window by *Lavers & Barraud*, 1866; uncharacteristic, not of their best.

MONUMENTS. Four good standing monuments, the best Bishop Hough †1743, by *L.F. Roubiliac*, 1744–7, his first major monument. Already a dramatic Rococo composition, i.e. one in which symmetry is artfully avoided. On the l. a fine standing female figure representing Religion raises a piece of drapery to reveal the relief on the sarcophagus; this shows the attempted expulsion of Hough from the Presidency of Magdalen College by order of James II, who wanted a Catholic president. On the r. a small seated cherub with portrait medallion of Mrs Hough. Above, on the sarcophagus, the bishop rises in a diagonal, or rather serpentine movement, against an obelisk background. – Bishop James Fleetwood †1683, attributed to *Thomas Cartwright I* (GF). Also black and white marbles, but the very reverse. No figures, just a reredos or aedicule, with two Corinthian columns and broken segmental pediment with heraldry. – Bishop Edward Stillingfleet †1699, attributed to *Grinling Gibbons* (GF). Grey marble, again reredos type, with gadrooned base. Two putto heads rather

86

*A large quantity of painted plaster debris, no doubt from Wulfstan's E end, was found during the excavations of 1986–7.

unconvincingly hold back the drapery from the inscription. – Sir Thomas Street †1695, but executed by *Joseph Wilton*, 1774. An exquisitely chaste reredos, with Ionic demi-pilasters and pediment, and Adamish urn like a wine-cooler. A splendid putto hovers above, holding a Cap of Liberty on a pole. – Also several tablets by *Joseph Stephens* (as elsewhere in the cathedral). The best, probably his though unsigned, is Rev. James Stillingfleet †1817; large, with altar with Ionic volutes pierced with drapery, and flaming urn. – Early C20 tablets with portrait roundels, e.g. Mrs Henry Wood, the popular novelist, †1887, by *D.S. Wise*, c. 1914.

South transept

Huge ORGAN CASE designed by *Scott*, 1873. Now mostly empty. Fine stencilling on the display pipes, various carved angels. Overwhelming like Lord Dudley, who insisted on having a nave as well as choir organ. – STAINED GLASS. Good s window, Queen Adelaide Memorial, by *George Rogers*, 1852–3: a Tree of Jesse in the style of c. 1200, designed by *Frederick Preedy*. – MONUMENTS. Mary Hall (of the Island of Jamaica and Bevere near this city) †1794, by *William Stephens*, perhaps his best work. Standing white monument with seated woman, pensively reading, leaning on an urn wreathed with ivy. – Small tablets include Henrietta Wrottesley †1719, by *Thomas White*.

Nave

PAVEMENT in nave and aisles, of Sicilian white and Kilkenny 21 black marbles, laid 1872–3 by *Joseph Wood & Son* of Worcester. Here *Scott* is said to have been inspired by Amiens; it is far more like Burlington and Kent's floors at York Minster. – Elaborate PULPIT by Scott, 1873–4, carved by *James Forsyth*; highly coloured marbles and alabaster, sculptured scenes of famous preachings. – STAINED GLASS. Great w window by *Hardman*, 1874–5, designed by *J.H. Powell*. Large roundels of the Six Days of Creation in the outer sections; Adam and Eve in the centre.

MONUMENTS. Beneath the N arcade, a late C14 Beauchamp knight and his lady, perhaps John Beauchamp of Powick and wife Elizabeth; sandstone, restored and repainted. Tomb-chest with shields of arms in ogee trefoil-headed panels. Impressive effigies, both with feet on greyhounds. His head rests on a helm with black swan crest; hers is cushioned by another black swan. – Opposite, Robert Wilde †1608 and wife Margaret. Recumbent effigies on tomb-chest with decorated floral strips instead of pilasters. Inscriptions removed. On the aisle wall nearby, the tablet that stood at the head of the tomb, dated 1608, with strapwork. – Dean Richard Eedes †1604 (w end, s). Effigy, his head on a book placed on a cushion; high sarcophagus tomb-chest with garish leaf decoration. Canopy with cambered heads on solid corner piers, each with two attached Corinthian columns, incorrectly detailed; vault with diagonal and ridge ribs. Strapwork cresting. – Opposite, Bishop John Thornborough †1641, but erected 1627. Not at all complete; what remains shows that this was much more correctly classical. Round-arched canopy with attached Corinthian columns. Wooden inscription board with strapwork frame.

Nave north aisle

The JESUS CHAPEL, originally Bishop Cobham's chantry chapel, used as a baptistery from *c.* 1756, restored by *R.A. Briggs*, 1899. His the crisp stone SCREEN in Perp style, two tiers with rood above, and wooden ALTAR with huge REREDOS; all carved by *H.H. Martyn & Co.* of Cheltenham. – Big ROYAL ARMS, of stone, later C17, probably brought in from outside. – SCULPTURE. Loose, a fine C13 corbel with two tumblers. – STAINED GLASS. N window, 1st bay from E. By *Lavers & Barraud*, 1864; slender stylized figures of Faith, Charity, and Hope. Very intense, the best Victorian glass in the cathedral. – Jesus Chapel. By *Wailes*, 1849; six ogee-headed panels of baptismal scenes, in two tiers, backgrounds removed. – N window, 6th bay. By *C.C. Powell*, 1932. – 8th bay, memorial to Sir Edward Elgar, by *A.K. Nicholson*, 1935. – W window by *Hardman*, 1895, Solomon in his Temple.

MONUMENTS (E to W). Bishop Nicholas Bullingham †1576. Recumbent effigy, its upper and lower parts sliced in half by a large block with heraldry and finely lettered inscription. He was, we read among other things, 'a painful preacher of the truthe'. The Perp base has probably nothing to do with the effigy; he originally lay in a recess on the N side of the sanctuary (cf. the Perp remains built into *Scott*'s screen). – In the seventh bay, three small C17 tablets: Robert Luddington †1625; Henry Bright †1627; and Elizabeth Powell †1697, perhaps by *Thomas White*. – John Moore †1613, wife, sons and daughters. Large kneeling figures, the three women behind the three men. Pendant-vaulted recess, with coupled Composite columns; flat canopy. The urns may be an C18 addition. – Abigail Goldsborough †1613, perhaps by *Samuel Baldwin*. Standing monument; she kneels, quite small, in a coffered-arched recess between Composite columns. – Monument to those who fell by the Sutlej river, in the Sikh Wars, 1845–6; by *R. Westmacott Jun.*, 1849. Classical, white marble. An officer stands, r. hand on his sword, l. on his breast, by a memorial tablet draped with regimental colours. – Cecily Warmstrey †1649. Tablet with Composite columns and wreathed oval medallion, originally with painted inscription. Below, a corpse in a winding sheet, yet propped up on one elbow. Broken segmental pediment, with two female mourners. – Martha Middleton †1705; good tablet, grey and white marbles. – Opposite, Bishop Richard Hurd †1808, by *Stephens & Co.* Simple classical, without figures, a little dry; sarcophagus above with mitre and crozier, sunburst, clouds and cross below. – Freestanding, Bishop Henry Philpott †1892, by *Sir Thomas Brock*. Of white marble. Life-sized figure, one hand raised, seated on an ornate throne.

Nave south aisle

FONT. By *G.F. Bodley*, 1891. Sandstone, octagonal, ogee niches with angels. Immensely tall pinnacled cover reaching to the vault (cf. Bodley's at Southwark Cathedral). – STAINED GLASS. S window, 1st bay from E. By *Lavers & Westlake*, 1894; rather tame. – 2nd bay. By *Herbert Bryans*, 1900. C14 fragments in the tracery lights, much restored by *Hardman*, 1868, as were similar fragments in other S aisle windows. – 3rd bay, good Arts and Crafts by *Christopher & Veronica Whall*, 1923–4. – 5th bay by *Hardman*, 1877. – W window by *Clayton & Bell*, also 1877.

MONUMENTS (E to W). Bishop William Thomas †1689, carved by *Thomas White c.* 1710. Brown and grey marbles, not large, very simple. No figures, no display, apart from his mitre and crook. – Thomas Jones †1804. Tablet with pair of urns. – Set in the first gabled recess, a late C14 prior, perhaps Walter de Legh †1388; tonsured head, feet on a lion. – Edward Corles †1866, by *J. Stephens*, with scene of the Good Samaritan. – The next bay has a similar C14 recess, the only other of the S aisle niches thus prepared to receive a monument. It now contains the recumbent alabaster effigy of Bishop Henry Parry †1616, re-set here 1872, with new front part of stone. – Big plain Late Perp tomb-chest, entirely renewed. – Good tablets nearby: Susannah Warren †1792, by *Ricketts* of Bath, with weeping putto; Mary Whitmore †1808, surrounded by the serpent of eternity; Catherine Palmer †1703, a cartouche attributed to *Francis Bird* (GF). – John Bromley †1674, by *William Stanton*. Narrow standing monument, urn on top. – Sir Thomas Lyttelton †1481. Tomb-chest of polished marble; octofoils with repainted heraldic shields. The brass effigy, in judicial robes, is missing. – Sir Thomas Lyttelton †1650 and wife Catherine †1666; signed *Stanton*, i.e. also probably *William Stanton*, mid-1670s. Black and white marble, again tall and narrow, attached Ionic columns. – Bishop Edmund Freake †1591, signed *Anthony Tolly*. High tomb-chest with caryatids and atlantes, coats of arms in broad strapwork cartouches. Pedimented back tablet; coffered arch with fluted Ionic pilasters. Has this never had an effigy? – Bishop Walter Blandford †1675, attributed to *Jasper Latham* (GF). Pinkish brown standing monument, of noble simplicity. Tall Ionic columns, broken curly pediment, no figures. – Col. Sir Henry Walton Ellis †1815 at Waterloo; by *John Bacon Jun*. Large, white, standing monument. He sinks from his horse to be received by the Angel of Victory with laurel wreath; kneeling soldier to the r. Obelisk background. – Richard Woolfe. Very good Renaissance-style tablet of 1879–80, of sgraffito, or rather *pietre dure*. – Richard Solly †1803. White standing monument, also by *Bacon Jun.*, 1804. His wife, with

85

their three young children, grieves by the sarcophagus. Gothic background. Very fine, as Bacon often could be. – Bishop John Gauden †1662, probably by *Joshua Marshall*. Black and white. Demi-figure with book, in an oval recess, beneath open segmental pediment. A little heavy and rather busy; the decoration nicely done. – Bishop James Johnson †1774. Standing monument, of white marble. The design, with sarcophagus etc., is by *Robert Adam*, with excellent bust on top carved by *Nollekens*.

THE CLOISTERS AND MONASTIC REMAINS

Worcester, a monastic cathedral at the centre of a very large medieval diocese, displays substantial remains of a major Benedictine priory. The cloisters are complete, together with the remarkable chapter house, E side, and the (restored) refectory, S. Of other parts there are only ruins, notably the Guesten Hall, E of the chapter house, and bits of the dormitory and reredorter, which lay in an exceptional position W of the W range, towards the River Severn.

Cloisters

The Norman CLOISTERS were mostly rebuilt in the late C14–early C15, beginning with the E walk between 1372 and c. 1395, probably in the 1380s. The DOORWAY from the aisle, at the E end of the N walk, with moulded capitals and fine arch mouldings with many fillets, looks c. 1300 at the latest. Smaller doorway at the W end of the N walk, Perp, with four-centred arch. The most striking motifs, chains of reticulation units in the window embrasures and squints between each bay, are applied to all walks but the western. As the cloister is not quite square, the slightly greater length of the E walk is disguised by transverse arches of similar reticulation chains, towards its N and S ends. The Perp panel tracery of the five-light WINDOWS is all by *Perkins*, 1865–7, and very successful; it replaced more basic tracery inserted 1762. The VAULT in all four walks is of the same type with central octagon of lierne ribs, though the W (perhaps not completed until the 1430s) differs slightly in detail. The BOSSES most distinguish walk from walk. In the E walk there are not over-many, and they are small, nearly all leaves and heads. The S walk, perhaps c. 1405, has the finest bosses, all figures and scenes. Centre bay with the Coronation of the Virgin, the Tree of Jesse further E, bishops and kings elsewhere. Their varying state of preservation seems to be due to the different types of stone used. The W walk again has small foliage bosses. The N walk's bosses are quite different, with large applied figures of angels (plus figures of the Trinity and Evangelist symbols at the centre) rather than real bosses. These suggest that this, rather the W walk, was the last to be vaulted, though rebuilding here may have begun in conjunction with

38

rebuilding the S nave aisle. The OUTER WALLS of much of the cloister remain substantially Norman, perhaps in parts even earlier, as a closer and more extensive examination of the ranges around will show. – Slate and stone PAVEMENT by *Perkins* (originally in the nave), laid 1873. – MONUMENT. Very weathered sandstone effigy of an ecclesiastic, N walk E end; perhaps John Fordham, prior 1409–38, under whom the cloisters were completed. – STAINED GLASS. Small historical scenes in the tracery lights: E and N walks 1916–23, mostly by *J. Eadie Reid*; W walk, 1930–40s by *A.J. Davies*. – Engraved window, S walk, by *Mark Cazalet*, 1999.

Monastic buildings on the east side of the cloisters

The E WALL begins with coursed rubble, apparently earlier than the ashlar Early Norman masonry immediately following, and keyed into it. Then the first room in the E range, the groin-vaulted SLYPE, now tea-room, entered through a continuously moulded C14 doorway, flanked by canopied niches, with reticulation in the arch. On entering, one is back in Wulfstan's time, with blind arcading, each of two bays of three arches, on either side. The S side has columns with block and single-scallop or single-trumpet capitals, just like the crypt; square abaci, arches with roll-moulded soffits. But the N side seems almost entirely of Anglo-Saxon masonry, with 'lathe-turned' capitals and bulbous bases. These are probably reused, although an overlap is not impossible; after all, Wulfstan was an Anglo-Saxon, not a Norman. The bulbous capitals are similar to C10 capitals in the Wipertus Crypt at Quedlinburg, also to C11 capitals at Great Paxton near Huntingdon. There are also a couple of bulbous bases, S side. Above the slype is the TREASURY, a series of vaulted rooms constructed *c.* 1377, with excellent contemporary tiled floors; it is entered from St John's Chapel, off the S chancel aisle.

After the slype the E range continues with two large rectangular RECESSES, probably receptacles for the Norman library (now housing redundant C14–C17 bells). The chapter house entrance belongs again to the late C14. Four-centred DOORWAY, Perp panel tracery above, quite possibly the earliest in the cathedral; pairs of canopied niches in the reveals, another reticulation chain in the arch.

But the CHAPTER HOUSE itself is again Norman, probably *c.* 1100–15, certainly no later than the 1120s; in any case, it is the earliest surviving example of that solely British speciality, the centrally planned chapter house. Worcester's is particularly memorable for being (originally) round inside and out – in ten sections, each with a single window. The lower inside wall still is round, but in the late C14, when the large four-light, four-centred Perp windows were made, the upper walls inside and the visible outer walls entirely were rebuilt straight-sided to form a decagon, with big stepped buttresses at the angles; Norman masonry, mixed red and white stone, seems to have been reused.* With its middle column supporting semicircular radial ribs, this building shared with Durham choir the Norman willingness to experiment with a major stone vault over a broad span (over 55 ft (17 metres) diameter here). The present central column, despite its elementary capital, is a reconstruction of *c.* 1240, see especially the waterholding base. The work of the C13 and late C14 suggests the original structural solution here was imperfect. But, although the vault may also have been interfered with since the early C12, essentially such a vault on such a column must have been here from the beginning. Behind the stone bench (now renewed) are shallow round-arched niches, some, N side, retaining traces of later wall painting;† above, an area of intersecting blank arcading with smaller sub-arches, with block or single-scalloped capitals, topped with billet frieze. The whole of this lower zone is patterned with alternate courses of white Cotswold and green Highley stone, but is otherwise not enriched as later Norman work would have been. Traces of the Norman doorway inside show it to have been on a slightly different alignment to its C14 replacement, but that it was not flanked by open bays to the cloister (in contrast, for example, to Winchester). *Perkins* restored the chapter house in 1862.

Continuing along the cloister, one passes a plain single-chamfered doorway, then, turning the corner, the C13–C14 doorway which leads into the usual tunnel-vaulted PASSAGE to the S. Its S exit has a portal of *c.* 1200; four orders of shafts with foliage capitals, round arch with an inner order of individual affronted small leaves, then roll mouldings, one with an order of pellets.

To the E of the E range and chapter house are the ruins of the GUESTEN HALL, of five bays, aligned N–S. All that survives is the E lateral wall, its windows exhibiting remains of flowing tracery of the first order, the best in the cathedral. Richard K. Morris suggests these imply a date near the end of Braunsford's priorate, i.e. *c.* 1338–9, rather than the traditional date, *c.* 1320. Two very tall S windows with transoms, plus part of the third; two N (dais end) higher up, with small doorway beneath. Here another building, probably the prior's chapel, adjoined the hall; the prior's lodging (demolished 1846) lay beyond. On the opposite side were four bays of windows plus a porch. The Guesten Hall was partly demolished in 1862, its fine roof given to Holy Trinity, Shrub Hill Road (itself demolished 1969); it is now at the Avoncroft Museum of Buildings (p. 608).

---

* A curving stone wall, concentric to the chapter house, about 10 ft (3 metres) outside it, was excavated in the late 1990s; its date and purpose are unknown. It predated the late C14 but not the Norman work.
† The ceiling vaults were probably painted from the outset, with an elaborate cycle of Old and New Testament subjects, plus perhaps the Tree of Jesse on the central column; cf. the C12 manuscript in the Cathedral Library.

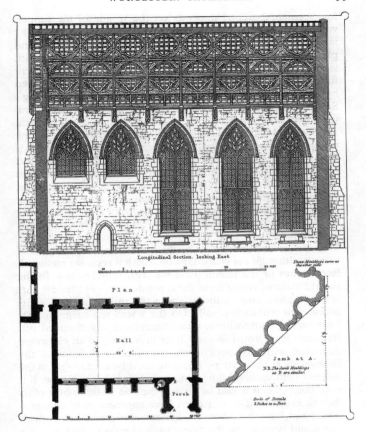

Worcester Cathedral, Guesten Hall.
Interior elevation and plan

Monastic buildings on the south side of the cloisters

The entire S side is occupied, as usual, by the REFECTORY, originally a large first-floor Early Norman hall, above an undercroft; the latter survives, the hall itself was rebuilt in the C14,
probably in the 1330s.* The cloister wall towards the refectory
cannot be deciphered with certainty. It is very thick, aligned
neither with the cathedral nor the other monastic buildings.
There are two large blocked Norman arches, plus a roll-
moulded doorway into the undercroft. The C14 refectory
doorway is near the W end: finely moulded with fillets, with
hoodmould with leaf and three small animals. The main
entrance to the Norman undercroft seems to have been the

---

*Dr Hopkins's C17 notebooks give the date 1372.

low segmental-arched doorway on the w side of the tunnel-vaulted passage leading s from the cloisters. The UNDERCROFT is now subdivided but retains its central row of squat piers and plain groined vaults; the three central piers are round with simple capitals, suggesting this part may have had a different function from the two ends. The refectory above was restored by *Ewan Christian*, 1885–7, as the College Hall of the King's School (which purpose it still serves); the five three-light lateral windows, either with ogee reticulation or three-petal pattern, are basically trustworthy. The high-set windows with flowing tracery either end are mostly C19 renewal. The main show is to the s, facing College Green, where the Norman undercroft has flat buttresses and a row of round-arched openings beneath a continuous dripmould. The present finely moulded entrance, sw, is of 1886–7. There was no medieval doorway here at ground level, though there may have been an upper door giving access from the octagonal kitchen (immediately sw, finally demolished 1845).

Inside the refectory HALL, the timber roof is entirely of 1886–7, although the wall-shafts on which it rests are medieval. Rere-arches of the lateral windows with fluted shafts. In the second window recess from the E, N side, survives the rear part of the vaulted stone canopy above the pulpit (as well as its access stair within the wall). On the E wall is a magnificently bold carved composition, unfortunately largely chopped off. Its centre is an over-life-size Christ in Majesty in an elongated quatrefoil with dogtooth in the surround and Signs of the Evangelists at the corners. The date must be *c.* 1220–30, as the drapery demonstrates. The composition is French in type. If it were complete, it would be among the two or three best of its date in England. The C14 must have appreciated it, or else it would not have been reused. Friezes above and below, with heads and beasts, also the thinly vaulted pairs of niches either side, are C14 additions. Traces of paint, especially red, survive in the backgrounds.

Monastic buildings on the west side of the cloisters

The w range of the cloister is exceptional amongst English monastic cathedrals in that the dormitory range ran E–W to a line far forward of the cathedral front. The normal position, on the upper floor of the E range, was precluded at Worcester by the unusual form of the chapter house; the arrangement here puts the reredorter close to the river for the convenience of the drains (cf. Durham). The infirmary range was also here, probably partly beneath the reredorter, partly in a separate building w or sw of the cathedral; its normal place would have been somewhere to the E of the E range. At Worcester there was more peace and quiet near the river.

In the w cloister, meanwhile, coming from the s walk, one sees first an inserted pointed doorway, leading to Nos. 14–14A College Green, an early C19 house mostly built against the cloister wall here, on the site of the Sub-Prior's Lodging. Then, conveniently close to the original refectory entrance, the wide two-bay monks' LAVATORIUM, C14 of course, probably c. 1395–6, but partly altered; its end walls have small arches on head- or lion-stops. The base of a C13 nook-shaft immediately N may be a remnant of an earlier lavatorium. Next to this, a small round-arched Late Norman doorway with continuous filleted rolls, probably an entrance to the dormitory sub-vault (see below); earlier blocked opening above. The main dormitory entrance (at least from the C15) is marked by a large and deep square-headed Perp niche, with wide four-centred doorway. Then various other openings, some of which must have lit the steps up to the dormitory, before the tall arch of its Early Norman predecessor, with big roll moulding on block capitals; the height of this doorway no doubt allowed for an earlier rising stair. Blocked four-centred doorway beneath it, presumably providing temporary access after 1377, until the new entrance was ready.* Finally Late Norman work reappears with the portal to the PASSAGE, or W slype (now the shop), in the N bay of the W range; this gave access to the infirmary. The pointed doorway has a continuous quarter-roll, sandwiched between keeled shafts with trumpet-scallop capitals; arch with undercut point-to-point chevron. It is reasonable to assume that this passage was built at the same time as the adjoining W bays of the nave. It is rib-vaulted in four bays, on triple corbels with scallop capitals; these do not rise from the same level, the middle one always starting a little lower. One capital has short broad leaves, compared by Neil Stratford to the nave at Abbey Dore, Herefs. Canted abaci, single-chamfered ribs. The W exit again has a continuous quarter-roll. Just within the passage, a blocked Norman opening, S, probably for a vanished stairway to the floor above; at the NW end, a blocked pointed doorway to the S aisle SW stair-turret, for access to the LIBRARY. This is in the roof space above the S aisle, prepared for this or some other purpose in the late C14 by raising the outer wall and introducing the small paired windows already observed.

Of the DORMITORY, and the sub-vault above which it stood, very little evidence remains: besides its E wall (i.e. the W side of the cloister), there is just the portion of the N wall shared with the infirmary passage, a fragment of the W end of the S wall, and more of the W wall, all thoroughly patched. The W side of the cloister wall (visible from the private garden of Nos. 13–14 College Green) is most obscure. It is of a kind of masonry not found anywhere else in the cathedral precincts, with irregular narrow bands of Lias between courses of mostly Highley stone; this could be of Saxon origin. The dormitory itself, 123 ft (38 metres) long by 63 ft (19 metres) wide, was rebuilt 1375–7, with two parallel roofs (there is no evidence as to how the interior was divided). It was rebuilt on the Norman

---

* The wall into which these various dormitory openings are cut may be Saxon (see below).

sub-vault, eight bays long, also subdivided into parallel naves, by oblong piers; its groin vaults and transverse arches of *c.* 1110–20 were remade *c.* 1375 with single-chamfered ribs. The REREDORTER (or latrine) formed the top floor of a three-storey range which ran W in line with the N half of the dormitory, projecting over the steep fall of the ground to the river. Remarkably much of it is preserved, partly visible from the public garden SW of the cathedral (though it is uncommonly difficult to work out these ruins). The tallest remaining part belonged to the reredorter S wall, with two pairs of deeply set small lancets still visible. This wall stood immediately N of the necessary drainage channel, with a parallel and presumably lower range to the S. The E wall, i.e. the W wall of the dormitory and its sub-vault, mostly of *c.* 1110–20, also partly survives as we have seen. Harold Brakspear (in 1912) argued that the two storeys or sub-vaults below the reredorter were parts of the infirmary (if so, hardly a satisfactory arrangement). The upper, perhaps the infirmary hall, was five by two bays in size; the parallel range, S, had four bays with Norman flat buttresses. Both of the lower sub-vaults mostly survive. The N one has two vessels divided by round columns with moulded capitals; single-chamfered ribs between cells made of very large stones, pairs of lancets in deep recesses in the N wall. The narrower sub-vault, S (visible from the steps between the two parts of the public garden) had an open arcade of wide semicircular arches, probably a kind of cloister walk; this was filled in and windows inserted in the C14 (when a further storey seems to have been added). The steps may occupy the site of the monastic prison, with a garderobe within the thickness of the wall to the W.

THE PRECINCTS

Worcester Cathedral has not got a real precinct, except on its S side where College Green, the former Great Court of the Benedictine priory, provides some sense of a close. Ever since a road was cut through its NE angle in 1794, that side has lost all seclusion; the channelling since the 1960s of through traffic along just that corner (College Street) has made things infinitely worse. The former Bishop's Palace (in Deansway) no longer has anything to do visually with the cathedral, except when seen from the Severn. It is just a large house behind a wall, next to the Worcester College of Technology (p. 726), beside that ferocious traffic route.

The north side: College Street and College Yard

A few trees shelter the NE aspect of the cathedral from COLLEGE STREET. Just NE of the NE transept stood a large octagonal C14 bell-tower, called Clocherium, free-standing (cf. Chichester), with steep conical roof or spire; demolished in the C17. Adjoining it, E, was the medieval parish church of St Michael;* stone

---

* Replaced by a church by *Eginton*, 1840, across College Street; demolished 1965.

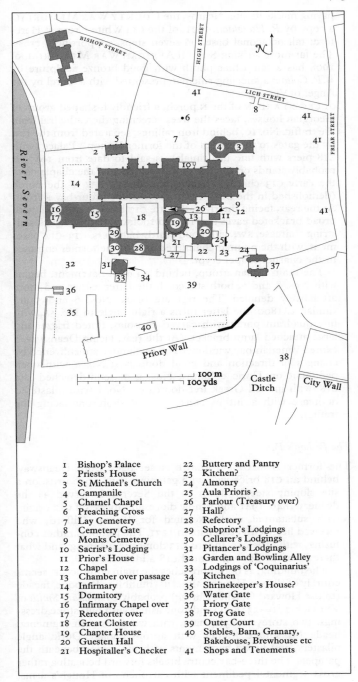

1	Bishop's Palace	22	Buttery and Pantry
2	Priests' House	23	Kitchen?
3	St Michael's Church	24	Almonry
4	Campanile	25	Aula Prioris ?
5	Charnel Chapel	26	Parlour (Treasury over)
6	Preaching Cross	27	Hall?
7	Lay Cemetery	28	Refectory
8	Cemetery Gate	29	Subprior's Lodgings
9	Monks Cemetery	30	Cellarer's Lodgings
10	Sacrist's Lodging	31	Pittancer's Lodgings
11	Prior's House	32	Garden and Bowling Alley
12	Chapel	33	Lodgings of 'Coquinarius'
13	Chamber over passage	34	Kitchen
14	Infirmary	35	Shrinekeeper's House?
15	Dormitory	36	Water Gate
16	Infirmary Chapel over	37	Priory Gate
17	Reredorter over	38	Frog Gate
18	Great Cloister	39	Outer Court
19	Chapter House	40	Stables, Barn, Granary,
20	Guesten Hall		Bakehouse, Brewhouse etc
21	Hospitaller's Checker	41	Shops and Tenements

Worcester Cathedral Priory precincts.
Plan of suggested medieval layout

paving marks its site. Nearby, the COUNTY WAR MEMORIAL, a copy by *R. Haughton*, 1921, of the C14 White Cross at Hereford: tall octagonal base, on seven steps, supporting a cross. The far more striking SOUTH AFRICAN WAR MEMORIAL of 1908 has a tall ashlar plinth with good bronze sculpture by *W.R. Colton*: a kneeling rifleman presented with a laurel by the Angel of Victory.

COLLEGE YARD, N of the N porch, a friendly L-shaped group of Georgian houses, faces the trees screening the cathedral from the traffic. No. 10, behind iron railings, separated from the rest by the gates to the garden of the former Bishop's Palace (with C18 piers with fine urn finials), is said to date from 1687. It probably stands on the site of the residence of the chaplains of the early C13 charnel chapel, immediately NW of the porch (demolished in the C17). Early C19 stuccoed four-bay E front. At the rear, facing the river, the late C17 brick is exposed, with broad bracketed eaves and hipped roof; contemporary closed-string staircase, SW, with good sturdy balusters. C13–C14 basement, with the pointed chamfered arch of the former entrance to the charnel chapel crypt.

The main L-plan group, behind a raised pavement, begins with Nos. 8 and 7, both stuccoed, the latter earlier and more attractively detailed. The rest are brick. Nos. 6 and 5 are similar, *c.* 1800; the latter turns a right angle to No. 5A, with fine quadrant porch with carved consoles, fluted frieze, and large attached lamp bracket. (At the rear, facing Deansway, a canted Venetian bay window.) The remainder are enlivened by changes of direction and good doorcases: No. 4 with open pediment on Doric columns; Nos. 2–3, semi-detached late C18, with incised Greek fret doorcases; No. 1 with pilastered doorcase with acanthus consoles (and shopfront facing the traffic).

The Bishop's Palace

The former BISHOP'S PALACE is set back from Deansway, behind an C18 brick wall with gatepiers with stone urns, on a site sloping steeply down to the Severn. It served as the deanery 1846–1941 and is now diocesan offices. Of C12 origin, with substantial work executed for Bishop Giffard, who received licence to crenellate in 1271. The layout is rather confusing, with little of standard C13 domestic planning, and what there is masked by substantial C18 additions.

The building, as one approaches the main entrance, E, seems entirely of Bishop Hough's time, its 'bumbling Baroque' façade (to use Howard Colvin's phrase) probably by *William Smith* of Warwick, 1719–23. Red sandstone ashlar with buff stone dressings, two storeys, 4+3+4 bays, with windows with segmental heads (in square frames with aprons), giant Doric angle pilasters, and broad battlements with big coving beneath the parapets. The three-bay centre breaks forward beneath a rather gross segmental pediment with cartouche of Hough's arms;

keyed oculus above the surprisingly insignificant round-arched doorway. The return sides, negotiating the slope, are confusing, but there is clearly much medieval masonry including an apparently Norman arch at low level, SW corner. The W front, facing the river, begins with a buttressed medieval section, with narrow lancets below, and two two-light windows of *c.* 1300 above, with Geometrical tracery (one partly blocked). Then a plain three-bay three-storey projection, of *c.* 1759–74, probably by *Stiff Leadbetter*, for Bishop Johnson. The medieval work reappears, beneath a half-hipped roof, with the large (mostly C19?) end window of the hall, with its five stepped trefoil-headed lancets, above the two-light C14 window of its undercroft. Finally the big canted bay window of the drawing room, added for Bishop Hurd, *c.* 1781–7, with open ground floor on three round arches.

Inside, one has at once a wide staircase with three balusters per tread, the central one with long shallow twist, and unusually richly carved tread ends with foliage above volutes. Move up that stair or down into the basement and you are in the C13 house, against the E side of which the C18 front range was built. The top landing probably stands on the site of the medieval porch. A doorway to its N opens into the GREAT HALL, set E–W, much redone, especially in the late C15. Roof with ovolo-moulded beams on arched braces and renewed corbels. At the E end, a large Perp doorway with steep arch with continuous mouldings and hoodmould. Early C17 chimneypiece with imported overmantel with broad strapwork and allegorical figures. The CHAPEL of the palace lies W of the landing (or porch), originally running parallel to the hall. What remains is only its chancel, reorientated N–S for Bishop Sandys in the 1560s; canted roof, trefoil-headed piscina below the five-light late Perp window in the S wall. Large blocked W arch to the former nave. C17 panelling and other fittings mostly introduced for Bishop Skinner, including the canopied bishop's pew. C18–C19 stained glass.

At basement level, below the landing, is an undercroft of one elongated rib-vaulted bay, with a late C13 N doorway into the splendid undercroft beneath the hall, now called the ABBOT'S KITCHEN. Four bays of rib vaulting, the ribs springing from moulded corbels and forming quadripartite bays, with a longitudinal ridge rib in addition; foliage bosses. One roll-moulded lancet, N. At the NE corner was the spiral staircase up to the hall. Blocked E window with roll mouldings with fillets; W window with similar mouldings. N of the W half of the undercroft are two smaller rib-vaulted C13 chambers, with E of them remains of a C15 room, probably the kitchen.

Beneath the S part of the building, two more fine rib-vaulted undercrofts, to an L-plan, two bays E–W and four N–S; this has the narrow lancets to the W, noticed outside. Above, all is altered. The library is lit by the two bar-traceried windows, which must have been part of the solar. Above the E–W part was probably the bishops' private hall, of Norman origin.

Former COACHHOUSE and STABLES, SE, probably again
c. 1719–23. Brick, ashlar quoins and bands, 3+1+3 bays, the
centre pedimented with keyed oculus.

College Precincts

COLLEGE PRECINCTS is the little pedestrian street facing the E
end of the cathedral and its E precinct wall, i.e. it is really in the
town: a row of small Georgian brick houses, varying in height
and forming a pretty picture. The first few are early to mid-C19.
The street narrows at No. 4 (BURGAGE HOUSE), six bays altogether with fluted keystones, probably originally two mid-C18
houses; later C18 pedimented doorway with palm-leaf capitals.
No. 7 is early C18, with moulded wooden cornice, and another
good later C18 doorway, with pilasters with lozenge decoration.
At No. 8 a modillion cornice and C19 bow window; at No. 9 a
pair of linked gables, probably denoting an earlier origin.

College Green

COLLEGE GREEN, the former monastic Great Court on the S
side of the cathedral, is, as has been said, the only fragment of
real precinct remaining at Worcester. Substantial sections of
the monastic boundary wall run along its E and S sides, behind
the C18–C19 buildings which now nearly all form part of the
King's School (*see* pp. 727–8), before returning N along the
bank of the Severn (*see* below). The picture is complicated by
the fact that WORCESTER CASTLE, of which virtually nothing
is left above ground, stood immediately S, on the site now occupied by the main school buildings. In 1084, after the Northern Rebellion, much of the Great Court was requisitioned to
enlarge the castle's outer bailey. This was returned to the Priory
in 1217. It is thus unclear whether the fragments of sandstone
walling incorporated into the buildings of College Green
belonged to the castle or to monastic outbuildings.

The Green is entered from the outside world by the EDGAR
TOWER, a gateway probably begun 1346–7 and completed
after licence to crenellate had been obtained in 1368–9. To the
outside, where all detail belongs to *Perkins*'s restoration (1869),
two polygonal turrets flank two two-light windows under
crocketed hoodmoulds; two tiers of canopied niches to l. and
r., three tiers between. The niches contain terracotta figures by
R. F. Wells of Chelsea, 1910. To the inner side the arrangement
is similar but simpler. The archway has continuous chamfers,
to the outside separated by the portcullis groove. Within, it
is subdivided by a cross-wall, alone making the distinction
between pedestrians and carriages, with the original battened
doors. Inner vault with diagonal and ridge ribs, the outer with
in addition liernes and murder holes. Inside, the turret rooms
have small rib vaults, with other rib-vaulted rooms to the S.
The main upper room (now King's School Library) has a small
doorway with shouldered lintel, the shoulders double-curved.

NW of Edgar Tower, on the site of the medieval Almoner's House, is No. 15 (THE GUESTEN), built by *William Stephens*, c. 1730–40; it was the Deanery from 1942 until the late C20. Seven by four bays, with prominent keystones and rusticated angle quoins; doorway with Gibbs surround and pediment. In the hallway, a panelled dado and pair of rear arches leading to the pretty open-well staircase, with slender turned balusters and closed string with carved tread ends. Rear addition by *William Wilkinson* of Oxford, 1869.

Opposite, No. 2, early C18 with simple Doric porch, its w side facing the Green. Then buildings for the King's School, keeping to the older scale. No. 4 was built in 1910 by *A. Hill Parker* as an extension to No. 3 (CHOIR HOUSE); of snecked stone, gabled and Tudorish. Internal alterations by *Associated Architects*, 2001, revealed by the sleek flat-roofed dormer. In 1908 *Parker* remodelled the more basic Tudor building set at right angles, the former Canons' Stables by *A.E. Perkins*, 1845.

The rest of the S SIDE, originally containing service buildings for the priory, is now mostly quiet Georgian houses: No. 5 with canted bay, No. 6 with big doorcase. The sandstone side wall of No. 6 is a significant fragment, perhaps late C12. Both houses were modified or rebuilt by *Parker* for the School (No. 6 with tile-hung top floor). His also the larger classroom block, 1898–9, brick with decorated gables, set back by the main entrance to the King's School (which reveals *Ewan Christian*'s School House, 1886–7, see p. 727).

In the SW corner of College Green, two good brick houses. No. 9, three bays, with slender wooden porch, is a late C18 refronting of a timber-framed house of the 1640s, with good late C17 staircase, NW. At right angles is No. 10, the present Deanery. Early C18, five bays with modillion cornice; much enlarged by *Perkins*, 1872–3. At the rear, where the ground drops away, the house stands on a tall platform of coursed stone, with five (later) relieving arches; this is probably the most substantial surviving fragment of the C12–C13 castle.

The rambling Nos. 12–12A, N of No. 10, are C16–C17 or earlier (the site was that of the monastic shrine keeper or tumbary), encased in C18–C19 painted brick. The more systematic S front is by *Harvey Eginton*; gabled Tudor Gothic, with diapered brickwork prominently dated 1844. No. 13, further NE, next to Nos. 14–14A and the former monastic refectory (p. 699), also has its date, 1847, proudly displayed in brickwork. Between the two, the ground slopes steeply down to No. 12B, the monastic WATER GATE of 1378. The brick and roughcast house on top is probably partly C17; beneath it the late C14 structure survives, shorn of detail. Four-centred chamfered arches, the outer, w, doubled to allow for the portcullis groove; two bays of vaulting, now without ribs. Along the river bank, N and S, extend long stretches of buttressed walling, of C14 origin, no doubt much rebuilt after the creation of the riverside path in 1844. Nestling upon the wall, S of the Water Gate, brick outbuildings of 1846 belonging to Nos. 12–12A.

1. Church of England

ALL SAINTS, Deansway. A fine introduction to Worcester, as one crosses the bridge from the W. Only some sandstone walling, S aisle W end, and the lowest stage of the W tower are medieval; the latter is mid-C15, with diagonal W buttresses but flat NE one with part of an apparently Norman arch. Also Perp the tall, characteristic arch to the nave. Large W window by *Aston Webb*, 1888–9. The upper stages of the tower and body of the church, all with round-arched windows with keystones and imposts, are of 1739–42. The most likely designer is the master mason *Richard Squire*, who rebuilt it with *William Davis* as master carpenter. The tower's second stage has paired rusticated pilaster strips, the bell-stage paired pilasters flanking unusual twinned bell-openings. Balustraded parapet with corner urns, renewed 1992. The church is of six bays, the chancel projecting just a little further. The main doorway, second bay from the W, N side, has fluted Doric pilasters, triglyph frieze, and segmental pediment. The E is the real façade (cf. St Swithin): very large window between coupled Doric pilasters with portions of frieze; broken-back triangular pediment with roundel with bust (said to be by *Thomas White*) of Bishop Hough, who contributed £1,000 towards the rebuilding. The aisles end in (former) E entrances, beneath large roundels. Inside, six-bay arcades with Doric columns on high bases, supporting a continuous straight entablature and almost semicircular vault; flat aisle ceilings.

REREDOS. Not high; tripartite, with Corinthian pilasters and segmental pediment. Altar by *C.F. Whitcombe*, 1903. – COMMUNION RAIL, *c.* 1740; close-set fluted balusters. – Good scrolly SWORD REST; wrought iron, mid-C18. – Otherwise most furnishings belong to *Aston Webb*'s restoration, 1888–9, though the PULPIT reuses C17 panels of the Evangelists. Webb extended the sanctuary one bay W, providing it with marble FLOOR, WALL PAINTINGS, now surviving only on the E wall (replacing a scheme of 1867 by *Josiah Rushton*), CHOIR STALLS, and gilt wrought-iron PARCLOSE SCREENS; the PEWS are also his. – N CHAPEL ALTAR by *Troyte Griffith*, 1912–13. – Stone and marble FONT of 1901, by *R. Haughton*. – Also a plain round font from St Andrew, perhaps C12. – STAINED GLASS. Good C15 fragments in the W and N aisle W windows. – In the S aisle W, a C17 heraldic oval. – The Evangelist roundels must be mid-C19, by *George Rogers*. – Murky E window by *Powell & Sons*, 1890. – N aisle NE, by *J.E. Nuttgens*, 1954; next but one W, *Christopher Webb*, 1964. – S aisle SE, *Reginald Bell*, 1933.

MONUMENTS. Edward Hurdman †1621 and wife. Two large kneeling figures at a prayer-desk, the context destroyed. – Many attractive TABLES, especially Samuel Mathews †1684; stiff frontal demi-figure beneath broken pediment on twisted columns. Another nearby also has twisted columns. – By

Richard Squire: James Smyth †1740 and Cocker Draper *c.* 1765, both with obelisks; Edward Lowbridge †1742, with pilasters and broken pediment (all N aisle). – By *W. Stephens*: John Williams †1793, with draped urn above scrolly pediment (nave W), and probably the similar one to Luke Spilsbury †1798 (S aisle E).

BOUNDARY WALL, with C19 brick piers by *George Truefitt*; railings removed.

HOLY TRINITY AND ST MATTHEW, Lichfield Avenue, Ronkswood. By *Maurice W. Jones*, by far his most interesting work; designed 1958, built to a slightly modified scheme 1964–5. Circular, windows only in the bottom half; the upper part, now rendered, originally had a striking chequerboard pattern. Concrete-framed but double-layered, the outer cylindrical, the inner a truncated cone, with the linking ring beams supporting a central spike; narrow clerestory strip at the top of the conical section. Inside, a concrete gallery above the narrow concentric aisle; small sanctuary recess between the glazed screens hiding its staircases. NE chapel and SE vestry, augmented, E, by an angular concrete-block hall of 1975, by *Snell & Thompson*. – WAR MEMORIAL CROSS outside, of 1919, from Holy Trinity, Shrub Hill.

ST ALBAN, Deansway (formerly Fish Street). Now a centre for the homeless. Small, Norman (or earlier), severely over-restored. Nave and chancel in one, plus N aisle; short W bellcote. The S wall has much Norman stonework, with various blocked openings; the doorway and two large windows are crude Neo-Norman, said to be of 1821, but probably dating from the restoration of 1850 by *Perkins*. He extended the N aisle at both ends and rebuilt the E.E. chancel (with stepped E triplet); circular SE window, 1920. Inside, the two W bays of the N arcade are genuine Late Norman: round piers, round abaci, capitals with scallops or flat-leaf decoration; later double-chamfered arches, hoodmould with coarse dogtooth. The two E bays are by *Perkins*. – MONUMENTS. Large tablet to Edmund Wyatt †1684, with drapery and gadrooned top with urn. – Tablets with heraldry: Francis Warmstry †1589; Marcia Wyatt †1595. – STAINED GLASS. E window by *Preedy*, *c.* 1858; also upper W rose (now blocked off), 1863. – N aisle NW by *Geoffrey Webb*, 1919.

ST ANDREW, Deansway. Only the Perp tower remains; the rest was demolished in 1949. It stands in a public garden, opened 1953. The three-stage tower carries an excellently slim ribbed spire, 155 ft (48 metres) high, a notable landmark known locally as the Glover's Needle; built or rebuilt by *Nathaniel Wilkinson*, 1751, with Corinthian capital at the top (replaced by a copy) instead of a finial. The original top is in the public garden. The spire is recessed behind a battlemented parapet which, together with the top stage, may also have been rebuilt in 1751; the whole tower was then refaced in limestone (the original red sandstone remains beneath). Five-light W window with stepped trefoil-headed lights. The aisles embraced the tower, as can be seen by surviving fragments of their W walls, the S set at an angle. High tower arches to E, N and S, with fine Perp mouldings. Lierne vault inside, with thirty-two good figured bosses. To the E, the springers of the first arcade bay.

ST BARNABAS, Church Road, Rainbow Hill. 1884–5 by *Ernest A. Day*; cost £3,931. Dour red brick, relieved by yellow string courses and stone dressings; banded tile roof. Nave and aisles, no tower, wide canted apse. Mostly lancet windows, five stepped beneath the W bellcote; basic plate tracery in the clerestory. Semi-detached NE vestry with hipped roof, by *C.F. Whitcombe*, 1908. Good spacious interior, exposed brick, stone used only for the tall chancel arch and arcades. These, three bays plus a slightly higher one for the shallow transepts, have round piers and roundels of saints in the spandrels, carved by *William Forsyth*. He also carved the bowl-shaped FONT. – Attractive encaustic chancel TILING, executed by *Webb* of Worcester; sanctuary refurnished 1960. – Stone PULPIT. 1890. – Open oak CHANCEL SCREEN by *A.H. Parker*, 1921. – STAINED GLASS. Apse E, 1894, flanked by windows of 1929, no doubt by *Pearce & Cutler*. – S transept E by *Edwin Horwood*, 1890.

VICARAGE, W, by *A.B. Rowe*, 1888; brick, timbered gables. – Plain PARISH HALL, NW, by *Maurice W. Jones*, 1940.

ST CLEMENT, Henwick Road. 1821–3 by *Thomas Lee Jun.*[*] The amazing thing is that it is emphatically Neo-Norman, a choice exceptional before 1830, fashionable only in the 1840s. Ornate, rather crude façade, faced in Roman cement; blunt W tower embraced by gallery staircase, N, vestries, S. The church stands on sloping ground, above an undercroft; two-light nave windows, in two stages to express the galleries. Sandstone chancel added by *Preedy*, 1878–9, still Neo-Norman, with stepped E window and S organ chamber. Pleasant interior, the three galleries preserved; again Norman in style, on iron columns. *Charles Nicholson* shortened them, E end, to provide new staircases, 1928–9, and converted the organ chamber to a S chapel.

PEWS, STALLS and stone PULPIT by *Preedy*. – Round FONT of 1885 (and alabaster REREDOS, 1890, now kept hidden) carved by *William Forsyth*. – SCREEN by *A. Hill Parker*, 1918–19: Neo-Norman, with added refinement. – STAINED GLASS. E window, 1890, and chancel SE, 1894, by *Hardman*. – S chapel E by *A.J. Davies*, 1951. – MONUMENTS. Early C19 tablets include two by *J. Stephens*, c. 1831–2, with draped altar or draped urn. – More striking that to the Rev. John Davis †1858, designed by *George Truefitt*: Caen stone and marble, early Gothic style, with big angel above the open Bible. – Good wrought-iron RAILINGS to Henwick Road.

ST CUTHBERT, Lower Wick. *See* p. 776.

ST GEORGE, St George's Square. 1893–5 by *Aston Webb*, a key work of his early and best period; placed spectacularly at the

---

[*] Replacing a medieval church, by the bridge, on the E bank of the river.

far end of the long square. Its façade is basically of the Windsor and King's College type, i.e. with large window flanked by turrets. But nothing, except the Dec-Perp window tracery, is really imitative. Of red Stonehouse brick with some stone bands. The w front, flanked by two low porches, has a centre with giant niche à la Tewkesbury, its arch almost round. On the entrance level the niche is filled by a doorway with attractive Free Style detail. The top of the façade is a straight stone band, the turret-tops standing above it, instead of one being fully prepared for them from the ground. Small recessed spires on the turrets; set-back central gable. Excellent interior, also *p. 73* brick and stone. Wide nave with three-bay arcades, their wide brick arches again almost round; short stone piers. Single thin triangular shafts runs up the piers to the roof. Each clerestory bay has two single-light windows, again divided by a stone shaft. Taller arches to the large transepts, each with two tall transomed two-light end windows. No chancel arch, the chancel being distinguished largely by a greater use of stone. Low side chapels separated by two-bay arcades, with moulded and panelled arches. Tracery of the five-light E window rather more personal than the w window. Narrow w narthex with low five-bay arcade, with segmental arches.

FURNISHINGS designed by *Webb* include the mosaic CHANCEL FLOOR; low CHANCEL SCREEN, with iron balusters and gates made by *Starkie Gardner & Co.*; and ROOD carved by *Forsyth. Webb*'s beautiful ORGAN CASE, delicately painted probably by *H. W. Lonsdale*, is of *c.* 1901–2. – Richly carved timber PULPIT added by *A. H. Parker*, 1905. – STALLS. 1932. – Gothic stone and marble REREDOS in the s chapel, probably by *Hopkins*, 1867, from the previous church.* STAINED GLASS. All by *Kempe* (later *Kempe & Co.*): chapels and w narthex, 1897–8; s aisle 1900; N aisle 1908; E window 1909. – Brick ENTRANCE PIERS, with ball finials and wrought-iron gates, by *Maurice W. Jones*, 1939.

ST HELEN, Fish Street. Perhaps the 'mother church' of Worcester. The present Geometrical Dec exterior is Victorian. The E façade, towards High Street, forms a vital part of its townscape: five-light E window by *Preedy*, 1863, aisle windows by *Aston Webb* (*see* below). Other details (e.g. buttresses and battlemented gable) are C18 or early C19 Gothick. Battlemented w tower rebuilt 1820–1, probably by *John Collingwood*. Other detail and the whole s front, with its timber porch, belong to *Webb*'s extensive restoration, 1879–80. The spacious interior is entirely Perp, mid-C15, with impressive, continuous six-bay arcades: piers with canted projections in the four main directions, double-chamfered arches. Contemporary tower arch. Most FURNISHINGS have been been removed (the building served as the County Record Office 1957–2002), but fragments of *Webb*'s mosaic SANCTUARY FLOORING survive. – Good

---

* A Gothic chapel of ease, to Claines, 1829–30, by *James Lucy*, completed by *Lewis Belling*.

alabaster REREDOS by *Preedy*, 1865. – FONT. 1855. – STAINED GLASS. E window (tracery lights only) by *Preedy*, 1863. – S aisle: easternmost by *Lavers, Barraud & Westlake*, 1879, another by *Ward & Hughes*, 1883. – One, N aisle, by *Hardman*, 1879 (from St Michael, College Street, *see* p. 702).

MONUMENTS. John Nash †1662. Standing monument with stiffly reclining figure; a provincial job, of some character. His head is propped on his r. arm, his l. hand marks his place in his book. Twisted columns, odd broken pediment with cartouche of arms, garlands, and small segmental pediment set in. Shallow back arch with putti in the spandrels. – Opposite, good tablets of *c.* 1605 and *c.* 1693; above these, Richard Cotton †1761, by *Richard Squire*, with obelisk. – N aisle: Anne Fleet †1600; kneeling figures, decorated pilasters. – Richard Nash †1825, by *J. Stephens*; draped urn. – S aisle. Philip Bearcroft †1728, by *Squire*, probably *c.* 1760, with putti and urn. – Dud Dudley, the Royalist and ironmaster, †1684; large, entirely redone 1911. – Other tablets include three from St Michael, beneath the tower: Nicholas Archbold †1640, demi-figure with skull; Margery Archbold †1615, with painted figure of Time; Stephen Maylard †1622, with inset kneeling brass.

PARISH HALL, SW, by *Lewis Sheppard*, 1890; brick, Gothic.

ST JOHN IN BEDWARDINE, St John's. The church of the medieval suburb W of the Severn; large, of sandstone. Norman in origin, though nothing of this is visible outside where the sturdy Perp W tower, said to be of 1461, dominates. It has diagonal buttresses, four-light W window, and battlements with renewed pinnacles and central spike. Perp also the E window (reused when *Ewan Christian* rebuilt and extended chancel and N chapel, 1884), and the S aisle and chapel. The aisle has three transverse gables, two filled with five-light windows with a Perp type of reticulated tracery. Below the third, the former entrance, replaced by a porch to its W, with stairs to the galleries, by *Lewis Belling*, 1840–1. His also the NW vestry (refaced and extended 1963–4). The N aisle, of greyer Ombersley stone, is a rebuilding (and widening) of 1861 by *A. E. Perkins*: W rose, two-light Dec-style N windows allowing for the former gallery, banded roof.

Inside, the three-bay N arcade is later C12: round piers, multi-scallop capitals, square abaci; the pointed arches are C19. Perp S arcade, with double-chamfered arches on piers with four canted projections; the E pier must be a chunk of Norman wall left standing. Perp chancel arch widened by *Christian*, who also reconstructed the two-bay arcade to the S chapel, with its continuous two-wave mouldings. The double-chamfered NW arch tells of a former transeptal chapel, removed by *Perkins* for his enlarged aisle; the E rose of this was re-set in the E wall of Christian's N chapel, which has bold two-bay openings to W and S.

Good carved, gilded oak REREDOS by *C. F. Whitcombe*, 1908, plus sanctuary panelling and plaster plaque above the sedilia. – By *Christian*, the STALLS, timber PULPIT (with some reused

Perp tracery), and carved stone and marble FONT. – W
GALLERY by *Perkins*.* – PEWS mostly by *Henry Rowe*, 1878. –
S CHAPEL ALTAR by *P.B. Chatwin*, 1933; also SCREENS to tower
and NE vestry, 1936–8. – STAINED GLASS. Chancel windows,
1884, and N chapel E, *c*. 1907, by *Clayton & Bell*; in the tops
of the chancel side windows, C15 fragments including two good
heads, SW. – S chapel windows 1884–8: E, *Burlison & Grylls*,
two S, *Lavers, Barraud & Westlake*. – S aisle SW by *A.J. Davies*,
1923. – MONUMENTS. Abel Gower †1669. Large tablet with
twisted Composite columns, two female allegorical figures
between them and the inscription; two putti on the broken
curly pediment. – Minor tablets include several of the mid C17,
crudely repainted (S chapel E), and one by *Bott & Stephens*,
c. 1763 (N aisle W). – In the porch, a former churchyard tomb
to two sons of A.M. Hopkins, by *Boulton*, 1872, with inset
photograph.

Attached to the church, NE, part of the former VICARAGE,
C17–C18, brick with a timbered gable; the rest rebuilt by
Christian, 1884–5, with tile-hung gables.

ST MARK, Orchard Street, Cherry Orchard. Simple mission
church of 1902–3 by *E.G. Jones* (*Yeates & Jones*); apsed chancel
and broad nave with W porch and bellcote, undercroft for
schoolrooms etc. Brick with stone bands and alternating voussoirs; grouped lancets, without carved embellishment apart
from the W front. Inside, simplified hammerbeam roof, and
mostly contemporary fittings.

ST MARTIN, Cornmarket; known as Old St Martin. Of 1768–72,
by *Anthony Keck*, though he may have followed the design of
Henry Keene, who was 'desired to prepare a plan' in 1765. Blue
Bewdley brick, with stone dressings. The E end, facing Cornmarket, is the main front, with large pediment all across: large
round-arched chancel window (with rather silly Gothic tracery
inserted by *Hopkins*, 1855–6), smaller ones for the aisles. Five-
bay sides with straight quoins, the N windows plain-arched, the
S with rusticated surrounds of alternating size; blocky rendered
porch. The W tower incorporates some stone fabric from its
medieval predecessor; lowest stage 1768–72, the upper two,
more elaborate, of different brick, added 1780. Balustraded
parapet with corner obelisks. Elegant interior (derived from St
Martin-in-the-Fields): five-bay arcades with slender unfluted
Ionic columns, on high bases, each with its own bit of entablature; this repeats on the aisle walls, supported on large brackets. Groin-vaulted aisles; flat nave ceiling with penetrations
from the arcades. Short sanctuary, with round chancel arch,
built into the nave.

WEST GALLERY. 1811, balustraded front; rebuilt 1836–7. –
Panelled DADO, made up from the C18 pews. – Other FIT-
TINGS either 1855–62 (by *Hopkins*), or early C20. Sanctuary
extended into the nave in 1900. – STAINED GLASS. Good S
aisle E by *Preedy*, 1857. – The rest by *Hardman*: E window 1857;

---

* N and S galleries were removed in 1974.

others 1861–5, apart from one N aisle, 1881, one S, 1876. – MONUMENTS. N aisle: two excellent cartouches with cherubs and draperies, William Johnson †1711 and John Hughes †1726; another, above the S door, to Richard Grismond. – Otherwise minor tablets, with an exceptional number of late C18–early C19 brass plates.

Small brick PARISH ROOM, SW, by *Henry Rowe*, 1881, on the site of the rectory.

ST MARTIN, London Road. By *G.H. Fellowes Prynne*, designed 1903–4, built 1909–11; apsed S chapel completed 1915. Large, Free Dec style; rock-faced Alveley sandstone, Bath ashlar dressings and banding. Tiled roof with no break between nave and chancel, their junction marked by a small copper-roofed turret. The E end stands above an undercroft. Well grouped to the S, despite the stump of the incomplete tower; twin-gabled transept. W baptistery and flanking porches by *F. Potter* of Birmingham, 1962, on Prynne's foundations. Fine spacious interior, brick banded with stone. Wide nave with five-bay arcades, their run not distinguishing between the narrow passage aisles and two-bay-deep transepts; their arches die against the tall diamond-plan piers. Panelled roofs. High-set rood instead of a chancel arch. Passageway, with gallery above, between chancel and S chapel; broad stairway, N, to the undercroft. – ORGAN CASE by *Nicholson & Co.*, 1928. – C19 Perp stone PULPIT, from St Andrew. – STAINED GLASS, S chapel, by *A. J. Davies*, 1927–31.

PARISH HALL, E, in Victoria Avenue; by *A. Hill Parker*, 1903–4. Also stone-banded brick; Free Tudor Perp. The upper floor served as a temporary church, the basement for vestry, schoolrooms etc.

ST MARY MAGDALENE, Sansome Walk. By *Frederick Preedy*, 1876–7; tall SW steeple added by his former assistant *J.S. Alder*, 1888–9. Redundant since 1977; converted to flats in the early 1990s. Of snecked Ombersley sandstone with Bath dressings. Aisled nave and chancel with S chapel (and N organ chamber-cum-vestry, 1883), mostly late C13 style; paired two-light Geometrical W windows with small rose above, three-light clerestory windows, otherwise mostly lancets, five stepped to the E. The spacious interior had five-bay arcades with short round piers, their foliage capitals carved by *Martyn & Emms*. SW tower with octagonal bell-stage with broad lancets; big octagonal corner pinnacles connect with the 195-ft (60-metre)-high spire, enlivened by sandstone bands: a prominent landmark at the N end of the city centre. Above its S doorway, small scene of Mary Magdalene with Christ, carved by *H.H. Martyn*.

Former SUNDAY SCHOOLS, E, in Northfield Street. 1884 by *Lewis Sheppard* (Preedy's clerk of works for the church); E.E.-style, with stepped lancets, in a similar, Bromsgrove, sandstone.

ST NICHOLAS, The Cross. Closed 1992; now a wine bar. Built 1730–5 by *Humphrey Hollins*, but it is unclear who provided the design; *Thomas White* has also been suggested. The W tower is in any case cribbed from an alternative design for St Mary-le-Strand, London, published by James Gibbs in his *Book of Architecture*, 1728. It is embraced by the two former staircase bays, so that the façade is given some grandeur, with its channelled stonework and giant Doric pilasters, doubled for the portal bay. The doorway (altered, after the removal of semicircular steps, by *P.B. Chatwin*, 1935) has attached Doric columns and broken-back triangular pediment; above, a blank horizontal oval. The side bays have niches with blank roundels over. The coupled pilasters carry a large segmental pediment, also broken-back with shield of arms, helping to confirm the Baroque feel. The tower has variety from stage to stage, the first square with stepped corners, the cornice curving up above the clock and side windows, the second also square but with recessed rounded corners, the bell-openings with triangular pediments; then an octagonal stage, and finally the double-curved cap with circular open Tuscan lantern. The body of the church (built above a spacious crypt, perhaps surviving from the late medieval church) is more basic; four bays, round-arched windows, the arches keyed in, balustrade above, apsed chancel. Disappointing interior, just a rectangle with simply moulded, coved ceiling, plus the apse. – Simple C18 Doric REREDOS. – Other FITTINGS mostly belong to *Hopkins*'s restoration, 1865–7: GALLERIES on three sides and PULPIT, both timber with wrought-iron infill (by *Skidmore & Co.*), and COMMUNION RAILS, wholly of iron. – STAINED GLASS. Apse windows by *George Rogers*, 1857. – MONUMENTS. Tablets at gallery level, the best the lively cartouches at the E ends, with fronds, draperies, wings, skulls: William Gower †1694 and John Burton †1708 are quite large, the other two smaller, that to Elizabeth Mills †1686 particularly leathery. – Also Joseph Berwick †1798, by *W. Stephens*; big strigilated sarcophagus, curly pediment.

St Nicholas, St Nicholas Lane, Warndon. *See* Warndon.

St Paul, Spring Gardens. Built, at a cost of £8,400, in 1885–6 by *Arthur Edmund Street*, his best church, still very much in the style of his famous father.* Large, red brick with vigorous blue-black patterning; nave with aisles, chancel with s chapel and n organ chamber and vestry. Double bellcote on the nave E gable. The windows, mostly of Bath stone, are grouped lancets or have bold plate tracery with Dec detailing; only the three stepped w windows exhibit bar tracery. Splendid interior, a synthesis of High and Late Victorian. High Victorian is the consistent decoration of exposed red and blue-black brick, with broad stone bands. The plan and proportions are decidedly Late Victorian: lofty five-bay arcades with continuously double-chamfered arches, with only a small cusp indicating the arch springing; narrow clerestory with paired lancets flanked by roundels; taller triple-chamfered chancel arch. The rest was subdivided *c.* 1988, by *Arnold Gurney*, for the Assemblies of

* It replaced a church by *Eginton*, 1835–6.

God. – Surviving fittings include the fine iron and brass CHANCEL SCREEN, executed by *Barford* of Maidenhead; octagonal FONT, carved by *Earp*; and timber PULPIT (on stone base), painted by *Bell & Beckham*. – STAINED GLASS. All but one by *Kempe* (or *Kempe & Co.*): E and S chapel E 1886–8; chancel side windows 1899; N aisle 1901; S aisle S 1905–7, W 1932. – N aisle NW window by *J.N. Comper*, 1932.

ST STEPHEN, St Stephen's Street, Barbourne. By *Frederick Preedy*, 1861–2; large, of snecked red sandstone. Gauche SW tower, with big buttresses and gargoyles, projecting parapet and blunt pinnacles; the intended spire is sorely missed. Windows mostly with muscular plate tracery, but the large E and W with Geometrical Dec bar tracery. Apsed S chapel added, very tactfully, by *A. Hill Parker*, 1913–15. Four-bay nave arcades with alternating octagonal and circular piers, their capitals vigorously carved (by *Earp*) with foliage and dragons. Each clerestory bay has two short two-light windows, separated by a stubby round detached shaft. Equally vigorous the chancel arch, with attached Purbeck shafts, and opening to the N organ chamber, with paired corbel shafts. High arch-braced roofs. – Mostly original FITTINGS: square alabaster and marble FONT; similar polygonal PULPIT and large REREDOS (now hidden); *Minton* encaustic TILING. – The true date of the LADY CHAPEL, S, is revealed by its plaster panelled ceiling; its W SCREEN is by *Pancheri & Son*, 1961. – STAINED GLASS. By *Preedy*, the E window, 1862, W, 1863, and N aisle NW, 1877. – Sanctuary N by *T.W. Camm*, 1899; S by *Heaton, Butler & Bayne*, 1894. – Chancel SW by *Clayton & Bell*, 1865. – S chapel apse and SE windows all by *A.J. Davies*, probably *c.* 1920. – The pictorial SW window here is the re-set S aisle E, by *Lavers, Barraud & Westlake*, 1870; also theirs no doubt the S aisle SE, *c.* 1883.

ST SWITHIN, Church Street, off High Street. By *Thomas & Edward Woodward* of Chipping Campden, 1734–6. Vested in the Churches Conservation Trust since 1977. The core of the W tower is C15, with diagonal buttresses. The Woodwards entirely refaced it with their nice combination of classical and Gothick; round-arched W doorway, with linked Y-traceried openings above beneath ogee gables; crocketed pinnacles, balustraded parapet. The S side has six narrowly spaced bays with giant fluted Doric pilasters and windows with keyed-in round arches; tall parapet. The E front is the real façade, similar to the same architects' St John the Baptist, Gloucester. Giant fluted pilasters, centre with broken-back pediment above a richly appointed Venetian window with Ionic detail. Pedimented clock on top.* The N side also retains medieval fabric. Marvellous interior. Aisleless, with segmental plaster vault with ribs which must be meant to be Gothic, for the little angel wall corbels on which they stand are imitation Perp. Bosses, also a Gothic motif, set in classical roundels. Larger roundel above

---

* Its drive-shaft runs the full length of the nave, above the ceiling; the mechanism is within the tower.

the chancel, the space of which is divided from the side areas (former E entrances) by half-height screen walls carrying fluted Doric columns. Floor paved almost entirely with C18 ledger stones. Discreet vestry additions by *William Weir* and *Gerald Cogswell*, 1912.

REREDOS with fluted pilasters, now without its pediment. – ALTAR. Grey marble top on beautiful wrought-iron supports. – COMMUNION RAILS with thin fluted balusters. – Panelled BOX PEWS, some family size; those against the side walls set longitudinally. – Wholly delightful three-decker PULPIT. It rises very high above the pews, reached by a winding staircase. Back wall and tester with plenty of frills. Above the tester a gilded Pelican, below it an anchor and serpent. – MAYOR'S CHAIR in his own pew below; rising from its curved back the scrolly wrought-iron CIVIC SWORD REST. – FONT. Oval marble bowl on a baluster, with the original mahogany cover. – Canted WEST GALLERY, on square fluted wooden pillars, supporting a late C17 ORGAN. – STAINED GLASS. In the E window, early C19 patterned glass by *W.R. Eginton*, inserted by his son *Harvey Eginton*, *c*. 1840, with new roundels by *George Rogers*. – MONUMENTS. Tower. Rebecca Ashby †1735, fluted Ionic pilasters. – Joseph Withers †1741 and wife, by *John Bacon Sen.*, *c*. 1770. Big putto, one hand on the double-profile medallion, the other holding a willow spray. The putto is placed before a draped urn against an obelisk background. – Nave. William Swift †1688. Corinthian columns flanked by kneeling children; broken segmental pediment. – Elizabeth Barker †1694, leathery cartouche extended by a pendant tablet of about the same date. – Henry Hope †1753, by *Richard Squire*. Corinthian pilasters, broken segmental pediment; conservative for its date.

2. Roman Catholic

ST GEORGE, Sansome Place. Rebuilt by *Henry Rowe*, 1828–9, but of his rectangular Grecian church little more than brick side walls remain. Remodelled 1880 by *S.J. Nicholl*, who added chancel and flanking chapels, and probably, in 1887, the ambitious ashlar façade of Roman Baroque type. This has three wide bays, the upper stage with Corinthian angle pilasters and pedimented windows; projecting centre with coupled attached columns and top pediment. Open, richly appointed interior. The plaster ceiling must be *Rowe*'s, also the WEST GALLERY, on Ionic columns. Similar columns flanking the straight-headed chancel opening were removed in 1907 by *Edmund Kirby & Sons* of Liverpool. Also of this date the *opus sectile* panels, by *Powell & Sons*, above the chapel entrances. All three altars, with marble and alabaster REREDOS, and the PULPIT, are of 1880, carved by *William Forsyth*. – Round marble FONT. 1918. – Large altar PAINTING, a copy of Raphael's Transfiguration by *Furse*, 1837, flanked by saints painted by *Joseph Bouvier*, 1880. – Richly enamelled STAINED GLASS, S chapel, by *W.R. Eginton*, 1813 (given by his daughter, 1889): the Mass of St Giles, after the painting of *c.* 1500 in the National Gallery, London. – Bronze resin PLAQUE nearby by *Faith Tolkien*, 1996.

PRESBYTERY, at right angles to the façade, NW, by *J.A. Hansom*, 1851; severely plain brick, originally two houses. – On the opposite side, S, a circular CHURCH HALL, with rectilinear lower wings, by *KKE Architects*, 2005–6.

3. Nonconformist

BAPTIST CHURCH, Sansome Walk. 1863–4 by *Pritchett & Son* of Darlington; yellow sandstone, with blue and white voussoirs, and patterned slate roof. A full-dress Geometrical Dec church; thin SW steeple, with tapering square tower and broach spire. Nave with aisles, large transepts. Open interior, the four-bay arcades with tall thin cast-iron columns with foliage capitals supporting timber arches; matching arch-braced roof. Deep W and transept galleries, 'chancel' with organ gallery above vestries. – FITTINGS mostly original.

Former CONGREGATIONAL CHURCH, Angel Place. Rebuilt 1858–9 by *Poulton & Woodman* of Reading, at a cost of nearly £6,000 (almost twice that of the Baptist church). Brick, with ashlar front of some grandeur; five bays dominated by a giant semicircular portico of four Corinthian columns; balustraded porches in the single bays either side, recessed central pediment. Closed *c.* 1980, now a nightclub. The splendid interior is all but intact beneath the glitzy fittings. It is square with rounded corners, the coved and panelled ceiling with a large twelve-sided central lantern and pendant ventilator. Curved gallery with panelled front around three walls, plus narrower cast-iron upper gallery, both supported on big iron brackets. Massive round-arched Corinthian organ recess sheltering the bulbous tripartite pulpit. A huge cast-iron spiral staircase provides access to this and the galleries from the vestries.

Former SUNDAY SCHOOLS, N, by *Aston Webb*, 1888; buff Ruabon brick with stone dressings. Now a community centre. Angled corner entrance, with gabled doorway and carved figure of a boy reading; octagonal flanking buttresses, more steeply gabled roof with shingled spike. Mostly Tudor cross-windows. Polygonal plan with small classrooms, plus larger canted one adjoining the church, around the central two-storey hall (with balustraded gallery on columns).

Former COUNTESS of HUNTINGDON'S CHAPEL, Deansway; now Huntingdon Hall. A notable example of a chapel that developed on a restricted site, with remarkably well-preserved fittings. Brick, of 1804 (replacing a smaller chapel of 1771–3), enlarged 1815; an odd T-plan is the result. Converted to a concert hall by the *Buttress Fuller Partnership*, 1980–7. The four-bay chapel of 1804, with hipped roof, stands at the end of a deep courtyard, with a terrace of three houses including the former manse on its S side, and former schoolrooms on the N, all of 1839, much altered and enlarged *c.* 1980–90. W front with three round-arched windows and central doorway, hidden by a mid-C19 stuccoed external staircase to the gallery. Round-arched windows also on the chapel's N and S sides; segment-headed windows below. The 1815 enlargement is a large oblong E transept, with apsed N and S ends. It has taller round-arched windows, the stuccoed N arm also a wooden Doric porch with fluted columns. Interior refitted 1815 (further amendments 1839). Continuous gallery on slender quatrefoil piers of cast iron; flat ceiling, lightly divided at the junction of the two parts by an additional tier forming a broad tripartite arch. – PULPIT. Square, with rounded corners, on eight fluted Doric columns, flanked by cast-iron eagle LECTERNS of 1871. It stands within an oval enclosure with (late C19) iron rails; matching stairs either side. – ORGAN, E gallery. 1840, rebuilt 1896. – Most of the panelled BOX PEWS survive. – STAINED GLASS. Two E windows 1858, probably mostly by *George Rogers*, incorporating medieval and C18–early C19 pieces.

FRIENDS' MEETING HOUSE, Sansome Place. Built 1701. Brick, originally all single-storeyed, with hipped slate roof. S front with brick platband above four large segmental-arched windows; central entrance with later pedimented porch. Interior partly refitted *c.* 1823; remodelled 1981–2 by *Rowe, Elliott & Partners*, who rebuilt the early C19 range to the E. – Attached C18 terrace, W, three two-storey cottages.

ST ANDREW'S METHODIST CHURCH, Pump Street. 1966–7 by *Norman Webster* (of *Shingler Risdon Associates*). Narrow entrance front with huge *dalle-de-verre* window, by *A. E. Buss* (of *Goddard & Gibbs*), 1968, set between concrete fins. Behind this, an open-well stair through three storeys. Hall and ancillary rooms on the first floor above the shops. The church is on the second floor, its big semi-octagonal end cantilevered out and faced in granite aggregate. Good spacious interior, clerestory-lit apart from the large end window.*

4. Cemetery

ASTWOOD CEMETERY, Astwood Road. By *Robert Clarke* of Nottingham, 1857–8; his lodges and linked E.E.-style chapels have been demolished, leaving a meaningless void at the centre of the Victorian part. Dispiriting brick CREMATORIUM added 1958–9; City Engineer *J. S. Williams*.

PUBLIC BUILDINGS

COUNTY HALL, Spetchley Road, in a semi-rural setting on the city's E edge. Built for the short-lived Hereford and Worcester County Council in 1974–8, by *Robert Matthew, Johnson-Marshall & Partners* (RMJM); partner in charge *Hugh Morris*, job architects *Raj Malik* and *Robin Booth*. Quiet, spreading, well-grouped pavilion plan. Crisp horizontal emphasis, two or   130

---

*Previous Wesleyan churches on the site, were of 1795, 1813, and 1901–2 (by *J. J. Green*).

three storeys above a basement, the frame clad in deep reddish-brown brick with recessed bands of windows; ground floors mostly further recessed, with smaller windows, supported on concrete pillars. Zinc-clad piecrust roofs, their centres rising higher, especially above the octagonal elm-panelled council chamber, NW. Offices mostly grouped to the E, civic and social areas to the W. The loose plan, providing a high level of natural lighting, was designed to allow for expansion, which never materialized; detached Record Office added *c.* 1984 on the site of the intended second phase (the Boiler House further E belongs to the original build). Brises-soleil to the S, where the entrance is set back behind a broad paved courtyard, approached up brick steps; a generous top-lit staircase fills most of the entrance block. An amphitheatre and small lake, W, forming a backdrop to the social areas, is linked by a formal, concrete-framed cascade to another lake, SW, enhancing the approach. *RMJM* also acted as landscape architects, partner in charge *Maurice Lee.*

To the E (off Swinesherd Way), beyond the traditional ST RICHARD'S HOSPICE by *Panton Sargent*, 2005, two slick office groups by *Level Seven Architects*: WILDWOOD, 2005, and THE TRIANGLE, 2006–7.

SHIRE HALL, Foregate Street. 1834–8 by *Charles Day.* Impeccable Grecian, in the Smirke taste, of fine ashlar. Giant portico of six fluted Ionic columns with pediment and excellent Schinkelish detail, flanked by single recessed bays with plain pilasters. Inside, all across the building, the large County Hall, now a waiting room for the courts. Plainly coffered segmental ceiling; large tripartite window each end, with central pediment, and heraldic stained glass of *c.* 1909. Balcony along the back wall, on console brackets, with iron handrail; central rear staircase with courtrooms either side: Court One is largely original; others re-fitted 1995. Extensive rear additions by *Henry Rowe*, of 1898 etc.; long side walls partly stucco, mostly bare brick.

Railed front COURTYARD, framed by two low, detached, single-storey blocks with plain pilasters, coming forward towards the street. In the centre, a white marble STATUE of Queen Victoria by *Thomas Brock*, 1887, on a grey granite plinth.

Attached to the rear, set back from Sansome Walk, the JUDGES' LODGINGS, also by *Charles Day.* Big, powerful brick composition, three bays, two-and-a-half storeys; recessed centre with fluted Greek Doric columns *in antis.* Tripartite windows throughout. Central hall with imperial staircase with cast-iron balusters, beneath an oval skylight. The glazed links either side belong to refurbishment by *Associated Architects*, 1995.

COUNTY BUILDINGS, corner of St Mary's Street and Sansome Place. Large Neo-Georgian quadrangular office block by *A. V. Rowe*. 1929–30 (heightened 1935). Brick, stone dressings, including three-bay Doric centrepieces to the both fifteen-bay fronts (i.e. facing St Mary's Street and the Shire Hall).

GUILDHALL, High Street. A fine town hall of 1721–4 (on the site of its medieval predecessor), as splendid as any of the C18 in England, but just a little barbaric in its Baroque splendour. The architect is traditionally claimed to be *Thomas White*, who submitted a design in 1718, and signed the carved trophy in the pediment. The attribution is, however, far from certain.*

Of brick with ample stone dressings, including even quoins. 74 3+3+3 bays plus three-bay wings, two bays deep. Main range of two storeys; wings slightly lower, of two-and-a-half. Windows all segment-headed, with rather clumsy roll-moulded surrounds and good keystone heads; aprons beneath, the lower ones with curved undersides, the upper with paired cartouches. Between the storeys, oblong panels with garlands and other carved motifs such as the mace and sword. Three-bay centre framed by giant Corinthian pilasters, carrying an enormous segmental pediment with the trumpet-blast of White's bellicose trophy, painted and gilded (dated 1722); three statues on top: Justice flanked by Peace and Plenty. Parapet with urns and further statues (Labour, i.e. Hercules, and Chastisement) at the corners; in the centre, an ogee-roofed octagonal cupola. Between the giant pilasters, a grand doorway with Composite columns against rustication and open triangular pediment, broken-backed, enclosing the city arms. Flanking the doorway, beneath oculi, niches with stodgy C17 statues of Charles I (repaired by *Richard Squire*, 1724) and Charles II (by *Stephen Baldwin*, 1661, re-cut by *White*); above it, also in a niche, an originally free-standing statue of Queen Anne, by *White*, 1709. The wings were added in 1725 (N) and 1727 (S); both were partially rebuilt at the extensive restoration of 1877–80 by the city architect *Henry Rowe* (consultant *Sir Gilbert Scott*).† They retain fine doorways at the angles, with spider-web fanlights. Wrought-iron railings, of 1751, to the shallow forecourt, said to be by *Robert Bakewell* of Derby; splendid central gates with scrolled overthrow, mostly renewed in 1880 by *W.H. Letheren* of Cheltenham.

The high, long entrance hall is disappointing; flat ceiling with simple modillion cornice. At the rear, NW, the (Sessions) Court Room, to the SW, the panelled Mayor's Parlour (created out of the Police Court in 1926), each with a canted end. Between them, a fine open-well staircase, with two plain balusters per tread and carved tread ends, rises to the more rewarding top floor. Here is the excellent Assembly Room, remodelled by *George Byfield*, 1791. Of his work all that remains are the shallow apses either end, with niches and delicate plasterwork, screened in Adam fashion by columns, now painted red, with gilded Ionic capitals. The coved and painted ceiling is of

---

* Though White did receive a substantial pension. There is no evidence that *William Smith* was involved, despite some similarity to his Bishop's Palace (p. 704).
† A competition of 1872 for a new town hall was won by *C.G. Wray*. In 1875 *Alfred Waterhouse* also prepared a Gothic design. At this stage, *Scott* spoke out in favour of retaining the early C18 building.

1877–80, octagonal-coffered decoration in a reasonably light Italian style. By *Scott & Rowe* also most of the fittings and the decoration of the Council Chamber above the Court Room.

MAGISTRATES' COURT and POLICE STATION, Castle Street. A huge linked pair of 2000–1 by *Worcestershire County Council Property Dept*, both mostly of brick with large windows and prominent round corner entrances. The Magistrates' Court, E, is the calmer, with two tiers of brises-soleil, plus a third at roof level, together with the continuous clerestory providing a strong horizontal emphasis. The Police Station, W, is like a more aggressive mirror-image, with restless, rather ungainly two-tier roof; the circular entrance here is more transparent. – Incorporated between restored early C19 houses: a semi-detached pair, with pedimented doorways, and a larger one with round-arched moulded doorway.

Former COUNTY POLICE STATION, Castle Street (opposite its successor). By *A.B. Rowe*, 1902–3. Also quite large, brick, terracotta trim, in loose Queen Anne style. Five-bay centre with doorway with pediment on green marble columns; hipped mansard roof with dormers. Four bays either side, but the asymmetry asserted by an additional section at the corner of Infirmary Walk, W, with gable and domed corner turret. Now Enterprise House, a centre for small businesses; rear additions and large detached block, with fashionable curved roofs and glossy cladding, all by *Johnson Blight & Dees*, 1999.

Former CITY POLICE HEADQUARTERS, Deansway (now Worcester College of Technology, St Wulstan's Building). Of 1939–41 by *Ivor Jones & Thomas* of Cardiff, i.e. *Percy Thomas* (appointed architect as early as 1936). Large brick Neo-Georgian block, two storeys, almost square. Eleven bays to Deansway, with stone quoins, central doorway and window above (fronting a good stone and marble staircase). Hipped roof with neatly domed open cupola, of timber.[*]

FIRE STATION, Deansway, S of the above (across Copenhagen Street). Also by *Percy Thomas*, 1939–41, similar, belonging to the same scheme. Two-and-a-half storeys, with central courtyard. Rounded corners, some ground-floor circular windows, big rectangular chimneys on its hipped roofs.

VICTORIA INSTITUTE, Foregate Street. Now museum, art gallery, and library. 1894–6 by *John W. Simpson & E.J. Milner Allen*. Red brick with terracotta dressings, a resourceful and animated composition in mixed Tudor and Baroque ('Queen Anne style with Italian modifications', according to *The Building News*). The front is artfully asymmetrical. Gabled centre topped with figure of Victory; broad Ionic entrance with pediment broken by an elaborate royal arms and, above, Tudor-arched window of 2+4+2 lights, between Corinthian

[*] Pevsner's comment in 1968 was: 'Those who object to the Technical College ought to answer honestly whether they prefer this anaemic Neo-Georgianism. Historicism is surely not the solution to building near a cathedral (or anywhere) in the mid C20'; cf. p. 726.

pilasters. This is continued, l., with windows of 4+4 lights, forming a long row; beneath them, a large Elizabethan nine-light window, its three middle lights under a round arch. To the r. of the centre, however, a wholly different rhythm, with smaller windows, another gable, and octagonal corner turret with ogee cap and spike. Lively return front, N, to the Shire Hall forecourt, mostly with Tudor transomed windows, excellently extended (E) 1935 by *Alfred G. Parker*; quieter return, S, to Taylor's Lane. Tunnel-vaulted entrance with convex iron gates. Square vestibule open to the first floor; Doric pillars below, green-faced Ionic columns above, balcony with sturdy balusters. Spacious stone staircase, S, of dog-leg form, up to the art gallery and museum.

At the rear, facing Sansome Walk, the former SCHOOL OF ART AND SCIENCE, by the same architects, indeed part of the same commission, at a total cost of £51,000. Façade even more asymmetrical, and just as successful. Off-centre entrance of two storeys, doorway with stubby columns and terracotta putti. Big terracotta-faced staircase window, l., followed by a plain projection; twin gables, r., with piquant battlemented corner turret with spike. The Science School was on the ground floor, the Art School above, hence the large gabled windows, N side. Converted to housing 2001. – At the SW end, in Taylor's Lane, a wing built for the GIRLS' SECONDARY SCHOOL, 1909–10, by *Alfred G. Parker*, closely following the style of 1894–6; doorway with good terracotta figures. Set in the wall nearby, a stone tablet to Richard Inglethorpe †1618, from the almshouses he founded *c.* 1620 in Sansome Street, rebuilt there 1648 and in Taylor's Lane *c.* 1730.

SWAN THEATRE, The Moors. 1963–5 by *Henry Gorst*. Brick, as light and inexpensive as if for an exhibition. Simply raked auditorium to the N; its E end wall has raised patterning, the W, facing the racecourse, simple corrugated cladding. Foyer etc., S, later extended.

Former WORCESTER ROYAL INFIRMARY, Castle Street. By *Anthony Keck*, 1766–70, at a cost of £6,085; probably based on *Luke Singleton*'s Gloucester Infirmary (1757–61; demolished). The original red brick building, two storeys above a basement, can best be appreciated from Infirmary Walk, NE, where it is set back behind C19 gatepiers and railings (mostly reused from the Arboretum Gardens, p. 752). E front of seven bays: pedimented three-bay centre, projecting two-bay wings; pedimented doorway approached up steps, segment-headed windows. The return fronts of the wings also with central pediments. Extra half-storey added by *Henry Day*, 1864–5. Entrance hall with stone flags and rear screen of two Tuscan columns. Behind this, the board room, extended W by *Henry Day* in 1849–50, when he added the Neo-Norman CHAPEL. Of red brick with purple and buff patterning; Neo-Norman stone pulpit, apsed sanctuary, stained glass by *George Rogers*. Later C19 alterations include the two pyramid-roofed service towers at the rear outer angles, by *Martin & Chamberlain*,

p. 724

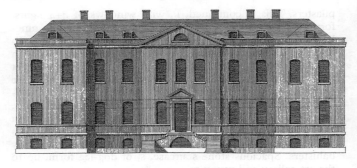

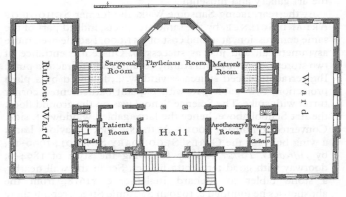

Worcester, former Royal Infirmary.
Elevation and plan of principal floor

1871–4. The SE wing received a similar tower when extended forward in 1887, by *Fell & Jones* of London. Functional NW wing (to Castle Street) by *Adams, Holden & Pearson*, 1932; extended *c.* 1966. Low outpatients' range along Castle Street, partly 1871–4, partly of 1912, with pediment, by *A. Hill Parker & Son*.

To the SE, along Infirmary Walk, the NURSES' HOME by *Lewis Sheppard & Son*, 1897–8. Neo-Georgian, lanky H-plan, with hipped roof and three-bay wings flanking the stone-framed centrepiece. This was superseded by a larger NURSES' HOME by *A. V. Rowe*, 1931–2, running S from the W end of the main block; more refined Neo-Georgian brick, thirteen bays, the centre rendered, with segmental pediment. Taller S cross-wings, *c.* 1940–50. Nearer Infirmary Walk, the late C18 WALNUT TREE HOUSE, three wide bays, with hipped roof and pedimented porch, and an early C20 lodge, no doubt again by *Rowe*.

The whole complex is scheduled to be converted (or partially rebuilt) for University College, Worcester, who commissioned *BDP* to prepare a master plan in 2006.

WORCESTERSHIRE ROYAL HOSPITAL, Charles Hastings Way. Huge spreading star-plan hospital built under the Private Finance Initiative, 1999–2001, by the American practice *RTKL Associates* (cf. Calderdale Royal Hospital, Halifax). Mostly three-storeyed, brick with much artificial stone trim, all rather mechanical-looking; the windows are either quite small or arranged horizontally, giving a somewhat Deco appearance. Very large central block, with curved rear; projecting ward wings set at an angle to the front corners. Between these the fully glazed entrance, facing SW towards Nunnery Wood, with large masts supporting its curved entrance canopy. Within, a very large concourse, an excellently modulated space, with tall, white-painted columns and glazed corridor gallery along its rear wall; the restaurant, at lower level, looks onto the central planted courtyard.

To the NE, by Newtown Road, the hospital approach is upstaged by three large chunky L-plan office blocks, by *Temple Cox Nicholls Ltd* of Birmingham, 2001–2, part of the PFI scheme; three-storeyed, much dark green glazing.

To the NW, now an integral part of the Worcestershire Royal, the former NEWTOWN HOSPITAL, begun as an isolation hospital, 1896. Of this date two severe gabled buildings by *H. Rowe & Son*. Large brick additions of the late 1970s. Along the W boundary, MALVERN VIEW, an attractive range of accommodation for doctors, by *John Carter* (of the *Pentan Partnership*, Cardiff), 2000: linked three-storey square units with overhanging hipped roofs with glazed cupolas. Further S, the striking CHARLES HASTINGS EDUCATION CENTRE, striped red and buff brick, by *Philip Proctor Associates*, 2001–2; two conjoined cylinders (the higher, N, the lecture hall, the S a restaurant), with angled NW teaching wing. Curved lobby (displaying a bust of Sir John Rushout by *J.F. Moore*, 1769, from the Royal Infirmary), answered by the curving medical museum.

SHRUB HILL STATION. Rebuilt 1863–4 for the GWR, probably by their engineer *Edward Wilson*. A remarkably good building, set back on an elevated forecourt above a stuccoed arcaded basement giving access to storage cellars (originally a Railway Institute). Entrance front of thirteen bays and two storeys, of Staffordshire blue engineering brick with stone dressings. Italianate detail, still indebted to Georgian: bold cornice, rusticated quoins, ground-floor windows with straight architraves. Five-bay centre with straight quoins and pedimented outer windows. Porte cochère on stalky iron columns. Most platform canopies renewed *c.* 1936. On the up platform, a remarkable waiting room survives, of cast-iron construction, with arched windows and foliated shafts; probably *c.* 1865, manufactured at the local *Vulcan Iron Works*. Elaborately faced with glazed ceramic tiles, vividly coloured, of Islamic and Renaissance inspiration, made by *Maw & Co*.

RAILWAY BRIDGE across the Severn, by *Stephen Ballard*, 1860, for the Hereford & Worcester Railway; approached, from Foregate Street station, by a gently curving viaduct of sixty-eight brick arches.* Sadly the two graceful segmental cast-iron river spans had to be replaced, in 1904 by *J.C. Ingles* for the GWR, by an unattractive lattice-girder construction.

SABRINA BRIDGE, just N of the above. Graceful cable-stayed suspension bridge for pedestrians, by *YRM Anthony Hunt Associates*, 1991. Supporting A-frame on the W bank only, with three pairs of cables quartering the 202-ft (62-metre) span.

WORCESTER BRIDGE. Rebuilt, a little downstream of its medieval predecessor, by *John Gwynn*, 1771–80. The cost, nearly £30,000, included the approach roads and quays (*see* Perambulation 2b), and a pair of ornamental domed toll houses, W side, now demolished. The present watered-down form of the bridge derives from reconstruction and widening, 1931–2, by the City Surveyor *C.I. Carey Walker*, with *L.G. Mouchel & Partners* as consultants. Sandstone, five segmental rusticated arches with tripled keystones and channelled undersides. Balustraded parapet with nice fluted lamp-posts with paired lanterns (made by *Hardy & Padmore* of Worcester). From the centre, an outstanding view of the cathedral.

Educational buildings

UNIVERSITY OF WORCESTER, Oldbury Road; see p. 778.

WORCESTER COLLEGE OF TECHNOLOGY, Deansway. By *Richard Sheppard, Robson & Partners*, begun 1960. A good design, looked at independently of its surroundings; it has the massiveness which became the hallmark of the 1960s, without gimmicks, unified by the consistent use of brown Hornton stone facing above a blue brindle engineering brick plinth. What turns one against it with some violence, however, is its position above the Severn, separated from the cathedral only by the former Bishop's Palace; it presses its C20 point home rather too forcibly.† Mostly of four storeys, in three parts, the first two to the S forming a compact T-plan. The earlier section, the three-storey St Andrew's Building, completed 1962, reads like a lower, larger N wing to Cathedral Building, opened 1966; this, boldly elbowing itself up against the Old Palace, expresses its rough concrete frame more clearly, and projects vigorously on two pilotis above an open public stairway down to the riverside. The third part, All Saints Building, two linked blocks completed 1973, is separated by St Andrew in its public garden. Chunkier, with cantilevered projections, but sitting rather more comfortably on its grassy slopes, at least when seen from the river. The front, with its entrance to Deansway

---

*Attached to the viaduct's N flank, part of the arcaded sloping embankment that took the former Butts Spur Line down to the quayside.

†Pevsner added that 'perhaps one does not like to be reminded that what in the past had been the force of the House of God is now that of the House of Technology'; but he preferred it to the Neo-Georgian buildings opposite, p. 722. Richard Sheppard had convinced the City Education Committee as early as 1957 that their new college should not be 'fake'.

emphasized by a flourish of exposed concrete, is more cramped, set too close to the road and to the C18 All Saints (p. 708).

ALICE OTTLEY SCHOOL, Upper Tything. A High School for girls, founded 1883. It took over BRITANNIA HOUSE, the most ambitious town house in Worcester; probably of *c.* 1730, perhaps by *Thomas White*, who certainly carved the figure of Britannia which gave the house its name. Brick, stone dressings. Two storeys, 2+1+2 bays, these divisions marked by rusticated pilaster strips. Central doorway with embryonic segmental pediment above lush carving of fronds and cherubs; fluted pilasters. Even lusher decoration of leaves and fruit round the window above. Tall panelled parapet raised segmentally in the middle to house the seated Britannia. Segmental-headed windows with aprons in the form of fluted segments (cf. St Mary, Castle Bromwich, Warwicks.). Spacious entrance hall with open-well mahogany staircase, three twisted and columnar balusters per tread; much original panelling. School hall etc. added at the rear by *Lewis Sheppard*, 1884.

The large classroom block of 3+3+3 bays adjoining, N, projecting slightly forward, is also by *Sheppard*, 1891–2. This was meant to match Britannia House in style and height, but seems more emphatic with its segmental gables flanked by urns and various other details. WHITSTONES, further NW, plain brick with sunflower frieze, was built as a private house by *J.H. Williams*, 1890.

Substantial brick and concrete-framed additions by *Michael Godwin* (*Godwin & Cowper* of Stourport) line the N boundary (with the Royal Grammar School, *see* below). The prominent COBHAM SPORTS HALL is of 1970–1. The range then continues E (with central infill of 1990) to the SCIENCE BLOCK, terminating, towards Tennis Walk, with polygonal laboratories, like a truncated cone, with raking concrete pilotis; this opened in 1978.

THE KING'S SCHOOL, College Green, was founded by Henry VIII *c.* 1541 in compensation for the loss of the Priory school. Its College Hall is the former monastic refectory (p. 699); most of the buildings around College Green also belong to the school. Its main site, immediately S, covers ground originally occupied by WORCESTER CASTLE, of which virtually nothing remains. The site of its great Norman motte, levelled 1823–43, is now a garden between school and river; remnants of sandstone walls incorporated into the buildings of College Green may have belonged to the C12–C13 castle (*see* pp. 706–7).

The dominant building is the huge SCHOOL HOUSE (the Headmaster's Boarding House) by *Ewan Christian*, 1886–7, raw red brick, with gables, big hipped roof, and tall chimneys. It overlooks, W, a neat terraced garden by *Hope Bagenal*, 1931, on the site of the motte; low brick walls, lead-covered fountain with column and statuette of Sabrina (by *Anne Acheson*). To its E, a classroom block by *H. Rowe & Son*, 1925, extended to an L-plan in 1936 and 1950 to form a small quad. To the NE, the

Neo-Georgian CHAPPEL HALL, by *A. V. Rowe*, 1925, closing the yard formed by the backs of College Green. Further E (more or less on the site of the mid-C18 County Gaol, demolished 1814), another yard with the chunky brick WOLFSON BUILDING, by *J.R. Wingfield (IDC Ltd)*, 1972, S side, and the WINSLOW BUILDING, standard curtain walling of 1958 by *Maurice W. Jones* on the E. At a lower level, along Severn Street, more late C20 buildings, mostly brick, including the THEATRE by *John Barnsley*, 1986, and ANNETT BUILDING by *Cassidy, Farrington & Dennys*, 1963–4, with strip glazing and projecting eaves.

ROYAL GRAMMAR SCHOOL, Upper Tything. Refounded 1561, the school moved here in 1868 from its former modest building in Church Street (p. 739). The site was that of the Cistercian nunnery of Whistones, called WHITELADIES, founded by Bishop Walter de Cantelupe *c.* 1240. Some fragments of its red sandstone chapel remain built into the walls of two Georgian houses at the S end of the site. PRIORY HOUSE faces the street: *c.* 1730, five bays, mottled brick with lighter red brick window surrounds (with fluted keystones) and quoins. In the wall of its rear addition, the chapel's W wall, with two blocked lancets set in chamfered relieving arches. Its E wall, with two large lancets and two (originally three) smaller recesses lower down, is preserved in the W return wall of WHITELADIES HOUSE. This, *c.* 1720, faces N: eleven bays, brick, with segmental-headed windows with contrasting headers, brick platbands, and hipped roof. Later C18 doorway, with open pediment on Ionic demi-columns. Large additions of 1904–10 for the school.

The first scholastic building here (now ELD HALL), by *A.E. Perkins*, 1867–8, faces the street further N. Tall Elizabethan Gothic, of Tewkesbury brick with Bath stone dressings; three rather tight bays, with large transomed windows under straight entablatures. Ornate shaped gables, central statue of Queen Elizabeth I by *R.L. Boulton*. The ends have five-light pointed windows. Tall timber lantern, with ogee top. Hammerbeam roof within; upper floor inserted *c.* 1981. Small N porch with attached classroom. The two-storey S extension, 1895–6 by *A. Hill Parker*, with carving by *W. Forsyth*, in matching but rather looser style, provided further classrooms linked by a cloistered passage.

Later buildings are by the same practice, the best, set back NE, the PERRINS HALL, by *A.H. Parker & Son*, 1913–15. This is Neo-Jacobean, quite bold in scale, of darker red brick with ample yellow Cotswold stone dressings. Asymmetrically arranged: centre with mullioned-and-transomed windows above a round-arched loggia, projecting S part with shaped gable above rounded oriel, N end with big canted apse. Elaborate segmental ceiling on scrolled brackets within; S gallery. The neat S return faces Whiteladies House across a large quadrangle. The LECTURE THEATRE (originally Biology Block), 1928, forms the rest of its N side, still with shaped central gable; the PERRINS LABORATORIES, 1922, fill the E side, their projecting ends yet again with shaped gables, above Venetian windows.

The Queen Elizabeth Almshouses (p. 760), at the corner of Upper Tything and Little London, form part of the same complex. Postmodern DESIGN CENTRE, N of Little London, by *Rowe, Elliott & Partners*, 1984.

RNIB NEW COLLEGE, Whittington Road. Founded, as Worcester College for the Blind, in 1866 (cf. p. 734). The first building on the present site is a long range of 1900–2 by *Richard Creed*, brick with rendered upper floor; small cupola above the porch, half-timbered and tile-hung gable, NW, hipped-roof projection, SE. L-plan rear wing, SW, with prominent gymnasium with hipped roof and flatter cupola, by *Elcock & Sutcliffe*, 1937–9; completed as a small quadrangle, plus chapel, in matching style, 1961. Later additions include residential blocks of 1987–9, nearer the road, still in Neo-vernacular style; THE GABLES, a large house of *c.* 1890, brick with timbered gables, is incorporated.

ST MARY'S CONVENT SCHOOL, Battenhall Avenue. *See* p. 771.

NUNNERY WOOD HIGH SCHOOL, Spetchley Road. By *E.B. Musman*, 1951–2, built as a secondary modern. Brick, with gabled entrance range and projecting hall with big glazed window; two-storey classroom ranges. Many later additions. – The nearby SIXTH-FORM COLLEGE was the Grammar School for Girls by *Musman & Cousens*, 1960–2; four storeys, straightforward brick with concrete frame.

KING'S ST ALBAN'S JUNIOR SCHOOL, Mill Street. The site is that of the St Alban's Home for Girls, founded by Cordelia Stillingfleet, 1859. Re-established here in an L-plan mid-C18 brick building, formerly assembly rooms associated with the Diglis Pleasure Gardens. The main room in the W wing has Venetian windows and ceiling with plaster rose. S wing much extended for the Home *c.* 1870–80, with tall range with hipped or half-hipped roofs. To the NW, a neat Neo-Georgian addition by *C.F. Whitcombe*, 1908. This adjoins the brick CHAPEL of 1873, probably by *Hopkins*: Geometrical windows, voussoirs of alternating stones. Some decoration of *c.* 1900 survives, with stained glass in the E window (probably by *Clayton & Bell*); side windows by *Hardman*: one opposing pair 1901, the other 1925–6. Plain brick buildings for the school, of the 1990s, complete the quadrangle, with gabled entrance-cum-library added to the inner S side by *DJD Architects*, 2002.

PERAMBULATIONS

The main spine of development at Worcester runs S–N, along the line High Street–The Cross–Foregate–Foregate Street–Tything–Upper Tything. This will be followed, in stages, below (Perambulations 2–3). Perambulations 1a and 1b are short excursions S and SE of the cathedral, the latter, in an area ravaged by C20 traffic management, with one outstanding building, The Commandery.

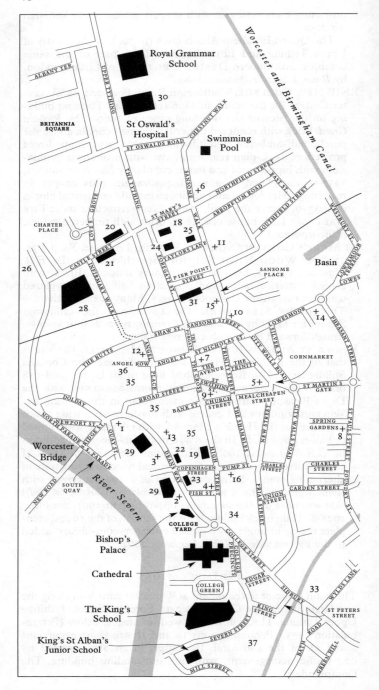

Royal Grammar School

St Oswald's Hospital

Swimming Pool

ALBANY TER.

BRITANNIA SQUARE

CHARTER PLACE

UPPER TYTHING

ST OSWALDS ROAD

THE TYTHING

CHESTNUT WALK

SANSOME WALK

NORTHFIELD STREET

EAST ST.

ARBORETUM ROAD

SOUTHFIELD STREET

WESTBURY ST.

ST MARY'S STREET

FOREGATE ST.

TAYLORS LANE

PIER POINT STREET

SANSOME PLACE

Basin

LOWESMOOR TERRACE

LOWES

LOVE'S GROVE

CASTLE STREET

INFIRMARY WALK

SHAW ST.

SANSOME STREET

LOWESMOOR

PHEASANT STREET

THE BUTTS

ANGEL PLACE

ANGEL ROW

ANGEL ST.

ST NICHOLAS ST.

SILVER ST.

CITY WALLS ROAD

CORNMARKET

DOLDAY

THE CROSS

BROAD STREET

ST SWITHINS ST.

THE AVENUE

THE TRINITY

ST MARTIN'S GATE

NORTH PARADE

NEWPORT ST.

QUAY ST.

BANK ST.

CHURCH STREET

MEALCHEAPEN STREET

NEW STREET

CITY WALLS ROAD

SPRING GARDENS

ST PAUL'S STREET

FOUNDRY ST.

Worcester Bridge

BRIDGE ST.

S. PARADE

DEANS WAY

COPENHAGEN STREET

HIGH STREET

THE SHAMBLES

PUMP ST.

CHARLES STREET

CHARLES STREET

River Severn

NEW ROAD

SOUTH QUAY

FISH ST.

UNION STREET

FRIAR STREET

CARDEN STREET

COLLEGE YARD

COLLEGE ST.

COLLEGE PRECINCTS

Bishop's Palace

Cathedral

COLLEGE GREEN

EDGAR STREET

SIDBURY

WYLDS LANE

33

ST PETERS STREET

The King's School

King's St Alban's Junior School

KING STREET

SEVERN STREET

MILL STREET

BATH ROAD

GREEN HILL

37

26   20   21   28   18   25   24   11   31   15   10   14

6   12   36   35   7   5   9   29   1   13   35   22   19   3   23   4   16   2   34   8   29   35   30

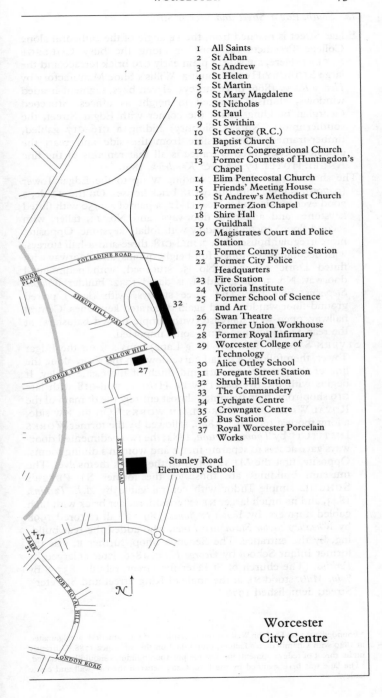

1 All Saints
2 St Alban
3 St Andrew
4 St Helen
5 St Martin
6 St Mary Magdalene
7 St Nicholas
8 St Paul
9 St Swithin
10 St George (R.C.)
11 Baptist Church
12 Former Congregational Church
13 Former Countess of Huntingdon's Chapel
14 Elim Pentecostal Church
15 Friends' Meeting House
16 St Andrew's Methodist Church
17 Former Zion Chapel
18 Shire Hall
19 Guildhall
20 Magistrates Court and Police Station
21 Former County Police Station
22 Former City Police Headquarters
23 Fire Station
24 Victoria Institute
25 Former School of Science and Art
26 Swan Theatre
27 Former Union Workhouse
28 Former Royal Infirmary
29 Worcester College of Technology
30 Alice Ottley School
31 Foregate Street Station
32 Shrub Hill Station
33 The Commandery
34 Lychgate Centre
35 Crowngate Centre
36 Bus Station
37 Royal Worcester Porcelain Works

Worcester
City Centre

1a. South: Edgar Street and Severn Street

Edgar Street is reached from the SE angle of the cathedral along
College Precincts (p. 706) or along the busy COLLEGE
STREET. Here, SW side, a plain early C19 brick terrace and the
large SIDBURY HOUSE, built as Willis's Shoe Manufactory by
Henry Rowe, 1866; three storeys, eleven bays, segment-headed
windows, clumsily reduced in height as offices. Stuccoed
Georgian buildings mark the corner with Edgar Street, the
southernmost (No. 34 Sidbury) hiding a C16–C17 gabled,
timber-framed house, visible from the side and rear; the
attached pedimented entrance is all that remains of the fine
ANGEL HOTEL by *Wood & Kendrick*, 1899.

The short EDGAR STREET, leading W up to the Edgar Tower
(p. 706), is lined with pretty C18 brick houses. On the N side, a
good even run includes Nos. 11–12, a pair of *c.* 1750 with fluted
keystones and adjoining doorways, and No. 13, taller, with
second-floor Venetian window with foliate keystone. Opposite,
more irregular houses: No. 7, mid-C18, three-and-a-half storeys,
with decorated keystones, full-height quoins, and doorway with
fluted Doric columns; No. 5, stuccoed, with pedimented
doorway. No. 3, the grandest, is dated 1732; builder *William
Stephens*. Five bays and three storeys, with (later) paired
ground-floor windows and again decorated keystones. Central
hallway, open-well staircase (with simple turned balusters) at
the rear, SE. Good panelling, some imported.

SEVERN STREET (formerly Frog Lane) runs S from the Edgar
Tower, then follows a broad curve down to the river, along the
line of the former rampart and ditch of the castle bailey. It
begins with the five-bay TOWER HOUSE, mid-C18 with late
C19 shopfront, then becomes almost entirely the domain of the
ROYAL WORCESTER PORCELAIN WORKS.* On the NW side,
a long modest terrace, *c.* 1880, followed by the former WORKS
INSTITUTE by *Thomas Sutton*, 1884; the two pedimented doorways gave access to separate men's and women's dining rooms.
Opposite, first the MUSEUM, then the works themselves. The
museum buildings are those of the former ST PETER'S
SCHOOL: simple Tudor with central gable by *A.E. Perkins*,
1843, and its much larger NE extension, redder brick with high
gabled dormers, by *Yeates & Jones*, 1891–2;† all restored 1998
by *Wheatley Taylor Stainburn Lines*, who added the rear building, by the entrance. The Seconds Shop, further E, was the
former Infant School by *George Hunt*, 1856, later enlarged by
Perkins. (The church of St Peter the Great, rebuilt 1837–8 by
John Mills, stood NE at the angle of King Street and St Peter's
Street; demolished 1976.)

---

*Founded 1751 by Dr John Wall on the riverside N of the cathedral; amalgamated
in 1840 with Chamberlain's factory, established on this site since 1788. Currently
under threat of redevelopment; most of the pre-1900 buildings should be retained.
†The lane was here spanned by the Frog Gate, between the city wall and castle
bailey.

The SHOWROOM (now restaurant), plus the range beyond, is of 1851–2 by *Robert Armstrong*, an Irish architect who worked in the Staffordshire Potteries. Stuccoed, with big channelled round-arched entrance, bracketed frieze, and urns over plain corner pilasters; top-lit interior. On its S side, a brick building dated 1840, continued E by the GRINDING SHOP, mostly also by *Armstrong*, with boiler house and hexagonal chimney added 1863, and grinding machinery *in situ*, a rare survival. To the W, all along the curve, are the LODGE and WAREHOUSES, by *Scrivener & Son* of Hanley, 1865, continued by *Thomas Sutton*, 1887–91: two-storeyed, red brick, with yellow brick pilasters rising to giant segment-headed arches; windows stone-framed, the lower segmental-, the upper round-arched. Other late C19 buildings mostly by *G.B. Ford* of Burslem; mid-C20 additions by *S.N. Cooke*.

Severn Street then narrows between unexciting late C20 buildings of the King's School, the main part of which occupies the castle site above (p. 727–8). The buttressed brick wall further on, S side, is the boundary of the former St Alban's Home, now the King's Junior School (p. 729). At the end, the mid-C18 DIGLIS HOTEL faces the river. Brick, four bays, the central two projecting with pediment; modillion cornice, fluted keystones. On the long side towards Severn Street, an Ionic doorcase; on the garden side, a Doric doorcase and pair of canted bays. Edward Leader Williams, chief engineer to the Severn Navigation Commission, lived here in the early C19; his son, the painter Benjamin Leader Williams, was born here in 1831.

1b. South-east: Sidbury

SIDBURY suffers severely from traffic, a dual carriageway feeding into City Walls Road, to the N. SW side entirely demolished; disjointed survivors on the NE side. No. 55 (DANESBURY HOUSE), rebuilt in red and yellow brick by *A.H. Parker*, 1889, is proudly labelled 'the early home of Mrs Henry Wood'. No. 57, partly of C16–C17 narrow studding, has two gables with original bargeboards with chains of quatrefoils. Then, a few more timber-framed houses, mostly refaced in C18 brick, and the stuccoed KING'S HEAD, by the site of the C13 Sidbury Gate (demolished 1768). Beyond the canal and its lock is the major C15–C18 survivor, The Commandery.

THE COMMANDERY, originally Hospital of St Wulfstan, is said to have been founded a few years before Wulfstan's death in 1095; a late C12 or early C13 origin is more likely. Standing just outside the city walls and run by Augustinian canons, it served as an almshouse as well as a place of hospitality for travellers. By the end of the C13 it had become known as the Preceptory or Commandery of St Wulfstan. The present building, largely of close-studding, is mostly late C15, much of it later clad with brick or rendered. It now forms an irregular extended H-plan, but was probably originally built round two courtyards, with

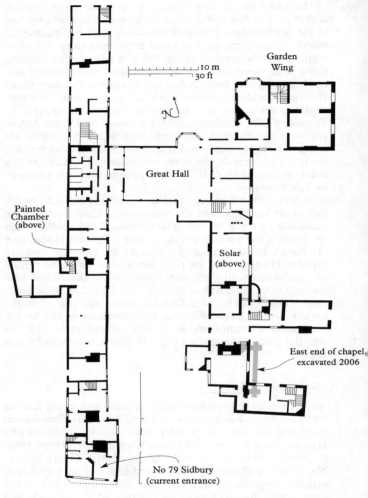

Garden
Wing

├─────────┤ 10 m
├─────────┤ 30 ft

Great Hall

Painted
Chamber
(above)

Solar
(above)

East end of chapel,
excavated 2006

No 79 Sidbury
(current entrance)

Worcester, The Commandery.
Plan

the chapel (St Godwald) close to Sidbury*. Suppressed 1540, the Hospital was acquired as a house by the clothier Thomas Wylde in 1545. It was bought by the Dandridge family in 1764 and subdivided. In 1843 a carriageway was cut through the Great Hall into the rear courtyard. The building was used as the College for the Blind in 1866–87, then as a printing works; the Hall was carefully reconstructed (eliminating the carriage-

---

*The chapel's C13 E end was excavated in 2006, together with the footings of a C15 N chapel.

way) in 1954. Worcester City Council purchased the site in 1973, restoring it as a museum (opened 1977). Further restoration by *F.W.B. & Mary Charles* in the late 1980s and by *S. T. Walker & Duckham*, 2006.

EXTERIOR. The entrance is now through the former No. 79 Sidbury, a two-storey late C15 house with close studding and first-floor overhang. Commandery Drive leads between the long S ranges to the screens-passage doorway at the W end of the hall range (with windows only on its upper floor). The E range, the S part of which, with two added E wings, later formed a separate house, was much altered in the C18, it E side refaced in brick, with sashes and rusticated doorway with pediment. NE of the hall range projects the hipped-roofed garden wing (built 1708) which also formed a separate late C18 dwelling; the main approach to the complex was then from this direction.* The N side of the Great Hall, between the NE garden wing and the mostly brick N end of the W range, has a large polygonal NE bay window. Above this and the adjoining end of the E range, large gables with carved bargeboards, originally balanced by a cross-gabled NW porch, at the N end of the screens passage. The W range has a long front towards the canal, mostly square-panelled framing, partly brick, especially the C16–C17 N extension. An early C19 industrial cross-wing, three storeys with passageway beneath, projects towards the canal; to its N, the prominent gable-end of the hall range.

INTERIOR. The GREAT HALL, of the 1470s, is impressive in size and detail. Four and a half bays, with moulded wall-shafts originally supporting hammerbeams, later converted to tie-beam construction. Tracery in the arched braces of both the tie- and collar-beams, as well as above; curved wind-braces, good carved bosses, also evidence for two louvres. The cross-passage is preserved, demarcated by a spere (probably originally with movable screen). The present screen, with plain muntins, is mostly reconstruction, apart from the panels between the spere-trusses and the walls, probably inserted in the early C17 when the W gallery was installed. The upper end 52 is lit by the fine large polygonal bay window, with arched lights and boarded ceiling with ribs and small bosses. Most lights have pretty late C15 stained glass with quarries of birds and plants with the inscription 'Emanuell'; coloured fragments higher up. Above the high table, a coved ceiling also with ribs and small bosses. At its entry from the bay window and from the staircase opposite, two fine bench ends carved with lions, *in situ*. Hall floor partly of C19 tiles, partly brick paving (where the carriageway was driven through).

Good STAIRCASE, SE, probably *c.* 1600; tapering square balusters, round-arched openings, newel posts with geometrical decoration. The E wing probably contained accommodation for the master and chaplains. On its upper floor, a fine

---

*In the garden here, three bases of late C13–early C14 quatrefoil piers, with fillets, perhaps from the chapel.

three-bay SOLAR, with similar detail to the hall: moulded wall-shafts, wall-plates and tie-beams, with tracery in the roof, and again carved bosses and wind-braces.* To its N (i.e. E of the upper level of the hall), two rooms with good C17–C18 panelling, the larger one with mid-C19 Jacobethan overmantel with religious scenes, and closet with peephole down into the hall. In the NW room of the garden wing, a relocated overmantel with arched panels and Wylde heraldry of *c.* 1594.

The w range is probably mostly contemporary with the hall cross-range, but of simpler construction; one room thick, the ground floor (the later printing shop) much altered. The chamber over the service end was modified when the gallery above the screens passage was constructed in the early C17. The upper-floor rooms to its s were linked by interconnecting doors. The most remarkable survival here is a PAINTED CHAMBER, with stencilled palmette decoration and eminently interesting wall paintings of religious subjects, probably *c.* 1490, rediscovered 1935. The ceiling is filled by a large representation of the Trinity, with inscriptions and emblems. N wall: St Michael weighing Souls, flanked by St Godwald and St Etheldreda; top part of a Crucifixion below the latter. s wall, the Martyrdom of St Erasmus flanked by St Roche and St Peter; below, the Martyrdom of St Thomas Becket, and St Anne teaching the Virgin.

In SIDBURY beyond The Commandery, modest C18 (or earlier) houses; opposite, Nos. 82–84, a CO-OP STORES by *Yeates & Jones*, 1916, banded brick and stone. This faces up Wylds Lane, at the beginning of which is the former ST PETER'S MISSION HALL by *Henry Rowe*, 1869, two-storey Tudor, with big windows; top storey, lopped off after a fire, rebuilt by *Walter Thomson*, 2005. Sidbury ends with the BARLEY MOW, a good Queen Anne pub by *Frederic Hughes*, 1898, with gables with plasterwork decoration, and No. 119, formerly the Loch Ryan Hotel. This is mid- to late C18, painted brick, with pedimented three-bay projection and urns above; doorway with open pediment on engaged Ionic columns.

Opposite, stranded by the late C20 Commandery Road, an attractive fragment of the Georgian brick BATH ROAD. Its w side is a continuous terrace, partly renewed. Nos. 8–10, dated 'JS 1740', has five bays of segment-headed windows with decorated keystones, and doorway with attached Doric columns. On the E, Nos. 11–15, a terrace of *c.* 1800 with fluted Doric doorcases, then a few pleasant early C19 villas.

More early C19 housing in GREEN HILL high above, with fine views back to the cathedral: four villas, E side, No. 12 with fancy valance-like bargeboards, No. 8 with bay windows and pretty iron porch; opposite, Nos. 1–6, a small-scale brick terrace with good columned porches.

---

* Foundations of a central bay window, facing the courtyard, were excavated in 2005.

2. The city within the walls

The area covered by Perambulations 2a–2c is almost exactly that which lay within Worcester's MEDIEVAL WALLS. Compared with such cities as York and Chester, or even Newcastle upon Tyne, there is little to be seen: just two or three low stretches alongside the late C20 City Walls Road (pp. 743, 746), a little more s of The Butts (p. 754). Nor is there much to see of other medieval stone remains: two churches more or less in medieval form (St Alban, St Helen), the steeple of a third (St Andrew), plus fragments incorporated into the city's four notable C18 churches; also one medieval undercroft. But there will be plenty of other C18 to early C20 compensations, and, particularly in Perambulation 2c, a fine display of C15–C17 timber framing.

2a. High Street and The Cross

Before starting along High Street, we must take in the extensive central redevelopment of 1965–7, the LYCHGATE CENTRE (now Cathedral Plaza). It is not easy to be fair to it, but as Pevsner pointed out in 1968, one should not forget that such a development in this place (obliterating the medieval street lines) was hara-kiri by the City Council, not murder by the architects: *Shingler Risdon Associates*, who made a reasonable enough job of it. The parts by the cathedral and the unfortunate roundabout are of only three storeys; their façades, all of dark red engineering brick, vary enough to prevent boredom, yet sufficiently to give each side a character: mostly glazed, N; boxy oriels, E, plus the section stepping down College Street, SE. The rectangular high block, set N–S and faced in ribbed concrete tiles, built as the Giffard Hotel (consultants *Russell, Hodgson & Leigh*), is, however, seven storeys high and, though set well back, very intrusive in all elevated views of the cathedral. The pedestrian shopping alleys (from the roundabout, from High Street, and from Pump Street, *see* below) converge at a small top-lit court, in the shadow of this higher block. Otherwise the design is neither gimmicky nor modish. This is perhaps more than can be said for the 1990s revamping of the High Street frontage by the *Stanley Bragg Partnerhip*, with unglazed terracotta tiling, wavy roof canopies and entrance with flared-out glazed oriel. The mildly Deco block incorporated further N, 1925–32, by *Yeates & Jones* for the drapers Russell & Dorrell, makes an interesting contrast.

So the whole SE end of HIGH STREET is this C20 development. The W side retains much C18–C19 work, often hiding timber-framed remnants. It starts with No. 106 (College Gates), *c.* 1700, with stuccoed early C19 front of 1+3+1 bays; at the rear a good open-well staircase with twisted balusters. Nicely restored 1974 for the Portman Building Society. Outside, a bronze STATUE of Sir Edward Elgar, by *Kenneth Potts*, 1980, facing s (across the traffic) towards his beloved cathedral. Then a few modest Georgian frontages up to and beyond St Helen (p. 711).

FISH STREET, along the S side of the church, is a pleasant enclave, varied C18 with timber-framed survivors. The FARRIER'S ARMS, C16 with some close studding and two over-hangs, the upper added *c.* 1666–78, is much restored; the early C17 No. 21, gable-end to the street, looks more authentic, with its jetties on scrolled brackets. The early to mid-C18 PLOUGH INN, of four rendered bays, belongs now rather to Deansway (*see* Perambulation 2b).

Back in HIGH STREET, No. 95, W side, is of 1877 by *Henry Rowe* for the wine merchants Stallard & Sons; good shopfront with polished granite shafts, foliage capitals carved by *H.H. Martyn*. Now a WATERSTONE'S bookshop (incorporating the brick tunnel-vaulted wine cellars). MARMION HOUSE, a standard block of 1965–6 by *John B. Day* of Bristol, has, beneath its rear, part of a C13 stone undercroft: one bay of octopartite vaulting with chamfered ribs, plus springers for another. By the entrance (now to Keystones Wine Bar) in COPENHAGEN STREET, a lively bronze carving of St John on horseback, by *Anita Lafford c.* 1966. Also on the S side here, No. 7, timber-framed, *c.* 1558, refaced in brick with shaped gable *c.* 1717 (and refenestrated *c.* 1792); and Nos. 9–11, brick, *c.* 1800, with mid-C19 stone ground floor, and good cantilevered staircase, top-lit from an elliptical skylight. Opposite, after the long C19 flank of the Guildhall (p. 721), the former POLICE STATION by *Rowe*, 1862, with a redder brick addition of *c.* 1900.

In HIGH STREET, E side, with rounded corner to Pump Street, is No. 25 (Compton Buildings), by *E.A. Day*, 1881; terracotta lintels with sunflower decoration. Most of the N side of PUMP STREET is contemporary, including a former side entrance to the MARKET HALL (originally by *Richard Morton*, 1804, mostly rebuilt 1857); dated 1881, with segmental pediment containing a carved basket of flowers. The S side, with St Andrew's Methodist Church (p. 719), belongs to the late 1960s scheme. Georgian fronts in High Street facing the Guildhall begin with No. 27, four bays with good late C19 shopfront. Then the wayward entry to CITY ARCADE, with cutaway corner, clock (of 1849, recycled from the Market Hall on the site), glazed first-floor prow and Art Nouveau-inspired steel gates; 2000–1 by *Lett & Sweetland* (executive architects *Glazzard Associates*). The stuccoed No. 31 has a little incised decoration. At No. 32, the former Golden Lion, the early C19 stuccoed front conceals a probably early C15 timber-framed hall house, of three bays, end-on to the street. The gabled front was sliced off, perhaps *c.* 1700, but the interior has been partly restored (by *F.W.B. Charles*, 1988). The entrance passage was on the S side, as now, probably with gallery above, alongside the lofty two-bay hall (with reconstructed high-set mullioned windows); arch-braced tie-beams with queenposts at the centre and arched wind-braces. Altered and floored, as usual, in the C17. No. 34, again stuccoed, has intermittently blocked fluted pilasters.

Of Georgian survivors on the W side (all of course with modern shopfronts, several hiding earlier fabric) the best is Nos. 83–84, early C18, five bays, with band courses and decorated keystones. No. 85 (once the Bull Inn) now forms a discreet entrance to the CROWNGATE SHOPPING CENTRE, by *Frederick Gibberd, Coombes & Partners*, 1989–92. In contrast to the Lychgate Centre, this is mostly plugged in to the existing townscape, with 'instant history' motifs, reasonably well done. It stretches back, mostly behind existing frontages, to Deansway, where it engulfs the former Countess of Huntingdon's Chapel (p. 718). Neatly inserted café at first-floor level, S of the chapel, by *Malcolm Booth* of *Associated Architects*, 1993–4. Sculptural interludes provided by *Kenneth Potts*, 1998. No. 78 High Street, with over-enthusiastic half-timbering, is a refacing of 1921 by *L.L. Bussault* for the Shakespeare Café; authentic C16 work survives inside. BOOTS has a neat Neo-Georgian Deco front of 1936, by their in-house architect *Percy J. Bartlett*. DEBENHAMS is much larger, concrete-framed, *c.* 1960, by *Healing & Overbury*; brick and curtain walling, with concrete fins.

Opposite, all is now also C20, a disparate mixture between the *retardataire* Neo-Georgian of MARKS AND SPENCER (by *Monro & Partners*, 1959–60) and the livelier Neo-Georgian of BARCLAYS BANK, with canted corner to Church Street; the latter, built for the grocers David Greig by *H. Rowe & Son*, 1930–1, was adapted for Martin's Bank by *E.C. Aldridge*, 1937.

In CHURCH STREET, E, half-hidden behind the tower of St Swithin (p. 716), the OLD GRAMMAR SCHOOL, or what is left of it; dated 1735, brick, single-storeyed, with three round-arched windows and plain timber turret.

High Street, E side, ends with two striking brick and terracotta buildings. Nos. 55–58, dated 1903, by *Clare & Ross* of London for Messrs Woodwards, topped with a balustrade and central pediment with obelisks, have shopfronts divided by green marble and brown tiling. Nos. 59–60 by *Lewis Sheppard & Son*, 1901–3, built as the Central Temperance Hotel, of brighter red brick with ampler orange terracotta trim, have broad gables and a big corner turret with ogee-domed copper roof.

The last section of the W side begins with No. 65, the former Old Bank, opened 1761: 2+1+2 bays, three storeys, the projecting centre stressed by even rusticated quoins and pediment. Restored 1860 by *John Billing*, who probably extended the front along Bank Street. Then plain late C18 houses up to No. 61, at the corner with Broad Street. This is early C18, with panelled keystones linked by a moulded band, quoins, pretty modillion cornice, and hipped roof with pedimented dormers; stone ground floor by *T.B. Whinney*, 1910, for the London, City & Midland Bank.

High Street now becomes THE CROSS, with notable buildings on its E side. It begins quietly with a brick and terracotta building, with polygonal corner turret, by *Henry Rowe & Son*, 1890, continuing along the N side of St Swithin Street. No. 2, fine early C18 brick, has four bays and three-and-a-half storeys, with quoins, windows with prominent acanthus-scroll keystones, swags below them on the upper two floors, another delicate modillion cornice, and hipped roof; later doorway, l., with Composite columns, fanlight, and open pediment. Then the former NATIONAL PROVINCIAL BANK by *Charles Heathcote & Sons* of Manchester, 1906–7, an excellent Portland stone façade of three bays, English Baroque style, with channelled rustication and recessed Ionic columns on the first floor.

The superb LLOYDS BANK, by *E. W. Elmslie*, 1861–2, was built as the head office of the Worcester City and County Bank, at a cost of *c.* £14,000; it represents the provincial bank at its most confidence-inspiring. An ashlar-faced palazzo, of three storeys, the upper two with five generously spaced bays. All the first-floor windows are in pedimented aedicules with Ionic columns and balustraded aprons. On the rusticated ground floor, the massive portal, with two pairs of Doric granite columns, is flanked by single, large, thickly framed windows. Carving by *W. Forsyth*. s return (to The Avenue) also impressive, with its gently swelling, off-centre bow. All interior detail has been boxed in. The former St Nicholas (p. 714) provides a splendid foil.

THE AVENUE leads to the odd-looking OLD TRINITY HOUSE, now a restaurant. Its front, behind wrought-iron gates between polygonal lodges, seems entirely of 1907, when the building was adapted as the Worcester Diocesan Church House. The rear elevation, however (*see* Trinity Street, p. 747), is mid-C18 Gothic Revival and wholly delightful. Closer inspection suggests that underlying the fanciful Edwardian work, with its broken pediment, obelisks, and rusticated porch with scrolled pediment, may be the shadow of an early C18 house with giant fluted pilasters and fluted keystones. The interior indeed retains much early to mid-C18 Rococo plasterwork and joinery, the former now too heavily gilded; cantilevered wrought-iron staircase presumably of *c.* 1907.

THE CROSS, w side, is far more humdrum; some C18 brick fronts punctuated by No. 29, by *E.A. Day*, 1893, with fancy gable and terracotta sunflower decoration. No. 32, with curved corner to Broad Street, of 1860, is typical of *Henry Rowe*.

2b. *West of High Street, via Broad Street, to the Severn*

BROAD STREET leads w from The Cross to the Severn. By the C16 it was second only to High Street in importance, with at least two substantial inns; like High Street, it is now pedestrianized. Little to note at first. No. 69, s side, standard C19 commercial, narrow and gabled, was built as offices for Lea & Perrins, of Worcestershire Sauce fame, by *Henry Rowe*, 1870; remnants of a high quality C15 roof at the rear. The bland HSBC opposite, by *Whinney, Son & Austen Hall*, 1968–9, replaced a dignified Italianate bank by *H.L. Florence*, 1875. The CROWN INN is part of a loose C18–early C19 stuccoed group (Nos. 10–12) of some twelve bays, the outer parts with flanking fluted pilasters, the centre with nice cast-iron balcony (and sensible shopping passage of 1984 by *Glazzard Associates*). At its rear, a first-floor assembly room with a little plasterwork and rounded ends with fluted Ionic pilasters, approached by an early C18 staircase.

Opposite, the best Georgian group. Most imposing are Nos. 59–60, mid-C18, four storeys, six bays altogether, brick with stone quoins and panelled keystones. No. 61, adjoining, is one of the collector's pieces at Worcester, also four-storeyed, perhaps a decade or so earlier. Only one bay wide, busy quoins emphasising its narrowness. Venetian window on each floor, all with human figure-head keystones; rounded gable above flanked by urns; on top, a little lead-domed belvedere with pointed windows in three directions and access to a gabled back room on the fourth. Within, much original joinery and plasterwork; the belvedere, entered through a trap door above the stairwell, has sparse Gothick decoration. The former UNICORN HOTEL (No. 55), with stuccoed seven-bay front of *c.* 1830, now forms an entrance to the Crowngate Shopping Centre (*see* above); excavations here, 1989, revealed the N line of the Saxon defences. Other Georgian frontages follow, their interiors sometimes revealing timber-framed origins.

Opposite, N side, opens ANGEL PLACE, its rounded SE corner with the Deco-classical premises of the Jap Furnishing Co., by *Yeates & Jones*, 1928, the SW with the DOLPHIN INN, painted brick, *c.* 1800. There follows a further shopping centre, of late 1960s vintage, revamped as part of the Crowngate Centre *c.* 1990; its N end stands on the site of the Dominican (Black-friars) Priory (*see* p. 753). More Georgian façades at the end, facing All Saints (p. 708), where, despite the Deansway traffic, some suggestion remains of the small marketplace that occupied this area.

The continuation of Broad Street (or rather Deansway) is BRIDGE STREET, part of *John Gwynn*'s designs of 1779 for the approaches to his Worcester Bridge (*see* p. 726). Work began 1780. The three-storey terraces, stepping down slightly in pairs, were not erected until 1788–92. They are remarkably well-preserved: three-bay houses with timber Doric doorcases with open pediments and good fanlights. The ends differ somewhat, the grandest house being nearest the bridge, NW, four storeys, with more prominent doorcase, and big curved end to its rear staircase. All restored and converted to flats 1981–3.

Gwynn also planned terraces along the riverside to N and S (where he also rebuilt the quays), but these never materialized. On NORTH PARADE now there is just the OLD RECTIFYING HOUSE, a half-timbered two-storey inn, rather like a boathouse, and the adjoining HOP WAREHOUSE (now flats), a lively mix of red and yellow brick with some terracotta, the most elaborate in Worcester. Both are by *Yeates & Jones*, 1897–8.

SOUTH PARADE begins with WARMSTREY COURT, warehousey-vernacular housing, *c.* 1985, by the *Panton Sargent Partnership*. Then (on SOUTH QUAY) a group of three real C19 warehouses, all now converted. GASCOYNE HOUSE, probably *c.* 1850–60, is particularly severe: four storeys, with curved corner, small windows, and two gabled hoists. Then a lower, earlier one, probably *c.* 1840, with C18 house at the rear (Quay Street, converted to Brown's Restaurant by *Associated Architects*, 1982). The third, BOND HOUSE, again four-storeyed, with corner hoist, is by *Henry Rowe*, 1870–1. Nearby a paved, computer-controlled FOUNTAIN of 2001, part of the Quayhead Project by *Chris Dobbs*, Worcester City Council Landscape Architect.

We can return to the cathedral via the traffic-laden confusion of DEANSWAY, with St Andrew and St Alban (p. 709), the latter cowering beneath the Worcester College of Technology (p. 726). This faces, in an uneasy stand-off, the Neo-Georgian Police and Fire Stations (p. 722). At the SE end, opposite the former Bishop's Palace (p. 704), one Georgian survivor, No. 5 Deansway, late C18, five bays and three storeys, with elaborate doorway; C19 shutters and cast-iron balconies, C19–C20 wings.

2c. East of High Street, along Friar Street and New Street

This expedition will reveal Worcester's best half-timbered houses. We start at the S end of FRIAR STREET, reached from College Street (Perambulation 1a). Its beginning is not promising, the W side almost entirely of 1965–6, dominated by a huge spiral concrete car-park ramp. The E side starts with the discreet entrance to the VUE CINEMA, by *Alistair Grills & Saunders*, 2000, with fashionable varied brickwork and curved roof. Older houses begin with Nos. 45–47 (once Nos. 11–13 Sidbury), painted brick, with reused C15 doorway with traceried spandrels. No. 43 (once No. 9 Sidbury), jettied and timber-framed with stuccoed front, is dated 1642 on a plaque with affronted dragons; rectangular eight-light oriel, with transom, on carved brackets. The following houses are mostly Georgian brick, their timber-framed skeletons, where revealed, much restored.

The W side now becomes more interesting. An excellent group, all with jettied upper floors, begins with Nos. 46–48, once a single early C16 house. At the rear of No. 46, a curious later structure, perhaps a single-bay workshop, originally separated by a few feet from the front block, now linked to it by the chimneystack. Within No. 44, gabled, perhaps early C17, the first-floor room has bold black-and-white acanthus leaf decoration (painted on the walls of the flanking buildings as it has no structural walls of its own). Nos. 38–42 (TUDOR HOUSE), four-bay late C16, have a particularly undulating overhang; close-studded first floor with four shallow oriels (restored 1910). The ground floor was probably originally divided into three, i.e. not respecting the bay divisions; this must be the reason for the two large hearths side by side within the present shop. In one first-floor room, a good early C17 plaster ceiling, ribbed, with small-scale detail. The rear wings, originally longer, housed weaving shops.

Opposite, at the angle with Union Street, the spacious
LASLETT'S ALMSHOUSES by *Lewis Sheppard & Son*, 1911–12;
brick, stone dressings, half-timbered upper floors. Main range
with central Free Perp chapel flanked by Board Room (E),
Chaplain's House (W); detached side ranges, forming an open
rectangular quadrangle, with pleasant garden. The almshouses
replaced the City Gaol of 1823–4 (by *Henry Rowe*, of semicircular plan), on the site of the FRANCISCAN FRIARY. The
Greyfriars came to Worcester early, between 1225 and 1230.
The old orders never liked their coming; Florence of Worcester wrote: 'O dolor, o plus quam dolor, o pestis truculenta.
Fratres minores venerunt in Angliam.' The Worcester house,
one of the most important in the West Midlands, occupying
sites within and outside the walls, was suppressed in 1539, but
not finally demolished until 1822.

By turning N or S along City Walls Road from the E end of Union
Street (the site of Friars' Postern Gate), one can see good surviving evidence of these CITY WALLS, probably not completed
until the C15, though their line seems to have been established
by 1216. To the N, the boundary wall of the almshouses rests
on a few sandstone courses and the sloping plinth of the C13
wall. A little S, a well-exposed section sits below the four curved
roofs of the Vue Cinema complex. For Fownes Hotel opposite,
see p. 748.

Now back to FRIAR STREET, W side, for Nos. 26–32, late
C15–early C16, with large square panels with tension braces,
and first-floor overhang; restored by *F. W. B. Charles*. The S gable
is half of a formerly two-bay structure; the central part with its
roof parallel to the street and the higher N gable formed
another. The latter had a wide through passage. The ground
floor of No. 32 was originally a shop; the ceiling of the room
behind is painted with a pretty strawberry trail, mostly brown
and red. A couple of Georgian houses follow, the finer, No. 22,
of *c.* 1726. Then Nos. 14–18, with jettied and close-studded 56
first floor and again two outer gables, the S tilting alarmingly.
This (No. 18) may be mid-C16. The rest, a separate dwelling,
is probably slightly earlier, though originally without the gable,
as its roof ran parallel. Restored 1956.

THE GREYFRIARS opposite is one of the finest timber-framed
buildings in the county. The name derives from the mistaken
belief that it was the guest-house of the Franciscan Friary. It
is now accepted that it was a private house, built *c.* 1480–90,
probably for the brewer Thomas Grene, substantially altered
early in the C17 for the Street family, who owned it 1565–1660.
Subdivided in the C18–early C19, the ground floor later converted into three shops. Saved from demolition in 1943, the
house was restored by Matley Moore and his sister Elsie, who
lived here from 1949. Donated to the National Trust in 1966,
it remains the best-kept of Worcester's much depleted stock of
framed buildings.

The shallow-curved façade, some 69 ft (21 metres) long, 56
consists of two central bays parallel to the street and gabled

cross-wings either end, all with a continuous jetty. Close-studded throughout, the first-floor jetty supported on coved brackets between finely moulded wall-posts; gables with remains of richly carved bargeboards. The long twelve-light central oriel, with transom and thicker central mullion, belongs to the Streets' C17 alterations (when the two rooms behind were probably thrown into one). Under the gables, similar four-light transomed oriels, mid-C20 but probably reproducing the C17 appearance. The ground-floor street wall is also not original; there were, before restoration, shop windows here. But an early C19 engraving published by John Britton shows that the building now looks very much as it did then. A broad archway into the small courtyard adjoins the N cross-wing; it has thin buttress-shafts, leaf spandrels, and foliage brackets with the initials TG and EG. Its rear is gabled above another wide, flat oriel; the entrance here into the main range looks convincingly late C15. Behind the cross-wings are short rear wings, both structurally distinct. The N rear wing, mostly early C17, may stand on the site of a late C15 great hall; the S wing, of uncertain date with very deep jetty, was extended in C18 brick.

The present HALL, occupying the centre of the ground floor, S of the archway, was originally two rooms, as revealed by the tenon joints for the partition, visible in the cross-beam. This accounts for the eccentric position of the moulded, four-centred C15 fireplace. Imported panelling and floor. In the rear wing, a small DINING ROOM, fitted up by the Moores with Georgian work from elsewhere. A broad early C17 staircase* leads up to the finest room, the central first-floor PARLOUR (not corresponding to the hall below, but partly above the archway). Good C17 panelling with pretty dragon frieze with the Streets' Catherine Wheel shield; imported overmantel dated 1616. The roll-moulded ceiling beams, however, are late C15; so the room was ceiled from the start, not open to the roof. Similar beams in the flanking rooms: LIBRARY, N, OAK BEDROOM, S, the latter the most authentic late C15 room, with contemporary fireplace. Beautiful enclosed garden, re-created from 1955, with small brick summerhouse decidedly of the 1950s.

Adjoining The Greyfriars is No. 7, a restored, square-panelled house, c. 1660, with overhang and two gables above shallow square oriels on brackets. Nos. 4–6 opposite, probably late C16, completes this exceptional display of half-timbering. The w side of Friar Street ends with the EAGLE VAULTS, early C18 brick, seven bays with hipped roof, but the ground floor entirely faced in faience, brown with bulgy green pilasters, by *Wood & Kendrick*, 1899; good pub interior of this date.

NEW STREET, the continuation of Friar Street, begins with PHOENIX HOUSE, for the corn merchant John Barnett, by *Yeates & Jones*, 1895–6: brick, stone dressings, shaped gables.

---

*On the side gallery, painted panels of *c.* 1540 from Ribbesford House; cf. p. 573.

Nos. 4–5, stuccoed early C19, five bays with nice central doorway, are followed by NASH'S HOUSE (Nos. 6–7), the tallest framed building in Worcester. It was being erected for Richard Nash when he died in 1605. Three bays and storeys with gabled attics, it is jettied on brackets at each floor, with close-timbered wall frame and continuous windows above the renewed ground floor. The window pattern consists of a large window in the centre of each bay flanked by high-level two-light openings. The mullions of many of these are original. Alterations for Richard Nash c. 1674 included two brick chimneys at the rear. The first-floor jetty was given additional support in the C19 by fluted cast-iron columns. Restored by *Henry Gorst*, 1966.

Opposite, the MARKET HALL by *Henry Rowe & Son*, 1849. Three broad stuccoed bays, the centre with fluted Greek Doric columns *in antis*; galleried interior with cast-iron railings and stairs. Plainer stuccoed front to THE SHAMBLES, now a mostly C20 shopping street parallel to High Street.

Back to the narrow NEW STREET, now mostly Georgian brick (sometimes masking earlier framing). The mid-C18 No. 9, adjoining Nash's House, has five bays and central pedimented doorway; at the rear, the Oddfellows Hall, mostly c. 1800. No. 10 masks timber-framing of c. 1600, visible from Nash's Passage. No. 11, three wide bays, with segmental-headed first-floor windows, was the former Methodist chapel, opened 1772; ground floor later converted to shops, of which one shallow early C19 bow window and adjoining doorway remain. Then NASH'S and WYATT'S COURT, almshouses rebuilt by *G. Raymond Acton*, 1964–5; severe brick front with leaded oriels, two parallel rear ranges facing a narrow court, marginally less severe. Nos. 16–17, four bays, have a good doorcase with open pediment. No. 18, the former Labour Club, is larger-scale mid-C20 Neo-Georgian.

Nos. 45–47 opposite, the Old Greyhound Inn, mostly rebuilt 1801–2, with tripartite upper windows, is now an entrance to Reindeer Court, modest and polite shopping infill of the late 1980s (*Stanley Bragg Partnership*).

The PHEASANT INN (No. 25), E side, probably late C16, four bays and three storeys, has a rather pretentious front with two overhangs, some herringbone decoration, and Ionic pilasters. The elaborate archway brackets must be later. No. 27, five-bay brick, is late C18, but at No. 28 (The Swan with Two Nicks), behind four wide bays of earlier C18 painted brick, is more late C16 timber framing.

KING CHARLES HOUSE, at No. 29, is the start of an originally timber-framed, L-plan group, turning the corner into CORN-MARKET: a merchant's house of 1577, with jettied and gabled upper storey added probably in the mid C17 when it was divided into two houses (No. 29 and Nos. 4–5 Cornmarket). No. 29 (perhaps originally a parlour) has two bays, its far-projecting gables restored after a fire in 1986; inside, imported panelling and elaborately carved chimneypiece with small figured scenes, dated 1634 (from Sidbury House). No. 30, and No. 4 Cornmarket, were rebuilt and heightened in brick, *c.* 1800: three bays to each street, and a splendid, continuously bowed shopfront, with fluted Composite columns. They probably stand respectively on the site of the late C16 hall and the corner shop with adjoining porch. Then, at No. 5 Cornmarket (the C16 kitchen and parlour?), framing, with herringbone strutting, reappears; the inscription, with date 1577 and initials of William Blagden and Richard Durant, was originally on the porch. Another good Late Georgian shopfront, with graceful Adamish doorway with swags, paterae, and urn.

Nos. 6–10 CORNMARKET, at right angles to No. 5, are all Georgian brick, Nos. 8–9, the most notable, largely reproduction: seven bays and three storeys; straight quoins, panelled keystones, fluted segmental aprons below the second-floor windows. If this last motif is reliable, the house can be attributed to *Thomas White* on the strength of his Britannia House, Upper Tything (p. 727).

On Cornmarket's W side stands St Martin (p. 713); the NE corner has been sliced off by CITY WALLS ROAD. A compensation is that the latter has revealed, behind Nos. 6–10 (S of the site of St Martin's Gate, demolished 1787), another longish stretch of the plinth and base of the medieval CITY WALLS, including the lower courses of a semicircular bastion. (For the buildings opposite, *see* Perambulation 2d).

MEALCHEAPEN STREET, leading W from the SW corner of Cornmarket, is an attractive C18 street, its W end focused on the splendid E façade of St Swithin (p. 716). Its begins, NE, with the ROYAL EXCHANGE, its ground floor with another display of pub tiling by *Wood & Kendrick*, 1900. Opposite, S side, Nos. 1–3 Cornmarket, early C18 painted brick, followed by almost continuous Georgian houses. No. 12 has an open-well staircase of *c.* 1768, with twisted balusters (visible at the rear of the shop); the five-bay No. 9, the former Reindeer Inn, provides another entrance to the eponymous small shopping development, incorporating its stable yard. Most of the rest of the S side was rebuilt after fire in 1765. The N side is more varied. Nos. 15–16 (the former Shades Inn) were rebuilt in 1748; No. 16, five bays, has quoins and central windows emphasized with ears and segmental pediment. Nos. 20 and 21, near the W end, conceal earlier timber framing, the latter, now stuccoed, unusually well documented. It was built for the card-maker William Bradley, 1635–9: *Henry Richards*, carpenter, constructed the four-storey, square-panelled frame; *George Drew*, mason, the cellar and chimney.

Now N up TRINITY STREET, cut through *c.* 1890, its corners marked by a spikily gabled 1988 revamp by *Glazzard Architects* for Cheltenham and Gloucester Building Society, and (NW to St Swithin Street) by another building with shaped gables by *Yeates & Jones*, 1891. Then a dour warehouse dated 1895 and St Swithin's House, the former printing works of E. Baylis & Sons, by *A. Hill Parker*, 1891. Opposite, a final timber-

framed building, restored 1995, a remnant of the extensive
ALMSHOUSES OF THE GUILD OF THE HOLY TRINITY, of
c. 1554, which ran along and across the line of the present
street. The small survivor, QUEEN ELIZABETH HOUSE, its NE
wing, was relocated a little S in 1891. A four-room unit of single
cells, with external upper gallery with timber posts supporting
two jutting gables; the glazed area below, r., marks the line of
the W–E route, now Trinity Passage and The Trinity. The
former is still spanned by BRIDGE HOUSE, its fake half-
timbered exterior concealing a genuine late C15 structure, the
original main entrance to the complex; it joined Trinity Hall,
S, to the Chapel, N. The half-timbered ST SWITHIN'S INSTI-
TUTE, in The Trinity, is by *H. Rowe & Son*, 1930–1.

Then (w side), behind a railed forecourt, the delightful rear (originally garden) façade of OLD TRINITY HOUSE, Worcester's
premier Gothick building, probably *c.* 1750. Two storeys and
three bays, brick with stuccoed quoins and window frames.
Projecting centre; its doorway and all windows Venetian, but
the higher middle light of each ogee-headed with finial. Ogee
tops also to the dormers. The basement has broad pointed
windows and gabled buttresses (and lattice-ribbed barrel
vault). The former TRINITY HALL on the N side of the forecourt is of 1907, the same date as the odd alterations to the
front, facing The Avenue (*see* p. 740).

Next door, continuing into ST NICHOLAS STREET, the brick
and stone premises of the WORCESTER CO-OPERATIVE
SOCIETY, with shaped gables and other lively detail; by *Yeates
& Jones*, 1888, extended in the 1890s; carving by Messrs
Haughton. Otherwise worth a glance in St Nicholas Street, N
side, are No. 35, the Old Yorkshire House inn, near the E end,
rebuilt 1899 by *Yeates & Jones*, with half-timbered gables and
broad central bow; and, further w, the former PACK HORSE
(No. 11, now The Courtyard), with fully half-timbered front by
Scott & Clark of Wednesbury, 1936. This contrasts with the
adjoining ROYAL BANK OF SCOTLAND (Nos. 5–9), built as a
Co-op Ladies' Fashion Store, 1958–62, by the CWS chief
architect, *G.S. Hay*; zigzag green curtain walling on the two
upper floors. Converted to a bank 1982. At the w end, S side,
on the corner with The Cross, the former St Nicholas (p. 714).

2d. East of City Walls Road

A postscript on the Blockhouse district immediately E of the city
walls, cut off from the city centre *c.* 1972 by City Walls Road;
for Lowesmoor further N, *see* p. 764. The area, formerly known
as Blockhouse Fields, filled with factories and small cottages
from *c.* 1820 (after completion of the Worcester & Birmingham
Canal, 1815). Now mostly a confused hotchpotch of C20 flats
and assorted industrial premises.

The most prominent building is St Paul (p. 715), at the corner
of Spring Gardens and St Paul's Street. To its NE, a large City
Council estate of the early 1970s, well grouped, with three- and

four-storey brick flats with angled roofs and weather-boarded staircase links, set round small courtyards. In Spring Gardens, W, the HEALTH CENTRE, by the City Architect *J.R. McKee*, 1969–70; pale brick with split-angled roofs. The higher STUD-DERT KENNEDY HOUSE, nearer City Walls Road, Postmod-ern, was added as a mental heath centre by the *County Council Property Services Design Unit* in 2003. N of this, squeezed between the road and a Postmodern multi-storey car park (by *Ardin & Brookes*, 1988), the citadel-like CITY YOUTH CENTRE, also by *McKee*, 1969–71, square-block construction, with the same split roofs. Further S, a huge BT SWITCHING CENTRE by the *Renton Howard Wood Partnership*, *c.* 1970; rec-tangular, three storeys, with chamfered brick piers between recessed bronze-tinted panelling.

St Paul's Street, further S, becomes FOUNDRY STREET, named after Hardy & Padmore's foundry, E side, established 1814; one sad later C19 fragment remains. More rewarding, at the CHARLES STREET corner, a remnant of WILLIAMSON & SONS' sheet-metal works, a two-storey front of 1893, brick with terracotta dressings, probably by *J.H. Williams*; five-bay centre, one-bay pediment. Then BLOCKHOUSE LOCK on the canal, its bridge crudely rebuilt in 1936, the plain brick lock-keeper's cottage surprisingly intact. PARK STREET, beyond the canal, really part of the Fort Royal area N of London Road (*see* p. 769), has a complete mid-C19 terrace, E side, with the former ZION CHAPEL (United Methodist), rebuilt 1845, at its centre. Three-bay front, painted brick, with parapet and quoins; pilastered doorway, flanked by windows with eared architraves linked over the two storeys.

Finally, in City Walls Road, S of Carden Street, one further C19 industrial remnant, the former Fownes Glove Factory (now FOWNES HOTEL), by *Yeates & Jones*, 1882–4, later enlarged. Red brick, blue trim, twenty-five bays and three storeys; segment-headed windows, pilasters, three-bay pediment, timber ventilation turrets.

3. The city centre, further north

Perambulations 3a–3c continue the leisurely progress N, resum-ing with the central spine, here The Foregate and Foregate Street, followed by diversions to E and W. Perambulation 3d covers the final part of the central spine.

3a. The Foregate and Foregate Street

THE FOREGATE, the last section of the S–N spine within the medieval city wall, continues The Cross (p. 739–40) with little change. Its E side is imposing commercial work, red brick with ample Doulton terracotta dressings, begun 1899. The N part, by *Alfred B. Rowe* (of *Henry Rowe & Son*), came first, built as the HOP MARKET and COMMERCIAL HOTEL, with former bank, S (No. 13); won in competition 1898, archway dated

1900. Shallow-bowed oriels, Venetian windows, Baroque corner cupola, also several Tudor touches, and a dash of the Loire in the gabled attic storey. Similar return front to Sansome Street, N, followed by the much plainer hop warehouses. The brick and half-timbered courtyard, nicely converted to shops, is also surprisingly plain. *Rowe*'s S continuation (No. 12), 1906–7, is more Baroque, with paired first-floor Ionic columns with linked blocking. Finally, in 1908–9, the City Architect *Alfred G. Parker* provided the yet more ornately Baroque section (No. 11) to the St Nicholas Street corner, with attractive turret with open dome.

On the W side, No. 19, stuccoed early to mid-C18 brick, five bays and three storeys, with giant fluted angle pilasters, was altered for W.H. Smith & Son, with applied armorial shields, by *Guy Pemberton*, 1927–8. Then, by the site of the Foregate (demolished 1702), on the corner of Shaw Street, BERKELEY'S HOSPITAL, a splendid early C18 almshouse group, slightly Dutch in appearance, endowed by Robert Berkeley (of Spetchley), 1692; chapel dated 1703, the complex completed *c*. 1710. To The Foregate, two five-bay two-storey blocks (for chaplain and warden), with hipped roofs with pedimented dormers; slightly mottled brick with stone dressings, moulded window surrounds. Small doorways, with broken curly pediments with foliage and the Berkeley arms, face the opening between the two blocks; fine rusticated gatepiers with animal finials, iron gates with overthrow. These lead into the courtyard, lined with the single-storey almshouses, originally six either side; each has a doorway with broken curly pediment and again the Berkeley arms, flanked by two windows. The upright CHAPEL stands in the middle of the far end. Five bays, round-arched windows, wide central doorway with broken segmental pediment on carved brackets. Above a round-arched niche with the statue of the founder, and composite curvy pediment. Quoins, and splayed hipped roof with ogee-domed lantern. The doorway enters the middle of one of the long sides, but the interior has been stripped out. Three rectangular windows to the rear.

FOREGATE STREET, now the richest in Georgian buildings, was already called 'a long fayre suburbe' by Leland in 1556; most of this was destroyed during the Civil War. During the later C18 it served as a fashionable promenade known as The Mall. Later the S part was unfortunately cut by the arch of the railway, a sign of what the free enterprise of railway building in the mid C19 was allowed to do to towns.

The W side starts with VICTORIA HOUSE (Nos. 63–66), once the Hop Pole Inn; plain late C18, ten bays and three-and-a-half storeys, quoins and prominent keystones the only emphases. Four-bay S return to Shaw Street. Set back there, the hotel's former ASSEMBLY ROOM, mid-C18, until 1840 with access only at first-floor level. Brick-arcaded ground floor, originally coachhouse and stables; upper floor mostly timber-framed, jettied and roughcast, with two Venetian windows. The assembly room is panelled, with fluted Doric pilasters. Paired Ionic pilasters carry pediments at either end; the w led to a gallery which could be hidden within the panelling. Chimneypieces originally faced both the Venetian windows. Restored 1994–5 by *Nick Joyce*.

Also in SHAW STREET two pairs of three-storeyed early C19 brick houses, each with combined doorway of three Greek Doric columns under one pediment (as the Greeks would not have done it). Nos. 3–4 are next to the Assembly Room. Nos. 6–7, further w at the corner of Farrier Street, have only three bays, so the doorways are off-centre; to Farrier Street, a separate single doorway.

FOREGATE STREET, e side, begins with a tall building with heavily detailed arched windows, by *Henry Rowe*, 1874–5, for the watchmaker and jeweller Franz Friedrich, hence the clock and barometer. Adjoining, at the start of Sansome Street, contemporary single-storey premises for the hop merchant S. Myer, by *Haddon Bros*; the pediment above the poorly remodelled frontage remains, carved with hop pickers by *William Forsyth*. Varied Georgian fronts follow (No. 4 with good stone shopfront dated 1903), until spoiled by the Post Office of 1953, characterless sub-Neo-Georgian, set back at No. 9.

Nos. 61–62, w side (WHITEHOUSE HOTEL, formerly the Star Hotel), are probably of *c.* 1820; nine bays, three-and-a-half storeys, but slightly higher than Victoria House. Extended one matching bay s, 1886; the first-floor balcony of florid cast-iron must also be late C19. Then the five-bay Nos. 59–60, plain late C18, and No. 58, convincing early Neo-Georgian by *J.H. Williams*, 1902.

Here the RAILWAY BRIDGE of *c.* 1860 intervenes. A valiant attempt to mitigate its impact was undertaken in 1908–9 when a panelled cast-iron screen was applied in the form of a segmental arch with pierced balustrade. At high level is FOREGATE STREET STATION, mostly brick, opened 1860.

Beyond the railway, w side, the large ODEON CINEMA by *H. W. Weedon*, 1938–9 (interior not completed until 1949, by *Robert Bullivant*); pale brick, recessed centre with columns and canopy, all rather insipid.[*] Opposite, flanking Pierpoint Street, are No. 15, late C18 (with large fluted Doric column at the corner), and the Neo-Georgian former TELEPHONE EXCHANGE, 1957–8, by *John Heald* for the *Office of Works* (now a pub), with curved corner. Facing its flank, at No. 14 Pierpoint Street, WORCESTER CHAMBERS, good, no-nonsense Italianate offices by *Henry Day*, 1866: brick, stone dressings, 3+3+3 bays, modillion cornice. (For the rest of Pierpoint Street, *see* p. 752.)

The e side of Foregate Street continues with modest C18 frontages, interrupted by the former GAUMONT CINEMA (now bingo), by *W.E. Trent & Ernest F.Tulley*, 1934–5: plain with a little brick decoration; stadium-plan interior originally with

---

[*] On the site of the Worcestershire Natural History Society Museum by *Fiddian & Newey*, 1835.

pseudo-Egyptian detailing. The Georgian houses have some nice doorways, the best (Doric) at No. 23, built 1792 for Rufus James, with much original plasterwork and joinery.

But it is the w side that has the best Georgian run, without significant interruption. The stuccoed No. 49, adjoining the Odeon, has giant Soanean incised pilasters and a nice first-floor wrought-iron balcony with heart and honeysuckle motifs. Nos. 45–46 are a mid-C18 pair with decorated keystones, those of No. 45 the more lively. No. 43, built c. 1761 by Dr John Wall (of the Royal Worcester Porcelain Works), probably to his own designs, is more ambitious; five bays, the windows with eared architraves, the surround of the middle one curving out to a blind balustrade at the foot. Three-bay pediment on fat consoles. No. 42 also has five bays, but crams in three-and-half storeys; stuccoed lower floors. Big doorcase with Doric columns and open pediment; within it an Apollo mask and sunburst, in William Kent taste, but nice Adamish detail otherwise. Good open-well rear staircase. Nos. 40 and 39 are both plain but stately late C18: the former with tall doorway, r., with sturdy Doric demi-columns, the latter with pretty wrought-iron balcony (similar to No. 49). No. 37, again early C18, is more ambitious though of only three bays; decorated keystones, wide pediment with central oculus, Doric doorcase, l. Panelled rooms within, and fine dog-leg rear staircase. No. 36 is a good Deco interloper of 1935, by *Briggs & Thornely* of Liverpool for the Royal Insurance Co. Then plainer frontages, but at No. 33, with late C18 tripartite ground-floor windows, a central doorcase with fluted Corinthian pilasters, apparently early C18, the best of all so far.

This has taken us to the corner of Castle Street, ignoring the remainder of the E side, where the dominant accents are the Victoria Institute (p. 722) and Shire Hall (p. 720). The end here is late C18: No. 28, three bays with good pedimented Doric doorcase and fanlight, and Nos. 29–30, nine bays arranged 2+3+2+2. The three bays project beneath a pediment, with Gibbs surround to the doorway, with Gothick fanlight; the two-bay inner s part (No. 29) has an equally fine doorway on large consoles, with intersecting fanlight. Restored after fire in 1996.

3b. East of Foregate Street, north–south along Sansome Walk

The N part of SANSOME WALK, dominated by the fine spire of St Mary Magdalene (p. 714), can be reached via St Mary's Street. Sansome Fields was a popular promenade from the late C18, and Sansome Walk its principal route (from c. 1815). Pleasantly tree-lined, with mostly late C19 houses or terraces, e.g. Nos. 29–37 (St Oswald's Terrace), w side, c. 1880.* This side, further s, is filled by the Judges' Lodgings and other out-

* Further N, the SWIMMING POOL, 1969–70 by *J.R. McKee*, and, in CHESTNUT WALK, earlier C19 houses; also, in the grounds of St Oswald's Hospital, p. 756, a late C18 obelisk marker.

posts of Shire Hall (p. 720), and the former School of Art and Science (p. 723).

On the E side, the best house is No. 24, THE LODGE, banded red and yellow brick with shaped gables, the sole survivor of the short-lived ARBORETUM GARDENS, opened 1859 to a design by *William Barrow*, closed as early as 1866. Lower-middle-class housing then gradually filled the estate. ARBORETUM ROAD has the best selection, with some semi-detached pairs (e.g. the sharply gabled Nos. 35–37, N side), but mostly floridly embellished, bay-windowed terraces; later C19 terraces (Nos. 2–8, Nos. 38–44) are more sober.*

Back in SANSOME WALK, assorted modest late C19 houses followed by the Baptist Church (p. 718); behind it, a large late C19 hop warehouse, half of it incorporating the walls and roof of a mid-C19 rackets court. Opposite, No. 15, early C18, five bays, altered *c.* 1886 when *Lewis Sheppard* added a single-storey tailor's shop, with shaped gable, further S.

The brick No. 8, E side, by *H. Rowe & Son*, 1904, tries hard, with its truncated shaped gable, patterned chimneys, and garden wall with terracotta decoration. Then, Nos. 4–6, formerly Sansome Lodge, a small mid-C18 country house built on the edge of the city for C.T. Withers. Two storeys, 2+3+2 bays, the centre projecting beneath a pediment (with lunette); segment-headed windows, hipped roof. Doorways with segmental pediments on brackets, that to the N part unaltered; behind this, the closed-string staircase. The S return, also of 2+3+2 bays, originally the garden front, now stares blankly at the railway embankment.

On the S side of PIERPOINT STREET, leading back W to Foregate Street, the early C19 No. 11, brick, with striking round-arched doorway, and No. 13, the former School of Art, built as a Mechanics' Institute by *Harvey Eginton*, *c.* 1839. Stuccoed, five bays and two storeys, with large pilasters; doorway also with pilasters, with discs, and shallow pediment with wreathed frieze on elongated brackets. On the N side, No. 8 (almost identical to No. 11 opposite), followed by a simple brick terrace.

Beyond the brick railway bridge, Sansome Walk, after a neat former P.O. SORTING OFFICE (by *H.E. Seccombe* of the *Office of Works*, 1935) becomes SANSOME PLACE. On its W side, behind a brick wall, the Friends' Meeting House (p. 719). On its E, a late C18 three-storey terrace development, to an L-plan. Nos. 8–14 run W–E, the taller Nos. 6–7 forming their W return with wrought-iron balcony; then, set back, the finer Nos. 3–5, with channelled stuccoed ground floors and doorways with fluted Doric columns. All are apparently shown on Young's map of 1779. Nos. 1–2 Sansome Place belong with St George (R.C., p. 717).

* The florid type continues into the neighbouring streets. Towards the canal, E, the terraces become much plainer, interspersed occasionally with large hop warehouses, the best that of J.W. Buckland & Co., Southfield Street, by *J.H. Williams*, 1892. In East Street, a former RAILWAY MISSION HALL by *Yeates & Jones*, 1896.

We can return to The Foregate along SANSOME STREET. On its
s side, before the warehouses adjoining the Hop Market and
Commercial Hotel (p. 749), No. 8, plain commercial of 1876,
with big bracketed cornice, for Caldicott & Sons, hop merchants, surprisingly by *W.J. Hopkins*; and No. 6, the former
Golden Hart inn, by *A. Hill Parker*, 1898, small, quite jolly, with
pretty carving.

3c. West of The Foregate and Foregate Street

The best place to start is ANGEL STREET, leading w from the s
end of The Foregate, i.e. just within the former city wall. On
the N side, two pubs: THE CRICKETERS (formerly Shakespeare Hotel), early C19 stuccoed, and HORN AND TRUMPET,
with ground-floor frontage by *Yeates & Jones*, 1916, but much
of its fabric of 1646–7 (for Robert Sterrop), the earliest datable
brick house in the city; original panelling, first floor.*

Next door, the former FRUIT AND VEGETABLE MARKET of
brick, 1920. Opposite, the former CORN EXCHANGE, a mighty
job of 1848 by *Henry Rowe & Son*. Only five bays, brick with
giant stuccoed pilasters, entablature with balustrade, but a
colossal centre with pairs of Tuscan columns *in antis* and attic
with wheat sheaves; round-arched windows either side. A small
warehouse at the rear, SE, incorporates the remains of a
C15–C16 stone hall, adapted and partly rebuilt in the C17–C18.
Two blocked four-centred openings in the w wall; the C17–C18
inserted a brick-vaulting cellar and added floors and attic
above.

The former SCALA THEATRE, curving round the corner
to Angel Place, was built as a cinema by *Essex & Goodman*,
1921–2; pale terracotta, embellished Ionic pilasters, festooned
windows, latticed parapet. PUBLIC CONVENIENCES adjoining, of the same date.

ANGEL ROW ahead is now filled by the BUS STATION, part of
extensive redevelopment of *c.* 1990 by *Gibberd, Coombes &
Partners* (*see* pp. 739 and 741), here mostly a remodelling of the
Blackfriars Shopping Centre (by *A. Maurice Tribich & Associates*, 1967–8). This occupies the site, just within the city walls,
of the DOMINICAN FRIARY, founded 1347, one of the latest
in England. The bus station plunges beneath the multi-storey
CAR PARK, which forms an effective backdrop, with brick walls
and stair-towers capped with timber gables or pyramidal roofs.
On the N, a fragment, with tall, tapering, brick chimney, of
Lewis Clarke & Co.'s BREWERY by *Scamell & Colyer*, 1890.

Now N along Angel Place, dominated by the former Congregational Church (p. 718), to THE BUTTS. Here, in the angle with
Infirmary Walk, is the PAUL PRY INN, an exceptionally well-
preserved example of 1901, by *Frederic Hughes* (for R. Allen &
Sons). Brick, stone trim, with two-storey angle bay, shallow

---

*Between, until 1961, stood the THEATRE ROYAL, rebuilt by *C.J. Phipps*, 1878,
reconstructed by *A.B. Rowe*, 1902–3.

oriels and carved friezes. Lavishly tiled two-way lobby, marble floors, Lincrusta ceilings, and etched glass and original woodwork in the bar and smoke room.

The s side of The Butts runs along the N face of the MEDIEVAL WALL; glimpses of its C13 lower courses, with later brick above, can be glimpsed between the C20 buildings. Further W, NORTHWALL HOUSE (No. 11), vigorously patterned brick of *c.* 1865, stands on the wall: tall one-bay centre with canted bay and gabled balcony, single-storey wings; tiled cornice friezes. The core of the centre is actually a three-bay late C18 house astride the wall (visible from the bus station). To the N, the site of the cattle market, awaiting redevelopment at the time of writing.

So back to the Paul Pry and NW along INFIRMARY WALK to ALDERMAN LEA'S ALMSHOUSES, by *Henry Rowe*, 1864. Their s side, brick with stone dressings, has something of the severity of Street or William White. The N, with blue brick trim, latticed windows and gabled dormers, is decidedly pretty; long L-plan, with larger house at right angles. Adjoining, the former ST NICHOLAS SCHOOLS, two-storeyed, by *Rowe & Son*, 1894.[*]

Beyond the railway, contrasting housing on the E side: WALSGROVE COURT, pale brick two-storey almshouses by *Maurice W. Jones*, 1965–70, with angled bays and tile-hanging; then simple roughcast cottage terraces of the early C20. Opposite, the former Worcester Royal Infirmary (pp. 723–4).

Infirmary Walk emerges at CASTLE STREET between the Infirmary and former County Police Station. On the N side, the current Police Station and Magistrates' Court (p. 722). In its W part, a former *Office of Works'* EMPLOYMENT EXCHANGE, 1939, and the surprisingly ambitious AUSTIN HOUSE, built as a garage by *John C.S. Soutar*, 1938–9. Brick, with central clock tower with tapering sides and pretty, rather Swedish open lantern with copper roof, flanked by large staggered wings with obelisk finials: showroom, E, car repair shop, W. It stands partly on the site of the County Gaol, by *Francis Sandys*, 1809–13 (later enlarged); this was castellated, giving the street its somewhat confusing name.

Behind, off Love's Grove, is CHARTER PLACE, an unusual, rather claustrophobic, oval layout of white-rendered, three-storey Postmodern houses by *N.O. Arbuthnott* (*ALP Architects* of Cirencester), 1991–2, with nice central garden. Similar, more confined housing of 1993–9 by the practice, mostly brick, extends back to Moor Street and W to Easy Row.[†]

At its E end CASTLE STREET rejoins the N end of Foregate Street.

---

[*] Replacing excellent schools by *E.W. Elmslie*, 1856.
[†] Further W, along the E side of SEVERN TERRACE, a continuous irregular brick terrace, *c.* 1830–40, two-and-a-half storeys, with round-arched doorways. A similar, smaller block in THE MOORS, further N, opposite the Swan Theatre, p. 723.

3d. The Tything and Britannia Square

After Castle Street, the N–S spine of Worcester becomes THE
TYTHING. The change is one of name only. Late Georgian
houses continue from Foregate Street, slightly more modest
and rather more varied in height. The best, Nos. 57–58, almost
immediately on the W side, has three-and-a-half storeys, with
keystones, quoins, moulded cornice, and nice iron balcony;
C19 shopfronts. Either side, dour premises by *Thomas Sutton*,
1891–6. Assorted houses follow, the lower Nos. 53–54 probably
disguising an earlier origin, the taller ones mostly early C19
(e.g. No. 51, the DRAGON INN).

The E side is in the same mode. No. 1, late C18, painted brick,
with pedimented doorcase, is slightly set back. Nos. 5–6, five-
bay earlier C18, were the premises of the sculptor *William
Forsyth*, who added the particularly ornate Victorian Gothic
shopfront. Then CLYDESDALE HOUSE, the former showrooms of Messrs Kay & Co., by *W. Braxton Sinclair*, 1938, Georgian imitation taken remarkably seriously. Eleven bays, the
centre recessed with tall stone doorway and pedimented
windows; reduced to a single storey 1949, after fire in 1941, so
that now all the first-floor openings are blind. Ornate flanking
lamp-posts.

Here the street curves slightly, for the first time since the Cathedral, with the best houses on the E side. Nos. 14–15, five bays
altogether, have paired central doorcases, nicely detailed;
No. 16, five bays, has a good wide Doric doorcase; Nos. 18–19
are an attractive interloper of 1910 by *Henry Rowe & Son*, with
a pair of two-storey oriels; Nos. 20–21, *c.* 1800, irregularly fenestrated; and No. 22, contemporary but taller, with grander
Doric doorcase with very nice fanlight.

Then the main premises of KAY & CO.'s Mail Order Stores (now
apartments) by *J. W. Simpson & Maxwell Ayrton*, 1907, perhaps
the best Edwardian building in Worcester; offices with warehouse behind, all brick with stone dressings. Compact façade,
as successful as the very long utilitarian side, both made true
architecture by subtle fenestration and gabling. The best detail
is the lettering over the entrance; above this a round-arched
window flanked by oriels, beneath the wide central gable. The
long side to St Oswald's Road continues the pretty wrought-
iron railings and is articulated by five gables, the last two an
addition of 1914 by the same architects.

A few Georgian details from the W side: Nos. 36–37 have a nice
frieze; Nos. 33–35, 1776–9 (much altered in the C19), retain
one fine Ionic doorcase with open pediment; No. 29,
c. 1820, a pedimented doorcase and wrought-iron balcony. At
the end the very tall Nos. 26–27, an early C19 pair with good
outer doorcases with open pediments, and the lower Nos.
24–25, with similar, central doorway.

These last face ST OSWALD'S HOSPITAL, spacious almshouses
of medieval origin, rebuilt 1873–4 by *Henry Rowe*. Brick, stone
dressings, rectangular plan, the upper storey with grouped
lancets and regularly disposed gables; multi-shafted brick

chimneystacks. Symmetrical front with central archway, the gable above with triple crocketed and pinnacled Dec openings, the middle one with large statue of St Oswald (by *W. Forsyth*); bellcote on the E gable. Equally regular lawned courtyard, mostly with stepped lancets on the upper storey, apart from the taller chaplain's house, NE, of 1875, with bay windows (and fine serpentine central staircase within). The open E side is all but filled by *Rowe*'s CHAPEL, 1877–8, the size of a small church, with polygonal apse. Geometrical Dec-style. The SW porch leads into a kind of narthex separated by a moulded arch with foliated corbel shafts. Similar but richer chancel arch; high, arch-braced nave roof. – STAINED GLASS. Mostly by *Hardman*: apse 1889–99, chancel S 1926; nave 1905–6 with one N of 1936. – Nave NW by *James Powell & Sons*, 1913; W window *c.* 1955. – Early C19 MONUMENTS from the previous church. – At the NE corner of the grounds, a late C18 OBELISK on a square base; it marked the N end of the Sansome Walk promenade (p. 751).

The splendid Britannia House (*see* p. 727), immediately N of St Oswalds, marks the start of UPPER TYTHING and hence Outer Worcester, here including the Royal Grammar School (p. 728) and its associated Almshouses (p. 760).

Opposite Britannia House one ought to turn W to see BRITAN-NIA SQUARE, the best Regency development in the city. It covers a large area with spacious central green in which the main house is placed. This and all the others are stuccoed, more or less in the same style, mostly two-storeyed with giant pilasters, though varying considerably in form: detached, semi-detached, or in short terraces. The first house apparently went up *c.* 1815. S and E sides were mostly complete by 1822, the W by 1826, the N side in the 1830s. The central house, SPRING-FIELD (now Alice Ottley Junior School), *c.* 1830, is the largest, three storeys and five bays. The entrance front, E, is divided into 2+1+2 bays by upper pilasters; simple round-arched doorway below, flanked by pairs of windows under blank segmental arches. Good wrought-iron entrance gates, S, with Grecian detailing.

Examination of the other houses can begin with the two sides completed first. On the E SIDE they are all detached. No. 53 has curved end gables, and windows with shell tympana derived from the later work of Nash. No. 52, five bays, has a little Grecian detailing. Nos. 51 and 50 again have shell tympana, the latter also a pretty veranda. The five-bay No. 49 has a Doric porch and another nice veranda.

Back then to the S SIDE, where the centre, Nos. 8–9 (ALBION HOUSE) is a palatial pair of three storeys and 1+2+1 bays, with giant Corinthian pilasters and central broken-back pediment with urn and ball finials. Fine tripartite doorcases under reeded segmental arches, set back in lower bays either side. To its E, detached or semi-detached villas, the latter rising to two-and-a-half storeys. To its W, a terrace of 2+4+2 bays (Nos. 10–13), with broad central pediment (with inset windows); canted single-storey bays added by *Hipkiss & Stephens*, 1908. Plain semi-detached examples adjoin, and fill most of the W SIDE, apart from a more varied group at its centre: Nos. 28–29, taller, No. 30 a nice villa with Doric porch, Nos. 31–33 a five-bay three-storey terrace. Doorcases vary: Soanean incised, Doric, Ionic.

The N SIDE, the most sylvan, has again larger detached houses, the earliest probably No. 37, five bays, with (later) Doric side porch. No. 39 has an attractive iron veranda; No. 40 rises to three storeys. The only semi-detached pair, Nos. 42–43, disguise that fact by sharing a central pediment. No. 45, at the end, has a two-storey bow window adjoining the doorway on its E return.

Further N, beyond the square, the E SIDE, with a two-and-a-half-storey pair like a short terrace (Nos. 47–48), is terminated, screen-like, by the thin-looking brick front of No. 46. On the W side here, the start of ALBANY TERRACE is No. 4, ALBANY HOUSE, a four-by-three-bay villa singled out for especially ornate treatment, though this betrays at once the provincial quality of the whole. Of channelled stucco, with broad Greek-key frieze and giant angle pilasters with incised decoration; the detail debased Greco-Egyptian, especially the capitals (cf. No. 49 Foregate Street). The matching porch has fluted columns, as have the outer tripartite windows of the longer garden elevation, S. This faces a rusticated two-storey terrace (Nos. 1–11, S side), also with tripartite windows. The remainder of the N side is filled by four-bay semi-detached villas, some linked by pretty set-back entrances. These are interrupted by YORK PLACE, brick terraces of 1831–5 clearly intended for humbler occupants.

From the W end of Albany Terrace, the Regency villas continue briefly at right angles, facing the racecourse. To the S, Nos. 35–37, a large semi-detached pair perhaps c. 1835–40, have already become Tudorish, with battlemented two-storey bay windows and big stepped gables with finials. In STEPHEN-SON TERRACE, N, No. 1 (SEVERN LODGE), probably by *John Mills*, 1838, three bays with pilasters and veranda, is immediately followed by assorted mid-to-late C19 brick houses.

OUTER WORCESTER

These outer districts can rarely make up continuous perambulations. The exceptions are to the N, where the Georgian ribbon development of The Tything continues into Barbourne Road (*see* 1a); to the E, the industrial area around Shrub Hill (*see* 2a); and perhaps the first part of London Road, SE (*see* 3a). Worcester W of the Severn (*see* 4) incorporates a medieval suburb and is rather different.

1. North

Most of this area belonged to Claines parish, already with a population of some 17,000 by 1833. The city boundary was extended northwards, in stages, from 1885.

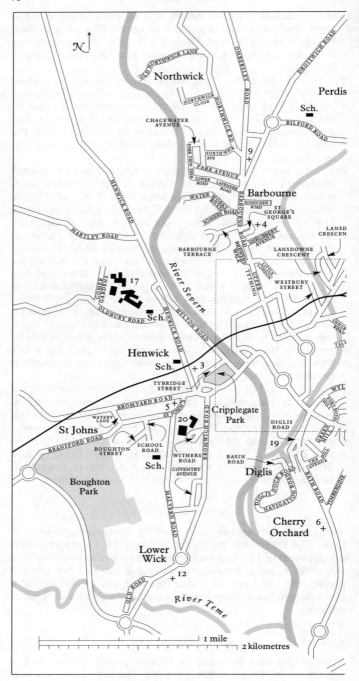

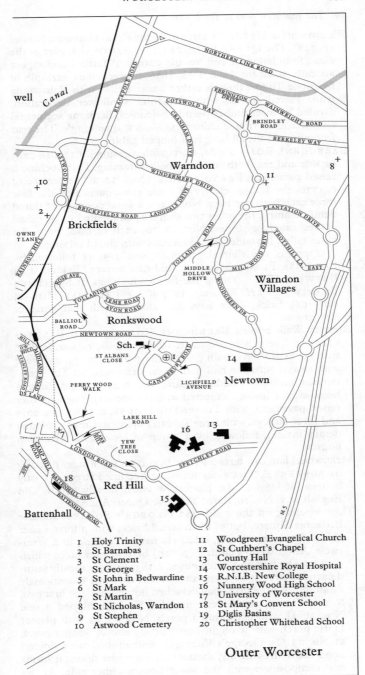

1 Holy Trinity	11 Woodgreen Evangelical Church
2 St Barnabas	12 St Cuthbert's Chapel
3 St Clement	13 County Hall
4 St George	14 Worcestershire Royal Hospital
5 St John in Bedwardine	15 R.N.I.B. New College
6 St Mark	16 Nunnery Wood High School
7 St Martin	17 University of Worcester
8 St Nicholas, Warndon	18 St Mary's Convent School
9 St Stephen	19 Diglis Basins
10 Astwood Cemetery	20 Christopher Whitehead School

Outer Worcester

1a. The southern part of Barbourne

We can start in UPPER TYTHING, by the Royal Grammar School
(p. 728). The QUEEN ELIZABETH ALMSHOUSES, part of the
same foundation, N end, on the corner of Little London, are
an early work by *Aston Webb*, 1876; a precocious example of
free-style Tudor, though rather basic. Brick, with Bath stone
trim. Paired gables with terracotta sunflower decoration,
divided by inset timber pseudo-balconies, flank the segmental
entrance arch; ribbed chimneys. Modest quadrangle. The rear
frontages, oddly, all have half-hipped gables.

BARBOURNE ROAD, E side, starts with a restored C17–C18 pair,
its side and rear with square-panelled framing. Then, behind a
raised pavement, PARADISE ROW (Nos. 12–20), a terrace of
c. 1770, the houses clearly of some consequence as the first
three each have five bays. No. 12 has a good doorway of fluted
demi-columns, the other two simpler pedimented ones; fluted
or decorated keystones. Nos. 18–20, each of three bays, the
latter taller, have identical doorways with fluted pilasters.

Opposite, C19 shaped gables at Nos. 1–5 are followed by
PARADISE PLACE, a modest mid-C19 terrace. Behind it in
BREWERY WALK, facing the former maltings of Spreckley's
Brewery (by *J.H. Williams*, 1887–8), is PARADISE HOUSE,
early C19 brick, three bays and storeys, with rear wing of
similar size.

Brewery Walk rejoins BARBOURNE ROAD by OLD BASKER-
VILLE, a late C18 house in its own grounds, two-and-a-half
storeys, 2+1+2 bays, with good Ionic porch with pretty frieze
with swags; entrance hall with open-well staircase. The semicircular mid-C19 building nearer the road was probably a
horse-engine house connected with the brewery. Then another
raised pavement, with THORNLOE HOUSE, *c.* 1780, five bays
and three storeys, with large Tuscan porch (and many original
details inside), followed by a group of lower Late Georgian
houses.

Meanwhile, late C19 terraces have begun on the E side, flanking
SHRUBBERY AVENUE, an attractive tree-lined street of costly
houses (at least at the plusher W end), mostly 1890s, Old
English (e.g. No. 10, dated 1892) or Queen Anne.

Then, opening off the E side, ST GEORGE'S SQUARE, another
Britannia Square, but of unstuccoed brick, with a form easier
to take in: long, oblong, relatively narrow, ending in a semicircle. Aston Webb's church (p. 710) here is a set piece which
could not be bettered. The houses, *c.* 1830–40, are mostly semi-
detached, three storeys and two bays each, some convincingly
disguised as large three-bay detached houses, e.g. the first two,
N side. These stand very upright, beneath hipped roofs:
Nos. 30–31 with good fluted porch, Nos. 28–29 with plainer
Doric porch with wrought-iron balcony above. Similar porch
at No. 23 (St George's Vicarage), embellished with domed
hood above the balcony, shutters on the upper floors; it forms
one composition with the lower houses either side. At the

curved E end, flanking the church, the N side has been rebuilt.
The S side has first No. 18 (Annesley), stuccoed, nicely
detailed, then alternately brick singletons and semi-detached
pairs, all more modest (and probably later) than on the N side.
The last pair, Nos. 1–2, must be mid-C19; their detail has
turned Italianate.

Back in Barbourne Road, the Deco styling of the former SEC-
ONDARY SCHOOL FOR GIRLS (now an outpost of the College
of Technology), by *William Ransom*, City Engineer, 1928–9,
makes an effective backdrop to the W end of the Square; long
brick front with stone dressings, more profuse in the five-bay
centre.

BARBOURNE TERRACE, off the W side, typifies the development
of this area. Nos. 1–3 are an early C19 six-bay brick terrace, its
first-floor windows with balconettes. Then No. 4, Lindisfarne
House, an Italianate villa by *Henry Day* (for the newspaper
proprietor Thomas Chalk), c. 1855: brick, stone trim, hipped
pantiled roofs, set-back tower. Italianate reappears further on
with Nos. 1–2 SELBORNE ROAD, the rest of which has large
patterned brick pairs, c. 1860–70. BARBOURNE CRESCENT, at
the end of Barbourne Terrace, was clearly intended to receive
large detached houses, but only a couple were built, plus a later
Queen Anne example.

*1b. Barbourne further north, and along the Droitwich
and Ombersley roads*

Of BARBOURNE generally, *The Builder*, 1866 noted that 'within
the last year or two a little town has sprung up'. Development
has continued remorselessly northward ever since. Only highlights can be mentioned here. The former WATERWORKS (now
Pump House Environment Centre), in Waterworks Road close
to the river, is a large pumping station in three parts, the earliest the W, by the water engineer *Thomas Hawksley*, 1857–8.
This, red brick with blue/black bands, is in an odd chunky
Franco-Jacobethan style; two-storeyed, giant pilasters. Matching E range, 1868. In between, a taller plainer centre of 1901–2
by *Thomas Caink*, still copying the eccentric details. Further N,
towards Tower Road, the base of the original circular WATER
TOWER of c. 1770 (demolished 1957).

In SUNNYSIDE ROAD, off Barbourne Road, E, No. 8 (Brook
House) is a sub-Voysey-style house of 1911, by *A. V. Rowe* for
himself (cf. Saints Hill, below): roughcast, three weather-
boarded gables, horizontally emphasized windows. GHELU-
VELT PARK, at the N end of Barbourne Road, opened as a war
memorial in 1922. Monumental brick gateway, and, along the
N boundary, dwellings for disabled servicemen by *A. Hill Parker
& Son*, 1920, meant to be picturesque in their variety. The
bandstand sits in the middle of a small lake. By the park
entrance, the road divides, to Ombersley and Droitwich.
Within the fork, a large rendered octagonal TOLL HOUSE by
John Collingwood, 1814.

The E side of DROITWICH ROAD is lined with early-to-mid-C19 villas, mostly detached, occasionally stuccoed. The w side has later C19 houses, the most notable No. 17, built for John Rouse, 1892, by *A. Hill Parker*. Much of its detail is still Gothic, but the bedroom floor of the broad canted bay is recessed to provide an angled balustraded balcony, with extravagant glazed tiling and carved decoration.

Further N, beyond St Stephen (p. 716), its former VICARAGE (No. 89) by *Lewis Sheppard*, 1892–3; big, brick, mildly Gothic. In BILFORD ROAD, off to the E, PERDISWELL PRIMARY SCHOOL, by the City Architect, *J.R. McKee*, 1969–70, a good, well-sited example of its date: brick, timber eaves bands, spreading single storey, apart from the higher hall.

Yet further N, E side, remnants of PERDISWELL HALL, built for Henry Wakeman by *George Byfield*, 1787–8; demolished 1956. The fine, tall rusticated GATEPIERS, now leading nowhere in particular, have beautiful *Coade*-stone reliefs of Navigation and Agriculture, dated 1788, and oval urn finials. Some distance NE, beyond the Park-and-Ride bus terminus, the former STABLES, stuccoed, 2+3+2 bays, centre pedimented above the wide carriage archway; blank arches round the side windows. Attached two-storey cottage, l. The stables stand in the shadow of large Postmodern office blocks by *Glazzard Architects Ltd*, 2002–5; jagged plans, of brick, with much tinted green glazing and curved, partly overhanging roofs.

PERDISWELL HOUSE (formerly Little Perdiswell, now a pub), on the main road nearby, is of *c.* 1840; Tudor Gothic, roughcast, with oriels and bargeboards.

Now OMBERSLEY ROAD. After the tollhouse are late C19 houses, paired or in short terraces, and the (WESLEYAN) METHODIST CHAPEL by *Yeates & Jones*, 1884: brick, stone bands, w window with bald bar tracery. To the w, facing the park, a good Queen Anne terrace, *c.* 1880–90, Nos. 2–12 LAVENDER ROAD. This, with Park Avenue further N, mostly built up *c.* 1886–98, leads to BARBOURNE PARK, an area of large late C19 houses close to the Severn, showing the influence of Norman Shaw's half-timbered Old English style. THE WILLOWS, Tower Road, is by *A.H. Parker*, 1882. The much finer CHACEWATER HOUSE, Chacewater Avenue, is by *J.H. Williams*, 1885. Others in Park View Terrace may also be his: No. 16, AVENBURY, with round corner turret, is dated 1890.

In OMBERSLEY ROAD further N, w side, a late C18 brick survivor, No. 59 (Barbourne Grange), 1+4 bays with fluted keystones, the doorway with open modillion pediment. Nearby, at the start of NORTHWICK ROAD, Nos. 1–2, a gabled, timber-framed, L-plan house of *c.* 1600; altered in the C18–C19, and again when converted into two dwellings *c.* 1920. Further w in NORTHWICK AVENUE, amongst council housing of the early 1920s, the large BARBOURNE WORKS, built as W.E. Tucker & Co.'s printing factory, 1898–9, by *R.A. Briggs*; reinforced concrete frame, dressed up in Neo-Georgian brick, with smart three-bay stone frontispiece: wide entrance with Doric paired columns, Ionic and Corinthian pilasters in correct order above, then a segmental pediment.

Of the OMBERSLEY ROAD houses further N, the most striking are the semi-detached Nos. 106–108, of 1902–3, at the corner of Penbury Street, with bay windows and much free, curvy detail; by *H. Percy Smith*, whose other work in this area is not unfortunately of this quality. Finally, a great surprise close to the edge of the city, the former NORTHWICK CINEMA of 1938, by *C. Edmund Wilford* of Leicester. Plain brick, retaining most of its mild Deco detail: canopy above the buff-tiled entrance, the cinema's name on a central fin-like projection with curved top, fluted friezes. The real Deco joy is the remarkable auditorium, a rare surviving scheme by *John Alexander*, designed 1936. This has fluted giant columns and much stencilled fibrous plasterwork on balcony, walls and stepped-up ceiling. Most astonishing are the ante-proscenium splays, with large mythological females, with looped-up hair and limited stylized drapery, standing in sloping chariots or galleons.

NORTHWICK, from the early medieval period until superseded by Hartlebury (q.v.), was the principal manor of the Bishops of Worcester. They relinquished it only in 1860, when it was still little more than a hamlet. Of this a few remnants survive: a couple of large stuccoed C19 houses in OLD NORTHWICK LANE (which led to an ancient Severn crossing), and a small green where this meets Northwick Road.

Most of the Worcester housing that swamped the area in the C20 is of no particular merit. NORTHWICK CLOSE, leading W off Northwick Road further S, has the exceptions. SAINTS HILL, at its W end, was built for himself in 1925 by the county architect *A. V. Rowe*, under the influence of Voysey (cf. No. 8 Sunnyside Road, above). White-painted brick, half-timbered porch, three steep weatherboarded gables; similar garden front, with oriels and bay windows. Smaller houses lined the Close from *c.* 1930, most on the N side probably also by *Rowe*; predominately white, with half-timbering or weatherboarding.

A little N of Saints Hill is COBTUN, a remarkable, ecologically designed house of 2000–1 by *John T. Christophers* (of *Associated Architects*), for Nicholas Worsley. A curving, earth-red, cob wall, with brick/stone base and corrugated aluminium capping, encircles the garden, before serving as the N wall of the single-storey house. Recessed entrance and circular lobby leading to a spreading U-plan, open to the W. Mostly timber-framed construction, clad in horizontal oak boarding, with projecting eaves and floor-to-ceiling glazing, apart from the blocky, white-rendered bathroom. ¹³²

2. East and north-east

This segment covers a large area, ranging from the C19 industrial development close to the centre to C20 and later commercial and residential growth further NE and E, the latter all but engulfing the tiny medieval village of Warndon (q.v.).

2a. Lowesmoor and Shrub Hill

Shrub Hill became the main industrial suburb of Worcester after the arrival of *Brunel*'s Oxford, Worcester & Wolverhampton Railway in 1850. The Worcester and Birmingham Canal, opened 1815, with a wharf at Lowesmoor closer to the city centre, had already begun this trend (cf. p. 747). A perambulation can follow this development from the edge of the city centre along Lowesmoor and onto Shrub Hill.

A good place to start is the surviving rump of SILVER STREET, across City Walls Road from Cornmarket (p. 746). Here the stuccoed Nos. 18–20 and timber-framed wing behind are the original premises of the Worcester Royal Infirmary (cf. p. 723), adapted from existing buildings in 1745–6; all altered apart from the central pedimented doorway. Behind, outlying remnants of the former VINEGAR WORKS (*see* below): extensive C19 brick-vaulted wine cellars (beneath County Furnishings); further s, a four-storeyed GRANARY with hipped roof.

LOWESMOOR retains many late C18–early C19 brick buildings, mostly above later shopfronts. The best are Nos. 13–17 at the start, N side, and No. 54 (The Appletree), s side, with thin Doric porch approached up six steps; shaped parapet at the side. This faces a remnant of St Martin's Street, the access to the VINEGAR WORKS of Hill, Evans & Co. (founded 1830). Its huge WAREHOUSE (or Filling Room), c. 1865–70, red brick with yellow voussoirs, pilasters and cornices, has thirteen by eleven bays, with two storeys of segment-headed windows. The ends have broad pediments, with five stepped round-arched openings. Re-roofed 1988. Other surviving buildings include nearby OFFICES dated 1859; brick with stone trim, squared-up Tudor with large oriels on brackets (now in poor condition).

Next to No. 54, ELIM PENTECOSTAL CHURCH, built for Wesleyans 1823, sold in 1836 to the Countess of Huntingdon's Connexion, who added the present façade of 1860 (builder: *Joseph Wood*); stuccoed, channelled pilasters, doorway flanked by large round-arched windows with moulded frames. Opposite, LOWESMOOR WHARF, with early C19 brick cottage at the entrance, and a few remaining later C19 warehouses, engulfed by C20 retail development; the wharf itself, partly infilled in the 1970s, now lies well back. The large wedge-shaped, stuccoed building adjoining the entrance is the sadly altered hulk of the Worcester New Concert Hall, a music hall of 1869, converted to a Salvation Army Citadel, 1889–90, by *J. W. Dunford*; now offices. A brief excursion NE along Lowesmoor Terrace, past the BRIDGE INN (1935, by *J. R. Wilkins* of Oxford), leads to WESTBURY STREET, where a fine brick RAILWAY BRIDGE of 1860 by *Charles Liddell* crosses the canal; big segmental arch over the water; low arch over the adjoining roadway, beneath a large circular hole to lessen the load. The short canal arm to the wharf leads off just to its s. On the SE side of Lowesmoor Terrace, scattered C19 brick remnants of the GAS WORKS.

Back to LOWESMOOR PLACE, with the WEST MIDLAND
TAVERN, vulgar classical, *c.* 1860, then SE along SHRUB HILL
ROAD. Its N side is filled by the enormous former WORCES-   116
TER ENGINE WORKS of 1864, by *Thomas Dickson* (of *Edward
Wilson*'s office); now little more than a shell for industrial units.
The works, closed by the early 1870s, were used for the Worcestershire Exhibition, 1882, then became Heenan & Froude's
engineering works (1903–84). All polychromatic brick: mostly
red, with pilasters, quoins, window frames and cornices of
yellow, bracketed cornices of blue; segmental- or round-arched
windows. The start, at the corner of Tolladine Road, is a square
two-storey block with Italianate clock tower, then a long single-
storey foundry, with large round-arched windows. The higher
main part has 10+5+10 bays, its centre with pediment above
three tall conjoined windows of equal height.*

ISAAC MADDOX HOUSE, filling the S side opposite, was built
as additional office accommodation for Heenan & Froude,
1937–8, by *Dyneley, Luker & Moore* of London: a good, externally unaltered building, in mild industrial Deco style. Stubby
stepped tower above the entrance, two storeys of long strip
windows either side. Matching NW extension, with canteen etc.
Then the GREAT WESTERN HOTEL, presumably contemporary with the station; also Italianate, in the Georgian tradition,
and of blue engineering brick. Five bays, two-and-a-half
storeys, with stuccoed and rusticated ground floor with central
Doric porch; paired moulded windows either side, sharing an
architrave on consoles. S side of plain red brick.

The station itself (p. 725), at the top of Shrub Hill, is dwarfed by
ELGAR HOUSE, a dire office slab by *Ashley & Newman*,
1965–6. At the corner of Tallow Hill stands NEEDLE POINT,
a tripod-like, pierced, stainless steel sculpture, by *Paul Juillerat*,
2002, claimed to be a symbol of Worcester past and present.
It does indeed provide a good view of the city, beyond a sea of
contemporary shopping parks. On the S side of TALLOW HILL
was the UNION WORKHOUSE, later Hillborough Hospital;
originally the House of Industry, by *George Byfield*, 1793–4,
mostly rebuilt by *Henry Rowe & Son*, 1893–4. All that survive
are the boundary wall, and Rowe's LODGE and BOARD ROOM
BLOCK (now a mosque). To their E, ST PAUL'S HOSTEL for
the homeless, brick with hipped roofs, by *Panton Sargent*, 1988,
when the S part of the site was developed for housing (Byfield
Rise). Further S, off Autumn Terrace, the former NURSES'
HOME (now Nightingale House), by *E.G. Jones* (*Yeates &
Jones*), 1928; successful Late Georgian pastiche: eleven bays,
the pedimented centre flanked by two-bay recessions; Doric
stone entrance.

MIDLAND ROAD leads S to the former MIDLAND GOODS
STATION, opened 1868, red brick with yellow trim. Seven

---

*Immediately E was Holy Trinity church, by *Hopkins*, 1863–5 (incorporating the
Guesten Hall roof, *see* p. 608); demolished 1969, its boundary wall remains. The
GWR workshops further NE were demolished in 1968.

gables above stepped blind windows alternating with segmental-headed archways; recessed six-bay office wing, s. Some distance further on, LEA & PERRINS WORCESTERSHIRE SAUCE FACTORY, by *William Henman*, 1896–7; brick, 5+4+5 bays, two storeys above a basement, the centre with intermittently blocked round-arched entrance flanked by paired Doric windows. Broad c17-style gable and clock turret rebuilt more or less in original form in 1966, after a fire. Within, offices and warehouses are set round a top-glazed courtyard. Opposite, facing w to Stanley Road, a good City Council ELEMENTARY SCHOOL by *Alfred Parker*, 1914–15. Single-storey, Neo-Georgian brick; square plan, with classroom ranges on three sides, all with central pediments, entrance block on the fourth, w, with rather Soanean turret.

2b. Further north-east, including Lansdowne Crescent

RAINBOW HILL is the NE continuation of Lowesmoor (p. 764). Just beyond the railway bridge, E side, is LOWESMOOR HOUSE, a neat brick villa, *c*. 1840–50, with Doric porch.

Opposite, LANSDOWNE CRESCENT leads off NW, a long string of stuccoed houses making use of the rising ground to obtain fine views of the city and Malvern Hills beyond (with originally Sansome Fields, *see* p. 751, across the canal, in the foreground). They were begun *c*. 1835, and vary as much as those of the earlier Britannia Square (p. 756). Many retain internal features: panelled shutters, fluted architraves, staircases with stick balusters. Set well back, behind ample sloping front gardens, their backs close to Lansdowne Crescent Lane, the former mews. The first four are semi-detached pairs. Then two singletons (Nos. 5 and 6), taller, with giant fluted pilasters with scrolled-shell motifs as capitals; No. 5 has a pretty tented veranda, with small grotto to its l. Nos. 7–9, disguised as one large villa with central Italianate tower, are as late as 1861–2; tripartite first-floor windows, fancy eared architraves below, doorway of Venetian type beneath the tower. The next five, probably 1840s–50s, are detached, though No. 12 (with Doric side porch) was converted from a semi-detached pair in 1878. No. 10, taller than the others, also has a Doric side porch, like No. 14 (with another attractive tented veranda). The end house, No. 16, by *Hopkins*, 1861, breaks the stuccoed chain. Built as St Nicholas's Rectory, it is Gothic with sharp gables, half-hipped dormers and canted bays, of brick with patterning; the road curves E here, so it can have a recessed N porch behind pierced spandrels, beneath steep pyramid-roofed tower.

Beyond, two more stuccoed houses of *c*. 1830–40, larger than the others, with giant pilasters and ground-floor windows with shell tympana. THE HOMESTEAD (No. 17) has an asymmetrical side elevation with canted bays and conservatory. The stately BISHOP'S HOUSE (No. 18, named after Bishop Gore, who lived here 1902–4 in preference to Hartlebury Castle) was built as the Worcester Female Asylum, 1830–1; converted to a house by 1850 when the architect and engineer *Richard Varden* was living here. 3+1+3 bays, the divisions emphasized by pilasters; Doric central porch, wrought-iron balcony above; square-headed first-floor windows.

Now back to Rainbow Hill. Only a little further N, off the E side, is RAINBOW HILL TERRACE, a similar, smaller development of *c.* 1835–45. The stuccoed S fronts are separated by a pathway from their front gardens; brick rears reached from Reservoir Lane. The nine houses vary rhythmically in height, Nos. 4–5 and 8–9 rising to three storeys. Details to note are the recessed doorway of No. 1, with Tuscan-style antae and columns *in antis* above; other doorways from thin Doric porches to the round moulded type; much wrought ironwork at Nos. 4–5; and the ornamental shell tympana of Nos. 8–9. No. 10, all but detached, has a fluted Doric porch.

The arrival of the railway in 1850, especially its extension to Hereford 1860, caused a change of gear in the development of Rainbow Hill. Everything further N is brick, nearly all built for a lower social class. In ASTWOOD ROAD, the continuation of Rainbow Hill, a Gothic BAPTIST MISSION HALL, 1881; the stuccoed VAUXHALL INN, with domed turret and green-glazed ground-floor tiling, *c.* 1897; and a CO-OP STORE by *A.H. Parker*, 1902, with nicely detailed gables. Further on, off the W side, is St Barnabas (p. 710). Then, trying with limited success to dominate the corner with Blackpole Road, the NEW CHEQUERS INN by *A.H. Parker & Son*, 1927–8; splayed plan, timbered gables.

Further NE, at BLACKPOLE and BRICKFIELDS, large areas of council housing of the early-to-mid 1930s, mostly brick semi-detached pairs, by the City Engineer *William Ransom*. The largest City Council scheme, the WARNDON ESTATE, lies further E. Begun *c.* 1955, *John S. Williams*, City Surveyor, again mostly semi-detached pairs, rather more spaciously planned. The spine roads are WINDERMERE DRIVE (W–E), and LANGDALE DRIVE and CRANHAM DRIVE (S–N); in the last, an attempt at a local centre, with shops (1963–4), small brick church (ST WULSTAN by *T.R. Bateman*), and ranks of three-storey flats.

Yet further N, between the B4639 and the canal, an extensive area of business parks, with the usual assortment of slick late C20 designs. The largest, both by *Peter Hing & Jones*, are in COTSWOLD WAY, either side of Ebrington Drive: MAZAK FACTORY, 1986, with much sleek black glazing and ribbed cladding, and WORCESTER BOSCH, 1990, its grey metallic cladding pierced by large hexagonal openings. Also worth a glance, two of *c.* 1994: WICKENS by *Jeffrey Roberts*, further up EBRINGTON DRIVE, with projecting roof supported on steel ties, all painted yellow; and, at the E end of WAINWRIGHT ROAD close to the M5, SOUTHCO by *John Hewitt* (of *Panton Sargent*), with big blue curved roof.

2c. East from Shrub Hill

Two roads lead E, beneath the railway at Shrub Hill, to further extensive areas of City Council housing, especially around TOLLADINE ROAD, the more northerly route. The most consistent, least altered layout is around ROSE AVENUE, N, by *William Ransom, c.* 1937. Here, at the corner of Rowan Avenue, is the TOLLY CENTRE, a gritty community centre by *Meadowcroft Griffin Architects,* 2005–6, wrapped round the N and E sides of the blocky brick Christ Church (by *H.S. Rogers & M.W. Jones,* 1940). Low with shallow monopitched roofs. Crèche and office have a 'cheese-grater' finish of galvanized steel mesh; youth club and entrance have green-rendered walls. Inviting foyer. A decided oddity are the slightly later council houses in TEME ROAD and AVON ROAD, S: abrupt flat-roofed pairs and terraces of six, with concrete-framed porches and windows. More appealing is the fragment of the proposed WORCESTER GARDEN SUBURB at BALLIOL ROAD, S, begun 1913 by *A. V. Rowe;* all that materialized, mostly by 1915, were a couple of roughcast houses with weatherboarded gables, matching bungalows around EARL GREY SQUARE, and one tree-lined side street (CHRISTCHURCH ROAD).

NEWTOWN ROAD, further S, leads past the GUN TAVERN by *Alfred Parker,* 1936, Neo-Georgian with good carved cannon above the doorway; and HARESFIELD HOUSE, a medical centre by *Bundred & Goode* of Stourbridge, 2006, three-storey brick with split-level roofs. Then uphill to the large RONKSWOOD ESTATE, mostly *c.* 1946–50, *H.A. Mackrill,* City Surveyor, distinguished only by the circular Holy Trinity and St Matthew (p. 709) at its centre, and by RONKSWOOD PRIMARY SCHOOL, by *Jackson & Edmonds,* 1950–3, on its W edge (in St Alban's Close). Orange-brown brick, with flat concrete roofs; glazed entrance, E, with blocky tower, flanked by the projecting dining hall, N, and large main hall, S, with curved corner. Further E, the extensive Worcestershire Royal Hospital (p. 725).

WARNDON VILLAGES, on the city's E boundary, is an extensive area of private housing, built 1988–2002 to guidelines laid down by *Worcester City Council.* The spine, WOODGREEN DRIVE, runs S to N, with most of the housing to its E. Their design is the usual late C20 builder's mix of patterned brickwork, half-timbering, tile-hanging, Victorian porches etc. The layout is exceptionally intricate, especially in the S part (landscaped by the *Derek Lovejoy Partnership,* 1989–90), with alternative footpath routes, and conservation of existing trees and buildings. The centre, off MILL WOOD DRIVE, incorporates LYPPARD GRANGE, restored C17–C19, now a pub, plus a Neo-vernacular square with weatherboarded shops and other buildings: a matching 'Essex-barn' TESCO store, W, and the PRIMARY SCHOOL (1998), to the E. Further N, a rural byway, TROTSHILL LANE, with some timber-framed cottages, has been preserved as if in aspic, leading SE to the early C19 TROT-

SHILL FARM (with small timber-framed GRANARY of *c.* 1700, on staddle-stones). Landmarks further N (landscape consultants *Mason Richards*) are the WOODGREEN EVANGELICAL CHURCH, Hastings Drive, by *Mayway Design Construction*, 1992–5, to a scheme by *Mike Auty* and *Chris Brain*, two-tone brick, with pantiled roofs and fancy sail-like spire; and, at the NE tip, Warndon church and its well-preserved surroundings (*see* p. 649).

3. South-east and south

Late C18–early C19 development has left more traces to the SE, around London Road, than in any other direction. These must often be sought out amongst later housing, especially in the W part, the only one that makes an easy perambulation. Diglis, off Bath Road, is in contrast almost entirely industrial.

3a. London Road, western end

From Sidbury (p. 736) LONDON ROAD climbs steeply up Wheatsheaf Hill; here, No. 21, *c.* 1800–20, of three bays and storeys, has a big bow-window oriel to the road.

First to the S up GREEN HILL, a fairly complete street of *c.* 1828–30. On its W side, Nos. 1–10, a false-ashlar stucco terrace: round-arched reeded doorways approached up steps with wrought-iron railings or through shared tented porches. Then two large stuccoed houses with giant pilasters: No. 11, set back; No. 12 with elegant iron porch with twisted columns. Opposite, a spacious brick pair and the matching four-bay ST HELENS, originally the vicarage for that church. GARICOITS HOUSE next door, big bald Queen Anne, was built as St Peter's vicarage, 1883–4, by *Yeates & Jones*.

Back to London Road, where the N side is dominated by FORT ROYAL PARK, opened 1915, previously a garden and deerpark belonging to The Commandery (p. 733). The rounded knolls on top, with fine views, are remnants of a large star-shaped fort of *c.* 1651 (captured in that year by the Parliamentarians at the Battle of Worcester). In and off FORT ROYAL HILL, running along its E side, several Late Georgian houses, notably the tall, stuccoed PARK HOUSE, at the end of Fort Royal Lane, said to have been built for the porcelain manufacturer Humphrey Chamberlain *c.* 1828: two bays, shell window tympana, giant pilasters with anthemion capitals. Of the later C19 housing, ST WULSTAN'S CRESCENT is worth a glance, with small-scale terraces and villas by *E.A. Day*, *c.* 1880–1.

Back again to LONDON ROAD, where continuous Late Georgian houses recommence with the stuccoed Nos. 63–67. Nos. 1–2 BATTENHALL PLACE opposite, S, are the best pair, perhaps 1790s, with stuccoed false ashlar fronts; five bays altogether, the central one blind, with a window with swags and the shell (or fan) motif above another with a lion's head; fine Adamish doorcases, carved with putti and musical instruments. SOUTHSIDE

nearby is by *E. G. Jones*, for himself, 1885. Set back in VICTO-
RIA PLACE, N side, a brick terraced group of *c.* 1800. Then more
Late Georgian brick houses (No. 73 with fluted Ionic porch)
before ROSE HILL leads N to ROSE HILL HOUSE (now St
Richard's Hospice), large, stuccoed, *c.* 1810, with later addi-
tions; Tuscan porch to the N, flanked by bow windows.

Next in LONDON ROAD, the twelve-bay ST MARY'S TERRACE
(Nos. 79–87), red brick, three storeys, set back behind front
gardens, the middle window of each house round-arched.
ROSE LAWN (No. 89), beyond Rose Avenue, detached, three
bays, in the same style, is set even further back. No. 101, now
South Bank Nursing Home, said to be of 1783, is again similar
(much expanded in the C20). Beside it, ROSE BANK leads N
to another good stuccoed villa, ROSE BANK HOUSE, of 1814.

On the S side of LONDON ROAD also several Late Georgian
houses, but none to single out. At the corner of Camp Hill
Road, a larger Early Victorian brick house, EDGEHILL
COURT, flat Tudor Gothic with steep bargeboarded gables and
fancy terracotta chimneys. Probably by *Henry Day*, who was
certainly responsible for ELDERSLIE, further E, now the centre
of a sub-Span estate of flat-roofed houses and flats (begun
1969 by *Ralphs & Mansell*). Elderslie is Italianate, its main
front facing S; taller tower-like centre with tripartite windows;
ground-floor windows round-arched. Opposite, on the N side
of London Road, is St Martin (p. 714).

3b. Battenhall

Battenhall, S of London Road, once a medieval deerpark belonging to the Priors of Worcester, was sold for development in
1884. Only a few of its affluent houses are noteworthy; late C20
infill has since eroded much of its secluded character.

The spine is the tree-lined BATTENHALL ROAD, running S from
London Road. Near the beginning, W side, a tall Queen Anne
terrace (Nos. 18–30) by *J. Cuddon Close*, 1889, perhaps heightened later; *see* the terracotta gable decoration and bulbous, Art
Nouveau-like, paired balconies over the doorways. The road
then turns SE, and the late C19 brick semi-detached pairs on
the NE side give way to single houses in secluded grounds,
mostly quite mundane. This is true even of No. 51 (Uplands)
by *Aston Webb*, 1878, built for the minister of the Congregational Church, Angel Place: severe, tall, brick, timbered gables.

On the SW side, gabled half-timbered houses of *c.* 1890, smarter
and larger, including a semi-detached pair with big coving,
probably by *J. H. Williams*. The best, after Timberdine Avenue,
include No. 60 (Battenhall Lodge) by *Wood & Kendrick*,
1896–7, which adds tile-hanging to the mix, plus a large Tudorish stone staircase window above doorway with radiating voussoirs; and No. 62 (Oaklands) by *J. H. Williams*, 1904, yet larger,
with ornately carved bargeboards and beams; entrance front
with three gables above deep red terracotta ground floor with
columned porch and big round bay.

Further on, in extensive grounds, is BATTENHALL MOUNT (since 1934 ST MARY'S CONVENT SCHOOL), an Italianate house of *c.* 1867 for William Spriggs, hugely enlarged in closely matching style in the 1890s for the Hon. Percy Allsopp (not surprisingly declared bankrupt in 1913). It is announced by a proud LODGE, at the corner of Battle Road, by *J.H. Williams*, 1893, florid Tudor Gothic with terracotta trim and half-timbered gables. The gateway, with fine iron gates (electrically operated from the beginning), is flanked by stunted turrets; another turret rises to full height, with ogee copper cap, from the side of the lodge. The drive curves uphill past *Williams*'s large STABLE BLOCK, mostly 1891–2, similarly florid. The HOUSE, of gault brick with yellow stone trim, seems rather dour in comparison. NW entrance front partly of *c.* 1867, with typically Italianate NW tower, partly (with pedimental attic gables) of *c.* 1892–4 by *J.H. Williams*, who provided much of the street front, NE (to Battenhall Avenue). More attractive, the long SW front, with bowed garden entrance, more pedimental gables, and five canted bay windows. This is mostly by *R.A. Briggs*, 1895–6, as is the SE front, with its broader Italianate tower with elaborate balcony, and adjoining apse with loggia above. Richly appointed INTERIORS, mostly by *Williams* in C17 style, with fine woodwork, especially the main staircase, and former dining room, with inglenook with Arthurian stained glass. The best are those by *Briggs*, notably the large music room along the SW front, with plaster compartment ceiling (by *Jackson & Sons*) and excellent Mannerist fireplace with inset tiling of Scylla and Charybdis, probably by *William de Morgan*. Parallel marble-floored hall (originally sculpture gallery), with glazed barrel-vaulted roof, ending in a stone minstrel gallery (beneath the SE tower). Almost as impressive is *Briggs*'s small chapel on the upper floor of the NE front (where its E apse appears as a rounded oriel); L-plan, with central dome, patterned marble floor, iron screens (by *Starkie, Gardner & Co.*), finely carved stalls, and stained glass by *Shrigley & Hunt*. – In the GROUNDS, to NW and SW, remains of balustrading of Italianate gardens.

In BATTENHALL AVENUE, opposite the NE flank of the house, more large brick and half-timbered houses, *c.* 1886–91, probably all by *J.H. Williams*; some, including Williams's own, have been demolished. On the SW side, beyond the school's 1960s classrooms and hall, a gardener's COTTAGE dated 1896 and one more large house by *Williams*, HIGHFIELD, 1886–7, mostly brick with much tile-hanging and terracotta patterning.

The roughcast MIDDLE BATTENHALL FARM, off the SE end of Battenhall Road, beyond the railway, is at least partly C17, on the site of the Priory grange. Within the gabled E wing, its timber framing perhaps relocated from Prior More's C16 house (on the moated site further S), are traces of green and red decorative painting. To the E, a good group of C17 former farm buildings.

3c. On and off London Road, eastern part

In PERRY WOOD WALK, off Wyld's Lane, the former METAL BOX FACTORY (now Crown Food). Original office block by *S.N. Cooke*, 1930–1, smooth brick, 4+1+4 bays, slight Deco detailing. The large, vigorous E extension, 1963–4 by *Howell, Killick, Partridge & Amis*, shows the restlessness typical of that decade, especially around the jagged entrance; long E flank with greater horizontal emphasis.

Lark Hill Road leads to LARK HILL, a small stuccoed development, like Britannia Square (p. 756) and the later Lansdowne Crescent (p. 766), still quite isolated in its elevated position beneath Perry Wood. Built *c.* 1819–24, intended to be much larger, with terraces and crescent. All that materialized was one detached villa (WOODSIDE) to the N, with elemental giant pilasters, broad Doric porch, and good interior detail, and four semi-detached pairs, S. These are approached by a rear mews (as at Lansdowne Crescent), their small stable yards more or less intact. The fronts face W to long gardens and a green lane; all have giant pilasters, and most pretty timber or iron verandas. Some bow windows on the return fronts.

HERON LODGE, below, W, of *c.* 1825, formed part of the scheme, but is now approached from London Road: five bays, giant pilasters, fluted and pedimented doorcase, first-floor shutters, mildly Gothick veranda on the W and S sides. SE extension by *A.H. Parker*, 1897, with billiard room with rounded bay window.

Further along London Road, isolated Late Georgian survivors. The best, N side, are No. 163, *c.* 1800, ashlar-faced, with Doric doorcase approached up steps; and, further up Red Hill (now in Yew Tree Close), RED HILL HOUSE, *c.* 1830, stuccoed, with cast-iron veranda with tented canopy. Opposite, in CROMWELL CRESCENT, a couple of roughcast, gabled, Voysey-inspired houses by *A.V. Rowe*: No. 3, 1908, and facing it, No. 4, 1910, with polygonal bay at its l. corner.

At Red Hill Top, London Road divides into Spetchley Road, leading E to County Hall (p. 719) past Nunnery Wood High School and Sixth Form College, and Whittington Road, to the SE, with RNIB New College (*see* p. 729).

3d. South, along the Bath Road

There is little to see in this direction, apart from industrial development by the Severn at Diglis, and minor housing on and off Bath Road. (For the extreme N end of Bath Road, *see* p. 736). From BATH ROAD, between canal-side apartments with fashionable curved roofs by *Boughton Butler*, 2002–4, and THE ALBION inn, brick, *c.* 1840, with rounded end, DIGLIS ROAD leads SW to the DIGLIS BASINS, the terminus of the 30-mile-long Worcester and Birmingham Canal. An act was passed in 1791, the canal completed in 1815, at a cost of £610,000, by far the most expensive in the Midlands. There are two basins,

the main N one with small warehouses, workshops, lock
cottage, and dry dock; good canalscape, but hardly bearing
comparison with Stourport (q.v.). Access to the Severn is
through two river locks, with holding basin between.

DIGLIS DOCK ROAD continues SW to the riverside, passing a
large rectangular TRANSHIPPING DOCK, built 1892–4 to
encourage sea-going ships to come up to Worcester. Further
on, the DIGLIS SEVERN LOCKS, part of *Edward Leader
Williams*'s scheme of *c.* 1840 to maintain at least a 6-ft (0.9-
metre) river depth between Stourport and Worcester; twin
locks with massive double gates. On DIGLIS ISLAND, W, a
painted-brick Tudor group dated 1844, with gabled and bargeboarded lock-keeper's house flanked by cottages. To its N, a
single-storey range of contemporary workshops; arched
windows with cast-iron frames.

Standard, scruffy industrial development all around. The exception, at the bend of NAVIGATION ROAD, is the former
WORCESTER ENGINEERING premises, of 1968–72, given a
striking E end, with offices and showrooms, in 1980–1 by the
Glazzard Partnership. Steel frame, covered in blue-painted, corrugated 'Floclad'; undulating sloping walls and roofs, staggered in height, strip windows at ground and clerestory level,
fully glazed end wall.

Back in BATH ROAD, W side, uphill from The Albion, three-
storey pairs of *c.* 1840 (Nos. 54–64) continue SW into FIELD
TERRACE, an attractive stuccoed group, with only footpath
access: two more pairs and a short terrace. Late C19 houses
opposite, uphill, and along The HILL AVENUE and neighbouring streets, mostly *c.* 1893. At the NE end of the former,
either side of Woolhope Road, three pairs (Nos. 34–44) with
timber balconies at attic level, and a group with lively terracotta detail (Nos. 46–62).

The largest house in BATH ROAD, at No. 139, SOUTHBANK By
G.G. Scott for Thomas Southall, 1866, was demolished
c. 1983 for a bland, brick BUPA Hospital; its plain brick LODGE
and some garden walls survive.

Little else to note in Bath Road, apart from St Mark, Cherry
Orchard (p. 713), set back, W side. At the S end, the former
TIMBERDINE FARMHOUSE (now a pub); late C16 floored hall
range with W cross-wing, mostly of close-studded. The broad
gable of the wing is jettied, with tie-beam and arch-braced
collar. Large E cross-wing, half-timbering above brick, added
by *F.S. Waller & Son* of Gloucester, 1879–80.

4. West of the Severn

Worcester W of the river began as the medieval suburb of ST
JOHN'S, incorporated into the city in 1837. This grew up around
St John in Bedwardine (p. 712), at a safe distance, from flooding, above the Severn bridge. Tybridge Street represents the
medieval bridge approach, New Road its replacement of *c.* 1780
(p. 726). Both now form part of a furious gyratory system around

CRIPPLEGATE PARK, opened 1922. Resited here, a fine cast-iron
FOUNTAIN, given to the city by Richard Padmore (of *Hardy &
Padmore*) in 1858; two diminishing basins with water-lily and lion-
mask ornamenation, gilded cherubs standing on a shaft of
twisted dolphins. Marooned in TYBRIDGE STREET, one brick
villa (No. 52), *c.* 1820, with central round-arched recess above its
Tuscan porch.

4a. Around St John in Bedwardine church and south along Malvern Road

Near St John's church Georgian brick houses remain, also a few
earlier timber-framed examples, mostly in the street called ST
JOHN'S. The best Georgian house, No. 25, is set back on the
SE side, E of the former vicarage (p. 713); mid-C18, five bays,
the keystones fluted above, panelled below; pedimented doorcase with fluted pilasters and triglyph frieze, arched window
above with big sunflower keystone. Good open-well staircase
with slender balusters. No. 23, also five bays, is disfigured by
a C20 shopfront. Minor Georgian frontages further E, No. 24
(N side), the former ANGEL INN, with good early C19 lettering. Then, stepping slightly downhill, the CO-OP SUPERMAR-
KET (*Glazzard Partnership*, 1979), brick with timber oriels,
followed at No. 6 by a renewed C16 timber-framed and jettied
gable, probably originally the E (service) cross-wing of a hall-
house. The continuation, BULL RING, has a corner shop by
A.H. Parker, 1902, and the little-altered BUSH INN by *Owen
& Ward* of Birmingham, 1898; opposite, S, a brick terrace of
c. 1800. Further progress is deterred by three twelve-storey *City
Council* POINT BLOCKS, *c.* 1967, the only ones in Worcester.
Their brick design is not unacceptable; their siting, between St
John's and the river, defies comprehension. At least the distant
view of the cathedral remains.

Back to the former vicarage and W along BROMYARD ROAD.
Opposite the church, N, its former INFANTS' SCHOOL (now
County Library) by *Perkins*, 1870, brick, stone trim. Central
gable and grouped trefoiled lancets; good arch-braced roof
within. NW wing by *A.B. Pinckney*, 1897. Then, S side, a varied
early C19 terrace (Nos. 5–17). Set back, N side, No. 28, *c.* 1800;
three bays and storeys, pedimented doorway.

The SW section of ST JOHN'S can be regained through the
churchyard. Several minor Georgian brick houses and, at Nos.
43–49, a notable timber-framed survivor, restored *c.* 1980. It
represents a two-bay hall house of *c.* 1500, its S cross-wing now
sheared off. Close-studded, with square panelling above;
renewed timber-mullioned windows. N of the doorway to the
screens passage was perhaps a shop; to the S, the hall, with
double-height window. Moulded stone chimneypiece of
c. 1600 within; on the upper floor to the N, a fragment of C16
wall painting depicting a crane amongst foliage trails. No. 54,
opposite, W side, was built as Cousens' Hygienic Machine
Bakery, by *A. Hill Parker*, 1897; brick, banded with stone, odd

Jacobethan detail high up, shaped gable above the entrance archway.

In MALVERN ROAD, the s continuation of St John's, a few more Late Georgian houses face the former St John's Green, at the junction with Bransford Road (*see* below). No. 1 (now Barclays Bank) is a stuccoed villa with Doric porch; Nos. 5–7 a late C18 brick pair, ten bays altogether, with segment-headed windows and doorway pediments on brackets. Then the CHRISTOPHER WHITEHEAD SENIOR SCHOOL by *Alfred G. Parker*, 1937–8. Brick, with stone trim; central hall with tall windows with jazzily stepped tops, flanked by turrets crowned with Vanbrughian arches; long classroom ranges either side. Contemporary railings.

Further s, pleasant later C19 development. On the w side, behind its high mid-C19 wall and Tudor Gothic lodge, is the early C19 PITMASTON HOUSE, five bays of orange brick, gothicized *c.* 1830–40 and later, apparently for the noted horticulturalist John Williams (1773–1853). His house received a battlemented porch with clustered shafts, plus gables and clustered chimneys; also a substantial N wing, with bay window and more battlements, balanced, s, by a large Gothick conservatory apparently of *Coade* stone. Classical entrance hall, with Ionic screen to the curving staircase. The grounds are now partly a park, partly filled by Pitmaston Primary School (by *Willis, Llewellyn Smith & Waters*, 1952–3; enlarged 1970).

In BROMWICH ROAD, further e, more or less parallel to Malvern Road, the former Bromwich House (Nos. 55–57), of 1810; stuccoed, with central porch with paired Doric columns, broad round-headed window recesses either side, wide pilasters above. Opposite, much half-timbering by *W.G. Lofthouse* of Bilston, including a whole bungalow estate of 1924–5, remarkably little altered, around Withers and Alexander roads. Further s, around Coventry Avenue, CITY COUNCIL HOUSING by *William Ransom*, *c.* 1925–30, predominates.

4b. Further west, to the city boundary

In BRANSFORD ROAD, leading w from St John's Green, OUR LADY QUEEN OF PEACE (R.C.), a small brick church by *G.R. Acton*, 1951: round-arched windows, large shaped gable above the entrance; glazed porch with upturned roof by *DJD Architects*, 2003. Then, scattered Late Georgian houses, the best No. 61 (Belmont House), s side, *c.* 1800: three storeys, pedimented doorway. BOUGHTON VILLA, at the corner of School Road, is stuccoed, *c.* 1820, with giant pilasters, fan-pattern window tympana, and Doric porch. A little s, in BOUGHTON STREET, a colony of modest villas was begun *c.* 1811; those that materialized include No. 45, brick with fluted Doric porch, and Nos. 46–47, a semi-detached pair of only two bays together, with side porches. Further along Bransford Road, at Nos. 103–111, more attractive, if modest development of *c.* 1800 or soon after.

In WATERY LANE, N, the large CINDERELLA SHOE WORKS of Messrs J.F. Willis Ltd., by *Brown & Mayor* of Northampton, 1914. Attractive front, with much blank wall above the windows, central Doric entrance; bold parapet lettering. Small square tower at the rear, NW.

BOUGHTON PARK, further along Bransford Road, in its own grounds (now a golf course), is of *c.* 1814, for the banker Elias Isaac. Rendered, 2+3+2 bays with fluted Doric porch, two-storeyed since a third was removed after a fire in 1948; new parapet and pediment by *H.W. Weedon & Partners*. Hall with two fluted Doric columns fronting the restored iron-balustraded staircase. The garden front, including service wing, SE, looks mostly mid-C19, with thicker detail; Doric veranda, balustraded parapet. Before the fire the house had a mansard roof and tower.

Set back at No. 250 Bransford Road, the enormous WAREHOUSE built for Kay & Co.'s mail-order business in 1969–70, designed by *Tarmac Building Ltd*, following the scheme of Herr *Pierau*. Concrete-framed, pale brick infill, only narrow glazing bands high up on each upper floor; flat stair-towers of darker brick. Windowless ribbed-metallic extension, E, *c.* 1985.

At the W end of BROMYARD ROAD, beyond the railway is MUDWALL (or ST JOHN'S) MILL, rebuilt 1869; brick, six bays and five storeys, it was steam-powered apart from one earlier water wheel. Altered in the 1890s and later. Opposite looms the rear of Kay's warehouse (originally approached from this side).

4c. Lower Wick

LOWER WICK, the SW extremity of Worcester City, retains a few remnants of the former hamlet; for Upper Wick, *see* p. 252. BENNETTS FARM, C16–C17 in origin but mostly *c.* 1800, big, square, brick with hipped roof, was the former manor house. Various outbuildings surround a scruffy courtyard facing Malvern Road. Behind the Manor Farm pub, a BARN incorporates the remains of the mid-C12 ST CUTHBERT'S CHAPEL (closed 1371). Its red sandstone S and E walls survive to a height of some 12 ft (3.7 metres), with buttresses demarcating a two-bay nave and single-bay chancel; openings now indistinct. Timber-framed C17 upper storey, with brick infill; further alterations of the later C19, including a brick W addition for grain storage. Hidden in trees, E, is LYTTLETON HOUSE, *c.* 1700, five bays of whitewashed brick, with platbands; later E bay and rear range.

OLD ROAD leads SW, past a couple of early C19 brick villas, to the former CITY ELECTRICITY WORKS, 1893–4 by the City Engineer, *S.G. Purchas* (succeeded by *Thomas Caink*), with *W.H. Preece* as consultant. It was the first permanent hydro-electric power station built by any English municipality; the waters of the River Teme generated some 400 kilowatts, supplemented as required by steam power. Red and yellow brick, gabled, with round-arched windows. The riverside range contained the boiler house, with tall, tapering, octagonal chimney at its SE end. The three water-driven turbines lay in the range across the river, behind the entrance (with small office wing to its NW). Converted to housing by *Lett & Sweetland*, 1999. The OLD BRIDGE nearby, C15–C16, of sandstone, has three segmental skew arches over the river, with angled cutwaters, plus two across the mill stream; their round arches are probably late C17 renewals after Civil War damage. Later brick repairs, including the whole parapet. The present POWICK BRIDGE, by *C.H. Capper* of Birmingham, 1836–7, is of Arley sandstone, with slight Gothic detail, * but with segmental cast-iron arch of Telford type (cf. Holt) across the river. Seven ribs underneath, latticed spandrels, pretty iron parapet railings with heraldic cartouche below; one smaller cast-iron, four-centred flood arch either side. The ironwork was by *Yates* of Birmingham.

4d. Henwick

HYLTON ROAD, running NW from Worcester Bridge alongside the Severn, is mostly scrappy C20, a wasted opportunity. Of note only BERROW'S NEWSPAPERS premises, by *Austin-Smith, Salmon, Lord*, 1964–5, two storeys of pre-cast concrete panels, with typical 1960s-looking angular staircases at the corners; staggered monopitch roofs. The former Colour Printing Works, N, by *Henry Gorst*, 1960–1, also has monopitched roofs, here a series of hyperbolic paraboloid shells; timber-clad office range.

In HENWICK ROAD leading N from St John's Late Georgian brick houses remain to the S of St Clement (p. 710), a few more N of the railway crossing. Then the former RECTORY (No. 60), basic Tudor Gothic, of diapered brick, by *Henry Rowe*, 1866–7. Opposite, W, first ST CLEMENT'S PRIMARY SCHOOL, simple low-key brick by *Henry Gorst*, 1975–6 and later. Then, in total contrast, the former ROYAL ALBERT ORPHANAGE (now Worcester YMCA), intimidating red brick Gothic of 1868–9 by *William Watkins* of Lincoln (with *S. Dutton Walker* of Nottingham). E-plan, three storeys, with gabled dormers and larger stepped gables to the centre and ends. The centre has a far-projecting canted bay supported on massive foliated pink columns; pyramid-roofed turret behind. Steep slate roofs bristling with fancy iron cresting. Matching wings, the S added 1885, the N 1900.

Nothing more until OLDBURY ROAD branches off to the W. Here, a former LODGE dated 1881, yellow brick with timbered gable. It led to HENWICK GROVE, which survives, hemmed in by late C20 housing, in Tollhouse Drive: latest classical, *c.* 1840–50, also yellow brick, with tripartite windows, stuccoed

---

* This was far more pronounced until *c.* 1950, when Gothic domes were removed from the eight octagonal turrets.

parts to the rear and sides. In its former grounds are OLDBURY PARK PRIMARY SCHOOL by *Jackson & Edmonds*, *c.* 1951 (cf. Ronkswood Primary School, p. 768), and the UNIVERSITY OF WORCESTER. This began as the City of Worcester Training College, by *Holland W. Hobbiss & Partners*, 1961–4; brick, with concrete-framed windows strips, undetermined whether to be modern or traditional. Entrance with three round-headed arches, with tall rectangular copper-roofed tower, r., plus low administrative block projecting forward; dining hall, l. Teaching accommodation built round two courtyards, divided by the main hall. Later buildings crowd in on all sides, the best the PEIRSON LIBRARY, SW of the entrance, by *J.R. McKee*, City Architect, 1970–1: white ribbed and projecting first floor; staggered brick rear section added 1998–9 by *Marson Rathbone Taylor*. Also two low, spreading, partly bomb-proofed ranges built *c.* 1940 for the Air Ministry's exile from London;* adapted for college use *c.* 1950. Nearby, domestic-style complexes of student accommodation: WYVERN HALL of 1988, with timber oriels and balconies; WORCESTER HALLS, NE, opened 1995, more insipid, with pantiled roofs.

COMER GARDENS, leading N from Oldbury Road, some distance W, began as an out-of-town suburb after the cholera epidemic of 1848; brick Institute of 1906, S end, various brick or roughcast villas of the 1850s further N, mostly in ample gardens.

Finally back to HENWICK ROAD, the N part of which, beyond the junction with Hylton Road, has a long early C19 range, E side, enjoying fine elevated views across the Severn. Interrupting, at Nos. 206–210, a striking group of four steel-clad gabled houses by *John Edwards* of Droitwich, 1997; two storeys with balconies above partly open ground floors for car parking. Of the larger mid-C19 houses further N only two remain. THE CEDARS (at Nos. 222–224) is Italianate Picturesque. HENWICK GRANGE (now a nursing home), in the continuing Hallow Road, is full-blown Tudor Gothic: diapered brick, gabled, tall chimneys.

WRIBBENHALL
Bewdley

ALL SAINTS, Kidderminster Road. 1878–9 by *Arthur W. Blomfield*; red rock-faced Alveley sandstone, in the style of *c.* 1300. Nave and chancel with S aisle and chapel, routine apart from the octagonal tower with pyramidal spire above the NE vestry. Quite high interior: five-bay S arcade on round piers, two-bay arcade with quatrefoil pier between chancel and chapel. – Wrought-iron CHANCEL SCREEN (made by *John C. Culwick* of Lichfield) and gilded wooden REREDOS by *R.A. Briggs*, 1899. *Blomfield*'s painted reredos is now above the N door. – Much

---

* A whole complex of such buildings survive on the DEFRA site, Whittington Road.

STAINED GLASS, the best two by *Heaton, Butler & Bayne*: E *c.* 1879, W 1886; also theirs, the nave NW, 1893. – By *Burlison & Grylls*, two chancel N lancets, 1884–6. – By *James Powell & Sons*, S chapel SW 1904 and S aisle S central, 1917. – Nave N by *Nick Bayliss*, 2000. – The rest by *Hardman*: nave NE 1879, four S aisle S 1901–11, S aisle W 1961. – From the former church (*see* below) the mid-C19 Perp FONT; also a Gothic TABLET to Col. Philip Wodehouse †1846, and C18 ROYAL ARMS (both S chapel).

LYCHGATE. By *Thomas Gordon*, 1891; cross-gabled, open tracery. – Large WAR MEMORIAL CROSS by *Godwin, Browett, Riley & Smith*, 1920.

BEWDLEY HIGH SCHOOL, Stourport Road. A secondary modern by *Yorke, Rosenberg & Mardall*, 1953–5; assistant architect *J. Sofaer*. A pleasant design, much wood-slatting in lieu of curtain walling, with bold concrete water tower; centre block and assembly hall largely of timber construction, the rest of reinforced concrete and load-bearing red brick. Curved classroom block, NE, by *Architype* of London, 1996.

BEWDLEY RAILWAY STATION, opened 1862, on an elevated site off Stourport Road; very well preserved by the Severn Valley Railway. Brick station house with round-arched windows, linked to the waiting room by the booking hall. Island platform added 1877–8 (for the Kidderminster branch).

PERAMBULATION

Wribbenhall, like Bewdley across the river, has three streets, one running straight from the bridge, two l. and r. along the Severn; only everything is on a smaller scale.

Starting then from the bridge (p. 142), RIVER SIDE NORTH has *p. 142* mostly mediocre C20 buildings, a wasted opportunity. Facing the bridge approach, difficult to see behind their long front gardens, a Georgian brick row, fifteen bays, with modillion cornice, hipped roof and pedimented dormers. It consists of three houses: GLENHURST, N, seven bays, early C18, the other two, WOOD EAVES and PLEASANT HARBOUR, three and five bays respectively, probably mid-C18; all have bolection-moulded doorways with flat architraves. Then BEALE'S CORNER, a good group: No. 7, dated 1623, restored narrow studding, with side gables flanking a brick chimney; Nos. 4–6 mid-C18 brick; No. 3 again timber-framed, early C17, lower with jettied gable. Behind the r. of its two five-light mullioned-and-transomed first-floor windows, a room with three C17 painted plaster panels on its S wall: rural scenes perhaps illustrating Aesop. SEVERN VIEW, at the corner, tall mid-C17 brick, has its gable-end towards the river, its main front, S, facing Kidderminster Road.

Before turning the corner, first into STOURPORT ROAD, continuing alongside the Severn, its sylvan river front contrasting to Bewdley's urban Severn Side opposite. No. 1, brick, five bays and three storeys with segment-headed windows, several blind, is dated 1735. Its warehouse, end-on to the road, is perhaps contemporary; more warehouses, N E (*see* below). Nos. 5–9 also seem C18 brick, with sashed windows, bargeboarded gables, and taller rendered gabled wing. Only the gable-end of No. 5 and framing high up on the wing's w side reveal that this is a major C14 house, possibly the manor house; Nos. 5–7 the two-bay open hall, No. 9 its two-bay cross-wing. The latter's roof comprises a cambered tie, with crown-post and scissor rafters. The hall's central truss, with base cruck, collar on cusped knee-braces, then crown-post and scissor rafters similar to the wing, has been dendro-dated to *c*. 1302–24.

Now KIDDERMINSTER ROAD, N side. Adjoining Severn View are Nos. 5–9 (SYDNEY PLACE), a short brick terrace of 1741; three storeys, six bays, straight rusticated quoins, plain pilasters dividing the houses (above the rendered ground floor). Nos. 11–19 are a Neo-Georgian police terrace of 1934 by *A. V. Rowe*, County Architect: two houses either side of the pedimented central station. Between these terraces, the narrow PEWTERERS' ALLEY leads N to the stuccoed, gabled VINE COTTAGE; then N E, to the diminutive ENA COTTAGE, late C18 Gothick. Further N, the MALT HOUSE, good C17 timber-framed, and the s end (Pleasant Harbour) of the fifteen-bay terrace noted above; its rear has projecting gabled brick wings.

A good group in KIDDERMINSTER ROAD, s side, begins with No. 6, early C17 timber-framed, with two moulded bressumers on console brackets. Remodelled 1723 when a rear range was added; open-well staircase with turned balusters, C17–C18 panelling. Nos. 8–10 are early C19 brick. The roughcast front of No. 12 hides C17 framing, with decorative cusping and carved bargeboards visible on the E gable-end. The BLACK BOY HOTEL, painted brick, L-plan, is part late C17, part early C19.

An alleyway alongside leads to LYCH GATE, the original nucleus of Wribbenhall around its former church. MINSTER HOUSE, early C18 painted brick, altered in the early C19, has a long attached warehouse, part of an elongated courtyard linking up with No. 1 Stourport Road; all now housing. Then the lychgate (of 1949) to the former churchyard of Christ Church, built 1701, demolished 1881; some of its stone was used for the CROSS here (partly renewed 1898). Opposite, the former NATIONAL SCHOOLS, delightful gabled Gothic by *Robert Robinson* of Stourbridge, 1850: purple brick, yellow dressings, grouped lancets; boys' and girls' schoolrooms at right angles, master's house at the centre. Then Lych Gate joins WESTBOURNE STREET, C18–C19 brick with some C17 timber-framing. Its N E end, flanked by small-scale mid to late C18 terraces, is dramatically framed by the skewed rusticated sandstone BRIDGE of the Severn Valley Railway; 1859–61 by *John Fowler* with *Henry Bridgeman*. A seven-arched viaduct continues this, S E, to Bewdley Station (p. 779). In its shadow, LOWE'S ROPE AND TWINE MANUFACTORY (established 1801), a modest industrial group mostly of 1866–70, behind a late C17 timber-framed cottage, all now converted to housing.[*]

Uphill in KIDDERMINSTER ROAD, some distance NE, is All Saints (p. 778). The return, SW, to the river, passes the former BRITISH SCHOOL, severe brick Gothic by *Robinson* of Darlington, 1881.

THE SUMMER HOUSE, further N, hidden in suburban housing off Gloucester Way, overlooks much of Bewdley. The original part, a short polygonal brick tower of *c.* 1740, was incorporated (as the centre of its SW front) into a gabled Tudor Gothic house, *c.* 1840–5, for the Sturge family; roughcast, tall brick chimneys. Contemporary STABLES.

HOARSTONE FARM, ¾ m. N, C17–C18, little altered. Brick-faced early C18 S front with projecting gabled wings, the E with attached two-storey gabled porch. W cross-wing, C17, with large lateral ashlar chimney-breast with star-clustered brick stacks: on each floor, a fine panelled room with good figured overmantel. The projecting early C17 rear wing, NE, has two storeys of large sandstone blocks, the upper slightly jettied, with mullioned windows; timber-framed, gabled second floor. Two five-bay BARNS: one, immediately W, brick, probably early C18; the other, a little SW, stone, with hipped roof, late C17.[†]

WASSELL WOOD HOUSE, 1 m. NNE. Gabled Tudor Gothic, *c.* 1840. Stuccoed brick; central three-bay ground-floor loggia, side entrance leading to an octagonal vestibule, top-lit stairs beyond. Jacobethan ribbed ceilings, Tudor Gothic fireplaces.

SPRING GROVE, ⅔ m. E, now within West Midland Safari Park. Built for Samuel Skey, 1787–90. Cemented S front of 2+3+2 bays, the centre projecting beneath a pediment. Balustraded porch with Ionic pilasters and short E extension ending in a simple Italianate three-storey tower, probably both *c.* 1840. Open-well staircase with cast-iron balustrade; octagonal dome above. Late C18 STABLES, S, now a café.

At BLACKSTONE, 1 m. S, two farms with good late C18 brick barns with hit-and-miss ventilators. BLACKSTONE FARM-HOUSE, by the Stourport Road, is also C18 brick, with off-centre gable. LOWER BLACKSTONE FARMHOUSE, nearer the river, mostly late C16 timber-framed, has a jettied S end-gable with oriel and carved consoles. Prattinton recorded a date 1589 over the back door.

On the sheer cliff face of BLACKSTONE ROCK, S of the latter, a single entrance gives access to a network of caves (cf. Redstone Rock, p. 112).

WYCHBOLD

Dodderhill

ST MARY DE WYCHE. Quite large, the major work of *Lewis Sheppard* of Worcester, built 1887–8 at the expense of John Corbett

---

[*] Its rope-walk has been reconstructed at the Bewdley Museum (p. 144).

[†] At LIGHTMARSH FARM, ⅓ m. W, there was a major Mesolithic site, *see* p. 11.

of Chateau Impney (p. 255). Random Malvern rubble, Late Dec style, no aisles but shallow transepts. Bold SE tower with battlements and pinnacles. Its S doorway seems genuine late C13 work, but its origin is unknown: sandstone shafts, moulded capitals, deeply moulded arch; the E lancet's trefoiled head also seems old. Well-proportioned interior, brick-faced, unfortunately painted above the string course; arch-braced roofs. Tilting floors, the result of subsidence caused by brine extraction. – Mostly original FURNISHINGS, with good mosaic PAVING in the chancel. – Oak Perp REREDOS by *J. Wippell & Co.*, 1946, worth comparing with that in the S transept chapel, with finely carved ALTAR, by the *Bromsgrove Guild*, 1948–9. – STAINED GLASS. E window, 1888, and nave NW, 1910, both *Clayton & Bell*. – Nave W by *Samuel Evans*, 1894. – Nave S: one, 1927, typical *A.J. Davies*; one by *F.W. Skeat*, 1965.

Former VICARAGE, ¼ m. SW, by *Sheppard*, 1900–1; brick, gabled, quite plain.

Some buildings of interest along the main A38 road. First, from the SW, the former CROWN INN (now The Poachers' Pocket) by *A.T. Butler*, 1914; half-timbered, roughcast infill, hipped roof. Then, opposite side, WYCHBOLD COURT, C16–C17 timber-framed, with matching mid-C19 S wing forming a U-plan; Corbett's ALMSHOUSES by *J.A. Cossins & Peacock*, 1895, 'for decayed salt makers or their widows', brick with half-timbered upper floor with paired gables; and the BBC TRANSMITTING STATION, opened 1934, its radio masts dominating the district.

ASTWOOD MANOR FARM, ½ m. SSE. Square-panelled framing, mostly early C17, with large sandstone chimney with three brick star-shafts on the front of the hall range; late C18 NW wing forming an H-plan. Good C18–C19 barns.

OLD ASTWOOD FARM, a little SE (in Hanbury parish), is mostly C18–C19 brick. The timber-framed central bay was the main (S) cross-wing of a house built by the Rev. Richard Vernon, called 'new built' in his will, 1627; its hall range and N wing have disappeared. Narrow studding, decorative bracing above; four rebuilt diagonal brick stacks, S. Squat C17 stone gatepiers with ball finials.

ASTWOOD COURT FARM, ¾ m. E, also H-plan, displays even finer, late C16, framing, though the S front was entirely refaced in brick *c.* 1790: gabled wings, slightly recessed centre with two gables, all windows segment-headed. Close studding on the three other sides, each with large sandstone lateral stack with three star-plan brick shafts. The N front's wings have big diagonal braces, with herringbone framing in the W (parlour-wing) gable.

Between the two parts of Astwood, a good stretch of the Worcester and Birmingham Canal: between two hump-backed brick BRIDGES of *c.* 1810, a rise of three LOCKS, separated by holding basins.

WYRE PIDDLE

ST ANNE. A chapelry of Fladbury, mostly rebuilt by *Hopkins*, 1888–9; Dec-style nave and chancel, timber NW porch. The only external medieval features are the double E.E. bellcote on the nave E gable, and re-set Perp W window. Inside, an Early Norman chancel arch with chamfered imposts, as elementary as any, flanked by rectangular squints, probably post-medieval. – FONT. The bowl is a replica of 1986; the original, lying in the sanctuary, resembles that at Abberton (q.v.). Norman, drum-shaped, with top band of vertical single zigzags; another below of normal zigzag. Circular stem, scallops beneath the bowl. – In the chancel, a C12 PILLAR PISCINA, with single-scallop capital; also a stone CREDENCE with E.E. stiff-leaf capital and moulded quatrefoil abacus. – Good C15 TILES, especially in the sanctuary. – SCULPTURE. In a display case (nave NW) some large-scale pieces, possibly Saxon. One appears to be a hood-mould stop: a beast-head with prominent teeth; another is an acanthus leaf capital. Discovered 1888, and presumably from a much more substantial building. – STAINED GLASS. W window: excellent C15 fragments including much of a Virgin and Child, St John's chalice, and fine head of Christ. – E window 1889, no doubt *Lavers, Barraud & Westlake*. – Porch: pretty quarries by *Francis Stephens*, 1960 (E and W), and by *Hardman*, 1975 (N).

The churchyard slopes down S towards the Avon.

WYRE HOUSE, NNW. Of *c.* 1840–50, faced in rusticated stucco ashlar. Straight-headed windows, Tudor-arched lights under hoodmoulds, pierced bargeboarded gables; recessed centre with cast-iron veranda. It resembles the larger, earlier Vandyke Court at Wick (p. 660).

Along CHURCH STREET, NE, a good row of C17 timber-framed houses, beginning with CHURCH COTTAGE; L-plan, with tall gabled dormer to the main range, and blocked ogee-headed doorway. THE COTTAGE next door has remains of a cruck in its E gable. AVONBANK FARM, H-plan, has a C17 W wing and centre (raised in the C18), and earlier close-studded E wing. More C17 thatched cottages further on. At the junction with Worcester Road, the VILLAGE CROSS, mostly by *J.P. St Aubyn*, 1844; two steps, high base and shaft.

Former WESLEYAN CHAPEL, ½ m. E, by the railway. Of 1840, with two-storey gabled front of 1890: patterned brick, wide lancets flanking the doorway, two-lighter above with chequer-tile tympanum.

WYRE MILL, ½ m., WSW. Double range of *c.* 1800, four by six bays; segment-headed windows, originally three waterwheels. Attached house, with late C19 extension, SW.

WYTHALL

Until 1911 part of Kings Norton, the rest of which now lies within Birmingham. Close to the city boundary, with its council tower *p. 43* blocks, is MAYPOLE COTTAGE (set back at No. 10 Crabmill Lane), a remarkable C17 timber-framed survivor; of two bays with a shorter smoke bay for an open hearth at the s end (with inserted C18 chimney). Further s much open country remains, with C16–C19 farmhouses.

ST MARY, Chapel Lane. Declared redundant 1991, now in commercial use. Nave with s aisle, crossing with short transepts, and chancel, by *Frederick Preedy*, 1861–2; N large vestry and
124 splendid central tower added by *W.H. Bidlake*, 1908. This last (paid for by the Misses Mynors of Weatheroak Hall) is outstanding: very high, providing a notable landmark. Of banded red brick to match the church, but of darker hue and less heavy in style. Upper, belfry stage entirely open so that one can see through it. On each side, two very tall bar-traceried openings, of two lights, with rich and elegant shafting. The top is a saddleback roof with sharp central lead flèche. Equally unusual, the stair-turret, NE corner, beginning as a cylinder, but in the upper part octagonal with thin engaged buttresses and open stone cap with pyramidal roof. The whole design is of exceptionally high quality, inspired no doubt from C13 Northern France or Normandy. *Preedy*'s Geometrical Dec-style church, his only major brick example, is in Butterfield's aggressively muscular style. Orange red brick, black brick and stone banding and patterning, stone dressings; window and door jambs emphasized by sawtooth brick cutting, good foliage carving by *Thomas Earp*.

Banded brick and stone patterning also inside, though nave and crossing are now horizontally subdivided. Three-bay s arcade with more notched arches; round stone piers with Early French Gothic foliage capitals. Crossing arches with coupled attached piers carved with large reptilian monsters. Above the chancel arch, a marble cross flanked by alpha and omega. – *Preedy*'s stone PULPIT survives; also a good carved stone REREDOS by *J.G. Bland*, 1866. – STAINED GLASS. s aisle w window by *Preedy*, 1862, originally the central light of the E window. – Nave w by *W. Holland & Son*, 1864, even more colourful. – By *Hardman*, the s transept windows (s 1871, E 1877) and nave NW, 1907. – s aisle SE by *Swaine Bourne*, c. 1875. – s aisle SW, excellent Birmingham Arts and Crafts work by *Geraldine Morris*, 1908–9. – All in the chancel by *Powell & Sons*: E 1895–6, SE 1901, others 1910.

SCHOOL (now PARISH HALL), s, dated 1840. Brick, six bays, centre two-storeyed with pedimental gable; pointed windows, cast-iron intersecting tracery. Altered 1892 (see the end windows), when the master's house was confined to the two-storey rear wing.

Further s, CHAPELGREEN FARM, timber-framed with tripled, star-shaped brick stack; early C17 T-plan, altered in the late C19. – A little NE, the OLD VICARAGE, c. 1860; three-bay brick, shallow hipped slate roof.

At Wythall Green, ⅓ m. N, the extensive chief offices of BRITANNIC ASSURANCE, 1994–6 by the *T.P. Bennett Partnership*.

Huge batwing plan, with two crescent façades, the N with the 131
entrance, the S longer, with offices facing excellently landscaped grounds. Three storeys, stone-faced piers, infilling of
grey-green curtain walling, clearer glazing at clerestory level;
stainless steel wave-form roofs on bifurcated stainless steel
columns. Restaurant (and plant room), W end, mostly stone-
and brick-faced. Circulation is via a full-height central rotunda
with atria either side. Displacement ventilation; engineers
Oscar Faber.

BLACKGREVES FARM, ½ m. NW. Probably the most interesting
of the outlying farmhouses, especially for its medieval double-
moated site; rectangular, the inner moat still wet. Modest
house, probably early C17: roughcast brick with central gabled
brick porch, of two storeys, dated 1827.

Extensive late C20 Birmingham suburbia has developed along and
especially E of ALCESTER ROAD, a little NE of the former
church. At its S end, WYTHALL INSTITUTE by *John Cotton*,
1888, brick with characteristic pilaster decoration. To its NE, the
BAPTIST CHAPEL, 1805, all but rebuilt 1837; roughcast, round-
arched windows, hipped slate roof, much C20 alteration.

A more significant Nonconformist survival is the KINGS-
WOOD MEETING HOUSE (originally Presbyterian, later
Unitarian) in Packhorse Lane, Hollywood, W of Alcester Road,
over 1 m. further N. Founded 1708, destroyed in the Priestley
Riots 1791, rebuilt in brick on this new site 1793. Of this building only the basic structure, especially the S wall with platbands
and doorways, remains. Alterations by *Henry Naden*, 1861, may
have included adding the present (N) chancel. The body of the
chapel was remodelled in 1874, with tall pairs of two-light Geo-
metrical-traceried windows either side. On the gabled S front,
a triple arcade: round-arched outer porches flank a two-storey
centre with notched segmental arch sheltering the tomb of the
Greves family; small rose windows above the doorways. Interior little altered, with sturdy open roof and fittings mostly of
1874. – The panelled PULPIT and much of the panelled dado
must be of 1793. – Four Grecian WALL TABLETS by *Peter
Hollins*, including Emma Greves †1842, with willow spray, and
Rebecca Lloyd †1849, with broken lily; also Rev. James Taplin
†1882, by *J. Roddis*, an unsubtle portrait roundel. – Attached
SCHOOLROOMS behind, 1890. – Large, tomb-packed burial
ground, with brick hipped-roofed PARSONAGE, also 1793, to
its E.

Schools are the best C20 buildings. The large WOODRUSH
HIGH SCHOOL, Shawhurst Lane, by *S. T. Walker*, 1955–7, is
brick with much curtain-walling; THE COPPICE PRIMARY
SCHOOL, nearby, of 1968, is a typically spreading example.
MEADOW GREEN PRIMARY SCHOOL, Meadow Road,
further S, 1963, looks equally friendly. The only housing noteworthy is the Bromsgrove RDC group around HOUNDSFIELD
CLOSE (corner of Hollywood and Houndsfield Lanes): ten
brick pairs by *H. T. W. Gough*, 1948, hipped-roofed, gabled two-
storey porches, with distant echoes of Garden City ideals.

BERRY MOUND, 2¼ m. NE close to the Solihull boundary. Univallate Iron Age hill-fort, oval in plan, enclosing some eleven acres. Rampart and ditch are best preserved to the SE, perhaps with original entrance; traces of an inturned N entrance.

BROOK PRIORY FARM, at the W end of Barkers Lane, Inkford, ⅝ m. SSE, is perhaps C15, with chimney inserted c. 1600, all encased in C19 brick. Above the hearth, within the brick shaft, is an unaltered bacon-smoking chamber, a rare survival.

At WEATHEROAK HILL, 1 m. WSW, the dominant accent is the early C19 WINDMILL, an odd profile as its base cone is topped with an early C20 water tower in matching brick. At the crossroads, E: WEATHEROAK HOUSE, gabled brick, partly by *John Cotton*, 1886, much altered; a bargeboarded lodge of 1835; then HALL FARM, externally brick, of 1827, with gabled porch added 1895. The interior proves it to be a C16 timber-framed hall and parlour (showing evidence for a jettied front), with probably earlier W cross-wing (later truncated). Brick farm buildings of 1829.

WEATHEROAK HALL (now Kings Norton Golf Club), ¼ m. N, probably succeeded Hall Farm as the manor house in the late C18. Rebuilt 1884–5 for the Rev. T.H. Mynors by *John Cotton*, his largest house. Florid Queen Anne W front: brick, stone dressings, five bays with projecting wings, the latter with Corinthian pilasters, Venetian-type upper windows with shell tympana, and vertical ovals in the gabled dormers. Recessed centre, its higher three-bay pedimented part flanked by blind balustrades; quoins, first-floor windows with fancy lintels, matching porch. Cotton's busy brick pilasters and string courses are everywhere; hipped green slate roofs. Big S extension for the golf club, 1969–70, when the garden front was completely obscured. Inside, a galleried entrance hall fills the centre. – Contemporary STABLES, N; brick GAZEBO by *W.A. Harvey*, 1911, NE; LODGE by *W.H. Bidlake*, 1896, NW.

Downhill, W of the windmill (in Alvechurch parish), two good timber-framed farmhouses. WEATHEROAK FARM, complex C16–C17, has probably at least four phases. Its most attractive features, the close studding and herringbone strutting of the main N range and central cross-wing, are probably early C17; late C17 S cross-wing.

MOORGREEN HALL, further W, late C17 L-plan, faced in heavy C19 roughcasting, has square-panelling visible only at the rear. Brick gatepiers with stone ball finials.

GLOSSARY

Numbers and letters refer to the illustrations (by John Sambrook) on pp. 796–803.

ABACUS: flat slab forming the top of a capital (3a).

ACANTHUS: classical formalized leaf ornament (4b).

ACCUMULATOR TOWER: *see* Hydraulic power.

ACHIEVEMENT: a complete display of armorial bearings.

ACROTERION: plinth for a statue or ornament on the apex or ends of a pediment; more usually, both the plinth and what stands on it (4a).

AEDICULE (*lit.* little building): architectural surround, consisting usually of two columns or pilasters supporting a pediment.

AGGREGATE: *see* Concrete.

AISLE: subsidiary space alongside the body of a building, separated from it by columns, piers, or posts.

ALMONRY: a building from which alms are dispensed to the poor.

AMBULATORY (*lit.* walkway): aisle around the sanctuary (q.v.).

ANGLE ROLL: roll moulding in the angle between two planes (1a).

ANSE DE PANIER: *see* Arch.

ANTAE: simplified pilasters (4a), usually applied to the ends of the enclosing walls of a portico *in antis* (q.v.).

ANTEFIXAE: ornaments projecting at regular intervals above a Greek cornice, originally to conceal the ends of roof tiles (4a).

ANTHEMION: classical ornament like a honeysuckle flower (4b).

APRON: raised panel below a window or wall monument or tablet.

APSE: semicircular or polygonal end of an apartment, especially of a chancel or chapel. In classical architecture sometimes called an *exedra*.

ARABESQUE: non-figurative surface decoration consisting of flowing lines, foliage scrolls etc., based on geometrical patterns. Cf. Grotesque.

ARCADE: series of arches supported by piers or columns. *Blind arcade* or *arcading*: the same applied to the wall surface. *Wall arcade*: in medieval churches, a blind arcade forming a dado below windows. Also a covered shopping street.

ARCH: Shapes *see* 5c. *Basket arch* or *anse de panier* (basket handle): three-centred and depressed, or with a flat centre. *Nodding*: ogee arch curving forward from the wall face. *Parabolic*: shaped like a chain suspended from two level points, but inverted. Special purposes. *Chancel*: dividing chancel from nave or crossing. *Crossing*: spanning piers at a crossing (q.v.). *Relieving or discharging*: incorporated in a wall to relieve superimposed weight (5c). *Skew*: spanning responds not diametrically opposed. *Strainer*: inserted in an opening to resist inward pressure. *Transverse*: spanning a main axis (e.g. of a vaulted space). *See also* Jack arch, Triumphal arch.

ARCHITRAVE: formalized lintel, the lowest member of the classical entablature (3a). Also the moulded frame of a door or window (often borrowing the profile of a classical architrave). For *lugged* and *shouldered* architraves *see* 4b.

ARCUATED: dependent structurally on the arch principle. Cf. Trabeated.

ARK: chest or cupboard housing the

tables of Jewish law in a synagogue.

ARRIS: sharp edge where two surfaces meet at an angle (3a).

ASHLAR: masonry of large blocks wrought to even faces and square edges (6d).

ASTRAGAL: classical moulding of semicircular section (3f).

ASTYLAR: with no columns or similar vertical features.

ATLANTES: see Caryatids.

ATRIUM (plural: atria): inner court of a Roman or C20 house; in a multi-storey building, a toplit covered court rising through all storeys. Also an open court in front of a church.

ATTACHED COLUMN: see Engaged column.

ATTIC: small top storey within a roof. Also the storey above the main entablature of a classical façade.

AUMBRY: recess or cupboard to hold sacred vessels for the Mass.

BAILEY: see Motte-and-bailey.

BALANCE BEAM: see Canals.

BALDACCHINO: free-standing canopy, originally fabric, over an altar. Cf. Ciborium.

BALLFLOWER: globular flower of three petals enclosing a ball (1a). Typical of the Decorated style.

BALUSTER: pillar or pedestal of bellied form. *Balusters*: vertical supports of this or any other form, for a handrail or coping, the whole being called a *balustrade* (6c). *Blind balustrade*: the same applied to the wall surface.

BARBICAN: outwork defending the entrance to a castle.

BARGEBOARDS (corruption of 'vergeboards'): boards, often carved or fretted, fixed beneath the eaves of a gable to cover and protect the rafters.

BAROQUE: style originating in Rome *c.*1600 and current in England *c.*1680–1720, characterized by dramatic massing and silhouette and the use of the giant order.

BARROW: burial mound.

BARTIZAN: corbelled turret, square or round, frequently at an angle.

BASCULE: hinged part of a lifting (or bascule) bridge.

BASE: moulded foot of a column or pilaster. For *Attic* base see 3b.

BASEMENT: lowest, subordinate storey; hence the lowest part of a classical elevation, below the *piano nobile* (q.v.).

BASILICA: a Roman public hall; hence an aisled building with a clerestory.

BASTION: one of a series of defensive semicircular or polygonal projections from the main wall of a fortress or city.

BATTER: intentional inward inclination of a wall face.

BATTLEMENT: defensive parapet, composed of *merlons* (solid) and *crenels* (embrasures) through which archers could shoot; sometimes called *crenellation*. Also used decoratively.

BAY: division of an elevation or interior space as defined by regular vertical features such as arches, columns, windows etc.

BAY LEAF: classical ornament of overlapping bay leaves (3f).

BAY WINDOW: window of one or more storeys projecting from the face of a building. *Canted*: with a straight front and angled sides. *Bow window*: curved. *Oriel*: rests on corbels or brackets and starts above ground level; also the bay window at the dais end of a medieval great hall.

BEAD-AND-REEL: see Enrichments.

BEAKHEAD: Norman ornament with a row of beaked bird or beast heads usually biting into a roll moulding (1a).

BELFRY: chamber or stage in a tower where bells are hung.

BELL CAPITAL: see 1b.

BELLCOTE: small gabled or roofed housing for the bell(s).

BERM: level area separating a ditch from a bank on a hill-fort or barrow.

BILLET: Norman ornament of small half-cylindrical or rectangular blocks (1a).

BLIND: see Arcade, Baluster, Portico.

BLOCK CAPITAL: see 1a.

BLOCKED: columns, etc. interrupted by regular projecting

blocks (*blocking*), as on a Gibbs surround (4b).

BLOCKING COURSE: course of stones, or equivalent, on top of a cornice and crowning the wall.

BOLECTION MOULDING: covering the joint between two different planes (6b).

BOND: the pattern of long sides (*stretchers*) and short ends (*headers*) produced on the face of a wall by laying bricks in a particular way (6e).

BOSS: knob or projection, e.g. at the intersection of ribs in a vault (2c).

BOWTELL: a term in use by the C15 for a form of roll moulding, usually three-quarters of a circle in section (also called *edge roll*).

BOW WINDOW: *see* Bay window.

BOX FRAME: timber-framed construction in which vertical and horizontal wall members support the roof (7). Also concrete construction where the loads are taken on cross walls; also called *cross-wall construction*.

BRACE: subsidiary member of a structural frame, curved or straight. *Bracing* is often arranged decoratively e.g. quatrefoil, herringbone (7). *See also* Roofs.

BRATTISHING: ornamental crest, usually formed of leaves, Tudor flowers or miniature battlements.

BRESSUMER (*lit.* breast-beam): big horizontal beam supporting the wall above, especially in a jettied building (7).

BRICK: *see* Bond, Cogging, Engineering, Gauged, Tumbling.

BRIDGE: *Bowstring*: with arches rising above the roadway which is suspended from them. *Clapper*: one long stone forms the roadway. *Roving*: *see* Canal. *Suspension*: roadway suspended from cables or chains slung between towers or pylons. *Stay-suspension* or *stay-cantilever*: supported by diagonal stays from towers or pylons. *See also* Bascule.

BRISES-SOLEIL: projecting fins or canopies which deflect direct sunlight from windows.

BROACH: *see* Spire and 1C.

BUCRANIUM: ox skull used decoratively in classical friezes.

BULL-NOSED SILL: sill displaying a pronounced convex upper moulding.

BULLSEYE WINDOW: small oval window, set horizontally (cf. Oculus). Also called *œil de bœuf*.

BUTTRESS: vertical member projecting from a wall to stabilize it or to resist the lateral thrust of an arch, roof, or vault (1c, 2c). A *flying buttress* transmits the thrust to a heavy abutment by means of an arch or half-arch (1c).

CABLE OR ROPE MOULDING: originally Norman, like twisted strands of a rope.

CAMES: *see* Quarries.

CAMPANILE: free-standing bell-tower.

CANALS: *Flash lock*: removable weir or similar device through which boats pass on a flush of water. Predecessor of the *pound lock*: chamber with gates at each end allowing boats to float from one level to another. *Tidal gates*: single pair of lock gates allowing vessels to pass when the tide makes a level. *Balance beam*: beam projecting horizontally for opening and closing lock gates. *Roving bridge*: carrying a towing path from one bank to the other.

CANTILEVER: horizontal projection (e.g. step, canopy) supported by a downward force behind the fulcrum.

CAPITAL: head or crowning feature of a column or pilaster; for classical types *see* 3; for medieval types *see* 1b.

CARREL: compartment designed for individual work or study.

CARTOUCHE: classical tablet with ornate frame (4b).

CARYATIDS: female figures supporting an entablature; their male counterparts are *Atlantes* (*lit.* Atlas figures).

CASEMATE: vaulted chamber, with embrasures for defence, within a castle wall or projecting from it.

CASEMENT: side-hinged window.

CASTELLATED: with battlements (q.v.).

CAST IRON: hard and brittle, cast in a mould to the required shape.

Wrought iron is ductile, strong in tension, forged into decorative patterns or forged and rolled into e.g. bars, joists, boiler plates; *mild steel* is its modern equivalent, similar but stronger.

CATSLIDE: *See* 8a.

CAVETTO: concave classical moulding of quarter-round section (3f).

CELURE OR CEILURE: enriched area of roof above rood or altar.

CEMENT: *see* Concrete.

CENOTAPH (*lit.* empty tomb): funerary monument which is not a burying place.

CENTRING: wooden support for the building of an arch or vault, removed after completion.

CHAMFER (*lit.* corner-break): surface formed by cutting off a square edge or corner. For types of chamfers and *chamfer stops see* 6a. *See also* Double chamfer.

CHANCEL: part of the E end of a church set apart for the use of the officiating clergy.

CHANTRY CHAPEL: often attached to or within a church, endowed for the celebration of Masses principally for the soul of the founder.

CHEVET (*lit.* head): French term for chancel with ambulatory and radiating chapels.

CHEVRON: V-shape used in series or double series (later) on a Norman moulding (1a). Also (especially when on a single plane) called *zigzag*.

CHOIR: the part of a cathedral, monastic or collegiate church where services are sung.

CIBORIUM: a fixed canopy over an altar, usually vaulted and supported on four columns; cf. Baldacchino. Also a canopied shrine for the reserved sacrament.

CINQUEFOIL: *see* Foil.

CIST: stone-lined or slab-built grave.

CLADDING: external covering or skin applied to a structure, especially a framed one.

CLERESTORY: uppermost storey of the nave of a church, pierced by windows. Also high-level windows in secular buildings.

CLOSER: a brick cut to complete a bond (6e).

CLUSTER BLOCK: *see* Multi-storey.

COADE STONE: ceramic artificial stone made in Lambeth 1769–c.1840 by Eleanor Coade (†1821) and her associates.

COB: walling material of clay mixed with straw. Also called *pisé*.

COFFERING: arrangement of sunken panels (coffers), square or polygonal, decorating a ceiling, vault, or arch.

COGGING: a decorative course of bricks laid diagonally (6e). Cf. Dentilation.

COLLAR: *see* Roofs and 7.

COLLEGIATE CHURCH: endowed for the support of a college of priests.

COLONNADE: range of columns supporting an entablature. Cf. Arcade.

COLONNETTE: small medieval column or shaft.

COLOSSAL ORDER: *see* Giant order.

COLUMBARIUM: shelved, niched structure to house multiple burials.

COLUMN: a classical, upright structural member of round section with a shaft, a capital, and usually a base (3a, 4a).

COLUMN FIGURE: carved figure attached to a medieval column or shaft, usually flanking a doorway.

COMMUNION TABLE: unconsecrated table used in Protestant churches for the celebration of Holy Communion.

COMPOSITE: *see* Orders.

COMPOUND PIER: grouped shafts (q.v.), or a solid core surrounded by shafts.

CONCRETE: composition of *cement* (calcined lime and clay), *aggregate* (small stones or rock chippings), sand and water. It can be poured into *formwork* or *shuttering* (temporary frame of timber or metal) on site (*in-situ* concrete), or *pre-cast* as components before construction. *Reinforced*: incorporating steel rods to take the tensile force. *Pre-stressed*: with tensioned steel rods. Finishes include the impression of boards left by formwork (*board-marked* or *shuttered*), and texturing with steel brushes (*brushed*) or hammers (*hammer-dressed*). *See also* Shell.

CONSOLE: bracket of curved outline (4b).

COPING: protective course of masonry or brickwork capping a wall (6d).

CORBEL: projecting block supporting something above. *Corbel course*: continuous course of projecting stones or bricks fulfilling the same function. *Corbel table*: series of corbels to carry a parapet or a wall-plate or wall-post (7). *Corbelling*: brick or masonry courses built out beyond one another to support a chimney-stack, window, etc.

CORINTHIAN: *see* Orders and 3d.

CORNICE: flat-topped ledge with moulded underside, projecting along the top of a building or feature, especially as the highest member of the classical entablature (3a). Also the decorative moulding in the angle between wall and ceiling.

CORPS-DE-LOGIS: the main building(s) as distinct from the wings or pavilions.

COTTAGE ORNÉ: an artfully rustic small house associated with the Picturesque movement.

COUNTERCHANGING: of joists on a ceiling divided by beams into compartments, when placed in opposite directions in alternate squares.

COUR D'HONNEUR: formal entrance court before a house in the French manner, usually with flanking wings and a screen wall or gates.

COURSE: continuous layer of stones, etc. in a wall (6e).

COVE: a broad concave moulding, e.g. to mask the eaves of a roof. *Coved ceiling*: with a pronounced cove joining the walls to a flat central panel smaller than the whole area of the ceiling.

CRADLE ROOF: *see* Wagon roof.

CREDENCE: a shelf within or beside a piscina (q.v.), or a table for the sacramental elements and vessels.

CRENELLATION: parapet with crenels (*see* Battlement).

CRINKLE-CRANKLE WALL: garden wall undulating in a series of serpentine curves.

CROCKETS: leafy hooks. *Crocketing* decorates the edges of Gothic features, such as pinnacles, canopies, etc. *Crocket capital*: *see* 1b.

CROSSING: central space at the junction of the nave, chancel, and transepts. *Crossing tower*: above a crossing.

CROSS-WINDOW: with one mullion and one transom (qq.v.).

CROWN-POST: *see* Roofs and 7.

CROWSTEPS: squared stones set like steps, e.g. on a gable (8a).

CRUCKS (*lit.* crooked): pairs of inclined timbers (*blades*), usually curved, set at bay-lengths; they support the roof timbers and, in timber buildings, also support the walls (8b). *Base*: blades rise from ground level to a tie- or collar-beam which supports the roof timbers. *Full*: blades rise from ground level to the apex of the roof, serving as the main members of a roof truss. *Jointed*: blades formed from more than one timber; the lower member may act as a wall-post; it is usually elbowed at wall-plate level and jointed just above. *Middle*: blades rise from half-way up the walls to a tie- or collar-beam. *Raised*: blades rise from half-way up the walls to the apex. *Upper*: blades supported on a tie-beam and rising to the apex.

CRYPT: underground or half-underground area, usually below the E end of a church. *Ring crypt*: corridor crypt surrounding the apse of an early medieval church, often associated with chambers for relics. Cf. Undercroft.

CUPOLA (*lit.* dome): especially a small dome on a circular or polygonal base crowning a larger dome, roof, or turret.

CURSUS: a long avenue defined by two parallel earthen banks with ditches outside.

CURTAIN WALL: a connecting wall between the towers of a castle. Also a non-load-bearing external wall applied to a C20 framed structure.

CUSP: *see* Tracery and 2b.

CYCLOPEAN MASONRY: large irregular polygonal stones, smooth and finely jointed.

CYMA RECTA and CYMA REVERSA: classical mouldings with double curves (3f). Cf. Ogee.

DADO: the finishing (often with panelling) of the lower part of a wall in a classical interior; in origin a formalized continuous pedestal. *Dado rail*: the moulding along the top of the dado.

DAGGER: *see* Tracery and 2b.

DALLE-DE-VERRE (*lit.* glass-slab): a late C20 stained-glass technique, setting large, thick pieces of cast glass into a frame of reinforced concrete or epoxy resin.

DEC (DECORATED): English Gothic architecture *c.* 1290 to *c.* 1350. The name is derived from the type of window tracery (q.v.) used during the period.

DEMI- or HALF-COLUMNS: engaged columns (q.v.) half of whose circumference projects from the wall.

DENTIL: small square block used in series in classical cornices (3c). *Dentilation* is produced by the projection of alternating headers along cornices or stringcourses.

DIAPER: repetitive surface decoration of lozenges or squares flat or in relief. Achieved in brickwork with bricks of two colours.

DIOCLETIAN OR THERMAL WINDOW: semicircular with two mullions, as used in the Baths of Diocletian, Rome (4b).

DISTYLE: having two columns (4a).

DOGTOOTH: E.E. ornament, consisting of a series of small pyramids formed by four stylized canine teeth meeting at a point (1a).

DORIC: *see* Orders and 3a, 3b.

DORMER: window projecting from the slope of a roof (8a).

DOUBLE CHAMFER: a chamfer applied to each of two recessed arches (1a).

DOUBLE PILE: *see* Pile.

DRAGON BEAM: *see* Jetty.

DRESSINGS: the stone or brickwork worked to a finished face about an angle, opening, or other feature.

DRIPSTONE: moulded stone projecting from a wall to protect the lower parts from water. Cf. Hoodmould, Weathering.

DRUM: circular or polygonal stage supporting a dome or cupola. Also one of the stones forming the shaft of a column (3a).

DUTCH or FLEMISH GABLE: *see* 8a.

EASTER SEPULCHRE: tomb-chest used for Easter ceremonial, within or against the N wall of a chancel.

EAVES: overhanging edge of a roof; hence *eaves cornice* in this position.

ECHINUS: ovolo moulding (q.v.) below the abacus of a Greek Doric capital (3a).

EDGE RAIL: *see* Railways.

E.E. (EARLY ENGLISH): English Gothic architecture *c.* 1190–1250.

EGG-AND-DART: *see* Enrichments and 3f.

ELEVATION: any face of a building or side of a room. In a drawing, the same or any part of it, represented in two dimensions.

EMBATTLED: with battlements.

EMBRASURE: small splayed opening in a wall or battlement (q.v.).

ENCAUSTIC TILES: earthenware tiles fired with a pattern and glaze.

EN DELIT: stone cut against the bed.

ENFILADE: reception rooms in a formal series, usually with all doorways on axis.

ENGAGED or ATTACHED COLUMN: one that partly merges into a wall or pier.

ENGINEERING BRICKS: dense bricks, originally used mostly for railway viaducts etc.

ENRICHMENTS: the carved decoration of certain classical mouldings, e.g. the ovolo (qq.v.) with *egg-and-dart*, the cyma reversa with *waterleaf*, the astragal with *bead-and-reel* (3f).

ENTABLATURE: in classical architecture, collective name for the three horizontal members (architrave, frieze, and cornice) carried by a wall or a column (3a).

ENTASIS: very slight convex deviation from a straight line, used to prevent an optical illusion of concavity.

EPITAPH: inscription on a tomb.

EXEDRA: *see* Apse.

EXTRADOS: outer curved face of an arch or vault.

EYECATCHER: decorative building terminating a vista.

FASCIA: plain horizontal band, e.g. in an architrave (3c, 3d) or on a shopfront.

FENESTRATION: the arrangement of windows in a façade.

FERETORY: site of the chief shrine of a church, behind the high altar.

FESTOON: ornamental garland, suspended from both ends. Cf. Swag.

FIBREGLASS, or glass-reinforced polyester (GRP): synthetic resin reinforced with glass fibre. GRC: glass-reinforced concrete.

FIELD: see Panelling and 6b.

FILLET: a narrow flat band running down a medieval shaft or along a roll moulding (1a). It separates larger curved mouldings in classical cornices, fluting or bases (3c).

FLAMBOYANT: the latest phase of French Gothic architecture, with flowing tracery.

FLASH LOCK: see Canals.

FLÈCHE or SPIRELET (lit. arrow): slender spire on the centre of a roof.

FLEURON: medieval carved flower or leaf, often rectilinear (1a).

FLUSHWORK: knapped flint used with dressed stone to form patterns.

FLUTING: series of concave grooves (flutes), their common edges sharp (arris) or blunt (fillet) (3).

FOIL (lit. leaf): lobe formed by the cusping of a circular or other shape in tracery (2b). Trefoil (three), quatrefoil (four), cinquefoil (five), and multifoil express the number of lobes in a shape.

FOLIATE: decorated with leaves.

FORMWORK: see Concrete.

FRAMED BUILDING: where the structure is carried by a framework – e.g. of steel, reinforced concrete, timber – instead of by load-bearing walls.

FREESTONE: stone that is cut, or can be cut, in all directions.

FRESCO: al fresco: painting on wet plaster. Fresco secco: painting on dry plaster.

FRIEZE: the middle member of the classical entablature, sometimes ornamented (3a). Pulvinated frieze (lit. cushioned): of bold convex profile (3c). Also a horizontal band of ornament.

FRONTISPIECE: in C16 and C17 buildings the central feature of doorway and windows above linked in one composition.

GABLE: For types see 8a. Gablet: small gable. Pedimental gable: treated like a pediment.

GADROONING: classical ribbed ornament like inverted fluting that flows into a lobed edge.

GALILEE: chapel or vestibule usually at the w end of a church enclosing the main portal(s).

GALLERY: a long room or passage; an upper storey above the aisle of a church, looking through arches to the nave; a balcony or mezzanine overlooking the main interior space of a building; or an external walkway.

GALLETING: small stones set in a mortar course.

GAMBREL ROOF: see 8a.

GARDEROBE: medieval privy.

GARGOYLE: projecting water spout often carved into human or animal shape.

GAUGED or RUBBED BRICKWORK: soft brick sawn roughly, then rubbed to a precise (gauged) surface. Mostly used for door or window openings (5c).

GAZEBO (jocular Latin, 'I shall gaze'): ornamental lookout tower or raised summer house.

GEOMETRIC: English Gothic architecture c. 1250–1310. See also Tracery. For another meaning, see Stairs.

GIANT or COLOSSAL ORDER: classical order (q.v.) whose height is that of two or more storeys of the building to which it is applied.

GIBBS SURROUND: C18 treatment of an opening (4b), seen particularly in the work of James Gibbs (1682–1754).

GIRDER: a large beam. Box: of hollow-box section. Bowed: with its top rising in a curve. Plate: of I-section, made from iron or steel plates. *Lattice*: with braced frame-work.

GLAZING BARS: wooden or some-times metal bars separating and supporting window panes.

GRAFFITI: *see* Sgraffito.

GRANGE: farm owned and run by a religious order.

GRC: *see* Fibreglass.

GRISAILLE: monochrome painting on walls or glass.

GROIN: sharp edge at the meeting of two cells of a cross-vault; *see* Vault and 2c.

GROTESQUE (*lit.* grotto-esque): wall decoration adopted from Roman examples in the Renaissance. Its foliage scrolls incorporate figur-ative elements. Cf. Arabesque.

GROTTO: artificial cavern.

GRP: *see* Fibreglass.

GUILLOCHE: classical ornament of interlaced bands (4b).

GUNLOOP: opening for a firearm.

GUTTAE: stylized drops (3b).

HALF-TIMBERING: archaic term for timber-framing (q.v.). Sometimes used for non-structural decorative timberwork.

HALL CHURCH: medieval church with nave and aisles of approxim-ately equal height.

HAMMERBEAM: *see* Roofs and 7.

HAMPER: in C20 architecture, a visu-ally distinct topmost storey or storeys.

HEADER: *see* Bond and 6e.

HEADSTOP: stop (q.v.) carved with a head (5b).

HELM ROOF: *see* 1c.

HENGE: ritual earthwork.

HERM (*lit.* the god Hermes): male head or bust on a pedestal.

HERRINGBONE WORK: *see* 7ii. Cf. Pitched masonry.

HEXASTYLE: *see* Portico.

HILL-FORT: Iron Age earthwork en-closed by a ditch and bank system.

HIPPED ROOF: *see* 8a.

HOODMOULD: projecting moulding above an arch or lintel to throw off water (2b, 5b). When horizontal often called a *label*. For label stop *see* Stop.

HUSK GARLAND: festoon of stylized nutshells (4b).

HYDRAULIC POWER: use of water under high pressure to work machinery. *Accumulator tower*: houses a hydraulic accumulator which accommodates fluctuations in the flow through hydraulic mains.

HYPOCAUST (*lit.* underburning): Ro-man underfloor heating system.

IMPOST: horizontal moulding at the springing of an arch (5c).

IMPOST BLOCK: block between abacus and capital (1b).

IN ANTIS: *see* Antae, Portico and 4a.

INDENT: shape chiselled out of a stone to receive a brass.

INDUSTRIALIZED or SYSTEM BUILDING: system of manufac-tured units assembled on site.

INGLENOOK (*lit.* fire-corner): recess for a hearth with provision for seating.

INTERCOLUMNATION: interval be-tween columns.

INTERLACE: decoration in relief simulating woven or entwined stems or bands.

INTRADOS: *see* Soffit.

IONIC: *see* Orders and 3c.

JACK ARCH: shallow segmental vault springing from beams, used for fireproof floors, bridge decks, etc.

JAMB (*lit.* leg): one of the vertical sides of an opening.

JETTY: in a timber-framed building, the projection of an upper storey beyond the storey below, made by the beams and joists of the lower storey oversailing the wall; on their outer ends is placed the sill of the walling for the storey above (7). Buildings can be jettied on several sides, in which case a *dragon beam* is set diagonally at the corner to carry the joists to either side.

JOGGLE: the joining of two stones to prevent them slipping by a notch in one and a projection in the other.

KEEL MOULDING: moulding used from the late C12, in section like the keel of a ship (1a).

KEEP: principal tower of a castle.

KENTISH CUSP: *see* Tracery and 2b.

KEY PATTERN: *see* 4b.

KEYSTONE: central stone in an arch or vault (4b, 5c).

KINGPOST: *see* Roofs and 7.

KNEELER: horizontal projecting stone at the base of each side of a gable to support the inclined coping stones (8a).

LABEL: *see* Hoodmould and 5b.

LABEL STOP: *see* Stop and 5b.

LACED BRICKWORK: vertical strips of brickwork, often in a contrasting colour, linking openings on different floors.

LACING COURSE: horizontal reinforcement in timber or brick to walls of flint, cobble, etc.

LADY CHAPEL: dedicated to the Virgin Mary (Our Lady).

LANCET: slender single-light, pointed-arched window (2a).

LANTERN: circular or polygonal windowed turret crowning a roof or a dome. Also the windowed stage of a crossing tower lighting the church interior.

LANTERN CROSS: churchyard cross with lantern-shaped top.

LAVATORIUM: in a religious house, a washing place adjacent to the refectory.

LEAN-TO: *see* Roofs.

LESENE (*lit.* a mean thing): pilaster without base or capital. Also called *pilaster strip*.

LIERNE: *see* Vault and 2c.

LIGHT: compartment of a window defined by the mullions.

LINENFOLD: Tudor panelling carved with simulations of folded linen. *See also* Parchemin.

LINTEL: horizontal beam or stone bridging an opening.

LOGGIA: gallery, usually arcaded or colonnaded; sometimes freestanding.

LONG-AND-SHORT WORK: quoins consisting of stones placed with the long side alternately upright and horizontal, especially in a Saxon building.

LONGHOUSE: house and byre in the same range with internal access between them.

LOUVRE: roof opening, often protected by a raised timber structure, to allow the smoke from a central hearth to escape.

LOWSIDE WINDOW: set lower than the others in a chancel side wall, usually towards its w end.

LUCAM: projecting housing for hoist pulley on upper storey of warehouses, mills, etc., for raising goods to loading doors.

LUCARNE (*lit.* dormer): small gabled opening in a roof or spire.

LUGGED ARCHITRAVE: *see* 4b.

LUNETTE: semicircular window or blind panel.

LYCHGATE (*lit.* corpse-gate): roofed gateway entrance to a churchyard for the reception of a coffin.

LYNCHET: long terraced strip of soil on the downward side of prehistoric and medieval fields, accumulated because of continual ploughing along the contours.

MACHICOLATIONS (*lit.* mashing devices): series of openings between the corbels that support a projecting parapet through which missiles can be dropped. Used decoratively in post-medieval buildings.

MANOMETER or STANDPIPE TOWER: containing a column of water to regulate pressure in water mains.

MANSARD: *see* 8a.

MATHEMATICAL TILES: facing tiles with the appearance of brick, most often applied to timberframed walls.

MAUSOLEUM: monumental building or chamber usually intended for the burial of members of one family.

MEGALITHIC TOMB: massive stonebuilt Neolithic burial chamber covered by an earth or stone mound.

MERLON: *see* Battlement.

METOPES: spaces between the triglyphs in a Doric frieze (3b).

MEZZANINE: low storey between two higher ones.

MILD STEEL: *see* Cast iron.

MISERICORD (*lit.* mercy): shelf on a carved bracket placed on the underside of a hinged choir stall seat to support an occupant when standing.

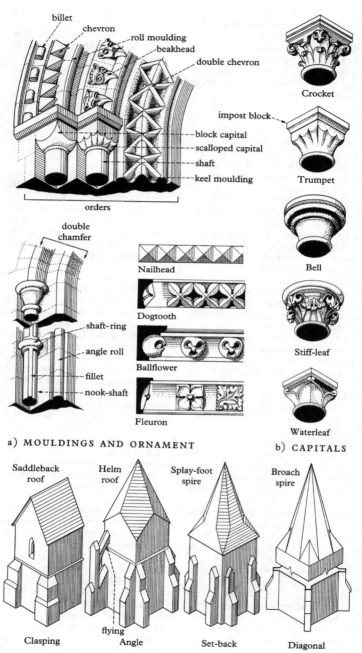

a) MOULDINGS AND ORNAMENT

b) CAPITALS

c) BUTTRESSES, ROOFS AND SPIRES

FIGURE I: MEDIEVAL

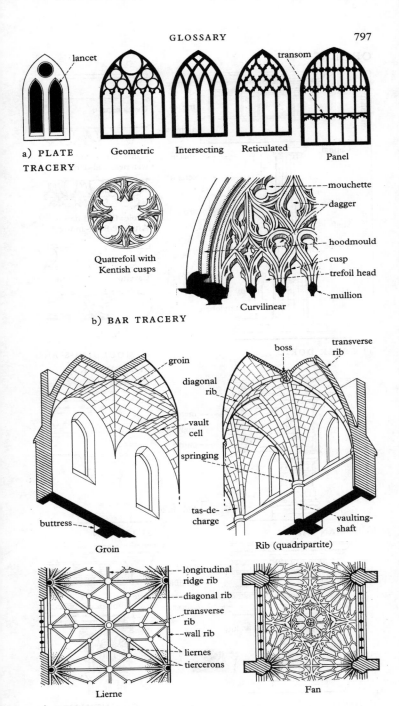

a) PLATE TRACERY

Geometric Intersecting Reticulated Panel

lancet

transom

b) BAR TRACERY

Quatrefoil with Kentish cusps

Curvilinear

mouchette
dagger
hoodmould
cusp
trefoil head
mullion

c) VAULTS

Groin

groin
diagonal rib
vault cell
springing
buttress

Rib (quadripartite)

boss
transverse rib
tas-de-charge
vaulting-shaft

Lierne

longitudinal ridge rib
diagonal rib
transverse rib
wall rib
liernes
tiercerons

Fan

FIGURE 2: MEDIEVAL

ORDERS

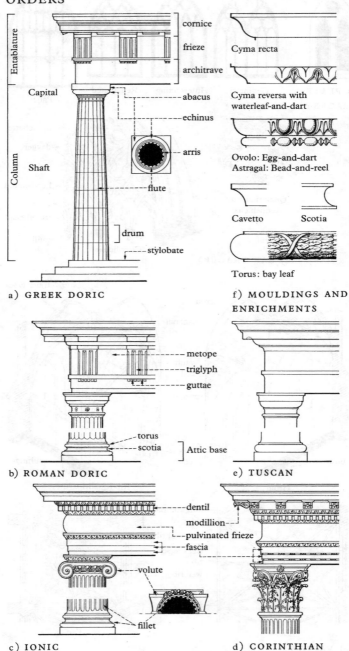

a) GREEK DORIC

- cornice
- frieze
- architrave
- abacus
- echinus
- arris
- flute
- drum
- stylobate

Entablature
Capital
Column
Shaft

Cyma recta

Cyma reversa with
waterleaf-and-dart

Ovolo: Egg-and-dart
Astragal: Bead-and-reel

Cavetto   Scotia

Torus: bay leaf

f) MOULDINGS AND
ENRICHMENTS

b) ROMAN DORIC

- metope
- triglyph
- guttae
- torus
- scotia   ] Attic base

e) TUSCAN

c) IONIC

- dentil
- modillion
- pulvinated frieze
- fascia
- volute
- fillet

d) CORINTHIAN

FIGURE 3: CLASSICAL

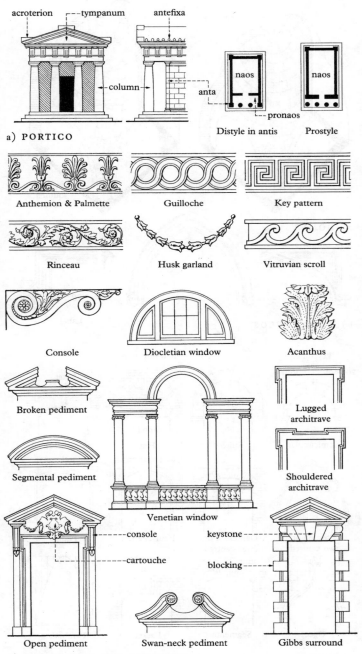

a) PORTICO

Anthemion & Palmette   Guilloche   Key pattern

Rinceau   Husk garland   Vitruvian scroll

Console   Diocletian window   Acanthus

Broken pediment

Segmental pediment

Venetian window

Lugged architrave

Shouldered architrave

Open pediment   Swan-neck pediment   Gibbs surround

b) ORNAMENTS AND FEATURES

FIGURE 4: CLASSICAL

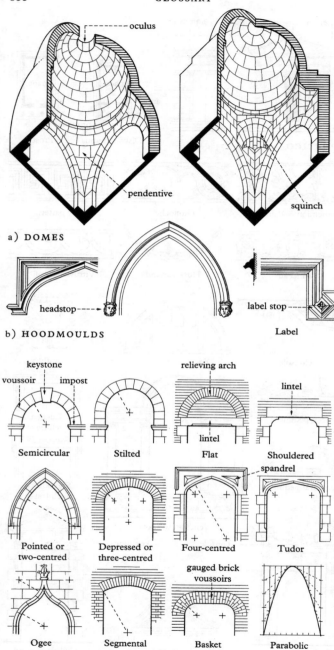

a) DOMES

b) HOODMOULDS

c) ARCHES

FIGURE 5: CONSTRUCTION

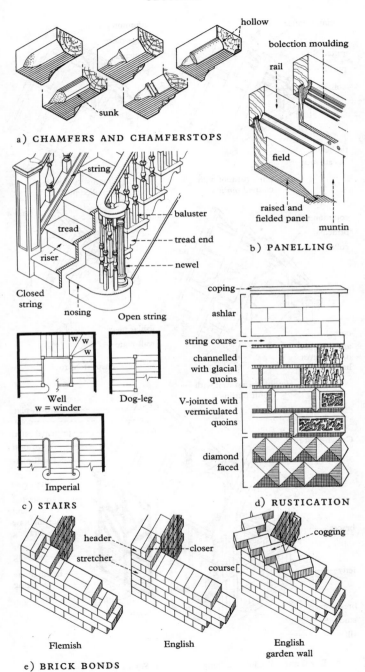

a) CHAMFERS AND CHAMFERSTOPS

hollow
bolection moulding
rail
field
raised and fielded panel
muntin

b) PANELLING

string
baluster
tread
tread end
riser
newel
Closed string
nosing
Open string

Well   w = winder
Dog-leg
Imperial

c) STAIRS

coping
ashlar
string course
channelled with glacial quoins
V-jointed with vermiculated quoins
diamond faced

d) RUSTICATION

header
closer
stretcher
course
cogging

Flemish   English   English garden wall

e) BRICK BONDS

FIGURE 6: CONSTRUCTION

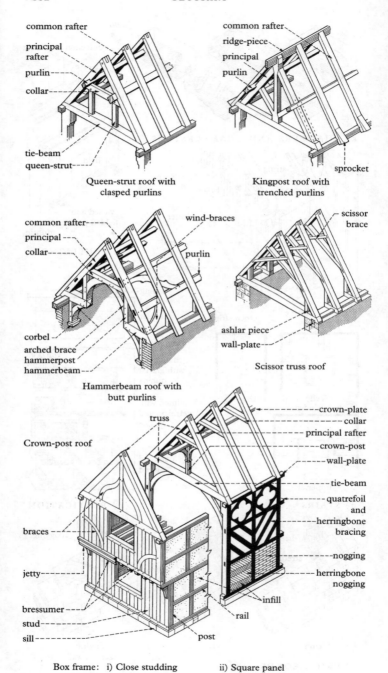

Queen-strut roof with
clasped purlins

Kingpost roof with
trenched purlins

Hammerbeam roof with
butt purlins

Scissor truss roof

Crown-post roof

Box frame: i) Close studding   ii) Square panel

FIGURE 7: ROOFS AND TIMBER-FRAMING

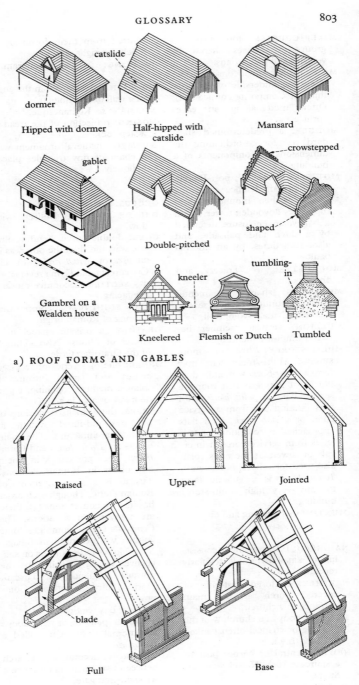

a) ROOF FORMS AND GABLES

b) CRUCK FRAMES

FIGURE 8: ROOFS AND TIMBER-FRAMING

MIXER-COURTS: forecourts to groups of houses shared by vehicles and pedestrians.

MODILLIONS: small consoles (q.v.) along the underside of a Corinthian or Composite cornice (3d). Often used along an eaves cornice.

MODULE: a predetermined standard size for co-ordinating the dimensions of components of a building.

MOTTE-AND-BAILEY: post-Roman and Norman defence consisting of an earthen mound (motte) topped by a wooden tower within a bailey, an enclosure defended by a ditch and palisade, and also, sometimes, by an internal bank.

MOUCHETTE: see Tracery and 2b.

MOULDING: shaped ornamental strip of continuous section; see e.g. Cavetto, Cyma, Ovolo, Roll.

MULLION: vertical member between window lights (2b).

MULTI-STOREY: five or more storeys. Multi-storey flats may form a *cluster block*, with individual blocks of flats grouped round a service core; a *point block*, with flats fanning out from a service core; or a *slab block*, with flats approached by corridors or galleries from service cores at intervals or towers at the ends (plan also used for offices, hotels etc.). *Tower block* is a generic term for any very high multi-storey building.

MUNTIN: see Panelling and 6b.

NAILHEAD: E.E. ornament consisting of small pyramids regularly repeated (1a).

NARTHEX: enclosed vestibule or covered porch at the main entrance to a church.

NAVE: the body of a church w of the crossing or chancel often flanked by aisles (q.v.).

NEWEL: central or corner post of a staircase (6c). Newel stair: see Stairs.

NIGHT STAIR: stair by which religious entered the transept of their church from their dormitory to celebrate night services.

NOGGING: see Timber-framing (7).

NOOK-SHAFT: shaft set in the angle of a wall or opening (1a).

NORMAN: see Romanesque.

NOSING: projection of the tread of a step (6c).

NUTMEG: medieval ornament with a chain of tiny triangles placed obliquely.

OCULUS: circular opening.

ŒIL DE BŒUF: see Bullseye window.

OGEE: double curve, bending first one way and then the other, as in an *ogee* or *ogival arch* (5c). Cf. Cyma recta and Cyma reversa.

OPUS SECTILE: decorative mosaic-like facing.

OPUS SIGNINUM: composition flooring of Roman origin.

ORATORY: a private chapel in a church or a house. Also a church of the Oratorian Order.

ORDER: one of a series of recessed arches and jambs forming a splayed medieval opening, e.g. a doorway or arcade arch (1a).

ORDERS: the formalized versions of the post-and-lintel system in classical architecture. The main orders are *Doric*, *Ionic*, and *Corinthian*. They are Greek in origin but occur in Roman versions. Tuscan is a simple version of Roman Doric. Though each order has its own conventions (3), there are many minor variations. The *Composite* capital combines Ionic volutes with Corinthian foliage. *Superimposed orders*: orders on successive levels, usually in the upward sequence of Tuscan, Doric, Ionic, Corinthian, Composite.

ORIEL: see Bay window.

OVERDOOR: painting or relief above an internal door. Also called a *sopraporta*.

OVERTHROW: decorative fixed arch between two gatepiers or above a wrought-iron gate.

OVOLO: wide convex moulding (3f).

PALIMPSEST: of a brass: where a metal plate has been reused by turning over the engraving on the back; of a wall painting: where one overlaps and partly obscures an earlier one.

PALLADIAN: following the examples and principles of Andrea Palladio (1508–80).

PALMETTE: classical ornament like a palm shoot (4b).

PANELLING: wooden lining to interior walls, made up of vertical members (muntins) and horizontals (rails) framing panels: also called wainscot. Raised and fielded: with the central area of the panel (field) raised up (6b).

PANTILE: roof tile of S section.

PARAPET: wall for protection at any sudden drop, e.g. at the wall-head of a castle where it protects the parapet walk or wall-walk. Also used to conceal a roof.

PARCLOSE: see Screen.

PARGETTING (lit. plastering): exterior plaster decoration, either in relief or incised.

PARLOUR: in a religious house, a room where the religious could talk to visitors; in a medieval house, the semi-private living room below the solar (q.v.).

PARTERRE: level space in a garden laid out with low, formal beds.

PATERA (lit. plate): round or oval ornament in shallow relief.

PAVILION: ornamental building for occasional use; or projecting subdivision of a larger building, often at an angle or terminating a wing.

PEBBLEDASHING: see Rendering.

PEDESTAL: a tall block carrying a classical order, statue, vase, etc.

PEDIMENT: a formalized gable derived from that of a classical temple; also used over doors, windows, etc. For variations see 4b.

PENDENTIVE: spandrel between adjacent arches, supporting a drum, dome or vault and consequently formed as part of a hemisphere (5a).

PENTHOUSE: subsidiary structure with a lean-to roof. Also a separately roofed structure on top of a C20 multi-storey block.

PERIPTERAL: see Peristyle.

PERISTYLE: a colonnade all round the exterior of a classical building, as in a temple which is then said to be peripteral.

PERP (PERPENDICULAR): English Gothic architecture c. 1335–50 to c. 1530. The name is derived from the upright tracery panels then used (see Tracery and 2a).

PERRON: external stair to a doorway, usually of double-curved plan.

PEW: loosely, seating for the laity outside the chancel; strictly, an enclosed seat. Box pew: with equal high sides and a door.

PIANO NOBILE: principal floor of a classical building above a ground floor or basement and with a lesser storey overhead.

PIAZZA: formal urban open space surrounded by buildings.

PIER: large masonry or brick support, often for an arch. See also Compound pier.

PILASTER: flat representation of a classical column in shallow relief. Pilaster strip: see Lesene.

PILE: row of rooms. Double pile: two rows thick.

PILLAR: free-standing upright member of any section, not conforming to one of the orders (q.v.).

PILLAR PISCINA: see Piscina.

PILOTIS: C20 French term for pillars or stilts that support a building above an open ground floor.

PISCINA: basin for washing Mass vessels, provided with a drain; set in or against the wall to the S of an altar or free-standing (pillar piscina).

PISÉ: see Cob.

PITCHED MASONRY: laid on the diagonal, often alternately with opposing courses (pitched and counterpitched or herringbone).

PLATBAND: flat horizontal moulding between storeys. Cf. stringcourse.

PLATE RAIL: see Railways.

PLATEWAY: see Railways.

PLINTH: projecting courses at the

foot of a wall or column, generally chamfered or moulded at the top.

PODIUM: a continuous raised platform supporting a building; or a large block of two or three storeys beneath a multi-storey block of smaller area.

POINT BLOCK: see Multi-storey.

POINTING: exposed mortar jointing of masonry or brickwork. Types include *flush, recessed* and *tuck* (with a narrow channel filled with finer, whiter mortar).

POPPYHEAD: carved ornament of leaves and flowers as a finial for a bench end or stall.

PORTAL FRAME: C20 frame comprising two uprights rigidly connected to a beam or pair of rafters.

PORTCULLIS: gate constructed to rise and fall in vertical grooves at the entry to a castle.

PORTICO: a porch with the roof and frequently a pediment supported by a row of columns (4a). A portico *in antis* has columns on the same plane as the front of the building. A *prostyle* porch has columns standing free. Porticoes are described by the number of front columns, e.g. tetrastyle (four), hexastyle (six). The space within the temple is the *naos*, that within the portico the *pronaos*. *Blind portico*: the front features of a portico applied to a wall.

PORTICUS (plural: porticūs): subsidiary cell opening from the main body of a pre-Conquest church.

POST: upright support in a structure (7).

POSTERN: small gateway at the back of a building or to the side of a larger entrance door or gate.

POUND LOCK: see Canals.

PRESBYTERY: the part of a church lying E of the choir where the main altar is placed; or a priest's residence.

PRINCIPAL: see Roofs and 7.

PRONAOS: see Portico and 4a.

PROSTYLE: see Portico and 4a.

PULPIT: raised and enclosed platform for the preaching of sermons. *Three-decker*: with reading desk below and clerk's desk below that. *Two-decker*: as above, minus the clerk's desk.

PULPITUM: stone screen in a major church dividing choir from nave.

PULVINATED: see Frieze and 3c.

PURLIN: see Roofs and 7.

PUTHOLES or PUTLOG HOLES: in the wall to receive putlogs, the horizontal timbers which support scaffolding boards; sometimes not filled after construction is complete.

PUTTO (plural: putti): small naked boy.

QUARRIES: square (or diamond) panes of glass supported by lead strips (*cames*); square floor slabs or tiles.

QUATREFOIL: see Foil and 2b.

QUEEN-STRUT: see Roofs and 7.

QUIRK: sharp groove to one side of a convex medieval moulding.

QUOINS: dressed stones at the angles of a building (6d).

RADBURN SYSTEM: vehicle and pedestrian segregation in residential developments, based on that used at Radburn, New Jersey, USA, by Wright and Stein, 1928–30.

RADIATING CHAPELS: projecting radially from an ambulatory or an apse (*see* Chevet).

RAFTER: see Roofs and 7.

RAGGLE: groove cut in masonry, especially to receive the edge of a roof-covering.

RAGULY: ragged (in heraldry). Also applied to funerary sculpture, e.g. *cross raguly*: with a notched outline.

RAIL: see Panelling and 6b; also 7.

RAILWAYS: *Edge rail*: on which flanged wheels can run. *Plate rail*: L-section rail for plain unflanged wheels. *Plateway*: early railway using plate rails.

RAISED AND FIELDED: see Panelling and 6b.

RAKE: slope or pitch.

RAMPART: defensive outer wall of stone or earth. *Rampart walk*: path along the inner face.

REBATE: rectangular section cut out of a masonry edge to receive a shutter, door, window, etc.

REBUS: a heraldic pun, e.g. a fiery cock for Cockburn.

REEDING: series of convex mouldings, the reverse of fluting (q.v.). Cf. Gadrooning.

RENDERING: the covering of outside walls with a uniform surface or skin for protection from the weather. *Limewashing*: thin layer of lime plaster. *Pebbledashing*: where aggregate is thrown at the wet plastered wall for a textured effect. *Roughcast*: plaster mixed with a coarse aggregate such as gravel. *Stucco*: fine lime plaster worked to a smooth surface. *Cement rendering*: a cheaper substitute for stucco, usually with a grainy texture.

REPOUSSÉ: relief designs in metalwork, formed by beating it from the back.

REREDORTER (*lit.* behind the dormitory): latrines in a medieval religious house.

REREDOS: painted and/or sculptured screen behind and above an altar. Cf. Retable.

RESPOND: half-pier or half-column bonded into a wall and carrying one end of an arch. It usually terminates an arcade.

RETABLE: painted or carved panel standing on or at the back of an altar, usually attached to it.

RETROCHOIR: in a major church, the area between the high altar and E chapel.

REVEAL: the plane of a jamb, between the wall and the frame of a door or window.

RIB-VAULT: *see* Vault and 2c.

RINCEAU: classical ornament of leafy scrolls (4b).

RISER: vertical face of a step (6c).

ROACH: a rough-textured form of Portland stone, with small cavities and fossil shells.

ROCK-FACED: masonry cleft to produce a rugged appearance.

ROCOCO: style current *c.* 1720 and *c.* 1760, characterized by a serpentine line and playful, scrolled decoration.

ROLL MOULDING: medieval moulding of part-circular section (1a).

ROMANESQUE: style current in the C11 and C12. In England often called Norman. *See also* Saxo-Norman.

ROOD: crucifix flanked by the Virgin and St John, usually over the entry into the chancel, on a beam (*rood beam*) or painted on the wall. The *rood screen* below often had a walkway (*rood loft*) along the top, reached by a *rood stair* in the side wall.

ROOFS: Shape. For the main external shapes (hipped, mansard, etc.) *see* 8a. *Helm* and *Saddleback*: *see* 1c. *Lean-to*: single sloping roof built against a vertical wall; lean-to is also applied to the part of the building beneath.

Construction. *See* 7.

Single-framed roof: with no main trusses. The rafters may be fixed to the wall-plate or ridge, or longitudinal timber may be absent altogether.

Double-framed roof: with longitudinal members, such as purlins, and usually divided into bays by principals and principal rafters. Other types are named after their main structural components, e.g. *hammerbeam*, *crown-post* (*see* Elements below and 7).

Elements. *See* 7.

Ashlar piece: a short vertical timber connecting inner wall-plate or timber pad to a rafter.

Braces: subsidiary timbers set diagonally to strengthen the frame. *Arched braces*: curved pair forming an arch, connecting wall or post below with tie- or collarbeam above. *Passing braces*: long straight braces passing across other members of the truss. *Scissor braces*: pair crossing diagonally between pairs of rafters or principals. *Wind-braces*: short, usually curved braces connecting side purlins with principals; sometimes decorated with cusping.

Collar or *collar-beam*: horizontal transverse timber connecting a pair of rafter or cruck blades (q.v.), set between apex and the wall-plate.

Crown-post: a vertical timber set centrally on a tie-beam and supporting a collar purlin braced to it longitudinally. In an open truss lateral braces may rise to the collar-beam; in a closed truss they may descend to the tie-beam.

Hammerbeams: horizontal brackets projecting at wall-plate level like an interrupted tie-beam; the inner ends carry *hammerposts*, vertical timbers which support a purlin and are braced to a collar-beam above.

Kingpost: vertical timber set centrally on a tie- or collar-beam, rising to the apex of the roof to support a ridge-piece (cf. Strut).

Plate: longitudinal timber set square to the ground. *Wall-plate*: plate along the top of a wall which receives the ends of the rafters; cf. Purlin.

Principals: pair of inclined lateral timbers of a truss. Usually they support side purlins and mark the main bay divisions.

Purlin: horizontal longitudinal timber. *Collar purlin* or *crown plate*: central timber which carries collar-beams and is supported by crown-posts. *Side purlins*: pairs of timbers placed some way up the slope of the roof, which carry common rafters. *Butt* or *tenoned purlins* are tenoned into either side of the principals. *Through purlins* pass through or past the principal; they include *clasped purlins*, which rest on queenposts or are carried in the angle between principals and collar, and *trenched purlins* trenched into the backs of principals.

Queen-strut: paired vertical, or near-vertical, timbers placed symmetrically on a tie-beam to support side purlins.

Rafters: inclined lateral timbers supporting the roof covering. *Common rafters*: regularly spaced uniform rafters placed along the length of a roof or between principals. *Principal rafters*: rafters which also act as principals.

Ridge, ridge-piece: horizontal longitudinal timber at the apex supporting the ends of the rafters.

Sprocket: short timber placed on the back and at the foot of a rafter to form projecting eaves.

Strut: vertical or oblique timber between two members of a truss, not directly supporting longitudinal timbers.

Tie-beam: main horizontal transverse timber which carries the feet of the principals at wall level.

Truss: rigid framework of timbers at bay intervals, carrying the longitudinal roof timbers which support the common rafters. *Closed truss*: with the spaces between the timbers filled, to form an internal partition.

See also Cruck, Wagon roof.

ROPE MOULDING: *see* Cable moulding.

ROSE WINDOW: circular window with tracery radiating from the centre. Cf. Wheel window.

ROTUNDA: building or room circular in plan.

ROUGHCAST: *see* Rendering.

ROVING BRIDGE: *see* Canals.

RUBBED BRICKWORK: *see* Gauged brickwork.

RUBBLE: masonry whose stones are wholly or partly in a rough state. *Coursed*: coursed stones with rough faces. *Random*: uncoursed stones in a random pattern. *Snecked*: with courses broken by smaller stones (snecks).

RUSTICATION: *see* 6d. Exaggerated treatment of masonry to give an effect of strength. The joints are usually recessed by V-section chamfering or square-section channelling (*channelled rustication*). *Banded rustication* has only the horizontal joints emphasized. The faces may be flat, but can be *diamond-faced*, like shallow pyramids, *vermiculated*, with a stylized texture like worm-casts, and *glacial* (frost-work), like icicles or stalactites.

SACRISTY: room in a church for sacred vessels and vestments.

SADDLEBACK ROOF: *see* 1C.

SALTIRE CROSS: with diagonal limbs.

SANCTUARY: area around the main altar of a church. Cf. Presbytery.

SANGHA: residence of Buddhist monks or nuns.

SARCOPHAGUS: coffin of stone or other durable material.

SAXO-NORMAN: transitional Romanesque style combining Anglo-Saxon and Norman features, current *c.* 1060–1100.

SCAGLIOLA: composition imitating marble.

SCALLOPED CAPITAL: *see* 1a.

SCOTIA: a hollow classical moulding, especially between tori (q.v.) on a column base (3b, 3f).

SCREEN: in a medieval church, usually at the entry to the chancel; *see* Rood (screen) and Pulpitum. A *parclose screen* separates a chapel from the rest of the church.

SCREENS or SCREENS PASSAGE: screened-off entrance passage between great hall and service rooms.

SECTION: two-dimensional re-presentation of a building, moulding, etc., revealed by cutting across it.

SEDILIA (singular: sedile): seats for the priests (usually three) on the S side of the chancel.

SET-OFF: *see* Weathering.

SETTS: squared stones, usually of granite, used for paving or flooring.

SGRAFFITO: decoration scratched, often in plaster, to reveal a pattern in another colour beneath. *Graffiti*: scratched drawing or writing.

SHAFT: vertical member of round or polygonal section (1a, 3a). *Shaft-ring*: at the junction of shafts set *en delit* (q.v.) or attached to a pier or wall (1a).

SHEILA-NA-GIG: female fertility figure, usually with legs apart.

SHELL: thin, self-supporting roofing membrane of timber or concrete.

SHOULDERED ARCHITRAVE: *see* 4b.

SHUTTERING: *see* Concrete.

SILL: horizontal member at the bottom of a window or door frame; or at the base of a timber-framed wall into which posts and studs are tenoned (7).

SLAB BLOCK: *see* Multi-storey.

SLATE-HANGING: covering of over-lapping slates on a wall. *Tile-hanging* is similar.

SLYPE: covered way or passage leading E from the cloisters between transept and chapter house.

SNECKED: *see* Rubble.

SOFFIT (*lit.* ceiling): underside of an arch (also called *intrados*), lintel, etc. *Soffit roll*: medieval roll moulding on a soffit.

SOLAR: private upper chamber in a medieval house, accessible from the high end of the great hall.

SOPRAPORTA: *see* Overdoor.

SOUNDING-BOARD: *see* Tester.

SPANDRELS: roughly triangular spaces between an arch and its containing rectangle, or between adjacent arches (5c). Also non-structural panels under the windows in a curtain-walled building.

SPERE: a fixed structure screening the lower end of the great hall from the screens passage. *Spere-truss*: roof truss incorporated in the spere.

SPIRE: tall pyramidal or conical feature crowning a tower or turret. *Broach*: starting from a square base, then carried into an octagonal section by means of triangular faces; and *splayed-foot*: variation of the broach form, found principally in the south-east, in which the four cardinal faces are splayed out near their base, to cover the corners, while oblique (or intermediate) faces taper away to a point (1c). *Needle spire*: thin spire rising from the centre of a tower roof, well inside the parapet: when of timber and lead often called a *spike*.

SPIRELET: *see* Flèche.

SPLAY: of an opening when it is wider on one face of a wall than the other.

SPRING or SPRINGING: level at which an arch or vault rises from its supports. *Springers*: the first stones of an arch or vaulting rib above the spring (2c).

SQUINCH: arch or series of arches thrown across an interior angle of a square or rectangular structure to support a circular or polygonal superstructure, especially a dome or spire (5a).

SQUINT: an aperture in a wall or through a pier usually to allow a view of an altar.

STAIRS: *see* 6c. *Dog-leg stair*: parallel flights rising alternately in opposite directions, without an open well. *Flying stair*: cantilevered from the walls of a stairwell, without newels; sometimes called a *Geometric* stair when the inner edge describes a curve. *Newel stair*: ascending round a central supporting newel (q.v.); called a *spiral stair* or *vice* when in a circular shaft, a *winder* when in a rectangular compartment. (Winder also applies to the steps on the turn.) *Well stair*: with flights round a square open well framed by newel posts. *See also* Perron.

STALL: fixed seat in the choir or chancel for the clergy or choir (cf. Pew). Usually with arm rests, and often framed together.

STANCHION: upright structural member, of iron, steel or reinforced concrete.

STANDPIPE TOWER: *see* Manometer.

STEAM ENGINES: *Atmospheric*: worked by the vacuum created when low-pressure steam is condensed in the cylinder, as developed by Thomas Newcomen. *Beam engine*: with a large pivoted beam moved in an oscillating fashion by the piston. It may drive a flywheel or be *non-rotative*. *Watt* and *Cornish*: single-cylinder; *compound*: two cylinders; *triple expansion*: three cylinders.

STEEPLE: tower together with a spire, lantern, or belfry.

STIFF-LEAF: type of E.E. foliage decoration. *Stiff-leaf capital see* 1b.

STOP: plain or decorated terminal to mouldings or chamfers, or at the end of hoodmoulds and labels (*label stop*), or stringcourses (5b, 6a); *see also* Headstop.

STOUP: vessel for holy water, usually near a door.

STRAINER: *see* Arch.

STRAPWORK: late C16 and C17 decoration, like interlaced leather straps.

STRETCHER: *see* Bond and 6e.

STRING: *see* 6c. Sloping member holding the ends of the treads and risers of a staircase. *Closed string*: a broad string covering the ends of the treads and risers. *Open string*: cut into the shape of the treads and risers.

STRINGCOURSE: horizontal course or moulding projecting from the surface of a wall (6d).

STUCCO: *see* Rendering.

STUDS: subsidiary vertical timbers of a timber-framed wall or partition (7).

STUPA: Buddhist shrine, circular in plan.

STYLOBATE: top of the solid platform on which a colonnade stands (3a).

SUSPENSION BRIDGE: *see* Bridge.

SWAG: like a festoon (q.v.), but representing cloth.

SYSTEM BUILDING: *see* Industrialized building.

TABERNACLE: canopied structure to contain the reserved sacrament or a relic; or architectural frame for an image or statue.

TABLE TOMB: memorial slab raised on free-standing legs.

TAS-DE-CHARGE: the lower courses of a vault or arch which are laid horizontally (2c).

TERM: pedestal or pilaster tapering downward, usually with the upper part of a human figure growing out of it.

TERRACOTTA: moulded and fired clay ornament or cladding.

TESSELLATED PAVEMENT: mosaic flooring, particularly Roman, made of *tesserae*, i.e. cubes of glass, stone, or brick.

TESTER: flat canopy over a tomb or pulpit, where it is also called a *sounding-board*.

TESTER TOMB: tomb-chest with effigies beneath a tester, either free-standing (tester with four or more columns), or attached to a wall (*half-tester*) with columns on one side only.

TETRASTYLE: *see* Portico.

THERMAL WINDOW: *see* Diocletian window.

THREE-DECKER PULPIT: *see* Pulpit.

TIDAL GATES: *see* Canals.

TIE-BEAM: *see* Roofs and 7.

TIERCERON: *see* Vault and 2c.

TILE-HANGING: *see* Slate-hanging.

TIMBER-FRAMING: *see* 7. Method of construction where the structural frame is built of interlocking timbers. The spaces are filled with non-structural material, e.g. *infill* of wattle and daub, lath and plaster, brickwork (known as *nogging*), etc. and may be covered by plaster, weatherboarding (q.v.), or tiles.

TOMB-CHEST: chest-shaped tomb, usually of stone. Cf. Table tomb, Tester tomb.

TORUS (plural: tori): large convex moulding usually used on a column base (3b, 3f).

TOUCH: soft black marble quarried near Tournai.

TOURELLE: turret corbelled out from the wall.

TOWER BLOCK: *see* Multi-storey.

TRABEATED: depends structurally on the use of the post and lintel. Cf. Arcuated.

TRACERY: openwork pattern of masonry or timber in the upper part of an opening. *Blind tracery* is tracery applied to a solid wall.
Plate tracery, introduced *c.* 1200, is the earliest form, in which shapes are cut through solid masonry (2a).
Bar tracery was introduced into England *c.* 1250. The pattern is formed by intersecting moulded ribwork continued from the mullions. It was especially elaborate during the Decorated period (q.v.). Tracery shapes can include circles, *daggers* (elongated ogee-ended lozenges), *mouchettes* (like daggers but with curved sides) and upright rectangular *panels*. They often have *cusps*, projecting points defining lobes or *foils* (q.v.) within the main shape: *Kentish* or *split-cusps* are forked (2b).
Types of bar tracery (*see* 2b) include *geometric(al)*: *c.* 1250–1310, chiefly circles, often foiled; *Y-tracery*: *c.* 1300, with mullions branching into a Y-shape; *intersecting*: *c.* 1300, formed by interlocking mullions; *reticulated*: early C14, net-like pattern of ogee-ended lozenges; *curvilinear*: C14, with uninterrupted flowing curves; *panel*: Perp, with straight-sided panels, often cusped at the top and bottom.

TRANSEPT: transverse portion of a church.

TRANSITIONAL: generally used for the phase between Romanesque and Early English (*c.* 1175–*c.* 1200).

TRANSOM: horizontal member separating window lights (2b).

TREAD: horizontal part of a step. The *tread end* may be carved on a staircase (6c).

TREFOIL: *see* Foil.

TRIFORIUM: middle storey of a church treated as an arcaded wall passage or blind arcade, its height corresponding to that of the aisle roof.

TRIGLYPHS (*lit.* three-grooved tablets): stylized beam-ends in the Doric frieze, with metopes between (3b).

TRIUMPHAL ARCH: influential type of Imperial Roman monument.

TROPHY: sculptured or painted group of arms or armour.

TRUMEAU: central stone mullion supporting the tympanum of a wide doorway. *Trumeau figure*: carved figure attached to it (cf. Column figure).

TRUMPET CAPITAL: *see* 1b.

TRUSS: braced framework, spanning between supports. *See also* Roofs and 7.

TUMBLING or TUMBLING-IN: courses of brickwork laid at right-angles to a slope, e.g. of a gable, forming triangles by tapering into horizontal courses (8a).

TUSCAN: *see* Orders and 3e.

TWO-DECKER PULPIT: *see* Pulpit.

TYMPANUM: the surface between a lintel and the arch above it or within a pediment (4a).

UNDERCROFT: usually describes the vaulted room(s), beneath the main room(s) of a medieval house. Cf. Crypt.

VAULT: arched stone roof (sometimes imitated in timber or plaster). For types see 2c.
Tunnel or *barrel vault*: continuous semicircular or pointed arch, often of rubble masonry.

Groin-vault: tunnel vaults intersecting at right angles. *Groins* are the curved lines of the intersections.

Rib-vault: masonry framework of intersecting arches (ribs) supporting *vault cells*, used in Gothic architecture. *Wall rib* or *wall arch*: between wall and vault cell. *Transverse rib*: spans between two walls to divide a vault into bays. *Quadripartite* rib-vault: each bay has two pairs of diagonal ribs dividing the vault into four triangular cells. *Sexpartite* rib-vault: most often used over paired bays, has an extra pair of ribs springing from between the bays. More elaborate vaults may include *ridge ribs* along the crown of a vault or bisecting the bays; *tiercerons*: extra decorative ribs springing from the corners of a bay; and *liernes*: short decorative ribs in the crown of a vault, not linked to any springing point. A *stellar* or *star* vault has liernes in star formation.

Fan-vault: form of barrel vault used in the Perp period, made up of halved concave masonry cones decorated with blind tracery.

VAULTING SHAFT: shaft leading up to the spring or springing (q.v.) of a vault (2c).

VENETIAN or SERLIAN WINDOW: derived from Serlio (4b). The motif is used for other openings.

VERMICULATION: *see* Rustication and 6d.

VESICA: oval with pointed ends.

VICE: *see* Stair.

VILLA: originally a Roman country house or farm. The term was revived in England in the C18 under the influence of Palladio and used especially for smaller, compact country houses. In the later C19 it was debased to describe any suburban house.

VITRIFIED: bricks or tiles fired to a darkened glassy surface.

VITRUVIAN SCROLL: classical running ornament of curly waves (4b).

VOLUTES: spiral scrolls. They occur on Ionic capitals (3c). *Angle volute*: pair of volutes, turned outwards to meet at the corner of a capital.

VOUSSOIRS: wedge-shaped stones forming an arch (5c).

WAGON ROOF: with the appearance of the inside of a wagon tilt; often ceiled. Also called *cradle roof*.

WAINSCOT: *see* Panelling.

WALL MONUMENT: attached to the wall and often standing on the floor. *Wall tablets* are smaller with the inscription as the major element.

WALL-PLATE: *see* Roofs and 7.

WALL-WALK: *see* Parapet.

WARMING ROOM: room in a religious house where a fire burned for comfort.

WATERHOLDING BASE: early Gothic base with upper and lower mouldings separated by a deep hollow.

WATERLEAF: *see* Enrichments and 3f.

WATERLEAF CAPITAL: Late Romanesque and Transitional type of capital (1b).

WATER WHEELS: described by the way water is fed on to the wheel. *Breastshot*: mid-height, falling and passing beneath. *Overshot*: over the top. *Pitchback*: on the top but falling backwards. *Undershot*: turned by the momentum of the water passing beneath. In a *water turbine*, water is fed under pressure through a vaned wheel within a casing.

WEALDEN HOUSE: type of medieval timber-framed house with a central open hall flanked by bays of two storeys, roofed in line; the end bays are jettied to the front, but the eaves are continuous (8a).

WEATHERBOARDING: wall cladding of overlapping horizontal boards.

WEATHERING or SET-OFF: inclined, projecting surface to keep water away from the wall below.

WEEPERS: figures in niches along the sides of some medieval tombs. Also called mourners.

WHEEL WINDOW: circular, with radiating shafts like spokes. Cf. Rose window.

WROUGHT IRON: *see* Cast iron.

INDEX OF ARCHITECTS, ARTISTS, PATRONS AND RESIDENTS

Names of architects and artists working in Worcestershire are given in *italic*. Entries for partnerships and group practices are listed after entries for a single name.

Also indexed here are the names/titles of families and individuals (not of bodies or commercial firms) recorded in this volume as having commissioned architectural work or owned or lived in properties in the area. The index includes monuments to members of such families and other individuals where they are of particular interest.

INDEX OF PLACES

Principal references are in **bold** type; demolished buildings are shown in *italic*.